The Marketing Book

The Marketing Book

Sixth Edition

Edited by
MICHAEL J. BAKER and SUSAN HART

AMSTERDAM • BOSTON • HEIDELBERG • LONDON • NEW YORK • OXFORD
PARIS • SAN DIEGO • SAN FRANCISCO • SINGAPORE • SYDNEY • TOKYO

Butterworth-Heinemann is an imprint of Elsevier

Butterworth-Heinemann is an imprint of Elsevier
Linacre House, Jordan Hill, Oxford OX2 8DP, UK
30 Corporate Drive, Suite 400, Burlington, MA 01803, USA

First edition 1987
Reprinted 1987, 1990 (twice)
Second edition 1991
Reprinted 1992, 1993
Third edition 1994
Reprinted 1995, 1997
Fourth edition 1999
Reprinted 2000, 2001
Fifth edition 2003
Sixth edition 2008

British Library Cataloguing in Publication Data
A catalogue record for this book is available from the British Library

Library of Congress Cataloging-in-Publication Data
A catalog record for this book is available from the Library of Congress

ISBN: 978-0-7506-8566-5

For information on all Butterworth-Heinemann publications visit
our web site at books.elsevier.com

Printed and bound in Great Britain
08 09 10 10 9 8 7 6

Working together to grow
libraries in developing countries

www.elsevier.com | www.bookaid.org | www.sabre.org

ELSEVIER   BOOK AID International   Sabre Foundation

Contents

Illustrations

Tables

Contributors

Tim Ambler is a Senior Fellow at London Business School. His main research covers dynamic marketing capabilities, how advertising works and the evaluation of marketing performance. He is currently also researching narrative disclosures in company annual reports as well as regulation and deregulation by the EU and UK governments. His books include *Marketing and the Bottom Line* (2000, 2003), *Doing Business in China* (2000, 2003), *The SILK Road to International Marketing* (2000) and *Marketing from Advertising to Zen* (1996). He has published several articles in the *Journal of Marketing, Journal of Marketing Research, International Journal of Research in Marketing, Psychology & Marketing, Journal of Advertising Research* and *International Journal of Advertising*. A member of the *Journal of Marketing, International Journal of Advertising* and Psychology & Marketing Editorial Review Boards and Economics Committee of the Advertising Association, he is a Fellow of the Institute of Chartered Accountants in England and Wales and previously Joint Managing Director of International Distillers and Vintners, now part of Diageo plc. During his various marketing roles in IDV, in the UK and internationally, he was involved in the launch of Baileys, Malibu and Archers and the development of Smirnoff vodka worldwide.

Michael J. Baker is Emeritus Professor of Marketing at the University of Strathclyde where he founded the Department of Marketing in 1971. He served as Dean of the Strathclyde Business School from 1978 to 1984, Deputy Principal of the University from 1984 to 1991 and Senior Adviser to the Principal from 1991 to 1994. He has served as Chairman of SCOTBEC, the Chartered Institute of Marketing and the Marketing Education Group, as a Governor of the CAM Foundation and Member of the ESRC and UGC. He is the author/editor of more than forty books of which the best known are *Marketing* (Westburn Publisher, 7th edition, 2006) and *Marketing Strategy and Management* (Palgrave, 4th edition, 2007) and *Product strategy and Management* with Susan Hart (Pearson, 2nd edition, 2007). A member of numerous editorial boards, he was also the Founding Editor of the *Journal of Marketing Management*. He has extensive international experience and has held Visiting Professorships in Australia, Canada, Egypt, France, Hong Kong, New Zealand and Qatar as well as acting as a consultant to numerous international companies. He is an Honorary Professor at Aberystwyth University and Special Professor at Nottingham University.

Alan Wilson is Professor of Marketing at the University of Strathclyde Business School. Prior to joining the University of Strathclyde, he held high level positions within leading London-based marketing research agencies and a management consultancy practice. He has written numerous articles on marketing research and has received a number of awards for his publications. His textbook, *Marketing Research: An Integrated Approach* is in its second edition. He is also a member of the executive editorial board of the *International Journal of Market Research*. He regularly acts as a marketing and market research advisor to a number of public and private organizations. He is also a full member of the Chartered Institute of Marketing, a Council member of The Market Research Society and he chairs the Society's Professional Development Advisory Board.

David Richard Bell is an Associate Professor at the Wharton School, University of Pennsylvania. He teaches marketing management and marketing strategy in the MBA and MBA for Executives programs. Bell is a recipient of the Miller-Sherrerd MBA Core Teaching Award, MBA Core Curriculum Award MBA and MBA for Executives Excellence in Teaching Awards (East and West). He also teaches in the PhD program, Advanced Management Program, and custom executive education programs for clients including AXA, AVIVA, Rohm and Haas, Shell Oil and Toyota. Previously, he taught at UCLA and was a visiting associate professor at the Sloan School of Management, MIT.

David's research focuses on quantitative analysis of consumer behaviour, retailing practices and spatial diffusion. Research on these topics has appeared in *Journal of Consumer Research, Journal of Marketing Research, Journal of Retailing, Marketing Science, Management Science, Quantitative Marketing and Economics,*

California Management Review and Sloan Management Review. He is a three-time finalist for the John D.C. Little Award for the best paper published annually in either Marketing Science or Management Science. He is also a recipient of Frank M. Bass Outstanding Dissertation Award.

David is a Senior Editor for the journal *Manufacturing & Service Operations Management* and on the editorial boards of *International Journal of Research in Marketing, Journal of Marketing Research, Journal of Retailing, Marketing Science and Foundations and Trends in Marketing*. He holds a PhD from the Graduate School of Business at Stanford University, an MS in Statistics from Stanford, an MCom (1st class honours) and BCom from the University of Auckland.

Stephen Brown is Professor of Marketing Research at the University of Ulster. Best known for *Postmodern Marketing* (1995), he has written or co-edited numerous books, including *Marketing Apocalypse* (1996), *Postmodern Marketing Two* (1998) and *Marketing – The Retro Revolution* (2001). His articles have been published in the *Journal of Marketing, Harvard Business Review, Journal of Advertising, Business Horizons, Journal of Retailing, European Management Journal* and many more.

Dave Chaffey, BSc, PhD, FCIM, MIDM (www.davechaffey.com) is a specialist Internet marketing trainer, consultant and author. He specialises in helping companies improve their E-communications including digital campaign planning, e-mail marketing, search engine marketing, and web analytics. He has run training courses on Internet marketing since 1997 for training providers such as the Chartered Institute of Marketing, Institute of Direct Marketing and E-consultancy. In-company training workshop clients include 3M, BP, Euroffice, Foviance, HBOS, HSBC, Orange, Siebel and Tektronix.

Dave is Director of Marketing Insights Limited (www.marketing-insights.co.uk), a consultancy and training company offering the WebInsights™ service for evaluation and recommendations on e-marketing strategy and execution. Dave has worked with companies including 3M, BP, EMI (KPM Music), HSBC, Intel Reseller Channel, NCH, Siebel and Tektronix to improve their e-marketing using this approach. He also works for cScape Strategic Internet Services (www.cscape.com) as an E-marketing consultant.

His books include: E-marketing Excellence; Total E-mail Marketing and Internet Marketing: Strategy, Implementation and Practice. He has been recognised by the CIM as one of 50 marketing gurus worldwide who has shaped the future of Marketing and by the Department of Trade and Industry as one of the leading individuals who have provided input and influence on the development and growth of E-commerce and the Internet in the UK over the last 10 years.

Leslie de Chernatony, BSc, PhD, FCIM, FMRS is Professor of Brand Marketing and Director of the Centre for Research in Brand Marketing at the Birmingham Business School, The University of Birmingham. After a career in the marketing departments of a few blue chip organizations, he completed his doctorate in brand marketing which laid the foundations for his research focus. With a substantial number of publications on brand management in American and European journals, Leslie is a regular presenter at international conferences. His papers have won best paper awards in journals and at conferences. He has written several books on brand management, the two most recent being *Creating Powerful Brands* and *From Brand Vision to Brand Evaluation*, both published by Butterworth–Heinemann. Winning several major research grants has helped support his research into factors associated with high performance brands and also strategies for succeeding with services brands. Leslie was Visiting Professor at Madrid Business School and is currently Visiting Professor at Thammasat University, Bangkok and Lugano University, Switzerland. He sits on the editorial boards of several scholarly journals. A firm believer of the importance of research having applied value, he acts as an international consultant to organizations seeking more effective brand strategies and has run numerous acclaimed branding seminars throughout Europe, Asia, the Far East and North America.

Tony Cram is Programme Director at Ashridge Business School, one of Europe's leading centres for Management Development. Tony designs and delivers executive programmes on business strategy and market innovation. A particular interest is in understanding Customer Value, developing brands and the dynamics of long term business relationships. He works internationally with experience in Europe, Asia and the Americas and has taught at Swedish Institute of Management, Vlerick Leuven Gent Management School, Stockholm School of Economics, PEF University, Vienna and University of Michigan, USA. He is Fellow of the Chartered Institute of Marketing.

Before joining Ashridge, Tony held a general management position with Manpower. As Director of Marketing Services at TSB Bank, he controlled £20 million marketing expenditure. Earlier, he spent 8 years with Grand Metropolitan at operating company board level. As a Marketing Director, he played a key part in the launch of Foster's Draught Lager into the UK. For two years, he had executive responsibility for 500 licensed retail outlets. His early career was spent with Andre Jamet, a French company in the leisure industry and in the motor industry with Unipart. He gained an MBA from Cranfield School of Management in 1980 (including study at the University of Washington, USA).

Tony has presented on competitive marketing and innovation at public conferences and company conventions in Buenos Aires, Budapest, Gothenburg, Istanbul, London, Paris, Stockholm and Warsaw. His publications include:

- *Smarter Pricing – how to capture more value in your market*, published by Financial Times/Prentice Hall, 2006. Available in four languages.
- The *Financial Times Handbook of Management*, 2004, contributor.
- *Customers that Count –How to build living relationships with your most valuable customers*, published by Financial Times/ Prentice Hall, 2001. Available in six languages.
- *Mastering Risk: Part One Concepts*, published by Financial Times, 2001. Contributor.
- The *Financial Times Handbook of Management 2000*. Contributor.
- *The Power of Relationship Marketing*, published by Pitman in 1996, Paperback edition, 2002.
- *Marketing Managers' Yearbook*, published by Chartered Institute of Marketing, 1992. Contributor.

Bill Donaldson is Professor of Marketing at Aberdeen Business School, The Robert Gordon University. He is responsible for research within the Marketing Division and is author of *Sales Management: Philosophy, Process and Practice*, 3rd edition, Palgrave (2007); *Strategic Market Relationships*, with Tom O'Toole, 2nd edition, John Wiley & Sons (2007) and *The Busy Manager's Guide to Marketing Juridical* (2007).

Pennie Frow is Senior Lecturer in Marketing at the University of Sydney and Visiting Fellow in the Marketing Group at Cranfield School of Management at Cranfield University. Pennie is a psychologist with a special interest in assisting organizations undergoing change. She worked for many years in The Cranfield Marketing Planning Centre. This work included all aspects of strategic planning, marketing planning and implementation. Before joining academia, Pennie was Managing Director of a distribution and manufacturing company in the USA and Chief Marketing Officer of a major British charity. Her research interests are in marketing planning, customer relationship management (CRM), customer retention, internal marketing and developing customer-centric organizations. She has extensive experience of consulting with clients such as Mercedes-Benz, Royal Mail, Cable & Wireless, The National Health Service and many professional service firms.

Mark Gabbott graduated from the University of Essex with a BA (Hons) in Economics followed by an MSc in Technology Management from Imperial College, University of London. After working in government for 6 years in consumer policy and protection, he joined the University of Stirling as a Research Fellow and completed a PhD in Marketing. He was Lecturer and then Senior Lecturer at Stirling researching and teaching in the areas of Electronic and Direct Marketing, Services Marketing, Consumer Behaviour and Consumer Policy. Mark joined Monash University in 1997 as Professor and was appointed Head of Department in 2000. He took up the position of Deputy Dean of the Faculty of Business and Economics in 2006.

Mark's current research interests are in services marketing, knowledge management, CRM, consumer behaviour and customer value. Mark has published four books and has published research in a variety of academic journals including the *Journal of Business Research*, *Journal of Public Policy and Marketing*, *European Journal of Marketing*, *Journal of Marketing Management* and *Journal of Healthcare Marketing*. He currently sits on the editorial boards of three international marketing journals. Mark is a member of the European Marketing Academy, The UK Academy of Marketing, past Chair of the American Marketing Associations Services Interest Group and President of ANZMAC.

Evert Gummesson is Professor of Marketing at the Stockholm University School of Business, Sweden. His interests embrace services, quality management, relationship marketing and CRM, and currently a network approach to a new logic of marketing, reflected in his latest book *Many-to-Many Marketing*. His article (with Christopher Lovelock) 'Whither Services Marketing?', in the *Journal of Service Research*, won the American Marketing Association's Award for Best Article on Services in 2004. He is the author of several articles on methodology and theory generation in marketing and the book *Qualitative Methods in Management Research*. He has also spent 25 years in business.

Lloyd C. Harris is Professor of Marketing and Strategy at Warwick Business School, Warwick University. Past research has focused on market orientation, the organizational culture/marketing interface, the initiation of strategic marketing, professional services marketing and other exploratory projects. Currently, he is working on variety of projects including studies on dysfunctional customer behaviour, some new surveys of market orientation, as well as a number of other culture-orientated projects. Over one hundred peer-reviewed pieces have been disseminated via a range of marketing, strategy, HRM and general management journals, including the *Journal of Retailing, Journal of the Academy of Marketing Science, Journal of Service Research, Human Resources, Human Resource Management, British Journal of Industrial Relations* and the *Journal of Management Studies*. He serves on the editorial boards of a number of journals and reviews papers in a wide field of disciplines.

Susan Hart is Professor of Marketing and Vice Dean (Research) of Marketing at the University of Strathclyde. After working in industry in France and the UK, she joined the University of Strathclyde as a researcher. She completed her PhD on the subject of product management and has published widely on subjects such as the contribution of marketing to competitive success, and product design and development in the manufacturing industry. Current research interests are in the development of new products and innovation, the contribution of marketing to company success, loyalty marketing and accounting for marketing performance.

Derek Holder is Founder and Managing Director, Institute of Direct Marketing. After graduating from Manchester University, Derek worked in marketing for two major multi-nationals – Ford and British Airways. He, then, held senior marketing positions at McGraw-Hill and Reader's Digest, where he gained wide experience in both consumer and business-to-business direct marketing. A consultant and trainer for multinationals around the world, Derek has developed undergraduate and postgraduate programmes in direct marketing. In 1981, he created the world's first Diploma in Direct and Interactive Marketing and has subsequently designed Certificates in Direct and Interactive Marketing, e-marketing and CRM. Recently, he pioneered the introduction of a Certificate and Diploma in Digital Marketing. He is also Co-Editor of the internationally recognized *Journal of Direct, Data and Digital Marketing*. He was voted the third most influential person in direct marketing over the past 15 years by the readership of Precision Marketing.

Piyush Kumar Sinha, Professor, Marketing, and Chairperson, Centre for Retailing, Indian Institute of Management Ahmedabad (IIMA), has over two decades of academic and Industry experience. He has also served as Dean, Mudra Institute of Communications, Ahmedabad (MICA), and has taught at leading business schools in India.

Dr. Sinha is active in research in the area of retailing and consumer behaviour. He is involved in qualitative research in the area of marketing in India and has several international publications to his credit.

Malcolm McDonald is Professor of Marketing and Deputy Director of the Cranfield School of Management. He is a graduate in English Language and Literature from Oxford University, in Business Studies from Bradford University Management Centre, has a PhD from Cranfield University and an honorary Doctorate of Letters from Bradford University. He has extensive industrial experience, including a number of years as Marketing Director of Canada Dry. During the past 20 years, he has run seminars and workshops on marketing planning in the UK, Europe, India, the Far East, Australasia and the USA. He has written thirty-seven books, including the best-seller *Marketing Plans: How to Prepare Them, How to Use Them* (Butterworth-Heinemann, 5th edition, 2002) and many of his papers have been published. His current interests centre around IT in marketing, the development of expert systems in marketing and key account management.

Luiz Moutinho is Professor of Marketing, University of Glasgow Business School. He completed his PhD at the University of Sheffield in 1982 and held posts at Cardiff Business School, University of Wales College of Cardiff, Cleveland State University, Ohio, USA, Northern Arizona University, USA and California State University, USA, as well as visiting Professorship positions in New Zealand and Brazil. Between 1987 and 1989, he was Director of the Doctoral Programmes at the Confederation of Scottish Business Schools and at the Cardiff Business School between 1993 and 1996. He has been Director of the Doctoral Programme at the University of Glasgow Department of Business and Management. In addition to publishing nineteen books and presenting papers at many international conferences, he also has had a vast number of articles published in international journals. He is also a member of the Editorial Board of several international academic journals. He has been a full-time Professor of Marketing since 1989 and was appointed in 1996 to the Foundation Chair of Marketing at the University of Glasgow.

Prathap Oburai is a faculty member of the Marketing area at IIM Ahmedabad. Prior to joining IIMA, Prathap taught at IIM Bangalore and worked as a tutor at the University of Strathclyde in Glasgow. Professor Oburai served as Visiting Professor at Asian Institute of Management, Manila, Philippines; Multimedia University, Cyberjaya, Malaysia; MICA, India and NID, India. He has been awarded several teaching excellence awards including the IIMA Poll of the Year 2006 and Poll of the Year 2007 awards.

Dr Oburai has a PhD in Marketing and an MSc in International Marketing from the Department of Marketing, University of Strathclyde, where he held a Commonwealth Scholarship from the Association of Commonwealth Universities, London. He has a graduate degree in computer science engineering from Jawaharlal Nehru Technological University, Hyderabad, and a Post-Graduate Diploma in Management from Indian Institute of Management, Ahmedabad.

Prof. Oburai, who believes in the pursuit of scholarship rooted in practice and application, has 7 years of managerial experience His research interests include Business-to-Business Marketing; Cooperative Marketing Strategies; Industrial Clusters and Policies; International Business Strategies; International Marketing; Marketing Research and Relationship Marketing.

Dr. Oburai presented research work at several major European and Indian conferences, and has published in journals, and in leading books such as The Encyclopaedia of Marketing. He is a member of the European Marketing Academy and the Academy of Marketing.

Lisa O'Malley is senior Lecturer in Marketing at the University of Limerick. Lisa's main teaching and research interests are in the areas of marketing theory, direct marketing and relationship marketing. She has published widely on relationship marketing including articles in the *Journal of Marketing Management*, the *European Journal of Marketing, Service Industries Journal, Journal of Business Research* and *Interactive Marketing*. These include critical works on RM in mass consumer markets as well as investigations on the role of relationships in professional services.

Adrian Payne is Professor of Marketing at the University of New South Wales in Australia and an adjunct Professor at the Cranfield School of Management in the UK. He has practical experience in marketing, market research, corporate planning and general management. His previous appointments include positions as chief executive for a manufacturing company and he has also held senior appointments in corporate planning and marketing. His is an author of six books on Relationship Marketing and CRM. His research interests are in Customer Retention Economics; the impact of IT on CRM and Marketing Strategy and Planning in Service Businesses. Adrian is a frequent keynote speaker at public and in-company seminars and conferences around the world. He also acts as a consultant and educator to many service organizations, professional service firms and manufacturing companies.

Ken Peattie is a Professor of Marketing and Strategy at Cardiff Business School, which he joined in 1986 following practical experience in marketing and information systems in the paper and electronics industries. His research interests are focussed on the implications of sustainability for business and business education, and on its impact on marketing strategies, theories and practices in particular. He is the author of two books and numerous book chapters on these topics, and has published in a range of journals including *California Management Review, Journal of Business Research, Journal of Public Policy and Marketing, Journal of Marketing Management, Industrial Marketing Management* and *European Management Journal*.

In 2001, he became Director of the ESRC-funded BRASS Research Centre, which specialises in researching issues relating to business sustainability and corporate social responsbility.

Angela da Rocha holds a PhD in Management from IESE Business School, University of Navarra, Barcelona, Spain. She received her MBA in Business Administration and her bachelor's degree in Economics from the Federal University of Rio de Janeiro. She is Professor of Marketing and International Business at the Coppead Graduate School of Business, The Federal University of Rio de Janeiro. She served as Dean of the School for two terms. Her research interests include the internationalization of firms from Emerging Economies and cross-cultural management.

Adrian Sargeant joined Indiana University as the Robert F Hartsook Professor of Fundraising in 2006. He is currently Visiting Professor of Non-profit Marketing at Bristol Business School and Henley Management College in the UK. He is also Adjunct Professor of Philanthropy at the Centre of Philanthropy and Non-profit Studies at Queensland University of Technology, Australia, where he won a Myer Fellowship in the Summer of 2005. Professor Sargeant is the Managing Editor of the *International Journal of Non-profit and Voluntary Sector Marketing* and a member of the Editorial Boards of the *Journal of Non-profit and Public Sector Marketing* and *Non-profit and Voluntary Sector Quarterly*. He has acted as a guest editor for *New Directions for Philanthropic Fundraising* and the leading *Journal of Business Research*. He has published 58 peer reviewed academic articles, 7 books and made over 100 conference appearances in the past 10 years. The majority of this output has focused on the topic of non-profit marketing and within that, fundraising management. He is the author of *Marketing Management for Non-profit Organizations* and *Fundraising Management*, published by Oxford University Press and Routledge, respectively.

Jorge Ferreira da Silva holds a PhD in Industrial Engineering from the Pontifical Catholic University of Rio de Janeiro and an MSc in Electronics from the Air Force Technological Institute. He also holds an MBA in Business Administration and a bachelor's degree in Electric Engineering from the Pontifical Catholic University of Rio de Janeiro, and a bachelor's degree in Statistics from the National School of Statistics. He is presently an Associate Professor of Strategy at the IAG Business School, The Pontifical Catholic University of Rio de Janeiro, after holding a number of top positions in large Brazilian corporations. He presently serves as Director of Graduate Studies at his school. His research interests are corporate strategy, including the impacts of strategy on business performance and strategic alliances.

Caroline Tynan is Professor of Marketing and Head of the Marketing Division at Nottingham University Business School, Chair of the Academy of Marketing, a member of the Academic Senate of the Chartered Institute of Marketing and Visiting Professor of Marketing at the University of Ljubljana, Slovenia. Her research interests include relationship marketing, particularly regarding issues related to its application within business-to-consumer and cross-cultural contexts, services marketing and marketing in transition economies. She has published in a number of journals, including *Journal of Business Research*, *European Journal of Marketing*, *Journal of Marketing Management* and *Journal of Strategic Marketing*, and she currently edits *The Marketing Review*.

Douglas West is Professor of Marketing at the University of Birmingham and Visiting Professor at Henley Management College. His interests include creative marketing, risk and strategic and high-tech marketing. His business experience includes market research at a subsidiary advertising agency of a leading multinational agency group and as an assistant marketing director at an international toy company. He has acted as a marketing consultant for a variety of companies in Britain and Canada and has taught executive programmes for a variety of companies. Amongst others his publications have appeared in the *European Journal of Marketing*, the *International Journal of Advertising*, the *International Marketing Review*, the *Journal of Advertising*, the *Journal of Advertising Research*, the *Journal of Business Research*, the *Journal of Forecasting* and the *Journal of Marketing Management*. He holds positions on several journal editorial boards and is Editor of the *International Journal of Advertising*. He is co-author of *Direct and Interactive Marketing* (Oxford University Press, 2001) and *Marketing Strategy: Creating Competitive Advantage* (Oxford University Press, 2006).

Robin Wensley is Professor of Strategic Management and Marketing and Deputy Dean at Warwick Business School. He was Chair of the School from 1989 to 1994 and Chair of the Faculty of Social Studies from

1997 to 1999. He was previously with RHM Foods, Tube Investments and London Business School, and was Visiting Professor twice at UCLA and once at the University of Florida. He is a Council member of the ESRC, having been a member of the Research Grants Board from 1991 to 1995. He is also Chair of the Council of the Tavistock Institute of Human Relations. His research interests include the long-term evolution of competitive markets and structures, the process of strategic decision making and the nature of sustainable advantages, and he has published a number of books, most recently the *Handbook of Marketing*, and articles in the *Harvard Business Review*, the *Journal of Marketing* and the *Strategic Management Journal*, and has worked closely with other academics both in Europe and the USA. He is joint editor of the *Journal of Management Studies* and has twice won the annual Alpha Kappa Psi Award for the most influential article in the US *Journal of Marketing*, as well as the *Journal of Marketing Management* Millennium Article award.

Yoram (Jerry) Wind is the Lauder Professor and Professor of Marketing at The Wharton School. He joined the Wharton faculty in 1967, with a doctorate from Stanford University. He is the founding director of The SEI Center for Advanced Studies in Management, the founding academic director of The Wharton Fellows Program and founding editor of Wharton School Publishing. From 1995 to 1997, he led the development of the Wharton globalization strategy. Dr. Wind led the reinvention of the Wharton MBA curriculum (1991–1993) and the creation of the Wharton Executive MBA Program (1974). Dr. Wind was the founding director of the Joseph H. Lauder Institute (1983–1988) and the Wharton International Forum (1987). He has served in editorial positions for many top marketing journals. He has published over 250 papers and articles and more than 20 books. Dr. Wind has consulted and conducted research for over 100 companies and has served as an expert witness in several intellectual property and antitrust cases. He is a member of the advisory boards for various entrepreneurial ventures and a trustee of the Philadelphia Museum of Art. He received all the major marketing awards including The Charles Coolidge Parlin Award (1985), AMA/Irwin Distinguished Educator Award (1993), the Paul D. Converse Award (1996) and the Elsevier Science Distinguished Scholar Award of the Society of Marketing Advances (2003). Dr. Wind is former Chancellor of the International Academy of Management, and co-founder of the Interdisciplinary Center, Herzliya (IDC) and chair of its academic council and university appointment and promotion committee.

Len Tiu Wright is Professor of Marketing and Research Professor at De Montfort University, Leicester and Visiting Professor at the University of Keele. She has held full-time appointments at the universities of Keele, Birmingham and Loughborough and visiting lecturing positions with institutions in the UK, for example Cambridge University and overseas. Len Tiu has consultancy and industrial experience and has researched in the Far East, Europe and North America. Her writings have appeared in books, in American and European academic journals, and at conferences where some have gained best paper awards. She is on the editorial boards of a number of leading marketing journals. She is Founding Editor of the *Qualitative Market Research*, An International Journal, an Emerald publication.

Tony Yeshin is currently Senior Lecturer in Marketing at the University of Greenwich. Prior to joining the University, his entire career was spent in the field of marketing communications, predominantly within advertising and Sales Promotion. In 1972, with a colleague, he started a company – The Above and Below Group – specifically designed to create integrated marketing communications (IMC) programmes for its diverse clients. Having worked on a wide range of both domestic and international accounts, his practical experience of developing and implementing marketing communications programmes is now combined with a solid academic background. He is the author of several books. His first, *Inside Advertising*, was published by the professional body, the Institute of Practitioners in Advertising. He is the co-author of the *Chartered Institute of Marketing Postgraduate Coursebook on Integrated Marketing Communications*, and the author of the text *Integrated Marketing Communications: The Holistic Approach* (Butterworth-Heinemann, 1998). He has recently written two in-depth texts on specific areas of marketing communications – Advertising (2005) and Sales promotion (2006).

Leigh Sparks has been professor at Stirling University since 1992. He has also been Head of the Department of Marketing, Director of the Institute for Retail Studies and Dean of the Faculty of Management. From July 2000 to July 2001, Leigh was Visiting Professor at Florida State University in Tallahassee, and from June to December, 2006 he was Visiting Professor at the University of Tennessee at Knoxville. He is Co-editor of the leading European retail journal, *The International Review of Retail,*

Distribution and Consumer Research, published by Taylor and Francis. Since January 2002, Leigh has been Director of the SHEFC funded Centre for the Study of Retailing in Scotland, a research centre based at the Institute for Retail Studies at the University of Stirling, but combining with excellence in retailing in other Scottish universities. In 2002–2004, he was the only academic member of the UK Department of Trade and Industry's Retail Strategy Group.

Andrea Prothero is Senior Lecturer in Marketing at University College Dublin, Ireland. Prior to this, she worked at universities in Soctland and Wales and also enjoyed a sabbatical period at Arizona State University in the USA. Dr Prothero's research interests focus on marketing's impact in society, and she has published widely in this area.

Arch G. Woodside (PhD in Business Administration, Pennsylvania State University) is Professor of Marketing, Carroll School of Management, Boston College. He is a Fellow of the American Psychological Association, American Psychological Society, Royal Society of Canada, the Society for Marketing Advances, and the International Academy for the Study of Tourism. His research reports include articles in the *Journal of Travel Research, Annals of Tourism Research, Tourism Management, Canadian Journal of Administrative Sciences, Tourism Analysis, Journal of Applied Psychology, Journal of Marketing, Psychology & Marketing, Journal of Marketing Research, Journal of Social Psychology*, and 32 additional research journals. He is the author, co-author, and editor of 32 books on research in culture, tourism, advertising, management, and marketing—*Market-Driven Thinking* (2005), *Brand Choice* (2006), *Innovation and Diffusion of Software Technology* (2008), and *Tourism Management* (2008) are example of these works. He teaches research methods workshops and courses for faculty members and Ph.D. students annually as an invited professor in Australia, South America, Europa and Asia; in 1997 this work includes a Ph.D. research methods course at Feng Chiu University, Taiwan; University of Innsbruck; and Auckland University of Technology.

Kathleen Ferris-Costa is a PhD student in marketing, at the University of Rhode Island College of Business Administration. In addition to Chapter 7 she has also co-authored several B2B chapters and articles in the industrial marketing and purchasing literature. Her research interests include word-of-mouth communications, behavioural science applications in marketing, and business-to-business marketing. One focus of her research is on the building of case-based reasoning models that move empirical positivists versus existential phenomenologists to a rapprochement via system dynamics modeling and mixed methods research strategies in B2B settings.

Preface to the sixth edition

The sixth edition of *The Marketing Book* is a testimony to both the continuing demand for an authoritative overview of the marketing discipline and the constantly changing nature of its subject matter. First published in 1987 to coincide with the Michael Baker's appointment as the first academic National Chairman of the Institute of Marketing, the original concept was:

> To produce an authoritative handbook setting out the scope and nature of the marketing function, its managerial applications and its contribution to corporate success.

To implement this concept, contributing authors were advised: '*The Marketing Book* should serve as first point of reference for experienced practitioners and managers from other functions, and as an introduction to those embarking on a career in marketing. In short, the kind of book which every member and student of the Chartered Institute of Marketing will find relevant and useful.'

The fact that the book has been continuously in print for 20 years and is now in its sixth edition is clear evidence that there is a continuing need for such a publication. However, at least two significant factors have influenced the preparation of this new edition. First, the original editor has retired from full-time involvement in the marketing academy and is now an Emeritus Professor. So, to ensure both continuity and currency, Professor Susan Hart, Professor of Marketing and Vice Dean Research in the Strathclyde Business School, has been invited to act as co-editor. Second, the international success of the book and its translation into other languages, together with the impact of globalization, have resulted in a reconsideration of the original remit which was that the contributors be drawn exclusively from the UK marketing community. For this edition, the publishers have encouraged us to include contributions from leading international experts and this we have done. As the majority of contributors are based in the UK, the current collection reflects a British view of what is important and relevant in the theory and practice of marketing. Obviously, this view recognizes and reflects international perspectives but, in a subject where so much published work is written from a purely American point of view, I consider it important that an alternative, albeit similar, interpretation be available. That said, there can be no doubt that this has been enhanced by the views of our international experts.

While it is unlikely that anyone other than the Editors and Publisher would wish to make an analysis of the content of successive editions, such a review would reveal that while some contributions have changed very little, others have been extensively updated, a few topics have been dropped and a significant number of new ones added. In parallel, the list of contributing authors has also changed markedly over the years. However, the present roll of contributors shares a common feature with all the preceding editions – the authors are all leading experts in their fields. All have published widely on the topics for which they are responsible and many of them have written one or more definitive and widely used textbooks on the subject of their contribution.

Four chapters have been dropped from the last edition, twelve chapters have new authors and four new chapters have been added. In every case, the reason for omitting these chapters is that their content is covered by other entries. Some of these are completely new and are evidence of the way in which the subject of marketing is developing, while others mirror the incorporation of what were emerging areas into mainstream marketing. All these chapters are, of course, still available in the fifth edition.

A number of chapters remain much the same as they appeared in the fifth edition. These are:

Chapter 1   'One more time – what is marketing?' by Michael J. Baker
Chapter 2   'Postmodern marketing' by Stephen Brown
Chapter 3   'Relationship marketing' by O'Malley and Tynan
Chapter 4   'The basics of marketing strategy' by Robin Wensley
Chapter 5   'Strategic marketing planning: theory and practice' by Malcolm McDonald
Chapter 10   'Quantitative methods for research in marketing' by Luiz Mouthino
Chapter 13   'New product development' by Susan Hart
Chapter 15   'Selling and sales management' by Bill Donaldson
Chapter 28   'Green marketing' by Ken Peattie

All these chapters have been updated with some new material, some quite radically, and more recent references where appropriate. They all meet the criteria that they give a clear and authoritative overview of their subject matter.

Given the strictures of our good friend and Publisher, Tim Goodfellow, not to exceed the limit of 450 000 words for this edition, we will restrict our comments on the content of this edition to a minimum necessary to give you a foretaste of the content.

Chapter 1: One more time – what is marketing? Right from the start, Baker's chapter robustly asserts that marketing as practised in British Industry bears as little relationship to professional marketing as over the counter potions of alternative therapies do to professional medical disciplines and practice. Having stated the position that marketing is, as medicine before, in a process of transition from an art to a profession with strong theoretical foundations, the chapter goes on to trace some of the underlying theories behind marketing as both managerial orientation and a business function. As managerial orientation, marketing is allied to the notion of product differentiation as a means of gaining competitive advantage, with a customer orientation as the driver of the distinguishing feature of the product or service. The chapter, then, goes on to outline the history of the function of marketing and its much reported (and greatly exaggerated) 'death'. In so doing, the advent of the Internet with its implications for marketing is discussed. There follows an expanded discussion regarding the nature of competition, drawing comparisons between the Anglo-Saxon models of capitalism and the Alpine Germanic, wherein the latter, adopting a long-term perspective, is the link to a more relational perspective on marketing. The derivation, diagnosis and prognosis for relationship marketing are considered before a direct comparison between the transactional and relational view of marketing is made. In the final section of the chapter, attention is turned to the debate surrounding 'a new model of marketing'. In reviewing the article by Vargo and Lusch (2004), the chapter concludes that the concept of marketing management may have paid insufficient attention to consumers wants, but it has done much in catering for their needs.

Chapter 2 'Postmodern marketing' by Stephen Brown was new to the last edition and discusses an important new trend in marketing thought. Since the Enlightenment of the eighteenth century, the dominant model for research has been positivistic. The defining characteristic of positivism has been a belief in the existence of an objective reality that can be defined, explained and understood through the application of scientific methods. In turn, this belief has given rise to 'modern' society, of which mass production, mass consumption and modern marketing are major manifestations. It would seem, therefore, that 'postmodern' must refer to the nature of society that has or is likely to evolve out of the 'modern' state. To establish, if this is or is not the case, we invited one of the most widely published and cited authorities on the subject – Stephen Brown – to contribute a chapter on the subject. Its positioning immediately after my own attempts to define modern marketing is deliberate.

It would be facile to try and summarize Stephen's chapter. However, in our view it provides one of the clearest expositions of what postmodern marketing is or is perceived to be. (It is also written in his own distinctive and entertaining style.) Whether or not you are converted to this perspective of marketing, it is important that you are aware of its defining characteristics as with the more traditional views contained in Chapter 1.

Chapter 3 deals with a topic – 'Relationship marketing' – that has been widely referred to in earlier editions (and in this edition). Several pages were given to the topic in Baker's introductory chapter in earlier editions and are retained in this one. However, relationship marketing (RM) has evolved to become the dominant paradigm in marketing and deserves an entry of its own.

While there are many distinguished authors that might have been approached to contribute this chapter, the choice of Lisa O'Malley and Caroline Tynan was an obvious one. As the authors make clear, relationship marketing has evolved over the past 30 years or so as a re-conceptualization of the *transactional* model of marketing, based upon the application of the marketing mix to the marketing of mass-produced products to large, homogeneous consumer markets. This model was seen to be inappropriate in industrial or business-to-business markets, and also to the marketing of services, and a new approach based on the creation and maintenance of relationships began to emerge. Accordingly, 'The purpose of this chapter is to begin to describe how the rich body of knowledge that is relationship marketing has come into being, what its major underpinning theories are, what defining moments occurred, and what might shape its future'.

In our view, it accomplishes this in a clear and scholarly way. Plainly, having evolved from a number of different, albeit complementary, research traditions, relationship marketing is not a single monolithic concept – 'Indeed, relationship marketing is less a coherent body of knowledge and more a collection of loosely aligned understandings'. To know what these are, how they have developed and how they might be applied in practice, this chapter is 'must' reading. And, for those wishing to dig deeper, the References are an invaluable resource in their own right.

Chapters 4 and 5 – 'On marketing strategy and strategic marketing planning' by Robin Wensley and Malcom McDonald – appeared in the First Edition and with appropriate updating remain classic introductions to the subject matter and a sound foundation for further study.

Chapter 6, 'Consumer behaviour', is by the 'new' author, Mark Gabbott of Monash University in Australia. Gabbott's overview of consumer behaviour begins with the often forgotten fact that nothing is more central to marketing than consumption, or as Adam Smith said in his 1776 *Wealth of Nations*, 'consumption is the sole and only purpose of production'. Acknowledging this central role in practice, however, the chapter equally notes that the definition of consumer behaviour at the core of consumption is extremely wide in scope and has produced numerous sub-fields which are often contradictory. The chapter traces the development of consumer behaviour studies and their intellectual origins, from the economic, through to the behavioural, presenting the key models of consumer behaviour. It, then, outlines the layers of actors involved in the process of consumer decision making before considering more contemporary perspectives of consumer behaviour.

Chapter 7 – 'Business-to-business marketing, organizational buying behaviour, interfirm relationships, and network behaviour' – is contributed by American authors Arch G. Woodside and Kathleen R. Ferris-Costa. As they point out, *Business marketing* is the practice of organizations, including commercial businesses, governments and institutions, facilitating the sale of their products or services to other companies or organizations that in turn resell them, use them as components in products or services they offer, or use them to support their operations. Also known as industrial marketing, business marketing is also called business-to-business marketing, or *B2B* marketing, for short. B2B marketing is larger in size of revenues than B2C (business-to-consumer) marketing because B2B marketing includes all inter-organizational transactions involving suppliers, manufacturers, agents, distributors, retailers, transportation firms, financial enterprises and government departments. Thus, learning how firms implement B2B strategies and attempt to evaluate and improve the effectiveness and efficiency of such strategies are worthy topics for training by executives and students.

The chapter serves as an introduction to the body of applied and scholarly work focusing on B2B marketing, organizational buying behaviour, relationships and networks. Aims of the chapter include stimulating the reader to seek out the sources of work that these pages summarize as well as to present a few core propositions for crafting and implementing effective strategies relevant for firms operating in B2B markets. To keep the present treatise to a reasonable length, the chapter mostly focuses on the following five topics:

1 Insights on how B2B is similar to and differs from B2C marketing-purchasing behaviour and strategies.
2 Deductive modelling of B2B marketing-purchasing behaviour.
3 Inductive modelling of B2B marketing-purchasing behaviour.
4 Innovation and diffusion decisions and strategy propositions.
5 B2B network research findings and strategy implications.

Wilson's overview of contemporary marketing research notes that the way in which information, information technology and more broadly, market knowledge is gathered, stored, accessed and used in marketing have significantly changed the role and nature of marketing research. The chapter, then, goes on to outline the key stages in the market research process and in so doing, explicitly deals with the agency/client interface in the writing of research briefs and proposals, including how agencies are selected for a particular piece of research. Discussion of the different types of research is provided, together with an overview of the kinds of decisions that require these different types of research. The chapter examines sources of secondary data, their purposes and gives an overview of the key factors governing the choices on data collection strategies employed. Finally, discussion turns to the consideration of ethics in market research, incorporating data protection and codes of practice.

Len Tiu Wright's chapter 'Qualitative research' is 'first' for the *Marketing Book* and complements Luiz Mouthino's wide ranging chapter on quantitative methods that has been a feature of the book since its first edition. The reason for the delay in giving explicit recognition to the importance of qualitative research in part reflects the influence of the Ford Foundation and Carnegie reports on business education in the 1950s which argued for a positivistic/scientific approach to research rather than the interpretivistic/judgemental methods widely used in the 'soft' social sciences. At the same time, it also reflected the original Editor's view that many, if not the majority of academics and practitioners, were more comfortable and familiar with qualitative research methods so that the need in a book of this kind was for a clear exposition of the wide range of quantitative methods available and their application to marketing research and practice.

While this belief still holds, and the chapter on Quantitative Methods which follows is one of the longest in the book, there has been growing recognition of the importance of qualitative methods as a means of gaining greater insight into the reasons *why* the actors in exchange relationships behave in the way they do in order to understand concepts like 'relationships' and 'loyalty'. In turn this has prompted growing interest in qualitative methods widely used in other social sciences such as ethnography, narrative and story telling and the use of grounded theory and case studies. So, as the author advises in the introduction to her chapter, it concerns:

> . . . the *importance of qualitative research in marketing*. It is not in the remit of this chapter to cover the numerous typologies and specialisms of qualitative research used in the social sciences. The chapter's orientation is directed at where some of the traditions and applications inherent in qualitative research are suited to marketing. Definitions and scope of qualitative research are provided. Background aspects are provided about the growth of qualitative research, theoretical underpinnings for and differences of qualitative and quantitative approaches, including what validity, reliability and triangulation mean in qualitative research. These are followed by reflections on existing traditional types of enquiry namely: autobiography, biography, ethnography, grounded theory, phenomenology and the case study. Data collection methods and the applicability of qualitative research to the broader realms of international marketing are examined. The chapter concludes with a brief prognosis for qualitative research in marketing.

So, if you are not sure what ontology and epistemology mean, or how ethnography or phenomenology might contribute to the development of more effective marketing strategies, this is the chapter for you. Furthermore, you will be introduced to a range of methods and their applications as well as important issues like validity and reliability.

Chapter 10, 'Quantitative methods in marketing', has appeared in every edition of the book, although on this occasion it is under the sole authorship of Luiz Mouthino of Glasgow University following the retirement of Arthur Meidan. **SH comment**
Market segmentation, together with targeting and positioning, is central to the development of marketing plans and the selection of the most effective marketing mix. Essentially, the marketing planner has the choice of two basic approaches – product differentiation and market segmentation. In the case of product differentiation, the supplier develops an offering that differs in some material and important way from other competitive offerings which, they believe, will attract customers to them but without any clear idea who they will be. Conversely, suppliers following a strategy of market segmentation start by identifying unsatisfied customer needs and develop new offerings to care specifically for these.

For over 30 years now, Yoram (Jerry) Wind has been recognized as an international expert on the subject of market segmentation and, in Chapter 11, he and co-author David Bell provide a clear, up-to-date and authoritative overview of the subject. While the authors acknowledge that many of the fundamental approaches to market segmentation have remained the same since the 1970s, they point out,

> Despite the underlying stability of the basic concept, recent advances in information technology and the trend towards globalization are introducing a discontinuous change to the adoption and implementation of segmentation strategies. The revolution in information technology and strategy makes possible the creation of databases on the entire universe and enormous advances in database marketing and innovative distribution approaches. It has also facilitated much of the development in flexible manufacturing with the consequent emergence of mass customization. In addition, the Internet has expanded not only the ability to implement market segmentation research more effectively, but also the portfolio of segmentation methods available for use (see e.g. Dahan and Srinivasan, 2004). These changes are leading to the creation of 'one-on-one marketing' or segments of one. The globalization of business expands the scope of operations and requires a new approach to local, regional and global segments.

In light of these changes, not only a re-appraisal of what we know about segmentation, and what works and does not work, but also a review of the segmentation area as part of an entirely new marketing and management paradigm.

Accordingly, the authors' objective is 'to introduce the reader to both the "best practice" in the segmentation area and the likely new developments. These observations are based on advances in marketing concepts, marketing science research and modelling tools, generalizations from empirical studies, successful practices of leading firms and the conceptual implications of operating in the global information age.'

To achieve their object, five issues are discussed in detail:

1 Use of segmentation in marketing and business strategy.
2 Decisions required for the implementation of a segmentation strategy.
3 Advances in segmentation research.
4 Impact of operating in the global information age on segmentation theory, practice and research.
5 Expansion of segmentation to other stakeholders.

Thus, this chapter is based on the premise that segmentation is the firm's response to a fundamental market feature – heterogeneity. The likely success (or otherwise) of the firm's segmentation strategy is assessed through a segmentation audit discussed next. The firm enacts the segmentation strategy through three factors: (1) data collection, (2) application of models and frameworks and (3) resource allocation and differential action based on segment (customer) value. The chapter concludes with a set of critical issues that provide the guidelines for the research agenda in this area.

This chapter meets exactly the objectives of *The Marketing Book*. For someone completely new to the subject, it provides a succinct summary of all the key issues; for someone wishing to update their knowledge of the latest development, it does just that and provides detailed references that can be followed up as required.

In 2003, the UK marketing academy lost one of its leading lights with the untimely death of Professor Peter Doyle. Peter's contribution to marketing thinking and practice was immense and his views on shareholder value as the responsibility of marketing value provides the vehicle for the marketing professional to have an increasing impact in the boardroom. The Editors debated omitting a chapter on the *Marketing Mix* but, given continuing interest in and use of the concept, decided this was not appropriate. Michael drew the short straw.

The marketing mix – specifically the 4Ps – is often considered the cause for embarrassment in marketing academia. This chapter traces the history of the 4Ps, making the point that, as an *aide-memoire*, the 4Ps are representative of many more factors of marketing decisions and these are also subject to a wide variety of influences. The chapter gives an overview of the components of the marketing mix and discusses their weaknesses and criticisms of the marketing mix, in particular that there should be a 1P extension to include *people*. Moreover, there is extensive discussion of key articles which have suggested that the marketing mix be left behind as a relic from a distant past, but the chapter also examines more recent work which seeks to establish a balanced perspective on the utility of the 4 or 5Ps model of the marketing mix.

Chapter 13, 'New product development', is contributed by Susan Hart, Professor of Marketing and Vice Dean Research, Strathclyde Business School. With more than two decades experience of researching and publishing internationally on issues covering all aspect of product strategy and management, and co-author of a definitive textbook on the subject, Susan is the obvious choice of 'expert witness'.

In this chapter, the activities, their sequence and organization required to develop new products are discussed in the light of an extensive body of research into what distinguishes successful from unsuccessful new products.

The focus of the chapter is exclusively on how new products are developed. Starting with the proposition that it takes more than a good idea to make a successful new product, the main activities needed to bring a new product to market successfully are described. In so doing, the main critical success factors for new product development (NPD) which have been revealed through research are woven into the discussion of the process models commonly exhorted as the blueprints for success. In turn, this discussion highlights the importance of market information to the successful completion of NDP projects, but it also shows that blind adherence to a model for NPD cannot be productive as the whole business needs to be characterized by flexibility and open to creativity from various sources within and outside companies. The principal argument is that information is a central thread of successful NPD. The NPD process is one of uncertainty reduction which requires information, constant evaluation of options, which requires information and integration of various functional perspectives, as well as the sharing of information. A review and critique of the current models reveals their contribution to and constraints on the process of developing new products and suggestions are derived from recent research as to how they might be improved and managed.

In his chapter, 'Pricing', Cram explains the importance of pricing as an element of marketing and gets to the heart of the problem: mismanagement. The chapter explains the reasons underlying its mismanagement and explores the consequences of over-simplified approaches to taking pricing decisions. The chapter then reviews the classic methods for setting prices, or for thinking about setting prices, and gives an overview of issues from the points of view of customers, competitors and the company taking the decisions. The chapter ends with a discussion of pricing effectiveness.

Chapter 15, 'Selling and sales management', by Bill Donaldson has been a feature of *The Marketing Book* for several editions. But, as the author observes, 'The role of selling is continuing to change and evolve in response to dramatic moves in the way buyers and sellers interact. Individual knowledge, skills and abilities are still required, perhaps more than ever, but teamwork and technology are also vital ingredients in an effective organizational response to the needs and demands of customers. The sales force have always been ambassadors for their firm, but in a turbulent business environment, the information and persuasion role of salespeople is being absorbed into their relationship role. Salespeople must take responsibility for creating, developing and maintaining profitable relationships with their customers. This being so, the paramount need is to focus on how to win, develop and retain customers to achieve the marketing and sales objectives of the firm. This puts the spotlight once again on the role of selling in the marketing mix and on the management of sales operations. Sales operations are the revenue generation engine of the organization and thus have a direct impact on the success of the firm. In this chapter, we consider how selling is changing and evolving. We examine the strategic nature of sales and the new role of salespeople and redefine the sales encounter in different exchange situations. We then address some of the key issues in managing the salesforce as they relate to marketing'.

Chapter 16, 'Brand building', is by Leslie de Chernatony, an international authority on the subject. Brands, branding and brand building are all terms of multiple interpretation, as the chapter acknowledges in its introduction. A comprehensive overview of different brand interpretations is given, including logos, legal instruments, a company, shorthand for a product, service or firm, to name but a few. These are clearly distinguished before a detailed exploration of how to build brands strategically using a model of brand planning, which takes the reader through a number of stages. These include articulating a brand vision, consideration of the organization's culture, setting brand objectives, auditing the brand, distilling brand essence, internal implementation and resourcing. The chapter finishes with a discussion of the evaluation of brands which encourage reflection on the achievements at each stage in the model.

Chapter 17, 'Integrated marketing communications', by Tony Yeshin appeared first in the previous edition and reflected a trend that has accelerated since. While the need to employ different communication techniques has long been recognized and is reflected in different specializations – advertising, sales promotion, public relations, etc. – it is only in the last two decades or so that explicit recognition has been given to the need to integrate these into a single communication strategy. As Yeshin observes,

> Integrated marketing communications is significant to the consumer, although they are unaware of the concept. They recognize integration and see it logically as making it easier for them to build an overall brand picture. In essence, links between the media are seen as:
>
> • providing short cuts to understanding what a brand stands for;
> • adding depth and 'amplifying' a particular message or set of brand values;
> • demonstrating professionalism on the part of the brand owner.

Given that the seller's primary concern is to position their brand clearly in the prospective customer's mind, the pressure to integrate their marketing communications is obvious and more so now with the emergence of new approaches including e-marketing, product placement, the organization of trade and consumer events, sponsorship activities and so on now abound. Individual specialist companies can now provide clients with inputs in areas such as the design and production of point-of-sale materials, the creation of trade and consumer incentives, pack design and guerilla marketing techniques, amongst many others. Even in the mainstream areas, agencies have become specialized in terms of youth or grey marketing, FMCG or retail marketing communications; dealing with pharmaceutical products or travel and tourism. And the specialisms continue.

As Yeshin notes, 'The essential requirement of the "new marketing" approach is the development of a close customer focus throughout the organization which, in turn, demands an understanding of customers as individuals in order to appreciate their perceptions, expectations, needs and wants. The increasing availability of tools to enable the marketer to achieve this deeper understanding of the consumer, similarly demands the re-evaluation of the ways in which the tools employed to communicate with those consumers are used'.

For persons seeking a clear explanation of the nature of IMC, of the strategic role it can play in managing the 'intangible side of business', through assisting in building relationships with customers and other stakeholders and in creating positive perceptions, attitudes and behaviours towards brands and of how to achieve integration, this chapter is a 'must read'.

As Yeshin points out, 'If all other things are equal – or at least more or less so – then it is what people think, feel and believe about a product and its competitors which will be important. Since products in many areas will achieve parity or comparability in purely functional terms, it will be the perceptual differences which consumers will use to discriminate between rival brands. Only through the use of sustained and IMC campaigns, will manufacturers be able to achieve the differentiation they require'.

Having defined the nature and origins of IMC in some detail, Yeshin reviews the factors that have precipitated the growing interest in the subject. The impact and benefits of IMC are, then, spelled out followed by a detailed review of the organizational issues involved in developing an integrated approach. Finally, the potential barriers to achieving IMC are discussed, as are the international implications.

Because of the major changes that have taken place in marketing communications in recent years reflected in Chapter 17, the chapters on *Promotion* and *Sales Promotion* that appeared in earlier editions have been omitted from this edition. In their place are chapters on *Mass Communication* and *Direct Marketing*.

Chapter 18, 'Mass communications', is by Professor Douglas West, Professor of Marketing in the Birmingham Business School and Editor of the *International Journal of Advertising*.

Despite the contemporary view that Mass Communications are of the past, this chapter by Douglas West does an excellent job of contextualizing mass communications' development within the multi-media one-to-one age. The chapter covers how to formulate mass media in terms of the audience, geographic area, seasonality and the creative proposition. The choice of media and media buying is given comprehensive coverage also, with detailed discussion of the print media, television, web, radio and cinema.

Chapter 19, 'What do we mean by direct, data and digital marketing?', provides a very accessible and authentic overview of direct, data and digital marketing by Professor Derek Holder FIDM Founder and Managing Director, Institute of Direct Marketing. Voted the third most influential person in direct marketing by readers of *Precision Marketing* and Co-Editor of the internationally recognized *Journal of Direct, Data and Digital Marketing*, it would be difficult to find someone better qualified for the task.

Since Lester Wunderman first coined the term 'direct marketing' in 1961, experienced marketing people are still arguing about what direct marketing is. From those early days, we have seen the rise of new (or enhanced) methodologies bearing descriptions such as 'database marketing', 'relationship marketing', 'interactive marketing' and 'digital marketing'. In this chapter, Holder sets out to set the record straight and discuss the essential similarities and differences between direct marketing and these newcomers.

In answering his rhetorical question, 'What do we mean by direct, data and digital marketing?', the author looks at the origins of direct marketing, its adoption by multichannel users and how its disciplines underpin all that has followed its inception. This includes a discussion of the four basic principles of direct marketing: Targeting, Interaction, Control and Continuity (TICC), and introduces the direct, data and digital marketer's information system, establishing its context within the company-wide information system.

The author concludes that whilst the term 'direct marketing' may still carry many prejudices and misunderstandings, the skill sets that direct marketers have honed over the years are even more vital to major businesses today. Direct marketing is still the most accountable form of marketing. Its concepts such as lifetime value help to determine the value of customer relationships and are as important as brand equity. Direct marketers are also better versed at managing the customer journey, understanding the touchpoints and building a one-to-one dialogue with customers. Equally, direct marketers understand profiling and customer value segmentation better than general marketers as it is based on the empirical customer data they maintain. Building, maintaining and utilizing customer databases are at the heart of direct marketing's strengths. Digital media has finally made one-to-one communications in real time possible.

Customer Relationship Management is a subject with a wide variation of meaning to different stakeholder groups, those investing in systems, those implementing the investments, those designing the systems and the customer. In the chapter, 'Customer relationship management', Payne and Frow take a strategic approach, addressing five inter-related cross functional processes: strategy development, value creation, multichannel integration, information management and performance assessment, each being a large area for research and practice in its own right.

A major criticism of marketing in the past has been that it lacks objective performance measures enabling assessment of its contribution to competitive success. Against this background, the Marketing Science Institute in the USA identified 'Marketing Metrics' as the most important research issue in its programme for the years 2000 to 2004. This, then, is the theme of Chapter 21 and who better to address it than Tim Ambler, Senior Fellow, London Business School who has written extensively on the subject. As he explains in his introduction, 'Marketers have long felt marginalized or at least under pressure to justify their plans. They may not look for accountability but there is increasing acceptance that quantification, preferably in financial terms, of plans and performance is an increasing factor in marketing . . . Marketing performance measurement has traditionally focused on top line financial metrics such as sales and sales growth (Clark, 1999). More recently, financial attention has shifted to the bottom line expressed as net cash flow, profits or shareholder value'.

This chapter is structured as follows. After reviewing the theoretical, empirical and brand equity measurement literature, management practice is explored first in terms of its presumed evolution and then metrics usage. From this, some lessons for good and bad practice can be drawn and specifically in three areas: discounted cash flow (DCF), return on investment (ROI) and the benchmarks used for performance metrics comparison. DCF methods include customer lifetime value, customer equity and brand valuation. The metrics used for planning purposes, for example, are not necessarily suitable for performance evaluation. Brand equity needs to be formally measured but, on the other hand, searching for a single financial performance indicator ('the silver metric') is misguided. After suggesting where future research is needed, the chapter concludes with a summary of the findings.

Lloyd C. Harris' entertaining chapter on how to implement strategic change begins with a broad ranging discussion of why it is difficult to implement strategic plans, especially those that require significant change, and gives numerous methods and examples of how change is resisted or subverted in organizations. The chapter discusses equally how these tactics might be successfully challenged and gives a perspective on ten levers for implementing change, linking these to ideas from within the research on internal marketing.

Services marketing – and marketing in general – is in turbulent flux. This claim constitutes the vantage point for chapter 23 contributed by Professor Evert Gummesson of Stockhom University entitled 'Exit *services* marketing – Enter *service* marketing'.

Evert is recognized internationally as one of the first researchers to inquire into the nature and importance of services marketing, and this chapter is a synthesis of research, practical experience as marketer and consumer, and personal ideas about where marketing is heading. As such it constitutes a highly original and up-to-date evaluation of current thinking on the subject. Those looking for a more complete overview of concepts, models, authors and cases in services marketing are referred to textbooks and other overviews listed in the Recommendations for Further Reading.

Given the nature of the chapter, it is probably wisest to let the author introduce it himself:

> When in the 1970s, services immigrated to Marketingland and applied for citizenship, it was in protest against the hegemony of goods marketing. The initial sections of the chapter elaborate on the distinction between services and goods marketing, bearing in mind that goods (things) and services (activities) always appear together. So far, research in marketing and textbooks have not been able to integrate this insight with general marketing theory. The chapter proposes that the time is ripe for a merger on a higher level of validity and relevance.
>
> Through the concept of the service-dominant logic (Vargo and Lusch, 2004a; Lusch and Vargo, 2006), a daring and constructive effort has been made to turn what we know so far into a tentative synthesis. Their logic opened up an international dialogue on the output of marketing as value propositions rather than as goods or services. By further appointing the customer co-creator of value, the roles of supplier and customer become blurred and require redefinition.
>
> The chapter further brings in the marketing mix and what it stands for today. It considers the mix and the well-known value chain as primarily supplier-centric. It dethrones the mix to the second level of marketing and elevates networks of relationships in which we interact to the first level. So far, relational approaches – relationship marketing, CRM and one-to-one marketing – have been primarily focused on the dyad, the customer-supplier relationship. The chapter suggests a transition from customer-centricity to a balanced centricity of the interests of multiple parties. This requires a network, many-to-many, approach to marketing. The chapter ends with a summary and an epilogue.

Chapter 24, 'International marketing', by Angela da Rocha and Jorge Ferreira da Silva begins by tracing the challenges and opportunities afforded by the forces of globalization that have had a profound effect on the way companies compete and the effect of this competition on the social and economic welfare of people around the world. In their wide-ranging chapter, the authors explore the cultural, social and economic, as well as the political and institutional environments as backdrops to a discussion of how firms internationalize. In dealing with the internationalization process of firms, the selection of foreign markets, choice of entry mode marketing strategies and marketing mix programmes are discussed.

Holder's earlier chapter on direct and interactive marketing provides a natural introduction to the chapter by Dave Chaffey on e-marketing. Given the spectacular failure of a number of dotcom companies in recent years, there is a need for a critical appraisal of the potential of e-marketing. This is provided in this chapter.

Opening with a set of clear definitions of various aspects of e-marketing, Chaffey, then, identifies the key communications characteristics of digital media as the basis for determining how these may be used to best effect. Once these are understood, it is possible to develop an e-marketing plan, and Chaffey proposes using his SOSTAC framework which embraces Situation analysis, Objectives and Strategy, Tactics, Action and Control. This structure is broadly consistent with other models of strategic marketing planning, as described by Malcolm McDonald in Chapter 5. Each of these elements is discussed in detail.

Chaffey concludes that while a minority of businesses have converted extensively to the use of the Internet, for most it simply represents another channel to the market. This chapter and Dave Chaffey's textbooks from which it has been developed provide comprehensive advice on how best to incorporate the Internet into more effective marketing practice.

In the last edition, separate chapters dealt with the subjects of cause-related marketing and social marketing. In this edition, these have been combined into a new chapter 'Marketing for non-profit organizations' by Adrian Sargeant, who is the Robert F Hartsook Professor of Fundraising, School of Public and Environmental Affairs, Indiana University.

Kotler and Levy (1969) are credited with opening the academic debate on the transferability of the marketing concept arguing that marketing had for too long been regarded as a narrow business function and rebuking both academics and practitioners for ignoring the broader relevance of our ideas. In the early 1980s, the first generic non-profit marketing textbooks appeared. Textbooks also began to appear in the specific fields of healthcare, education, the Arts, the marketing of ideas, social marketing and most recently, fundraising. In parallel, a wide range of scholarly journals was launched and it was also not unusual to find journals from other disciplines printing studies from the field of non-profit marketing.

Many marketing ideas, models and frameworks have as much relevance to the non-profit as the for-profit domain. Indeed, the eminent marketer scholar Shelby Hunt argued that a profit/non-profit dichotomy would only be valuable until:

1   The broadening of the marketing concept was no longer regarded as controversial.
2   The non-profit sector and the issues that must be addressed therein was completely integrated into all marketing courses and not treated as a separate subject.
3   Non-profit managers perceived their organizations as having marketing problems.
4   Non-profits established marketing departments (where appropriate) and employed marketing personnel.

Since the adoption of marketing ideas in the non-profit arena is no longer controversial and many non-profits now employ marketing personnel to address marketing issues, the second of Hunt's tests seems the only area of difficulty. Non-profit marketing has yet to be properly integrated into 'mainstream' marketing courses, quite possibly because it is seen as being of less interest to the majority of marketing students and/or employers. While this may seem intuitive, it fails to reflect the pattern of the majority of modern careers, where many individuals will now work for a variety of employers and quite possibly in a variety of different contexts. The need for a broader perspective on the subject has, therefore, never been greater.

However, Sargeant argues cogently that the subject of marketing for non-profits has now grown to the extent that it could not really be accommodated with a generic marketing course and deserves recognition as a subject in its own right. The reasons for adopting this view are explained in detail in this chapter which provides an excellent introduction to and overview of the topic and makes a strong case why the adaptation of marketing thought is essential. As his review shows, blindly applying for-profit ideas is at best counter-productive and at worst may actually injure the organization the marketer is attempting to assist.

While ethical issues are touched on in many of the individual chapters, in this edition we felt it important to deal with them in a chapter of their own which is contributed by Andrea Protheroe. Chapter 27 opens by setting the context for a discussion of ethics in marketing by considering related ideas in business ethics and corporate social responsibility, observing that, from earliest times, philosophers have been concerned with ethical questions in all walks of life, public and private. While noting the way in which business ethics are questioned in contemporary culture, in books, films and documentaries, the chapter focuses on marketing ethics and the fact that marketing is a business function frequently associated with unethical behaviour. Looking at all marketing decisions through an ethical lens is linked to the concepts of macro- and micromarketing, defined as looking at marketing from a macro, or societal level, in the case of the former, or from a micro or firm level, in the case of the latter. Marketing's sins can be seen as operating at both levels, examples of which are also given. In addition, there are the sins of consumers, including consumer fraud, theft and counterfeiting. In contrast, many consumers actively pursue ethical consumption, boycott products and services of organizations they believe to be unethical which in turn leads to a response – in many, if not all, cases – by those organizations.

Professor Ken Peattie of Cardiff Business School opens his chapter, 'Green marketing' with the following statement:

In the wake of the Earth Summits at Rio in 1992 and Johannesburg in 2002, the World's governments and major corporations have generally adopted the pursuit of sustainability as a strategic goal. The challenge lies in turning these good intentions into meaningful progress in the face of powerful vested interests, an entrenched and environmentally hostile dominant social (and management) paradigm and a global economy with tremendous momentum on a trajectory that pursues conventional economic growth.

For marketing, the challenge is two-fold. In the short-term, ecological and social issues have become significant external influences on companies and their markets. Companies are having to react to changing customer needs, new regulations and a new social zeitgeist which reflects increasing concern about the socio-environmental impacts of business. In the longer term, the pursuit of sustainability will demand fundamental changes to the management paradigm which underpins marketing and other business functions (Shrivastava, 1994).

Accordingly, the author sets out to illustrate how the 'green challenge' is exerting an influence on current marketing practice, and how its implications will eventually require a more profound shift in the marketing mindset, if marketers are to continue delivering customer satisfaction at a profit. But '[t]he concept of sustainability allows the apparently paradoxical integration of environmental concern (which traditionally involves encouraging conservation), with the discipline of marketing (which is based on seeking to stimulate and facilitate consumption). A sustainable approach to consumption and production involves enjoying a material standard of living today, which is not at the expense of the standard of living and quality of life of future generations'.

This is a deceptively simple concept involving two key principles:

1   Using natural resources at a rate at which environmental systems or human activity can replenish them (or in the case of non-renewable resources, at a rate at which renewable alternatives can be substituted in).
2   Pollution and waste at a rate which can be absorbed by environmental systems without impairing their viability.

Putting this into practice can be extremely difficult. That said, Peattie's chapter covers all the major issues and offers much thoughtful advice on what is possibly the most important challenge facing marketing today – sustainable consumption.

Chapter 29, 'Marketing in emerging economies', by Piyush Kumar and Prathap Oburai of the Indian Institute of Management, Ahmedebad (India's top business school) is a completely new chapter in this edition.

While developments in the so-called BRIC countries (Brazil, Russia, India and China) have been apparent for some years now, it is only since the beginning of the millennium that the impact of these has been fully felt. With China and India set to overtake the USA as the world's largest economy before the middle of the century, an understanding of these countries and their markets is essential. Such an understanding is provided by this chapter, which

1   establishes the nature of the different terrain that marketers in the emerging economies have to deal with;
2   describes the phenomenon of emerging economies;
3   discusses their characteristics;
4   highlights the difference between emerging and emergent economies as well as among the emerging economies;
5   postulates a different development route using the case of India as an example;
6   suggests an approach to marketing in such economies.

Finally, in Chapter 30, Professor Leigh Sparkes of Stirling University takes a wide-ranging look at retailing.

Retailing, as Sparks notes in his introduction, accounts for a large portion of the European – and other – economies, provides employment for millions of workers, is hugely varied in terms of the kinds of businesses it comprises, is increasingly global, and is embedded in culture and leisure, a fact which provokes much criticism. The chapter deals with both the consumer and cultural aspects of retailing as well as the variety of management issues associated with retailing. Culture and consumer behaviour are comprehensively explored, covering aspects of local, national and international cultures, as well as sub-cultures, and these are considered for their implications for retailers. The chapter then goes on to discuss the nature of the decisions involved with retail locations and outlets, their geographic spread, retail managers and contractual arrangements for retail management, product sourcing, branding and distribution, the increased focus on business relationships and loyalty, merchandizing and selling. The chapter concludes first with a review of the contemporary retail world, summarizing the key changes taking place in retailing, including the expanding nature of the retail outlet into superstores and shopping centres of various kinds, retail differentiation, scale and power and the effect of internationalization on international- and national-based retailing. The final section offers a view of the future of retailing, including the need to cope with concerns about ethical and environmental factors and the impact of the Internet.

Compiling a contributed book of this kind is not without its challenges. While it is true that if you want to get something done you should ask a busy person, it is also true that busy people have many compelling calls on their time and writing a chapter for a book may not be their top priority! That said, we are greatly indebted to all the contributors who have, with great good humour, responded to our pleas to meet pressing deadlines. Together, we think, we have achieved our original objective and compiled an original and authoritative handbook that addresses most of, if not all, the key issues and challenges faced by the marketing profession today. We hope you agree.

Michael J. Baker & Susan Hart
Strathclyde University

Part One
Organization and Planning for Marketing

CHAPTER 1

One more time: what is marketing?

MICHAEL J. BAKER

The enigma of marketing is that it is one of man's oldest activities and yet it is regarded as the most recent of the business disciplines.
Michael J. Baker, *Marketing: Theory and Practice*, 1st edn, Macmillan, 1976

Introduction

As a discipline, marketing is in the process of transition from an art which is practised to a profession with strong theoretical foundations. In doing so it is following closely the precedents set by professions such as medicine, architecture and engineering, all of which have also been practised for thousands of years and have built up a wealth of descriptive information concerning the art which has both chronicled and advanced its evolution. At some juncture, however, continued progress demands a transition from description to analysis, such as that initiated by Harvey's discovery of the circulation of the blood. If marketing is to develop it, too, must make the transition from art to applied science and develop sound theoretical foundations, mastery of which should become an essential qualification for practice.

Adoption of this proposition is as threatening to many of today's marketers as the establishment of the British Medical Association was to the surgeon–barber. But, today, you would not dream of going to a barber for medical advice.

Of course, first aid will still be practised, books on healthy living will feature on the bestsellers list and harmless potions will be bought over the counter in drug stores and pharmacies. This is an amateur activity akin to much of what passes for marketing in British industry. While there was no threat of the cancer of competition it might have sufficed, but once the Japanese, Germans and now the emerging economies invade your markets you are going to need much stronger medicine if you are to survive. To do so you must have the courage to face up to the reality that aggressive competition can prove fatal, quickly; have the necessary determination to resist rather than succumb, and seek the best possible professional advice and treatment to assist you. Unfortunately, many people are unwilling to face up to reality. Even more unfortunate, many of the best minds and abilities are concentrated on activities which support the essential functions of an economy, by which we all survive, but have come to believe that these can exist by themselves independent of the manufacturing heart. Bankers, financiers, politicians and civil servants all fall into this category. As John Harvey-Jones pointed out so eloquently in the 1986 David Dimbleby lecture, much of our wealth is created by manufacturing industry and much of the output of service industries is dependent upon manufactured products for its continued existence. To assume service industries can replace manufacturing as the heart and engine of economic growth is naive, to say the least.

But merely to increase the size of manufacturing industry will not solve any of our current problems. Indeed, the contraction and decline of our manufacturing industry is not directly attributable to government and the City – it is largely due to the incompetence of industry itself. Those that survive will undoubtedly be the fittest and all will testify to the importance of marketing as an essential requirement for continued success.

However, none of this preamble addresses the central question 'What is marketing?' save perhaps to suggest that it is a newly emerging discipline inextricably linked with manufacturing. But this latter link is of extreme importance because in the evangelical excess of its original statement in the early 1960s, marketing and production were caricatured as antithetically opposed to one another. Forty years later most marketers have developed sufficient self-confidence not to feel it necessary to 'knock' another function to emphasize the importance and relevance of their own. So, what is marketing?

Marketing is both a managerial orientation – some would claim a business philosophy – and a business function. To understand marketing it is essential to distinguish clearly between the two.

Marketing as a managerial orientation

> Management . . . the technique, practice, or science of managing or controlling; the skilful or resourceful use of materials, time, etc.
> *Collins Concise English Dictionary*

Ever since people have lived and worked together in groups there have been managers concerned with solving the central economic problem of maximizing satisfaction through the utilization of scarce resources. If we trace the course of economic development we find that periods of rapid growth have followed changes in the manner in which work is organized, usually accompanied by changes in technology. Thus from simple collecting and nomadic communities we have progressed to hybrid agricultural and collecting communities accompanied by the concept of the division of labour. The division of labour increases output and creates a need for exchange and enhances the standard of living. Improved standards of living result in more people and further increases in output accompanied by simple mechanization which culminates in a breakthrough when the potential of the division of labour is enhanced through task specialization. Task specialization leads to the development of teams of workers and to more sophisticated and efficient mechanical devices and, with the discovery of steam power, results in an industrial revolution. A major feature of our own

industrial revolution (and that of most which emulated it in the nineteenth century) is that production becomes increasingly concentrated in areas of natural advantage, that larger production units develop and that specialization increases as the potential for economies of scale and efficiency are exploited.

At least two consequences deserve special mention. First, economic growth fuels itself as improvements in living standards result in population growth which increases demand and lends impetus to increases in output and productivity. Second, concentration and specialization result in producer and consumer becoming increasingly distant from one another (both physically and psychologically) and require the development of new channels of distribution and communication to bridge this gap.

What of the managers responsible for the direction and control of this enormous diversity of human effort? By and large, it seems safe to assume that they were (and are) motivated essentially by (an occasionally enlightened) self-interest. Given the enormity and self-evident nature of unsatisfied demand and the distribution of purchasing power, it is unsurprising that most managers concentrated on making more for less and that to do so they pursued vigorously policies of standardization and mass production. Thus the first half of the twentieth century was characterized in the advanced industrialized economies of the West by mass production and mass consumption – usually described as a production orientation and a consumer society. But changes were occurring in both.

On the supply side the enormous concentration of wealth and power in super-corporations had led to legislation to limit the influence of cartels and monopolies. An obvious consequence of this was to encourage diversification. Second, the accelerating pace of technological and organizational innovation began to catch up with and even overtake the natural growth in demand due to population increases. Faced with stagnant markets and the spectre of price competition, producers sought to stimulate demand through increased selling efforts. To succeed, however, one must be able to offer some tangible benefit which will distinguish one supplier's product from another's. If all products are perceived as being the same then price becomes the distinguishing feature and the supplier becomes a price taker, thus having to relinquish the important managerial function of exercising control. Faced with such an impasse the real manager recognizes that salvation (and control) will be achieved through a policy of *product differentiation*. Preferably this will be achieved through the manufacture of a product which is physically different in some objective way from competitive offerings but, if this is not possible, then subjective benefits must be created through service, advertising and promotional efforts.

With the growth of product differentiation and promotional activity social commentators began to complain about the materialistic nature of society and question its value. Perhaps the earliest manifestation of the consumerist movement of the 1950s and 1960s is to be found in Edwin Chamberlin and Joan Robinson's articulation of the concept of imperfect competition in the 1930s. Hitherto, economists had argued that economic welfare would be maximized through perfect competition in which supply and demand would be brought into equilibrium through the price mechanism. Clearly, as producers struggled to avoid becoming virtually passive pawns of market forces they declined to accept the 'rules' of perfect competition and it was this behaviour which was described by Chamberlin and Robinson under the pejorative title of 'imperfect' competition. Shades of the 'hidden persuaders' and 'waste makers' to come.

The outbreak of war and the reconstruction which followed delayed the first clear statement of the managerial approach which was to displace the production orientation. It was not to be selling and a sales orientation, for these can only be a temporary and transitional strategy in which one buys time in which to disengage from past practices, reform and regroup and then move on to the offensive again. The Americans appreciated this in the 1950s, the West Germans and Japanese in the 1960s, the British, belatedly in the late 1970s (until the mid-1970s nearly all our commercial heroes were sales people, not marketers – hence their problems – Stokes, Bloom, Laker). The real solution is marketing.

Marketing myopia – a watershed

If one had to pick a single event which marked the watershed between the production/sales approach to business and the emergence of a marketing orientation then most marketing scholars would probably choose the publication of Theodore Levitt's article entitled 'Marketing myopia' in the July–August 1960 issue of the *Harvard Business Review*.

Building upon the trenchant statement 'The history of every dead and dying "growth" industry shows a self-deceiving cycle of bountiful expansion and undetected decay', Levitt proposed the thesis that declining or defunct industries got into such a state because they were product orientated rather than customer orientated. As a result, the concept of their business was defined too narrowly. Thus the railroads failed to perceive that they were and are in the *transportation* business, and so allowed new forms of transport to woo their customers away from them. Similarly, the Hollywood movie moguls ignored the threat of television until it was almost too late because they saw themselves as being in the cinema industry rather than the *entertainment* business.

Levitt proposes four factors which make such a cycle inevitable:

1 A belief in growth as a natural consequence of an expanding and increasingly affluent population.
2 A belief that there is no competitive substitute for the industry's major product.
3 A pursuit of the economies of scale through mass production in the belief that lower unit cost will automatically lead to higher consumption and bigger overall profits.
4 Preoccupation with the potential of research and development (R&D) to the neglect of market needs (i.e. a technology push rather than market pull approach).

Belief number two has never been true but, until very recently, there was good reason to subscribe to the other three propositions. Despite Malthus's gloomy prognostications in the eighteenth century the world's population has continued to grow exponentially; most of the world's most successful corporations see the pursuit of market share as their primary goal, and most radical innovations are the result of basic R&D rather than product engineering to meet consumer needs. Certainly the dead and dying industries which Levitt referred to in his analysis were entitled to consider these three factors as reasonable assumptions on which to develop a strategy.

In this, then, Levitt was anticipating rather than analysing but, in doing so, he was building upon perhaps the most widely known yet most misunderstood theoretical construct in marketing – the concept of the product life cycle (PLC).

The PLC concept draws an analogy between biological life cycles and the pattern of sales growth exhibited by successful products. In doing so it

Figure 1.1 The product life cycle

distinguishes four basic stages in the life of the product: introduction; growth; maturity; and decline (see Figure 1.1).

Thus at birth or first introduction to the market, a new product initially makes slow progress as people have to be made aware of its existence and only the bold and innovative will seek to try it as a substitute for the established product which the new one is seeking to improve on or displace. Clearly, there will be a strong relationship between how much better the new product is, and how easy it is for users to accept this and the speed at which it will be taken up. But, as a generalization, progress is slow.

However, as people take up the new product they will talk about it and make it more visible to non-users and reduce the perceived risk seen in any innovation. As a consequence, a contagion or bandwagon effect will be initiated as consumers seek to obtain supplies of the new product and producers, recognizing the trend, switch over to making the new product in place of the old. The result is exponential growth.

Ultimately, however, all markets are finite and sales will level off as the market becomes saturated. Thereafter sales will settle down at a level which reflects new entrants to the market plus replacement/repeat purchase sales which constitutes the mature phase of the PLC. It is this phase which Levitt rightly characterizes as self-deceiving. Following the pangs of birth and introduction and the frenetic competitive struggle when demand took off, is it surprising that producers relax and perhaps become complacent when they are the established leaders in mature and profitable markets? But consumers, like producers, are motivated by

self-interest rather than loyalty and will be quite willing to switch their allegiance if another new product comes along which offers advantages not present in the existing offering. Recognition of this represents a market opportunity for other innovators and entrepreneurs which they will seek to exploit by introducing their own new product and so initiating another new PLC while bringing to an end that of the product to be displaced.

The import of the PLC is quite simple, but frequently forgotten – *change is inevitable*. Its misunderstanding and misuse arise from the fact that people try to use it as a specific predictive device. Clearly, this is as misconceived as trying to guess the identity of a biological organism from the representation of a life cycle curve which applies equally to gnats and elephants.

Life cycles and evolution

As noted earlier, the PLC concept is based upon biological life cycles and this raises the question as to whether one can further extend the analogy from the specific level of the growth of organisms and products to the general case of the evolution of species and economies. At a conceptual level this seems both possible and worthwhile.

Consider the case of a very simple organism which reproduces by cell division placed into a bounded environment – a sealed test tube containing nutrients necessary for the cell's existence. As the cell divides the population will grow exponentially, even allowing for the fact that some cells will die for whatever reason, up to the point when the colony reaches a ceiling to further growth imposed by its bounded environment. What happens next closely parallels what happens in PLCs, industry life cycles and overall economic cycles – a strong reaction sets in. Discussing this in a biological context, Derek de Solla Price cites a number of ways in which an exponentially growing phenomenon will seek to avoid a reduction in growth as it nears its ceiling. Two of these, 'escalation', and 'loss of definition', seem particularly relevant in an economic context.

In the case of escalation, modification of the original takes place at or near the point of inflection and '. . . a new logistic curve rises phoenix-like on the ashes of the old'. In other words, the cell modifies itself so that it can prosper and survive despite the constraints which had impeded its immediate predecessor. In marketing, such a phenomenon is apparent in a strategy of product rejuvenation in which either new uses or new customers are found to revitalize demand.

In many cases, however, it is not possible to 'raise the ceiling' through modification and the cell, or whatever, will begin to oscillate wildly in an attempt to avoid the inevitable (the 'hausse' in the economic cycle which precedes crisis and depression). As a result of these oscillations the phenomenon may become so changed as to be unrecognizable, that is it mutates or diversifies and recommences life in an entirely new guise. Alternatively, the phenomenon may accept the inevitable, smoothing out the oscillations and settling in equilibrium at a stable limit or, under different circumstances, slowly decline to nothing.

Over time, therefore, civilizations (and economies) rise and fall but the overall progression is upwards and characterized by periods of rapid development and/or stability when conditions are favourable and of decline when they are not. Observation would also seem to suggest that not only is change inevitable but that its pace is accelerating.

While it is often difficult to analyse the major causes and likely effect of major structural change when one is living in the midst of it, it seems likely that future historians will regard the 1960s and 1970s as a period of hausse in our economic and social evolution. Certainly economic forecasters are inclined in this direction through their interest in 'the long wave' or Kondratieff cycle in economic development. Similarly, management writers of the standing of Drucker talk of 'turbulence' while Toffler speaks of the third wave which will bring about Galbraith's post-industrial society.

And what has this to do with marketing? Quite simply, everything. For the past 200 years the advanced industrial economies have prospered because the nature of demand has been basic and obvious and entrepreneurs have been able to devote their energies to producing as much as possible for as little as possible. But, in a materialistic society, basic demand for standardized and undifferentiated products has become saturated and the ability to off-load surpluses onto Third World developing economies is limited by their inability to pay for these surpluses. Product differentiation and an emphasis upon selling provide temporary respite from the imbalance but the accelerating pace of technological change rapidly outruns these. Indeed, in the short run the substitution of technology for unskilled and semi-skilled labour has resulted in a rich working population, with much higher discretionary purchasing power than ever before, and a poor, unemployed and aging sector with limited or no discretionary purchasing power at all.

All the indications would seem to point to the fact that we are in an age of transition from one order to another. In terms of personal aspirations many people are growing out of materialism and want, in Maslow's terminology, to 'self-actualize' or 'do their own thing'. As a consequence we are moving towards a post-industrial, post-mass consumption society which is concerned with quality not quantity and the individual rather than the mass. To cope with this we need a complete rethink of our attitudes to production, distribution and consumption and it is this which marketing offers.

Marketing starts with the market and the consumer. It recognizes that in a consumer democracy money votes are cast daily and that to win those votes you need to offer either a better product at the same price or the same product at a lower price than your competitors. Price is objective and tangible but what is 'a better product'? Only one person can tell you – the consumer. It follows, therefore, that a marketing orientation starts and ends with consumers and requires one to make what one can sell rather than struggle to sell what one can make. But marketing is not a philanthropic exercise in which producers give away their goods. Indeed, the long-run interest of the consumer requires that they do not, for otherwise as with eating the seed corn, we will eventually finish up with nothing at all. Producers are entitled to profits and the more value they add and the greater the satisfaction they deliver, the more the customer will be prepared to pay for this greater satisfaction. Marketing therefore is all about mutually satisfying exchange relationships for which the catalyst is the producer's attempt to define and satisfy the customer's need better.

Marketing misunderstood

The emphasis thus far, and of the chapter as a whole, has been upon the need for a new approach to managing production and distribution in response to major environmental changes. The solution proposed is the adoption of a marketing orientation which puts the customer at the beginning rather than the end of the production–consumption cycle. To do so requires a fundamental shift of attitude on the part of all those concerned with production and consumption. Unfortunately, while this concept seems both simple and obvious to those who have subscribed to it there is ample evidence that it is widely misunderstood and hence misapplied.

In 1970, Charles Ames drew attention to this in an article in the *Harvard Business Review* entitled 'Trappings versus substance in industrial marketing'. The thesis of this was that industrial companies that complained marketing was not working for them as it appeared to do so for the consumer good companies had only themselves to blame as they had not understood the substance of the marketing concept but had merely adopted some of its superficial trappings. At worst, they had merely changed the name of their personnel from 'sales' to 'marketing'.

More recently in the *Journal of Marketing Management* (1985), Stephen King diagnosed at least four different misinterpretations of marketing in the UK as follows:

1 *Thrust marketing* – this occurs when the sales managers change their name to marketing managers. But the emphasis is still upon selling what we can make with an emphasis upon price and cost cutting but little attention to fitness for purpose, quality and value for money. In other words, it ignores what the customer really wants.
2 *Marketing department marketing* – indicated by the establishment of a bolt-on specialized department intended to remedy the lack of customer understanding. Some improvement followed in markets where change was slow and gradual but it did not address the critical areas where radical innovation was called for. A sort of 'fine tuning' of the customer service function but based on existing products and customers.
3 *Accountants marketing* – prevalent where chief executive officers have no direct experience of selling or marketing and concentrate upon short-term returns to the neglect of long-run survival. This approach was pungently criticized by Hayes and Abernathy in their 1980 *Harvard Business Review* article 'Managing our way to economic decline', which has been echoed many times since. Accountants marketing neglects investment in R&D, manufacturing and marketing and leads to a vicious downward spiral.
4 *Formula marketing* – in which control is seen as more important than innovation. This emphasizes sticking to the tried and true and reflects a

risk-averse strategy. It appears professional (many MBAs) and concentrates on managing facts and information but its consumer research bias tends to tell you more about the past than the future.

Failure of these approaches suggests that *real* marketing has four essential features:

1 Start with the customer.
2 A long-run perspective.
3 Full use of *all* the company's resources.
4 Innovation.

The marketing function

From the foregoing it is clear that without commitment to the concept there is little likelihood that the marketing *function* will be executed effectively. It is also clear that the size and nature of the marketing function will vary enormously according to the nature of the company or organization and the markets which it serves.

Basically, the marketing function is responsible for the management of the marketing mix which, at its simplest, is summarized by the four Ps of product, price, place and promotion.

While much more elaborate formulations containing a dozen or more elements are to be found in the marketing textbooks such fine distinctions are not central to the present inquiry into the nature of marketing. As a function marketing has as many quirks and mysteries as research and development, finance and production but the important point to establish here is that the adoption of a marketing orientation does not mean nor require that the marketing function should be seen as the largest or the most important. In fact, in a truly marketing-orientated organization the need for a specialized marketing function is probably far less than it is in a sales- or production-dominated company. Appreciation of this fact would do much to disarm the resistance of other functional specialists who equate the adoption of a marketing orientation with a diminution in their own organizational status and influence.

Ideally, of course, such functional divisions would not exist. Perhaps, if everyone were marketing orientated would they disappear to our continuing competitive advantage?

During the late 1980s and early 1990s there was considerable evidence to suggest that the marketing orientation had become so widely accepted that commentators were beginning to question the need for a separate marketing function to assume responsibility for it. Marketing's 'mid-life crisis' caused more than a frisson of anxiety amongst marketing academics and practitioners alike!

'Elegy on the death of marketing'

With the sub-title 'Never send to know why we have come to bury marketing but ask what you can do for your country churchyard' Holbrook and Hulbert (2002) take a whimsical look at the past, present and future of marketing and conclude that while the marketing concept may survive the marketing function is dead.

Citing numerous authorities, no doubt prompted by McKinsey's (1993) pronouncement of marketing's 'mid-life crisis', Holbrook and Hulbert begin by reviewing 'What is or was marketing?' First, there is the managerial school of marketing epitomized by Philip Kotler and endorsed by the American Marketing Association (AMA) in its 1985 official definition:

> Marketing (management) is the process of planning and executing the conception, pricing, promotion and distribution of ideas, goods and services to create exchanges that satisfy individual and organisational objectives.

Central to this definition, as in my own earlier (1975) attempt, is the notion of exchange which is then developed by reference to a rarely cited paper by McInnes (1964) that describes the evolution of exchange beginning with barter and craft industry. Of course the defining characteristic of such exchanges is that they are direct between producer and consumer, a characteristic that becomes uncommon with the division of labour and industrialization associated with mass manufacturing. As a result a 'gap' develops between consumer and producer. Holbrook and Hulbert identify this as essentially a physical separation and only indirectly acknowledge that this gap is also psychological given the lack of dialogue between consumer and producer as to what the former really wants. At worst there is no dialogue at all – 'I know what is good for you' – or attenuated as interpreted by intermediaries who have emerged to help close the physical gap.

As a result of further technological advances, and a slowing down of population growth in the industrialized economies with the discretionary purchasing power to absorb this increased output, growth in the consumption of homogeneous, mass produced goods competing on price begins to stall. To compensate for this producers, like General Motors, begin to appreciate the underlying logic of downward sloping demand curves and recognize that demand is not homogeneous and that different customers are prepared to pay different prices for goods that are differentiated and more closely match their personal needs. Segmentation, targeting and positioning become the new goal whose achievement is to be secured through the manipulation of the elements of the marketing mix.

Pursued to its ultimate conclusion every consumer becomes a potential customer in their own right. Initially, this possibility is driven by further advances in manufacturing technology that make mass customization possible but it is the information revolution that transforms it into a reality. Day and Montgomery (1999) are cited as saying:

> The rapid rise of the Internet has changed the rules of interactive marketing by enabling addressability and two-way interaction. It is a uniquely responsive and interactive medium. There is also an affinity between the Internet and mass customisation strategies that use dialogue to help customers articulate their needs, find the option that best fits those needs, and then makes an order.

And herein lies the problem – as Mark Twain famously observed when told that his obituary had been published 'Rumours of my death are greatly exaggerated'. Holbrook and Hulbert were writing at a time when Internet hysteria and the talk of a 'new economy' dominated people's thinking. As we now know, advances in ICT (Information and Communication Technology) have had and are having a significant effect on our everyday lives but, like other technological breakthroughs before them, they will take time to get adopted and diffuse through the population to the point that they displace current ways of doing things – including the practice of marketing.

However, the ability of potential customers to establish direct contact with potential producers does not automatically lead to the elimination of the marketing function as Holbrook and Hulbert assume when they write:

> . . . instead of an emphasis on marketing, a premium will be placed on engineering skills, manufacturing flexibility and on logistic efficiency. The job of running the company will fall to those expert in operations management, inventory control and transportation logistics.

Essentially, the authors believe that powerful search engines will automatically connect the precisely defined needs of individuals with sources able to match them exactly. Fat chance! To begin with intending consumers can rarely define precisely what it is they want and, even if they could, most could not afford the cost of something tailored precisely to their needs. Savile Row may not be short of customers for its suits but Savile Row's output of such garments is a miniscule fraction of the total supply of such items for the simple reason that the price is far beyond the purchasing power of the average individual. But then, as behavioural scientists (?), perhaps the authors have not heard of the economies of scale and experience associated with large scale production?

In a 'commentary' on Holbrook and Hulbert's paper (McCole, 2004) makes this point when he observes:

> Thus the diversity existing among businesses in terms of the products or services they offer means that whereas some will be able to take advantage off new developments in light of the information era (i.e. the Internet), others will not – or will not have to, and thus will have to depend upon the traditional marketing function to 'market' their business to consumers.

So the consumers (and producers) of low-cost, frequently purchased goods are likely to continue to favour traditional retail outlets, whereas the new channel of communication will favour exchanges where the value proposition is intangible or informational.

This is not to say that the Internet will not have a major impact on the marketing function. Clearly, access to and availability of more and better information will lead to greater transparency in markets and to increased competition between efficient and less efficient suppliers. In turn, this is likely to lead to changes in the marketing function calling for modifications in marketing and these are already apparent as, for example, in the growing emphasis on direct communication and a decline in mass media advertising. Similarly, enhanced understanding of buyer behaviour is likely to lead to more sophisticated segmentation techniques and consequential improvements in targeting and positioning rather than their disappearance as marketing tools.

In rejecting Holbrook and Hulbert's thesis, McCole asserts that even in the very unlikely event that e-marketing was to displace traditional marketing many functions would still remain that might properly be regarded as 'marketing' functions. Among these may be numbered:

- Management of the 4Ps
- Management of the value/supply chains
- Management of a marketing intelligence function
- Management of service delivery

Further, as McCole points out in order to be able to modify the marketing function to adjust to the demands of a new channel of communication/ distribution (the Internet), one must first understand what it is that may be changed. In other words, we need to start with an understanding of 'traditional' marketing. And, more important, we need to stop being apologetic for managing a function which adds value to the great majority of consumers because a small minority of critics believe that they know better how to control their buying decisions and behaviour.

In retrospect it seems that the collapse of communism in the late 1980s had a significant effect on managerial perceptions of marketing and highlighted the need to reconsider its role and function. During the years following World War II, politics and economics were dominated by the 'super powers' – the USA and the Soviet Union – each of which represented a quite different ideology and approach to economic organization – capitalism and communism. An essential difference between the two is that the former believes in and encourages competition in free markets while the latter is founded on central control and an absence of competition in the marketplace.

The fall of the Berlin Wall and the disintegration of the Soviet Union which followed it would seem to confirm the view that competition is necessary to encourage change and progress. But the collapse of communism created the kind of dilemma addressed by Chamberlin and Robinson in the 1930s which led to the articulation of the theory of imperfect competition. Prior to this economists had focused analysis on the polar opposites of monopoly (no competition) and perfect competition with only limited attention given to intermediate conditions such as oligopoly. Clearly, there are many degrees of competition in the real world which lie between the polar extremes and it was these that came to be designated as imperfect.

The analogy may be extended if one considers communism to represent monopoly and the 'free' market as perfect competition. It was against this background that the dominant model of competition post-1950 was modelled on the US and gave rise to what we now distinguish as the marketing management paradigm immortalized in Levitt's (1960) article, 'Marketing myopia', McCarthy's 4Ps and Kotler's seminal (1967) *Marketing Management: Analysis, Planning and Control*. Because of its primacy few gave much attention to free markets subject to varying degrees of regulation despite the fact that these probably, like imperfect competition, represented the majority. All that was to change in 1989!

In a penetrating analysis entitled *Capitalisme contre Capitalisme* Michel Albert (1991) pointed out that there is no single, monolithic definition of capitalism just as there is no single model of competition. Dussart (1994) elaborated on this and contrasted the American, Friedmanite model of unfettered competition practised in the USA and UK (Anglo-Saxon competition) with a modified form to be found in many social democracies in which a degree of market control is exercised by the state to moderate the excesses of big business. This Alpine/Germanic model of competition is strongly associated with most West European economies, and also with Japan and the 'tiger' economies of South East Asia, most of which have achieved a consistently better economic performance than the USA and UK since 1950.

The essential difference between the Anglo-Saxon/marketing management approach and the Alpine/Germanic style of competition is that the former takes a short-term, zero-sum adversarial view based on one-off transactions while the latter adopts a long-term perspective which promotes win–win relationships.

Relationship marketing

According to Möller and Halinen-Kaila (1997) relationship marketing or RM was the 'hot topic' of the marketing discipline during the 1990s, but 'the rhetoric is often characterized more by elegance than by rigorous examination of the actual contents' (p. 2/3). The debate raises at least four critical questions:

1 Will RM replace the traditional marketing management school?
2 Will RM make marketing management theory obsolete?
3 Is RM a completely new theory, or does it derive from older traditions?
4 Do we need different theories of RM depending on the type of exchange relationships?

Möller and Halinen-Kaila seek to answer these questions. In doing so they stress the need to look back as well as forward and link new ideas with existing knowledge. They see the current interest in RM as deriving from four basic sources – marketing channels, business-to-business marketing (inter-organizational marketing), services marketing and direct and database marketing (consumer marketing).

The dominant marketing management paradigm founded on the manipulation of the mix began to be questioned in the 1970s as it provided an inadequate explanation of the marketing of services. Such a challenge was unsurprising given that services had become the largest sector in the advanced industrial economies. Specifically, services marketing calls for recognition of both buyer and seller in the exchange process. Developments in information technology during the 1980s made it possible to both model and operationalize individual relationships through the use of databases.

However, the different research approaches are derived from different perspectives and conceptual frames of reference and provide only partial explanations which have yet to be synthesized and integrated into a holistic meta-theory. Meta-theory is derived from meta-analysis which follows one of two closely related approaches – profiling or typology development. The latter tends to be abstract, the former descriptive, and it is this procedure which is followed by Möller and Halinen-Kaila who develop a detailed comparison matrix in which they examine the four traditions specified earlier across a number of dimensions, as illustrated in Table 1.1. While the authors acknowledge that such a matrix glosses over many details, nonetheless it provides useful generalization of the ways in which the different research traditions handle exchange relationships. To reduce the complexity of their comparison matrix with its four traditions, the authors collapse these into two categories – consumer and inter-organizational relationships – and summarize their salient characteristics as in Table 1.1.

Although relationships are recognized as existing on a continuum in terms of closeness/involvement of the parties, the definition of the two categories is seen as helpful in 'anchoring' the ends of this continuum. This distinction is reinforced when one considers the different viewpoint or perspective taken in terms of the underlying assumptions on which consumer and inter-organizational relationships have been evaluated – the former

Table 1.1 Comparison matrix of research approaches to marketing exchange relationships

Characteristics / Research tradition	Database and direct consumer marketing	Services marketing	Channel relationships	Interaction and networks
Basic goals	Enhance marketing efficiency through better targeting of marketing activities, especially marketing communications – channels and messages. Strong managerial emphasis, integrated marketing communications (IMC) an important agenda.	Explain and understand services marketing relationships and services management. Managerial goal: enhance the efficiency of managing customer encounters and customer relationships through managing the perceived quality of the service offer and relationship.	Theoretical goal: explain governance structures and dyadic behaviour in the channel context. Normative goal: determine efficient relational forms between channel members.	Three interrelated sets of goals: (i) understand and explain inter-organizational exchange behaviour and relationship development at a dyadic level in a network context, (ii) understand how nets of relationships between actors evolve and (iii) understand how markets function and evolve from a network perspective. Managerial goal: gain a more valid view of reality through network theory.
View of relationship	Organization–personal customer relationships, often distant and generally comprising discrete transactions over time, handled through customized mass communication.	Personal customer relationships attended by service personnel and influenced through other marketing activities. Earlier a strong focus on the service encounter, later expanded to include the life cycle of relationships.	Inter-organizational business relationships characterized by economic exchange and use of dependent power. Actors are on each other and behave reciprocally.	Relationships exist between different types of actors: firms, government and research agencies, individual actors. Not only goods, but all kinds of resources are exchanged through relationships. Relationships are seen as vehicles for accessing and controlling resources, and creating new resources.
Questions asked	How to provide value for the customer, how to develop loyal customers, how to adapt marketing activities along the customer's life cycle, how to retain customers?	How to provide value and perceived quality for the customer, how to manage service encounters, how to create and manage customer relationships?	What forms of governance are efficient for what types of channel relationships, how is the use of power related to relationship efficiency, how can the more dependent party safeguard against the dominant party, in what way is the dyadic relationship contingent on the larger channel context?	How are relationships created and managed, how do nets of relationships evolve, how can an actor manage these relationships and create a position in a net?
Disciplinary background	No disciplinary background; driven by information technology, marketing communication applications and consultants.	No clear disciplinary background early phase a response to 'traditional marketing management', later consumer behaviour applications, human resource perspective and general management outlook. Empirically – and theory-driven with heavy managerial orientation.	Primarily theory-driven, attempts to combine the economic and political aspects (power, dependency) of channels. The tradition relies on transaction cost theory, relational law, social exchange theory, political economy, power and conflict in organizational sociology.	Both empirically and theory-driven; earlier influenced by channels research, organization buying behaviour, resource dependency theory, social exchange theory and institutional economics; later by institutional theory, dynamic industrial economics, organizational sociology and resource-based theory.

	Column 1	Column 2	Column 3	Column 4
World view and assumptions about relationships	Pragmatic – no explicit assumptions; implicitly assumes competitive markets of customers; S-O-R view with feedback the marketer is active, plans the offers and communications on the basis of customer status (profile) and feedback. Relatively weak dependency between buyer and seller, as the goods exchanged are relatively substitutable and many buyers and sellers exist.	Primarily the management perspective; dyadic interactive relationship but customers often seen as objects; that is, the marketer is generally the active party. Interdependence between the seller and the customer varies from weak to relatively strong. The basic service is often relatively substitutable, but the service relationship can be differentiated and individualized.	Both parties can be active and reciprocally interdependent; the basic interest is in economic exchange and its efficiency. The relationship is unique, its substitutability depends on the availability of alternative buyers and sellers and the amount of switching costs related to relationship-specific investments.	Depending on the research goals, the relationship perspective can be dyadic, focal firm or network type. Any actor can be active, actors are generally seen as subjects. There is often relatively strong inter-dependency between actors, caused by heterogeneity of resources which makes substitution difficult.
Topics/concepts important for RM	Customer retention, share of customer, database as a device for managing direct communications, integrated use of channels.	Service encounters, experience and expectations, service and relationship quality, life-time value of the customer, internal marketing, empowerment of personnel.	Bases of power, uses of power and conflict behaviour, interdependence, goal congruity, decision domains, environmental influence on dyadic behaviour; transaction-specific investments, switching costs, dyadic governance, dyad outcomes: efficiency, satisfaction, relational norms.	Interaction processes, adaptation and investments into relationships, phases of relationships, actor bonds, ties, activity chains and relationship outcomes; resource nets and networks of relationships; network dynamics and embeddedness.
Level/unit of analysis and contextuality	Individual consumer; a group of consumers (segment); in applications customers are practically always aggregated into groups (segments). No conscious assumptions about the contextuality of the customer relationships; the competitive situation is the general contextuality perspective.	Individual customer, group or segment, service provider–client relationship. Little emphasis on contextuality, sometimes the history of a relationship is emphasized – generally handled through 'experience'; generally implicit assumption about the market as the dominant environmental form.	Firm, dyadic relationship in the channel context. Contingency perspective: dyadic behaviour and efficient forms of governance are dependent on the channel context. Well developed 'environment' theory.	Actor (organization, person), dyadic relationship, net of relationships. Transactions episodes in the long-term relationship. The emphasis is on the embeddedness of relationships in nets and networks, and their history – no understanding of the present situation without history.
Time orientation, focus on structure versus process	Rhetoric emphasizes the long-term view, no published tools for handling long-term issues of relationships. The focus is on the content of a customer profile, little emphasis/conceptual effort on tackling the dynamism of customer development.	Earlier emphasis on short-term encounters, now shifting to a more enduring relational perspective. The process aspect is evident, but empirical research is primarily on the content of relationship characteristics.	Emphasis on efficient forms of channel relationships ranging from market-like transactions to long-term reciprocal relationships. Theoretically dynamic, but the majority of empirical research is static; the focus is on structure not process.	Time is an essential phenomenon. Dynamic perspective, focus on both structure (content) and processes (how dyads, nets and networks evolve).
Methodological orientation	No conscious methodology, primarily cross-sectional analysis of survey data and customer databases.	Divided methodology; North American emphasis on explanation through hypothesis testing by multivariate analysis; Nordic emphasis on understanding through qualitative research.	Hypothetical – deductive reasoning, explanation through hypothesis testing by multivariate analysis.	Divided methodology, European emphasis (IMP Group) on understanding through historical case analysis; North American emphasis on explanation through hypothesis testing by multivariate analysis (this is primarily limited to dyads).

Source: Möller and Halinen-Kaila (1997, p. 10).

following a market perspective, the latter a network/systemic perspective.

In identifying two distinct streams of thought within the RM literature Möller and Halinen-Kaila recognize that they may be 'swimming against the fashionable stream of RM as the general marketing theory rhetoric!'(p. 16). If so, they are not alone as Mattsson (1997) is clearly of a similar opinion as is the author for, otherwise, he would have promoted an alternative perspective. That said, by adopting the Möller and Halinen-Kaila approach and identifying the key characteristics of the different schools of thought, it becomes possible to recognize both similarities and differences in much the same way that the concepts of pure competition and monopoly enabled the emergence of a theory of imperfect competition which reflects messy reality rather than theoretical purity. As Möller and Halinen-Kaila point out, the key managerial challenge in both forms of RM is how to manage a portfolio of exchange relationships. Within the domain of consumer or 'limited' RM, numerous approaches and techniques have evolved which are highly relevant to addressing this problem. Indeed, with the developments in information technology in recent years many of these have become of practical rather than theoretical interest. We should not lightly discard these methods.

In the domain of inter-organizational relationships their complexity is likely to limit the extent to which 'packaged' solutions may be applied. While useful generalizations will have an important role to play, the situation-specific nature of most problems will continue to require decision makers to use experience and judgement in coming up with effective solutions.

A new model of marketing ?

A recent article in the *Journal of Marketing* has prompted extensive debate about the need for a new model, or paradigm, of the domain of marketing. This proposition has been the subject of extensive debate with special sessions at many academic conferences, like ANZMAC 2005 and 2006, given to arguments for and against the adoption of this new model. In the absence of agreement on the subject, it is clear that it would be premature to argue for or against the model when documenting the evolution of the accepted wisdom about marketing. On the other hand, when discussing the nature of marketing, an overview of the arguments is clearly important for those new to the subject.

The article that precipitated the debate is entitled 'Evolving to a new dominant logic of marketing' by Stephen L. Vargo and Robert F. Lusch (**68**(1), 2004). In the *Abstract* the authors write:

'The purpose of this article is to illuminate the evolution of *marketing* thought toward a new dominant logic. . . . Briefly, *marketing*, has moved from a goods-dominant view, in which tangible output and discrete transactions were central, to a service-dominant view, in which intangibility, exchange processes, and relationships are central.'

The authors then stress that their interpretation of 'service-centred' should not be equated with current conceptualizations of services as a residual (i.e. not a tangible good) something to add value to a good – value-added services; or service 'industries like health care and education. They state:

'Rather, we define services as the application of specialised competences (knowledge and skills) through deeds, processes, and performances to the benefit of another entity or the entity itself . . . Thus, the service-centred dominant logic represents a reoriented philosophy that is applicable to all *marketing* offerings, including those that involve tangible output (goods) in the process of service provision'.

In order to justify and sustain the case for a new model or paradigm of marketing involves a closely argued case running to 17 pages of text, and supported by 4 pages of references. To begin with Vargo and Lusch's analysis starts with a summary of the evolution of marketing thought that reflects the overview provided here and mirrors that to be found in most standard marketing textbook. So, we are agreed on the point of departure, and know 'where we are'. The need for a new 'worldview' or dominant logic is predicated on the proposition that 'Marketing inherited a model of exchange from economics, which had a dominant logic based on the exchange of "goods", which usually are manufactured output. The dominant logic focused on tangible resources, embedded value and transactions'. However, this view is not seen as appropriate today.

Over the past 50 years or so the focus on resources as 'stuff' that is to be acquired and used by humans – what we would normally think of as natural and physical resources – has changed to a view that incorporates intangible and dynamic functions calling for human ingenuity and appraisal. 'Everything is neutral (or perhaps even a resistance) until humankind learns what to do with it (Zimmerman, 1951). Essentially, resources are not; they become'.

To explain this distinction the authors introduce the distinction between *operand* and *operant resources* (my emphasis). Operand resources are those on which some act or operation has to be performed to produce an effect while, operant resources are those that produce effects. Increased interest in operant resources 'began to shift in the late twentieth century as humans began to realise that skills and knowledge were the most important types of resources'. Although prior reference had been made to the work of Malthus (1798), and his conclusion that the continued growth of population would result in the exhaustion of natural resources, no explicit link is made by the authors to numerous forecasts in the 1960s of the inevitable truth of this prediction, unless humankind could make them go further. Thus it was publications such as the Club of Rome's *Limits to Growth* that precipitated the recognition of the primacy of operant over operand resources.

The logic and importance of this is manifest in Vargo and Lusch's statement that:

> 'Operant resources are often invisible and intangible; often they are core competences or organisational processes. They are likely to be dynamic and infinite (sic) and not static and finite, as is usually the case with operand resources. Because operant resources produce effects, they enable humans both to multiply the value of natural resources and to create additional operant skills'.

If, then, this primacy is the defining characteristic of the new 'service-centered logic' few would challenge it; whether they would describe it as a service-centred logic is another matter. Vargo and Lusch believe that this perceived shift (hint: they perceive it; I'm not sure yet) has important implications for marketing and they start with an examination of the 'Goods versus Services' schools of thought.

Traditional marketing is seen as focusing on operand resources, is goods centered and concerned with the notion of utility(ies). Service-centered marketing is seen as comprising four elements which are summarized as:

1 Identify or develop core competences, the fundamental knowledge and skills of an economic entity that represent potential competitive advantage.
2 Identify other entities (potential customers) that could benefit from these competences.
3 Cultivate relationships that involve the customers in developing customized, competitively compelling value propositions to meet specific needs.

4 Gauge marketplace feedback by analysing financial performance from exchange to learn how to improve the firm's offering to customers and improve firm performance.

This view is grounded in and largely consistent with resource advantage theory. It is customer centric and market driven.

Vargo and Lusch then proceed to compare the two views and identify six differences between them, all centered on the operand/operant distinction. These attributes are then analysed in the context of eight foundational premises (FPs). These premises are:

1 The application of specialized skills and knowledge is the fundamental unit of exchange.
2 Indirect exchange masks the fundamental unit of exchange.
3 Goods are distribution mechanisms for service provision.
4 Knowledge is the fundamental source of competitive advantage.
5 All economies are service economies.
6 The customer is always a co-producer.
7 The enterprise can only make value propositions.
8 The service-centered view is customer oriented and relational.

Each of these premises is discussed and evaluated in some detail.

In sum, I believe that the logic of the service-centered approach reflects the logic and intentions of the marketing era as distinguished from the production era that preceded it. Where I have difficulty with Vargo and Lusch's proposal is that in order to recognize the importance of services/operant activities they seem to think it is necessary to deny the role of physical resources and technology in creating physical objects that are necessary to realize the value of those service activities. In other words, without operand or physical resources to work with we would soon all die of starvation.

In their *Discussion* the first issue appears to concern the degree of customization incorporated into physical goods. I have to confess to having some difficulty in following their argument, especially in terms of their definition of 'normative qualities'. According to Vargo and Lusch 'The goods-centered view implies that the qualities of manufactured goods (e.g. tangibility), the separation of production and consumption, standardisation, and nonperishability are normative qualities (Zeithaml, Parasuraman and Berry, 1985)'. As a consequence, 'From what we argue the *marketing* perspective should be, the qualities are often neither valid nor desirable'.

I have great difficulty in accepting this claim, which is almost as bad as the academic economist's view that to purchase on the basis of emotional beliefs, rather than giving precedence to price, is 'irrational'. In the great majority of purchase decisions our survival does not depend on buying anything – we can always take it or leave it. Furthermore, the existence of producers attempting to satisfy picky customers has led to greater choice and variety than has ever existed before. What the authors see as the service-centred view of exchange is what, since 1987, has been known as 'mass customization' in which producers like Dell involve customers directly in specifying the attributes and features that they desire in their computer. Now, with a complex product such as this, if I know precisely what I want then I can become a co-producer but what if I can't? Or what about my motor car when I only wish to order a limited number of 'extras' because otherwise the standard model meets virtually all of my needs? Or what about canned vegetables? The activities involved in getting these to my preferred retail outlet are extensive, complex and expensive. There is a huge variety on offer, and keen competition between suppliers of the same product category. And, if you are dissatisfied with the manufacturers attempt to satisfy your need you can always go to the Farmer's Market and buy 'the real thing' for a much higher price. Or, better still why not become a producer yourself and find out if the time involved improves your overall standard of living?

To be fair, many of the attributes of the service-centered view recognize that marketing should be about 'mutually satisfying exchange relationships' in which both producer and consumer have a role to play and in which supply should be determined by demand. In my opinion, these are the distinguishing features of the marketing concept and a marketing orientation, which has taken rather longer to put into practice than one would have liked. On the other hand those organizations that have bought into the concept and are marketing oriented are more successful. Ultimately, natural selection and the 'invisible hand' will prevail. In this sense Vargo and Lusch may be seen as seeking to accelerate the process and, as they say, they are looking for 'reorientation rather than reinvention' (p. 14).

As with any debate, the proponents have to exaggerate their case to make their point. So we would agree that the marketing management concept has paid insufficient attention to the wants of consumers. On the other hand it has done very well in catering to their needs. What is called for is more fine tuning to ensure that the goods and services created cost effectively by producers/sellers match ever more closely the needs of buyers/consumers. As we have said, mass customization has recognized the benefits of doing this, as has the emphasis on customer relationship management and getting closer to the customer. But producers have an important role to play too. Giving the customer what they (think) they want is not necessarily the way to ensure the optimum utilization of scarce physical resources. In solving the basic economic problem of maximizing satisfaction through the use of scarce resources both producer and consumer have an equal role to play. Handing over 'dominance' to users does not appear to be the best way to achieve this.

So much for my views. In the same issue of the *Journal of Marketing* there are also invited commentaries from some much better known marketing scholars. You should read these too if you intend to study marketing in greater detail. For the time being, however, the jury is out.

Summary

In this introductory chapter we have attempted to trace the evolution of exchange relationships and provide at least a partial answer to the question 'What is marketing?' In the process we have established that exchange is at the very heart of human development in both economic and social terms. Until recently, however, the desirability of enhancing consumer satisfaction through the provision of more and better goods and services has been so self-evident that little consideration has been given as to how to define 'more' and 'better', or the processes by which such evaluations are made. As Adam Smith observed in his *Wealth of Nations* (1776), 'Consumption is the sole end and purpose of production'. Having stated the obvious the remainder of his great work is devoted wholly to issues of improving supply with no consideration of demand *per se*.

As we have seen, it is only with the stabilization of populations in advanced economies, and the continuous and accelerating improvements in productivity attributable to technological innovation, that a preoccupation with supply side problems has given way to demand side considerations. Modern marketing, dating from the 1950s, reflects this transition. But, as we have attempted to show, the marketing management model which emerged was itself a purely transitional response to managing the changing balance between sellers and buyers. Initially, the marketing management model was concerned with what sellers needed to do to retain control over the transaction, with consumers seen as passive participants in the process. With the evolution of service dominated economies, so the balance of power changed and supply was now seen to be subservient to demand and consumer sovereignty.

As we noted in the last edition prepared in 2002, the problem with the change in emphasis is that it still sees exchange as a zero-sum game. While buyers are winners, sellers are losers! As predicted then, the dangers of this adversarial approach to exchange are readily apparent, especially in the manufacturing sector, where the greatest potential for growth and added value exist. Thus, the outsourcing of manufacturing by the wealthier economies to the newly industrializing and emerging economies has tended to exaggerate rather than reduce the unequal distribution of wealth between these economies. This gloomy scenario is compounded when one recognizes that the concentration of much of the world's wealth in the hands of a minority of the world's population was undoubtedly a factor in the horrific events of 11 September 2001 and the wave of conflict and terrorism that has followed. While it would be overly simplistic to attribute these events solely to envy and resentment of the disproportionate consumption of resources by the American people, it is clear that Americans, and others, are having difficulty in adjusting to the fact that such win–lose situations engender such feelings among the 'losers'.

What is needed is a proper appreciation of the true marketing concept of exchange based on *mutually satisfying relationships* in which both parties get what they want – a true win–win situation. Such a concept reflects the 'Golden Rule' central to most religious ideologies – 'Do unto others as you would be done by'. While it would be unrealistic to expect those enjoying high standards of living to reduce these radically overnight, it should not be impossible to promote a more equitable global society by encouraging the win–win outcomes advocated by the marketing concept and its emphasis on mutually satisfying relationships.

In our view, implementation of this concept/ orientation demands the existence of a marketing function and the management of the marketing mix. The remainder of *The Marketing Book* draws on the expertise of leading thinkers and practitioners to see how we might achieve this desired state.

References

Albert, M. (1991) *Capitalisme contre Capitalisme*, Seuil, L'Historie Imm' ediate, Paris.

Ames, C. (1970) Trappings versus substance in industrial marketing, *Harvard Business Review*, July–August, 93–103.

Baker, M. J. (1976) *Marketing: Theory and Practice*, Macmillan, London.

Day, G. S. and Montgomery, D. B. (1999) Charting new directions for marketing, *Journal of Marketing*, **63**(Special Issue), 3–13.

Dussart, C. (1994) Capitalism versus capitalism, in Baker, M. J. (ed.) *Perspectives on Marketing Management*, Vol. 4, John Wiley & Sons, Chichester.

Hayes, R. and Abernathy, W. (1980) Managing our way to economic decline, *Harvard Business Review*, July–August, 67–77.

Holbrook, M. B. and Hulbert, J. M. (2002) Elegy on the death of marketing, *European Journal of Marketing*, **36**(5/6), 706–732.

King, S. (1985) Has marketing failed or was it never really tried? *Journal of Marketing Management*, **1**(1), Summer, 1–19.

Kotler, P. (1967) *Marketing Management: Analysis, Planning and Control*, Prentice-Hall, Englewood Cliffs, NJ.

Levitt, T. (1960) Marketing myopia, *HarvardBusiness Review*, July–August, 45–60.

Mattsson, L.-G. (1997) 'Relationship marketing' and the 'markets-as-networks approach' – a comparative analysis of two evolving streams of research, *Journal of Marketing Management*, **13**, 447–461.

McCole, P. (2004) Commentary, marketing is not dead: a response to 'Elegy on the death of marketing', *European Journal of Marketing*, **38**(11/12), 1349–1354.

McInnes, W. (1964) A conceptual approach to marketing, in Cox, R., Alderson, W. M. and Shapiro, S. J. (eds), *Theory in Marketing*, Richard D. Irwin, Homewood, IL, pp. 51–67.

Möller, K. and Halinen-Kaila, A. (1997) *Relationship Marketing: Its Disciplinary Roots and Future Directions, Working Papers*, W-194, Helsinki School of Economics and Business Administration, Helsinki.

Vargo, S. L. and Lusch, R. F. (2004) Evolving to a new dominant logic of marketing, *Journal of Marketing*, **68**(1), 1–17.

Further reading

Baker, M. J. (2006) What is Marketing? Chapter 1 in *Marketing: An Introductory Text*, 7th edn, Westburn Publishers, Helensburgh.

CHAPTER 2

Postmodern marketing

STEPHEN BROWN

In August 2004, a one-day symposium was held in Boston, MA, as part of the American Marketing Association's annual summer conference. Entitled *Does Marketing Need Reform?* it featured the crème de la crème of US marketing scholarship, everyone from Philip Kotler and Fred Webster to Jerry Wind and Jagdish Sheth. Over a fraught 12-hour period, the leading lights of American academia earnestly debated the parlous state of theory and practice. Marketing, most delegates agreed, is facing a fundamental crisis of confidence and, more worryingly, authority (Sheth and Sisodia, 2006). It is disdained by today's consumers, who are growing wise to marketers' nefarious wiles. It is disdained by senior managers, who feel that marketing is failing to deliver on its much-trumpeted transformational promises. It is disdained, at least implicitly, by academicians who are talking to themselves rather than communicating with key constituents like practitioners and policy makers. The inevitable upshot of this near universal loathing is that marketing is losing touch with its markets and, if not quite plummeting into the pit of eternal damnation, the discipline's definitely teetering on the edge of an intellectual abyss.

According to Evert Gummesson (2001), it takes approximately 10 years for marginal ideas to penetrate the mainstream. Postmodern marketing is a textbook example of Gummesson's rule of thumb. The existential crisis that is currently exercising Kotler, Webster, Wind, Sheth and analogous highly placed 'reformers' is exactly the same existential crisis that postmodern marketers identified 10 years earlier, much to the amusement of the mainstream (e.g. Piercy, 1997). In the early- to mid-1990s, postmodernists were the whipping boys (and girls) of the marketing academy, a bunch of crazies spouting strange predictions about the imminent collapse of the discipline and the need to rethink our field's most fundamental premises. A decade on, the postmodernists' doom-laden predictions appear remarkably prescient. Their cries in the wilderness have finally forced themselves onto the agenda of the heavy hitters, leading lights and, let's be frank, fat cats of marketing thought. It is deeply ironic, is it not, that the people who are loudly making the case for reform are the very same people who laid down the principles that now need reforming. Irony, however, is a signature feature of postmodernism, so the present state of affairs shouldn't surprise us.

Postmodern marketing may be moving toward the mainstream, but what exactly is it? This is a very good question, one that has perplexed many marketers in the 10–15 years since 'PoMo' appeared at the edge of the academic radar. However, as with so many marketing topics and terminologies – for example, the definitions of 'brand', 'globalization' or 'marketing' itself – there is no single, simple, clear-cut answer that is universally accepted. There are, nonetheless, two crucial things to bear in mind about 'the postmodern' in its many and varied manifestations. First, it is a critique not a concept. It does not provide an alternative to existing marketing concepts. It simply informs us that there is something wrong with established ideas and understandings. Although it tells us that the emperor has got no clothes, it doesn't attempt to tailor a new outfit. It doesn't so much think outside the box as think *about* the box.

The second key point is that the postmodern is a pan-disciplinary movement. The concerns raised by card-carrying postmodernists are not confined to marketing. Postmodern irruptions have occurred in many academic domains, everything from archaeology and geography to theology and zoology (see Appignanesi and Garratt, 1995; Calás and Smircich, 1997; Ward, 1997; Best and Kellner, 2001; Crews, 2001). In this respect, it is noteworthy that sociologists, anthropologists and cultural studies specialists – the fields which have most fully embraced postmodern modes of thought – regard marketing as one of the distinguishing characteristics of the postmodern condition. Consumer society and postmodern society are considered synonymous, near enough (e.g. Featherstone, 1991; Bocock, 1993; Falk and Campbell, 1997; Warde, 2002). Thus, the past 10 years have witnessed a bizarre scholarly situation where the marketing mainstream was mocking the lunatic fringe of postmodern marketers, while non-marketers were holding marketing up as the epitome of postmodernism! Marketing's moment of academic glory had arrived and nobody noticed, except a few crazies of the lunatic fringe of our field. Ironic, or what?

In the beginning was the word

The postmodern, then, has come in from the cold. Its concerns are now widely recognized by the marketing community and, if not being acted on with commendable dispatch, they're undoubtedly attracting the attention of the great and good (Sheth and Sisodia, 2006). Does this mean that early adopters should pull up their tents and disappear into the sunset, whistling a merry tune? No. Categorically not. The problem with postmodernism's ostensible entry into the mainstream is that the problems it poses are being tackled by the self same mainstream 'reformers' who got marketing into its current crisis. Are they up to the task? Are they prepared to dismantle what they built? Are they willing to wipe their own slate clean and start from scratch?

Before we answer such irreverent questions, it is necessary to step back and take a brief look at the intellectual gorilla in our midst. Perhaps the best way of making sense of the postmodern is to recognize that the word itself is multi-faceted. It is a signifier with many signifieds. That is to say, it's an umbrella term, four ribs of which can be tentatively identified.

Postmodernism

For many commentators, postmodernism is primarily an aesthetic movement, a revolt against the once shocking subsequently tamed 'modern' movement of the early- to mid-twentieth century. (In fact, some scholars reserve the term 'postmodernism' for developments in the cultural sphere.) To cite but three examples: in architecture, PoMo is characterized by the eschewal of the austere, unembellished, 'glass box' International Style of Le Corbusier and Mies van der Rohe, and a return to inviting, ornamented, mix 'n' matched, vernacular or pseudo-vernacular forms, as found in the work of Venturi, Portman, Jencks and Gehry. In literature, likewise, the spare, experimental, and, as often as not, inaccessible writings of the giants of high modernism – Joyce, Proust, Eliot, etc. – have given way to the parodic, reader-friendly vulgarities of Martin Amis, Will Self and Bret Easton Ellis. In popular music, moreover, the 'modern' era of The Beatles, Rolling Stones, Beach Boys and Bob Dylan (albeit there is some debate over the existence of modernist pop/rock), has sundered into a multiplicity of modalities – house, jungle, techno, rap, roots, world, drum 'n' bass, speed garage and the like – many of which are parasitic upon (sampling, scratch), pastiches of (the tribute group phenomenon) or cross-pollinated with existing musical forms (alt.county, nu-metal, neo-disco *et al.*).

Postmodernity

A second rib of the postmodern umbrella rests on the economic base, rather than the aesthetic superstructure. The world, according to this viewpoint, has entered a whole new, qualitatively different, historical epoch; an epoch of multinational, globalized, ever-more rapacious capitalism, where traditional ways of working, producing, consumption and exchange have changed and changed utterly. Frequently described by the epithet 'postmodernity', this is the world of the world wide web, 24/7 day-trading, satellite television, soundbitten and spindoctored politics, mobile phoneophilia, pick 'n' mix lifestyles, serial monogamy and relentless McDonaldization. It is a world of ephemerality, instability, proliferation, hallucination and, above all, chaos. It is a world where the beating of a butterfly's wings in South America can cause a stock market crash in Hong Kong or swerve the ball into the net at Wembley Stadium. It is a world of unexpected, unpredictable, uncontrollable, unremitting, some would say unnecessary, upheaval.

The postmodern condition

Paralleling the transformations that are taking place in the aesthetic and economic spheres, a postmodern turn in the nature of knowledge and thought has transpired. The so-called Enlightenment Project, which commenced in western Europe during the eighteenth century and comprised a systematic, rigorous, supposedly dispassionate search for objective knowledge, universal laws, meaningful generalizations and absolute truths, has run slowly but irreversibly into the sand. Its replacement, to some extent at least, is a low-key postmodern worldview, which emphasizes the boundedness of knowledge, the limits to generalization, the lack of universal laws, the prevalence of disorder over order, irrationality rather than irrationality, subjectivity instead of objectivity and passionate participation as an alternative to dispassionate spectatorship. Thus, the 'grand narratives' of the project of modernity – progress, freedom, profit, utopia, liberalism, truth, science etc. – have been superseded by an awareness of the lack of progress, the absence of freedom, the price of profit, the dystopia that is utopia, the illiberalism of liberalism, the fiction that is truth and the artistry of science.

Postmodern apocalypse

Another, and in certain respects the most straightforward, way of grasping the postmodern is to eschew the idea that it is an 'it'. It's 'itness', after all, assumes a referential model of language (i.e. that there are 'things' out there in the world that the word 'postmodern' refers to), which is something card-carrying postmodernists are loath to concede. Postmodernism, rather, is better regarded as an attitude, a feeling, a mood, a sensibility, an orientation, a way of looking at the world – a way of looking askance at the world. A pose, if you prefer. As noted in the introduction, irony, parody, playfulness, irreverence, insolence, couldn't-careless cynicism and a refusal to defer to those holding the levers of power are postmodernism's distinguishing features. Hence, the progressive, optimistic, forward-looking, ever-onward-ever-upward worldview of the modern era has been replaced by a pessimistic, almost apocalyptic, sense of apprehension, anxiety, apathy and anomie. The postmodern, then, is suffused with an air of exhaustion, ending, crisis and (calamitous) change. Its characteristic attitude is a 'mixture of worldweariness and cleverness, an attempt to make you

think that I'm half-kidding, though you're not quite sure about what' (Apple, 1984, p. 39).

Physician, heal thyself

Now, it doesn't take a great deal of cleverness, let alone world-weariness, to recognize that many of these postmodern modalities are discernible in today's marketing and consumer environment. Consider shopping centres. The archetypal Arndale developments of the 1960s – all reinforced concrete, flat roofs, straight lines, low ceilings and oozing mastic – have been eclipsed by postmodern shopping malls, which are bright, airy, eclectic, ornamented, extravagantly themed, unashamedly ersatz and invariably welcoming. Instead of a glowering, intimidating, brutalist bulk, a blot on the cityscape that seemed to say, 'enter if you dare, go about your business and get out as quickly as possible', postmodern centres suggest that shopping is a pleasure not a purgatorial experience. They say, in effect, 'enjoy yourself, call again, bring the family, fulfil your fantasies, relive your childhood, imagine yourself in another world or another part of the world, or both' (Shields, 1992; Goss, 1993; Maclaran and Brown, 2001).

In advertising, likewise, the straightforward marketing pitch of tradition – 'this product is good, buy it' – is almost unheard of these days (except when it's used ironically). Contemporary commercials are invariably sly, subtle, allusive, indirect, clever, parodic, insouciant, self-referential (ads about ads), cross-referential (ads that cite other cultural forms – soap operas, movies, etc.) and made with staggeringly expensive, semi-cinematic production values. They not only presuppose a highly sophisticated, advertising- and marketing-literate audience, but work on the basic premise that advertising-inculcated images (cool, sexy, smart and the like) are the essence of the product offer. Products, in fact, are little more than the campaign's tie-in merchandise, along with the videos, CDs, PR hoopla and media coverage of the ad agency's self-serving endeavours (Davidson, 1992; Goldman and Papson, 1996; Berger, 2001).

Consumers, too, are changing. As Chapter 6 explains, the certainties, uniformities and unambiguities of the modern era – where mass production produced mass marketing which produced mass consumption which produced mass production – are being trumped by the individualities, instabilities and fluidities of the postmodern epoch.

Postmodernity is a place where there are no rules only choices, no fashion only fashions, the Joneses are kept well away from and anything not only goes but it has already left the building. It is a place where 'one listens to reggae, watches a western, eats McDonalds food for lunch and local cuisine for dinner, wears Paris perfume in Tokyo and retro clothes in Hong Kong' (Lyotard, 1984, p. 76). It is a place where 'we have literally shopped 'til we dropped into our slumped, channel-surfing, couch-potatoed position, with the remote control in one hand, a slice of pizza in the other and a six-pack of Australian lager between our prematurely swollen ankles' (Brown *et al.*, 1997). It is a place, as the irascible novelist Will Self notes, where anti-capitalist, anti-globalization, anti-marketing protesters 'take global airlines so that they can put on Gap clothes to throw rocks at Gap shops' (Dugdale, 2001, p. 37).

Let there be light

Marketing, it's clear, is permeated by purportedly postmodern practices. But what does it all mean? Well, there have been many more or less successful attempts to make sense of the PoMo phenomenon. Perhaps the most compelling was made back in 1995 by two prophets of the postmodern turn: A. Fuat Firat and Alladi Venkatesh. In a lengthy article on the 're-enchantment of consumption', they contend that postmodern marketing is characterized by five main themes: *hyperreality, fragmentation, reversed production and consumption, decentred subjects* and the *juxtaposition of opposites* (Table 2.1).

Hyperreality

Exemplified by the virtual worlds of cyberspace and the pseudo worlds of theme parks, hotels and heritage centres, hyperreality involves the creation of marketing environments that are 'more real than real'. The distinction between reality and fantasy is momentarily blurred, as in the back lot tour of 'working' movie studios in Universal City, Los Angeles. In certain respects, indeed, hyperreality is *superior* to everyday mundane reality, since the unpleasant side of 'authentic' consumption experiences – anti-tourist terrorism in Egypt, muggings in New York, dysentery in Delhi – magically disappears when such destinations are recreated in Las Vegas, Busch Gardens, Walt Disney World or the manifold variations on the theme park theme.

Ironically, however, the perceived superiority of the fake is predicated upon an (often) unwarranted stereotype of reality, and the reality of the fake – for example, the queues in Disneyland – may be much worse than anything the average visitor would actually experience in Egypt, New York, Delhi or where-ever. But such is the cultural logic of postmodern marketing.

Fragmentation

Consumption in postmodernity is unfailingly fast, furious, frenetic, frenzied, fleeting, hyperactive. It is akin to zapping from channel to channel, or flicking through the pages of the glossies, in search of something worth watching, reading or buying. Shopping on Speed. This disjointedness is partly attributable to the activities of marketers with their ceaseless proliferation of brands, ever-burgeoning channels of distribution, increasingly condensed commercial breaks and apparent preparedness to make use of every available surface as advertising space (sidewalks, urinals, foodstuffs, orbiting satellites, human flesh, fifties sitcoms and so forth). It is also due to the disconnected postmodern lifestyles, behaviours, moods, whims and vagaries of contemporary consumers. A product of profusion with a profusion of products, the prototypical 'postmodern consumer' performs a host of roles – wife and mother, career woman, sports enthusiast, fashion victim, DIY enthusiast, culture vulture, hapless holidaymaker, websurfing Internet avatar and many more – each with its requisite brand name array. These identities or selves, furthermore, are neither sequential nor stable, but fluid, mutable and, not least, negotiable. Pick 'n' mix personae are proliferating. Off-the-shelf selves are available in every conceivable size, style, colour, fit and price point. Made to measure selves cost extra.

Reversed production and consumption

This fragmented, hyperrealized, postmodern consumer, it must also be stressed, is not the unwitting dupe of legend, who responds rat-like to environmental stimuli of Skinnerian caprice. Nor is the postmodern consumer transfixed, rabbit-like, in the headlights of multinational capital. Nor, for that matter, is he or she likely to be seduced by the sexual textual embeds of subliminal advertisers, though (s)he might pretend to be. On the contrary, the very idea that consumers have something

Table 2.1 Postmodern conditions and their main themes

Hyperreality	Fragmentation	Reversal of production and consumption	Decentred subjects	Juxtaposition of opposites
Reality as part of symbolic world and constructed rather than given	Consumption experiences are multiple, disjointed	Postmodernism is basically a culture of consumption, while modernism represents a culture of production	The following modernist notions of the subject are called into question:	Pastiche as the underlying principle of juxtaposition
Signifier/signified (structure) replaced by the notion of endless signifiers	Human subject has a divided self	Abandonment of the notion that production creates value while consumption destroys it	Human subject as a self-knowing, independent agent	Consumption experiences are not meant to reconcile differences and paradoxes but to allow them to exist freely
The emergence of symbolic and the spectacle as the basis of reality	Terms such as "authentic self" and "centered connections" are questionable	Sign value replaces exchange value as the basis of consumption	Human subject as a cognitive subject	Acknowledges that fragmentation, rather than unification, is the basis of consumption
The idea that marketing is constantly involved in the creation of *more real than real*	Lack of commitment to any (central) theme	Consumer paradox:	Human subject as a unified subject	
The blurring of the distinction between real and nonreal	Abandonment of history, origin, and context	Consumers are active producers of symbols and signs of consumption, as marketers are	Postmodernist notions of human subject:	
	Marketing is an activity that fragments consumption signs and environments and reconfigures them through style and fashion	Consumers are also objects in the marketing process, while products become active agents	Human subject is historically and culturally constructed	
	Fragmentation as the basis for the creation of body culture		Language, not cognition, is the basis for subjectivity	
			Instead of a cognitive subject, we have a communicative subject	
			Authentic self is displaced by made-up self	
			Rejection of modernist subject as a male subject	

Source: Firat and Venkatesh (1995).

'done' to them by marketers and advertisers no longer passes muster. Postmodern consumers, in fact, do things with advertising; they are active in the production of meaning, of marketing, of consumption. As Firat and Venkatesh (1995, p. 251) rightly observe,

> It is not to brands that consumers will be loyal, but to images and symbols, especially to images and symbols that *they* produce while they consume. Because symbols keep shifting, consumer loyalties cannot be fixed. In such a case a modernist might argue that the consumers are fickle – which perhaps says more about the modernist intolerance of uncertainty – while the postmodernist interpretation would be that consumers respond strategically by making themselves unpredictable. The consumer finds his/her liberatory potential in subverting the market rather than being seduced by it.

Decentred subjects

This idea of a multiphrenic, fragmented, knowing consumer is further developed in Firat and Venkatesh's notion of decentred subjectivity. The centredness that is characteristic of modernity, where individuals are unambiguously defined by their occupation, social class, demographics, postcode, personalities and so on, has been ripped asunder in postmodernity. Traditional segmentation criteria *may* be applied to such people, and marketing strategies formulated, but it is increasingly accepted that these fleetingly capture, or freeze-frame at most, a constantly moving target market. Even the much-vaunted 'markets of one', in which marketing technologies are supposedly adapted to the specific needs of individual consumers, is doomed to fail in postmodernity, since each consumer comprises a multiplicity of shopping homunculi, so to speak. The harder marketers try to pin down the decentred consuming subject, the less successful they'll be. Today's consumers are always just beyond the reach of marketing scientists, marketing strategists, marketing tacticians, marketing technologists, marketing taxonomists and all the rest. In the words of leading marketing authority, Alan Mitchell (2001, p. 60),

> There is nothing wrong with trying to be scientific about marketing; in trying to understand cause and effect. And stimulus-response marketing has chalked up many successes. Nevertheless, it now faces rapidly diminishing returns. Consumers are becoming 'marketing literate'. They know they

are being stimulated and are developing a resistance to these stimuli, even learning to turn the tables. Consumers increasingly refuse to buy at full price, for example, knowing that a sale is just around the corner. They have fun 'deconstructing' advertisements. The observed has started playing games with the observer. Buyers are starting to use the system for their own purposes, just as marketers attempted to use it for theirs.

Juxtaposition of opposites

Although it is well-nigh impossible to 'target' or 'capture' the inscrutable, amorphous, unpindownable entity that is the postmodern consumer, it is still possible to engage with, appeal to or successfully attract them. The key to this quasi-conversation is not ever-more precise segmentation and positioning, but the exact opposite. An open, untargeted, ill-defined, ambiguous approach, which leaves scope for imaginative consumer participation (e.g. ironic advertising treatments where the purpose, pitch or indeed 'product' is unclear), is typical of postmodern marketing (Brown, 2006). This sense of fluidity and porosity is achieved by pastiche, by bricolage, by radical juxtaposition, by the mixing and matching of opposites, by combinations of contradictory styles, motifs and allusions, whether it be in the shimmering surfaces of pseudo-rococo postmodern buildings or the ceaseless cavalcade of contrasting images that are regularly encountered in commercial breaks, shop windows or roadside billboards. Occasionally, these succeed in exceeding the sum of their parts and combine to produce a sublime whole, an ephemeral spectacular, a fleeting moment of postmodern transcendence, as in *Riverdance*, *Shrek* or Celine Dion at Ceasar's Palace. Well, okay, maybe not.

The sweet bye and bye

While few would deny that Firat and Venkatesh have done much to explain the postmodern marketing condition, their analysis is not without its weaknesses. Many commentators would contest their inventory of overarching themes and, indeed, the very idea of clearly identifiable overarching themes. Little is accomplished by reciting such shortcomings. It is sufficient to note that all manner of alternative interpretations of postmodern marketing are now available and all sorts of signature 'themes' have been suggested. Cova (1996),

Table 2.2 Anything but the present

America has no now. We're reluctant to acknowledge the present. It's too embarrassing.

Instead, we reach into the past. Our culture is composed of sequels, reruns, remakes, revivals, reissues, re-releases, re-creations, re-enactments, adaptations, anniversaries, memorabilia, oldies radio and nostalgia record collections. World War Two has been refought on television so many times, the Germans and Japanese are now drawing residuals.

Of course, being essentially full of shit, we sometimes feel the need to dress up this past-preoccupation, as with pathetic references to reruns as 'encore presentations'.

Even instant replay is a form of token nostalgia: a brief visit to the immediate past for reexamination, before slapping it onto a highlight video for further review and re-review on into the indefinite future.

Our 'yestermania' includes fantasy baseball camps, where aging sad sacks pay money to catch baseballs thrown by men who were once their heroes. It is part of the fascination with sports memorabilia, a 'memory industry' so lucrative it has attracted counterfeiters.

In this the Age of Hyphens, we are truly retro-Americans.

Source: Carlin (1997, p. 110).

for example, considers it to be about the 'co-creation of meaning'. Thompson (2000) regards 'reflexivity' as the be all and end all. O'Donohoe (1997) draws attention to the importance of 'intertextuality'. And Sherry (1998) sets great store by PoMo's preoccupation with 'place'. The important point, however, is not that any of these readings is 'right' or 'wrong' but that postmodern marketing is itself plurivalent and open to multiple, highly personal, often irreconcilable interpretations.

For my own part, I reckon that *retrospection* is the defining feature of the present postmodern epoch and acerbic comedian George Carlin concurs (Table 2.2). The merest glance across the marketing landscape reveals that retro goods and services are all around. Old-fashioned brands, such as Atari, Airstream and Action Man have been adroitly revived and successfully relaunched. Ostensibly extinct trade characters, like Mr Whipple, Morris the Cat and Charlie the Tuna, are cavorting on the supermarket shelves once more. Ancient commercials are being re-broadcast (Ovaltine, Alka-Seltzer); time-worn slogans are being resuscitated (Britney Spears sings 'Come Alive' for Pepsi); and long-established products are being re-packaged in their original, eye-catching liveries (Blue Nun, Sun Maid raisins). Even motor cars and washing powder, long the acme of marketing's new-and-improved, whiter-than-white, we-have-the-technology world-view, are getting in on the retrospective act, as the

success of the BMW Mini Cooper and Colour Protection Persil daily remind us (Hedberg and Singh, 2001).

The service sector, similarly, is adopting a time-was ethos. Retro casinos, retro restaurants, retro retail stores, retro holiday resorts, retro home pages and retro roller coasters are two a penny. The movie business is replete with sequels, remakes and sequels of prequels, such as the recent Star Wars trilogy, to say nothing of historical spectaculars and postmodern period pieces like *Moulin Rouge* and *Gladiator*. *The Producers, Kiss Me Kate, Mama Mia* and analogous revivals are keeping the theatrical flag flying; meanwhile television programming is so retro that reruns of classic weather reports can't be far away. The music business, what is more, is retro a-go-go. Madonna is back on top. Queen are the champions once again. The artist formerly known as Prince is known as Prince, like before. Simple Minds are promising another miracle. Pink Floyd are rebuilding the wall, albeit temporarily. And U2 have reclaimed their title as the best U2 tribute band in the world.

Above and beyond the practices of retromarketing, this back-to-the-future propensity has significant implications for established marketing principles. As Brown (2001a, b) explains (after a fashion), it involves abandoning modern marketing's 'new-and improved' mindset and returning to the retro ethic of 'as good as always'. It spurns the dispassionate, white-coated, wonder-working laboratories of marketing science in favour of the extravagant, over-the-top hyperbole of pre-modern marketers like P.T. Barnum (consider the postmodern publicity stunts of retro CEO, Richard Branson). It eschews the chimera of customer-orientation for a marketing philosophy predicated on imagination, creativity and rule breaking. It refuses to truck with the guru du jour and goes back to the marketing giants of yesteryear – Wroe Alderson, Ralph Breyer, Melvin Copeland and all the rest. It gets back to basics by acknowledging that, for all the fancy folderol and academic huffing and puffing, marketing boils down to 'selling stuff'. No more, no less.

Crying in the wilderness

The retromarketing revolution is all very well, but the postmodern paradigm of which it is part poses a very important question for marketing and consumer researchers. Namely, how is it possible to understand, represent or describe postmodern marketing phenomena, when postmodernism challenges the very premises of conventional research? The logic, order, rationality and model building modalities of the modernist research tradition seem singularly inappropriate when addressing postmodern concerns. Now, this is not to suggest that established tools and techniques *cannot* be applied to postmodern artefacts and occurrences. There are any number of essentially modernist portrayals of the postmodern marketing condition (what is it?, what are its principal characteristics?, what can we 'do' with it?). Yet the relevance of such approaches remains moot. Is it *really* possible to capture the exuberance, the flamboyance, the incongruity, the energy, the playfulness of postmodern marketing in a standard, all-too-standard research report?

On the surface, this may seem like a comparatively trivial matter – if we jazz up our reports and use expressive language, everything will be okay – but it goes to the very heart of why we do what we do, how we do it and who we do it for. The decision facing marketing, as it has faced other academic disciplines grappling with postmodern incursions (and will continue to face marketing, regardless of the recommendations of the 'reformers'), is whether we should strive to be postmodern marketing researchers or researchers of postmodern marketing. The former implies

that the modalities of postmodernism should be imported into marketing research, that we should endeavour to 'walk the talk', to *be* postmodern in our publications, presentations and what have you. The latter intimates that researchers should confine themselves to applying proven tools and techniques to the brave old world of postmodern marketing. Just because the market has changed, or is supposed to have changed, it does not necessarily follow that tried and trusted methods of marketing research must change as well.

Although this choice is nothing if not clear-cut, a moment's reflection reveals it to be deeply divisive at best and potentially ruinous at worst. After all, if one group of marketing researchers works in a postmodern mode, a mode that is unlike anything that has gone before, it is fated to 'fail' when conventional standards of assessment are applied. Postmodern marketing research *cannot* meet the criteria – rigour, reliability, trustworthiness and so on – that are accepted, indeed *expected*, by champions of established methods and used to judge the worth, the contribution, the success or otherwise of a particular piece of work. For many commentators, then, postmodern marketing research does not constitute 'research' as such (other terms, invariably pejorative, are usually applied). However, as academic careers depend upon the publication of research findings, the potential for internecine conflict is self-evident. True, the etiquette of intellectual discourse emphasizes mutual tolerance, openness to opposing points of view, the community of scholars and suchlike, but the practicalities of academic politics belie the placid facade. Insurgence, in-fighting and intolerance are the order of the day. And the next day. And the day after that . . .

It would be excessive to imply that this latter-day postmodern dalliance has precipitated a civil war in the marketing academy – as we have seen, the mainstream is taking postmodern diagnoses on board, if not its prescriptions – but the PoMo fandango undoubtedly carries connotations of crisis, of uncertainty, of catastrophe, of intellectual meltdown. Indeed, if there is one word that captures the postmodern mindset that word is crisis. Almost every commentator on the postmodern condition refers to an oppressive atmosphere of 'crisis'. Denzin (1997), for instance, describes three contemporary crises facing the citadels of cerebration:

- *crisis of representation*, where established modes of depicting 'reality' (e.g. theories, metaphors, textual genres) are inadequate to the task;

- *crisis of legitimacy*, where conventional criteria for assessing research output (validity, reliability, objectivity etc.) leave a lot to be desired; and
- *crisis of praxis*, where academic contributions signally fail to contribute to the resolution, or even clarification, of practical problems.

Although formulated with regard to the human sciences generally, these concerns are highly relevant to the state of twenty-first-century marketing and consumer research. Our models are outmoded, our theories undertheorized, our laws lawless. Reliability is increasingly unreliable, the pursuit of reason unreasonable, and there are mounting objections to objectivity. Practitioners often fail to see the point of scholarly endeavour, despite the enormous amount of energy it absorbs, and get absolutely nothing of worth from the principal journals. The fact that the editorial boards of these journals are dominated by the very people who are planning to 'reform' marketing does not bode well for our field.

Be fruitful and multiply

The picture, however, isn't completely bleak. The postmodern manoeuvre in marketing and consumer research has brought benefits as well as costs. Scholarly conflict, remember, is not necessarily a 'bad thing'. On the contrary, a host of thinkers, from Nietzsche to Feyerabend, has observed that conflict can be a force for the good, since it helps avoid intellectual disintegration, dilapidation and decline (Collins, 1992; Brown, 1998).

Be that as it may, perhaps the greatest benefit of this postmodern pirouette is that it has led to dramatic changes in the methodology, domain and source material of marketing research (see Belk, 1991, 1995; Sherry, 1991; Hirschman and Holbrook, 1992). Methodologically, it has opened the door to an array of qualitative/interpretive research procedures predicted on hermeneutics, semiotics, phenomenology, ethnography and personal introspection, to name but the most prominent. In terms of domain, it has focussed attention on issues previously considered marginal to the managerial mainstream of brand choice and shopper behaviour (e.g. gift giving, compulsive consumption, obsessive collecting, grooming rituals, the meaning of personal possessions) and which has further encouraged researchers' interest in the tangential,

peripheral or hitherto ignored (homelessness, drug addiction, consumer resistance, anti-globalization movements, conspicuous consumption in the developing world etc.). With regard to source material, moreover, it has given rise to the realization that meaningful insights into marketing and consumption can be obtained from 'unorthodox' sources like novels, movies, plays, poetry, newspaper columns, comedy routines and so forth. Few would deny that restaurant critic Jonathan Meades' portrayal of the Hamburger Hades, colloquially known as *Planet Hollywood*, is just as good, if not better, than anything currently available in the academic literature (Table 2.3).

The outcome of the postmodern kafuffle is summarized in Table 2.4, though it is important to reiterate that this rupture is not as clear-cut as the columns suggest. Truth to tell, modernist approaches remain very deeply engrained in marketing, even though the postmodern lunatics are in the process of taking over the asylum (or having their straightjackets removed, at least). Similarly, the preferred stance of postmodern marketing researchers is by no means consistent or devoid of internal discord. Although the postmodern/post-positivist/interpretive/qualitative perspective (the terms themselves are indicative of intraparadigmatic wrangling) is often depicted in a monolithic manner, albeit largely for political purposes of the 'us against them' variety, postmodernism itself is unreservedly pluralist. It is a veritable monolith of pluralism.

Some 'postmodern' marketing researchers, for example, employ qualitative methods that are overwhelmingly 'scientific' in tenor (e.g. grounded theory), whereas others utilize procedures that hail from the liberal wing of the liberal arts (personal introspection). Some surmise that such research should be evaluated according to conventional, if adapted, assessment criteria (trustworthiness, reliability *et al.*), while others contend that entirely different measures (such as verisimilitude, defamiliarization or resonance) are rather more appropriate. Some say that the vaguely voguish term 'postmodern' has been usurped by scholarly trendies and bandwagon-boarders, although all such attempts to palisade the unpalisadable are themselves contrary to the unconditional postmodern spirit. Some, indeed, say it is impossible to 'do' postmodern research, since the attendant crisis of representation renders all theoretical, methodological and textual representations untenable. Postmodernism is nothing if not contradictory.

Table 2.3   Hurray for Planet Hollywood

The genius of Planet Hollywood is that it is a restaurant which replicates the way tracksuit bottoms eat at home. It gives a new meaning to home cooking. You can come here and eat couch-potato-style grot whilst gaping at a screen. Just the way you do at home. And you don't even have to button-punch. Your minimal attention span is addressed by the commensurate brevity of the clips. Planet Hollywood is ill named. Planet MTV would be apter. Planet Trash would be aptest. One wonders if the whole tawdry show is not some elaborate experiment being conducted by a disciple of the loopy behaviourist B.F. Skinner. The Hollywood it celebrates is not that of Welles or Siodmark or Sirk or Coppola, but that of aesthetic midgets with big budgets.

You fight your way (with no great enthusiasm) past merchandising 'opportunities' up a staircase to a world of operatives with clipboards – keen, smiley people who may or may not be victims of EST. They are frighteningly keen, alarmingly smiley. Our waiter, or customer chum, or whatever, was called Mike. He cared. He really cared about whether we were enjoying the whole experience. He kept asking. The pity of it is that he probably did care – he was so hyped up by the Planetary geist that he sought salvation through kiddy approbation.

He offered a trip of the premises. Politely declined. Close inspection is not liable to improve them. Over there is the sci-fi section within zoomorphic megagirders. Look that way and you've got the James Bond room, whose entrance apes the camera shutter device those mostly tiresome films used to use in their titles. Above us slung from the ceiling was a motorbike apparently used in a film I'd not even seen. It looked dangerous and I kept thinking that there would be no more pathetic way to die than by being crushed in so dreadful a place.

Source: Meades (1997).

Table 2.4   Modern and postmodern research approaches

Modern	Postmodern
Positivist	Non-positivist
Experiments/surveys	Ethnographies
Quantitative	Qualitative
A priori theory	Emergent theory
Economic/psychological	Sociological/anthropological
Micro/managerial	Macro/cultural
Focus on buying	Focus on consuming
Emphasis on cognitions	Emphasis on emotions
American	Multicultural

Source: Belk (1995).

Behold a pale horse

Irrespective of internal debates, it is not unreasonable to conclude that the postmodern fissure has opened up a significant intellectual space within the field of marketing research. Perhaps the clearest evidence of this 'space' is the way in which marketing scholarship is communicated. Traditional research reports and academic articles have been supplemented with works of poetry, drama, photoessays, videography, netnography, musical performances and many more (Stern, 1998; Brown, 2005). Conventional modes of academic discourse – unadorned, passive voiced, third personed, painfully pseudo-scientific prose – are being joined by exercises in 'experimental' writing, where exaggeration, alliteration and flights of rhetorical fancy are the order of the day. The success of such experiments is moot, admittedly and many mainstream marketing scholars are understandably appalled by such egregious exhibitions of self-indulgence. If nothing else, however, they *do* draw attention to the fact that writing in a 'scientific' manner isn't the only way of writing about marketing. There is no law that says marketing discourse must be as-dry-as-dust, though a perusal of the principal academic journals might lead one to think otherwise.

Be that as it may, the inexorable rise of postmodern marketing leaves one significant question unanswered. If, as postmodernists loudly proclaim, the old marketing model is broken, and beyond repair, what should be put in its place? This is a critical issue, one that many postmodernists prefer to avoid, usually by contending that PoMo is a critique not a concept. The only problem is that without a workable alternative, most people will (understandably) stick with what they know, even if it doesn't work as well as it ought to. People will attempt to patch up the current model, and who can blame them?

In truth, there is no shortage of solutions to marketing's manifold ills, though most of these comprise the cogitations of consultants rather than academics. The business sections of high street bookstores are heaving with works that challenge the received marketing wisdom and contend that it is time for a change. As with the postmodernists, this emerging school of marketing thought is highly variegated and somewhat contradictory. However, the principal contributions can be quickly summarized under the following Eight Es:

- *Experiential* – ecstasy, emotion, extraordinary experience (e.g. Schmitt, 1999);
- *Environmental* – space, place and *genius loci* (Sherry, 1998);
- *Aesthetic* – beauty, art, design (Dickinson and Svensen, 2000);
- *Entertainment* – every business is show business (Wolf, 1999);
- *Evanescence* – fads, buzz, the wonderful word of mouth (Rosen, 2000);
- *Evangelical* – spirituality, meaning, transcendence (Finan, 1998);

- *Ethical* – buy an eye shadow, save the world (Roddick, 2001);
- *Effrontery* – shock sells, who bares wins, gross is good (Ridderstrale and Nordstrom, 2000).

E-type marketing is many and varied, yet its espousers share the belief that marketing *must* change, as do the aforementioned reformers. Nowhere is this ebullient ethos better illustrated than in John Grant's *New Marketing Manifesto*. 'New Marketing', he argues, is predicated on creativity; it treats brands as living ideas; it is incorrigibly entrepreneurial; it favours change over conservatism; it is driven by insight not analysis; and it is humanist in spirit rather than 'scientific'. Granted, Grant's final chapter reveals that New Marketing isn't so new after all (retro rides again) and at no point does he align his precepts with postmodernism, but the simple fact of the matter is that he's singing from the postmodern marketing hymnbook (Grant, 1999, p. 182).

> New Marketing is a challenge to the pseudo-scientific age of business. It is a great human, subjective enterprise. It is an art. New Marketing needs New Market Research. Old market research was largely there to objectify and to justify – to support conventions. New Marketing is here to challenge and seek the unconventional.

The postmodernists couldn't put it better. Whether our self-appointed reformers can put things right is another matter entirely . . .

The end is nigh

For some, 'postmodern' is just one among many pseudo-intellectual buzz-words which attain prominence for a moment, only to pass swiftly into merciful obscurity. However, postmodernism's 15 minutes of Warholesque fame is dragging on a bit. Postmodern intrusions are evident across the entire spectrum of scholarly subject areas, marketing and consumer research among them. Indeed, the flotsam, jetsam and general detritus of consumer society are widely regarded, by non-business academics especially, as the very epitome of postmodernity.

'Postmodern', admittedly, is an umbrella term which shelters a number of closely related positions. These range from latter-day developments in the aesthetic sphere, most notably the blurring of hitherto sacrosanct boundaries between high culture and low, to the re-emergence of counter-enlightenment proclivities among para-intellectuals and academicians.

The multi-faceted character of postmodernity is equally apparent in marketing milieus. The phenomenon known as the postmodern consumer, which comprises gendered subject positions indulging in playful combinations of contrasting identities, roles and characters (each with its requisite regalia of consumables) is now an accepted socio-cultural artefact, as is the so-called 'post-shopper'. The latter shops in a knowing, cynical, been-there-done-that-didn't-buy-the-souvenirs manner or loiters in the mall looking at other consumers looking at them. For Firat and Venkatesh, indeed, the essential character of postmodern marketing is captured in five main themes – *hyperreality, fragmentation, reversed production and consumption, decentred subjects* and *juxtaposition of opposites* – though these categories are not clear-cut and other commentators see things differently.

Above and beyond empirical manifestations of the postmodern impulse, the field of marketing and consumer research has been revolutionized by postmodern methodologies, epistemologies, axiologies, ontologies, eschatologies (any ologies you can think of, really). Although there is some debate over what actually constitutes postmodern marketing research, it is frequently associated with the qualitative or interpretive turn that was precipitated by the Consumer Odyssey of the mid-80s and academics' attendant interest in non-managerial concerns. Perhaps the clearest sign of 'postmodernists at work', however, is the convoluted, hyperbolic and utterly incomprehensible language in which their arguments are couched, albeit their apparently boundless self-absorption is another distinctive textual trait. Does my brand look big in this?

In fairness, the postmodernists' linguistic excesses and apparent self-preoccupation serve a very important purpose. Their language mangling draws attention to the fact that 'academic' styles of writing are conventions not commandments, decided upon not decreed, an option not an order. But, hey, don't take my word for it; check out the further reading below . . .

References

Appignanesi, R. and Garratt, C. (1995) *Postmodernism for Beginners*, Icon, Trumpington.

Apple, M. (1984) *Free Agents*, Harper & Row, New York reprinted in McHale, B. (1992), *Constructing Postmodernism*, Routledge, London, pp. 38–41.

Belk, R. W. (ed.) (1991) *Highways and Buyways: Naturalistic Research from the Consumer Behavior Odyssey*, Association for Consumer Research, Provo.

Belk, R. W. (1995) Studies in the New Consumer Behaviour, in Miller, D. (ed.), *Acknowledging Consumption*, Routledge, London, pp. 58–95.

Berger, W. (2001) *Advertising Today*, Phaidon, London.

Best, S. and Kellner, D. (2001) *The Postmodern Adventure*, Guildford, New York.

Bocock, R. (1993) *Consumption*, Routledge, London.

Brown, S. (1998) Slacker Scholarship and the Well Wrought Turn, in Stern, B. B. (ed.), *Representing Consumers*, Routledge, London, pp. 365–383.

Brown, S. (2001a) *Marketing – The Retro Revolution*, Sage, London.

Brown, S. (2001b) Torment your customers (they'll love it), *Harvard Business Review*, **79**(9), 82–88.

Brown, S. (2005) *Wizard! Harry Potter's Brand Magic*, Cyan, London.

Brown, S. (2006) Ambi-brand culture: on a wing and a swear with Ryanair, in Schroeder, J. E. and Salzer-Morling, M. (eds), *Brand Culture*, Routledge, London, pp. 50–66.

Brown, S., Bell, J. and Smithee, A. (1997) From genesis to revelation – introduction to the special issue, *European Journal of Marketing*, **31**(9/10), 632–638.

Calás, M. B. and Smircich, L. (eds) (1997) *Postmodern Management Theory*, Ashgate, Dartmouth.

Carlin, G. (1997) *Brain Droppings*, Hyperion, New York.

Collins, R. (1992) On the Sociology of Intellectual Stagnation: the Late Twentieth Century in Perspective, in Featherstone, M. (ed.), *Cultural Theory and Cultural Change*, Sage, London, pp. 73–96.

Cova, B. (1996), What postmodernism means to marketing managers, *European Management Journal*, **14**(5), 494–499.

Crews, F. (2001) *Postmodern Pooh*, North Point, New York.

Davidson, M. (1992) *The Consumerist Manifesto: Advertising in Postmodern Times*, Routledge, London.

Denzin, N. K. (1997) *Interpretive Ethnography: Ethnographic Practices for the 21st Century*, Sage, Thousand Oaks.

Dickinson, P. and Svensen, N. (2000) *Beautiful Corporations: Corporate Style in Action*, Pearson, London.

Dugdale, J. (2001) Diary, *The Sunday Times*, Culture, 28 January, 37.

Falk, P. and Campbell, C. (eds) (1997) *The Shopping Experience*, Sage, London.

Featherstone, M. (1991) *Consumer Culture and Postmodernism*, Sage, London.

Finan, A. (1998) *Corporate Christ*, Management Books, Chalford.

Firat, A. F. and Venkatesh, A. (1995) Liberatory postmodernism and the reenchantment of consumption, *Journal of Consumer Research*, **22**(December), 239–267.

Goldman, R. and Papson, S. (1996) *Sign Wars: The Cluttered Landscape of Advertising*, Guilford, New York.

Goss, J. (1993) The magic of the mall: an analysis of form, function and meaning in the contemporary retail built environment, *Annals of the Association of American Geographers*, **83**(1), 18–47.

Grant, J. (1999) *The New Marketing Manifesto*, Orion, London.

Gummesson, E. (2001) Are current research approaches in marketing leading us astray? *Marketing Theory*, **1**(1), 27–48.

Hedberg, A. and Singh, S. (2001) Retro chic or cheap relics? *Marketing Week*, 18 October, 24–27.

Hirschman, E. C. and Holbrook, M. B. (1992) *Postmodern Consumer Research: The Study of Consumption as Text*, Sage, Newbury Park.

Lyotard, J.-F. (1984 [1979]), *The Postmodern Condition: A Report on Knowledge*, trans. Bennington, G. and Massumi, B. Manchester University Press, Manchester.

Maclaran, P. and Brown, S. (2001) The future perfect declined: utopian studies and consumer research, *Journal of Marketing Management*, **17**(3/4), 367–390.

Meades, J. (1997) Eating out, *The Times Magazine*, Saturday 20 December, 33.

Miles, S., Anderson, A. and Meethan, K. (eds) (2002) *The Changing Consumer: Markets and Meanings*, Routledge, London.

Miller, D. (ed.) (1995) *Acknowledging Consumption: A Review of New Studies*, Routledge, London.

Mitchell, A. (2001) *Right Side Up: Building Brands in the Age of the Organized Consumer*, HarperCollins, London.

O'Donohoe, S. (1997) Raiding the pantry: advertising intertextuality and the young adult audience, *European Journal of Marketing*, **31**(3/4), 234–253.

Piercy, N. (1997, 2002) *Market-Led Strategic Change*, Butterworth-Heinemann, Oxford.

Ridderstrale, J. and Nordstrom, K. (2000) *Funky Business: Talent Makes Capital Dance*, FTCom, London.

Roddick, A. (2001) *Business as Unusual: The Triumph of Anita Roddick*, Thorsons, London.

Rosen, E. (2000) *The Anatomy of Buzz*, HarperCollins, London.

Schmitt, B. (1999) *Experiential Marketing*, Free Press, New York.

Sherry, J. F. (1991) Postmodern Alternatives: the Interpretive Turn in Consumer Research, in Robertson, T. S. and Kassarjian, H. H. (eds), *Handbook of Consumer Research*, Prentice-Hall, Englewood Cliffs, pp. 548–591.

Sherry, J. F. (ed.) (1998) *Servicescapes: The Concept of Place in Contemporary Markets*, NTC Books, Chicago.

Sheth, J. and Sisodia, R. (2006) *Does Marketing Need Reform?: Fresh Perspectives on the Future*, M.E. Sharpe, Armonk.

Shields, R. (ed.) (1992) *Lifestyle Shopping: The Subject of Consumption*, Routledge, London.

Stern, B. B. (ed.) (1998) *Representing Consumers: Voices, Views and Visions*, Routledge, London.

Thompson, C. J. (2000) Postmodern Consumer Goals Made Easy!!!, in Ratneshwar, S., Mick, D. G. and Huffman, C. (eds), *The Why of Consumption: Contemporary Perspectives on Consumer Motives, Goals and Desires*, Routledge, London, pp. 120–139.

Ward, G. (1997) *Teach Yourself Postmodernism*, Hodder Headline, London.

Warde, A. (2002) Setting the Scene: Changing Conceptions of Consumption, in Miles, S., Anderson, A. and Meethan, K. (eds), *The Changing Consumer: Markets and Meanings*, Routledge, London, pp. 10–24.

Wolf, M. J. (1999) *The Entertainment Economy*, Penguin, London.

Further reading

Modesty forbids, you understand, but you might find the following of interest:

Brown, S. (1995) *Postmodern Marketing*, Routledge, London. Summarizes the major strands of postmodern thought, coupled with a critique of 'modern' marketing theory.

Brown, S. (1998) *Postmodern Marketing Two: Telling Tales*, International Thomson, London. Extends the first book by arguing that art, aesthetics, storytelling *et al.* offer a possible way forward for 21st century marketing scholarship.

Brown, S. (2001) *Marketing – The Retro Revolution*, Sage, London. Rummages through the dustbin of marketing history and comes up with an alternative to the 'modern' marketing paradigm.

Brown, S. (2003) *Free Gift Inside!!*, Capstone, Oxford. Challenges the customer-centric model of marketing and puts forward an alternative based on marke*tease*.

CHAPTER 3

Relationship marketing

LISA O'MALLEY and CAROLINE TYNAN

Marketing as a body of knowledge and an academic discipline owes a great deal to what Bartels (1976) calls the period of re-conceptualization where the marketing concept and the mix management paradigm (4Ps), introduced in the 1950s and 1960s, defined the nature and content of marketing management (O'Malley and Patterson, 1998). This approach focused predominately on the marketing of products to large homogeneous consumer markets (as existed in the USA). Underpinning this approach are assumptions from micro-economics that markets are efficient, buyers and sellers are anonymous, previous and future transactions are irrelevant and that the price and quality function contains all of the information needed for consumers to make a rational decision (Easton and Araujo, 1994). However, even within this *transactional* approach to marketing it is obvious that these assumptions are questionable given the increasing importance of marketing communications, branding and relationships in consumers' decision making in the last 50 years.

The mix management approach focuses on the sale of products to consumers. However, a great deal of marketing occurs in situations other than this, for example when the object of exchange is a service rather than a product and when the buyer is a company rather than an individual consumer. The mix management paradigm had very little to offer in situations other than mass consumer product markets and therefore new approaches sensitive to specific contexts and cultures needed to be developed (see Shostack, 1977; Håkansson, 1982;

Gummesson, 1987). This resulted in a new approach to marketing, based on the creation and maintenance of relationships, becoming popular. This approach, known as relationship marketing, is the focus of this chapter.

The purpose of this chapter then is to begin to describe how the rich body of knowledge that is relationship marketing has come into being, what its major underpinning theories are, what defining moments occurred and what might shape its future. The chapter begins by defining what is commonly understood by relationship marketing. Next, a brief review is offered of the development of relationship marketing in the key areas of services marketing, business-to-business and consumer marketing. In a chapter such as this only a brief overview of the field can be offered and thus, readers are directed towards the seminal works in each area. Included in the chapter are discussions of customer relationship management (CRM), brand consumer relationships (BCRs) as well as a broad overview of the models of relationship development and a consideration of the relationship success variables. Finally, some possible research opportunities are identified as a basis for further work in this rich and exciting area.

Relationship marketing defined

The broadest understanding of what we mean when we talk about relationship marketing (RM) is provided by Gummesson (1994, p. 12) who regards RM as 'marketing seen as relationship, networks and interactions'. Interestingly, this view of marketing has become so prevalent that the whole of marketing has now been re-defined in terms of relationships. For example, the American Marketing Association definition published in 2004 is cited, and critically reviewed from an RM perspective, by Grönroos (2006, p. 397). It states:

> 'Marketing is an organizational function and a set of processes for creating, communicating and delivering value to customers and for managing customer relationships in ways that benefit the organization and its stakeholders'.

Given this understanding, it is generally agreed that when we talk about relationship marketing we are referring to commercial relationships between economic partners, service providers and customers at various levels of the marketing channel and the broader business environment. This recognition results in a focus on the creation, maintenance and termination of these commercial relationships in order that parties to the relationship achieve their objectives (mutual benefit). Profit remains an underlying business concern and relational objectives are achieved through the fulfilment of promises. An acceptance of a service-centred view of marketing which concentrates on intangible resources such as skills, information and knowledge, and the co-creation of value between relational partners through interactivity and connectivity in ongoing relationships, has re-emphasized the importance of relationship orientation in successful marketing (Vargo and Lusch, 2004).

History of relationship marketing

One of the most interesting things about the body of knowledge that has come to be known as relationship marketing is that it emerged independently at the end of the 1970s in different research contexts and in several different countries. In other words, relationship marketing was discussed, defined and explored in different research 'silos' with very little consideration of what was taking place elsewhere. This section will briefly review the motivation, contribution and important concepts to emerge in services and business-to-business research. For a more detailed review of the history interested readers are directed to Möller and Halinen (2000) and Harker and Egan (2006).

The relational paradigm has a relatively long history within the management literature (Levine

and White, 1961; Evan, 1966; Van de Ven, 1976). In marketing, this approach to understanding business markets became popular among the IMP group in Europe in the mid-1970s with their network or interaction approach, and received some attention in North America within the marketing channels literature (Anderson and Narus, 1984) and later in the buyer–seller literature (Dwyer *et al.*, 1987). Since the late 1980s, inter-firm relationships have become more strategic (Wilson, 1995) and there has been an increasing emphasis on networks (Thorelli, 1986) for securing sustainable competitive advantage (Jarillo, 1988). Thus, by the mid-1990s, the literature on inter-organizational marketing relationships was characterized by a dual emphasis on single dyadic relationships (the relational paradigm) and on relationships within the context of networks (the network paradigm). Through a review of the contributions from each sector, it becomes obvious how 'interaction, relationships and networks' have come to dominate contemporary understandings of marketing.

Contributions from business-to-business marketing

A great deal of academic research has been conducted in the area of business-to-business marketing, and, from this, a number of distinct research streams have emerged which foreground inter-organizational relationships. Most notable here, is the work of the IMP group in Europe and work on buyer–seller relationships in the USA. These are briefly reviewed below.

The IMP group is a loose network of European researchers who have been involved in research on business relationships in Europe since the mid-1970s. Interestingly, researchers within the IMP fail to agree on the exact meaning of the acronym with some suggesting that it is the Industrial Marketing and Purchasing Group and others referring to the International Marketing and Purchasing Group (see Ford, 1997). The problem occurs because industrial (or business-to-business) marketing in Europe is, by definition, international. IMP researchers relied primarily on qualitative methodologies (observation, interviewing managers and archive data) within a number of case studies in order to explore inter-organizational exchange. This work resulted in the recognition that relationships are important to the facilitation of inter-organizational exchange (often more important than price) and that the *interaction* between buyer and seller organizations was integral to the formation and maintenance of relationships. A detailed review of the interaction approach was published in a very influential book (Håkansson, 1982). Indeed, this view of interaction and relationships is integral to the subsequent development of the relational paradigm. The major contribution of the interaction paradigm was the recognition (contra to the mix management paradigm) that buyers and sellers could be equally active in pursuing exchange. Equally the work identified the influence of the business environment and atmosphere on both short-term exchange episodes and long-term relationships affecting co-operation, adaptation and institutionalization (Håkansson, 1982). Although the interaction approach was commended for advancing understanding of exchange in a business-to-business context, it was also criticized for (a) taking a single actor (buyer or seller) perspective (see Ford, 1997) and (b) being too difficult to operationalize (see Wilson, 1995). Whilst the latter problem has not been overcome, the early focus on dyadic interaction (one buyer and seller pair) was later superseded by the network approach which look at webs of linked relationships (see Andersson and Söderlund, 1988; Ford, 1997).

The major contributions of the interaction approach to our present understanding of relationship marketing include the following issues:

- Both buyers and sellers have similar roles in forming, developing and operating relationships (Håkansson, 1982; Ford, 1990).
- The match between supplier capability and customer need is accomplished by interaction between the two parties, and adaptation by one or both of them (Håkansson, 1982).
- Personal contacts are frequently used as a mechanism for initiating, developing and maintaining relationships (Turnbull, 1979; Cunningham and Homse, 1986).
- Interaction with other companies is the force that unifies the company and gives it the capability to perform its activities (Ford, 1990).
- Each party to a relationship may take the initiative in seeking a partner, and either party may attempt to specify, manipulate or control the transaction process. Thus, 'this process is not one of action and reaction: it is one of interaction' (Ford, 1997, p. xi).

- The relationship between buyer and seller is frequently long term, close and involves complex patterns of interactions.
- The links between buyer and seller often become institutionalized into a set of roles that each party expects the other to perform.
- Both parties are likely to be involved in adaptations of their own processes or product technologies to accommodate the other, and neither party is likely to make unilateral changes to its activities without consultation or at least consideration of the reaction of their opposite number in the relationship.

In the USA, research was also underway on business-to-business exchange, although initially at least this remained within the dominant mix management and adversarial paradigm. Earlier research had demonstrated the importance of power and conflict particularly in channel research (El-Ansary and Stern, 1972; Wilkinson, 1973, 1979; Etgar, 1976) and, in the early 1980s there was the beginning of a recognition that co-operation might prove to be a more important explanatory variable. In the latter part of the 1980s two significant events occurred. Firstly, within the business environment generally, the impact of Japanese business systems particularly 'just-in-time' was having an important impact on the competitiveness of US and European companies (see Spekman, 1988, Webster, 1992). One of the major sources of competitive advantage enjoyed by the Japanese was assumed to be the strength of business relationships and the nature of their distribution systems where the major Japanese companies 'sit in a web of strong permanent relationships with its major creditors, suppliers, key customers and other important stakeholders . . . bound together by complex and evolving ties of mutual benefit and commercial interest' (Doyle and Stern, 2006, p. 14). This propelled an interest in relationships generally (Webster, 1992; Möller and Wilson, 1995). Secondly, Dwyer *et al.* (1987) wrote a seminal paper that employed social exchange theory (SET) to offer insights into the motivation and process of relationship formation. A major contribution of this paper was the suggestion that, like business markets, consumer markets might also benefit from attention to the conditions that foster relational bonds. Thus, this important paper legitimized relationship marketing in business markets and opened up the possibility that it might be an appropriate vehicle to engender customer retention in mass consumer markets.

The major contributions of US researchers include:

- Interaction between organizations must be understood in terms of economic, behavioural and political influences (Stern and Reve, 1980).
- Explicit consideration of SET in conceptualizing relationship development (Anderson and Narus, 1984, 1990; Dwyer et al., 1987).
- Creation of models of relationship development explained in terms of increasing commitment and trust (Anderson and Narus, 1984, 1990; Dwyer et al., 1987). This underpinned the later work of Morgan and Hunt (1994).
- The recognition that co-operation and communication lead to trust which in turn leads to greater levels of co-operation. (Anderson and Narus, 1984, 1990).

Contributions from services marketing

The 1970s saw the emergence of services marketing as a distinct aspect of marketing. Early attempts to apply marketing techniques were dismissed as being essentially product focused and failing to deal with the unique characteristics of services (see Shostack, 1977). Essentially, the unique characteristics of services – inseparability, intangibility, heterogeneity and perishability (Zeithaml et al., 1985) highlight the importance of people in the service experience. Although one hopeful contribution to the services literature in terms of extending the marketing mix to 7Ps was offered by Booms and Bitner (1981) this proved to be less compelling than a focus on the service encounter (Solomon et al., 1985) and upon interaction (Grönroos, 1983). The recognition that customer retention was central to services marketing, focused attention on the notion of creating service relationships (Grönroos, 1983, 1989, 1994; Gummesson, 1987) and led Berry (1983) to coin the term relationship marketing. To ensure that service delivery personnel were fully trained and motivated to build and maintain service relationships, internal marketing was developed. It rested on the recognition that 'a service must be successfully marketed to the personnel so that the employees accept the service offering and thoroughly engage in performing their marketing duties' (Grönroos, 1978, p. 594).

Contributions to the relational paradigm from services marketing include the development and understanding of service encounters (Solomon

et al., 1985), internal marketing (George, 1977; Grönroos, 1978; Berry, 1981; Gummesson, 1987), service design (Shostack, 1984) and service quality (Parasuraman et al., 1985). Although viewed as distinct research streams within services marketing (Fisk et al., 1993), they share many common themes. In particular, there is an emphasis on the interaction process (relationship marketing, service encounter and service design), and on creating and understanding quality from the point of view of the customer (service quality and internal marketing). Specific contributions from research in services marketing which develop our understanding of relationship marketing include the following conclusions:

- Service provision can be customized to suit the specific requirements of the buyer (Lovelock, 1983).
- The development of formal, ongoing relationships is a viable strategy in attempting to engender and build customer loyalty (Lovelock, 1983).
- The nature of services forces the buyer into intimate contact with the seller (Grönroos, 1978).
- The service encounter (interaction) has an important impact on customers' perceptions of, and satisfaction with, the service (Grönroos, 1983, 1994).
- Service encounters facilitate the development of social bonds (Crosby and Stephens, 1987; Berry and Parasuraman, 1991).
- The SERVQUAL gap model emerged as a useful managerial tool that distinguishes between *actual quality* and *customer-perceived quality* (Parasuraman et al., 1985, 1988).
- Customers assess services on the basis of both *technical* quality (the quality of the service itself) and *functional* quality (the quality of the service delivery process) (Gummesson, 1987; Grönroos, 1990).
- The importance of *part-time marketers* (i.e. those individuals who are service providers but probably not marketing personnel) was recognized and highlighted (Gummesson, 1987).
- Internal marketing is using a marketing approach within the business to target employees was recognized as an important tool in ensuring service quality (Gummesson, 1987; Grönroos, 1994; Berry, 1995) and was posited as integral to relationship management.
- Not all service encounters are necessary relational, only those which are extended, emotive or intimate (Crosby et al., 1990; Price et al., 1995).

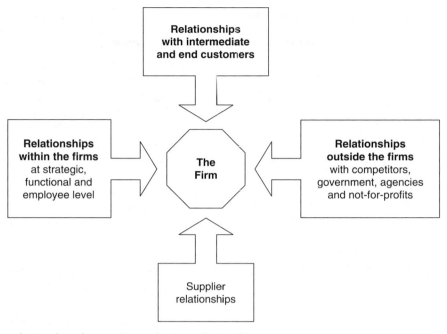

Figure 3.1 The relational exchanges in marketing relationship
Source: After Morgan and Hunt (1994, p. 21).

Focal relationships

The relational paradigm drives an organization to focus on relationships. Strategically, this involves identifying which relationships are to be pursued and how they are to be managed (Gummesson, 1994; Morgan and Hunt, 1994). In terms of the first issue, identifying marketing relationships, there are a number of competing views. One essentially suggests that relationships are not chosen, rather relationships exist and the choice is whether to manage them explicitly or not. Within this perspective, Gummesson (1999) considers 30 relationships to be important resulting in a broad organizational remit for the firm. In contrast, Morgan and Hunt (1994) limit their definition of relationships more precisely within the conventional business domain (see Figure 3.1). They suggest four broad categories of relationships: supplier partnerships, lateral partnerships, customer partnerships and internal partnerships. Within each of these categories the authors further specify a number of particular relationships. These include supplier relationships (with goods and service suppliers), internal relationships (with employees, etc.), lateral relationships (with government, competitors, etc.) and buyer relationships (with immediate and ultimate customers).

As we can see Morgan and Hunt (1994) and Christopher *et al.* (1991) extended the focus of RM beyond buyer–seller relationships to include stakeholders as partners. As a result, it is now generally accepted that firm–employee relationships, firm–public agency relationships, firm–investor relationships, firm–competitor firm relationships are all within the domain of RM, including the upstream and downstream supplier–customer relationships. While some authors consider that marketers should focus only on the consumer, others adopt a multiple stakeholder perspective and argue that marketers should adopt a more strategic role in the organization and take responsibility for any relationship that influences the ultimate sale (Payne and Holt, 2001). Berry (1995, p. 242) defines relationship marketing in terms of a means–end equation: 'in effect, companies must establish relationships with non-customer groups (the means) in order to establish relationships with customers (the end)'. This definition effectively re-focuses marketing in terms of end-customer relationships. This position is consistent with other definitions that assume that the aim of marketing is the development of customer relationships (cf. Ford, 1980; Berry, 1983; Jackson, 1985). Grönroos' (1994) definition does mention customers, but also acknowledges the importance of 'other partners'. However, this position identifies a very broad domain for marketing.

Equally it is important to consider how each relationship should be managed, that is, should all customers be treated equally, what resources should be invested in each relationship, how should the portfolio of relationships be managed? These issues are encapsulated into what Håkansson (1982) refers to as handling problems and limitation problems.

The interpersonal relationship metaphor and use of social exchange theory (SET)

Most marketers today view their interaction with customers in terms of a relationship. While many such interactions share similarities with close interpersonal relationships, and some interactions between, say, customers and their service providers can be actual interpersonal relationships, others are simply associations which occur with repeated transactions. However, relationship is a value laden word. It conjures up visions of closeness, mutuality, intimacy, caring and sharing. In describing all such interactions as relationships we have been able to borrow ideas from SET and also from our own understanding of interpersonal relationships. So while the word is used metaphorically we have reified it and see all relationships in relationship marketing as having the characteristics of an interpersonal relationship. This could explain the emphasis, some would argue over-emphasis, placed in RM research of variables related to interpersonal relationships, namely trust, commitment and communication (O'Malley *et al.*, 2008).

Relationship marketing in consumer markets

Relationship marketing developed in industrial and service marketing contexts as a reaction against the limitations of mainstream (transactional) marketing. Initially, eschewed by manufacturers interested in mass consumer markets because of the efficiency of the mix management paradigm, changes in the competitive climate, new technology and better customer information in the latter part of the 1980s and early 1990s propelled the interest in relationship marketing in mass consumer markets. Indeed, it may be useful to conceptualize considerations of relationship marketing in mass consumer markets in terms of four phases: obscurity, discovery, acceptance and popularity

(see O'Malley and Tynan, 2000). Prior to the mid-1980s (obscurity) there was little consideration of the need for customer retention (cf. Rosenberg and Czepiel, 1984). In the latter part of the 1980s technology developments fuelled the growth of direct and database marketing (Fletcher *et al.*, 1991; Evans *et al.*, 1996) which Dwyer *et al.* (1987) argued could usefully form the basis of relationship marketing in mass consumer markets. This, together with other academic considerations of direct and database marketing marked the period of discovery for relationship marketing (O'Malley and Tynan, 2000). Essentially, the recognition that customer retention is far less costly and significantly more profitable than a focus on customer acquisition (Rosenberg and Czepiel, 1984; Reichheld and Sasser, 1990) cemented the business argument justifying a new approach. Acceptance is largely attributed to the work of Sheth and Parvatiyar (1995) who not only argued the benefits of relationship marketing in a consumer context but, more importantly, re-framed relationship marketing within the extant consumer behaviour literature. Thus, although there were some suggestions that relationship marketing might not be appropriate in a consumer context (e.g. Barnes, 1994, 1995; Grönroos, 1994) marketing practitioners were already doing relationship marketing – often in the form of loyalty or retention programmes. Relationship marketing became increasingly popular throughout the latter part of the 1990s and is still hugely popular today.

Customer relationship management

Whilst there is a suggestion that relationships between consumers and organizations (see Sheth and Parvatiyar, 1995) and consumers and their brands (see Fournier, 1998) have always been important, it is also recognized that, today, such relationships must be facilitated or at least supported by technology (Dwyer *et al.*, 1987; Blattberg and Deighton, 1991). As a result, the focus within consumer markets has recently evolved from RM to CRM, with CRM (customer relationship management) being defined as 'information-enabled relationship marketing' (Ryals and Payne, 2001, p. 3). Although philosophically in line with relationship marketing, the focus in CRM is on the technology, particularly on that technology which attempts to manage all customer touch points and facilitate the integration of various database systems to provide a single picture of the customer (Peppers and Rogers, 1995; Ryals and Knox, 2001).

This picture encompasses the customers' needs, preferences, buying behaviour and price sensitivity and allows the CRM business to focus on building customer retention and profitability. However, underpinning both approaches is the understanding that CRM is a technology tool which facilitates interaction between different databases and different interaction media in order to facilitate segmentation and communication (see Ryals and Knox, 2001). In their introduction to the *Journal of Marketing* special section, editors Boulding *et al.* (2005) offer a thorough reappraisal of the history, definition, current position and pitfalls of CRM.

As previously outlined, the relationship marketing ideal developed out of the study of exchange in intra-organizational and high-contact services markets. The observed value of relationships in these markets drove attempts to implement similar ideals in mass consumer markets (e.g. Dwyer *et al.*, 1987), where traditional marketing techniques were being questioned and customer expectations and competitive pressures were increasing (Sisodia and Wolfe, 2000). However, the operationalization of the relationship marketing ideal in consumer markets requires the exploitation of information technology if it is to be extended beyond application only to most valued customers, as it was originally conceived (Rogers and Peppers, 1997). Information on customers is critical to developing and maintaining customer relationships (Boulding *et al.*, 2005). While small organizations with very few customers find it relatively easy to collect and use relevant information in building customer relationships, larger organizations with mass markets find this practically impossible to do. Thus, information technology, initially in the form of the database was regarded as 'an agent of surrogacy to be enlisted to help marketers to re-create the operating styles of yesterday's merchants' (Sisodia and Wolfe, 2000, p. 526).

Vast reductions in the cost of information technology brought the promise that relational strategies might be extended to all customers. Unfortunately, the application of technology in these markets has not been unproblematic, perhaps because focus has shifted to technology, at the cost of remembering the ideal it was supposed to support (O'Malley *et al.*, 1997; Fournier *et al.*, 1998; Mitussis *et al.*, 2006). Moreover, the limited understanding of *relating* to customers means that, contrary to the insight of the IT literature (e.g. Feeny *et al.*, 1997), information systems were imposed that could be incompatible with a firms culture, capabilities and systems (e.g. Piercy, 1998).

The ability to develop successful customer relationships lies in an organization's capacity to understand and respect its customers, their individual preferences, expectations and changing needs. While today's markets are so complex that such customer intimacy may be precluded (Di Tienne and Thompson, 1996) the database is employed by contemporary marketers to try to overcome this problem. In the absence of both intimate knowledge of individual customers and interpersonal contact with them, the database promised an opportunity to capture information on customers in a useful and accessible fashion (Shani and Chalasani, 1992), enabling them to identify individual customers, monitor their buying behaviour (Blattberg and Deighton, 1991) and to communicate with them on an individual basis, often with personalized offers. Although these are essentially the basic elements of database marketing, RM should use such data 'to build a long-term connection between the company and consumer' (Copulsky and Wolf, 1990, p. 17).

The creation of a 'special status' between company and customers (Czepiel, 1990; Rowe and Barnes, 1998) relies on fostering customer intimacy (Jackson, 1985). In order to achieve this, data on transactions is held in the customer database and this is overlaid with demographic, geodemographic, lifestyle data and a range of other data sources including country court judgements (CCJs), electoral register, etc. The data are fused and held in a data warehouse where 'biographic data' (Evans, 1999) on individual customers can be viewed. Thus, within an RM strategy, the database becomes a key knowledge tool for the organization (Di Tienne and Thompson, 1996; Evans *et al.*, 2004) and is used to simulate indicia of intimacy and connectedness. In addition to databases, other technologies have developed that 'can give companies a host of opportunities for communicating with the customer and have information on hand to engage, inform and direct each customer with complete knowledge as to the customers' preferences and behaviours' (Gordon, 2000, p. 512). These developments include the Internet, telecoms and computer telephony in call centres. These technological developments have served to make systems that are supposed to make RM more affordable and, perhaps, more effective for companies operating in mass markets (Rapp and Collins, 1990; Sisodia and Wolfe, 2000).

Some of the new technologies have opened up new channels of dialogue, which can be customer initiated as well as organization initiated.

This being the case, efforts must be made to capture data at all interactions and make that information available for subsequent conversations. This is possible when technology is used at the customer interface to secure real-time or near real-time interaction (Gordon, 2000). This has resulted in a need to move beyond the customer database as the basis of RM and to link the central information centre with call-centre software and Internet systems that allow direct interaction, as well as into other functions that contain histories of customer interaction (such as accounts and product service departments).

However, if relationship management support systems develop *ad hoc* from product unit customer databases a number of different CRM programmes may be implemented within a single organization (O'Malley and Mitussis, 2002). These systems might reflect the various organizational silos (e.g. product or brand divisions, direct marketing) or different channels (particularly true when Internet channels are introduced). As a result, customers may obtain a very different experience, offer or outcome depending on when, why and with whom in the organization they interact. Thus, rather than treating each customer with the consistency, fairness and respect one might expect in a relationship (Sheaves and Barnes, 1996; Boulding *et al.*, 2005), customers often get competing relational offers from different parts of the organization. This can lead to an exacerbation of privacy issues with customers becoming increasingly concerned with organizational intrusion (Patterson *et al.*, 1999) a perception that might actually translate into a reduction in consumer trust (O'Malley *et al.*, 1997; Fournier *et al.*, 1998). From a more pragmatic viewpoint, there is little reduction in marketing costs because several divisions are incurring direct communication costs, and may continue to maintain their own databases. Finally, the inconsistencies (in communication style, offer content and occasionally salutation) demonstrate to customers that they are unimportant (whilst simultaneously advocating a 'meaningful' relationship). Thus, as O'Malley and Mitussis (2002) demonstrate there are several problems that result when RM is overlaid onto the existing organizational structure and systems without any consideration for how relationships might be appropriately pursued and developed (i.e. relationship development process). 'Organizations continue to approach relationship marketing using the same structures that were appropriate for the marketing era, a time when product, price, promotion

and distribution channels were discrete, pre-established and one-way. In short, today's organization is often designed for the technologies and processes appropriate for transactions, not relationships' (Gordon, 2000, p. 506). Thus, (relationship) language structures consumers' expectations (e.g. Mitussis and Elliott, 1999) but (transaction) technology structures their experiences. It is important that to employ CRM effectively, due attention is paid to both customer and competitive data, evolving technologies and customer-focused organizational forms. Therefore implementation requires difficult integration of channels, technologies, customers and employees as the basis of competitive advantage (Boulding *et al.*, 2005).

Many problems stem from the fact that, because RM 'in mass markets is a relatively new topic for research, very little is known about how an organizations' relationship marketing efforts affect . . . customer satisfaction, the perceived future value of the relationship, trust and related behaviours' (Bhattacharya and Bolton, 2000, p. 340). In any case, such problems simply magnify the importance of ensuring that there is an appropriate customer-centric culture and employee skill-set prior to the introduction of a relational strategy (Crosby and Johnson, 2001). These observations are reinforced by Gruen (2000), who argues that companies that have successfully implemented RM have done so by trial and error rather than on the basis of any theory. Despite such problems with CRM implementation, the concept of relationships has also become hugely popular within the branding literature. That is, marketers are not content to develop relationships between consumers and organizations, but are also keen to nurture relationships between consumers and their brands as is discussed below.

Brand–consumer relationships

In recent years there have been a number of calls within the branding literature for a consideration of brand–consumer relationships (BCRs) and certainly the term *relationship* is fast infiltrating the branding literature (Patterson and O'Malley, 2006). Some commentators (e.g. Blackston, 1992) have even suggested that a focus on BCRs can more usefully provide concrete assistance to brand management programmes than can brand image research. In investigating mass-market brands Blackston (1992) compares the BCR to a relationship between a doctor and patient and, in extending his analysis to corporate brands, concepts from SET such as trust begin to emerge. Furthermore, Blackston (1992) makes explicit the link between BCRs and RM. Consequently, Palmer (1996, pp. 253–254) argues that 'individuals have an underlying need for an emotional bond with high-involvement products that they buy. Brand development and relationship development are complementary and substitutable strategies towards this bonding'. Moreover, Dall'Olmo Riley and de Chernatony (2000, p. 140) propose that 'the concept of the brand has evolved from a name given to differentiate a firm's products, to that of a relationship based on trust'. This evolution is predicated on the fact that brands possess meaning for consumers above and beyond their functional characteristics, they have personalities described in much the same way as human personalities, and, thus, we can have relationships with them.

Fournier (1998) recognizes that for a BCR to exist the brand must be a living entity because relationships exist between active and interdependent partners. That is, if brands were living entities, they would have personalities, would grow and develop over time and, therefore, it would be possible to have *relationships* with them. However, personification of the brand is insufficient for the brand to be considered a legitimate relational partner. Rather, for this to happen, brands need to be anthropomorphized, or humanized (Fournier, 1998). While brands can be animated through brand characters or are somehow possessed by the spirit of a past or present others, complete anthropomorphization of the brand involves imbuing it with human qualities such as emotion, thought and volition. Fournier (1998) argues that marketers perform this transmogrification through their everyday activities, particularly those conducted under the rubric of interactive marketing. The conceptual leap made here is that BCRs can be treated *as if* they were interpersonal relationships a leap criticized by some (Dowling, 2002). Fournier and Yao (1997) make explicit reference to their use of the *interpersonal relationship* metaphor in analysing the bonds between consumers and the brands they use. Furthermore, although they acknowledge their failure to test the relevance of the relationship frame against other frames, they do call for the abandonment of research on brand loyalty in favour of relational perspectives.

Following from understandings from services marketing where the consumption experience of customer A affects that of customer B (Langeard *et al.*, 1981), it may be that customers who have a relationship with a particular brand will develop relational links with other relational customers of that brand. The members of the brand community thus formed will have a relationship with the brand, with the firm and also with each other; a series of complex, interlocking and interdependent relationships which need careful management.

Models of relationship development

Process models of relationships

The dynamic nature of marketing relationships is captured in a number of *process* models of relationship development (e.g. Gummesson, 1977; Ford, 1980; Dwyer *et al.*, 1987; Borys and Jemison, 1989; Wilson, 1995; Parvatiyar and Sheth, 2000). Consistent with the recognition that relationships evolve and change over time, as a result of interaction between parties, the notion of an exchange relationship *life cycle* is employed within the literature. The life-cycle metaphor comes from studies of ecology and, consistent with the use of metaphor, the assumptions employed in the source domain (ecology) transfer to the target domain (exchange relationships) (Hunt and Menon, 1995; O'Malley and Tynan, 1999). In the case of the life-cycle metaphor, these assumptions include recognition of a deterministic, inevitable evolution from one stage to another (Van de Ven, 1992). For example, Ford (1980) depicts relationship development in terms of a pre-relationship stage, an early stage, a development stage, a long-term stage and a final stage. Similarly, Dwyer *et al.* (1987) conceptualize these phases as awareness, exploration, expansion, commitment and dissolution. Although labelled differently, these models essentially describe the same process and implicitly or explicitly rely on SET. Furthermore, while the models present relational development as a series of discrete stages, it is generally accepted that, in reality, exchange relationships are more likely to be characterized by 'wigwag movements of strengthening and weakening forces, maybe even with intermittent disconnections, impacting the dynamics and quality of relationships' (Hedaa, 1993, p. 191). However, researchers have had difficulty capturing the extent to which the nature of the relationship changes over time (Hedaa, 1993; Dabholkar *et al.*, 1994). Nonetheless, it is assumed that exchange relationships become progressively closer and deeper (Halinen, 1997) and exhibit increasing degrees of

	Ford (1980)	Frazier (1983)	Dwyer et al. (1987)	Borys and Jemison (1989)	Wilson (1995)
Pre-relationship	Pre-relationship stage	Review	Awareness		Search and selection
Attraction	Early stage		Exploration	Defining purpose	Defining purpose
Formation	Development stage	Implementation	Expansion	Setting boundaries	Setting boundaries
Expansion	Long-term stage	Outcomes	Commitment	Value creation	Value creation
Ending	Final stage			Hybrid stability	Hybrid stability
			Dissolution		

Table 3.1 Process models of relationship development

trust and commitment (Ford, 1980; Dwyer *et al.*, 1987) (Table 3.1).

Pre-relationship

In the pre-relationship stage there may be very little interaction between the organizations but they may be aware of each others existence. The distance between them is affected by distance in terms of social and cultural distance, geography, technology and time. The situation is characterized by a high level of inertia and high levels of uncertainty (Ford, 1980).

Attraction

The concept of *attraction* seems to play a fundamental role in explaining relationship development (Dwyer *et al.*, 1987; Grönroos, 2000). Derived from SET, attraction explains why relationships are initiated and developed (see Kelley and Thibaut, 1978). Some degree of attraction is a necessary precondition for the commencement of interaction, while ongoing attraction determines whether parties are motivated to maintain a relationship (Dwyer *et al.*, 1987; Halinen, 1997).

Halinen (1997, p. 59) defines attraction as 'a company's interest in exchange with another, based on the economic and social reward–cost outcomes expected from the relationship over time'. More recently, Morgan (2000) suggests that the basis

for relational exchange should be expanded to incorporate access to resources. For, in order to develop competitive advantage, parties to a relationship need access to resources that they do not currently possess (Van de Ven and Walker, 1984). Thus, Harris *et al.* (2003, p. 12) define attraction as *'the extent to which relational partners perceive past, current, future or potential partners as professionally appealing in terms if their ability to provide superior economic benefits, access to important resources and social compatibility'*.

Harris *et al.* (2003) demonstrate that relationships are unlikely to be initiated unless at least one party finds the other attractive. Furthermore, the level of attraction is likely not only to stimulate investment initiatives but also to influence the *level* of those investments (Halinen, 1997). Hence, investment refers to 'the amount of time, money and life chances that are expended in forming and maintaining relationships' (Sheaves and Barnes, 1996, p. 217) some of which are unrecoverable, regardless of the success or failure of the relationship, and must be regarded as a sunk cost.

Formation

In the early stages, the relationship is fragile and termination simple. It is the stage at which the partners gauge and test the integrity, capability and performance of the other (Dwyer *et al.*, 1987). The partners test and probe each other with early

Table 3.2 Relationship ending	
Termination	One party deliberately ends the relationship.
Dissolution	The ending process irrespective of whether an ending decision has been made.
Switching	Ending where the supplier (or the customer) is substituted for another.
Exit	A single channel member's disengagement from a system of relationships.

Source: Tähtinen and Halinen (2002).

trial purchases and early attempts at co-creation of value develop. During these formation stages, partners negotiate the benefits each will offer the other and agree their mutual obligations. This process of bargaining offers an opportunity to make disclosures to the partner as a basis on which a reciprocal relationship can develop. It is important to consider the issues of power and justice to ensure that agreed concessions and rewards are commensurate with notions of fairness and justice (Dwyer *et al.*, 1987). Norms of behaviour and expectations are developed which set the ground rules for the future relationship and are vital in areas where conflicts of interest may emerge.

With a successful relationship, experience reduces uncertainty over time, interdependence gradually increases, additional gratifications are sought from the current exchange partner and so a larger share of the partners overall spend is earned.

Expansion

After the formation process, the expansion stage addresses management and governance processes (Sheth and Parvatiyar, 2000). The process of communication, bargaining, norm and expectation development will continue but this stage is characterized by extensive contractual mechanisms and/or shared value systems which ensure sustained interdependence. Partners adapt to work in a mutually collaborative manner with conflict resolution taking place where necessary. The inputs by both parties are necessarily both significant and consistent to ensure this stage progresses.

This stage is characterized by an increase in the range and depths of rewards partners supply to each other (Scanzoni, 1979). This can be achieved through customization of outputs and the integration of the customer into planning, provision and innovation activities (Bruhn, 2003) so that they can evaluate ideas, provide feedback and test concepts to achieve mutual value.

Ending

Relationship ending has only recently attracted attention within the marketing literature. It is best described as a process in its own right (Gadde and Mattsson, 1987; Tähtinen and Halinen, 1999) rather than simply an end point. Indeed, it is likely that the relationship may not totally end, but that bonds between key players may be maintained, and, in some cases, the relationship may even be restored at a later stage (Havila, 1996; Havila and Wilkinson, 1997). When referring to this stage of the relationship researchers use a variety of different words including: switching, exit, dissolution, termination, fading, defection, disengagement, breakup, divorce and relationship demarketing. This proliferation of terminology is problematic in that these terms are often used interchangeably, prompting Tähtinen and Halinen (2002) to propose that the term 'ending' be used to broadly describe this stage of a relationship. 'Ending would cover all kinds of relationship breakups, in all types of relationships, no matter what the reasons for their ending are. In this way, terms such as "termination", "dissolution", "switching" and "exit" could be defined as specific types of relationship ending, which would help to specify the focus of research and to further our understanding of the various ending processes' (Tähtinen and Halinen, 2002, p. 183). In this regard, 'ending' is the process, and dissolution is the end state. As Tähtinen and Halinen-Kaila, 1997, p. 560) outline: 'a relationship is dissolved when all activity links are broken and no resource ties and actor bonds exist between the companies'. Thus, it may take some time for this state to be achieved, and in some cases, although relationships end, they do not dissolve (Table 3.2).

Relationship ending clearly represents an important research area and is equally important whether the relationship is between two organizations, between a service provider and a client or between a mass marketer and a consumer.

Ending, whether decided unilaterally or agreed bilaterally, is important in practical terms because how relationship ending is managed may impact upon a firm's reputation and upon subsequent efforts to renew relationships. In this regard, 'beautiful exits' are what relationship participants should aim for: 'A beautiful exit is achieved by a strategy that minimises damage occurring to the disengager, the other party and the connected network' (Alajoutsijärvi *et al.*, 2000, p. 1272).

Motivation for relationships and relational success variables

Håkansson (1982) suggests that relationships are developed to reduce uncertainty and/or add value. More recent work emphasizes the co-creation of value through interactions between partners, rather than 'adding' value by exchanging 'ready-made' value embedded in products (Grönroos, 2006). In terms of reducing uncertainty, Håkansson (1982) highlights improvements in the firm's forecasting abilities. In contrast, Möller and Wilson (1995, p. 40) take a broader perspective, and argue that 'firms generally develop business relationships for multiple reasons that are not based on any singular dimension'. They suggest that relationship development can be motivated by the need for economic gains, the quest for stability or predictability; the search for reciprocity; the quest for efficient and effective operations, to establish legitimacy; or, because the firm lacks resources, or wishes to utilize an asymmetrical power base (Möller and Wilson, 1995). In services marketing, the organization seeks relationships with customers in order to enhance loyalty. Within this context, consumers are believed to seek relationships in order to minimize risk (Berry, 1995) or routinize choice and thus save time and effort in buying and consuming situations (Sheth and Parvatiyar, 1995).

Relationship marketing represents an incredibly broad area of marketing thought and has been strongly influenced by empirical evidence from several business sectors as well as by theories and concepts from diverse disciplines. Indeed, concepts such as retention, loyalty, commitment, trust, mutuality, reciprocity, structural bonds, relationship quality, relationship satisfaction and attraction are central to understanding relationships. These concepts have their origins in economics, sociology, SET, small group behaviour, psychology and elsewhere and have been borrowed, refined and

Table 3.3 Summary of variables of relationship success models	
Commitment	Social bonds
Trust	Structural bonds
Co-operation	Summative constructs
Mutual goals	Shared technology
Interdependence/ power imbalance	Non-retrievable investments
Performance satisfaction	Comparison level of alternatives
Adaptation	

Source: Wilson (1995).

moulded by contemporary understandings of service relationships, business relationships and consumer behaviour. Add to this understandings of market-related behaviours influenced by contemporary readings of postmodernism, critical theory, branding, consumer literacy, organizational networks and we begin to understand how this intricate and influential body of thought has been woven, such that it is difficult to divide new from old marketing theory, and marketing from other aspects of management which consider business structures and business networks as aspects of its core. In a useful and very thorough literature review, Wilson (1995) attempts to identify those concepts that are most widely used. These are identified in Table 3.3.

Depending on the specific context, these variables are likely to be more or less important. However, it is worth noting that of these, trust, commitment, co-operation and mutual benefit have attracted the most empirical attention and are considered fundamental to understanding and creating commercial relationships (Dwyer *et al.*, 1987; Anderson and Narus, 1990; Crosby *et al.*, 1990; Czepiel, 1990; Grönroos, 1990; Heide and John, 1990; Moorman *et al.*, 1992; Rusbult and Buunk, 1993; Barnes, 1994; Morgan and Hunt, 1994).

It is acknowledged that not all customers are profitable as relationship customers (Ford, 1980; Håkansson, 1982; Reichheld and Sasser, 1990; Berry, 1995; Reinartz and Kumar, 2002). Thus, a first stage of relationship management must clearly be the identification of relationship potential. Even then, not all customers will necessarily be interested in, or merit, the same level of investment, and thus a relationship specification phase must be included. This specification phase may occur before, after or simultaneous to the relationship initiation phase. Furthermore, while some definitions incorporate enhancing and maintaining relationships as distinct stages this is an unnecessary distinction. Some relationships will require continual enhancement in order to be maintained, whereas others will not. Thus, it is argued that it is implicit in the relationship maintenance concept that relationship investments, enhancements and communication are likely to be required. Equally, the nature of the relationship may change, and a reduction in resources or a redefinition (re-specification) of the norms of the relationship may be most appropriate. Finally, there may come a time when the relationship is no longer appropriate at all, and thus there is clearly a phase of relationship ending. The phases that have just been described clearly need more refinement. However, it is recognized that they are dynamic and ongoing and are unlikely to reflect a linear process. Therefore, a matrix or building block approach to defining relationship development stages seems most appropriate. This process is, therefore, seen to include: identification of relationship potential; specification of relationship format; relationship initiation; relationship development; relationship maintenance and relationship ending.

Critique and emerging issues

Conceptually, relationship marketing continues to be understood in different and often very interesting ways. Whilst this provides richness and diversity to the literature it is difficult to share research findings between different empirical contexts and conceptual frameworks. For new researchers entering the field, attention to the original works will offer particular insights and understanding which will in turn inform their understanding and critique of current developments. Thus, for a review of the history and development of relationship marketing, a number of treatments are essential reading. These include Sheth and Parvatiyar (1995); Grönroos (1994); Aijo (1996); Möller and Halinen (2000) and Harker and Egan (2006). Furthermore, the special issue of the *Journal of the Academy of Marketing Science* (Cravens, 1995) provides a series of insightful commentaries on relationship marketing in different

empirical contexts. Added to this, the relational perspective as discussed by the IMP group (Håkansson, 1982; Turnbull and Valla, 1985; Ford, 1997) and services researchers (Grönroos, 1978; Berry, 1983; Shostack, 1984; Parasuraman *et al.*, 1985; Solomon *et al.*, 1985; Gummesson, 1987, Grönroos, 2006) are equally important.

The richness and conceptual diversity of relationship marketing results in a lack of understanding and agreement as to how relationship marketing should be implemented. Thus, a number of issues require further conceptual and empirical work. The following is not an exhaustive list of such issues, but merely serves to highlight the numerous gaps in our knowledge.

Identification and assessment of relational partners

Definitions of relationship marketing suggest that marketing is concerned with developing relationships with key customers and other parties (Grönroos, 1994; Möller and Wilson, 1995; O'Malley *et al.*, 1997), indeed that relationship marketing 'refers to all marketing activities directed towards establishing, developing and maintaining successful relational exchanges' (Morgan and Hunt, 1994, p. 23). However, little attention has been paid to how potentially successful relational partners might be identified. This is important, given the limitation problems that exist for organizations in terms of the portfolio of relationships with which they can be involved (Håkansson, 1982). It is also recognized that there is an opportunity cost, and potential downsides (Blois, 1997), associated with each relationship, and thus great care must be taken in selecting relational partners. Within consumer markets the concept of life-time value is being used. However, this approach focuses only on the potential dyad, and ignores the network, the limitation problems and opportunity costs involved. Clearly, further research is required in this area.

Customer relationship managers

What management training is required to facilitate the implementation of relationship marketing? Wilson (1995) suggests that relationships are now more difficult to develop and manage given that the race for relationship partners has accelerated.

In consumer markets there is often the simplistic assumption that all that is required to enhance customer value is a database and direct communications. However, it is likely that more attention needs to be paid to developing relational skills in customer-facing staff. Services marketers may be more advanced than others in terms of managing interaction given the importance of the co-creation of value and the centrality of the customer contact employee in service delivery. This has led, amongst others, to the development and utilization of service quality analysis and management systems based on the gap model – SERVQUAL (Parasuraman *et al.*, 1985, 1988), the employment of service blueprinting to better design and manage service delivery (Shostack, 1984), the use of techniques like the Critical Incident Technique (Gremler, 2004) to identify satisfying and dissatisfying service encounters. This experience may provide some useful guidelines for training.

It is important that relationship marketers also learn to balance their dual commitment to the company that employs them and to their customer. This is particularly difficult for boundary spanning personnel, predominantly in B2B situations. The nature of this role offers potential for conflict with choices at one extreme of satisfying the partner at the expense of their employer, and at the other of satisfying their employer but not their partner. Setting parameters for negotiations and training go someway towards offering solutions.

Relationship policy

How should organizations devise relationship policies? Relationship policy refers to the management of a portfolio of relationships. As such, it is concerned with both handling and limitation problems (Håkansson, 1982), and with positioning strategies within the network (Andersson and Söderlund, 1988). Research is required to address issues such as relationship investments and adaptation, how individual relationships should be managed, the avoidance of institutionalization and how the integral elements of relationships can be fostered with exchange partners (O'Malley *et al.*, 1997; Fournier *et al.*, 1998).

Relationship seeking

In what circumstances, or situations, do customers want relationships? There is currently a tendency to assume that relationships are seen as desirable, and are sought by customers (Sheth and Parvatiyar,

1995). Christy *et al.* (1996) deal with this issue to some extent in consumer markets. Other literature in consumer markets implicitly questions this assumption (Barnes, 1995; Tynan, 1997, 1999; Fournier *et al.*, 1998; O'Malley and Tynan, 1999, 2000). It may well be the case that relationships are desirable, but research that supports this is clearly needed. In particular, it should identify the types of situations or circumstances when relationships are especially sought by customers.

If marketing is now about managing relationships, but that this job is too important to remain in the marketing department, what is the current function of marketing? This is another particularly problematic issue that has yet to be resolved. The literature suggests that 'the traditional ways of organizing the marketing function, and of thinking about marketing activity must be re-examined' (Wilson, 1995, p. 10). The problem revolves around the broad gamut of relationship partners that have been identified (Gummesson, 1994; Morgan and Hunt, 1994). In services it has long been understood that close links between marketing, operations and HR are essential to deliver the offer. However, responsibility for this extended and extensive range of relationships tends to fall outside the existing domain of marketing, and as a result, it has been argued by IMP researchers that many of these are organizational strategy rather than marketing issues. This view is echoed by Webster *et al.* who noted that marketing competence needed to be dispersed across the firm rather than simply residing in the marketing department (Webster, 1992; Webster *et al.*, 2005). The value proposition can be communicated via a single marketing function, but the fulfilment of that proposition requires wider co-operation usually with the organizational functions (Grönroos, 2006). The problem is exacerbated when the interface between the company and its customers is primarily through part-time marketers (Gummesson, 1987). As a result, the role of marketing must be identified within the relational paradigm, as this has important implications for developing a framework for implementation, for devising relationship policy and for dealing with training requirements.

Exploring relationship variables

What are the antecedents of trust, commitment, etc.? The integral elements of successful relationships have been identified (Wilson, 1995) and discussed. However, further research investigating the antecedents of these elements is clearly desirable. Taking greater account of the contextual elements surrounding dyadic relationships would substantially enhance this. Thus, the incorporation of broader underpinning theory, other than just SET would be useful here. While occasional examples of the use of a wider range of theoretical perspectives is evident (see e.g. Arnett *et al.*'s work employing identity theory 2003) there is little real evidence of innovation in this regard.

Do bonds create relationships or do relationships create bonds? Andersson and Söderlund (1988, p. 65) suggest that 'relationships can create bonds of technical, planning, knowledge, social and legal content'. Since much of the other literature suggests that bonds, in fact, create relationships, research illuminating the direction of causality would be beneficial. Understanding of causal direction would also be particularly relevant as an input into managerial training. Alternatively, it may be that causal directions cannot be identified as a result of the integrative and interactive nature of relationship variables, the context in which the research occurs, and the expectations of the parties concerned.

The importance of the social within relationship marketing

It is not always possible to identify where professional relationships end and social relationships begin (Harris *et al.*, 2003). This is substantiated by the work of Wright (1988, p. 370) who found that 'virtually all close friendships involve shared interests and activities, various kinds of intimacy, including self-disclosures and the sharing of confidences, emotional support, small talk, shop talk and exchanges of tangible favours'. There is evidence to indicate that RM is more effective when relationships are built with an individual person rather than with a firm more generally (Palmatier *et al.*, 2006). As a result, the academy could usefully re-focus research interest on the social aspect of business relationships. However, it must be acknowledged that this complicates Morgan's (2000) distinction between the economic, resource and social content of relationships. In practice, these three components are inextricably interwoven and it is difficult to identify where one element begins and the other ends. As Hutt *et al.* (2000, p. 51) outline, 'many alliances fail to meet their promise because little attention is given to nurturing the close working relationships and interpersonal connections that unite partnering organisations'. In order to foster organizational social capital and

thus enable future co-operation (Gulati, 1999), organizational resources must be allocated not only to the development of working relationships but, more fundamentally, to interpersonal connections which are best achieved in natural rather than contrived settings (Hutt *et al.*, 2000). Furthermore, in choosing individuals from partnering organizations to work together, strategic attention must be given to the matching process. While this might be assumed to emphasize similarity (e.g. in age, experience and position in organizational hierarchies), it needs also to accommodate complementarity.

Domain of relationship marketing

Questions remain over the domain of relationship marketing (Saren and Tzokas, 1998). Relationship marketing has not been subjected to sufficient critical scrutiny and has been indiscriminately applied to any issue where traditional marketing has proved useful. As discussed in the chapter above, the theoretical roots of relationship marketing are firmly grounded in business-to-business and services marketing. However, its wholesale extension into business-to-consumer markets and not-for-profit contexts has been of questionable value. The issues of power and conflict, which have been so carefully explored in other contexts, are ignored in business-to-consumer marketing (see Fitchett and McDonagh, 2000; Smith and Higgins, 2000). Can a single, individual consumer really have a relationship with a huge, multinational company? If the customer does recognize a relationship in such a situation, is the relationship with the service delivery employee not with the firm itself? Does not the sheer size and marketing budget of the firm make the possibility of a mutually beneficial relationship unlikely, if not impossible? For the consumer there are likely to be only a few possible providers of a particular offer, whereas for the firm there are likely to be millions of potential customers for their offer, so there is no equity in the issue of power or importance.

Technology and relationship marketing (CRM)

The interface between marketing and CRM is another field where there is substantial need for research. CRM is based upon sound marketing principles through identifying customer needs, segmentation, offering superior customer value and customer retention all of which processes are enabled by the application of sophisticated technology. However, the processes by which this is specified and managed and whether that is controlled by technologists or marketers is as yet an issue of some debate and little empirical knowledge (Sisodia and Wolfe, 2000; O'Malley and Mitussis, 2002). Issues relating to consumer privacy are likely to be exacerbated within this new environment and may ultimately undermine consumer trust (O'Malley *et al.*, 1997). Moreover, there needs to be greater consideration of how consumer information should be acquired and used. Ultimately, it must be remembered that the objective is to build relationships, not databases. This is achieved through dialogue (see Grönroos, 2000) and not one-way communication.

Relationship marketing in cross-cultural contexts

Despite the importance of international RM, insufficient attention is being paid to exploring and theorizing RM in an international context (Samiee and Walters, 2003).

Relationship marketing is frequently applied in cross-cultural contexts but the theoretical and empirical work upon which it is grounded has been largely conducted in Scandinavia, Britain, North America and more recently Australia. Unfortunately, these regions share many cultural similarities exhibiting high individualism with low power distance, uncertainty avoidance, long-term orientation and context communication scores (Hall, 1960, 1973; Hofstede, 2001). Even where RM theory has been tested cross-culturally it has been within similar cultures for example Friman *et al.*'s (2002) study in Sweden, Australia and the UK. So it is more than possible that our understandings of relationship marketing will not be relevant to cultures that are more collectivist, more hierarchical, with a lower tolerance for uncertainty, a long-term orientation and where understanding communication is highly dependent upon the context in which it takes place. Some initial work has been conducted on these issues, largely from the perspective of the Chinese system of Guanxi (Ambler, 1995; Ambler and Styles, 2000; Leung *et al.*, 2005) but much remains to be done on a wider geographical basis.

Operationalizing relationship marketing

It is surprising how little research has been conducted which sheds light upon suitable approaches to operationalizing relationship marketing. It is impossible to support or refute particular approaches to developing a relationship marketing strategy, implementing it or assessing its performance. While there appears to be agreement that a processual view of RM practice is appropriate, there are huge gaps in our understanding of the way in which the RM offer is enabled, created and delivered in a way which co-creates value rather than simply delivering pre-produced value. Furthermore, the processes by which relational partners should be identified, the appropriate levels of investment in the relationship established, the portfolio of simultaneously relationships appropriately managed or the termination of an unprofitable relationship achieved without rancour, are all unknown. As yet we have no metrics by which the success or failure of relationship marketing approaches can be evaluated. There is much research and theorizing to be done before we can make strategic use of relationship marketing.

Staff retention and empowerment

Additionally, our understanding of issues concerning staff retention and empowerment have largely been developed in the field of services marketing and to some extent small business marketing. There is little research available on the importance of employees in the relationship, their training and retention which had been specifically conducted in the context of a relational view of marketing. Whether this will prove to be an important issue cannot be established until more research has been conducted.

Conclusion

This chapter has reviewed the history, definition and core concepts that are part of the emerging understanding of relationship marketing. Central to this is the recognition that, although there is some shared understanding, relationship marketing is also shaded by the empirical context and by the nature of the parties in the relationship. It is clear that understandings which emerge from services marketing research differ from that which has emerged in a business-to-business context for example. Relationship marketing is also influenced by underpinning theories such that integration can never be possible. So, although there will never be one agreed definition, one common approach, one single understanding there is much to learn from these many and various strands of research on the topic. For example, insights can be gained into why firms to develop a relational approach, what the range of relationships they focus on, what are the success variables and how the interaction process is managed. We can also learn, from the many models of relationship development, what might promote and what might impede relationship formation, development and maintenance.

There is much to understand about this innovative and developing paradigm. This chapter has drawn attention to the many unknowns in this field, to the questions, the critiques and the under-researched issues. As such, it offers some suggestions for new researchers as to possible topics and issues for exploration. Hopefully, you will find the topic as interesting and exciting as we do.

References

Aijo, T. S. (1996) The theoretical and philosophical underpinnings of relationship marketing: environmental factors behind the changing marketing paradigm, *European Journal of Marketing*, **30**(2), 8–18.

Alajoutsijärvi, K., Möller, K. and Tähtinen, J. (2000) Beautiful exit: how to leave your business partner, *European Journal of Marketing*, **34**(11/12), 1270–1290.

Ambler, T. (1995) Reflections in China: reorienting images of marketing, *Global Marketing*, **4**(1), 22–30.

Ambler, T. and Styles, C. (2000) The future of relational research in international marketing: constructs and conduits, *International Marketing Review*, **17**(6), 492–508.

Anderson, J. C. and Narus, J. A. (1984) A model of the distributor's perspective of distributor–manufacturer working relationships, *Journal of Marketing*, **48**, Fall, 62–74.

Anderson, J. C. and Narus, J. A. (1990) A model of distributor firm and manufacturer firm working partnerships, *Journal of Marketing*, **54**, January, 42–45.

Andersson, P. and Söderlund, M. (1988) The network approach to marketing, *Irish Marketing Review*, **3**, 63–68.

Arnett, D. B., German, S. B. and Hunt, S. D. (2003) The identity salience model of relationship marketing success: the case of nonprofit marketing, *Journal of Marketing*, **67**, April, 89–105.

Barnes, J. G. (1994) Close to the customer: but is it really a relationship? *Journal of Marketing Management*, **10**, 561–570.

Barnes, J. G. (1995) Establishing relationships – getting closer to the customer may be more difficult than you think, *Irish Marketing Review*, **8**, 107–116.

Bartels, R. (1976) *The History of Marketing Thought*, GRID Inc., Columbus, OH.

Berry, L. L. (1981) The employee as customer, *Journal of Retail Banking*, March, 33–40.

Berry, L. L. (1983) Relationship Marketing, in Berry, L. L., Shostack, G. L. and Upah, G. D. (eds), *Perspectives on Services Marketing*, American Marketing Association, Chicago, pp. 25–28.

Berry, L. L. (1995) Relationship marketing of services – growing interest, emerging perspectives, *Journal of the Academy of Marketing Science*, **23**(4), 236–245.

Berry, L. L. and Parasuraman, A. (1991) *Marketing Services – Competition Through Quality*, Free Press, New York.

Bhattacharya, C. B. and Bolton, R. N. (2000) Relationship Marketing in Mass Markets, in Sheth J. N. and Parvatiyar, A. (eds), *Handbook of Relationship Marketing*, Sage Publications, Inc., Thousand Oaks, CA, pp. 327–354.

Blackston, M. (1992) Observations: building brand equity by managing the brand's relationships, *Journal of Advertising Research*, May/June, 79–83.

Blattberg, R. C. and Deighton, J. (1991) Interactive marketing: exploiting the age of addressability, *Sloan Management Review*, Fall, 5–14.

Blois, K. (1997) Are business-to-business relationships inherently unstable? *Journal of Marketing Management*, **13**(5), 367–382.

Booms, B. H. and Bitner, M. J. (1981) Marketing Strategies and Organisational Structures for Service Firms, in Donnelly, J. H. and George, W. R. (eds), *Marketing of Services*, American Marketing Association, Chicago.

Borys, B. and Jemison, D. B. (1989) Hybrid arrangements as strategic: theoretical issues in organisational combinations, *Academy of Management Review*, **14**(2), 234–240.

Boulding, W., Staelin, R., Ehret, M. and Johnston, W. J. (2005) A customer relationship management roadmap: What is known, potential pitfalls and where to go, *Journal of Marketing*, **69**, October, 155–166.

Bruhn, M. (2003) *Relationship Marketing: Management of Customer Relationships*, FT Prentice Hall, Harlow, UK.

Christopher, M., Payne, A. and Ballantyne, D. (1991) *Relationship Marketing: Bringing Quality, Customer Service and Marketing Together*, Butterworth-Heinemann, Oxford.

Christy, R., Oliver G. and Penn, J. (1996) Relationship marketing in consumer markets, *Journal of Marketing Management*, **12**, 175–187.

Copulsky, J. R. and Wolf, M. J. (1990) Relationship marketing: positioning for the future, *Journal of Business Strategy*, July/August, 16–26.

Cravens, D. W. (ed.) (1995) Special issue on relationship marketing, *Journal of the Academy of Marketing Science*, **23**(4).

Crosby, L. A. and Johnson, S. L. (2001) Technology: friend or foe to customer relationships? *Marketing Management*, **10**(4), 10–11.

Crosby, L. A. and Stephens, N. (1987) Effects of relationship marketing on satisfaction, retention, and prices in the life insurance industry, *Journal of Marketing Research*, **24**, November, 404–411.

Crosby, L. A., Evans, K. R. and Cowles, D. (1990) Relationship quality in services selling: an interpersonal influence perspective, *Journal of Marketing*, **54**, July, 68–81.

Cunningham, M. T. and Homse, E. (1986) Controlling the marketing-purchasing interface: resource development and organisational implications, *Industrial Marketing and Purchasing*, **1**(2), 3–27.

Czepiel, J. A. (1990) Service encounters and service relationships: implications for research, *Journal of Business Research*, **20**, 13–21.

Dabholkar, P. A., Johnston W. and Cathay, A. S. (1994) The dynamics of long-term business to business exchange relationships, *Journal of the Academy of Marketing Science*, **22**(2), 130–145.

Dall'Olmo Riley, F. and de Chernatony, L. (2000) The service brand as relationship builder, *British Journal of Management*, **11**, 137–150.

Di Tienne, K. B. and Thompson, J. A. (1996) Database marketing and organisational learning theory: toward a research agenda, *Journal of Consumer Marketing*, **13**(5), 12–34.

Dowling, D. (2002) Customer relationship management: in B2B marketing, often less in more, *California Management Review*, **44**(3), 87–104.

Doyle, P. and Stern, P. (2006) *Marketing Management and Strategy*, 4th edn, Financial Times-Prentice Hall, Harlow, England.

Dwyer, R. F., Schurr, P. H. and Oh, S. (1987) Developing buyer–seller relationships, *Journal of Marketing*, **51**, April, 11–27.

Easton, G. and Araujo, L. (1994) Market exchange, social structures and time, *European Journal of Marketing*, **28**(3), 72–81.

El-Ansary, A. I. and Stern, L. W. (1972) Power measurement in the distribution channel, *Journal of Marketing*, **38**(1), 47–52.

Etgar, M. (1976) Channel domination and countervailing power in distributive channels, *Journal of Marketing Research*, **13**, August, 254–262.

Evan, W. (1966) The Organisational Set: Toward a Theory of Inter-Organisational Relations, in Thomson, J. (ed.), *Approaches to Organisation Design*, The Free Press, New York.

Evans, M., O'Malley, L. and Patterson, M. (1996) Direct marketing communications in the UK: a study of growth, past, present and future, *Journal of Marketing Communications*, **2**, 51–65.

Evans, M., O'Malley, L. and Patterson, M. (2004) *Exploring Direct & Customer Relationship Marketing*, 2nd edn, International Thomson Business Press, London.

Evans, M. J. (1999) Market Segmentation, in Baker, M. (ed.), *The Marketing Book*, Heinemann Professional, Oxford, pp. 209–236.

Feeny, D. F., Earl, M. J. and Edwards, B. (1997) Information Systems Organization: The Roles of Users and Specialists, in Willcocks, L., Feeny, D. and Islei, G. (eds), *Managing IT as a Strategic Resource*, McGraw-Hill, London, pp. 151–168.

Fisk, R. P., Brown, S. W. and Bitner, M. J. (1993) Tracking the evolution of the services marketing literature, *Journal of Retailing*, **69**(1), 61–94.

Fitchett, J. A. and McDonagh, P. (2000) A citizen's critique of relationship marketing in risk society, *Journal of Marketing Strategy*, **8**(2), 209–222.

Fletcher, K., Wheeler, C. and Wright, J. (1991) Database marketing: a channel, a medium, or a strategic approach, *Marketing Intelligence and Planning*, **10**(6), 18–23.

Ford, D. (1980) The development of buyer–seller relationships in industrial markets, *European Journal of Marketing*, **14**(5/6), 339–354.

Ford, D. (1990) *Understanding Business Markets: Interaction, Relationships, Networks*, Academic Press, Harcourt Brace and Co. Publishers, London.

Ford, D. (1997) *Understanding Business Markets: Interaction, Relationships, Networks*, 2nd edn, Academic Press, Harcourt Brace and Co. Publishers, London.

Fournier, S. (1998) Consumers and their brands: developing relationship theory in consumer research, *Journal of Consumer Research*, **24**(4), 343–371.

Fournier, S. and Yao, J. L. (1997) Reviving brand loyalty: a reconceptualisation within the framework of consumer–brand relationships, *International Journal of Research in Marketing*, **14**, 451–472.

Fournier, S., Dobscha, S. and Glen Mick, D. (1998) Preventing the premature death of relationship marketing, *Harvard Business Review*, January–February, 42–51.

Frazier, G. L. (1983) Inter-organisational exchange behaviour in marketing channels: a broadened perspective, *Journal of Marketing*, **47**, Fall, 68–71.

Friman, M., Garling, T., Millett, B., Mattsson, J. and Johnston, R. (2002) An analysis of international business-to-business relationships based on the commitment-trust theory, *Industrial Marketing Management*, **31**(5), 403–409.

Gadde, L. E. and Mattsson, L.-G. (1987) Stability and change in network relationships, *International Journal of Research in Marketing*, **4**(1), 29–41.

George, W. R. (1977) The retailing of services: a challenging future, *Journal of Retailing*, **53**(3), 85–98.

Gordon, I. (2000) Organizing for relationship marketing, in Sheth, J. N. and Parvatiyar, A. (eds), *Handbook of Relationship Marketing*, Sage Publications, Inc., Thousand Oaks, CA, pp. 505–523.

Gremler, D. D. (2004) The critical incident technique in service research, *Journal of Service Research*, **7**, August, 65–89.

Grönroos, C. (1978) A service-orientated approach to marketing of services, *European Journal of Marketing*, **12**(8), 588–601.

Grönroos, C. (1983) *Strategic Management and Marketing in the Service Sector*, Marketing Science Institute, Cambridge, MA.

Grönroos, C. (1989) Defining marketing: a market-orientated approach, *European Journal of Marketing*, **23**(1), 52–60.

Grönroos, C. (1990) Relationship approach to marketing in service contexts: the marketing and organisational behaviour interface, *Journal of Business Research*, 20, January, 3–11.

Grönroos, C. (1994) From marketing mix to relationship marketing: towards a paradigm shift in marketing, *Management Decision*, **32**(2), 4–20.

Grönroos, C. (2000) Creating a relationship dialogue: communication, interaction and value, *The Marketing Review*, **1**(1), 5–14.

Grönroos, C. (2006) On defining marketing: finding a new roadmap for marketing, *Marketing Theory*, **6**, 395–417.

Gruen, T. W. (2000) Membership Customers and Relationship Marketing, in Sheth, J. N. and Parvatiyar, A. (eds), *Handbook of Relationship Marketing*, Sage Publications, Inc., Thousand Oaks, CA, pp. 355–380.

Gulati, R. (1999) Network location and learning: the influence of network resources and firm capabilities on alliance formation, *Strategic Management Journal*, **20**(5), 397–420.

Gummesson, E. (1987) The new marketing – developing long-term interactive relationships, *Long Range Planning*, **20**, 10–20.

Gummesson, E. (1994) Making relationship marketing operational, *International Journal of Service Industry Management*, **5**(5), 5–20.

Gummesson, E. (1997) Relationship marketing as a paradigm shift: some conclusions from the 30R approach, *Management Decision*, **35**(4), 267–272.

Gummesson, E. (1999) *Total Relationship Marketing*, Butterworth-Heinemann/The Chartered Institute of Marketing, Oxford, UK.

Håkansson, H. (1982) *International Marketing and Purchasing of Industrial Goods*, Wiley, New York.

Halinen, A. (1997) *Relationship Marketing in Professional Services: A Study of Agency Client Dynamics in the Advertising Sector*, Routledge, London.

Hall, E. T. (1960) The silent language of overseas business, *Harvard Business Review*, May–June, 87–96.

Hall, E. T. (1973) *Beyond Culture*, Anchor Books, New York.

Harker, M. J. and Egan, J. (2006) The past, present and future of relationship marketing, *Journal of Marketing Management*, **22**, 215–242.

Harris, L., O'Malley, L. and Patterson, M. (2003) Professional interaction: exploring the concept of attraction, *Marketing Theory*, **3**(1), 9–36.

Havila, V. (1996) When does an international business relationship become non-existent? in *Proceedings of the 25th EMAC Conference*, Budapest.

Havila, V. and Wilkinson, I. (1997) The principle of the conservations of relationship energy: or many kinds of new beginnings, in *Proceedings of the 13th International Conference on Industrial Marketing and Purchasing*, Lyon.

Hedaa, L. (1993) Distrust, uncertainties and disconfirmed expectations, *International Business Review*, **2**(2), 191–206.

Heide, J. B. and John, G. (1990) Alliances in industrial purchasing: the determinants of joint action in buyer–seller relationships, *Journal of Marketing Research*, **27**, February, 24–36.

Hofstede, G. (2001) *Culture's Consequences*, 2nd edn, Sage, Thousand Oaks, California.

Hunt, S. D. and Menon, A. (1995) Metaphors and competitive advantage: evaluating the use of metaphors in theories of competitive strategy, *Journal of Business Research*, **33**, 81–90.

Hutt, M. D., Stafford, E. R., Walker, B. A. and Reingen, P. H. (2000) Defining the social network of a strategic alliance, *Sloan Management Review*, Winter, 51–62.

Jackson, B. B. (1985) Build customer relationships that last, *Harvard Business Review*, November–December, 120–128.

Jarillo, J. C. (1988) On strategic networks, *Strategic Management Journal*, **9**, 31–41.

Kelley, H. H. and Thibaut, J. W. (1978) *Interpersonal Relationships: A Theory of Interdependence*, John Wiley & Sons, New York.

Langeard, E., Bateson, J., Lovelock, C. and Eiglier, P. (1981) *Marketing of Services: New Insights from Consumers and Managers*, Report No. 81–104, Marketing Sciences Institute, Cambridge, MA.

Leung, T. K. P., Kee-hung, L., Chan, R. Y. K. and Wong, Y. H. (2005) The roles of xinyong and guanxi in Chinese relationship marketing, *European Journal of Marketing*, **39**(5/6), 528–558.

Levine, S. and White, P. E. (1961) Exchange as a conceptual framework for the study of inter-organisational relationships, *Administrative Science Quarterly*, **5**, 583–601.

Lovelock, C. H. (1983) Classifying services to gain strategic marketing insights, *Journal of Marketing*, **47**, Summer, 9–20.

Mitussis, D. and Elliott, R. (1999) Representations, text and practice: a discourse-analytic model of the consumer, *Advances in Consumer Research*, **26**(1), 312–319.

Mitussis, D., O'Malley, L. and Patterson, M. (2006) Mapping the re-engagement of CRM with relationship marketing, *European Journal of Marketing*, **40**(5/6), 572–589.

Möller, K. and Halinen, A. (2000) Relationship marketing theory: its roots and direction, *Journal of Marketing Management*, **16**, 29–54.

Möller, K. and Wilson, D. T. (eds) (1995) *Business Marketing: An Interaction and Network Perspective*, Kluwer Academic Publishers, Norwell, MA.

Moorman, C., Zaltman, G. and Deshpande, R. (1992) Relationships between providers and users of market research: the dynamics of trust within and between organisations, *Journal of Marketing Research*, **29**, August, 314–329.

Morgan, R. H. (2000) Relationship Marketing and Marketing Strategy, in Sheth, J. N. and Parvatiyar, A. (eds), *Handbook of Relationship Marketing*, Sage Publications, Thousand Oaks, CA, pp. 481–504.

Morgan, R. M. and Hunt, S. D. (1994) The commitment-trust theory of relationship marketing, *Journal of Marketing*, **58**, July, 20–38.

O'Malley, L. and Mitussis, D. (2002) Relationships and technology: strategic implications, *Journal of Strategic Marketing*, **10**(3), 225–238.

O'Malley, L. and Patterson, M. (1998) Vanishing point: the mix management paradigm reviewed, *Journal of Marketing Management*, **14**(8), 829–852.

O'Malley, L. and Tynan, A. C. (1999) The utility of the relationship metaphor in consumer markets: a critical evaluation, *Journal of Marketing Management*, **15**, 487–602.

O'Malley, L. and Tynan, A.C. (2000) Relationship marketing in consumer markets: rhetoric or reality? *European Journal of Marketing*, **34**(7), 797–815.

O'Malley, L. and Tynan, A. C. (2001) Reframing relationship marketing for consumer markets, *Interactive Marketing*, **2**(3), 240–246.

O'Malley, L., Patterson, M. and Evans, M. J. (1997) Intimacy or intrusion: the privacy dilemma for relationship marketing in consumer markets, *Journal of Marketing Management*, **13**(6), 541–560.

O'Malley, L., Patterson, M. and Kelly-Holmes, H. (2008) Death of a Metaphor: Reviewing the 'Marketing as Relationships' Frame, *Marketing Theory*, in press.

Palmatier, R. W., Dant, R. P., Grewal, D. and Evans, K. R. (2006) Factors influencing the effectiveness of relationship marketing: a meta-analysis, *Journal of Marketing*, **70**, October, 136–153.

Palmer, A. (1996) Integrating brand development and relationship marketing, *Journal of Retailing and Consumer Services*, **3**(4), 251–257.

Parasuraman, A., Zeithaml, V. A. and Berry, L. L. (1985) A conceptual model of service quality and its implications for further research, *Journal of Marketing*, **49**, Fall, 41–50.

Parasuraman, A., Zeithaml, V. A. and Berry, L. L. (1988) SERVQUAL: a multiple-item scale for measuring consumer perceptions of service quality, *Journal of Retailing*, **64**(1), 12–40.

Parvatiyar, A. and Sheth, J. N. (2000) The domain and conceptual foundations of relationship marketing, in Sheth, J. N. and Parvatiyar, A. (eds), *Handbook of Relationship Marketing*, Sage Publications, Thousand Oaks, CA, pp. 3–38.

Patterson, M. and O'Malley, L. (2006) Brands, consumers and relationships: a critical review, *Irish Marketing Review*, **18**(1/2), 10–20.

Patterson, M., Evans, M. J. and O'Malley, L. (1999) UK attitudes toward direct mail, *Journal of Database Marketing*, **7**(2), 157–172.

Payne, A. and Holt, S. (2001) Diagnosing customer value: integrating the value process and relationship marketing, *British Journal of Management*, **12**, 159–182.

Peppers, D. and Rogers, M. (1995) A new marketing paradigm, *Planning Review*, **23**(2), 14–18.

Piercy, N. F. (1998) Barriers to implementing relationship marketing: analysing the internal market-place, *Journal of Strategic Marketing*, **6**(3), 209–222.

Price, L. L., Arnould, E. J. and Tierney, P. (1995) Going to extremes: managing service encounters and assessing provider performance, *Journal of Marketing*, **59**, April, 83–97.

Rapp, S. and Collins, T. (1990) *The Great Marketing Turnaround: The Age of the Individual – and How to Profit from It*, Prentice-Hall, Englewood Cliffs, NJ.

Reichheld, F. F. and Sasser Jr., E. W. (1990) Zero defections: quality comes to services, *Harvard Business Review*, **69**, September–October, 105–111.

Reinartz, W. and Kumar, V. (2002) The mismanagement of customer loyalty, *Harvard Business Review*, July, 86–94.

Rogers, M. and Peppers, D. (1997) Making the transition to one-to-one marketing, *Inc.* **19**(1), 63–65.

Rosenberg, L. J. and Czepiel, J. (1984) A marketing approach for customer retention, *Journal of Consumer Marketing*, **1**, Spring, 45–51.

Rowe, G. W. and Barnes, J. G. (1998) Relationship marketing and sustained competitive advantage, *Journal of Market Focused Management*, **2**, 281–297.

Rusbult, C. E. and Buunk, B. P. (1993) Commitment processes in close relationships: an interdependent analysis, *Journal of Social and Personal Relationships*, **10**, 175–204.

Ryals, L. and Knox, S. (2001) Cross-functional issues in the implementation of relationship marketing through customer relationship management, *European Management Journal*, **19**(5), 534–542.

Ryals, L. and Payne, A. F. T. (2001) Customer relationship management in financial services: towards information-enabled relationship marketing, *Journal of Strategic Marketing*, **9**, March, 1–25.

Samiee, S. and Walters, P. (2003) Relationship marketing in an international context: a literature review, *International Business Review*, **12**(2), 193–214.

Saren, M. J. and Tzokas, N. X. (1998) Some dangerous axioms of relationship marketing, *Journal of Strategic Marketing*, **6**, 187–196.

Scanzoni, J. (1979) Social Exchange and Behavioral Interdependence, in Burgess, R. L. and Huston, T. L. (eds), *Social Exchange in Developing Relationships*, Academic Press, New York.

Shani, D. and Chalasani, S. (1992) Exploiting niches using relationship marketing, *Journal of Business Strategy*, **6**(4), 43–52.

Sheaves, D. E. and Barnes, J. G. (1996) The fundamentals of relationships: an exploration of the concept to guide marketing implementation, *Advances in Services Marketing and Management*, **5**, 215–245.

Sheth, J. N. and Parvatiyar, A. (1995) Relationship marketing in consumer markets: antecedents and consequences, *Journal of the Academy of Marketing Science*, **23**(4), 255–271.

Sheth, J. N. and Parvatiyar, A. (eds) (2000) *Handbook of Relationship Marketing*, Sage Publications, Thousand Oaks, CA.

Shostack, L. G. (1977) Breaking free from product marketing, *Journal of Marketing*, **45**, April, 73–80.

Shostack, L. G. (1984) Designing services that deliver, *Harvard Business Review*, **62**, January–February, 133–139.

Sisodia, R. S. and Wolfe, D. B. (2000) Information Technology, in Sheth, J. N. and Parvatiyar, A. (eds), *Handbook or Relationship Marketing*, Sage Publications, Thousand Oakes, California, pp. 525–563.

Smith, W. and Higgins, M. (2000) Reconsidering the relationship analogy, *Journal of Marketing Management*, **16**, 81–94.

Solomon, M. R., Suprenant, C., Czepiel, J. A. and Gutman, E. G. (1985) A role theory perspective on dyadic interactions: the service encounter, *Journal of Marketing*, **49**, Winter, 99–111.

Spekman, R. E. (1988) Strategic supplier selection: understanding long-term buyer relationships, *Business Horizons*, **31**(4), 75–81.

Stern, L. W. and Reve, T. (1980) Distribution channels as political economies: a framework for comparative analysis, *Journal of Marketing*, **44**, Summer, 52–64.

Tähtinen, J. and Halinen, A. (1999) A business divorce. How does it happen? in *Proceedings of Australian and New Zealand Marketing Academy Conference*, Sydney.

Tähtinen, J. and Halinen, A. (2002) Research on ending exchange relationships: a categorisation, assessment and outlook, *Marketing Theory*, **2**(2), 165–188.

Tähtinen, J. and Halinen-Kaila, A. (1997) The death of business triads: the dissolution process of a net of companies, in *Proceedings of the 13th IMP International Conference*, Lyon, 553–590.

Thorelli, H. B. (1986) Networks: between markets and hierarchies, *Strategic Management Journal*, **7**, 37–51.

Turnbull, P. (1979) Roles of personal contacts in industrial export marketing, *Scandinavian Journal of Management*, **7**, 325–339.

Turnbull, P. and Valla, J. P. (eds) (1985) *Strategies for International Industrial Marketing*, Croom Helm, London.

Tynan, A. C. (1997) A review of the marriage analogy in relationship marketing, *Journal of Marketing Management*, **13**, 695–703.

Tynan, A. C. (1999) Metaphor, marketing and marriage, *Irish Marketing Review*, **12**(1), 17–26.

Van de Ven, A. (1976) On the nature, formation, and maintenance of relations among organisations, *Academy of Management Review*, October, 24–36.

Van de Ven, A. H. (1992) Suggestions for studying strategy process, *Strategic Management Journal*, **13**, Summer, 169–188.

Van de Ven, A. and Walker, G. (1984) The dynamics of inter-organizational coordination, *Administrative Science Quarterly*, **29**, 598–621.

Vargo, D. L. and Lusch, R. F. (2004) Evolving to a new dominant logic for marketing, *Journal of Marketing*, **68**(1), 1–18.

Webster, F. E. (1992) The changing role of marketing in the corporation, *Journal of Marketing*, **56**, October, 1–17.

Webster, F. E., Malter, A. J. and Ganesan, S. (2005) The decline and dispersion of marketing competence, *MIT Sloan Management Review*, **46**(4), 35–43.

Wilkinson, I. F. (1973) Power and influence structures in distribution channels, *European Journal of Marketing*, **7**(2), 119–129.

Wilkinson, I. F. (1979) Power and satisfaction in channels of distribution, *Journal of Retailing*, **55**, Summer, 79–94.

Wilson, D. T. (1995) An integrated model of buyer–seller relationships, *Journal of the Academy of Marketing Science*, **23**(4), 335–345.

Wright, P. H. (1988) Interpreting research on gender differences in friendship: a case for moderation and a plea for caution, *Journal of Social and Personal Relationships*, **5**, 367–373.

Zeithaml, V. H., Parasuraman, A. and Berry, L. L. (1985) Problems and strategies in services marketing, *Journal of Marketing*, **49**, 33–46.

CHAPTER 4

The basics of marketing strategy

ROBIN WENSLEY

Marketing strategy sometimes claims to provide an answer to one of the most difficult questions in our understanding of competitive markets: how to recognize and achieve an economic advantage that endures. In attempting to do so, marketing strategy, as with the field of strategy itself, has had to address the continual dialectic between analysis and action, or in more common managerial terms between strategy formulation and strategic implementation. At the same time, it has also had to address a perhaps more fundamental question: how far at least from a demand or market perspective can we ever develop general rules for achieving enduring economic advantage.

Strategy: from formulation to implementation

From the late 1960s to the mid-1980s at least, management strategy seemed to be inevitably linked to issues of product–market selection and hence to marketing strategy. Perhaps ironically this was not primarily or mainly as a result of the contribution of marketing scholars or indeed practitioners. The most significant initial contributors, such as Bruce Henderson and Michael Porter, were both to be found at or closely linked to the Harvard Business School, but were really informed more by particular aspects of economic analysis: neo-marginal economics[1] and Industrial

Organizational (IO) Economics, respectively. However, in various institutions the marketing academics were not slow to recognize what was going on and also to see that the centrality of product–market choice linked well with the importance attached to marketing. This expansion of the teaching domain had a much less significant impact on the research agenda and activity within marketing itself, where the focus continued to underplay the emerging importance of the competitive dimension (Day and Wensley, 1983). Hence the relatively atheoretical development continued into the process of codification of this new area, most obviously in the first key text by Abell and Hammond (1979), which was based on a, by then, well-established second year MBA option at Harvard.[2]

In retrospect this period was the high point for the uncontested impact of competitive market-related analysis on strategic management practice. With the advantage of hindsight, it is clear that a serious alternative perspective was also developing, most obviously signalled by Peters and Waterman (1982), which was to have a very substantial impact on what was taught in strategic management courses and what was marketed by consultancies. It was also a significant book in the sense

---

[1] Labelling the intellectual pedigree for Bruce Henderson and the Boston Consulting Group is rather more difficult than for Michael Porter. This is partly because much of the approach developed out of consulting practice (*cf.* Morrison and Wensley, 1991) in the context of a broad rather than focus notion of economic analysis. Some of the intellectual pedigree for the approach can be found in Henderson and Quant (1958) but some basic ideas such as dynamic economies of scale have a much longer pedigree (see, for instance, Jones (1926)).

[2] The book itself is clearly influenced by the work related to the PIMS project, as well as work in management consultancies such as McKinsey, ADL and, perhaps most importantly, Boston Consulting Group, whose founder, Bruce Henderson had close links with Derek Abell. The MBA course itself started in 1975 with a broad notion of 'filling the gap' between what was seen then as the marketing domain and the much broader area of Business Policy, so encompassing issues relating to Research and Development, Distribution and Competitive Costs. The course itself was a second year elective and rapidly expanded to four sections with a major commitment on development and case writing in 1976 and 1977. For a more historical analysis of the ways in which the case method has been used to incorporate new issues in management whilst avoiding some central concerns about the nature of power and influence see Contardo and Wensley (2004).

that, although not widely recognized as so doing, it also attempted to integrate at least to some degree earlier work by other relevant academics such as Mintzberg (1973), Pettigrew (1973) and Weick (1976).

As the decade progressed, it was inevitable that at least to some degree each side recognized the other as a key protagonist. Perhaps one of the most noteworthy comments is that in which Robert Waterman challenged the value of a Michael Porter-based analysis of competition Waterman (1988) argued that the Porter approach does not work because 'people get stuck in trying to carry out his ideas'[3] for three reasons: the lack of a single competitor, the actual nature of interfirm co-operation as well as competition and, finally, the fact that competitors were neither 'dumb nor superhuman'[4].

Equally, the economists did not take such attacks lying down: Kay (1993) attempted to wrest back the intellectual dominance in matters of corporate strategy and Porter (1990) extended his domain to the nation–state itself. The story, of course, has also become complicated in other ways, many of which are outside the scope of this chapter. In terms of key perspectives, Tom Peters has become more and more polemical about the nature of success,[5] C. K. Prahalad has refined his original notion of dominant logic to reflect in general terms the importance of transferable capabilities and technological interdependencies in the development of strategic advantage[6] whilst Gary Hamel who started his work with C. K. Prahalad on Strategic Intent (1989) has moved on to espousing radical and revolutionary change (2000) and, of course, Peter Senge (1992) reiterated the importance of information structures and Hammer and Champy (1993) introduced a 'new' approach labelled business process analysis.

In terms of the disciplinary debate, what was originally broadly a debate between economists and sociologists, now also involves psychologists, social anthropologists and, if they are a distinct discipline, systems theorists.

However, the key change in emphasis has been the one from analysis to process, from formulation to implementation. Perhaps the single most important contributor to this change has been Henry Mintzberg, who has developed over the period an extensive critique of, what he calls the 'Design School' in Strategic Management, culminating in his 1994 book. In this he even challenges the notion of planning in strategy:

> "Thus we arrive at the planning school's grand fallacy: Because analysis is not synthesis, strategic planning is not strategy formation. Analysis may precede and support synthesis, by defining the parts that can be combined into wholes. Analysis may follow and elaborate synthesis, by decomposing and formalizing its consequences. But analysis cannot substitute for synthesis. No amount of elaboration will ever enable formal procedures to forecast discontinuities, to inform managers who are detached from their operations, to create novel strategies. Ultimately the term 'strategic planning' has proved to be an oxymoron."
>
> (1994, p. 321)

Since then, he has extended his critique to the who domain of management teaching, particularly MBAs, rather than just strategic planning. (Mintzberg, 2004).[7]

Overall, whilst his approach and indeed critique of strategy analysis is itself rather polemical and overstated,[8] there is little doubt that he is broadly correct in that the general emphasis in strategic management has shifted significantly towards implementation and away from formulation and planning.

The nature of the competitive market environment

As our analysis of marketing strategy has developed over the last 35 years, so our representation of the marketing context has also changed.

Thirty years ago the marketing context was presented with what would now seem as a number of major omissions. In particular there was little recognition of competitors and distribution was

---

[3] It is noteworthy that the very representation of the five-forces diagram for instance is one which emphasizes that the firm is under pressure from all sides.

[4] This is a particular and rather colourful way of representing the notion of 'rational expectations' (Muth, 1961; Simon, 1979) in economics to which we will return later in this chapter.

[5] Indeed to the extent of arguing in one interview that innovative behaviour now depends on ignoring rather than exploiting market evidence.

[6] For instance, see Bettis and Prahalad (1989), Prahalad and Hamel (2000) and Prahalad and Bettis (1986).

[7] As often, his approach has also been subject to critique and challenge (see Shepherd, 2005).

[8] In fact Mintzberg himself goes on to argue three roles for 'corporate planning': (1) a more refined approach in traditional contexts, (2) a focus on techniques which emphasize the uncertain and emergent nature of strategic phenomena and/or (3) a more creative and intuitive form of strategic planning (see Wensley, 1996).

clearly seen as a solely logistical function. On top of this, customers were very much represented as 'at a distance' in that advertising and market research were the intermediary activities between the firm and its customers.

More recently marketing has recognized much more explicitly this further range of issues including the key role of competition and the importance of a longer-term so-called relationship perspective particularly in the context of customers. On top of this various entities in the distribution chain are now clearly seen as very active intermediaries rather than just passive logistics agents.

However, the development of this more complex dynamic representation of the competitive market, which can be seen broadly in the marketing strategy triangle of the 3Cs: customers, competitors and channels, also implies a more fluid and complex context for systematic modelling purposes.

Customers, competitors and channels

The early more static model of the nature of the competitive market, which informed many of the still current and useful tools of analysis was both positional and non-interactive. It was assumed that the market backcloth, often referred to as the product–market space, remained relatively stable and static so that at least in terms of first order effects, strategies could be defined in positional terms. Similarly, the general perspective, strongly reinforced by the earlier representations, was that actions by the firm would generally not create equivalent reactions from the relatively passive 'consumers'. This perspective on the nature of marketing which might be fairly labelled the 'patient' perspective (Wensley, 1990) is to be found rather widely in marketing texts and commentaries despite the continued espousal of slogans such as 'the customer is king'.

With the adoption of the more interactive and dynamic perspective implied in the 3Cs approach the nature of market-based strategy becomes much more complex. At the same time we must be wary of the temptation to continue to apply the old tools and concepts without considering critically whether they are appropriate in new situations. They represent in general a special or limiting case that quite often requires us to distort the nature of environment that we are attempting to characterize. The key question as to how far this distortion is, as our legal colleagues would say, material is another but frequently unresolved matter. This notion of materiality is really linked to impact on actions rather than just understanding and the degree to which in practice particular forms of marketing strategy analysis encourage actions that are either sub-optimal or indeed dysfunctional.

Lacking further experimental or research evidence on this question, this chapter is mainly written around the assumption that we need to recognize in using these simplifying approaches that (i) the degree to which they actually explain the outcomes of interest will be limited, particularly when it is a direct measure of individual competitive performance and (ii) the ways in which the underlying assumptions can cause unintentional biases.

The evolution of analysis, interpretation and modelling in marketing strategy from customers to competitors to channels

Given that the underlying representation of the competitive market environment has changed so, not surprisingly, have our processes of analysis, interpretation and modelling. Initially the key focus was on customer-based positioning studies in a particular product–market space. Such work remains a key component in the analysis of much market research data but from the marketing strategy perspective, we need to recognize that the dimensionality of the analytical space has often been rather low, indeed in some situations little more than a single price dimensions which has been seen as highly correlated with an equivalent quality dimension.[9]

The increased emphasis on the analysis of competitors has also required us to make certain compromises. One, of course, relates to the balance between what might be termed, respectively, public information, legitimate inference and private information. The other to the fact that our colleagues in business strategy now give emphasis to two rather different perspectives on the nature of competitive firms, one essentially based on similarities (strategic groups: McGee and Thomas,

---

[9] There are undoubtedly good reasons for adopting such a low dimensionality approach in the name of either stability, which is clearly a critical issue if strategic choices are going to be made in this context, and/or a hierarchy of effects in which strategic choices at this level dominate later more complex choices in a higher dimension perceptual space, but it is often doubtful whether either or both of these rationales are based on firm empirical evidence in many situations.

1986) the other on differences (resource-based perspective: Wernerfeld, 1984, 1995a).[10] Sound competitor analysis should at least enable us to avoid making inconsistent assumptions particularly in the context of public data, like, for instance, assuming that we will be able to exploit an opportunity which is known to all, without a significant amount of competitive reaction.

Finally there is the question of channels or, in more general terms, supply chains. The issue of retailers in particular as independent and significant economic intermediaries rather than just logistical channels to the final consumer has been an important consideration in consumer marketing, at least since the 1970s. Similarly in industrial markets the issue of the supply chain and the central importance of some form of organization and co-ordination of the various independent entities within the chain has been seen as an increasingly important strategic issue. Both these developments have meant that any strategic marketing analysis needs to find ways to evaluate the likely impact of such independent strategies pursued by intermediaries, although in many cases our tools and techniques for doing this remain rather limited and often rely on no more than an attempt to speculate on what might be their preferred strategic action.[11]

The codification of marketing strategy analysis in terms of three strategies, four boxes and five forces

What can now be regarded as 'traditional' marketing strategy analysis was developed primarily in the 1970s. It was codified in various ways, including the strategic triangle developed by Ohmae (1982) but perhaps more memorably, the most significant elements in the analysis can be defined in terms of the three generic strategies, the four boxes (or perhaps more appropriately strategic contexts) and the five forces.

These particular frameworks also represent the substantial debt that marketing strategy owes to economic analysis; the three strategies and the

five forces are directly taken from Michael Porters influential work, which derived from his earlier work in IO economics. The four contexts were initially popularized by the Boston Consulting Group (BCG) under Bruce Henderson, again strongly influenced by micro-economic analysis. Whilst each of these approaches became a significant component in much marketing strategy teaching (see Morrison and Wensley, 1991), we also need to recognize some of the key considerations and assumptions that need to be considered in any critical application.

The three strategies

It could reasonably be argued that Porter really reintroduced the standard economic notion of scale to the distinction between cost and differentiation to arrive at the three generic strategies of focus, cost and differentiation. Indeed in his later formulation of the three strategies they really became four in that he suggested, rightly, that the choice between an emphasis on competition via cost or differentiation could be made at various scales of operation.

With further consideration it is clear that both of these dimensions are themselves not only continuous but also likely to be the aggregate of a number of relatively independent elements or dimensions. Hence scale is in many contexts not just a single measure of volume of finished output but also of relative volumes of sub-assemblies and activities that may well be shared. Even more so in the case of 'differentiation', where we can expect that there are various different ways in which any supplier attempts to differentiate their offerings. On top of this, a number of other commentators, most particularly John Kay (1993), have noted that not only may the cost–differentiation scale be continuous rather than dichotomous but it also might not be seen as a real dimension at all. At some point this could become a semantic squabble but there clearly is an important point that many successful strategies are built around a notion of good value for money rather than a pure emphasis on cost or differentiation at any price. Michael Porter (1980) might describe this as a 'middle' strategy but rather crucially he has consistently claimed that there is a severe danger of getting 'caught in the middle'. In fact it might be reasonable to assume that in many cases being in the middle is the best place to be: after all, Porter never presented significant systematic evidence to support his own assertion (*cf.* Wensley, 1994)

---

[10] More recently it would seem that the differences approach in the form of the RBV is in the ascendancy.
[11] It should also be noted that the very complexities of modelling and interpreting competitive and intermediary response have led some marketing scholars to suggest that it would be better to focus on so-called monopoly models and ignore issues of competitive reaction (Shugan, 2002).

and more recent work has suggested that such systematic empirical evidence is indeed lacking (Campbell-Hunt, 2000).

The four contexts

The four boxes (contexts) relates to the market share/market growth matrix originally developed by BCG under Bruce Henderson. Although there have inevitably been a whole range of different matrix frameworks which have emerged since the early days, the BCG one remains an outstanding exemplar not only because of its widespread popularity and impact, more recently even University vice-chancellors have been heard to use terms such as 'cash cow', but because there was an underlying basic economic logic in its development. Other similar frameworks often adopted the rather tautologous proposition that one should invest in domains which were both attractive and where one had comparative advantage!

The market growth/market share matrix, however, still involved a set of key assumptions that were certainly contestable. In particular, alongside the relatively uncontroversial one that in general over time the growth rate in markets tends to decline, there were the assumptions that it was in some sense both easier to gain market share in higher growth rate markets, and also that the returns to such gains were likely to be of longer duration.

This issue which can be seen as assumptions about first the cost and then the benefit of investment in market share, and has been discussed and debated widely in marketing over the last 25 years (see Jacobson and Aaker, 1985; Jacobson, 1994). The general conclusions would appear to be that:

(i) Market share as an investment is not on average under-priced, and may just as well be over-priced.
(ii) The cost of gaining market share is less related to the market growth rate and much more to the relationship between actual growth rates and competitors expectations.
(iii) Much of the benefit attributed to market share is probably better interpreted as the result of competitive advantages generated by more specific resources and choices in marketing activities or other corporate areas.

On this basis, it would seem that the bias implied in the BCG matrix towards investment in market share at the early stages of market growth is not really justified particularly when one takes into account that at this stage in market development many investments are likely to be somewhat more risky as well.[12] However, companies can benefit from a focus on market share position when it encourages them to place greater emphasis on the marketing fundamentals for a particular business.

More generally, the matrix as an analytical device suffers from some of the problems which we illustrated for the three strategies approach: an analysis which is essentially based on extreme points when in practice many of the portfolio choices are actually around the centre of the diagram. This implies that any discrimination between business units needs to be on the basis of much more specific analysis rather than broad general characteristics.

The five forces

The five forces analysis was originally introduced by Michael Porter to emphasize the extent to which the overall basis of competition was much wider than just the rivalries between established competitors in a particular market. Whilst not exactly novel as an insight, particularly to suggest that firms also face competition from new entrants and substitutes, it was presented in a very effective manner and served to emphasize not only the specific and increasing importance of competition as we discussed, but also the extent to which competition should be seen as a much wider activity within the value chain as Porter termed it.

Porter used the term value chain when in essence he was concentrating more on the chain of actual costs.[13] Whilst ex post from an economic point-of-view, there is little difference between value and cost, it is indeed the process of both competition and collaboration between various firms and intermediaries that finally results in the attribution of value throughout the relevant network. In this sense, as others have recognized, a supply chain is an intermediate organization form where there is a higher degree of co-operation

---

[12] We do, however, need to be clear between the simple trade-off between risk and return and the undoubted fact that in more risky situations, it may be more advisable to make optional investments, that is to look at what are termed 'real options' (see Dixit and Pindyck, 1995; Adner and Levinthal, 2004a and further commentaries and reply (Adner and Levinthal, 2004b)).

[13] More recent commentators such as McGee (2002) maintain a distinction between the value chain which represents those activities undertaken by a firm, and the supply chain, of which the value chain is a subset, which refers to all the activities leading up to the final product for the consumer.

between the firms within the chain and a greater degree of competition between the firms within different chains. In this context, Porter's analysis has tended to focus much more clearly on the issue of competition rather than co-operation. Indeed, at least in its representational form it has tended to go further than this and focus attention on the nature of the competitive pressures on the firm itself rather than interaction between the firm and other organizations in the marketplace.[14]

The search for generic rules for success amidst diversity

As we have suggested above, the codification of marketing strategy was based on three essential schema. This schemata, whilst it was based on some valid theoretical concepts did not really provide a systematic approach to the central question: the nature of sustained economic performance in the competitive marketplace. Whilst such an objective was clearly recognized in the so-called search for Sustainable Competitive Advantage (Day and Wensley, 1988), there remained some central concerns as to whether such a notion was realistic given the dynamic and uncertain nature of the competitive marketplace (Dickinson, 1992).

Indeed, not only is it dynamic and uncertain but it is also diverse: firms are heterogeneous and so is the nature of demand. A useful way of looking at demand side heterogeneity is from the user perspective directly. Arguably from its relatively early origins marketing, or at least the more functional focused study of marketing management, has been concerned with managerial effective ways of responding to this heterogeneity, particularly in terms of market segmentation. Indeed it would be reasonable to suggest that without a substantial level of demand heterogeneity, there would be little need for marketing approaches as they are found in most of our textbooks. Whilst there remains a substantial debate about the degree to which this market-based heterogeneity is indeed 'manageable' from a marketing perspective (*cf.* Saunders, 1995; Wensley, 1995), to which we will partly return later in this chapter, our concern at the moment is merely to recognize the substantial degree of heterogeneity

and consider the degree to which such diversity on both the supply and demand side facilitates or negates the possibility of developing robust 'rules for success'.

To address this question, we need to consider the most useful way of characterizing the competitive market process. This is clearly a substantial topic in its own right with proponents of various analogies or metaphors along a spectrum including game theory, sports games and military strategy.

To illustrate this issue, let us consider the field of ecology[15] where we observe wide diversity in terms of both species and habitat. There are two critical aspects that must inform any attempt to transfer this analogy into the field of strategy. The first is the interactive relationship between any species and its habitat, nicely encapsulated in the title of the book by Levins and Leowontin (1985): *The Dialectical Biologist*. Particularly in the context of strategy it is important to recognize that the habitat (for which read market domain) evolves and develops at least as fast as the species (for which, rather more problematically, read the individual firm).[16]

The second aspect addresses directly our question of 'rules for success'. How far can we identify particularly through the historical record, whether there are any reliable rules for success for particular species characteristics? Of course, it is very difficult to address this question without being strongly influenced by hindsight and most specific observations can be seen as contentious.[17]

It would seem that we should at least be very cautious in any search for rules for success amidst a world of interactive diversity. Hence we should hardly be surprised that marketing strategy analysis does not provide for consistent and sustainable individual success in the competitive marketplace. However, we do have a set of theoretical frameworks and practical tools that at least allow us to represent some of the key dynamics of both customer and competitive behaviour in a way that ensures we avoid errors of inconsistency or simple naiveté.

---

[14] In particular, others have emphasized the importance of co-operative as well as competitive behaviour, particularly in terms of knowledge flows (see Cooke, 2002) and strategic alliances (Todeva and Knoke, 2005).

[15] This links to an interest in co-evolutionary processes but much of the strategy-related writing in this area has focused on interactions between organizations rather than between organizations and users (see Volberda and Lewin, 2003).

[16] For a much more developed discussion of the application of such notions as species to competitive strategy at the firm level see McKelvey (1982).

[17] Stephen Jay Gould (1987, 1990) has perhaps most directly considered this issue in his various writings, in particular the analysis of the Burgess Shale, and come to the uncompromising conclusion that it is difficult if not impossible to recognize any species features or characteristics that provided a reliable *ex ante* rule for success.

As we have discussed above, most analysis in marketing strategy is informed by what are essentially economic frameworks and so tend to focus attention on situations in which both the competitive structure of the market and the nature of consumer preferences are relatively well established. As we move our attention to more novel situations these structures tend to be at best indeterminate and therefore the analytical frameworks are less appropriate. We encounter the first of many ironies in the nature of marketing strategy analysis. It is often least applicable in the very situations in which there is a real opportunity for a new source of economic advantage based on a restructuring of either or both the competitive environment and consumer preferences.[18]

Models of competition: game theory versus evolutionary ecology

To develop a formal approach to the modelling of competitive behaviour we need to define:

1 The nature of the arena in which the competitive activity takes place.
2 The structure or rules that govern the behaviour of the participants
3 The options available in terms of competitor behaviour (when these consist of a sequence of actions through time, or over a number of 'plays', then they are often referred to in game theory as strategies).

In this section, however, we particularly wish to contrast game theory approaches which in many ways link directly to the economic analysis to which we have already referred, and analogies from evolutionary biology which raise difficult questions about the inherent feasibility of any systematic model building at the level of the individual firm.

Game theory models of competition

A game theory model[19] is characterized by a set of rules which described (1) the number of firms competing against each other, (2) the set of actions that each firm can take at each point in time, (3) the profits that each firm will realize for each set of competitive actions, (4) the time pattern of actions – whether they occur simultaneously or one firm moves first? and (5) the nature of information about competitive activity – who knows what, when? The notion of rationality also plays a particularly important role in models of competitive behaviour. Rationality implies a link between actions and intentions but not common intentions between competitors. Models describing competitive activity are designed to understand the behaviour of 'free' economic agents. Thus, these models start with an assumption of 'weak' rationality – the agents will take actions that are consistent with their longer-term objectives. The models also assume a stronger form of rationality – the intentions of the agents can be expressed in terms of a number of economic measures of outcome states such as profit, sales, growth or market share objectives.

Do the results of game theory model indicate how firms should act in competitive situations? Do the models describe the evolution of competitive interactions in the real world? These questions have spawned a lively debate among management scientist concerning the usefulness of game theory models. Kadane and Larkey (1982) suggested that game theory models are conditionally normative and conditionally descriptive. The results do indicate how firms should behave given a set of assumptions about the alternatives, the payoffs and the properties of an 'optimal' solution (the equilibrium). Similarly, game theory results describe the evolution of competitive strategy but only given a specific set of assumptions.

The seemingly unrealistic and simplistic nature of the competitive reactions incorporated in game theory models and nature of the equilibrium concept led some marketers to question the managerial relevance of these models (Dolan, 1981). However, all models involve simplifying assumptions and game theory models,[20] whilst often highly structured underpin most attempts to apply economic analysis to issues of competition among

---

[18] However, some detailed work on customer perceptions of market structure actually suggests that in even relative stable contexts such as autos and motor cycles, the structures maybe quite dynamic (Rosa *et al.* 1999; Rosa and Porac, 2002).

[19] A wider and comprehensive review of the application of game theory to marketing situations can be found in Moorthy (1985). For a more recent but broader and rather patchy review see Chatterjee and Samuelson (2001).

[20] A good coverage of game theory approaches is to be found in Kreps (1990), but as indeed Goeree and Holt (2001) note, there remain some significant problems with the predictive power of game theory models when they are compared with actual behaviour most obviously in asymmetric pay-off situations, which raises questions about the underlying notion of rationality.

a limited number of firms. Indeed, as Goeree and Holt (2001) observe:

> 'Game theory has finally gained the central role . . . in some areas of economics (e.g. IO) virtually all recent developments are applications of game theory' (2001 p. 1402)

As discussed above, IO economics provides one way of extending basic game theory approaches by examining the nature of competitive behaviour when assumptions about homogeneous firms and customers are relaxed. IO economists, especially Richard Caves (1980) and Michael Porter (1981) directed the development of IO theory to strategic management issues. The concepts of strategic groups and mobility barriers were key elements in this new IO perspective (Caves and Porter, 1977). As Richard Caves indicates, 'the concepts of strategic groups and mobility barriers do not add up to a tight formal model. Rather, they serve to organize predictions that come from tight models and assist in confronting them with empirical evidence – a dynamized add-on to the traditional structure–conduct–performance paradigm' (1984).

Evolutionary ecological analogies

Evolutionary ecology has also emerged as a popular analogy for understanding the types of market-based strategies pursued by companies (Coyle, 1986; Lambkin and Day, 1989; Summut-Bonnici and Wensley, 2002). These analogies have been previously used to describe both the nature of the competitive process itself (Henderson, 1983) as well as the notion of 'niche' strategy (Hofer and Schendel, 1977). Organizational theorists and sociologists have adopted an ecological model, describing the growth of a specie in an ecology, to describe the types of firms in an environment.

r- and k-strategies

From an ecological perspective, there is an upper limit on the population of a specie in a resource environment. When the population of a specie is small, the effects of the carrying capacity are minimal and the growth is an exponential function of the natural growth rate. The carrying capacity only becomes important when the population size is relatively large relative to the carrying capacity. The parameters of the standard growth model have been used to describe two alternatives strategies: r-strategies and k-strategies. r-Strategists enter a new resource space (product–market space)

at an early stage when few other organizations are present, while k-strategists join later when there are a larger number of organizations in the environment. Once a particular type of organization established itself in an environment, it resists change for various reasons. The number of firms in an environment at one point time, referred to as the population density, is a proxy for the intensity of competition.

Based on this perspective, the initial entrants into an environment are usually r-strategist-small, new firms that are quick to move and not constrained by the inherent inertia confronting firms established in other environments. While r-strategists are flexible, they are also inefficient due to their lack of experience. After several r-strategists have entered a new environment, established organizations, k-strategists, overcome their inertia, enter the environment and exploit their advantage of greater efficiency based on extensive experience. The characteristics of the environment and particularly the viable niches that emerge determine whether these successive entrants can coexist.

A niche is defined as the specific combination of resources that is needed support a specie or type of organization. Niche width indicates whether this combination of resource is available over a broad range of the resource source space or whether it is only available in a narrow range of the space. A generalist is able to operate in a broad range while a specialist is restricted to a narrow range. The nature of a particular environment favours either generalists or specialists.

Environments are described by two dimensions: variability and frequency of environmental change. In a highly variable environment, changes are dramatic, and fundamentally different strategic responses are required for survival. In contrast, strategic alterations are not required to cope with an environment of low variability. A specialist strategy in which high performance occurs in a narrow portion of the environment is surprisingly more appropriate when environmental changes are dramatic and frequent. Under these conditions, it is unlikely that a generalist would have sufficient flexibility to cope with the wide range of environmental conditions it would face, whilst the specialist can at least out-perform it in a specific environment.[21] A generalist strategist is most

---

[21] For a more detailed discussion of this analysis see Lambkin and Day (1989), as well as an introduction to more complex strategy options involving polymorthism and

appropriate in an environment characterized by infrequent, minor changes because this environment allows the generalist to exploit its large-scale efficiencies.

Comparing the key elements in different models of competition[22]

The strategic groups and mobility barriers in the IO economics approach recognize the critical asymmetries between competing firms. It identifies three methods by which firms can isolate themselves from competition: (1) differentiation, (2) cost efficiency and (3) collusion although the later issue has tended to be ignored. The developments within the IO paradigm have therefore tended to usefully focus on the nature and significance of various mechanisms for isolating the firm from its competition. The evolutionary ecological analogy, on the other hand, focuses on the notion of scope with the general distinction between specialists and generalists. The ecological approach also raises interesting questions about the form, level and type of 'organization' that we are considering. In particular, we need to recognize most markets as forms of organization in their own right, as those who have argued the 'markets as networks' approach have done, and question how far we can justify an exclusive focus on the firm as the key organization unit. Finally, the analogy raises more directly the concern about the interaction between various different units (species) and their evolving habitat. The marketplace, like the habitat, can become relatively unstable and so both affect and be affected by the strategies of the individual firms.

As we have suggested, any analogy is far from perfect, as we would expect. The limitations are as critical as the issues that are raised because they give us some sense of the bounds within which the analogy itself is likely to be useful. Extending it outside these bounds is likely to be counter-productive and misleading.

The IO approach in practice tends to neglect the interaction between cost and quality. We have already suggested that while the notion 'focus' within this analogy is an attempt to recognize this problem; it is only partially successful because it subsumes a characteristic of any successful competitive strategy into one generic category. We must further consider the extent to which we can reasonably reliably distinguish between the various forms of mixed strategies over time and the extent to which the strategic groups themselves remain stable.

The limitations of analogies from evolutionary ecology are more in terms of the questions that are not answered than those where the answers are misleading. The nature of 'competition' is both unclear and complex, there is confusion as to the level and appropriate unit of analysis, and the notion of 'niche' which has become so current in much strategy writing overlooks the fact that by definition every species has one anyway.

Characterizing marketing strategy in terms of evolving differentiation in time and space

Central to any notion of competition from a marketing strategy viewpoint is the issue of differentiation in time and space. In a 'real' market (i) demand is heterogeneous, (ii) suppliers are differentiated and (iii) there are processes of feedback and change through time. Clearly these three elements interact significantly, yet in most cases we find that to reduce the complexity in our analysis and understanding we treat each item relatively independently. For instance, in most current treatments of these issues in marketing strategy we would use some form of market segmentation schema to map heterogeneous demand, some notion of the resource-based view (RBV) of the firm to reflect the differentiation amongst suppliers and some model of market evolution such as the product life cycle to reflect the nature of the time dynamic.

Such an approach has two major limitations that may act to remove any benefit from the undoubted reduction of analytical complexity by looking at three sub-systems rather the whole system. First, it assumes implicitly that this decomposition is reasonably first order correct: that the impact of the individual elements is more important than their interaction terms. To examine this assumption critically we need some alternative

portfolios. Achrol (1991) also develops this approach further with some useful examples. In strategy language, we recognize that the ability to adapt in a more rapidly changing or turbulent environment is out down to being a 'learning organization' or having so-called 'dynamic capabiities' (Teece *et al.* 1997).

[22] In this analysis we have left out two other generic types of competitive analogy that are commonly used: sports games and military conflict. Whilst in general these can both be illuminating and informative, they represent in many ways intermediate categories between game theory and evolutionary ecology.

form of analysis and representation, such as modelling the phenomena of interest as the co-evolution of firms and customers in a dynamic phase space, which allows for the fact that time and space interact. Second, it assumes that the ways of representing the individual elements that we use, in particular market segmentation and product life cycle concepts, are in fact robust representations of the underlying phenomena. In terms of the adequacy of each element in its own terms, we need to look more closely at the ways in which individual improvements may be achieved and finally we might wish to consider whether it would be better to model partial interactions, say, between two elements only rather than the complete system.

Differentiation in space: issues of market segmentation

The analysis of spatial competition has, of course, a long history back at least to the classical Hotelling model of linear competition such as that faced by the two ice-cream sellers on the seafront. The basic Hotelling model, however, did capture the two critical issues in spatial competition: the notion of a space dimension that separated the various competitive suppliers as well as the fact that these suppliers themselves would have some degree of mobility. In traditional economic terms Hotelling was interested in establishing the equilibrium solution under these two considerations, whereas in marketing we are often more concerned with the impact and likelihood of particular spatial moves, although some notion of the stable long-term equilibrium, if it exists, is obviously important. The Hotelling model provides us with the basic structure of spatial competition: a definition of the space domain, some model of the relationship between the positioning of the relevant suppliers within this space and their relative demands.

In marketing, the competitive space is generally characterized in terms of market segmentation. Market segmentation has, of course, received considerable attention in both marketing research and practice, but there remain some critical problems. In particular:

1 We have evidence that the cross-elasticities with respect to different marketing mix elements are likely to be not only of different orders, but actually imply different structures of relationship between individual product offerings.
2 Competitive behaviour patterns, which after all in a strict sense, determine the nature of the

experiment from which the elasticities can be derived, seem to be, to use a term coined by Leeflang and Wittick (1993), 'out of balance' with the cross-elasticity data itself.

The topic of market segmentation is covered in much greater depth elsewhere in this book but for the purposes of this chapter we wish to concentrate on the specific question as to how far segmentation provides us with an appropriate definition of the space within which competition evolves. In this sense, the key questions are, as we discussed above, about the dimensionality of the space concerned, the stability of the demand function and the degree of mobility for individual firms (or more correctly individual offerings) in terms of repositioning.

These are in practice very difficult questions to deal with for two critical reasons:

(i) The nature of the choice process is such that for many offerings, individual consumers chose from a portfolio of items rather than merely make exclusive choices, and, hence, in principle it is difficult to isolate the impact of one offering from the others in the portfolio.
(ii) The dimensions of the choice space are often inferred from the responses to current offerings and therefore it is difficult to distinguish between the effects of current offerings and some notion of an underlying set of preference structures.

Segmentation and positioning

In principle, we can describe the nature of spatial competition in a market either in demand terms or in supply terms. Market segmentation represents the demand perspective on structure, whilst competitive positioning represents the supply perspective.

Market segmentation takes as its starting point assumptions about the differing requirements that individual customers have with respect to bundles of benefits in particular use situations. Most obviously in this context it is an 'ideal' approach in that it is effectively assumed that each customer can/does specify their own ideal benefit bundle and their purchase choice in the relevant use situation is based on proximity to this ideal point. In consumer psychology this is equivalent to an assumption that individuals have strong and stable preferences.

The competitive positioning approach uses consumer judgements, normally on an aggregate basis, on the similarities and differences between specific competitive offerings. In principle this provides an analytical output roughly equivalent to the spatial distribution in the Hotelling model. Such an analysis can also be used to provide an estimate of the dimensionality of the discriminant space, but in many situations for ease of presentation the results are presented in a constrained 2D format. Equally benefit segmentation studies can be used along with techniques such as factor analysis to try and arrive at an estimate of the dimensionality of the demand side.

We can be reasonably certain that the attitude space for customers in any particular market is generally, say, $N > 3$: factor analytical studies might suggest at least four or five in general and that of competitive offerings is of at least a similar order. Indeed, in the later case if we considered the RBV of the firm very seriously we might go for a dimensionality as high as the number of competitors.[23]

Of more interest from a strategy point-of-view is how we represent what happens in terms of actual purchase behaviour in a competitive market through time. Although there is relatively little high-quality empirical and indeed theoretical work in this area, so far there are intriguing results to suggest that the dimensionality of the market space for this purpose can be much reduced, although we may still then have problems with some second order effects in terms of market evolution. There have been a number of attempts to apply segmentation analysis to behavioural data with much less information as to attitudes or intention. In one of the more detailed of such studies, Chintagunta (1994) suggested that the dimensionality of the revealed competitive space was two dimensional but even this might be really an over-estimate.[24] In his own interpretation of the results he focuses on the degree to which the data analysis reveals interesting differences in terms of brand position revealed by individual purchase patterns through time.

In terms of second order anomalies, we can also consider some of the issues raised by so-called 'compromise effect' in choice situations where the choice between two alternatives depends on other, less attractive, alternatives. In an intriguing paper, Wernerfeld (1995b) argues that this effect can be systematically explained by the notion that consumers draw inferences about their own personal valuations from the portfolio of offerings. However, it may be that a compromise effect could also be seen as the result of mapping an $N > 1$ attribute and preference space on to an $N = 1$ set of purchase decisions.[25]

A simple model of spatial competition might therefore be one in which a considerable amount of competition can be seen as along a single dimension, in circumstances in which multiple offerings are possible, and where there is no reason to believe a priori that individual offerings will be grouped either by common brand or specification, with a fixed entry cost for each item and a distribution of demand which is multi-modal. To this extent it may actually be true that the very simplifications that many criticize in the Porter ' three generic strategies' approach may be reasonably appropriate in building a first order model of competitive market evolution (see Campbell-Hunt, 2000). In the short-run, following the notion of 'clout' and 'vulnerability' (Cooper and Nakanishi, 1988), we might also expect changes in position in this competitive dimension could be a function of a whole range of what might often be seen as tactical as well as strategic marketing actions.

Cooper extended his own approach to understanding market structures by marrying two different data types – switching probabilities and attribute ratings (Cooper and Inoue, 1996). Despite the fact that the models developed appear to perform well against the appropriate statistical test, there remain basic issues which link to the issue of the time dynamic evolution of the market or demand space. When the model is applied to the well-established dataset on car purchase switching behaviour (Harshman et al., 1982), it is clear that it provides an interesting and informative analysis of the ways in which various customer 'segments' have evolved over time both in terms of their size and attribute preferences. However, given the nature of the data and the form of analysis the dynamic process whereby customer desires change in response to both new

---

[23] Since the RBV approach focuses particularly on the nature of idiosyncratic and difficult to imitate resources in each individual firm. For a thorough presentation and analysis of the RBV approach see Barney and Clark (2007).

[24] In fact, on closer inspection, it is clear that we can achieve a high level of discrimination with the one-dimensional map where there are two distinct groupings, and one intermediate brand and one 'outlier' brand. It is significant that these groupings are not either brand or pack-sized based but a mixture. In fact, the only result in moving from the one-dimensional to the two-dimensional analysis, is that one brand has become less discriminated (see Wensley, 1997). Hence it would appear that we can rather surprisingly reduce the effective competitive space to a single dimension with the possibility of only some second order anomalies.

[25] The classical Victorian monograph 'Flatland' (Abbott, 1992) provided an early illustration of many perceptual problems of moving between spaces of different dimensions.

competitive offerings and other endogenous and exogenous factors can only be seen it terms of changes in attributes and specific switching decisions. We must now consider, however, particularly in the context of understanding the time-based nature of market strategies, how we might incorporate in more detail a longer-term time dimension with a stronger customer focus.

Differentiation in time: beyond the PLC – characterizing the nature of competitive market evolution

'Few management concepts have been so widely accepted or thoroughly criticized as the product life cycle'

(Lambkin and Day, 1989, p. 4)

The product life cycle has the advantage that it does represent the simplest form of path development for any product (introduction, growth, maturity, decline) but as has been widely recognized, this remains a highly stylized representation of the product sales pattern for most products during their lifetime. Whilst it is reasonably clear that it is difficult if not impossible to propose a better single generic time pattern, any such pattern is subject to considerable distortion as a result of interactions with changes in technology as well as both customer and competitor behaviour.

Lambkin and Day (1989) suggested that an understanding of the process of product–market evolution required a more explicit distinction between issues of the demand system, the supply system and the resource environment. However, they chose to emphasize the nature of the demand evolution primarily in terms of diffusion processes. This approach tends to underestimate the extent to which demand side evolution is as much about the way(s) in which the structure of the demand space is changing as the more aggregate issue of the total demand itself. Lambkin and Day (1989), themselves, treat these two issues at different levels of analysis with 'segmentation' as an issue in market evolution which is defined as the resource environment within which the process of the product life cycle takes place.

Beyond this, more recent research, on the process of market evolution, partly building on some of the ideas developed by Lambkin and Day (1989), has attempted to incorporate some insights from, amongst other areas, evolutionary ecology. In particular, work on the extensive disk-drive database, which gives quarterly data on all disk-drive manufacturers has allowed Christensen (1997) and Freeman (1997) to look at the ways in which at the early stages in the market development, the existence of competitive offerings seems to encourage market growth whereas at later stages the likelihood of firm exit increases with firm density. Other computer-related industries have also provided the opportunity for empirical work on some of the issue relating to both the impact of standardization, modularization and the nature of generation effects (Sanchez, 1995), although in the later case it must be admitted that the effects themselves can sometimes be seen as a result of marketing actions in their own right.[26]

The nature of research in marketing strategy: fallacies of free lunches and the nature of answerable research questions

Distinguishing between information about means, variances and outliers

As we indicated at the start of this chapter, much research in marketing strategy has attempted to address what is in some senses an impossible question: what is the basic generalizable nature of a successful competitive marketing strategy. Such a question presumes the equivalent of a free lunch: we research to find the equivalent of a universal money machine. Before we explore this issue further we need to establish a few basic principles. The competitive process is such that:

(i) Average performance can only produce average results which in the general nature of

---

[26] Much of the market shift towards standardization as it evolves can be seen as analogous to more recent work on the mathematics of chaos and particular questions of the nature of boundaries between domains of chaos and those of order: often labelled the phenomena of complexity (Cohen and Stewart, 1995). Whether we can use such models to provide a better understanding of the nature of market evolution beyond the basic analogy remains an important question for empirical research.

There have been more recent attempts to apply spatial competition models which demonstrate some level of chaotic or complexity characteristics either to competitive behaviour in a retailing context (Krider and Weinberg, 1997) or to multi-brand category competition (Rungie, 1998) and competition between audit service providers (Chan *et al.*, 1999). Whilst these approaches suggested that such models may be able to give us significant new insights as to the nature of competitive market evolution, there has been little further progress.

a competitive system means that success is related to above average and sometime even outlier levels of performance.

(ii) We can expect our competitors to be able on average to interpret any public data to reveal profitable opportunities as well as we can. In more direct terms it means that on average competitors are as cleaver or as stupid as stupid as we are. A combination of public information and the impact of such basic rational expectations approaches, therefore, means that the route to success cannot lie in simply exploiting public information in an effective manner, although such a strategy may enable a firm to improve its own performance.

(iii) The basis of individual firm or unit performance is a complex mix of both firm, competitor and market factors. We therefore can expect that any attempt to explain performance will be subject to considerable error given that it is difficult or not impossible to identify an adequate range of variables which cover both the specifics of the firms own situation and the details of the market and competitor behaviour.

For these reasons research in marketing strategy, as in the strategy field as a whole, has almost always tended to be in one of the two categories:

1 Quantitative database analysis which has relied on statistical and econometric approaches to produce results which indicate certain independent variables which on average correlate with performance. As McCloskey and Ziliak (1996) indicated more generally in econometric work, there is a danger that we often confuse statistical significance for what they term economic significance. This notion of economic significance can, from a managerial perspective, be decomposed into two elements: first, the extent to which the relationship identified actually relates to a significant proportion of the variation in the dependent variable and second, the extent to which even if it does this regularity actually enables one to produce a clear prescription for managerial action.[27]

2 Case study-based research on selected firms, often based on the notion of some form of outliers, such as those that perform particularly well. Here the problems are the extent to which the story that is told about the particular nature of the success concerned can be used to guide action in other organizations. In practice this often results in managerial prescriptions that are rather tautological and at the same time not adequately discriminating.

Market share and ROI: the 10 per cent rule in practice

One of the most famous results from the Profit Impact of Market Strategy (PIMS) database was that first reported by Bob Buzzell, Brad Gale and Ralph Sultan in the Harvard Business Review in 1976 under the title 'Market Share – A Key to Profitability'. They reported on the relationship between Return on Investment (ROI) and market share on a cross-sectional basis within the then current PIMS database. Although over the years estimates of the R^2 of this relationship have varied, it generally shows a value around 10 per cent up to a maximum of 15 per cent. We can start by simulating the original data that was used (Figure 4.1).

The chart is a scatter plot of 500 datapoints (notional observations) where the relationship between the two implied variables is actually the equivalent of an R2 of 0.12 or 12 per cent.[28] In their original article Buzzell, Gale and Sultan 'removed' much of the variation: by calculating cohort means. We can do the same and also use more typical modern computer-generated graphics to represent the results (Figure 4.2).

The cohort mean approach, although now not commonly used in strategy research of this sort will show, as above, some deviations from the straight line trend at sample sizes such as 500 but as samples get even larger the deviations get, on average, even smaller: indeed, some textbook representations of the results go as far as merely illustrating the trend with no deviations at all. Hence in the process of producing a clearer message from

[27] As they recognize this is not an issue of statistical significance of individual coefficients. For samples of only 50, we can roughly speaking achieve a significant result, using the 'normal' $p < 0.05$ criterion, and yet only have about 5 per cent of the variability 'explained'. For a further and broader discussion on both the issues of statistical reliability and research inference in management research see Starbuck (2004).

[28] Because of the statistical nature of the data distribution in the PIMS database: the fact that it is not strictly normal, it is only possible to simulate a dataset which has either the right range or the right slope within the correct proportion of variance explained. This simulation is based on the right range of values so that the extreme points are estimated correctly as a result however the actual slope is underestimated (see Roberts, 1997; Wensley, 1997a, b).

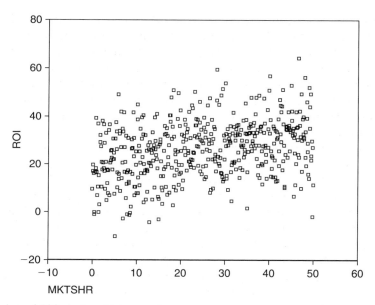

Figure 4.1   A scatter plot of 500 notional observations

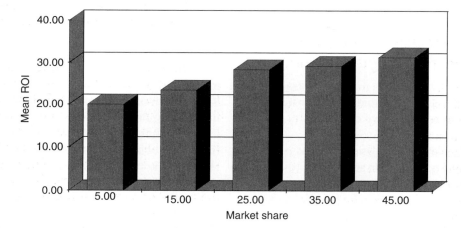

Figure 4.2   A chart of the Cohort Means

the data we have nearly eliminated nine tenths of the variability in our performance variable.

How does one explain the 'unexplained' 90 per cent?

If we return to the scatter diagram and treat it as if it represented the current performance of 500 business units within a single corporate portfolio in terms of the relationship between ROI and market share, then we can see some of the problems that arise when we try and make managerial evaluations. The first set of problems relates to the nature of the data itself and the way in which the axes are measured. In most analysis of this

sort, and in the PIMS data as we discussed above, the data is essentially cross-sectional, that is, it is either annual of averaged out over a longer-fixed period. It therefore excludes any lead or lag effects and also compensates for particular one-off effects only to the extent that they are already discounted from the input data that is normally based on management accounts. The nature of the axes in a standard market share/ROI analysis is a problem in that they are both ratios. There are very considerable advantages that accrue from using ratios in this situation: most obviously the fact that it is possible to plot on the same graph units of very different absolute sizes but we do then have the problem of measurements errors in both the numerator and denominator for both axes.

Finally, the basic data is also inevitably limited in the extent to which it can measure the specifics of any particular business unit situation. Using basic financial and accounting data we cannot take into account issues such as managerial effectiveness as well as the degree of integration to achieve scale economies and efficiencies in terms of marketing and other activities.

However, we must also put this overall critique of 'market share/return' analysis in context. We should not underestimate the original impact of the 'market share' discovery. Even if it only 'explains" around 10 per cent of financial performance, this is still a considerable achievement. The problem is that, as we have seen, even at this level we face difficult interpretation problems. In the end, one perhaps concludes that its greatest impact was merely that it legitimized debate and discussion about key competitive market assumptions in any strategy dialogue.

Getting to management action: the additional problem of economics

Even if we can identify the source of a particular success or indeed the cause of a particular failure it is a big jump to assuming that suitable action can be taken at no cost or even at a cost which is justified by the subsequent benefits.

We therefore need to overlay our notion of practical significance with one of economic significance: a factors or set of factors which explain a significant proportion of success and can also be used as a decision rule for subsequent successful management action. This is a big jump. To return to the market share/ROI relationship even if we conclude that there is a significant correlation between market share and profitability we have to make two further assumptions to justify an economic rule of 'investing' in market share. First, we have to move from the more general notion of 'correlation' or 'explanation' to the much more specific one of 'causation' and second, we have to assume that whatever its benefits, market share is somehow under-priced. If our first assumption is correct then broadly it can only be under-priced if either our competitors, both current and potential, have a different view or, for some unspecified reason, happen to value the asset (market share) significantly lower than we do. In fact, in specific situations this latter assumption may be rather less unlikely than it at first appears: our competitors could indeed value the benefits differently given their differing

portfolio of assets and market positions but it all depends on the specifics and the details of the individual situation rather than the general.

In the end, it is likely that the continued search for general rules for strategic success via statistical analysis and large databases will prove illusory. This does not make the research effort worthless, we merely have to be realistic about what can and cannot be achieved. After all, the in-depth case study narrative approach[29] often results in another type of economic rule: the truth that is virtually impossible to apply. Perhaps the best example is to be found in Peters and Waterman's original work. Amongst many memorable criteria for success to be found in In Search of Excellence was that undeniable one: the achievement of simultaneous 'loose–tight' linkages. To those who thought that this might seem contradictory Peters and Waterman provided the helpful observation that:

> 'These are the apparent contradictions that turn out in practice not to be contradictions at all'
>
> (1982:320)

More recently in marketing strategy, as in strategy as a whole, there has been a move away from analysis based on real substantive recommendations for management action towards a concern more for processes, people and purposes rather than structure, strategies and systems.[30] Whilst this shift can be seen as a reasonable response to our lack of substantive generalizable knowledge about the nature of successful marketing strategies in a competitive marketplace, as we have discussed above, it should also be seen as one which itself has rather limited evidence to support it. In marketing strategy in particular, two areas can be identified where this trend has been very evident and we will look critically at both of these: the shift towards a focus on networks and relationship marketing and the increased emphasis on marketing processes within the firm.

Markets as networks

It is clear, as Easton (1990) has indicated that actual relationships between one firm and another must

---

[29] Perhaps the best example of both the value but also the risks of relying on an in-depth case study lies in the continuing debates about the interpretation of the story of Honda and their entry into the American motor cycle market (Mintzberg, 1996; Mair, 1999).

[30] Bartlett and Ghoshal (1995) in their influential Harvard Business Review article played a key role in this change in emphasis.

be seen on a spectrum between outright competition at one end and collusion at the other. At the very least, such a self-evident observation raises the issue of the firm (or business unit) as the basic, and often only, unit of analysis: in certain circumstances we might more appropriately consider an informal coalition of such firms as the key unit:

> 'Earlier, the border of the company was seen as the dividing line between co-operation and conflict – co-operation within the company and conflict in relation to all external units. The corresponding means for co-ordination are hierarchy and the market mechanism. The existence of relationships makes this picture much more diffuse. There are great opportunities for co-operation with a lot of external units forming, for example, coalitions. Thus, it is often more fruitful to see the company as a part of a network instead of a free and independent actor in an atomistic market'
>
> (Hakansson, 1987, p. 13)

However, the recognition that there is a network of relationships is merely the first step. Approaches need to be developed for the analysis of the network. Hakansson has, for instance, suggested that the key elements of any network are actors, activities and resources. He also suggests that the overall network is bound together by a number of forces including functional interdependence, as well as power, knowledge and time-related structure.

There is a danger in confusing a detailed descriptive model with a simple but robust predictive one, let alone one that aids the diagnostic process. The basic micro-economic framework which underlies the 'competitive advantage' approach, central to much marketing strategy analysis, should not be seen as an adequate description of the analytical and processual complexities in specific situations. It is a framework for predicting the key impacts of a series of market-mediated transactions: at the very least outcomes are the joint effect of decisions themselves and the selection process. In this sense the only valid criticisms of the application of such a model is that either the needs of the situation are not met by the inherent nature of the model or that the model fails to perform within its own terms.

Relationship marketing

Beyond this there has been a broader attempt to introduce what has become known as relationship marketing. Whilst the relationship perspective rightly moves our attention away from individual transactions towards patterns of interaction over longer-time periods it often seems to assume that the motivations of each party are symmetric. In practice in both consumer (Fournier et al., 1998) and industrial markets (Faria and Wensley, 2002) this may prove to be a very problematic assumption.

Equally, we may wonder how far the new-found concern for relationship marketing is indeed new at all. The recognition that customers faced switching costs and that therefore the retention of existing customers was clearly an effective economic strategy is certainly not new. One can therefore sympathize with Baker when he commented:

> 'For example, the propositions that companies need to understand the industry infrastructure and/or that working closely with customers is likely to improve product development success rates have been known and accepted many years now, and are embedded in the curricula of most business schools'.
>
> (Baker, 1993)

on the book by Regis McKenna (1992) entitled Relationship Marketing.

Mattsson (1997) has considered much more critically the relationship between the underlying approaches in the 'markets as networks' and relationship marketing perspectives. He rightly observed that much of the problem lay in the various different approaches claiming to represent relationship marketing:

> 'My conclusion is that if we take the limited view of relationship marketing, we come close to be first extreme position stated in the beginning of this article: relationship marketing and the network perspective have very little in common. Some relationship marketing aspects are even contradictory to basic views in the network perspective. Relationship marketing in its limited interpretation is just a marketing strategy aimed to increase customer loyalty, customer satisfaction and customer retention. Relationship marketing is aided by modern information technology that makes it possible to individualize communication with customers in a mass market. In that sense relationship marketing is just a basic application of the marketing management thinking.
>
> However, let us consider the extended view that the relationship marketing means true interaction between the parties over time, a relatively high mutual dependency between seller and buyer and a major concern for how individual relationships are interconnected in nets and networks. Then we will come much closer to my second initial position that relationship marketing and the network

perspective have much to gain from more research interaction and mutual awareness than what is presently the case. Relationship marketing research would benefit from the following aspects of network perspective research: more focus on embeddedness of actors and relationships, more consideration of the buyers point of view, more descriptive studies on interaction and relationships over time, more concern at the meso and macro levels in the governance structure, more use of longitudinal research methods, including case studies. Obviously, both relationship marketing and the network perspective must become increasingly aware of, and contribute to, research developments in a broader social science framework where the focus is on the function of relationships between economic actors'.

More recently, Vargo and Lusch (2004) developed the argument further on the assumption of a dominant trend from the marketing of goods to the provision of services. They argued that *inter alia* all economies are service economies, and that the customer is always a co-producer and that the enterprise can only make value propositions.[31] In a sense, however, to describe, as they do the trend as being from goods dominant to service dominant perspectives over a period of around 100 years is to describe a genuine shift in perspective but a less clear shift in the underlying realities.

The whole development might remind one rather more of M. Jourdain in Moliere's *The Bourgeoise Gentilhomme* who discovers, he has been effortlessly speaking prose all his life. The proposed move towards a more relational and service-based perspective reflects more a changing view of the nature of the customer: from consumer to co-producer than the fact that those who used to be characterized as consumers are now in some objective way more co-producers.[32] We would do well to remember that memorable expression of Ivan Illich (1981); 'shadow work' to describe real work which we do not see because of the nature of our measurement or value systems. Arnould (2006) notes the clear potential link between the approach advocated by Vargo and Lusch, and consumer culture theory but also notes that these aspects are less well developed in their initial presentation. Moreover, Schembri (2006) suggests that the approach adopted still remains somewhat rooted in the more traditional goods centred logic, and needs to engage more with approaches focused around the nature of the customer experience.

It may well be that the relationship marketing movement will in the end have a rather similar impact on marketing as the market share one did in the seventies and early eighties. As such the renewed emphasis on the nature of the customer relationship, which is self-evidently important in industrial markets, will encourage retail marketers to take their customers more seriously even to regard them as intelligent and rational agents. To do so, however, would also mean to recognize severe scepticism about some of the various developments in relationship marketing such as 'loyalty' cards and one-to-one targeting.[33]

However, it may also be true that the relationship and network perspective will, in the longer run change our perception of the critical strategic questions faced by firms as they and their 'markets' evolve and develop. Easton et al. (1992), for instance, suggest that the notion of competition and markets is really only appropriate at specific stages in the life cycle of the firm or business unit. Indeed, their approach could be taken further to suggest that at the time when there is significant indeterminacy in terms of competitor and customer choice, this way of characterizing strategic choice is, of itself, of limited either theoretical or practical value. Almost by definition, the product technology and market structure needs to be relatively stable for such strategic choices to be formulated yet by this stage the feasible choice set itself may be very restricted.[34]

Emergent or enacted environments

The notion of emergent phenomena has itself emerged as a key concept in organizational strategy. Much of the credit for this must go to Mintzberg (1994) but ironically his analysis of the concept itself has been perhaps rather more limited

---

[31] For a generally constructive and useful set of commentaries on the Vargo and Lusch approach see the special issue of Marketing Theory (Aitken *et al.*, 2006).

[32] And in this sense another long-running debate in marketing (Wensley, 1990).

[33] And also perhaps a more critical look at the overall and very central issue of branding. For instance, whilst some commentators see the new service logic as consistent with many aspects of a traditional view on branding (Brodie *et al.*, 2006), others would argue that the developing nature of active customers communities imply the need to rethink the whole nature of branding (Ahonen and Moore, 2005).

[34] The argument is, of course, rather more complicated than this and relates to the previous debate between Child (1972) and Aldrich (1979) on the more general issue of strategic choice, as well as to some degree the wide field of Actor-network theory (Latour, 2005).

than it could have been. Indeed in his more recent work, he has tended to define the nature of emergent phenomena in a rather idiosyncratic manner:

> 'Much as planners can study and interpret patterns in the organization's own behavior to identify its emergent strategies, so too can they study and interpret patterns in the external environment to identify possible opportunities and threats (including as already noted, the patterns of competitors actions in order to identify their strategies)'
>
> (1994, p. 375)

This implies that emergent phenomena are such that they can ex post be related to intentions or actions through time of the individual actors.[35] However, a more common use of the term emergence incorporates some notion of interpretation at different levels of aggregation.[36] After all, for instance, as a number of authors have previously commented, markets themselves are emergent phenomena. It was originally Adam Smith's insight that each actor in a market following there own interest could under certain conditions create an overall situation of welfare maximization: in this sense the invisible hand was much more effective than any attempts at local or even global optimization.

Others have paid much greater attention to this the nature of emergent properties, but we also need to recognize a further distinction between what have been termed emergent and enacted environments. In a number of relevant areas, such as information systems, there is no overall agreement on the nature of the differences (see Mingers, 1995) but in the absolute an emergent environment is one in which there are a set of rules but they are generally undetermining of the outcome states or at least the only way in which an outcome state can be predicted is by a process of simulation whereas an enacted environment is one in which the nature of the environment is itself defined by the cognitive patterns of the constituents.

This distinction is particularly important when we consider the possible of 'markets-as-networks' as a perspective to understand the nature of competitive market phenomena. If we understand the nature of the phenomena we are trying to understand as essentially emergent, then there

remains considerable value in attempting to model the relevant structure of rules or relationships that characterize the environment.[37] If on the other hand, we are more inclined to an enactive view of the relationship between organizations and their environment, we need to consider the degree to which the structure of the network is not more than a surface phenomena resulting itself from other deeper processes: in this analysis we need to consider the phenomena that Giddens (1979) identifies in terms of 'structuration'. In this process agents and organizations are simultaneously both creators of structures but also have their action constrained by these structures.

However, even if we are willing to give a relatively privileged ontological status to the detailed network structure in a particular context,[38] we may still face insurmountable problems in developing high-level regularities from a more detailed analysis. As Cohen and Stewart assert:

> 'We've argued that emergence is the rule rather than the exception, and that there are at least two distinct ways for high-level rules to emerge from low-level rules – simplexity and complicity.[39] Can we write down the equations for emergence? The short answer is no . . . Essentially what is needed is a mathematical justification for the belief that simple high-level rules not only can, but usually do, emerge from complex interactions of low-level rules. By 'emerge' we mean that a detailed derivation of the high-level rules from the low-level ones would be so complicated that it could never be written down in full let alone understood'
>
> (1995, p. 436)

It seems that whilst Cohen and Stewart warn convincingly about the dangers of drowning in the

---

[35] In many ways, issues of intention and anticipation are both central to any analysis of strategic behaviour but also complex and multi-faceted (see Wensley, 2003).

[36] For a broader discussion of emergence see Johnson (2002).

[37] Actually even this statement incorporates another critical assumption. As Mingers notes in commenting on assumptions about the nature of social systems and the degree to which they can be seen as self-producing (autopoietic), even those who develop such an analysis define the nature of the organizations and their environment in unexpected ways:
'Luhmann . . . in conceptualizing societies as autopoietic . . . (sees them) as constituted not by people but by communications. Societies and their component subsystems are networks of communicative events, each communication being triggered by a previous one and leading in turn to another . . . People are not part of society but part of its environment' (p. 211).

[38] A position that others such as Margaret Archer would indeed challenge (Archer, 1995).

[39] Cohen and Stewart use specific meanings for both 'simplexity' and 'complicity' which roughly describe phenomena where in the former case similar low-level rules create high level similar structures whereas in the later case 'totally different rules converge to produce similar features and so exhibit the same large-scale structural patterns' (p. 414). As they emphasize, in the case of complicity one of the critical effects is the way in which 'this kind of system ... *enlarges the space of the possible*' (original emphasis).

detail of low-level rules they give only limited useful advice as to the practical nature of the alternatives. There continues to be a spate of interest in mathematically approaches under the general title of 'Complexity'. In the context of the economics of forms of market organization, perhaps the most obvious is that due to Kaufmann (1995):[40]

> 'Organizations around the globe were becoming less hierarchical, flatter, more decentralized, and were doing so in the hopes of increased flexibility and overall competitive advantage. Was there much coherent theory about how to decentralize, I wondered. For I was just in the process of finding surprising new phenomena, that hinted at the possibility of a deeper understanding of how and why flatter, more decentralized organizations – business, political or otherwise – might actually be more flexible and carry an overall competitive advantage'
>
> (pp. 245–246)

Kaufmann goes on to discuss the logic of what he calls a 'patch' structure in which at various levels the form of organization involves a series of relatively autonomous sub-units which under certain conditions are more effective at achieving a system wide performance maxima compared with the more extreme options which he terms rather controversially, the fully integrated 'Stalinist' system, or the fully autonomous 'Italian leftist' system![41]

However, despite the fact that some of these general notions have been seen in the mainstream of strategic management thought for some considerable time (see Stacey, 1995), we should remain cautious. Horgan (1997) suggests that we should be cautious of the likely advances to be made in the field that he has dubbed 'chaoplexity':

> 'So far, chaoplexologists have created some potent metaphors, the butterfly effect, fractals, artificial life, the edge of chaos, self-organized criticality. But they had not told us anything about the world that is both concrete and truly surprising, either in a negative, or in a positive sense. They have slightly extended the borders of our knowledge in certain areas, and they have more sharply delineated the boundaries of knowledge elsewhere'
>
> (p. 226)

[40] With a fine, if totally unintentional sense of irony, the chapter in Kauffman's book which addresses these questions has the same title as the infamous Peters and Waterman classic 'In Search of Excellence'. Interestingly, however, Kauffman is drawing a distinction between the 'lesser' criteria of 'excellence' compared with 'optimality'!

[41] One can see analogies between this argument and Herb Simon's (1969) explanation of the robustness of modular systems of assembly.

Marketing processes

Not surprisingly, the 1990s saw a renewed interest in the marketing process and particular in the nature of the processes that support the development of a marketing orientation. This approach had been encouraged by the renewed attempts to model the nature of marketing orientation due to both Narver and Slater (1990) and Kohli and Jaworski (1990). In essence the shift is one that Simon (1979) recognized in his original distinction between substantive and procedural rationality in which he suggested that an appropriate response to the problem of bounded rationality was to focus attention more on the appropriate process for arriving at a particular choice rather than developing a general analytical approach to make that choice in any particular situation.

Much empirical research, in particular that based on key informant surveys, has been undertaken to establish the extent to which various operational measures of marketing orientation are correlated with commercial success. On top of this there has been work to establish some of the possible antecedents for such orientation including measures related to the accumulation and organizational dispersion of market research data. The results remain somewhat contradictory, but it seems likely that some level of association will finally emerge, although whether it will achieve the minimum 10 per cent target which we considered earlier is rather another question.

It is also important to note that the two approaches to measuring market orientation focused on substantial different approaches; one essentially related to a more organizational 'cultural' or attitude measure and the other related to an information processing perspective around market-based data. Hult et al. (2005) reported on a study still based primarily on survey data which not only incorporated both of these measures but also attempted to overcome one of the common criticisms of much of the other empirical work in that they used independent and leading performance measure.[42]

On top of this, we need to address more fundamental questions about the underlying logic of procedural rationality in this context. As we have suggested above, it is reasonable to argue that some consideration in any marketing context of

[42] Admittedly the performance measure was only leading by 1 year but this was clearly an improvement on most cross-sectional studies which even when they try and incorporate time effects have to rely on informant recall.

approach which really depends on analysis of means or averages leaves us with a further dilemma: not only does any relative 'usable' explanation only provide us with a very partial picture where there is much unexplained rather than explained outcomes, but also the very notion of a publicly available 'rule for success' in a competitive market is itself contradictory except in the context of a possible temporary advantage.[46] We can try and resolve the problem by looking at the behaviour of what might be called successful outliers but here we face a severe issue of interpretation. As we have seen, as we might expect the sources of such success are themselves ambiguous and often tautological: we end up often really asserting either then to be successful one needs to be successful or that the route to success is some ill-defined combination of innovation, effectiveness and good organization.

It may well be that the best we can do with such analysis is to map out the ways in which the variances of performance change in different market contexts: just like our finance colleagues we can do little more than identify the conditions under which variances in performance are likely to be greater and therefore through economic logic the average performance will increase to compensate for the higher risks.

Finally, we may need to recognize that the comfortable distinction between marketing management, which has often been framed in terms of the more tactical side of marketing and marketing strategy is not really sustainable. At one level all marketing actions are strategic: we have little knowledge as to how specific even brand choices at the detailed level impact or not on the broad development of a particular market so we are hardly in a position to label some choices as strategic in this sense and others as not. On the other hand, the knowledge that we already have and are likely to develop in the context of the longer-term evolutionary patterns for competitive markets will not really also enable us to engage directly with marketing managerial actions and choices at the level of the firm: the units of both analysis and description are likely to be different. In our search for a middle way which can inform individual practice, it may well be that some of the thinking tools and analogies that we have already developed will prove useful but very much as means to an end rather than solutions in their own right.

References

Abell, D. and Hammond, J. (1979) *Strategic Marketing Planning: Problems and Analytical Approaches*, Prentice Hall, Englewood Cliffs, NJ.

Abbot, E. A. (1992) *Flatland: A Romance of Many Dimensions*, Dover Publications: Mineola NY (first published by Seeley and Co Ltd., London 1884).

Achrol, R. S. (1991) Evolution of the marketing organisation: new forms for turbulent environments, *Journal of Marketing*, **55**(4), 77–93.

Adner, R. and Levinthal, D. A. (2004a) What is not a real option: considering boundaries for the application of real options to business strategy. *Academy of Management Review*, **29**, 74–85.

Adner, R. and Levinthal, D. A. (2004b) Reply: real options and real tradeoffs, *Academy of Management Review*, **29**(1), 120–126.

Ahonen, T. and Moore, A. (2005) *Communities Dominate Brands: Business and Marketing Challenges for the 21st Century*, Futuretext, London.

Aitken, R., Ballantyne, D., Osborne, P. and Williams, J. (2006) Introduction to the special issue on the service-dominant logic of marketing: insights from The Otago Forum, *Marketing Theory*, **6**, 275–280.

Aldrich, H. E. (1979) *Organizations and Environments*, Prentice-Hall, Englewood Cliffs.

Archer, M. (1995) *Realist Social Theory: The Morphogenetic Approach*, CUP, Cambridge.

Arnould, E. J. (2006) Service-dominant logic and consumer culture theory: natural allies in an emerging paradigm, *Marketing Theory*, **6**, 293–297.

Baker, M. (1993) Book review, *Journal of Marketing Management*, **9**, 97–98.

Barney, J. and Clark, D. (2007) *Resouce-Based Theory: Resources, Capabilities, and Sustained Competitive Advantage*, OUP, Oxford.

Bartlett, C. A. and Ghoshal, S. (1995) Changing the role of top management: beyond systems to people, *Harvard Business Review*, **73**(3), May–June, 132–142.

Bettis, R. A. and Prahalad, C. K. (1995) The dominant logic: retrospective and extension, *Strategic Management Journal*, **16**, 5–14.

---

[46] Indeed it would appear that in very rapid response markets such as currency markets this temporal advantage is itself measured only in seconds: it is reasonable to assume it is somewhat longer in product and service markets!

Brodie, R. J., Glynn, M. S. and Little, V. (2006) The service brand and the service-dominant logic: missing fundamental premise or the need for stronger theory? *Marketing Theory*, **6**, 363–379.

Brownlie, D. (1998) Marketing Disequilibrium: On Redress and Restoration, in Brownlie, D., Saren, M., Wensley, R. and Whittington, R. (eds), *Rethinking Marketing*, Sage, London.

Buzzell, R. D., Gale, B. T. and Sultan, R. G. M. (1975) Market share – a key to profitability, *Harvard Business Review*, **53**, January–February, 97–106.

Campbell-Hunt, C. (2000) What have we learned about generic competitive strategy: a meta-analysis, *Strategic Management Journal*, **21**(2), February, 127–154.

Caves, R. E. (1980) Industrial organization, corporate strategy and structure, *Journal of Economic Literature*, **43**, March, 64–92.

Caves, R. E. (1984) Economic analysis and the quest for competitive advantage, *American Economic Association Papers and Proceedings*, May, 130.

Caves, R. E. and Porter, M. E. (1977) From entry barriers to mobility barriers: conjectural decisions and contrived deterrence to new competition, *Quarterly Journal of Economics*, **91**, May, 241–262.

Chan, D. K., Gerald, A. F. and Dan, A. S. (1999) *A Spatial Analysis of Competition in the Market for Audit Services*, August, (available at http://www.ecom.unimelb.edu.au/accwww/seminars/Papers99/paper30.pdf)

Chang, M.-H. and Harrington, Jr. J. E. (2003) Multi-market competition, consumer search, and the organizational structure of multi-unit firms, *Management Science*, **49**, 541–552.

Chatterjee, K. and Samuelson, W. F. (2001) *Game Theory and Business Applications*, Kluwer Academic Publishers, Massachusetts.

Child, J. (1972) Organisational structure, environment and performance: the role of strategic choice, *Sociology*, **6**, 1–22.

Chintagunta, P. (1994) Heterogeneous logit model implications for brand positioning, *Journal of Marketing Research*, **XXX1**, May, 304–311.

Christensen, C. M. (1997) *The Innovator's Dilemma*, Harvard Business School Press, Boston.

Cohen, J. and Stewart, I. (1995) *The Collapse of Chaos*, Penguin Books, USA.

Contrado, I. and Wensley, R. (2004) The Harvard Business School Story: avoiding knowledge by being relevant, *Organization*, **11**, 211–231.

Cooke, P. (2002) *Knowledge Economics: Clusters, Learning and Co-operative Advantage*, Routledge, London.

Cooper, L. and Nakanishi, M. (1988) *Market Share Analysis: Evaluating Competitive Marketing Effectiveness*, Kluwer Academic Press, Boston.

Coyle, M. L. (1986) *Competition in Developing Markets: The Impact of Order of Entry*, the Faculty of Management Studies Paper, University of Toronto, June.

Davis, J. P., Eisenhardt, K. M. and Bingham, C. B. (2006) *Complexity Theory, Market Dynamism, and the Strategy of Simple Rules*, Working Paper, Stanford University available at http://www.stanford.edu/~jpdavis/complexity.pdf (accessed 12 October 2006).

Day, G. S. (1994) The capabilities of market-driven organizations, *Journal of Marketing*, **58**(4), October, 37–52.

Day, G. S. and Wensley, R. (1983) Marketing theory with a strategic orientation, *Journal of Marketing*, Fall, 79–89.

Day, G. S. and Wensley, R. (1988) Assessing advantage: a framework for diagnosing competitive superiority, *Journal of Marketing*, **52**, April, 1–20.

Dickinson, P. R. (1992) Toward a general theory of competitive rationality, *Journal of Marketing*, **56**(1), January, 68–83.

Dixit, A. K. and Pindyck, R. S. (1995) The options approach to capital investment, *Harvard Business Review*, **73**(3), May/June, 105–115.

Dolan, R. J. (1981) Models of competition: A Review of Theory and Empirical Findings, in *Review of Marketing*, Enis, B. M. and Roering, K. J. (eds) Chicago: American Marketing Association, 224–234.

Easton, G. (1990) Relationship Between Competitors, in Day, G. S., Weitz, B. and Wensley, R. (eds), *The Interface of Marketing and Strategy*, JAI Press, Conneticut.

Easton, G., Burell G., Rothschild, R. and Shearman, C. (1993) *Managers and Competition*, Blackwell, Oxford.

Feldman, M. S. (2000) Organizational routines as a source of continuous change, *Organizational Science*, **11**(6), November–December, 611–629.

Fournier, S., Dobscha, S. and Mick, D. G. (1998) Preventing the premature death of relationship marketing, *Harvard Business Review*, January–February, 42–50.

Freeman, J. (1997) Dynamics of market evolution, *European Marketing Academy. Proceedings of the 26th Annual Conference*, May, Warwick University: Warwick.

Galunic, D. C. and Kathleen, M. E. (1996) The evolution of intracorporate domains: divisional charter losses in high-technology, multidivisional corporations, *Organization Science*, **7**, 255–282.

Giddens, A. (1979) *Central Problems in Social Theory: Action, Structure and Contradiction in Social Analysis*, Macmillan, London.

Goold, M. (1996) Learning, planning and strategy: extra time, *California Management Review*, **38**(4), 100–102.

Goeree, J. K. and Holt, C. A. (2001) Ten little treasures of game theory and ten intuitive contradictions, *The American Economic Review*, **91**(5) December, 1402–1422.

Gould, S. J. (1987) *Time's Arrow, Time's Cycle: Myth and Metaphor in the Discovery of Geological Time*, Harvard University Press, Cambridge, MA.

Gould S. J. (1990) *Wonderful Life: The Burgess Shale and the Nature of History*, Hutchinson Radius, London.

Hakansson, H. (1987) *Industrial Technological Development: A Network Approach*, Croom Helm, London.

Hamel, G. (2000) *Leading the Revolution*, Harvard Business School Press: Harvard MA.

Hammer, M. and Champy, J. (1993) *Reengineering the Corporation: A Manifesto for Business Revolution*, Brealey, London.

Harland, C. and Wensley, R. (1997) *Strategising Networks or Playing with Power: Understanding Interdependence in Both Industrial and Academic Networks*, Working Paper presented at Lancaster/Warwick Conference on 'New Forms of Organization', Warwick, April.

Henderson, B. (1980) *Strategic and Natural Competition*, BCG Perspectives, 231.

Henderson, B. D. (1983) The anatomy of competition, *Journal of Marketing*, **2**, 7–11.

Henderson, J. M. and Quant, R. E. (1958) *Microeconomic Theory: A Mathematical Approach*, McGraw Hill, New York.

Hofer, C. W. and Schendel, D. (1977) *Strategy Formulation: Analytical Concepts*, West Publishing, St Paul MN.

Horgan (1997) *The End of Science*, Broadway Books, New York.

Hult, G. T. M., Ketchen, Jr. D. J. and Slater, S. F. (2005) Market orientation and performance: an integration of disparate approaches, *Strategic Management Journal*, **26**, 1173–1181.

Hunt, M. S. (1972) Competition in the Major Home Appliance Industry, 1960–1970. Unpublished doctoral dissertation, Harvard University.

Hunt, S. D. (2000a) *A General Theory of Competition: Resources, Competences, Productivity and Economic Growth*, Thousand Oaks CA: Sage Publishing.

Hunt, S. D. (2000b) A general theory of competition: Too eclectic or not eclectic enough? Too Incremental or not incremental enough? Too neoclassical or not neoclassical enough? *Journal of Macromarketing*, **20**(1), June, 77–81.

Illich, I. (1981) *Shadow Work*, Marion Boyars, London.

Ishibuchi H., Ryoji S. and Tomoharu N. (2001) Evolution of unplanned coordination in a market selection game," *IEEE Transactions on Evolutionary Computation*, **5**, 5.

Jacobson, R. (1992) The 'Austrian' School of Strategy, *Academy of Management Review*, October, 782–807.

Jacobson, R. (1994) *The Cost of the Market Share Quest*, Working Paper, University of Washington, Seattle.

Jacobson, R. and Aaker, D. (1985) Is market share all that it's cracked up to be?, *Journal of Marketing*, **49**(4), Fall, 11–22.

Johnson, S. (2002) *Emergence: The Connected Lives of Ants, Brains, Cities and Software*, Penguin, London.

Jones, H. J. (1926) *The Economics of Private Enterprise*, Pitman and Sons, London.

Kadane, J. B., and Larkey, P. D. (1982) Subjective probability and the theory of games, *Management Science*, **28**, February, 113–120.

Kaufmann, S. (1995) *At Home in the Universe*, Oxford University Press, New York.

Kay, J. (1993) *Foundations of Corporate Success*, Oxford University Press, Oxford.

Kohli, A. K. and Jaworski, B. J. (1990) Market orientation: the construct, research propositions and managerial implications, *Journal of Marketing*, **54**(2), April, 1–18.

Kotler, P. (1991) Philip Kotler explores the new marketing paradigm, *Marketing Science Institute Review*, Spring.

Kreps, D. (1990) *Game Theory and Economic Modelling*, Oxford University Press: Oxford.

Krider, R. E. and Weinberg, C. B. (1997) Spatial competition and bounded rationality: retailing at the edge of chaos, *Geographical Analysis*, **29**(1), January, 17–34.

Lambkin, M. and Day, G. (1989) Evolutionary processes in competitive markets: beyond the product life cycle, *Journal of Marketing*, **53**(3), July, 4–20.

Latour, B. (2005) *Reassembling the Social: An Introduction to Actor-network-theory*, Oxford University Press, Oxford.

Leeflang, P. S. H. and Wittick, D. (1993) Diagnosing Competition: Developments and Findings, in Laurent, G., Lillien, G. L. and Pras, B. (eds),

Research Traditions in Marketing, Kluwer Academic, Norwell, MA.

Levins, R. and Leowontin, R. (1985) *The Dialectical Biologist*, Harvard University Press, Cambridge, MA.

Mair, A. (1999) The business of knowledge: Honda and the strategy industry, *Journal of Management Studies*, **36**(1), January, 25–44.

Mattsson, L.-G. (1997) 'Relationship marketing' and the 'markets-as-networks approach' – a comparative analysis of two evolving streams of research, *Journal of Marketing Management*, **13**, 447–461.

McCloskey, D. N. and Ziliak, S. T. (1996) The standard error of regressions, *Journal of Economic Literature*, **XXXIV**, March, 97–114.

McGee, J. and Thomas, H. (1986) Strategic groups: theory, research and taxonomy, *Strategic Management Journal*, **7**, 141–160.

McKelvey, B. (1982) *Organisational Systematics: Taxonomy, Evolution, Classification*, University of California Press, Berkley, CA.

McKenna, R. (1992) *Relationship Marketing*, Century Business, London.

Mingers, J. (1995) *Self-Producing Systems*, Plenum Press, New York.

Mintzberg, H. (1973) *The Nature of Managerial Work*, Harper and Row, New York.

Mintzberg, H. (1994) *The Rise and Fall of Strategic Planning*, Prentice-Hall.

Mintzberg, H. (1996) CMR Forum: the Honda Effect revisited, *California Management Review*, **38**(4), 78–79.

Mintzberg, H. (2004) *Managers not MBAs*, Berrett-Koehler Publishers, Inc: San Francisco, CA.

Moorthy, J. S. (1985) Using game theory to model competition, *Journal of Marketing Research*, **22**, August, 262–282.

Morrison, A. and Wensley, R. (1991) A short history of the growth/share matrix: boxed up or boxed in?, *Journal of Marketing Management*, **7**(2), April, 105–129.

Muth, J. F. (1961) Rational expectations and the theory of price movements, *Econometrica*, 29 July.

Narver, J. C. and Slater, S. F. (1990) The effect of market orientation on business profitability, *Journal of Marketing*, **54**(4), October, 20–35.

Ohmae, K. (1982) *The Mind of the Strategist*, McGraw Hill, London.

Peters, T. J. and Waterman, R. H. (1982) *In Search of Excellence*, Harper and Row, New York.

Pettigrew, A. M. (1973) *The Politics of Organisational Decision Making*, Tavistock, London.

Porter, M. E. (1979) The structure within industries and companies' performance, *Review of Economics and Statistics*, **61**, May, 214–227.

Porter, M. E. (1980) *Competitive Strategy*, Free Press, New York,

Porter, M. E. (1981) The Contribution of Industrial Organization to Strategic Management, *Academy of Management Review*, **6**, 609–620.

Porter, M. E. (1985) *Competitive Advantage*, Free Press, New York.

Porter, M. E. (1990) *The Competitive Advantage of Nations*, Free Press, New York.

Prahalad, C. K. and Bettis, R. A. (1989) The dominant logic: A new linkage between diversity and performance, *Strategic Management Journal*, **10**(6), 523–552.

Prahalad, C. K. and Hamel, G. (1990) The core competence of the corporation, *Harvard Business Review*, May–June, 79–91.

Roberts, K. (1997) Explaining success – hard work not illusion, *Business Strategy Review*, **8**(2), 75–77.

Rosa, J. A., Porac, J. F., Runser-Spanjol, J. and Saxon, M. S. (1999) Socio cognitive dynamics in a product market, *Journal of Marketing*, **63**, 64–77.

Rosa, J. A. and Porac, J. F. (2002) Categorization bases and their influence on product category knowledge structurer, *Psychology and Marketing*, **19**(6) 503–531.

Rumelt, R. P. (1996) The many faces of Honda, *Californian Management Review*, **38**(4), 103–111.

Rungie, C. (1998), *Measuring the Impact of Horizontal Differentiation on Market Share*, Working Paper, Marketing Science Centre, University of South Australia, November.

Sanchez, R. (1995) Strategic flexibility in product competition, *Strategic Management Journal*, **16**(Special Issue), 135–159.

Santos, F. M., and Eisenhardt, K. M. (2005) Organizational boundaries and theories of organization, *Organization Science*, **16**, 491–508.

Saunders, J. (1995) Invited response to Wensley, *British Journal of Management*, **6** (Special Issue).

Schembri, S. (2006) Rationalizing service logic, or understanding services as experience? *Marketing Theory*, **6**, 381–392.

Senge, P. (1992) *The Fifth Discipline: The Art and Practice of the Learning Organization*, Century Business, London.

Shepherd, J. (ed.) (2005) Special book review: Henry Mintzberg: managers not MBAs, *Organisation Studies*, **26**(7), 1089–1109.

Shugan, S. M. (2002) Editorial: marketing science, models, monopoly models, and why we need them, *Marketing Science*, **21**(3), Summer, 223–228.

Simon, H. A. (1969) *The Sciences of the Artificial*, MIT Press, Cambridge, MA.

Simon, H. A. (1979) Rational decision making in business organizations, *American Economic Review*, September.

Stacey, R. D. (1995) The science of complexity: an alternative perspective for strategic change processes, *Strategic Management Journal*, **16**(6), September.

Starbuck, W. H. (2004) Vita contemplativa: why I stopped trying to understand the real world, *Organization Studies*, **25**(7), 1233–1254.

Summut-Bonnici, T. and Wensley, R. (2002) Darwinism, probability and complexity: market-based organizational transformation and change explained through the theories of evolution, *International Journal of Management Reviews*, **4**, September, 291–315.

Teece, D. J., Pisano, G. and Shuen, A. (1997) Dynamic capabilities and strategic management, *Strategic Management Journal*, **18**(7), August.

Tesfatsion, L. (2001) "Guest editorial: agent-based modelling of evolutionary economic systems" *IEEE Transactions on Evolutionary Computation*, **5**, 5.

Todeva, E. and Knoke, D. (2005) Strategic alliances and models of collaboration, *Management Decision*, **43**(1), 123–148.

Volberda, H. W. and Lewin, A. Y. (2003) Co-evolutionary dynamics within and between firms: from evolution to co-evolution, *Journal of Management Studies*, **40**(8), December, 2111–2136.

Waterman, R. H. (1988) *The Renewal Factor*, Bantam Books, London.

Weick, K. E. (1976) Educational organizations as loosely coupled systems, *Administrative Science Quarterly*, **21**, 1–19.

Wensley, R. (1982) PIMS and BCG: new horizon or false dawn, *Strategic Management Journal*, **3**, 147–153.

Wensley, R. (1990)'The voice of the consumer?' Speculations on the limits to the marketing analogy, *European Journal of Marketing*, **24**(7), 49–60.

Wensley, R. (1994) Strategic Marketing: A Review, in Baker, M. (ed.), *The Marketing Book*, Heinemann: Butterworth, London, pp. 33–53.

Wensley, R. (1995) A critical review of research in marketing, *British Journal of Management*, **6**(Special Issue), December, S63–S82.

Wensley, R. (1996) Book review: Henry Mintzberg and Kevin Kelly, BAM Newsletter, Spring, 4–7.

Wensley, R. (1997a) Explaining success: the rule of ten percent and the example of market share, *Business Strategy Review*, **8**(1), Spring, 63–70.

Wensley, R. (1997b) Rejoinder to 'hard work, not illusions', *Business Strategy Review*, **8**(2), Summer, 77.

Wensley, R. (1997c) Two Marketing Cultures in Search of the Chimera of Relevance, Keynote address at joint AMA and AM seminar 'marketing without borders', Manchester, July 7.

Wenseley, R. (2002) "Marketing for the New Century". *Journal of Marketing Management*, **18**(1), February, 229–238.

Wensley, R. (2003) Strategy as Intention and Anticipation, in Wilson, D. and Cummings, S. (eds), *Images of Strategy*, Blackwell, Oxford.

Wensley, R. (2007) Beyond rigour and relevance: the underlying Problematic of Management Research, *British Journal of Management* (forthcoming).

Wernerfeld, B. (1984) A resource-based view of the firm, *Strategic Management Journal*, **5**(2), 171–180.

Wernerfeld, B. (1995a) The resource-based view of the firm: ten years after, *Strategic Management Journal*, **16**, 171–174.

Wernerfeld, B. (1995b) A rational reconstruction of the compromise effect, *Journal of Consumer Research*, **21**, March, 627–633.

Winter, S. G. (2003) Understanding dynamic capabilities, *Strategic Management Journal*, **24**(10), October.

Zahra, S. A., Sapienza, H. J. and Davidsson, P. (2006) Entrepreneurship and dynamic capabilities: a review, model and research agenda, *Journal of Management Studies*, **43**(4), 917–955.

Zander, I. and Zander, U. (2005) The inside track: on the important (but neglected) role of customers in the resource-based view of strategy and firm growth, *Journal of Management Studies*, **42**(8), 1519–1548.

CHAPTER 5

Strategic marketing planning: theory and practice

MALCOLM McDONALD

Summary

In order to explore the complexities of developing a strategic marketing plan, this chapter is written in three sections.

The first describes the strategic marketing planning process itself and the key steps within it.

The second section provides guidelines for the marketer which will ensure that the input to the marketing plan is customer-focused and considers the strategic dimension of all of the relationships the organization has with its business environment.

The final section looks at the barriers which prevent organizations from reaping the benefits which stem from a well-considered strategic marketing plan.

Introduction

Although it can bring many hidden benefits, like the better co-ordination of company activities, a strategic marketing plan is mainly concerned with competitive advantage – that is to say, establishing, building, defending and maintaining it.

In order to be realistic, it must take into account the organizations' existing competitive position, where it wants to be in the future, its capabilities and the competitive environment it faces. This means that the marketing planner must learn to use the various available processes and techniques which help to make sense of external trends, and to understand the organization's traditional ways of responding to these.

However, this poses the problem regarding which are the most relevant and useful tools and techniques, for each has strengths and weaknesses and no individual concept or technique can satisfactorily describe and illuminate the whole picture. As with a jigsaw puzzle, a sense of unity only emerges as the various pieces are connected together.

The links between strategy and performance have been the subject of detailed statistical analysis by the Strategic Planning Institute. The PIMS (Profit Impact of Market Strategy) project identified from 2600 businesses, six major links (Buzzell 1987). From this analysis, principles have been derived for the selection of different strategies according to industry type, market conditions and the competitive position of the company.

However, not all observers are prepared to take these conclusions at face value. Like strategy consultants Lubatkin and Pitts (1985), who believe that all businesses are unique, they are suspicious that something as critical as competitive advantage can be the outcome of a few specific formulae. For them, the PIMS perspective is too mechanistic and glosses over the complex managerial and organizational problems which beset most businesses.

What is agreed, however, is that strategic marketing planning presents a useful process by which an organization formulates its strategies,

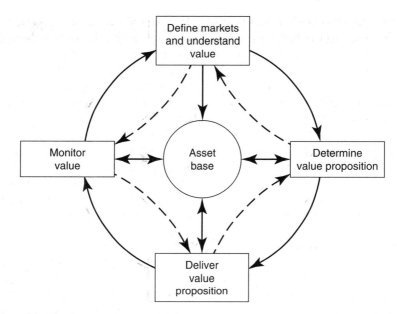

Figure 5.1 Overview of marketing

providing it is adapted to the organization and its environment.

Let us first, however, position strategic marketing planning firmly within the context of marketing itself.

As can be deduced from Chapter 1, marketing is a process for:

- defining markets,
- quantifying the needs of the customer groups (segments) within these markets,
- determining the value propositions to meet these needs,
- communicating these value propositions to all those people in the organization responsible for delivering them and getting their buy-in to their role,
- playing an appropriate part in delivering these value propositions to the chosen market segments monitoring the value actually delivered.

For this process to be effective, we have also seen that organizations need to be consumer/customer-driven.

A map of this process is shown in Figure 5.1. This process is clearly cyclical, in that monitoring the value delivered will update the organization's understanding of the value that is required by its customers. The cycle is predominantly an annual one, with a marketing plan documenting the output from the 'understand value' and 'determine value proposition' processes, but equally changes throughout the year may involve fast iterations around the cycle to respond to particular opportunities or problems.

It is well known that not all of the value proposition delivering processes will be under the control of the marketing department, whose role varies considerably between organizations.

The marketing department is likely to be responsible for the first two processes, 'Understand value' and 'Determine value proposition', although even these need to involve numerous functions, albeit co-ordinated by specialist marketing personnel. The 'Deliver value' process is the role of the whole company, including, for example, product development, manufacturing, purchasing, sales promotion, direct mail, distribution, sales and customer service. The marketing department will also be responsible for monitoring the effectiveness of the value delivered.

The various choices made during this marketing process are constrained and informed not just by the outside world, but also by the organization's asset base. Whereas an efficient new factory with much spare capacity might underpin a growth strategy in a particular market, a factory running at full capacity would cause more reflection on whether price should be used to control demand, unless the potential demand warranted further capital investment. As well as physical assets, choices may be influenced by financial, human resources, brand and information technology assets, to name just a few.

Thus, it can be seen that the first two boxes are concerned with strategic marketing planning processes (in other words, developing market strategies), whilst the third and fourth boxes are concerned with the actual delivery in the market of what was planned and then measuring the effect.

Input to this process will commonly include:

- the corporate mission and objectives, which will determine which particular markets are of interest;
- external data such as market research;
- internal data which flow from ongoing operations.

Also, it is necessary to define the markets the organization is in, or wishes to be in, and how these divide into segments of customers with similar needs. The choice of markets will be influenced by the corporate objectives as well as the asset base. Information will be collected about the markets, such as the market's size and growth, with estimates for the future.

The map is inherently cross-functional. 'Deliver value proposition', for example, involves every aspect of the organization, from new product development through inbound logistics and production to outbound logistics and customer service.

The map represents best practice, not common practice. Many aspects of the map are not explicitly addressed by well-embedded processes, even in sophisticated companies.

Also, the map is changing. One-to-one communications and principles of relationship marketing demand a radically different sales process from that traditionally practised. Hence exploiting new media such as the Internet requires a substantial shift in thinking, not just changes to IT and hard processes. An example is illuminating. Marketing managers at one company related to us their early experience with a website which was enabling them to reach new customers considerably more cost-effectively than their traditional sales force. When the website was first launched, potential customers were finding the company on the Web, deciding the products were appropriate on the basis of the website, and sending an e-mail to ask to buy. So far so good. But stuck in a traditional model of the sales process, the company would allocate the 'lead' to a salesperson, who would phone up and make an appointment perhaps 3 weeks' hence. The customer would by now probably have moved on to another online supplier who could sell the product today, but those

that remained were subjected to a sales pitch which was totally unnecessary, the customer having already decided to buy. Those that were not put off would proceed to be registered as able to buy over the Web, but the company had lost the opportunity to improve its margins by using the sales force more judiciously. In time the company realized its mistake: unlike those prospects which the company identified and contacted, which might indeed need 'selling' to, many new Web customers were initiating the dialogue themselves, and simply required the company to respond effectively and rapidly. The sales force was increasingly freed up to concentrate on major clients and on relationship building.

Having put marketing planning into the context of marketing and other corporate functions, we can now turn specifically to the marketing planning process, how it should be done and what the barriers are to doing it effectively. We are, of course, referring specifically to the second box in Figure 5.1. See Chapters 11 and 27 for more detail on market segmentation.

Part I The marketing planning process

Most managers accept that some kind of procedure for marketing planning is necessary. Accordingly they need a system which will help them to think in a structured way and also make explicit their intuitive economic models of the business. Unfortunately, very few companies have planning systems which possess these characteristics. However, those that do tend to follow a similar pattern of steps.

Figure 5.2 illustrates the several stages that have to be gone through in order to arrive at a marketing plan. This illustrates the difference between the process of marketing planning and the actual plan itself, which is the output of the process.

Experience has shown that a marketing plan should contain:

- A mission statement.
- A financial summary.
- A brief market overview.
- A summary of all the principal external factors which affected the company's marketing performance during the previous year, together with a statement of the company's strengths and weaknesses vis-à-vis the competition. This is what

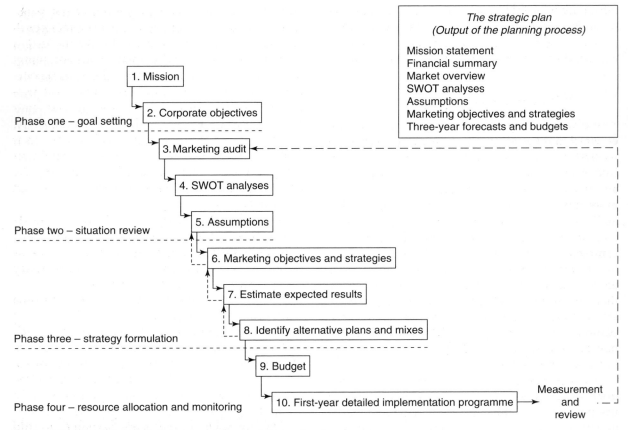

Figure 5.2   The 10 steps of the strategic marketing planning process

we call SWOT (strengths, weaknesses, opportunities, threats) analyses.
● Some assumptions about the key determinants of marketing success and failure.
● Overall marketing objectives and strategies.
● Programmes containing details of timing, responsibilities and costs, with sales forecasts and budgets.

Each of the stages illustrated in Figure 5.2 will be discussed in more detail later in this chapter. The dotted lines joining up stages 5–8 are meant to indicate the reality of the planning process, in that it is likely that each of these steps will have to be gone through more than once before final programmes can be written.

Although research has shown these marketing planning steps to be universally applicable, the degree to which each of the separate steps in the diagram needs to be formalized depends to a large extent on the size and nature of the company. For example, an undiversified company generally uses less formalized procedures, since top management tends to have greater functional knowledge and

expertise than subordinates, and because the lack of diversity of operations enables direct control to be exercised over most of the key determinants of success. Thus, situation reviews, the setting of marketing objectives, and so on, are not always made explicit in writing, although these steps have to be gone through.

In contrast, in a diversified company, it is usually not possible for top management to have greater functional knowledge and expertise than subordinate management, hence planning tends to be more formalized in order to provide a consistent discipline for those who have to make the decisions throughout the organization.

Either way, there is now a substantial body of evidence to show that formalized planning procedures generally result in greater profitability and stability in the long term and also help to reduce friction and operational difficulties within organizations.

Where marketing planning has failed, it has generally been because companies have placed too much emphasis on the procedures themselves and the resulting paperwork, rather than on generating information useful to and consumable by management. But more about reasons for failure later. For now, let us look at the marketing planning process in more detail, starting with the marketing audit.

What is a marketing audit?

Any plan will only be as good as the information on which it is based, and the marketing audit is the means by which information for planning is organized. There is no reason why marketing cannot be audited in the same way as accounts, in spite of its more innovative, subjective nature. A marketing audit is a systematic appraisal of all the external and internal factors that have affected a company's commercial performance over a defined period.

Given the growing turbulence of the business environment and the shorter product life cycles that have resulted, no one would deny the need to stop at least once a year at a particular point in the planning cycle to try to form a reasoned view of how all the many external and internal factors have influenced performance.

Sometimes, of course, a company will conduct a marketing audit because it is in financial trouble. At times like these, management often attempts to treat the wrong symptoms, most frequently by reorganizing the company. But such measures are unlikely to be effective if there are more fundamental problems which have not been identified. Of course, if the company survived for long enough, it might eventually solve its problems through a process of elimination. Essentially, though, the argument is that the problems have first to be properly defined. The audit is a means of helping to define them.

Two kinds of variable

Any company carrying out an audit will be faced with two kinds of variable. There is the kind over which the company has no direct control, for example economic and market factors. Second, there are those over which the company has complete control, the operational variables, which are usually the firm's internal resources. This division suggests that the best way to structure an audit is in two parts, external and internal. Table 5.1 shows areas which should be investigated under both headings. Each should be examined with a view to building up an information base relevant to the company's performance.

Many people mistakenly believe that the marketing audit should be some kind of final attempt to define a company's marketing problems, or, at best, something done by an independent body from time to time to ensure that a company is on the right track. However, many highly successful companies, as well as using normal information and control procedures and marketing research throughout the year, start their planning cycle each year with a formal, audit-type process, of everything that has had an important influence on marketing activities. Certainly, in many leading consumer goods companies, the annual self-audit approach is a tried and tested discipline.

Occasionally, it may be justified for outside consultants to carry out the audit in order to check that the company is getting the most out of its resources. However, it seems an unnecessary expense to have this done every year.

Objections to line managers doing their own audits usually centre around the problem of time and objectivity. In practice, a disciplined approach and thorough training will help. But the discipline must be applied from the highest to the lowest levels of management if the tunnel vision that often results from a lack of critical appraisal is to be avoided.

Where relevant, the marketing audit should contain life cycles for major products and for market segments, for which the future shape will be predicted using the audit information. Also, major products and markets should be plotted on some kind of matrix to show their current competitive position.

The next question is: what happens to the results of the audit? Some companies consume valuable resources carrying out audits that produce very little in the way of results. The audit is simply a database, and the task remains of turning it into intelligence, that is, information essential to decision making.

It is often helpful to adopt a regular format for the major findings. One way of doing this is in the form of a SWOT analysis. This is a summary of the audit under the headings of internal strengths and weaknesses as they relate to external opportunities and threats. There will be a number of SWOT analyses for each major product for market to be included in the marketing plan.

The section containing SWOT analyses should, if possible, contain no more than four or five pages of commentary, focusing only on key factors. It should highlight internal strengths and weaknesses measured against the competition's, and key external opportunities and threats. A summary of

Table 5.1 Conducting an audit

External audit	Internal audit
Business and economic environment Economic political, fiscal, legal, social, cultural Technological Intra-company	*Own company* Sales (total, by geographical location, by industrial type, by customer, by product) Market shares Profit margins, costs

The market
Total market, size, growth and trends (value volume)
Market
  characteristics, developments and trends; products, prices, physical distribution, channels, customers, consumers, communication, industry practices
	Marketing
	  information
	  research
	Marketing mix
	  variables: product management, price, distribution, promotion, operations and resources
	Key strengths and weaknesses

Competition Major competitors Size Market share coverage Market standing and reputation Production capabilities Distribution policies Marketing methods Extent of diversification Personnel issues International links Profitability	

reasons for good or bad performance should be included. It should be interesting to read, contain concise statements, include only relevant and important data and give greater emphasis to creative analysis.

It is important to remember at this stage that we are merely describing the process of marketing planning as outlined in Figure 5.2. The format of the strategic marketing plan itself (i.e. what should actually appear in the written plan) is given in Table 5.2 (p. 87).

Having completed the marketing audit and SWOT analyses, fundamental assumptions on future conditions have to be made. It would be no good receiving plans from two product managers, one of whom believed the market was going to increase by 10 per cent and the other who believed it was going to decline by 10 per cent.

An example of a written assumption might be: *'With respect to the company's industrial climate, it is assumed that over-capacity will increase from 105 to 115 per cent as new industrial plants come into operation, price competition will force price levels down by 10 per cent across the board; a new product will be introduced by our major competitor before the end of the second quarter.'* Assumptions should be few in number. If a plan is possible irrespective of the assumptions made, then the assumptions are unnecessary.

Setting marketing objectives and strategies

The next step is the writing of marketing objectives and strategies. This is the key to the whole process and undoubtedly the most important and difficult of all stages. If this is not done properly, everything that follows is of little value.

It is an obvious activity to follow on with, since a thorough review, particularly of its markets,

Table 5.2   What should appear in a strategic marketing plan

1 Start with a mission statement.
2 Here, include a financial summary which illustrates graphically revenue and profit for the full planning period.
3 Now do a market overview:
   Has the market declined or grown?
   How does it break down into segments?
   What is your share of each?
   Keep it simple. If you do not have the facts, make estimates. Use life cycles, bar charts and pie charts to make it all crystal clear.
4 Now identify the key segments and do a SWOT analysis for each one:
   Outline the major external influences and their impact on each segment.
   List the key factors for success. These should be less than five.
   Give an assessment of the company's differential strengths and weaknesses compared with those of it competitors. Score yourself and your competitors out of 10 and then multiply each score by a weighting factor for each critical success factor (e.g. CSF 1 = 60, CSF 2 = 25, CSF 3 = 10, CSF 4 = 5).
5 Make a brief statement about the key issues that have to be addressed in the planning period.
6 Summarize the SWOTs using a portfolio matrix in order to illustrate the important relationships between your key products and markets.
7 List your assumptions.
8 Set objectives and strategies.
9 Summarize your resource requirements for the planning period in the form of a budget.

should enable the company to determine whether it will be able to meet the long range financial targets with its current range of products. Any projected gap has to be filled by new product development or market extension.

The important point to make is that this is the stage in the planning cycle at which a compromise has to be reached between what is wanted by various departments and what is practicable, given all the constraints upon the company. At this stage, objectives and strategies should be set for 3 years ahead, or for whatever the planning horizon is.

An objective is what you want to achieve, a strategy is how you plan to achieve it. Thus, there can be objectives and strategies at all levels in marketing, such as for service levels, for advertising, for pricing and so on.

The important point to remember about marketing objectives is that they are concerned solely with products and markets. Common sense will confirm that it is only by selling something to someone that the company's financial goals can be achieved; pricing and service levels are the means by which the goals are achieved. Thus, pricing, sales promotion and advertising

objectives should not be confused with marketing objectives.

The latter are concerned with one or more of the following:

- Existing products in existing markets.
- New products for existing markets.
- Existing products for new markets.
- New products for new markets.

They should be capable of measurement, otherwise they are not worthwhile. Directional terms, such as 'maximize', 'minimize', 'penetrate' and 'increase' are only acceptable if quantitative measurement can be attached to them. Measurement should be in terms of sales volume, value, market share, percentage penetration of outlet and so on.

Marketing strategies, the means by which the objectives will be achieved, are generally concerned with the 'four Ps':

1 *Product*: deletions, modifications, additions, designs, packaging, etc.
2 *Price*: policies to be followed for product groups in market segments.

3   *Place*: distribution channels and customer service levels.
4   *Promotion*: communicating with customers under the relevant headings, that is, advertising, sales force, sales promotion, public relations, exhibitions, direct mail, etc.

There is some debate about whether or not the four Ps are adequate to describe the marketing mix. Some academics advocate that people, procedures and almost anything else beginning with 'P' should be included. However, we believe that these 'new' factors are already subsumed in the existing four Ps.

Estimate expected results, identify alternative plans and mixes

Having completed this major planning task, it is normal at this stage to employ judgement, experience, field tests and so on to test out the feasibility of the objectives and strategies in terms of market share, sales, costs and profits. It is also at this stage that alternative plans and mixes are normally considered.

General marketing strategies should now be reduced to specific objectives, each supported by more detailed strategy and action statements. A company organized according to functions might have an advertising plan, a sales promotion plan and a pricing plan. A product-based company might have a product plan, with objectives, strategies and tactics for price, place and promotion, as required. A market or geographically based company might have a market plan, with objectives, strategies and tactics for the four Ps, as required. Likewise, a company with a few major customers might have a customer plan. Any combination of the above might be suitable, depending on circumstances.

There is a clear distinction between strategy and detailed implementation of tactics. Marketing strategy reflects the company's best opinion as to how it can most profitably apply its skills and resources to the marketplace. It is inevitably broad in scope. The plan which stems from it will spell out action and timings and will contain the detailed contribution expected from each department.

There is a similarity between strategy in business and the development of military strategy. One looks at the enemy, the terrain, the resources under command, and then decides whether to attack the whole front, an area of enemy weakness, to feint in one direction while attacking in another or to attempt an encirclement of the enemy's position.

The policy and mix, the type of tactics to be used and the criteria for judging success, all come under the heading of strategy. The action steps are tactics.

Similarly, in marketing, the same commitment, mix and type of resources as well as tactical guidelines and criteria that must be met, all come under the heading of strategy. For example, the decision to use distributors in all but the three largest market areas, in which company sales people will be used, is a strategic decision. The selection of particular distributors is a tactical decision.

The following list of marketing strategies (in summary form) cover the majority of options open under the headings of the four Ps:

1   Product:
    ● Expand the line.
    ● Change performance, quality or features.
    ● Consolidate the line.
    ● Standardize design.
    ● Positioning.
    ● Change the mix.
    ● Branding.
2   Price:
    ● Change price, terms or conditions.
    ● Skimming policies.
    ● Penetration policies.
3   Promotion:
    ● Change advertising or promotion.
    ● Change selling.
4   Place:
    ● Change delivery or distribution.
    ● Change service.
    ● Change channels.
    ● Change the degree of forward integration.

Formulating marketing strategies is one of the most critical and difficult parts of the entire marketing process. It sets the limit of success. Communicated to all management levels, it indicates what strengths are to be developed, what weaknesses are to be remedied and in what manner. Marketing strategies enable operating decisions to bring the company into the right relationship with the emerging pattern of market opportunities which previous analysis has shown to offer the highest prospect of success.

The budget

This is merely the cost of implementing the strategies over the planning period and will obviously be deducted from the net revenue, giving a marketing contribution. There may be a number of iterations of this stage.

The first year detailed implementation programme

The first year of the strategic marketing plan is now converted into a detailed scheduling and costing out of the specific actions required to achieve the first year's budget.

What should appear in a strategic marketing plan?

A written marketing plan is the back-drop against which operational decisions are taken.

Consequently, too much detail should be avoided. Its major function is to determine where the company is, where it wants to go and how it can get there. It lies at the heart of a company's revenue-generating activities, such as the timing of the cash flow and the size and character of the labour force. What should actually appear in a written strategic marketing plan is shown in Table 5.2. This strategic marketing plan should be distributed only to those who need it, but it can only be an aid to effective management. It cannot be a substitute for it.

It will be obvious from Table 5.2 that not only does budget setting become much easier and more realistic, but the resulting budgets are more likely to reflect what the whole company wants to achieve, rather than just one department.

The problem of designing a dynamic system for setting budgets is a major challenge to the marketing and financial directors of all companies. The most satisfactory approach would be for a marketing director to justify all marketing expenditure from a zero base each year against the tasks to be accomplished. If these procedures are followed, a hierarchy of objectives is built in such a way that every item of budgeted expenditure can be related directly back to the initial financial objectives.

For example, if sales promotion is a major means of achieving an objective, when a sales promotion item appears in the programme, it has a specific purpose which can be related back to a major objective. Thus every item of expenditure is fully accounted for.

Marketing expense can be considered to be all costs that are incurred after the product leaves the 'factory', apart from those involved in physical distribution. When it comes to pricing, any form of discounting that reduces the expected gross income – such as promotional or quantity discounts, over-riders, sales commission and unpaid

invoices – should be given the most careful attention as marketing expenses. Most obvious marketing expenses will occur, however, under the heading of promotion, in the form of advertising, sales salaries and expenses, sales promotion and direct mail costs.

The important point about the measurable effects of marketing activity is that anticipated levels should result from careful analysis of what is required to take the company towards its goals, while the most careful attention should be paid to gathering all items of expenditure under appropriate headings. The healthiest way of treating these issues is through zero-based budgeting.

We have just described the strategic marketing plan and what it should contain. The tactical marketing plan layout and content should be similar, but the detail is much greater, as it is for 1 year only.

Requisite strategic marketing planning

Many companies with financial difficulties have recognized the need for a more structured approach to planning their marketing and have opted for the kind of standardized, formalized procedures written about so much in textbooks. Yet, these rarely bring any benefits and often bring marketing planning itself into disrepute.

It is quite clear that any attempt at the introduction of formalized marketing planning requires a change in a company's approach to managing its business. It is also clear that unless a company recognizes these implications, and plans to seek ways of coping with them, formalized strategic planning will be ineffective.

Research has shown that the implications are principally as follows:

1 Any closed-loop planning system (but especially one that is essentially a forecasting and budgeting system) will lead to dull and ineffective marketing. Therefore, there has to be some mechanism for preventing inertia from setting in through the over-bureaucratization of the system.
2 Planning undertaken at the functional level of marketing, in the absence of a means of integration with other functional areas of the business at general management level, will be largely ineffective.
3 The separation of responsibility for operational and strategic planning will lead to a divergence of the short-term thrust of a business at the operational level from the long-term objectives of

the enterprise as a whole. This will encourage preoccupation with short-term results at operational level, which normally makes the firm less effective in the longer term.

4 Unless the chief executive understands and takes an active role in strategic marketing planning, it will never be an effective system.

5 A period of up to 3 years is necessary (especially in large firms) for the successful introduction of an effective strategic marketing planning system.

Marketing planning systems design and implementation

While the actual process of marketing planning is simple in outline, a number of contextual issues have to be considered that make marketing planning one of the most baffling of all management problems. The following are some of those issues:

- When should it be done, how often, by whom, and how?
- Is it different in a large and a small company?
- Is it different in a diversified and an undiversified company?
- What is the role of the chief executive?
- What is the role of the planning department?
- Should marketing planning be top-down or bottom-up?
- What is the relationship between operational (1 year) and strategic (longer-term) planning?

Let us be dogmatic about requisite planning levels. First, in a large diversified group, irrespective of such organizational issues, anything other than a systematic approach approximating to a formalized marketing planning system is unlikely to enable the necessary control to be exercised over the corporate identity. Second, unnecessary planning, or over-planning, could easily result from an inadequate or indiscriminate consideration of the real planning needs at the different levels in the hierarchical chain. Third, as size and diversity grow, so the degree of formalization of the marketing planning process must also increase. This can be simplified in the form of a matrix, Figure 5.3.

It has been found that the degree of formalization increases with the evolving size and diversity of operations (see Figure 5.3). However, while the degree of formalization will change, the need for an effective marketing planning system does not. The problems that companies suffer, then, are a function of either the degree to which they have

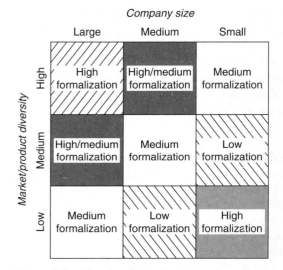

Figure 5.3   Planning formalization

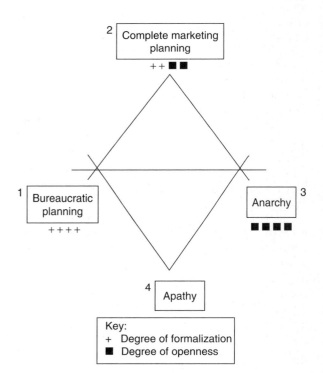

Figure 5.4   Four key outcomes

a requisite marketing planning system or the degree to which the formalization of their system grows with the situational complexities attendant upon the size and diversity of operations.

Figure 5.4 shows four key outcomes that marketing planning can evoke. It can be seen that systems 1, 3 and 4 (i.e. where the individual is totally subordinate to a formalized system, or where there is neither system nor creativity), are less successful than system 2, in which the individual is allowed to be entrepreneurial within a total system. System 2, then, will be an effective marketing planning system, but one in which the degree of formalization will be a function of company size and diversity.

One of the most encouraging findings to emerge from research is that the theory of marketing planning is universally applicable. While the planning task is less complicated in small, undiversified companies and there is less need for formalized procedures than in large, diversified companies, the fact is that exactly the same framework should be used in all circumstances, and that this approach brings similar benefits to all.

How far ahead should we plan?

It is clear that 1- and 3-year planning periods are by far the most common. Lead time for the initiation of major new product innovations, the length of time necessary to recover capital investment costs, the continuing availability of customers and raw materials and the size and usefulness of existing plant and buildings are the most frequently mentioned reasons for having a 3-year planning horizon.

Many companies, however, do not give sufficient thought to what represents a sensible planning horizon for their particular circumstances. A 5-year time span is clearly too long for some companies, particularly those with highly versatile machinery operating in volatile fashion-conscious markets. The effect of this is to rob strategic plans of reality.

The conclusion to be reached is that there is a natural point of focus into the future beyond which it is pointless to look. This point of focus is a function of the relative size of a company. Small companies, because of their size and the way they are managed, tend to be comparatively flexible in the way in which they can react to environmental turbulence in the short term. Large companies, on the other hand, need a much longer lead time in which to make changes in direction. Consequently, they tend to need to look further into the future and to use formalized systems for this purpose so that managers throughout the organization have a common means of communication.

How the marketing planning process works

As a basic principle, strategic marketing planning should take place as near to the marketplace as possible in the first instance, but such plans should then be reviewed at higher levels within an organization to see what issues may have been overlooked.

It has been suggested that each manager in the organization should complete an audit and SWOT analysis on his or her own area of responsibility. The only way that this can work in practice is by means of a hierarchy of audits. The principle is simply demonstrated in Figure 5.5. This figure illustrates the principle of auditing at different levels within an organization. The marketing audit format will be universally applicable. It is only the detail that varies from level to level and from company to company within the same group.

Figure 5.6 illustrates the total corporate strategic and planning process. This time, however, a time element is added, and the relationship between strategic planning briefings, long-term corporate plans and short-term operational plans is clarified. It is important to note that there are two 'open-loop' points on this last diagram. These are the key times in the planning process when a subordinate's views and findings should be subjected to the closest examination by his or her superior. It is by taking these opportunities that marketing planning can be transformed into the critical and creative process it is supposed to be rather than the dull, repetitive ritual it so often turns out to be.

Since in anything but the smallest of undiversified companies it is not possible for top management to set detailed objectives for operating units, it is suggested that at this stage in the planning process strategic guidelines should be issued. One way of doing this is in the form of a strategic planning letter. Another is by means of a personal briefing by the chief executive at 'kick-off' meetings. As in the case of the audit, these guidelines would proceed from the broad to the specific, and would become more detailed as they progressed through the company towards operating units.

These guidelines would be under the headings of financial, manpower and organization, operations and, of course, marketing.

Under marketing, for example, at the highest level in a large group, top management may ask for particular attention to be paid to issues such as the technical impact of microprocessors on electromechanical component equipment, leadership and innovation strategies, vulnerability to attack from the flood of Japanese, Korean and Third World products and so on. At operating company level, it is possible to be more explicit about target markets, product development and the like.

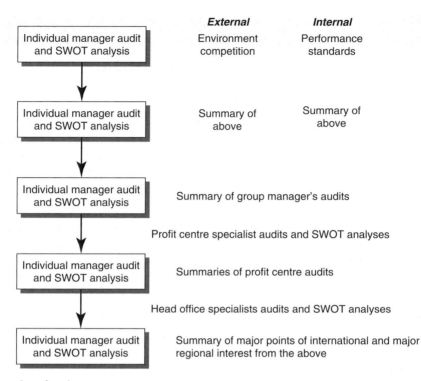

Figure 5.5   Hierarchy of audits

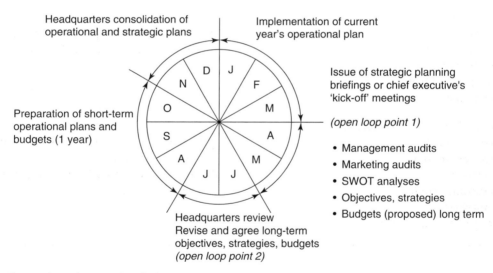

Figure 5.6   Strategic and operational planning

Part I Conclusions

In concluding this section, we must stress that there can be no such thing as an off-the-peg marketing planning system and anyone who offers one must be viewed with great suspicion. In the end, strategic marketing planning success comes from an endless willingness to learn and to adapt the system to the people and the circumstances of the firm. It also comes from a deep understanding about the nature of marketing planning, which is something that, in the final analysis, cannot be taught.

However, strategic marketing planning demands that the organization recognizes the challenges that face it and their effect on its potential for future success. It must learn to focus on customers and their needs at all times and explore every

Table 5.3   Change and the challenge to marketing

Nature of change	*Marketing challenges*
Pace of change • Compressed time horizons • Shorter product life cycles • Transient customer preferences	• Ability to exploit markets more rapidly • More effective new product development • Flexibility in approach to markets • Accuracy in demand forecasting • Ability to optimize price setting
Process thinking • Move to flexible manufacturing and control systems • Materials substitution • Developments in microelectronics and robotization • Quality focus	• Dealing with micro-segmentation • Finding ways to shift from single transaction focus to the forging of long-term relationships • Creating greater customer commitment
Market maturity • Over-capacity • Low margins • Lack of growth • Stronger competition • Trading down • Cost-cutting	• Adding value leading to differentiation • New market creation and stimulation
Customer's expertise and power • More demanding • Higher expectations • More knowledgeable • Concentration of buying power • More sophisticated buyer behaviour	• Finding ways of getting closer to the customer • Managing the complexities of multiple market channels
Internationalization of business • More competitors • Stronger competition • Lower margins • More customer choice • Larger markets • More disparate customer needs	• Restructuring of domestic operations to compete internationally • Becoming customer-focused in larger and more disparate markets

avenue which may provide it with a differential advantage over its competitors.

The next section looks at some guidelines which lead to effective marketing planning.

Part 2 Guidelines for effective marketing planning

Although innovation remains a major ingredient in commercial success, there are nevertheless other challenges which companies must overcome if they wish to become competitive marketers. While their impact may vary from company to company, challenges such as the pace of change, the maturity of markets and the implications of globalization need to be given serious consideration. Some of the more obvious challenges are shown in Table 5.3.

To overcome these challenges the following guidelines are recommended to help the marketer to focus on effective marketing strategies.

Twelve guidelines for effective marketing

1 Understanding the sources of competitive advantage

Guideline 1 (p. 94) shows a universally recognized list of sources of competitive advantage. For small firms, they are more likely to be the ones listed on the left. It is clearly possible to focus on highly individual niches with specialized skills and to develop customer–focused relationships to an extent not possible for large organizations. Flexibility is also a potential source of competitive advantage.

Wherever possible, all organizations should seek to avoid competing with an undifferentiated product or service in too broad a market.

The author frequently has to emphasize to those who seek his advice that without something different to offer (required by the market, of course!), they will continue to struggle and will have to rely on the crumbs that fall from the tables of others. This leads on to the second point.

2 Understanding differentiation

Guideline 2 takes this point a little further and spells out the main sources of differentiation. One in particular, superior service, has increasingly become a source of competitive advantage. Companies should work relentlessly towards the differential advantage that these will bring. Points 1 and 2 have been confirmed by results from a 1994 survey of over 8000 small- and medium-sized enterprises (SMEs).

3 Understanding the environment

Guideline 3 spells out what is meant by the term environment in the context of companies. There is now an overwhelming body of evidence to show

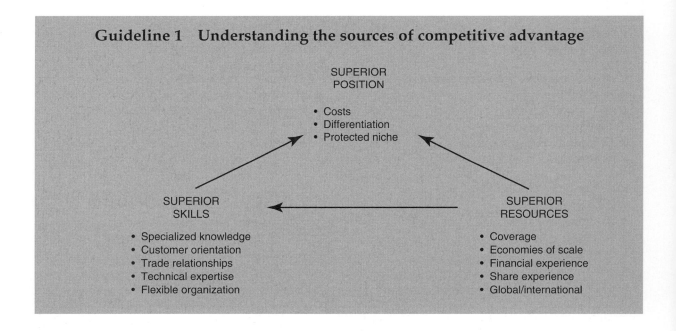

Guideline 1   Understanding the sources of competitive advantage

SUPERIOR
POSITION

- Costs
- Differentiation
- Protected niche

SUPERIOR
SKILLS

- Specialized knowledge
- Customer orientation
- Trade relationships
- Technical expertise
- Flexible organization

SUPERIOR
RESOURCES

- Coverage
- Economies of scale
- Financial experience
- Share experience
- Global/international

Guideline 2   Understanding differentiation

- Superior product quality
- Innovative product features
- Unique product or service
- Strong brand name
- Superior service (speed, responsiveness, ability to solve problems)
- Wide distribution coverage

Continuously strive to serve customer needs more effectively

Guideline 3   Understanding the environment (opportunities and threats)

1   MACRO ENVIRONMENT
- Political/regulatory
- Economic
- Technological
- Societal

2   MARKET/INDUSTRY ENVIRONMENT
- Market size and potential
- Customer behaviour
- Segmentation
- Suppliers
- Channels
- Industry practices
- Industry profitability

Carry out a formal marketing audit.

Guideline 4   Understanding competitors

- Direct competitors
- Potential competitors
- Substitute products
- Forward integration by suppliers
- Backward integration by customers
- Competitors' profitability
- Competitors' strengths and weaknesses

Develop a structured competitor monitoring process. Include the results in the marketing audit.

that it is failure to monitor the hostile environmental changes that is the biggest cause of failure in both large and small companies. Had anyone predicted that IBM would lose billions of dollars during the last decade, they would have been derided. Yet it was the failure of IBM to respond sufficiently quickly to the changes taking place around them that caused their recent problems.

Clearly, marketing has a key role to play in the process. For all organizations, this means devoting at least some of the key executives' time and resources to monitoring formally the changes taking place about them. Guidelines 3, 4 and 5 comprise the research necessary to complete a marketing audit. This leads on naturally to the next point.

4 Understanding competitors

Guideline 4 is merely an extension of the marketing audit. Suffice it to say that if any organization, big or small, does not know as much about its close competitors as it knows about itself, it should not be surprised if it fails to stay ahead.

5 Understanding strengths and weaknesses

Guideline 5 sets out potential sources of differentiation for an organization. It represents a fairly comprehensive audit of the asset base. Together with written summaries of the other two sections of the marketing audit (Guidelines 3 and 4), there should be a written summary of all the conclusions.

Guideline 5   Understanding strengths and weaknesses

Carry out a formal position audit of your own product/market position in each segment in which you compete, particularly of your own ability to:

- Conceive/design
- Buy
- Produce
- Distribute
- Market
- Service
- Finance
- Manage
- Look for market opportunities where you can utilize your strengths

Include the results in the marketing audit.

Guideline 6   Understanding market segmentation

- Not all customers in a broadly-defined market have the same needs.
- Positioning is easy. Market segmentation is difficult. Positioning problems stem from poor segmentation.
- Select a segment and serve it. Do not straddle segments and sit between them.
  1 Understand how your market works (market structure)
  2 List what is bought (including where, when, how, applications)
  3 List who buys (demographics; psychographics).
  4 List why they buy (needs, benefits sought)
  5 Search for groups with similar needs.

If the sources of the company's own competitive advantage cannot be summarized on a couple of sheets of paper, the audit has not been done properly. If this is the case, the chances are that the organization is relying on luck. Alas, luck has a habit of being somewhat fickle!

6 Understanding market segmentation

Guideline 6 looks somewhat technical and even esoteric, at first sight. Nonetheless, market segmentation is one of the key sources of commercial success and needs to be taken seriously by all organizations, as the days of the easy marketability of products and services have long since disappeared for all but a lucky few.

The ability to recognize groups of customers who share the same, or similar, needs has always come much easier to SMEs than to large organizations. The secret of success, of course, is to change the offer in accordance with changing needs and not to offer exactly the same product or service to everyone – the most frequent product-oriented mistake of large organizations. Closely connected with this is the next point.

7 Understanding the dynamics of product/market evolution

Although at first sight Guideline 7 looks as if it applies principally to large companies, few will need reminding of the short-lived nature of many retailing concepts, such as the boutiques of the late 1980s. Those who clung doggedly onto a concept that had had its day lived to regret it.

Few organizations today will need to be reminded of the transitory nature of their business success.

8 Understanding a portfolio of products and markets

Guideline 8 suggests plotting either products/services or markets (or, in some cases, customers)

Guideline 7   Understanding the dynamics of product/market evolution

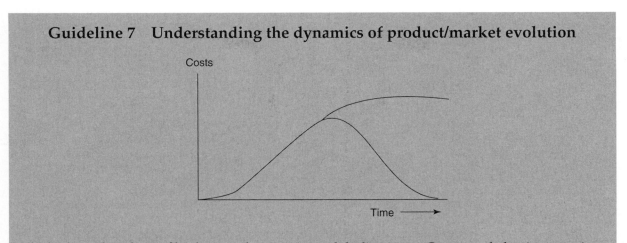

The biological analogy of birth, growth, maturity and decline is apt. Corporate behaviour, particularly in respect of the marketing mix, must evolve with the market. Share-building in mature markets is difficult and often results in lower prices. Those with lower costs have an advantage at the stage of maturity. Life cycles will be different between segments.

Guideline 8   Understanding a portfolio of products and markets

You cannot be all things to all people. A deep understanding of portfolio analysis will enable you to set appropriate objectives and allocate resources effectively. Portfolio logic arrays competitive position against market attractiveness in a matrix form.

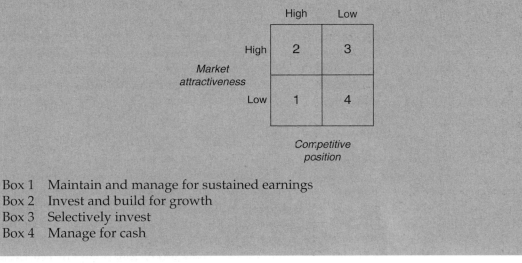

Box 1   Maintain and manage for sustained earnings
Box 2   Invest and build for growth
Box 3   Selectively invest
Box 4   Manage for cash

on a vertical axis in descending order of market attractiveness. (The potential of each for the achievement of organizational and commercial aims and objectives should be used as a criterion as, clearly, they cannot all be equal.) The organization will obviously have a greater or lesser strength in serving each of these 'markets', and this will determine their competitive position. For each location on the graph, a circle, representing the size of current sales, should be drawn.

The graph is divided into a four-box matrix, and each box assessed by management as suggested in the figure. This will give a reasonably accurate 'picture' of the business at a glance and will

Guideline 9   Setting clear strategic priorities and sticking to them

- Focus your best resources on the best opportunities for achieving continuous growth in sales and profits.
- This means having a written strategic marketing plan for 3 years containing:
  - A mission statement
  - A financial summary
  - A market overview
  - A SWOT on key segments
  - A portfolio summary
  - Assumptions
  - Marketing objectives and strategies
  - A budget
- This strategic plan can then be converted into a detailed 1-year plan.
- To do this, an agreed marketing planning process will be necessary.
- Focus on key performance indicators with an unrelenting discipline.

Guideline 10   Understanding customer orientation

- Develop customer orientation in all functions. Ensure that every function understands that they are there to serve the customer, not their own narrow functional interests.
- This must be driven from the board downwards.
- Where possible, organize in cross-functional teams around customer groups and core processes.
- Make customers the arbiter of quality.

indicate whether or not it is a well-balanced portfolio. Too much business in any one box should be regarded as dangerous.

9 Setting clear strategic priorities and sticking to them

Guideline 9 suggests writing down the results in the form of a strategic marketing plan with all those benefits outlined in Part 1 of this chapter.

Commercial history has demonstrated that any fool can spell out the financial results they wish to achieve. But it takes intellect to spell out how they are to be achieved. This implies setting clear strategic priorities and sticking to them.

10 Understanding customer orientation

Guideline 10 will be familiar to all successful companies. Quality standards, such as ISO 9001 and the like, although useful for those with operations such as production processes, have, in the past, had little to do with real quality, which, of course, can only be seen through the eyes of the customer.

(It is obvious that making something perfectly is something of a pointless exercise if no one buys it.)

It is imperative today to monitor customer satisfaction, so this should be done continuously, for it is clearly the only real arbiter of quality.

11 Being professional

Guideline 11 sets out some of the marketing skills essential to continuous success. Professional management skills, particularly in marketing, are becoming the hallmark of commercial success in the late 1990s and the early twenty-first century. There are countless professional development skills courses available today. Alas, many directors consider themselves too busy to attend, which is an extremely short-sighted attitude. Entrepreneurial skills, combined with hard-edged management skills, will see any company through the turbulence of today's markets.

12 Giving leadership

Guideline 12 sets out the final factor of success in the 1990s − leadership. Charismatic leadership,

Guideline 11 Being professional

Particularly in marketing, it is essential to have professional marketing skills, which implies formal training in the underlying concepts, tools and techniques of marketing. In particular, the following are core:

- Market research
- Gap analysis
- Market segmentation/positioning
- Product life cycle analysis
- Portfolio management
- Database management
- The four Ps
  - Product management
  - Pricing
  - Place (customer service, channel management)
  - Promotion (selling, sales force management, advertising, sales promotion)

Guideline 12 Giving leadership

- Do not let doom and gloom pervade your thinking.
- The hostile environment offers many opportunities for companies with toughness and insight.
- Lead your team strongly.
- Do not accept poor performance in the most critical positions.

however, without the 11 other pillars of success, will be to no avail. Few will need reminding of the charisma of Maxwell, Halpern, Saunders and countless others during the past decade. Charisma, without something to sell that the market values, will ultimately be pointless. It is, however, still an important ingredient in success.

Part 2 Conclusions

Lest readers should think that these 12 guidelines for success are a figment of the imagination, there is much recent research to suggest otherwise. The four ingredients listed in Figure 5.7 are common to all commercially successful organizations, irrespective of their national origin.

From this it can be seen, first, that the core product or service on offer has to be excellent.

Secondly, operations have to be efficient and, preferably, state-of-the-art.

Thirdly, research stresses the need for creativity in leadership and personnel, something frequently discouraged by excessive bureaucracy in large organizations.

Finally, excellent companies do professional marketing. This means that the organization

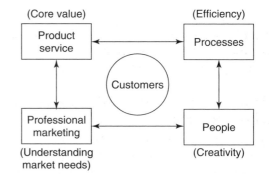

Figure 5.7 Business success

continuously monitors the environment, the market, competitors and its own performance against customer-driven standards and produces a strategic marketing plan which sets out the value that everyone in the organization has to deliver.

Part 3 Barriers to marketing planning

As we have seen, the marketing planning process is quite rational and proposes nothing which, on the surface at least, is risky or outrageous. Similarly,

---

Table 5.4 Barriers to the integration of strategic marketing planning

1 Weak support from the chief executive and top management.
2 Lack of a plan for planning.
3 Lack of line management support due to any of the following, either singly or in combination:
   - hostility
   - lack of skills
   - lack of information
   - lack of resources
   - inadequate organizational structure.
4 Confusion over planning terms.
5 Numbers *in lieu* of written objectives and strategies.
6 Too much detail, too far ahead.
7 Separation of operational planning from strategic planning.
8 Once-a-year ritual.
9 Failure to integrate marketing planning into total corporate planning system.
10 Delegation of planning to a planner.

---

the guidelines for marketing competitiveness are built on current good practice and common sense. It is extremely surprising, therefore, that when confronted by an unfriendly economic environment, a majority of business people perpetuate an essentially parochial and short-term strategy as a coping mechanism.

By their own admission 80 per cent of companies in recent research studies did not produce anything approximating to an integrated, co-ordinated and internally consistent plan for their marketing activities.

Marketing's contribution to business success lies in its commitment to detailed analysis of future opportunities to meet customer needs. In other words, identifying what products or services go to which customers. It rewards those managers with a sense of vision who realize that there is no place for 'rear view mirror' planning, that is, extrapolations from past results. Of course, it is wise to learn from history, but fatal for businesses to attempt to relive it.

It is clear that any attempt to introduce formalized marketing planning systems will have profound implications for the business in terms of its organization and behaviour. Until these implications are recognized and addressed, it is unlikely that strategic marketing planning will be effective. Moreover, the task of designing and implementing sensible planning systems and procedures becomes progressively more complex as the size and diversity of the company grows.

The author's research has identified the items in Table 5.4 as the most frequently encountered barriers to successful marketing planning.

This final section will discuss each of these design and implementation problems.

Weak support from chief executive and top management

Since the chief executive and top management are the key influences in the company, without their active support and participation any formalized marketing planning system is unlikely to work. This fact emerged very clearly from the author's research. Their indifference very quickly destroyed any credibility that the emerging plans might have had, led to the demise of the procedures, and to serious levels of frustration throughout the organization.

There is a depressing preponderance of directors who live by the rule of 'the bottom line' and who apply universal financial criteria indiscriminately to all products and markets, irrespective of the long-term consequences. There is a similar preponderance of engineers who see marketing as an unworthy activity and who think of their products only in terms of their technical features and functional characteristics, in spite of the overwhelming body of evidence that exists that these are only a part of what a customer buys. Not surprisingly, in companies headed by people like this, marketing planning is either non-existent, or where it is tried, it fails. This is the most frequently encountered barrier to effective marketing planning.

Lack of a plan for planning

The next most common cause of the failure or partial failure of marketing planning systems is the belief that, once a system is designed, it can be implemented immediately. One company achieved virtually no improvement in the quality of the plans coming into headquarters from the operating companies over a year after the introduction of a very sophisticated system. The evidence indicates that a period of around 3 years is required in a major company before a complete marketing planning system can be implemented according to its design.

Failure, or partial failure, then, is often the result of not developing a timetable for introducing a new system, to take account of the following:

1 The need to communicate why a marketing planning system is necessary.
2 The need to recruit top management support and participation.
3 The need to test the system out on a limited basis to demonstrate its effectiveness and value.
4 The need for training programmes, or workshops, to train line management in its use.
5 Lack of data and information in some parts of the world.
6 Shortage of resources in some parts of the world.

Above all, a resolute sense of purpose and dedication is required, tempered by patience and a willingness to appreciate the inevitable problems which will be encountered in its implementation.

This problem is closely linked with the third major reason for planning system failure, which is lack of line management support.

Lack of line management support

Hostility, lack of skills, lack of data and information, lack of resources and an inadequate organizational structure, all add up to a failure to obtain the willing participation of operational managers.

Hostility on the part of line managers is by far the most common reaction to the introduction of new marketing planning systems. The reasons for this are not hard to find, and are related to the system initiators' lack of a plan for planning.

New systems inevitably require considerable explanation of the procedures involved and are usually accompanied by pro formas, flow charts and the like. Often these devices are most conveniently presented in the form of a manual. When such a document arrives on the desk of a busy line manager, unheralded by previous explanation or discussion, the immediate reaction often appears to be fear of their possible inability to understand it and to comply with it, followed by anger and finally rejection. They begin to picture headquarters as a remote 'ivory tower', totally divorced from the reality of the marketplace.

This is often exacerbated by their absorption in the current operating and reward system, which is geared to the achievement of current results, while the new system is geared to the future. Also, because of the trend in recent years towards the frequent movement of executives around organizations, there is less interest in planning for future business gains from which someone else is likely to benefit.

Allied to this is the fact that many line managers are ignorant of basic marketing principles, have never been used to breaking up their markets into strategically relevant segments, nor of collecting meaningful information about them.

This lack of skill is compounded by the fact that there are many countries in the world which cannot match the wealth of useful information and data available in the USA and Europe. This applies particularly to rapidly growing economies, where the limited aggregate statistics are not only unreliable and incomplete, but also quickly out of date. The problem of lack of reliable data and information can only be solved by devoting time and money to its solution, and where available resources are scarce, it is unlikely that the information demands of headquarters can be met.

In medium- and large-sized companies, particularly those that are divisionalized, there is rarely any provision at board level for marketing as a discipline. Sometimes there is a commercial director, with line management responsibility for the operating divisions, but apart from sales managers at divisional level, or a marketing manager at head office level, marketing as a function is not particularly well-catered for. Where there is a marketing manager, he tends to be somewhat isolated from the mainstream activities.

The most successful organizations are those with a fully integrated marketing function, whether it is line management responsible for sales, or a staff function, with operating units being a microcosm of the head office organization. Without a suitable organizational structure, any attempt to implement a marketing planning system which requires the collection, analysis and synthesis of market-related information is unlikely to be successful.

Confusion over planning terms

Confusion over planning terms is another reason for the failure of marketing planning systems. The initiators of these systems, often highly qualified, frequently use a form of planning terminology that is perceived by operational managers as meaningless jargon.

Those companies with successful planning systems try to use terminology which will be familiar to operational management, and where terms such as 'objectives' and 'strategies' are used, these are clearly defined, with examples given of their practical use.

Numbers *in lieu* of written objectives and strategies

Most managers in operating units are accustomed to completing sales forecasts, together with the associated financial implications. They are not accustomed to considering underlying causal factors for past performance or expected results, nor of highlighting opportunities, emphasizing key issues and so on. Their outlook is essentially parochial, with a marked tendency to extrapolate numbers and to project the current business unchanged into the next fiscal year.

Thus, when a marketing planning system suddenly requires that they should make explicit their understanding of the business, they cannot do it. So, instead of finding words to express the logic of their objectives and strategies, they repeat their past behaviour and fill in the data sheets provided without any narrative.

It is the provision of data sheets, and the emphasis which the system places on the physical counting of things, that encourages the questionnaire-completion mentality and hinders the development of the creative analysis so essential to effective strategic planning.

Those companies with successful marketing planning systems ask only for essential data and place greater emphasis or narrative to explain the underlying thinking behind the objectives and strategies.

Too much detail, too far ahead

Connected with this is the problem of over-planning, usually caused by elaborate systems that demand information and data that headquarters do not need and can never use. Systems that generate vast quantities of paper are generally demotivating for all concerned.

The biggest problem in this connection is undoubtedly the insistence on a detailed and thorough marketing audit. In itself this is not a bad discipline to impose on managers, but to do so without also providing some guidance on how it should be summarized to point up the key issues merely leads to the production of vast quantities of useless information. Its uselessness stems from the fact that it robs the ensuing plans of focus and confuses those who read it by the amount of detail provided.

The trouble is that few managers have the creative or analytical ability to isolate the really key issues, with the result that far more problems and opportunities are identified than the company can ever cope with. Consequently, the truly key strategic issues are buried deep in the detail and do not receive the attention they deserve until it is too late.

Not surprisingly, companies with highly detailed and institutionalized marketing planning systems find it impossible to identify what their major objectives and strategies are. As a result they try to do too many things at once, and extend in too many directions, which makes control over a confusingly heterogeneous portfolio of products and markets extremely difficult.

In companies with successful planning systems, there is system of 'layering'. At each successive level of management throughout the organization, lower-level analyses are synthesized into a form that ensures that only the essential information needed for decision-making and control purpose reaches the next level of management. Thus, there are hierarchies of audits, SWOT analyses, assumptions, objectives, strategies and plans. This means, for example, that at conglomerate headquarters, top management have a clear understanding of the really key macro issues of company-wide significance, while at the lower level of profit responsibility, management also have a clear understanding of the really key macro issues of significance to the unit.

It can be concluded that a good measure of the effectiveness of a company's marketing planning system is the extent to which different managers in the organization can make a clear, lucid and logical statement about the major problems and opportunities they face, how they intend to deal with these and how what they are doing fits in with some greater overall purpose.

Once-a-year ritual

One of the commonest weaknesses in the marketing planning systems of those companies whose planning systems fail to bring the expected benefits, is the ritualistic nature of the activity. In such cases, operating managers treat the writing of the marketing plan as a thoroughly irksome and unpleasant duty. The pro formas are completed, not always very diligently, and the resulting plans are quickly filed away, never to be referred to again. They are seen as something which is required by headquarters rather than as an essential tool of management. In other words, the production of the marketing plan is seen as a once-a-year ritual, a sort of game of management bluff. It is not surprising that the resulting plans are not used or relegated to a position of secondary importance.

In companies with effective systems, the planning cycle will start in month three or four and run through to month nine or ten, with the total 12-month period being used to evaluate the ongoing progress of existing plans by means of the company's marketing intelligence system. Thus, by spreading the planning activity over a longer period, and by means of the active participation of all levels of management at the appropriate moment, planning becomes an accepted and integral part of management behaviour rather than an addition to it which calls for unusual behaviour. There is a much better chance that plans resulting from such a system will be formulated in the sort of form that can be converted into things that people are actually going to do.

Separation of operational planning from strategic planning

Most companies make long-term projections. Unfortunately, in the majority of cases these are totally separate from the short-term planning activity that takes place largely in the form of forecasting and budgeting. The view that they should be separate is supported by many of the writers in this field, who describe strategic planning. Indeed, many stress that failure to understand the essential difference between the two leads to confusion and prevents planning from becoming an

integrated part of the company's overall management system. Yet it is precisely this separation between short- and long-term plans which the author's research revealed as being the major cause of the problems experienced today by many of the respondents. It is the failure of long-term plans to determine the difficult choices between the emphasis to be placed on current operations and the development of new business that lead to the failure of operating management to consider any alternatives to what they are currently doing.

The almost total separation of operational or short-term planning from strategic or long-term planning is a feature of many companies whose systems are not very effective. More often than not, the long-term strategic plans tend to be straight-line extrapolations of past trends, and because different people are often involved, such as corporate planners, to the exclusion of some levels of operating management, the resulting plans bear virtually no relationship to the more detailed and immediate short-term plans.

This separation positively discourages operational managers from thinking strategically, with the result that detailed operational plans are completed in a vacuum. The so-called strategic plans do not provide the much needed cohesion and logic because they are seen as an ivory tower exercise which contains figures in which no one really believes.

The detailed operational plan should be the first year of the long-term plan, and operational managers should be encouraged to complete their long-term projections at the same time as their short-term projections. The advantage is that it encourages managers to think about what decisions have to be made in the current planning year, in order to achieve the long-term projections.

Failure to integrate marketing planning into a total corporate planning system

It is difficult to initiate an effective marketing planning system in the absence of a parallel corporate planning system. This is yet another facet of the separation of operational planning from strategic planning. For unless similar processes and time scales to those being used in the marketing planning system are also being used by other major functions such as distribution, production, finance and personnel, the sort of trade-offs and compromises that have to be made in any company between what is wanted and what is practicable and affordable, will not take place in a rational way. These trade-offs have to be made on the basis of the fullest possible understanding of the reality of the company's multifunctional strengths and weaknesses and opportunities and threats.

One of the problems of systems in which there is either a separation of the strategic corporate planning process or in which marketing planning is the only formalized system, is the lack of participation of key functions of the company, such as engineering or production. Where these are key determinants of success, as in capital goods companies, a separate marketing planning system is virtually ineffective.

Where marketing, however, is a major activity, as in fast-moving industrial goods companies, it is possible to initiate a separate marketing planning system. The indications are that when this happens successfully, similar systems for other functional areas of the business quickly follow suit because of the benefits which are observed by the chief executive.

Delegation of planning to a planner

The incidence of this is higher with corporate planning than with marketing planning, although where there is some kind of corporate planning function at headquarters and no organizational function for marketing, whatever strategic marketing planning takes place is done by the corporate planners as part of a system which is divorced from the operational planning mechanism. Not surprisingly, this exacerbates the separation of operational planning from strategic planning and encourages short-term thinking in the operational units.

The literature sees the planner basically as a co-ordinator of the planning, not as an initiator of goals and strategies. It is clear that without the ability and the willingness of operational management to co-operate, a planner becomes little more than a kind of headquarters administrative assistant. In many large companies, where there is a person at headquarters with the specific title of marketing planning manager, they have usually been appointed as a result of the difficulty of controlling businesses that have grown rapidly in size and diversity, and which present a baffling array of new problems to deal with.

Their tasks are essentially those of system design and co-ordination of inputs, although they are also expected to formulate overall objectives and strategies for the board. In all cases, it is lack of line management skills and inadequate organizational structures that frustrates the company's marketing efforts, rather than inadequacies on the part of the planner. This puts the onus on planners themselves to do a lot of the planning, which is, not surprisingly, largely ineffective.

Two particularly interesting facts emerged from the author's research. Firstly, the marketing planning manager, as the designer and initiator of systems for marketing planning, is often in an impossibly delicate political position vis-à-vis both their superior line managers and more junior operational managers. It is clear that not too many chief executives understand the role of planning and have unrealistic expectations of the planner, whereas for their part the planner cannot operate effectively without the full understanding, co-operation and participation of top management, and this rarely happens.

This leads on naturally to a second point. For the inevitable consequence of employing a marketing planning manager is that they will need to initiate changes in management behaviour in order to become effective. Usually these are far reaching in their implications, affecting training, resource allocation and organizational structures. As the catalyst for such changes, the planner, not surprisingly, comes up against enormous political barriers, the result of which is that they often become frustrated and eventually ineffective. This is without doubt a major issue, particularly in big companies.

The problems which are raised by a marketing planning manager occur directly as a result of the failure of top management to give thought to the formulation of overall strategies. They have not done this in the past because they have not felt the need. However, when market pressures force the emerging problems of diversity and control to the surface, without a total willingness on their part to participate in far-reaching changes, there really is not much that a planner can do.

This raises the question again of the key role of the chief executive in the whole business of marketing planning.

Part 3 Conclusions

Consultants have learned that introducing change does not always mean forcing new ideas into an unreceptive client system. Indeed, such an approach invariably meets resistance for the organization's 'anti-bodies' whose sole purpose is to protect the *status quo* from the germs of innovation.

A quicker and more effective method is to remove or reduce the effect of the barriers which will stop the proposed improvement from becoming effective. Thus, any attempt to introduce systematic strategic marketing planning must pay due concern to all the barriers listed in this section.

Of course, not all of them will be the same for every organization, but without a doubt the most critical barrier remains the degree of support provided by the chief executive and top management. Unless that support is forthcoming, in an overt and genuine way, marketing planning will never be wholly effective.

Summary

Strategic marketing planning, when sensibly institutionalized and driven by an organization's top management, can make a significant contribution to the creation of sustainable competitive advantage. It is, however, important to distinguish between the *process* of marketing planning and the *output*. Indeed, much of the benefit will accrue from the process of analysis and debate amongst relevant managers and directors rather than from the written document itself.

Twelve guidelines were provided which have been shown to be significant contributors to determining an organization's competitiveness.

Finally, there are many human organizational and cultural barriers which prevent an organization deriving the maximum benefit from strategic marketing planning. Being aware of what these are will go some way to helping organizations overcome them.

References

Burns, P. (1994) Growth in the 1990s: winner and losers, Special Report 12, 31 European Enterprise Centre, Cranfield School of Management, UK.

Buzzell, R. D. and Gale, B. T. (1987) *The PIMS Principles: Linking Strategy to Performance*, Free Press, New York.

Lubatkin, M. and Pitts, M. (1985) The PIMS and the policy perspective: a rebuttal, *Journal of Business Strategy*, Summer, 85–92.

McDonald, M. (1994) *Marketing – the Challenge of Change*, Chartered Institute of Marketing, Maidenhead.

Porter, M. (1980) *Competitive Strategy: Techniques for Analysing Industries and Competitors*, Free Press, New York.

Saunders, J. and Wong, V. (1993) Business orientations and corporate success, *Journal of Strategic Marketing*, **1**(1), 20–40.

Further reading

Brown, S. (1996) Art or Science? Fifty Years of Marketing Debate, *Journal of Marketing Management*, **12**, 243–267. This fascinating and highly readable paper discusses the eternal debate about whether marketing is more art than science. It is recommended here because readers should never lose sight of the need for strategic marketing plans and the process that produces them to be creative as well as diagnostic.

Leppard, J. and McDonald, M. (1987) A reappraisal of the role of marketing planning, *Journal of Marketing Management*, **3**(2). This paper throws quite a considerable amount of light onto why marketing planning is rarely done. It examines the organization's context in which marketing planning takes place and gives a fascinating insight into how corporate culture and politics often prevent the marketing concept from taking hold.

McDonald, M. (1996) Strategic marketing planning: theory; practice; and research agendas, *Journal of Marketing Management*, **12**(1–3), Jan./Feb./March/April, 5–27. This paper summarizes the whole domain of marketing planning, from its early days to the current debate taking place about its contribution. It also explores forms of marketing planning other than the more rational/scientific one described in this chapter.

McDonald, M. (2007) *Marketing Plans: How to Prepare Them; How to Use Them*, 6th edn, Butterworth-Heinemann, Oxford. This book is the standard text on marketing planning in universities and organizations around the world. It is practical, as well as being based on sound theoretical concepts.

Part Two
The Framework of Marketing

CHAPTER 6

Consumer behaviour

MARK GABBOTT

There is nothing more central to marketing than consumption, and nothing more central to consumption than consumers. Without individuals behaving as consumers, there would not be a market, there would not be marketing, and our society would look very different. The study of consumer behaviour is important to marketers because it impacts upon how marketing strategy is developed and implemented. For instance, understanding how consumers will react to a new product offering, a new advertising campaign, the withdrawal of certain services, a new channel of delivery or the provision of web-based information. But it is not just marketers who are interested since consumer behaviour can inform the way governments and policy makers act. For instance, the format and provision of food labelling, the introduction of restrictions on gambling, the design and execution of road safety campaigns or delivery of improved health screening. All of these need some understanding of people, and how they consume. By way of definition, consumer behaviour is the study of individuals, groups or organizations, and the processes they use to select, secure, use and dispose of goods, services, experiences and ideas which are associated with the satisfaction of their needs and the impact of these processes upon consumers, organizations and society.

Given the scope of this definition it is very difficult to write succinctly about consumer behaviour, it comprises a multitude of different subcomponents which, depending upon how you configure them, can provide quite contrasting understandings. The economic behaviourist has a very different understanding of how consumers operate in the economy when compared to a psychologist or a post-modern sociologist. Yet, these perspectives are all valid interpretations of 'what is known'. Much like natural science, the study of consumer behaviour has reflected constant revision with early assumptions and understandings of consumer behaviour being challenged by a series of crises of falsification (a process observed by Kuhn, 1962). Simply, what we thought we knew did not match up to what we observed and as a result we needed new explanations.

My problem is how to reflect what is known about consumer behaviour without reflecting a particular theoretical stance through selection or exclusion? In order to partially protect objectivity, this chapter will be structured around three perspectives or paradigms, each providing its own illumination on human consumption behaviour. The first is a focus upon the individual and the internal psychological processes associated with consumption behaviour. The second approach seeks to understand consumption by viewing the individual not as an isolated decision-maker but as a social being subject to influence from others. Finally, the third perspective sees consumers as reactive to context and consumption environments. Each will be considered separately but each is an important part of understanding and appreciating the complexity of consumer behaviour.

Before considering each of these, I am going to digress and spend some time looking at the history of consumer behaviour as a way of introducing some of the main ideas, and explaining how they fit into the three perspectives.

Consumer behaviour underpinnings

Prior to 1945 most of the theories of human behaviour were based upon a philosophy which was consistent with market-based economics. Simply if you accepted the attractiveness of neo-classical economic models, then you also had to accept that individuals were calculating, rational and self-motivated. More specifically, the assumptions about consumers within the neo-classical tradition were focused upon three key drivers of behaviour (see Ackerman, 1997);

- Asocial individualism: Consumers desires and preferences were not affected by social or economic institutions, interactions with others or the observation of others consumption.
- Insatiability: That a consumer has a multiplicity of insatiable material desires, the more 'goods' we consume the more satisfied we are and that provides some innate motivation to consume.
- Commodity orientation: Consumer preferences consist of well-informed desires for specific goods and services, they have perfect knowledge of all that is available to them.

Although an early work by Veblen (1899) had indicated that purely economic explanations of consumer behaviour were inadequate, it was not until post-1945 that a number of influential authors started to challenge the assumptions directly, most notably Duesenberry (1949), Liebenstein (1950) and Galbraith (1958). Their economic commentary suggested that consumers were not asocial at all but that social factors had a marked impact upon their consumption decisions. This thread of thinking added to the already substantial criticism of insatiability put forward by Marshall (1920) and Keynes (1930). Work was already underway to question the commodity orientation which started to gain ground through the extensive work of Lancaster (1966). This debate in economics is still continuing today as behavioural and radical economists pursue means to adapt the main economic understanding of human behaviour.

A second developmental thread was occurring in the psychology discipline, as the work of Freud indicated that human behaviour was highly dependent upon repressed desires and unconscious wishes. In a sense overt behaviours were a function of hidden and subconscious drives. The publications of *The Interpretation of Dreams* (Freud, 1899) *The Ego and The Id* (1923) and *Totem and Taboo* (Freud, 1923) were markers for a psychoanalytic stream of research which eventually found application to consumption by Dichter (1964) in his study on consumer motivation. To this work was added the emergent understandings of personality originated by Allport (1937), which examined differences between individual behaviour suggesting the existence of different personality types and inconsistent behavioural responses to the same stimuli. Other notable events during this period include the publication by Maslow (1943) on human needs, the emergence of humanist psychology in the early 1900s (see Watson, 1913; Pavlov, 1927) followed by Skinner (1938), which examined how cognition and learning were structured. Haire's study (1950) of responses to new products also marked a significant shift towards the application of psychology to the domain of consumption.

Putting these two threads together we can see that the economic view, which was decidedly 'inhuman', was significantly extended by psychologists who started to illustrate some underlying human motives and emergent social psychologists who were beginning to see the significance of context. The importance for Marketers of the emergence of this new thinking about human behaviour should not be underestimated. Our discipline emerged at this time, a time when current economic understandings about consumption and consumer behaviour were going through a period of re-examination. The new 'marketing concept' required organizations to understand their customers, preferably be able to predict how they would behave and more importantly identify unmet opportunities for new products. Neo-classical economics was looking a little unreliable in providing the level of understanding about consumer behaviour that would make for sound business decisions. Psychology was showing some promise but was itself emerging from a period dominated by behaviourism and psychoanalytical models, and was still developing. In fact, marketing had an almost unique opportunity to craft a new cross-disciplinary approach, taking and adapting knowledge from very many different disciplines to help understand human behaviour related to consumption.

If anything is distinctive about the study of consumer behaviour in marketing, it is this freedom from a single paradigm, the inclusive theoretical and methodological approach driven by our eclectic development and the willingness to re-examine assumptions in the light of actual behaviour. Perhaps more significant is that consumer behaviour in marketing has the benefit of being applied to a specific set of behaviours which provides a basis for theory development. Having looked briefly at how the discipline emerged, the next section examines its early development.

Marketing and consumer behaviour

In 1961, the Ford Foundation commissioned a report on the study of marketing at US Business Schools (see Howard, 1963). Two chapters of the foundation report summarized available research from economics and psychology which was relevant to understanding consumer behaviour. This first codification did much to stimulate the development of marketing research, including the development of the product life cycle. More specifically, subsequent studies in conjunction with General Foods and Nestle provided some face validity for a generalized model of consumer behaviour based upon some recurring features of existing knowledge. In other words, a single model that summarized how consumers arrived at a purchase. The format of these models, or grand theories, was a series of boxes connected by arrows to explain sequences, processes and relationships. Early works by Andreassen (1965) Nicosia (1966), Engel and Kollatt (1968) and Howard and Sheth (1969) all had a common format. Simply, that the individual receives information from a variety of different sources which is filtered through the five senses. The interpreted information influences internal processes such as the formation of opinions, likings and attitudes. These prompt search and evaluation behaviour in the external environment directed towards a purchase and ultimately ownership.

The Engel Model was perhaps the most elegant of these grand theories for three reasons. First, it identified the individual as the central control mechanism engaged in an almost constant process of problem solving. The individual receives stimuli from the environment which is significative (i.e. descriptive), symbolic (e.g. advertising communication or brand information) or social (e.g. from friends or by observation of others), and utilizes this information with that already held in memory, to help identify products in the external environment which can satisfy needs. Second, this model is notable because it included external influences on the problem solving process (such as family, references groups, society and government). This was a key shift in how consumer behaviour was represented. Finally, the model was significant because it provided for a feedback loop. This suggested that individuals learn from activity and experience, and these understandings are used again in subsequent problem solving.

While the intention was to provide a comprehensive exposition of how consumers behave, in actual fact these models proved difficult to use and embodied a view of consumers that was confining for researchers (see Foxall, 1980). Many of the relationships were untestable, and where testable produced conflicting results. Ultimately, their contribution was not so much as a theory, but more a schematic representation which served to order and categorize known elements of behaviour. These in turn spawned specific research agendas which are still evident today. For our purposes, though, the relevance of this early work was to focus attention on three key components:

- The individual: This deals with their psychological processes, their underlying needs and drives, how they handle information, interpret communications, derive attitudes and beliefs, and make choices.
- The Social Environment: This includes information provision and communication, the influence of family and other consumers, marketing activity, regulations and suppliers.
- The Physical Environment: The only thing we really know about consumers is how they actually behave. We cannot observe attitudes, the network of memory and selective information, the reasons why some friends are more influential than others or the causes of reaction to external stimuli. We observe that people behave differently in different settings and respond to their environments in different ways. This would suggest that physical surroundings may drive consumption.

While these three components are very obvious, they provide a good structure for the rest of this chapter since each embodies a particular consumer behaviour paradigm. In the first case, focusing upon the individual allows us to examine the information processing view of consumer behaviour, so influential in the academic literature for the last 25 years. It also allows us to examine the consumer decision-making framework which has been applied as part of this approach. The second theme focuses upon the social context of consumers and reflects a growing practitioner and academic view that consumer behaviour can only be understood by examining the social context of consumption. Our final section on the market environment draws together a number of themes from the first two and looks at the impact of the market environment on behaviour. In this area we will be looking at the environmental psychology literature on consumer behaviour, as well as post-modern expositions on consumer behaviour with its reliance upon decoding and re-interpreting what we experience in our every day lives. While I will consider these separately for ease of exposition, it should be clear that they are intimately connected to each other in fully understanding consumer behaviour.

The individual

Following the delineation of the comprehensive models of behaviour in the 1960s, a number of key underlying propositions were evident. The first was that psychological processes associated with individual consumption behaviour were goal directed. In other words, the behaviour which was observed was the outcome of some internal and unobservable psychological process focused upon achieving something. The Engel-Kollatt model also made it clear that the consumer's decision process was an entirely rational and goal directed one. In that sense, we could understand the behaviour we observed (purchase) as the outcome of a series of sequential steps where the consumer made rational and conscious decisions to acquire consume.

A number of models were put forward to describe this hidden process. Although there were variations in the precise construction, the main steps were considered to be the following: recognizing needs, information search, evaluation of alternatives, purchase and post purchase evaluation. This series of sequential tasks is the core of consumer behaviour and while the process was influenced by a range of internal, external and situational variables, the sequence of activity and the impact of such activity upon marketing communications is still recognized today. Because of the dominance of this model, it is worth spending some time examining the steps.

Recognize needs

The first step, and one which starts the consumer on their consumption journey, is the recognition of needs and wants. To make a cursory distinction, needs are things you feel you cannot do without, but wants are more abstract desires for things, events or experiences. The process of recognition asserts that these needs and wants are continuously present, but remain at a low and tolerable level for us until some event causes them to become acute. For instance, your need for food to sustain you is a continuous need. However, it is likely to be irrelevant just after a meal. As time goes by, you will start noticing hunger and then you will be prompted to satisfy that hunger with food. There are also symbolic needs associated with how we perceive ourselves, such as the need to belong to a group, to display certain behaviours, or to have status or recognition. Finally, there may also be needs which are hedonic, in other words they reflect our desires, such as novelty, enjoyment, sensory pleasure and play. Needs are not always driven from latent to acute just by the physiological processes of the body but are driven by feelings of loneliness, failure, excitement or celebration, reactions to communications, environments or imagination.

There is no way we can categorize or summarize all the various needs and wants that consumers have. However, we can point to a number of their characteristics:

1 Needs and wants exist in some sort of hierarchy, in other words some are more important to us than others, and their predominance reflects both psychological processes and situational circumstances.
2 Multiple needs and wants may be activated simultaneously and any associated behaviour may satisfy none, some or all those activated.
3 Needs are dynamic and are never fully satisfied; they can become acute or latent at different times and in different circumstances.
4 Needs may often conflict with each other such that we must make trade-offs. For example, eating high calorie foods because they taste so good at the same time as wanting to lose weight.
5 Needs can be aroused as the result of both internal reflection and externally. An internal decision to 'sort out your life' after a set back can trigger needs as well as the smell of fresh bread, or perfume, the viewing of an advertisement, or reading a magazine.

There is some uncertainty as to how needs and wants operate, but for marketers the identification and stimulation of customer needs and wants and the associated presentation of satisfiers of those needs and wants are considered to be one of the core functions of marketing. The debate about whether needs can be created where they do not previously exist is one which is unresolvable, as is the suggestion that individuals have no control over need activation and their subsequent behaviours. If you see food and start to feel hungry is that because you were hungry anyway but did not recognize it? Or, were you not hungry and the food made hungry?

Information search and evaluation

Once need activation has occurred, the second step in the generalized model of consumer decision-making is to collect information. When considering needs above, we had implicitly assumed that a need could be readily associated with a satisfying behaviour; however, in many cases it cannot. How many times have you felt some drive to do something but not known exactly what? This may be because we recognize that our information about alternatives may be out of date, that we have not undertaken this type of purchase before, or we have specific requirements. There are generally two sources of information – those held internally by the individual in the form of memory and those which are external. In simple terms, memory not only is drawn upon to aid the current decision activity but can also provide a framework for how information is interpreted. If we walk into a building and it looks like a restaurant, then this frames the way we interpret information. We will wait to be seated, we will expect certain things of the environment, the service process and the people in that space. These will be different if we framed the space as a store, or a private house, or an office.

Internal information is drawn from memory, and research has focused specifically upon how consumers recall product attributes, previous product evaluations, previous experiences and brand communications to derive understanding about the decision facing them. It may also help direct additional information search in the external environment. We know from psychology that the human brain processes huge volumes of information on a daily basis. It manages to select key bits of information to hold in memory to associate bits of information together and alters or updates information stored on the basis of new information. In the context of the individual consumer, some purchase decisions will be relatively routinized and the individual will rely upon habit and memory. Other decisions will be so new that the individual recognizes that they have no information directly relevant and this will prompt extensive information search.

Clearly the accumulation of information associated with a prospective purchase is made with the intention of optimizing the purchase decision. In consumer theory, the purchase decision is characterized as a choice between competing alternatives. A judgement based upon the information available as to which product or service is most likely to satisfy the aroused needs or wants. The mechanics of evaluation are presented as highly complex and as highly diverse, which when you consider what we are trying to understand is not a surprise. We do know that search and evaluation take place simultaneously and that some tasks require extensive evaluation and others almost none. Complex tasks are not immediately self-evident and certainly can not be conclusively categorized by the type of product or service. Some consumers may find it difficult to evaluate different cars, others find that same task no problem at all. Some consumers can choose a newspaper or a chocolate bar without even noticing it, yet others will deliberate for some time. In general terms we know that some evaluations are difficult and some are simple but we do not know precisely which is to be purchased, for any particular group of consumers. We also know that consumer learning allows for the configuring and adapting of evaluation rules such as buying the most expensive, the one made in Europe or a particular brand. There is also some complexity represented by evaluating alternatives which are substantially different (for instance comparing a holiday with a new TV). In this case there are no common product attributes but nevertheless the alternatives need to be evaluated comparatively on more abstract benefits.

Purchase and post purchase evaluation

The actual purchase is the culmination of these previous phases, but it would appear that the process of purchase can also encapsulate more decision-making. New products that have not been found before, the impact of service personnel, alternatives which were not considered, pricing and payment circumstances, different channels to use in acquisition, etc. The specialist consumer behaviour texts skim over purchase as something which everyone knows about and there is not much to say but increasingly, as services dominate the experiences associated with purchase become major considerations for marketers. This is especially true when we consider the emotional, cognitive and physical resources needed to consummate a purchase. We will return to a consideration of the purchase environment later in this chapter.

It should be evident that the decision process does not end once a purchase has been made since the consumer will continue to evaluate the product or service in use. This evaluation will feed into subsequent decisions. If the product is not satisfying, then it will not be considered again or if the product becomes superseded, cannot be used due to the unavailability of peripherals or replenishment, its performance will be compromised. There are also some processes that the individual consumer uses to come to terms with their purchase. How many times have you checked the price of a product you have just purchased in different stores just to reassure yourself you got a good deal? How many product reviews have you read hoping that the product you purchased is highly rated? This is all part of the post-purchase evaluation. Clearly the outcome of this phase of our generalized decision model will impact upon future purchases, loyalty and brand equity.

Depending upon how you break down the various stages in the decision model, you will have differing numbers of steps but the elements will be roughly the same. This consumer decision-making framework, which emerged from the early literature and the comprehensive models, was an important step forward. It not only focused upon the individual as the key to consumer behaviour, but it also served as an agenda for subsequent research. This was characterized with a focus upon the details of how consumers' psychological process operated and it became known as the information processing approach which dominated consumer behaviour research through the 1970s (see Bettman, 1979).

The key assumptions of the information processing approach are that individual consumers engage in both active and conscious information processing when making choices. Second, that the rules (which dictate how the information is managed) can be modelled. Remember that we can not actually observe this phenomenon so the early modelling had to rely upon inference. In practice consumers were asked to talk through what they were thinking during a decision-making event. While these early studies proved instructive, it was the adoption of research from psychology that really started to put some weight behind an information processing view of the consumer. By understanding the ways in which information is stored, organized and retrieved, consumer behaviour researchers could examine how decisions and

evaluations were conducted. Three cognitive operations were critical. First, how consumers managed to associate new information with what they already held (specifically the role of rehearsal in strengthening new associations). Second, how information is encoded so that it is stored and retrieved. Third, how information is structured so that data could be retrieved together.

Information processing was important because it was predicted that the outcome of this information activity fed directly into individual consumer beliefs and attitudes about products. Beliefs are those things which consumers believe to be true or factually correct. For example, I might believe that Ariel is a well-known soap powder, or that Heinz products are available in every supermarket. By contrast, attitudes are evaluations of a product. For example, I think Ariel is too expensive, or I do not like the packaging of Heinz products. The importance from the information processing perspective is that our beliefs and attitudes combine together to form intentions which are then translated into purchases.

The elegance of the information processing approach is in the detailed modelling and extensive experimentation used to infer cognitive processes. But there were also two problems. The first was that while the processing models were elegant, they were all based upon individual experimentation. There were some significant problems caused by aggregation where it became evident that individual consumers were not very alike. The second and probably more significant problem was that attitudes, intentions and actual behaviour seemed to have very little correlation. In other words, when it got to observable behaviour, the theory did not stack up. A contribution by Fishbein and Ajzen (1975) went someway towards retrieving this desperate situation by focusing not on attitudes towards a particular product or object, but shifted the focus by measuring attitude towards a behaviour. In other words, rather than looking for attitudes towards an object (product) as a means to predict behaviour, measure attitude towards the behaviour in terms of the object (buying it). In the past, researchers had asked people what they thought about a product and then used these evaluations to predict purchase. The Fishbein approach asked consumers about their attitude towards buying a particular product on their next shopping trip. A development of this research incorporated a subjective norm component with attitude to determine behavioural intentions. The resulting Theory of Reasoned Action (1975, 1980) and the Theory of Planned Behaviour (1985) are still used as the basis for research today.

Before we leave the domain of the individual, we should also mention current consumer behaviour research. A major thread is the increasing focus upon experiential consumption by individuals. This suggests that individual consumer behaviour is motivated not by rational decisions but by emotions and experiences. In the last two decades, marketing researchers have started to study the emotions prompted by products and brands (Holbrook and Hirschman, 1982). These studies have examined consumers' emotional responses to advertising (e.g. Derbaix, 1995), and the role of emotions in customer satisfaction (e.g. Phillips and Baumgartner (2002), complaining (Stephens and Gwinner, 1998), service failures (Zeelenberg and Pieters, 1999) and attitudes (Dube *et al.*, 2003). While the marketing literature is still developing, this thread of consumer research shows some promise in understanding the often volatile and unpredictable responses of consumers to marketing efforts. In the next section we leave the domain of the individual operating in isolation and turn to the social context of consumer behaviour.

The social context of consumption

Now that we have built our understanding of the individual we can start to appreciate that the development of consumer behaviour was almost exclusively focused upon psychological processes as a means of predicting an individuals purchase. While this provides us with a framework for understanding how a consumer makes decisions and resolves problems, even the early comprehensive models recognized that consumers operate within a social context. Other people have a part to play in determining our needs and wants, providing us with information, helping us evaluate different offerings, directing our purchase behaviour and even determining how satisfied we are after a purchase. In this section I will briefly consider social influences and the discussion will be framed within two recognized social structures: family and social/reference groups. The third social influence is culture which is a study in its own right.

Family

It has been argued that the family is the most important consumption unit in the economy because the household is a cohesive and interdependent consumption unit in its own right, and many of the consumption behaviours by individuals are in fact concerned with household not individual consumption. There is a degree of confusion about the definitions of household and family but we can distinguish them for the purpose of this discussion. A household comprises all the people who live within a single place, which can be a single person ranging to multiple persons such as a shared house. Families are two or more cohabiting people connected by means of marriage, partnership, blood or legal relationship but excluding financial relationships. If we take a traditionally structured nuclear family, we can determine consumption decisions taken by the individual members of that family, for example by a parent, child or either partner. However, of more interest to this discussion are consumption decisions taken on behalf of the family by one party, decisions which are taken jointly by the family unit, and the various decision roles adopted. The reason why this is of importance is that often the buyer of a product or service is not the ultimate consumer. Consider that within a family, men and women may undertake different roles and be responsible for different purchase decisions. Within some decisions children or other family members may have a substantial influencing role, especially where the decision is collective such as a family holiday.

We can also track the influence of different family members depending upon the stage of the decision. Kirchler (1981) tracked family decision-making using diaries and determined that individuals adopt different roles. The initiator starts the process by defining the problem, such as running out of tea, or the need for a new TV, and may suggest the type or style or brand. The influencer may approve or disapprove of the need, or the choice and suggest alternative solutions. The decision-maker is the person who finally decides or, at least, determines the range of alternatives to be considered. The buyer is the one who goes to the shop and buys the product. The users are those who actually consume the products benefits. For marketing, it is important to understand this process as it allows more targeted communications and delivery decisions. The early work by Sheth (1974) suggested that middle class families took more joint (syncratic) decisions, while upper class families took more individual decisions. Lower class families had more strictly defined purchase roles. In other words, the purchase of particular products or services was the responsibility of a defined member of the family. Sheth also found that the stage of the family life cycle was also important in that young families took more joint decisions and took longer to make a decision. This research is somewhat undermined by the rapidly changing family structures evident today. The high divorce rate, blended and re-structured families, children remaining at home longer and single and communal living arrangements have all made the simple family/household decision scenario more complex. For further research on this topic especially the influencing roles, see Corfman and Lehmann (1987) and Carlson and Grossbart (1988).

Social and reference groups

Outside the family the individual consumer operates within a social environment dominated by groups of others. These social groups to which an individual consumer belongs impact the behaviour of its members through the determination of group norms, the development of group values and also the exchange of information. Group norms are the collective opinions about how people should behave in certain circumstances, for example a formal board meeting versus a meeting over a coffee. The group may enforce its norms through sanctions such as overt disapproval or even rejection from the group. Clearly some groups require more conformity than others and the individual may have to trade conformity with individualism. For instance, the membership of a sporting club may impose certain expectations about what type of sports equipment you should purchase. It may require attendance at certain sporting events, the adoption of certain political or social views or the adoption of certain behaviours.

Group values are associated with group norms to the extent that they represent how the group views the world. A particular social group may have clear environmental values, or clear lifestyle values or even child rearing values. These values may be the reason why an individual is attracted to them (such as membership of Amnesty International or Greenpeace) or they may be learned and adopted over time. The operation of group values and norms can have a significant influence upon purchase behaviour. You need only ask a member of generation Y what clothing brands are acceptable and why, and which are not, to get some idea of the impact of social groups in product selection.

Leibenstein (1950) identified two consumption effects emanating from social groups. The first was the 'bandwagon effect' which simply describes how within a particular group, the more people who own a product the more pressure is exerted on non owners to conform by purchasing. The second effect was called the 'Veblen effect' and describes how group members may purchase expensive or high status products to display their own wealth or success and achieve status within the group. This social influence on consumption is communicated and expressed in a myriad of different ways. It might be through a dominant member exerting authority, it might through modelling behaviour on other group members, it may involve sanctions (such as being laughed at) or rewards (such as more intense social connections). Social groups can be categorized according to their formality with high formality groups exhibiting formalized structures and operations such as societies or clubs. Social groups may vary according to their degree of attraction for the individual which may range from very positive (aspiration or affiliation groups) to very negative (dissociative groups).

There is increasing attention being paid to the impact of word of mouth communication in marketing. Not least because it provides a relatively believable source of information in todays information rich environment. More significantly, though, is the impact of technology is providing consumers with greater access to each other and to an information source (the Internet). As consumers become more connected to each other, the opportunity to engage in word of mouth communication also increases. Weblogs (Blogs) provide the opportunity to tell others about purchase and consumption experiences. The rise in negative or defamatory websites put up and managed by consumers is also making the consumer to consumer information environment more transparent and relying less upon social and physical co-location.

Situation and environmental consumption effects

The predominant view of consumer behaviour is focused upon cognitive psychology. Specifically, before people buy, they engage in a cognitive process involving information held and information gained from the environment. This is either a complex or simple process depending upon the task. The outcome of this cognitive processing of information (choice/preference), then, directs purchase behaviour. This view reflects the idea that the 'core' of decision-making is the individual's conscious deliberations. The consumer negotiates purchasing behaviour by carefully evaluating the pros and cons of every purchase.

An alternative view is that consumers are subconsciously reactive and are influenced by their perception of both the physical environment and the behaviour of others within it. Donovan *et al.* (1994) make the point that consumer's emotional responses to environments are directly related to their willingness to engage with it by spending time, money and effort. The design of an environment to enhance positive emotions increases the likelihood that consumers will be receptive.

Mehrabian and Russell (1974) were the first to focus upon an individual's emotional response to a physical environment, something referred to as environmental psychology. They categorized the range of emotional responses to a physical place as pleasure, arousal and dominance. Pleasure responses can be verbally described as feelings of happiness/unhappiness, satisfaction/dissatisfaction and content/discontent. Arousal responses are verbally described as feelings stimulated/unstimulated, excited/relaxed and wide-awake/sleepy. Dominance responses are verbally described as controlling/controlled, influential/influenced and overwhelmed/in control. The emotional responses mediate overt behaviour such as staying in the environment or space, how the individual relates to other and search behaviours. For a more complete discussion, see Foxall and Greenley (1999) and Dawson *et al.* (1990).

A competing view and one gaining credibility is that consumers often react mindlessly to certain environmental stimuli. This fact had caused a degree of difficulty for the information processing adherents since it challenged the whole basis of rational consumption. While a partial solution was to point to 'instantaneous' evaluation and impulse behaviours, it did not accommodate the increasing evidence of an emotional and highly malleable set of experience-based effects. Cialdini (2001) provided powerful evidence through a range of experiments for a 'click-zoom' response. In other words, certain environmental cues elicited almost instant behaviour change in certain settings. This was supported by the work of Wheeler and Petty (2001), who suggest that perception of the social environment will automatically cause the consumer to behave consistently. The range of

response varies from simple mimicry such as facial expression, or physical disposition (see Chartrand and Bargh, 1999; Johnston, 2002) through to goal contagion (see Aarts *et al.*, 2004) where consumers subconsciously adopt observed behaviours and their associated outcomes. The implications of this work are far reaching as it suggests that consumers are highly susceptible to their perception and understanding of their immediate environment. This places environmental design, atmospherics and emotional responses at the very forefront of influencing a range of behaviours, that is not the purchase of specific bundles of product benefits, but the consumption of a purchase experience. North, Hargreaves and McKendrick (1997) found that playing French music in a supermarket increased the sales of French wine, while playing German music increased the sales of German wine. The theoretical basis of this work provides support for the wide range of research experiments on the effects of music, smell and temperature on buyer behaviour.

At this juncture we move to the final consideration in this chapter which falls somewhere between the society and the environment. The idea of a post-modern perspective on consumer behaviour is gaining adherents. The voluminous and insightful commentaries from Brown (1998) as well as the research by Belk (1988), McCracken (1990), Richins (1994) and Cova (1997) drew together a modern sociological stance on consumption. The Frankfurt School of Critical Theory, and particularly the work of Marcuse (1964) and Fromm (1976), was instrumental in developing a humanistic perspective on consumption behaviour. In simple terms a consumer is characterized by what they consume. The individual 'self' constructs a reality through the acquisition of goods, services and experiences. For the purposes of this chapter, observed consumer behaviour is dependent upon the model of 'self' which has, or is being, constructed by the individual.

According to Shove and Warde (2003), three clear developments led to the current explosion of interest in the philosophy of consumption. The first was the role of consumption behaviour in the process of social differentiation with Bourdieu's (1984) analysis generating a wealth of activity around the relationship between social position and aspects of lifestyle and consumption. The second development was the concept of collective consumption, particularly institutional theory and the nature of social capital (Castells, 1977 [1972]).

The third development was the emergence of cultural studies and multi-disciplinary approaches to analysing the use and meanings of goods and artefacts in everyday life.

The observation that we now inhabit a social world where consumption has replaced work as people's central life interest (Moorhouse, 1983; Offe, 1985) is already being subjected to critical analysis with western consumer culture being criticized on a number of fronts. These include the exclusion of large sections of the population of the world from the benefits associated with consumption. Material prosperity seemingly fails to bring happiness or improved satisfaction, materialism compromises social and spiritual values and leads to isolationism and a scarcity mentality; mass culture is vulgar, degrading and panders to the lowest denominator, etc. But perhaps the most current concern is the impact of our expanding levels of consumption upon our natural environment (e.g. Gabriel and Lang, 1995). This criticism is largely associated with globalization and the increasing prevalence of consumer culture. This reflective stance from consumer behaviourists may yet cause the study of consumption to change its focus from improving or enhancing consumption to reducing and minimizing the impact of consumption.

Conclusion

As stated at the beginning of this chapter, consumer behaviour is a particularly challenging field of study. Not only does it require consideration of a wide range of theoretical material and perspectives, but, like any aspect of human behaviour, it is very difficult to deal in absolutes. That having been said it is also one of the most interesting, dynamic, challenging and frustrating areas of study.

The contribution that marketing has made to our understanding is often overlooked. Without marketing and its need to understand how consumers behave, there is no reason to believe that the economic, psychological or sociological disciplines would have turned their attention to the study of mere customers. Marketing researchers are approaching a time when their efforts will be increasingly recognized due to the general applicability of their work on consumption. The application of marketing principles in non-traditional spheres of health, public policy, not for profit, international aid, environmental protection and security, provides increasing demand for more applied understanding of consumers and their consumption behaviour.

References

Aarts, H., Gollwitzer, P. and Hassin, R. (2004) Goal contagion: perceiving is for pursuing, *Journal of Personality and Social Psychology*, **87**, 23–37.

Ackerman, F. (1997) Consumed in theory: alternative perspectives on the economics of consumption, *Journal of Economic Issues*, **31**(3), 651–664.

Allport, G. W. (1937) *Personality: A psychological interpretation*, Holt, Rinehart and Winston, New York.

Andreassen, A. R. (1965) Attitudes and Customer Behaviour: A Decision Model, in Preston, L. E. (ed.), *New Research in Marketing*, Institute of Business and Economic Research, University of California, Berkeley.

Belk, R. (1988) Possessions and the extended self, *Journal of consumer Research*, **15**(September), 139–168.

Bettman, J. R. (1979) *An Information Processing Theory of Consumer Behaviour*, Addison-Wesley, Mass.

Bourdieu, P. (1984) *Distinction: A Social Critique of the Judgement of Taste*, Routledge-Keegan Paul, London.

Brown, S. (1998) *Postmodern Marketing Two: Telling Tales*, Thomson Press, London.

Carlson, L. and Grossbart, S. (1988) Parental style and the consumer socialisation of children, *Journal of Consumer Research*, **15**, 77–94.

Castells, M. (1977 [1972]) *The Urban Question: A Marxist Approach*, Edward Arnold, London.

Chartrand, T. L. and Bargh, J. A. (1999) The chameleon effect: the perception behaviour link and social interaction, *Journal of Personality and Social Psychology*, **76**, 893–910.

Cialdini, R. B. (2001) *Influence: Science and Practice*, Harper Collins, New York.

Corfman, K. and Lehmann, D. (1987) Models of cooperative group decision making and relative influence: an experimental investigation of family purchase decisions, *Journal of Consumer Research*, **13**, 1–13.

Cova, B. (1997) Community and consumption: toward a definition of the linking value of product or services, *European Journal of Marketing*, **31**(3/4), 297–316.

Dawson, S., Bloch, P. and Ridgeway, N. (1990) Shopping motives, emotional states and retail outcomes, *Journal of Retailing*, **66**(4), 408–428.

Derbaix, C. (1995) The impact of affective reactions on attitudes toward the advertisement and the brand: a step toward ecological validity, *Journal of Marketing Research*, **32**(4), 470–480.

Dichter, E. (1964) *Handbook of Consumer Motivations: The Psychology of the World of Objects*, McGraw-Hill, New York.

Dijksterhuis, A., Smith, P., van Baaren, R. and Wigboldus, D. (2005) The unconscious consumer: effects of environment on consumer behaviour, *Journal of Consumer Psychology*, **15**(3), 193–202.

Donovan, R., Rossiter, J., Marcoolyn, G. and Nesdale, A. (1994) Store atmosphere and purchase behaviour, *Journal of Retailing*, **70**, 283–294.

Dube, L., Cervellon, M. C. and Han, J. (2003) Should consumer attitudes be reduced to their affective and cognitive bases? Validation of a hierarchical model, *International Journal of Research in Marketing*, **20**(3), 259–272.

Duesenberry, J. S. (1949) *Income, Saving and the Theory of Consumer Behavior*, Harvard University Press.

Engel, J. F., Kollatt, D. J. and Blackwell, R. D. (1968) *Consumer Behaviour*, Dryden Press, New York

Fishbein, M. and Ajzen, I. (1975) *Belief, Attitude, Intention and Behaviour: An Introduction to Theory and Research*, Addison-Wesley, Mass.

Foxall, G. (1980) Marketing models of consumer behaviour: a critical review, *European Research*, **8**, 195–206.

Foxall, G. and Greenley, G. (1999) Consumers' emotional responses to service environments, *Journal of Business Research*, **46**, 149–158.

Freud, S. (1899) The Interpretation of Dreams, in Marinelli, L. and Andreas, M. A. (2003) *Dreaming by the Book: A History of Freud's 'The Interpretation of Dreams' and the Psychoanalytic Movement*, Other Press, New York.

Freud, S. (1913) *Totem and Taboo* (first published in German in 1913 as *Totem und Tabu: Einige Übereinstimmungen im Seelenleben der Wilden und der Neurotiker* 1913).

Freud, S. (1920) *Beyond the Pleasure Principle* (first published in German in 1920 as *Jenseits des Lustprinzips*)

Freud, S. (1923) *The Ego and The Id* (first published in German Das Ich and Das Es).

Fromm, E. (1976) *To Have or To Be?* Jonathan Cape, London.

Gabriel, Y. and Lang, T. (1995) *The Unmanageable Consumer: Contemporary Consumption and Its Fragmentation*, Sage, London.

Galbraith, J. K. (1958) *The Affluent Society*, Riverside Press, Cambridge.

Haire, M. (1950) Projective techniques in marketing research, *Journal of Marketing*, **XIV**(5),April, 649–657.

Holbrook, M. and Hirschman, E. (1982) The experiential aspects of consumption: fantasies feelings and fun, *Journal of Consumer Research*, **9**(2), 132–139.

Howard, J. (1963) *Executive and Buyer Behaviour*, Columbia University Press, New York.

Howard, J. and Sheth, J. N. (1969) *Theory of Buyer Behaviour*, John Wiley & Sons, New York.

Johnston, L. (2002) Behavioural mimicry and stigmatization, *Social Cognition*, **20**, 18–35.

Keynes, J. M. (1930) Economic Possibilities for Our Grandchildren, in *Essays in Persuasion*, W. W. Norton, New York.

Kirchler, E. (1981) Diary reports on daily economic decisions of happy versus unhappy couples, *Journal of Economic Psychology*, **9**, 327–357.

Kuhn, T. S. (1962) *The Structure of Scientific Revolutions*, Chicago University Press, Chicago, IL.

Lancaster, K. (1966) Change and innovation in the technology of consumption, *American Economic Review*, **56**, 14–23.

Liebenstein, H. (1950) Bandwagon, snob and veblen effects in the theory of consumers' demand, *Quarterly Journal of Economics*, **64**, 198–207.

Marcuse, H. (1964) *One Dimensional Man*, Beacon, Boston.

Marshall, A. (1920) *Principles of Economics*, Macmillan, London.

Maslow, A. (1943) A theory of human motivation, *Psychological Review*, **50**, 370–396.

McCracken, G. (1990) *Culture and Consumption*, Indiana University Press, Bloomington.

Mehrabian, A. and Russell, J. A. (1974) *An Approach to Environmental Psychology*, MIT Press, Cambridge.

Moorhouse, H. (1983) American automobiles and workers dreams, *Sociological Review*, **31**(3), 403–426.

Nicosia, F. M. (1966) *Consumer Decision Processes: Marketing and Advertising Implications*, Prentice-Hall, New Jersey.

North, A., Hargreaves, D. J. and Mckendrick, J. (1977) In store music affects product choice, *Nature*, **390**, 132

Offe, C. (1985) *The Future of Work in C Offe Disorganised Capitalism*, Polity Press, Cambridge. Quoted in Shove and Warde (2004)

Pavlov, I. P. (1927) *Conditioned Reflexes: An*

Investigation of the Physiological Activity of the Cerebral Cortex (translated), Oxford University Press, London.

Phillips, D. and Baumgartner, H. (2002) The role of consumption emotions in the satisfaction response, *Journal of Economic Psychology*, **12**(3) 243–252.

Richins, M. (1994) Valuing things: the public and private meanings of possessions, *Journal of Consumer Research*, **21**(December), 504–521.

Sheth, J. (1974) A Theory of Family Buying Decisions, *Models of Buyer Behaviour*, Harper Row, New York.

Shove, E. and Warde, A. (2003) *Inconspicuous Consumption: The Sociology of Consumption and the Environment*, Department of Sociology, Lancaster University, Lancaster, UK, at http://www.comp.lancs.ac.uk/sociology/papers/Shove-Warde-Inconspicuous-Consumption.pdf (accessed 19 January 2007).

Skinner, B. F. (1938) *The Behavior of Organisms: An Experimental Analysis*, Appleton Century, New York.

Stephens, N. and Gwinner, K. (1998) Why don't some people complain? A cognitive–emotive process model of consumer complaint behaviour, *Journal of the Academy of Marketing Science*, **26**(3), 172–189.

Veblen, T. (1899) *The Theory of the Leisure Class: An Economic Study of Institutions*, Viking Press, New York.

Watson, J. B. (1913) Psychology as the behaviorist views it, *Psychological Review*, **20**, 158–177.

Wheeler, S. and Petty, R. (2001) The effects of stereotype activation on behaviour, *Psychological Bulletin*, **27**(6) 797–826.

Zeelenberg, M. and Pieters, R (1999) Comparing service delivery to what might have been: behavioural responses to regret and disappointment, *Journal of Services Research*, **2**(1), 86–98.

CHAPTER 7

Business-to-business marketing, organizational buying behaviour, interfirm relationships and network behaviour

ARCH G. WOODSIDE and KATHLEEN R. FERRIS-COSTA

Introduction

Business marketing is the practice of organizations, including commercial businesses, governments and institutions, facilitating the sale of their products or services to other companies or organizations that in turn resell them, use them as components in products or services they offer, or use them to support their operations. Also known as industrial marketing, business marketing is also called business-to-business marketing, or *B2B* marketing, for short (http://en.wikipedia.org/wiki/Business_marketing, 2007). B2B marketing is larger in size of revenues than B2C (business-to-consumer) marketing because B2B marketing includes all inter-organizational transactions involving suppliers, manufacturers, agents, distributors, retailers, transportation firms, financial enterprises and government departments. Thus, learning how firms implement B2B strategies and attempt to evaluate and improve the effectiveness and efficiency of such strategies are worthy topics for training by executives and students.

Three organizations are particularly noteworthy in their focus on increasing knowledge and skills in performing B2B marketing and buying strategies: the Business Marketing Association (http://www.marketing.org/), the Institute for the Study of Business Markets (http://www.smeal.psu.edu/isbm) and the Industrial Marketing and Purchasing Group (http://www.impgroup.org/about.php). The Internet sites of each of these organizations offer informative reports on advancing effective planning and implementing of B2B marketing and purchasing strategies. For example, the paper by Ford *et al.* (2002) on *Managing Networks* is available at the IMP Group Internet site (go to http://www.impgroup.org/uploads/papers/4198.pdf). *Managing Networks* provides a tutorial that deepens readers' understanding on how B2B networks operate and shows why B2B network research is a major focus of members of the IMP Group (the IMP Group includes B2B researchers from 45+ countries). Ford *et al.* (2002) provide a basic model on how to manage B2B networks that builds on the following observations:

> A network consists of companies and the relationships between them. A network is not restricted to the set of companies with which a *single* company deals, or even to the companies that they deal with. Nor is a network simply the set of companies with

which a company has formal or informal agreements about some co-operation. Any view of a network centred on a single company, or defined by the company itself is inevitably restricted and biased and gives an incomplete view of the world surrounding that company. A company-centred view of the network provides an inadequate basis for understanding the dynamics within that world or for helping the company to understand the pressures that are or may affect the company or the opportunities open to it.

(Ford *et al.*, 2002, p. 3)

An important early work covering major B2B marketing–purchasing studies by members of the IMP Group as well as by leaders of the ISBM is particularly noteworthy – *Understanding Business Markets* – this edited book by David Ford (1990) includes 33 articles and book chapters on B2B buyer–seller relationships, international marketing, 'an interaction approach to industrial purchasing' and network implemented strategies.

The present chapter serves as an introduction to the body of applied and scholarly work focusing on B2B marketing, organizational buying behaviour and relationships, and networks. Aims of the chapter include stimulating the reader to seek out the sources of work that these pages summarize as well as to present a few core propositions for crafting and implementing effective strategies relevant for firms operating in B2B markets. To keep the present treatise to a reasonable length, the chapter mostly focuses on the following five topics:

- Insights on how B2B is similar and differs from B2C marketing–purchasing behaviour and strategies.
- Deductive modelling of B2B marketing–purchasing behaviour.
- Inductive modelling of B2B marketing–purchasing behaviour.
- Innovation and diffusion decisions and strategy propositions.
- B2B network research findings and strategy implications.

How thinking by marketing and purchasing executives is similar to – and departs from – thinking by household consumers

Whether or not executives and household consumers exhibit similarities or differences in their decision making is useful to consider. Critical nuances in conversations, thought processes and behaviours associated with individual business and consumer case studies support the view that every decision process is unique (see Woodside, 1996). Yet a compelling need to categorize and simplify exists in both theory and management practice that results in grouping cases into a manageable number of processes. Effective thinking requires building and comparing typologies and categories, for example, associating unique decision processes with executive versus consumer problem solving implies two process categories that differ meaningfully. This compelling need is to achieve deep understanding of what is happening, what outcomes are likely to occur and not occur, and the reasoning (i.e. the implicit 'mental models' being implemented by the decision makers) (see Senge, 1990) supporting the observed decision processes. Our review of relevant literature leads to two central conclusions: (1) Noteworthy similarities in executive and consumer decision processes are useful to describe and test empirically to achieve greater sense making of both processes. (2) For every similarity proposition, stating a relevant departure proposition may be supportable empirically. Consequently, the study of similarities and departures in such decision processes presents multiple meanings and cues – the answer most useful to the principal issue is that both similarities and departures should be expected in studies of thinking, deciding and behaviours among executives and consumers.

Several differences in decision making between executives and consumers can be identified in B2B and consumer behaviour literatures. Here are some noteworthy examples:

- Formal, written, rules for searching for suppliers and evaluating vendor proposals are created for many categories of decisions within organizations but rarely by consumers.
- Formal performance audits by external audit professionals occur annually for purchasing and in many marketing organizations, but rarely are such audits done for consumer decisions.
- For many categories of decisions, documentation of deliberations and decision outcomes is more extensive in business organizations compared to consumer households.

This section describes five formal propositions of *similarities* (S) and *departures* (D) of thinking by executives and consumers. The discussion for this section closes with implications of the propositions for improving sense making to help plan and implement decisions that achieve desired outcomes.

S_1: automatic and controlled thinking; D_1: meta-thinking

Bargh (1989, 1994) and Bargh *et al.* (1996) empirically support the proposition that most thinking, deciding and doing processes include combining bits and pieces of automatic and conscious processes. Consequently, all decision makers can only partly report the motivations and steps taken in their thoughts and actions because they are only partly aware of their own decision processes. 'All decision makers' would include marketers and buyers in organizations and consumers in households. Such a view has profound implications for theory, research and marketing practice. Evidence supporting this viewpoint is available in the field of business and industrial marketing (see Woodside, 1987; Woodside and McMurrian, 2000) as well as household buying behaviour (Cohen, 1966; Thelen and Woodside, 1997).

> S_1: Thinking, deciding and actions by marketing and purchasing executives and household consumers often include automatic as well as conscious processing of information.

Meta-thinking is thinking about how thinking occurs including how thinking should occur. Meta-thinking by decision makers is a higher form of conscious thought compared to conscious thoughts directly relevant to immediate issues. Here is an example of meta-thinking versus first-level conscious thinking:

> Meta-thinking: What supplier performance attributes really make a difference in my own purchasing performance?
> First-level conscious thinking: Does our major supplier provide on-time delivery consistently?

The creation of written checklists, such as safety procedures that must be followed by a pilot before lift-off is an example of meta-thinking. While written procedures on how to think and act with customers and suppliers are often proscribed in industrial marketing and purchasing departments, written guidelines of purchasing procedures are not found in households.

Written evaluation methods using weighted compensatory models are required in some industrial purchasing departments (see Woodside and Wilson, 2000) but likely are rarely available in households. In the US, the National Association of Purchasing Managers (NAPM) offers short courses and educational certification programmes to train managers on how to think and act effectively as buyers and purchasing managers; more than 30000 professional buyers are 'Certified Purchasing Managers'. Similar certification programmes for training household consumers do not appear to be available.

> D_1: Evidence of business and industrial marketers and purchasers engaging in meta-thinking is more substantial compared to household consumers.

S_2: use of simplifying categorization rules; D_2: formalizing such rules

Both executives and consumers appear to use a few framing rules when deciding the nature of the problem or opportunity before them. Learning these problem/opportunity framing rules has important implications for influencing the thinking and subsequent actions of both managers and consumers. For example, if a buyer perceives an upcoming purchase as a standard re-order from current suppliers, a new vendor may need to influence the buyer to reframe the purchase as a 'new task buy' (Howard and Sheth, 1969) before the buyer will consider the new vendor's product or service. This implication follows from the related proposition that the amount of effort in searching for alternatives and in evaluating alternatives is likely to be influenced by how decision makers frame problems.

> S_2: Both executives and consumers apply simplifying categorizing rules for defining decision contexts.

Three problem dimensions may dominate how decision makers frame a problem/opportunity (see Wilson *et al.*, 2000): familiarity, financial commitment and technical complexity. Assuming two levels are used as a way of simplifying each of these three dimensions, then eight framing categories may be identified. Both the industrial and consumer research literatures note such problem framing thoughts (see Woodside, 1992; Payne *et al.*, 1993).

> D_2: For repetitive decision-making contexts, categorization rules are more often formalized in writing by executives but not by consumers.

Several rationales may be suggested for written problem/opportunity framing rules occurring for executives but not for consumers. The formal requirements listed in the occupational specialty often require written order routines that differ by product categories (i.e. raw materials versus maintenance, repair, and operating (MRO) items) for purchasers and buyers in firms but not in households. Most household consumers may view the purchase of low-priced consumer goods to be peripheral actions not worth the effort of creating and following written guidelines. Training of new professional buyers is facilitated often by detailed written order routines for all product categories; such written order routines may be prepared rarely for household consumers because training in buying is more informal and one-on-one, for example, parent-to-child and sibling-to-sibling.

D_3: Formal, written, evaluation and choice rules are created and applied more often by professional buyers compared to household consumers.

Industrial marketers should be aware that the final evaluations from customers' written weighted compensatory rules often do not reflect the final choices and purchase agreements (see Woodside and Wilson, 2000) – the outcomes of using the weighted compensatory rules may be revised to account for seemingly idiosyncratic preferences in the organization. See Woodside and Sherrell (1980) for such choice behaviour examples. Nevertheless, buyers using weighted compensatory rules report that doing the necessary calculations are helpful because the approach forces them to consider more product and service attributes than they would consider without the use of such rules.

S_3: use of simplifying evaluation/choice rules; D_3: formalizing evaluation/choice rules

S_3: All decision makers appear to create and use simplifying decision rules when faced with two or more alternatives.

For example, both professional buyers and household consumers create and use simple conjunctive rules to eliminate all but a few possible suppliers or brands when faced with many alternatives (i.e. more than seven or so). A conjunctive rule sets minimum levels of performance that must be met or surpassed in the product provided as well as supplier service performance. Consequently, a 'short list' or 'consideration set' of three to five alternatives is formed for more in-depth evaluation using some other evaluation and choice rule. A weighted compensatory or lexicographic rule may be applied for evaluating the alternatives in the short list (consideration set). See Payne *et al.* (1993) for a discussion of these heuristics.

Thus, a combination of evaluation and choice rules may occur often for both executives and household consumers when faced with many alternatives to evaluate, even though printed forms using weighted compensatory rules for evaluating competing vendors likely are printed only among industrial firms not households. Consequently, organizational buyers and household consumers depart from each other in the degree of formalization in creating weighted compensatory heuristics.

S_4: meetings for evaluating alternative products and suppliers; D_4: formalizing rules of discussion and application of group choice rules

S_4: Decisions are often made in groups of two or more persons both in industrial organizations and households.

Even when all members of a group name one person as the sole decision maker, other members of the group and group discussion are likely to influence the choices made (Wilson *et al.*, 1991).

D_4: Formal procedures are enacted often within industrial firms but not in households for meetings to frame problems/opportunities, develop rules for evaluating alternatives, evaluate alternatives and make choices.

Written procedures of discussion, and minutes of conversations and decision outcomes (including formal purchase agreements), often follow from cross-departmental meetings in business organizations more often than in meetings of household members. To achieve wiser decisions and savings in bulk purchases, meetings for the purpose of evaluating and selecting suppliers may extend across several manufacturing locations for an industrial firm on an annual basis for several product categories (see Woodside and Samuel, 1981). Such meetings may be held rarely by adult siblings living in separate households.

S$_5$: evaluating outcomes of buying transactions and quality-in-use experiences; D$_5$: formal performance audits

S$_5$: Post-experience evaluations and assessments of (dis)satisfaction occur often among both industrial firms and households.

Some judgements influence intentions towards suppliers as well as buying specific products. Consequently, industrial and consumer marketers often design marketing information systems to measure customer satisfaction with use of products and services – including services provided by salespersons.

D$_5$: Performance audits of suppliers, products purchased and the professional buyers/marketers employed by the organized are done more frequently by industrial firms and rarely, if ever, done by households.

Written guidelines are available on how to evaluate the performance of marketers, professional buyers and the strategy of the organization for industrial firms; much of the popular business literature is devoted to reports of such performance audits (see Woodside and Sakai, 2001). Compared to the B2B literature and the activities, the written reports on the effectiveness and efficiency of buying decisions by households are less extensive.

Implications for business and industrial marketing strategy

The five sets of identified similarities and departures are not intended to be exhaustive. Many additional sets may be described. For example, feedback loops exist in both executive and consumer decision processes that are often unrecognized by both parties. However, in many industrial contexts, systems analyses (e.g. mathematical modelling and simulations) have been applied for identifying key leverage points affecting outcomes desired by executives (e.g. see Hall, 1984), such work does not appear to be available in the consumer research literature. Taking the time, making the effort, to study feedback loops may be critical for achieving deep sense making of how our decisions/actions result in desired and undesired outcomes (see Senge, 1990).

Also, many executives in industrial firms and household consumers resist adoption of products/services built on new technology platforms proven to be superior to installed products/services (see Ram, 1987; Woodside, 1996). However, such resistance may lead to decline and death of business organizations (see Christensen, 1997) but rarely among household consumers.

The main benefit from studying and comparing both the industrial and consumer research literatures may be gaining deep understanding of the subtleties and unexpected interdependencies in thinking, deciding, talking and actions of decision makers. Most likely, sense making skills are improved from learning the similarities and departures in the processes of both categories of decision making. Thus, the issue of what similarities and departures in decisions and actions occur among business executives and household consumers may be more useful than advocating that the study of decision making by executives is distinct from the study of decision making by consumers.

Business and industrial strategists are likely to increase their skills in making effective decisions from studying both the industrial marketing and the consumer research literature. Too often the thought is expressed, 'My company's situation is unique – it would not be useful to consider the behaviour of other firms, let alone household consumers, in similar situations because the situation is really unique to my company'. Expressing such a mental model often indicates an inability to create and learn from analogies. Better to start by casting a wider net: let us admit that important similarities in decisions and behaviours do exist between business firms and household consumers, while recognizing that success lies also in studying the nuances occurring in the unique combinations of events in each case study (see Ragin, 1987 for a complete development of points relating to research on conjunctive processes).

Deductive modelling of B2B marketing–purchasing behaviour

A *deductive model* is a set of propositions that builds from insight and knowledge of relevant literature; the propositions include theoretical statements for testing via data collection and analysis. Deductive models of marketing and purchasing behaviour are useful for building what-if scenarios and testing whether or not specific antecedents

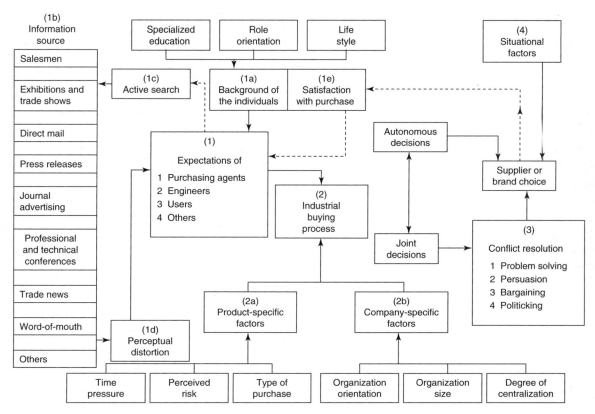

Figure 7.1 An integrative model of industrial buyer behaviour
Source: Sheth (1973), Figure 1, p. 51.

affect how problems/opportunities are found, framed and handled by executives. Deductive models focus on identifying variables and how they are likely to relate to one another – such models predict and explain processes that are likely to occur and the conditions that likely bring about outcomes of interest.

The Sheth (1973) model of organizational buying behaviour is an early and widely referenced example of a general deductive model. The Webster and Wind (1972) model is another example of a deductive model. Figure 7.1 is a summary of Sheth's model.

Sheth's deductive model is useful for suggestions, propositions and identifying issues relevant for B2B buying behaviour. For example, the Sheth model proposes that the backgrounds of individuals involved in industrial buying affect their expectations and their expectations affect the buying process itself. The model proposes that a key issue in the buying process is whether/when buying problems are handled autonomously by one person (e.g. a buyer) or handled jointly by two or more persons. Note that the model in Figure 7.1 shows that 'product-specific factors'

and 'company-specific factors' are also antecedent factors in possibly influencing the industrial buying process.

Campbell (1985, p. 37) criticizes the Sheth model (as well as the Webster and Wind model) for not incorporating the interplay of marketing and purchasing strategies and their antecedents. 'Another disadvantage of both models is that they concentrate on the buyer's side'. Scant attention is paid to the seller's influence on buyer behaviour. By contrast, the interaction model developed by the IMP Group stresses the interaction between two active parties, and the model proposed here (see Figure 7.2) gives equal weight to buyer and seller characteristics.

According to Campbell (1985), Figure 7.2 includes three groups of variables – the characteristics of the buyer, the supplier and the product. Note Figure 7.2 includes three possible types of buyer and seller interaction strategies: competitive, cooperative and command. A joint occurrence of competing strategies in a buyer–seller interaction is likely when both parties have nearly equal power in their bargaining positions – both are similar in importance to each other and the switching

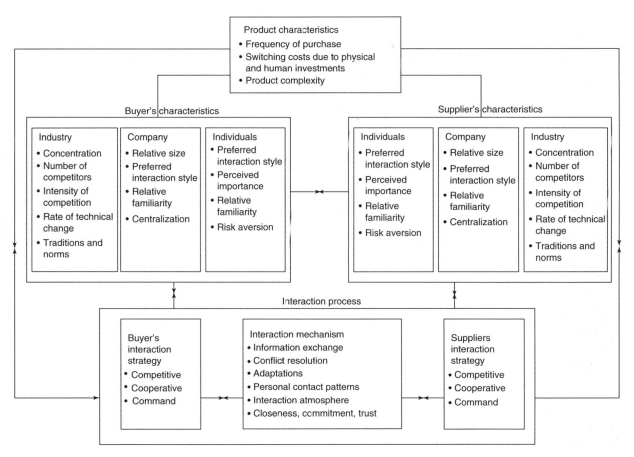

Figure 7.2   Buyer–seller interaction model
Source: Campbell (1985), Figure 2, p. 39.

costs to other suppliers/customers are about equal. Command buying (where the buyer has more power than the vendor) is more likely to occur when the buyer is larger than the supplier; command selling is more likely when the vendor is much larger than the buyer. Cooperative interaction processes are most likely to occur consistently between manufacturers and distributors of the manufacturers' products.

Table 7.1 includes predictions of conditions favouring each of the three interaction processes for buying behaviour. Note that while insightful, the value of such observations includes two important limits. First, the favouring conditions that Table 7.1 describes are predictions and not empirical findings; how consistently such predictions actually represent in real-life buyer–seller interactions is still an open question. Second, such deductive model presentations do not capture the details of real-life interaction processes – they are not thick descriptions and do not provide much understanding of the complexity, delays, interruptions and looping-back behaviour that occur in real-life marketing–buying behaviour.

Inductive modelling of B2B marketing–purchasing behaviour

Inductive model building in B2B marketing and buying behaviour focuses on reporting the details of real-life decisions and observable behaviour to deepen understanding and accuracy of descriptive reports of what actually happened. The objectives of inductive modelling usually include providing thick descriptions of real-life processes with frequent discussions focusing on explaining the meaning of events, conversations, behaviours, decisions and outcomes in the descriptions. Sometimes inductive modelling includes building system dynamic models and running simulations of alternative conditions for a given real-life process – such system dynamics modelling represents

Table 7.1 Conditions favouring different buying strategies

	Competitive buying	Cooperative buying	Command buying
Product characteristics	• Low or high frequency of purchase • Low switching costs (standardized product) • Product performance can be precisely specified	• High frequency of purchase • High switching costs (customized product) • Product performance difficult to specify	• High frequency of purchase • High switching costs
Industry characteristics	• Supplier's industry fragmented • Intense price competition among suppliers • High rate of technical change • Tradition of competitive buying	• Both industries are concentrated • Stable competitive situation in each industry • Low rate of technical change • Tradition of cooperative buying	• Buyer's industry concentrated but supplier's industry fragmented • Average level of competition • Low rate of technical change • Tradition of command buying
Company characteristics	• Buying company is larger than supplier • Buying company prefers competitive buying • Buying company lacks familiarity with product (new buy) • Centralized buying organization	• Both companies are similar in size • Both companies seek a cooperative relationship • Both companies are familiar with each other and respect each other's technical knowledge • Organizational structures are similar	• Buying company much larger than supplier • Buying company prefers to dominate supplier's costs and technology • Buying company is familiar with suppliers • Buyer has more professional organization than supplier
Individual characteristics	• Product perceived as important by buyer • Buyer is not risk averse for this purchase • Individuals who interact do not know each other well • Buyer prefers competitive buying approach	• Product is perceived as important by both parties • Buyer is risk averse for this purchase • Individuals who interact know each other • Both buyer and seller prefer a cooperative relationship	• Product is important to buyer • Buyer is risk averse for this purchase • Individuals know each other personally • Buyer prefers a command strategy and supplier accepts cooperative role

Source: Campbell (1985), Table 2, p. 43.

advanced inductive modelling (e.g. see Huff *et al.*, 2000; Sterman, 2000).

The following reports are a few major milestones in the literature on inductive model building involving B2B behaviour. Cyert *et al.* (1956) present the classic thick description of real-life B2B buying behaviour that captures the complexity, delays, personality influences and restarts (i.e. feedback loops) occurring when a firm attempts to buy a main frame computer for the first time. Witte (1972) inductively examines the deductive 'phase theorem' model that predicts that decisions follow a sequence of five phases: problem recognition, gathering of information, development of alternatives, evaluation and choice. Witte's report includes no support for the sequence among 233 buying processes for data processing equipment and he notes that searching, developing alternatives, making evaluations and choice occur in each of 10 time periods when he divided up each process in 10 equal time units. Witte's article often receives credit for originating the 'revised phase theorem' proposition that processes never really end – systems is what life is about – whereby all variables are both antecedents and consequences (also see Senge, 1990). In 1976, Mintzberg, Raisinghani and Theoret proposed the need for research on structuring unstructured decision processes and how to go about doing such structuring. By crafting and analysing thick descriptions of 25 mostly B2B marketing–buying processes Mintzberg *et al.* (1976) provide the following conclusions:

> The results of this study suggest that the design of a custom-made solution is a complex, iterative procedure, which proceeds as follows: the designers may begin with a vague image of some ideal solution. They factor their decision into a sequence of nested design and search cycles, essentially working their way through a decision tree, with the decisions at each node more narrow and focused than the last. Failure at any node can lead to cycling back to an earlier node. Thus a solution crystallizes, as the designers grope along, building their solution brick by brick without really knowing what it will look like until it is completed.
>
> (Mintzberg *et al.*, 1976, p. 256)

Additional milestones on inductive model building include the call by Howard *et al.* (1975) to map actual decision processes. Figure 7.3 is an example of such mapping research. Such a decision systems analysis (DSA) as the pricing decision process in Figure 7.3 provides the benefit of predicting outcomes of alternative antecedent states that affect path choices by decision makers through the process. DSA includes developing a model structure of relationships among events, decisions and outcomes. DSA is sometimes an intermediary step between a thick description in the form of text and a system of equations that are used to create a system dynamics model and to perform simulation runs of a process.

Figure 7.3 does not illustrate a system dynamics model but does represent a forecasting model of whether or not a firm will increase, maintain or decrease price in response to competitors' pricing behaviour. Taking the time and effort to understand the contingency paths in Figure 7.3 is worthwhile because (1) such contingency thinking depicts real-life processing of information in making a decision and (2) such models bridge description, understanding and prediction. Box 1 in Figure 7.3 calls for watching the wholesale price of the initiator (a large competitor) in the current time period in a local market. Box 2 asks the question if the initiator has changed price – if not, the pricing decision maker continues to watch the competitor. If the competitor's price does change, the model says to go to box 3. The paths in Figure 7.3 indicate that deciding to reduce price is more complicated than deciding to increase price in this model. Please study Figure 7.3 to see the different levels of complexity. (A marketer might have a natural preference to increase price – all other things remaining the same.)

Figure 7.4 is an example of the contingency nature of a small manufacturing firm's buying behaviour of industrial solvents – almost always buying from a large chemical manufacturing firm. Note that when a local distributor does offer a lower price to this customer that the customer gives the big supplier a 'second look' and the opportunity to match the lower price. How is the large supplier likely to respond when receiving such information? Unfortunately for the local distributor, the larger supplier is usually able to retain 100 per cent of this customer's purchasing requirements. See Woodside and Wilson (2000) for further details of contingency inductive modelling of pricing and bidding decision processes.

Innovation and diffusion decisions and strategy propositions

Recent decades show how the introduction of superior new products manufactured on new technology platforms cause dramatic changes in

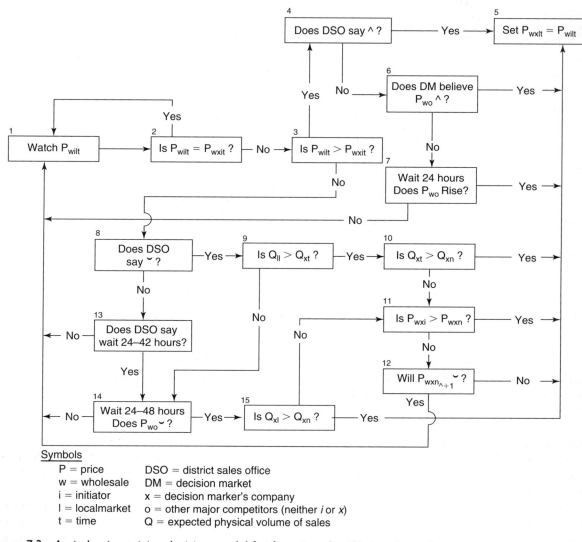

Figure 7.3 An inductive pricing decision model for firms in a distribution channel
Source: Adapted from Howard and Morgenroth (1968).

market share among firms in an industry and often result in death for prior leading firms because these leaders fail to envision and buy into the new reality (for evidence, see Christensen, 1997; Golder, 2000; McDermott and O'Connor, 2002). The main reasons for such failure include combinations of poor sense making and unwillingness to innovate; high profits for existing core customers giving a false sense of security; perception of high risk and low rewards in adopting new technologies; most organizational power being in the hands of supporters of the currently dominating logic that rejects the new technology and failure to provide a unique organization structure to nurture product development built on the new technology platform.

While a consensus does not exist regarding a formal definition of *radical innovation* (McDermott and O'Connor, 2002), Green *et al.* (1995) provide a reliable and valid measure that includes four dimensions associating with the concept:

1 technological uncertainty;
2 technical inexperience;
3 business inexperience;
4 technological costs.

Radically new products and services are high in all four dimensions. Examples include the shift from typewriters and electric–mechanical calculators to personal computers and shifting from invasive surgical procedures to endoscope procedures. Key

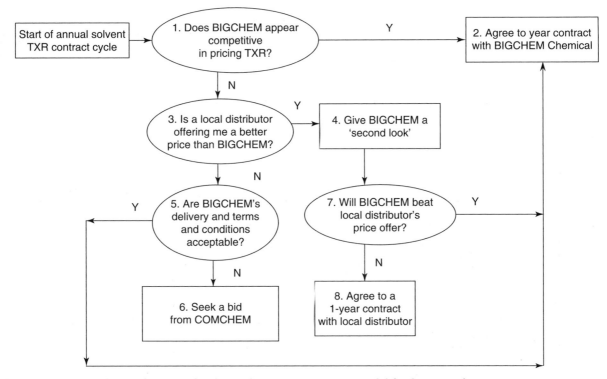

Figure 7.4   A small manufacturing firm's purchasing contingency model for buying solvents
Source: Woodside and Wilson (2000), Figure 5, p. 362.

empirical findings on radically new product development (NPD) include: long-term commitments (10+ years from first working model to widespread market adoption, see Morone, 1993); numerous stops and starts, deaths and revivals (i.e. feedback loops and delays) before such projects are ultimately commercialized successfully (Rice *et al.*, 1998; McDermott and O'Connor, 2002) and almost certain failure of firms manufacturing products based on the existing, older, dominant technology to maintain leadership following the shift to adopting new products based on the radically new technology (e.g. rejection of radically new products and explicit attacks against their adoption by manufacturers and customers advocating the older dominating technology, see Christensen, 1997). These three key findings suggest the need for longitudinal research (e.g. historical method, see Golder, 2000) rather than cross-sectional surveys, recognizing and examining the nuances of failure–success feedback loops and how breakouts from these loops occur (Sterman, 2000; Repenning, 2001), and for theory that describes and leads to useful prescriptions for improving the interactions among radically new *i*nnovation creation, *m*anufacturing, B2B *d*iffusion and *a*doption/*r*ejection – many superior new

technologies are initially rejected by large customers buying competing products manufactured on older technology platforms (i.e. IMDAR modelling, see Woodside and Voss, 1999).

This chapter advocates adopting system dynamics modelling to inform theory and to prescribe executive actions for successfully managing new products built using radically new technologies (see Huff *et al.*, 2000; Sterman, 2000). While the literature offers separate descriptions of processes such as innovation, manufacturing, diffusion and adoption/rejection, an integrated study of these processes, with attention to how these processes link together in series of events and feedback loops, contributes to understanding and improves managerial relevance of the findings.

Based on a review of case research field studies that provide thick descriptions of NPD built on radically new technological platforms (for one example of such a review see Woodside *et al.*, 2005), Figure 7.5 summarizes a general IMDAR model. Figure 7.5 is a general framework that illustrates frequently occurring repeating loops in IMDAR processes. Note in Figure 7.5 that each of the five stages in IMDAR includes a combination of unique and generalized micro-stages. The IMDAR framework includes the specific propositions that

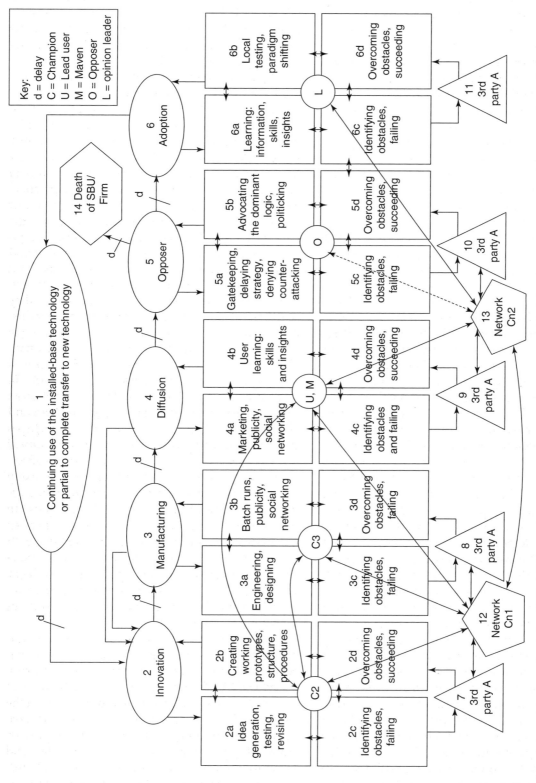

Figure 7.5   Innovation, manufacturing, B2B diffusion, adoption/rejection of superior new product/services built on a new technological platform

Source: Adapted from Woodside and Biemans (2005), Figure I, p. 383.

obstacles and failing occur within each of the five major IMDAR stages; searching/finding/using the help of third parties (Biemans, 1989) occurs for each IMDAR stage, including the rejection stage. For example, in the rejection stage, advocates of the installed-base technology may seek the help of third-party inspectors and trade association leaders to prevent the testing of a really new product based on a revolutionary new technology; overcoming such a powerful combination of advocates for the existing installed-base technology usually requires consorted efforts by the advocates of the superior new technology (Woodside, 1996).

Note in Figure 7.5 that some degree or form of rejection of a radically new product process occurs before adoption occurs. Powerful forces rise up to prevent, delay and subvert the testing and acceptance of a really new product developed using a superior new technology. To overcome such formidable obstacles often requires dramatic 'organizational improvisation' (Gemünden, 1985; Gemünden et al., 1992) and participation by a combination of on-site senior executives, performance testing the new technology (Woodside, 1996).

Figure 7.5 includes the presence of several types of champions: product champions within four of the five specific IMDAR stages, with mavens shown as a product champion in the diffusion stage and opposer representing an anti-champion in the rejection stage. In addition, opinion leaders and network champions play supportive roles. Mavens stimulate others to adopt the superior new product based on their expertise and communication abilities – even if mavens do not seek the role of championing the adoption of the superior new product, others seek them out for advice and demonstration. Mavens represent Rogers' (1995) consumer innovators and mavens relate to von Hippel's (1986) lead users concept. Lead users are very advanced mavens – they are consumers who recognize how a new technology offers unique benefits versus the currently available products built on the currently dominating technology. Lead users also envision potential designs for a new product built using the new technology. Lead users are often frustrated engineers working for manufacturing firms whose senior executives are ignoring their advice to begin research on developing new products built on the new technology platform; such lead users often quit and form their own companies with the help of third parties (Biemans, 1991; Christensen, 1997). Opposed to these champions of the new product, rejecters are persons championing the status quo;

they stress financial, performance and personal risks of adopting the new product and often are responsible for lengthy delays and outright rejection of the new product in many customer firms – particularly the large users of products manufactured using the older and still dominating technology (Woodside, 1996).

Opinion leaders are not mavens; an opinion leader is vigilant of decisions implemented by mavens and seeks mavens out for advice about adopting new technologies. The opinion leader often relishes her early adopter and community leader roles in communicating the superior performance benefits and lower total lifetime costs of adopting new products. Mavens focus on personal satisfaction and internal company recognition of doing things better, faster and cheaper using the new-technology-based products. Network champions (Woodside, 1996) serve as communication and support functions across organizations and IMDAR stages. While network champions can emerge from more than one organization, they often include a supply chain executive or an industrial manufacturer agent who stimulates unique multi-organizational meetings and special financing to demonstrate the superior performance of the new product to customers in local markets. In some cases, innovative and entrepreneurial users may also act as network champions (see Lettl and Gemünden, 2005). Note that Figure 7.5 includes two network champions to indicate the difficulty of any one party to span all the IMDAR stages effectively. The presence of network champions likely reduces the time necessary to achieve market take-off for the radically new product from several to one or two decades. Figure 7.5 includes death as an end node possibility to illustrate the point that both manufacturers and customer firms do face extinction if they effectively reject superior new products. Underwood, the leading typewriter manufacturer in 1923 in the USA, is an excellent case study of such behaviour (see Golder, 2000).

Senge's (1990) core proposition that the world consists of circle relationships instead of linear relationships is a central proposition of the proposed IMDAR framework. Senge (1990) points to the need for systems thinking and research on the causes and nature of system do-loops to achieve deep understanding on the restraints keeping us from adopting superior new technologies and behaviour. His call for finding the powerful, hidden levers occurring within systems needs to be answered with the adoption of dynamic grounded theories of IMDAR processes, and a combination of data collection methods using longitudinal research designs.

B2B network research findings and strategy implications

Probably the most salient part of the environment of all firms is other firms. Interfirm relations receive surprisingly short shrift in marketing, industrial organization economics and organization theory. 'The point here is that the entire economy may be viewed as a network of organizations with a vast hierarchy of subordinate, criss-crossing networks' (Thorelli, 1986, p. 38).

The involvement of customers' customers, that is users of a manufactured workpiece (a 'workpiece' is a unit of output from a manufacturing process, including machines to make other machines, as well as bolts, trucks, drinking water, machines to dry paint on metal, motor drives and even MBA candidates), and especially third parties (e.g. electronic technology (ET), experts, government agencies, electric utilities, and consulting engineers (CE)) are vital for successful diffusion and adoption of the new, proven manufacturing technologies (von Hippel, 1986; Biemans, 1990, 1991). The necessary involvement of third parties in the adoption by manufacturing firms of new technologies demonstrates the theoretical and research need to include diagonal relationships in network analyses of innovation adoption (Biemans, 1989, 1991). Research that confirms and extends the importance of third parties in B2B networks in the adoption of innovations would suggest the need to extend the concept of co-marketing alliances. Bucklin and Sengupta (1993, p. 32) define co-marketing alliances as 'lateral relationships between firms at the same level in the value-added chain and represent a form of "symbiotic marketing"' (see also Adler, 1966; Varadarajan and Rajaratnam, 1986). The results of additional research that this section discusses do support the following revision to the definition of the co-marketing alliances: lateral and diagonal relationships among two or more firms at possibly several levels in related value chains, representing a form of symbiotic marketing.

Network champions

The presence and realized strategies of third parties in innovation adoption networks may require the development of new concepts for understanding and explaining network behaviour. For example, the concept of *network champion* (Woodside and Wilson, 1994) is helpful for explaining the behaviour of the enterprise serving as a catalyst to build new linkages among multiple firms that have previously not communicated with one another. Creating the new linkages is necessary in assisting a manufacturing firm in the process of replacing its existing manufacturing technology with an ET manufacturing process.

The concept of network champions extends the work on the product champion concept (Schön, 1967; Maidique, 1980; Burgelman, 1983) and the organizational champion concept (Burgelman, 1983; Hutt *et al.*, 1988). The *product champion* is the member of an organization who creates, defines or adopts an idea for a technological innovation and is willing to assume significant risk (e.g. in terms of position or prestige) to make possible the successful implementation of the innovation (Maidique, 1980); the presence and nurturing activities of product champions is found for almost all successful innovations (Peters and Waterman, 1982). An *organizational champion* is a decision maker who provides sponsorship or impetus for a project within the management structure of an enterprise (Burgelman, 1983). In a detailed case study, Hutt *et al.* (1988) document the existence and roles organizational champions play; for example, one marketing manager in the firm they studied nurtured the marketing–R&D interface. Similarly, *network champions* are likely to serve, in part, as marriage brokers and deal makers to bring about new relationships among enterprises at multiple levels who must interact for the adoption of new ETs in manufacturing processes. The present section describes processes of how new networks of relationships emerge among multiple firms during processes of adoptions of new, proven, ET manufacturing processes. The following discussion reports details of how emerging networks are created within US industrial manufacturing firms in one industry. An analogy to the biological research on anatomies is used for mapping who is involved in such networks (i.e. the nodes of the networks) and the communication links among these parties.

Uncovering networks of vertical and diagonal marketing relationships is analogous to the study of anatomy. Anatomy is the art of separating the parts (e.g. of an animal) in order to learn their position, relations, structure and function. Marketing anatomy is the detailed examination of what is actually occurring in the marketing–buying

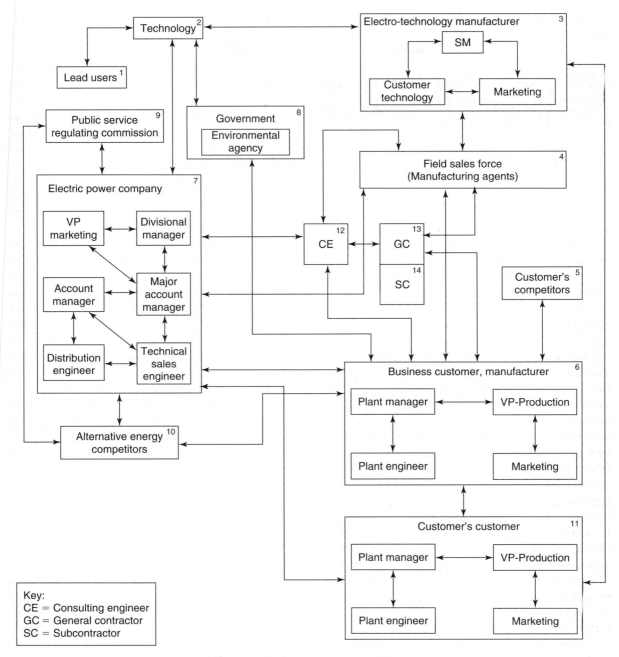

Figure 7.6. Key participants in the diffusion and adoption of a new ET
Source: Adapted from Woodside (1994), Figure 9, p. 61.

process, including who is doing what, when and with what outcomes. The research objectives include replicating and expanding the research reported by Biemans (1989, 1990, 1991); Biemans's work is based on research on network anatomies in marketing–purchasing of innovations in the Dutch medical equipment industry. Here we examine the B2B networks related to adoption processes of a new, proven ET manufacturing process, electric motor drives (EMDs). The worldwide paradigm

shift to EMDs from mechanical motor drives represents a large-scale industrial application of the new, ET manufacturing processes. In 1994 EMDs achieved a small market share penetration (less than 20 per cent) in the USA compared with the old technologies, which they are replacing.

Figure 7.6 is a composite marketing anatomy of the principal participants in the industrial adoption process of the new ETs and the key relationships among these participants. Figure 7.6 is a composite in that this illustration is not intended to describe one particular network involved in customer acceptance of one new ET. The composite is a summary of the principal parties often found to be involved in many such networks. For many specific customer adoptions of one of the new ETs not all the participants shown in Figure 7.6 will be found. Thus the marketing anatomy Figure 7.6 summarizes is a composite of the structure often found in many, but not all, customer adoptions of one of the new ETs.

Lead users are shown in box 1 of Figure 7.6. *Lead users* are the first 1–2 per cent of customers who apply the new technology commercially in a new application in a defined market (see von Hippel, 1986), for example, the very early adopters of ozone generators in water treatment plants in 1982 in the USA and the use of radio-frequency technology for processing infectious medical wastes in 1991 (Woodside and Wilson, 1994). Lead users tend to be leading experts in the technology and in applying the technologies; thus this strong link between lead users and technology is depicted by the double-arrow line in Figure 7.6. Lead users are a very special category of business customers (shown in boxes 6 and 11). Lead users work closely with a manufacturer of the new technology (box 3) who is committed to developing new uses for it. Thus, manufacturers committed to applying the new ET to lead users' manufacturing requirements need to find one another and work closely together to field-test the technology.

After several field applications of the new ET are completed successfully (5–10 years of testing being required), the Environmental Protection Agency (EPA) or other government agencies (box 8) may set new industry regulations that can be met only by the large group of industrial customers (box 6), by applying the new ET in their manufacturing/process/fabricating operations.

Meanwhile, other manufacturers of the new ET (box 3) are developing a field sales force (box 4) and marketing strategies to reach the decision makers (boxes 12, 13 and 6) on buying and installing (box 14) the new ET. Also, customers' demand (box 11) for higher delivered-product quality that can only be achieved by including the new ET in vendors' manufacturing operations. Five to ten years after the early, successful applications of the new ET, a new stage of rapid installation growth – which includes the first-time use of the new ET by up to 10 per cent of customers – for the new ET occurs, for example, infrared heating and curing applications in the late 1980s.

Between 10 and 20 years after its early commercial application, the successful adoption of the new ET by competitors of the business customer (box 5) is an additional force helping to initiate adoption among 20–40 per cent of customers (box 6). Thus, several forces create increasing influence for the widespread adoption of the proven new ET: competitive pressures (box 5), continued tighter customer quality requirements (box 11), government regulations (box 8), the marketing efforts of the new ET manufacturers (boxes 3 and 4) and the marketing efforts of electric power companies to assist business customers in adopting the new ET (box 7).

Often the electric power company needs to gain approval from a public service regulating commission (box 9) to implement marketing tools to assist business customers in adopting the new ET. Alternative energy competitors (box 10) seek to prevent the use of marketing tools by the electric power company and to slow the rate of customers' conversions to the new ET. Four persons are included within each customer firm (boxes 6 and 11) to emphasize that the adoption and conversion process of the new ET requires several persons in several functional areas to be made aware of the new ET and become convinced that their company should convert to the new ET. Such a marketing and buying process takes time – many delays and roadblocks usually occur.

Two key points from the marketing anatomy of the new ETs

First, with all the network participants involved in marketing the new ETs as Figure 7.6 depicts, the explicit creation and implementation of network strategic alliances to help to design and use marketing tools helps to eliminate delays and accelerate the adoption process. Second, for several reasons, the enterprises, which are best located to act as network champions may be electric power companies (box 7). Electric power companies have the financial and human resources for industrial marketing of the new ETs; they have an ongoing service- and trust-based relationship with their customers; they have, or can develop, the technical expertise in the new ETs, to work closely with CEs and ET manufacturers; and they can gain substantial returns on their new ET marketing investments.

The findings that this section presents confirm and extend the work of Biemans (1989, 1990, 1991) and Woodside and Wilson (1994) that intricate third-party relationships occur in the adoption of new manufacturing technologies and B2B relationships in general. In cases of radical new product adoption, third-party network champions work to nurture relationships among other network members. This nurturing role may include financing the purchase of new manufacturing equipment for the customer, hiring CEs, joint sales calls and introductions of manufacturer and distributor representatives to potential customers, hiring of experts in manufacturing using the new technologies to direct customer-training programmes and field tests of local applications of the new technologies. Biemans's (1991) general conclusion in his research on new technology adoptions in the Dutch medical equipment industry likely is generalizable to other settings. By seeking possible network members and working together, manufacturers, customers, CEs, electric power companies and other third-party participants facilitate and accelerate the adoption processes of new, proven and disruptive technologies.

Conclusion

Advances in crafting effective marketing strategies and in crafting marketing theory are occurring in both B2B and B2C subfields of the discipline. Given the large economic size and necessity of B2B marketing, the field deserves direct attention in the study of marketing processes and decision making. This chapter shows that B2B marketing theory and practice are similar and also depart from B2C marketing theory and practice. Rich insights and skills await students, executives and scholars who study both areas rather than focusing only on one subfield.

Alternative deductive theories of B2B behaviour are useful for seeing broad and deep views of possible antecedents, intervening variables, moderators and outcomes that might occur when firms interact. Inductive model building of B2B behaviour provides thick descriptions and deep meanings of how real-life interfirm relationships occur. B2B system dynamics modelling builds from inductive modelling of B2B processes. The work on innovation, manufacturing, diffusion and adoption/rejection of superior, radically new, products indicates that such IMDAR processes are a blend of mayhem and meticulous planning with frequent delays, interrupts and restarts. The chapter emphasizes the need to not only build knowledge and

skills in understanding marketing relationships between firms but also of networks of firms and individuals. Not only do new product champions and B2B third-party facilitators occur in interfirm relationships but also B2B network champions arise during successful diffusing of superior, radically new products.

Personal study and nurturing system dynamics views and modelling skills for simulating dynamic models of B2B relationships hold great promise for achieving effective sense making and effective decision making in B2B marketing. The works by Christensen (1997), Huff *et al.* (2000) and Sterman (2000) are particularly useful for accomplishing these objectives. Applying the historical method (as Christensen, 1997; Golder, 2000 illustrate) and system dynamics modelling (as Huff *et al.*, 2000; Sterman, 2000 illustrate) advances B2B marketing knowledge and skills that relate to describing, understanding, predicting and controlling (influencing) interfirm behaviour – combining the two research approaches represents a superior, disruptive, technological platform for acquiring and applying B2B knowledge and decision-making skills.

References

Adler, L. (1966) Symbiotic marketing, *Harvard Business Review*, **44**, November–December, 59–71.

Bargh, J. A. (1989) Conditional Automaticity: Varieties of Automatic Influence in Social Perception and Cognition, in Uleman, J. S. and Bargh, J. A. (eds), *Unintended Thought*, Guilford Press, New York, NY, pp. 3–51.

Bargh, J. A. (1994) The Four Horsemen of Automaticity, in Wyer, R. S. and Srull, T. K. (eds), *Handbook of Social Cognition*, Erlbaum, Hillsdale, NJ, pp. 1–40.

Bargh, J. A., Chen, M. and Burrows, L. (1996) Automaticity of social behavior: direct effects of trait construct and stereotype activation on action, *Journal of Personality and Social Psychology*, **71**(2), 230–244.

Biemans, W. G. (1989) *Developing Innovations within Networks*, Technische Universiteit, Eindhoven.

Biemans, W. G. (1990) The managerial implications of networking, *European Management Journal*, **8**, December, 529–540.

Biemans, W. G. (1991) User and third-party involvement in developing medical equipment innovations, *Technovation*, **11**(3), 163–182.

Bucklin, L. P. and Sengupta, S. (1993) Organizing successful co-marketing alliance, *Journal of Marketing*, **57**, April, 32–47.

Burgelman, R. A. (1983) A process model of internal corporate venturing in the diversified major firm, *Administrative Science Quarterly*, **28**(3), 223–244.

Campbell, N. C. G. (1985) An interaction approach to organizational buying behavior, *Journal of Business Research*, **13**(1), 35–48.

Christensen, C. M. (1997) *The Innovator's Dilemma*, Harvard Business School Press, Cambridge, MA.

Cohen, L. (1966) The level of consciousness: a dynamic approach to the recall technique, *Journal of Marketing Research*, **3**(2), 142–148.

Cyert, R. M., Simon, H. A. and Trow, D. B. (1956) Observation of a business decision, *The Journal of Business*, **29**(4), October, 237–248.

Ford, D. (1990) *Understanding Business Markets: Interaction, Relationships and Networks*, Academic, London.

Ford, D., Gadde, L. E., Hakansson, H. and Snehota, I. (2002) *Managing Networks*. Paper presented at *IMP Congress 2002*. http://www.impgroup.org/uploads/papers/4198.pdf

Gemünden, H. G. (1985) 'Promoters' – key persons for the development and marketing of innovative industrial products, *Proceedings of the Annual Conference 1985 of the European Marketing Academy*, Bielefeld, Germany, 10–12 April, pp. 402–425.

Gemünden, H. G., Heydebreck, P. and Herden, R. (1992) Technological interweavement: a means of achieving innovation success, *R&D Management*, **22**, 359–376.

Golder, P. N. (2000) Historical method in marketing research with new evidence on long-term market share stability, *Journal of Marketing Research*, **37**, May, 156–172.

Green, S., Gavin, M. and Aiman-Smith, L. (1995) Assessing a multidimensional measure of radical technological innovation, *IEEE Transactions on Engineering Management*, **42**, 203–214.

Hall, R. I. (1984) The natural logic of management policy making: its implications for the survival of an organization, *Management Science*, **30**, 905–927.

Howard, J. A. and Morgenroth, W. M. (1968) Information processing model of executive decision, *Management Science*, **14**, March, 416–428.

Howard, J. A. and Sheth, J. N. (1969) *The Theory of Buyer Behavior*, Wiley, New York, NY.

Howard, J. A., Hulbert, J. and Farley, J. U. (1975) Organizational analysis and information systems design: a decision-process perspective, *Journal of Business Research*, **3**(2), 133–148.

Huff, A. S., Huff, J. O. and Barr, P. S. (2000) *When Firms Change Direction*, Oxford University Press, Oxford.

Hutt, M., Reingen, P. H. and Ronchetto Jr., J. R. (1988) Tracing emergent strategy formation, *Journal of Marketing*, **52**, January, 4–19.

Lettl, C. and Gemünden, H. G. (2005) The entrepreneurial role of innovative users, *Journal of Business and Industrial Marketing*, **20**, 339–346.

Maidique, M. A. (1980) Entrepreneurs, champions and technological innovations, *Sloan Management Review*, **21**, Spring, 59–76.

McDermott, C. and O'Connor, C. C. (2002) Managing radical innovation: an overview of emergent strategy issues, *Journal of Product Innovation Management*, **19**, 424–438.

Mintzberg, H., Raisinghani, D. and Theoret, A. (1976) The structure of 'unstructured' decision processes, *Administrative Science Quarterly*, **21**, June, 246–275.

Morone, J. (1993) *Winning in High Tech Markets*, Harvard Business School Press, Boston.

Payne, J. W., Bettman, J. and Johnson, E. (1993) *The Adaptive Decision-Maker*, Cambridge Press, New York, NY.

Peters, T. J. and Waterman Jr., R. H. (1982) *In Search of Excellence*, Harper and Row, New York, NY.

Ragin, C. C. (1987) *The Comparative Method*, University of California Press, Berkeley, CA.

Ram, S. (1987) A Model of Innovation Resistance, in Wallendorf, M. and Anderson, P. (eds), *Advances in Consumer Research*, Vol. 14, Association for Consumer Research, Provo, UT, pp. 193–197.

Repenning, N. P. (2001) Understanding fire fighting in new product development, *Journal of Product Innovation Management*, **18**, 285–300.

Rice, M. P., O'Connor, G. C., Peters, L. S. and Morone, J. G. (1998) Managing discontinuous innovation, *Research-Technology Management*, **7**, 52–58.

Rogers, E. M. (1995) *Diffusion of Innovations*, 4th edn, Free Press, New York, NY.

Schön, D. A. (1967) *Technology and Change*, Delacotte Press, New York, NY.

Senge, P. M. (1990) *The Fifth Discipline*, Doubleday, New York, NY.

Sheth, J. N. (1973) A model of industrial buying behavior, *Journal of Marketing*, **37**(4), October, 50.

Sterman, J. (2000) *Business Dynamics*, McGraw-Hill/Irwin, Boston.

Thelen, E. M. and Woodside, A. G. (1997) What evokes the brand or store? *International Journal of Research in Marketing*, **14**, November, 125–143.

Thorelli, H. B. (1986) Networks: between markets and hierarchies, *Strategic Management Journal*, 7, 37–51.

Varadarajan, P. R. and Rajaratnam, D. (1986) Symbiotic marketing revisited, *Journal of Marketing*, 50, January, 7–17.

von Hippel, E. (1986) Lead users: a source of novel product concepts, *Management Science*, 32, July, 791–805.

Webster, F. and Wind, Y. (1972) *Organizational Buying Behavior*, Prentice-Hall, Englewood Cliffs, NJ.

Wilson, E. J., Lilien, G. L. and Wilson, D. T. (1991) Developing and testing a contingency paradigm of group choice in organizational buying, *Journal of Marketing Research*, 28, November, 452–466.

Wilson, E. J., McMurrian, R. C. and Woodside, A. G. (2000) How Business-to-Business Buyers Frame Problems and the Influence of Value-Added Customer Services (VACS) on Supplier Choice, in Arch, G. W. (ed.), *Designing Winning Products*, Elsevier Science, Amsterdam, pp. 245–254.

Witte, E. (1972) Field research on complex decision processes, *International Studies of Management and Organization*, 2, 156–182.

Woodside, A. G. (1987) Customer awareness and choice of industrial distributors, *Industrial Marketing & Purchasing*, 2(2), 47–68.

Woodside, A. G. (ed.) (1992) *Mapping How Industry Buys*, JAI Press, Stamford, CT.

Woodside, A. G. (1994) Network anatomy of industrial marketing and purchasing of new manufacturing technologies, *The Journal of Business and Industrial Marketing*, 9(3), 52–63.

Woodside, A. G. (1996) Rejecting Superior New Technologies, in Shaw, S. A. and Hood, N. (eds), *Marketing and Evolution*, Macmillan, London, pp. 96–142.

Woodside, A. G. and Biemans, W. (2005) Managing relationships, networks, and complexity of innovation, diffusion, and adoption processes, *The Journal of Business and Industrial Marketing*, 20(7), 335–228.

Woodside, A. G. and McMurrian, R. C. (2000) Automatic Cognitive Processing and Choice of Suppliers by Business-to-Business Customers, in Woodside, A. G. (ed.), *Designing Winning Products*, Elsevier Science, Amsterdam, pp. 245–254.

Woodside, A. G. and Sakai, M. (2001) *Meta-Evaluation*, Sagamore Publishing, Champaign, IL.

Woodside, A. G. and Samuel, D. M. (1981) Observations of corporate procurement, *Industrial Marketing Management*, 10, 191–205.

Woodside, A. G. and Sherrell, D. C. (1980) New replacement part buying, *Industrial Marketing Management*, 9, 123–132.

Woodside, A. G. and Voss, G. (1999) Causal modeling innovation, manufacturing, diffusion, and adoption/rejection (IMDAR) processes for new, superior medical technologies, *International Journal Technology and Management*, 1, 200–208.

Woodside, A. G. and Wilson, E. J. (1994) Tracing Emergent Networks in Adoptions of New Manufacturing Technologies, in Sheth, J. N. and Parvatiyar, A. (eds), *Relationship Marketing: Theory, Methods and Applications*, Goizueta Business School, Amory University, Atlanta, GA.

Woodside, A. G. and Wilson, E. J. (2000) Constructing thick descriptions of marketers' and buyers' decision processes in business-to-business relationships, *Journal of Business and Industrial Marketing*, 15(5), 354–369.

Woodside, A. G., Pattinson, H. M. and Miller, K. E. (2005) Advancing hermeneutic research for interpreting interfirm new product development, *The Journal of Business and Industrial Marketing*, 20, 364–379.

CHAPTER 8

Marketing research

ALAN WILSON

Introduction

Marketing research is defined as the collection, analysis and communication of information to assist decision making in marketing (Wilson, 2006). Whatever the type of organization, information on customers, competitors and markets is critical if strategic goals are to be achieved and customer needs are to be met effectively. This chapter looks at the changing nature and sources of such marketing information and the implications for marketing research. The chapter then considers the main steps in the marketing research process and considers the ethical issues impacting on the collection of information. The following two chapters will then look at qualitative and quantitative research in more detail.

The changing marketing research environment

Traditionally information on customers, their behaviours, awareness levels and attitudes was only available to organizations by using marketing research to observe or survey customers. Organizations did hold limited information on their customers but what they held was frequently in the form of invoices, files and salespersons' reports. The material was generally difficult to access, patchy in its coverage and rarely up-to-date. Over the past 10–15 years, significant improvements in computerization, data capture and database management have meant that many organizations now hold significant amounts of data on their customers. For example, a grocery store operating a loyalty card scheme will have details on each cardholder (Wilson, 2006) relating to:

- their home address;
- the frequency with which they visit the store;
- the days and times they visit the store;
- the value of their weekly grocery shopping;
- the range of products purchased;
- the size of packages purchased;
- the frequency with which they use promotional coupons;
- the consistency with which they purchase specific brands;
- the extent to which they trial new products;
- the extent to which purchasing behaviour is influenced by the timing of advertising campaigns.

In addition, their purchases may indicate whether they have a family, live alone, have pets, are vegetarian or tend to snack between meals.

The availability of such information has changed the role and nature of marketing research in many organizations. Research is beginning to focus more on awareness and attitudes rather than behaviour, and may focus more on potential rather than existing customers. Customer databases may also be used to assist in identifying potential respondents or topics for research. In addition, customers who are known to the organization and have an ongoing relationship with them may be more willing to take part in research on a regular basis. Also, budgets that were used solely for marketing research may now be split between the managing of a database and marketing research.

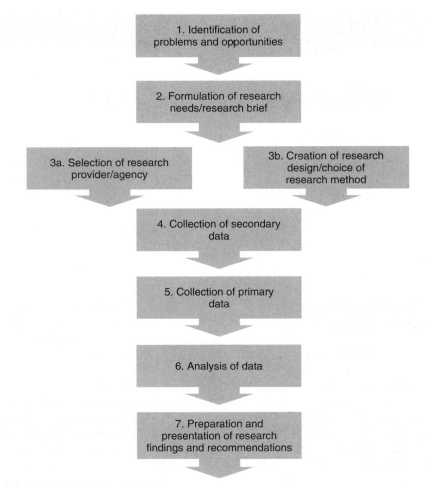

Figure 8.1 The marketing research process
Source: Wilson (2006).

These interrelationships between customer databases and marketing research mean that many organizations are starting to adopt an integrated approach to the collection, recording, analysing and interpreting of information on customers, competitors and markets. This has to be done with care to ensure that marketing research is not involved in collecting personal data that will be used in selling or marketing activities directed at the individuals who have participated in a research survey. Marketing research is dependent on respondents voluntarily providing information on their attitudes and opinions. Respondents may not be willing to provide such information if they think the information is likely to be misused for purposes other than research. Organizations undertaking marketing research must therefore understand their dual role of providing integrated information to marketing decision-makers while protecting the rights of their main information resource, the respondent.

The marketing research process

There are a number of key steps involved in undertaking and managing a marketing research project. These steps represent the marketing research process, the sequence of activities that require to be addressed if a marketing research project is to provide information that is valuable to the marketing decision maker. This marketing research process is shown in Figure 8.1.

Stage 1: identification of problems and opportunities

An organization's marketing environment is constantly changing and therefore marketing managers have to address new issues which may create opportunities or challenges for their organizations. For example, the development of a new advertising campaign may offer potential opportunities to develop business or may simply result in major costs in terms of finance and corporate reputation. A drop in sales may mean that the advertising campaign is not working and needs to be redesigned, or it may have come about as a result of short-term price-cutting by the competition. Issues such as these raise questions that need to be answered before decisions can be made. Marketing research may help to provide the answers to some of these questions.

The precise definition of the problem aids in understanding the information that will be needed and therefore helps in identifying the marketing research objectives. The organization should assess the nature or 'symptoms' of the issue that it is currently facing. These may stem from what is known about:

- market conditions;
- competitors' activities;
- the organization's own strategic objectives, plans and capabilities;
- market share and sales performance;
- previous marketing initiatives;
- the nature of the existing and new products or services;
- the awareness, attitudes and behaviour of customers.

Stage 2: formulation of research needs/research brief

In formulating the specific research needs of a project, it is important to consult all of the departments and managers that will be involved in making and implementing the decisions that will flow from the research results. Their input at this early stage will ensure the research is appropriate for the final marketing decisions that have to be made.

In particular, the consultation should focus on understanding:

1 *The context in which the need for marketing research was required.* If an organization wishes to look at customer attitudes as a result of a significant decline in sales then they may require greater urgency and detail than would be the case if customer attitudinal data is simply required as an input into an organization's regular performance measurement programme. It is also important to be aware of any internal tensions or politics within an organization which may influence the decisions that have to be taken. Any tensions that may exist may influence the type and quality of the information that will be required.

2 *The boundaries that exist around the problem.* If all of the potential courses of action relate to communication objectives, then that is where the focus should be. There can often be the danger of decision-makers taking the opportunity to add peripheral research questions, for example, about other topics such as distribution or pricing that can significantly change the nature of the project. As a result, the research can lose focus and fail to address the information requirements of the core decision area.

3 *The information components that are required to evaluate the alternative courses of action.* Understanding the information that is required behind a decision is critical. If a company wishes to consider the suitability of opening a new grocery store in a particular city, it is not appropriate to simply ask city residents if they would like a new store as they are all likely to say 'yes, that would be nice'. Instead the decision needs to be based on information such as the disposable income of city residents, the stores residents currently visit, the perceived strengths and weaknesses of competing stores.

4 *The time scale for the decisions that have to be taken.* It may not be appropriate to plan a large marketing research study if a decision is required within the next 15 days. Alternatively, where a final decision is not required for 9 months, it may be more appropriate to establish a phased approach to the gathering of information.

5 *The budget available for obtaining the information.* The scale of the available budget for the research will have a direct influence on the scale and type of information that can be obtained.

6 *The suitability of marketing research for some or all of the information that is required.* Information may be gathered from a variety of sources, some may be available in an organization's records or customer database. Other information may be in readily available reports or on the Internet. Alternatively some of the information requirements may not even relate to marketing but may relate to more technical information about logistics or manufacturing. It is important to determine the most reliable and economic sources for all of the information that is required for the decisions that have to be taken.

The consultation is usually managed by establishing a small project team which represents all of the interested parties within the organization (e.g. it may include representatives from marketing, research and development, operations, distribution, sales, corporate strategy, etc.). Alternatively, where the number of interested individuals and departments is large, it is easier to have a small core team who have discussions and meetings with all of the interested parties, and who then filter the information from these meetings to determine the specific research requirements.

This team would also be responsible for determining the extent to which the information targets can be achieved with information that already exists on customer databases and elsewhere within the organization. If relevant internal data does exist it can reduce the cost and time involved in undertaking the research and it may also help to formulate the specific information targets and identify the most appropriate respondents for the research.

The research brief

If marketing research is required, the project team will normally develop a written research brief setting out the organization's requirements. This will provide the specification against which the researchers will design the research project. A written brief in comparison with a verbal briefing of the researchers allows the specifics of the briefing to be circulated and assists in:

1 ensuring that the information obtained will be relevant and of sufficient scope for the decisions that need to be taken;
2 verifying that the need for the research is genuine and is not simply:
   - a way of using up this year's marketing research budget, in order to guarantee similar levels of funding on marketing research next year;
   - supporting a decision that has already been made as a way of reassuring the management team that they have made the correct decision;
   - a way of stalling a decision that management do not wish to make;
   - reiterating information that already exists within the organization.

Unfortunately, it is often the case that the desire of managers to move things forward, results in the development of the brief not being given proper attention. The tendency to short circuit the formulation of the research needs is unfortunate, as it can be very costly. A considerable amount of time, money and effort can be wasted in pursuit of inappropriate research questions.

The contents of the research brief are therefore very important; the typical structure for such a brief is set out in Table 8.1.

Stage 3a: selection of research provider/agency

This stage of the research process is the selection of the researchers who are to do the research. The research could be undertaken by an in-house marketing research department within the organization or by an external research agency. Larger organizations are more likely to have formal marketing research departments.

In many organizations, the marketing research department primarily manages the research activity of external agencies rather than undertaking projects on its own. Many related considerations influence the decision to go outside and use external agencies. Wilson (2006) states the most common of these as being:

- Internal personnel may not have the necessary skills or experience. Few but the very largest companies can afford to have specialists in the full range of research techniques.
- It may be cheaper to go to an agency that has encountered similar studies with other clients and is therefore more likely to be more efficient at tackling the research.
- Agencies may have special facilities or competencies (a national field force; group discussion facility with one-way mirrors; a telephone research call centre) which would be costly to duplicate for a single study.
- Internal politics within the organization (e.g. the product under investigation is the pet project of a particular senior manager) may dictate the use of an objective outside agency whose credentials are acceptable to all parties involved in an internal dispute. The internal research department may be well advised to avoid being on one side or the other of a sensitive issue.
- If the research is to be undertaken on an anonymous basis without the name of the sponsoring organization being divulged then an external agency may need to be used.

Selection of external research agencies

Initially, it is necessary to identify a shortlist of three or four agencies to be briefed on the organization's

Table 8.1 Contents of the research brief

The research brief

1 *Background*
  - This section should set out a brief explanation of what is happening within the organization, the nature of its products or services as well as current market trends.

2 *Project rationale*
  - This section sets out the reasons for the research being required. What areas of decision will be addressed by the research and what are the implications of these decisions to the organization?

3 *Objectives*
  - The objectives set out the precise information needed to assist marketing management with the problem or opportunity. They should be clear and unambiguous, leaving little doubt as to what is required.

4 *Outline of possible method*
  - This section should only give a broad indication of the approach to be undertaken in the research. The researcher, once briefed, should be allowed to use his or her experience to develop the most appropriate research design.

5 *Reporting and presentational requirements*
  - This section of the brief sets out the organization's requirements in terms of the nature of the written documents required from the researchers such as the research proposal, any interim reports produced during the research and the final report. It should also highlight what formal stand-up presentations will be required when the proposals are submitted and also for the final results at the end of the project.

6 *Timing*
  - This section sets out the time scales for the submission of the proposal and the completion of the research.

research requirements. Without prior experience, it is difficult to prejudge the effectiveness and likely research output of an agency. Like any service, there are few tangible cues to assist in the selection of the shortlist. Therefore, the shortlist is normally drawn up on the basis of the following factors (Wilson, 2006):

- previous experience in appropriate market sector (cars, groceries, advertising, etc.);
- previous experience in appropriate geographical market (for international research);
- appropriate technical capabilities (e.g. able to undertake telephone research – in the UK, the Market Research Society (MRS) produces an annual Research Buyer's Guide which lists agencies and their expertise);
- appropriate research facilities and field force (e.g. call centre, national field force, group discussion facilities);
- reputation for quality of work and keeping to time scales;

- evidence of professionalism (membership of professional bodies such as the MRS, adoption/compliance with recognized quality standards, etc.);
- communication skills (both written and verbal);
- financially stable/well established.

Once a shortlist of three or four agencies has been drawn up, briefing of each of the agencies should take place using the written brief supported by a meeting between the organization's project team and the agency. This will enable the agency personnel to fully understand the organization's requirements, allowing them to develop a research proposal.

The research proposal

In response to the brief, the research proposal is the submission prepared by the research agency specifying the research to be undertaken. On the

Table 8.2 Contents of the research proposal
The research proposal
1   Background
2   Objectives
3   Approach and method
4   Reporting and presentation procedures
5   Timing
6   Fees
7   Personal CVs
8   Related experience and references
9   Contract details
Source: Wilson (2006).

basis of the research proposal, the client will select an agency to undertake the research. The proposal then becomes the contract between the agency and the client company. The typical structure for such a research proposal is set out in Table 8.2.

The content of the various sections is similar to the research brief.

1 *Background:* This demonstrates that the agency understands the context of the research by briefly describing the client organization, its markets and products, and the rationale for doing the research.
2 *Objectives:* The objectives are similar to those in the brief, although they may in certain cases be more precisely defined.
3 *Approach and method:* This section sets out the methodology of the research approach, highlighting the types of research to be used, the sample, the method of analysis and any limitations of the proposed approach.
4 *Reporting and presentation procedures:* This section highlights the likely structure of the final report and the agency's proposals for interim and final presentations.
5 *Timing:* This should set out the time the project will take from time of commissioning and highlight any phasing of the research.

6 *Fees:* This should set out the total fees for the project. Expenses (e.g. travel, room hire, etc.) may be charged separately or be incorporated into the fees.
7 *Personal CVs:* Sets out details about the background and experience of the key researchers who will be involved in this project.
8 *Related experience and references:* Sets out the background on the research agency, outlining what experience it has had in projects similar to or relevant to this one. Certain clients may also require the agency to provide references from previous clients.
9 *Contract details:* If the proposal is accepted by the client, it will become the contract for the research that is to be carried out. As such, it is common for contractual details to be enclosed at the end of the proposal.

Presentation of proposals

In addition to the written proposal, agencies will generally be asked to present their proposals verbally in a form of 'beauty parade'. From the client organization's perspective, this has three major advantages. Firstly, it demonstrates the competence of the individuals in the agency. Secondly, it provides a check on the quality of their presentational skills and materials. This obviously gives an indication of their communication skills, but in addition it gives an impression of the care and attention that they put into their work. Finally it allows the organization to question the agency on their justification for the proposed approach.

Selection criteria to determine the successful agency

Agencies will be judged on a whole range of criteria, but Wilson (2006) suggests that the core criteria should include:

1 the agency's ability to comprehend the research brief and translate it into a comprehensive proposal;
2 the compatibility of the agency staff with the members of the client's project team (as they are going to have to work together on this project);
3 evidence of innovative thinking in the proposal (the research has been designed for this client and is not a standard off-the-shelf solution);
4 evidence of the agency understanding both the market in which the client organization operates and the specific problem facing the organization;

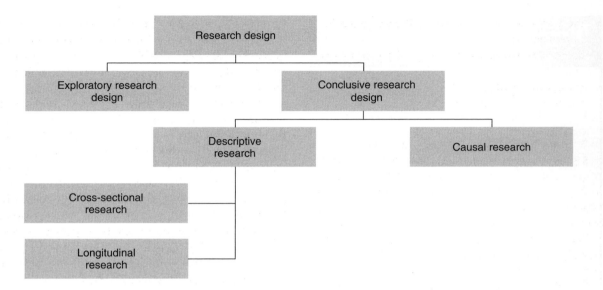

Figure 8.2   Types of research design
Source: Wilson (2006).

5   confidence in the ability of the agency to deliver
    and communicate actionable results that meet
    the decision-maker's requirements;
6   sound and appropriate methodology for the
    specific research needs;
7   meeting the organization's requirements in terms
    of time scale and budgets;
8   relevant past experience and references.

Once the successful agency has been selected, the
agency and client organization will confirm that
the proposal or a revised version of the proposal
meets the client's needs. The proposal then becomes
the contract for the completion of the research.

Stage 3b: creation of research design/choice of research method

In developing the research proposal, the agency
will have been involved in designing the project
and identifying the appropriate sources of data for
the study. Where the research is being undertaken
by a marketing research department, the process
of research design will also have to be undertaken.
In determining the design, it is important to be
aware of the broad types of information required
and the resultant decisions to be made (Figure 8.2).
There are three main categories of marketing
research that are undertaken:

1   exploratory research;
2   conclusive – descriptive research (cross-sectional
    or longitudinal);
3   conclusive – causal research.

Exploratory research

Exploratory research is research intended to
develop initial ideas or insights and to provide
direction for any further research needed (Wilson,
2006). It is a preliminary investigation of a situation
involving a minimum expenditure of cost and time.
Normally, there is little prior knowledge on which
to build. It may be used to assist in the definition
of detailed objectives for a subsequent marketing
research programme, or to examine whether it is
valuable to undertake further research at all. The
research may be aimed at exploring whether there
is any interest in a new product idea or at examining a new market that an organization wishes to
enter. The research may involve a small programme
of qualitative research or even telephone research.
Overall, exploratory research tends to be flexible
and unstructured reflecting the tentative nature of
the research objectives at this stage.

Conclusive research

All other research that is not exploratory in
nature and that is aimed at evaluating alternative
courses of action or measuring and monitoring
the organization's performance is described as
conclusive research. Conclusive research can provide information that is inherently descriptive in
nature or causal in nature.

Looking first at descriptive information about
a market, examples are:

● the proportion of the population buying a
  particular brand of toothpaste;

- the customers' attitudes towards an organization's new products;
- the level of awareness of a particular sponsorship activity;
- the extent to which customers are satisfied with the service they receive.

Descriptive information of this type is gathered using descriptive research. It provides the answers to the who, what, where, how and when of marketing research. The research outcomes describe what is happening; they generally do not explain why it is happening. Descriptive research is appropriate when the research objectives include the description of the characteristics, frequency or prediction of marketing phenomena.

If descriptive research of this type is undertaken in relation to one point in time, it is called a cross-sectional study and involves the research being undertaken once to explore what is happening at that single point in time. Alternatively, if research intends to measure trends in awareness, attitudes or behaviour over time, it is called a longitudinal study. This may involve asking the same questions on a number of occasions of either the same respondents or of respondents with similar characteristics. The cross-sectional survey is aimed at obtaining a picture of a marketplace at one point in time. However, longitudinal studies, such as panel surveys, do enable researchers to go back to the same respondents again and again to detect ongoing changes in behaviour, awareness and attitudes in response to advertising campaigns, pricing changes or even through changes in the economy. The cost and complexity of maintaining a group of respondents for a longitudinal study tends to be greater than for one-off cross-sectional projects.

Descriptive research can tell us that two variables seem to be somehow associated, such as discounting and sales, but cannot provide reasonable proof that high levels of discounting result in high sales. Research that does examine information on relationships and the impact of one variable on another is called causal research. This addresses research questions such as:

- the relationship between disposable income and expenditure on luxuries;
- the relationship between time listening to radio and expenditure on music downloads;
- the relationship between awareness of sponsorship activity and purchasing behaviour.

Causal research provides the type of evidence necessary for making inferences about the relationships between variables; for example, whether one variable causes or determines the value of another variable.

Causal research and descriptive research should not be seen as mutually exclusive, as some studies will incorporate elements of both causal and descriptive research. Conclusive projects should be seen as falling along a research continuum with 'purely descriptive studies' at one extreme and 'purely causal with strict manipulation and testing of relationships' at the other. Virtually all marketing research projects fall somewhere along this continuum, although the point where descriptive ends and causal begins is subjective and somewhat arbitrary.

Studies that are nearer to the causal end of the continuum will require an experimental research design in comparison to more standard data gathering for a descriptive study. Experimental research allows changes in behaviour or attitudes to be measured while systematically manipulating one marketing variable (e.g. price) and holding all other variables constant.

Although in pure science a completely controlled experiment can indicate for sure whether something is caused by something else, in marketing practice complete control is rarely possible. Therefore seldom can causation be conclusively established in practical settings, although most experimental research designs will provide an indicative set of findings.

In addition to the determination of the data collection method, the research design phase will also consider the nature and number of respondents (sampling) to be included in the research as well as aspects such as the timing and scheduling of the research.

Stage 4: collection of secondary data

Secondary data is information that has been previously gathered for some purpose other than the current research project. There are two main sources of secondary data: data available within the organization (internal data) and information available from published and electronic sources originating outside the organization (external data). Internal data may include information from customer loyalty cards, sales reports and information in the internal marketing information system. External data may include government reports, newspapers, published research reports and the Internet.

Secondary data is used in many studies because it can be obtained at a fraction of the cost and time involved in primary data collection. It is most commonly obtained prior to the primary research as it:

- can help to clarify or redefine the research requirements. For example, internal data held on customers may provide more information on the detail of customer behaviour and may therefore clarify which customers or which product offerings should be researched further;
- may actually satisfy the research needs without the requirement for further primary research;
- may alert the marketing researcher to potential problems or difficulties. Secondary information about previous research studies may identify difficulties in accessing respondents through, for example, the Internet and therefore may persuade a researcher to switch to some other data collection method.

Stage 5: collection of primary data

Primary data will be collected by a programme of observation, qualitative or quantitative research, either separately or in combination. Each of these types of research and their application will be discussed in detail in later chapters. In this chapter, it is sufficient to signpost their existence and define them (Wilson, 2006):

Observation research is a data gathering approach where information is collected on the behaviour of people, objects and organizations without any questions being asked of the participants. The researcher becomes the witness of behaviour and events rather than the collector of information second-hand from others about their perceptions and recollections of behaviour and events. Events may be witnessed by human observers or using equipment such as security cameras, cookies on websites, electronic scanners, automatic counting devices at the doors of shops or buildings or other forms of recording device.

Observation only measures behaviour – it cannot investigate reasons behind behaviour, it cannot assess the participant's attitudes towards the behaviour and it cannot measure the likelihood of the participant repeating the behaviour. Also, only public behaviour is observed; private behaviour in people's homes or offices is generally beyond the scope of observation studies unless permission has been obtained to install recording devices in an individual's home. The types of behaviour that can be measured are physical actions such as shopping patterns or television viewing, spatial patterns such as traffic flows on roads and in-store, temporal patterns such as the amount of time spent queuing, verbal behaviour such as conversations with customer service personnel and physical objects such as the brands of products in a consumer's kitchen cupboard.

The major advantage of observation research over surveys of respondents is that the data that is collected does not have distortions or inaccuracies as a result of memory error or social desirability bias. The data that is recorded is the actual behaviour that took place. Often facts are only brought to light by means of natural settings only. The interviewee is not conscious of them and they are therefore not easy to get at by questioning. People may not remember which shelves they looked at when going around a supermarket, however, a video camera can capture every movement.

Observation overcomes the high refusal rates that may exist for some survey research. Respondents may be willing to provide their attitudes in a survey but may be less willing to spend a large amount of time listing their behaviours and purchases. Observation can gather this behavioural information without inconveniencing the participant and in certain cases without the participant even being aware that it is happening.

Qualitative research uses an unstructured research approach with a small number of carefully selected individuals to produce non-quantifiable insights into behaviour, motivations and attitudes. It is a mistake to consider qualitative and quantitative research as two distinctly separate bodies of research – many studies encompass both approaches, with qualitative research being used to explore and understand attitudes and behaviour, and quantitative research being used to measure how widespread these attitudes and behaviours are. However, in comparison to quantitative research:

- the data gathering process in qualitative research is *less structured* and more flexible than quantitative research and does not rely on the predefined question and answer format associated with questionnaires;
- qualitative research involves *small samples* of individuals who are not necessarily representative of larger populations, however, great *care is taken in the selection of respondents* owing to the time and effort that will be spent on researching the views of each of them;

- the qualitative researcher obtains *deeper and more penetrating insights* into topics than would be the case with a questionnaire or a more structured interview;
- the qualitative data produced is *not quantifiable* and is not statistically valid – qualitative research is concerned with understanding things rather than with measuring them.

The most commonly used forms of qualitative research are the individual depth interview and the group discussion.

The individual depth interview

Individual depth interviews are interviews that are conducted face-to-face, in which the subject matter of the interview is explored in detail using an unstructured and flexible approach. As with all qualitative research, depth interviews are used to develop a deeper understanding of consumer attitudes and the reasons behind specific behaviours. This understanding is achieved through responding to an individual's comments with extensive probing. The flexibility of this probing sets this interview approach apart from other questionnaire-type interviews. Although there is an agenda of topics (topic list) to be covered, the interviewers will use their knowledge of the research objectives, the information gained from other interviews and the comments of the respondent to select which parts of the dialogue with the respondent to explore further, which to ignore and which to return to later in the interview. Not only is the depth interview flexible, it is also evolutionary in nature. The interview content and the topics raised may change over a series of interviews as the level of understanding increases.

Group discussions

Group discussions (also known as focus groups or group depth interviews) are depth interviews undertaken with a group of respondents. In addition to the increased number of respondents, they differ from individual interviews in that they involve interaction between the participants. The views or contribution of one person may become the stimulus for another person's contribution or may initiate discussion, debate and even arguments. The interaction between group members, commonly called *group dynamics*, is critical to their success and is their principal asset. Group discussions can provide the researcher with a richer and more detailed knowledge of a subject. It can also highlight the dynamics of attitudes, by showing how participants change their opinions in response to information or stimulus introduced by

others. Information about the triggers that change opinions is of particular importance to advertisers. They generally take the form of a moderator holding an in-depth discussion with 8–12 participants on one particular topic. A discussion guide is used that outlines the broad agenda of issues to be explored and indicates at which point stimulus materials such as advertisements or new product designs should be introduced. Traditionally, group discussions were held in locations where participants felt most comfortable, such as individual homes located in the same area as the respondents or hotels for business people. These locations have no special facilities apart from the researcher using a voice recorder. Although the majority of group discussions are still undertaken in such venues, there are also a growing number of specialist viewing rooms or viewing facilities in cities and large towns throughout the world which have one-way mirrors or CCTV systems to allow researchers and clients to view the discussions taking place.

Quantitative research uses a structured approach with a sample of the population to produce quantifiable insights into behaviour, motivations and attitudes. Data is generally gathered through the structured questioning of participants and the recording of responses. These tasks can be undertaken verbally, in writing or via computer-based technology. An interviewer may be used to administer the survey over the telephone or through face-to-face contact in the home, street or place of work. They may involve the use of paper-based questionnaires or computer terminals (laptops and notepads). Alternatively, the respondent may complete a survey on his or her own. This second type of survey is known as a self-completion or self-administered survey and can be delivered and collected from respondents by post, by hand, by fax, by the Internet, by e-mail or potentially by a web-enabled WAP phone (Figure 8.3).

The advantages and disadvantages of the main approaches are set out on the following pages.

In addition to the selection of the research approach and depending on the type of research being carried out, this phase is also likely to involve the development of data collection forms (questionnaires), the determination of the sample of respondents to take part in the research and the actual collection of the data.

Developing data collection forms

Primary data is frequently collected through questionnaires, but in some instances, it is also gathered

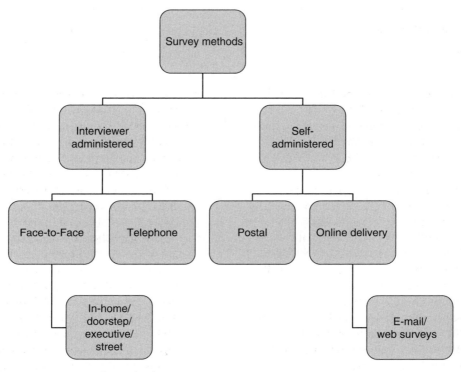

Figure 8.3   Quantitative research methods

Personal interviews

Advantages

- you can motivate a respondent to take part time and answer difficult questions when there is direct face-to-face interaction;
- you can convince the respondent that the research and the interviewer are genuine;

- you can check and ensure respondent eligibility before the interview is conducted;

- you can assist a respondent with a more complex questionnaire or set of questions;

- you can judge the interest, impatience and the seriousness with which a respondent is answering a questionnaire;
- it improves understanding of the interviewer and the respondent through non-verbal communication.

Disadvantages

- it is generally seen as being a more costly and consuming approach;

- interviews need to be clustered within specific geographical areas (e.g. cities, town centres, etc.)
  if interviewers are to be used efficiently. Therefore, people in more remote locations are less likely to be interviewed;
- quality control is more difficult as supervisors have to travel around a dispersed set of interviewers to ensure that proper interviewing standards are being met;
- it is more difficult to motivate interviewers than is the case, for example, in a centralized telephone call centre.

Telephone interviews

Advantages

- The interviewers can be briefed and trained in one location. Their calls can be monitored using unobtrusive monitoring equipment that allows supervisors to listen in on interviews and correct or replace interviewers who are interviewing incorrectly.
- Unlike personal interviews, the interviewers do not need to be located near the respondents and the interviews can be undertaken nationally or internationally from one central location.
- Some of the interviewer bias that may exist with personal interviewers is also reduced, first, through the tighter supervision, which ensures that questions are asked correctly and responses are recorded accurately, and second, through the interviewer's selection of respondents being dictated by the names and/or numbers supplied rather than the approachability of different types of respondent.
- The telephone also has the advantage of reaching people who otherwise may be difficult to reach through any other means, such as businesspeople travelling around or people who live in flats with entry-phones.
- The other major benefit of telephone interviews is speed. Interviewers can be briefed and be conducting interviews within hours of the questionnaire being developed. It would take much longer to brief a team of personal interviewers.

Disadavantages

- The biggest disadvantage relates to respondent attitudes towards the telephone. Over the past 15 years, there has been a major growth of telephone usage for telemarketing purposes throughout Europe. Home improvement companies, financial service organizations, catalogue marketers and even charities use the telephone to generate sales/funds, either directly or by arranging for a sales representative to visit prospective purchasers. Many are persistent and relatively aggressive callers and in certain situations some disguise their approach as being marketing research. This activity is called 'sugging' (selling under the guise of research) by the marketing research industry. Refusal rates are therefore increasing.
- Although some telephone interviews can last 25–30 minutes, they are normally much shorter and certainly shorter than face-to-face interviews.
- Certain types of question such as complex ranking questions or questions with a large number of multiple-choice responses are also more difficult to undertake over the phone.
- In international telephone surveys, there may be specific problems in undertaking interviews. One of these relates to low levels of telephone ownership, particularly in many of the developing countries in Africa and Asia. Even in developed countries there may be problems relating to the coverage of telephone networks owing to the growth of the use of mobile phones and people choosing to rely solely on mobile rather than land line networks (e.g. students, people on low incomes).

Postal surveys

Advantages

- Questionnaires can be sent to a geographically dispersed sample at low cost. For each completed questionnaire from a geographically dispersed sample, postal surveys are likely to be around one-third of the cost of a typical telephone survey and less than a ninth of the cost of a typical face-to-face interview.
- No interviewer bias.
- The respondents can complete the questionnaire at their own speed when they want and can confer with other members of their household or refer to files, documents, etc.
- The questionnaire can piggyback on the back of other correspondence such as bank statements, warranty registrations and newsletters, reducing the cost further.

Disdavantages

- Very low response rate, which can lead to a high cost per completed interview. Those who respond may not be representative of the population. It may be that only those who have strong opinions or have links with the organization being researched take the time and effort to complete the questionnaire.
- It is difficult to control the manner in which the questionnaire is completed. As a result sections may be left blank and it is not unknown for managers to get their secretaries or parents to get their children to complete the questionnaires.
- It is difficult to get respondents to write down full answers to open-ended verbatim-type questions. Therefore most questions should simply involve ticking boxes, and open-ended questions should be limited to a very small proportion of the total.
- From time of despatch, it can take 2–3 weeks until all completed questionnaires are returned. There may even be the odd questionnaire drifting in up to 12 weeks after the survey was despatched. Postal or telephone reminders with incentives may be needed to get respondents to return questionnaires.

Online surveys

Advantages

- The costs are even less than for a postal survey as there are no photocopying and postage costs.
- There are a growing number of online survey software packages and survey hosting sites that make the design and analysis of online surveys very straightforward. Therefore online surveys can be designed, despatched and analysed very quickly.
- Online surveys can be personalized with only the most relevant questions being asked of each respondent. In addition, respondents can pause and resume the survey at their convenience.
- Online surveys can access business people and wealthy individuals who may be difficult to reach through the telephone, post or face to face.

Disdavantages

- E-mail addresses are constantly changing and it can be difficult to obtain an up-to-date sample list. Alternatively you need to approach potential respondents when they visit your website.
- Response rates are similar to postal surveys and may deteriorate further as respondents receive large quantities of 'junk' e-mail as well as more and more requests to undertake on-line surveys.
- There are still segments of the population who do not have access to the Internet and do not have an e-mail address.

through observation and through qualitative research. Regardless of the data collection method used, some instrument or form must be designed to record the information being collected. This is a skilled task requiring careful thought and planning. A poorly designed questionnaire can jeopardize response rates and provide incomplete or inaccurate data. With the growth of computer-assisted interviewing and web-based surveys where respondents' answers are fed directly into a computer terminal or through the Internet, computing skills may also be critical.

Determination of the sample

Determining the sample involves specifying the types of respondent to be included in the research, the numbers of respondent required and the method by which individual respondents will be selected. There are a large number of sampling approaches and their selection is influenced by factors such as the level of accuracy required, the nature of the project, the characteristics of the potential respondents, as well as time and cost constraints.

Collection of the data

Once the data collection form and the sample design are prepared, the data can be collected. If the research involves observation, then different types of equipment may be used. If it is qualitative, researchers need to use specific skills and techniques to gather detailed information from respondents. Quantitative research may require significant logistical management activity to co-ordinate the dispatch of large postal surveys, the management of geographically dispersed field force interviewers or the operations of a telephone call centre. Quality control is critical at this stage to ensure that the research approach is implemented in a manner which will ultimately address the research objectives.

Stage 6: analysis of data

The types of analysis undertaken in a project depend on the nature of the data and the specific data collection method used, as well as on the use to be made of the findings. In particular, there are significant differences between the analysis approaches adopted for qualitative research and those used for quantitative research.

Stage 7: preparation and presentation of research findings and recommendations

Generally, most projects involve the preparation of a formal written report and an oral presentation. Often the presentation and communication of the research findings is as important, if not more important, than is the research itself. It is difficult for client organizations to take research findings seriously if they are confusing, inaccurate or lack relevance to the key marketing decision-makers. There is a need to understand the requirements of the audience for any research report or presentation, and to develop quality materials to match these needs.

Managing the client/agency relationship

Throughout the marketing research process, it is important that the project team in the client organization and the researchers work as a unit in order to maintain the quality and relevance of the research. This means that the project team should seek regular meetings during the project in order to maintain their awareness of what is going on and also to suggest alternative courses of action if the research is encountering problems, such as high refusal rates among respondents or the sample lists provided by the client being inaccurate. It may be worthwhile phasing the research into different stages and having interim presentations at various points throughout the research. At these presentations, decisions could be taken as to whether to continue with the proposed research, make amendments to the research design or abort the project.

Ethics in marketing research

Marketing research ethics refers to the moral guidelines or principles that govern the conduct of behaviour in the marketing research industry. Ethics is particularly important in marketing research, as the industry is dependent on (Wilson, 2006):

- *Goodwill:* The goodwill of the individual respondents for their willingness to volunteer information on their awareness, attitudes and behaviours. Any practice that erodes that goodwill makes future marketing research studies more difficult to undertake.

- *Trust*: Marketing decision-makers trust researchers to provide accurate information that has been collected in a professional manner. Researchers also trust decision makers to divulge all information that may have an impact on the completion of a marketing research study.
- *Professionalism*: If respondents are to answer questionnaires in a serious and thoughtful manner, they have to feel that the research is going to be used in a professional manner.
- *Confidentiality*: Respondents are more willing to express their views and opinions, if they know that the information is going to be used in a confidential manner (in other words, taking part in marketing research will not result in the respondent becoming subject to sales calls).

The behaviour of marketing researchers is controlled by the data protection laws enforced by the government of the country in which the research is being carried out and also by the relevant self-regulatory codes of conduct drawn up by the professional bodies that represent the marketing research industry.

Data protection legislation

Individual European countries each have their own national legislation on data protection. These all tend to fit within the framework of the European Union Directive on Data Protection. This Directive was passed in 1995 and required Member States to implement the Directive into national legislation during 1998. Although the intention was to have a common data protection law for Europe, each country has added to or changed the detailed meaning of some parts. This means that researchers undertaking research in non-domestic markets should always check the specific laws of the country in which they are researching.

Despite the different nuances of the different laws, the guiding principles are common and these are:

- *Transparency*: Individuals should have a very clear and unambiguous understanding as to why their personal data (i.e. data that identifies a living, individual, natural person) is being collected and for what purpose it will be used.

- *Consent*: At the time when their personal data is being collected, individuals must give their consent to it being collected and they should also, at this time, have the opportunity to opt out of any subsequent uses of their personal data.

It is important to note that data protection legislation only covers data (including audio and video records) that identifies a living, individual, natural person. Once any identifiers linking data to a specific person have been removed then it no longer constitutes 'personal data' and is therefore not covered by the legislation. Information about companies is also outwith the remit of the legislation unless it identifies information about individuals within the companies.

Codes of marketing and social research practice

In addition to legislation, there are professional codes of marketing and social research practice. These are self-regulatory codes of conduct developed by the professional bodies responsible for the research industry. The first such code was published in 1948 by the European Society for Opinion and Marketing Research (ESOMAR). In the UK, the Market Research Society Code of Conduct was first introduced in 1954. Other national marketing research societies and the International Chamber of Commerce (ICC), which represents the international marketing community, produced their own codes. In 1976, ESOMAR and the ICC produced a single international code instead of two differing ones, and the joint ICC/ESOMAR code was established. This has been revised on a number of occasions since. National organizations such as the MRS in the UK have also been revising their own codes during this time, to the extent that most European national codes are now fully compatible with the ICC/ESOMAR International Code of Marketing and Social Research Practice.

It is important to note that these codes are self-regulatory and are not controlled by law. Breaches of these codes can only result in disciplinary action relating to an individual's membership of the relevant professional body. Such disciplinary action may involve membership being withdrawn, demoted or suspended and the publication of information about such actions.

In addition to the formal code of conduct, ESOMAR, MRS and other national marketing research societies provide written guidelines to their members on specific areas and issues involving the practice of marketing research such as:

- research among children and young people;
- Internet research;
- qualitative research;
- mystery shopping research;
- questionnaire design;
- maintaining distinctions between marketing research and direct marketing.

These are regularly updated and can be obtained from the MRS (www.mrs.org.uk) and ESOMAR (www.esomar.org) websites.

Summary

The marketing concept promotes the idea that the whole of the organization should be driven by the goal of serving and satisfying customers in a manner which enables the organization's financial and strategic objectives to be achieved. Marketing decision makers therefore require the best customer, competitor and market information available when deciding on future courses of action for their products and organizations. As such, the source of the information is less important than the quality of information. There is a growing trend towards a blended approach to information gathering where database information and Internet sources are used at any of the stages of the research process to satisfy the information needs of the project and assist in the design and the execution of the research. In doing so, however, care must always be taken to ensure that the data obtained about and from individuals is protected within the parameters established by the relevant data protection legislation and the self-regulatory codes of conduct established by the research industry. Marketing research is dependent on the goodwill of the individual respondents for their willingness to volunteer information on their awareness, attitudes and behaviours. It is therefore important that the whole of the marketing research process is undertaken in an ethical and professional manner.

This chapter has set out the research process highlighting the stages that guide a research project from conception through to final recommendations. Great care must be taken in the early stages of a project to formulate what is expected from the research, and a research brief should be written to act as a specification against which researchers will be able to design the research project.

The research proposal is the submission prepared by the researchers for a potential client specifying the research to be undertaken. The proposal is also critical in the agency selection process and sets out the detail of the research design.

The later sections of the research process, such as collection of secondary data, primary research, analysis of data and the presentation of research findings are also outlined.

Marketing research does not in itself make decisions; it simply enables better in informed decision-making to take place. Managers still need to use judgement and intuition when assessing marketing information. The growth in information sources as a result of computerization and the Internet means that managers need more guidance in validating and selecting the most appropriate information to access and use. The marketing research industry with its detailed understanding of information collection and analysis, should be the best qualified to provide this guidance.

Reference

The material in this chapter is based on extracts from:

Wilson, A. (2006) *Marketing Research: An Integrated Approach*, 2nd edn, FT Prentice Hall, Harlow, UK.

CHAPTER 9

Qualitative research

LEN TIU WRIGHT

Introduction

There is a long tradition in the social sciences of observing, studying and recording what it is that people do and how they live. Qualitative research is rooted firmly in this tradition drawing from the various social science disciplines, such as those of anthropology, education, history, linguistics, psychology, sociology and the practices of business, management and politics, with which to inform its own brand of study. This is why qualitative research has been described as both art and science, informed through an approach that consists of being naturalistic, humanistic, holistic and speculative (Mariampolski, 2001, p. 7–9), represented and interpreted by many, such as those of academics, filmmakers, essayists, writers and social critics (Denzin and Lincoln, 2005, p. 4). Humans are subject to received wisdom as they are to infinite thirst for knowledge and imaginary leaps of faith, so qualitative researchers are unbounded by conventional wisdom in seeking new interpretations and challenges to advance knowledge in the human race.

While this gives qualitative research its unique and timeless quality, it has to be said that there is a caveat to qualitative research. It is to be expected that there are differences in the abilities of the people conducting qualitative research as there are variations in the quality of the material being researched. In addition, there are individual value judgements in interpretations giving rise to differences in research techniques and reported controversies, examples of which are discussed under the subheading of ethnography.

What is important to recognize is that there is much good qualitative research being carried out. Its steady growth in marketing and market research in the last 67 years attests to this. In this chapter no distinction is made between qualitative research in marketing and market research as it has become an indispensable part of both their activities. When Neil Borden introduced the term 'the marketing mix' in his seminal publication (1964) he included market research as one of the 12 components of the mix. Since then the market research industry has grown to be a large and important industry in its own right, as evidenced by the European Society for Opinion and Marketing Research (ESOMAR) publications of annual reports on turnover and spend in the market research industry. See website (2005).

In 1997, ESOMAR put the size of the world research market at more than 10.4 billions euros. It listed amongst 'the top 10 research groups worldwide' those companies that were also amongst the top 10 in the European Union. The European Union (41 per cent) and the United States (37 per cent) accounted for the largest shares of world turnover for qualitative research (ESOMAR, 1998). By 2003 a global industry report (Tarran, 2004) gave the overall worth of the global market research industry as US $18.9 billion (£11.6 billion). The breakdown distribution of spend was given as: Middle East and Africa ($246 million); Asia Pacific ($2569 million); Central and South America ($685 million); North America ($7137 million) and Europe ($48 285 million). Compared to quantitative studies with their larger samples and higher costs qualitative research accounts for a much smaller percentage of the overall figure, in general between 10 and 20 per cent.

For matured research markets Goodyear (2000, p. 379) put qualitative research at about 20 per cent of revenues with a lower figure in less mature markets.

This chapter concentrates on the *importance of qualitative research in marketing*. It is not in the remit of this chapter to cover the numerous typologies and specialisms of qualitative research used in the social sciences. The chapter's orientation is directed to where some of the traditions and applications inherent in qualitative research are suited to marketing. Definitions and scope of qualitative research are provided. Background aspects are provided about the growth of qualitative research, theoretical underpinnings for and differences of qualitative and quantitative approaches, including what validity, reliability and triangulation mean in qualitative research. These are followed by reflections on existing traditional types of enquiry, namely: autobiography, biography, ethnography, grounded theory, phenomenology and the case study. Data collection methods and the applicability of qualitative research to the broader realms of international marketing are examined. The chapter concludes with a brief prognosis for qualitative research in marketing.

There are a number of reasons why qualitative research in marketing thrives. It is not only the preserve of the marketing and market research industries. All kinds of organizations and their consultants conduct qualitative investigations in many and different fields, such as for academia, charities, media, public relations and government departments, which conduct qualitative research to find out the attitudes or opinions, behaviour and motivations of targeted groups and individuals. In the twenty-first century the creation of new industries and markets, goods and services replacing many old products from manufacturing and old service industries has led to new types of consumption and user behaviour, for example for the new products and services of modern electronics, telecommunications and entertainment sectors. There are proponents of more qualitative research to enable greater 'nuance-based audience definitions' away from static measurement, as in an Indian example by Nye and as quoted by Mackenzie (2005, p. 8). The increasing number of universities and practitioner institutions worldwide teaching qualitative research as part of marketing and market research courses can be seen in trawling through their specific websites or conducted through various search engine sites, for example *Google* and *Yahoo*. In the academic and practitioner spheres there are informative and instructive books on qualitative research, examples of which are included in the references at the end of this chapter.

Definition and traditions of qualitative research

Qualitative research is an overall term to describe the work researchers do in formulating their interpretations of the subjects of their studies and giving representations of these interpretations in order to add to a body of knowledge. For current examples of new knowledge see the table on *'Examples of practitioner contributions from the MRS Conference 2006'*. Perhaps qualitative research needs to carry a health warning. The very wide scope of what is loosely interpreted as qualitative research means that there are as many different definitions as there are researchers depending on the qualifications, training and backgrounds that researchers come from. A variety of explanations for the theoretical understanding of qualitative research is given in this section.

Within the humanities the sociological and educational perspectives are expounded by Denzin and Lincoln (2005, p. 2) who defined qualitative research as *'a field of inquiry in its own right'*, being a *'complex, interconnected family of terms, concepts and assumptions'* associated with *'methods connected to cultural and interpretive studies'*. Qualitative research is further described by the authors as crosscutting eight historical moments of North American traditions: the traditional (1900–1950); the modernist/golden age (1950–1970); blurred genres (1970–1986); the crisis of representation (1986–1990); the postmodern (1990–1995); postex-perimental enquiry (1995–2000), the methodologically contested present (2000–2004) and the fractured future (from 2005). For explanations of these terms see Denzin and Lincoln (2005, p. 3–8).

Ontology

The sense of tradition, place, time and 'of being' are echoed in qualitative research. The deep philosophical position of ontology is the concern with the nature of being or existence, as envisioned by Descartes' phrase *cogito ergo sum* (*I think*, therefore *I am*) and which have been present in one form or another within the principles about life, as taught by philosophers through the centuries as in the examples of Aristotle (384 BC) and

Confucius (551 BC). Within the terms of what Byrne (2001, p. 372) described as qualitative research, 'contextually laden, subjective and richly detailed', such a description can be applied to the writings in marketing studies. What people wear, their mannerisms and their proximity to others, what they say with inflections of tone and volume, what they show by body movements and mannerisms or in their stillness, what they see or not see and appreciate or not appreciate about the contents within physical settings and the contexts of an occasion within each setting all convey rich data to qualitative researchers. The procedural nature for valuable or good qualitative research can be established by following the rules of epistemology.

Epistemology

As defined by the ongoing publications of the Longman Dictionary of the English Language, epistemology is the study or theory of the nature, grounds, methods and limits of experience, belief and knowledge. In producing knowledge there is debate and scepticism, given the different claims to knowledge. Since epistemology primarily addresses the questions: 'what is knowledge and how is knowledge acquired?'.

These are inevitable debates. What people think they understand as knowledge is dependent on the perspectives they take, or how much they are able to analyse the nature of such knowledge in order to link these to their beliefs. It is not enough for a researcher to state that an inductive reasoning process, as based on observation and experience, has taken place because this logical line of reasoning needs to be evident to others and also capable of being judged by other researchers as to its credibility. 'Analytic logic' and its 'interpretive authority' (Morse, 1997, p. 121) requires making clear what the researcher 's reasoning is, from *'the inevitable forestructure to the interpretations and knowledge claims made on the basis of what was learned in the research'*. Interpretive authority stems from the requirement that researchers should make statements founded upon observations which are not prejudicial, but objective. Therefore, qualitative researches are considered 'good or excellent' when they can be justified on these grounds.

Realism and interpretivist traditions

There is a richness in qualitative studies in throwing much light on the way respondents think, feel

and behave. Qualitative researchers, according to Silverman (2005, p. 9), look for details in the *'precise particulars of such matters as people's understandings and interactions ... a non-positivist model of reality'*. Realism and the interpretivist traditions are generally held up as alternative approaches to positivism (see next section). Philosophical realism is a belief that reality exists independently of observers, while critical realism extends this to the proposition that while some of what we see and sense around us relating to external objects and eventscan be taken to be accurate representations, there are other sense data which may not be accurately portrayed. We see plentiful examples of this in marketing. One example is the gulf between the advertising agencies and public relations people with the consuming public caught in the middle, see Bell (2005, p. 21): *'The truth is the ad industry thinks that PR men are idiots, a waste of time, good at lunch and not much else ... PR men think that ad men are grossly overpaid, whilst producing far too much rubbish and that for an industry that reaps billions of dollars its vast output has no effect on anything'*. It is not surprising that in critical and postmodern marketing writings there is a sense of gaps in marketing theory and limitations of marketing methodologies. However, while both critical marketers and postmodernists have raised awareness of shortcomings in their critiques of marketing, there has been very little that is of relevance in terms of their establishing any alternative new marketing theories or new methods for marketing applications.

The generalized nature of the interpretivist approach to qualitative research has usually been contrasted to positivism (see the next section), because the interpretivist researcher looks for hidden meanings beyond the external façades of people or in their dealings with their peer and reference groups, for example contemporaries and family members, or in society as a whole. Body language, movements, looks, speech or inflections of voice, verbal anecdotes, jokes and story telling all contain subtle meanings which need to be explored. At the sub-conscious level individuals interacting with others have hidden intentions and meanings that may mean more on interpretivist examination than realism, that is the realist perspective of what is seen represented in the world.

Discourse analysis for studying language, verbal and textual, also looks for layers of meaning and reference points, for example, how many times a key work or phrase was used and what meaning these same key words tell us of the writer or speaker and the characters he or she chooses to use. However, as Black (2006) puts it, *'how can words fully express the meaning inherent in our observations, personal interviews and pictures when so much of it is subtle, hidden and contextually bound?'* So qualitative researchers can also apply a variety of methods such as the examination of film and personal photographs to observe their subjects (Holbrook, 1995). Interpretivists see their strength as being able to go beyond the surface complexities to uncover hidden layers, for example, in marketing this might be the deeper meanings of consumption situations to people.

Qualitative research, according to Bill Schlackman (1999), started out as motivational research with its roots in psychology and owed credit for its initial popularization to Dr Ernest Dichter in the USA. Schlackman has been widely credited with introducing qualitative research in the UK in the 1960s. He saw motivational research lose its title to become 'qualitative research' which he thought was a more accurate description. In Britain, as on the Continent, much pioneering work came from social reformers and early consumer groups which undertook limited social and market studies in efforts to persuade their governments, influential ruling classes and business corporations that there were cases for reform. Social class divisions with their impact on poverty amongst the working classes, limited provision of education, poor living conditions and low welfare standards were items for reform on their agendas. Governments in expanding their public sector commitments set up more national corporations such as those overseeing broadcasting and public transport. After the Second World War the expanding public and private sectors provided much work for market research agencies.

Qualitative researchers can come from any discipline, from the social sciences and other more mathematical fields as represented in the persona of Bronislaw Malinowski. He was the founder of *Mass Observation* who had a background in mathematics and who applied scientific logic to the traditional field of ethnography. He disagreed with the traditional view of ethnography that was reliant on believing what people said they did. His view was that ethnography should be about observing what others did. *Mass Observation* was started in the 1930s when he led a group of young researchers to study the cultures of working men and women in the north of England (BBC Four, 2007). It was the start of a social phenomenon when market research uncovered the attitudes and behaviour of working people at a time when politicians were becoming aware of consumer research as a growing force for change. *Mass Observation* became one vehicle by which government agencies listened to their publics, helping to establish it as one of the best known in market research.

Qualitative research associations are at the forefront of pushing the discipline in the United States and Europe. They include qualitative consultants from all kinds of social science backgrounds. The UK professional body for qualitative researchers, the Association of Qualitative Research (AQR), holds annual conferences and opportunities for networking for its members. Such bodies are normally practitioner dominated, as is the Market Research Society (MRS) in the UK. Annual conferences for academics, such as those run by the Association for Consumer Research in the USA, the Academy of Marketing in the UK, the European Marketing Academy and the American Marketing Association all include tracks for papers that have qualitative content. The Worldwide Biennial Conference on Qualitative Research (WBCQR) is a joint venture of the two leading associations representing the discipline, the Association for Qualitative Research (AQR) in the UK and the Qualitative Research Consultants Association (QRCA) based in the USA. The common aim is to create a forum to showcase best thinking and practices, to reflect all aspects of qualitative research from the perspectives of those who commission, design, execute and apply the findings of research studies. The WBCQR also creates numerous opportunities for networking with the discipline's leaders, as well as with prospective clients and business partners by scheduling diverse types of sessions and sponsoring a social programme that takes advantage of the diverse international locations for its conferences.

Theory and application

A wide ranging and inclusive list of the versatility of the qualitative researcher's toolkit is offered by Gummesson (2007). His choice of *'interactive research…includes case study research (recognizing complexity, context and ambiguity); grounded theory (letting reality tell its story on its own terms); anthropology/ethnography (the importance of being there); action research (making it happen and reflecting); narrative research (making reality come alive) . . . network theory (addressing complexity, context and dynamism), not limited to social network theory but including recent developments in natural sciences'.* These are amongst the *most commonly used theoretical research paradigms,* as stated by Creswell (1998, p. 11) and in part by Richards and Morse (2007, p. 12), namely: autobiography, biography, ethnography, grounded theory, phenomenology and the case study.

Autobiography and biography

The intellectual strands of autobiographical and biographical writings have their roots in literary and social science disciplines. Internet searches reveal extensive numbers of autobiographies and biographies providing varied and interesting contents, such as those written by and about past American presidents.

Some writers are stimulated to compile biographies of other people, even when these people are alive and might not have consented to the work being done or have divorced themselves from it. For example, biographies of Princess Diana were written of her when she was alive and after her death. They are annually sold by publishers each year with the excuse of satisfying consumer demand. Some biographers write about their subjects out of personal interest. However, there are biographies written to tap into the markets where there exist potential readerships and hence profits to the publishers marketing the books.

An autobiography is a life story of a person written by the same person. A politician's memoirs followed by a full autobiography of himself or herself can invoke feelings of anticipation or distaste, depending on one's view of his or her abilities while holding public office. In the 1980s one such politician in the cabinet of the then UK Prime Minster, Mrs Thatcher, had a re-run showing of his memoirs in 2006, as adapted for television audiences. There are radio interviews and dedicated Internet websites for the rich and famous, including infamous ones which seek to provide insights for the consuming public. For qualitative researchers both autobiographies and biographies provide rich sources of secondary, historical, anthropological and ethnographic data. The fascination with past famous figures by modern writers and consumers who buy their writings has helped to keep a whole genre of film and book suppliers in strong marketing and subsequent good financial health.

Phenomenology

This is a method largely developed by Edmund Husserl (1859–1938). The first step of phenomenological reduction is to suspend all preconceptions about experience. The phenomenologist describes the invariant essences of objects rather than the consideration of their objective states. Transcendental phenomenology is based on insights from the exploration of how knowledge comes into being. It is interpretive, based on intention and vivid attention to description. Existential phenomenology regards human reality as a reciprocal relationship between the researcher and the phenomena of all the thoughts, moods and actions, that are lived experiences. Hermeneutical phenomenology includes the arts, myths, religion and symbols in cultures. Linguistic phenomenology finds meanings residing within the language, binding it to historical and cultural contexts. Qualitative market research has shown there are phenomena of lifestyle changes with specific groups, in-group behaviour and out-group behaviour carried out with observation and in-depth interviewing techniques. Such researches of people's past and present live experiences have led to the creation of advertising campaigns around the 'desirability' of product brands to consumers. Recent work carried out by a small group of qualitative marketing researchers led by Henry and Caldwell of Sydney University included filming the events of heavy rock music groups to investigate the influence of music on consumption lifestyles and vice versa as in the Cliff Richard Fan Club in Melbourne. Recognition of such qualitative in-depth marketing studies came with a European film award in 2006 for 'Living Doll' (title of a Cliff Richard's song) which was based around the topic of fandom or fan worship of specific celebrities.

Grounded theory

This starts from the intention to generate, or to discover a theory by studying how people interact in response to a particular phenomenon. Theoretical propositions are developed from interview data and field research. Grounded theory is often about looking at how people are seen to react and the signs or cues in their individual and group behaviour. It is about defining, refining categories and revisiting the questions arising from the research repeatedly until specific, tenable propositions arise. These propositions or theories are then developed for further research. There has been confusion as to how the method of grounded theory has been used. This originates from individual researchers with varied research experience and skills, with extensive or not extensive understanding of the contexts-laden aspects of a situation, hence affecting their interpretations of the many clues in the field. However, for grounded theory the theoretical basis for the coding of data and the methods for coding has lent itself to computer software analysis, as explained in the section, *Using computers in qualitative research*. Where it is difficult to research overseas markets, for example where western theories about female emancipation and effects on female lifestyles will not fit with Muslim societies' treatment of the issue, then a grounded theorist perspective could be justifiable as a research approach over other approaches.

Ethnography

Ethnography is the description, or interpretation, of the observable and learned patterns of behaviour in a social group or setting. The researcher immerses himself or herself in a variety of ways into the culture of the group to be studied. For example, he or she might live with the community, experiencing their day-to-day lives and pursuing one-to-one interviews with members of the group. By doing this, the researcher experiences at first hand how the subjects of the study are living, working and behaving, while taking notes and observing or being a participant (researcher immersion) in the subjects' community living. Some historical ethnographers' studies are open to controversy, for example the evidence presented by Margaret Mead in her book, *Coming of Age in Samoa* and Freeman's dispute of her theories in his book *Coming of Age in Samoa: Making and Unmaking of a Myth*. Mead gave her account as evidence that Samoan teenagers were not prone to the pain and stress of growing up compared to American teenagers.

These theories were disproved by Derek Freeman who publicized evidence disproving her theories in his book and in subsequent writings. The moral of this story is that the scientific basis about racial difference rests on shaky ground. Early ethnographers went from the West to remote island or village communities to justify supposed differences in race. Marketing studies found that 'within group' differences caused by genetic variations within the same race groups and those found between groups representing different races do not need to get in the way of branding. For example, the global brand with one global message and brand image are part of our modern history (e.g. Coca Cola, IBM, Sony). The global brand is sold to the human race which would consume or use the product in the way it is marketed by the company, whatever anyone's race.

International marketing and market segmentation studies concerning geodemographics and psychographic or lifestyle data about the targeted segments or consumer groups concentrate on attitude and usage data. They generally do not focus on the challenges of 'race'. So much of what we consume is international in one way or another, as grown in Africa, made in Indonesia, mass produced in China and used in similar ways from the industrialized Western countries to newly developing economies. For example, teas and coffees from PG Tips, toothpaste and detergents from Proctor and Gamble, Nike and Reebok clothing and shoes are sold to markets all over the world.

Case study

Such examples of marketing studies have contributed to a huge case load, as published by many academic writers and institutions. A case study about an event, an activity or individuals builds a scenario with contrasting individual perspectives and managerial implications. Qualitative research contributes to case studies by finding out detailed and intimate information about people using multiple perspectives to build up a picture of individuals and their contributions to a particular situation.

The case study is a theoretical or simulated way of presenting information to others by telling an account, a narrative or story involving various people and their roles. Creswell (1998, p. 61) explained case research as an 'exploration of a 'bounded system' or a case (or multiple cases) over time through detailed, in-depth data collection involving multiple sources of information rich in context'. In marketing teaching and research the case study has a specific role for the instructor of the case and the students set to work on the problems of the case. It is the educational value of teaching the case study that keeps a research study alive for years to come.

Validity and reliability

Confusion about what is validity and reliability and the interchangeability of these terms in popular use usually results from misunderstandings over how to justify the small sample sizes and choices of method. In qualitative research it is important to recognize that there is 'no one size to fit all'. Take for example the thick descriptions envisaged by ethnographers who craft their own reports from verbatim accounts of their data or grounded theorists who use selective criteria for their coding in field research. The bases for inductive reasoning and making judgements are based on observations and past experiences that involve statements which have different levels of validity. It is important to distinguish between prejudicial and objective statements while the latter are more acceptable if they are based on many observations and supported by general opinion from other researchers and experts in the field, a process of consultative validity. Validity of results in marketing describes how the information and recommendations from qualitative studies are considered to be defensible or logically sound and are of use to the clients paying for the studies about their markets. Validity is a truth or belief. While Table 9.1 is not intended to show all the different types of validity it nevertheless represents common types of validity, found in qualitative research.

When qualitative studies use small samples, as in marketing, it can be hard sometimes to justify the reliability of the researches undertaken. So long as there is some relationship to one or more types of validity and, provided that the processes of research and results can be extrapolated to other groups, then reliability can be justified.

Reliability presupposes that the particular theoretical approach to inform a given method has taken place and that the findings uncovered by such a method can be duplicated if the study were repeated with other groups. In doctoral research 'the contribution to knowledge' is ingrained in the expectation that there will be some originality in the work. This could be new theories, new methods or new findings. In general, most research studies tend to add a little to existing knowledge rather than the big breakthroughs in innovations. Examiners of the doctoral work need to see whether the work stands up to scrutiny if applied in more than one study. Reliability adds consistency of approach with an external dimension, whether or not a researcher 's study is revisited by the same researcher or other external researchers assigning the same principles or categories and getting similar or fairly similar types of results. Of course, one has to bear in mind that 'revisions' are a normal part and parcel of research work in adapting to change.

Triangulation

The origin of triangulation is a mathematical concept in measuring elements to determine a network of triangles or trigonometric operation to discover a position from two fixed points, a known distance apart. In qualitative research *triangulation* involves a combination of finding out the data to validate a conclusion, by combining for example asking industry experts with direct questioning of users and applying projective techniques. Sequential triangulation reflects the strong links between qualitative and quantitative research.

Table 9.1   Validity types

(a) Theoretical validity, where research procedures are justified from established theoretical perspectives or where original work has led to new theories being established.

(b) Instrumental validity, when the procedural method generated matches with the data generated.

(c) Consultative validity, when others knowledgeable in the field are consulted and have given their feedback in terms of validating what is done.

(d) Internal validity where there is coherence in the fit between data and results.

(e) External validity, where the results produced match the kinds of information accepted by others.

Source: Adapted from Sykes in Wright and Crimp (2000).

For example, in the pharmaceutical industry both types of researches are necessary before a new drug is marketed. So a pharmaceutical company would conduct field trials with doctors, nurses and patients to gather observations and measurements in order to determine whether the intervention of the drug for a particular treatment is justifiable or not. Given this context the application of triangulation becomes another form of validating the credibility of both qualitative and quantitative studies.

In qualitative research the word *triangulation* takes on a separate meaning from the mathematical one, to refer to a combination of several methods, such as observation and interviews in researching the same phenomenon. It is also another way of proving reliability. For example, in marketing studies multiple points of view can be gathered about a particular type of marketing theory, method, product or service concept. A simplified version would be to ask three observers selected for their different types of expertise or background about a particular phenomenon to determine how far their three statements coalesce. In revisiting this at a later stage, the judgement about reliability would be whether this position would still hold? The degree of agreement can then be assessed. In marketing studies determining the extent of competition and market risk can be difficult. The resultant conclusion of this process becomes a compromise in using multiple frames of reference sourced from expert views, consumer responses and backed up by secondary data sources. The skill of the qualitative researcher in using triangulation is in balancing multiple perspectives in the research design and multiple realities from the research data, thereby reducing the risks of avoiding biases and prejudices.

Differences in research traditions: qualitative and quantitative approaches

The variety of qualitative approaches, as discussed in the previous section, remains in stark contrast to quantitative research. The theoretical paradigm of positivism is a label generally applied to quantitative research. The theoretical stance of *Positivism*, postulated by Auguste Comte in 1856, stated that the only authentic knowledge is scientific knowledge, which comes from positive affirmation of theories tested through strict scientific methods of investigation. This is a view propounded by technocrats and others in scientific and mathematical circles, who regard scientific progress as the means of gathering knowledge applicable to standing up to the rigours of validity and reliability in research design and outcomes.

The structured approach of closed-ended questioning and multiple numbers of questions allows quantitative researchers to send questionnaires via the post, telephone and computer to hundreds and thousands of people simultaneously in order to conduct large-scale surveys. The quantitative research approach has the comfort of numbers giving the advantage of reliability in producing statistical evidence for such surveys. The biggest examples of such surveys are by national governments conducting censuses to help their planning and forecasting. International agencies collect information on matters of global concern, such as on world health and environmental issues in order to mobilize support from world leaders and the public. The data gathered are subjected to mathematical analysis and modelling to explain national and global phenomena by showing their key constructs, their inter-relationships and their relative strengths within these inter-relationships. So decisions can be based on statistically proven facts with known margins of error.

Critics of qualitative research point to the problem of replicating studies, given the labour intensive nature of qualitative enquiry and therefore the relatively small sample sizes involved, in comparison to quantitative work. However, there remain weaknesses in the quantitative approach when questions and answers are limited to tight designs and controlled by predetermined constructs. Quantitative research has been criticized for 'scraping the surface of peoples' attitudes and feelings'. The complexity of the human soul is 'lost' through the counting of numbers, giving rise to the failure to follow unexpected clues or to research a topic in greater detail through deeper probing and understanding of respondents' motivations and behaviour during a research investigation. Our mental faculties allow us to use our five senses of hearing, sight, smell, taste, touch and what those which 'sense' the paranormal might think of, as our sixth sense. Respondents differ in how they feel or not feel concerning issues, what they like or dislike about data presented to them and whether they can treat researchers with rudeness or charm. So many factors and influences affect people in their everyday lives that when qualitative researchers set out to understand the complexities surrounding the underlying causes of behaviour, qualitative enquiry in such cases, may be more appropriate than quantitative research methods.

It makes sense to utilize both the qualitative and quantitative approaches to solve marketing or social problems. Both have strengths in their inductive and deductive approaches and when used together can work well in reducing risks and complementing each other's strengths. Academic institutions and large marketing firms accommodate both. Qualitative exploratory research is commonly used as a precursor to conducting expensive quantitative surveys, helping to get the right questions asked. Broadly, three types of sequential triangulation from qualitative to quantitative based upon qualitatively derived measures, interventions and relationships enables managers to have three types of valid bases upon which to fine tune their go/no go decisions in marketing. The final decisions that client managers take are inevitably qualitative.

Using computers in qualitative research

Using computers has helped to narrow the division between qualitative and quantitative approaches. The computer is a great equalizer. It is inanimate and yet both parties can point to their software use to legitimize the procedures in analysing data. The manual processes of content analysis of texts transferred to the setting of the computer with the added sophistication of coding and structure, the speed of multiple data entries and linking of data have revolutionized the ways in which qualitative researchers can now work. Larger numbers of interviews and data can be added, coded, categorized, stored and revisited. It is the case now that computers with higher specifications, that is faster speed of processor and greater capacities of hard drive and memory, are cheaper relative to 5 years ago so that more people can afford to turn to computers for qualitative data analysis.

Since the early 1980s the popularly known CAQDAS (Computer Assisted Qualitative Data AnalysiS) has been used in social research (Seidel and Clark, 1984). Although in the market research industry CAQDAS was reportedly rarely used (Nancarrow *et al*, 1996), what a difference 10 years make in computing life. There is now a variety of institutions and agencies which run introductory,

intermediate and advanced courses, such as those run by the CAQDAS Networking Project at Surrey University (http://caqdas.soc.surrey.ac.uk) for: ATLAS.ti, NVivo, Qualrus and MAXqda. For clear and step by step explanations about CAQDAS, see Searle's work on 'Using computers to analyse qualitative data' (Silverman, 2005). In practice, experienced users can view the applications of software in terms of a computer-assisted strategy to expedite and to generally enhance the qualitative research process. In this respect such a strategy is an additional way to add rigour to data handling and evaluation by qualitative researchers.

There are, of course, limitations with any method, including the use of the computer which distances the researcher from the data, prompting the researcher to follow an established pattern of behaviour instead of noticing the little nuances in the data itself. Some authors have pointed to the risks of using CAQDAS in creating too many codes (Roberts and Wilson, 2002) or confusing coding with analysis (Coffey *et al.*, 1996) or creating bias towards grounded theory (Lonkila, 1995). However, it can be said that the computer has its many uses, such as its renowned ability to handle data search and large data sets, hypotheses testing and generating information for clients of research in professional looking, presentational formats.

Not all researchers use computers though. In the market research industry CAQDAS packages have been reportedly rarely used (Nancarrow *et al.*, 1996; Ereuat *et al.*, 2002). Clients often want quick results for their money and turnaround time for qualitative studies in markets can be very short. If computer coding cannot take place, someone has to do the laborious work of inputting data and when speed is of the essence, then the tried and trusted way of transcribing data is used. If even this method is not fast enough or too expensive there are other methods such as videoing or tape recording. A focus group discussion in a room that has a one-way mirror system, where the market researcher and the client can view the proceedings without the members of the focus group being able to see them, is a quick and efficient method to get fast turnaround of results. For small qualitative research agencies without many resources and for individual researchers who wish to spend more time in the field taking and analyzing notes the computer is not a favoured solution.

From the marketing perspective the view of the practitioner is aptly put by Goodyear (2000, p. 374–375) who sees the focus of qualitative researchers as representing the consumer and his or her world 'as accurately as possible for deci-sion-makers in marketing or social policy'. The job of the qualitative researcher is 'to act as an interpreter between the consumer and the client'. For example, by interacting and talking with the consumer the researcher is able to make detailed and at times more intimate discoveries about the consumer. The researcher interprets these in a manner suitable for answering the client's market-ing questions. As Goodyear stated, within the world of advertising this is colloquially known as 'bringing the consumer into the agency'. Here the particular value of qualitative research is to add value to creative development in advertising or in general to developing marketing communications. This is because by understanding the specifics of consumer likes and dislikes about brands, adver-tising, companies, media and film celebrities, etc., suppliers gain knowledge about the general mar-keting environments in which consumers spend their money. Intricate demands are placed on researchers to be good at writing and communicat-ing, to be able to disseminate findings and to have strategies in place to make recommendations.

Many companies, particularly larger ones, through their researches and interactions with their consumers and their business customers already have big resources of information to draw upon, especially when supplemented with updated field research or secondary data. In this situation they do not need to reinvent the wheel. In these departments qualitative researchers work within the remits of their organization's resources and parameters, such as gathering and evaluating feedback from consumers, retailers and distribu-tors about new product launches.

The global nature of the marketing industry is seen by the American Marketing Association as incorporating the *business perspective* with its emphasis on strategy and organization and the *consumer perspective* with focus on consumer needs Imaginative use of qualitative enquiry extends to getting people to imagine what they would do given past, present and future scenarios.

As an example, researchers employed by busi-nesses can ask consumers to imagine the condi-tions under which they would buy the revamped brands that were old brand leaders three and four decades ago.

Take for example 'Prell' shampoo, 'Smash' potato mash, the fashion label 'Biba' and the 'Commodore' computer logo, now adorning MP3 players. These brands have been revived by their companies in connection with other new products.

Individual interviews and focus group dis-cussions with consumers are the qualitative mar-keters' tried and tested means of elucidating information about consumer habits and prefer-ences. These can be seen with regard to asking questions about current shoppers' intentions con-cerning their purchases and use of goods and services, or in contributing ideas for new product development and new marketing promotions.

Data collection methods

Unlike quantitative research which collects data for statistical analysis, the data gathered in quali-tative research ranges from the unstructured to the semi-structured kind. In the unstructured form the qualitative research approach can rely on innumerable tangible and intangible forms of self-expression by respondents. For example, qualitative researchers can get respondents to see, smell and touch tangible artefacts or other physical objects and pictures in order to let the respondents describe how they feel about them. Or they can challenge the respondents to imagine in an intangible way what it feels like to be in a particular situation or to lose a favourite brand. Both forms of enquiry are used to allow respon-dents to describe their feelings and emotions. To capture these moments researchers often rely on one or more of note taking, tape recording, cam-era surveillance and the computer to capture the data. Such data include similarities and peculiar-ities of respondents' facial expressions, behaviour and their verbal answers. The semi-structured kind normally involves a questionnaire as the research instrument where respondents are asked to tick boxes for their preferences and to rate or rank a product, service or corporate entity, usu-ally in terms of whether the respondents think favourably or not favourably towards these. It gives flexibility where numbers are required for coding either manually or electronically by quali-tative software. The semi-structured question-naire has spaces for comments with each main question where respondents are encouraged not only to give factual answers, but also to dig deeper into their consciousness and to project their feelings. For example, marketing managers when interviewed could be asked about their marketing decisions and the impact they have had on others involved, such as competitors, dis-tributors and consumers.

Table 9.2 Commissioned research from client sectors	
Food and non-alcoholic drinks	Government and public bodies
Media	Household products
Public services and utilities	Alcoholic drinks
Financial services	Travel and tourism
Pharmaceutical companies	Advertising agencies
Health and beauty	Household durables and hardware
Vehicles	Tobacco
Business and industrial retailers	Other direct clients for particular researches
	Other, mainly sub-contracted fieldwork

Source: Adapted from Wright and Crimp (2000).

Qualitative research can be undertaken to check that the appropriate questions are asked through an initial exploration of the market to product launch into a new market. When marketing managers are seeking answers to marketing problems and investigating opportunities the qualitative approach has much to contribute. Mistakes are costly and there are not only financial risks inherent in new developments of products and services. There is also the risk of market share loss in alienating consumers, as Coca Cola found in the 1980s with its unpopular variation of its long established recipe for its product and in the 1990s when its new range of carbonated water was introduced into the market.

Test decisions for new product and service introductions are informed from qualitative feedback of users and experts in many markets investigated, see Table 9.2.

The flexibility of qualitative research with its small samples means that observing and asking questions of respondents can take place anywhere on a one-to-one or small group basis. A typical small focus group can be around 6–10 or 8–12 individuals depending on the extent of the topic and researcher preferences. The study can take place anywhere by interviewing respondents in their homes, on the street in shopping malls and in public places, including hiring halls to get respondents to try out or test new products. They can take place in business premises where researchers and their client managers can observe respondents' behaviour and interactions through specially adapted viewing facilities for studying respondents. Researchers can conduct mystery shopping where they visit stores to observe behaviour without letting the subjects of their study

know their identities. Researchers and respondents' interactions for research can be conducted via Internet, audio and visual links using headsets and webcams.

Questionnaires types

In an industrial society the common prevalence of the use of the questionnaire method means that it is difficult for people to avoid participating in questionnaires about themselves, in applications for financial services products such as mortgages and insurance policies or to take part in direct marketing mailshots linked to sales promotions. Most people become familiar with the notion of questionnaires before they reach adulthood, having disclosed information on themselves in applications for example, to study at educational establishments or membership of sports and travel clubs.

Consequently, there are many questionnaires put forth by organizations and individuals which vary between two basic types. These take the form of being fully structured with closed questions at one extreme to being completely unstructured with open-ended questions at the other extreme. A compromise is the semi-structured questionnaire which incorporates a mix of the two.

Unstructured questionnaire: most of the questions are open ended. The interviewer is free to change the order of asking questions and to explain them. The questionnaire may take the form of a checklist for discussion. The unstructured questionnaire is used in 'depth' interviews, group discussions and in non-domestic surveys. The interview

Table 9.3 Stimulus material

Concept boards: single boards showing visual or written ideas for a product, pack or advertising.

Storyboards: with key frames shown as in comic strips and commercials.

Animatics: where key frames are drawn and filmed with sound tracks added.

Admatics: where animatics have their graphic images generated by the computer so that the finished version resembles a commercial.

Photomatics: where animation for photographs is used instead of drawing key frames, to give a more realistic appearance.

can be respondent-led, particularly if the interview is with an expert in the field so that the observations and expertise of the respondent can be taken account of.

Semi-structured questionnaire: this usually constitutes a mixture of closed or fixed response questions, quick response ranking or rating scales for measuring attitudes, organizational and product attitudes and open-ended questions or spaces for respondents to fill in their comments. Semi-structured questionnaires are useful in enabling the interviewer to 'stage-manage' the interview by making sure that all questions are covered with room for the interviewee or respondent to comment on the specific questions already asked.

Stimulus materials

Stimulus materials are used as aids in the data collection process. Various types of stimulus materials are used in marketing to prompt and to test respondents, whether in a group discussion or an extended face-to-face interview. The choice of material, including degree of finish, demands professional judgement based on experience and training in the behavioural sciences. Examples of stimulus materials are given in Table 9.3.

Pushing boundaries in marketing

In the UK local government authorities and the central government including their agencies, for example Warwickshire's youth forums and Tony Blair 's government during the last 11 years, have used both quantitative and qualitative research,

to find out public opinions on a broad range of government provisions and issues of widespread concern. For example, the recent British Crime Survey reported on the UK news media in January 2007 was carried out by the British Market Research Bureau (BMRB) for the Home Office. The participants were chosen by random sampling with questioning undertaken in their homes at their convenience. The interview using the questionnaire was activated on the computer and the results collected for quantitative analyses. Feedback to the public included leaflets and news reports showing responses of people in percentage terms to questions. Government departments and their agencies also have qualitative individual and focus group information to complement their data collection.

Qualitative research processes are continually evolving in uncovering and interpreting meanings behind people's thoughts, behaviours and motivations either through non-participant study or via participant interactions with the people they are studying or by a mix of both. It lends itself to the analyses of attitudes, lifestyles and people's preferences for what they purchase and consume. The three most common data collection methods are observations, personal in-depth interviews and group discussions. Lees and Broderick (2007) pointed to the power of modern technology when they showed the importance of eye tracking technologies to observation research.

With the advent of the Internet, e-mail and website provisions data collection methods have extended to other forms of enquiry, such as comparisons of offline and online buying behaviour, online focus group interviewing and gathering feedback from Internet chat rooms and individual 'blogs' containing personal statements linked to the web. See examples in Table 9.4. The forcefulness

Table 9.4   Examples of practitioner contributions from the MRS Conference 2006
A paper by Simon Chadwick (Cambiar LLC) and Ed Keller, co-author of 'The Influentials', on 'Is WOM just a Buzz?' examined how WOM works. The authors had access to a three million strong Internet panel that had been very aptly recruited virally – member get member … showing the power of viral marketing.
Paul Marsden of Enterprise LSE, 'Measuring the Success of Word of Mouth' suggests that market research can actually create WOM by listening to, involving and engaging customers driving business performance by turning respondents into WOM advocates.
Blogs are 'demystified' by Carmen Aitken of IPSOS Mori and Will Corry of The Marketing Blog where many consumers now rely on Blogs for accurate information and exchange of product/service experiences and therefore marketers need to consider them as part of the communication mix. There can undoubtedly be an anti-big business element to these Blogs and the speakers will address the issue of online detractors and critics as well as suggesting how to combine a website with a Blog that will produce a creative interaction with consumers … with an expert briefing from Simon Andrews (Big Picture) on 'Knowing your Blogs from your Pods'.
A training workshop on The Art and Science of Webnography led by Anjali Puri (AC Neilsen ORG-MARG, India) concerns the web as a social forum, webnography being a virtual ethnography … as qualitative research moves increasingly towards 'natural' contexts – observation over interrogation, ethnography over focus groups, then insights culled from everyday conversations on the web have even greater value.

Source: Based on Nancarrow, C. (2006).

of word of mouth (WOM) effects, blogging and webnography are provided in thought provoking papers and workshops from practitioners at the MRS Annual Conference in the UK in July 2006. Its theme, 'Connections', was connecting business or policy, people and ideas, and to strengthen links between the research industry's various stakeholders.

Today's generation of young children and teenagers are exposed to the Internet revolution and consequently are targets for more qualitative research. In the education sector both primary and secondary school children are introduced to a connected world where computers, mobile phones and handheld video and voice sets are connected for downloading music, games, films and Internet content. This provides a multi-media landscape where increasingly 'multi-dimensional entertainment experiences' are introduced by suppliers looking to maximize their profits in selling such technological products and downloadable contents. In the public domain the qualitative implications of the success of YouTube, an Internet showcase for musical talent and other performing arts, has been discussed on the UK television channel (Channel 4, 2007).

Conclusion

Qualitative research has much to contribute as the discussion of the theoretical traditions and methods have shown. While there are differences in approaches between the various disciplines of the social sciences, it can be said that there is also much common ground between them. This is in terms of the importance placed on 'understanding' the respondent and the individual consumer and 'interpretation of his or her actions' in order to 'inform' an aspect of social policy and market need. The use of the Internet and computer software has helped to create new opportunities for generating and analysing data.

There are risks for organizations in providing the social and marketing infrastructures to 'grow' services or brands. There are also potentially great rewards to companies involved in managing and marketing them because of satisfying the needs of their constituencies. There is a complex web of cultural and market differences plus international regulation and competition faced by marketing companies. Researching the consumer domestically and internationally has fuelled the growth of the market research industry and the proliferation of brands by companies. The marketplace is constantly evolving with innovative firms pursuing new ways such as webnography in pushing boundaries. The power of qualitative research is that it is supported by the long tradition of social science research and the extensive body of knowledge about the study of people.

References

BBC Four (2007) Tales from the jungle, *Bronislaw Malinowski*, **22**, January, 9pm–10pm.

Bell, L. (2005) Industry talk, *Research*, January, 21–23.

Black, I. (2006) Viewpoint: the presentation of interpretivist research, *Qualitative Market Research – An International Journal*, 9(4), 319–324.

Borden, N. (1964) The concept of the marketing mix, *Journal of Advertising Research*, June, 2–7.

Byrne, M. (2001) Disseminating and presenting qualitative research findings, *AORN Journal*, **74** (5), 372.

Channel 4 (2007) Channel 4 News, including YouTube, **30**, January, 7.00pm–7.30pm.

Creswell, J. (1998) *Qualitative Inquiry And Research Design*, Sage Publications Inc., USA, p. 11.

Denzin, N. and Lincoln, Y. (2005) *The Sage Handbook of Qualitative Research*, Sage Publications Inc., USA, p. 4.

ESOMAR (1998) ESOMAR Annual Study on the Market Research Industry 1997, 1–4.

ESOMAR (2005) Annual report on turnover and spend in the market research industry, http://dev.prezenz.com/esomar/gmr2005/index.php

Goodyear, M. (2000) Qualitative Research, in Wright, L. T. and Crimp, M. (eds), *The Marketing Research Process*, FT Prentice Hall, UK, pp. 374–375, 379.

Gummesson, E. (2007) Access to reality: observations on observational methods (invited commentary), *Qualitative Market Research – An International Journal*, **10**(2), 130–134.

Holbrook, M. B. (1995) *Consumer Research: Introspective Essays on the Study of Consumption*, Sage Publications Inc., USA.

Lees, N. and Broderick, A. (2007) Guest editorial: the past, present and future of observational research in marketing, *Qualitative Market Research – An International Journal*, 10(1), 121–129.

Lonkila, M. (1995) Grounded Theory as an Emerging Paradigm for Computer-Assisted Qualitative Data Analysis, in Kelle, U. (ed.), *Computer-Aided Qualitative Data Analysis: Theory, Methods and Practice*, Sage Publications Ltd., London.

Mackenzie, Y. (2005) BBC man takes issue with TV research in India, *Research*, January, 8.

Mariampolski, H. (2001) *Qualitative Market Research*, Sage Publications Inc., USA, pp. 7–9.

Morse, J. (1997) *Completing a Qualitative Project*, Sage Publications Inc., USA, p. 121.

Nancarrow, C., Moskvin, A. and Shankar, A. (1996) Bridging the great divide – the transfer of techniques, *Marketing Intelligence and Planning*, **14** (6), 27–37.

Richards, L. and Morse, J. (2007) *User's Guide To Qualitative Methods*, Sage Publications Inc., USA, p. 12.

Roberts, K. A. and Wilson, R. W. (2002) ICT and the research process: issues around the compatibility of technology with qualitative data analysis, *Forum Qualitative Social Research*, **3** (2), available at: http://www.qualitative-research.net/fqs-texte/2-02/2-02robertswilson-e.htm

Schlackman, B. (1999) The history of UK qualitative research, according to Bill Schlackman, *The AQRP Directory and Handbook of Qualitative Research 1989–1999*, p. 16.

Seidel, J. and Clark, J. (1984) The ethnograph: a computer programme for the analysis of qualitative data, *Qualitative Sociology*, **7** (1 and 2), 110–125.

Silverman, D. (2005) *Doing Qualitative Research*, Sage Publications Ltd., UK.

Sykes, W. (2000) Different Types of Validity, in Wright, L. T. and Crimp, M. (eds), *The Marketing Research Process*, FT Prentice Hall, UK.

Tarran, B. (2004) Developing markets carry global MR turnover to almost $19 bn, *Research*, October, 6.

Wright, L. T. and Crimp, M. (2000), *The Marketing Research Process*, 5th ed, FT Prentice Hall.

Further reading

Qualitative Market Research – An International Journal, Emerald, UK, for regular issues on qualitative research.

CHAPTER 10

Quantitative methods in marketing

LUIZ MOUTINHO[1]

Introduction

Marketing was one of the last of the major functional areas of management activity to be entered by quantitative methods and techniques in a systematic way, and only in the last four decades or so was any significant progress achieved. This relative lag of quantitative methods progress in marketing was attributed to a number of factors:

1 *The complexity of marketing phenomena.* This is due to the fact that when stimuli are applied to the environment, the responses tend to be non-linear, to exhibit threshold effects (a minimum level of stimulus needs to be applied before response occurs), to have carry-over effects (e.g. response to this period of advertising will occur in future) and to decay with time in the absence of further stimulations.

2 *Interaction effects of marketing variables.* This means that the impact of a single controllable marketing variable is difficult to determine due to interactions of the variable with the environment and also with other marketing variables. Indeed, most of the variables in marketing are interdependent and interrelated.

3 *Measurement problems in marketing.* It is often difficult to measure directly the response of consumers to certain stimuli and therefore indirect techniques are often used. An example is the use of recall measures to ascertain the effectiveness of advertisements.

4 *Instability of marketing relationships.* The relationship between marketing responses and marketing decision variables tends to be unstable due to changes in taste, attitude, expectations and many others. These factors make continuous market measurements and revision of decisions crucial to marketing.

There are several ways in which quantitative methods can be used in marketing. One of these is through the classification of marketing into decision areas which confront the marketing manager and which include product development, pricing, physical distribution, sales force, advertising and consumer behaviour. However, it is thought to be more appropriate first to classify the techniques which are used in marketing and to fit in the situations where these models are used most frequently.

In this way, most of the models and techniques can be analysed. Their validity can be judged from their usage, how accurately they represent the problem environment, their predictive power and the consistency and realism of their assumptions.

In selecting an appropriate method of analysis, two major factors should be taken into consideration: first, whether the variables analysed are dependent or interdependent and, second, whether the input data are of a metric or non-metric form. Metric data are measured by interval or ratio

[1] The author would like to thank Professor Arthur Meidan, Emeritus Professor of Marketing, University of Sheffield, for his outstanding contribution to the previous editions of this chapter.

scales, while non-metric data are only ordinal scaled. The dependent variables are those which can be explained by other variables, while inter-dependent variables are those which cannot be explained solely by each other.

Marketing variables are usually interdependent. For example, a firm's objectives are usually interdependent with marketing mix variables; profits usually depend on sales; market share depends on sales; firms' growth depends on profits and sales and vice versa, etc. Also, firms' marketing mix variables, such as price, promotion, distribution and product are interdependent.

Since marketing research is very often a multivariate analysis involving either dependent or interdependent variables, the major groups of techniques that can be used are as shown in Figure 10.1.

1 *Multivariable methods*, so-called because the various techniques attempt to investigate the relationships and patterns of marketing decisions that emerge as a result of the interaction and interdependence among main variables at the same time.
2 *Regression, correlation and forecasting techniques* are methods that can be employed in inferring the relationships among a set of variables in marketing. 'Forecasting methods' are mainly applied in forecasting sales and market demand. Sales forecasting methods are a function of an aggregation of non-controllable environmental variables and marketing effort factors, which have to be taken into consideration.
3 *Simulation methods* are a group of techniques which are appropriate to use when the variables affecting the marketing situation (such as competition) require complex modelling and are not amenable to analytical solutions. The importance of the simulation technique in marketing is that it offers a form of laboratory experimentation by permitting the researcher to change selected individual variables in turn and holding all the others constant.
4 *Fuzzy sets* could be used for modelling consumer behaviour, marketing planning, new product testing, etc., by determining the rank and size of the possible outcomes.
5 *Artificial intelligence (AI) techniques* are relatively very recent tools for simulating human logic. There are two main models in this set of techniques: expert system – requiring user intervention to accommodate changes within the model; and neural network (NN) – less 'rigid' than expert system, facilitating 'retraining' (mainly via addition of new input and output data).

6 *Statistical decision theory or stochastic methods* represent stochastic or random responses of consumers, which allow a multitude of factors that might affect consumer behaviour to be included in the analysis. This means that market responses can be regarded as outcomes of some probabilistic process. Essentially, there are two main uses of these methods: to test structural hypotheses and to make conditional predictions.
7 *Deterministic operational research methods* are OR techniques looking for solutions in cases where there are many interdependent variables and the research is trying to optimize the situation. A classical example of such a situation in marketing is when a company producing various products (or parts) is selling them through two different channels which vary with respect to selling costs, typical order sizes, credit policies, profit margins, etc. Usually in such cases the company's major objective is to maximize total profits by establishing optimal sales target volumes and marketing mixes for the two channels (or customer segments) subject to the existing limiting constraints.
8 *Causal model* consists of two main analytical models for *testing* causal hypotheses (path analysis (PA) and LISREL). *PA* is used on those occasions when some of the variables are unobservable or have modest reliabilities. (This tool should not be confused with the critical path method (CPM), which is one of the networking programming models discussed below.) LISREL is of paramount importance in marketing situations, when we want to investigate both measurement and cause, that is, structural components, of a system (e.g. in a consumer behaviour study).
9 *Hybrid models* are methods that combine deterministic and probabilistic (stochastic) properties (e.g. dynamic programming, heuristic programming and stock control). These models are particularly useful in handling distribution problems, as explained below.
10 *Networking programming models* are generally used for planning, scheduling and controlling complex projects. There are two fundamental analytical techniques: the CPM, and the performance evaluation and review technique (PERT). The differences between the two are, first, that the PERT acknowledges uncertainty in the times to complete the activities, while the CPM does not. Second, the PERT restricts its attention to the time variable while the CPM includes time–cost trade-offs. These two together are also called critical path analysis (CPA) techniques.

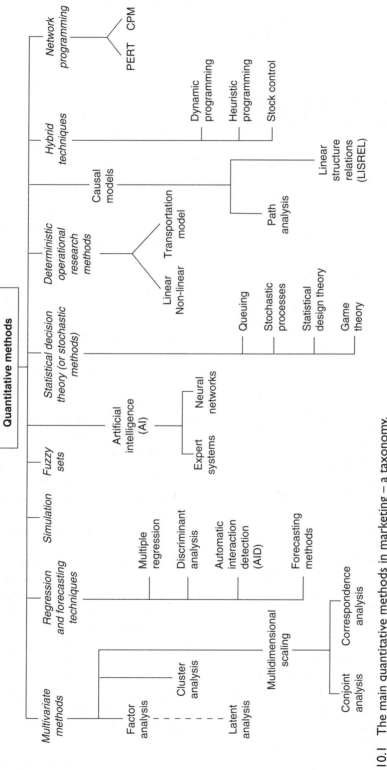

Figure 10.1 The main quantitative methods in marketing – a taxonomy.

The ten sets of methods above in no way exhaust the quantitative methods in marketing. The selection of techniques presented in this chapter is based either on their particular current relevance of handling many marketing problems or/and because of their potential in marketing research and analysis.

Multivariate methods

The multivariate methods in marketing are probably the predominant techniques of the last three decades, not only because of the wide variety of flexible techniques available in this category, but mainly because they answer the most pressing need of marketing research, which is to obtain the ability to analyse complex, often interrelated and interdependent data. There are six main multivariate sets of methods: factor analysis; latent analysis; cluster analysis; multidimensional scaling; conjoint analysis and correspondence analysis.

Factor analysis

Factor analysis (FA) is primarily a tool to reduce a large number of variables to a few interpretable constructs. The method is used for exploration and detection of patterns in the data with the view to obtaining data reduction, or summarization, which could be more amenable for reaching decisions and taking marketing management actions. The software for FA is readily available and is standard in any SPSS (Statistical Package for Social Science) package. The input data are collected from respondents and the main limitations are how many factors to extract and the labelling of the emerging factors. FA could be used for analysing consumer behaviour, market segmentation, product/service attributes, company images, etc.

Latent analysis

Latent structure analysis (LA) is a statistical technique somewhat related to FA, which can be used as a framework for investigating causal systems involving both manifest variables and latent factors having discrete components. LA shares the objective of FA, that is, first, to extract important factors and express relationships of variables with these factors and, second, to classify respondents into typologies.

The latent class model treats the manifest categorical variables as imperfect indicators of underlying traits, which are themselves inherently unobservable. The latent class model treats the observable (manifest) categorical variables as imperfect indicators of underlying traits, which are themselves inherently unobservable (latent). This technique is appropriate for the analysis of data with discrete components.

Essentially, LA attempts to 'explain' the observed association between the manifest variables by introducing one (or more) other variables. Thus, the basic motivation behind latent analysis is the belief that the observed association between two or more manifest categorical variables is due to the mixing of heterogeneous groups. In this sense, latent analysis can be viewed as a data-unmixing procedure. This assumption of conditional independence is directly analogous to the assumption in the factor-analytic model.

The main advantage of latent analysis is that it could be used for investigating causal systems involving latent variables. A very flexible computer program for maximum likelihood LA, called MLLSA, is available to marketing researchers. Latent class models have great potential and no doubt will be used more frequently in marketing investigations in the future.

One of the major limitations related to LA concerns the estimation problem, which previously made this class of models largely inaccessible to most marketing researchers. This problem was later solved by formulating latent class models in the same way as in the general framework of log-linear models. LA models have been used in segmentation research, consumer behaviour analysis, advertising research and market structure analysis.

One of the best papers in this field is by Dillon and Mulani (1989). A number of latent structure models have been developed (DeSarbo, 1993) for problems associated with traditional customer response modelling (e.g. for more regression, conjoint analysis, structural equation models, multidimensional scaling (MDS), limited dependent variables, etc.). Such latent structure models simultaneously estimate market segment membership and respective model coefficients by market segment, to optimize a common objective function.

Cluster analysis

Cluster analysis is a generic label applied to a set of techniques in order to identify 'similar' entities

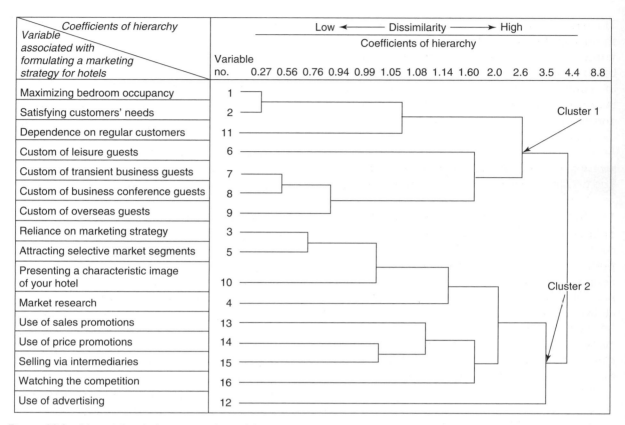

Coefficients of hierarchy / Variable associated with formulating a marketing strategy for hotels	Variable no.	Low ◄──── Dissimilarity ────► High Coefficients of hierarchy
		0.27 0.56 0.76 0.94 0.99 1.05 1.08 1.14 1.60 2.0 2.6 3.5 4.4 8.8
Maximizing bedroom occupancy	1	
Satisfying customers' needs	2	
Dependence on regular customers	11	
Custom of leisure guests	6	
Custom of transient business guests	7	
Custom of business conference guests	8	
Custom of overseas guests	9	
Reliance on marketing strategy	3	
Attracting selective market segments	5	
Presenting a characteristic image of your hotel	10	
Market research	4	
Use of sales promotions	13	
Use of price promotions	14	
Selling via intermediaries	15	
Watching the competition	16	
Use of advertising	12	

Figure 10.2   Hierarchical clustering of variables associated with a marketing strategy for hotels
Source: Adapted from Meidan (1983).

from the characteristics possessed by these entities. The clusters should have high homogeneity within clusters and high heterogeneity between clusters, and geometrically the points within a cluster should be close together, while different clusters should be far apart.

Cluster analysis is, in a sense, similar to FA and to MDS in that all three are used for reduced-space analysis. That is, all three methods could facilitate the presentation of the output data in a graphical two-dimensional format that is easier to comprehend and analyse. Cluster analysis is primarily used for segmentation and for decisions on marketing strategies towards different segments and markets (Saunders, 1994), or insituations which involve grouping products, brands, consumers, cities, distributors, etc. The main limitations of this technique are that there are no defensible procedures for testing the statistical significance of the emerging clusters and often various clustering methods yield differing results. There are several types of clustering procedures. In Figure 10.2 a hierarchical clustering of variables associated with a marketing strategy for hotels is presented (Meidan, 1983). The diagram presents the (level of) aggregation (or

clusters) of variables that are product (i.e. hotels) characteristics of a strategy, as defined by the suppliers (i.e. hotel managers). Cluster 2 strategy includes variables that indicate that hotels adopting this strategy are more 'aggressive' using, to a larger extent, marketing tools and techniques, while cluster 1 strategy is more 'passive'. Low coefficients of hierarchy (or low dissimilarity) indicate high relationships or high similarity. For example, variables 1 and 2 are highly correlated, that is, they aggregate early, at a coefficient of 0.27. In contrast, variable 12 (use of advertising) is highly dissimilar to other variables and associates with the remaining coefficients in cluster 2 only at the 3.5 level. A possible explanation of this could be that hotels adopting the marketing strategy indicated by cluster 2 use an alternative communication mix and/or other marketing tools (e.g. variables 13, 14, 15, 4, 5, 10, etc.).

Multidimensional scaling

MDS is a set of data analysis techniques that display the structure of distance-like data as a geometrical picture.

MDS has its origins in psychometrics, where it was proposed to help understand people's judgements of the similarity if members of a set of objects.

MDS pictures the structure of a set of objects from data that approximate the distances between pairs of the objects. The data are called similarities, dissimilarities, distances or proximities. We use the term *similarity* generically to refer to both similarities (where large numbers refer to great similarity) and to dissimilarities (where large numbers refer to great dissimilarity).

In addition to the traditional human similarity judgement, the data can be an 'objective' similarity measure or an index calculated from multivariate data. However, the data must always represent the degree of similarity of pairs of objects (or events).

Each object or event is represented by a point in a multidimensional space. The points are arranged in this space so that the distances between pairs of points have the strongest possible relation to the similarities among the pairs of objects. That is, two similar objects are represented by two points that are close together, and two dissimilar objects are represented by two points that are far apart. The space is usually a two- or three-dimensional Euclidean space, but may be non-Euclidean and may have more dimensions.

MDS is a generic term that includes many different specific types. These types can be classified according to whether the similarities data are qualitative (called non-metric MDS) or quantitative (metric MDS). The number of similarity matrices and the nature of the MDS model can also classify MDS types. This classification yields classical MDS (one matrix, unweighted model), replicated MDS (RMDS) (several matrices, weighted model).

MDS is a class of procedures for representing perceptions and preferences of respondents spatially by means of a visual display. Perceived or psychological relationships among stimuli are represented as geometric relationships among points in a multidimensional space. These geometric representations are often called special maps. The axes of the spatial map are assumed to denote the psychological bases or underlying dimensions respondents use to form perceptions and preferences of stimuli. For example, MDS has been used in marketing to identify the following:

1   The number and nature of dimensions consumers use to perceive different brands.
2   The positioning of brands on these dimensions.

3   The positioning of consumers' ideal brand on these dimensions.

Information provided by MDS has been used for a variety of marketing applications, including:

- *Image measurement.* Comparing the customers' and non-customers' perceptions of the firm with the firm's perception of itself.
- *Market segmentation.* Brands and consumers can be positioned in the same space and thus groups of consumers with relatively homogeneous perceptions can be identified.
- *New product development.* Gaps in a spatial map indicate potential opportunities for positioning new products. MDS can be used to evaluate new product concepts and existing brands on a test basis to determine how consumers perceive the new concepts. The proportion of preferences for each new product is one indicator of its success.
- *Assessing advertising effectiveness.* Spatial maps can be used to determine whether advertising has been successful in achieving the desired brand positioning.
- *Pricing analysis.* Spatial maps developed with and without pricing information can be compared to determine the impact of pricing.
- *Channel decisions.* Judgements on compatibility of brands with different retail outlets could lead to spatial maps useful for making channel decision.
- *Attitude scale construction.* MDS techniques can be used to develop the appropriate dimensionality and configuration of the attitude space.

The important statistics and terms associated with MDS include the following:

Similarly judgements. Similarity judgements are ratings on all possible pairs of brands or other stimuli in terms of their similarity using a Likert-type scale.

Preference rankings. Preference rankings are rank orderings of the brands or other stimuli from the most preferred to the least preferred. They are normally obtained from respondents.

Stress. Stress is a lock-of-fit measure; higher values of stress indicate poorer fits.

R-square. R-square is a squared correlation index that indicates the proportion of variance of the optimally scaled data that can be accounted for by the MDS procedure. This is a goodness-of-fit measure.

Spatial map. Perceived relationships among brands or other stimuli are represented as geometric relationships among points in a multidimensional space.

Coordinates. Coordinates indicate the positioning of a brand or a stimulus in a spatial map.

Unfolding. The representation of both brands and respondents as points in the same space.

MDS is a measurement technique concerned mainly with the representation of relationship, differences, dissimilarities (or similarities), substitutability, interaction, etc. among behavioural data such as perceptions, preferences and attitudes. The input data on various objects (variables) which are to be analysed are collected from the subjects (respondents) by a number of direct or indirect questions. The questions can be either of Likert type (i.e. a five-point scale questionnaire indicating the level of agreement or disagreement to statements) or, alternatively, asking each of the respondents to rank the variables to be investigated (e.g. products, brands, characteristics, etc.). When the number of variables investigated is n, the number of all possible relationships among these variables (along k dimensions) is $n(n-1)/2$. In order to visualize and quantify the overall attitudinal data of these respondents with regard to the n variables investigated along (k) dimensions, the data should be inputted onto one of the available software packages.

The solution (output) of the MS computer program is of a metric nature, consisting of a geometric configuration, usually in two or three dimensions. The distances between the variables (objects) and/or respondents (subjects) investigated, which are presented as points in the configuration, represent the (dis) similarity, substitutability, relationship, etc. MDS is used particularly in its non-metric version, non-metric multidimensional scaling (NMS). The advantage of NMS in relation to, say, factor or cluster analyses is the ability to see the entire structure of variables together and to obtain metric output from attitudinal (non-metric) input data. In addition, NMS enables easy comprehension of the results, since the decision maker can visualize and assess the relationships among the variables.

MDS and NMS, in particular, have been successfully applied in investigating various marketing problems (e.g. market research, sales and market share, market segmentation, determination of marketing mix, consumer buyer behaviour, brand positioning, branch preference, export marketing, etc.). An introduction to MDS is presented by Diamantopoulos and Schlegelmilch (1997). Discussion on when to use NMS techniques in marketing research is offered by Coates *et al.* (1994).

Classical MDS

The identifying aspect of classical MDS (CMDS) is that there is only one similarity matrix.

Metric CMDS. The first major CMDS proposal was metric (i.e. the similarities had to be quantitative). Torgerson's development required the data to be at the ratio level of measurement, although this was soon generalized to the interval level. While the data could contain random error, this early type of MDS required that the data be dissimilarities (not similarities), complete (no missing values) and symmetric (the dissimilarity of objects I and J had to equal that of objects J and I). These CMDS proposals also required the distance model to be Euclidean.

For metric CMDS the distances D are determined so that they are as much like the dissimilarities S as possible.

E is a matrix of errors (residuals) that in the least-squares optimization situation, we wish to minimize. Since the distances D are a function of the coordinates X, the goal of CMDS is to calculate the coordinates X so that the sum of squares of E is minimized, subject to suitable normalization of X.

Non-metric CMDS. The second major CMDS proposal was non-metric. That is, the data could be at the ordinal level of measurement. In addition, the data S could either be complete or incomplete; symmetric or asymmetric and similarities or dissimilarities.

These non-metric CMDS proposals extend the distance model to the Minkowski case and generalized the relation between similarities and distances. They enable defining

$$m\{S\} = D + E,$$

Where $m\{S\}$ is read 'a monotonic transformation of the similarities'. If S is actually dissimilarities then $m\{S\}$ preserves order, whereas if S is similarities, it reverses order. Thus, for non-metric CMDS, we need to solve for the monotonic (order-preserving) transformation $m\{S\}$ and the coordinates X. which together minimize the sum of squares of the errors E (after normalization of X). The non-metric optimization represents a much more difficult problem to solve than the metric problem and is an important breakthrough in MDS.

Replicated MDS

The next major development, RDMS, permitted the analysis of several matrices of similarity data simultaneously. There are m matrices S, one for each subject k, $k = 1, \ldots, m$.

RDMS uses the same distance models as CDMS, but uses them to describe several similarity matrices rather than one. The data may be similarities or dissimilarities and may be at the ratio or interval levels, just as in metric CDMS.

Weighted MDS

The next major MDS development, *weighted MDS* (WMDS), generalized the distance model so that several similarity matrices S_k could be assumed to differ from each other in systematically non-linear or non-monotonic ways. Whereas RMDS only accounts for individual differences in response bias, WMDS incorporates a model to account for individual differences in the fundamental perceptual or cognitive processes that generate the responses. For this reason, WMDS is often called *individual differences scaling* (INDSCAL) and is often regarded as the second major breakthrough in MDS.

WMDS invokes the following definition of weighted Euclidean distance:

$$d_{ij} = \left[\sum_a w_{ka}(x_{ia} - x_{ja})^2 \right]^{1/2}$$

Which, in matrix algebra is

$$d_{ij} = [(x_i - x_j) W_k (x_i - x_j)']^{1/2}$$

Where W_k is a $r \times r$ diagonal matrix. The diagonal values, which must not be negative, are weights for subject k on each of the r dimensions.

WMDS is appropriate for the same type of data as RMDS. However, RMDS generates a single distance matrix D, while WMDS generates m unique distance matrices D_k, one for each data matrix S_k.

While WMDS incorporates the RMDS notion of individual differences in response bias, the important aspect of WMDS is that it provides specific parameters for individual variation in cognitive or perceptual processes. These parameters are the weights. The weights are interpreted as the importance, relevance or salience of each dimension to each individual, a small weight means the dimension is unimportant.

MDS can be considered to be an alternative to FA. In general, the goal of the analysis is to detect meaningful underlying dimensions that allow the researcher to explain observed similarities or dissimilarities (distances) between the investigated objects. In FA, the similarities between objects (e.g. variables) are expressed in the correlation matrix. With MDS one may analyse any kind of similarity or dissimilarity matrix, in addition to correlation matrices.

Logic of MDS

In general, MDS attempts to arrange 'objects' in a space with a particular number of dimensions so as to reproduce the observed distances. As a result, we can 'explain' the distances in terms of underlying dimensions.

Orientation of axes. As in FA, the actual orientation of axes in the final solution is arbitrary. Thus, the final orientation of axes in the place or space is mostly the result of a subjective decision by the researcher, who will choose an orientation that can be most easily explained.

Measures of goodness-of-fit: Stress. The most common measure that is used to evaluate how well (or poorly) a particular configuration reproduces the observed distance matrix is the stress measure. The raw stress value *Phi* of a configuration is defined by:

$$Phi = \sum {}_{[d_{ij} - f(\delta_{ij})]^2}$$

In this formula, d_{ij} stands for the reproduced distances, given the respective number of dimensions, and δ_{ij} (*delta$_{ij}$*) stands for the input data (i.e. observed distances). The expression $f(\delta_{ij})$ indicates a *non-metric*, monotone transformation of the observed input data (distances). Thus, it will attempt to reproduce the general rank-ordering of distances between the objects in the analysis.

There are several similar related measures that are commonly used; however, most of them amount to the computation of the sum of squared deviations of observed distances (or some monotone transformation of those distances) from the reproduced distances. Thus, the smaller the stress value, the better is the fit of the reproduced distance matrix to the observed distance matrix.

Shepard diagram. One can plot the reproduced distances for a particular number of dimensions against the observed input data (distances). This scatterplot is referred to as a *Shepard* diagram. This plot shows the reproduced distances plotted on the vertical (Y) axis versus the original similarities plotted on the horizontal (X) axis (hence, the

Table 10.1 Main multivariate methods and their marketing applications

Method	Based on	Marketing applications	Main advantages	Main limitations
Factor analysis	Identification of relationships among variables and establishing the 'weight' (factor loadings) for these variables	Determine corporate marketing images, consumer behaviour and attitudes	Data reduction, identification of the main constructs (factors that underline the data characteristics)	Applicable only to interval-scaled data
Latent analysis	Investigation of both manifest and latent factors by estimating these latent parameters	Segmentation research, market structure analysis (Dillon and Mulani, 1989)	Could be used for investigating causal systems involving latent variables	Difficulties in estimating the latent variables
Cluster analysis	Developing similarity or dissimilarity measures (coefficients), or distance measures, to establish clusters association	Primarily for segmentation studies and strategy (Saunders, 1994)	Enables classification of brands, products, customers, distributors, etc.	Different clustering methods could generate different clusters
Multidimensional scaling	Calculating the proximity (or, alternatively, of dominance) among attributes/variables and respondents	Market research, market share analysis (Coates et al., 1994), market segmentation, brand positioning, etc.	Presents the entire structure of variables, making it easier to visualize and interpret relationship/similarities among data	Different software packages required for different types of data input
Conjoint analysis	Measurement of psychological judgements by measuring the joint effect of two or more independent variables on the ordering of a dependent variable	Consumer research (Vriens, 1994), advertising evaluations (Stanton and Reese, 1983)	Enables calculation of preferences. Suitable for product design and attitude measurement	Measures first utility rather than behaviour
Correspondence analysis	Graphical technique for representing multidimensional tables. For procedures, see Figure 9.3	Selling functions in bank branches (Meidan and Lim, 1993), market segments, track brand images	Can be used for analysing binary, discrete and/or continuous data. Facilitates both within- and between-set squared distance comparison. Fast, easy to interpret	Limited applications in marketing because of lack of suitable software

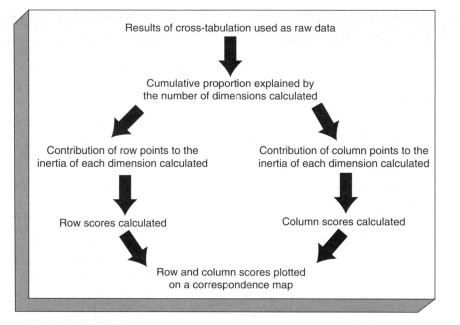

Figure 10.3 Procedural steps for CA

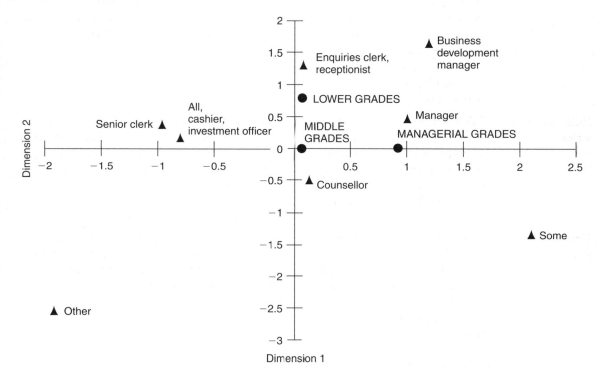

Figure 10.4 External perceptions of the different grade levels on the issue of identifying customer needs
Source: Adapted from Meidan and Lim (1993).

relationships, attitude measurement, promotional congruence testing, the study of functional versus symbolic product characteristics, and to rank a hypothetical product against existing competitors already in the market and suggest modifications to existing products which would help to strengthen a product's performance.

The limitations of conjoint analysis are quite clear when, for example, we are using this technique to predict trial rate. These include:

1 Utility measurement rather than actual purchase behaviour is used as the predictor.
2 The configuration of elements used in the concepts may not be complete.

3   In the case of a new product that differs substantially from its principal competitors, the same elements cannot be used for aggregating utilities.
4   The effects of promotion and distribution effort on competitive reaction are not considered.
5   Perceptions from a concept statement and those from the actual product may differ.
6   New products may take several years to reach the market, during which time customer preferences and competitive products may have undergone substantial changes. Conjoint analysis has been applied widely on consumer research (Vriens, 1994), in advertising evaluation (Stanton and Reese, 1983) and other commercial uses (Cattin and Wittink, 1982).

Correspondence analysis

Correspondence analysis (CA) is a visual or graphical technique for representing multidimensional tables. It can often be impossible to identify any relationships in a table and very difficult to account for what is happening. CA unravels the table and presents data in an easy-to-understand chart. One approach for generating maps uses cross-classification data (e.g. brands rated as having or not having a set of attributes) as a basis (Hoffman and Franke, 1986). In this approach both brands and attributes are simultaneously portrayed in a single space. This technique is particularly useful to identify market segments, track brand image, position a product against its competition, and determine who non-respondents in a survey most closely resemble. CA shows the relationships between rows and columns of a correspondence or a cross-tabulation table. This method can be used for analysing binary, discrete or/and continuous data. CA belongs to the family of MDS techniques and could be employed to scale a matrix of non-negative data to represent points (described by rows or columns) in a lower dimensional space. It facilitates both within- and between-set squared distance comparisons (Carroll *et al.*, 1986), and the results can be represented graphically and used as such in marketing investigations.

CA and management

There are several reasons why a management researcher could be attracted to CA:

- CA is an appropriate method for the analysis of categorical data; it avoids the unease of using traditional multivariate techniques such as FA on such data.
- It produces a visual representation of the relationships between the row categories and the column categories in the same space.
- The technique is versatile: it can be used with frequency data, with percentages, with data in the form of ratings and with heterogeneous datasets.
- CA can suggest unexpected dimensions and relationships in the tradition of exploratory data analysis even if, in this post-empiricist age, no-one expects 'theory' to emerge automatically from the data.
- Although 'model-free' itself, the results of CA are often a useful preliminary to a more structured and traditional multivariate modelling of categorical data.

Figure 10.3 shows the different stages of CA. The results of a cross-tabulation are used as raw data in a CA. The specific mathematics involved in CA can be found in Greenacre (1984).

Figure 10.4 presents the output of a study that maps out how bank branch personnel in various roles see themselves (internal perceptions) and what are their colleagues' (external) perceptions with regard to the 27 selling bank branch functions identified (Meidan and Lim, 1993). The figure represents the output of a study where respondents were asked who they felt were mainly responsible for the selling function of 'Identifying customers' needs' in a bank. The responses of various function holders are indicated by the triangular signs on the map (e.g. counsellor, manager, business development officer, etc.). The respondents themselves were grouped into three categories indicated by the circles (e.g. lower grades (cashier, statements clerk), middle grades (counsellors, officers), managerial grades (branch managers, etc.)).

The interpretation of data output is fairly straightforward, although not all dimensions could be labelled. The closer two points are on the map, the closer the relationship. For example:

1   Lower grades tend to believe that the enquiries clerk and receptionist are mainly responsible for identifying customer needs.
2   Middle grades, however, are more inclined to see this as mainly the counsellor's responsibility. Some middle grades also tend to consider it the responsibility of cashiers, investment officers or everyone (all).
3   Managerial grades believe that this function is mainly their own responsibility. These beliefs of

various role players within the branch are, of course, of paramount importance, as it might lead to under-training for certain function(s) at grade levels, where customer contact is higher. Therefore, this kind of study could focus the training efforts and needs for specific selling functions and certain grade levels/roles.

The six multivariate methods described above are summarized in Table 10.1.

Partial correlation

Introduction

Whereas the product moment or simple correlation is a measure of association describing the linear association between two variables, a *partial correlation coefficient* measures the association between two variables after controlling for or adjusting for the effects of one or more additional variables. This statistic is used to answer the following questions:

- How strongly are sales related to advertising expenditures when the effect of price is controlled?
- Is there an association between market share and size of the sales force after adjusting for the effect of sales promotion?
- Are consumers' perceptions of quality related to their perceptions of prices when the effect of brand image is controlled?

Key features

As in these situations, suppose one wanted to calculate the association between X and Y after controlling for a third variable, Z. Conceptually, one would first remove the effect of Z from X. To do this, one would predict the values of X based on knowledge of Z by using the product moment correlation between X and Z, r_{xz}. The predicted value of X is then subtracted from the actual value of X. In a similar manner, the values of Y are adjusted to remove the effects of Z. The product moment correlation between the adjusted values of X and the adjusted values of Y is the partial correlation coefficient between X and Y, after controlling for the effect of Z, and is denoted by r_{xyz}. Statistically, because the simple correlation between two variables completely describes the linear relationship between them, the partial correlation coefficient can be calculated by knowledge of the

simple correlations alone, without using individual observations.

$$r_{xy.z} = \frac{r_{xy} - (r_{xz})(r_{yz})}{\sqrt{1 - r_{xz}^2}\sqrt{1 - r_{yz}^2}}$$

Examples

The example, suppose the research wanted to calculated the association between attitude towards the city, Y, and duration of residence, X_1, after controlling for a third variable, importance attached to weather, X_2. The simple correlations between the variables are:

$$r_{xy_1} = 0.9361 \quad r_{xy_2} = 0.7334 \quad r_{x_1 x_2} = 0.5495$$

The required partial correlation be calculated as follows:

$$r_{yx_1.x_2} = \frac{0.9361 - (0.5495)(0.7334)}{\sqrt{1 - (0.5495)^2}\sqrt{1 - (0.7334)^2}}$$
$$= 0.9386$$

As can be seen, controlling for the effect of importance attached to weather has little effect on the association between attitude towards the city and duration of residence.

Partial correlations have an order associated with them. The order indicates how many variables are being adjusted or controlled. The simple correlation coefficient, r_1 has a zero-order, as it does not control for any additional variables when measuring the association between two variables. The coefficient $r_{xy.z}$ is a first-order partial correlation coefficient, as it controls for the effect of one additional variable, Z. A second-order partial correlation coefficient controls for the effects of two variables, a third-order for the effects of three variables and so on. The higher-order partial correlations are calculated similarly. The $(n + 1)$th-order partial coefficient may be calculated by replacing the simple correlation coefficients on the right side of the preceding equation with the nth-order partial coefficients.

Partial correlations can be helpful for detecting spurious relationships. The relationship between X and Y is spurious if it is solely due to the fact that X associated with Z, which is indeed the true predictor of Y. In this case, the correlation between X and Y disappears when the effect of Z is controlled. Consider a case in which consumption of a cereal brand (C) is positively associated with income (I), with $r_{ci} = 0.28$. Because this brand was popularly priced, income was not expected to be a significant factor. Therefore, the researcher suspected that this relationship was spurious. The sample results also indicated that income is positively associated with household size (H), $r_{hi} = 0.48$, and that household size is associated with cereal consumption, $r_{ch} = 0.56$. These figures seem to indicate that the real predictor of cereal consumption is not income but household size. To test this assertion, the first-order partial correlation between cereal consumption and income is calculated, controlling for the effect of household size. The reader can verify that this partial correlation, $r_{ci.h}$, is 0.02, and the initial correlation between cereal consumption and income vanishes when household size was controlled. Therefore the correlation between income and cereal consumption is spurious. The special case when a partial correlation is larger than its respective zero-order correlation involves a suppressor effect.

Another correlation coefficient of interest is the *part correlation coefficient*. This coefficient represents the correlation between Y and X when the linear effects of the other independent variables have been removed from X but not from Y. The part correlation coefficient, $r_{y(x.z)}$, is calculated as follows:

$$r_{y(x.z)} = \frac{r_{xy} - r_{yz}r_{xz}}{\sqrt{1 - r_{xz}^2}}$$

The part correlation between attitude towards the city and the duration of residence, when the linear effects of the importance attached to weather have been removed from the duration of residence, can be calculated as:

$$r_{y(x_1.x_2)} = \frac{0.9361 - (0.5495)(0.7334)}{\sqrt{1 - (0.5495)^2}}$$
$$= 0.63806$$

Conclusion

The *partial correlation coefficient* is a measure of the association between two variables after controlling or adjusting for the effects of one or more additional variables.

The *partial correlation coefficient* is a measure of the correlation between Y and X when the linear effects of the other independent variables have been removed from X but not from Y.

The interclass correlation coefficient

Introduction

Most of the correlation measures are all measures of *interclass* correlation – measures of the relationship between two or more variables based on a number of observations of the corresponding values of these variables. However, in many instances, observations of a particular variable are taken in groups, or subsamples, that are later combined to form one aggregate sample. For example, where a number of interviewers were sent out to collect data on the planned vacation expenditures of families. The interviews made by each interviewer form a subsample, all of these five subsamples being combined later into one large sample to arrive at the overall results of the survey. Now, if a random sampling procedure has been employed, the data obtained from the interviews are influenced by two major considerations: random sampling fluctuations, and any particular bias on the part of each interviewer in the selection process, as well as other non-random effects, if they exist.

Sometimes we are not able to measure the bias. In other words, we can determine, with a certain degree of confidence, whether or not it exists but we cannot determine to what *extent* it exists. The measurement of this bias is the subject of the present discussion.

Key features

The bias, or degree of relationship, between subsamples or classes of the same sample is known as *interclass correlation*. The measure of this bias is known as the *interclass coefficient*, which we shall denote by r_c. In population, the interclass correlation coefficient is defined as

$$r_c = \frac{\text{Variance due to subsamples}}{\text{variance due to subsamples} + \text{random sampling variance}}$$

Like the other correlation measures, the intraclass correlation coefficient varies between -1 and $+1$. Where no intraclass correlation is present, r_c is 0. Perfect intraclass correlation, when r_c is ±1, means that all members of the class or subsample are identical, the values of at least two classes differing from each other; r_c is negative when the sampling variance exceeds the variance between classes, though in most practical problems r_c is positive. The intraclass correlation coefficient is based on one important assumption, that is, that the variance due to the subsample is unrelated to the random sampling variance. However, this assumption is not very restrictive, as it is generally valid in practice.

For computational purposes, it is necessary to have estimates of the two variances in the formula for the intraclass correlation coefficient. The estimate of the random sampling variance is taken to be the variance within classes, as in the previous analysis-of-variance (ANOVA) problems. If we denote X_{ij} as the jth value in the ith class, or subsample, then the variance within classes (σ_ω^2) is defined as

$$(\sigma_\omega^2) = \frac{\sum_i \sum_j \left(X_{ij} - \bar{X}_i\right)^2}{k(n-1)}$$

where X_i is the mean value of the ith class, there being k different classes with n members, or interviews, in each class.

The variance due to the classes or subsamples (σ_ω^2) is the difference between the variance between classes (σ_ω^2) and the variance within classes (the sampling variance (σ_ω^2)) divided by the size of each class. In other words

$$\sigma_c^2 = \frac{\sigma_b^2 - \sigma_\omega^2}{n}$$

$$\sigma_b^2 = \frac{n\sum_i \left(\bar{X}_i - \bar{X}\right)^2}{k-1}$$

The reason for this definition of the variance due to classes is not difficult to see. Since (σ_ω^2) measures the influence of the random sampling variation on the sample members, the extent to which non-random influences affect the various classes is reflected by the excess of the variance between classes over the random sampling variance. This difference is divided by the size of the class[1] because it is the variation in the class means that is being examined.

If the classes vary in size, an average value n_0 is used instead of n. It is computed from the following formula:

$$n_o = \frac{1}{k-1}\left(\sum k - \frac{\sum k^2}{\sum k}\right)$$

Making the above substitutions in the definitional formula and clearing fractions yields the usual computational form for the interclass correlation coefficient

$$r_c = \frac{\sigma_b^2 - \sigma_\omega^2}{\sigma_b^2 + (n-1)\sigma_\omega^2}$$

Since r_c is generally computed in connection with ANOVA problems, the required variances are merely copied into the formula from the ANOVA table constructed for that particular problem.

The following approximation formula may be used to compute r_c directly from the sample data:

$$r_c = \frac{kA - (k-1)B - C}{A + n(k-1)B - C}$$

where

$$A = \sum_i \left(\sum_i X_{ij}\right)^2$$

$$B = \sum_i \sum_i X_{ij}^2$$

$$C = \left(\sum_i \sum_i X_{ij}^2\right)$$

Thus, only three produce sums are required: the sum of squares of all the observations (B), the sum of the squared totals of the observations in each class (A) and the square of the sum of all the observations (C). With an automatic calculator, all three product sums may be computed in a single operation.

Example

For example, suppose it is desired to compute r_c for the interviewer problem and we σ_b^2 find that is 17.00 and σ_ω^2 is 10.97. Since each interviewer obtained data from eight families we have

$$r_c = \frac{17.00 - 10.97}{17.00 + (8-1)(10.97)} = 0.064$$

In this case, the sampling variation within each class is very large relative to the variation from class (mean) to class (mean). The low value of r_c indicates that the correlation between classes is very small, if it actually exists, and hence that the results obtained by the different interviewers not seem to differ appreciably from each other.

Once the intraclass correlation coefficient is computed from sample data, the next problem becomes to determine the significance of r_c. The value of r_c computed from a sample drawn from a population in which no intraclass correlation is present will obviously not be zero because of random sampling variations. Given a sample-computed intraclass correlation coefficient, the question becomes: Does this value indicate the presence of intraclass correlation in the population, or could it arise from a population with zero intraclass correlation purely as a result of random selection? The answer is simple, for the relevant significant test is the same F test. The F ratio tests the *presence* of bias or other non-random factors, or, in other words, of intraclass correlation. Therefore, the significance of an intraclass correlation coefficient is determined by the significance of the appropriate F ratio. For example, in the case of the interviewer-bias problem, the computed value of F had been found to be not significant. Hence, it was a foregone conclusion that the corresponding value of the intraclass correlation coefficient would be due to sampling fluctuations.

Conclusion

Because the significance of an intraclass correlation coefficient can be determined without having to know its actual value, the procedure in such cases is generally the reverse of that used in other correlation problems. The usual procedure is to compute the value of the particular correlation coefficient and then test its significance. However, in an intraclass correlation problem, it is more economical first to carry out the analysis of variance, which would be required in any event, and test the significance of the compute value of F. If the F-test indicates the presence of intraclass correlation, r_c is then computed as the measure of the degree of this correlation. If the value of F is not significant, indicating that the apparent intraclass correlation merely reflects normal sampling variations, the value of r_c becomes superfluous and need not be computed.

Regression and forecasting techniques

Multiple regression

Regression analysis attempts to investigate the nature (and strength) of relationships, if any, between two or more variables in marketing phenomena. It can be used, for example, to establish the nature and form of association between sales and, say, the number of customers, the nature of competitive activity, the amount of resources spent on advertising, etc. The association between Y (sales) – which is the dependent variable – and the independent variables affecting sales are usually expressed in a mathematical function of the type:

$$Y = f(\chi_1, \chi_2, \chi_3, \ldots, \chi_n)$$

The purpose of regression is to make predictions about scores on the dependent variable based upon knowledge of independent variable scores (Speed, 1994).

Regression provides measures of association, not causation; yet regression (and correlation analysis) could assist marketing managers in better understanding the implicit relationships among various independent and dependent variables (e.g. age, income, education and amount of credit card usage, or various forms of salespeople's incentives and their sales calls, or the number of new orders obtained, etc.).

Generalized linear models

Generalized linear models (GLMs) have a number of advantages over more traditional 'hypothesis testing' statistics:

- They are constituents of a unified theory of data analysis (this makes the whole process of choosing a test and understanding the analyses easier).
- They model rather than hypothesis test (they can therefore be used for both description and prediction).
- They provide significant advantages over the more traditional bivariate tests and in many cases can replace them.
- GLMs can be used to analyse most of the data we are likely to collect in the social sciences.

It is these advantages which make GLMs perhaps the most important set of statistical tests in the social sciences.

What are GLMs?

Basically, they are methods which model data using linear relationships. Linear relationships are important due to the ease with which they can be described mathematically. However, not all relationships between variables are linear and able to be adequately described in this way. In such cases we can still take advantage of linear methods

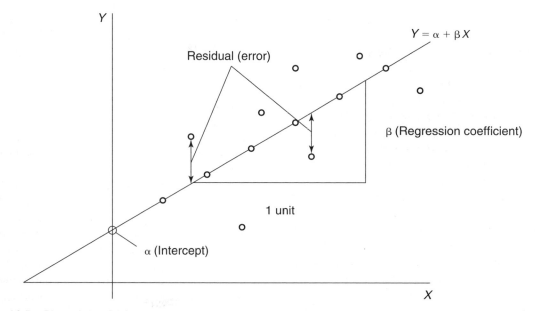

Figure 10.5   Plot of the OLS regression equation

by modelling the relationship between variables using a linear model, but including transformations which approximate non-linear relationships to linear ones.

The techniques that fall under the GLM umbrella include a number of popular techniques:

- Ordinary least-squares (OLS) regression.
- Logistic regression.
- Log-linear modelling.

By way of an introduction we will begin with OLS regression, a technique which is very common and fairly easy to understand.

OLS regression

Simple OLS regression

Simple OLS regression attempts to represent the relationship between two variables using a line. This line is computed using the least-squares method and provides a line of best fit. For two variables, the OLS regression equation is equivalent to $Y = \alpha + \beta X = \varepsilon$ (Figure 10.5).

Using this graph, we are able to define the relationship between the two variables Y and X, and also how strong the relationship is.

The important thing to note from this demonstration is that GLMs can be used to model non-linear relationships even though they are linear techniques. This makes the techniques particularly useful in the social sciences, where relationships are rarely linear.

Multivariate OLS regression

OLS regression can also be used when there are more than two variables. It is important to be able to include a number of variables into a model, as more than one source of information is often required to account for a particular variable.

Take, for example, a situation where a particular company employs on the basis of educational achievement and not on the basis of gender. If this company recruits in a region where males and females do not have equal access to education, it is likely that a simple regression model that predicts wages from gender will show a significant relationship between the two. On the basis of this relationship, it would appear that the company is breaking the law, as it is paying different rates to males and females. This conclusion might be unjust in this case, as it is possible that it is a bias in the provision of education that has resulted in males being more highly educated and, consequently, better paid. In this case, the relationship between gender and wage is a consequence of the relationship between gender and education. To adequately model wages, both pieces of information need to be included in a model. Such a model can be represented in the form of a Venn diagram (Figure 10.6).

Many variables can be added to a regression analysis. We merely add more terms into the model. A multiple OLS regression model with k variables can be represented by the equation:

$$Y = \alpha + \beta_1 X_1 + \beta_2 X_2 + \beta_2 X_2 + \beta_3 X_3 + \beta_4 X_4 + \cdots + \beta_k X_k + \varepsilon$$

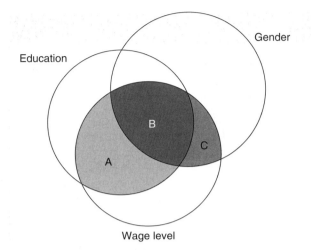

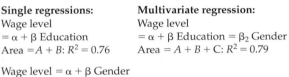

Single regressions:
Wage level
$= \alpha + \beta$ Education
Area $= A + B$: $R^2 = 0.76$

Wage level $= \alpha + \beta$ Gender
Area $= B + C$: $R^2 = 0.47$

Multivariate regression:
Wage level
$= \alpha + \beta$ Education $= \beta_2$ Gender
Area $= A + B + C$: $R^2 = 0.79$

Figure 10.6 Venn diagram representing multivariate OLS regression

In the above equation, the variable Y is predicted using information from all of the X variables. This could be wages predicted by gender, education, type of work, location, experience, etc. The effect that each variable has on wage is assessed whilst controlling for all other variables. The output from an OLS regression is given in Tables 10.2 and 10.3, and shows how such a model can be interpreted.

Which data can be used in OLS regression?

OLS regression can be used to model response variables (Y variables) which are recorded on at least an interval scale (i.e. continuous variables such

as age, output and wages). Explanatory variables (the X variables) can be continuous or ordered and unordered categorical data provided that they are coded appropriately). In short, OLS regression is used to model continuous data from all other types of data.

Conclusions

- OLS regression uses linear equations, as these are relatively easy to formulate and work with.
- Non-linear relationships can be modelled using linear equations if transformations are applied to the data.
- When there are a number of factors affecting the variable we wish to model, a multiple regression can be used.
- Response variables need to be interval, but with appropriate coding, any explanatory variables can be included.

Logistic regression

Quite often we may wish to model a binary variable, such as male–female, etc. For such analyses, it is not appropriate to use OLS regression as the data are not linear – we have to use logistic regression.

Similar to OLS regression, a whole range of useful statistics can be computed, including standard errors, confidence and prediction intervals. We are not limited by the traditional statistics which can only provide group comparisons.

The logistic regression model

As with OLS regression, we can use any number of explanatory variables, variables which can be interval or categorical. The same considerations apply to the data as with multiple OLS regression. All the power that is available in traditional OLS

Table 10.2 ANOVA[1]

Model	Sum of squares	df	Mean square	F	Significance
1 Regression	123.581	8	15.448	9.919	0.000[2]
Residual	722.617	464	1.557		
Total	846.199	472			

[1] Dependent variable: SSAT.
[2] Predictors (constant): SH_TESC, REGR factor score 3 for analysis 1, REGR factor score 2 for analysis 1, SH_SOLO, SH_ASDA, REGR factor score 4 for analysis 1, REGR factor score 1 for analysis 1, SH_SAINS.

Table 10.3 Coefficients[a]

Model	Unstandardized coefficients		Standardized coefficients beta	t	Significance
	B	Standard error			
I (Constant)	4.888	0.102		48.115	0.000
Quality	0.308	0.061	0.234	5.017	0.000
Other services	−3.06E-03	0.062	−0.002	−0.050	0.961
Value brands	4.524E-03	0.059	0.003	0.077	0.939
Car facilities	−3.44E-02	0.064	−0.026	−0.534	0.594
SH_ASDA	0.851	0.277	0.142	3.076	0.002
SH_SAINS	0.795	0.214	0.178	3.710	0.000
SH_SOLO	9.928E-02	0.253	0.018	0.393	0.694
SH_TESC	0.725	0.137	0.270	5.297	0.000

[a] Dependent Variable: SSAT.

Table 10.4 Model, block and step data

	Chi-square	df	Significance
Model	41.781	7	0.0000
Block	41.781	7	0.0000
Step	41.781	7	0.0000

regression is also available in logistic regression – there should be no need to ever compute a test which assesses group differences (*t*-test, Mann–Whitney, Wilcoxon, ANOVA, etc.).

The basic form of the model is identical to OLS regression. The only difference is in the interpretation of the parameters. A logistic regression can be represented as:

$$Y = \alpha + \beta_1 X_1 + \beta_2 X_2 + \beta_2 X_2 + \beta_3 X_3 + \beta_4 X_4 + \cdots + \beta_k X_k + \varepsilon$$

An example of a logistic regression

The data in Tables 10.4–10.6 are taken from a recent study into consumer behaviour. The variables have been selected for the purpose of demonstration and not to provide a 'good' model.

Conclusions

- Binary response variables have a non-linear S-shaped distribution.
- This distribution can be modelled using a linear equation once it has been transformed.
- The model-building approach of the logistic regression provides much more detailed analysis of data than can be obtained using a *t*-test, ANOVA, Mann–Whitney or Kruskal–Wallis.
- The linear component of the model is the same as that used for the OLS regression.

Log-linear analysis

GLMs can also be used to model categorical data (i.e. data in the form of contingency tables). The traditional method of analysing such data is to interpret bar charts and to use the chi-square statistic as part of the cross-tabs procedure. These methods have severe limitations as they can only deal with two variables and cannot model the data to provide predictions. The same considerations apply to contingency table data as applied to OLS regression regarding the problems of interaction variables (e.g. wages, education and gender).

Table 10.5   Classification table for SH_TESC (the cut value is 0.50)

			Predicted				Per cent correct
			0.00 0		1.00 1		
Observed							
0.00	0		174		90		65.91
1.00	1		97		120		55.30
					Overall		61.12

Table 10.6   Variables in the equation

Variable	B	S.E.	Wald	df	Significance	R	Exp (B)
FI_QUAL	0.3573	0.1099	10.5612	1	0.0012	0.1137	1.4294
F2_OTHER	−0.0296	0.1018	0.0844	1	0.7715	0.0000	0.9709
F3_CHOIC	−0.2022	0.0989	4.1801	1	0.0409	−0.0574	0.8169
F4_CAR	0.2799	0.1018	7.5586	1	0.0060	0.0916	1.3231
DIS_CAT			7.6330	3	0.0542	0.0497	
DIS_CAT(1)	0.6929	0.8451	0.6722	1	0.4123	0.0000	1.9996
DIS_CAT(2)	1.2199	0.8257	2.1825	1	0.1396	0.0166	3.3869
DIS_CAT(3)	1.5018	0.9169	2.6824	1	0.1015	0.0321	4.4896
Constant	−1.3027	0.8175	2.5393	1	0.1110		

A log-linear analysis enables much more information to be obtained from the data and also enables statistics to assess the overall fit of the model. As the log-linear name suggests, it is a technique which makes use of the linear model and a transformation involving the natural log. Similar to OLS and logistic regression, the form of model is a linear combination:

$$\ln(\text{cell count}) = \alpha + \beta_1 X_1 + \beta_2 X_2 + \beta_3 X_3 + \beta_k X_k$$

The form of the log-linear model is very similar to the previous models discussed – the only difference is that we are now modelling cell counts. In effect, all of the terms in the model have been moved to the right-hand side of the equation. Parameters from the model are similar to the other models, but are interpreted slightly differently.

Conclusions

- The log-linear model is very similar to the OLS and logistic regression models.
- All of the advantages of OLS regression, such as being able to compute model fits, make predictions and investigate complex interactions, also apply to log-linear.
- It enables analysis of multicategory, multigroup data – something not possible using chi-square.

Discriminant analysis

Like regression analysis, discriminant analysis (DA) uses a linear equation to predict the dependent variable (say, sales). However, while in regression analysis the parameters (coefficients) are used to minimize the sum of squares, in DA the parameters are selected in such a way as to maximize the ratio:

$$\frac{\text{Variance between group means}}{\text{Variance within groups}}$$

DA is used in marketing for predicting brand loyalty and buying or attempting to predict consumer behaviour in general; this classification method can be used when the data (the independent variables) are interval scales.

Discriminant analysis

Introduction

DA is a technique for analysing data when the criterion or dependent variable is categorical and the predictor or independent variables are interval in nature. For example, the dependent variable may be the choice of a brand of personal computer (brand A, B or C) and the independent variables may be ratings of attributes of PCs on a seven-point Likert scale. The objectives of DA are as follows:

1   Development of *discriminant functions*, or linear combinations of the predictor or independent variables, which will best discriminant between the categories of the criterion or dependent variable (groups).
2   Examination of whether significant differences exist among the groups in terms of the predictor variables.
3   Determination of which predictor variables contribute to most of the intergroup differences.
4   Classification of cases to one of the groups based on the values of the predictor variables.
5   Evaluation of the accuracy of classification.

DA techniques are described by the number of categories possessed by the criterion variable. When the criterion variable has two categories, the technique is known as *two-group discriminant*. When three or more categories are involved, the technique is referred to as *multiple discriminant analysis (MDA)*. The main distinction is that in the two-group case, it is possible to derive only one discriminant function. In MDA, more than one function may be computed.

Key features

DA Model

The *DA model* involves linear combinations of the following form:

$$D = b_0 + b_1 X_1 + b_2 X_2 + b_3 X_3 + \cdots + b_k X_k$$

Where
  D = discriminant score
  Bs = discriminant coefficients or weights
  Xs = predictors or independent variables

The coefficients, or weights (b), are estimated so that the groups differ as much as possible on the values of the discriminant function. This occurs when the ratio of between-group sum of squares to within-group sum of squares for the discriminant scores is at maximum. Any other linear combination of the predictors will result in a smaller ratio. Several statistics are associated with DA.

Statistics Associated with DA

The important statistics associated with DA include the following:

Canonical correlation. Canonical correlation measures the extent of association between the discriminant scores and the groups. It is a measure of association between the single discriminant function and the set of dummy variables that define the group membership.

Centroid. The centroid is the mean values for the discriminant scores for a particular group. There are as many centroids as there are groups, as there is one for each group. The means for a group on all the functions are the *group centroids*.

Classification matrix. Sometimes also called *confusion* or *prediction matrix*, the classification matrix contains the number of correctly classified and misclassified cases. The correctly classified cases appear on the diagonal, because the predicted and actual groups are the same. The off-diagonal elements represent cases that have been incorrectly classified. The sum of the diagonal elements divided by the total number of cases represents the *hit ratio*.

Discriminant function coefficients. The discriminant function coefficients (unstandardized) are the multipliers of variables, when the variables are in the original units of measurement.

Discriminant scores. The understandardized coefficients are multiplied by the values of the variables. These products are summed and added to the constant term to obtain the discriminant scores.

Eigenvalue. For each discriminant function, the eigenvalue is the ratio of between-groups to within-group sums of squares. Large eigenvalues imply superior functions.

F-values and their significance. These are calculated from a one-way ANOVA, with the grouping variable serving as the categorical independent variable. Each predictor, in turn, serves as the metric dependent variable in the ANOVA.

Group means and group standard deviations. These are computed for each predictor for each group.

Pooled within-group correlation matrix. The pooled within-group correlation matrix is computed by averaging the separate covariance matrices for all the groups.

Standardized discriminant function coefficients. The standardized discriminant function coefficients are the discriminant function coefficients and are used as the multipliers when the variables have been standardized to a mean of 0 and a variance of 1.

Structure correlations. Also referred to as *discriminant loadings*, the structure correlations represent the simple correlations between the predictors and the discriminant function.

Total correlation matrix. If the cases are treated as if they were from a single sample and the correlations computed, a total correlation matrix is obtained.

Wilks' λ. Sometimes also called the *U* statistic, Wilks' λ for each predictor is the ratio of the within-group sum of squares to the total sum of squares. Its value varies between 0 and 1. Large values of λ (near 1) indicate that group means do not seem to be different. Small values of λ (near 0) indicate that the group means seem to be different.

The assumptions in DA are that each of the groups is a sample from a multivariate normal population and all of the populations have the same covariance matrix. The role of these assumptions and the statistics just described can be better understood by examining the procedure for conducting DA.

Estimate the discriminant function coefficients

Once the analysis sample has been identified, we can estimate the discriminant function coefficients. Two broad approaches are available. The *direct method* involves estimating the discriminant function so that all the predictors are included simultaneously. In this case, each independent variable is included, regardless of its discriminating power. This method is appropriate when, based on previous research or a theoretical model, the researcher wants the discrimination to be based on all the predictors. An alternative approach is the stepwise method. In *stepwise DA*, the predictor variables are entered sequentially, based on their ability to discriminate among groups. This method is appropriate when the researcher wants to select a subset of the predictors for inclusion in the discriminant function.

Determine the significance of discriminant function

It would not be meaningful to interpret the analysis if the discriminant functions estimated were not statistically significant. The null hypothesis that, in the population, the means of all discriminant functions in all groups are equal can be statistically tested. In SPSS, this test is based on Wilks' λ. If several functions are tested simultaneously (as in the case of MDA), the Wilks' λ statistic is the product of the univariate λ for each function. The significance level is estimated based on a chi-square transformation of the statistic. In SAS, an approximate *F* statistic, based on an approximation to the distribution of the likelihood ratio, is calculated. A test of significance is not available in MINITAB. If the null hypothesis is rejected, indication significant discrimination, one can proceed to interpret the results.

Interpret the results

The interpretation of the discriminant weights, or coefficients, is similar to that in multiple regression analysis. The value of the coefficient for a particular predictor depends on the other predictors included in the discriminant function. The signs to the coefficients are arbitrary, but they indicate which variable values result in large and small function values and associate them with particular groups.

We can obtain some idea of the relative importance of the variables by examining the absolute magnitude of the standardized discriminant function coefficients. Generally, predictors with relatively large standardized coefficients contribute more to the discriminating power of the function, as compared with predictors with smaller coefficients, and are, therefore, more important.

Some idea of the relative importance of the predictors can also be obtained by examining the structure correlations, also called *canonical loadings* or *discriminant loadings*. These simple correlations between each predictor and the discriminant function represent the variance that the predictor shares with the function. The greater the magnitude of a structure correlation, the more important the corresponding predictor. Like the standardized coefficients, these correlations must also be interpreted with correlation.

Discriminant analysis

The results from simultaneously entering all variables in DA are presented in the table. The rank order of importance, as determined by the relative magnitude of the structure correlations, is presented in the first column. Satisfaction with the job and promotional opportunities were the two most important discriminators, followed by job security. Those who stayed in the company found the job to be more exciting, satisfying, challenging and interesting than those who left.

Examples

Note that in this example, promotion was identified as the second most important variable based on the structure correlations. However, it is not the second most important variable based on the absolute magnitude of the standardized discriminant function coefficients. This anomaly results from multicollinearity.

Another aid to interpreting DA results is to develop a *characteristic profile* for each group by describing each group in terms of the group means for the predictor variables. If the important predictors have been identified, then a comparison of the group means on these variables can assist in understanding the intergroup differences. However, before any findings can be interpreted with confidence, it is necessary to validate the results.

Home bodies and couch potatoes

Two-group DA was used to assess the strength of each of five dimensions used in classifying individuals as TV users or non-users. The procedure was appropriate for this use because of the nature of the predefined categorical groups (users and nonusers) and the interval scales used to generate individual factor scores.

Two equal groups of 185 elderly consumers, users and non-users (total $n = 370$) were created. The discriminant equation for the analysis was estimated by using a subsample of 142 respondents from the sample of 370. Of the remaining respondents, 198 were used as a validation subsample in a cross-validation of the equation. Thirty respondents were excluded from the analysis because of missing values.

The canonical correlation for the discriminant function was 0.4291, significant at the $p < 0.0001$ level. The eigenvalue was 0.2257. The table summarizes the standardized canonical discriminant coefficients. A substantial portion of the variance is explained by the discriminant function. In addition, as the table shows, the home orientation dimension made a fairly strong contribution to classifying individuals as users or non-users of television. Morale, security and health, and respect also contributed significantly. The social factor appeared to make little contribution.

The cross-validation procedure using the discriminant function from the analysis sample gave support to the contention that the dimensions aided researchers in discriminating between users and non-users of television. As the table shows, the discriminant function was successful in classifying 75, 76 per cent of the cases. This suggests that the consideration of the identified dimensions will help marketers understand the elderly market. Although it is very important for marketers to know and understand the elderly market, the Generation Xers (those born between 1961 and 1981) are also a group that should be overlooked by marketers. Due to technological advances with the Internet and television, a revolutionary form of interactive TV (ITV) has been created. By 2003, ITV services will be fully deployed and operational and will combine the Internet and broadcasting with software programs and hardware components to give consumers Internet access, online shopping, music downloads and an interactive broadcast programme all through their television. By 2006, it is predicted that 61.5 million people will be interacting with their televisions through ITV. With such a prosperous looking forecast for ITV, who better to target this revolutionary form of television than Generation Xers? DA can again be used to determine who amongst Generation Xers are users or non-users of ITV and to market ITV services successfully.

The extension from two-group DA to MDA involves similar steps.

Conclusion

DA is useful for analysing data when the criterion or dependent variables are interval scaled. When the criterion has two categories, the technique is known as two-group DA. MDA refers to the case when three or more categories are involved.

Conducting DA is a five-step procedure. First, formulating the discriminant problem requires identification of the objectives and the criterion and predictor variables. The sample is divided into two parts. One part, the analysis sample, is used to estimate the discriminant function. The other part, the holdout sample, is reserved for validation. Estimation, the second step, involves developing a linear combination of the predictors, called discriminant functions, so that the groups differ as much as possible on the predictor values.

Determination of statistical significance is the third step. It involves testing the null hypothesis that, in the population, the means of all discriminant functions in all groups are equal. If the null hypothesis is rejected, it is meaningful to interpret the results.

The fourth step, the interpretation of discriminant weights or coefficients, is similar to that in multiple regression analysis. Given the multicollinearity in the predictor variables, there is no unambiguous measure of the relative importance of the predictors in discriminating between the groups. However, some idea of the relative importance of the variables may be obtained by examining the absolute magnitude of the standardized discriminant function coefficients and by examining the structure correlations between each predictor and the discriminant function represent the variance that the predictor shares with the function. Another aid to interpreting DA results is to develop a characteristic profile for each group, based on the group means for the predictor variables.

Validation, the fifth step, involves developing the classification matrix. The discriminant weights estimated by using the analysis sample are multiplied by the values of the predictor variables in the holdout sample to generate discriminant scores for the cases in the holdout sample. The cases are then assigned to groups based on their discriminant scores and an appropriate decision rule. The percentage of cases correctly classified is determined and compared to the rate that would be expected by chance classification.

Two broad approaches are available for estimating the coefficients. The direct method involves estimating the discriminant function so that all the predictors are included simultaneously. An alternative is the stepwise method, in which the predictor variables are entered sequentially, based on their ability to discriminate among groups.

Automatic interaction detection

The regression analysis mentioned above attempts to identify association between the dependent and the independent variables, one at a time. In addition, the assumption is that the data are measured on interval scales. In many other marketing research situations we need a method able to handle nominal *or* ordinal data and to identify *all* the significant relationships between the dependent and the independent variables. AID is a computer-based method for interactively selecting the independent variables in order to be able to predict the dependent variables. It splits the sample of observations into two groups on a sequential routine, trying to keep the subgroups that emerge as homogeneous as possible, relative to the dependent variable. The homogeneity is measured by minimizing the sum-of-square deviations of each subgroup member from its subgroup mean. AID is used in marketing for market segments analysis, analysing the effect of advertising levels on retail sales, predicting consumption/sales and brand loyalty.

This method is not as powerful as regression analysis and, since the minimum subgroup size should be no less than 30, the original sample of objects required must be fairly large (1000 or more).

Three of the regression and forecasting techniques described above are summarized in Table 10.7.

Forecasting methods

Forecasting methods are mainly applied in forecasting sales and market demand. Chambers *et al.* (1979) classify them into three categories: qualitative techniques, time-series analysis and causal models. In each category there is a series of models; some are suitable for forecasting initial sales and others for forecasting repeat purchases. Consequently, one should make clear the differentiation between diffusion and adoption models, although, unfortunately, the space available here is not sufficient for a detailed presentation.

Probably the most well-known forecasting techniques are the time-series methods. These rely on historical data and, by definition, are of limited application to the forecasting of new product sales.

In order to select a forecasting technique for new products, the first principle is to match the methodology with the situation. The degree of newness of the product, for example, is crucial, as are product and market characteristics, the forecaster's ability, the cost, the urgency and the purpose for which the forecast is needed.

The second principle is that at least two methods should be used and one of these should always be the subjective judgement of the forecaster, who must override the formal technique decision when information coming from outside the model clearly shows that the technique's forecast may be at fault. There are powerful arguments for combining

Table 10.7 Regression, AD and discriminant analysis – a comparison

Method	Based on	Marketing applications	Main advantages	Main limitations
Regression analysis	Developing a function expressing the association (or relationship) between dependent and independent variables	For segmentation, consumer behaviour analysis, sales forecasting (Speed, 1994)	Enables predictions about a dependent variable (say, sales figures). Provides measures of association between independent variables and certain important marketing dependent variables	Requires fitting a regression line and determining the parameters. This could be quite complex and lead to certain errors
AD	A computer-based sequential routine attempting to classify objects into groups as possible, by minimizing the within-group sum of squares	For market segments analysis, assess the effects of advertising on retail sales, predict brand loyalty sales prediction, etc.	Suitable for identifying the different variables affecting market segments; determining the importance of each independent variable and the form in which it affects the dependent variable	Less powerful than regression. Minimum group size should be no less than 30, and the original sample size should be quite large
Discriminant analysis	Maximize the ratio of variance between group means, not within-group variance	Predicting brand loyalty, consumer innovators, like/dislike of a service (or product), etc.	Enables predictions of dependent variables	Identifying the statistical significance of the discriminant function; multiple discriminant analysis requires a computer program

forecasts by different techniques. Methods are selective in the information they use, so that a combination of methods would incorporate more information and improve accuracy. Doyle and Fenwick (1976) advocate this and produce evidence of improved accuracy.

Simulation methods

The cost, the time involved and other problems associated with field experimentation often preclude a method as a source of information for particular situations. In such instances it is often desirable to construct a model of an operational situation and obtain relevant information through the manipulation of this model. This manipulation, called simulation, describes the act of creating a complex model to resemble a real process or system and experimenting with this model in the hope of learning something about the real system.

Simulations represent a general technique which is useful for studying marketing systems and is one of the most flexible methods in terms of application. Simulation models have been formulated to serve two management functions:

1 Planning.
2 Monitoring and controlling operations.

Marketing simulations can be conveniently divided into three classes (Doyle and Fenwick, 1976). The first deals with computer models of the behaviour of marketing system components, the second with computer models on the effect of different marketing instruments on demand and the third with marketing games.

A firm wanting to adopt a simulation model would have to take into account the market characteristics of the environment it operates in and model on this basis.

Fuzzy sets

The fuzzy set theory is a relatively new approach that has been growing steadily since its inception in the mid-1960s. In the fuzzy set theory, an abstract concept such as a sunny day can be considered as a fuzzy set and defined mathematically by assigning to each individual in the universe of discourse, a value representing its grade of membership in the fuzzy set. This grade corresponds to the degree to which that individual is similar or compatible with the concept represented by the fuzzy set. Thus, individuals may belong in the fuzzy set to a greater or lesser degree as indicated by a larger or smaller membership grade. These membership grades are very often represented by real member values ranging in the closed interval between 0 and 1. Thus, a fuzzy set representing our concept of sunniness might assign a degree of membership 1 to a cloud cover of 0 per cent, 0.8 to a cloud cover of 20 per cent, 0.4 to a cloud cover of 30 per cent and 0 to a cloud cover of 75 per cent. These grades signify the degree to which each percentage of cloud cover approximates our subjective concept of sunniness, and the set itself models the semantic flexibility inherent in such a common linguistic term. Vagueness in describing many consumer behaviour constructs is intrinsic, not the result of a lack of knowledge about the available rating. That is why a great variety of definitions in marketing exist and most of them cannot describe the fuzzy concepts completely. So long as the semantic assessment facets in the construct can be quantified and explicitly defined by corresponding membership functions, the initial steps of the mathematical

---

Example: Definition – 'consumer involvement'

Consumer involvement can be construed as a fuzzy set. It is a family of pairs $(A_i, \mu_{Ai}(y))$, where for each i in the index set is a fuzzy set ϑ, A_i is a fuzzy set of assessment facet and μ_{Ai} is a membership function from A_i to the unit interval $[0,1]$ which describes the behaviour of the fuzzy set A_i, $\mu_{Ai}(y)$ is the membership function of the assessment facet that takes value on $[0,1]$ for all y in A_i, that is,

Consumer involvement $= \{A_i, \mu_{Ai}(y)|\mu_{Ai};$ $A_i \to [0,1]_3 \mu_{Ai}(y)[0,1]_{3yAi}\}$

and i, ϑ, A_i is a fuzzy set of assessment facet.

---

definition of marketing constructs are achieved. Recognizing the difficulty of accurate quantification of the semantic assessment facets like product interest, hedonic value and others, some researchers utilize the fuzzy mathematical method (Zimmerman, 1991; Klir and Yuan, 1995) to quantify the assessment facets by membership functions so that the results obtained are more accurate than the traditional statistical methods and more suitable for the semantically modified assessment facets.

The benefits of using fuzzy sets are:

1 The membership function is deliberately designed in fuzzy set theory to treat the vagueness caused by natural language. Therefore, using membership functions to assess the semantically defined measuring facets is more reliable and accurate than using the traditional statistical methods – score points or scatter plot.
2 The membership function standardizes the semantic meaning of assessment facets so that we can compare the degree of the definition of marketing constructs regardless of the differences of timing, situation, consumer and so on.
3 The membership functions are continuous functions which are more accurate in measuring the assessment facets than the traditional discrete methods.
4 The fuzzy mathematical method is easier to perform than the traditional method, once the membership of assessment facets is defined.

Some of the main characteristics, advantages, limitations and applications of simulation and fuzzy sets in marketing are presented in Table 10.8.

Table 10.8	Uses of simulation and fuzzy sets in marketing (the method, advantages, limitations and when recommended to use)			
Method	*Based on*	*Marketing applications*	*Main advantages*	*Main limitations*
Simulation	Conducting experiments using a model to simulate working conditions of the real system	(a) Marketing planning (b) Monitoring and controlling (Kotler and Schultz, 1970), marketing operations (c) Distribution, consumer behaviour, retailing, staffing, advertising (d) Marketing training (Kotler and Schultz, 1970)	(a) A very felxible and simple method easily understood by managers (b) Saves time and resources (c) Simulation has found wide applications in the field of marketing	(a) Tedious arithmetical calculations (b) Rather costly in computer time
Fuzzy sets	The technique is essentially a factual modelling process that attempts to fine tune the expression of knowledge. It does this by using a linguistic scale describing the characteristics under each of the main dimensions of the model to form fuzzy sets; a hierarchical aggregation of information based on fuzzy aggregation operators; and a conceptual hypercube to determine the rank and ranking size of the outcomes. Includes the concept of membership function (between 0 and 1)	Modelling consumer behaviour, marketing planning, new product testing, perceived price testing, marketing communication effects research (Zimmerman, 1991)	Flexibility which accommodates a degree of uncertainty or fuzziness, in diagnosis. This fuzziness is indeed lauded as realistic in expressing human judgement	Difficult measurement scaling and estimation of the bipolar descriptors. Linguistic scale for characteristics description. Description of the values for the parameters of the model

Fuzzy decision trees

Inductive decision trees were first introduced in 1963 with the Concept Learning System Framework. Since then, they have continued to be developed and applied. The structure of a decision tree starts with a root decision node, from which all branches originate. A branch is a series of nodes where decisions are made at each node, enabling progression through (down) the tree. A progression stops at a leaf node, where a decision classification is given.

As with many data analysis techniques (e.g. traditional regression models), decision trees have been developed within a fuzzy environment. For example, the well-known decision tree method ID3 was developed to include fuzzy entropy measures. The fuzzy decision tree method was introduced by Yuan and Shaw (1995) to take account of cognitive uncertainty (i.e. vagueness and ambiguity).

Central to any method within a fuzzy environment is the defining of the required membership functions. Incorporating a fuzzy aspect (using membership functions) enables the judgements to be made with linguistic scales.

Summary of fuzzy decision tree method

In this section a brief description of the functions used in the fuzzy decision tree method are exposited. A fuzzy set A in a universe of discourse U is characterized by a membership function μ_A, which take values in the interval $[0, 1]$. For all $\mu \in U$, the intersection $A \cap B$ of two fuzzy sets is given by $\mu_{A \cap B} = \min(\mu_A(u), \mu_A(u))$.

A membership function $\mu(x)$ of a fuzzy variable Y defined on X can be viewed as a possibility distribution of Y on X, that is, $\pi(x) = \mu(x)$, for all $x \in X$. The possibilistic measure of ambiguity – $E_\alpha(Y)$ – is defined as:

$$E_\alpha(Y) = g(\pi) = \sum_{i=1}^{n} (\pi^*_i - \pi^*_{i+1}) \ln[i],$$

where $\pi^* = \{\pi^*_1, \pi^*_2, \ldots, \pi^*_n\}$ is the permutation of the possibility distribution $\pi = \{\pi(x_1), \pi(x_2), \ldots, \pi(x_n)\}$, sorted so that $\pi^*_i \geq \pi^*_{i+1}$ for $i = 1, \ldots, n$, and $\pi^*_{n+1} = 0$

The ambiguity of attribute A is then:

$$E_\alpha(A) = \frac{1}{m} \sum_{i=1}^{m} E_\alpha(A(u_i)),$$

where $E_\alpha(A(u_i)) = g(\mu_{Ts}(u_i)/\max_{15j5s}(\mu_{Tj}(u_i)))$, with T_j the linguistic scales used within an attribute.

The fuzzy subsethood $S(A, B)$ measures the degree to which A is a subset of B (see Kosko, 1986) and is given by:

$$S(A, B) = \frac{\sum_{u \in U} \min(\mu_A(u), \mu_B(u))}{\sum_{u \in U} \mu_A(u)}$$

Given fuzzy evidence E, the possibility of classifying an object to Class C_i can be defined as:

$$\pi = \hat{E}(C_i | E) = \hat{E} \frac{S(E, C_i)}{\max_j S(E, C_j)}$$

where $S(E, C_i)$ represents the degree of truth for the classification rule. Knowing a single piece of evidence (i.e. a fuzzy value from an attribute), the classification ambiguity based on this fuzzy evidence is defined as:

$$G(E) = g(\pi(C | E))$$

The classification ambiguity with fuzzy partitioning $P = \{E_1, \ldots, E_k\}$ on the fuzzy evidence F, denoted as $G(P | F)$, is the weighted average of classification ambiguity with each subset of partition:

$$G(P|F) = \sum_{i=1}^{k} W(E_i | F)G(E_i \cap F),$$

where $G(E_i \cap F)$ is the classification ambiguity with fuzzy evidence $E_i \cap F$, $w(E_i | F)$ is the weight which represents the relative size of subset $E_i \cap F$ in F:

$$W(E_i | F) = \frac{\sum_{u \in U} \min(\mu_{Ei}(u), \mu_F(u))}{\sum_{j=1}^{k} \left[\sum_{u \in U} \min(\mu_{Ej}(u), \mu_F(u)) \right]}$$

The fuzzy decision tree method considered here utilizes these functions. In summary, attributes are assigned to nodes based on the lowest level of ambiguity. A node becomes a leaf node if the level of subsethood (based on the conjunction (intersection) of the branches from the root) is higher than some truth value β assigned to the whole of the decision tree. The classification from the leaf node is to the decision class with the largest subsethood value.

The results of the decision tree are classification rules, each with an associated degree of truth in their classification. These rules are relatively simple to read and apply.

Artificial intelligence

AI models have emerged in the last few years as a follow-up to simulation, attempting to portray, comprehend and analyse the reasoning in a range of situations. Although the two methods of AI (expert systems and NNs) are, in a certain sense, 'simulations', because of the importance and the potential of these methods, we have introduced them under a separate stand-alone heading.

Expert systems

Simply defined, an expert system is a computer program which contains human knowledge or expertise which it can use to generate reasoned advice or instructions. The knowledge base is usually represented internally in the machine as a set of IF . . . THEN rules and the 'inference engine' of the expert system matches together appropriate combinations of rules in order to generate conclusions.

In determining whether a particular marketing domain is suited for this methodology the following checklist is useful:

- Are the key relationships in the domain logical rather than computational? In practical terms, the answer requires an assessment of whether the decision area is knowledge-intensive (e.g. generating new product areas) or data-intensive (e.g. allocating an advertising budget across media).
- Is the problem domain semi-structured rather than structured or unstructured? If the problem is well structured, a traditional approach using sequential procedures will be more efficient than an expert system approach. This would be true, for example, when the entire problem-solving sequence can be enumerated in advance.
- Is knowledge in the domain incomplete? If the problem is well structured, a traditional approach using sequential procedures will be more efficient than an expert system approach. This would be true, for example, when the entire problem-solving sequence can be enumerated in advance. Moreover, for highly unstructured domains, expert system performance may be disappointing because the available problem-solving strategies may be inadequate.
- Is knowledge in the domain incomplete? In other words, is it difficult to identify all the important variables or to specify fully their

interrelationships? Expert systems are particularly applicable in domains with incomplete knowledge.
- Will problem solving in the domain require a direct interface between the manager and the computer system? A direct interface may be necessary in situations calling for on-line decision support. Such situations are generally characterized by a high level of decision urgency (e.g. buying and selling stocks) or complexity (e.g. retail site selection). Expert systems are particularly useful in these contexts because of their flexible and 'friendly' user interaction facilities, coupled with their ability to explain their reasoning (Rangaswamy *et al.*, 1989). A number of expert systems in marketing have been developed over the years, in particular focusing on the following domains: marketing research, test marketing, pricing, generation of advertising appeals, choice of promotional technique, selection of effective sales techniques, negotiation strategies, site selection, allocation of marketing budget, promotion evaluation, strategic positioning, strategic marketing, assessment of sales territories, brand management, marketing planning, international marketing, bank marketing, tourism marketing and industrial marketing (see Curry and Moutinho, 1991).

The greatest single problem with regard to the effectiveness and applicability of expert system models in the marketing context concerns the construction and validation of the knowledge base.

Neural networks

NNs are designed to offer the end user the capability to bypass the rigidity of expert systems and to develop 'fuzzy logic' decision-making tools. Several authors claim that NNs provide the user with the ability to design a decision-support tool in less time and with less effort than can be accomplished with other decision-support system tools. NNs have been successfully applied in the following marketing areas: consumer behaviour analysis (Curry and Moutinho, 1993), market segmentation, pricing modelling (Ellis *et al.*, 1991), copy strategy and media planning (Kennedy, 1991).

NNs use structured input and output data to develop patterns that mimic human decision making. Input data are compared to relative output data for many data points. The relationships between the input data and output data are used to develop a pattern that represents the decision-making style of the user. The development of

Table 10.9 Applications of artificial intelligence methods in marketing (basic content, advantages, limitations and when recommended to use)

Method	Content	Marketing applications	Advantages	Limitations
AI	A computer program to express the reasoning process by modelling relationships among various variables (see checklist in text)	Marketing research, test marketing, pricing, site selection, tourism marketing and international marketing (Curry and Moutinho, 1991)	Flexible, able to explain reasoning of interactions	Difficulties in construction of the expert system model
Neural networks	Use of structured input and output data to develop patterns that mimic human decision making. Employs a statistically based procedure of iteratively adjusting the weights	Consumer behaviour (Curry and Moutinho, 1993), price modelling (Ellis *et al.*, 1991), media planning (Kennedy, 1991) and market segmentation	Capable of retraining. Able to bring together psychometric and econometric analyses	Low accuracy. More difficult to interpret than the expert systems above

patterns from data points eliminates the need to build rules that support decision making. Unlike expert systems, which require user intervention to accommodate variable changes within the model, the NN is capable of retraining, which is accomplished through the addition of new input and output data.

An important strength of this method is its ability to bring together psychometric and econometric analyses, so that the best features of both can be exploited. Whereas expert systems are good at organizing masses of information, NNs may prove capable of duplicating the kind of intuitive, trial and error thinking marketing managers typically require. The accuracy of the NN is not as high as of other methods, yet it has the ability to learn from increased input/output facts and the ability to address data that other decision-support systems cannot handle logically.

Table 10.9 presents the main applications, advantages and limitations of expert systems and NNs.

Statistical decision theory or stochastic methods

In this category there are a number of methods, all of which are useful in solving marketing problems.

Queuing

This method is of importance to large retailing institutions such as supermarkets, petrol stations, airline ticket offices, seaports, airports and other areas where services are available through queuing. A notable problem in retailing institutions is that of making sales force decisions, the reason being the high cost incurred in hiring sales clerks whose services are almost irreplaceable. Since these sales clerks work in situations which can be systematically regulated and accurately observed, techniques can be used to provide management with information so that the optimal size of the sales force can be ascertained. A queuing model to determine the optimum number of sales clerks to be assigned to a floor in a department store so as to maximize profitability can be determined. Attention should be focused on five main variables:

1 The number of potential customers arriving and requesting service per unit time.
2 The amount of time required by a sales clerk to wait on a customer.
3 The number of items purchased per customer per transaction.
4 The incremental value to the retail establishment of each item sold (i.e. profits).
5 The amount of time the customer is willing to wait for service.

Most research articles state that the use of queuing theory is mainly concentrated on solving problems in retailing institutions, where the model helps management to decide on the size of their sales force. Perhaps it was the successful application of this technique in this area of marketing that has contributed to its vast improvements and wide applications. There are, however, limitations to this technique, one of which is that queuing systems must be operated over a sufficiently long period to achieve a steady-state solution, and it is often difficult to predict the length of time required to achieve this.

Self-organizing maps

The Kohonen self-organizing map

Following Gurney (1997), for example, we define a NN as a collection of interrelated nodes. Definitions of this nature remove the need to rely on analogies of the brain and take us into more general domains, in which the nodes amount to what are known more familiarly as variables. NN techniques have become an accepted part of the 'toolkit' available to researchers in numerous fields. There are other less well-known NN techniques which also hold much potential, and perhaps the most notable of these is the Kohonen SOM. Neelakanta (1999) described self-organization as the 'progressive formation within the system of sequential, ordered relationships between the interacting dynamic variables'. One might also describe the phenomenon as 'adaptation'. The SOM provides, quite literally, a picture or map of a set of data, but it does so in an adaptive or 'intelligent' way. On the other hand, NNs in general, including those which apply supervised learning, are also self-organizing in a similar sense: for

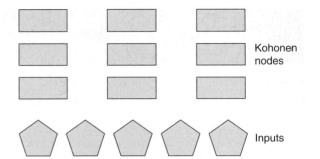
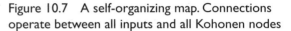

Figure 10.7　A self-organizing map. Connections operate between all inputs and all Kohonen nodes

example, the hidden nodes in perceptron models provide approximations to an underlying function and can act to filter the data.

The SOM amounts to a relationship between a set of input nodes and a set of nodes connected to these inputs which perform the operations of transformation and grouping.

There is no output node serving the role of predicted or target value and hence in NN terminology we have 'unsupervised learning'. Specifically, these 'Kohonen' nodes are arranged in a two-dimensional grid, with each node being connected to each of the inputs, as shown in Figure 10.7.

Interestingly, the actual spacing of the Kohonen nodes has no meaning: what is important is their grouping together. This is because each node is regarded as a 'prototype', a set of cognate values of the attributes of the input data. An equivalent term is 'reference vector'. These values are the weights of the node. As discussed below, each vector of observed values, which may be continuous, discrete or categorical, will be closest in terms of Euclidean distance to one particular prototype node. The latter nodes serve to classify or cluster inputs, but the proximity of each node to its neighbours in the grid is a key element, which distinguishes the SOM from conventional statistical clustering techniques. Whereas cluster analysis (CA) operates in the space of actual data values, the SOM operates within its own two-dimensional grid. Standard methods of CA are almost invariably designed to produce non-overlapping clusters (Everitt, 1993), but the prototypes of the SOM are not mutually exclusive. This means that the final feature map, instead of showing several distinct clusters with differing characteristics, shows neighbouring nodes which have many similar characteristics but differ perhaps on one or two, or in the degree of intensity of characteristics.

In the terminology of the SOM, the grid preserves the 'topological structure' of the data or alternatively may help us *uncover* such structure. The *Concise Oxford Dictionary* (1999) defines topology as 'the study of geometrical properties and spatial relations left unchanged by the continuous change of shape or size of the figure'. The topological structure emerges as a 'feature map' in which the prototypes are related and subject to potential overlaps. Topology preservation implies that input vectors close together in input space map to close nodes in the grid. Thus, not only are the prototypes intended to reflect 'typical' values of the inputs in their respective neighbourhoods, but their grid positions reflect the relative positioning and density of the original data. No such ordering exists for the clusters which emerge from CA.

We have noted how, once 'trained', the network classifies a data point by identifying the nearest Kohonen node. As regards the training process, a similar principle is adopted. As is common in NN operation, data points are presented randomly to the network, and at each stage the nearest Kohonen node is identified. This is referred to as the 'winning' node and the learning mechanism itself as 'competitive learning' or 'winner takes all learning'. The weights of the winning node are adjusted so as to move towards the current data point, in which case the training process involves allowing the weights of each node to reflect or describe the data. The topological structure of the data is preserved because not only is the winning node updated, but also its neighbouring nodes. The shape of the neighbourhood may take various forms, such as square or diamond. It is also possible to model the proximity of nodes by a Gaussian decay function.

More formally, we denote the input data by an $m \times n$ matrix $\mathbf{X}$, each row of which contains a data point comprising observed values of the n inputs. Each node k in the SOM grid is characterized by a $1 \times n$ vector $\mathbf{w}^{(k)}$ of weights. The Euclidean distance between the kth node and the jth input vector is then given by:

$$D = \sum_i (W_i^{(k)} - X_{ji})^2$$

where the observed values of the attributes of each data vector are indexed by i.

During training, the winning node is that with the smallest distance from the current data vector. The distance is in fact modified to allow for the frequency with which nodes have previously been 'winners', a so-called 'conscience mechanism' through which an additional egality is inserted.

The adjusted distance is given by:

$$D^* = D - \gamma(NF_k - 1)$$

where N is the number of Kohonen nodes, F_k is the relative frequency with which the kth of these nodes has been the winning node, and γ is a constant between zero and unity. For nodes whose frequency is the average for all nodes, that is, $1/N$, the adjustment is zero. Nodes winning with higher or lower frequencies have the distances adjusted downwards or upwards, respectively. The frequency values are estimates adjusted at each iteration.

The weight adjustment process involves finding the node nearest to the data vector in terms of adjusted distance D^*, and this node, p say, has its weights updated. The actual adjustment used is such that the change in each weight of the prototype is proportional to the Euclidean distance between the current weights and the current input vector. The adjustment proportion λ is referred to as the learning constant. Hence we have:

$$W(p_i)^* = W(p_i) + \lambda(X_{ji} - W(p_i))$$

where $W(p_i)^*$ and $W(p_i)$ respectively denote new and old weight values.

An interesting presentation of this learning rule is given by Kohonen (1995) and Ritter *et al.* (1992). Who make an analogy with data compression techniques, in which the primary aim is subsequent reconstruction of the data with minimal error. They show that the SOM has a similar interpretation, whereby the learning procedure amounts to a search for a set of weights to minimize the expected reconstruction error. The learning rule embodies the principle of gradient descent and there is, therefore, an element of similarity with back-propagation. Also, as well as being an independent statistical procedure in its own right, the SOM may be used as a pre-filter to other forms of NN, for instance to a standard multiplayer perceptron using back-propagation.

Business applications

SOMs have been shown to be useful in different types of business applications. Mazanec (1995) analysed positioning issues related to luxury hotels, using SOMs based on the discrete-value neighbourhood technique. Using data on perceptions of hotels and customer satisfaction, he showed that the non-parametric nature of this analysis allowed for compression of binary profile data.

Cottrell *et al.* (1998) applied the SOM in a forecasting context, with the nodes in the Kohonen layer used to store profiles describing the shapes of various trends, as opposed to relying solely on traditional parameters such as mean and standard deviation.

Serrano Cimca (1998) examined strategic groupings among Spanish savings banks, using a combination of SOMs and CA. The idea of the strategic group is often used to explain relationships between firms in the same sector, but here the groups were identified using only data from published financial information, thus giving groups of firms that followed similar financial strategies, with similar levels of profitability, cost structures, etc. The methodology allowed the visualization of similarities between firms in an intuitive manner, and showed up profound regional differences between Spanish savings banks.

The Kohonen SOM is a form of NN, which shares with other networks an origin in models of neural processing. As with other NNs, applications of such methods tend to take us into the realm of statistics, with the SOM operating as a new and interesting variant on CA. The aim is to provide a 'topology preserving' data transformation onto a two-dimensional grid, in which the location of the nodes *vis-à-vis* each other is important.

The SOM has some similarities with CA, in the sense that both involve 'unsupervised learning', where there is no dependent variable. Most clustering techniques involve attempts to find non-overlapping groups, so that each data point belongs uniquely. In the SOM, however, each data point is associated with the nearest prototype, but this does not exclude an association with others. Indeed, the fact that Kohonen nodes are spatially related in defined 'neighbourhoods' is an important feature of the approach. Clustering and SOMs tend to show us different aspects of the data. Clustering, by its concentration on differences, points out the observations that do not conform, while SOMs concentrate on similarities and gradual changes in the data. The relationships between prototypes are a key part of the model. One may navigate between them, and important attributes of the data set may be found in groups of prototypes.

It is also possible to employ the SOM in a predictive format, involving supervised learning. It can be used in this way as a pre-filter to a predictive NN using methods such as back-propagation. The model first of all derives a Kohonen map, and then applies supervised learning as a second step.

Stochastic processes

A stochastic process is a random experiment which occurs over time, the outcome of which is determined by chance. From these random experiments some attributes of interest are observed and numerical values can be given to these attributes according to the probability law. The stochastic process method is commonly used in building brand-choice models of consumers. In all, there are three basic types of stochastic process methods – the zero-order, Markovian and learning models – and each has its own set of assumptions.

The zero-order model assumes that past brand choice has no effect on future brand choice. There are studies on the existence of brand or store loyalties using the zero-order model approach which have defined brand loyalty as a proportion of total purchases within a product class that a household devotes to its favourite or most frequently purchased brand.

The Markov model assumes that only the most recent purchases affect the brand-choice decisions. Using the Markovian model, one can measure the expected number of periods before an individual would try a particular brand. Markov models should be used for dynamic market predictions such as equilibrium market shares, average time to trial, which is a measure of the attractive power of the brand, and for evaluating the success of new product introduction. One other area where Markovian analysis has been employed in marketing is in making personal selling decisions, where it is used in the modelling of sales-effort allocation to customers.

The third of the stochastic process methods is the learning model, which postulates that brand choice is dependent upon a complete history of past brand purchases, as the effect of purchasing a brand is cumulative. Therefore, when applied in the brand-switching complex, this will mean that purchase of a brand will ultimately increase the probability of purchasing the same brand again. This model may be used in monitoring consumer behaviour.

Statistical decision theory

Decision theory is often used to evaluate the alternative outcomes of different decisions and to find the best possible decision. Associated with the statistical decision theory is the decision tree diagram, which portrays the various alternative decisions and their consequences. Game theory, discussed below, is commonly regarded as an analytical approach to decision making involving two or more conflicting individuals, each trying to minimize the maximum loss (minimax criterion).

One other application of game theory is for formulating advertising budget decisions. In statistical decision theory, probabilities of each outcome are based upon either past data or subjective estimates. Pricing decisions in advertising are another area where decision theory can be applied. The main disadvantage of this method is the subjective estimation of the probability for each decision.

Decision trees can also be used to decide whether or not to test-market a new product before launching it. Cadbury-Schweppes Ltd used this technique to help in deciding the feasibility of test-marketing a new chocolate product. By carrying out a test-market programme of the new chocolate, the earnings obtained exceeded those of embarking on a national launch without prior test-marketing. This method has been used for making merchandising decisions, such as finding the optimum mix of sizes and widths of fashion shoes to be ordered, especially when the possible alternative choices were numerous and carried high costs.

Game theory

Game theory, when compared with decision theory, has found limited applications in marketing. Nevertheless, it has been applied to retailing institutions in making product decisions. Game theory helps management to decide on its advertising budgets without any prior knowledge of competitors' budgeting decisions.

In pricing advertisements, Higgins (1973) used game theory to provide solutions. The total reward for all the firms included in the pricing decision study was considered fixed, the decision resting on which product price to lower to generate more sales so as to minimize the maximum loss.

A summary of the major stochastic methods, their possible applications in marketing (with some references), advantages and limitations is presented in Table 10.10.

Deterministic operational research methods

Deterministic techniques are those in which chance plays no part and solutions are determined by sets of exact relationships.

Rough set theory

Rough set theory (RST) is a fairly new approach to decision making in the presence of uncertainty and vagueness (Pawlak, 1997). RST was first introduced by Zdzislaw Pawlak in the early 1980s, as a new mathematical tool to deal with vagueness and uncertainty. This approach seems to be of fundamental importance to AI and cognitive sciences, especially in the areas of machine learning, knowledge discovery from databases, expert systems, decision-support systems, inductive reasoning and pattern recognition. One of the main advantages of RST is that it does not need any preliminary additional information about data, such as probability distributions or basic probability assignments, which means RST has numerous real-world applications (Pawlak *et al.*, 1995).

The main concept of RST is an indiscernibilty relation normally associated with a set of attributes. The key problem in this description is the informal term 'normally associated'. In real life, such an association does not exist until additional assumptions are made. The subjectivity issue is more complicated than in other methods for managing uncertainty, therefore RST is potentially an important tool in the analysis of data with important applications in data mining and knowledge discovery. However, claims of its superiority (objectivity) over other approaches remains to be substantiated by scientific evidence (Koczkodaj *et al.*, 1998). The results of RST are a set of 'if . . . then' rules which enable prediction of classification of objects.

The critical issues of data mining were examined by Lingras and Yao (1998), who used the theory of rough sets, which is a recent proposal for generalizing classical set theory. The Pawlak rough set model is based on the concept of an equivalence relation. Research has shown that a generalized rough set model need not be based on equivalence relations axions. Lingras and Yao (1998) demonstrated that a generalized rough set model could be used for generating rules from incomplete databases. These rules are based on plausibility functions. These authors also emphasized the importance of rule extraction from incomplete databases in data mining.

An RST approach was used by Dimitras *et al.* (1999) to provide a set of rules able to discriminate between healthy and failing firms in order to predict business failure. The evaluation of its predictive ability was the main objective of the study. The results were very encouraging, compared with

Table 10.10 Applications of statistical decision theory or stochastic methods in marketing (approaches, advantages, limitations and when recommended to use)

Method	Based on	Marketing applications	Advantages	Limitations
Queuing	Probability distribution analysis of data (empirically gathered on how the major factors/ variables will affect the situation-problem under analysis). It is an analysis of queuing systems attempting to determine service levels/performance	(a) Optimize: sales force (Paul, 1972), number of checkouts, number of attendants, etc. (b) Minimize inventory-carrying costs; suitable and widely used by chain stores, supermarkets, department stores, petrol stations, airline ticket offices, ports, airports, etc.	(a) Predicts how different marketing systems will operate (b) Gives explicit expression relating the design of a system to the length and frequency of queues, waiting time, etc.	(a) Must be operated a sufficient length of time to achieve a steady-state solution (b) Manager's reluctance to have confidence in this method
Stochastic process	A random experiment which occurs over time and whose outcome is determined by chance. This is an analysis of systems with variable/ uncertain components	(a) For building choice, models checking on customers' loyalty (b) Predict buying decisions and future purchasing probabilities	Might predict flow of customers and future purchase probabilities	Suitable for short-run predictions only
Statistical decision theory	This is an analysis of decision-making processes where outcomes are uncertain. Probability of each outcome – based upon past data or subjective estimates – is given adequate weight and is taken into consideration for decision making	For decision making on: budgeting, advertising, pricing, test-marketing, new product development, merchandising, optimum mix, etc.	Simplifies the level of analysis and suggests a number of possible outcomes	Subjective estimation of the probability for each decision might affect the results' validity

Table 10.10 Continued

Method	Based on	Marketing applications	Advantages	Limitations
Game theory	Constant sum game solution, use of a maximum criterion to determine, for example, budget/ resources allocation. Theoretical analysis of competition/ collusion between organizations	For decision making by retailing firms, mainly on: pricing (Higgins, 1973), product stock determination and advertising, budget allocations, also for better decision on negotiation processes	(a) Aids management in decision making (b) Suggests a useful analytical approach to competitive problems, such as: pricing, advertising outlay and product decisions	Does not have much predictive power compared with other quantitative techniques

those from discriminate and logit analyses, and proved the usefulness of the method. The rough set approach discovers relevant subsets of characteristics and represents in these terms all important relationships between the key constructs. The method analyses only facts hidden in the input data and communicates with the decision maker in the material language of rules derived from his or her experience.

A recent development in RST is the variable precision rough set (VPRS) model, by Ziarko (1993a, b). Unlike RST, which constructs deterministic rules (i.e. 100 per cent in correct classification by a rule), the VPRS model enables a level of confidence in correct classification by a rule. That is, they are probabilistic rules.

Dissatisfied customers pose numerous potential problems for any organization – for example, negative word of mouth, reduced change of repeat lower brand loyalty. All of these problems will negatively affect the measurements of any business (e.g. profits and market shares). Therefore, assessing customer satisfaction level and more importantly why they are dissatisfied has great benefits to any company. This is particularly true in high competitive globalized markets, where search costs are low and the cost of switching supplier negligible.

Variable precision rough sets

A further RST innovation has been the development by Ziarko (1993a, b) of a VPRS model, which incorporates probabilistic decision rules. This is an important extension since, as noted by Kattan and Cooper (1998), when discussing computer-based decision techniques in a corporate failure setting, 'In real world decision making, the patterns of classes often overlap, suggesting that predictor information may be incomplete . . . This lack of information results in probabilistic decision making, where perfect prediction accuracy is not expected'.

An *et al.* (1996) applied VPRS (which they termed 'enhanced RST') to generating probabilistic rules to predict the demand for water. Relative to the traditional rough set approach, VPRS has the additional desirable property of allowing for partial classification compared to the complete classification required by RST. More specifically, when an object is classified using RST it is assumed that there is complete certainty that it is a correct classification. In contrast, VPRS facilitates a degree of confidence in classification, invoking a more informed analysis of the data, which is achieved through the use of a *majority inclusion* relation.

This paper extends previous work by providing an empirical exposition of VPRS, where we present the results of an experiment which applies VPRS rules to the corporate failure decision. In addition, we mitigate the impact of using the subjective views of an expert (as employed in previous studies) to discretize the data, by utilizing the sophisticated FUSINTER discretization technique, which is applied to a selection of attributes (variables) relating to companies' financial and non-financial characteristics. The discretized data, in conjunction with other nominal attributes, are

Table 10.11 Example of a decision table

| Objects | Condition attributes (C) | | | | | | Decision attribute D |
	c_1	c_2	c_3	c_4	c_5	c_6	d
o_1	1	0	1	1	0	1	L
o_2	1	0	0	0	0	0	L
o_3	0	0	1	0	0	0	L
o_4	1	0	1	1	0	1	H
o_5	0	0	0	0	1	1	H
o_6	1	0	1	1	0	1	H
o_7	0	0	0	0	1	0	H

then used in this new VPRS framework to identify rules to classify companies in a failure setting.

To facilitate a comparison of our experimental VPRS results with those of existing techniques, we present the predictive ability of classical statistical methods – logit analysis and MDA – together with two more closely related non-parametric decision tree methods, RPA and the Elysee method, which utilizes ordinal DA.

An overview of VPRS

VPRS (as with RST) operates on what may be described as a decision table or *information system*. As is illustrated in Table 10.11, a set of objects $U(o_1, \ldots, o_7)$ are contained in the rows of the table. The columns denote *condition attributes* $C(c_1, \ldots, c_6)$ of these objects and a related *decision attribute* $D(d)$. A value denoting the nature of an attribute to an object is called a *descriptor*. As noted above, a VPRS data requirement is that it must be in discrete or categorical form. Table 10.11 shows that, with this particular example, the condition attribute descriptors comprise zeros and ones (e.g. denoting yes and no answers), and the decision attribute values are L and H (e.g. denoting low and high). The table shows that the objects have been classified into one of these decision values, which are also referred to as *concepts*.

For the condition attributes in this example, all of the objects (U) can be placed in five groups: $X_1 = \{o_1, o_4, o_6\}$, $X_2 = \{o_2\}$, $X_3 = \{o_3\}$, $X_4 = \{o_5\}$ and $X_5 = \{o_7\}$. The objects within a group are indiscernible to each other, so that objects o_1, o_4 and o_6 in X_1 have the same descriptor values for each of the condition attributes. These groups of objects are referred to as *equivalence classes* or *conditional classes* for the specific attributes. The equivalence classes for the decision attribute are: $Y_L = \{o_1, o_2, o_3\}$ and $Y_H = \{o_4, o_5, o_6, o_7\}$. The abbreviation of the set of equivalence classes for the conditional attributes C is denoted by $E(C) = \{X_1, X_2, X_3, X_4, X_5\}$ and for the decision attribute it is defined $E(D) = \{Y_L, Y_H\}$.

VPRS measurement is based on ratios of elements contained in various sets. A case in point is the conditional probability of a concept given a particular set of objects (a condition class). For example:

$$\Pr(Y_L \,|\, X_i) = \Pr(\{o_1, o_2, o_3\} \,|\, \{o_1, o_4, o_6\})$$
$$= \frac{|\{\mathbf{o_1}, \mathbf{o_2}, \mathbf{o_3}\} \cap \{\mathbf{o_1}, \mathbf{o_4}, \mathbf{o_3}\}|}{\{o_1, o_4, o_6\}}$$
$$= \mathbf{0.333}$$

It follows that this measures the accuracy of the allocation of the conditional class X_1 to the decision class Y_L. Hence for a given probability value β, the β-positive region corresponding to a concept is delineated as the set of objects with conditional probabilities of allocation at least equal to β. More formally:

$$\beta\text{-positive } \textit{region of the set } Z \subseteq U{:}POS_P^\beta(Z)$$
$$= \underset{\Pr(Z\,|\,X_,) \geq \beta}{\cup} \{X_i \in E(P)\} \text{ with } P \subseteq C.$$

Following An *et al.* (1996), β is defined to lie between 0.5 and 1. Hence for the current example, the condition equivalence class $X_1 = \{o_1, o_4, o_6\}$ have a majority inclusion (with at least 60 per cent majority needed, i.e. $\beta = 0.6$) in Y_H, in that most objects (two out of three) in X_1 belong in Y_H. Hence X_1 is in $POS_C^{0.6}$ (Y_H). It follows $POS_C^{0.6}$ (Y_H) = $\{o_1, o_4, o_5, o_6, o_7\}$.

Corresponding expressions for the β-boundary and β-negative regions are given by Ziarko (1993a) as follows:

β-boundary *region of the set* $\mathbf{Z} \subseteq \mathbf{U}:BND_P^\beta(\mathbf{Z})$

$= \underset{1-\beta \langle \Pr(Z|X_i)\langle\beta}{\cup} \{\mathbf{X}_i \in \mathbf{E}(\mathbf{P})\}$ with $\mathbf{P} \subseteq \mathbf{C}$,

β-negative *region of the set* $\mathbf{Z} \subseteq \mathbf{U}:NEG_P^\beta(\mathbf{Z})$

$= \underset{\Pr(Z|X_i)\leq 1-\beta}{\cup} \{\mathbf{X}_i \in (\mathbf{P})\}$ with $\mathbf{P} \subseteq \mathbf{C}$.

Using $\mathbf{P}$ and $\mathbf{Z}$ from the previous example, with $\beta = 0.6$, then $BND_C^{0.6}(\mathbf{Y}_H) = 0$ (empty set) and $NEG_C^{0.6}(\mathbf{Y}_H) = \{o_2, o_3\}$. Similarly, for the decision class $\mathbf{Y}_L$ it follows that $POS^{0.6}_C(\mathbf{Y}_L) \{o_2, o_3\}$, $BND_C^{0.6}(\mathbf{Y}_L) = 0$ and $NEG_C^{0.6}(\mathbf{Y}_L) = \{o_1, o_4, o_5, o_6, o_7\}$.

VPRS applies these concepts by firstly seeking subsets of the attributes, which are capable (via construction of decision rules) of explaining allocations given by the whole set of condition attributes. These subsets of attributes are termed β-*reducts* or *approximate reducts*. Ziarko (1993a) states that a β-reduct, a subset $\mathbf{P}$ of the set of conditional attributes $\mathbf{C}$ with respect to a set of decision attributes $\mathbf{D}$, must satisfy the following conditions: (i) that the subset $\mathbf{P}$ offers the same quality of classification (subject to the same value) as the whole set of condition attributes $\mathbf{C}$ and (ii) that no attribute can be eliminated from the subset $\mathbf{P}$ without affecting the quality of the classification (subject to the same β value).

The quality of the classification is defined as the proportion of the objects made up of the union of the β-positive regions of all the decision equivalence classes based on the condition equivalence classes for a subset $\mathbf{P}$ of the condition attributes $\mathbf{C}$.

As with decision tree techniques, *ceteris paribus*, a clear benefit to users of VPRS is the ability to interpret individual rules in a decision-making context (as opposed to interpreting coefficients in conventional statistical models). Hence VPRS-generated rules are relatively simple, comprehensible and are directly interpretable with reference to the decision domain. For example, users are not required to possess the technical knowledge and expertise associated with interpreting classical models. These VPRS characteristics are particularly useful to decision makers, who are interested in interpreting the rules (based on factual cases) with direct reference to the outcomes they are familiar with.

Dempster–Shafer theory

The Dempster–Shafer theory (DST) of evidence originated in the work of Dempster (1967) on the theory of probabilities with upper and lower bounds. It has since been extended by numerous authors and popularized, but only to a degree, in the literature on AI and expert systems, as a technique for modelling reasoning under uncertainty. In this respect, it can be seen to offer numerous advantages over the more 'traditional' methods of statistics and Bayesian decision theory. Hajek (1994) remarked that real, practical applications of DST methods have been rare, but subsequent to these remarks there has been a marked increase in the applications incorporating the use of DST. Although DST is not in widespread use, it has been applied with some success to such topics as face recognition (Ip and Ng, 1994), statistical classification (Denoeux, 1995) and target identification (Buede and Girardi, 1997). Additional applications are centred on multisource information, including plan recognition (Bauer, 1996).

Applications in the general areas of business decision making are in fact quite rare. An exception is the paper by Cortes-Rello and Golshani (1990), which although written for a computing science/ AI readership, does deal with the 'knowledge domain' of forecasting and marketing planning. The DST approach is as yet very largely unexploited.

Decision analysis relies on a subjectivist view of the use of probability, whereby the probability of an event indicates the degree to which someone believes it, rather than the alternative frequentist approach. The latter approach is based only on the number of times an event is observed to occur. Bayesian statisticians may agree that their goal is to estimate objective probabilities from frequency data, but they advocate using subjective prior probabilities to improve the estimates.

Shafer and Pearl (1990) noted that the three defining attributes of the Bayesian approach are:

1 Reliance on a complete probabilistic model of the domain or 'frame of discernment'.
2 Willingness to accept subjective judgements as an expedient substitute for empirical data.
3 The use of Bayes' theorem (conditionality) as the primary mechanism for updating beliefs in light of new information.

However, the Bayesian technique is not without its critics, including among others Walley (1987), as well as Caselton and Luo (1992), who discussed the difficulty arising when conventional Bayesian analysis is presented only with weak information sources. In such cases, we have the 'Bayesian dogma of precision', whereby the information concerning uncertain statistical parameters, no matter how vague, must be represented by conventional, exactly specified, probability distributions.

Some of the difficulties can be understood through the 'Principle of Insufficient Reason', as illustrated by Wilson (1992). Suppose we are given a random device that randomly generates integer numbers between 1 and 6 (its 'frame of discernment'), but with unknown chances. What is our belief in '1' being the next number? A Bayesian will use a symmetry argument, or the Principle of Insufficient Reason, to say that the Bayesian belief in a '1' being the next number, say $P(1)$, should be 1/6. In general, in a situation of ignorance, a Bayesian is forced to use this principle to evenly allocate subjective (additive) probabilities over the frame of discernment.

To further understand the Bayesian approach, especially with regard to the representation of ignorance, consider the following example, similar to that in Wilson (1992). Let *a* be a proposition that:

'I live in Byres Road, Glasgow'.

How could one construct $P(a)$, a Bayesian belief in *a*? First, we must choose a frame of discernment, denoted by Θ and a subset A of Θ representing the proposition *a*; we would then need to use the Principle of Insufficient Reason to arrive at a Bayesian belief. The problem is there are a number of possible frames of discernment Θ that we could choose, depending effectively on how many Glasgow roads can be enumerated. If only two such streets are identifiable, then $\Theta = \{x_1, x_2\}$, $A = \{x_1\}$. The Principle of Insufficient Reason then gives $P(A)$ to be 0.5, through evenly allocating subjective probabilities over the frame of discernment. If it is estimated that there are about 1000 roads in Glasgow, then $\Theta = \{x_1, x_2, \ldots, x_{1000}\}$ with again $A = \{x_1\}$ and the other x values representing the other roads. In this case, the 'theory of insufficient reason' gives $P(A) = 0.001$.

Either of these frames may be reasonable, but the probability assigned to A is crucially dependent upon the frame chosen. Hence one's Bayesian belief is a function not only of the information given and one's background knowledge, but also of a sometimes arbitrary choice of frame of discernment. To put the point another way, we need to distinguish between uncertainty and ignorance. Similar arguments hold where we are discussing not probabilities *per se* but weights which measure subjective assessments of relative importance. This issue arises in decision-support models such as the analytic hierarchy process (AHP), which requires

that certain weights on a given level of the decision tree sum to unity (see Saaty, 1980).

The origins of DST go back to the work by Dempster (1967, 1968), who developed a system of upper and lower probabilities. Following this, his student, Shafer, in his 1976 book *A Mathematical Theory of Evidence*, added to Dempster's work, including a more thorough explanation of belief functions. Even though DST was not created specifically in relation to AI, the name DST was coined by Barnett (1981) in an article which marked the entry of the belief functions into the AI literature. In summary, it is a numerical method for evidential reasoning (a term often used to denote the body of techniques specifically designed for manipulation of reasoning from evidence, based upon the DST of belief functions; see Lowrance *et al.*, 1986).

Following on from the example concerning Glasgow roads in the previous section, one of the primary features of the DST model is that we are relieved of the need to force our probability or belief measures to sum to unity. There is no requirement that belief not committed to a given proposition should be committed to its negation. The total allocation of belief can vary to suit the extent of our knowledge.

The second basic idea of DST is that numerical measures of uncertainty may be assigned to overlapping sets and subsets of hypotheses, events or propositions, as well as to individual hypotheses. To illustrate, consider the following expression of knowledge concerning murderer identification adapted from Parsons (1994).

Mr Jones has been murdered, and we know that the murderer was one of three notorious assassins, Peter, Paul and Mary, so we have a set of hypotheses, that is, frame of discernment, $\Theta = \{$Peter, Paul, Mary$\}$. The only evidence we have is that the person who saw the killer leaving is 80 per cent sure that it was a man, that is, $P(\text{man}) = 0.8$. The measures of uncertainty, taken collectively, are known in DST terminology as a 'basic probability assignment' (*bpa*). Hence we have a *bpa*, say m_1 of 0.8, given to the focal element {Peter, Paul}, that is, $m_1(\{$Peter, Paul$\}) = 0.8$; since we know nothing about the remaining probability, it is allocated to the whole of the frame of the discernment, that is, $m_1(\{$Peter, Paul, Mary$\}) = 0.2$.

The key point to note is that assignments to 'singleton' sets may operate at the same time as assignments to sets made up of a number of propositions. Such a situation is simply not permitted in a conventional Bayesian framework, although it is possible to have a Bayesian assignment of prior probabilities for groups of propositions (since conventional probability theory can cope with joint probabilities). As pointed out by Schubert (1994), DST is in this sense a generalization of the Bayesian theory. It avoids the problem of having to assign non-available prior probabilities and makes no assumptions about non-available probabilities.

The DS/AHP method allows opinions on sets of decision alternatives and addresses some of the concerns inherent within the 'standard' AHP:

- The number of comparisons and opinions are at the decision maker's discretion.
- There is no need for consistency checks at the decision alternative level.
- There is an allowance for ignorance/uncertainty in our judgements.

We remind the reader that the direction of this method is not necessarily towards obtaining the most highest ranked decision alternative, but towards reducing the number of serious contenders.

Linear programming

Linear programming (LP) is a mathematical technique for solving specific problems in which an objective function must be maximized or minimized, considering a set of definite restrictions and limited resources. The word 'programming' stands for computing or calculating some unknowns of a set of equations and/or inequalities, under specific conditions, mathematically expressed.

Before the LP technique can be employed in the solution of a marketing problem, five basic requirements must be considered (Meidan, 1981):

1 *Definition of the objective.* A well-defined objective is the target of the solution and the answer to the problem must satisfy the requirements. Objectives such as reduced costs, increased profits, matching of sales force effort to customer potential or improved media selection can be handled.
2 *Quantitative measurement of problem elements.* A quantitative measurement is needed for each of the elements described in the problem, which is an essential condition for applying mathematical models such as hours, pounds (£), etc.
3 *Alternative choice.* It must be possible to make a selection for reaching a solution which satisfies the objective function.
4 *Linearity.* The term 'linearity' describes the problem and its restrictions. Equations and inequalities must describe the problem in a linear form.
5 *Mathematical formulation.* Information must be compiled in such a manner that it is possible to translate the relationships among variables into a mathematical formulation capable of describing the problem and all the relations among variables.

A number of techniques are available for solving a formulated linear programme. A graphical solution is possible when there are three variables only. An example showing the use of LP in determining the best allocation and mix of marketing effort is presented in detail by Meidan (1981).

One is faced with four kinds of difficulties in using LP models:

1 The first difficulty is in describing the problem mathematically. In an industrial situation one must know exactly how much one can use the production resources, such as manpower, raw materials, time, etc.
2 The second problem lies in the interpretation and proper use of the objectively obtained optimum solution. One may need to analyse additional business considerations, over and above the ones used in describing and formulating the problem.
3 Even if the problem has been correctly stated and formulated, technical limitations may exist, such as the amount of data a computer can handle or that no solution exists (e.g. the number of constraints and/or variables may be too large).
4 A further limitation lies in the reliability of the proposed solution. This could arise when a linear assumption is taken for real non-linear behaviour of the component.

Physical distribution

Designing an optimal physical distribution system is dependent on choosing those levels of services that minimize the total cost of physical distribution, whose objective function might read: $C = T + F + I + L$, where C = total distribution cost, T = total freight cost, F = total fixed warehouse cost, I = total inventory cost and L = total cost of lost sales.

Given the objective function, one seeks to find the number of warehouses, inventory levels and modes of transportation that will minimize it, subject to at least three constraints:

1 Customer demand must be satisfied.
2 Factory capacity limits must not be exceeded.
3 Warehouse capacity cannot be exceeded.

The LP model has been used in solving distribution problems, particularly in the transportation of finished goods to warehouses. The aims were to minimize transport costs subject to certain constraints, such as warehouse costs (Kotler, 1972). Other uses of LP models in marketing include site location, physical distributions and blending products.

Warehouse location

Chentnick (1975) discusses the various methods of locating warehousing systems which are of interest as their usefulness is indicated, thus suggesting the advantage of LP in comparison to other methods. Broadly, the function of a warehouse can be broken down into five areas:

1 Storage.
2 Assembling of customer orders.
3 Service of customers.
4 Economies of scale by bulk buying and delivery.
5 Processing and final packaging.

There are two definable sets which characterize the two methods of solution to the warehouse location problem (Meidan, 1978):

1 The infinite set assumes that the warehouse can be positioned anywhere on the map – obvious slight adjustments can be made later to allow for rivers, mountains, etc. A main assumption is that transport costs are directly proportional to distance (as the crow flies), and this is questionable in many situations.
2 The feasible set assumes a finite number of possible locations, and both costs of buildings and haulage can be calculated with a high degree of precision.

Media selection

One area in marketing where LP models have been extensively used is in advertising decisions, especially in media mix decisions in a market segment. Higgins (1973), for example, proposed the use of this model for deciding on the optimum paging schedule for colour supplements of newspapers.

Marketing mix decisions and budget allocations

The marketing mix refers to the amounts and kinds of marketing variables the firm is using at a particular time, and includes price, advertising costs and distribution expenditures, each of which could be subdivided into further variables.

Product mix and the multiproduct marketing strategy problem

The problem of product mix, that is, variety and quantity of products produced, is commonly encountered by almost all multiproduct firms during the planning period. Here the objective is to maximize current profits subject to the various constraints, such as capacity, demand levels and quality. Such problems necessitate the use of LP.

Other marketing management applications for LP

Wilson (1975) cites a number of potential applications of LP, including new product decisions, resolving conflict in market segmentation and the choice of a new market from a set of possible alternatives, and gives an example of its use in allocating a sales force to new products. Goal programming, on the other hand, may be used when a minimum knowledge of the situation and realistic objectives are available. Here the subjective constraints placed on the model give direction to an objective and hence an area of solutions (i.e. constraints become goals).

The transportation model

The transportation model is a specialized class of LP model. Like the LP models, its aim is to optimize the use of resources, with the exception that it requires separate computational techniques not normally used in other models.

The transportation model seems to have limited application, and the area of marketing where it has been used is in making distribution decisions. This limited usage is the result of the way in which the model is formulated. The major deterministic operational research techniques and their marketing applications, limitations and advantages are summarized in Table 10.12.

Causal models

Under this heading we have two main techniques: PA and structural equation modelling (SEM), linear structural relations (LISREL). Both these methods are relatively new to marketing. Of the two, LISREL is more widely applied because of its versatility.

Table 10.12 Some major deterministic operational research techniques applicable in marketing (the methods, advantages, limitations and when recommended to use)

Method	Based on	Marketing applications	Main advantages	Major limitations
Linear programming	Objective and constraint linear functions	(a) Advertising (Higgins, 1973), space, optimal media mix allocations (b) Distribution problems, site location (Kotler, 1972) (c) Budget allocation, new product decision (Wilson, 1975) (d) Blending product mixes (e) Marketing mix decisions	(a) Maximizes profitability of allocations, subject to constraints (b) Minimizes costs (c) Aids management in decision making	(a) Difficult to obtain and formulate the various functions (b) Constraints must be altered as soon as external and/or internal factors change
Transportation model	Transportation/ allocation matrix ascertaining the minimum costs, routes, quantities supplied, etc.	To allocate resources, supply etc. by reducing transportation costs. Suitable particularly for department stores, truck rental firms, transport companies	Very suitable for managerial decision making	Inaccurate in the longer run as a result of changes in costs
Non-linear programming	Non-linear objective functions and non-linear constraint relationships	To find the maximum return to a new product search, subject to budget constraint	(a) When the relationships are non-linear (b) When the objective function is non-linear while the constraints are non-linear	Difficult to establish non-linear relationships

Path analysis

PA is a method for studying patterns of causation among a set of variables, which was popularized in the sociological literature (Hise, 1975). Though path diagrams are not essential for numerical analysis, they are useful for displaying graphically the pattern of causal relationships among sets of observable and unobservable variables. PA provides means for studying the direct and indirect effects of variables. PA is intended not to accomplish the impossible task of deducing causal relations from the values of the correlation coefficients, but to combine the quantitative information given by the correlations with such qualitative information as may be at hand on causal relations, to give quantitative information.

Path analytic models assume that the relationships among the variables are linear and additive. Path coefficients are equivalent to regression weights. Direct effects are indicated by path coefficients. Indirect effects refer to the situation where an independent variable affects a dependent variable through a third variable, which itself directly or indirectly affects the dependent variables. The indirect effect is given by the product of the respective path coefficients.

In a recent example, developed for a tourism marketing study (McDonagh *et al.*, 1992), PA was used to measure the effects of three major environmental factors (exogenous variables) – preservation of local landscape, preservation of architectural values and overcrowding – as a direct causal impact on two critical endogenous variables: (1) concern towards a policy of global conservation and (2) preservation of cultural values.

Structural equation modelling LISREL

LISREL is a method of SEM that allows the researcher to decompose relations among variables and to test causal models that involve both observable (manifest) and unobservable (latent) variables. PA and LISREL models are two important analytical approaches for testing causal hypotheses. Essentially, the analyst wants the reproduced correlations to be close to the original correlations. The LISREL model allows the researcher to simultaneously evaluate both the measurement and causal (i.e. structural) components of a system.

LISREL allows for a holistic, more realistic conception of social and behavioural phenomena. It recognizes that measures are imperfect, errors of measurement may be correlated, residuals may

be correlated and that reciprocal causation is a possibility. *A priori* theory is absolutely necessary for covariance structure analysis. An important strength of SEM is its ability to bring together psychometric and econometric analyses.

Many applications of LISREL modelling can be seen in such areas as consumer behaviour, personal selling, new product adoption, marketing strategy, organizational decision making, distribution channels, advertising research and international marketing. For a detailed example of an application of LISREL, see Moutinho and Meidan (1989). Table 10.13 summarizes the applications of the two causal models in marketing.

Hybrid models

Under this category there are three different types of methods used in solving marketing problems: dynamic programming; heuristic programming and stock control models.

Dynamic programming

As stated by Budnick *et al.* (1977), dynamic programming is a recursive approach to optimization problems which works on a step-by-step basis utilizing information from the preceding steps. The model has been used to aid decision making in areas such as distribution (i.e. the minimization of transportation costs), the distribution of salespeople to various territories (in such a way that maximum profits will be obtained) and determining the best combination of advertising media and frequency under a budgetary constraint.

Heuristic programming

Heuristics is commonly defined as the use of rule of thumb for solving problems. Therefore, heuristic programming techniques are based on an orderly search procedure guided by these rules of thumb and are mainly applied to problems when mathematical programming techniques are either too expensive or complicated. However, they do not guarantee optimal solutions. In the past, heuristic programming has been applied fairly extensively in certain areas of marketing.

Taylor (1963) devised a graphical heuristic procedure to derive solutions to the problems of media scheduling that suggested the optimal number of advertisements to be placed in each medium

Table 10.13   Applications of causal models in marketing (the techniques, advantages, limitations and when recommended to use)

Model	Content	Marketing applications	Advantages	Limitations
Path analysis	Provides the means for studying the direct and indirect effects of variables, by offering quantitative information on the basis of qualitative data on causal relations	Tourism marketing (McDonagh et al., 1992), other applications (Wasserman, 1989)	Displays graphically the pattern of causal relationships	Assumes relationships among variables are linear
LISREL (linear structural relations)	A structural equation modelling, that enables one to decompose relations among variables and test causal models that involve both observable and unobservable variables	Consumer behaviour, personal selling, marketing strategy, international marketing (Moutinho and Meidan, 1989)	Provides an integral approach to data analysis *and* theory construction. The method easily handles errors in measurement. Ability to bring together psychometric and econometric analyses	Requires an *a priori* theory for structure analysis

and the size of each insertion. The number of insertions was determined by graphical methods, which attempted to find the point where the marginal returns to the last insertion equalled the marginal cost of the advertisements for each medium.

A summary of the main characteristics, advantages, limitations and applications of dynamic and heuristic models in marketing is presented in Table 10.14.

Stock control models

The distribution side of marketing has been successfully modelled using quantitative methods for a number of years. The objective of the distribution system is to get the right goods to the right places at the right time for the least cost, and involves decisions on such problems as the number, location and size of warehouses, transportation policies and inventories. In this section the inventory decision will be discussed, but it must be realized

that inventory represents only one part of the local distribution network, a complete analysis of which is outside the scope of this chapter. The inventory decision has two parts to it: when to order (order point) and how much to order (order quantity). These are not independent and can be deduced from a stock control model. The ordering of goods involves costs, such as transportation and handling, which increase the number of orders placed.

On the other hand, the storage of goods also involves costs such as storage space charges, insurance costs, capital costs and depreciation costs. The first two decrease and the last two types of costs increase with the order quantity.

The simplest model assumes that demand is constant, shortages are not allowed (no stockouts), immediate replacements of stocks and a regular order cycle. If C = cost of holding of one unit of stock/unit time, C_o = cost of placing an order, d = demand rate (units/unit time), q = order quantity in units and t = order cycle time (order point),

Table 10.14 Applications of dynamic, heuristic and network programming in marketing (the methods, advantages, limitations and when recommended to use)

Model	Based on	Marketing applications	Advantages	Limitations
Dynamic programming	Recursive optimization procedure; optimizing on a step-by-step basis	Solving media selection problems; distribution (minimization of transportation costs; distribution of salespeople to various sales territories)	(a) Maximizes the objective over the planning period (b) Introduces new factors, for example, 'forgetting time', 'accumulation or intersections' (c) Wide potential application in industry	The programming procedure is rather complex; computational difficulties
Heuristic programming	Orderly search procedure guided by the use of rule of thumb. Based on 'marginal approach' or trial and error	Media selection and scheduling; warehouse location; sales force allocation; decision on the number of items in a product line; suitable for making product promotion decisions	(a) Good, flexible, simple and inexpensive method (b) Combines the analysis into the style of decision making and the reasoning used by managers	Does not guarantee optimal solution
Network programming (PERT and CPM)	Presents the wide range of critical activities that must be carried out and co-ordinated. PERT acknowledges uncertainty in the times required to complete activities while CPM does not. PERT deals only with the time factor. CPM refers to the time-cost trade-offs as well	Planning, scheduling and controlling complex marketing projects (Bird *et al.*, 1973), for example, building new stores, new product development (Robertson, 1970), product commercialization, advertising–sales relationships (Johansson and Redinger, 1979), distribution planning (LaLonde and Headon, 1973)	(a) Sequences and times of activities are considered, responsibilities allocated and co-ordinated in large/complex marketing projects (b) Project time can be forecast and completion time may be shortened	(a) Difficulties in estimating costs and times accurately, particularly for new projects (b) Of use only when functions and activities can, in fact, be separated

mathematical analysis shows that the total costs (ordering plus stockholdings) are minimized when the following order quantity is used:

$$q* = dt* = \sqrt{\frac{C_o d}{C}}$$

$C_o d\ C\ q*$ = is often referred to as the economic order quantity (EOQ). The simplest model can be improved by relaxing some of the assumptions.

Network programming models

Network programming models are the methods usually used for planning and controlling complex marketing management projects. There are two basic methods: the CPM and the PERT. The two methods together are also called CPA techniques.

Critical path analysis

CPA, in its various forms, is one of the techniques developed in recent years to cope with the increased need for planning, scheduling and controlling in all functions of management. For a number of reasons, this technique is particularly applicable for use in marketing management. First, marketing management, by definition, involves the co-ordination of many other functions and activities: advertising; distribution; selling; market research; product research and development. Second, much of the work in marketing can be of a project nature (e.g. new product launch, organization of a sales promotion, setting up of a new distribution system).

CPA is based on the assumption that some of the activities of a marketing project are in a concurrent relationship and take place simultaneously. The advantages to be gained from CPA in marketing are similar to those obtained in other functions, except that the centrality of the marketing function, particularly in some consumer goods firms, increases its desirability.

There are a large number of possible applications of PERT and CPM: for new product launch (Robertson, 1970), distribution, planning (LaLonde and Headon, 1973), sales negotiations, purchasing (Bird *et al.*, 1973), launching a marketing company/project/department, sales promotions, conference organization, advertising campaigns, new store openings, realigning sales territories, etc.

Budnick *et al.* (1977) proposed using network planning for product development, while others suggest the use of the CPM to co-ordinate and plan the hundreds of activities which must be carried out prior to commercialization of a new product. Johansson and Redinger (1979) used PA to formulate an advertising–sales relationship of a hairspray product.

Chaos theory

Chaos theory has the potential to contribute valuable insights into the nature of complex systems in the business world. As is often the case with the introduction of a new management metaphor, 'chaos' is now being 'discovered' at all levels of managerial activity (Stacey, 1993).

What is chaos theory?

Chaos theory can be compactly defined as 'the qualitative study of unstable aperiodic behaviour in deterministic non-linear dynamical systems' (Kellert, 1993, p. 2). A researcher can often define a system of interest by representing its important variables and their interrelationships by a set of equations. A system (or, more technically, its equations) is dynamical when the equations are capable of describing changes in the values of system variables from one point in time to another. Non-linear terms involve complicated functions of the system variables such as: $y_t + 1 = x_t y_t$.

Chaos theorists have discovered that even simple non-linear sets of equations can produce complex aperiodic behaviour. The most familiar example is the logistic equation of the form: $x_{t+1} = rx_t(1 - x_t)$, where x lies between 0 and 1. This system is deterministic in the sense that no stochastic or chance elements are involved. Figure 10.8 depicts the behaviour of this system for varying levels of r.

At values of $r < 2$, iterating over the logistic equation will result in the system stabilizing at $x = 0$ (Figure 10.8a). Between $r = 2$ and $r = 3$, the system reaches equilibrium at progressively higher values of x (Figure 10.8b). At around $r = 3$, the system is seen to bifurcate into two values. The steady-state value of x alternates periodically between two values (Figure 10.8c). As r continues to increase, it continues to increase in periodicity, alternating between 2, then 4, 8 and 16 points. When r is approximately 3.7, another qualitative change occurs – the system becomes chaotic. The output ranges over a seemingly infinite (non-repeating) range of x values (Figure 10.8d).

Chaotic systems are also unstable, exhibiting a sensitive dependence on initial conditions.

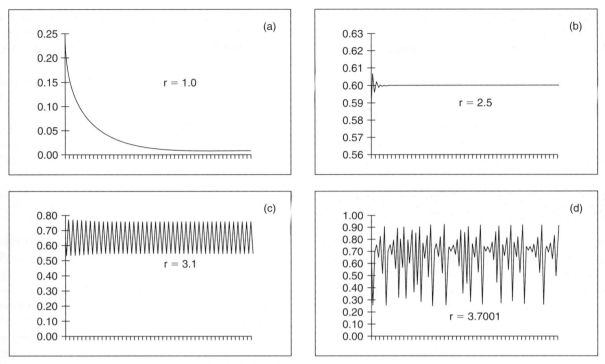

Note: Graphs represent output of the logistic equation: $X_{t+1} = rx_t(1-x_t)$, where $x_0 = 0.5$

Figure 10.8   Output of logistic equation for varying.

The Lyapunov exponent is a mathematically precise measure of the degree of sensitive dependence on initial conditions. The Lyapunov exponent takes the one-dimensional form $e^{\lambda t}$. If $\lambda < 0$, then the initial differences will converge exponentially. If $\lambda = 0$, then the displacements will remain constant over time, while if $\lambda > 0$, small differences will magnify over time. All chaotic systems have a lambda value that is greater than zero.

Initially, the system of interest would have to be specified in terms of non-linear dynamical equations. Few researchers in the social sciences have attempted to identify non-linear deterministic behaviours in their systems of interest. In the main, quantitative research in the social sciences has tended to be both statistical and linear in nature. Of course, it is possible that the appeal of chaos theory may excite an interest in developing non-linear models.

The researcher would also need to demonstrate that the system was capable of chaotic behaviour over some valid region of its parameters. By running digital simulations of the non-linear systems, researchers would hope to discover regions of chaos in the models that could be linked with phenomena in the observed world. Ideally, the Lyapunov exponent could then be calculated and found to be greater than zero.

Conclusion

The marketing research literature does not specify which quantitative method is most 'popular'. One can only conclude that the multivariate methods, as well as the stochastic and hybrid techniques and models, are widely used. CA is a method with much potential in marketing, as it displays all the benefits of multidimensional scaling and can be used with a variety of data inputs. The flexibility of both simulation and heuristic programming models mean that they can be applied to almost any situation where other models fail to give satisfactory results. In the last few years, causal models – in particular, LISREL – and AI techniques have been widely used. The fuzzy sets technique is a new method that has been applied in marketing only very recently. Expert systems are currently systematically applied in many marketing problem areas. Queuing theory, network planning and transportation models are more restricted in their applications in marketing, as they are formulated to solve problems in specific areas. Regarding deterministic techniques, these are suitable for finding optimum solutions to problems, particularly when set relationships exist between the variables. In summary, the usage of different types of models depends largely on the problem under investigation, as well as on the type of data available and their level of interrelationships.

This chapter has attempted to present the application of the main quantitative methods in marketing. A taxonomic structure was adopted and all the techniques were broadly classified under nine headings: multivariate methods; regression and forecasting techniques; simulation and fuzzy sets methods; operational research techniques; causal models; hybrid techniques and network programming models. Also discussed were GLMs, fuzzy decision trees, self-organizing maps (SOMs), RST, VPRS, DST and chaos theory. Advantages and limitations in the usage of each of these methods were discussed. However, the use of different types of methods depends largely on the marketing management situation of the problem under consideration.

References

An, A., Shan, N., Chan, C., Cercone, N. and Ziarko, W. (1996) Discovering rules for water demand prediction: an enhanced rough-set approach, *Engineering Applications in Artificial Intelligence*, **9**(6), 645–653.

Barnett, J. A. (1981) Computational methods for a mathematical theory of evidence, *Proceedings of the 7th International Joint Conference on Artificial Intelligence (IJCAI)*, Vancouver, **II**, 868–875.

Bauer, M. (1996) A Dempster–Shafer approach to modeling agent preferences for plan recognition, *User Modeling and User-Adapted Interaction*, **5**, 317–348.

Bird, M. M., Clayton, E. R. and Moore, L. J. (1973) Sales negotiation cost planning for corporate level sales, *Journal of Marketing*, **37**(2), April, 7–11.

Benzecri, J. P. (1992) *Correspondence Analysis Handbook*, Marcel Dekker, New York.

Buede, D. M. and Girardi, P. (1997) A target identification comparison of Bayesian and Dempster–Shafer multisensor fusion, *IEEE Transaction on Systems, Man and Cybernetics Part A: Systems and Humans*, **27**(5), 569–577.

Carroll, J., Green, E. and Schaffer, M. (1986) Interpoint distance comparisons in correspondence analysis, *Journal of Marketing Research*, **23**, August, 271–290.

Caselton, W. F. and Luo, W. (1992) Decision making with imprecise probabilities: Dempster–Shafer theory and applications, *Water Resources Research*, **28**(12), 3071–3083.

Cattin, P. and Wittink, D. R. (1982) Commercial use of conjoint analysis: a survey, *Journal of Marketing*, Summer, 44–53.

Chambers, J. D., Mullick, S. K. and Smith, D. D. (1979) How to choose the right forecasting technique, *Harvard Business Review*, July–August, 45–74.

Chentnick, C. G. (1975) Fixed facility location technique, *International Journal of Physical Distribution*, **4**(5), 263–275.

Coates, D., Doherty, N. and French, A. (1994) The New Multivariate Jungle, in Hooley, G. J. and Hussey, M. K. (eds), *Quantitative Methods in Marketing*, Academic Press, pp. 20–220.

Concise Oxford Dictionary (1999) Oxford University Press, Oxford.

Cortes-Rello, E. and Golshani, F. (1990) Uncertain reasoning using the Dempster–Shafer method: an application in forecasting and marketing management, *Expert Systems*, **7**(1), 9–17.

Cottrell, M., Girard, B. and Rousset, P. (1998) Forecasting of curves using a Kohonen classification, *Journal of Forecasting*, **17**, 429–439.

Curry, B. and Moutinho, L. (1991) Expert systems and marketing strategy: an application to site location decisions, *Journal of Marketing Channels*, **1**(1), 23–27.

Curry, B. and Moutinho, L. (1993) Neural networks in marketing: modelling consumer responses to advertising stimuli, *European Journal of Marketing*, **27**(7), 5–20.

Dempster, A. P. (1967) Upper and lower probabilities induced by a multi-valued mapping, *Annals of Mathematical Statistics*, **38**, 325–339.

Dempster, A. P. (1968) A generalization of Bayesian inference (with discussion), *Journal of the Royal Statistical Society Series B*, **30**(2), 205–247.

Denoeux, T. (1995) A k-nearest neighbour classification rule based on Dempster–Shafer theory, *IEEE Transactions on Systems, Man and Cybernetics*, **25**(5), 804–813.

DeSarbo, W. S. (1993) A lesson in customer response modeling, *Marketing News*, **27**(12), June, H24–H25.

Diamantopoulos, A. and Schlegelmilch, B. B. (1997) *Taking the Fear out of Data Analysis*, Dryden Press, London, pp. 209–218.

Dillon, W. R. and Mulani, N. (1989) LADI: a latent discriminant model for analysing marketing research data, *Journal of Marketing*, **26**, February, 15–29.

Dimitras, A. I. R., Slowinski, R., Susmaga, R. and Zopoundis, C. (1999) Business failure prediction using rough sets, *European Journal of Operational Research*, **11**(4), April, 263–280.

Doyle, P. and Fenwick, I. (1976) Sales forecasting using a combination of approaches, *Long Range Planning*, June, 61–64.

Ellis, R., LeMay, S. and Arnold, D. (1991) A transportation backhaul pricing model: an application of neural network technology, in Johnson, C., Krakay, F. and Laric, M. (eds), *Proceedings of the AMA Microcomputers in the Marketing Education Conference*, San Diego, CA, August, pp. 1–11, 15–17.

Everitt, B. S. (1993) *Cluster Analysis*, Edward Arnold, London.

Greenacre, M. J. (1984) *Theory and Applications of Correspondence Analysis*, Academic Press, New York.

Gurney, G. (1997) *An* Introduction to Neural Networks, University College Press, London.

Hajek, P. (1994) Systems of conditional beliefs in Dempster–Shafer theory and expert systems, *International Journal of General Systems*, **22**, 113–124.

Higgins, J. C. (1973) Some applications of operational research in advertising, *European Journal of Marketing*, **7**(3), 166–175.

Hise, D. R. (1975) *Causal Analysis*, Wiley, New York.

Hoffman, L. and Franke, R. (1986) Correspondence analysis: graphical representation of categorical data in marketing research, *Journal of Marketing Research*, **23**, August, 213–227.

Ip, H. H. S. and Ng, J. M. C. (1994) Human face recognition using Dempster–Shafer theory, *ICIP 1st International Conference on Image Processing*, **2**, 292–295.

Johansson, J. K. and Redinger, R. (1979) Evaluating advertising by path analysis, *Journal of Advertising Research*, 29–35.

Kattan, M. W. and Cooper, R. B. (1998) The predictive accuracy of computer-based classification decision techniques, *A Review and Research Directions OMEGA*, **26**(4), 467–482.

Kellert, S. H. (1993) *In the Wake of Chaos: Unpredictable Order in Dynamical Systems*, University of Chicago Press, Chicago.

Kennedy, M. S. (1991) Artificial intelligence in media planning: an exploration of neural networks, in Gilly, M. C. *et al.* (eds), *Enhancing Knowledge Development in Marketing, AMA Educators' Summer Conference Proceedings*, San Diego, CA, **2**, pp. 390–397.

Klir, J. G. and Yuan, B. (1995) *Fuzzy Sets and Fuzzy Logic: Theory and Application*, Prentice-Hall, New York, NY.

Koczkodaj, W. W., Orlowski, M. and Marek, V. W. (1998) Myths about rough set theory, *Communications of the ACM*, **41**(11), November, 102–103.

Kohonen, T. (1995) *Self Organisation and Associative Memory*, 2nd edn, Springer, New York.

Kosko, B. (1986) Fuzzy entropy and conditioning, *Information Science*, **30**, 165–174.

Kotler, P. (1972) *Marketing Management, Analysis Planning and Control*, Prentice-Hall, Englewood Cliffs, New Jersey, p. 364.

Kotler, P. and Schultz, R. L. (1970) Marketing simulations: review and prospects, *Journal of Marketing*, July, 237–295.

LaLonde, B. and Headon, R. (1973) Strategic planning for distribution, *Long Range Planning, Academy of Marketing Science Annual Conference*, December, 23–29.

Lingras, P. J. and Yao, Y. Y. (1998) Data mining using extensions of the rough set model, *Journal of the American Society for Information Science*, **49**(5), April, 415–422.

Lowrance, J. D., Garvey, T. D. and Strat, T. M. (1986) A framework for evidential-reasoning systems, *Proceedings of the 5th National Conference on Artificial Intelligence (AAAI-86)*, Philadelphia, 896–901.

Mazanec, J. A. (1995) Positioning analysis with self-organising maps: an exploratory study on luxury hotels, *Cornell Hotel and Restaurant Administration Quarterly*, **36**, 80–95.

McDonagh, P., Moutinho, E., Evans, M. and Titterington, A. (1992) The effects of environmentalism on the English, Scottish, Welsh and Irish hotel industries, *Journal of Euro-marketing*, **1**(3), 51–74.

Meidan, A. (1978) The use of quantitative techniques in warehouse location, *International Journal of Physical Distribution and Materials Management*, **8**(6), 347–358.

Meidan, A. (1981) *Marketing Applications of Operational Research Techniques*, MCB University Press, p. 86.

Meidan, A. (1983) Marketing strategies for hotels – a cluster analysis approach, *Journal of Travel Research*, **21**(4), Spring, 17–22.

Meidan, A. and Lim, I. (1993) The role of bank branch personnel in the sales process – an investigation of internal and external perceptions within the branch, *Proceedings of the 1993 MEG Conference: Emerging Issues in Marketing*,

Loughborough Business School, Academy of Marketing Science Annual Conference, **2**, July, pp. 660–670.

Moutinho, L. and Meidan, A. (1989) Bank customers' perceptions, innovations and new technology, *International Journal of Bank Marketing*, **7**(2), 22–27.

Neelakanta, P. S. (1999) *Information Theoretic Aspects of Neural Networks*, CRC Press, Boca Raton, FL.

Parsons, S. (1994) Some qualitative approaches to applying the Dempster–Shafer theory, *Information and Decision Technologies*, **19**, 321–337.

Paul, R. J. (1972) Retail store as a waiting line model, *Journal of Retailing*, **48**, 3–15.

Pawlak, Z. (1997) Rough set approach to knowledge-based decision support, *European Journal of Operational Research*, **99**(1), May, 48–57.

Pawlak, Z., Grzymala-Busse, J., Slowinski, R. and Ziarko, W. (1995) Rough sets, *Communications of the ACM*, **38**(11), November, 88–95.

Rangaswamy, A., Eliahberg, J. B., Raymond, R. and Wind, J. (1989) Developing marketing expert systems: an application to international negotiations, *Journal of Marketing*, **53**, October, 24–39.

Ritter, H., Martinetz, T. and Schulten, K. (1992) *Neural Computation and Self-Organising Maps*, Addison-Wesley, Reading, MA. Robertson, A. (1970) Looking out for pitfalls in product innovation, *Business Administration*, June, 39–46.

Saaty, T. L. (1980) *The Analytic Hierarchy Process: Planning, Priority Setting, Resource Allocation*, McGraw-Hill, New York.

Saunders, J. (1994) Cluster Analysis, in Hooley, G. J. and Hussey, M. K. (eds), *Quantitative Methods in Marketing*, Academic Press, London, pp. 13–28.

Schubert, J. (1994) *Cluster-Based Specification* Techniques in Dempster–Shafer Theory for an Evidential Intelligence Analysis of Multiple Target Tracks, Department of Numerical Analysis and Computer Science Royal Institute of Technology, S-100 44 Stockholm, Sweden.

Serrano Cimca, C. (1998) From financial information to strategic groups: a self-organising neural network approach, *Journal of Forecasting*, **17**(5–6), 415–428.

Shafer, G. (1976) *A Mathematical Theory of Evidence*, Princeton University Press, Princeton.

Shafer, G. and Pearl, J. (1990) *Readings in Uncertain Reasoning*, Morgan Kaufman, San Mateo, CA.

Speed, R. (1994) Regression Type Techniques and Small Samples, in Hooley, G. J. and Hussey, M. K. (eds), *Quantitative Methods in Marketing*, Academic Press, London, pp. 89–104.

Stacey, R. D. (1993) *Strategic Management and Organisational Dynamics*, Pitman, London.

Stanton, W. W. and Reese, R. M. (1983) Three conjoint segmentation approaches to the evaluation of advertising theme creation, *Journal of Business Research*, June, 201–216.

Taylor, C. J. (1963) Some developments in the theory and applications of media scheduling method, *Operational Research Quarterly*, 291–305.

Vriens, M. (1994) Solving Marketing Problems with Conjoint Analysis, in Hooley, G. J. and Hussey, M. K. (eds), *Quantitative Methods in Marketing*, Academic Press, London, pp. 37–56.

Walley, P. (1987) Belief-function representations of statistical evidence, *Annals of Statistics*, **10**, 741–761.

Wasserman, D. (1989) *Neural Computing: Theory and Practice*, Van Nostrand Reinhold, New York.

Wilson, J. M. (1975) The handling of goals in marketing problems, *Management Decision*, **3**(3), 16–23.

Wilson, P. N. (1992) Some theoretical aspects of the Dempster–Shafer theory, PhD Thesis, Oxford Polytechnic.

Yuan, Y. and Shaw, M. J. (1995) Induction of fuzzy decision trees, *Fuzzy Sets and Systems*, 125–139.

Ziarko, W. (1993a) Variable precision rough set model, *Journal of Computer and System Sciences*, **46**, 39–59.

Ziarko, W. (1993b) Analysis of uncertain information in the framework of variable precision rough sets, *Foundations of Computing and Decision Sciences*, **18**, 381–396.

Zimmerman, H. J. (1991) *Fuzzy Set Theory and its Applications*, 2nd edn, Kluwer Academic, Boston, MA.

Further reading

Bland, J.M. and Altman, D. G. (1990) A note on the use of the intraclass correlation coefficient in the evaluation of agreement between two methods of measurement, *Computers in Biology and Medicine*, **20**(5), 337–340.

Brave, G. and Potvin, L. (1991) Estimating the Reliability of Continuous Measures with Cohen, J., S. G. West, L. Aiken and P. Cohen (2002), *Applied Multiple Regression/Correlation*

Analysis for the Behavioral Sciences, Lawrence Erlbaum Associates, Mahwab, New Jersey.

Cramer, H. (1999) *Mathematical Methods of Statistics*, Princeton University Press, Princeton, New Jersey.

Diamantopoulos, A. and Schlegelmilch, B. B. (1997) *Taking the Fear Out of Data Analysis*, Dryden Press, London. This is an excellent text, easy to read, refreshing and amusing, yet introducing a very robust content.

Ferber, R. (1979) *Market Research – Statistical Techniques in Market Research*, McGraw-Hill, New York.

Finerty, J. J. (1971) Product pricing and investment analysis, *Management Accounting*, December, 21–37.

Glen, J. J. (2001) Classification accuracy in discrimination analysis: a mixed integer programming approach, *The Journal of the Operational Research Society*, **52**(3), March, 328.

Greenacre, M. J. (1984) *Theory and Applications of Correspondence Analysis*, Academic Press, London.

Hooley, G. J. and Hussey, M. K. (1994) *Quantitative Methods in Marketing*, Academic Press, London. This is a good book, introducing a collection of different quantitative research methods ranging from LISREL to neural networks. A new edition was published in 1999.

Kane, G., Richardson, F. and Meade, N. (1998) Rank transformation and the prediction of corporate failure, *Contemporary Accounting Research*, **15**(2), 145–166.

Kemsley, E. K. (1998) *Discriminant Analysis and Class Modelling of Spectroscopic Data*, John Wiley & Sons, New York.

Kinnear, T. C. and Taylor, J. R. (1996) *Marketing Research: An Applied Approach*, 5th edn, McGraw-Hill, New York. An excellent textbook for introductory marketing research.

Lachenbruch, P. A. (1997). *Discriminant Analysis*, Hafner Press, New York.

Lillien, G. L. and Rangaswamy, A. (1998) *Marketing Engineering* – Computer-Assisted Marketing Analysis and Planning, Addison-Wesley, Harlow, UK. Excellent new text on quantitative and computer modelling techniques with CD-ROM included. Techniques range from cluster analysis and conjoint analysis to AHP and neural networks.

Malhotra, N. K. (2004) *Marketing Research: An Applied Orientation*, 4th edn, Pearson-Prentice Hall, Upper Saddle River, New Jersey.

Mazanec, J. A. (1994) A priori and a posteriori segmentation: heading for unification with neural network modelling, in Chias, J. and Sureda, J. (eds), *Marketing for the New Europe: Dealing with Complexity, 22nd European Marketing Academy Conference Proceedings*, Barcelona, Spain, **I**(25–28), May, 889–917.

Meidan, A. (1981) Optimising the Number of Salesmen, in Baker, M. J. (ed.), *New Directions in Marketing and Research*, University of Strathclyde, Glasgow, pp. 173–197.

Moutinho, L. and Curry, B. (1994) Consumer perceptions of ATMs: an application of neural networks, *Journal of Marketing Management*, **10**(1), 191–206.

Moutinho, L., Goode, M. H. and Davies, F. F. (1998) *Quantitative Analysis in Marketing Management*, Wiley, Chichester. This is a very recent text which includes chapters on statistical analysis, forecasting, decision theory and new quantitative methods, among others.

Sharma, S. (1996) *Applied Multivariate Techniques*, Wiley, Chichester. Very good book on the topic. Issues covered range from factor analysis, cluster analysis and discriminant analysis to logistic regression, MANOVA and covariance structure models.

Walters, D. (1975) Applying the Monte Carlo simulation, *Retail and Distribution Management*, February, 50–54.

Zimmerman, H. J. (1991) *Fuzzy Set Theory and its Applications*, 2nd edn, Kluwer Academic. This is probably the best and most up-to-date text on fuzzy sets theory and applications.

CHAPTER 11

Market segmentation

YORAM (JERRY) WIND and DAVID R. BELL

All markets are heterogeneous. This is evident from observation and from the proliferation of popular books describing the heterogeneity of local and global markets. Consider, for example, *The Nine Nations of North America* (Garreau, 1982), *Latitudes and Attitudes: An Atlas of American Tastes, Trends, Politics and Passions* (Weiss, 1994) and *Mastering Global Markets: Strategies for Today's Trade Globalist* (Czinkota *et al.*, 2003). When reflecting on the nature of markets, consumer behaviour and competitive activities, it is obvious that no product or service appeals to all consumers and even those who purchase the same product may do so for diverse reasons. The Coca Cola Company, for example, varies levels of sweetness, effervescence and package size according to local tastes and conditions. Effective marketing and business strategy therefore requires a segmentation of the market into homogeneous segments, an understanding of the needs and wants of these segments, the design of products and services that meet those needs and development of marketing strategies, to effectively reach the target segments. Thus focusing on segments is at the core of organizations' efforts to become customer driven; it is also the key to effective resource allocation and deployment. The level of segment aggregation is an increasingly important issue. In today's global economy, the ability to customize products and services often calls for the most micro of segments: the segment of one. Following and implementing a market segmentation strategy allows the firm to increase its profitability, as suggested by the classic price discrimination model which provides the theoretical rationale for segmentation.

Since the early 1960s, segmentation has been viewed as a key marketing concept and has been the focus of a significant part of the marketing research literature. The basic concept of segmentation (as articulated, e.g. in Frank *et al.*, 1972) has not been greatly altered. And many of the fundamental approaches to segmentation research are still valid today, albeit implemented with greater volumes of data and some increased sophistication in the modelling method. To see this, consider the most compelling and widely used approach to product design and market segmentation – conjoint analysis. The essence of the approach outlined in Wind (1978) is still evident in recent work by Toubia *et al.* (2007) that uses sophisticated geometric arguments and algorithms to improve the efficiency of the method. Other advances use formal economic theory to specify optimal consumer trade-offs – see Iyengar *et al.* (2007) for an application to non-linear pricing.

Despite the underlying stability of the basic concept, recent advances in information technology and the trend towards globalization are introducing a discontinuous change to the adoption and implementation of segmentation strategies. The revolution in information technology and strategy makes possible the creation of databases on the entire universe and enormous advances in database marketing and innovative distribution approaches. It has also facilitated much of the development in flexible manufacturing with the consequent emergence of mass customization. In addition, the Internet has expanded not only the ability to implement market segmentation research more effectively, but also expanded the portfolio of segmentation methods available for use (see, e.g. Dahan and Srinivasan, 2000). These changes are leading to the creation of 'one-on-one marketing' or segments of one. The globalization of business expands the scope of operations and requires a new approach to local, regional and global segments. Moreover, businesses that have not traditionally embraced marketing in general or segmentation in particular, see it as imperative for success and even survival. Consider the current enormous effort by the leading financial services firms to understand how to segment the global at-retirement market fuelled by the baby boomers in North America and Western Europe. Finally, it is important to recognize a subtle but pervasive shift in the *bases* for segmentation. Historically, marketers segment the market according to characteristics (e.g. demographics), preferences, usage rates, etc. Increasingly, it is difficult to fully articulate a segmentation strategy without an accompanying discussion of customer lifetime value (CLV) and a thought process that makes the CLV calculation explicit (see Gupta and Lehmann, 2003).

These changes require not only an appraisal of what we know about segmentation, and what works and does not work, but also a review of the segmentation area as part of an entirely new marketing and management paradigm.

Therefore, the purpose of this chapter is to introduce the reader to both the 'best practice' in the segmentation area and the likely new developments. These observations are based on advances in marketing concepts, marketing science research and modelling tools, generalizations from empirical studies, successful practices of leading firms and the conceptual implications of operating in the global information age. This discussion of the best segmentation practices and likely advances encompasses five areas:

1 Use of segmentation in marketing and business strategy.
2 Decisions required for the implementation of a segmentation strategy.
3 Advances in segmentation research.
4 Impact of operating in the global information age on segmentation theory, practice and research.
5 Expansion of segmentation to other stakeholders.

Thus, this chapter is based on the premise that segmentation is the firm's response to a fundamental market feature – heterogeneity. The likely success (or otherwise) of the firm's segmentation strategy is assessed through a segmentation audit discussed next. The firm enacts the segmentation strategy through: (1) data collection, (2) application of models and frameworks and (3) resource allocation and differential action based on segment (customer) value. The chapter concludes with a set of critical issues that provide the guidelines for research agenda in this area.

Use of segmentation in marketing and business strategy

Conceptually any business strategy should be based on understanding, meeting and even exceeding the needs of target segments. Figure 11.1 illustrates the centrality of segmentation and the progression of fundamental questions to address. At the core is the identification of the existing and potential customer base, an understanding of underlying heterogeneity and the evolving needs and wants of target segments. Next is the response to segmentation, namely guidelines for the development of products and services, and their associated positioning to meet the evolving needs of the target segments. Finally, the product positioning provides the foundation for the rest of the marketing strategy and the processes, resource allocation decisions and other activities of the firm.

Numerous published and unpublished case studies attest to the value of segmentation. For example, Bell *et al.* (1998) show how segmentation of store choice decisions of supermarket shoppers reveals fundamental differences in store attractiveness, conditional on a shoppers preferred shopping style. The model illustrates how one store format can capture market share from another. It is important to recognize that applications of segmentation cover a diversity of business contexts. In an industrial buying setting, Gensch *et al.* (1990) provide compelling evidence of the positive consequences of segmentation of electrical equipment buyers. In a 1-year test segmentation applied in two of three geographic districts, sales increased 18 and 12 per cent – while sales declined 10 per cent in the district in which model-based segmentation was not applied and 15 per cent for the industry. The firm reports continuous market share increases from the application of the segmentation approach. This is not an isolated case. The popular business press and the conference circuit are full of anecdotal cases in which creative segmentation has paid off. In fact a growing number of firms do use segmentation as the basis of their marketing strategy.

Yet despite the general acceptability of segmentation and its value, too many firms are not segmenting their markets effectively and are not

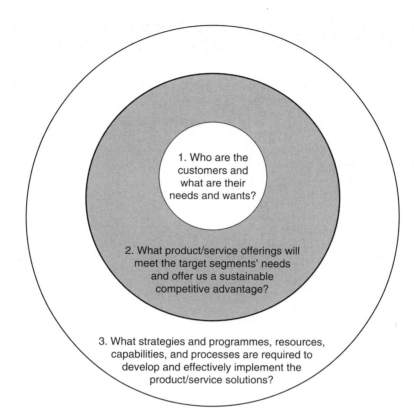

Figure 11.1 Focus on market-driven strategy

basing their strategies on the evolving needs of target segments. The experience of the more successful firms in consumer and industrial markets alike suggests, however, that effective segmentation is a must. The likelihood of a positive response to the firm's offerings is increased, the cost of reaching customers and chances of new product and service failures are reduced. The need to 'rediscover' the centrality of segmentation is made forcefully in a recent article by Yankelovich and Meer (2006).

A segmentation audit can help a firm make an initial determination as to whether it uses an effective segmentation strategy. We propose three interrelated approaches in decreasing order of complexity and time commitment. Table 11.1 presents a fairly comprehensive audit template (based on an actual audit for a large computer manufacturer). In scoring this particular audit it is important to note that effective segmentation requires a positive answer to each question. Any lower score on any of these dimensions requires correction.

A second approach is the *'Five Question' (5Q) method* which requires the firm to articulate an answer to each of the following:

1 *Who* are my market segments? This descriptive approach forces management to try and first identity the observable characteristics of individuals or firms thought to be in the target market segments. A firm unable to effectively answer this question is likely to have considerable trouble not only locating existing segments, but also predicting the evolution of new market segments.

2 *What* do my segments think and feel? An attitudinal evaluation of segments focuses on pyschographics and underlying segment preferences. A firm that cannot develop an answer to this question is unlikely to be able to communicate effectively with target segments. An understanding of perceptions, preferences and attitudes towards the firm and its competitors are necessary conditions for being able to tailor marketing messages and talk in the appropriate 'language'.

3 *How* do my segments behave? This question forces the firm to think about usage, demand and consumption patterns, and the reaction to changes in the marketing mix (product, price, promotion and distribution).

4 *Where* are my segments going? Here, the firm must attempt to map out the trajectory of segment growth. All segments follow a life cycle and this question forces the firm to address

Table 11.1 A segmentation audit				
Practice	*Completely describes us*	*Somewhat describes us*	*Does not describe us at all*	*Do not know*
1 Our business strategies recognize the need to prioritize target segments				
2 Our marketing plans include specific plans for each of the selected segments				
3 We have specific product offerings for each target segment				
4 We have a process for updating the information on our segments on an ongoing basis				
5 Our segments balance the unique country needs with potential synergies across countries				
6 We have an effective process for implementing segmentation research				
7 We have an effective process for implementing segmentation strategies				
8 We have P&L reports and accountability by segment				
9 We have detailed information about segments, including: • Current size of segment • Potential size of segment • Key business needs of the segment • Information systems needs of the segment • Their prioritized needs/benefits sought • Their prioritized preference for product and service features • Demographic characteristics of the segments • Product/system ownership and usage • Competition's strength in each segment • Perceived positioning of each competitor by the members of the segment				
10 Information about the target market segments are incorporated effectively into the following strategies: • Positioning • Product and service offerings • Pricing • Promotion • Advertising • Distribution • Sales force				

dynamics, and thereby understand long-term viability of segments.

5   *What* are my individual customers (and segments) worth? This final question stipulates that the firm must attempt to place a financial value on market segments. The inability to answer this question is likely to hamper firm efforts to effectively allocate marketing resources and maximize marketing return on investment (ROI).

A third exercise which is less time intensive, but can nevertheless reveal fundamental strengths and weaknesses in the current segmentation strategy is the '*Product by Segment Matrix*' (PSM). To create the PSM, the firm simply lists as rows of a matrix, the distinct products and services currently on offer. The columns of the matrix are a list of the segments thought to be addressed by the firm. At the very least, this exercise will provide some insight into the firm's view of market structure. For example, if all the matrix entries fall on the diagonal, each product is addressing a different market segment. A 'full row' implies that one of the firm's products is serving the needs of multiple segments simultaneously. Such a product is clearly of key strategic importance. Similarly, a 'full column' implies the presence of a segment with a deep level of attachment to the firm's product line.

These three different but complementary approaches to the segmentation audit illustrate important principles to keep in mind. First, effective segmentation requires a good deal of effort and attention. Cognitive effort, financial resources and time commitment from top management are prerequisites to the development of a viable segmentation strategy. A firm with limited commitment is unlikely to simply happen upon an effective strategy. Second, all good segmentation approaches seek to 'triangulate' – or converge on understanding segments through a different lens (description, attitude, behaviour, movement, value). Third, segmentation and the product/service portfolio must reflect and reinforce each other.

Decisions required in implementing a segmentation strategy

While poor segmentation can result from flawed thinking or conceptions of segmentation, it is our experience that many segmentation efforts fall flat because of poor execution and implementation.

Effective segmentation strategy requires *detailed* answers to the following sets of questions:

1   How to segment the market?
2   What research procedure to use to develop a segmentation strategy?
3   What segment(s) to target?
4   How to allocate resources among the segments?
5   How to implement the segmentation strategy?

Segment identification decision

The determination of which set of variables – *basis* – to use for segmentation of the market is critical. Conceptually, the guiding principle is fairly obvious. A good segmentation variable is one that explains variation in use of the firm's products and services. If a proposed segmentation variable has no correlation to choice or other important behaviours, it is clearly of little value. Practically, the approach is quite involved and requires consideration of the following issues. Should we segment on product usage patterns (e.g. users versus non-users or heavy versus light users)? Should we segment based on benefits sought (e.g. product performance versus convenience versus price sensitivity)? Should we use some other measure of consumer response to marketing variables (e.g. likelihood of buying a new product concept, response to price promotion, participation in a loyalty programme)? The 'best practice' in this area suggests three propositions:

1   An *effective basis* for segmentation should allow one to differentiate among segments based on their response to marketing variables; thus buyers versus non-buyers or price sensitive versus non-price sensitive are possible bases for segmentation. Age, sex, marital status, psychographic characteristics or other general characteristics of the consumer may not be good bases for segmentation since they do not assure differential response to marketing variables.
2   The *selected basis* for segmentation should be directly related to the strategic purpose of the segmentation effort. In general, there are two types of segmentation with two different underlying rationales:
    ● A general segmentation of the market which allows the organization to organize itself around the selected target segments. As an increasing number of companies shift from a product management organization to a market-driven organization or a matrix organization of product by market (as might

be implied by the PSM analysis), it is critical to identify relatively stable and large segments which could serve as strategic business units. Examples of such segments, in the case of a financial service firm, are the 'Delegators' – individuals who prefer to have a money manager take complete control over the management of their financial affairs, and the 'Electronic DIY' – who prefer to do it themselves using direct computer trading. To reach these two segments effectively the firm needs distinctly different strategies. Members of each of these strategic segments share some common financial/investment needs, yet each of these segments may still be quite heterogeneous with respect to other needs and, thus, could benefit from further sub-segmentation into more homogeneous groups.

● Specific segments for specific marketing and business decisions. For example, in the introduction of a new product, this may mean a focus on the segment that has the highest likelihood of buying the product. In the launch of a new online electronic shopping service, it could involve a focus on time-constrained individuals with high-speed Internet access at home. Other specific segments and their associated characteristics can be developed for each of the marketing mix decisions. Notice that in the following examples the informational requirements (and therefore basis for segmentation) differs systematically from issue to issue:

  ● *For positioning*: product usage, product preference, benefits sought or a hybrid of the variables above.
  ● *For new product concepts (and new product introduction)*: intention to buy, preference over current brand, benefits sought.
  ● *For pricing decisions*: price sensitivity, deal proneness, price sensitivity by purchase/usage patterns.
  ● *For advertising decisions*: benefits sought, media usage, psychographic/lifestyle. A hybrid of the variables above with or without purchase/usage patterns.
  ● *For distribution decisions*: store loyalty and patronage, benefits sought in store selection.
  ● *For general understanding of a market*: benefits sought, or in industrial markets, the criterion used is purchase decision, product purchase and usage patterns,

needs, brand loyalty and switching patterns or a hybrid of the above variables.

3   To gain a better understanding of the various segments and their characteristics, it is critical to profile the segment's key discriminating characteristics. These include the complete segment profile on demographic, psychographic, product usage, perceptions and preferences, attitudes and the like. In the case of industrial (business-to-business) segmentation, these variables should include both the characteristics of the organization and each of the key members of the relevant buying centre. Table 11.2 identifies a list of variables commonly used as a basis for segmentation and as segment descriptors. It is important to note that variables not used as a basis for segmentation can become descriptors of segments that are developed based on other bases.

Selecting a research programme

The quality of a segmentation programme depends largely on the quality of information used in developing the scheme. Segmenting any market requires information on the characteristics of the market including:

● *Attractiveness*: The size and growth of the market segment(s).
● *Decision making*: The evaluation and choice criteria used by individuals (or buying centres in business-to-business marketing contexts), including the benefits they seek and problems they try to solve.
● *Perceptions and preferences*: The perceptions of preference for attitudes towards and usage of the products and services of the firm and its competitors.
● *Characteristics*: The demographic characteristics of the segment members or other relevant stable characteristics of the buying centre in the case of business-to-business markets.
● *Attitudes/feelings*: The psychographic profile (lifestyle, personality and other psychological and attitudinal characteristics).
● *Responsiveness*: Reaction and sensitivity to the marketing actions of the firm and its competitors.

To collect data on these variables and to analyse and interpret them requires a systematic research programme. Historically, segmentation research centred on customer surveys. Yet there are a number of additional approaches that should be considered. Figure 11.2 outlines the range of options. Formal primary research and especially surveys on

Table 11.2 Variables commonly used as basis for segmentation and as descriptors of segments

Basis for segmentation	Descriptors of segments
Organizational • Share • Trial • Purchase/adoption • Source loyalty • Price sensitivity • Customers of key competitors • Etc. **Buying Centre** • Buying process • Informational search • Criteria/benefits sought • Negotiation style • Application • Decision • Post-purchase evaluation • Etc. **Individual** • Awareness • Knowledge • Perceptions, preferences, attitudes towards the brand • Preference • Recommendation • Purchase • Usage • Loyalty • Etc.	**External** • Socioeconomic, political environment (culture, technology, economic, political, regulatory, legal) • Behaviour towards competitors • Etc. **Organizational** • Industry type (e.g. SIC) • Size • Degree of centralization • Capabilities (technical, financial, etc.) • Geographic location (country, region, city, etc.) • Etc. **Buying centre** • Size • Composition • Buying situation • Influence • Consensus among the members • Buying process • Buying organization and policies • Relations with suppliers • Etc. **Individual** • Demographic (age, sex, family life cycle, income, education, social class, etc.) • Psychographics (personality, lifestyle, activities, interest opinions, etc.) • Etc.

a sample of customers and prospects have been the most common approach to segmentation research. Recent developments of databases on the entire universe have changed the nature of segmentation research. Consider, for example, the pharmaceutical industry. Here a number of firms are developing databases on the entire industry. These databases include hundreds of thousands of physicians, thousands of hospitals and thousands of managed care organizations.

A second type of formal research includes secondary data analysis using geo-demographic data which can be used both for segmentation research as well as for experimentation. Adaptive experimentation (Wind, 2007) is another approach which

could yield insights into the characteristics of various market segments and their response to marketing activities. One of the most important developments of recent years is the adaptation of traditional marketing research methods for application on the Internet. Dahan and Srinivasan (2000), for example, show which conjoint analysis replicates on the Internet. Of equal importance is the work by Dahan and Hauser (2002) that documents new research methods which are facilitated by the unique communication capabilities afforded by the Internet.

The third approach is input from ongoing business activities. In this case, we include both data on the market response to various strategies

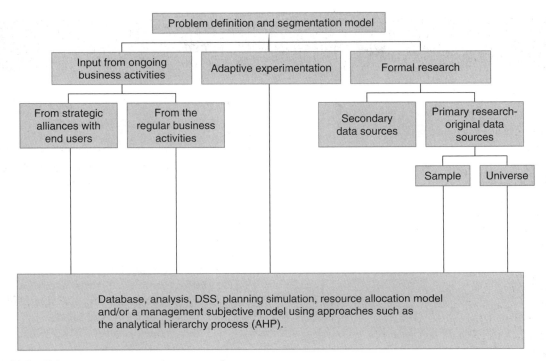

Figure 11.2   Selecting a segmentation research programme

and insights gained from strategic alliances with customers. This latter approach is especially critical in the new product development area when the firm works closely with its customers on the development of new products and service. "Best research practices" would include using a number of these approaches, integrating the resulting data in a database, continuously updating the database and having it as part of a decision-support system (DSS).

Selecting target segments

Having segmented a market it is often not desirable or possible to pursue all segments. Thus, a critical decision is the selection of target market segments. If more than one segment is to be addressed, then consideration needs to be given to the order in which each will be targeted. Moreover, all segments have to meet four conditions: measurability (ability to measure the size and characteristics of the segment); substantiality (having a minimum profitable size); accessibility (ability to reach and serve the segments) and actionability (ability to implement strategies to serve the segments) (Kotler and Keller, 2005). Beyond these fundamental requirements, the selection of target market segments requires answers to the questions given below. (Note the relationship between these questions for selecting segments, and those for segmenting the market itself, given previously.)

- *Relative Attractiveness:* What is the size of the segment in terms of the revenues and profits it is likely to generate?
- *Responsiveness:* What is the likely response to the firm's offering, including response to the positioning of the firm's products and services?
- *Competencies:* Do we have the required offerings and competencies to effectively develop, reach and serve the selected segments?
- *Exogenous factors:* What is the likely impact of changes in relevant environmental conditions (e.g. economic conditions, lifestyle, regulations, etc.) on the potential response of the target market segment?
- *Accessibility:* Can the segment be reached (via controlled media and distribution or via a self-selection strategy)?
- *Cost:* What are the likely costs of effectively reaching the target segment?
- *Competition:* What are the current and likely competitive activities directed at the target segment?
- *Portfolio management:* How many segments can be managed effectively? What synergies or relationships exist among the segments?

These and related criteria often require information that is not always available from market research. In addition, it is important that any information collected through marketing research or other

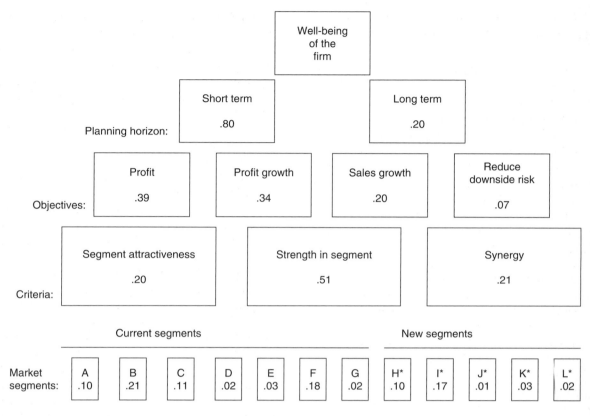

Note: The numbers are the composite priorities of each item.

Figure 11.3   An illustrative output of an AHP designed to select a portfolio of market segments

sources is structured in a way that is amenable to action. Consequently, a decision-support framework is needed to aid managerial decision making. This framework should utilize both managerial experience and available data. At the minimum it should include: identifying relevant criteria, and evaluating the segments on the selected criteria.

Following the logic of product and business portfolio analysis, a portfolio of current and potential market segments can be constructed (Wind and Robertson, 1983). Figure 11.3 illustrates a portfolio of segments in which each segment is evaluated on its attractiveness, on the firm's expected strength in the segment and on synergy. The first two criteria are the same dimensions used in the GE/McKinsey portfolio matrix. These dimensions can be based on a single criterion or represent a composite of multiple criteria. For example, segment attractiveness could include such factors as the segment's size and growth, risk factors and the cost of reaching the segment. Segment strength could include such factors as current and expected share in the segment and expected profitability. The specific criteria and their relative weights can be determined by management judgement and marketing research input.

The segment selection procedure illustrated in Figure 11.3 utilized the analytic hierarchy process (AHP). The AHP (Wind and Saaty, 1980; Saaty, 1992) is a measurement approach and process that helps quantify management subjective judgements. The essential steps in implementing an AHP include: (1) setting up the decision problem by the relevant management group as a hierarchy of interrelated decision elements, (2) evaluating the various elements of the hierarchy by pair-wise comparisons and (3) using a mathematical method to estimate the relative weights of decision elements. The *Decision Lens* (http://www.decisionlens.com) process and software greatly facilitates the implementation of an AHP and its extension to the Analytic Network Process (ANP).

The application of AHP or ANP to segment selection involves bringing together the key executives and presenting to them all available marketing research information. This provides input to the deliberation and evaluation of the various segments, in a pair-wise comparison, against each of the chosen criteria. The results for the prioritization of the segments from our illustrative example are given in Figure 11.3. An examination of this illustrative hierarchy suggests a number of segmentation-related conclusions:

- Management established three criteria (segment attractiveness, strength in segment and synergy) which vary in their importance with respect to the firm's ability to achieve their four objectives (profit, profit growth, sales growth and downside risk). The objectives, in turn, vary in their importance under short- or long-term conditions (not shown in the figure). The overall importance of the four objectives, assuming an 80–20 weight for short versus long term is presented in Figure 11.3. The seven current segments when evaluated against the three criteria (segment attractiveness, strength and synergy), which in turn are weighted by their importance to the accomplishment of the four objectives (weighted by their importance for the short- and long-term well-being of the firm), suggest that three of the segments – D, E and G – are not very attractive and should be considered as candidates for deletion, or at least destined to receive no incremental resources.
- Five new segments were identified. When evaluated on the three criteria, two of the segments – H and I – were viewed as candidates for inclusion in the portfolio and three – j, K and L – as candidates for exclusion.
- As a result of the process, a new portfolio of segments was established with segments A, B, C, F, H and I.
- The outcome also suggests how resources should be allocated to each segment. Since the dimensions included in the hierarchy encompass both the expected benefits from each segment as well as the cost of reaching them and risk, the priorities can be used as a rough guide for resource allocation. This would lead to the following allocation: A = 11 per cent, B = 24 per cent, C = 13 per cent, F = 21 per cent, H = 11 per cent and I = 20 per cent.

This example reinforces the idea that the identification and selection of market segments not only requires explicit structure, but also quantification and prioritization wherever possible.

Allocating resources among segments

The selection of target segments and the allocation of resources among segments are interrelated and iterative decisions. For example, in the preceding section, AHP was utilized to select a portfolio of segments. It also provided guidelines for resource allocation among the segments. Allocation of resources typically involves not only the allocation among segments, but also the allocation of resources to the marketing mix variables – product, price, distribution, promotion and advertising.

The basic problem of resource allocation is to decide on the mix of resources that generates optimal response (sales, profitability, etc.). Estimating and modelling the sales response of each segment to the various marketing resources is critical. How, for example, should sales persons currently covering a market be allocated across segments to optimize their return? A comprehensive set of analytical tools for how to answer such questions have been developed in Lilien and Rangaswamy (2002). Other traditional approaches, typically based on conjoint analysis studies among current and potential customers, have been applied to a wide range of situations including computers, telecommunications products and services, pharmaceuticals, etc. (Green and Krieger, 1985; Krieger *et al.*, 2004). In the cases in which empirically based market response functions are not available, management's subjective judgement, using either decision calculus methods (Little, 1979) or the AHP (Wind and Saaty, 1980), can be employed. Above all else, these approaches stress the importance of structure and managerial input. The principles underlying successful adoption and execution of marketing science models are clearly articulated by Lodish (2001) aptly titled *Building Marketing Models that Make Money*. The complexity and importance of the resource allocation decision suggests the advisability of employing a methodology such as the AHP that incorporates managerial judgement, empirical data derived from econometric market response models and experiments, consumer studies and decisions models.

Implementing a segmentation strategy

The most difficult aspect of any segmentation project is the translation of the study results into marketing strategy and programmes. No rules can be offered to assure a successful translation and, in fact, little is known (in the published literature) on how this translation occurs. However, informal discussions with executives and observations from our own experience of 'successful' and 'unsuccessful' translations suggest a few general conclusions on the conditions likely to increase successful implementation.

1 *Involvement:* All relevant decision makers (e.g. product managers, new product developers, advertising agency, sales management, etc.) must be involved in the problem definition, research design, strategy generation and evaluation.

2 *Texture:* The segment characteristics used in the analysis should be rich enough to provide the basis for innovative product positioning and product, pricing, communication and distribution decisions.

3 *Direction:* The segment characteristics should also provide guidelines for the generation of creative executions of the selected strategy.

4 *Ownership:* Given the oftentimes non-marketing orientation of product management, it can be desirable to shift the responsibilities for segmentation strategy to segment-driven managers and teams.

5 *Science:* Since vital information on the cause and effect relationship between marketing resource allocation and response is often absent, it is vital that firms undertake to explicitly measure and monitor outcomes. For example, linking market response to media and distribution systems.

Advances in segmentation research

Many of the papers published by academics and practitioners in *Marketing Science*, *Management Science* and the *Journal of Marketing Research* offer specific advances in segmentation research and modelling. Moreover, *Interfaces* offers in-depth case studies of marketing science tools that demonstrably improve the bottom line for the client firm. While the approaches outlined in these articles are necessarily diverse and sometimes focused in their application, they nevertheless are centred around six sets of key segmentation 'tools'. We list the tools below in approximate increasing order

Classification methods

Classification methods for segmenting markets are especially critical for clustering-based segmentation approaches and for hybrid designs. A *clustering-based segmentation design* involves determining the number, size and characteristics of the segments based on the results of clustering of respondents on a set of 'relevant' variables. Benefit, need and attitude segmentation are examples of this type of approach. Significant advances have been made in the clustering area. *Hybrid segmentation design*

includes those cases in which *a priori* segmentation design such as product purchase or usage, loyalty or customer type is augmented by some cluster-based segmentation on variables such as benefits sought. Hybrid designs are especially common in business-to-business segmentation.

Approaches such as macro and micro segmentation (Wind and Cardozo, 1974) and sequential clustering (Peterson, 1974) are often used in practice. Sequential clustering, for example, clusters on some market-based demographics followed by attitude (or benefit) clustering within each demographic segment. In both cluster-based design and hybrid design, the size and other characteristics (demographics, socioeconomic, purchase, etc.) of the segments are estimated. Classification procedures based on cluster analysis and variants thereof are especially useful in providing management with a data-driven view of segmentation. A 'classic' illustration of this value is given in Moriarty and Reibstein (1986) who use clustering methods to reveal a view of the market segments of the personal computer market that challenged management intuition about the way the market was thought to be structured. In particular, they are able to show how benefit segmentation relates to firm descriptors such as size and industry classification.

Discrimination methods

Discrimination methods employed to establish the profile of the segments commonly use multiple discriminant analyses or regression analysis. Such statistical methods are often augmented with graphic packages that graphically display the profile of the segments. These methods are especially useful when the goal is to assign new individuals (e.g. 'Prospects') into groups based on their likely disposition to use the firm's products and services. In recent years, discriminant-based techniques have fallen out of favour due to an absence of effective solutions to implementation and interpretation problems such as those documented in Eisenbeis (1977).

Simultaneous evaluation

One area receiving more attention from academic researchers involves application of sophisticated multidimensional scaling and multivariate statistical analyses in order to *jointly* locate segments and products in a consistent market map. One early development was the componential segmentation approach proposed by Green and DeSarbo (1979).

This method shifts the emphasis of the segmentation model from the partitioning of a market to a prediction of which person type (described by a particular set of demographic and other psychographic attribute levels) will be most responsive to what type of product feature. Componental segmentation is a logical extension of conjoint analysis and orthogonal arrays to cover not only product features but also person characteristics. In componental segmentation the researcher is interested in parameter values for various respondent characteristics (demographic, product usage, etc.) in addition to those for the product stimuli.

In a typical conjoint analysis approach to market segmentation, a matrix of subjects by utilities is developed. This matrix can serve as the input to the determination of the profile of some *a priori* segments (e.g. product users versus non-users) or alternatively as the input to a clustering programme which would result in a number of benefit segments. In componental segmentation, the same design principles which guide the selection of (product) stimuli are applied also to the selection of respondents. For example, in a study for a new health insurance product, four sets of respondent characteristics were identified on the basis of previous experience and management judgement: age, sex, marital status and current insurance status. Employing an orthogonal array design, one screens respondents to select those who meet the specific profiles specified by the design. Each respondent is then interviewed and administered the conjoint analysis task for the evaluation of a set of hypothetical health insurance products (also selected following an orthogonal array design).

Having completed the data collection phase, the researcher would have a matrix of averaged profile evaluations of the product stimuli by the groups of respondents. This data matrix is then submitted to any number of componental segmentation models, which decompose the matrix into separate parameter values (utilities) for each of the levels of the product feature factors (comprising the stimulus cards) and separate parameter values (saliences) for each of the levels of the customer profile characteristics (describing the respondents) which indicate how much each profile characteristic contributes to variation in the evaluative responses.

Given these two sets of parameters, the researcher can make predictions about the relative evaluation of any of the possible product features by any of the respondent types. The results are used with a simulation to estimate: (1) for each respondent segment the frequency of first choices for each of the new product combinations considered, and (2) for each new product combination, the frequency of first choices across segments. Componental segmentation offers a new conceptualization of market segmentation in that it focuses on the building blocks of segments and offers simultaneously an analysis of the market segment for any given product offering and an evaluation of the most desirable product offering (or positioning) for any given segment. The concept and algorithm of componental segmentation can be extended to cover not only two data sets (product feature and respondent characteristics) but three or more data sets by adding, for example, the components of usage situations and distribution options.

Other studies have used the output of logit and nested logit choice models to the simultaneous estimation of segment size, characteristics and choice probabilities to uncover market structure. Examples of this work can be seen in Bucklin and Gupta (1992) and other approaches documented in Grover and Srinivasan (1987, 1992). Elrod and Keane (1995) use panel data to simultaneously uncover latent attributes and consumer preferences. More recently, Moe and Fader (2001) use a stochastic modelling approach which allows clusters of products to draw from a fixed population of underlying segments. One advantage of this approach is that it simultaneously considers rates of purchase within segments and the mix of segments that interact with different clusters of products.

A conceptually related, but methodologically different stream of research has sought under the decision rules used by members of different market segments. Kamakura *et al.* (1996) illustrate that segments are not only heterogeneous in preferences, but also in information processing and consideration of product attributes. In that study, members of the 'Brand-type' segment focus first on brand, then on product form; 'Form-type' segment members reverse this process. Gilbride and Allenby (2004) show how to uncover and test for non-compensatory and compensatory decision rules using only choice data.

Simulation and optimization

Simulation and optimization are at the core of models for selection of a target portfolio of segments. These models are typically based on conjoint analysis studies. Among the most powerful of these approaches is flexible segmentation. In contrast to *a priori* segmentation in which the segments are determined at the outset of the study and clustering-based segmentation in which the selected segments are based on the results of the clustering analysis, the flexible segmentation model offers a dynamic approach to the problem. Using this approach, one can develop and examine a large number of alternative segments, each composed of those consumers or organizations exhibiting a similar pattern of responses to new 'test' products (defined as a specific product feature configuration). The flexible segmentation approach is based on the integration of the results of a conjoint analysis study and a computer simulation of consumer choice behaviour.

The simulation model in a flexible segmentation approach uses three data sets:

1 Utilities for the various factors and levels for each respondent.
2 Perceptual ranking or rating of the current brands on the same set of attributes.
3 A set of demographics and other background characteristics.

The active participation of management is also required to design a set of 'new product offerings' (each defined as a unique combination of product features – specific levels on each factor included in the conjoint analysis study). Management participation can be on a real-time basis in which managers interact directly with the computer simulation. Research suggests that cross-functional teams should also have input into the conjoint simulator approach. For example, Srinivasan *et al.* (1997) leverage inputs from marketing, design and manufacturing in order to offer 'customer-ready' prototypes to respondents.

The choice simulator is based on the assumption that consumers choose the offering with the highest utility and is designed to establish the consumer's share of choices among the existing brands, which can be validated against current market share data if available; and the consumer's likely switching behaviour upon the introduction of any new product. This phase provides a series of brand-switching matrices. Within each matrix management can select any cell or combination of cells as a possible market segment (e.g. those consumers remaining with brand *i* versus those who switched to new brand, etc.). Once the desired segments (cell or cell combination) have been selected, the demographic, lifestyle, product purchase and usage, and other relevant segment characteristics can be

determined by a series of multivariate statistical analyses which can be incorporated into the simulation. Some of the more significant developments in the segmentation area in the last two decades began with advances in simulation and optimization procedures and associated user-friendly software. Early developments by Green and Krieger (1991, 1994) greatly facilitate the task of selecting an optimal (or close to optimal) set of segments, and have now been incorporated into Adaptive Conjoint Analysis (ACA) routinely implemented by Sawtooth Software, one of the leading industry suppliers in the US (see e.g. Bryan Orme's *Introduction to Market Simulators for Conjoint Analysis*). A rigorous practitioner-oriented account of recent developments and applications can also be found in Krieger *et al.* (2004) and Green *et al.* (2003).

One of the more promising lines of research in simulation and optimization is emerging from the joint efforts of researchers in operations research and marketing. Camm *et al.* (2006) provide an exact algorithm to identify the new product concept that will maximize the number of respondents for whom that product exceeds a particular utility threshold. This is an important development as prior research in marketing was only able to identify heuristics for this task and therefore could not guarantee global optimality.

Bayesian methods

One important development in segmentation research is the application of Bayesian methods to segmentation problems. Bayesian methods allow researchers to estimate individual-level response parameters and therefore connect the modelling approach to the conceptual notion of 'one-to-one' or 'customized' marketing. These methods have become increasingly prevalent in a host of segmentation-related studies that cover issues ranging from coupon response (Rossi *et al.*, 1996), advertising effectiveness (Schweidel *et al.*, 2006), price response and new product design (Sandor and Wedel, 2005; Evgenio *et al.*, 2005). Review articles on the impact of Bayesian methods and the implications for market segmentation are given in Allenby and Rossi (1999) and Rossi and Allenby (2003).

Customer-to-customer interaction

One fundamental shift in the practice of segmentation involves the harnessing of 'customer-to-customer' interactions for segment involvement and development. Customer-to-customer interactions facilitate the evolution of new segments and the transmission of product-relevant information and preference data. These interactions are explicit in evolving social networks (e.g., MySpace, YouTube, LinkedIn) and will be increasingly important to firms of all types. Consider, for example, 1800diapers.com which has grown from a start-up with no customers to over 100,000 registered customers in the space of a few months. A particularly important segment for this business is the cluster of customers who respond to the incentive to recruit other customers. This notion of employing existing customers and segments to create new ones is analysed formally using data-mining methods (see subsequent section in this chapter) by Hill *et al.* (2006) in their application to telecommunications data. Among other things, the authors find that customers linked to a prior customer adopt new services of the firm at a rate that is three to five times higher than baseline groups that were selected according to the firm's existing best practices. The relationship between physical and virtual proximity is also likely to influence customer acquisition and segmentation strategies for firms that have spatially dispersed clienteles. In examining trials of a new online grocery service, Bell and Song (2007) find that 'neighbourhood effects' play an important role in generating new customers, even after controlling for typical demographic and other location specific variables.

Linking segmentation findings with management subjective judgements

Given the complexity of deciding on the portfolio of segments to target, it is helpful to use a framework and methodology that captures managements subjective judgement while allowing the incorporation of findings from various segmentation studies. The AHP, as illustrated in Figure 11.3, and the more general ANP is ideally suited for this task.

Addressing the problems

In addition to methodological advances in these seven areas, some of the more interesting advances in segmentation research are those developed to address three of the criticisms of segmentation research. Namely, that it: (1) has too narrow a focus, (2) is static and deterministic and (3) is poorly integrated with strategy. The advances in addressing these problems are briefly discussed in the following section.

Too narrow a focus

This criticism encompasses five areas that can be addressed using specific advances in modelling technologies:

1 The traditional focus on '*one segment per customer*' (the assignment of individuals to mutually exclusive and collectively exhaustive segments) is too narrow. This problem can be overcome by the use of overlapping clustering using a clustering procedure that allows for an individual to belong to more than one segment. For a discussion of this method, see Arabie *et al.* (1981) and Chaturvedi *et al.* (1994). One could also argue that it is more appropriate to *jointly* model product-segment relationships as Moe and Fader (2001). Moreover, the interrelationships among product purchases across multiple product categories also provide insight into *which* customers are most worth pursuing. For an application of this method see Kamakura *et al.* (2004).

2 *One segmentation scheme fits all.* This problem of trying to fit one segmentation scheme for all marketing decisions can be solved by employing the flexible segmentation approaches or by developing a number of segmentation schemes and linking them. Moreover, the results from multiple schemes should be complementary and convergent. While traditional segmentation approaches focus on uncovering differences in behaviours and preferences, it may also be important to consider other possible segmentation approaches. This includes variation in decision-making rules or heuristics adopted by customers (see Gilbride and Allenby, 2006).

3 *Neglect of sub-segments.* With the exception of segments of one, most segments are heterogeneous. It is important to recognize this and augment the basic segmentation with additional sub-segmentation. This is the concept underlying hybrid segmentation models and is increasing in its popularity. In this context, it is also helpful to develop a hierarchy of segments. A byproduct of this research is the development of measures on the segmentability of each market (and the degree of homogeneity of selected segments). Several methods have been developed to deal with within-segment heterogeneity. These include the multi-mode Bayesian methods of Allenby *et al.* (1998) and the empirical Bayes approach of Kamakura and Wedel (2004).

4 *Individual as the unit of analysis.* Most segmentation studies use data on individuals. However, few

decisions are made by a single individual. Most households and industrial (business-to-business) decisions are made by a buying centre. An important advance in segmentation research is the shift in the unit of analysis from individuals to buying centres, which may be a pair of individuals in a family unit, or a more complex set of relationships within an organization. Recognizing the heterogeneity within a buying centre, the use of key informants as representative of the buying centre is often not appropriate. A better approach would be to identify all the members of the buying centre and collect the information on a subset of the buying centre members. This allows an assessment of the level of consensus among members of the buying centres. The level of consensus as well as the composition of the buying centres can be used as a basis for, or descriptors of, segments. Choffray and Lilien (1978) demonstrate critical differences in decision criteria among members of buying centres for industrial heating and cooling equipment. In addition, Wilson et al. (1991) describe and test the best ways to combine the preferences of individuals and buying centre members when trying to determine how the buying centre is most likely to act. Individual preference formation and the integration of preferences in a group process are analysed in Arora and Allenby (1999). The authors show that the method also facilitates revelation of 'high influence individuals' as part of the estimation and segmentation process. A more recent paper by Aribarg et al. (2002) examines the separate processes of preference formation and consensus building and shows how the two interplay to produce final decisions. Finally, state of the art work by Arora (2006) shows that one may in fact impute joint preference using smaller and more cost effective datasets using 'sub-sampling'. A formal treatment of sub-sampling – or the repeated sampling from observations which exhibit dependence – is given in Politis et al. (1999).

5 *The segmentation of the month.* Segmentation area has not escaped other management fads and has had its share of 'segment of the month' promise and advocates. To avoid this trap, one must attempt theory-driven segmentation. It also helps to keep the focus on market response variation as bases for segmentation and to include all other variables as segment descriptors. A recent conceptual article on 'marketing malpractice' illustrates that segmentation schemes can become cumbersome, a-theoretic and consequently, ineffectual (see Christensen et al., 2005).

Static and deterministic perspective

A major limitation of many of the segmentation studies is their neglect of the dynamic aspects of segmentation. Static/deterministic segmentation tends to ignore segment change and market dynamics; ignoring such changes often has several consequences. Johnson and Lilien (1994) provide a conceptualization and model-based approach to deal with segment dynamics. The Internet is one environment in particular that requires special attention to dynamics and several authors have addressed this issue. A recent example is given in Reutterer et al. (2006) in which the authors develop a dynamic model built from purchase history information provided by a loyalty programme. In general, to address the issue of dynamics one can do the following:

- Define bases for segmentation that focus on change.
- Monitor changes in segment composition over time.
- Focus on strategies that will change segment membership (from non-users to users, light to heavy users).
- Incorporate competitive actions and reactions, since the desirability of a segment depends not only on the segment's characteristics and our own strategies but also on competitive actions and reactions.

A second major weakness of much of the segmentation research is the missing stochastic component. While early and seminal methods of segmentation (e.g. Kamakura and Russell, 1989) explicitly recognize that classification into segments is a probabilistic outcome, many applications seem to gloss over this important fact. One new direction in this area addresses the 'stochastic' component of the segmentation problem directly by explicit introduction of estimates of segment size and characteristics. The academic research world has also examined fuzzy clustering (see, e.g. Wedel and Steenkamp, 1991; Rayward-Smith, 2002), although this method has yet to be widely embraced and applied in the marketing community.

Poor integration with strategy

To address the problem that segmentation studies are often not reflected in the resulting strategy, a number of actions can be taken. These include:

1 *Analysis.* Carefully map the results of all studies such as copy, concept, product, distribution and other marketing studies at the segment level. To

the extend possible, develop empirical generalizations regarding your target segments.

2 *Targeting.* Avoid infrequent and expensive large base-line segmentation studies and instead include in all marketing and business studies a segmentation analysis.

3 *Linking.* Link the segmentation to positioning and its associated marketing mix strategies. Specifically recognize the interdependence between the two. Given a positioning, what is the best segment(s)? Given a segment, what is the best positioning(s)? Having fixed on a segment/positioning, it is critical to develop a marketing strategy that will meet the needs of the selected segment and reflect the target positioning.

4 *Implementation.* Carry the segmentation efforts to the sales force level by encouraging each sales person to segment his/her market. In addition, segmentation methods can also be very helpful in segmenting the sales force (or other aspects of the distribution channel).

5 *Selection.* Carry through the segmentation strategies to the business and corporate level by focusing on a portfolio of segments and by using the portfolio of segments as the core of the business and corporate strategy.

Segmentation in the global information age

The information revolution has been the subject of an increasing number of scholarly studies that has captivated the imagination of scholars, managers and the population at large. This revolution is greatly affecting the ways in which firms are managing their operations and is likely to change dramatically the way in which business is conducted. Information strategy is at the heart of most recent efforts to reengineer and reinvent the corporation and is leading to the creation of a new management and associated marketing paradigm.

In the new management and marketing paradigm (Wind, 2005) information is having a profound effect on: (a) the nature and quality of management decisions; (b) the nature of business strategies and (c) the creation of innovative communication and distribution systems.

Management decisions

Management decisions are affected by the availability and use of databases on the entire population

and their linkage to decision-(and executive-) support systems (DSS/ESS) and dashboards, which in turn can include expert/knowledge-based systems. In this context, many advances in segmentation research and modelling can be incorporated in the DSS; moreover, much of our knowledge of segmentation can be developed as rules for a knowledge-based system that could help management to select target segments.

Some of the advances in this area include the ability to have 'live' databases in which one can update on an ongoing basis the customer database. Consider, for example, Citibank's interactive intelligent DSS which guides all interactions with the customer. These interactions include the delivery of a direct mail or telephone sales message targeted by the system which also coordinates a number of customer interactions. The coordinated interactions create a 'dialogue' to follow the consumer with the appropriate intervention at each touch-point of contact of the consumer with Citibank. The touch points include subsequent telephone enquiries, ATM use, bank teller interactions and receipt of statements. This system is based on a new relationship model with household and not only on the traditional banking focus on accounts.

Data mining

Data mining (e.g. Lewinson, 1994) offers enormous potential for empirically driven insights. 'Data mining' refers to a number of pattern recognition models that may use neural nets or fractal technology to discover patterns in the data. These methods have been employed commercially to identify segments of customers most likely to buy a given product (in banking, e.g.) and to the identity of customers most likely to leave (cellular telephones, e.g.). These approaches, although intriguing, are still in their infancy and require further validation. Some marketing researchers have combined data-mining methodologies with more traditional statistical models. Cooper and Giuffrida (2000), for example, utilize data mine the residuals of a traditional segment-based model of response to promotions and use this combined model to improve sales forecasts. A notable exception in this area is the work of Levin and Zahavi (2001) who compare several segmentation methods used in a predictive modelling context – several supervised-learning segmentation methods involving decision trees, and a couple non-supervised methods involving judgemental FRM and FRAT methods. This line of work is promising and adds power to segmentation research and modelling.

Whereas the Citibank example illustrates future development, much of the work today relies more on the traditional geo-demographic segmentation based on consensus and other data. An example of this type of effort is the Claritas Prizm lifestyle segmentation. This segmentation divides the USA into 62 clusters. These clusters are further divided into 15 groups that vary with respect to the type of location – rural, town, suburb or urban – and with respect to level of affluence. The Prizm lifestyle clusters can be related to any target group of interest. Geo-demographic information continues to generate new applications and has been shown to be especially useful in customer targeting (see e.g. Sleight, 2004). Much of this work also signals a new interface between geography and marketing and how data sources and concepts can be combined for more effective segmentation and targeting (Harris *et al.*, 2005).

Information strategies

Information strategies are relatively recent additions to the traditional set of marketing strategies. One of the early and most effective information-based strategies was the 'capture the client' strategy of America Hospital Supply's direct link between hospital computers and AHS computers, eliminating the need for human interaction in the straight rebuy case. 'Capture the clients' strategies, such as the direct computer link between P&G and Walmart, are increasing in popularity.

New communication and distribution options

Information technology is also dramatically changing the nature of the communication and distribution options. Electronic shopping developed at a much faster pace than was ever expected (see, e.g. Blattberg *et al.*, 1994; Rangaswamy and Wind, 1994) and online business-to-consumer (B2C) sales in 2006 in the US alone were estimated at $212 billion (*US Department of Commerce*).

These changes affect all aspects of our lives and are altering the concept of segmentation. In the new marketing paradigm the traditional mass market is being replaced with segments including, at the extreme, segments of one. In a breakthrough book, *The One to One Future*, Peppers and Rogers (1993) presented a vision of their one-to-one paradigm which includes and focuses on:

- share of customers not share of market;
- collaborating with customers to create products and relationships;
- customizing products, services and promotional efforts for each customer;
- economics of scope;
- engaging the customers in dialogues – the interactive individualization of media is here.

The shift to segments of one requires a rethinking of the segmentation concept as well as the development and utilization of sophisticated databases, marketing analysis, modelling and strategy. The trend towards such developments is inevitable and is accompanied by another discontinuous trend – the globalization of business. The early vision exemplified in the work of Peppers and Rogers has recently been augmented by the notion of the 'Long Tail' – a phrase coined by Chris Anderson and popularized in his 2006 book. In the long tail a multitude of 'low demand' products are targeted at small segments of customers – such that their collective share outweighs that of traditional 'blockbuster' products. Effective segmentation is at the heart of delivering in long tail markets.

Globalization

Increasing numbers of industries are global. To succeed in this environment, firms have to shift from a domestic perspective to considering the world as the arena of operations both with respect to the consumer markets for products and services as well as for the resources markets for raw material, R&D, manufacturing, human and capital resources.

The globalization of industries is also accompanied by trends towards regional economic integration – the European Union, NAFTA and the various other efforts for regional integration in Asia and Latin America. The implication of these developments for segmentation is that management has to consider portfolios of segments that include:

- global segments;
- regional segments;
- segments within specific countries.

Added to this complexity is the need to consider as the unit of analysis not just countries but countries by mode of entry, since the risk and attractiveness of a country depend on the mode of entry. The selection and implementation of a portfolio of segments which includes global segments, regional segments and segments within countries (by mode of entry) requires a significant amount of information on all relevant markets around the world. The creation and maintenance of such a data/knowledge base is not a trivial undertaking and is one of the major obstacles to the development of global segmentation strategies.

Creation of processes for the development and maintenance of country, regional and world databases is a high priority undertaking for all global firms. Yet the development of effective segmentation can take place even without such databases if the firm will proceed in an iterative bottom–up and top–down segmentation. This process involves three bottom–up steps:

1 Segmentation of the market in each country (by mode of entry).
2 Examination of the resulting segments in all the selected countries to identify common segments across countries – clustering of country segments.
3 The creation of a global portfolio based on various clusters of segments.

The resulting portfolio of segments should be compared to a desired (top–down) conceptual portfolio of segments. The comparison and contrast of the two portfolios should be driven by the concept of global operation which balances the need to develop strategies that best meet the needs of the local markets (given the idiosyncratic market, competitive and environmental conditions), while at the same time trying to achieve economies of scale and scope by focusing on cross-country segments in a number of markets. The AHP framework and methodology can and has been used in this context to help make such decisions, even in the absence of the needed 'hard' market data. As data become available, both from the firm's own experience and from other sources, the data can be integrated in a database and used as input to the AHP process.

The segmentation of global markets offers enormous opportunities but is still one of the neglected areas of segmentation. It does offer intellectual and methodological challenges and is critical from a management point of view. The literature presents scattered examples of global segmentation. Helsen *et al.* (1993) offer a proposed segmentation of multinational diffusion patterns, while Ter Hofstede *et al.* (2002) extend this notion to include explicit modelling of spatial aspects of cross-national segmentation schemes. A conceptual overview of how to think about cross-national segmentation is given in Steenkamp and Ter Hofstede (2002). Interestingly, very recent research by Ter Hofstede and Park (2007) suggests that spatial or geographic differences across countries provide considerable explanatory power for segmentation schemes. This result holds in an analysis of European Union consumers that controls for differences in other critical variables including culture and socioeconomic status. As global firms continue to struggle with the appropriate mix of 'customization' and 'standardization' there is enormous potential for important conceptual and methodological breakthroughs in this area.

Extending the segmentation concept

In the marketing literature, in practice and in the discussion so far, segmentation has been limited to 'customer' markets. Yet the concept applies to all heterogeneous populations and can and should be extended to the other stakeholders in the firm – all those who have a 'stake' in its survival and growth.

Consider, for example, the firm's own sales force. Most large firms employ thousands of sales people who vary considerably in their performance. The 20/80 rule often applies to them as it does to the customers (i.e. 20 per cent of the sales force often accounts for 80 per cent of the profits). In multi-product firms, different sales people often tend to sell different mixes of products. They differ in their family life cycle stages and hence have different financial and time needs (some are still worried about college education for their kids while others are single, etc.). These and other differences among the sales persons of any firm suggest that the traditional approach, in which a single sales strategy and compensation is employed, is suboptimal. To benefit fully from one's sales force, it is critical to segment it.

The segmentation of the sales force based on needs, benefits sought, expertise, perceptions and preference or any other relevant characteristics could lead to the identification of homogeneous segments and the design of separate strategies towards them. In fact in any situation where management relies heavily on a sales force a dual marketing strategy should be developed – one for the (target segments of) customers and a corresponding one for the (segments of the) sales force. Obviously, these two strategies should be coordinated and integrated. Furthermore, a segmented strategy towards compensation is also desirable. To implement it while avoiding discriminatory practices requires the use of a compensation system with a number of options relying on a self-selection strategy in which the various sales people could select the option most appropriate for their needs. While the segmentation of the sales force and the resulting segmented strategies are likely to meet with considerable resistance, future research needs to address whether the benefits outweigh the difficulties and cost involved.

Similarly, a segmentation strategy can benefit the firm's dealings with its other stakeholders. Wind (1978) described a segmentation of security analysts and portfolio managers that led to better understanding by a firm of the criteria used in the evaluation of firms in their industry and the perceptions of the given firm and its competitors. Following a segmentation/positioning study, a strategy was developed to meet the needs of a target segment of security analysts that resulted in a spectacular increase in the P/E ratio of the given firm.

Other stakeholders such as suppliers, customer service personnel, competitors, government agencies and the firm's own shareholders are often heterogeneous. In all of these cases, understanding the key segments and selecting desired target segment(s) can greatly enhance the firm's effectiveness. In fact, as the cost of doing business in today's environment increases, a segmented strategy may be essential for any organization concerned with the return of their marketing investments.

Issues and associated research agenda

In one of the author's introduction to the *Journal of Marketing Research* special issue – segmentation research (Wind, 1978), the following conclusions were presented:

> 'Market segmentation has served as the focal point for many of the major marketing research developments and the marketing activities of most firms. Yet, too many segmentation researchers have settled on a fixed way of conducting segmentation studies. This tendency for standardization of procedures is premature and undesirable. Given the current state of the art, we offer the following 12-question areas as particularly ripe for new undertakings'.

Of particular importance seems to be research on the following areas:

1 *Conceptualization.* New conceptualizations of the segmentation problem.
2 *Theory.* Re-evaluation and operationalization of the normative theory of segmentation with special emphasis on the question of how to allocate resources among markets and products over time.
3 *New variables.* The discovery and implementation of new variables for use as bases for segmentation (i.e. new attitudinal and behavioural constructs such as consumption-based personality inventories and variables which focus on likely change in attitude and behavioural responses to the marketing variables) of the markets for products, services and concepts.
4 *Research design.* The development of new research designs and parallel data collection and analysis techniques which place fewer demands on the respondents (i.e. data collection which is simpler for the respondent and data analysis procedures capable of handling missing data and incomplete block designs).
5 *Analytic methods.* The development of simple and flexible analytical approaches to data analysis capable of handling discrete and continuous variables and selected interaction at a point in time and over time.
6 *Boundary conditions.* Evaluation of the conditions under which various data analytical techniques are most appropriate.
7 *Generalizations.* The accumulation of knowledge on successful bases for segmentation across studies (product, situations and markets). This could entail meta-analytic work to identify success drivers for different bases and methodologies.
8 *Validation.* Undertaking external validation studies to determine the performance of segmentation strategies which were based on findings of segmentation studies.
9 *Data generation techniques.* Designing and implementing multi-trait, multi-method approaches to segmentation research aimed at both the generation of more generalizable (reliable) and valid data.
10 *Cross-functional applications.* Integration of segmentation research with the marketing information system of the firm.
11 *Translation.* Exploring alternative approaches to the translation of segmentation findings into market strategies.

12 *Implementation.* Studies of the organizational design of firms which were successful and unsuccessful in implementing segmentation strategies.

As noted in this chapter, numerous innovative approaches to segmentation have evolved over the past 20 years. The centrality of the segmentation concept within the marketing field is still paramount, yet further work on the new conceptual and methodological aspects of segmentation should be undertaken. Review of some of the issues and current advances in segmentation research indicates that despite the great advances in the management of and research practice of segmentation numerous frontiers still require creative and systematic study. Furthermore, despite the advances in academic research during the past 30 years, we still do not have satisfactory solutions for many of the issues raised in the 1978 research agenda (Wind, 1978); yet new issues have emerged as well. The changes in the business environment and especially the implications of operating in a global information age, the emergence of empowered consumers and social networks do suggest, however, the need to challenge our mental models of segmentation (Wind *et al.*, 2004) and add a few additional items to the research agenda. These include:

1 *Problem orientation.* Reconceptualization of segmentation *problems* in light of the impact of operating in the global information age and the emergence of segments of one seems a useful first step. Many of the issues raised in this review from trends in customer-to-customer interaction to the application of sophisticated Bayesian and data-mining methodologies suggest that strong conceptualization is still a necessary condition for effective segmentation.

2 *Decision support.* Development of expert system/knowledge-based systems to help management to select and manage the portfolio of segments seems vital. Such systems would ideally be incorporated in an effective DSS. The key to this is the development of a set of rules summarizing our current understanding of market segmentation. These *rules* can reflect the empirical generalizations in this area and can be aided by appropriate meta-analyses. In addition, more thought needs to be given to the psychological and other impediments to use and implementation (see e.g. Hoch and Schkade, 1996).

3 *Management and implementation.* Development of the processes and organizational architecture required to assure effective adaptation and management of segmentation. This includes adoption of the segmentation concept as the foundation of all marketing and business decisions (as outlined in Figure 11.1) as well as the development of guidelines for effective management of segmentation.

4 *Implicit segmentation.* The effect of the Internet on within and across customer information transmission and demand aggregation is enormous (as acknowledged earlier in this chapter). It is therefore critical that firms understand and utilize *customer-to-customer* interactions as part of the segmentation process and allow customers to self-select and engage in mutually beneficial patterns of influence (consider the earlier example of 1800diapers.com). Such approaches may be more effective and leveraged than attempts to explicitly segment the market, regardless of the quality of the underlying data and statistical methods.

Addressing these newer challenges and continuing to build our knowledge concerning the items identified in the 1978 research agenda is critical in order to increase the value of segmentation. Continuous innovation and improvement in segmentation research and modelling for generating and evaluating segmentation strategies is necessary, but not sufficient. Real progress in this area requires rethinking the role of segmentation in the global information age and concentrated efforts by management to develop and implement innovative and effective segmentation strategies.

The obstacles to effective segmentation are not methodological, nor even the lack of data, but rather the ability and willingness of management to undertake a segmentation strategy and establish the processes and resources required for successful implementation. The concept of segmentation, once adjusted to reflect the impact of the information revolution and the globalization of business, is sound and valid. It is the *practice* of segmentation that is fraught with problems. These problems are solvable but the solutions require revision and alteration to most of the current approaches used to segment markets. If we have the conviction and courage to re-examine the traditional segmentation concept and approaches, we shall be able to significantly increase the value of our segmentation efforts in creating value to our customers and other stakeholders.

References

Allenby, G. M., Arora, N. and Ginter, J. L. (1998) On the heterogeneity of demand, *Journal of Marketing Research*, **35**(3), 384–389.

Allenby, G. M. and Rossi, P. E. (1999) Marketing models of consumer heterogeneity, *Journal of Econometrics*, **89**, 57–78.

Anderson, C. (2006) *The Long Tail: Why the Future of Business is Selling Less of More*, Hyperion.

Arabie, P., Douglas, C. J., DeSarbo, W. S. and Wind, J. (1981) Overlapping clustering: a new method for product positioning, *Journal of Marketing Research*, **18**, 310–317.

Aribarg, A., Arora, N. and Onur Bodur, H. (2002) Understanding the role of preference revision and concession in group decisions, *Journal of Marketing Research*, **39**(3), 336–349.

Arora, N. (2006) Estimating joint preference: a subsampling approach, *International Journal of Research in Marketing*, **23**(4), 409–421.

Arora, N. and Allenby, G. M. (1999) Measuring influence of individual preference structures in group decision making, *Journal of Marketing Research*, **36**(4), 476–487.

Blattberg, R., Glazer, R. and Little, J. (1994) *The Marketing Information Revolution*, Harvard Business School Press, Harvard.

Bell, D. R., Ho, T.-H. and Tang, C. S. (1998) Determining where to shop: fixed and variable costs of shopping, *Journal of Marketing Research*, **35**(3), 352–369.

Bell, D. R. and Song, S. (2007) Neighborhood effects and trial on the internet: evidence from online grocery retailing, *Quantitative Marketing and Economics*, forthcoming.

Bucklin, R. E. and Gupta, S. (1992) Brand choice, purchase incidence, and segmentation: an integrated modeling approach, *Journal of Marketing Research*, **XXIX**, May, 201–215.

Camm, J. D., Cochran, J. J., Curry, D. J. and Kannan, S. (2006) Conjoint optimization: an exact branch-and-bound algorithm for the share-of-choice problem, *Management Science*, **52**(3), 435–447.

Chaturvedi, A., Douglas, C. J. and Green, P. E. (1994) *Market Segmentation via Overlapping K-centroids Clustering*, Working Paper, Wharton School, University of Pennsylvania, Pennsylvania, May, 1–21.

Choffray, J.-M. and Lilien, G. L. (1978) A new approach to industrial market segmentation, *Sloan Management Review*, **19**(3), Spring, 17–30.

Christensen, C., Cook, S. and Hall, T. (2005) Marketing malpractice: the cause and cure, *Harvard Business Review*, HBR Reprint 2386.

Cooper, L. G. and Giuffrida, G. (2000) Turning datamining into a management science tool, *Management Science*, **47**(2), 249–264.

Czinkota, M. R., Ronkainen, I. A. and Donath, B. (2004) *Mastering Global Markets: Strategies for Today's Trade Globalist*, South-Western, Mason, OH.

Dahan, E. and Hauser, J. R. (2002) The virtual customer, *Journal of Product Innovation Management*, **19**(5), 332–347.

Dahan, E. and Srinivasan, V. (2000) The predictive power of internet-based product concept testing using visual depiction and animation, *Journal of Product Innovation Management*, **17**, 99–109.

Eisenbeis, R. A. (1977) Pitfalls in the application of discriminant analysis in business, finance, and economics, *Journal of Finance*, **33**(3), 875–900.

Elrod, T. and Keane, M. P. (1995) A factor-analytic probit model for representing the market structure in panel data, *Journal of Marketing Research*, **32**(1), 1–16.

Frank, R., Massy, W. and Wind, J. (1972) *Market Segmentation*, Prentice Hall, Englewood Cliffs, NJ.

Garreau, J. (1982) *The Nine Nations of North America*, Houghton Mifflin, Boston.

Gensch, D., Aversa, N. and Moore, S. (1990) A choice modeling market information system that enabled ABB Electric to expand its market share, *Interfaces*, **20**, January–February, 6–25.

Gilbride, T. J. and Allenby, G. M. (2004) A choice model with conjunctive, disjunctive, and compensatory decision rules, *Marketing Science*, **23**(3), 391–406.

Gilbride, T. J. and Allenby, G. M. (2006) Estimating heterogeneous EBA and economic screening rule choice models, *Marketing Science*, **25**(5), 494–511.

Green, P. E. and DeSarbo, W. S. (1979) Componential marketing in the analysis of consumer trade-offs, *Journal of Marketing*, **43**, 83–91.

Green, P. E. and Krieger, A. M. (1985) Models and heuristics for product line selection, *Marketing Science*, **4**, Winter, 1–19.

Green, P. E. and Krieger, A. M. (1991) Segmenting marketing with conjoint analysis, *Journal of Marketing*, **55**, October, 20–31.

Green, P. E. and Krieger, A. M. (1994) *An Evaluation of Alternative Approaches to Cluster-Based Market Segmentation*, Working Paper, Wharton School, University of Pennsylvania, Pennsylvania.

Green, P. E., Krieger, A. M. and Wind, Y. (2003) Buyer Choice Simulators, Optimizers and Dynamic Models, in Wind, J. and Green, P. E. (eds), *Market Research and Modeling: A Tribute to Paul E. Green*, Kluwer Academic Publishers, Norwell, MA.

Grover, R. and Srinivasan, V. (1987) A simultaneous approach to market segmentation and market structuring, *Journal of Marketing Research*, **24**, May, 139–153.

Grover, R. and Srinivasan, V. (1992) Evaluating the multiple effects of retail promotions on brand loyal and brand switching segments, *Journal of Marketing Research*, **29**(1), 76–89.

Gupta, S. and Lehmann, D. R. (2003) Customers as assets, *Journal of Interactive Marketing*, **17**(1), 9–24.

Harris, R., Sleight, P. and Webber, R. (2005) *Geodemographics, GIS and Neighborhood Targeting*, Wiley, Hoboken, NJ.

Helsen, K., Jedidi, K. and DeSarbo, W. S. (1993) A new approach to country segmentation utilizing multinational diffusion patterns, *Journal of Marketing*, **57**, October, 60–71.

Hill, S., Provost, F. and Volinksy, C. (2006) Network-based marketing: identifying likely adopters via consumer networks, *Statistical Science*, **22**(2), 256–276.

Hoch, S. J. and Schkade, D. A. (1996) A psychological approach to decision support systems, *Management Science*, **42**(1), 51–64.

Iyengar, R., Jedidi, K. and Kohli, R. (2007) A conjoint approach to multi-part pricing, *Journal of Marketing Research*, forthcoming.

Johnson, B. and Lilien, G. L. (1994) *A Framework and Procedure for Assessing Market Segment Change*, Penn State ISBM Working Paper, Penn State University, University Park, PA.

Kamakura, W. and Russell, G. J. (1989) A probabilistic choice model for market segmentation and elasticity structure, *Journal of Marketing Research*, **26**(4), 379–390.

Kamakura, W. and Wedel, M. (2004) An empirical Bayes procedure for improving individual-level estimates and predictions from finite mixtures of multinomial logit models, *Journal of Business and Economic Statistics*, **22**(1), 121–125.

Kamakura, W., Kim, B.-D. and Lee, J. (1996) Modeling preference and structural heterogeneity in consumer choice, *Marketing Science*, **15**(2), 152–172.

Kamakura, W., Kossar, B. S. and Wedel, M. (2004) Identifying innovators for the cross-selling of new products, *Management Science*, **50**(8), 1120–1133.

Kotler, P. and Keller, K. L. (2005) *Marketing Management*, Prentice Hall, Englewood Cliffs, NJ.

Levin, N. and Zahavi, J. (2001) Predictive modeling using segmentation, *Journal of Interactive Marketing*, **15**(2), Spring, 2–22.

Lewinson, L. (1994) Data mining: tapping into the mother code, *Database Programming and Design*, February, 50–56.

Lilien, G. and Rangaswamy, A. (2002) *Marketing Engineering: Computer-Assisted Marketing Analysis and Planning*, Trafford, Victoria, BC.

Little, J. D. C. (1979) Decision support systems for marketing managers, *Journal of Marketing*, **43**(3), 9–26.

Lodish, L. (2001) Building marketing models that make money, *Interfaces*, **31**(3), 45–55.

Moe, W. W. and Fader, P. S. (2001) Modeling hedonic portfolio products: a joint segmentation analysis, *Journal of Marketing Research*, **38**(3), 376–385.

Moriarty, R. T. and Reibstein, D. J. (1986) Benefit segmentation in industrial markets, *Journal of Business Research*, **14**(6), 463–486.

Peppers, D. and Rogers, M. (1993) *The One to One Future*, Doubleday, New York.

Peterson, R. A. (1974) Market structuring by sequential cluster analysis, *Journal of Business Research*, **2**, July, 249–264.

Politis, D., Romano, J. P. and Wolf, M. (1999) *Subsampling, Springer Series in Statistics*, Springer-Verlag, New York, NY.

Rangaswamy, A. and Wind, Y. (1994) *Don't Walk In, Just Log In! Electronic Commerce on the Information Highway*, Working Paper, Wharton School, February.

Rayward-Smith, V. (2002) Fuzzy cluster analysis: methods for classification, data analysis and image recognition, *The Journal of the Operational Research Society*, **51**(6), 769–780.

Reutterer, T., Mild, A., Natter, M. and Taudes, A. (2006) A dynamic segmentation approach for targeting and customizing direct marketing campaigns, *Journal of Interactive Marketing*, **20**(3/4), 43–52.

Rossi, P. E. and Allenby, G. M. (2003) Bayesian statistics and marketing, *Marketing Science*, **22**(3), 304–328.

Rossi, P. E., McCulloch, R. E. and Allenby, G. M. (1996) The value of purchase history data in target marketing, *Marketing Science*, **15**(3), 321–340.

Saaty, T. L. (1992) *Decision Marketing for Leaders*, RWS Pittsburgh Publications, Pittsburgh.

Sandor, Z. and Wedel, M. (2005) Heterogenous conjoint designs, *Journal of Marketing Research*, **42**(2), 210–220.

Schweidel, D. A., Bradlow, E. T. and Williams, P. (2006) A feature-based approach to assessing advertising similarity, *Journal of Marketing Research*, **43**(2), 237–243.

Sleight, P. (2004) *Targeting Customers*, 3rd edn, World Advertising Research Council (WARC), London.

Srinivasan, V., Lovejoy, W. S. and Beach, D. (1997) Integrated product design for marketability and manufacturing, *Journal of Marketing Research*, **34**(1), 154–163.

Steenkamp, J.-B. E. M. and Ter Hofstede, F. (2002) International market segmentation: issues and perspectives, *International Journal of Marketing Research*, **19**, 185–213.

Ter Hofstede, F., and Park, K. (2007) *On the Spatial Structure of Consumer Needs: Cross-National Evidence from the European Union*, Working Paper, Coombs School of Business, UT Austin.

Ter Hofstede, F., Wedel, M. and Steenkamp, J.-B. E. M. (2002) Identifying spatial segments in international markets, *Marketing Science*, **21**(2), 160–177.

Toubia, O., Hauser, J. R. and Garcia, R. (2007) Probabilistic polyhedral methods for adaptive choice-based conjoint analysis: theory and application, *Marketing Science*, forthcoming.

Wedel, M. and Steenkamp, J.-B. E. M. (1991) A clusterwise regression method for simultaneous fuzzy market structuring and benefit segmentation, *Journal of Marketing Research*, **XXVIII**, November, 385–396.

Weiss, M. (1994) *Latitudes of Altitudes: An Atlas of American Tastes, Trends, Politics and Passions*, Little Brown and Company, Boston.

Wilson, E. J., Lilien, G. L. and Wilson, D. T. (1991) Developing and testing a contingency paradigm of group choice in organizational buying, *Journal of Marketing Research*, **28**, November, 452–466.

Wind, Y. (1978) Issue and advances in segmentation research, *Journal of Marketing Research*, **XV**, August, 317–337.

Wind, Y. (2007, forthcoming) The power of adaptive experimentation, *Marketing Research*.

Wind, Y. and Cardozo, R. N. (1974) Industrial marketing segmentation, *Industrial Marketing Management*, March, 153–165.

Wind, Y. and Robertson, T. (1983) Marketing strategy: new directions for theory and research, *Journal of Marketing*, Spring, 12–25.

Wind, Y. and Saaty, T. L. (1980) Marketing applications of the analytic hierarchy process, *Management Science*, **26**, July, 641–658.

Wind, Y., Crook, C. and Gunther, R. (2004) *The Power of Impossible Thinking: Transform the Business of Your Life and the Life of Your Business*, Wharton School Publishing, Upper Saddle River, NJ.

Yankelovich, D. and Meer, D. (2006) Rediscovering market segmentation, *Harvard Business Review*, **84**(2), 122–132.

Part Three
Managing the Marketing Function

CHAPTER 12

The marketing mix*

MICHAEL J. BAKER

Introduction

In common with many other professions, the practice of marketing is often made complex and difficult due to the sheer diversity of the problems with which it is confronted. To a large degree, this diversity is due to the fact that the principal actors in exchange processes are people, or organizations comprised of people, and so exhibit the dynamic and interactive behaviour associated with human beings. If human beings rarely became unwell only from a small range of causes, we would have a need for many fewer doctors than at present. Similarly, if disagreements between parties leading to litigation were limited in their origins, then we would have a need for many fewer lawyers. However, like marketing, these two professions have to deal with an enormous variety of factors which might give rise to a need for medical care or litigation. Accordingly, all professions have a need for diagnostic frameworks which help them isolate the most likely causes of the problem to be solved, so that these may become the focus of detailed examination.

In marketing, one such conceptual framework that is particularly useful in helping practitioners structure their thinking about marketing problems is the so-called 'marketing mix'. To devise a product or service which will be seen as different in the eyes of prospective customers, to the point where they will prefer it to all competing substitutes, is obviously the ultimate objective of the marketer. In devising this unique selling proposition or bundle of benefits, the marketer has four basic ingredients which they can combine in an almost infinite number of ways to achieve different end results. These four basic ingredients are frequently referred to as the 4 'Ps' of marketing, following the classification first proposed by McCarthy. These 4 'Ps' – Product, Price, Place (or distribution) and Promotion – are the subject of separate treatment in later chapters. At this juncture, our primary aim is to review how they may be combined to create a distinctive marketing mix.

According to John O'Shaughnessey (1984), 'Product, price, promotion and distribution are factors that, within limits, are capable of being influenced or controlled. Marketing strategy can be viewed as reflecting a marketing mix of these four elements. Every market has its own logic whereby excellence on one element of the mix, whether product, price, promotion or distribution, is often a necessary condition for success . . . Knowing the key factor in the marketing mix is crucial in drawing up a marketing strategy since it means knowing what to emphasize' (p. 54).

The evolution of the marketing mix concept

Although marketers have always experimented with different combinations of product, price, place and promotion, it is only comparatively recently that serious attempts have been made to see if any particular combinations give better or

* This Chapter draws extensively on Baker (2006) and Baker (2007).

worse results than others. Clearly, if this is the case, then such combinations are to be preferred or avoided as the case may be. One of the earliest studies of this kind was undertaken by the Harvard Business School Bureau of Business Research in 1929 which sought to determine if there were any common relationships to be found in the expenses on various marketing functions of a sample of food manufacturing companies.

Almost two decades later, James Culliton set out to discover whether a bigger sample and more careful classification of companies would yield a different result from that found in the earlier study (in the 1929 study, no common figures had been found which could be used for predictive purposes). Despite Culliton's more rigorous and larger-scale investigation, the results were the same, and it was this which led Culliton to describe the business executive as a 'decider', 'an artist' and a 'mixer of ingredients who sometimes follows a recipe to the ingredients immediately available, and sometimes experiments with or invents ingredients no-one else has tried'. This description of a marketing executive as a mixer of ingredients appealed greatly to his fellow Harvard Professor, Neil Borden, who began to use the term 'marketing mix' to describe the results. Borden wrote that 'Culliton's description . . . appealed to me as an apt and easily understandable phrase, far better than my previous references to the marketing man as an empiricist seeking in any situation, to devise a profitable "pattern" or "formula" of marketing operations from among the many procedures and policies that were open to him. If he was a "mixer of ingredients", what he designed was a "marketing mix"!' Given this idea of a marketing mix, it follows that the next step is to identify and classify the various ingredients available to the marketer and the uses to which they may be put.

In his original conceptualization, Borden suggested the following list of market forces bearing upon the marketing mix:

1 Consumer Attitudes and Habits
   (a) Motivation of users
   (b) Buying habits and attitudes
   (c) Important trends bearing on living habits and attitudes
2 Trade Attitudes and Methods
   (a) Motivation of trade
   (b) Trade structure
   (c) Trade practices and attitudes
   (d) Trends in trade procedures, methods and attitudes

3 Competition
   (a) Is competition on a price or non-price basis?
   (b) What are the choices afforded consumers?
       (1) In product?
       (2) In price?
       (3) In service?
   (c) What is the relation of supply to demand?
   (d) What is your position in the market – size and strength relative to competitors? – number of firms – degree of concentration.
   (e) What indirect competition versus direct competition?
   (f) Competitors' plans – what new developments in products, pricing or selling plans are impending?
   (g) What moves will competition be likely to make to actions taken by your firm?
4 Governmental controls
   (a) Over product
   (b) Over pricing
   (c) Over competitive practices
   (d) Over advertising and promotion

Identification and listing of the ingredients of the marketing mix ranges from the very simple to the very complex. At one end of the spectrum, there is Eugene McCarthy's (1978) 4 Ps of product, price, place and promotion, while at the other there is the much longer listing of Borden (1975) himself which is reproduced as Table 12.1.

While McCarthy's 4 Ps still enjoy considerable currency, most observers would agree that at the very least they need to be extended to include consideration of People, that is the most basic but probably most complex of the mix ingredients, and to acknowledge the importance of research in determining both the nature of the ingredients to be used and the most appropriate recipe.

These ingredients of the mix are valid in most situations. Nonetheless, there are environments in which the mix ingredients must be adapted to the specific needs of the market-place. For a cosmetic manufacturer, packaging and advertising may be so important that they deserve classification as separate marketing activities, while storage may be so unimportant as not to deserve separate classification. Each marketer should set up their own classification of marketing activities, emphasizing those important to the operation's success and de-emphasizing others.

Majaro (1982) identifies three of the factors which help the marketer to make a decision as to whether a specific ingredient deserves a separate existence in the mix.

Table 12.1   Elements of the marketing mix

1. Merchandising – product planning:
   (a) Determination of product (or service to be sold – qualities, design, etc.). To whom, when, where and in what quantities?
   (b) Determination of new product programme – research and development, merger
   (c) Determination of marketing research programme

2. Pricing:
   (a) Determination of level of prices
   (b) Determination of psychological aspects of price (e.g. odd or even)
   (c) Determination of pricing policy (e.g. one price or varying price, use of price maintenance, etc.)
   (d) Determination of margins: freedom in setting

3. Branding:
   (a) Determination of brand policy (e.g. individual brand or family brand)

4. Channels of distribution:
   (a) Determination of channels to use, direct sale to user, direct sale to retailers or users' sources of purchase (e.g. supply houses, sale through wholesalers)
   (b) Determination of degree of selectivity among dealers
   (c) Devising of programmes to secure channel cooperation

5. Personal selling:
   (a) Determination of burden to be placed on personal selling and methods to be employed
       (1) For manufacturer's organization
       (2) For wholesalers
       (3) For retailers
   (b) Organization, selection, training and guidance of sales force at various levels of distribution

6. Advertising:
   (a) Determination of appropriate burden to be placed on advertising
   (b) Determination of copy policy
   (c) Determination of mix of advertising
       (1) to trade
       (2) to consumers
   (d) Determination of media

7. Promotions:
   (a) Determination of burden to place on special selling plans or devices and formulation of promotions
       (1) to trade
       (2) to consumers

8. Packaging:
   (a) Determination of importance of packaging and formulation of packages

9. Display:
   (a) Determination of importance and devising of procedures

10. Servicing:
    (a) Determination of importance of service and devising of procedures to meet consumer needs and desires

11. Physical handling, warehousing, transportation and stock policy

12. Fact-finding and analysis – marketing research

Source: Neil Borden (1964).

1   The level of expenditure spent on a given
    ingredient

    Every ingredient involving a significant
    expenditure would normally earn its separate
    identity. Basically, it is a question of resources
    allocated to each ingredient which matter. Thus, a
    firm that spends an insignificant amount of money
    on packaging would not bother to give this
    ingredient a separate existence, but will attach it
    to the product or the 'promotional' mix,
    whichever appears more appropriate in the
    circumstances.

2   The perceived level of elasticity and consumer
    responsiveness

    When the marketer knows that a change in
    the level of expenditure (up or down) of a given
    ingredient will affect results, it must be treated as
    a separate tool in the mix. For example, if the
    marketer is able to alter the supply–demand
    relationship through price changes, this element
    deserves a separate place in the mix. On the
    other hand, for a firm enjoying a monopoly or
    where the price is fixed by government edict, the
    price will be less important or may be removed
    from the mix.

3   Allocation of the responsibilities

    A well-defined and well-structured marketing
    mix reflects a clear-cut allocation of
    responsibilities. Thus, when the firm requires the
    services of a specialist to help developing or
    designing new packaging, as in the case of
    cosmetics firms, it is perfectly proper to say that
    'packaging' is an important and integral part of the
    mix and deserves a separate existence therein.

So, while the ingredients of the mix described
above are valid in most situations, the mix elements
and their relative importance may differ
from industry to industry, from company to company
and quite often during the life of the product
itself. Furthermore, the marketing mix must
take full cognizance of the major environmental
dimensions that prevail in the marketplace. This
latter point adds a dynamic flavour to the marketing
mix in so far as it has to be changed from
time to time in response to new factors in the
marketing scene.

Generally, in striving to maintain or improve
their profit position, the marketer is an empiricist
trying changes in the several procedures and policies
which make up what we call a 'marketing
programme'. Success depends to a large extent on
understanding the forces of the market which
bear upon any product or product line and skill in
devising a 'mix' of marketing methods that conforms
and adjusts to these forces in ways that produce
a satisfactory net profit figure.

A study of the marketing programmes or
mixes that have been evolved under this empirical
approach shows a tremendous variation in their
patterns. This variation is reflected in the operating
statements of manufacturers (e.g. Profit and Loss
Account and Balance Sheets). As Culliton found
among such statements there is little uniformity,
even among manufacturers in the same industry.
There are no common figures of expense that
have much meaning as standards, as holds true for
many retail and wholesale trades, where the methods
of operation tend to greater uniformity.
Instead, the ratios of sales devoted to the various
functions of marketing are widely diverse. This
diversity in methods and in expenditures by
categories even within an industry is accounted
for largely by the fact that products, the volume of
sales, the market covered and the other facts that
govern operations of each company tend to be
unique and not conducive to uniformity with the
operational methods of other companies, although
there are tendencies towards uniformity among
companies whose product lines are subject to the
same market forces. As noted, in any category of
expenses the percentage of sales spent may cover
wide ranges. For instance, the advertising expense
figure, which reflects the burden placed upon
advertising in the marketing programme, will be
found to vary among manufacturers from almost 0
to over 50 per cent. Similarly, the percentages of
sales devoted to personal selling will cover a wide
range among different businesses.

To illustrate, proprietary medicine manufacturers
often have no sales force at all. Advertising
is used to sell the product to consumers and
advertising literally 'pulls' the product through
the channels of distribution. At the retail level,
little or no effort is made to secure selling support.
In contrast, manufacturers of other types of products,
for example heavy machinery, often put relatively
little of the burden of marketing upon
advertising and rely primarily on the 'push' of
personal selling by either sales force or the sales
force of distributors.

The part played in the marketing programme
by the distributive trades varies markedly. Sometimes
the trade plays a considerable part in the
sales programme, and the close support and
co-operation of the trade is sought, as has generally
been true with heavy appliances. In other
instances, the part played by the trade is not highly

important, and little effort is devoted to securing trade support, as is true among the proprietary medicine companies cited above. Likewise, the employment of sales promotional devices and of point of purchase effort in marketing programmes varies widely.

In the matter of both pricing and pricing policy, wide variation is likely to be found. In some instances, competition is carried out largely on price and margins are narrow. In other instances, prices are set with wide margins and competition is carried out on non-price bases, such as product quality or services or advertising. In some instances, resale prices are maintained; in others they are not. Similarly, it is possible to go on citing wide differences in the practices of branding, packaging and servicing that have been evolved.

In short, the elements of marketing programmes can be combined in many ways. Or, stated another way, the 'marketing mixes' for different types of products vary widely, and even for the same class of product, competing companies may employ different mixes. In the course of time, a company may change its marketing mix for a product, for in a dynamic world the marketer must adjust to the changing forces of the market. The goal of business in any instance is to find a mix that will prove profitable. To attain this end, various elements have to be combined in a logically integrated programme to conform to market forces bearing on the individual product. To summarize, the concept of the marketing mix is a schematic plan to guide analysis of marketing problems through utilization of:

1 A list of the important forces emanating from the market which bear upon the marketing operations of an enterprise.
2 A list of the elements (procedures and policies) of marketing programmes.

The marketing mix, thus, refers to the apportionment of effort, the combination, the designing and the integration of the elements of marketing into a programme or 'mix' which, on the basis of an appraisal of the market forces, will best achieve the objectives of an enterprise at a given time.

Management of the marketing mix

In the earlier editions of *The Marketing Book*, the late Professor Peter Doyle provided a clear exposition of the key issues involved in managing the marketing mix. As he points out, 'There are two key decisions which are central to marketing management: the selection of target markets which determine where the firm will compete and the design of the marketing mix (product, price, promotion and distribution method) which will determine its success in these markets'.

To this point, the emphasis has been upon defining the context within which exchange or marketing occurs; of the forces – economic, behavioural, technological, political and legal – which shape and influence the exchange process; and of procedures for analysing and interpreting all these factors as a basis for developing a coherent and viable strategy. But, as we have seen, strategy identifies future objectives to which the firm aspires and those which are likely to be modified due to changing circumstances. Thus strategy charts a direction to be followed to achieve a destination that will probably be changed as we approach it. However, to ensure that we remain on course, we will set a series of sub-objectives which represent points along the way from where we are to where we want to be. Given the convention of reporting financial performance on an annual basis, it has also become conventional to set performance targets on an annual basis and develop short-term plans for their achievement. In turn, short-term (1 year) plans are usually a sub-set of a medium-term (3–5 years) plans.

Short-term plans and, to a lesser extent, medium-term plans are clearly the domain of operational management. It is this operational management which is responsible for translating the strategy into plans and for devising marketing mixes for their realization. Where a firm is practising undifferentiated or concentrated marketing, it will have only a single marketing mix but, where it is practising differentiated marketing, it will have several. Irrespective of whether it has one or several mixes, the objective is the same – to develop and maintain a sustainable differential advantage (SDA). In order to do this, it is necessary to undertake the several kinds of analysis described in earlier chapters.

Simply analysing problems is not enough – as we have observed on several occasions, it is a necessary, but not sufficient, condition for success. Marshalling evidence is a precondition for analysis but it does not follow that all decision makers will draw the same conclusion from a given data set (selective perception strikes again!). What matters is the quality of the plan devised by the manager based upon his analysis and the quality of the implementation. Central to all is the understanding and deployment of the mix elements. Doyle (1999) provides a useful diagram to illustrate the nature of the matching process which ensures that the marketing mix is consistent with the needs of customers in the target market (see Figure 14.4).

Peter Doyle's discussion of the marketing mix in the last (Fifth) edition is essentially a synopsis of the thinking developed in detail in his best-selling text book *Value-based Marketing: Marketing Strategies for Corporate Growth*. The most recent edition of this book is in collaboration with Phil Stern and is an essential reading for anyone concerned with strategic marketing planning. Similarly, Doyle's chapter in the fifth Edition is well worth re-visiting but, for our purposes here, citation of his *Summary* will have to suffice:

1   The marketing mix is at the core of marketing. The marketing mix consists of the key decisions where marketing managers should exhibit their greatest expertise and professionalism. It has become common to summarize the elements of the marketing mix in the 4 Ps – product, price, promotion and place. Some writers have suggested adding a fifth P – people – to highlight the service element in marketing.

2   However, there is a crucial weakness in the way marketing authors and managers themselves have approached the marketing mix. It has never been clear in marketing theory or practice what the objective is in determining the mix. Without a clear goal, it is impossible to design an optimal marketing mix.

3   Marketing professionals have tended to assume that the objective was to design a mix that meets purely marketing criteria – notably customer satisfaction or market share. But setting prices, communications budgets or designing products that maximize sales or customer satisfaction is a sure route to financial disaster, because it invariably result in negative cash flow and a failure to cover the cost of capital. Consumers will always perceive value in lower prices, more features and high customer-support investments.

4   Equally fallacious is the view of many accountants that the marketing mix should be used to increase profits. This short-termism will usually produce immediate profit improvements but the cost, as many firms have discovered, is a

long-term erosion in their market shares and the value investors place on the company.

5   In the private sector, the right marketing mix is the one that maximizes shareholder value. Shareholder value as an objective avoids the focus on short-termism of the accountancy because it leads managers to take into account all future cash flows. Long-term performance is almost always a much more important determinant of shareholder value than the profits earned in the next few years. It also avoids the fallacy of the market-led approach by emphasizing that the purpose of the firm is not market share but to create long-term financial value.

6   Though applying the shareholder value approach has, of course, many problems associated with forecasting future sales and cash flows (e.g. Day and Fahey, 1988, pp. 55–56; Doyle, 2000, pp. 64–66), it does provide a clear, rational direction for research and decision making.

7   Finally, shareholder value provides the vehicle for marketing professionals to have an increasing impact in the boardroom. In the past, senior managers have often discounted the recommendations of their marketing teams, because the marketing mix and strategies for investment have lacked a rational goal. Marketers have not had the framework for translating marketing strategies into what counts for today's top executives – maximizing shareholder value. Value-based marketing provides the tools for optimizing the marketing mix.

Writing in the *Journal of Business Strategy* (2005), Wise and Sirohi address the question of the best way to identify and implement the marketing mix. In their view, the emphasis on growth and spending apparent in the annual reports of many leading companies has focused attention on marketing expenditures 'perhaps the last significant elements on the income statement without explicit links to revenues and profits'. In turn, this requires marketers to identify and use appropriate metrics to ensure that the optimum mix is achieved. Accordingly, 'Marketing budgets should be viewed as a portfolio of investments, each of which has a different growth potential and resource requirements. Proven ROI techniques can help marketers make the best tradeoffs by identifying the right data to track, the best metrics to use, and the right comparisons to make'. Implicit in this recommendation is that one has a view of what marketing activities are associated with growth and how to establish the best combination (mix) of these activities.

Some criticisms of the marketing mix

While the marketing mix has become one of the best known models in marketing, described in detail in every basic marketing text and widely used in practice, the concept is not without its critics. Writing in the *Companion Encyclopedia of Marketing* (Baker, 1999), van Waterschoot (1999) identifies a number of deficiencies in the concept which may be summarized as follows:

1 It focuses on what marketers do *to* customers rather than *for* them.
2 It is externally directed and ignores the internal market.
3 It says nothing about interactions between the mix variables.
4 It takes a mechanistic view about markets.
5 It assumes a transactional exchange rather than a relationship.

In a nutshell, these five criticisms may all be seen to be dimensions of the same failing – a neglect of the people factor. It would seem appropriate, therefore, that we should extend and modify the 4 Ps model of marketing to include a fifth P – People.

Putting people into marketing is essential for many reasons. Within the limits of a small chapter of this kind, we may only consider three of the more important ones.

First, marketing is a professional practice – it is something which people do. While it is perfectly feasible to theorize about marketing in the abstract, like many other academic disciplines, the main reason people study the subject is to provide a basis for success, for practice. Like medicine, engineering and architecture, marketing is what we have described as a synthetic discipline. Not 'synthetic' in the pejorative sense of 'a poor substitute for the real thing' but synthetic in the sense defined by the Concise Oxford Dictionary as 'the process or result of building up separate elements, especially ideas, into a connected whole, especially into a theory or system'. Thus, in marketing, we incorporate and integrate the best insight, and ideas from core disciplines such as economics, psychology and sociology and synthesize them into implementable practices. Market segmentation, targeting and positioning are examples of how marketing reconciles the economist's assumptions of homogeneous demand with the psychologist's perception of every individual differing from every other in some degree, and provides a practical solution of creating choice at an affordable cost. Marketing is something done for people by people.

The second reason for putting people into the marketing mix is that increasingly it is the people who provide the basis of differentiation between competing suppliers on which buyers make their choices. Traditionally, differentiation between competing suppliers has tended to rest upon the creation of objective differences through technological innovation. Nowadays, such objective differences are rapidly eroded by competition (it is relatively easy to benchmark your competitors' product to see how they have improved it) or else overtaken by the ever quickening pace of new product development. It is this trend which has led to the recognition that long-term competitive success depends on building relationships rather than seeing marketing management as responsible for ensuring that the seller gets the better of the buyer in a series of independent transactions each of which must be profitable to the seller. In turn, this recognition has highlighted the importance of internal marketing and the fact that in an increasingly knowledge-based society, people (human capital) are the organization's greatest asset.

Finally, the third reason for putting people into the marketing mix is because it is people who plan and devise marketing mixes, it is people who implement such plans. Further, a great deal of research into competitiveness in recent years has confirmed beyond doubt that in the final analysis, it is the quality of implementation that distinguishes between success and failure. In *Marketing and Competitive Success* (Baker and Hart, 1989), a rigorous survey into a matched sample of successful and less successful firms in six industries indicated that very few of the so-called critical success factors were present in successful firms and absent from unsuccessful firms, that is, you could not infer that they were related to improved performance. On reflection, the reasons are not hard to find.

To begin with, nobody wants to fail. Accordingly, management staff in less successful organizations are just as ambitious as their opposite members in successful firms in studying for professional qualifications, reading management books, attending seminars and seeking advice from experts. In other words, *they know what to do*. It follows that if they are less successful, it is due to the quality of execution and, possibly, a little luck. The view confirms with Napoleon's expressed wish for lucky generals. Other things being equal, we must assume that the military commanders who become generals must both understand the principles of warfare and have demonstrated skill in their practice or they would not have been promoted to command an army. In warfare, however, we have the extreme form of competition as a zero-sum game with a winner and a loser, so what determines the outcome? People! In the words of the song, 'It ain't what you do, it's the way that you do it'.

But, even with the addition of 'people', many still believe that the mix concept has outlived its usefulness. Among the more recent, best documented and certainly most readable criticisms is an article by Lisa O'Malley and Maurice Patterson, which appeared in the 1998 *Journal of Marketing Management*. ('Vanishing Point: The Mix Management Paradigm Reviewed', 14, November). Taking the view that theory development is an evolutionary process and one of displacement where new ideas supersede the old, O'Malley and Patterson utilize a road metaphor in the guise of a road movie to trace the origins and development of the marketing mix concept to support their view that it should now be left behind as we move towards more attractive destinations.

In tracing the evolution of marketing theory and practice, it is pointed out that the 'mid-life crisis of marketing' identified by McKinsey in 1993 is not the first time that the discipline has reached a crossroads where it has had to determine the direction it has to take in future. As noted by O'Malley and Patterson, 'The philosophical position of early marketing scholars was heavily influenced by the historical approach to economics and was more concerned with pressing social issues than business practice'. The catalyst for shifting emphasis to the managerial implications of marketing '. . . can no doubt be attributed to an expansion of large scale enterprise, an increase in the number of affluent buyers (Benton, 1987) and widespread employment of marketing techniques in industrialized societies (Fullerton, 1988)'.

As we saw in Chapter 1, the marketing management approach evolved during the 1950s in the US when the economic system was in danger of collapse as supply rapidly began to overtake demand. A similar imbalance had precipitated the great depression of the late 1920s and early 1930s and, as we have seen, an emphasis upon high-pressure selling had been insufficient to overcome this imbalance. Clearly, a more sophisticated approach was called for which, in turn, resulted in

a demand for marketing education and a change in focus to '[t]he extension, refinement and evaluation of marketing as an organizational or management technology rather than on macro level social issues, concerns, and problems'. (Benton, 1987, p. 240). As O'Malley and Patterson note, 'This shift in philosophical position is encapsulated in the mix management paradigm'.

Underlying criticism of the marketing mix mode, in our opinion, is the mistaken view that it was ever intended as a 'theory' of marketing rather than a currently useful generalization (CUG) or helpful learning and teaching tool. Certainly, Borden in his original conceptualization which, as we have seen, contains 12 variables, did not regard this as either a comprehensive or exhaustive list. It is also equally important that when McCarthy reduced the 12 mix elements to 4 – product, price, place and promotion – he, too, was more concerned with memorability than completeness.

Given that at least two generations of professional marketers have survived and, indeed, prospered believing in the marketing mix as a useful approach to the management of the marketing function, we should not now reject this approach on the grounds that its interpretation and implementation are flawed in terms of the philosophical intentions of the marketing concept itself. This point is highlighted by O'Malley and Patterson when they write,

> In terms of customer orientation, 'the marketing concept . . . calls for most of the effort to be spent on discovering the wants of a target audience and then creating goods and services to satisfy them', (Kotler and Zaltman, 1971, p. 5). However, far from being concerned with a customer's interests, the view implicit in the 4 Ps approach implies that the customer is somebody *to* whom something is done rather than somebody *for* whom something is done (Dickson and Blois, 1983). The managerial approach to marketing, therefore, concentrates on the seller, and subordinates the customer to a passive as opposed to a pivotal role (Grönroos, 1994). Rather than the function of marketing being dynamic and market oriented, it is instead a rather clinical, production oriented approach (Laylock, 1983; Grönroos, 1994).

As a result of the emphasis upon manipulation of the 4 Ps, the marketing management function became dominant resulting in the establishment of formal marketing departments. As we now know, this concentration of responsibility for marketing within a single department was a mistake as the essence of marketing was defined in Drucker's (1954) original statement that 'Concern and responsibility for marketing must permeate all areas of the enterprise'. This is certainly the view that prevails today and is reflected in the disestablishment of formal marketing departments, the growth of internal marketing and the recognition that all members of a successful business organization need to be marketing orientated.

Other failings associated with the marketing mix concept include:

1   The inherent assumption that the firm is independent of its environment (Andersson and Soderlund, 1988).
2   The view that the seller is active and the buyer is passive (Grönroos, 1994).
3   The assumption that markets are homogeneous and amenable to the application of a standardized marketing mix.
4   The emphasis on marketing as a transaction which sees buyers and sellers as separate entities.

To accommodate these criticisms, many authors have increased the number of Ps, as we have ourselves by suggesting the inclusion of people. Of course, by doing this they may just increase the complexity of the basic model and thereby reduce its memorability.

Fundamentally, however, the essential criticism of the marketing mix model by marketing scholars is that it is positivistic and prescriptive and so communicates an overly simplistic view of a complex reality. The fact that this chapter and several which have preceded it and will follow it contain discussions of alternative hypotheses and criticisms of prevailing models should be sufficient to convince the reader that while the authors may have their own view as to how things are or ought to be, the reader is perfectly entitled to form an alternative viewpoint.

While debate on the application of the marketing mix model is to be welcomed, one should be careful not to discard it prematurely because of perceived weaknesses in it. In line with our own preferred definition of marketing as being concerned with 'mutually satisfying exchange relationships', we must be careful not to tip the balance too much in favour of the buyer. The relationship between seller and buyer can only be mutually satisfying if both parties receive the benefit or satisfaction which they looked for in entering into the relationship in the first place. In

the case of the seller, this invariably means that income received exceeds the costs involved so that the selling organization can survive, prosper and deliver benefits to the stakeholders who depend upon it. It follows that those responsible for the management of the selling organization must have a clear view as to how they can manage the resources under their control to achieve this outcome. It further follows that they need to have a view on what to do when entering into relationships with customers. If we also take the view that customers know what they are doing when they enter into a relationship with a seller, then perhaps we can also assume that they are not as easily manipulated as critics of the marketing mix paradigm would have us believe. Thus, while we willingly accept that many of the conditions that prevailed when the marketing mix model was first formulated – mass marketing practised by large divisionalized, hierarchical, and functional organizations – have declined in importance, marketing is still concerned with time, place and consumption utilities and these are still very much determined by product, price, place and promotion.

Although O'Malley and Patterson claim that 'The marketing mix is a myth', the reader will have to decide for themselves if this is the case (you should read the article in full before coming to any conclusions). For our part, we can only point out that since time immemorial people have believed in myths and this has and continues to have a significant impact on the way they lead their lives. Given that this book is as much about the practice of marketing as the theory which underpins it, the author's view is that the 4 Ps model is a useful, simplifying device to enable marketing managers to impose some structure and direction on the tasks which they must perform. It is in this belief that succeeding chapters deal with the key policies associated with the 4 Ps of product, price, place and promotion.

In July 2006, the *Journal of Marketing Management* contained a substantial article on the subject of the marketing mix by Efthymios Constantinides together with a commentary on it by distinguished scholar Kristian Moller. Based on an extensive review of the literature (over 100 references), Constantinides ' assesses the current standing of the 4Ps Marketing Mix framework as the dominant marketing management paradigm' and major criticisms of it emanating from five 'traditional' marketing areas – consumer, relationship, services, retail and industrial marketing as well as from the emerging field of electronic Marketing. Based on this review, the author identifies a number of limitations and concludes that it is time to replace it with a more up-to-date analytical approach. In a nutshell, Moller disagrees! Clearly, both these articles should be read as, at the time of writing, they represent the latest discussions of the topic. Meantime, the following represents my own interpretation of the essence of their arguments.

Constantanides declares 'the objective of the study is to present a realistic picture on the current standing of an old and ongoing debate about the merits of the 4P marketing mix as a present and future marketing management conceptual platform' (2006, p. 409). As limitations to his study, the author acknowledges that his research is limited to the writings of academics and to the six spheres of activity identified earlier. The first limitation is mediated by the inclusion of normative prescriptions of the kind to be found in major textbooks, while the second could be easily addressed by extending the search/analysis to other sub-fields of marketing.

Since the articulation of the mix concept in 1964, Constantinides identifes several important landmarks in the evolution of marketing management theory:

- The 'broadening' of the marketing concept in the 1970s.
- The emphasis on transactions in the 1980s
- The development of Relationship marketing and Total Quality Management (TQM) in the 1990s.
- The emergence of Information and Communication Technologies (ICT) in the 2000s.

> 'At the same period the consumer behaviour has also evolved[sic]; one of the noticeable changes has been the gradual evolution from the mass consumer markets of the 60s (Wolf, 1998) towards increasingly global, segmented, customized or even personalized markets of today (Kotler *et al.*, 2001) where innovation, customization, relationships building and networking have become issues of vital significance'.

Taken together these changes have led to the emergence of more-and-more specialized sub-fields of marketing and it is proponents of these who are seen as most strident in their criticisms of the application of the 4Ps framework to their area of interest. Constantinides then proceeds to summarize major contributions to the debate originating in his six chosen sub-fields. (While some sources reviewed date to the 1980s, the majority are

post-1990.) Among the major reasons advanced for rejecting or possibly modifying the mix paradigm are the following:

1. The concept has an internal focus, that is, it concentrates on what the firm should do or needs to do. It is a production orientation rather than a customer orientation.
2. It lacks an appreciation of the need to interact with customers.
3. The absence of 'strategic' elements.
4. It is 'offensive' rather than collaborative in nature. This is a variant of 1 in that the focus on what the firm should do *to* the customer rather than *for* him.
5. It ignores the distinguishing features of services, especially the role of the individual delivering the service, the need for interaction (*qv.* 2), and the one-to-one nature of service marketing.
6. It neglects the importance of factors such as physical evidence, shopping experience and atmosphere which are salient in retailing. (It will be noted that these criticisms are very similar to those of van Waterschoot cited earlier).

Despite these criticisms emanating from the 'traditional sub-fields it appears that in the newly emerging area of e-commerce commentators are largely in favour of its use and application. Further, from the detail contained in the six Tables in which the main contributions to each sub-field are documented, there seems to be a propensity for the critics recommending rejection of the 4Ps to propose its replacement with a new framework of their own that has the same intention and underlying framework – perhaps a case of a rose by another name?'

Based on their introduction and summary of *Rethinking Marketing: Developing a New Understanding of Markets* (2004), Hakansson and Waluszewski (2005) developed a paper in which they 'offer a critical analysis of existing marketing models, which mainly originate from the marketing mix (the 4Ps model), which in turn has a clear micro economic "allocation of resources" background'.

In their article, the authors trace the origins of marketing mix model to Rasmussen (1955), McCarthy (1960) and Kotler (1967). Clearly, this differs somewhat from our own 'genealogy' outlined earlier and illustrates well the problems that still bedevil much of what passes for research in business and marketing. Basically this problem is an inadequate awareness of work being published in other places and, to a lesser degree, in other languages. (While English has become the main business language, there are still important contributions being made that are not published in this language.) Given the Rasmussen's book was published in 1955, it is unlikely that either McCarthy or Kotler was aware of it and so was following the Culliton/Borden conceptualization described earlier. While the latter was presented as a simplifying framework to structure problems of resource allocation between various marketing activities to develop an effective marketing plan, the former appears to have been founded much more firmly on economic theory and it is this interpretation that Hakansson and Waluszewski analyse in their paper.

In essence, the authors perceive that the original model is one of economic resource allocation based on the assumption that 'the relevant resources engaged in the exchange process, including the products, are homogeneous' (p. 111). Understandably, the 'fit' between this theoretical model and the real world experienced by marketing decision makers is poor, and it is for this reason that many writers have recommended that the model be dropped. While acknowledging that the dynamic nature of marketing and the focus on interaction need to be factored in, Hakansson and Waluszewski consider that the 4Ps model still has its merits; what is needed is a more explicit recognition of the heterogeneous nature of the mix elements and their interaction with each other when devising a unique marketing plan to address a unique problem in a dynamic environment.

Before turning to Moller's comments, my personal views are as follows:

1 Practitioners like the 4Ps approach because 'it does what it says on the tin'. It provides a relatively simple analytical framework that can be easily extended (remember Borden had 12 elements in his original conceptualization) and adapted to address the specific problem under consideration.

2 Of course, marketing management want to know what they can do to persuade potential customers to prefer them over the competition – that is what competition is all about.

3 It is naïve to the point of stupidity to assume that practitioners are not fully aware of the need to understand the potential customer as the starting point for creating an original solution or recipe that will appeal to them.

4 The whole point of the mix approach is to remind the practitioner what tools are at their disposal to enable them to craft a differentiated marketing strategy. In order to do so, it is self-evident that they need to gather intelligence about the macro-environment, competition and customer needs and wants. It is for this reason that discussions of the marketing mix are embedded within comprehensive treatments of the kind represented in this book.

So what does Kristian Moller have to say?

To begin with, he acknowledges that since the 1990s marketing theorists have been engaged in a 'paradigm shift' from a tansactional view of marketing to one founded on relationships. Nonetheless, in the process it is important that we recognize the contribution of notions like the marketing mix to the evolution of marketing theory. And, second, 'I think there is too little reflection on the theoretical foundations of the normative advice found in abundance in the textbooks'. Accordingly, while Constantinides' review is to be welcomed, it should not be allowed to pass without comment.

Moller's aim is 'to examine the Mix approach from a theoretical perspective; this involves uncovering the cognitive goals, theoretical driving forces, underlying assumptions, and the insights which the Mix offers to the marketing discipline' (2006, p. 439).

While acknowledging the scope of Constantanides' review, Moller feels that he failed to dig down and explore its meta-theoretical underpinnings. In this sense, it might be regarded as superficial (my word). Further, while examining the application of mix thinking in a number of difffferent sub-fields is considered 'excellent' in that, it explores a number of different contexts Moller is concerned about the status of the six sub-fields (contexts) that are discussed. If these sub-fields are considered to be 'practical fields', then the analysis is acceptable. However, if Constantinides considers them to reflect sub-theories of topics like bank marketing, health care marketing, etc. then he is confusing practice with theory as the view that such sub-fields call for separate theories is outdated. In sum, 'I am afraid that Constantinides and many of the authors he cites, are misreading the Mix and consequently drawing misleading conclusions of the Mix as well' (2006, p. 441).

Moller's summary of the major criticisms contained in Constantanides' article are very similar to my own. His analysis and discussion of them is more rigorous and documents clearly why criticisms of the mix arise from an insufficient/ incomplete understanding of the origins and foundations of the concept which, in turn, lead to the misleading conclusions referred to earlier.

A broadly based book of this kind is not the place to rehearse the detail of Moller's arguments and you should consult the original for these. However, the essence of Moller's comments is that one needs to consider the mix as an element in the thinking of the Managerial School of Marketing (MSM) epitomized by Philip Kotler's seminal *Marketing Management: Analysis, Planning and Control* (1967). In Kotler's, and many others' view, the problem to be solved by the marketing manager is that of devising an optimal combination of product, place, price and promotion (as shorthand for all the tools and ingredients available) to achieve the organization's objectives. As Moller observes, 'In sum, the deriving of an optimal marketing Mix involves solving a market segmentation problem, being able to carry out marketing positioning analysis, and finally being able to differentiate the Mix from the competitors' offers using the target customers (segment) preferences as criteria' (2006, p. 442).

With the current pre-occupation with relationship marketing and e-marketing, it is appropriate that one should question the applicability of theory and tools developed at an earlier time when a different emphasis prevailed. However, as a recognized authority on the subject of relationship marketing, Moller's view that MSM still provides the 'best approach and toolkit for those marketing management decision contexts where there exist a market of customers or a set of customer relationships, which can be characterized by market like exchange conditions,' (2006, p. 445) carries considerable weight. It is certainly a view that I endorse.

While many criticisms of the mix have claimed that it is outdated and unsuited to the dynamics of modern markets, this is not the view taken by Carolyn Siegel in her textbook *Internet Marketing*. Indeed, Module III of her book comprising four chapters is concerned with 'The Internet Marketing Mix'. It opens with this introductory paragraph:

or 4Ps of product, price, place
promotion are known to any-
ken an introductory marketing
any attempts have been made
id the Ps, they've endured as an
or organising the major tactical

tools marketers can deploy in a competitive marketplace. Just as the 4Ps have an enduring place offline, their importance online is equally compelling. Many dot com failures can be attributed to weak or non-existent attention to the planning, implementation, and control of the marketing mix, and the essential details that mean the difference between profitability and bankruptcy.

References

Andersson, P. and Soderlund, M. (1988) The network approach to marketing, *Irish Marketing Review*, **3**, 63–68.

Baker, M. J. (1999) *The IEBM Encyclopedia of Marketing*, Thomson Learning, London.

Baker, M. J. (2006) *Marketing*, 7th edn, Westburn Publishers Limited, Helensburgh.

Baker, M. J. (2007) *Marketing Strategy and Management*, 4th edn, Palgrave, Basingstoke.

Baker, M. J. and Hart, S. J. (1989) *Marketing and Competitive Success*, Philip Allan, London.

Borden, N. (1964) The concept of the Marketing Mix, *Journal of Advertising Research*, **4**, June.

Borden, N. H. (1975) The Concept of the Marketing Mix, in McCarthy, E. J. *et al.* (eds), *Readings in Basic Marketing*, Homewood, Ill., Irwin, pp. 72–82.

Constantanides, E. (2006) The marketing mix revisited: towards the 21st century marketing, *Journal of Marketing Management*, **22**, 407–438.

Day, G. and Fahey, L. (1988) Valuing market strategies, *Journal of Marketing*, **52**, July, 45–57.

Doyle, P. (1999) Managing the Marketing Mix, Chapter 11, in Baker, M. J. (ed.), *The Marketing Book*, 4th edn, Butterworth Heinemann, Oxford.

Doyle, P. (2000) *Value-based Marketing: Marketing Strategies for Corporate Growth and Shareholder Value*, Wiley, Chichester.

Drucker, P. (1954) *The Practice of Management*, Harper & Row, New York.

Grönroos, C. (1994) From marketing mix to relationship marketing: towards a paradigm shift in marketing, *Management Decision*, **32**(2), 4–20.

Hakansson, H. and Waluszewski, A. (2005), Developing a new understanding of markets: reinterpreting the 4Ps, *The Journal of Business and Industrial Marketing*, **20**(2/3), 110–117.

Hakansson, H., Harrison, D. and Waluszewski, A. (eds) (2004) *Rethinking Marketing: Developing a New Understanding of Markets*, John Wiley, Chichester.

Kotler, P. (1967) *Marketing Management*, 1st edn, Prentice-Hall, Englewood Cliffs, New Jersey.

Kotler, P., Armstrong, G., Saunders, J. and Wong, V. (2001) *Principles of Marketing*, Third European Edition, Prentice-Hall, Pearson Education Limited, Harlow.

Majaro, S. (1982) *Marketing in Perspective*, George Allen & Unwin, London, pp. 20–21.

McCarthy, E. J. (1978) *Basic Marketing: A Managerial Approach*, 6th edn, Homewood, Ill., Irwin, pp. 7–8.

Moller, K. (2006) Comment on: the marketing mix revisited: towards the 21st century marketing, *Journal of Marketing Management*, **22**, 439–450.

O'Malley, L. and Patterson, M. (1998) Vanishing point: the mix management paradigm revisited, *Journal of Marketing Management*, **14**, November.

O'Shaughnessey, J. (1984) *Competitive Marketing: A Strategic Approach*, Allen & Unwin, Winchester, Mass.

Rasmussen, A. (1955) *Pristeori eller Parameterteori*, Handelshojskolen Forlag, Copenhagen.

Siegel, C. F. (2005) *Internet Marketing*, 2nd edn, Houghton Mifflin Company, Boston, MA.

van Waterschoot, W. (1999) The Marketing Mix, in Baker M. J. (ed.), *The IEBM Encyclopedia of Marketing*, International Thomson Business Press, London, pp. 319–330.

Wise, R. and Sirohi, N. (2005) Finding the best marketing mix, *The Journal of Business Strategy*, **26**(6), 10–11.

Wolf, D. B.(1998) Developmental relationship marketing (connecting messages with mind: an empathetic marketing system), *Journal of Consumer Marketing*, **15**(5), 449–467.

CHAPTER 13

New product development

SUSAN HART

Introduction

Today's successful organizations learn and re-learn how to deal with the dynamics of consumers, competitors and technologies, all of which require companies to review and reconstitute the products and services they offer to the market. This, in turn, requires the development of new products and services to replace current ones, a notion inherent in the discussion of Levitt's (1960) *Marketing Myopia*. Over the years, much research has reported success rates for product innovation as between 35 per cent and 75 per cent, with a very recent study of the innovative practices in the UK showing an average success rate of 65 per cent (Hart *et al.*, 2007). Although the success rates differ across different industries, technologies and states of product–market maturity, the persistence of significant levels of failure remains a concern for those developing new products and services alike.

In this chapter, the activities, their sequence and organization required to develop new products are discussed in the light of an extensive body of research into what distinguishes successful from unsuccessful new products. The chapter starts by introducing the new product development (NPD) process model before going onto a general discussion of the usefulness of models in the NPD context. It then develops an integrating model of NPD and finally, issues identified in current research regarding organizational structures for NPD are considered.

The process of developing new products

In retrospect, some innovations often seem like such good ideas that their successes appear as inevitabilities. Take mobile music gadgets, from the walkman to the MP3 and 4. Might they have failed? What is the basic idea? Portable, personal audio entertainment. How else might the idea have been made real? And might this realization have taken place less successfully than the products we now find so familiar and convenient? Alternative forms for personal audio entertainment include, a bulkier headset which contains the tape-playing mechanism and earphones; a small hand held player, complete with carrying handle, attached to earphones via a cord; a 'backpack' style player with earphones, player device attached to spectacles, sunglasses or forms of head gear? All of these ideas would have delivered to the idea of 'portable, personal audio entertainment', but which if any of these would have enjoyed the same success as the Walkman, Discman, Flashdrives, iPod, to name but a few?

A second 'good idea' is the lightweight, low-pollution, low-cost, easily parked town car. Now imagine one realization of the idea: 3-wheeled, battery-run (with 80 kilometre worth of charge only), and, for the British weather, an *optional* roof. This realization is, of course, the widely quoted failure, the C5. Yet the *idea* remains a good one.

Examples such as these serve to remind us that good ideas do not *automatically* translate into workable, appealing products. The idea has to be given a physical reality (in the case of products) or a deliverable reality (in the case of services) which performs the function of the idea and which potential customers find an attractive alternative to what is currently available to them and for which they are prepared to pay the asking price. This task requires NPD to be managed actively, working through a set of activities which ensure that the eventual product is makeable, affordable, reliable and attractive to customers.

The activities carried out during the process of developing new products are well summarized in various NPD models. These are templates or maps which can be used to describe and guide those activities required to bring a new product from an idea or opportunity, through to a successful market launch. NPD models take numerous forms, including those developed by Booz Allen Hamilton (1982), Cooper (1993) and PRTM (2004). The process steps are somewhat similar and research reports that firms do carry out key stages such as idea generation, screening, concept development and testing, business analysis, product development and testing, market testing and launch (Hart *et al.*, 2007). The Booz Allen Hamilton model is shown in Figure 13.1.

This model has been re-formulated and shaped over several decades, with the influential derivative from Cooper (1990) known as the Stage-Gate™ process, shown in Figure 13.2.

In the US, the Best Practice Study (1997) showed that 60 per cent of firms used some form of Stage-Gate process whilst the study in the UK by Hart *et al.* (2007) reported 'variable recognition' of the different stage gates in the NPD process. Despite the fact that the foundations of these models were laid down over two decades ago, a recent report by Booz Allen Hamilton posted in 2004 on their website (www.boozallen.com) also noted that, contrary to the common view that what makes a successful new product is a 'killer idea', the really important capabilities are to do with controlling the NPD process to ensure the efficient use of scarce resources. In other words, the development of capabilities often embedded within the frameworks of NPD models.

These capabilities are described briefly with respect to each of the key stages of the process models, below.

The stages of the NPD process

New product strategy

A specific new product strategy explicitly places NPD at the heart of an organization's priorities, and sets out how NPD will satisfy the competitive requirements of the company's overall strategy. The strategy of a company dictates how it

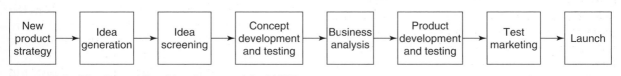

Figure 13.1   The Booz Allen Hamilton model of NPD

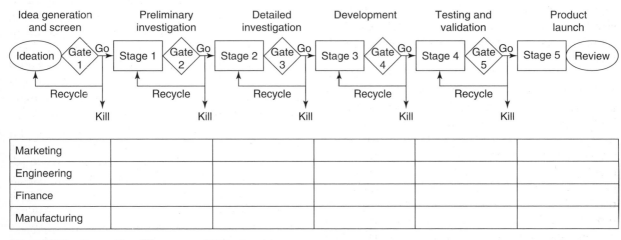

Figure 13.2   Stage-Gate™ process NPD process

will operate internally, and how it will approach the outside world. To be successful, NPD must be guided by, that is be derived from, the corporate goals of the canon company, and therefore there is a need to set clearly defined objectives for NPD projects. A new product strategy ensures that product innovations become a central facet of corporate strategies, that objectives are set and that the 'right' areas of business are developed. Thus, a critical success factor for NPD is the extent to which a specific strategy is set for guiding NPD efforts. The NPD benchmarking study by Cooper *et al.* (2004) found that more of the best performing companies defined the strategic arena for NPD, clearly identified NPD goals, took a long-term view of NPD and strategically allocated resources to portfolios of NPD projects. While it is often argued that NPD should be guided by a new product strategy, it is important that the strategy is not so prescriptive as to restrict, or stifle, the creativity necessary for NPD. Getting the balance right is not straightforward. The history of Cannon's success is one described by Hamel and Prahalad (2005) as one where their strategic intent ('beat Xerox') was broken down into a series of product (and market) development tasks, including competitive study and technology licensing to gain experience, developing technology in-house, selective market entry to exploit the weakness of competition, before going onto to develop completely new technological solutions in the form of disposable cartridges. This development in particular changed the rules of engagement in the photocopy market, reducing market prices by around 30 per cent making the threat from competitive imitation much less. The issue to note from this example is that with the overall target destination is in mind, each of the steps towards the destination is given a purpose and a structure, thereby promoting the effective use of resources. These examples show how the strategic focus, given by top management, is important for NPD success. Yet Beerens *et al.* (2004), in a report for Booz Allen Hamilton found that most companies have difficulty in controlling their product development activities. Symptoms included ignorance of the NPD roles and responsibilities, frequent reprioritizing of projects and the discovery of projects by top management previously unknown to them, lack of robustness in the process and its management. In other words, a lack of a strategic focus on product innovation. The ramifications of practices like these include working on projects that are

unlikely to make money, overloading R&D people, not meeting schedules and increasing the chances of failure. Setting a clear strategy for NPD, on the other hand, not only provides guidelines for resource allocation, but also sets up the key criteria against which all projects can be managed through to the market launch. The well-known assault by Komatsu on Caterpillar through the 70s and 80s was comprised of numerous strategies, amongst which features the frequent launch of new products developed to extend the product lines, future new products based on envisioning programmes and a period of matching increased product variety with efficiency gains. New product strategy, which has also been called the Product Innovation Charter (Crawford, 1984) and Protocol (Cooper, 1993) and whatever its title, the strategic stage is effective because it helps provide the standard against which a development project might be judged, particularly in the early phases. One key element of the protocol, PIC or new product strategy for new product projects, relates to the extent of 'newness' to be pursued.

A majority of 'new' products and services are not entirely 'new'. The new product strategy specifies how innovative the firm intends to be in its NPD and how many new product projects should be resourced at any one time. In their study of NPD practices, Tzokas and Hart (2001) found that only 13 per cent of the new product innovations they studied were 'new to the world'. Similarly, research by Cooper *et al.* (2004) reported from the American Productivity and Quality Centre study of best practices in product development, that new to the world products made up 10.2 per cent of the innovations they surveyed. So, how do companies decide how innovative they want to be and why is this important? The seminal work of Booz, Allen and Hamilton in 1968 and in 1980 revealed the importance of this specification. In their 1968 study, an average of 58 new product ideas were required to produce one successful new product. By 1982, a new study showed this ratio had been reduced to seven to one. The reason forwarded for this change was the addition of a preliminary stage: the development of an explicit, new product strategy that identified the strategic business requirements new products should satisfy. Effective benchmarks were set up so that ideas and concepts were generated to meet strategic objectives; 77 per cent of the companies studied had initiated this procedure with remarkable success. Although written in the early 80s, the lessons to be learned from the work of Booz, Allen and Hamilton are still relevant. According to Andrew and Sirkin (2003) many companies go down the route of generating many new product ideas, setting up new business ventures, floating venture capital funds, nurture corporate intrapreneurs in the belief that return on innovation investment will rise if only more ideas are forthcoming. This is a false assumption, leading to losses.

While it is often argued that NPD should be guided by a new product strategy, it is important that the strategy is not so prescriptive as to restrict, or stifle, the creativity necessary for NPD. In addition to stating the level of newness, a new product strategy should encompass the balance between technology and marketing, the level and nature of new product differentiation, the desired levels of synergy and risk acceptance. Each of these is discussed below:

Technology and marketing   One of the most prevalent themes running throughout the contributions on setting new product strategy the balance between technical and marketing emphases. There is now broad acceptance that there should be a *fusion* between technology- and market-led innovations at the strategic level (Johne and Snelson, 1988; Dougherty, 1992). The examples of both Komatsu and Cannon, above, show how, at various times in their pursuits to topple the market leaders, both market and technology orientations have played their part. Similarly, problems can be found if one approach is allowed to dominate, despite competitive market and technological conditions. Companies such as Kodak, although dominant in analogue photography has been less able when making the change to digital camera technology.

Product differentiation   The literature refers to new product strategies which emphasize the search for a differential advantage, through the product itself (Cooper, 1984). Product advantage is of course a subjective and multi-faceted term, but may be seen as comprising the following elements: technical superiority, product quality, product uniqueness and novelty, product attractiveness and high performance to cost ratio (Hultink and Hart, 1998). In their attempt to rise to the competitive challenge of IT-based play products, the makers of iconic board games such as Scrabble and Monopoly, Hasbro, has launched Hasbro Interactive. This new format began by converting Hasbro products to an interactive format and went on to develop video games bought on license from TV shows before finally investing in a new Internet platform, games.com (Govindarajan and Trimble, 2005).

Synergy   A further consideration for those developing new product strategies, identified in the literature, is the relationship between the NPD and existing activities, known as the synergy with existing activities. High levels of synergy are typically less risky, because a company will have more experience and expertise, although perhaps this contradicts the notion of pursuing product differentiation. With Hasbro, for example, the switch to interactive technology at first kept some synergies by sticking to the traditional games for which the company was known. Once the new interactive versions were successful, the company could then move to unfamiliar (less synergistic) games, before combining the completely new games with a new technological platform. Even then, there was a need for learning, as the corollary of less synergy is lack of knowledge. The Hasbro management team did not know whether it could turn other companies' video games into successes as it had done with its own games, nor did the team have any knowledge of how quickly video game players might switch to the Internet (Govindarajan and Trimble, 2005).

Risk acceptance   Finally, the creation of an internal orientation or climate which accepts risk is highlighted as a major role for the new product strategy. Although synergy might help avoid risk associated with lack of knowledge, the pursuit of product differentiation and advantage must entail acceptance that some projects will fail. An atmosphere that refuses to recognize this tends to stifle activity and the willingness to pursue something new. Again, the Hasbro example reveals some insights here. The original switch to interactive platform took place back in 1997, and results for 97/98 were strong. On the basis of early successes, the investment in the new platform was initiated but results in both 1999 and 2000 were disappointing. Risk was accepted, but almost blindly, since according to Govindarajan and Trimble (2005), there was a reluctance to make predictions, or plan, based on the idea that both would be wrong anyway, and that first to market was the key to success. There was therefore a lack of planning, lack of learning, which meant that little attempt was made to ditch the initiatives that were not succeeding and focusing more resource on those that were doing well.

Once the general direction for NPD has been set, the process of developing new ideas, discussed below, can become more focused.

Idea generation

This is a misleading term, because, in many companies, ideas do not have to be 'generated'. They do, however, need to be managed. This involves identifying sources of ideas and developing means by which these sources can be activated. The aim of this stage in the process is to develop a bank of ideas that fall within the parameters set by 'new product strategy'. Sources of new product ideas exist both within and outside the firm. Inside the canon company, technical departments such as research and development, design and engineering work on developing applications and technologies which will be translated into new product ideas. Equally, commercial functions such as sales and marketing will be exposed to ideas from customers and competitors. Otherwise, many company employees may have useful ideas: service mechanics, customer relations, manufacturing and warehouse employees are continually exposed to 'product problems' which can be translated into new product ideas. Outside the company, competitors, customers, distributors, inventors and universities are fertile repositories of information from which new product ideas come. Products launched with extensive consumer research include Ryvita Minis, the relaunched Hovis pack and Bliss (*Marketing*, 2004, p. 40).

Screening

The next stage in the product development process involves an initial assessment of the extent of demand for the ideas generated and of the capability the company has to make the product. At this, the first of several evaluative stages, only a rough assessment can be made of an idea, which will not yet be expressed in terms of design, materials, features or price. Internal company opinion will be canvassed from R&D, sales, marketing, finance and production, to assess whether the idea has potential, is practical, would fit a market demand and could be produced by existing plant and to estimate the payback period. In their 2004 benchmarking study, Cooper, Edgett and Kleinschmidt showed that the 'best performers did significantly more initial idea screening than other firms in their sample.

The net result of this stage is a body of ideas which are acceptable for further development.

Concept development and testing

Once screened, an idea is turned into a more clearly specified concept and testing this concept begins for its fit with company capability and its fulfilment of customer expectations. Developing the concept from the idea requires that a decision be made on the content and form of the idea. Concept variations may be specified and then subjected to concept tests. Internally, the development team needs to know which varieties are most compatible with current production plant, which require plant acquisition and which require new supplies, and this needs to be matched externally, in relation to which versions are more attractive to customers. The latter involves direct customer research to identify the appeal of the product concept, or alternative concepts to the customer. Concept testing is worth spending time and effort on, collecting sufficient data to provide adequate information upon which the full business analysis will be made. Increasingly, concepts are presented via the Internet.

Business analysis

At this stage, the major 'go–no go' decision will be made. The company needs to be sure that the venture is potentially worthwhile, as expenditure will increase dramatically after this stage. The analysis is based on the fullest information available to the company thus far. It encompasses:

1 A market analysis detailing potential total market, estimated market share within specific time horizon, competing products, likely price, break-even volume, identification of early adopters and specific market segments.
2 Explicit statement of technical aspects, costs, production implications, supplier management and further R&D.
3 Explanation of how the project fits with corporate objectives.

The sources of information for this stage are both internal and external, incorporating any market or technical research carried out thus far. The output of this stage will be a development plan with budget and an initial marketing plan.

Product development and testing

This is the stage where prototypes are physically made. Several tasks are related to this development. First, the finished product will be assessed regarding its level of functional performance. Until now, the product has only existed in theoretical from or mock-up. It is only when component parts are brought together in a functional form that the validity of the theoretical product can be definitively established. When the founders of Innocent Smoothies were thinking of going into business, they bought £500 worth of fresh fruits and 'product tested' them at a music festival (*Marketing*, 2004, p. 40). Second, it is the first physical step in the manufacturing chain. Whilst manufacturing considerations have entered into previous deliberations, it is not until the prototype is developed that alterations to the specification or to manufacturing configurations can be designed and put into place. Third, the product has to be tested with potential customers to assess the overall impression of the test product. Some categories of product are more amenable to customer testing than others. Capital equipment, for example, is difficult to have assessed by potential customers in the same way as a chocolate bar can be taste-tested, or a dishwasher evaluated by an in-house trial. One evolving technique in industrial marketing, however, is called 'Beta-testing', practised informally by many industrial product developers.

Test marketing

The penultimate phase in the development cycle, test marketing, consists of small-scale tests with customers. Until now, the idea, the concept and the product have been 'tested' or 'evaluated' in a somewhat artificial context. Although several of these evaluations may well have compared the new product to competitive offering, other elements of the marketing mix have not been tested, nor has the likely marketing reaction by competitors. At this stage the appeal of the product is tested amidst the mix of activities comprising the market launch: salesmanship, advertising, sales promotion, distributor incentives and public relations.

Test marketing is not always feasible, or desirable. Management must decide whether the costs of test marketing can be justified by the additional information that will be gathered. Further, not all products are suitable for a small-scale launch: passenger cars, for example, have market testing complete before the launch, while other products, once launched on a small scale, cannot be withdrawn, as with personal insurance. Finally, the delay involved in getting a new product to market may be advantageous to the competition, who can use the opportunity to be 'first-to-market'. Competitors may also wait until a company's test market results are known and use the information to help their own launch, or can distort the test results using their own tactics. In addition, for some services, the relative cost of launching a new product is lower, because there are fewer tangible elements in which to invest, so a direct market entry (perhaps on a limited scale) is a viable alternative. Particularly in the fashion industry a fabric, design, cut will be launched directly into stores and, if popular, more designs using the same fabric, ideas and other features will be added.

Some of the problems faced as a result of test marketing have encouraged the development and use of computer-based market simulation models, which use basic models of consumer buying as inputs. Information on consumer awareness, trial and repeat purchases, collected via limited surveys or store data, are used to predict adoption of the new product.

Commercialization or launch

This final stage of the initial development process and is very costly. Decisions such as when to launch the product, where to launch it, how and to whom to launch it will be based on information collected throughout the development process. With regard to timing, important considerations include:

- seasonality of the product;
- whether the launch should fit any trade or commercial event;
- whether the new product is a replacement for the old one;
- whether it is advantageous to be first to market (much debate exists regarding this decision).

Location will, for large companies, describe the number of countries into which the product will be launched and whether national launches will be simultaneous or roll out from one country to another (Chryssochoidis and Wong, 1998). For smaller companies the decision will be restricted to a narrower geographical region. The factors upon which such decisions will be based depend upon the required lead-times for product to reach all the distributive outlets and the relative power and influence of channel members.

Launch strategy encompasses any advertising and trade promotions necessary. Space must be booked, copy and visual material prepared, both for the launch proper and for the pre-sales into the distribution pipeline. The sales force may require extra training in order to sell the new product effectively.

The final target segments should not, at this stage, be a major decision for companies who have developed a product with the market in mind and who have executed the various testing stages. Attention should be more focused on identifying the likely early adopters of the product and on focusing communications on them. In industrial markets, early adopters tend to be innovators in their own markets. The major concern of the launch should be the development of a strong, unified message to promote to the market. Once accepted by the market, the company will elicit feedback to continue the improvement and redevelopment of the product.

Research by Hultink *et al.* (2000) has shown the importance of having the tactics of the launch consistent with the level of innovativeness in the new product. In other words, the commercialization of the new product cannot successfully make claims for it that are dubious. The most successful launches they studied were innovations aimed at carefully selected niche markets, supported by exclusive distribution and pricing.

This explanation of the NPD process has used the model forwarded by Booz Allen Hamilton as an example; there are numerous other models, which are similar in their representation of a series of activities necessary to bring new products to market. The next section of this chapter considers two related concepts that are central to the process of NPD: Uncertainty reduction and the role of information.

Uncertainty and information roles in NPD

At the heart of the notion of the process of developing new products is the notion that the beginning of the process concerns an idea for a new product or service and at its end an actual product or service is designed for, delivered to and appreciated by a market. On the journey from idea to finished product, many questions will be raised and answered, relating to the market (its receptivity, size, congestion), the technologies (if they can be developed, how, with what resources and up against which competitors) and the commercial skills that may be required to sell the new product effectively. This requires progressive uncertainty reduction and indeed the whole procedure has been described as one of information processing (see Hart *et al.*, 2004) whose aim is to continually reduce the uncertainties which pervade the process and whose nature varies at every stage.

Uncertainty

Tzokas identifies six types of uncertainty found throughout the NPD process, namely, market, technological, competitive, resource, product policy and organizationally based uncertainties. These can be illustrated and slotted into the NPD process as shown in Table 13.1.

Of course, the primary input to uncertainty reduction is the collection, dissemination and use of information throughout the NPD process, which is dealt with below.

Information

The role which information can play in facilitating an efficient NPD *process* and achieving *functional co-ordination* is implicit in the literature on success in NPD. The notion of reducing uncertainty as the main objective of the project development activities is reiterated throughout the literature: project activities *'can be considered as discrete information processing activities aimed at reducing uncertainty. . .'* (Moenaert and Souder, 1990, p. 92). These activities include gathering and disseminating information and making decisions based upon this information, which must include evaluations of *both the market and technical aspects* of the development project. Indeed, it is ultimately this information which is evaluated during the NPD process review through the 'gates'.

In order to reduce uncertainty, it is not sufficient that information be processed, it also has to be transferred between different functions (Moenaert and Souder, 1990). In this way the uncertainty perceived by particular functions can be reduced. At the same time the efficient transfer of quality information between different functions encourages their co-ordination (Moenaert and Souder, 1990).

Information, therefore, is a base currency of the NPD process; evaluative information is crucial and must be efficiently disseminated to facilitate communication. It is even possible to analyse the various factors which have been shown to correlate with NPD success in such a way as to reveal the information needs of the process for greater success. An example of the information elements implied by the numerous studies into success and failure is given in Table 13.2.

Table 13.1 Types of uncertainty

Types of uncertainty	Stages in process		
	Idea-Concept	Development	Launch
Market based			
Is there customer need for the product?		X	
How stable is the need in the long term?		X	X
How strongly is the need felt?		X	X
Is the market big enough?		X	
Do we have access to distribution?	X		
Do we have experience in this market?		X	
Do customers perceive value in use?	X	X	X
Technology based			
Can the chosen technology deliver the benefit?		X	
Will the technology become the standard?		X	
Do we have knowledge of the chosen technology?		X	
Do we have manufacturing capability for the chosen technology?		X	
Which OEMs/suppliers do we collaborate with?		X	
Competitive based			
What would be the reaction of our immediate competitors?			X
What would be the new competitive products?			X
What is the threat of technologies from other industries?		X	
Resource based			
Do we have the resources to complete NPD on time?			X
Do we have the resources to support the product in the market?			X
Product policy based			
What would be the effects on other products of the firm?		X	
What would be the effects on resources for other NPD projects?		X	
Organizational based			
Do we have the support of top management?			
Are there any interdepartmental conflicts?		X	
Is there integration among the departments involved?		X	

Source: Adapted from Tzokas (2000).

Research by Maltz (2000) has shown that the way in which information is communicated has a profound effect on its perceived quality and therefore use. Specifically, his study showed that across functions involved in NPD, the frequency of communications needs to be above a threshold level before information is absorbed. Moreover, routine e-mail, contributing as it does to the often unnecessary buzz and obscuring the substantive, is unlikely to be viewed as quality information. Scheduled telephone calls were shown to be of greater value, and *impromptu* face-to-face conversations are associated with higher levels of perceived information quality. Although it is clear that information management is central to NPD and that the models for NPD provide a framework

Table 13.2 The role of market information in achieving critical success factors

Success factor	Studies citing importance	Operationalization of success factors	Expected market information elements
Strategic success factors			
Product advantage	Cooper (1990), Cooper and Kleinschmidt (1987, 1990)	Excellent relative product quality in comparison to competitive offerings; good value for money (perceived by the customer); excellence in meeting customer needs; inclusion of benefits perceived by the customer as useful; benefits which are obvious to the customer; superior price/performance characteristics; unique attributes.	Customer perceptions of competitive offerings; technological dimensions of competitive offerings; customer perceptions of new product's attributes and benefits; feedback from customers after trial; feedback on customer understanding of the message; perceptual maps – based on customer data; technical specifications, product design information; attributes and features specifications.
Well specified protocol	As above; Rothwell (1972), Rothwell et al. (1974), Rubenstein et al. (1976)	Firm's knowledge and understanding, prior to development, of the target market; customer needs, wants, preferences; the product concept; product specifications and requirements.	Research information detailing market demographics/psychographics; customer needs, wants and preferences; technical specifications, product design information, attributes and features specifications (prior to development).
Market attractiveness	Maidique and Zirger (1984), de Brentani (2001)	High growth rates, high market need for product type; stability of demand; relative price insensitivity; high trial of new products.	Economic market data; economic trends; level of employment; income levels; inflation rates.
Top management support	McDonough (1986)	Levels of risk aversion; aspects of corporate culture.	Risk involved; identification of product champions; power and influence distribution among mangers.
Synergy/familiarity	Rothwell et al. (1972, 1974), Maidique and Zirger (1984)	Knowledge of technology; relevance to other projects; access to scientific institutes and laboratories.	Extent of new knowledge involved; technology centres where knowledge resides; key scientists; technological networks of firms.
Development process issues			
Proficiency of pre-development activities.	Cooper and Cooper and Kleinschmidt, Rubenstein et al. (1976), Voss (1985))	Proficiency of concept screening; preliminary market and technical assessment; preliminary business analysis; technical assessment.	Research on customer perceptions, gap analysis, needs analysis, concept tests; market size potential, market segments; technical feasibility, preliminary costs; market size, likely price, profit, break even, etc.
Proficiency of marketing activities	Rothwell et al. (1972, 1974), Roberts and Burke (1974), Cooper (1979, 1980), Maidique and Zirger (1984), Link (1987)	Proficiency of concept, product and market tests, service, advertising, distribution and elements of market launch.	Market information for the acceptance of alternative product concepts or designs, customer preference data; market profile information, information concerning the distribution channels of interest.
Proficiency of technological activities	Rothwell et al. (1972, 1974), Maidique and Zirger (1984)	Proficiency in physical product development; in-house and in-use test iterations; trial production runs; technology acquisition.	Technical solutions to functional and marketing problems; technical information on test performance; information on production costs and problems; information on suppliers' developments and adjacent technologies.
Integration of R&D and Marketing	Rubenstein et al. (1976){AQ1}; Maidique and Zirger (1984), Takeuchi and Nonaka (1986), Gupta and Wilemon (1990), Rochford and Rudelius (1992)	Amount of information shared; agreement on decision-making authority; functional involvement at each stage.	Relevance, novelty, credibility, comprehensibility of information; timeliness of information provision.
Speed in development	Takeuchi and Nonaka (1986), Dumaine (1992), Cooper and Kleinschmidt (1994)	Time-to-market; product launched on schedule; number of competitors on market at time of launch.	Timeliness of information exchange; competitive information.

for evaluation and control of information flows, there is considerable discussion regarding their utility, to which we now turn.

Usefulness of models

The usefulness of the process models, such as that by Booz, Allen and Hamilton, lies in the way in which they provide an indication of the magnitude of the project required in order to develop and launch a new product. Recent research by Cooper *et al.* (2004) showed that using a 'roadmap' for product development, while not widespread among US businesses in general, was more often used by best performers (38 per cent using) than the worst performers (19 per cent using). NPD models are usually templates or maps which can be used to describe and guide those activities required to bring a new product from an idea or opportunity, through to a successful market launch. Like all models, they attempt to capture the essence of the tasks required to complete a project, they are therefore general in their orientation and often criticized for not being applicable to specific situations. For example, it has been argued that the development of new services requires different stages and emphases on stages when compared to product development, or that hi-tech product development does not follow the same steps as for fast-moving consumer goods, or that 'really new products' are a category of development all on their own. That said, it is also true that NPD models take numerous forms and have evolved in their level of prescription over the years. Early depictions of NPD models were rather blunt tools compared to those we have today. Often they described the NPD process by focusing on the departments or functions that hold responsibility for various tasks carried out. In a business to business, technology-based context, the ideas were often assumed to arise in the R&D department; design of the new product carried out by the design department with the engineering function responsible for prototyping, followed by production who tended the manufacturing problems, in front of marketing which planned and carried out the launch. These representations are rather outmoded. It is now accepted that the 'pass-the-parcel' or 'relay' approach to NPD from one department to the next is not only unnecessarily time consuming, but does nothing to foster ownership of, or strategic responsibility for, new products,

and there is nothing in the way of market feedback, since marketing is presented with the product to market. These models have been largely abandoned by the literature which examines NPD and by major companies such as Air Products and Chemicals, Bausch and Lomb, Kraft Foods, to name three reported by Cooper *et al.* (2004). The various stage models have also developed into those focusing on the stages of decision taken after each set of activities, and major exemplars of these models include PACE (Product and Cycle Time Excellence) and the Stage-Gate model devised by Cooper (1993).

These processes consist of stages of activity, followed by review points, or gates, where the decision to continue (or not) with the development is made. This approach clarifies the reality and importance of feedback loops, which although not impossible within the framework of the simpler activity-stage models, are usually not highlighted either. With the decision-stage models, each stage is viewed in terms of its potential output.

The models can provide a useful framework on which to build a complete picture of the development, particularly with regard to the potential advantage of the product viewed from the customers' perspectives. They do, however, suffer from a number of criticisms:

NPD processes are idiosyncratic

The NPD process is idiosyncratic to each individual firm and to the new product project in question. Its shape and sequence depend on the type of new product being developed and its relationship with the firm's current activities (Johne and Snelson, 1988). In addition to the need to adapt the process to individual instances, it should be stated that in real situations there is no clear beginning, middle and end to the NPD process.

For example, from one idea, several product concept variants may be developed, each of which might be pursued. Also, as an idea crystallizes, the developers may assess the nature of the market need more easily and the technical and production costs become more readily identified and evaluated.

NPD processes go through many iterations

The iterative nature of the NPD process results from the fact that each stage or phase of

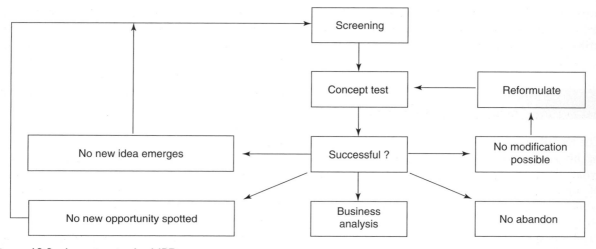

Figure 13.3   Iteration in the NPD process

development can produce numerous outputs which implicate both previous development work and future development progress. Using the model provided by Booz, Allen and Hamilton, if a new product concept fails the concept test, then there is no guidance as to what might happen next. In reality, a number of outcomes may result from a failed concept test, and these are described below and depicted in Figure 13.3.

- *A new idea.* It is possible that although the original concept is faulty, a better one is found through the concept tests; it would then re-enter the development process at the screening stage.
- *A new customer.* Alternatively, a new customer may be identified through the concept testing stage, since the objective of concept testing is to be alert to customer needs when formulating a new product. Any new customers would then feed into the idea generation and screening process.

Related strands of development

A further point in relation to the sequencing of product development tasks is the existence of related strands of development. These related strands of development refer to marketing, technical (design) and production tasks or decisions that occur as the process unwinds. Each strand of development gives rise to problems and opportunities within the other two. For example, if, at the product development stage, production people have a problem which pushes production costs up, this could affect market potential. The marketing and technical assumptions need to be reworked in the light of this new information. A new design

may be considered, or a new approach to the marketplace may be attempted. Whatever the nature of the final solution, it has to be based on the interplay of technical, marketing and manufacturing development issues, meaning that product development activity is iterative, not only between stages, but also within stages. The crucial issue here is that the activity- and decision-stage models do not adequately communicate the horizontal dimensions of the NPD process.

This shortcoming has resulted in the advancement of the idea of 'parallel processing', which acknowledges the iterations between and within stages, categorizing them along functional configurations. The idea of parallel processing is highly prescriptive: it advises that major functions should be involved from the early stages of the NPD process to its conclusion. This, it is claimed, allows problems to be detected and solved much earlier than in the classic task-by-task, function-by-function models. In turn, the entire process is much speedier, which is now recognized to be an important element in new product success. It should be mentioned that a substantial amount of what has been written about the concept of parallel processing is in the engineering domain.

Although greater integration through parallel processing has been attempted by various technical disciplines (e.g. manufacturing and engineering) the market perspective still appears to be 'tacked on' in the technical and engineering literature. True multi-disciplinary integration, embracing technical and commercial functions, is seen as crucial to the outcome of new products and will be considered later in the chapter. Examination of different projects at Hewlett Packard led Rivas and

Gobeli (2005) to conclude that freely distributed information, across multi-functional teams where there were clearly identified roles are crucial lessons for success.

The inclusion of third parties in the process

Another criticism of the 'traditional' process model forwarded by Booz, Allen and Hamilton and others is that it fails to show the importance of parties external to the firm who can have a decided impact on the success of new product development. Several studies have shown the importance of involving users in the NPD process to increase success rates (Thomke and von Hippel, 2002; Hillebrand Biemans, 2004). Equally, there is growing interest in the need for greater supplier involvement, in order to benefit from the advantages of supplier innovation and just-in-time (JIT) policies. The role of suppliers is growing in the quest for speed to market. For example, Dell shifted much of its component design work – laptop screens, optical drives to supplier partners Doolan (2005). Similarly, when Whirlpool decided to invest in a range of products for domestic garages, it decided to outsource much of the manufacturing (Andrew and Sirkin, 2003).

These shortcomings emphasize that the management of the NPD process is more than simply the number and sequencing of its activities. The extent to which the activities can or cannot be effectively carried out demands attention to the *people, or functions*, within the process. It is to these issues that we now turn our attention.

People

People involved in the NPD process and the way in which these people are organized are critical factors in the outcome of NPDs. In order to combine technical and marketing expertise, a number of company functions have to be involved: R&D, manufacturing, engineering, marketing and sales. As the development of a new product may be the only purpose for which these people meet professionally, it is important that the NPD process adopted ensures that they work well and effectively together. Linked to this is also the need for the voice of the customer to be heard, as well as that of suppliers, where changes to supply may be required or advantageous.

The Stanford Innovation Project (Maidique and Zirger, 1984) identified functional co-ordination as a critical factor contributing to the development of *successful* new products. Support for the importance of functional co-ordination is to be found in numerous studies, including Pinto and Pinto (1990), who found that the higher the level of cross-functional co-operation, the more successful the outcome of NPD. The benefits of a close relationship between functional co-ordination and an integrated set of NPD activities have already been highlighted, including the reduction of the development cycle time, cost savings and closer communication so that potential problems are detected very early in the process (Larson, 1988). Although integration of all the relevant functional specialisms into the NPD process is necessary, one particular interface has been given more attention in research studies: the R&D/marketing interface, due to the impact of this interface on the success with which a technological development can be made to match customer need.

Although a host of issues pertain to the integration of the R&D and marketing functions, one of the most powerful is that of how information is exchanged and acted upon throughout the NPD process.

The foregoing discussion of the usefulness of existing models shows that while it is useful to have a checklist of the crucial tasks needed to ensure that new products meet customer needs, any useful framework must allow for numerous inputs from a variety of functions both within and outside the company and must allow for both vertical and horizontal flows of market and technical information across these functions throughout the NPD project. Below an alternative framework for NPD is discussed, called the multiple convergent approach (Hart and Baker, 1994).

In suggesting a way forward in NPD research which builds on process models but which also takes account of the lessons to be learned from studies of success and failure in NPD, the multiple convergent process attempts to break-down research-discipline boundaries, which has direct and explicit consequences for people. This model is conceptually derived from the idea of parallel processing, and is shown in Figure 13.4.

Although models based on parallel processing were an improvement on earlier versions, there was an inherent problem in their parallelism. Definitions of 'parallel' refer to 'separated by an equal distance at every point' or 'never touching or intersecting', and while there are references to

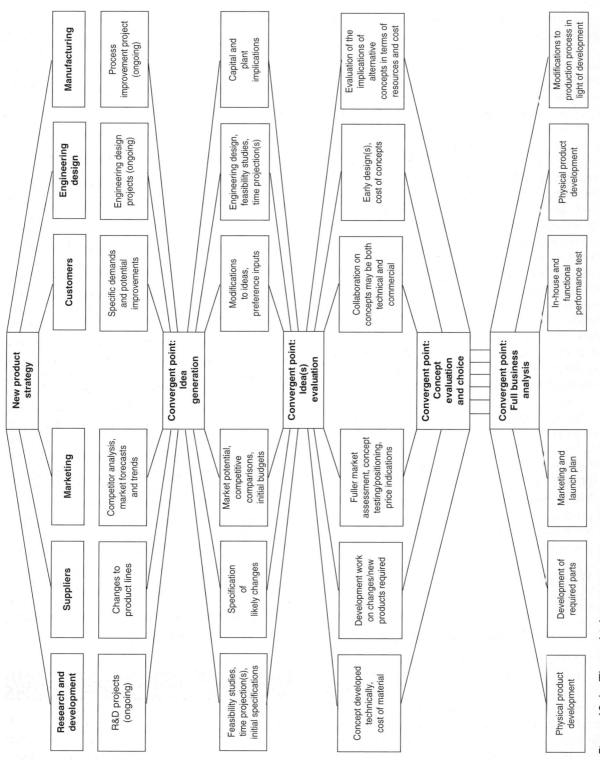

Figure 13.4 The multiple convergent process

simultaneity, it is a somewhat troublesome notion that suggests functional separation, when all the performance indicators in NPD point to the need for functional integration. On the other hand, 'to converge' is defined as 'to move or cause to move towards the same point' or to 'tend towards a common conclusion or result', and is therefore, a more precise indicator of what is required of NPD management.

Realizing, however, that there are still functionally distinct tasks which must be carried out at specific points throughout the NPD process, it is clear that the tasks will be carried out simultaneously at some juncture and that the results must *converge*. Due to the iterations in the process, this convergence is likely to happen several times, culminating at the time of product launch. As previously mentioned, the process is a series of information gathering and evaluating activities, and as the new product develops from idea to concept to prototype and so on, the information gathered becomes more precise and reliable and the decisions are made with greater certainty. Therefore as the development project progresses, there are a number of natural points of evaluation and a number of types of evaluation (market, functional) which need to be carried out in an integrated fashion. These convergent points can be set around decision outputs required to further the process.

The advantages of viewing the process this way are as follows:

1 Iterations among participants within stages are allowed for.
2 The framework can easily accommodate third parties.
3 Mechanisms for integration throughout the process among different functions are set in the convergent points.
4 The model can fit into the most appropriate NPD structures for the company.

Iterations within stages

As the relevant functions are viewed in terms of their contribution to each stage in the process by their specialist contribution, the cross-functional linkages between stages are incorporated. The extent of involvement of different bodies or outside parties will be determined by the specific needs of each development in each firm. Thus, within stage iteration can benefit from both task specialization which will increase the quality of

inputs and integration of functions via information sharing and decision making.

Accommodation of third parties

Several studies have shown the importance of involving users in the NPD process to increase success rates (Biemans, 1992). Equally, there is growing interest in the need for supplier involvement, in order to benefit from the advantages of supplier innovation and JIT (Ragatz *et al.*, 1997).

Mechanisms for Integration

Although the need for cross-functional integration has been widely claimed, there is some evidence to suggest that, in practice, this is not easy to achieve. In Biemans' study, most of the companies showed an understanding of the need to integrate R&D and marketing activities, although the desirability of this is not considered to be automatic, based on the evidence of the companies surveyed. A key element in integration is the amount of information sharing, and the multiple convergent process offers the opportunity for information sharing which is neglected by other models. Clearly, a host of other factors are likely to influence the amount of cross-functional information sharing, including organizational climate and structure. This said, the multiple convergent model carries within it the impetus for information sharing through the convergent points that can be located liberally throughout the process.

However, in studies stress that the appropriate level of integration must be decided upon, and that this level is dependent upon organizational strategies, environmental uncertainty, organizational factors and individual factors. This requires attention, not only to the process of developing new products, but also to the mechanisms used to manage the people responsible for bringing new products and services to the market and therefore to organizational design for NPD.

Organizational design for NPD

The process of developing successful new products needs to match technological competence with market relevance. Based on our discussions thus far, numerous inputs are required to achieve these twin goals. Much research has been carried out into various aspects of 'co-ordination' and 'integration' of the perspectives of different disciplines in NPD. This research is confusing, however, not only because of the sheer number of aspects of functional co-ordination which have been investigated, but also because of the variety of terms used to refer to what this article calls 'functional co-ordination'. Pinto and Pinto (1990, p. 203) make an informative summary of the different terms which have been used. Whatever the precise definition, it is important for companies to institute NPD processes and design structures which promote integration and co-ordination, at the same time as preserving the efficiencies and expertise within functional speciality. A recent article, by Olson *et al.* (1995) identified seven types of new product structure, or co-ordination mechanisms, which they describe in terms of four structural attributes: complexity, distribution of authority, formalization and unit autonomy. These are shown in Table 13.3 and discussed below, briefly.

- *Bureaucratic control.* This is the most formalized and centralized and the least participative

mechanism, where a high level general manager co-ordinates activities across functions and is the arbiter of conflicts among functions. Each functional development operates with relative autonomy within the constraints imposed by hierarchical directives, and, therefore most information flows vertically within each department. In such a mechanism, the different functional activities work sequentially on the developing product.
- *Individual liaisons.* Individuals within one functional department have to communicate directly with their counterparts in other departments. Therefore they supplement the vertical communication found in bureaucracies.
- *Integrating managers.* In this co-ordination structure, an additional manager is added to the functional structure, responsible for co-ordinating the efforts of the different functional departments, but without the authority to impose decisions on those departments. Thus, such integrating managers have to rely on persuasion and on their ability to encourage group decision making and compromise to achieve successful results.
- *Matrix structures.* Whereas all the previous mechanisms maintain the primacy of the

Table 13.3 Attributes of interfunctional co-ordination mechanisms

Structural and process variables	Types of co-ordination mechanisms						
	Bureaucratic control	Individual liaisons	Temporary task forces	Integrating managers	Matrix structures	Design teams	Design centres
Structural attributes							
Complexity	Simple structures		→				Complex structures
Distribution of authority	Centralized		→				Decentralized
Formalization	High; more reliance on rules and standard procedures		→				Low; fewer rules and standard procedures
Unit autonomy	Low		→				High

Source: Olson *et al.* (1995).

functional departmental structure, a matrix organization structures activities not only according to product or market focus, but also by function. Thus, individuals are responsible to both a functional manager and a new product manager.

According to this research, two newer structural forms have appeared in order to improve the timeliness and the effectiveness of the product development efforts within rapidly changing environments. These forms are:

- *Design teams.* Like the matrix structure, design teams are composed of a set of functional specialists who work together on a specific NPD project. The difference is that such teams tend to be more self-governing and have greater authority to choose their own internal leader(s) who have more autonomy to establish their own operating procedures and to resolve internal conflicts.
- *Design centres.* These centres have many of the same characteristics as a design team. However, such a centre is a permanent addition to an organization's structure, and members of the centre are involved in multiple development projects over time.

As one moves from bureaucratic control toward more organic and participative structures, the structural complexity of the mechanisms increases. Authority becomes more decentralized, rules and procedures less formalized and less rigidly enforced, and the individual units tend to have more autonomy. Consequently, members of relatively organic structures are more likely to share information across functional boundaries and to undertake interdependent tasks concurrently rather than sequentially.

In other words, as we move from left to right, structures become less 'mechanistic' and more 'organic'. Relatively organic mechanisms such as design teams have some important potential advantages for co-ordinating product development. Indeed, the participative decision-making, consensual conflict resolution and open communication processes of such a structure can help reduce barriers between individuals and functional groups. Such participative structures can also create an atmosphere where innovative ideas are proposed, criticized and refined with a minimum of financial and social risk. Besides, by facilitating the open exchange of creative ideas across multiple functions, the likelihood of producing innovative products that successfully address the market desires as well as technical and operational requirements is increased.

Finally, reduced functional barriers help ensure that unanticipated problems that appear during the development process can be tackled directly by the people concerned. This reduces the possibility that vital information may be delayed, lost or altered.

On the other hand, more participative structures have also some potential disadvantages, especially in terms of costs and temporal efficiency. Creating and supporting several development teams can lead to overabundance in personnel and facilities. The main reason for this is that employees have less relevant experience when developing innovative product concepts and then depend more heavily on other functional specialists for the expertise, information and other resources needed to achieve a creative and successful product. And these flows of information and resources are facilitated by less formal participative co-ordination structures. Thus, there is potential for stagnation in the process if the locus of control is unclear. To shed light on what structures might be used in industry, research was undertaken by Tzokas and Hart (2001), reported, in brief, below.

Structures used by industry

Many studies of innovation and product development give evidence of the 'structures' used to organize the process. Dyer *et al.* (2001) found that US firms which are 'first-to-market' tend to use project co-ordinators most often, followed by matrix and then dedicated team structures. They also found that dedicated teams are more successful whilst project co-ordinators and matrix structures are rated to be less successful. Research by Tzokas and Hart (2001) investigated the use of six alternative structures used by industry; results are shown in Figure 13.5.

This study, together with previous work, suggest that structures may exist either within or outside what might be termed 'existing line functions', although this is not always made explicit. For example, Tzokas and Hart's research (2001) shows that the most common mechanism used for NPD is that of a 'multi-disciplinary team', but this was used in combination with other mechanisms, such as a new product manager (process owner) and new product departments. At the risk of over-simplification, we can classify venture

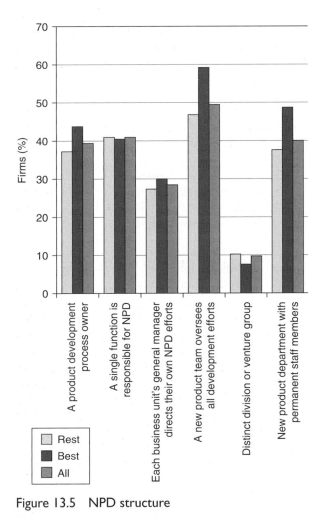

Figure 13.5   NPD structure

groups and new product departments as existing completely outside the normal functional lines, such as marketing, R&D or engineering.

Venture teams   tend to be a permanent 'maverick' group, with high status and separate budgets, reporting to the MD. Their responsibilities can vary, but include opportunity, identification and feasibility studies through to management of the NPD. The advantages are that, freed from the 'humdrum' of current business, creativity can be encouraged, and the development has high level support. On the other side, they can turn into acquisition hunters, may be prone to get into unrelated areas and can be seen as a waste of time if they acquire such information from inside the company, which might occur if they get involved with the development of existing products.

New product departments or divisions   have the same status as functional divisions and are essentially outside the 'mainstream' of business. They are usually staffed by a combination of

factors. They may be used in different ways: as idea hunters, where ideas are passed to the 'mainstream' for development, or as developers, who manage the new product from idea through to the market launch. In the latter instance, the 'handover' of the product will take place at the launch, which may engender feelings of 'not invented here'. However, the rationale for the complete segregation of new product activity is to encourage new ideas for products not contaminated by the vested interests of those managing the current business. If, however, new product activity does need to draw on experience of current technologies in current markets, then some linkage with those managing the current business is clearly beneficial.

Multi-disciplinary teams, new products' committees, new product teams, product managers and new product managers   are all limited – some more directly than others – to the existing line structures. Indeed Page's study showed that the line functions most involved in NPD were marketing, R&D and engineering. The various teams, committees or individuals may be given 'part-time' responsibility for NPD.

There is an inevitable tension between the need for integration and existing authority and responsibility lines. Due to this tension, many firms will locate responsibility for NPD in one function, and bring others in as and when required. This, of course, raises problems in that development work may be in conflict with the management of current business. This would be manifested in time pressures, whereby development work is squeezed by existing product management, and in stifled creativity, owing to procedures already being in place for existing products; finally, fresh business perspectives may be lacking in people who are expert in managing the current business.

Alternatively, a post of new products manager may be created in marketing or technical departments. The part-time option can suffer from time pressures and conflict of roles as besets much matrix structures and, worse, NPD can become something of a secondary goal. In addition, the individual new product manager tends not to be interdisciplinary, which forces negotiation with other departments, as opposed to collaboration. As a result, there tends to be a 'pass the parcel' approach to the development project, which gets shunted around from one department to the next. Finally, this mechanism tends to be low level with little leverage for important resource decisions, leading to an incremental approach to NPD and a new product committee. This is made up of senior managers from salient functions, and has the purpose of encouraging cross-functional co-operation at the appropriate senior level. However, these mechanisms may suffer from a remote perspective, as the line managers are not really carrying out the task.

Location of new product activity inside or outside existing functions requires a trade-off. Since autonomous structures are designed to allow the unfettered development of new ideas with greater levels of advantage, without much reliance on the existing business, it follows logically that this type of development is precisely what they should carry out.

Once these autonomous units become involved with what Johne and Snelson call 'old product development', their inevitable reliance on those within the line function may cause a conflict. In any case, perhaps the efficiency of an autonomous unit to redevelop current lines is questionable. Indeed, the research by Olson *et al.* (1995) showed that 'organic, decentralized participative co-ordination mechanisms *are* associated with better development performance . . . *but only when* used on projects involving innovative or new to the world concepts with which the company has little experience on which to draw' (p. 61).

Looking at product development at Ciba Vision, a Unit of the Swiss pharmaceutical company Cibe-Geigy (now Novartis) provides an interesting example of the issues. Ciba Vision's management realized that radical new products were required to grow the company (and even to fend off decline) at the same time as continuing to make money from its more conventional portfolio of contact lens and eye care products. The decision was taken to launch six formal development projects aiming at revolutionary change, two in manufacturing processes and four in new products. Many smaller R&D projects, aimed at on-going product improvement were cancelled to release cash for the more ambitious R&D imperatives. Traditional business sections were still able to pursue incremental innovations of their own, but the R&D budget was dedicated to the development of real breakthroughs. These, however, were freed from the structures of the old organization and instead autonomous units for the new projects were developed, each with its own R&D, finance and marketing functions.

This section has introduced some of the complexities involved in designing mechanisms which provide the appropriate balance between creativity and innovation on the one hand, and building on the expertise accumulated with regard to technologies and markets on the other. Although the success literature points to the need for cross-functional teams, the extent to which these should be autonomous will depend, among other things, on the type of NPD being pursued.

There is however, another set of issues which impact upon the management of product and service innovation projects, namely, the extent to which this now takes place in networks that cross firms' traditional boundaries.

Managing networks for NPD

Research has highlighted the importance of 'inter-organizational collaboration', 'innovation networks' (e.g. Gnyawali and Madhavan, 2001; Pyka, 2002; Powell *et al.*, 2005). Indeed, the successes of companies such as Wal-Mart and Microsoft has been attributed to their system of networks (Iansiti and Levien, 2004) Due to the emphasis on speed in the NPD process, together with the fact that it is a resource-hungry activity, firms will have to be engaged in learning races, requiring the capacity to work with specialized companies in their networks so that all participants get better and faster (Powell, 1998). In addition, due to the many different technologies involved in NPD it will need networks to leverage the functional integration required for success (Hakansson *et al.*, 1999; Owen-Smith and Powell, 2004).

Powell (1998) argues that in order to reduce the inherent uncertainties associated with new products or markets, inter-organizational learning in firm's networks plays a crucial role in creating a firm's competitive advantages. Eisenharkt and Martin (2000) define 'dynamic capability' as *'the firm's processes that use resources to integrate, reconfigure, gain and release resources – to match and even create market change . . . by which firms achieve new resource configurations. . . .'* (p. 1107). Dynamic capabilities consist of processes such as alliancing, product development by which managers combine varied skills and functional backgrounds through inter-firm collaboration. Moreover, 'dynamic capabilities', by achieving new resource configurations, turns the inter-organizational relationships in NPD networks into another important topic: 'the changing dynamics of competition and cooperation'. Knowledge creation and transferring are two important topics in studying inter-firm learning in NPD networks, although an in-depth treatment is beyond the scope of this book. That said, the ensuing chapters will make to firms working in alliances and networks to carry out their NPD activities.

Summary

This chapter has focused exclusively on how new products are developed. Starting with the proposition that it takes more than a good idea to make a successful new product, it has described the main activities needed to bring a new product to market successfully. In so doing, the main critical success factors for NPD which have been revealed through research have been woven into the discussion of the process models commonly exhorted as the blueprints for success. This discussion has, in turn, highlighted the importance of market information to the successful completion NPD projects but it has also shown that blind adherence to a model for NPD cannot be productive as the whole business needs to be characterized by flexibility and open to creativity from various sources within and outside companies. The argument has presented information as a central thread of successful NPD. The NPD process is one of uncertainty reduction which requires information, constant evaluation of options, which requires information and integration of various functional perspectives, also requiring the sharing of information. A review and critique of the current models is given, revealing their contribution to and constraints on the process of developing new products and suggestions have been derived from recent research as to how they might be improved and managed.

References

Andrew, J. P. and Sirkin, H. L. (2003) Innovating for cash, *Harvard Business Review*, September, 76–83.

Baker, M. J. and Hart, S. J. (2007) *Product Strategy and Management*, Pearson, London.

Baker, M. J. and Hart, S. J. (1994) Learning from success: multiple convergent processing in new product development, *International Marketing Review*, **11**(1), 77–92.

Beerens, J., Van Boetzelaer, A. *et al.* (2004) The road towards more effective product/service development, Booz Allen Hamilton.

Biemans, W. (1992) *Managing Innovations Within Networks*, Routledge, London.

Booz, E., Allen, J. and Hamilton, C. (1968) *Management of New Products*, Booz Allen & Hamilton, Chicago.

Booz Allen Hamilton (1982) *New Products Management for the 1980s*, Booz Allen Hamilton, New York.

Chryssochoidis, G. M. and Wong, V. (1998) Rolling out new products across country markets: an empirical study of the causes of delays, *Journal of Product Innovation Management*, **15**(1), 16–41.

Cooper, R., Edgett, S. and Kleinschmidt, E. (2004) Benchmarking best NPD practices – I, *Research Technology Management*, **47**(1), 31–43.

Cooper, R. G. (1979) The dimensions of industrial new product success and failure, *Journal of Marketing*, **43**(1), Spring, 44–54.

Cooper, R. G. (1984) How new product strategies impact on performance, *Journal of Product Innovation Management*, **1**, 5–18.

Cooper, R. G. (1993) *Winning at New Products; Accelerating the Process from Idea to Launch*, Addison-Wesley, Reading, MA.

Crawford, C. M. (1984) Protocol: new tool for product innovation, *Journal of Product Innovation Management*, **2**, 85–91.

De Brentani, U. (2001) Innovative versus incremental new business services: different keys for achieving success, *Journal of Maroduct Innovation Management*, **18**, 169–187.

Doolan, K. (2005) Speed, the new X factor, *Forbes*, **176**(13), 74.

Dougherty, D. (1992) A practice-centred model of organisational renewal through product innovation, *Strategic Management Journal*, **13**, 77–92.

Eisenhardt, K. and Martin, J. (2000) Dynamic capabilities: what are they?, *Strategic Management Journal*, **21**, 1105–1121.

Gnyawali, D. and Madhavan, R. (2001) Cooperative networks and competitive dynamics: a structural embeddedness perspective, *The Academy of Management Review*, **26**(3), 431.

Govindarajan, V. and Trimble, C. (2005) Building breakthrough businesses within established organization, *Harvard Business Review*, May, 58–68.

Hakansson, H. *et al.* (1999) Learning in networks, *Industrial Marketing Management*, **28**, 443–452.

Hamel, G. and Prahalad, C. K. (2005) Strategic intent, *Harvard Business Review*, July–August, 148–161.

Hart, S. J. and Baker, M. J. (1994) The multiple convergent process of new product development, *International Marketing Review*, **11**(1), 77–92.

Hart, S. *et al.* (2004) Navigating the new product development process, *Industrial Marketing Management*, **33**, 619–636.

Hart, S. *et al.* (2007) *Marketing in the Innovative Firm*, Unpublished Report to Scottish Enterprise.

Hillebrand, B. and Biemans, W. (2004) Links between internal and external cooperation in product development: an exploratory study, *Journal of Product Innovation Management*, **21**(2), 110.

Hultink, E. and Hart, S. (1998) The world's path to the better mousetrap: myth or reality? an empirical investigation into the launch strategies of high and low advantage new products, *European Journal of Innovation Management*, **1**(3), 106.

Hultink, E. J., Hart, S., Robben, S. J. and Griffin, A. (2000) Launch decisions and new product success: an empirical comparison of consumer and industrial products, *Journal of Product Innovation Management*, **17**(1), 5–23.

Iansiti, M. and Levien, R. (2004) Strategy as ecology, *Harvard Business Review*, **82**(3), 68.

Industry Week (1996) 16 December, 45.

Johne, A. F. and Snelson, P. (1988) Marketing's role in new product development, *Journal of Marketing Management*, **3**, 256–268.

Larson, C. (1988) Team tactics can cut development costs, *Journal of Business Strategy*, **9**(5), September/October, 22–25.

Levitt, T. (1960) Marketing myopia, *Harvard Business Review*, July–August, 45–56.

Maidique, M. A. and Zirger, B. J. (1984) A study of success and failure in product innovation: the case of the US electronics industry, *IEEE Transactions on Engineering Management*, **31**, 192–203.

Maltz, E. (2000) Is all communication created equal?: an investigation into the effects of communication mode on perceived information quality, *Journal of Product Innovation Management*, **17**(2), 110–127.

Moenaert, R. K. and Souder, W. E. (1990) An information transfer model for integrating marketing and R&D personnel in NPD projects, *Journal of Product Innovation Management*, **7**(2), 91–107.

Olson, E. M., Walker, O. C. and Ruekert, R. W. (1995) Organizing for effective new product development: the moderating influence of product innovativeness, *Journal of Marketing*, **59**, 48–62.

Owen-Smith, J. and Powell, W. (2004) Knowledge networks as channel and conduits: the effects of spillovers in the Boston biotechnology community, *Organisational Science*, **15**(1), 5–21.

Pinto, M. B. and Pinto, J. K. (1990) Project team communication and cross-functional co-operation in new product development, *Journal of Product Innovation Management*, **7**(3), September, 200–212.

Powell, W. (1998) Learning from collaboration: knowledge and networks in the biotechnology and pharmaceutical industries, *California Management Review*, **40**(3), 228–240.

Powell, W., White, D., Koput, K. W. and Owen-Smith, J. (2005) Network dynamics and field evolution: the growth of interorganizational collaboration in the life sciences, *The American Journal of Sociology*, **110**(4), 1132–1205.

PRTM (2004) PRTM.com

Pyka, A. (2002) Innovation networks in economics: from the incentive-based to the knowledge-based approaches, *European Journal of Innovation Management*, **5**(3), 152–163.

Ragatz, G. L., Handfield, R. B. and Scannell, T. V. (1997) Success factors for integrating suppliers into new product development, *Journal of Product Innovation Management*, **14**(3), 190–202.

Rivas, R. and Gobeli, D. H. (2005) Accelerating innovation at Hewlett-Packard: a case study identifies significant enablers as well as barriers to innovation, along with management lessons for speeding the process, *Research-Technology Management*, **48**(1), 32–39.

Soulsby, D. (2004) Products launched with consumer research, *Marketing*, 2 September, 40.

Thomke, S. and von Hippel, E. (2002) Customers as innovators: a new way to create value, *Harvard Business Review*, **80**(4), 74.

Tzokas, N. (2000) *Critical Information and the Quest for Customer Relevant NPD Processes*, Report to EU Marie-Curie Fellowship Programme.

Tzokas, N. and Hart, S. (2001) *Critical Information and the Quest for Customer Relevant NPD Processes*, Unpublished report for the EU, University of Strathclyde.

Further reading

Dahan, E. and Srinivasan, V. (2000) The predictive power of internet-based concept testing using visual depiction and animation, *Journal of Product Innovation Management*, **17**(2), 99–109.

de Meyer, A. (1985) The flow of technological innovation in an R&D department, *Research Policy*, **14**, 315–328.

Dwyer, L. M. and Mellor, R. (1991) Organization environment, new product process activities and project outcomes, *Journal of Product Innovation Management*, **8**(1), March, 39–48.

Dyer, B., Gupta, A. K. and Wilemon, D. (1999) What first-to-market companies do differently, *Research-Technology Management*, **42**(2), 15–21.

Eisenhardt, K. M. and Tabrizi, B. N. (1994) Accelerating adaptive processes: product innovation in the global computer industry, *Administrative Science Quarterly*, **40**(1), March, 84–110.

Griffin, A. (1997) *Drivers of NPD Success: The 1997 PDMA Report*, PDMA, Chicago.

Gupta, A. K. and Wilemon, D. (1988) The credibility – co-operation connection at the R&D marketing interface, *Journal of Product Innovation Management*, **5**, 20–31.

Harryson, S. J. (1997) How Canon and Sony drive product innovation through networking and application-focused R&D, *Journal of Product Innovation Management*, **14**(3), 288–295.

Hart, S., Tzokas, N., Hultink, E. J. and Commandeur, H. (1998) How companies steer the new product development process, *Proceedings of the Annual Conference of the Product Development Management Association*, Atlanta, Georgia, pp.

Hart, S., Tzokas, N., Hultink, E. J. and Commandeur, H. (2003) Industrial companies' evaluation criteria in new product development gates, *Journal of Product Innovation Management*, **20**(1), 22–36.

Hauser, J. and Zettelmeyer, F. (1997) Metrics to evaluate R,D,&E, *Research Technology Management*, **40**(4), 32.

Hill, P. (1988) The market research contribution to new product failure and success, *Journal of Marketing Management*, **3**(3), 269–277.

Hultink, E. J., Griffin, A., Hart, S. and Robben, H. S. J. (1997) Industrial new product launch strategies and product development performance, *Journal of Product Innovation Management*, **14**, 246.

Montoya-Weiss, M. and O'Driscoll, T. (2000) Applying performance support technology in the fuzzy front end, *Journal of Product Innovation Management*, **17**(2), 143–161.

Page, A. L. (1993) Assessing new product development practices and performance: establishing crucial norms, *Journal of Product Innovation Management*, **10**, September, 273–290.

Riek, R. F. (2001) Capturing hard-won NPD lessons in checklists, *Journal of Product Innovation Management*, **18**(5), 324–342.

Von Hippel, E. (1978) Successful industrial products from customer ideas – presentation of a new customer-active paradigm with evidence and implications, *Journal of Marketing*, January, 39–49.

Workman, Jr. J. P. (1993) Marketing's limited role in NPD in one computer systems firm, *Journal of Marketing Research*, **30**, 405–421.

CHAPTER 14

Pricing

TONY CRAM

Introduction

Pricing is crucial, often mismanaged, feared, challenging, yet ultimately an opportunity. This chapter will illustrate methods of setting prices, how best to understand and influence customer's perspectives on value, how to behave towards competitors and critically how to capture value for the firm. Finally it will give pointers to measuring price performance.

Pricing impact and challenge

Pricing is crucial. Arguably, pricing is the most significant element of the marketing mix after the product itself. An agreed price permits a transaction to take place, which is the core of the marketing process. Marketing focuses on creating value for a customer through developing a product or service to meet a need; price is the mechanism that captures a share of that value for the seller. Thus price is a significant lever in obtaining a profitable return. The case is long proven – in 1992, a McKinsey survey of 2483 companies calculated that a 1 per cent increase in prices improved operating profit by 11.1 per cent – greatly exceeding the impact of a 1 per cent improvement in fixed costs (+2.3 per cent), volume (+3.3 per cent) or even variable costs (+7.8 per cent). Furthermore, the price positions a brand more quickly and credibly than any advertisement – a buyer knows from its price tag that a Hagen Dazs is not an everyday ice cream.

Pricing is often mismanaged. J. Dean (1947), writing in 'Planning the price structure',

observed that pricing is the 'last stronghold of medievalism in modern management'. Foremost advertising guru, David Ogilvy (1983) wrote in his book *Ogilvy on Advertising* that 'pricing is guesswork. It is usually assumed that marketers use scientific methods to determine the price of their products. Nothing could be further from the truth'. A 2003 report by the consultants McKinsey & Company suggested that 80–90 per cent of poor pricing decisions featured under-pricing. Finally Mark Ritson, an assistant professor of marketing at London Business School, is quoted in the *Financial Times* (2002): 'Pricing is the worst managed of all marketing areas. How prices are decided is often a mixture of voodoo and bingo'.

Pricing is feared. Pricing is the explosive business variable. The wrong price can prejudice sales and damage commercial prospects rapidly and decisively. Price also generates powerful emotions. Low prices can lead to accusations of dumping and predatory pricing judgements. It can tarnish a brand with the label of cheapskate. At the other end of the scale, apparently high prices result in charges of gouging, fleecing, unfairness and rip-off. Getting the wrong price carries with it relationship and reputation dangers beyond profit shortfall.

Pricing is challenging. First, there is the surfeit of data. Wide product ranges, sold in numerous markets and bought by myriads of customers, result in huge quantities of data. Analysing sales can be like drinking from a fire hydrant. Added to this, a firm will have manifold competitors – direct and indirect – whose actions may impact on the relative perceptions of customers. A further factor in the pricing equation is the margin effect of changing cost prices: ingredients, packaging, labour, storage, insurance, transportation, advertising and merchandizing. Internally, there are many players in the pricing process. Accounts department will track costs, Sales will consider customers, the marketing department will research consumers and competitors, legal department will ensure regulatory compliance, production and distribution set supply constraints. Conflicting objectives need resolution when the finance department's view on margin calls for higher prices and the sales team focus on revenue and share growth demands lower prices. In the experience of McKinsey consultants, Eugster *et al.* (2000), 'Companies often base prices on the anecdotal evidence of a few vocal sales people or product managers'. Finally it is hard to set measurable objectives for pricing. High prices may mean lost sales. Low prices may mean margin left on the table. The true measure of pricing is the minimization of profit foregone through under- or over-pricing, which is difficult to calibrate in a balanced scorecard (Figure 14.1).

As a result of these challenges, many organizations silently delegate pricing decisions to their customers and competitors. They simply react to pressures and opportunities in the marketplace as they arise.

Yet, ultimately pricing is an opportunity. Commerce began when primitive man first bartered or exchanged goods of equivalent value. The cowry shell was the first form of money in China and elsewhere by 1200 BC. Metal coins were minted in Greece in 680 BC and the concept rapidly spread around the old world. The invention of money simplified transactions and price truly entered the consciousness of human kind. Determining the right price is a challenge. The right price gives value to the customer, differentiates from the competitor and gives a commercial return to the seller. This is the pricing opportunity.

Three methods for devising prices

There are three pointers for devising prices. The first method is to look at costs and mark up an acceptable margin. As a rule of thumb, this may be used, for example, by an industrial wholesaler who obtains numerous items from different sources. The appeal of this approach is based on hard facts – your costs are certain and a margin based on marking-up costs ensures that all products are contributing to profitability. However, costs are an internal matter. 'The customer does not care about the firm's costs . . . only about the value he/she is getting' (Diamantopoulos, 1995). A focus on costs ignores the value offered to the market. Pop-corn is bought in cinemas for £4.00 per tub, yet the raw materials of corn, sugar and card all cost a matter of pence. Cost-based prices are unlikely to capture an appropriate share of the potential value of the marketplace. Mark-up pricing tends to leave money on the table (Figure 14.2).

The second method is to study competitors. In this situation, companies set prices primarily with reference to one or more other players in the market. Frequently, this applies to follower brands whose prices are set at a discount to the leading brand. This ongoing reactive approach commoditizes products and services. It assumes that your goods are identical to competitors, with price as the only basis for choice. It downplays differentiation and may miss the value created for the buyer.

The third method is to see what the market will bear. This approach identifies the amount a buyer is able and willing to pay for the product or service. An auction website such as eBay is an example of a means whereby a seller can assess how much a customer values a product – prospective buyers see descriptions and illustrations of products and then bid competitively until the auction closes. This method comes closer to

Challenges in setting prices

Mass of sales and transaction data

Interplay of internal players: finance, sales, marketing, top management

Range of competitors direct/indirect

Multiple sources of costs

Challenge in setting pricing objectives

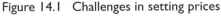

Figure 14.1   Challenges in setting prices

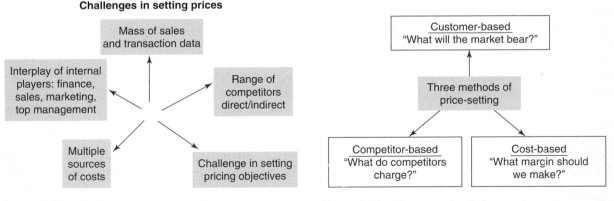

Figure 14.2   Three methods for setting prices

capturing full value because it tests how much a bidder values the auction lot. The more competitive the bidding is, the more effective is the value capture. However, for most companies with wide product ranges that serve large numbers of customers, an auction or an individual negotiation is impractical. They, therefore, need other means to discover what the market will bear.

Pricing – customer perspective

The objective of pricing is to optimize the company's economic value by capturing the value the customer sees in the proposition. This implies identifying the point at which the greatest revenue (and profit) can be achieved (see Figure 14.3).

Price-setting should begin with establishing how the customer values the product or service and what they are willing to pay. Yet, few companies use pricing research effectively. A survey quoted by Kent B. Monroe and Jennifer L. Cox (2001), writing in *Marketing Management*, found that 88 per cent of companies did little or no serious pricing research – only 8 per cent of companies could be classified as conducting professionally pricing research to support developing an effective pricing strategy.

Pricing research

Customers seem unable to answer honestly the question: How much would you pay for this?

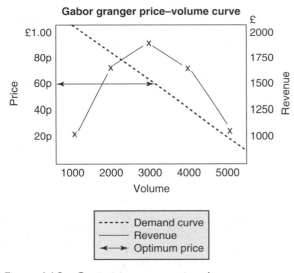

Gabor granger price–volume curve

- ----- Demand curve
- —— Revenue
- ◄——► Optimum price

Figure 14.3   Optimizing economic value

David W. Lyon's (2002) article 'The Price is Right (or is it?)', published in *Marketing Research*, explains the difficulty. He writes, 'hearing such a question, many respondents immediately shift into bargaining mode and produce opening offers that aren't even remotely reflective of what their real world behaviour would be'. A simple but more reliable direct question is the 'Buy Response Question'. Known as Gabor–Granger technique after the economists who invented it in the 1960s, the method is to describe or demonstrate a product with its features, mentioning the price in context. The customer is asked, 'Would you buy it?' The price should be presented unobtrusively, so it is seen as just one of the features of the product. To gauge price sensitivity, it is essential to test different price options. Obviously, if a single respondent were presented with a second option – a package identical apart from a price change – then he/she will be sensitized to price and revert to bargaining mode. Sequential tests may be appealing in terms of reducing research costs, but they actually destroy meaning. Therefore, monadic tests are used – each respondent is asked once only.

A more sophisticated approach was devised by the Dutch psychologist Peter van Westendorp in the 1970s. This is most often used for new products where there is no obvious value benchmark or competitor equivalent. The Van Westendorp Price Sensitivity Meter (PSM) describes or demonstrates the product as before and then poses four questions:

1   At what price would you consider this product to represent good value?
2   At what price would you say this item is getting expensive, but you would still consider buying it?
3   At what price would you consider this product to be too expensive to consider buying it?
4   At what price would you consider this product to be priced so cheaply that you would worry about quality?

There is an intersection point where the number of respondents who regard the product as too expensive exactly equal the number who see it as too cheap. This intersection is the recommended price.

Finally, trade-off or conjoint analysis is a statistical technique developed by Luce , a mathematical psychologist and Tukey, a statistician (described in Green and Srinivasan, 1978; Green *et al.*, 1981). This technique compels respondents to make 'either/or' choices that effectively rank benefits and benefit combinations against different price points. Respondents are invited to choose between different paired offers. The offers consist of various attributes and for each attribute a number of levels. For example, one attribute of a laptop computer might be portability and the levels might be three specified weights. Another attribute might be processing speed with three levels, and similarly for style and price. Each offer pairs a higher level of one attribute and a lower level of another at different price points. By giving a significant number of choices to a representative sample – in excess of 200 for statistical significance – it is possible to develop a robust model of the price people are prepared for potential combinations of benefits. Customers' preferences for different offers are ranked and then decomposed in order to determine the person's inferred 'utility function' or value for each element of the benefit package. Respondents' choices show the trade-offs they would make and convey the relative importance of each attribute in numerical terms. Conjoint analysis can be administered cost effectively online, once the sample has been qualified by telephone recruitment.

Probing intentions and preferences around price has perils. Research techniques risk that predicted behaviour may not occur in practice. For this reason, the most reliable findings come when real people are making normal decisions in a familiar environment. If it is possible to use actual behaviour as the guide, then do so. Hence, historical sales data, panel data, store scanner data and price tests are often used to establish reactions to price in practice. Writing in *Fast Company*, Charles Fishman (2003) describes the research conducted for DHL by the Texas-based pricing consultancy Zilliant. Their software runs numerous experiments, testing slightly changed prices on real customers, measuring the response of cells of customers. Tests covered prices for all weights of package across 43 different markets. With thousands of data points, the software measured customers who called, asked for a price and then did not ship. These failed prices indicated the price ceiling. Lower prices calibrated the potential for volume increase. The results showed that DHL – with its strong international reputation – did not need to match lower-priced rivals, UPS and Fedex. Hundreds of prices were changed. Some prices were lowered slightly, still maintaining a premium over competitors while gaining volume, revenue and profit. The critical pricing dimension is the amount that the customer is willing to pay.

Price sensitivity

Price levels will impact on the number of customers buying. When a price rises, fewer people are able or willing to buy and the remaining buyers may decrease their purchasing quantity or frequency. Higher tax on cigarettes raises prices to discourage smoking. When prices fall, more buyers enter the market or buy more often. As the price of DVD players has fallen, more and more households have bought them. Economists call this relationship the Price Elasticity of Demand (PED). This measures the percentage change in a product's unit sales as a result of a change in price. The demand elasticity, 'E' is normally a negative number because positive price changes (or increases) usually result in sales declines. Price sensitivity varies between categories and products. It may also vary over time. Innovative customers and early adopters tend to be less price sensitive when they discover new and unique products. The first buyers of iPods paid a price premium. As markets mature, novelty fades, customers become more familiar with product characteristics and price often becomes a greater factor in purchases.

Thomas T. Nagle and Reed K. Holden (2002), writing in *The Strategy and Tactics of Pricing*, identify nine 'effects' that influence willingness to pay and result in buyers being more or less price-sensitive.

1 *Reference price effect.* Willingness to pay is influenced by the perceptions buyers have of the relative cost of an alternative. If customers are unaware of substitutes, they will be less price-sensitive. If they are aware of an alternative, they will use this as a benchmark. Memory of previous purchases will give an understanding of acceptable value. Where they see comparisons side by side in a retail store, this will also encourage confidence in making a purchase and shape the resultant behaviour.
2 *Difficult comparison effect.* Willingness to pay is influenced by the ease of making valid comparisons. If the product or service alternative is difficult to evaluate (e.g. legal services – then customers will be less price-sensitive about buying from a trustworthy firm or brand).
3 *Switching cost effect.* The greater the amount of cost or effort in changing supplier, the less price-sensitive will be the customers. Barriers to exit may be financial or involve psychological switching costs (Cram, 2001).

4 *Price–quality effect.* Prestige signified by high price counteracts price sensitivity. Halving the list price of a Rolex would make it much less effective in conveying to others the wealth of the owner. Some other products, wine for example, which are hard to judge unopened, may be bought using price as a signal of relative quality.

5 *Expenditure effect.* Buyers will be more price-sensitive when the expenditure involved represents a greater portion of their available income. Higher spending means more focus on price. Thus, a snack bought as a single item may be purchased spontaneously, whereas the same snack bought as part of the weekly supermarket shop will be subject to closer price scrutiny.

6 *End-benefit effect.* When an item purchased is a component part of a bigger decision, the price sensitivity will be influenced by the proportion of the item's cost relative to the whole ensemble. For instance, a colleague, renowned for his search for value in other areas of his life, placed a deposit on a new Porsche Boxster at an agreed price. The day the order came to be confirmed, the salesman asked if he wanted leather seats. In the context of the whole package, the £2000 cost seemed relatively small. An hour later, the buyer commented, 'That's the fastest £2000 I ever gave away!'

7 *Shared cost effect.* The portion of the price paid by a buyer will influence their price sensitivity. Items may be subsidized by an employer or be tax deductible, or the cost may be shared in a joint venture.

8 *Fairness effect.* Willingness to pay is strongly affected by an emotional perception of fairness. This is a strongly subjective area. Perceived fairness is linked to assumptions about the seller's profit margin and their motives. A feeling that a very large company is increasing prices to vulnerable individuals might be seen as unfair.

9 *Framing effect.* Framing is linked to prospect theory. People frame purchases as a bundle of gains and losses. Kahneman and Tversky (1979) identified that individuals tend to be more sensitive to the prospect of a loss than the prospect of a gain. They are more price-sensitive when they perceive a price as a 'loss' to them rather than a foregone gain.

There are other factors that influence willingness to pay. For example, buyers who cannot store a product are less price-sensitive, and products that cannot be stored – like phone calls – will be less subject to price scrutiny than inventory items. This may be a pricing opportunity for 'just-in-time' suppliers.

Price discrimination

Price sensitivity will vary between customers. Yet, an average price assumes that customers value the product identically. The single price brings two negative concepts:

1 Some customers valued the product more highly than the single price. They would have paid more and money was left on the table.
2 Other customers cannot or will not afford the single price. They would, however, have bought at a lower price that still delivered a return above the cost price. Profitable sales were lost.

In Figure 14.4, a price of £50 is chosen. Half the customers were willing to pay more and their value is not captured by the single price. However, half the customers would only purchase at a lower price and their sales potential has been lost at £50. A single price policy loses potential profit and potential sales. It also risks attack from smart competitors who pick off profitable segments. Historically, credit card companies have overcharged low risk customers and therefore new entrants can segment their approach and skim off the most attractive customers with a better proposition.

Where different customers or groups of customers value products differently, the route to capturing this value is through differential pricing. Successful price discrimination requires that sellers find credible and sustainable ways to serve different segments at different prices. Economist

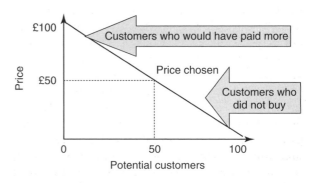

Figure 14.4 One price policy problem

Arthur Pigou (1920) labelled three degrees of price discrimination:

1 *First degree.* This occurs when there is a unique price for every customer. An auction is an example. Haggling in a bazaar is designed to identify the highest price each buyer will bear. Many business-to-business services will be based on bespoke prices per customer, driven by an assessment of economic value and a negotiated agreement.
2 *Second degree.* This is a rule-based approach which is evident when there is a visible and obvious relationship between the volume purchased and the price as in bulk-buying and group terms. Time-based pricing is another form of second degree discrimination with early-bird discount, 'Happy Hours' and last minute standby seats at theatres.
3 *Third degree.* This occurs when a segmented market permits watertight sales to one group at one price and to another group at another level with no arbitrage or transfer taking place between the segments. Gender-based segmentation is an example where women pay more for haircutting. Another form occurs when different prices are charged through different sales channels. The Internet may offer lower prices than a retail store. For third degree discrimination to succeed, it must be acceptable to legal jurisdictions and either be invisible to customers or if visible to appear justifiable. The simplest form of price segmentation is effort based. Cost-conscious consumers will take time to read, understand and clip coupons from advertisements, carrying them in their wallets until the moment they are able to exchange them at point of purchase. Less price-sensitive customers will not be prepared to take the trouble and pay full price. Imposing effort for discounts will screen out the lazy, the busy and the price insensitive. Some companies offer a brand per segment. Volkswagen Group cover four segments with brand variants: a base model under the Skoda marque, a mainstream model under the VW brand, a SEAT sporty model and an Audi status version.

Pricing can shape customer behaviour

The pricing strategy adopted by a company can inadvertently train its customers to behave in unprofitable ways. For example, Thomas T. Nagle and George E. Cressman (2002) criticize business-to-business companies who operate a reactive pricing processes. Without formal pricing structures and lacking strict criteria for discounts, these companies allow price negotiation as long as deals meet some minimum profit level. The intention is to be flexible and responsive to changing market dynamics. The result can be expensive. Regular customers soon learn that aggressive negotiating achieves larger and more frequent discounts. Smart buyers institute policies that drive deeper discounts – requiring sales people to deal with procurement departments, limiting supplier contact with satisfied users. They allocate wedges of business to competitors to increase leverage. They form buying co-operatives. The company has taught its customers the benefits of price resistance – rewarding them with discounts if they will not agree immediately. 'Good customers' have been incentivized to become 'bad customers'. Similarly in consumer goods companies, regular price promotions can teach customers that there is a benefit in delaying purchase until the next promotion. Srinivasan *et al.* (2002) studied 7 years of supermarket scanner data to establish that the long-term benefit of retail price promotions was zero.

However, it is also possible to use price to encourage profitable customer behaviour. Historically, water supply to domestic households in the UK was always charged at a flat rate based indirectly on property values. Without a correlation between usage and the amount charged, customers saw no incentive to conserve water. Thus, in drought periods, emergency action had to be taken to restrict usage by all consumers. In the 1980s, pricing began to be used as a mechanism to encourage responsible behaviour. Water companies began requiring water meters in all new homes. Existing households were encouraged to install water meters, and a long-term programme began to bring about linking usage and payment to encourage profitable behaviour.

Penalizing waste is another technique to improve behaviour. The Oriental City Food Court, 399 Edgware Road in North London offers an open Chinese buffet with self-service for a fixed meal price of £15 per head. The factor most impacting on profit, once the price has been set, is the degree of wasted food. Therefore, the restaurant has a second dimension to its pricing scale: wastage above a token amount on any plate is charged at £5 per 200 gm. With a penalty for wasting food, diners tend to take small portions and refill with dishes they enjoy. Good behaviour is supported by the pricing structure.

Falling prices of successive generations of electronic equipment has given a perverse incentive to prospective customers to hold back until the price comes down. The Carphone Warehouse – one of the UK's leading retailers of mobile phones – has identified this barrier to purchase, overcoming it with a creative approach: the ultimate price promise. Ninety days after a sale, the company's computer compares the price paid and the current price. If the price has fallen, a voucher for the difference will automatically be e-mailed to the buyer. This voucher can be redeemed in store for a phone accessory or put towards a larger transaction. The customer has the reassurance to buy today.

Pricing – competitor perspective

Monopoly suppliers have no competition and need only assess the customer perspective. Do their potential customers have the ability to buy? What is their willingness to pay? How will price influence the level of their demand? But companies are rarely alone in their market with their customers. They must also consider the competitor perspective. Competitor offerings allow customers to make comparisons.

Positioning

With more than one product on offer, customers will position brands relative to each other. Is a brand 'up-market' or 'down-market'? The position that a brand occupies in customers' minds will, therefore, partly be defined by competitors. A credible premium position is associated in the mind of a customer with a higher price. For example, Miele advertisesits washing machines with the slogan 'Anything else is a compromise' and hence their price is higher than mainstream Hotpoint branded washing machines. Aspirational brands and exclusive luxury brands need high relative prices to position them. Both entry brands and volume brands need accessible pricing. Price plays a key role in positioning. It is a clear and ascertainable aspect and it instantly places a brand on the field.

Price competition

Beyond positioning, price is a key weapon in competitive marketing. Price has a strong impact on market share and it is the variable in the marketing mix which can be more quickly changed. Unlike changes to the other elements of the marketing mix, price changes do not require additional marketing investment. It is, therefore, tempting to use price as a marketing tactic in a competitive activity. There are two factors which should inhibit this approach:

1 Price reductions have a disproportionate impact on profits. A small price reduction has a disproportionate impact on profit. With a straightforward price cut of 5 per cent typically, an increase in volume of 18–20 per cent is needed to recover operating profit. In addition, a sudden expansion in volume will have ramifications for variable costs of warehousing, inventory and delivery, plus possible advertising costs to communicate the cut. Volume surges on this scale are implausible.
2 Competitors are often equally able to use price changes and may react swiftly to price cuts. In markets where customers are very responsive, a series of price changes can rapidly lead to a price war.

Most price wars simply pass value from producers to customers and do not capture value for the producer. The US Air Transport Association has recorded more than 100 bankruptcies since deregulation in 1988, including the once proud Pan Am who led the way with trans-Atlantic flights and the jumbo-jet. Yet, whenever an airline goes bust, someone buys the planes and plans ways to put them back into the sky again. Warren Buffet has observed acidly that airlines as a whole have not netted a dime since 1903. Price wars have destroyed value for 100 years.

Contrary to management opinion, most price wars are not strategic exploitation of market growth potential or cost advantage. Most start where one company misinterprets a competitor's actions or acts and fails to consider the likely response of rivals. The price war may begin when Company A cuts prices in one district to clear obsolete stock and Company B sees this as an industry-wide price assault and responds aggressively. Both will believe that the other started the war.

Price war strategies

To capture value and achieve optimal profits, the aim must be to avoid price wars if at all possible.

Strategic approaches to support this objective are covered in Chapter 8 of *Smarter Pricing* (Cram, 2006b):

1 Create marketing communication strategies that emphasize value delivery and benefits rather than price.
2 Ensure that pricing strategies are clear, so that rivals understand the position and do not misinterpret actions as price aggression. Price guarantees – public statements that any competitor cuts will be matched can discourage rivals from launching price assaults.
3 Launch new and superior products at a price premium. Failing to do this may result in dramatic sales losses by competitors who then retaliate with severe price cuts.
4 Do not over-react to apparent signs of price activity from rivals. First check and corroborate all the facts. Reflect on the consequences before making any riposte.

If a price war is inevitable, there are ways to mitigate the severity or duration of the war. If the facts are checked and a competitor has initiated hostile price activity, there are four options:

1 *Do nothing.* the action may be temporary, it may affect you less than the competitor hopes and reaction by you may encourage the competitor to go further.
2 React with a non-price response. Rao *et al.* (2000) have suggested four types of non-price action: service enhancement, alerting customers to risks of supply change, highlighting negative consequences or negotiating support from government or a channel partner in the distribution chain.
3 React with a creative price response. This might be a specific category cut or a stock-loading promotion or the introduction of a new discount pack size.
4 Match the price cut head-on and aim to bring the war to a rapid conclusion.

The first three options should be evaluated and exhausted before a company joins the fray.

Fighting may not be the only option. Price wars take time and management focus and money resource. There is a strategic approach. Consider ceding the commodity market to discount players and build new businesses through innovation and opportunity evaluation. In the 1980s, Hochtief was one of the leading building firms in Germany, benefiting from the rebuilding bonanza following German reunification. The boom ended in 1995, German building output halved, three-quarters of workers lost their jobs and a price war broke out. Hochtief's biggest rival, Phillip Holzmann, went bankrupt in 2002, despite a government-backed rescue attempt. Walter Bau, the third largest German building firm, became insolvent in 2005. Yet, Hochtief avoided this disaster and thrived by moving out of its heartland. In 1995, its culture, history and four-fifths of its business was within Germany. By 2005, four-fifths of its business was outside Germany. Hochtief ceded domestic contracts to rivals and embraced an international strategy, buying Turner, a large US builder, in 1999 and moving into facilities management.

Pricing – company perspective

Setting the right price is crucial. Over-pricing happens but it is normally quickly corrected when sales disappoint. Under-pricing occurs significantly more often and damages brands when profits are foregone and products are positioned at a lower level in the marketplace.

There is a three-stage process to getting the price exactly right: considering customers, considering competitors and considering company objectives and aspirations. Ashridge's Steve Watson (2003), author of *The Long and the Short of Pricing*, expressed it lucidly: 'Pricing decisions are made where the key pricing forces meet. This is the interface between the three main players: the buyer, the seller and the competitor'. It is an iterative process, informed by pricing research, pricing experience and good judgement for the future.

Integrating all three factors

Effective price-setting combines all three factors. Establishing what the customer will pay is the first element in terms of capturing the potential value of a market. However, the relative price of competing products influences customer perceptions. In addition, the price chosen must be affordable from the vendor's viewpoint, so costs need to be considered. The process is dynamic. For example, calibrating what a customer will pay could influence the design or amount that can be invested in production. Figure 14.5 represents the forces impacting on the price-setting process.

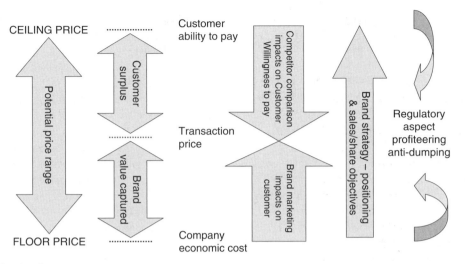

Figure 14.5 Pricing forces

Floor and ceiling prices: These define the potential price range. The floor price is driven by the full economic cost to a company including the allocation of associated costs. For long-term business success, it would not be possible to sell below this price. In some circumstances, products may be launched at prices below the current total economic costs in the expectation that costs will fall as a result of the learning curve, with the product moving into profit after the launch phase.

The ceiling price is the notional maximum price a customer is able to pay and still obtain value. Many businesses underestimate the price ceiling. An exercise to estimate this asks experienced salespeople to envisage a situation where they needed to quote a 'walk-away' price. Perhaps in a stock shortage, they wish to quote a price safe in the knowledge that it will *just* discourage a buyer from purchasing, without seeming wholly out of order. This price range defines the scope of the price to be set.

Transaction price, customer surplus and brand value captured: The transaction price will fall between the floor and ceiling prices. The difference between the ceiling price and the transaction price is known as the 'Customer surplus'. It is this benefit that encourages a buyer to exchange money for the product or service. An agri-chemicals company identified a product that could stunt the growth of fruit trees without diminishing the yield. The cost of production was minimal. The value to the fruit grower was substantial.

It saved both time and labour costs in picking and pruning the trees and allowed greater intensity of planting. The chemical company calculated the full financial benefit to the fruit grower and then selected a price that equated to 35 per cent of this value. This discount made the purchase of the chemical very attractive to the grower. It factored in a risk element and provided a certain return. The pricing was successful.

The margin between the transaction cost and the total economic cost is the brand value captured.

Competitor comparison and brand marketing activities: Customers take note of competing options and alternative propositions before they buy. Hence, the price that can be charged is influenced by rival products or services. Perceptions of relative value can be influenced by brand marketing activities to differentiate or highlight unique brand qualities.

Brand strategy, positioning and brand objectives: The brand strategy will determine wherein the potential price spectrum, a price should be placed. For a higher level positioning, a premium price would apply. For aggressive sales growth, a discount price platform may be set.

Legal considerations: Legislation may inhibit predatory prices designed to drive competitors from markets. High prices that are seen by legislators as excessive may result in 'windfall' taxes or other government intervention. Colluding with competitors to fix market prices in cartel activity is illegal.

Lifecycle pricing

There are three potential lifecycle pricing strategies:

1 *Premium pricing.* High launch prices position a brand for aspiration, luxury or high quality, and the continuing price strategy maintains the premium level. For example, the lager, Stella Artois, in UK has a high relative price which is underscored by the tag line, 'reassuringly expensive'. Premium pricing strategies often work effectively when demand is relatively inelastic.

2 *Skimming.* A relatively high launch price meets the expectations of selective customers who are eager to have a new product or service ahead of others and willing to pay a premium for this novelty. As demand from these early adopters is fulfilled, the company lowers the price progressively, encouraging more mainstream customers to buy the product and thereby widening demand. This strategy delivers a return on development/launch costs and also sets the reference price high enough to make subsequent prices appear particularly good value. An example is the Gillette razor company which has successively introduced innovative shaving systems at relatively high launch prices. These prices have normalized during the product life cycle (PLC). Skimming price strategies work effectively when initial demand is relatively inelastic, and mass demand is more elastic.

3 *Penetration.* A low initial price is set to encourage very speedy build up of demand. This price may even be below initial cost of production when there is an expectation that higher volumes will allow a firm to progress rapidly down the experience curve and quickly lower production costs to achieve medium term profitability. This can act as a barrier to a prospective following brand. Competitors have little time to react as the brand establishes itself in the minds of customers. The online retailer Amazon is an example of successful penetration pricing. Penetration strategies succeed when demand is elastic (*Figure 14.6*).

It is not a viable option to pitch prices low initially and then hope to raise prices subsequently. Prices are remarkably inflexible upwards. Customers quickly gain an impression of the benchmark or 'fair' price. They resist any attempt to move brands upmarket by raising price levels. Unless there is a well-founded and deliberate choice of the penetration strategy, it is a self-limiting strategy to under-price at the outset.

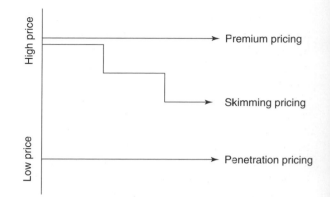

Figure 14.6   Lifecycle pricing

Price structures

Price structures are refinements of fixed prices to address customer price sensitivity and provide incentives to particular behaviours in a matrix that appeals to customers, represents value compared with competition and delivers profitable return to the vendor. There are two categories:

1 Price scales (second degree discrimination)
2 Segment criteria (third degree discrimination).

Quantity discounts. These are non-linear pricing scales, where a single item is priced at one level and multiple items are charged at discounted levels. Examples are bulk purchase discounts incentivizing customers to buy a greater requirement and store the surplus. For example, rail travellers with First Great Western can buy carnets or sets of ten tickets for the price of nine. The lower price reflects reduced packaging, less administration and staff time for the company. The customer pays a lower price unit price but bears the risk that some of the higher quantity may not be used.

Multi-dimensional pricing. This technique offers two or more variables so that the price paid can reflect and reward the dynamics of the marketplace. For example, a daily mileage limit for rental cars surcharges drivers who impose greater wear and tear on vehicles.

Time-based terms. These discounts can be used to capture value from more price-sensitive customers. Some restaurants have two editions of menus: same dishes, different prices. The social diners who want to eat after 7.30 pm will pay more. The more cost-conscious can be persuaded with lower prices to eat out at a less convenient time. This utilizes the facilities of the restaurant and fills capacity for a lengthier period.

Pricing by segment. Different types of customers often value a product more or less than others. Subject to customer perceptions of fairness, prices can be designated for certain segments. Examples are lower-priced admission to cinemas for children and discounted travel for senior citizens. To sell the same or similar products to different segments at different prices, it is usually necessary to use alternative channels and/or brand names. Black & Decker sells power tools in consumer markets under the Black & Decker brand name. The parent company sells similar tools under the DeWalt brand name through trade channels to independent tradespeople. Each brand has its own price structure, product range, distribution channel and promotional strategy.

The same brand can be sold to different segments at different price levels where the customer chooses the package that suits them with propositions such as price stairways and bundling.

Price stairways. In price-sensitive markets with a high elasticity, entry prices are crucial in the battle to gain the attention of customers. If the advertised price is not competitive, then the customer rejects this brand and moves to consider other brands. A competitive entry price can be accompanied by a menu of extras and upgrades that allow them to match their needs for additional services and capture potential value.

Tied consumable model. Competitors may sometimes be held at bay through separating two elements of a package. This is a tied consumables model. A subsidized master product, say an electric toothbrush, is offered that requires a consumable part, say a brushing head. The master product is patent protected such that other manufacturers are precluded from consumables that fit this system.

Bundling. Another form of pricing captures value from customers through the bundle. Customers are persuaded to buy a package of goods or services rather than a single item. The car industry has used bundled pricing structures to raise the value of its sales (Cram, 2004). The Mini One is advertised at a price, on top of which a choice of three option packs, branded Salt, Pepper or Chilli, tempts buyers to 'spice up' their chosen vehicle. The packs include cosmetic features, as well as features known to be advantageous when reselling cars – seat height adjustment, for example. For some customers, then, the extras become an obligatory part of the purchase and the company gains revenue from the bundled price.

Unbundling. Nagle and Cressman (2002) cite a printing company offering high-level services bundled in with their sales of units of printing. The company was faced with lower-priced competitors who did not offer the same added value services. Potential customers would challenge prices with quotations from these rivals. The result, costs were high and profits disappointing. The solution for this company was to identify which of their added value services made a difference to customers and charge for these services separately. Adapting to late delivery of files and scheduling jobs at peak times were two of the examples. The result was that customers either paid extra costs willingly or changed their behaviour in ways that saved costs for the company. By unbundling, the company became more price-competitive.

Confusion pricing

The furthest extremity of price structures is confusion pricing. Where customers are able readily to compare prices, they are expected to choose the lower prices. Brands in price-sensitive markets with low switching costs like telecommunications attempt to obstruct these comparisons with confusion pricing. Each brand develops different and complex price structures. Each supplier can make a 'lowest price' claim for one or other package. For example, prices for phone calls will vary by time of day, day of week, call length and caller destination or network. Up to a threshold calls will be included within the monthly rental payment. Six different parameters mean that the customer would need to understand precisely their own future usage mix to calculate which supplier represented best value. The disadvantage of confusion pricing is that consumers know they are being confused and their trust in suppliers diminishes. Less trust means less loyalty and a risk of defection to other suppliers who appear to be more transparent.

Communicating prices

The way prices are expressed can influence perceptions. Price may be presented as a single annual amount, or a monthly or daily sum. Irrationally, presenting the daily sum can create a lower price perception. Marn *et al.* (2004) give an instance where a term insurance provider offered options: US $360 per year or US $30 per month or

US $1 per day. Quoting monthly amounts resulted in three times higher take-up and daily sums were ten times more popular. This held true even when the actual payments were made every 180 days for all the options.

There are a number of pricing cues that buyers understand. The most obvious is the word "SALE" alongside product in retail outlets. Research by Anderson and Simester (2003) shows that displaying 'sale' besides the price of an item in an e-mail order catalogue (with or without actually varying the price) can increase demand by more than 50 per cent. Of course, retailers can (and some do) mislead consumers with non-genuine sale offers. Misuse of this tactic is controlled by legislation, media attention and the limits of consumer credibility. A small number of 'SALE' signs will increase customer purchases. Too many 'SALE' signs will diminish overall sales.

Another common pricing cue is using a 9 at the end of the price to signify a bargain. Academic research identified this effect in the 1950s and 1960s. M. A. Stiving (2000) proposed an economic model where firms wishing to convey quality with high prices should use the digit 0 as the rightmost digit and those operating in low-quality segments should use the digit 9 for their price endings.

Sandra Naipaul and H. G. Parsa (2001) applied this hypothesis to dining out, studying prices on 231 restaurant menus. Of 3290 menu items from the 62 high-end restaurants, only 13per cent ended with the digit 9. Looking at low-end restaurants, 63 per cent of menu items ended in the digit 9. The conclusions of Naipaul and Parsa support signalling theory. This states that sellers know the quality of their goods and services prior to the sale and prospective buyers are less well informed. Therefore, sellers convey quality through signals which are interpreted and used by the buyers in making decisions.

Research by Anderson and Simester (2003) showed signalling to be remarkably effective in retail pricing. Specifically, in a women's clothing catalogue, sales rose by a third when a dress originally priced at US $34 was increased to US $39. A further test with the price raised to US $44 showed the same demand as at US $34.

Higher prices may be a positive signal to customers who are risk-averse. Where the outcomes of a series of exchanges are predictable as an overall average, but unpredictable for any specific transaction, most people prefer to avoid the risk of making a loss, rather than take the chance of making a gain. This is explored further in 'Why

pay more' (Business Strategy Review, Cram, 2006a).

Pricing cues are most effective where customers' knowledge of prices is poor. This occurs where items are purchased infrequently, or prices vary seasonally or where goods are targeted at new buyers.

When prices are presented in price lists, adjustments to the price scale will be included, perhaps discounts for quantity or surcharges for urgent deliveries. These are also a key part of price communication. Prospect theory implies that surcharges will attract proportionately more negative attention than the positive effect of discounts. Therefore, the conventional advice is to present top-end prices and then allow discounts off these amounts, rather than presenting low-end prices and adding surcharges. There is an exception to this rule. If the surcharge added will direct blame to another party, it can underline a company's commitment to good value. Easyjet advertise low come-on prices, such as flights for £4.99. As the booking process progresses, taxes are added to these low prices (blame the government), charges are added (blame the airports) and credit card fees are added (blame the banks). Lufthansa adds a kerosene surcharge to send the blame to the oil companies.

Managing prices

Pricing decisions and execution must be co-ordinated across functions. Top management, for example, reflect revenue and profit aspirations in their targeted prices. With an eye to shareholders' expectations, they are eager to grow margins and may be bullish about pricing targets. By contrast, the sales force is often focused on short-term targets of sales volume or share of major customer purchases. Their view of pricing reflects the need to win the business. Trade promotions flex pricing strategies in order to achieve short-term volume targets. Their daily contact is with customers. Procurement teams deprecate quality arguments, challenge a price rise, demand discounts and threaten to buy elsewhere. For this reason, sales people may be pessimistic about pricing targets. The danger is that price increases implemented by management may be discounted away by sales people. Therefore, price discipline is vital to achieve results in practice.

In industrial markets, pricing committees of up to ten members facilitate price planning. Research by Richard Lancioni (2005) indicates that

68 per cent of industrial companies use this approach. He found that the functions of the committees varied from company to company, but generally they include responsibility for developing pricing strategies (58 per cent), administering those strategies (88 per cent) and addressing and analysing competitive threats in markets (87 per cent). A minority decide new product pricing (27 per cent) and sales incentive programmes (12 per cent). A strong recommendation of Marn *et al.* (2004) is that pricing is owned by an executive champion within each business unit. This champion would lead a specialized pricing group. In their view, the role of the group is to make actual pricing performance visible and continuously look for untapped opportunities to do even better.

Price discipline

Price discipline requires a full picture of allowances given to customers. Looking only at average discounts and invoiced terms understates the full extent of all allowances. McKinsey consultants Michael Marn and Robert Rosiello (1992) have called this effect the 'Pocket Price Waterfall'. From the dollar list price, order size discounts and competitive discounts are typically applied to produce the invoiced price. It is at this price that organizations normally measure price performance. However, further allowances are deducted: payment terms allowance, annual volume bonus, off-invoice promotions, co-operative advertising allowances and so on. The final net price is the 'pocket price'. Examples from Marn and Rosiello include a pocket price 16.7 per cent below invoiced price for a consumer packaged goods company, 17.7 per cent below for a commodity chemical company and 28.9 per cent below for a lighting products supplier. It is at the pocket price that valid pricing measurement should be carried out. Yet, accounting systems hide the customer-specific figures in general budgets – co-operative advertising funds are often incorporated in overall advertising budgets, emergency freight costs for one customer will be lost among other business transportation expenses. These hidden costs must be clarified so that true margins are explicit.

Measuring pricing effectiveness

Measuring pricing success is challenging. Using measures like volume sales growth and market share gains may demonstrate that prices are optimal ... or that they are too low, leaving money on the table. Measuring improvement in margin or contribution could mean that prices are optimal ... or that they are too high, failing to make profitable sales available in the market.

In theory, the true determinant of pricing success is the small size of the sum of money left on the table. The perfect price captures just less than the full value provided to the customer, leaving a small bonus or 'customer surplus' such that they feel they have made a beneficial transaction. It is partly economics and partly psychology. And both customer economics and psychological perceptions will move as market dynamics change, as new products appear and as competitors increase or reduce prices.

In practice, we measure the customer behaviour that illustrates their estimation of value.

1 *The 'Look to Book' ratio.* The first key indicator is the 'Look to Book" ratio. What proportion of potential customers asking for a quotation, proceed to place the order? How many enquirers follow on to make the purchase? If the strike rate is rising, the price may be too low. If the strike rate is falling, the price may be too high.
2 *The Sound of Silence.* Customers will complain vociferously if prices are too high. Listen for the sound of silence. Few grumbles about price may suggest that prices are too low.
3 *The Switching Rate.* The third key indicator is the switching rate. What percentage of last year's customers are not buying this year? How many existing customers have switched to other suppliers? If the churn rate of customers is declining, the price may be too low. If the churn rate is rising, then the price may be too high. If sales information by customer is not available, for example at a retailer, it can be possible to research sample groups of customers to establish this information at a macro-level.
4 *Market Share Movement.* The fourth indicator is market share change. Sodhi and Sodhi (2005) describe how an industrial equipment manufacturer monitored pricing effectiveness with a monthly review.
Vice-presidents of marketing, sales and finance and their direct reports scrutinized pricing performance by region and transaction size. Specifically, they looked for increasing average transaction value (to meet agreed internal objectives), fewer pricing exceptions to the scale of guidelines and finally to a maintenance of

market share. If share is being lost to comparable competitors, then prices may be too high. If share is being gained from these competitors, then prices may be too low. An exception is where pricing is being deployed as part of a corporate aim to grow market share. In this instance, the consistency of share growth is the indicator.

5 *Fixed Costs per Unit Sold.* The fifth indicator is an internal ratio looking at fixed costs per unit sold. Eugster *et al.* (2000) recommend this as a further way of assessing a market. They suggest that a decreasing fixed cost per unit sold is a sign of prices that are too low. Conversely, an increasing fixed cost per unit sold could warn that prices are too high. In their view, lack of quick pricing or volume swings show that prices are at an optimal rate.

Successful pricing needs time and attention. It combines customer insight, competitive context, a clear view of strategic aims and a solid knowledge of tools and techniques. Good judgement is needed, integrating fact-based inputs and less quantifiable elements that are nevertheless equally important. Most of all, pricing demands a sound understanding of the attitudes and emotions that make a customer willing to pay.

Summary

Pricing is crucial. It is a critical profit lever, with a powerful impact on customer perceptions, customer behaviour, relativities with competitors and finally on company sales and profits. As a result of the significance of pricing decisions, the discipline is often mismanaged, with sellers leaving money on the table, rather than risking the loss of sales to customers or the loss of market share to competitors.

The objective of pricing is to optimize the company's economic value by capturing the value the customer sees in the proposition. Therefore, this chapter has considered the challenges for those making pricing decisions and recommends three dimensions to effective pricing:

1 *Customer perspective.* Successful pricing requires a close understanding of the customers' willingness to pay. Pricing research and analysis of actual behaviour can contribute to an appreciation of the price sensitivity of customers. Since different customers may display differing sensitivities, price discrimination is a means to capture value from customer segments. Interestingly, pricing can shape customer behaviour negatively or positively.

2 *Competitor perspective.* Competitor offerings allow customers to make comparisons. Price plays a key role in positioning; as a clear ascertainable aspect, it instantly places a brand on the field. Price is a key weapon in competitive marketing. It has a strong impact on market share and it is the variable in the marketing mix which can most quickly be changed. This makes it tempting to use price as a marketing tactic in competitive activity. However, this creates a danger that price wars may break out and destroy value for all the industry players.

3 *Company perspective.* In setting prices, the company integrates the lessons of customers' willingness to pay, competitor comparison and company objectives. It also ensures that price behaviour is legally compliant. Company brand objectives will determine which of three lifecycle options best fit the product. A price structure can then be established. As structures become more elaborate, the risks and opportunities of customer confusion arise. Companies need to take into account the way that price is communicated in order to meet their objectives. Price discipline is important to ensure that price strategies are implemented in practice.

Finally, as with any management and marketing discipline, it is essential that performance is monitored. This is particularly difficult in the pricing arena since the obvious measure of margin may inhibit sales and the alternative measure of sales may damage margins. Five additional measures are suggested. Successful pricing needs time, attention and the judgement to integrate facts and opinions in a balanced approach to capturing value.

References

Anderson, E. and Simester, D. (2003) Mind your pricing cues, *Harvard Business Review*, September pp. 96–102.

Cram, T. (2001) *Customers that Count – How to Build Living Relationships with Your Most Valuable Customers*, *Financial Times* Prentice Hall.

Cram, T. (2004) Boost brand and profit with the right price, *Financial Times*, 6 August, London.

Cram, T. (2006a) Why pay more, *Business Strategy Review*, Autumn. *Financial Times* p. 11.

Cram, T. (2006b) *Smarter Pricing – How to Capture More Value in Your Market*, *Financial Times* Prentice Hall. *Business Strategy Review* pp. 30–33.

Dean, J. (1947) *Research approach to pricing, in planning the price structure, Marketing series No. 67*, American Management Association, New York.

Diamantopoulos, A. (1995) Pricing in Baker, M. J. (ed.), *Marketing Theory and Practice*, 3rd edn, Macmillan, London.

Eugster, C. C., Kakkar, J. T. and Roegner, E. V. (Winter 2000) in Bringing discipline to pricing, *McKinsey Quarterly*, p. 133.

Fishman, C. (2003) *Which price is right, Fast Company*, March pp. 92–101.

Green, P. and Srinivasan, V. (1978) Conjoint analysis in consumer research: issues and outlook, *Journal of Consumer Research*, **5**(September), 103–123.

Green, P., Carroll, J. and Goldberg, S. (1981) A general approach to product design optimization via conjoint analysis, *Journal of Marketing*, **43**(Summer), 17–35.

Kahneman, D. and Tversky, A. (1979) Prospect theory: an analysis of decision under risk, *Econometrica*, **47**(March), 263–291.

Lancioni, R. A. (2005) A strategic approach to industrial product pricing: the pricing plan, *Industrial Marketing Management*, **34**, 177–183.

Lester, T. (2002) How to ensure the price is exactly right, *Financial Times*, January 30, London p. 15, quoting Ritson, M.

Lyon, D. W. (2002) The price is right (Or is it?), *Marketing Research*, Winter, 8–13.

Marn, M. and Rosiello, R. L. (1992) Managing price, gaining profit, *Harvard Business Review*, September/October, 84–94.

Marn, M., Roegner, E. and Zawada, C. C. (2004) *The Price Advantage*, Wiley, Hobuken, NJ.

Monroe, K. B. and Cox, J. L. (2001) Pricing practices that endanger profits, *Marketing Management*, September, 42–46.

Nagle, T. T. and Cressman, G. E. (2002) Don't just set prices, manage them, *Marketing Management*, November/December, 29–33.

Nagle, T. T. and Holden, R. K. (2002) *Strategy and Tactics of Pricing*, Prentice Hall, Upper Saddle River, NJ.

Naipaul, S. and Parsa, H. G. (2001) Menu price endings that communicate value and quality, *Cornell Hotel and Restaurant Administration Quarterly*, February, 26–37.

Ogilvy, D. (1983) *Ogilvie on Advertising*, Pan, London.

Pigou, A. C. (1920) *Economics of Welfare*, Macmillan & Company, London.

Rao, A. R., Bergen, M. E. and Davis, S. (2000) How to fight a price war, *Harvard Business Review*, March/April, 107–116.

Sodhi, M. S. and Sodhi, N. S. (2005) Six Sigma pricing, *Harvard Business Review*, May, 135–142.

Srinivasan, S., Pauwels, K., Hanssens, D. M. and Dekimpe, M. (2002) Who benefits from price promotions, *Harvard Business Review*, September, 22–23.

Stiving, M. A. (2000) Price ending: when price signals quality, *Journal of Management Science*, **46**(12), December, 1616–1629.

Watson, S. (2003) The long and the short of pricing Directions – the Ashridge Journal, Summer 4–11.

Further reading

Cram, T. (2006) *Smarter Pricing – How to Capture More Value in Your Market*, *Financial Times* Prentice Hall.

Marn, M., Roegner, E. and Zawada, C. C. (2004) *The Price Advantage*, Wiley, Hobuken, NJ.

Nagle, T. and Holden, R. K. (2002) *Strategy and Tactics of Pricing*, Prentice Hall, Upper Saddle River, NJ, London.

CHAPTER 15

Selling and sales management

BILL DONALDSON

The role of selling is continuing to change and evolve in response to dramatic moves in the way buyers and sellers interact. Individual knowledge, skills and abilities are still required, perhaps more than ever, but teamwork and technology are also vital ingredients in an effective organizational response to the needs and demands of customers. The sales force have always been ambassadors for their firm, but in a turbulent business environment, the information and persuasion role of salespeople is being absorbed into their relationship role. Salespeople must take responsibility for creating, developing and maintaining profitable relationships with their customers. This being so, the paramount need is to focus on how to win, develop and retain customers to achieve the marketing and sales objectives of the firm. This puts the spotlight once again on the role of selling in the marketing mix and on the management of sales operations. Sales operations are the revenue generation engine of the organization and thus have a direct impact on the success of the firm. In this chapter, we consider how selling is changing and evolving. We examine the strategic nature of sales and the new role of salespeople and re-define the sales encounter in different exchange situations. We then address some of the key issues in managing the sales force as they relate to marketing.

The changing role of salespeople

Selling and sales management is undergoing something of a transformation in terms of its role, organization and mangement. Some of this is driven by structural and industry changes. For example, in grocery products 56 per cent of all purchases are sourced through just 4 buying points (Mintel, 2006) with the result that the size of the sales force has reduced dramatically and also changed in the nature of the tasks to be performed. Yet, numbers in sales continue to rise. In 2003, there were 766 000 full-time sales professionals within field sales operations, an increase of 9 per cent since 1993 (Benson Payne Ltd/MSSSB, 2006). In some industries such as pharmaceuticals and financial services, the numbers have risen dramatically. Fortis, a major European bank, employs some 686 business devlopment managers with many others in managerial and support staff roles across their operations. Hence, the need to adopt a different perspective for integrating sales and other forms of communication with the operational side of the business. Driven by an urgency arising from more complex supply chains, fewer and larger purchase points, the availability and use of information technology (IT) in customer contact operations, relative increased costs of labour and the continuing internationalization of business, sales operations are now different. These factors contribute positively to the need for more efficient exchange and communication systems between firms and their customers, predicated by increases in the costs of acquiring new customers, and the need to retain the existing customer base and stimulate the purchasing power of those customers already on the books.

Personal selling can be defined as the personal contact with one or more purchasers for the purpose of making a sale. To be effective, marketing management need to integrate personal selling with other promotional elements, with other organizational functions such as distribution and production, and with the customer and competitive structures prevailing in the market. The importance of personal selling is such that expenditure on the sales force usually exceeds the budget for all other marketing communications activities added together, with the possible exception of advertising in large, fast-moving consumer goods companies or direct marketing organizations.

Personal selling has several interrelated roles within the communications mix. The information role is part of a two-way process whereby information about the company's product or offer needs to be communicated to existing and potential customers and, in the reverse direction, customers' needs are correctly interpreted and understood by management. Salespeople impart knowledge about products or services which provide benefits to customers and also a range of information on promotional support, finance, technical advice, service and other elements which contribute to customer satisfaction. Salespeople are also the face-to-face contact between purchasers and the company and, for good reason, are referred to as 'the eyes and ears of the organization' since senior management's customer contact may be limited.

The second role salespeople must fulfil is persuasion. The importance of correctly identifying customers' needs and market opportunities cannot be overstated. Nevertheless, in competitive markets, prospective customers are usually faced with an abundance of choice. As a result, adoption of the marketing concept can be no guarantee of competitive advantage. Purchasers will have to be convinced that the company has correctly identified their needs and that the offer provides benefits over any other firm. Salespeople are part of this process through persuasion and service.

The third role is relationship building, and salespeople must initiate, build and develop relationships between the firm and its customers. Owing to their boundary-spanning role, the sales force of a company has traditionally been a vital link between the firm and its customers and a prime platform for communicating the firm's marketing message and the voice of the customer to the firm. In the high-tech world, it is easy to overlook the importance of personal relationships and how the interaction with customers has changed, if at all. Salespeople have always realized the importance of relationships, but there is now added recognition that salespeople are

critical to gaining the maximum value from each customer. Therefore, the management task is to re-engineer sales practices to maximize the value generation potential of the sales force in this new environment.

As a result, the nature of the personal selling task is continuing to change in that selling to customers has been replaced by cooperating with customers. The goals and objectives for the salesperson have also changed from achieving or exceeding target, selling X products in Y period and maximizing earnings, to building repeat business with the firm's existing and potential customer base. The emphasis has shifted from 'closing' the singular sale to creating the necessary conditions for a long-term relationship between the firm and its customers that breed successful sales encounters in the long run. This shift renders obsolete the currently available management practices, the sales philosophy and culture that have driven the development of the sales management field for decades. It also questions sales performance measures based on individual criteria and sales management practices which reflect recruitment, training and rewards based on sales volumes rather than relationship performance. The role of the salesperson seems to have moved away from traditional aggressive and persuasive selling to a new role of 'relationship manager' and, in practice, we are witnessing a tendency to change the sales lexicon from sales force to business development managers, customer account representatives or sales consultants. Perhaps the change in the title is designed to facilitate the transition of the sales force's tasks from selling to advising and counselling, from talking to listening and from pushing to helping, as suggested by Pettijohn *et al.* (1995). This transition is not only a matter of title. The new reality of relationship marketing directs salespeople and sales managers to develop long-lasting relationships with their customers based on mutual trust and commitment (Morgan and Hunt, 1994).

The costs of personal selling

According to industry sources, the average cost of an outside salesperson is in excess of £60 000 per annum, yet the time actually spent face to face with customers is typically around 20–30 per cent of working hours. This raises the question of what form of communication is both effective and efficient in today's marketplace. The most significant difference between selling and other elements in the marketing communications mix is the personal contact, but this comes with a relatively high price tag. The need for this personal contact will vary depending on such factors as the scale of risk, size of investment, type of customer, frequency of purchase, newness of product and many other factors. In some situations, the information or persuasion role can be achieved by impersonal means of communication, particularly advertising.

Advertising is impersonal, indirect and aimed at a mass audience, whereas selling is individual, direct and much more adaptable. With advertising the message is more limited, cheaper per contact but unidirectional, relying on a pull approach rather than personal selling which is two-way, but employs a push strategy and is relatively expensive per contact. Today, yet another dimension needs to be considered. This is the role and position of both direct marketing and electronic marketing as a form of communications. In Table 15.1, we compare advertising, direct marketing and personal selling.

Therefore, a primary task of management is to be clear on the role of personal selling and what exactly it is we want salespeople to do. Information technology is the set of technologies related to the processing and communication of information including computer and electronic databases, advanced telecommunications, CD-ROMs and the Internet. These technologies have led to new and powerful ways to reach customers and are changing the way firms interact.

The use of marketing databases, telemarketing and the Internet are having a significant impact on how sales operations are managed and will continue to do so. For example, the Internet is a powerful tool for providing information and an important means of buyer–seller communication. Many traditional intermediaries, particularly those who do not stock a physical product, now find that consumers empower themselves to collect information and make the purchase decision. This changes the information role of salespeople, and travel agencies, car dealerships and financial intermediaries appear to have been the most affected by such a process. The demand for secondary sources of information thus passes from a number of individual and independent sources to software programs which can browse the Internet and report the findings directly to users. Information itself is the market opportunity and the facilitation between source and consumer becomes the new challenge.

The incredible success of the Internet in terms of access and users has not always been matched by sales effectiveness. If anything, the telephone is more essential and powerful at present. In terms

Table 15.1 Choice of communication: comparing advertising, direct marketing and personal selling

Personal selling	Direct marketing	Advertising
Individual directionality	Individual directionality	Mass audience directionality
Personal, direct contact	Personal, indirect contact	Impersonal, indirect contact
Highly adaptable	Adaptable but relatively fixed format	Fixed format
Working in-depth	Working on one-to-one	Working in breadth
Two-way	Two-way	One-way
Direct feedback	Indirect feedback	Organized feedback (MIS, market research)
Expensive per contact	Inexpensive per contact	Relatively inexpensive (cost per 1000 criteria)
Push effect	Pull effect	Pull effect

of information provision, the Internet is unrivalled. It can reach an audience cheaply with the message you want to convey and allow full interaction – the ultimate in communication. However, unless the website is properly designed and maintained and linked with other communication points in the organization, it may prove damaging. To be effective, a website needs to identify the information you want to communicate and which the users will need, combined with effective links to other databases and that as a communication vehicle, it conveys the image as well as the content you wish to get across.

Just as telemetry (automatic reordering) and electronic data interchange (bar coding, etc.) have removed many mundane order processing tasks such as stock checking, inventory management and order filling and processing, the Internet is removing much of the more mundane information role that salespeople perform. The result will be a changing role for salespeople to a more highly skilled, more well-informed, computer literate person operating as customer account manager and coordinating the difficult interface between customer and company.

What do we expect salespeople to do? – the sales process

Despite what has been said, the correct approach and technique in selling is still, and always has been, vitally important. While cautioning against the idea of the one best or universal way to sell, nevertheless there are some appropriate guidelines that can be recommended in sales encounters.

Stage 1. Generating leads and identifying prospects

Most salespeople create sales with existing customers, and relationship maintenance is a key role. Nevertheless, the job also entails gaining new customers. The first step in achieving this is to identify suitable prospects. Many companies provide leads for salespeople from formal sources (Glenigan is one example from the building industry) or perhaps from response enquiries as a result of trade shows, direct e-mailing, telemarketing or advertising. Salespeople will also generate their own leads from lists/directories,

through personal contacts, newspapers or by telephone prospecting. However, a lead is a suspect that has to be qualified to become a prospect. To qualify a lead, it is important to ensure that the potential customer needs the product or service in question or has a problem to be solved and that they have the resources and authority to influence or decide on the purchase. Further, the potential account will be profitable.

Stage 2. Pre-call planning

An old rule of thumb suggests that a good sales process is 40 per cent preparation, 20 per cent presentation and 40 per cent follow-up. Regardless of the accuracy of these percentages, there is no doubt that success can be linked to preparation. All sales calls should have an objective, preferably with a specific outcome or action on the part of the prospect. Pre-call planning involves setting objectives, gathering information about the buyer and their company, deciding what questions to ask and what you intend to say. Remember that situation questions are important in the sales process, but you do not want to ask questions you can and should have known from other sources. Information such as the size of the firm, their products and services, their competitors, names of people in important executive positions, current and previous sales history should be part of pre-call preparation. Further information, such as the customer's buying processes, their current suppliers and their future plans can be identified in the initial stages of the sales interview. Ways to establish credibility and trust for the salesperson and their company with the buyer should be part of the pre-call preparation.

Stage 3. The approach

Getting an audience with a prospect can often be difficult and indeed harrowing for the inexperienced salesperson. Although the role of selling should not be technique driven, there is a skill in getting to see the right people so that your message can be communicated and understood. Ultimately, it will be on what you do and how you do it that builds long-term customer relationships, but getting there in the first place can be difficult. Experienced salespeople will recommend the importance of getting past the gatekeeper (receptionist, secretary or personal assistant) and building a relationship not only with the buyer but their gatekeepers and other influencers in the buying process. Making appointments is, in most cases, essential to establishing a professional approach, but letters of introduction and using third-party references can also be crucial. Establishing rapport, whether on the basis of similarity or expertise, is necessary before exchange takes place. For larger sales and new products, where the risk for the buyer is greater, establishing credibility is vital. A well-known company has a distinct advantage in this stage and the salesperson from a less well-known company has to work doubly hard to reassure the buyer.

Stage 4. The presentation

As Rackham's work has shown, the ability to ask questions and the right type of question differentiates successful and less successful salespeople (Rackham, 1995). Nevertheless, too often salespeople overemphasize the oral presentation and ignore the written sales proposal, the quotation or the subsequent follow-up, which technically can also be considered part of the presentation. It is vital to ensure that the buyer's needs have been correctly identified, that the solution offered is as expected and, if possible, that the customer's expectations are exceeded rather than merely satisfied. Further, in the right circumstances the use of visuals can reassure the buyer and instil confidence in the salesperson, their product and their company. Most experienced salespeople rate canned and stylized presentations much less important than the well-organized and individually tailored presentations (Hite and Bellizzi, 1986). Research in manufacturing has also shown that there is a need to segment customers and target your demonstration depending on the type of product. Many demonstrations were too long for the product and customer, in other words overselling (Heiman *et al.*, 1998). In business-to-business, buyers are looking for credibility, reliability, responsiveness and the ability to provide solutions from salespeople, rather than the more traditional aggressive or persuasive approach (Tzokas and Donaldson, 2000).

Stage 5. Overcoming objections

It is human nature that a buyer may stall and raise objections to a sales presentation. Again, experienced salespeople will claim that objections are to be welcomed since they confirm the buyer's interest in the product or service, although the idea of

questions is to reveal real needs so that surprises are kept to a minimum. Good salespeople differentiate between types of objections. Some objections are no more than clarifying questions and should be welcomed. However, there are also objections that express real concerns. The advice here is to listen carefully to the problem, clarify that both parties understand the real issue and agree how it can be solved. Listening enhances trust in the salesperson and leads to anticipation of future interaction (Ramsey and Sohi, 1997). Traditionally, salespeople have put too much emphasis on the ability to overcome resistance by technique instead of by sound solutions that meet the buyers' real needs and provide clear benefits. In other words, salespeople have been overly concerned with a performance orientation rather than a learning orientation, but those who learn, and learn how to adapt, will increase their performance. Effective communication helps the customer learn (Wernerfelt, 1996).

Stage 6. Closing

Since most selling is repeat business to existing and known customers, closing is a bad idea. Nevertheless, the salesperson has set an objective and achievement of this objective is necessary to progress the relationship. Very often, salespeople just simply forget to ask for the order. They are so busy with their presentation that asking for commitment is neglected or forgotten. In some cases, adding on extra features and advantages that the buyer may not be interested in loses the sale by not asking for a decision at the right time. Effective closing means agreeing on the objectives that both parties are trying to meet and which take the relationship forward to further integrated activities.

Stage 7. Follow-up

Vital to the customer-driven business is what happens after the sale. Most buyers object when promises are not delivered and the salesperson does not do what is expected. In the modern business, this is fatal – where building relationships and the ability to deliver as promised, go the extra mile and delight the customer, are at the heart of what a business should be about. The most important question a salesperson can ask is, 'What do I need to do, Mr or Mrs Customer, to get more of your business?'

Sales management issues

Sales management must also adapt to changes in market conditions. The need for closer, more demanding relationships with selected customers brings new problems and opportunities in the organization and deployment of salespeople. Traditional approaches to determining sales force size, territory deployment and call patterns can be brought into question. As a result, sales force size may need to be assessed on an estimate of the future revenue stream expected from a customer and the service that customer will require. Call rates, travel patterns and frequency of visits may change. In some cases, companies may have permanent staff on their customers' premises. Marketing orientation would suggest such customer-based sales solutions to be appropriate, but the cost-effectiveness of sales operations may need to be even more carefully assessed than in the past.

Similarly, traditional means of setting sales targets on sales volume and revenue may need to be replaced by measures which reflect the new customer-relationship job to be done. More appropriate targets are likely to be the retention rate of customers, the contribution these customers make and the satisfaction level they have in doing business with the firm. This is in keeping with a customer-focused, quality-based strategy that leading-edge firms pursue. This has implications for the kind of people to be recruited, who need to be relationship orientated, financially aware, marketing trained, computer literate and skilled negotiators. Individual ability and technique will still be important but this must be coupled with sound management, particularly in the areas of recruitment, training, leadership, remuneration and control. These issues are considered in the following sections.

Recruitment and selection

Recruiting and selecting suitable applicants is one of the most important and difficult jobs the sales manager can undertake. Formally addressing the recruitment process will help in defining the job, attracting the most suitable applicants and avoiding unnecessary problems and costs. The time and expense in recruiting is not insignificant, including advertising, selection procedures, and first and second interviews. Add to this other costs, including induction training, the potential cost of lost sales, the costs of dismissal if the wrong applicant is selected and the cost of repeating the process. Recruitment costs can be a major headache for sales managers as well as for the recruits themselves.

To overcome some of these difficulties, recruitment should be seen as part of a process which includes job analysis, manpower planning, job description, job specification, recruitment, screening and selection. This process should be systematic and thorough, and a planned approach will increase the success rate in selection, build a reputation as a desirable, progressive employer and sharpen the firm's competitive edge, thus improving effectiveness and efficiency in sales operations. The starting point in recruitment is job analysis. Job analysis specifies the tasks involved in a particular job and the factors which affect job performance, including reporting relationship, the role and tasks necessary to perform effectively, the environment in which the job operates including policies on sales, distribution and competitors and company rules and regulations. Sales managers should be careful not to be too intuitive in their job analysis. Of course, the job should reflect corporate ethos, marketing strategy and the specific reporting relationships, but job analysis also requires assessment of what existing salespeople do.

The second stage is manpower planning, which has both qualitative and quantitative dimensions. Initially, an assessment should be made as to how adequate and effective the current sales force is in meeting sales objectives. What characteristics are considered necessary to do the particular selling job? These are the knowledge, skills and abilities an individual should possess. The second factor is the turnover in personnel. That is, people may be recruited to add to the sales force, while others will be recruited to replace those who are promoted, leave, retire or are dismissed. A measure of turnover is the number of people who leave per annum divided by the total number in the sales force.

The next stage is to write a job description for an individual in a sales position, including the integration of the job into a team or organizational unit. The job analysis is the cornerstone on which the job description for the salesperson is based. Therefore, the job description should begin with repeating the main duties, tasks and responsibilities of the job. The key areas can vary but a job title, the main purpose of the job, key and secondary activities and performance measures should be included. It is preferable to be specific in the job description about job functions and duties. For example, indications can be given on time allocated to prospecting, travelling, merchandizing, servicing, reporting as well as selling time. The approach should cover the most important aspects of the job, the most essential and preferable criteria, the necessary education, qualifications, experience and other attributes and an assessment of the validity and reliability of previous methods.

A variety of potential sources can be used to recruit new salespeople. These sources can vary as to their adequacy and consistency in obtaining the best possible candidates for sales positions. Good recruitment policies will take a planned approach to this problem. For example, turnover rates will indicate how many and how often replacements are likely to be required. Further, analysis of previous recruits can indicate more and less productive sources. This analysis can be extended to discriminate between high, average and low performers. There is a need to link sources of recruits in sales to the selling style. For example, recruitment for missionary selling jobs favours employment agencies. For trade selling, sources are primarily from advertisements and educational institutions, while for technical selling, recruiters rely more on personal contacts. The use of different sources is, and should be, related to job and company specific criteria, as well as the matching characteristics between buyer and seller.

When the number and type of salespeople has been determined and the various sources have been selected to obtain the necessary applicants, it is then essential to evaluate these in order to recruit the best, that is those most suitable to the job and the firm. One possible cause of high turnover in sales personnel is that badly suited applicants are recruited in the first place. Turnover rates (i.e. number who leave per annum over number in sales force), which are above industry averages or seem to be increasing over previous periods, indicate a problem and an unnecessary cost. Related to the turnover level are the costs of recruiting, selecting, training and supervising new recruits who are poor performers. In addition to these costs, a salesperson leaving the company may well have a negative effect on sales in their territory and, if joining a competitor, business may be lost. The average lost sales multiplied by the number who leave will represent the total cost of lost business.

Commensurate with cost is the time factor. From a decision to recruit or replace through sourcing, interviewing, screening, second or third interviews, checking references, medical, to placing and accepting an offer may take several months.

Training and coaching

In addition to recruiting the most appropriate people for the job based on the job specification, every sales manager must try and improve their subordinates' individual effectiveness by appropriate training. Much training is wasted because it covers areas that the person already knows about. For this reason, it is important to separate induction training for new recruits from that suggested for existing staff. Again, planning is important, so the first stage, prior to training, is to conduct some audit of training requirements. This is stage one in the process, determine needs; stage two is designing the programme; stage three is conducting the training and finally evaluating the results.

Many firms realize, particularly in a relationship context, the importance of coaching. Somewhere between formal training and inspired leadership lies the importance of coaching. Sales coaching is a series of conversations and activities that provide ongoing feedback and encouragement to a salesperson or sales team member with the goal of improving that person's performance (Corcoran *et al.*, 1995, p. 118). To be effective, it requires salesperson trust in their supervisor/coach and accurate feedback and role modelling. It requires also frequent interaction to discuss account relationships, account potential and economic returns, thus developing insight rather than behaviours in a sales call. The salesperson must keep a diary of their interactions which analyses data for every call and describes the progress and problems encountered in the account. The sales manager should encourage insight by asking self-reflective questions that will enable improvement for future sales calls. The role of the coach is no longer that of teacher on 'how to do it' but to facilitate the digestion and interpretations of event that happened during a customer interaction so that the salesperson continually enhances their knowledge about how to manage their customer relationships in an account.

Leadership and supervision

The ability to get the best from subordinates is a valued characteristic and is referred to as leadership quality. However, leadership is best explained in the context in which it is exercised, and sales managers should assess their leadership style and its appropriateness to the people and circumstances in which it is applied.

In today's organization where rationalizing, downsizing and restructuring are being implemented, sales managers must encourage their people to adapt and be flexible. Such movers and shakers have been called transformational leaders who can get their salespeople to perform beyond typical expectations. However, in most situations, sales managers who have not proved themselves by having previously been a successful salesperson will find it hard, if not impossible, to be convincing in this role. Qualities thought to be important in sales managers vary and often extend to a variety of characteristics, usually ending with an ability to walk on water and other superhuman powers.

Perhaps more revealing are studies that reflect how salespeople feel about their boss. The major complaints usually focus on the following:

1 Managers do not spend enough time with their salespeople.
2 They do not listen to salespeople's concerns.
3 They do not take these concerns seriously.
4 They do not follow up to resolve problems.

Again, the difficulty may be that many sales managers have not been trained in management or prepared for the new skills and tasks that they are now asked to perform.

Remuneration

Arguably, the most influential factor in the motivational mix is remuneration, which can incorporate basic financial rewards and special incentives. Financial incentives are a popular means used to motivate sales personnel. Sales managers can remunerate salespeople using salary, commission, bonus or a combination of these. Most sales managers, based on their experience, seem to feel that a balance of types of remuneration is most appropriate. A recent study found that most UK companies offer combination remuneration comprising salary and commission or salary and some form of bonus, especially performance-related pay (Donaldson, 1998). This research also found that a number of salespeople consider job security of higher value than the level of remuneration. The variety of payment plans in operation, even within similar industry and sales situations, suggests that management do not fully understand the effect of payment on their employees' motivation. If a company's main objectives were on relationship building and long-term customers, a higher salary and lower incentive component

would be recommended. The difficulty with such rules is that within any one sales force, there is no one remuneration package that suits everyone and we have to settle for one that best meets the needs of most of our sales force.

Evaluation and control

Setting targets and quotas for salespeople has a direct effect on their motivation. Targets not only direct sales effort and provide evidence for performance evaluation but they can also act as an incentive and motivator. It is not only the target and system of control that is important but the way the target is determined, communicated and applied. For this reason, a system of management by objectives based on the participation and involvement of salespeople themselves is an appropriate option (Donaldson, 2007).

A problem already identified is that sales tasks and sales effort often can have an indirect rather than a direct effect on sales performance. Missionary or specification selling, such as pharmaceuticals, is particularly prone to this difficulty. For others, organizational complexity or dual effort with intermediaries may confuse the sales process and its effect on performance. Nevertheless, accurate and timely feedback for salespeople has a positive effect on job performance and job satisfaction. At one level, evaluation of salespeople is easy – they either make target or do not! The problem with the link between sales effort and sales response is that it is neither simple nor direct. Most companies do conduct some form of evaluation but few do this in a formal way that evaluates causes as well as outcomes. Part of the problem with evaluation is that to do it properly, far from being easy, it is time-consuming, costly and downright difficult. At the individual salesperson level evaluation, it is necessary to identify above and below average performers and to identify possible candidates for promotion or dismissal, and to identify areas of weakness in salespeople in carrying out their tasks in meeting sales objectives. For management, evaluation is necessary to assess the efficacy of sales management practices such as territory deployment, recruitment, training, remuneration and so on. Again, our starting point is an audit of current performance.

How organizations evaluate sales performance has been categorized into five classes of sales performance evaluation methods (Boles *et al.*, 1995). Class one evaluation is output only relying on results as the criteria for evaluation and can include objective measures such as sales volume or value or subjective measures such as 'achieving sales objective'. Class two methods use input objectives with measures such as calls made or sales skills measures against performance goals. In other words, on activities rather than on accomplishments. Class three, individual evaluation, relies on both input and output usually combining objective and subjective measures. Ratios can be determined and some order of preference is possible. Class four use both input and output measures against explicit standards and is evaluated through supervisory evaluation and statistical methods. Finally, class five is similar but evaluates against not the average but the 'best-in-class'. A necessary requirement to achieve sales force excellence.

Conclusion

Personal selling and sales operations are still key to the effective implementation of marketing plans. The role of personal selling is changing as new and different ways such as the telephone, electronic interchange and the Internet can be found to inform and persuade customers. The salesperson must adapt, and there is evidence that marketing and sales roles are becoming not only interdependent but also interchangeable. Positions such as business development manager, customer account manager and category manager reflect that salespeople must be better trained and qualified, able to work in teams and be capable of coordinating within their firm and at the boundary between the firm and their customer. The traditional sales process still applies in many exchange situations, but the key role for salespeople is to build, maintain and promote long-term profitable relationships with customers. This puts an additional burden on management to recruit, train, lead, reward and monitor effective sales performers since this role is crucial to the prosperity of their business.

References

Boles, J. S., Donthu, N. and Lothia, R. (1995) Salesperson evaluation using relative performance efficiency: the application of data envelop analysis, *Journal of Personal Selling and Sales Management*, **XV**(3), 31–49.

Corcoran, K. J., Petersen, L. K., Baitch, D. B. and Barrett, M. F. (1995) *High Performance Sales Organisations: Creating Competitive Advantage in the Global Marketplace*, McGraw Hill, New York.

Donaldson, B. (1998) The importance of financial incentives in motivating industrial salespeople, *Journal of Selling and Major Account Management*, **1**(1), July, 4–16.

Donaldson, B. (2007) *Sales Management: Philosophy, Process and Practice*, 3rd edn, Macmillan, Basingstoke.

Heiman, S., Sanchez, D. and Tuleja, T. (1998) *The New Strategic Selling*, Warner Books, London.

Hite, R. E. and Bellizzi, J. A. (1986) A preferred style of sales management, *Industrial Marketing Management*, **15**(3), 215–223.

Mintel (2006) *Food Retailing in the UK, November*, Mintel Group, London.

Morgan, R. M. and Hunt, S. D. (1994) The commitment–trust theory of relationship marketing, *Journal of Marketing*, **58**, July, 20–38.

Pettijohn, C., Pettijohn, L. and Taylor, A. (1995) The relationship between effective counselling and effective behaviors, *Journal of Consumer Marketing*, **12**(1), 5–15.

Rackham, N. (1995) *Spin Selling*, Gower, Aldershot.

Ramsey, R. P. and Sohi, R. S. (1997) Listening to your customers: the impact of perceived salesperson listening behaviour on relational outcomes, *Journal of the Academy of Marketing Science*, **25**(2), 127–137.

Tzokas, N. and Donaldson, B. (2000) A research agenda for personal selling and sales management in the context of relationship, *Management journal of Selling and Major Account Management*, **2**(2), 13–30.

Wernerfelt, B. (1996) Efficient marketing communication: helping the customer learn, *Journal of Marketing Research*, XXXIII, May, 239–246.

Further Reading

Bosworth, M. (1995) *Solution Selling*, McGraw Hill, New York.

Donaldson, B. (2007) *Sales Management: Philosophy, Process and Practice*, 3rd edn, Palgrave, Basingstoke.

Donaldson, B. and O'Toole, T. (2007) *Strategic Market Relationships*, 2nd edn, John Wiley & Sons, Chichester.

Ingram, T., LaForge, R., Avila, R., Schwepker, C. and Williams, M. (2001) *Sales Management Analysis and Decision-Making*, 4th edn, Hartcourt, Orlando, Florida.

MSSSB/Benson Payne, http://www.msssb.org (accessed 12 December 2006).

Rackham, N. and DeVincentis, J. R. (1999) *Rethinking the Sales Force: Redefining Selling to Create and Capture Customer Value*, McGraw Hill, New York.

Zoltners, A. A., Sinha, P. and Lorimer, S. E. (2004) *Sales Force Design for Strategic Advantage*, Palgrave Macmillan, Basingstoke.

CHAPTER 16

Brand building

LESLIE de CHERNATONY

Brands are clusters of functional and emotional values which promise stakeholders unique and welcome experiences. The functional values are less sustainable than the emotional values. Good product or service functionality is now a taken for granted expectation amongst stakeholders. Emotional values, delivered through sources such as staff interactions, represent a source of sustainable competitive advantage. Many organizations recognize that good externally focused communications raises stakeholders' expectations about brand promises, yet in many instances staff represent the brand. A well co-ordinated, committed group of employees enables an organization to deliver a welcomed difference based on what the consumer receives (functional values) and how they receive it (emotional values).

Introduction

Brands are intangible assets and because of their etheral nature, interpretations of a firm's brand can vary between members of the management team. Without surfacing diverse interpretations, a management team may have about their brand, it is likely that different parts of the organization will be "pulling in different directions", due to diverse views. This chapter therefore opens with a review of the different meanings of the brand concept.

Historically brand management primarily focused on consumers. This was based on the assumption that efficient production processes could be managed to guarantee the brand's functional values and that creative use of promotions resources, such as advertising and packaging, could promise emotional values. In today's competitive environment, where the services sector is far more dominant, there is a realization that attention needs to focus on consumers *and* staff. Advertising performs a useful role promoting a brand promise and enrobing a product or service with emotional values, but it is staff who deliver the promise. Without sufficient understanding and commitment, staff may not be delivering the brand promise. To encourage a more co-ordinated, pan-company approach to delivering the brand, there has been a move towards teams of senior managers planning and co-ordinating brand building activity. As a consequence of these issues, this chapter will also look at the importance of internal branding and culture. It will explain a strategic brand building procedure that facilitates a more integrated, pan-company approach which should engender a greater likelihood of brand coherence.

The chapter opens by reviewing the spectrum of brand interpretations. A sequential iterative process for building and sustaining brands is overviewed. Each block of this process is then explained, showing how a more integrated approach to branding can be enacted.

Spectrum of brand interpretations

Brands are conceived in brand plans but ultimately they reside in consumers' minds. They exist by virtue of a continuous process whereby the co-ordinated activities across an organization concerned with delivering a cluster of values are integrated and internalized by consumers in such

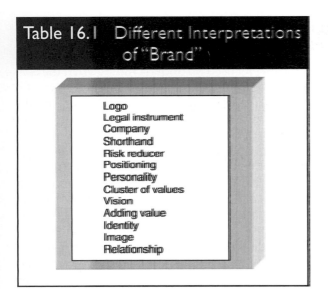

Table 16.1   Different Interpretations
of "Brand"

Logo
Legal instrument
Company
Shorthand
Risk reducer
Positioning
Personality
Cluster of values
Vision
Adding value
Identity
Image
Relationship

a way that reflects their functional and emotional needs. Consumers' buying behaviour provides feedback about their likes/dislikes of particular brands and responding to this through change programmes enhances the likelihood of brand success.

With a clear appreciation of the vision for the brand, a cluster of functional and emotional values can be devised and delivered through co-ordinated, pan-company processes. This leads to the development of a positioning statement to communicate the brand's functional values and a personality to act as a metaphor for the brand's emotional values. Ideally, these should be perceived by consumers as congruent with their self-image, matching their functional and emotional needs and thus generating goodwill from a trusted relationship which grows consumer confidence in the brand over time.

A review of the literature and interviews with leading edge consultants advising clients about their brands showed a variety of interpretations about brands (de Chernatony and Dall'Olmo Riley, 1998). Table 16.1 shows the variety of interpretations encountered which will be considered.

Brand as a logo

One of the more established definitions of a brand was proposed by the American Marketing Association (AMA) in 1960. This stresses the importance of the brand's logo and visual signifiers primarily as a basis for differentiation purposes, that is,

> A name, term sign, symbol or design, or a combination of them, intended to identify the goods or

services of one seller or group of sellers and to differentiate them from those of competitors.

The unique shape of Coca Cola's bottle, the distinctive "golden arch" of McDonald's, the blue and white roundel of BMW and the spectrum coloured, part-eaten apple of the Apple PC are notable examples of brands instantly identifiable through their logos. Organizations invest considerable resources on their logos as they can become powerful recognition devices. Through long-term investment logos give rise to a familiar set of associations favourably influencing brand selection decisions.

While this interpretation represents an important ingredient of brand building, it should not be the primary emphasis. Brand differentiation is more than making a brand distinctive. At its most basic, it is finding an attribute important to consumers then seeking to sustain this unique characteristic in a profitable manner. Developing the logo for the brand should be done strategically, rather than tactically. In other words the vision for what the brand is to become should drive ideas about the core essence of the brand, which should then be used as the brief for designers. Whether the colour or the type of font is appropriate can then be judged against how these will help the brand on its journey.

Brand as legal instrument

One of the simpler interpretations of a brand is that of ensuring a legally enforceable statement of ownership. Branding represents an investment and thus organizations seek legal ownership of title, as protection against imitators. As part of its brand strategy, Absolut Vodka stresses the importance of continually monitoring competitors' brand activity to quickly stop any firm adopting the name or bottle design.

Effective trademark registration offers some legal protection (e.g. Blackett, 1998) but 'look-alike' own labels in retailing exemplify the problem of being over reliant on legislation as a barrier against competitors (e.g. Lomax *et al.*, 1999). Kapferer (1995) devised an innovative procedure to help evaluate the extent to which a competitor had infringed a brand's equity. Consumers are invited to sit in front of a PC screen and are presented with an unfocused picture of the packaging of the copycat product. They are asked if they want to state what the brand is. Then, in an incremental manner, the picture gradually becomes clearer. At each step of increasing clarity, the consumer is asked if they can

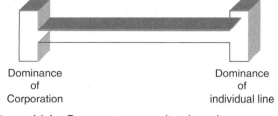

Dominance   Dominance
of   of
Corporation   individual line

Figure 16.1   Corporate versus line branding

state the brand. The measure of confusion is based on the proportion of consumers who stated they had seen the original brand when they actually had the copy.

Brand as company

One way of considering the nature of a brand is to think about the spectrum shown in Figure 16.1. At one extreme is corporate branding where any branding is based around the vision, culture and ethics represented by the corporation. This is prevalent in financial services (e.g. AXA, HSBC) where the corporate values are thought capable of stretching across the diverse product groups. At the other extreme, the brand is a 'stand alone' entity with its unique cluster of values and it has no immediately recognizable links with its parent. For example, Ariel Color and Fairy Liquid which are both from Procter & Gamble.

Considering a corporate brand solely from a nomenclature basis overlooks the rich meaning of this concept. A corporate brand is a projection of the amalgamated values of a corporation that enable it to build coherent, trusted relationships with stakeholders. Besides unifying staff, a corporate brand signals expectations to staff about desired forms of behaviour through a set of values that bond an organization. A successful corporate brand flags to stakeholders a set of principles that the organization stands for and which add value to the on-going relationships.

If the corporate brand has gained respect from its stakeholders it leads to a partnership mentally, whereby each stakeholder does not take a price driven, short-term transaction perspective, but rather adopts a more flexible attitude recognizing that both parties need a win–win outcome. From time to time either the corporation or its stakeholders entrusts a process or a decision to the other party, confidently knowing that the principled corporation's behaviour will be consistent with its espoused values.

Ultimately corporate brands should inspire staff to treat their stakeholders in a consistently

similar manner. The outcome should be stakeholder's confidence in extending their purchasing to a broader range from the seller's portfolio. By being focused on understanding what the corporate brand stands for and the way it projects its values, external stakeholders and staff should have pride from their partnered approach to growing each other.

For a variety of reasons there is a move towards corporate branding, for example the need to curtail the increasing costs of promoting individual line brands, and the prevalence of category management, where priority is given to promoting product sectors to retailers, rather than individual line brands. Mitchell (1997) provides a more complete picture. We have moved from the industrial age, which stressed tangible assets, to the information age which seeks to exploit intangibles such as ideas, knowledge and information. The new branding model is therefore one which emphasizes value through employees' involvement in relationship building. Internally brand management is becoming culture management and externally it is consumer interface management. In the new branding mode corporate branding internally signals messages about the desired culture and externally it reduces the information overload problems from line branding, decreasing consumers' information processing costs. Corporate branding facilitates consumers' desires to look deeper into the brand and assess the nature of the corporation. A further reason for corporate branding is that through building respect and trust with one of the corporation's offerings, consumers are more likely to accept the corporation's promises about other offerings.

Corporate branding thus provides the strategic focus for a clear positioning, facilitates greater cohesion in communication programmes, enables staff to better understand the type of organization they work for and thus provides inspiration about desired styles of behaviour.

Managing corporate brands needs a different approach to classic line branding. Individual line branding primarily focuses on consumers and distributors. By contrast, corporate branding is about multiple stakeholders interacting with many staff from numerous departments and important objectives are ensuring a consistent message and uniform delivery across all stakeholders groups. In line branding, consumers mainly assess the brand's values from advertising, packaging, distribution and the people using the brand. Yet in corporate branding, while values are partly inferred from corporate communication campaigns, stakeholders' interactions with staff are also important.

In the early days of some corporate brands (e.g. Virgin, Body Shop and Hewlett Packard) strong personality entrepreneurs had a philosophy about their brand making the world a better place and recruited staff with similar values to theirs. With a low number of staff in regular contact with each other, stakeholders were likely to perceive a consistent corporate brand. Success resulted in growth and more staff. The more successful firms communicated their brand philosophy through a culture that enshrined particular core values, allowing peripheral values and practices to adapt over time. New staff could appreciate from the culture how to contribute as brand builders. In less successful corporations, new managers were uncomfortable with the issues of corporate culture and brand visions and over time lost sense of their core values. New staff were less confident about the corporation's core values and different styles of behaviour evolved, causing disparate perceptions amongst stakeholders.

In corporate branding, staff are not only critical contributors to the brand's values, but represent evaluative brand cues. As such, the HR Director should be a key member of the brand's team, since they devise policy that impacts on brand building, such as recruitment, induction and training. At Waterstone's, the Marketing Director's view is 'Recruitment is a branding exercise, it's part of the management of the corporate brand' (Ind, 1998, p. 325). For successful corporate branding staff must understand the brand's vision, be totally committed to delivering it and more emphasis should be placed on internal communication.

In corporate branding, the CEO is responsible for the corporate brand's health and their leadership needs to enable all employees recognize the importance of the corporation's values. An advantage of focusing everything behind a common name is not only to provide clear direction for staff, but also to achieve a coherent focus for the portfolio and communicate a consistent message to all stakeholders. The disadvantage is that problems with the organization's reputation can taint the image of the whole portfolio.

Brand as shorthand

There are finite limits to our abilities to seek, process and evaluate information. Yet surfing the web, or considering other forms of advertising quickly makes one aware of the emphasis many organizations place behind the quantity, rather than the quality of information. To protect their limited cognitive capabilities people have developed methods for processing such large quantities of information. Miller (1956) carried out research into the way the mind encodes information and his research, along with that of Jacoby et al. (1977) plus Bettman (1979) help us to appreciate what happens. If we compare the mind with the way computers work, we can evaluate the quantity of information facing a consumer in terms of the number of 'bits'. All the information on the packaging of a branded grocery item would represent in excess of 100 bits of information. Researchers have shown that the mind can only simultaneously process between 5 and 9 bits of information.

To cope with this deluge of marketing information, the mind aggregates bits of information into larger groups, or 'chunks', which contain more information. An analogy may be useful. The novice yachtsman learning morse code, initially hears 'dit' and 'dot' as information bits. With experience, they organize these bits of information into chunks (letters), then mentally builds these chunks into larger chunks (words). In a similar manner, when first exposed to a new brand of convenience food, the first scanning of the label would reveal an array of wholesome ingredients with few additives. These would be grouped into a chunk interpreted as 'natural ingredients'. Further scanning may show a high price printed on a highly attractive, multicolour label. This would be grouped with the earlier 'natural ingredients' chunk to form a larger chunk, interpreted as 'certainly a high quality offering'. This aggregation of increasingly large chunks would continue until final eye scanning would reveal an unknown brand name but, on seeing that it came from a well-known organization (e.g. Nestle, Heinz, etc.), the consumer would then aggregate this with the earlier chunks to infer that this was a premium brand; quality contents in a well-presented container, selling at a high price through a reputable retailer, from a respected manufacturer known for quality. Were the consumer not to purchase this new brand of convenience food, but later that day to see an advertisement for the brand, they would be able to recall the brand's attributes rapidly, since the brand name would enable fast accessing of a highly informative chunk in the memory.

The task facing the marketer is to facilitate the way consumers process information about brands, such that ever larger chunks can be built in the memory which, when fully formed, can then be rapidly accessed through associations from brand names. Frequent exposure to advertisements containing a few claims about the brand should help the chunking process. What is important, however, is to reinforce attributes with the brand name rather than continually repeating the brand name without at the same time associating the appropriate attributes with it.

Conceiving brands as shorthand devices forces managers to think about the way they emphasize quality of information rather than quantity of information in any brand communication. As our minds cannot cope with more than seven bits of information at once, one test to apply to any brand communication is whether there are more than seven bits of information.

Brand as risk reducer

When people choose between brands they do not always base their decision on choosing the brand which maximizes their utility, as economic theory suggests. Rather there are situations where consumers perceive risk, for example the perceived risk of friends disapproving of a particular style of clothing. It is not uncommon to find consumers choosing between competing brands according to the extent to which they perceive least risk. Bauer (1960) was one of the early writers to suggest this notion and a stream of research has since evolved showing the importance of perceived risk, that is, the uncertainty consumers perceive that buying a particular brand will result in a favourable outcome.

While risk can be conceived as an objective concept, consumers use their perceptual processes to make any assessment. As such, due to their diverse backgrounds and the context in which they make assessments, it is likely that the perceived risk choosing a brand will vary between consumers.

Consumers perceive risk along several dimensions such as:

● performance risk (will the brand meet the functional specifications?);
● financial risk (will the consumer get good value for money from the brand?);
● time risk (will the consumer have to spend more time evaluating unknown brands and if the brand proves inappropriate, how much time will have been wasted?);
● social risk (what associations will the consumer's peer group link with them as a result of their

brand choice and will this enhance or weaken their views about the consumer?);
● psychological risk (does the consumer feel right with the brand in so far as it matches their self-image?).

Brands are more likely to succeed when the brand team delve deeper to understand what dimensions of perceived risk consumers are most concerned about. From this analysis a way needs to be found of presenting the brand to minimize consumers' perceptions of risk along the dimensions that particularly concerns them. For example, if research surfaced that potential car buyers were reticent about considering a new car brand because of its futuristic design, it would be wise to consider a communications strategy that seeks to reduce social risk through the use of peer group endorsement.

To capitalize on the brand as a risk reducer, marketers should segment consumers by similar risk perceptions. If any one of the segments has sufficient consumers and if the firm is profitably capable of developing the brand as a risk reducer to meet the segment's needs, this strategy should be considered.

Brand as positioning

Another perspective managers adopt when interpreting brands is in terms of positioning, that is, ensuring consumers instantly associate a brand with a particular functional benefit, or a very low number of functional benefits. For example, BMW as performance and Volvo as safety. In the information age people are bombarded with large amounts of data and choice. For example, it has been estimated that the weekend edition of a quality newspaper has more information than someone would have been exposed to in the seventeenth century. In a grocery superstore the consumer is faced with over 30 000 lines. To cope with this notable quantity of data people's perceptual processes take over. In effect these raise 'barriers' protecting the mind against accepting just any type of data, and perceptual vigilance then focuses attention on particular data which is selectively comprehended and retained in memory. One of the implications of the perceptual process is that consumers may interpret a brand differently from that intended by the organization. For this reason some managers interpret a brand as a device that enables them to establish a key functional association in the consumer's mind.

Successful brands represent a point of view and their positioning reinforces this. For example, innocent, the smoothies from the innocent drink company, questioned why healthy subsistence had to be dull and boring. They stand for putting fun back into a healthy diet with their frequently changing labels that are designed to raise a smile. Virgin is positioned as the challenger which questions whether consumers are being fairly treated, regardless of the market. Identifying a brand's differential advantage is but one part of a process that needs to establish the brand in the consumer's mind.

There are several characteristics of a powerful brand positioning strategy. Firstly, it should be centred ideally around one functional attribute; or if necessary a couple since the more attributes included the more difficult it is to get these registered in consumers' minds. Secondly, it should be recognized, as Ries and Trout (1986) stressed, that positioning is not what is done to a brand, but rather what results in the consumer's mind. In other words it is myopic to just focus on brand development. Rather there should be a balanced perspective, evaluating what the consumer registers about the brand, then fine tuning the brand until there is better alignment between the intended positioning and the resultant positioning, as shown in Figure 16.2.

Thirdly, the brand positioning should focus on functional benefits valued by consumers, rather than those valued by managers. It is too easy to focus on features which have more to do with reflecting the organization's competencies, rather than taking time to involve the consumer in the development process.

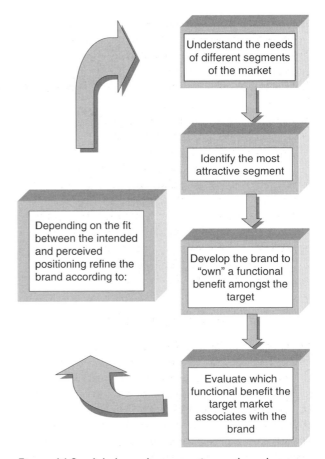

Figure 16.2 A balanced perspective on brand positioning

Brand as personality

With advancing technology and sufficient investment, competitors can emulate and surpass the functional advantage of a leading brand. One way to sustain a brand's uniqueness is through enrobing it with emotional values, which users sometimes value beyond the brand's functional utility. Consumers rarely undertake a thorough review of a brand to identify its emotional values, as can be appreciated from the early discussion about perceptual processes. By using the metaphor of the brand as a personality, manifest sometimes through a celebrity in brand advertisements, consumers find it much easier to appreciate the emotional values of the brand.

A brand's emotional values are also inferred from its design and packaging, along with other marketer controlled clues such as pricing and the type of outlet selling the brand. However, it should be realized that, particularly for conspicuously consumed brands, people form impressions according to the type of people using the brand and this is less easy for the marketer to control. There are some examples of successfully capitalizing on the people consuming a brand, for example the launch of the alcopop drink Hooch in Sweden. One of the emotional values of this brand is a distinctively independent attitude. In its early days, staff from the Swedish importer went to popular holidaying skiing slopes and watched young skiers. Those who had a more flamboyant skiing style were approached and asked if they would like to invite friends to a party that evening at a local bar where Hooch was being promoted. This proved to be a successful way of getting the brand associated in its early days with people whose emotional values echoed those of the brand.

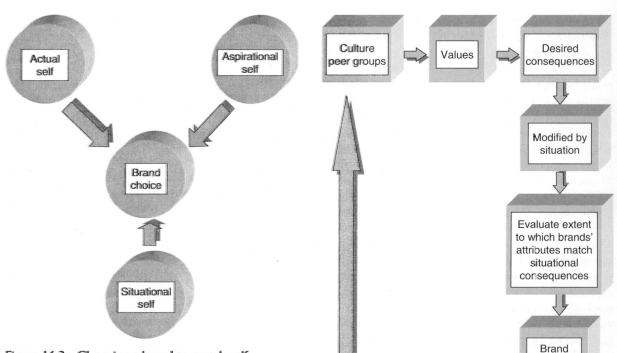

Figure 16.3   Choosing a brand to match self

Figure 16.4   How values influence behaviour
Source: Adapted from Gutman (1982).

This interpretation of the brand has given rise to a considerable amount of research into brands as symbolic devices with personalities that users welcome. When choosing between competing brands consumers assess the fit between the personalities of competing brands and the personality they wish to project, as shown in Figure 16.3.

According to the situation they are in, this may be

- the self they believe they are (e.g. the brands of clothing selected by a manager for daily wear in the office);
- the self they desire to be (e.g. the brand of suit worn by a young graduate going for interviews immediately after completing their degree);
- the situational self (e.g. the brands of clothing worn by a young man who is to meet for the first time the parents of his fiancé);
- the rejected self (e.g. rejecting an automotive brand because the consumer perceives it as being brash and does not want to have this type of association).

When therefore seeking to communicate the emotional values of the brand it is important to understand the emotional role potential consumers expect of the brand.

Brand as a cluster of values

In this interpretation, a brand is considered as a cluster of values. For example, the Virgin brand is a cluster of five values, that is, quality, innovation, value for money, fun and a sense of challenge. Conceiving a brand as a cluster of values provides a basis for making the brand different from others. Thus while there are several brands of off the road four wheel drive vehicles, Land Rover is distinctive because of its values of individualism, authenticity and freedom.

One of the key reasons for the interest in values is because they influence behaviour, as can be appreciated from Figure 16.4.

As a result of the society and the peer groups people come into regular contact with, so they develop their individual values. These lead to anticipations of particular types of outcomes, albeit varying by situation. For example, someone with the value of honesty may leave their door unlocked because they live in close proximity with neighbours who share the same value, yet when staying in a hotel the door is locked because of uncertainty about the values of other guests. Ultimately though values affect brand choice.

Consider the example of a lady who has a value of wanting to be fashionable. She is going out for dinner with her husband and will be meeting his colleagues for the first time. As such, when going through her dresses in the wardrobe her choice is based on rejecting those dresses which are over a year old, and because of the company she will be keeping she also rejects those that are not conservative in style. If at the end of the evening she is complemented on her good taste in clothes this will reinforce her association between the chosen dress and the value of being fashionable. One of the reasons for the success of the First Direct bank was because, in its early days, its values of consumer respect, openness and getting it right first time resonated with the values appreciated by numerous people.

The challenge managers face when interpreting brands as clusters of values is to understand what values are particularly important to their target market, then ensuring they are able to deliver these. If some staff do not believe in these values this will show in their behaviour and consumers will change to another brand.

Brand as vision

Another perspective noted about managers' interpretations of brands is akin to a beacon, whose rays provide a clear sense of direction for the traveller. In other words, brands are about a vision senior managers have for making the world a better place. As a result of this vision, a role can be defined for the brand. Within this perspective, brand management is about the senior team taking time to envision a world they want to bring about through their brand. Thus Apple PCs is about enabling more creativity, Benetton is about a world of social harmony and Versace is about a pleasurable life based on beauty and joy.

This interpretation is more strategic and takes courage from the brand's team. Gone are incremental extrapolations and instead the team takes time to envision long-term scenarios that they boldly want to bring about through their brand.

Without a well-defined vision a brand could be in danger of drifting and when faced with an unforeseen threat a short-term solution may result which could shift the brand's direction. A good brand vision spurs managers, staff and consumers towards greater things. Nike's consumer advertising campaign, 'You don't win silver. You lose gold' is a good example of the way the brand vision encourages a particular course of action.

Brand as adding value

This perspective on brands is akin to considering the extra benefits over and beyond the basic product or service that are added and which buyers value. These extra benefits could either be functionally based, albeit more difficult to sustain over time, or emotionally based. A functional example is a garage in a commuting town north of London displayed a banner proclaiming, 'We go the extra mile'. They do so through providing an extra service to consumers who bring their cars to the garage for maintenance, driving their consumers to and from the train station a mile away. By contrast, different brands of watches tell different stories about their owners. The emotional component of a fine chronometer can account for a notable component of the prize.

Added value is a relative concept that enables consumers make a purchase on the basis of superiority amongst competing brands. It can also be judged by consumers in terms of how the brand has improved over time, for example the pleasant surprise a car owner experiences when trading in their model for a newer model of the same marque. Interviews with branding consultants (de Chernatony *et al.*, 2000) showed that unless there has been a breakthrough in technology creating a new market, added values should not be conceived in terms relative to the core commodity form, but rather relative to competition or time.

As a result of the saying 'value is in the eyes of the beholder', if a brand is to thrive, its added values need to be relevant to consumers, and not just to managers. An engineer may believe they have helped in the branding process by developing a computer chip which repeatedly tells an unbelted car driver 'your belt is not fastened'. Yet to hear of the caravanning enthusiasts saying they would pay to have this removed as it is so irritating when jumping in and out of a car reversing a caravan onto a small pitch at a camp site provides some indication of its worth to consumers!

One way to identify added value opportunities is to accompany consumers both on their shopping trip and when they are using the brand. This enables identification of the stages they go through when choosing and using a brand. By then talking with consumers about each of the incidents, and getting them to identify what they liked and disliked, how different brands provide different benefits at each of the stages, ideas begin to surface about ways of enhancing the brand.

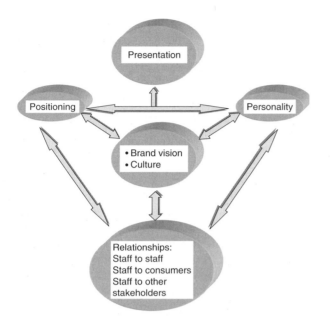

Figure 16.5   The components of brand identity

Brand as identity

The concept of brand as identity has attracted the interest of researchers in marketing, organizational behaviour and strategy. Drawing on the review by Hatch and Schultz (2000), brand identity is the distinctive or central idea of a brand and how the brand communicates this idea to its stakeholders. Particularly when the organization brands its offerings with its corporate name, or the brand is strongly endorsed by the corporation, this involves a lot of internal 'soul searching' to understand what the firm stands for and how it can enact the corporate values across all its range. Managers and staff become engrossed in surfacing consensus above who the organization is and what it stands for. For example, Apple believes in increasing people's productivity through challenging inborn resistance to change. Its corporate identity of the bitten apple epitomizes this – the forbidden fruit with the colours of the rainbow in the wrong order. Communication is not directed just at consumers, but also at staff, so they can appreciate how they must behave to be the embodiment of the brand.

This perspective of the brand is in sharp contrast to that of the brand as a 'legal instrument' and a 'logo', since the emphasis is on the brand as a holistic entity. Regarding a brand as a 'logo' or 'legal instrument' leads to almost a checklist mentality regarding the elements necessary to create a brand, whereas an emphasizes on the brand's identity encourages more integrated thinking about several component parts, as shown in Figure 16.5.

Brand identity can be appreciated from the model shown in Figure 16.5. Central to any brand is its vision which provides a clear sense of direction about how it is going to bring about a better future. To achieve this stretching future depends on a culture with staff who believe in particular values and managers who have a common mental model about how their market works and therefore how the brand must be developed. The core thinking behind the brand can now be translated into a positioning strategy that manifests the brand's functional values and a personality which brings the brand's emotional values to life. Underpinning all of this is a clear understanding amongst staff about the types of relationships they need to have with each other, with consumers and other stakeholders to enact the brand's values. If there is a unified form of internal behaviour, the organization can be more confident about presenting the brand to stakeholders with a design and promotional support that differentiates the brand in a manner which stakeholders welcome. Figure 16.5 shows the different interactions between the five components of a brand's identity and the challenge for managers is to find ways of blending these components to gain maximum internal reinforcement.

This interpretation may help managers reinforce a meaning behind a brand for consumers, and also communicate the essence of the brand to other stakeholders. The concept of brand identity offers the opportunity to develop the brand's positioning better, and encourages a more strategic approach to brand management. A carefully managed identity system also acts as a protective barrier against competitors.

One of the weaknesses of this perspective is that managers focus on the internal aspect of branding, thinking predominantly about the desired positioning. Thought also needs to be given to the way consumers perceive the brand, since their perception (brand image) may be different from the intended projection (brand identity). One of the problems with seeking to develop a brand through minimizing the gap between brand identity and brand image, is that image refers to a consumer's perception at a specific point in time and thus leads to short-term fluctuations. By contrast, reputation relates to perceptions about a brand over time and as a consumer based measure is more stable. Thus, brands could be managed by developing a brand identity, then regularly fine tuning the brand identity components to minimize the gap with the brand's reputation amongst stakeholders, as shown in Figure 16.6.

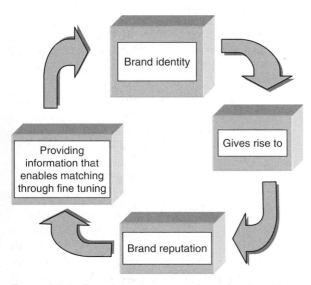

Figure 16.6 Brand management through minimizing gaps

Brand as image

People do not react to reality but to what they perceive to be reality. This perspective encourages a more consumer-centred approach. Brands are regarded as the set of associations perceived by an individual, over time, resulting from direct or indirect experience of a brand. These may be associations with functional qualities, or with individual people or events. It is unlikely for two people to have exactly the same image of a brand (since no two people have the same experiences), but their images may have common features. These features constitute, for example, 'the sociable image' of a particular brand of beer.

Adopting an image perspective forces management to face the challenge of consumers' perceptions, that is, due to their perceptual processes, the sent message is not necessarily understood as was intended. It therefore necessitates checking consumers' perceptions and taking action to encourage favourable perceptions.

Evaluating a brand's image needs to take into consideration consumers' levels of involvement with the category (Poiesz, 1989). For those categories where consumers are actively involved in spending time and effort seeking out and processing brand information, it has been argued (e.g. Reynolds and Gutman, 1984) that brand image relates to a network of information stored in memory that helps the consumer define their self. As consumers are so involved in the brand selection process it is appropriate to use an involved procedure when measuring brand image, for example means-end chaining. In this approach consumers are first asked what they see as being the difference between the brand in question and a couple of competing brands in the category. Having elicited a functional attribute, which acts as the anchor point, consumers are then asked why such an attribute might be important to them. They are then asked why this reason is important, and through repeatedly probing about why the reason is important, a value emerges. While this takes time to administer, it provides a rich insight to the brand's image.

For low involvement categories, where consumers habitually buy the brand, or undertake minimal information searching, brand image is a holistic impression of the brand's position relative to its perceived competitors. To identify the brand's image a low involvement evaluation procedure would be appropriate, for example mental mapping. Consumers are asked which brands they believe a particular brand competes against. The brand under attention and the other named brands are then written on cards. These are shuffled, given to the person who is asked to arrange all the cards on a desk in such a way that those brands perceived to be similar are placed close to each other. After photographing the way the cards were arranged, the respondent is asked to explain their map, and from this insight is provided about the brand's image.

Brand as relationship

The interpretation of a brand as a relationship is a logical extension of the idea of a brand's personality: if brands can be personified, then consumers can have relationships with them. Research has shown (e.g. Fournier, 1998) that relationships are purposive and enable both parties to provide meanings. Consumers choose brands in part because they seek to understand their self and to communicate aspects of their self to others. Through engaging in a relationship, albeit briefly, consumers are able to resolve ideas about their self and, with the brand metaphorically akin to an active member of a dyad, it helps legitimize the consumer's thoughts about themselves. Within this perspective managers consider how the brand's values should give rise to a particular type of relationship.

The interpretation of brands as relationships enables managers to involve staff more in the branding process. Some people find the concept of brand values difficult to understand, but they feel more confident about the idea of describing relationships. One way of getting employees to consider the implications of their brand's values is to use a variant on the party game, 'in the manner of the word'. Members of a department are brought together and someone is asked to leave the room with their manager. That person chooses one of the brand's values and spends a few moments thinking about what this means in terms of the relationship they should be building with their clients to reinforce the brand. They return to the room and in front of their colleagues mime a series of activities. As these are taking place their colleagues shout out the value they think is being enacted and terms to describe the relationship. A facilitator writes on a flip chart what is being shouted and the miming continues until the 'actor' feels someone has correctly mentioned both the value and the relationship implications they are acting. Besides being a fun activity, it surfaces lots of assumptions about the brand's values and relationships. As staff have used their own phrases and their own scenarios, it enables their manager to build on their frames of reference and help them develop more appropriate relationships in their daily working tasks.

When considering what the relationship implications are from the brand's values, it is important to recognize that relationships come about because of reciprocal exchanges between at least two individuals. While the organization may wish to use its brand to develop a close relationship with its consumers, they may prefer instead to have a more distant relationship. It is therefore important that once a relationship has been identified that research be undertaken with consumers to evaluate their view about the desired relationship. Through understanding what consumers want from a relationship, then revising the relationship strategy there is a greater likelihood of brand success. This process is depicted in Figure 16.7 where a continual process of feedback is used to refine and better develop the brand relationship.

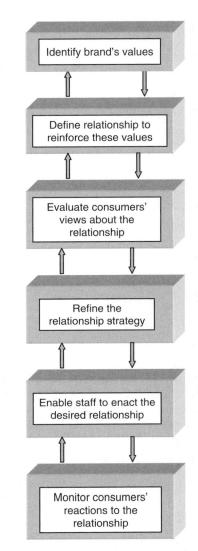

Figure 16.7 The interactive process to develop a relationship which reinforces the brand's values

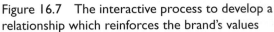

able to appreciate amongst which team members there are conflicting views and then can spend time enabling a consensus to be reached about the nature of the brand. Undertaking this work should contribute to a more coherent branding approach.

Surface diversity

From the material reviewed in this chapter, it is apparent that there are different interpretations of 'a brand' and if a firm is to ensure its brand thrives, it must encourage members of the brand's team to clarify their assumptions about the nature of their brand. By taking time to surface the taken for granted assumptions amongst the brand's team about the nature of their brand, they will be

A model for strategically building brands

As brand management is a company wide activity, there may be a lack of integration between different departments. An integrated brand necessitates detailed co-ordination. This can be aided by a planned approach, enabling staff to appreciate the brand objectives and the role they need to

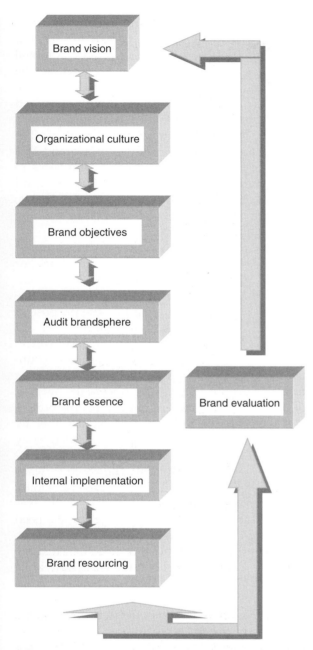

Figure 16.8 The process of building and sustaining brands

play in supporting the brand. Figure 16.8 shows one approach to planning for brand success.

The model is based on an iterative process that forces managers continually to reconsider whether their brand assumptions were appropriate. It is founded on the belief that brand planning should emanate from a multi-disciplinary senior management team. As the management team work through the model, so the emphasis moves from strategy to tactics to implementation. Once a brand has been developed (or an existing brand

fine tuned), instigating a performance monitor ensures that feedback is provided, from which further enhancements can be planned. Each of the blocks in the model will be considered in more detail.

Brand vision

A powerful brand vision indicates the long term, stretching intent for the brand which must excite staff, encourage their commitment and enable them to interpret how they can contribute to success. Kotter (1996) argues that there are three ways of managing. The first approach is to manage by authoritarian decree, but this gives rise to a fear culture and inhibits staff proposing innovations. The second approach is micro-management, specifying exactly how staff should work. This necessitates a notable investment in supervisory staff. The third way is visionary management which gains staff commitment through everyone believing in the future the firm wants to bring about and people being motivated to find more creative ways of solving problems. This model is based on visionary management.

Developing a brand vision can engender more committed employees if they have been involved in some of the brand visioning workshops. Brand visioning is typically a team-based activity based upon a process of amending drafts through a combination of analytical thinking and dreaming. It should result in a statement that is simple to understand and can be easily communicated. One of the challenges the senior team have to face when involving staff is that they are raising expectations that staff's views will be incorporated in the final decision. For some cultures, particularly those that are bureaucratic or autocratic, engaging staff in the process may make senior managers feel uncomfortable since they are not used to having their ideas questioned. Some relaxation of control could help these types of organizations to capitalize on staff participation. In an era of greater brand similarity, having a company wide approach to brand visioning may provide a stronger competitive advantage from staff who are committed to delivering the brand.

There are three components of a brand vision, as Figure 16.9 indicates. The first component, the envisioned future, encourages managers to think about the future environment they would like to bring about 10 years ahead. By saying '10 years ahead' this discourages incremental projections and encourages a more challenging, lateral view

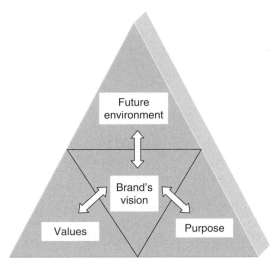

Figure 16.9   The three components of a brand's vision

about the future. Managers should not be dogmatic about a '10 year' horizon, rather they should have a long time period that reflects the dynamics of the market. This period may be wise for a stable market, but for a rapidly changing market (e.g. high technology products) a shorter period (e.g. 5 years) may be more appropriate.

To be appreciated, a brand should bring about *welcomed* change and by thinking a long way into the future, managers should not consider themselves to be shackled by the current constraints under which they operate. Specifying a long-term horizon encourages managers to think about discontinuities that will result in step changes in the market.

By employing a Delphi technique among the brand's team, different assumptions can be surfaced about the desired future. Through subsequent workshops, the attractiveness of different futures can be harnessed into a consensus view (Ritchie, 1999). The challenge is to recognize the barrier from mangers having entrenched mental models that they are reticent to re-assess (Huff, 1990). In this situation, stimulus to change can be helped by drawing on Hamel and Prahalad's (1994) questions:

- Are these managers' ideas based predominantly on information that has circulated within the firm, rather than externally generated information?
- Has their thinking been based predominantly on current and anticipated contracts?

The second component, the brand purpose, considers how the world could be a better place as

a consequence of the brand – and will this enthuse and guide staff? A particularly inspirational brand purpose is that of Federal National Mortgage Company, that is, to strengthen the social fabric of society by democratizing home ownership. A brand purpose must go beyond statements about profitability. Making a profit is taken for granted, just as we must breath air. The Co-op Bank is a good example of a brand that thinks beyond just making money and seeks to contribute to the world. Nike's purpose is a good example of inspiring staff and consumers, that is, to experience the emotion of competing, winning and crushing competitors.

One way of identifying the brand's purpose is to open a debate within the organization. For example, Oechsle and Henderson (2000) documented how in the early 1990s Shell's CEO encouraged the organization to question the purpose of the Shell brand. This had been around for 100 years, yet had no explicit brand purpose. Thirty-two workshops were undertaken in many countries amongst staff to elicit their views about the brand's purpose. Out of this emerged the purpose of the Shell brand, that is, helping people build a better world. The intent was to achieve this 'by creating communities of people who relentlessly pursue challenge with an unwavering commitment to be the best' (p. 76). The route forward became clearer as a result of this exercise. Firstly the internal programme, 'Count on Shell', was launched to get employees to recognize the need to be able to count on each other. Without a team approach the future would be uncertain and the initiative was strengthened by linking individual and team performance to support behaviours consistent with the brand's purpose. A communication's programme was then devised, which in the first phase was directed at specific publics to inform them of the new campaign. A national campaign was then launched to provoke dialogue on key issues.

Another way of stimulating staff to make explicit their views about the brand's purpose is the '5 whys' method proposed by Collins and Porras (1996). Employees are brought together in a workshop and the facilitator encourages debate around the question 'We are all involved in producing and delivering this brand. Why is it important?' As each reply is received, and discussed, the facilitator continues to probe 'why is it important?' After around five rounds of probing some indication of the brand's purpose should become clear. For example, a market research agency, which had devised a proprietary statistical analysis technique, may argue initially that their brand is important because it provides the best data available. After several rounds of further probing, the purpose of the brand starts to emerge as contributing to consumers' success by helping them understand their markets better.

The resulting brand purpose can be tested through questioning:

- Will this purpose make a real change and bring about a better world?
- Does this excite staff?
- Does it provide a clear sense of direction for staff?

The third component of the brand vision is the brand's values. A particularly clear definition has been advanced by Rokeach (1973), that is, a value is an enduring belief that a specific mode of conduct or end state of existence is personally or socially preferable to an opposite or converse mode of conduct or end state of existence. Values drive staff behaviour as they 'walk the talk', delivering the brand promise. For example, the Red Cross values of humanity, unity and independence motivate staff to go into disaster-stricken areas to help others. They provide the basis for brand differentiation. For example, a different greeting is given by the cabin crew of Virgin Atlantic compared with British Airways, as the first brand relates to fun and the second to being responsible.

Powerful brands are built on a low number of values. One of the reasons for this is that staff find it difficult to remember a large number of values and become unsure about how they should act in particular situations, thereby leading to brand inconsistency. A low number of values also makes it easier for consumers to recognize the unique benefits of the brand (Miller, 1956). Alas, regardless of the number of values, some managers espouse values yet act in a contrary manner, reducing staff loyalty (Martin, 1992). Surfacing differences between espoused and enacted values can help ensure greater consistency in brand delivery (Hatch and Schultz, 2001).

As they make explicit their values, some organizations do not differentiate sufficiently between category values and brand values, as depicted in Figure 16.10.

In each market, a brand must have category values as an 'entry price' to compete in that market. To then attract, and repeatedly serve consumers, the brand must additionally have unique

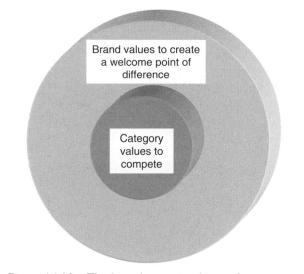

Figure 16.10 The brand as an amalgam of category values and its own unique values

brand values. This may be one of the reasons as to why there are so few successful financial services brands. An examination of financial services advertisements shows many firms majoring on generic category values, such as reliability, security and performance, yet few portray unique brand values. It is not inconceivable to encounter a mature market with discerning consumers who take for granted the category values of delight consumers and excellence when being served.

There are a variety of ways to unearth values. Laddering (Reynolds and Gutman, 1988) is one way and is based on the theory that a brand's attributes have consequences for a person which in turn reinforce their personal values. It progresses through a facilitator asking an employee to state a key attribute of their firm's brand and, by probing why this is important, a value can be revealed. An alternative is the Mars group method (Collins and Porras, 1996) in which exemplars among staff work together in a group of five people on the challenge of recreating the best of their organization on the planet Mars. By probing to surface their individual beliefs, insights about brand values are revealed.

Organizational culture

One of the components of a powerful vision is the brand's values and these are recognized as being part of the organization's culture. A clearly understood organizational culture provides a basis for differentiating a brand in a way which is often welcomed by consumers. Earlier it was clarified that

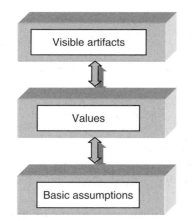

Figure 16.11   The three levels of culture
Source: Schein (1984).

Figure 16.12   Assessing the suitability of the current culture

a brand can be considered as being a cluster of functional and emotional values. With competitors being able to emulate functional values, a more sustainable route to brand building is through emotional values. In other words, it is not so much *what* the consumer receives, but rather *how* they receive it. When two organizations provide similar functional brand benefits, for example British Airways and Thai International, the discriminator that may influence consumers is the way the service is delivered. Organizational cultures are unique and provide a stimulus for staff behaving in ways unique to the organization.

Organizational culture can act as a 'glue' uniting staff in disparate locations to act in a similar manner. It can motivate staff and through coherence of employees' behaviour it can help engender a feeling of consistency about a brand. Furthermore, a strong organizational culture can increase the level of trust stakeholders have in a brand, encouraging better brand performance.

Organizational culture can be analysed at three levels (Schein, 1984), as shown in Figure 16.11. The most visible level is to look at the artifacts that reflect an organization's culture. This would include the office layout, manner of dress, the way people talk, any documentation, the firm's technology, etc. While this data is relatively easy to collect, it proves challenging to draw inferences about why a group behaves in a particular way. Seeing an open plan office layout may indicate the firm's belief in open access to information, but it may also suggest a concern about cutting costs.

A better appreciation of people's behaviour comes through understanding values. However, people can publicly exhort *espoused* values, yet behave in a manner which indicates an additional set of core values. To better understand the concealed reasons for behaviour there is a need to dig even deeper into the basic assumptions people hold. Individuals have mental maps, or schema (Schwenk, 1988) which are the rules they have formed to make sense of their business environment and to predict outcomes, given certain factors. For example, some managers might have as their basic assumption increasing advertising leads to higher levels of awareness and therefore greater sales. By contrast other managers might have as their basic assumption advertising works by building a reservoir of goodwill and that all is needed is just to have a continual trickle of expenditure to keep the pressure head of goodwill above a critical level.

By undertaking an audit of the organizational culture, then evaluating this against the brand vision, as shown in Figure 16.12, the appropriateness of the current culture can be assessed and changes identified. One of the problems though is that the shared mental model (*cf.* assumptions) of managers may engender resistance to change. A period of 'unlearning' (Bettis and Prahalad, 1995) has been suggested by writers, whereby the team is taken away from the office (leaving the incorrectly supporting artifacts) and they work with consultants to recognize the weakness of old assumptions and formulate more appropriate assumptions.

Setting brand objectives

From the brand vision should emerge a sense of direction for the brand. To transform the brand vision into quantified objectives, it may be helpful to think of a two-stage process. A long-term brand objective is set, which is broken down into a series of shorter-term objectives. Together those should sum to the long-term brand objective. For example, Starbucks set themselves the long-term brand objective of being the most recognized and respected brand in the world. The shorter-term objectives to achieve this could include rapidly expanding its retail operations, grow its speciality

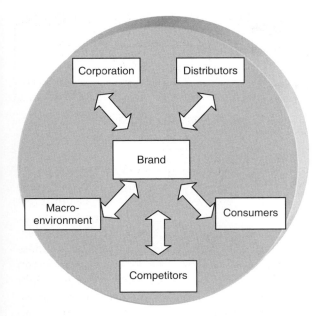

Figure 16.13 The five forces of the brandsphere

sales and introduce new products and develop new distribution channels.

Partly because of organizational bureaucracy, employees' actions become deflected from the central objective and, while a lot of work is done, this makes few strides towards the goal. One way to focus attention on achieving the brand objectives is through catalytic mechanisms (Collins, 1999). These are painful consequences which come into play when an activity is undertaken that does not support the long-term brand objective. For example, Granite Rock had the objective of providing outstanding service. After delivering crushed stones to road building contractors, it presents rather novel invoices. On these are boldly printed a statement that if the consumer is not satisfied, they should cross out the sum due, attach a cheque for a lower amount, with a brief note explaining this. Upon receipt of this information, this is rapidly routed to the appropriate managers so they can change matters. To focus everyone's attention on activities critical to achieving the brand objectives, catalytical mechanisms can prove helpful.

Auditing the forces enhancing/impeding

As Figure 16.13 shows, there are five key forces that can enhance or impede a brand. By auditing each of the forces separately, more powerful strategies can be devised which capitalize on the positive forces and circumvent the retarding forces.

Inside the *corporation* a variety of issues need considering. For example:

- How well are brand building activities being co-ordinated?
- To what extent do employees' values concur with those of the organization and the brand they are working on?
- Do each of the departments' cultures align with the desired organizational culture?
- To what extent do staff understand and feel committed to the brand?
- How appropriate is the brand's heritage in the modern world?
- How strongly do staff identify with the organization and its brands?

Having completed this evaluation of the impact that different corporation factors can have on the brand, the brand's team need to arrive at an overall assessment. After reviewing each of these issues, the team needs to decide whether *overall* they result in the corporation force enhancing or impeding the likelihood of brand success. If it is felt that overall the corporation force enhances the likelihood of brand success, a score of one should be given. However, if this force is thought to impede brand success, it gets a zero score. By forcing this one/zero decision it necessitates the team evaluating whether the *critical issues* overall work for or against the brand.

If a brand goes through *distributors*, some of the following factors need addressing:

- To what extent do the brand's objectives marry with each distributor's objectives?
- Are there some distributors who are using their economic power to demand unreasonably large discounts?
- Does each distributor have a consumer profile that matches the desired brand user profile?
- Are all the distributors supporting the brand with the right level of activity?

Once the distributor analysis is completed, a one/zero score needs to be assigned, reflecting whether this force works for or against the brand.

When considering the third force, that of *consumers*, some of the factors to take into consideration include:

- How closely does the brand match consumers' particular needs?

- Does the amount of brand information reflect consumers' involvement in the decision-making process?
- To what extend does the brand reduce any perception of risk?
- If there is an expectation of the brand making statements about the consumer, are these the right sorts of associations?

An analysis of the extent to which the consumer force impacts upon the brand enables the brand's team to consider potential changes.

The fourth force that impacts on the well being of a brand is *competitors*. Some of the issues to assess include:

- the extent to which competitors are differentiated;
- the objectives of competing brands and the impact these might have;
- the strategic direction of competitors;
- the resources backing competitors.

Undertaking an overall assessment, using a zero/one approach, helps appreciate whether or not this force might challenge the brand's growth.

Finally the macro-environment needs monitoring to appreciate how future political, economic, social and technological changes might impact on the brand.

Brand essence

As the model in Figure 16.8 is followed, analysis becomes combined with creative insights to conceive the core of the brand, ideally summarized in a brief statement about a promise. Hallmark is about caring shared and to enact this creativity and thinking 'out of the box' are critical. While the car breakdown organization, the RAC, used to conceive its brand in terms of providing breakdown services this was also claimed by the AA, who had a particularly powerful campaign positioning itself as the fourth emergency service. After much analysis the RAC reconceived itself around managing people's journeys and enacted this by repositioning in terms of total mobility and journey management.

One way of deriving the nature of the brand promise is to use the brand pyramid, as shown in Figure 16.14.

When managers devise a new brand, they are initially concerned with finding unexploited gaps in markets, then majoring on their core competencies to devise a brand supported by a novel

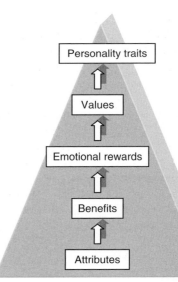

Figure 16.14   Brand pyramid summarizing the nature of the brand promise

technology, or process, that delivers unique attributes. However, consumers are less concerned with attributes, for example multi-function remote controller for a videocassette recorder, and more attentive to the benefits from these attributes (e.g. ease of recording a TV programme). With experience, consumers begin to understand the brand better and the benefits lead to emotional rewards. For example, one of the benefits of Emirates Airline, as an early innovator, installing individual TV screens in front of each economy class seat in all their aircraft is in-flight entertainment, leading to the emotional reward of fun during the flight. If the emotional reward is to be appreciated, it must lead to a value which is welcomed by consumers. Thus the emotional reward of fun could lead to the value of autonomy. For these passengers valuing 'what they want to watch when they want to watch', this value of autonomy could be the key reason for some passengers travelling with one airline rather than another. Consumers rarely spend long seeking and interpreting information about brands, therefore, at the top of the pyramid is a personality representing the personality traits associated with the values of the brand. By using a personality who exhibits the traits of the brand to promote the brand, consumers draw inferences that the brand has some of the values of the promoting personality.

One of the benefits of the brand pyramid is simplifying internal communication about the characteristics of the brand. Since consumers' choice decisions are based on a low number of attributes (Miller, 1956), only the three most important attributes are to be included at the base of the pyramid. Once these have been identified from consumer research, the brand's team then need to work together in a workshop to develop the three 'ladders'. Focusing on the first attribute, the team need to consider what rational benefit this leads to, then what emotional reward arises from this, followed by a debate about which values result and finally what personality traits arise from this value. This laddering is repeated for the other two attributes, resulting in three unique chains. Finally, by then examining the personality traits, the brand's team need to consider which well-known person might represent the elicited personality traits.

There is an advantage of undertaking this work with the brand's team together, rather than as a series of individual exercises. It requires people to 'spark off' each other and a more creative environment results from the team being together, drawing on their diverse backgrounds. Working together as a group, the brand pyramid can stimulate ideas about creatively positioning the brand (from the lower levels of the brand pyramid) and developing the brand's personality (from the upper level of the pyramid).

Internal implementation

To implement the brand essence a suitable value delivery system is needed to support both the functional and emotional aspects of the brand. By focusing first on the functional aspects of the brand, value chain analysis (Porter, 1985) enables a production flow process to be instigated, and for services brands, a services blueprint (Zeithaml and Bitner, 1996) captures the operational flow process. By referring back to the brand essence, an appropriate balance can be struck between outsourcing some activities and keeping others in-house to strengthen the firm's core competencies (Quinn and Hilmer, 1994).

The emotional values of the brand can be supported by recruiting staff according to the extent to which their personal values align with the brand's values (Kunde, 2000). A further way of engendering employee commitment is to encourage some degree of empowerment, which is increasingly common (Buchanan and Huczynski, 1997). To decide upon the level of empowerment, consideration must be given to the brand's values, the organization's culture, the business strategy and the types of staff (Bowen and Lawler, 1992).

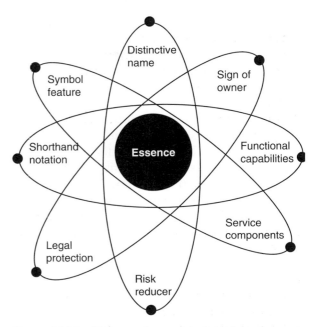

Figure 16.15 The atomic model of the brand

An outcome from the mechanistic and humanistic components of the value delivery system is that it engenders a unique relationship between consumers and the brand. As thinking becomes more refined in the flow model of Figure 16.8, so eventually a genuine relationship of trust and respect should emerge, bonding consumers to the brand. Alas same organizations have become overly attached to the cost savings from IT. There still remains a need for some staff interaction with consumers, even just having an empathetic telephone helpline team; otherwise the firm is erected barriers impeding bonding between consumers and its brands (Pringle and Gordon, 2001).

Brand resourcing which characterizes the brand

Just as the marketing mix enables a marketing strategy to be enacted, so the atomic model, shown in Figure 16.15, enables the brand essence to be realized by helping managers to identify the most appropriate combination of resources.

At the nucleus of the model is the brand essence which was covered earlier in this chapter. Succeeding the brand essence are the eight resourcing components. Progressing in a clockwise manner, the first two components relate to brand naming. To what extent is the brand's name going to exhibit the name of the company owning it (sign of ownership) and to what extent will the brand have the freedom to bear its unique name (distinction name)? The functional capability component summaries the functional advantages of the brand, for example performance, reliability and aesthetics. Provision needs to be made for after sales service, through the service components. Engendering consumer confidence by allaying particular worries is the task which the risk reducer component addresses. Questions to be resolved here include the extent to which the brand should major on reducing performance risk or time risk, or social risk, or psychological risk, or financial risk. The legal protection component focuses on providing the brand with rights to prosecute counterfeiters. The shorthand notation component forces the brand's team to simplify the brand presentation so there is more emphasis on quality, rather than quantity of information. Finally, the symbol feature component considers how the brand's values can be brought to life through associations with a personality, or lifestyle.

Brand evaluation

By following the flow chart in Figure 16.8, there is a greater likelihood of developing an integrated brand which is respected by all stakeholders. Brands are complex multi-dimensional entities and thus to use just one measure, for example sales, gives a superficial evaluation of brand performance.

Instead brand metrics are needed that monitor the suitability of the internal supporting systems along with the external favourability of the brand's essence and the degree of satisfaction generated by the eight components of the brand.

The nature of the brand metric will depend on the ideas that emerged from the model in Figure 16.8, as the nature of the brand emerged. By revisiting the decisions that were made by the brand team as they progressed through the planning process of Figure 16.8, a monitoring system can be developed which addresses issues such as:

Brand vision

- What progress is being made to bring about a welcomed envisioned future?
- To what extent is the brand making its market domain a better place?
- How much do stakeholders recognize and appreciate the brand's values?

Organizational culture

- How well do the artefacts, values and assumptions of the organizational culture support the brand vision?

- Are there any damaging internal counter subcultures?
- How appropriate is the organizational culture for the environment?

Brand objectives

- How stretching are the brand objectives?
- How aware and committed are staff to achieving the brand's objectives?
- To what extent is the brand under- or over-achieving on its objectives?

Brand essence

- How aware are staff of the elements of the brand pyramid and how committed are they to delivering the inherent brand promise?
- How well do consumers' perceptions of the brand pyramid match the planned pyramid?

Implementation and brand resourcing

- How appropriate is the value delivery system for the brand?
- How aware are stakeholders of the brand and its associations?
- What degree of commitment do stakeholders have for the brand?
- Do stakeholders perceive any conflicts between the brand's promise and their experiences with the brand?

Through undertaking regular monitors of a brand's health, the brand's team is better equipped to refine their thinking as they continue the cyclical process around the brand building model shown in Figure 16.8.

Summary

This chapter has provided the reader with knowledge about two critical topics in brand management, that is, characterizing interpretations about the concept of brands and providing a model which encourages a more integrated approach to brand building. Brands are valuable intangible assets. It is their intangible nature that necessitates all members of the brand's team to be clear about what they understand as being the defining characteristics of their brand. Time spent surfacing individual views about the nature of a team's brand is time well spent, since it enables everyone to not only understand the brand, but also helps them to appreciate how they can better contribute to the success of the brand.

The brand planning model shows how a logical, iterative process can be employed to focus thinking about brand building. Brand management is about understanding consumers and staff. Brand promises are delivered by staff and unless they understand and are committed to delivering brand benefits, they are unlikely to give the brand the support it demands. Brand building is a pan-company activity and the model enables a greater likelihood of a more coherent brands. By deliberately encouraging managers to adopt a visionary approach, not only do the resulting brands represent a clear sense of direction, but they also can more rapidly refine their supporting strategy when faced with greater competitive challenges.

The material covered in this chapter is addressed in far more detail in the author's book, *From Brand Vision to Brand Evaluation*, published by Butterworth-Heinemann.

References

Bauer, R. (1960) Consumer Behaviour as Risk Taking, in Hanckok, R. (ed.), *Dynamic Marketing for a Changing World*, American Marketing Association, Chicago, pp. 389–398.

Bettis, R. and Prahalad, C. K. (1995) The dominant logic: retrospective and extension, *Strategic Management Journal*, **16**(1), 5–14.

Bettman, J. (1979) *An Information Processing Theory of Consumer Choice*, Addison Wesley, Reading, MA.

Blackett, T. (1998) *Trademarks*, Macmillan, Basingstoke.

Bowen, D. and Lawler, E. (1992) The empowerment of service workers: what, why, how and when, *Sloan Management Review*, **33**(3), 31–39.

Buchanan, D. and Huczynski, A. (1997) *Organisational Behaviour*, Prentice Hall, Hemel Hempstead.

Collins, J. (1999) Turning goals into results: the power of catalytic mechanisms, *Harvard Business Review*, July–August, 70–82.

Collins, J. and Porras, J. (1996) Building your company's vision, *Harvard Business Review*, September–October, 65–77.

de Chernatony, L. and Dall'Olmo Riley, F. (1998) Defining a 'brand': beyond the literature with experts' interpretations, *Journal of Marketing Management*, **14**(5), 417–443.

de Chernatony, L., Harris, F. and Dall'Olmo Riley, F. (2000) Added value: its nature, roles and sustainability, *European Journal of Marketing*, **34**(1/2), 39–56.

Fournier, S. (1998) Consumers and their brands: developing relationship theory in consumer research, *Journal of Consumer Research*, **25**(4), 343–373.

Hamel, G. and Prahalad, C. K. (1994) *Competing For the Future*, Harvard Business School Press, Boston.

Hatch, M. J. and Schultz, M. (2000) Scaling the Tower of Babel, in Schultz, M., Hatch, M. J. and Larsen, M. H. (eds), *The Expressive Organisation*, Oxford University, Press, Oxford.

Hatch, M. J. and Schultz, M. (2001) Are the strategic signs aligned for your corporate brand? *Harvard Business Review*, February, 1–8.

Huff, A. (1990) *Mapping Strategic Thought*, Wiley, New York.

Ind, N. (1998) An integrated approach to corporate branding, *Journal of Brand Management*, **5**(5), 323–332.

Jacoby, J., Szybillo, G. and Busato-Sehach, J. (1977) Information acquisition behaviour in brand choice situations, *Journal of Consumer Research*, **3**, March, 209–216.

Kapferer, J.-N. (1995) Stealing brand equity: measuring perceptual confusion between national brands and 'copycat own labels', *Marketing and Research Today*, **23**, May, 96–103.

Kotter, J. (1996) *Leading Change*, Harvard Business School Press, Boston.

Kunde, J. (2000) *Corporate Religion*, Pearson Education, Harlow.

Lomax, W., Sherski, E. and Todd, T. (1999) Assessing the risk of consumer confusion: some practical test results, *Journal of Brand Management*, **7**(2), 119–132.

Martin, J. (1992) *Cultures in Organizations: Three Perspectives*, Oxford University Press, Oxford.

Miller, G. (1956) The magic number seven plus or minus two: some limits on our capacity for processing information, *Psychological Review*, **63**(2), 81–97.

Mitchell, A. (1997) *Brand Strategies in the Information Age*, Financial Times Business Ltd., London.

Oechsle, S. and Henderson, T. (2000) Identity: an exploration into purpose and principles at shell, *Corporate Reputation Review*, **3**(1), 75–77.

Poiesz, T. (1989) The image concept: its place in consumer psychology, *Journal of Economic Psychology*, **10**, 457–472.

Porter, M. (1985) *Competitive Advantage*, The Free Press, New York.

Pringle, H. and Gordon, W. (2001) *Brand Manners*, John Wiley, Chichester.

Quinn, J. and Hilmer, F. (1994) *Strategic Outsourcing*, *Sloan Management Review*, **35**(4), 43–55.

Reynolds, T. and Gutman, J. (1984) Advertising is image management, *Journal of Advertising Research*, **24**, 27–37.

Reynolds, T. and Gutman, J. (1988) Laddering theory, method, analysis and interpretation, *Journal of Advertising Research*, **28**, February–March, 11–31.

Ries, Al. and Trout, J. (1986) *Positioning: The Battle for Your Mind*, McGraw Hill, New York.

Ritchie, J. (1999) Crafting a value-driven vision for a national treasure. *Tourism Marketing*, **20**(3), 273–282.

Rokeach, M. (1973) *The Nature of Human Values*, The Free Press, New York.

Schein, E. (1984) Coming to a new awareness of organisational culture, *Sloan Management Review*, Winter, 3–16.

Schultz, M., Hatch, M. J. and Larsen, M. (eds) (2000) *The Expressive Organization*, Oxford University Press, Oxford.

Schwenk, C. (1988) *The Essence of Strategic Decision Making*, Lexington Books, Lexington.

Zeithaml, V. and Bitner, M. (1996) *Services Marketing*, McGraw Hill, New York.

Further reading

Barwise, P. and Meehan, S. (2004) *Simply Better*, Harvard Business School Press, Boston.

de Chernatony, L. (2006) *From Brand Vision to Brand Evaluation*, Butterworth-Heinemann, Oxford.

de Chernatony, L. and Cottam, S. (2006) Internal factors driving successful financial services brands, *European Journal of Marketing*, **40**(5/6), 611–633.

de Chernatony, L. and McDonald, M. (2003) *Creating Powerful Brands*, Butterworth-Heinemann, Oxford.

de Chernatony, L., Drury, S. and Segal-Horn, S. (2003) Building a services brand: stages, people and orientations, *The Services Industries Journal*, **23**(3), 1–21.

Ind, N. (2001) *Living the Brand*, Kogan Page, London.

Jones, R. (2001) *The Big Idea*, Harper Collins Business, London.

Mikunda, C. (2004) *Brand Lands, Hot Spots & Cool Spaces*, Kogan Page, London.

Morgan, A. (2004) *The Pirate Inside*, J. Wiley & Sons, Chichester.

CHAPTER 17

Integrated marketing communications

TONY YESHIN

The importance of integrated marketing communications

It must be remembered that advertising does not exist in isolation of the other tools of marketing communications. Whilst for many, advertising still remains the lead tool of the marketing communications mix (although even that position is being challenged by some, as alternative forms of communication become more important) there are few campaigns in which advertising is used on its own. More frequently, campaigns consist of a number of elements such as public relations, sales promotion, direct marketing used alongside advertising.

A major debate over recent years has been the significance of ensuring the integration of these tools of marketing communications. A paper by Caywood *et al.* in 1991 commenced a process of academic and professional discussion that continues today.

The study conducted by Schultz and Kitchen published in 1997 indicated that even then 75 per cent of all agencies in the USA devoted 25 per cent of their client time to integrated marketing communications (IMC) programmes. Interestingly, the smaller the size of the agency (and presumably, their client base) the greater the percentage of time devoted to achieving IMC.

Whilst the numbers of interviews was relatively small, it revealed that 59 per cent of small agencies devoted 50 per cent or more of their time to IMC programmes. This compares with 45 per cent amongst medium-sized agencies and 36 per cent amongst large agencies.

In contrast to the opinions of Schultz and Kitchen (1997), Duncan and Everett (1993) suggest that IMC is not a new issue in that smaller communications agencies have been doing co-ordinated planning for their clients for years. Furthermore, on the client side, small marketing departments have also had a quasi-integrated approach by the mere fact that all of them knew what was going on because all of them were involved with major communications programmes.

IMC is significant to the consumer, although they are unaware of the concept. They recognize integration and see it logically as making it easier for them to build an overall brand picture. In essence, links between the media are seen as:

- providing short cuts to understanding what a brand stands for;
- adding depth and 'amplifying' a particular message or set of brand values;
- demonstrating professionalism on the part of the brand owner.

The blurring of the edges of marketing communications

Recent years have seen significant changes in the way that marketing communications campaigns have been developed and implemented. In the

1960s and 1970s, the primary source for the development of all forms of marketing communications activity was the advertising agency. At that time, separate departments within the agency provided their clients with advice in all of the appropriate areas.

Since then, two strands of change have taken place. Firstly, the wider appreciation of the techniques themselves are the need for specialist personnel to develop them, have both resulted in the creation of specialist companies which deal with specific areas of marketing communications. The consequence has been a progressive fragmentation of provisions within the area. Initially, there was an emergence of specialists in each of the major fields of marketing communications, in areas such as sales promotion, public relations, direct marketing and so on.

Today, that specialism has been taken even further. Companies which deal with e-marketing, product placement, the organization of trade and consumer events, sponsorship activities and so on now abound. Individual specialist companies can now provide clients with inputs in areas such as the design and production of point-of-sale materials, the creation of trade and consumer incentives, pack design and guerilla marketing techniques, amongst many others. Even in the mainstream areas, agencies have become specialized in terms of youth or grey marketing, FMCG or retail marketing communications; dealing with pharmaceutical products or travel and tourism. And the specialisms continue.

Secondly, and in contradiction, there has been an increasing tendency for this wide variety of specialists to provide inputs which encompass a range of executional devices. Today, several different companies will have the ability and expertise to develop campaigns utilizing a wide range of marketing communications formats. Moreover, few marketing communications campaigns utilize a single component or element. Rather marketers will tend to employ several different devices that, previously, were the domain of dedicated and specialist companies.

The consequence has been a distinct blurring of the divisions between previous specialist practitioner areas. 'Discipline overlap is blurring long standing distinctions. It's becoming increasingly difficult to categorise work as sales promotion or direct marketing. Most direct marketing offers contain some form of sales promotion or vice versa. And with the growth of direct response press and TV advertising, direct marketing is moving closer to conventional advertising' Cook (1994).

The strategic challenges facing organizations

Marketing, and for that matter, marketing communications, are being re-addressed by major corporations to determine the values which they derive from the adoption of their principles. Indeed, the very nature of these principles is being challenged and re-evaluated to determine their relevance to the challenges being faced by companies at the start of the new millennium.

Nilson (1992) suggested that marketing had 'lost its way'. Despite employing high quality management, organizations have in many instances seemed unable to face the challenges which they face in the broader environment. Growth has come more from acquisition than brand development. The consequence of chasing niche markets has been the continued and growing failure of new products to attract substantial and profitable audiences. The continued growth of private label products in a wide variety of market sectors evidences the fact that retailers are often more successful in their identification and satisfaction of consumer needs. New and innovative competitors have stolen share from the large multinational FMCG companies, despite their comparatively smaller scale which should have precluded their entry into the market.

The essential requirement of the 'new marketing' approach is the development of a close customer focus throughout the organization which, in turn, demands an understanding of customers as individuals in order to appreciate their perceptions, expectations, needs and wants. The increasing availability of tools to enable the marketer to achieve this deeper understanding of the consumer, similarly demands the re-evaluation of the ways in which the tools employed to communicate with those consumers are used.

Strategic marketing communications

Schultz *et al.* (1992) argue that marketing communications often presents the only differentiating feature that can be offered to potential consumers. By recognizing the fact that everything a company does consists, in some form, as part of the communication that takes place between itself and its customers, it becomes aware of the increasingly important role of marketing communications as a strategic tool.

Just as the premise of the 'new marketing' places the consumer at the centre of all activity, so too, marketing communications must be considered from the essential perspective of understanding consumer behaviour. This implies a consideration of more than just the content of the message itself. Close attention needs to be paid to the context of the message (the vehicle used to communicate with the target audience), as well as the timing and tone of the message. The underlying imperative is the need for an identification of clear, concise and measurable communications objectives that will enable the selection of the appropriate communications tools to achieve the tasks set.

By developing an understanding of the identity of the consumer, and their particular needs and wants, we can determine the nature of the behaviour which the communications programme will need to reinforce or change. And, in turn, the specific nature of the message that will affect that behaviour, and the means by which we can reach them.

The strategic role that marketing communications can play is increasingly evidenced by the impact of specific campaigns. These not only affect the way in which consumers think about the particular products and services which are offered to them, but the very way in which they consider the categories in which those products and services exist.

The integration of marketing communications

A major contemporary issue in the field of marketing communications is the drive towards integrated activity. There are a number of reasons for this fundamental change of thinking which need to be examined.

The marketing methods businesses used in the 1980s are no longer working and have lost their value as competitive weapons, such as the constant focus on new products, generic competitive strategies, promotional pricing tactics and so on. Today's marketing environment has been described as an age of 'hyper-competition' in which there exists a vast array of products and services, both new and variations on existing themes. A casual look in the supermarket will confirm this view.

Many of the fastest growing markets are rapidly becoming saturated with large numbers of competitors. And, each competitor has similar

technology. The consequence is that, as Schultz *et al.* (1995) put it, sustainable competitive advantage has been eroded away. In many categories new products and services are copied in days or weeks rather than years. And, significantly, anything a company can do, someone else can do it cheaper.

Consumers are searching for more than a single element in any transaction. Instead, they seek to buy into the array of relevant experiences which surround the brand. Successful marketing in the 2000s will require total consumer orientation. It means communication with the individual, creating long-term relationships, quality driven, and the aim is customer satisfaction, not just volume and share.

Many writers on the subject, most notably Schultz (1999), argue that IMC is the natural evolution of mass-market media advertising towards targeted direct marketing. Schultz sees IMC as a logical and natural progression within the field of marketing communications. As he describes is 'it appears to be the natural evolution of traditional mass-media advertising, which has been changed, adjusted and refined as a result of new technology.' This author concurs with those who believe that IMC is significantly more than 'merely a management fashion' as attested by Cornellisen *et al.* (2000). Many companies strive to achieve total integration of their marketing communications efforts, recognizing the undeniable benefits which derive from the practice, not least of which is the ability to deliver consistency in their messages to their target audiences.

Integration, however, is not a new phenomenon, as the following quote from J. Walter Thompson in 1899 illustrates:

> We make it our business as advertising agents to advise on the best methods of advertising, in whatever form . . . as the best combination of work, such as we give, is the cheapest, as it brings the best results

Proctor and Kitchen (2002) argue that the brand is the hub of all marketing communications and depict this as the 'Wheel of integration'.

Defining IMC

Much debate surrounds the very nature of IMC, with the consequence that several alternative definitions have been proposed. Cornellisen *et al.* (2000) argue that one of the problems with the interpretation of IMC is the lack of a consensus

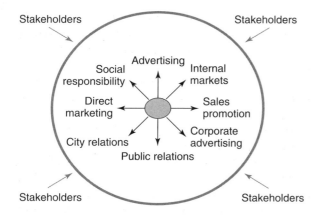

decision as to what the phrase actually means in practice. They point to the fact that various writers have argued about the move away from the traditional distinction between 'above-the-line' and 'below-the-line' to 'through-the-line', and 'zero-based' communications. What they fail to recognize is that the practitioners within the field operate as brands and seek to provide a distinctive offering to their clients. Hence, the adoption of a variety of nomenclatures for the practice of IMC.

They argue that the theoretical concept of IMC is ambiguous and 'provides the basis for researchers to adopt whichever interpretation of the term best fits their research agendas at any given time'.

There appears to be a discordancy between academic thinking and practice in the marketplace. Schultz and Kitchen (1997) argue that most marketing communications activities in the past have focused on breaking down concepts and activities into even more finite specialisms. Few marketing communications approaches have involved integration or holistic thinking. Whilst it is acknowledged that the pace of change towards the adoption of a holistic approach has been relatively slow, nonetheless, many practitioners and clients have moved progressively towards a focus on IMC.

Schultz in Jones (1999) defines IMC as 'a planning approach that attempts to co-ordinate, consolidate and bring together all the communications messages, programmes and vehicles that affect customers or prospects for a manufacturer or service organization's brands'.

Jeans (1998) provides greater clarity by proposing that 'IMC is the implementation of all marketing communications in such a way that each project, as well as meeting its specific project objects also

- conforms with the brand platform,
- is synergistic with all other projects related to the brand,

- actively reinforces the agreed brand values in any dialogue with the market,
- and is measured by short- and long-term effects on consumer behaviour'

Shimp (1996) suggests that the marketer who succeeds in the new environment will be the one who co-ordinates the communications mix so tightly that you can look from medium to medium and instantly see that the brand is speaking with 'one voice'. The one voice definition refers to an organizational effort to unify brand and image advertising, direct response, consumer sales promotions and public relations into a 'single positioning concept'.

Brannan (1995) argues that 'Our communications are fully integrated when we identify a single, core message which leads to one great creative idea which is implemented across everything we do'.

However, perhaps the clearest definition of IMC is that of the American Association of Advertising Agencies:

> A concept of marketing communications planning that recognizes the added value of a comprehensive plan that evaluates the strategic roles of a variety of communications disciplines and combines them to provide clarity, consistency and maximum communications impact through the seamless integration of discrete messages.
>
> The American Association of Advertising Agencies (1993)

The important dimension of this definition is the recognition of the need for a *comprehensive* plan that considers the strategic aspects of each of the tools of marketing communications in a holistic manner, rather than the development of them as separate elements. This approach represents a substantial shift in the underlying planning process, since it aims to ensure cohesion and the delivery of a single-minded message to the target audience.

Paul Smith writing in Admap (1996) states 'Integrated marketing communications is a simple concept. It brings together all forms of communication into a seamless solution. At its most basic level, IMC integrates all promotional tools so that they work together in harmony'.

Key to the issue is the fact that the consumer does not see advertising, public relations, sales promotion and other marketing communications techniques as separate and divisible components. As the receivers of a variety of messages from an equally wide range of sources they build up an image of a company, its brands and its services – both favourable and unfavourable. As far as they are concerned, the source of the message is unimportant. What they will be concerned with is the content of the message.

> A surge of interest by marketers in integrated communications strategies, where promotional messages are co-ordinated among advertising, public relations and sales promotion efforts, brings with it the implicit acknowledgement that consumers assimilate data about popular culture from many sources.
>
> Solomon and Englis (1994)

Equally, according to Lannon (1994) 'Consumers receive impressions of brands from a whole range of sources – first hand experience, impressions of where it can be bought, of people who use it or people who do not, from its role in cultural mores or rituals, from movies, literature, television, editorial, news, fashion, from its connections with events and activities and finally from paid advertising media'.

A parallel consideration is the fact that the communicator desires to achieve a sense of cohesion in the messages which the company communicates. If, for example, advertising is saying one thing about a brand and sales promotion something different, a sense of dissonance may be created with the consumer left in some confusion as to what the brand is really trying to say.

There is little doubt that marketing communications funds spent on a single communications message will achieve a far greater impact than when a series of different or contradictory messages are being sent out by the brand. And, with the pressure on funds, marketers desire to ensure that they are presenting a clear and precise picture of their products and services to the end consumer.

Few companies are specifically concerned with issues of whether to spend their money on advertising, sales promotion, public relations or elsewhere. They are concerned with ensuring that they develop a cohesive marketing communications programme that most effectively communicates their proposition to the end consumer. The particular route of communication is far less important than the impact of the message. And, in budgetary terms, companies need to consider where their expenditure will best achieve their defined objectives. The previous notions of separate and distinct advertising, sales promotion, public relations and other budgets fails to appreciate that the considerations of the overall marketing communications budget needs to be addressed as a matter of priority.

But at the heart of the debate is the recognition that the consumer must be the focus of all marketing communications activity. If we consider the Chartered Institute of Marketing's definition of marketing, we can see that the primary need is the anticipation and satisfaction of consumer wants and needs. It is the development of an understanding of the consumer and his or her wants and needs that will ensure that marketing communications works effectively to achieve the objectives defined for it. This represents a fundamental change of focus. A shift from the functional activity of creating marketing communications campaigns to an attitudinal focus in which the consumer's needs are at the heart of all marketing communications planning. And, with it a change from a focus from the product itself to the ultimate satisfaction of the end consumer. Of course, there are functional implications.

Above all else, there is an increasing recognition that companies need to identify what position their product or service occupies in the minds of the consumer relative to that of other products or services. Only when they have gained that knowledge can they begin the process of planning marketing communications either to alter or enhance that position:

> As choice becomes an ever greater factor for consumers, both in the products they use and the way they learn about those products, it is increasingly clear that no marketer can rely on advertising alone to deliver its message. Integration permits us to focus the power of all messages. It holds the greatest, most exciting promise for the future.
>
> George Schweitzer, Senior Vice President, Marketing and Communications, CBE's Broadcast Group

In general, some consistent themes may be drawn from prominent IMC definitions identified in the literature, including:

- a sound knowledge of the organization's stakeholders, acquired through two-way interaction with these parties;
- the selection of communication tools which promote the achievement of communications objectives; are reasonable in regard to the organization's resources, and are favourable to the intended recipient;

- the strategic co-ordination of various communication tools in a manner consistent with the organization's brand positioning, and which maximizes their synergistic effect so as to build strong brands and stakeholder relationships;
- the use of appropriate, timely and data-driven evaluation and planning to determine the effectiveness of this process;
- strong inter-functional and inter-organizational relationships with those responsible for implementing marketing communications campaigns;
- impact on customer relationships, brand equity and sales.

IMC is recognized increasingly for the strategic role it can play in managing the 'intangible side of business', through assisting in building relationships with customers and other stakeholders and in creating positive perceptions, attitudes and behaviours towards brands (Reid, 2003).

One of the difficulties with many definitions of IMC is the narrow ambit which they suggest. For the most part, authors concentrate on the primary tools of marketing communications, rather than the broader aspects which impact on their target audiences. Since, to reiterate the notion of David Ogilvy (1993), that everything that a company does, communicates, then the notion of IMC should realistically embrace every dimension of company activity.

Some authors do stretch the definitions somewhat. Much contemporary thinking can be depicted as in the diagram below:

The promotional outlook of IMC (Yeshin, 2006)

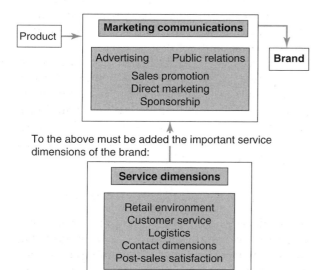

To the above must be added the important service dimensions of the brand:

Short-term IMC perspective

Short-term IMC perspective

However, for IMC to become the significant factor that it should be, it must go further. It must embrace the reputational facets of the company's behaviour. We are increasingly witnessing concerns voiced by the consumer about the reputation of the company with whom they do business. Whether or not they buy the brands of that company will depend as much on how they regard the organization as the efficacy of the products and services it provides. Whilst what is depicted above might be considered as a 'short-term' perspective of IMC, a longer-term view would encompass a number of other significant variables which mould the way that consumers and others view the organization. These new dimensions can be depicted graphically:

The reputational outbook of IMC (Yeshin, 2006)

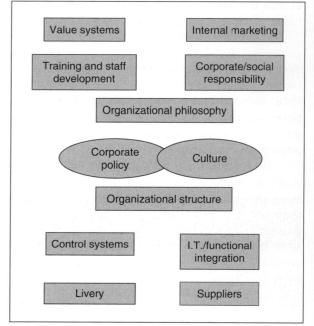

This notion is reinforced by the writing of Pickton and Hartley (1998) who assert 'Integration should not just involve the marketing communications activities, but all the messages delivered by the company'.

Dimensions of IMC

- Need for internal communications to ensure consistency of activities.

- Clearly identified marketing communications objectives which are consistent with other organizational objectives.
- Cohesive and planned approach encompassing all dimensions of marcom activity in a synergistic manner.
- Range of target audiences.
- Management of all forms of contact which may form the basis of marketing communications activity.
- Effective management and integration of all promotional activities and people involved.
- Incorporates all product/brand and corporate marketing communications efforts.
- Range of promotional tools including personal and non-personal communications.
- Range of messages derived from a single consistent strategy. This does not imply a single, standardized message. The IMC effort should ensure that all messages are determined in such a way as to work to each other's mutual benefit and minimize incongruity.
- Range of media including any vehicle capable of transmitting marketing communications messages (Pickton and Hartley, 1998).

The search for integration should not be taken to infer creative uniformity. Creative treatments need to be mutually consistent but it is perfectly acceptable to implement a range of different messages targeted at different audiences. The essential is to avoid confusion and inconsistency.

The impact of external factors on marketing communications

External and environmental factors have forced marketers to undertake a fundamental re-think both of marketing strategies and the positioning of products and this, in turn, must impact on the process of marketing communications.

Information overload

The consumer is continuously bombarded with vast quantities of information. According to Dan O'Donoghue (1997), whereas the average consumer was subjected to about 300 commercial messages a day in 1995, today that figure has risen to around 3000. Whether the information is orchestrated by the marketer or the media in general is less relevant than the fact that there is simply too much information for the average consumer to process effectively. The inevitable consequence is that much of the material is simply screened out and discarded. The result is that the consumer may make purchasing decisions based on limited knowledge, or even a misunderstanding of the real facts. The individual is far less concerned with the average advertising message which makes the task of ensuring appropriate communications with the target audience an event more daunting prospect.

An important dimension of the screening process is what I have described elsewhere as the 'submarine mentality'. In essence, since none of us can absorb all of the information around us, we establish personal defence mechanisms to screen out unwanted or irrelevant information. The analogy would be that of a submarine which goes underwater and, hence, avoids the surface bombardment. At periodic intervals, the submarine lifts its periscope to examine particular aspects of the world around it. And when it has finished gathering the new information, it descends again – oblivious to any changes which might be taking place.

As consumers, our awareness of specific advertising messages is treated in a similar way. Some form of trigger mechanism is usually required to encourage us to pay attention to the variety of marketing communications messages. Usually, this is an internal recognition of an unfulfilled need which heightens the levels of awareness of pertinent advertising and other information. The principle can be commonly observed. If, for example, you have recently purchased a new car, your awareness of the marque will be enhanced and you will immediately become aware of similar vehicles all around you.

However, in the process of attempting to find better and more effective ways of communicating, we have also gained a greater appreciation of the nature of marketing communications itself. Much work has been done in the area of model construction and theoretical examination which has helped us to enhance areas of implementation.

The discerning consumer

Recent decades have seen the progressive improvement in levels of education which, in turn, has made consumers both more demanding concerning the information they receive and more discerning in their acceptance of it. Marketing communications propositions developed in the 1950s and 1960s would be treated with disdain by today's more aware consumers. Specious technical claims and pseudo-scientific jargon which were at the heart of many product claims are no longer given quite the same credence.

This change is reflected in the comment of Judy Lannon (1994) 'Consumers have changed from being deferential and generalized to personal and selective'. She argues that we need to re-examine the way in which consumers use sources of commercial information. A particular issue to be addressed is, as she describes it, the 'credibility dimension' which involves not only the underlying credibility of the message, but the credibility of the sponsor delivering the message.

To this must be added the desire, amongst many, for a more healthy lifestyle. And manufacturers are being increasingly forced both by governmental initiatives and by changes in public opinion to respond both in the products they offer and the claims they make for them.

A contradiction

The inability to store and process new information, coupled with the demand for a greater focus in marketing communications messages, has resulted in the consumer relying more on perceptual values than on factual information. All consumers build up a set of 'values' which they associate with a company or a brand. Some of these values will be based on personal experience, or the experience of others. Much of it will be based, however, on a set of 'short-handed conclusions' based on overheard opinions, the evaluation of third party organizations, even the misinterpretation of information. These two factors combine to create a new dynamic for marketing communications.

However these thought processes are developed, and however the information is received, is less important than the fact that for the individual their views represent the truth. A product which is perceived to be inferior (even though there is factual evidence to contradict this view) is unlikely to be chosen in a normal competitive environment. The imperative, therefore, is to understand the process of perceptual encoding and relate it to the task of marketing communications. A simple example will suffice.

Most consumers are responsive to a 'bargain' proposition. And certain assumptions are made particularly in relation to well known and familiar brands. If a potential consumer sees a product on sale in a market environment, there is some expectation that the price will be lower than, say, in the normal retail environment. If the brand name is well established, then it is likely that they will be able to draw from it the confidence and reassurance which will be necessary to the making of a purchase decision. Indeed, there is considerable evidence that these perceptual factors, influenced by the environment, will for some consumers induce them to make a purchase even though they might have been able to purchase the same product at a lower price elsewhere.

Many retailers have recognized this situation and have adopted a positioning relative to their competitors of low price. By marking down the prices of a narrow range of products, they encourage the consumer to believe that all products are similarly discounted. The result is that the consumer will decide to make all of his or her purchases at that outlet based on the perceptions derived from a limited comparison of those brands upon which the retailer has focused marketing communications activity. Since few consumers are in a position to make objective comparisons across a wide range of comparable outlets, these perceptions are accepted and become the reality.

The situation is compounded by the fact that price is only one consideration in a purchase decision. Most people have an ideal view of a price and quality combination. Needless to say, such a view is highly personal and subjective but becomes the basis of making subsequent purchase decisions for that individual. Thus reputation, both for retailers and brands, will be an important consideration in the purchase selection.

Changes in family composition

Long gone are the notions of the family comprising two adults and 2.4 children.

In all countries, the notion of family itself has different meanings. Some communities perceive the family as a small integrated unit, others adopt a model of the extended family with the elder children having responsibility for ageing members of the family – either parents or grandparents. The increasing levels of divorce and the growing acceptance, by some, that marriage is not a norm to which they wish to comply, has resulted in growing numbers of single parent families. In all these situations, their needs and expectations will be substantially different from each other, and effective marketing communications needs to recognize and respond to these underlying changes in society.

The ageing population

In many countries, the improved standards of living and better health care have resulted in two parallel changes. On the one hand, in order to sustain living standards, people are deferring having children or are having fewer of them. On the other, life expectancy is improving as medical care is enhanced. These forces have resulted in a progressively ageing population in most developed markets. And with it, a change in the values, needs and wants which consumers exhibit about products and services.

The green imperative

Increasing numbers of consumers are concerned with the environmental impact of the products and services they consume. The abandonment of CFC's, the reduction in the volume of packaging waste, the consumption of scarce and irreplaceable resources and similar factors have all impacted on the consumers perceptions of desirable products and services.

No longer is the single focus of their attention the efficacy or otherwise of the products they might buy. They require reassurance that not only do the products perform in the way that they expect, but they also contribute to a better environment.

The changing face of media and the growth of narrow casting

The advent of an increased number of media channels – land based, cable and satellite television, an increasing number of radio networks and a mammoth explosion in the number of 'specialist' magazine titles – have resulted in a fundamental shift in terms of media planning. Where once the advertiser had to recognize that the use of a chosen media might, whilst providing excellent coverage of the desired target audience, carry with it a substantial wastage factor, the situation has now changed somewhat. Consumer groups can be targeted with a far higher level of precision. A specific message can be developed to appeal to a sub-group of users accessed by the nature of the television programmes they watch or the magazines they read. And, the increasing use of direct marketing techniques has resulted in the possibility

of one-to-one marketing – where the proposition can be tailored specifically to respond to the individual needs of the single consumer.

> Mass media advertising dominated marketing communications for decades, however, the nineties have seen companies place a greater emphasis on alternative communications mediums.
>
> Lannon (1996)

Most people are aware of the increasing fragmentation of media channels. However, perhaps more importantly, there is a wide variety of new channels of communication which can be used by brand owners to communicate with potential consumers and others – postcards; mobile Internet; till receipts; fuel pumps, hoardings around sports grounds; product placement; to name but a few. Research must be capable of monitoring the impact and ability of all of these communications channels to influence the 'viewer'.

Franz (2000) argues that the proliferation of new media adds complexity to the media landscape, since these new media channels rarely replace old media. Rather they tend to complement each other. What is significant is the way that media is used. Consumers tend to be more selective in their use of media, both because of time and money. The consequence is that media selection tends to be more specific than ever before.

The growth of global marketing

The changes brought about, substantially, by mass communications have, to some degree, encouraged the movement towards global marketing. With the recognition that national and cultural differences are growing ever fewer, major manufacturers have seized upon the opportunity to 'standardize' their marketing across different markets.

It is now possible to purchase an ostensibly similar product with the same name, same identity and similar product ingredients in many different markets. From the ubiquitous Coca Cola, now available in almost every different country, to products like the Mars Bar, manufacturers are seizing the opportunity to ensure a parity of branding throughout all of the markets they serve, and to extend the territories in which they operate. The latter company has unified its branding of the Marathon Bar to Snickers and Opal Fruits to Starburst to achieve international parity. Similarly, Unilever recently consolidated the various names of Jif and Vif into Cif for the same reasons.

There are few markets (although the product contents may well be different) which would not recognize the Nescafe coffee label or what it stands for. The big M means McDonalds in any language, and Gillette run the same copy platform for its series range of male shaving preparations in many different countries.

Non-verbal communications

We have already seen that the emergence of new media has enabled a more precise focus on target groups of consumers. But it has also demanded a new approach to the execution of marketing communications propositions, particularly on television.

Increasingly, satellite channels are unrestricted in their availability. The same programmes can be watched simultaneously in France and Finland, Germany and Greece. And, if that is true of the programming, it is equally true of the advertising contained within. Whilst programmers have the opportunity to overcome language and other barriers to communication within their formats, the same is not so readily true for the advertiser.

The response has been a growth in the recognition that visual communication has a vital role to play in the overall process. Increasing numbers of television commercials are being made with a Pan European or Global audience in mind. The emphasis is less on the words being used than the impact of the visual treatments employed.

Gillette, for example, use a constant visual treatment to support their Series range of products across diverse markets. Here, the voice over is modified to verbalize the proposition in each marketplace. In fact, the company has adopted an integrated approach for their long-running campaign embracing everything the company does. 'It is a much more single minded strategic platform for the brand', according to Bruce Cleverly, General Manager for Gillette Northern Europe, 'It is the strategic premise of the entire Gillette grooming business'.

Other companies have gone considerably further. The verbal component of the proposition has been minimized with the storyline being developed entirely, or almost so, in visual form. Television commercials for Dunlop, Levi's and Perrier are examples of this approach.

Speed of information access

Not only has the growth of information technology meant that information can be processed more rapidly, it has also meant that access to that information can be made far more speedily than at any time in the past. This has significant import for the marketer.

Census information which was previously tabulated by hand, or on comparatively slow computers – and which was substantially out of date by the time it was made available – is now available within a relatively short period of time. Marketers can determine with far greater precision than at any time in the past, the likely audience for their propositions, and can more readily segment markets into groups of users, rather than communicating with them as an aggregation.

At the same time, of course, this improved level of communication has a direct impact on the consumer. An increased level of media coverage of consumer-related issues means that any problem with a product or service is almost bound to receive media exposure. News stories about product withdrawals, the focus on product deficiencies within programmes like 'Watchdog', all ensure that large groups of consumers become aware of these issues within days, or even hours of the occurrence.

The widespread use of the Internet and the increasing number of Blogs expressing consumer views concerning product performance (or the lack of it) adds to the pressure on manufacturers to respond speedily to consumer concerns.

The driving forces behind the growth of IMC

Various studies have focused on the factors which are encouraging the adoption of IMC programmes (Yeshin, 1996; Duncan and Everett, 1993; Grein and Ducoffe, 1998; Kitchen and Schultz, 1999, 2000).

A further dimension of the study by Kitchen and Schultz (1999) was an identification by respondents of the forces driving the move towards IMC:

- call for synergy among promotional tools,
- rapid growth and development of database marketing,
- recognition that agency's future success depends on helping clients develop IMC programmes,
- emergence of a variety of compensation methods,
- rapid growth of IMC importance,
- fragmentation of media markets,
- shift in marketplace power from manufacturers to retailers,

- escalating price competition,
- traditional advertising too expensive and not cost effective.

Duncan and Everett (1993) identify several factors underlying the pressure to integrate marketing communications:

- agency mergers and acquisitions,
- increasing sophistication of clients and retailers,
- increasing cost of traditional advertising media,
- increased global competition,
- increasing pressure on organizations' bottom lines,
- decreasing effectiveness of traditional media,
- decreasing cost of database usage,
- trends such as zapping, zipping, media fragmentation and loss of message credibility.

Value for money: The recession of recent years and increasing global competition have brought about substantial changes in the way that client companies are managed. On the one hand, there has been the impact of shrinking marketing departments, in which fewer people are allocated to the management of the products and services which the company produces. On the other, the pressure on margins has encouraged clients to become tougher negotiators. Companies are keen to gain the maximum value for money and the maximum impact from all relevant disciplines.

Increasing pressure on organizations' bottom lines: The inevitable consequence of the variety of economic pressures has resulted in a close focus on company profitability. As all forms of cost increase, so companies seek to make compensatory savings throughout all of their activities.

Increasing client sophistication: This is particularly true of areas such as an understanding of retailers, customers and consumers. There has been an increasing confidence in the use of other marketing communication disciplines, especially sales promotion, and the greater ability to take the lead in terms of their strategic direction.

A disillusionment with advertising: It has resulted in clients turning to other disciplines in the search to improve customer relationships and more sales.

A disillusionment with agencies: Advertising agencies, in particular, which were often the primary source of strategic input for the clients with whom they worked, have lost significant ground in this respect. Specialist consultancies and other are now being retained by client companies to advise them of the strategic directions they should

be taking, with the agency role becoming progressively smaller in many instances.

The fragmentation of media channels: As we have seen earlier, the changing face of the media scene is demanding the re-evaluation of the contribution that the variety of media channels can make to the delivery of the message. With new ways of communicating with the target audiences, new approaches are necessary to achieve maximum impact from marketing communications budgets.

Traditional advertising too expensive and not cost effective: There is an increased recognition that, for many companies, the use of traditional forms of advertising no longer provides the means of achieving cost-effective reach of their target audiences. As media costs escalate, many companies are turning to other forms of marketing communications to achieve their objectives.

The rapid growth and development of database marketing: The increasing availability of sophisticated database techniques has enabled manufacturers and service providers alike with a more precise means of targeting consumers. The move away from traditional mass marketing towards closely focused communications techniques is a reflection of the increasing cost of traditional advertising techniques.

Power shift towards retailers: In most consumer markets, comparatively small numbers of retailers have come to dominate their respective categories. In the grocery field, for example, the major supermarket chains – Tesco, ASDA, Sainsbury and Safeway (now part of Morrisons), account for a substantial part of the retail business. Together, these four companies account for some two-thirds of retail sales. Inevitably, this has resulted in their taking the initiative in terms of the marketing to consumers. To a large degree, even major manufacturers have to bow to the demands of the retailers or face the prospect of their products being de-listed from their shelves.

Escalating price competition: As brands increasingly converge in what they offer to consumers, companies are striving to overcome the debilitating impact of the downward price spiral. The recognition that marketing communications is often the only differentiating factor between competing brands has led to an increased focus on how the tools can be used to achieve brand distinction.

Environmental factors: Consumers are becoming increasingly concerned with the way in which products impact on the general environment. In turn, companies have been forced to adopt a more environmentally friendly approach or risk consumers rejecting their products in favour of those which they consider to be more responsive to these broader concerns.

Emergence of a variety of compensation methods: Where once agencies were bound by a compensation based on commission (a fixed percentage of the monies spent on advertising), today's marketing communications companies are rewarded in many different ways. The most important impact of this change has been to free them (and the perception of their income) as being tied to recommendations to increase their clients' spend.

Agency mergers and acquisitions: Responding to the needs of the marketplace and, in particular, to pressures from their clients, agencies are increasing merging to form larger groups. Partly, this has been driven by the need to provide client services across a variety of territories. However, a further dimension has been the desire to provide a comprehensive service to clients across the variety of areas encompassed by marketing communications. The large agency groups exist as holding companies controlling operational companies in all of the relevant communications fields.

Increased global competition: The drive towards globalization has increased the necessity to achieve synergy between all forms of marketing communications. Where once a brand might be sold in a single country, today's mega-brands are available across the globe. Significant savings can be achieved through the implementation of a constant communications campaign across all of the territories in which the product is sold.

The impact on marketing communications

We have already seen that marketing communications need to focus on the end user rather than on the nature of the product or service provided. But, it is suggested, marketing communications needs to respond more rapidly to these underlying changes in the social and environmental framework.

In their important work on IMC, Schultz *et al.* (1992) propose that it is time to abandon the principles of the four Ps for the four Cs.

> Forget **P**roduct. Study **C**onsumer wants and needs. You can no longer sell whatever you make. You can only sell something that someone specifically wants to buy.

> Forget **P**rice. Understand the consumer's **C**ost to satisfy that want or need.

> Forget **P**lace. Think **C**onvenience to buy.

> Forget **P**romotions. The word in the 90s is **C**ommunications.

If marketing communications is to be effective, it is vitally important that we move from a situation of specialization – in which marketers are experts in one area of marketing communications – to people who are trained in all marketing communications disciplines.

At the same time, as we have already seen, the process of change requires us to look at focused marketing approaches rather than adopt the litany of the 60s – that of mass marketing. With the recognition that all consumers are different and, hence have different needs and wants – even of the same product or service – there is the need to ensure that we are able to communicate with them as individuals rather than as a homogenous unit. The increasing concern is the desire to communicate with ever small segments of the global market and, in an ideal world, reach a position where we can communicate with them individually. This desire manifests itself in the increasing drive towards direct marketing techniques, the most rapidly growing sector of the marketing communications industry.

There needs to be a clear statement of the desired outcomes of marketing activity as a whole. This requires a totally new approach since most people working within marketing have been brought up in a disintegrated environment.

Objectives need to be longer term and expressed more strategically than would be the case for the short-term objectives of more individual marketing tactics.

Schultz (1999) argues that as the tools of marketing communications are progressively diffused into a variety of specialisms, there has been a natural inclination for those individual specialists to focus entirely within their own area – often to the detriment of the brand or communication programme. The consequence has been a natural drift towards less integrated, less co-ordinated, less concentrated marketing communications activities.

The task of IMC is to strategically co-ordinate the various elements of the promotional mix in order to achieve synergies and to ensure that the message reaches and registers with the target audience.

Novak and Phelps (1994) have suggested that there are several important dimensions to the process of integration:

- The creation of a single-theme and image.
- The integration of both product image and relevant aspects of consumer behaviour in promotional management, as opposed to a focus on one or the other of these two.
- The co-ordinated management of promotion mix disciplines.

Similarly, Low (2000) identified four components that contribute to the co-ordination of marketing communications activities:

1 Planning and executing different communications tools as one integrated project.
2 Assigning responsibility for the overall communications effort to a single manager.
3 Ensuring that the various elements of the communications programme have a common strategic objective.
4 Focusing on a common communications message.

Relationship marketing

A development of the marketing communications process, as it moves through the early 2000s, is the area known as relationship marketing. With the ability to reach consumers on a highly segmented or even one-to-one basis, so too has come the recognition that the process itself can become two-way. Hitherto, marketing communications primarily concerned itself with the process of communicating *to* the end consumer. By encouraging the process of feedback, we can now communicate *with* the consumer.

Increasingly, companies such as Nestle and Heinz have announced moves into club formats which enable the establishment of a direct relationship between the manufacturer and the consumer. Many loyalty programmes, such as the Frequent Flyer and Frequent Stayer programmes now run by most international airlines and hotel groups, have a similar objective of establishing a relationship with the consumer, to their mutual benefit. The increasing use of customer loyalty programmes within the major retail chains is further evidence of the desire to establish direct contact with the customer base – for long-term advantage. The encouragement of a 'feedback' loop is a facet of

marketing communications which is destined to grow apace over the next few years and, as companies perceive the benefits of encouraging a positive relationship with their customers, their consumers, their suppliers and others, so we will witness the growth of developed two-way marketing communications programmes.

It has to be recognized that contemporary marketing is more complex than at any other time in the past. No longer is it sufficient to rely on the traditional marketing mix variables to achieve differentiation between manufacturers. Areas such as product design and development, pricing policies, distribution in themselves, are no longer capable of delivering the long-term differentiation required. With an increasing level of convergent technologies, product innovation may be going on in parallel between rival manufacturers even without their knowing what the other is doing. And, even where this is not the case, any new feature can rapidly be copied by the competition. Where once, a new feature, ingredient, or other product attribute would enable a manufacturer to achieve a unique stance for an extended period, today this is no longer the case. One has only to look at the area of the rapid innovation within the soap powder and detergent markets to see just how speedily rival manufacturers catch up with each other.

With the concentration of distribution into relatively few hands, the opportunities for achieving solus distribution of brands is minimized. Indeed, the retailers themselves represent an increasing threat to the manufacturers' brands as their packaging moves ever closer to that of the manufacturers own.

Pricing, once a major area of differentiation, similarly provides less scope. The pressure on margins brought about by the increasingly competitive nature of retailers own products, has restricted the scope to use price to differentiate effectively. Clearly, this is particularly true of fast moving consumer goods where price dissimilarity can only operate over a very narrow range. Other products, such as perfumes and toiletries, and luxury goods ranging from hi-fi's to cars still have more flexibility in the area of price.

We are left, therefore, with only one of the four marketing mix variables which can be utilized to achieve effective brand discrimination – marketing communications. Schultz *et al.* (1992) argue that the area of marketing communications will, increasingly, be the only opportunity of achieving sustainable competitive advantage.

If all other things are equal – or at least more or less so – then it is what people think, feel and believe about a product and its competitors which will be important. Since products in many areas will achieve parity or comparability in purely functional terms, it will be the perceptual differences which consumers will use to discriminate between rival brands. Only through the used of sustained and IMC campaigns, will manufacturers be able to achieve the differentiation they require.

To appreciate the impact of this statement, it is worth looking at a market which replicates many of the features described above. In the bottled water market, several brands co-exist, each with unique positionings in the minds of the consumer. Yet, in repeated blind tastings, few consumers can identify any functional characteristics which could be used as the basis for brand discrimination.

'The increasing need to manage relationship building has brought forth a variety of 'new generation' marketing approaches – customer focused, market-driven, outside-in, one-to-one marketing, data-driven marketing, relationship marketing, integrated marketing and integrated marketing communications (Duncan and Moriarty, 1998).

The benefits of IMC

Undeniably, the process of integration affords a great number of benefits to the companies which adopt it. Linton and Morley (1995) suggest nine potential benefits of IMC:

1 creative integrity,
2 consistent messages,
3 unbiased marketing recommendations,
4 better use of media,
5 greater marketing precision,
6 operational efficiency,
7 cost savings,
8 high-calibre consistent service,
9 easier working relations.

Similarly, Kitchen and Schultz (1999) identified a series of benefits which could be derived from IMC programmes. These included:

- increased impact,
- creative ideas more effective when IMC used,
- greater communications consistency,
- increases importance of one brand personality,
- helps eliminate misconceptions,

- provides greater client control over communication budget,
- provides clients with greater professional expertise,
- enables greater client control over marketing communications,
- helps eliminate miscommunications that result from using several agencies,
- enables greater control over budgets,
- provides client with greater professional expertise,
- IMC necessitates fewer meetings,
- enables client consolidation of responsibilities,
- agencies can provide faster solutions,
- provides method of effective measurement,
- reduces cost of Marcom programmes,
- greater agency accountability.

Consistency of message delivery: By approaching the planning process in a holistic manner, companies can ensure that all components of the communications programme deliver the same message to the target audience. Importantly, this demands the adoption of an overall strategy for the brand, rather than developing individual strategies for the separate tools of marketing communications. The avoidance of potential confusion in the minds of consumers is a paramount consideration in the development of effective communications programmes.

Corporate cohesion: For the company, IMC can be used as a strategic tool in communicating its corporate image and product/service benefits. This has important consequences both on an internal and an external level. As consumers increasingly gravitate towards companies with whom they feel comfortable, it becomes important to ensure that the overall image projected by the organization is favourably received. This demands, in turn, the development of a cohesive communications programme within the organization – to ensure that all people working for the company fully understand the organizations' goals and ambitions – and externally – to present the company in the most favourable light.

Mike Reid of Monash University (2003) argues that there is an interesting and positive relationship between IMC and different types of brand-related performance. In an analysis of the performance of a number of Australian organizations he indicates that those with high performance exhibit better communications practices and a higher level of integration in the management of marketing communications.

Client relationships: for the agency, it provides the opportunity to play a significantly more important role in the development of the communications programme, and to become a more effective partner in the relationship. By participating in the totality of the communications requirements, rather than having responsibility for one or more components, the agency can adopt a more strategic stance. This, in turn, yields significant power and provides important advantages over competitors.

Interaction: IMC ensures better communication between agencies and creates a stronger bond between them and the client company. By providing a more open flow of information it enables the participants in the communication programme to concentrate on the key areas of strategic development, rather than pursue individual and separate agenda's.

Motivation: IMC offers the opportunity to motivate agencies. The combined thinking of a team is better than the sum of the parts (and unleashes everyone's creative potential).

Participation: Everyone owns the final plan, having worked together on the brainstorming and implementation, avoiding any internal politics. Potentially, this can overcome the divisive nature of individual departments 'fighting their own corner'.

Perhaps the most important benefit is the delivery of better measurability of response and accountability for the communications programme.

The process of achieving integration

The task of developing and implementing marketing communications campaigns is becoming increasingly divergent. No longer is the task is one pair of hands. As the specialist functions develop further, the marketer must seek and co-ordinate the input from a number of different sources. Many organizations will retain an advertising agency, a public relations consultancy, a sales promotion company and, perhaps, even a media specialist. Ensuring that all of these contributors work to the same set of objectives and deliver a cohesive message to the consumer is a task which is an increasingly challenging one.

The key requirement is the establishment of a feedback mechanism between all elements of the strategic development process and, importantly, the consideration of all of the tools of marketing communications designed to fulfil the promotional objectives established for the campaign. It is the adoption of a holistic approach to campaign development which is at the heart of integration, a fundamental shift from the practice of developing each of the elements on a piecemeal basis.

> Integrated marketing communications offers strategic and creative integrity across all media.
>
> Linton and Morley (1995)

This ensures that the company maintains a constant theme and style of communication which can be followed across all applications. In turn, this provides for a strong and unified visual identity in all areas of communication.

This does not imply that all material should have the same copy and visual execution, however all items used must serve to tell the same story and to reinforce the overall message to the consumer. This enables each element of a campaign to reinforce the others and to achieve the maximum level of impact on the target audience. The best platforms for integrated campaigns are ideas that can be spread across the whole marketing communications mix, for example American Express 'Membership Has Its Privileges' and Gillette's 'The Best A Man Can Get' will work in any discipline.

Andrex has, for many years, used the image of a Labrador puppy in its advertising to symbolize softness. More recently, however, the device has been extended into other promotional areas. Its 'Puppy Tales' campaign offered a series of books about the adventures of a puppy, which was featured on-pack and in television advertising. The promotion gained editorial coverage both for the promotion itself and by way of reviews of the author, Gerald Durrell. All of these devices reinforced the brand message.

Some companies go further. They produce a visual identity manual to which all items produced on behalf of the company must comply. This establishes a series of specific requirements which may cover the typefaces used, the positioning of the logo and other important visual elements which provides a high level of commonality in all materials produced. Often this is associated with a re-design of the corporate image. When the author was working with the Prudential Corporation, Woolf Olins were engaged to re-design the company look and, as part of the package, created a corporate ID manual which covered all of the above areas, and to which all agencies were required to comply.

An essential part of IMC is the process of ensuring that the message conveyed is consistent.

Whereas this is achievable in the context of a single agency which produces all of the materials required by its client, in the vast majority of case, companies will employ several different agencies, often independent of each other. Indeed, some of the material will be produced by the company in-house. In this instance, someone must take overall responsibility for ensuring the consistency of the various items to ensure that there is an overall coherence in what is produced. This means that the person or department must consider not only the obvious items such as advertising, point of sale and direct mail pieces, but everything else which is prepared to support the brand. This may include product leaflets and other literature, presentations and audio-visual material, sales training items, exhibition stands and so on.

A key area within the requirement of IMC is the need for recommendations which are without structural bias. Historically (and still to a large degree) it was inevitable that agencies promoted their own particular corners. Advertising agencies would often present advertising solutions, promotions companies would offer sales promotion responses and so on.

The move towards IMC has been hastened by the desire for agencies to become more accountable for their recommendations. Inherently, agencies have to be confident, as far as it is possible to be so, that the recommendations they make are those most likely to achieve the outcome desired by the client company.

To many writers on the topic, the central part of the IMC process is the maintenance of an effective database. Not only does this provide the opportunity to gain a greater understanding of existing customers, from an examination of their profiles (and using those profiles to identify similar target groups) it is possible to achieve a greater degree of precision in all subsequent communications activity.

At the conceptual level, integration is about capturing a single thought which expresses what we wish the brand to stand for and of ensuring that this thought is expressed, whatever the medium. At the process level, it is about ensuring that the development and implementation of communications lives up to that brand thought, and drives forward the relationship between the brand and the consumer.

As John Farrell, then Chief Executive of DMB&B (now incorporated into Leo Burnett) said 'Unless there is close involvement of senior client personnel who truly have a full communications

perspectives, it's simply unfair on the agencies involved to expect them to drive the integration process from the outside.' Clients do not need specialist implementation functions within their businesses, rather at a conceptual stage there has to be a structure and attitude which actively encourages the agency to recommend the most appropriate media solution to solve the particular problem.

Integration is not just about execution. It is about the single brand thought that expresses the essence of the brand personality and then interpreting that thought for the appropriate audience without changing of denigrating it. Integration extends to the point where the client and agency work together as a single team. The total team across all communications requirements is fully integrated with the customer and brand requirements and that is what drives the focus of the team.

Winston Fletcher (1998) seeks to make the distinction between good and bad integration. He argues that badly done integrated marketing campaigns squeeze different communications media into strait-jackets which minimize their individuality. 'To force all types of communications to use the same message, instead of allowing them to deploy their own strengths and complement each other, is direly inefficient.'

Van Raaij (1998) summarizes the differences between classic forms of marketing communications with the IMC approach as follows:

Classic communications	Integrated communications
Aimed at acquisition	Aimed at retention and relationship management
Mass communications	Selective communications
Monologue	Dialogue
Information is sent	Information is requested
Information provision	Information self-service
Sender takes initiative	Receiver takes initiative
Persuasive 'hold-up'	Provide information
Effect through repetition	Effect through relevance
Offensive	Defensive

Hard sell	Soft sell
Salience of brand	Confidence in brand
Transaction oriented	Relationship oriented
Attitude change	Satisfaction
Modern, linear, massive	Post-modern, cyclical, fragmented

Organizational approaches to integration

Increasingly, attempts are being made by companies to co-ordinate some, if not all, of the marketing functions to benefit from the resultant synergy. In this regard, many companies adopt a 'consistency' approach to ensure that the brand messages created by different marketing activities do not conflict with the agreed strategic positioning of the brand. In some instances, much more compete integration is achieved by ensuring that a similar device is used across all marketing activities – for example, Coca Cola advertise their sponsorship of various events, especially football, and also use them as the basis of sales promotion activities.

Very few companies have really developed a comprehensive approach towards integration where the overall responsibility for all communication functions is lodged in a single location, either internally or externally.

A survey by Duncan and Everett (1993) found that, at that time, there was a relatively low familiarity with the concept of IMC. However, once the concept was defined, most regarded it as a valuable concept.

They identified that a significant number of companies were co-ordinating the functions of marketing communications both internally and externally. An increasing number of clients stated that they were likely to hire agencies with an understanding of IMC and believed that IMC would grow within their organizations.

The way in which companies are organized into different departments which reflect the various functions of marketing communications is a key cause of disintegrated communications where different messages are communicated to consumers about the same brand. In the worst case scenario, the messages delivered by marketing communications may actually contradict each other (Alanko, 2000). Some writers suggest that the most efficient means of achieving integration is to appoint a single agency which is responsible for all aspects of the campaign, contracting out certain areas. The reality, except for a relatively few number of companies, is that such an approach is generally not possible. The need for specialist services in the wide variety of areas which make up the tools of marketing communications requires staff who are skilled in those specialisms.

Research by Gronstedt and Thorson (1996) suggest that integrated approaches are necessary because most work related to communications cuts across different knowledge and skills domains, whilst Schultz *et al.* (1992) argue that IMC results in the creation of communications programmes that are both tonally and visually coherent.

The question of how to organize external communications disciplines has been a continuing source of debate within the arena of marketing communications (Cornellisen *et al.*, 2001). The conundrum is whether organization should be of a functional nature, that is, with the various departments merged together to create a single entity which can deal with all communications requirements or whether, as suggested by Gronstedt (1996) it is more about integrating the processes of marketing communications. Schultz *et al.* (1992) argue that the different mind-sets of professionals operating within the various disciplines inhibit the level of cross-functional operation and the ways in which the disciplines can contribute to the achievement of the desired objectives.

Gronstedt and Thorson (1996) suggest five possible models for an integrated organizational structure:

1   *The consortium.* One agency performs the role of main contractor to a consortium of specialist agencies. The main agency helps its client to develop a strategy and decides which persuasive tools to use. It typically executes traditional advertising but sub contracts other tools. The account team at the main agency co-ordinates the specialist agencies to ensure that messages and timing are integrated.
2   *Consortium with a dominant agency.* Agencies that have the capacity to plan an integrated campaign and execute traditional advertising as well as some other communications tools. The main agency has various combinations of in-house services and outside suppliers.

3 *Corporation with autonomous units*: All the specialists are brought in-house as separate and autonomous units. The specialist units are separate profit centres, sometimes with separate names and in separate buildings.

4 *The matrix organization*. Agencies not only have specialists in-house but they are integrated in a matrix structure. The matrix design combines functional division and cross-functional task force teams. The matrix structure requires that professionals work across functions whilst maintaining the functional division.

5 *The integrated organization*. All disciplines are incorporated into the advertising agency structure rather than forming separate units for each persuasive tool. The agency is no longer structured by functional departments but by accounts. Each person works for a particular client not for a direct marketing or sales promotion department. Each account group comprises personnel who are capable of handling all communications disciplines.

Duncan and Everett (1993) suggest four agency client relationships which could foster integration:

1 The client and its agencies collectively establish strategies, then each communications function is executed by a different agency.

2 The client and its agency establish the strategies, then the 'integrated' agency is responsible for the executions of all or most of the communications functions.

3 The client determines overall strategies and assigns individual functions to individual agencies, but requires that all of these suppliers stay in touch with each other.

4 The client alone determines overall strategies, then each communications function is executed by a different agency.

Grein and Gould (1996) identify five factors which, they suggest, impact on the organizational dimensions and affect its effective implementation:

1 Inter-office co-ordination.

2 Co-ordination of promotional disciplines across country offices.

3 The degree of centralization.

4 The frequency of inter-office communication.

5 The use of information technology.

Jeans (1998) argues that the most likely route to achieving IMC is in team-building, rather than any hierarchical or matrix method of control. Since the necessary practitioner skills are unlikely to be embodied in any single individual, a team of people will be essential to provide the necessary inputs.

A study by McArthur and Griffin published in 1997 demonstrated the extent to which marketing organizations perceived integration to have been fulfilled. Almost half of the companies surveyed indicated that all marketing communications activities of their companies were co-ordinated either by a single person or as a result of some reporting relationship. A further quarter co-ordinated the majority of their marketing communications programmes. Interestingly, and confirming the results of other studies, the areas of business which indicated the highest level of co-ordination of activities were Retail and Business to Business.

The study identified a series of 'inconsistencies' in the sourcing of activities across the different business types. Their study revealed, for example, that consumer marketers tended to use external suppliers for creative input more extensively than others. The business-to-business (B2B) sector relied more heavily on their advertising agencies for all communications activities. Retailer marketers were significantly more prone to source activities in-house.

There are sound historical reasons for these differences in practice sometimes, but not always, related to the level of marketing communications expenditures within specific categories. Within the consumer sector, budgets tend to be large and activities more extensive. Inevitably, companies involved with these programmes seek high levels of expertise within the respective fields and source suppliers who, in the main, have a demonstrable track record of being able to deal with the market sector. Elsewhere, where budgets are somewhat lower, companies tend to rely more heavily on a single supplier to achieve economies across the range of activities which they implement. The retail sector, by contrast, inevitably demands a greater speed of response and, hence, is more prone to produce material in-house where those with the specialist skills can be located.

Nor should it be presumed that IMC is the exclusive province of FMCG and branded manufacturers. Alanko (2000) argues that integration in B2B goes beyond co-ordinating media and other communications channels and their messages. It 'enters the heart of the enterprise and its core processes, customer acquisition, retention and development'.

He makes the point that, as with other forms of business, integration within the B2B sector occupies a strategic role and must involve senior management.

Interesting differences in the global acceptance and implementation of IMC are seen in various recent works.

A survey conducted by Griffin and McArthur (1997) sought to identify the extent to which IMC was practiced within companies. Respondents were shown a series of seven marketing communications functions (including creative, media, sales promotion, etc.) and asked to indicate the nature of co-ordination between them and the extent of that co-ordination.

The results were as follows:

	Business focus				
	All (%)	Consumer (%)	B to B (%)	Service (%)	Retail (%)
Companies where all activities co-ordinated	46.2	46.2	62.5	34.5	50.0
By a single person	24.0	30.8	31.3	17.2	15.0
Through a reporting relationship	22.1	15.4	31.3	17.2	35.0
Companies where 5 to 6 activities co-ordinated	28.7	33.3	18.8	20.7	35.0
By a single person	7.7	5.1	6.3	3.4	20.0
Through a reporting relationship	21.0	28.2	12.5	17.2	15.0
Companies where 3 to 4 activities co-ordinated	18.3	12.8	12.5	31.0	15.0
By a single person	12.5	7.7	12.5	27.6	–
Through a reporting relationship	5.8	5.1	–	3.4	15.0

A study conducted by Kitchen and Schultz (1999) indicated the extent to which the premise of IMC had been adopted in a number of countries:

Amount of time devoted to IMC programmes for clients					
Amount of time (%)	USA (%)	UK (%)	New Zealand (%)	Australia (%)	India (%)
75% or more	25	11	21	5	–
50–74%	25	32	11	–	–
25–49%	25	25	25	26	23
10–24%	15	30	37	37	46
10% or less	10	11	5	32	31

A further aspect of their research was the amount of client budgets devoted to IMC activities:

Country	% of budget
USA	52
UK	42
New Zealand	40
Australia	22
India	15

The study showed significant differences between the five countries surveyed. In response to a question about the amount of time devoted to IMC programmes for client firms, for those indicating more than 50 per cent of their time, the percentages were 50 per cent for the US; 43 per cent UK; 32 per cent NZ; 5 per cent Australia; 0 per cent India. From the expenditure perspective, respondents were asked to identify the percentage of their overall budgets devoted to IMC activities, with similar results. US 52 per cent; UK 42 per cent; NZ 40 per cent; Australia 22 per cent; India 15 per cent.

According to Kitchen and Schultz (1999) 'whilst IMC is recognized as offering significant value and importance to clients and agencies alike, the fact that no clear proposal, method or acceptable disposition of measurement and evaluation has been offered and/or found widespread acceptance weakens conceptual application in a global sense'.

Picton and Hartley (1998) summarize the different dimensions of integration:

- Promotional mix integration – synergy between the individual promotional elements.
- Promotional mix with marketing mix integration – synergy between the elements of the marketing mix with those of the marketing communications mix, since each element of the marketing mix has a communications value of its own.
- Creative integration – themes, concepts and messages across all marcom activities.
- Intra-organization integration – all relevant internal departments, individuals and activities within the organization.
- Inter-organization integration – all external organizations involved in marketing communications on behalf of the organization.
- Information and database systems – databases are rapidly becoming the primary management tool that drives the organization's business strategy.

- Integration of communication targeted towards internal and external audiences – a variety of audiences need to be considered within the context of IMC, both internal and external. They will represent a variety of potentially disparate groups.
- Integration of corporate and brand/product communications – corporate communications is often considered as a separate entity and, often, has different people who have the responsibility as 'corporate guardians'. Organizations must recognize the strategic and tactical impact of corporate identity on their other marketing communications activities.
- Geographical integration – integration cross both national and international boundaries.

The barriers to integration

Despite the undeniable advantages afforded by integration, an examination of the market situation suggests that relatively few companies have yet reached the stage of fully integrating their communications campaigns.

Various studies (Mitchell, 1995; Yeshin, 1996; Kitchen and Schultz, 1999, 2000) have described the progressive adoption of the philosophy of IMC across many major and sophisticated client companies. Nonetheless, many barriers continue to exist.

These studies indicate that, whilst much has been written on the topic, the subject remains largely misunderstood by many of those responsible for its implementation. This is clearly seen by the diversity of 'definitions' provided for IMC by the respondents.

> Co-ordinating all of the tools of promotion to ensure a consistent message

> Rolling out a single creative theme across all executions

> Using a single agency to deliver all requirements

Clearly there is considerable confusion as to the nature of IMC, with some respondents regarding it as a process; others perceiving it as a facility for 'one stop' shopping, whilst for others it was a means whereby cohesion might be achieved between creative executions and strategies, even if provided by a multiplicity of suppliers.

Several factors can be identified as presenting barriers to the integration process, both of an internal and an external nature.

Internally, the lack of management understanding of the benefits of IMC; the short-term outlook adopted towards much of the planning process; the inherent nature of the 'political' battles between departments battling for supremacy; the fear of departmental budget reductions with the consequence of staff reductions; together with the turnover of staff and the fear of losing expertise in specialist areas, were all identified as contributing to the general lack of adoption of IMC within companies. Externally, issues such as agency ego's, the agency's fears of losing control, the lack of expertise in the individual areas of communications, the concern over reductions in the scale of the communications budget and the problems of the system of remuneration were further restrictions of the progress of integration.

Structurally, few companies are in a position to ensure integration. Often various functions compete with each other for the responsibility of briefing and implementation of the tools of marketing communications. These include the brand manager, the marketing manager, the marketing director, in a few instances, a communications director, together with a variety of 'specialist' heads of departments covering public relations, sales promotion and so on. Often these individuals represent 'vested' interests and are protective of their own sectors to the preclusion of an integrated approach. Most importantly, few companies have truly recognized the issue of responsibility for the custodianship of the brand and the negative implications of divisive communications messages. '. . . In practice, the situation is even worse. Company structures perpetuate this division, giving each 'speciality' a different owner, based on technical skills required to execute, rather than conceptual skills required to plan' (Lannon, 1994).

Undeniably, there are significant problems for the client in terms of commissioning and managing several different agencies, especially in the context of the reduction in the size of marketing departments. The temptation for many of the integrated one-shop concept is overwhelmingly appealing. The attraction of using several different agencies is the possibility of selecting the best people in each field.

Moreover, there is a general lack of experienced people within the field of marketing communications, who exhibit expertise in the variety of fields which make up the total communications process. The need for individuals with a 'broad perspective' and an understanding of the contribution which each of the marketing communications disciplines can provide is underlined by a study by Cleland (1995).

The study by Kitchen and Schultz (1999) identified a number of barriers, real or perceived, to achieving IMC:

- Requires staff to be more generalist.
- Integrated agencies do not have talent across all marcom areas.
- IMC means staff have to develop new skills.
- IMC give a few individuals too much control.
- Client staff lack expertise to undertake IMC programmes.
- Client centralization difficulties.
- Client organizational structures constrain IMC.

Lannon (1994) asserts that most company communications policies are rooted in an outmoded past, when competition was less intense and the retailer was not anything like the powerful force it is today.

- the discontinuities of the 80s and into the 90s have fractured and fragmented not only the conventional media scene, but also the corporate structures and cultures of a more stable past.
- differing agendas of clients and agencies have eroded productive and trusting relationships between clients and their agencies.

Perhaps the most significant barrier to integration is the approach to communications budgeting. In most cases budgets are substantially determined on an 'historic' basis – considering what has been spent in the past – rather than against an evaluation of specific objectives. Often, individual departments are required to argue for budget tenure or an increase if the situation demands it. In the majority of cases, budgets are considered on a line-by-line basis, rather than holistically.

According to Kitchen (2005) the real weakness inherent in IMC is the failure of firms to invest major resources into the marketing and communications process. This failure results in IMC being used as a tactical device rather than making a strategic contribution.

Despite this, some market sectors are more advanced than others in the adoption of an integrated approach. Two, in particular, stand out as having made significant progress in the integration of their campaigns – the financial sector and retailers. In both cases, there has been a more widespread recognition of the benefits of integration. Campaigns by many of the commercial banks together with high street retailers underpin the advantages of integration. Certainly, most companies agree that the process of integration will increase apace, as much because of the need to deal with substantial communications budgets in a more positive manner, as from the drive towards global considerations where the desire for a common communications policy and the obvious financial benefits are of major importance.

The consumer and IMC

At the heart of the debate is the undeniable need to ensure the clear and effective communication of brand messages to consumers and others. The process demands a change of focus from share and volume to a detailed understanding of the extent to which the manufacturer can satisfy the needs and wants of consumers. The essential focus has to be on customers, relationships, retention levels and satisfaction.

Several authors have suggested that IMC, as well as benefiting the manufacturers of products and services, also works for the consumer. David Iddiols (2000) suggests that IMC works on three levels for the consumer.

1 It provides short-cuts to understanding what a brand stands for.
2 It adds depth and amplification to a particular message or set of brand values.
3 It demonstrates professionalism on the part of the brand owner.

Iddiols identifies three potential mechanics for providing integration across activities:

1 The use of some form of mnemonic device, such as the red telephone used by Direct Line.
2 A consistent proposition reinforced across all communications activities, such as Tesco's 'Every Little Helps'.
3 Conveying a consistent set of brand values, as in the examples of Coca Cola, Guinness or Levi's.

Further, he identifies three ways in which integration represents a coherent approach as far as consumers are concerned:

> Values driven – Guinness, Coca Cola, Halifax, Levi's
> Proposition driven – BT, Royal Mail
>
> Mnemonic driven –Direct Line, Scottish Widows, Walker's Crisps; Orange

Values: Conveying a consistent set of values is the strongest approach.

Proposition: Consistently delivering a proposition is important when establishing or shifting a brand's identity. This is apparent, for example,

with the Tesco line 'Every Little Helps' or L'Oreal's 'You're Worth It'.

Mnemonic: Employing a mnemonic device, such as the Red Phone for Direct Line or the Orange colour for Orange mobile phones, enabled both brands to establish an identity and gain a place in the publics' consciousness.

A key contributor to the achievement of effective and IMC is the appropriate use of market research – both to gain greater insight and understanding of consumer behaviour, as well as to achieve an understanding of the contributions of the individual tools of marketing communications.

The difficulty, as many writers acknowledge, is changing the focus of market research from a disintegrated mode into a holistic practice. Archer and Hubbard (1996) suggest that the vast bulk of market research carried out continues to reflect the outdated theories and structures of disintegrated marketing communications. They argue that a more holistic approach needs to be adopted to measure the aggregate outcomes of all marketing activity whilst, at the same time, monitoring the specific actions which contribute to that outcome.

The clear advantages of a more holistic approach to research are that it is more comprehensive, embracing all activities and both short- and long-term objectives; It provides the used with greater flexibility; and it is more realistic in that it measures the end result of all activities on the target audience.

International dimensions of IMC

Recent works reflect the increasing growth and impact of global marketing communications. Grein and Gould (1996) have suggested that the concept of IMC should be broadened and re-named Global Integrated Marketing Communications. Since, increasingly, manufacturers seek to implement communications campaigns across national boundaries, IMC requires integration beyond that of disciplines to encompass global management of campaigns. The management of international brands demands that strategic marketing decisions are integrated and co-ordinated across all relevant global markets.

They offer a new definition to incorporate the international dimension:

> A system of active promotional management which strategically co-ordinates global communications in all of its component parts both horizontally in

terms of countries and organizations and vertically in terms of promotion disciplines

A study conducted by Grein and Ducoffe (1998) revealed the extent to which advertising agencies in particular are becoming global enterprises, reflecting the needs of their, increasingly global, clients. They indicated that clients wish to use more standardized campaigns, which are easier and cheaper to administer, have proven track records in some countries, and result in a unified brand image and position around the world. For many companies, these benefits were considered sufficient to outweigh the less than perfect outcomes in some operating countries.

A direct consequence, confirmed by the study is a reduction in the extent of local creativity on international accounts. Once campaigns have been developed, usually in one country, they are implemented with relatively few variations on a worldwide basis.

However, as indicated by the work of Grein and Gould (1996), the level of inter-office communications made the task of effective integration difficult to achieve.

Summary

Using the analogy of Kitchen and Schultz (1999) who considered the state and acceptance of IMC against the product life cycle, it can be reasonably concluded that IMC is a marketing concept which is still emerging. As such, it might be positioned somewhere between its introduction and growth stage.

A point of issue is the difference between academic understanding of the concept and its role in the context of the practitioner. Kitchen argues that IMC, from the academic standpoint, is just over 10-years old, pointing to the work of Caywood *et al.* (1991) as the starting point for academic study.

In practice, the notion of IMC – albeit not the words – has been around for a considerably longer period. The author of this chapter was responsible for the establishment of a marketing communications agency, The Above and Below Group, in 1972 whose existence was founded on the provision of integrated communications activities to its clients.

However, several important dimensions of the practice of IMC can be recognized:

- IMC is an increasingly importance facet of the practice of marketing communications.
- An increasing number of client companies and their agencies strive to achieve deeper and better integration of their marketing communications activities.
- It reflects both an underlying conceptual as well as a practical change in the way in which marketing communications programmes are developed and implemented.
- The desire to achieve global presence for their brands drives companies towards the achievement of consistent imagery for their brands, and coherent messages in their communications programmes.
- In contrast to the views of Cornellisen *et al.* (2000), IMC is not a management fad.
- A continued inhibition to the development of IMC remains the internal structure of client companies and the defence of departmental independence.
- IMC will require the emergence of a new breed of communicators who can command a generalistic overview of all of the tools of marketing communications from a brand management perspective.
- Whilst it remains true that some brands can still achieve effective communications despite disintegration, 'all of the evidence points to the fact that it will take longer and runs the risk of confusing the very people you wish to sell to along the way' (Iddiols, 2000).

The way forward is summarized in the paper prepared by the American Productivity and Quality Centre Study in 1998. The Study identifies a series of key best practice issues which focus on the achievement of excellence in terms of brand development and communication. Those companies which most exemplified best practice:

- Concentrate on a few key brands and provide streamlined and sophisticated brand support.
- Provide the leadership and support of senior management in developing and sustaining successful brands.
- Provide the consumer and customer-led informational infrastructure to achieve an all-round view of the brand network.
- Define their brands in terms of core values, promise and personality that provide guidance, meaning and focus for all brand-related activities.
- View communication as an opportunity to project a unified image, not just of individual brands, but also of the company itself.

- Have started to move towards the financial measurement of brands and related communications activities.

Kitchen and Schultz (2000) argue for the imperative of IMC and suggest that it will become the essence of competitive advantage:

- because of the four goals of business – to increase, accelerate, stabilize cash flows and build shareholder value;
- because firms with strong brand relationship have significant competitive advantages, including getting a higher 'share of wallet' and obtaining price premiums, both of which result in increased revenues;
- because of the long-term effects of building brand equity and shareholder value;
- because of their contribution to business goals.

Similarly, Reid (2003) argues that IMC is 'not only about doing better marketing communications, but having a broader link to establishing a basis for competitive advantage'.

References

Alanko, J. (2000) The case for integration in B2B marketing, *Admap*, September.

American Association of Advertising Agencies (1993) *Marketing News*, 18 January.

Archer, J. and Hubbard, T. (1996) Integrated tracking for integrated communications, *Admap*, February.

Brannan, T. (1995) *A Practical Guide to Integrated Marketing Communications*, Kogan Page.

Caywood, C., Schultz, D. and Wang, P. (1991) *Integrated Marketing Communications: A Survey of National Consumer Goods Advertisers*, Northwestern University Report, June.

Cleland, K. (1995) A lot of talk, little action on IMC, *Business Marketing*, March.

Cook, W. (1994) The end of the line, *Marketing*, 24 February.

Cornellisen, J. P., Lock, A. R. and Gardner, H. (2000) Theoretical concept or management fashion, examining the significance of IMC, *Journal of Advertising Research*, **40**(5).

Cornellisen, J. P., Lock, A. R. and Gardner, H. (2001) The organisation of external communications disciplines: an integrative framework of dimensions and determinants, *International Journal of Advertising*, **20**(1).

Duncan, T. and Everett, S. (1993) Client perceptions of integrated marketing communications, *Journal of Advertising Research*, **33**(3).

Duncan, T. and Moriarty, S. E. (1998) A communication-based marketing model for managing relationships, *Journal of Marketing*, **62**(2).

Fletcher, W. (1998) Marketing skills can make sweet music together, *Marketing*, 12 February.

Franz, G. (2000) Better media planning for integrated communications, *Admap*, January

Grein, A. and Ducoffe, R. (1998) Strategic responses to market globalisation amongst advertising agencies, *International Journal of Advertising*, **17**(3).

Grein, A. F. and Gould, S. J. (1996) Globally integrated marketing communications, *Journal of Marketing Communications*, **2**(3).

Griffin, T. and McArthur, D. N. (1997) A marketing management view of integrated marketing communications, *Journal of Advertising Research*, September/October.

Gronstedt, A. and Thorson, E. (1996) Five approaches to organise an integrated marketing communications agency, *Journal of Advertising Research*, **36**(2).

Gronstedt, T. A. (1996) How agencies can support integrated communications, *Journal of Business Research*, **37**(3).

Iddiols, D. (2000) Marketing superglue: client perceptions of IMC, *Admap*, May.

Jeans, R. (1998) Integrating marketing communications, *Admap*, December.

Kitchen, P. (2005) New paradigm – IMC – under fire, *Communications Research*, **15**(1).

Kitchen, P. J. and Schultz, D. E. (1999) A multi-country comparison of the drive for IMC, *Journal of Advertising Research*, January/February.

Kitchen, P. J. and Schultz, D. E. (2000) The status of IMC: a 21st century perspective, *Admap*, September.

Lannon, J. (1994) What brands need now, *Admap*, September.

Lannon, J. (1996) Integrated marketing communications from the consumer end, *Admap*, February.

Linton, I. and Morley, K. (1995) *Integrated Marketing Communications*, Butterworth Heinemann.

Low, G. S. (2000) Correlates of integrated marketing communications, *Journal of Advertising Research*, May.

McArthur, D. N. and Griffin, T. (1997) A marketing management view of integrated marketing communications, *Journal of Advertising Research*, **37**(5).

Mitchell, H. (1995) *Client Perceptions of Integrated Marketing Communications*, Cranfield.

Nilson, T. S. (1992) *Value Added Marketing*, McGraw Hill.

Novak, G. J. and Phelps, J. (1994) Conceptualizing the integrated marketing communications phenomenon: an examination of its impact on advertising practices and its implications for advertising research, *Journal of Current Issues and Research in Advertising*, **16**(1).

O'Donoghue, D., writing in Cooper, A. (1997) *How to Plan Advertising*, 2nd edn, Cassell.

Ogilvy, D. (1993) *Ogilvy on Advertising*, Prion Books.

Picton, D. and Hartley, B. (1998) Measuring integration: an assessment of the quality of integrated marketing communications, *International Journal of Advertising*, **17**(4).

Pickton, D. and Hartley, B. (1998) Measuring integration: an assessment of the quality of integrated marketing communications, *Journal of Advertising*, November.

Proctor, T. and Kitchen, P. (2002) Communication in post-modern integrated marketing, *Corporate Communications*, **7**(3).

Reid, M. (2003) IMC – performance relationship. Further insight and evidence from the Australian marketplace, *International Journal of Advertising*, **22**(2).

Schultz, D. E., writing in Jones, J. P. (1999) *The Advertising Business*, Sage.

Schultz, D. E. and Kitchen, P. J. (1997) Integrated marketing communications in US advertising agencies: an exploratory study, *Journal of Advertising Research*, **37**(5).

Schultz, D. E., Tannenbaum, S. I. and Lauterborn, R. F. (1992) *Integrated Marketing Communications: Putting It Together and Making It Work*, NTC Business Books.

Schultz, D. E., Tannenbaum, S. I. and Lauterborn, R. F. (1995) *The Marketing Paradigm – Integrated Marketing Communications*, NTC Business Books.

Shimp, T. A. (1996) *Advertising Promotion: Supplemental Aspects of Integrated Marketing Communications*, Harcourt.

Smith, P. (1996) Benefits and barriers to integrated marketing communications, *Admap*, February.

Solomon, M. R. and Englis, B. G. (1994) The big picture: product complementarity and integrated communications, *Journal of Advertising Research*, January/February.

Van Raaij, W. F. (1998) Integration of Communication: Starting from the Sender or Receiver? in *Effectiveness in Communication Management*.

Yeshin, T. (1996) *The Development and Implications of Integrated Marketing Communications*, DMB& B Study.

Yeshin, T. (2006) *Advertising*, Thomson.

CHAPTER 18

Mass communications

DOUGLAS WEST

Introduction

As a term, 'mass communications' refers to particular media that can convey information to relatively large segments of the population, namely: press, TV, Web, posters and transport, radio and cinema. In the advertising business, these media are sometimes referred to as 'above-the-line' (ATL) as they are all media which offer commission. This chapter examines the key trends amongst the mass communications media including the shift from 'push' to 'pull', regulations and intrusiveness and the growing importance of measurement. Mass media strategy is then assessed in terms of whom to reach, where to reach them, when to reach them and finally what to say. Within this framework, the key elements in media class choice are reviewed related to creative scope, media history, distribution channels, budget and competitor activity and media vehicles in terms of costs, frequency and impact. The mass media are then considered in turn starting with the press. Each section examines types of media, spaces offered, audiences and audience research, pricing and effectiveness.

Key trends

Over the past 10 years or so, there has been a significant shift from 'push' to 'pull' marketing strategies that have had a significant impact on the mass media. The concept of 'push' is when marketers place information in order to influence members of an audience, whereas 'pull' is when members of an audience pull information towards themselves. Push is when a good or service is produced and offered to the market, whereas pull is when buyers order or configure products under their own initiate. The shift from push to pull represents a shift in power to the consumer which may be regarded as 'bad news' for marketers. However, there are a number of benefits such as only supplying goods and services when required which often leads to a reduction in inventory being carried and also the ability of producers to identify individual customers and target and tailor goods and services at a micro rather than macro level, so the shift is partly a necessary one as well as an opportunity. The result has been a general shift away from mass communications, leading to what might be loosely termed 'demassification' and a tendency to integrate with integrated marketing communications (IMC) (McGrath, 2005). As mass audiences have migrated away from the major TV networks and newspapers towards the Web, DVDs, cable and satellite, etc., even the classic mass media have fragmented towards more narrowcast formats. Major advertisers have increasingly shifted their marketing communications (MARCOMS) budgets away from the mass media towards sharper market focusing such as in-store video networks, the Web and specialist magazines and often attempts to create 'buzz' (Thomas, 2004). In response, the mass media have fragmented at a rapid rate. Creatively the role of the mass media has shifted, to some extent, from being the primary element in communications to a supporting role. For example, the use of TV commercials to encourage people to use particular websites rather than as stand-alone communications. Chang and Thorson (2004) conducted a set of experiments to test the existence of different synergy effects between the Web and TV and compared the information-processing model of synergy with that of repetition. They found television–Web synergy leads to significantly higher attention, higher perceived message credibility and a greater number of total and positive thoughts than did repetition. Also, people under synergistic conditions formed brand attitudes through the central processing route, whereas people under repetitive conditions formed brand attitudes through the peripheral route. Finally in the general context of changes, it should be noted that as the mass audience has began to evaporate, 'guerrilla' approaches have developed within ATL media to build audiences such as product placement in TV shows and films (e.g. *Minority Report* featured Nokia, the *Matrix Reloaded* featured Cadillac and *Casino Royale* featured Omega, Sony and Ford) and a variety of other ways such as attempts to raise interactivity with the use of voting through text messaging.

Regulation is an increasingly important component in the shift from push to pull. There are a variety of regulations and voluntary codes which protect the public, legislators, the media and advertisers (advertisers frequently use legislation to challenge the claims of rivals) across the world. Legislation tends to be generally successful with issues that can be more easily discerned such as banning particular products such as cigarette advertising, the advertising of junk food or what might or might not be claimed for product. However, voluntary codes work well across the UK, Germany, Canada, New Zealand and South Africa when it comes to 'grey areas' involving such matters as decency and taste which are more difficult to legislate for. Mistakes can still occur but scripts are often pre-vetted to ensure that they do not transgress any laws or codes before an agency goes into production. The link to push and pull is that much of advertising, particularly TV commercials, is seen as intrusive and irritating. People have reacted badly to the increased volume of commercials, the number of ads, the diverse range of advertisers (which means relatively few strike a chord with individuals) and often low budgets and production values (Speck and Elliott, 1997). Despite these issues, there is some evidence that homes with digital video recorders watch slightly more commercials than those without, despite being able to effectively zip through them. This is partly because households with digital video recorders

(DVRs) tend to watch more television than those without and partly because time shifting simply means that they watch the commercials later. A study by the UK media regulator, Ofcom, using in-home cameras in eight households found the vast majority of viewers with DVRs still watched programmes in real time and even when they did fast-forward recordings they still recognized the commercials.

Advertisers have no interest in switching off their audiences. The mass media are used as advertising tools with specific objectives in mind, primarily to reach cognitive, affective and/or conative objectives (Vakratsas and Ambler, 1999). The key trend here has been a general movement to measure results, particularly in terms of return on investment (ROI). However, this development has mitigated against the mass media because their value is notoriously difficult to measure and generally mainly the long-run, which is even harder to establish and the mass media are extremely effective at creating brand presence even if there is considerable wastage (Ambler and Hollier, 2004). For example, major network TV advertising for L'Oreal has greatly enhanced the brand over several years, but is difficult to measure in the immediate duration or 'halo' of the campaign. Having said that other more measurable media such as the Web are prone to problems. In particular, online 'pay per click' frauds have been found to cost advertisers US $100 million as even the most vigilant search engine will have trouble unearthing fraud. Returning to the mass communications media, rating points are the common currency to measure the exposure obtained, but this is not the same as measuring impact. A rating point measures the percentage of the potential audience exposed at a given time or over the life of a campaign. Points can relate to the audience as a whole or to a particular demographic segment, for example in the UK on a combined daily basis ITV1, C4 and Five reach about 55 per cent of men, 60 per cent of women and nearly 35 per cent of children. The main aspect is that advertisers normally need to look more closely at ratings than the general figures and the size of the universe watching at any particular time. A show with a low overall rating may be better than a show with a much larger rating at reaching a particular segment that they might be aiming for. In the US, both the Fox Network and HSBC have been successful at delivering relatively small, but highly sought after demographics. New measurement systems are underway, and last year Unilever and Proctor & Gamble joined forces in the US with project Apollo in an attempt to develop close to single-source data. The project is a pilot involving AC Nielsen and Arbitron covering 14 000 individuals who carry around mobile phone-sized people meters which record their exposure to all electronic media, TV, radio, iPods, cinema and the web with exposure to print and direct marketing covered by surveys and all are linked to purchasing data.

Mass media strategy

However, the essence of media strategy involves a number of 'rights'. That is to ensure that a clients' message is seen or heard by the right people, in the right place, in the right environment, with the right frequency and weight and at the right price and spending has to be targeted by buyer characteristics, geography and season. Classically, the process involves the four Ws:

1 *Who*: Establish the audience (e.g. '45–54-year-old women. . .').
2 *Where*: Identify the geographic area (e.g. 'Glasgow').
3 *When*: Establish the seasonality and timing of the purchase (e.g. 'the 4 weeks following Christmas').
4 *What*: Establish the creative proposition (e.g. 'the easiest folding bike on the market').

Specialists dominate media planning and buying. At the time of writing, the biggest is WPP's MediCom with over £800 millions in billings recorded in 2005 from clients such as BSkyB and T-Mobile. Another WPP media shop, MindShare, is close behind, thanks to winning Unilever's media spend in 1994. Other media shops worthy of note are Carat, part of the Aegis group; Starcom UK, part of Publicis; and ZenithOptimedia (also part of Publicis). Such is the importance of such media shops that, in a reversal of common practice, clients are increasingly briefing their media agency before they establish the creative brief.

Media shops make two kinds of decision: between media *classes* and media *vehicles*. A media class refers to the vertical decision involving media type, be it press, TV, radio, posters, cinema or the Web. Table 18.1 provides a breakdown of advertising expenditures by media. One of the most important aspects in choosing between classes is how well the chosen medium *reaches* the chosen audience (Abratt and Cowan, 1999). Generally,

Table 18.1　Total advertising expenditure by medium, 2005

	£million	%
Press	8589	43.6
Television	5543	28.2
Direct Mail	2371	12.0
Web	1366	6.9
Posters	1043	5.3
Radio	579	2.9
Cinema	188	1.0
Total:	19 679	100.0

Source: Advertising Association, *Advertising Statistics Yearbook 2006* (2006).

most media classes have a good reach of the population. In the case of television, only a tiny percentage of households do not have a television set, however; the number of readers of newspapers and magazine is slowly, but steadily, falling each year; the cinema audience is much more likely to be made up of younger people; posters tend to reach urban audiences more than rural; commercial radio tends to be more downmarket than its BBC (non-commercial) counterparts.

Creative scope is another element to consider. How does the chosen medium use audio and/or visual communications and with what context? The first issue is simply whether the strategy needs sound, movement or a still picture/printed word for impact? If so, different media can offer these either singularly or in combination. Whereas context refers to the primary location of the receiver and the time allocated. For example, most people watch television in their homes with family or friends, newspapers are often read while commuting or at work alone, and posters are seen singularly or in groups in the community at large. Such issues can affect choices. For example, car companies normally use posters to 'announce' new cars to the community. A further issue is timing. Some media classes set the time for the message to be decoded by the receiver, whereas others allow the receiver to decide upon the time allocated. Thus, if a full page ad is placed in the *Daily Mail*, the reader can flick over it or give it their full attention. A TV commercial by contrast sets the time whatever the requirements of the receiver.

The conventional strategy is to place ads for 'boring' products in media where the advertiser can determine the time.

Media history is a straightforward issue. The questions are what has been used before and what worked? Risk-averse advertisers in particular are inclined to use familiar classes of media. Occasionally, a risk is taken and it can pay of spectacularly well as when Whiskas switched much of its budget away from broadcast media to direct marketing, but this is rare.

The *location* of the audience located also needs to be considered. Thus, if you are targeting a specific district within Bristol or Manchester, local media will be more cost-effective. National/Pan-Regional campaigns require media with larger coverage.

Distribution channels may play an important role in choice too. If there is a channel in the distribution chain, how will they react to your choice of media class? Try telling a major supermarket chain that you want a significant amount of shelf space for a new shampoo and that you are going to spend a lot of money on advertising the product on match boxes! The chain will likely expect to see a heavy weight TV campaign.

Finally, the size of the *budget* will affect the strategy. How big is your budget? What is the threshold for the effective use of the chosen medium? If you have just about enough money to produce a TV commercial or a large poster, but little left over to buy the needed frequency, it might be best to consider a cheaper medium. Budgets are generally subject to the whims of the marketplace and the environment. For example, the hurricanes of 2005 in the US led to an enormous increase in spending by insurance companies (up by about a third in 2004) in the mass communications media, whereas the 2006 football World Cup had hardly any effect on UK advertising spends. In real terms, advertisers are spending more on both press and TV in terms of cost-per-viewer reached over the last 10–15 years, according to a variety of industry observers.

The final question to ask is what media class *competitors* are using? They might have made the right choice (or not!). Planners generally recommended going into similar classes if you can match competitors' budgets, but target different ones if not. For example, a company with a limited budget might use *Sky* magazine to reach customers of a rival product who advertise on television.

The extent of effectiveness between different media remains context dependent as much as on the circumstances and what you want to achieve. Some small insight has been provided by Dertouzoz and Garber (2006) who examined the effectiveness of advertising by the US. Army to promote enlistments using data between 1981and 1984. They examined advertising effects separately for television, radio, magazines and newspapers. Advertising–sales ratios were consistent with general advertising practices and they found that the advertising did work in that enlistment was achieved. Their work suggested that if an advertiser only has a relatively small budget, then print media should be used first, then radio and television added as budgets expand. Given the time frame and the restricted use of media, these suggestions need to be treated cautiously.

Media *vehicle* choice concerns the choice within the chosen class, for example if the press is chosen, will it be the *Telegraph* or the *Daily Mirror*? Or, if TV is chosen, what programmes will be targeted? The choice of media vehicles will depend on a number of quantitative and qualitative issues. Media planners and buyers will seek the most effective vehicles for their clients within the chosen medium. One of the key analyses to make is the 'cost per thousand' (CPT) – the cost of reaching a thousand people through the vehicle in comparison with other vehicles:

$$\frac{\text{Unit cost of a message}}{\text{Audience sixe}} \times 1000$$

or:

$$\frac{\text{Unit cost of a message}}{\text{Audience size}/1000}$$

Much depends on who is being compared in that advertisers rarely want to buy an entire audience so there will be considerable wastage in buying vehicles simply because they reach big audiences. A much better calculation is the CPT of the relevant target market, but decisions cannot be left to numbers. Thus, the numbers might suggest a particular tabloid 'red-top' newspaper for a luxury car advertiser. However, qualitatively the car company's brand might not benefit from the association with the red-top and a quality daily (with a less cost-effective audience than the red-top) will be the preferred choice. Also, editorial content and positioning count with media vehicles. Aspects such as the amount of editorial devoted to cooking or motoring might be important, or specific editorial content, the graphics used, and in the press such aspects as editorial excellence, political stance, consistency of press run quality, match and balance of colour.

Having lined-up the choice of vehicle, the key decisions involve frequency and impact and each issue will impact the other. With limited resources, agencies and their clients are forced to trade-off one against the other. If you double the frequency, without the commensurate doubling of the budget, the spaces purchased will inevitably have to be halved and impact consequently reduced. The key strategic issue here is the advertisers' decay rate.

The concept of the decay rate refers to the implication of stopping all advertising activity (Ray and Webb, 1986; Broadbent, 1999). If you stop MARCOMS tomorrow, what happens to the brand's awareness and positive attitudes? What would it look like in a week, a month or in 6 months time? Powerful brands like IBM and Max Factor would have extremely slow decay rates and would likely be well known after years of no MARCOMS. However, lesser brands that are not top-of-mind in their product categories may soon be forgotten. If awareness and positive attitudes play a major role in their sales, then they will be in considerable trouble if they stop the campaign. Such brands get 'hit' twice in the marketplace. They have to maintain some presence, but the need to maintain this may mean that they have to take smaller spaces and are probably going to be less visible. Bigger brands can use MARCOMS between intervals of non-activity and so not only have more resources to devote to MARCOMS, but can purchase bigger/higher impact spaces as a consequence. Strategically all that smaller advertisers can do is to attempt to maximize their creativity so that their smaller budgets can have a higher impact than the often bland communications of market leaders.

Mass communications exposures can take some time to 'wearin', but they also eventually 'wearout' (Ray and Webb, 1986). Conventional wisdom dictates that the response function to MARCOMS tends to be concave, that is, with each subsequent impression the response is reduced (Broadbent, 1999). The idea being that most impact is made with the first impression and thereafter the impact diminishes. The implication is that wearin is fast and wearout is continuous. It is certainly commonsense that once you have paid attention to a piece of MARCOMS, you are unlikely to give the same degree of attention subsequently. For example, if you read an ad in a newspaper giving

details about a new camera, you would be unlikely to bother to read it again in its entirety. Strategically it means that clients, all things being equal, need to produce a piece of MARCOMS that is so creative and entertaining that it can be seen again and again and still be enjoyed (as with the Guinness surfing commercial). Another related consideration is polychronic behaviour whereby people juggle several media in real time (Bluedorn et al., 1992; Pilotta and Schultz, 2005). It is obviously nothing new as people have commonly read a newspaper or a book while watching television; yet, new media have taken polychronic time to a new level such as watching television, surfing the web and playing music all at the same time.

At a macro level, clients with high awareness can afford to use high-impact bursts of MARCOMS expenditure as they will not be forgotten in the intervening periods. On the other hand, clients with low awareness may need a more continuous ('drip') spend to maintain their presence. Timing of purchase may also play a role. Car companies face seasonality of purchases, but also know that a new car is a considered purchase so that they need continual presence in the marketplace as there is a long gestation period in decision making. Micro level considerations involve timings during the week or month. For example, most household goods are purchased on Fridays and over the weekends, so a lot of clients aim to reach their audiences on Wednesdays and Thursday just prior to consumer spending.

The media

Press

The origins of today's advertising business lay with the press, and across the world more money is still spent on the press than any other medium (see Table 18.1). Newspapers come in a variety of formats (see Figure 18.1). Dailies are issued every day such as the *Sun*, *The Times* and *USA Today*. Sundays tend to have the same standing as dailies such as the *Sunday Times*, *Sunday Telegraph* or *People*. Weeklies tend to be less prestigious and more local than the nationals such as the *Henley Standard*. The UK is unusual in the strength of its national press as most countries only have one or two national newspapers (e.g. the *Globe and Mail* in Canada). Recent years have seen the emergence of the *Herald Tribune* and the *Financial Times* as

Figure 18.1   Newspaper formats
Source: www.backissuenewspapers.co.uk/

'international newspapers' with a growing readership across the world (though the FT is conscious of remaining 'connected' to its UK base). Digital printing technology has enabled newspapers to publish anywhere in the world where production and distribution facilities allow and markets exist.

In terms of format, newspapers come in three sizes: broadsheets like the *Telegraph* (60 mm × 38 cm), tabloids like the *Daily Mirror* (38 cm × 30 cm) and Berliner like the *Guardian* (47 cm × 31.5 cm). The number of sections being offered has grown with alacrity over the years with Sunday quality newspapers offering 8–10 sections. The vast majority of newspapers are 'printing' simultaneously online and some newspapers are purely online with subscribers able to identify what interests them and how they want to see the layout, though this remains a largely minority activity as yet with most people preferring hard copies of their papers. Traditionally, the nationals only offered spot colour (one colour only) but now full colour is available across all newspapers.

Circulation is the number of copies distributed and should not be confused with the number of copies sold or read. For example, the *Sun* has a circulation of around 2.9 millions (Audit Bureau of Circulation ABC), but is read by about 8 million people a day and the *Telegraph* around 0.8 million and 2 millions, respectively (National Readership Survey NRS). Overall readership is in long-term decline for most newspapers across the UK (and across most of the Western world).

According to the ABC, between 1999 and 2005 the circulation of popular dailies has fallen from 10 to 9 millions, quality dailies from 2.5 to 2 millions, popular Sundays have fallen from 10 to 9 millions and quality Sundays from 13 to 11 millions (all figures rounded up or down). Some of the biggest recent downward trends have affected the *Sun*, down by over 700 000; the *Daily Mirror* which lost about 500 000 readers and the *Daily Star* whose readership fell by over 100 000 towards the end of 2005, according to the NRS. However, the qualities benefited from some revamps over the period between 2005 and 2006, in particular a move to smaller format which saw *The Times* increase its readership by just over 150 000.

The UK has around a 1000 regional newspapers which are mainly published on a weekly basis and are either paid for such as the *Evening Standard* or the *Yorkshire Post* or distributed free as with the various metro editions such as in London and Manchester. The battle for commuters in London is particularly frantic with both News International and Associated Newspapers introducing free papers and aiming for circulations of around 400 000 amongst passing workers and shoppers in 2006 (which brings the number of London papers to five). Overall, there has been a great deal of consolidation amongst publishers of regionals led by Trinity Mirror, Newsquest, Johnstone Press, Northcliffe and Associated Newspapers.

There are around 2500 consumer magazines and 5000–6000 business, trade and professional publications. It is worth pointing out that many of the UK's professional magazines have considerable standing and prestige around the world with publishing houses such as Oxford University Press and the like, as well as business magazines such as the *Economist*. Magazines are published weekly and bi-weekly (women's, TV and Radio, current affairs and special interest), monthly and bi-monthly (mainly special interest such as *Empire* or *FHM*) or quarterly (mainly professional and academic journals) and mainly overall circulate nationally, but a minority of magazines are regional and sometimes local. Consumer magazines such as *Vogue* and the *Radio Times* are generally purchased over the counter at local newsagents, supermarkets or WH Smith. TV and Radio are the concerns of the biggest circulating magazines for example, *Sky* has a circulation of nearly 7 millions. Some magazines such as *Time* have international editions, but the editorial is tailored to global regions such as Asia and Europe.

By contrast, business magazines circulate to some extent by subscription, but often are free if readers meet criteria set by the magazine concerned. For example, *Marketing* the weekly trade journal for marketers is sent free to high-profile marketers. The variety of magazines in both the consumer and business marketplaces is enormous. They can be divided into 'horizontal' magazines which appeal across industries (e.g. *Accountancy Age* and the *Finance Director*) or 'vertical' with an appeal within a specific industry only (e.g. the *British Medical Journal* or *Trucking*).

Research into press readership is relatively well advanced in the UK compared to many countries. Newspaper and major magazine readership research is undertaken by the NRS which measures average readership from the age of 15+. Regional newspaper research is undertaken for the Newspaper Society and together both surveys provide a significant amount of data about who is reading what. They indicate, for example, that just under half of all adults read a daily newspaper at least once a week, just over half for the Sundays, similar figures for regional weeklies, falling to a third for general weekly magazines and just over a fifth for any woman's weekly. It is also possible to relate readership figures to a wide range of products and brands using the Target Group Index (TGI) which surveys a panel of people about their media and buying habits. However, the surveys cannot provide aggregate data on how much of a newspaper is read or what the impact of the advertising is, hence the advertising

business talks about audiences having opportunities to see (OTS) advertising rather than their impact, as noted above. The surveys do not prove that the advertising was seen and read simply that particular demographics are reading particular newspapers and magazines providing the aforementioned OTS. A study investigating issues associated with the dimensional representation of memory for print advertisements and the antecedent factors that relate to those dimensions was conducted by Leigh *et al.* (2006) and questioned whether memory for print advertising is unidimensional or multidimensional, as assessed by aided recall and recognition methods. They found that recall was influenced by cognitive and, to a lesser extent, by effective factors, whereas recognition is primarily influenced by affective factors. Moorman *et al.* (2002) conducted a study of the effects of context-induced psychological responses on the processing of magazine advertisements. Test ads were placed in the circulation of three magazine titles and a representative sample of subscribers were interviewed. The results show that magazine-induced liking and positive feelings had a positive influence on attitude towards the ad. Furthermore, thematically congruent advertisements were better remembered than incongruent advertisements. Indeed, it is interesting to note that despite much of the gloom around press readership declines over the past few years that Procter & Gamble (P&G) decided to shift about 3 per cent of its TV budget into the press in 2006 in support of big spending brands Olay and Pantene. It is not entirely clear why the shift was made, though effectiveness must have been an underlying factor.

When it comes to pricing, newspaper space is sold by the single column centimetre (SCC) in the UK with larger spaces being sold as quarter, half or single pages. Rate cards are provided for publications in considerable detail by British Rate and Data (BRAD). For example, a colour page in the *Sun* costs around £50 000 and £59 000 in the *Daily Telegraph*. However, published rates are the starting point for negotiation and depending on how many insertions requested, the time of year, day of week and location within the newspaper, the final price paid may vary considerably. At this point, it should be pointed out that there is a significant difference between the national and regional press in types of advertiser. Nationals primary advertising business emanates from display advertising (65–80 per cent), whereas the regionals are much more focused on classified which can

Figure 18.2   Sun local and 'Print Your Own' daily telegraph

account for up to 50 per cent of their revenue. Thus, the regionals have particularly suffered in competition with the Web with the growth of career and job websites. The nationals have begun to erode the regional advertising base as 2006 saw News Corporation's *Sun* newspaper launch a free classified site called 'Sun Local' and increasing use of web technology with downloadable papers (see Figure 18.2).

Normally, the copy and the images are produced separately and merged in a digital format and, to some degree, can be produced by novices. However, in practice it takes considerable skill and expertise, especially when producing full colour advertisements for glossy magazines where light, shade and tone need to be balanced to best effect. Costs can be reduced by centralizing production and doing volume deals with studios, although several large circulation newspapers have designated studios that they trust to produce the needed format and this can raise prices.

Buying space in magazines is largely about pages single or DPS (double-page spread) and subdivisions of pages rather than SCCs. Placing within newspapers is a sensitive issue but it is even more acute in magazines and their rate cards normally reflect this. Premiums are paid for outside and inside covers, pages early in the magazines and generally pages on the right hand side of the magazine where it is found readers glance more intently than on the left. Colour is mainly what magazines are about, though it is possible to buy black & white spaces which, many argue, have an impact by their contrast. Another popular space option is to buy a 'bleed page' – one that does not have a white border around it which has been found to be more effective in being read (though bleed pages are so common in magazines, they are hardly worth mentioning). Examples of pricing would be £17 320 for a colour page in *Cosmopolitan*, £10 752 for the same space in *BBC Top Gear* and £5750 in *Marketing Week*.

TV

The structure and nature of viewing commercial television has changed dramatically. From its *terrestrial* origins in the 1950s TV has developed *satellite*, *cable* and *digital* and *web* TV broadcast media with options to watch on TVs, personal computers (PCs) and, on the near horizon, mobile phones and personal digital assistants (PDAs). Since the 1980s, there has been a growth of cable and satellite television. Increasingly, speciality channels have emerged covering specific categories such as music (e.g. MTV). Also, there has been a shift towards more 'opting in' behaviour with entire channels devoted to selling such as QVC and the Home Shopping Network.

Terrestrial TV is dominated by the non-commercial BBC with BBC1 and BBC2 and then

ITV1, Channel 4 and Five (first broadcast in 1997). ITV1 comprise 15 regional licenses in the UK and is the most popular of all commercial stations reaching about 45 million people a week with the largest programming budget in Europe of about £1 billion and broadcasts about 6000 hours of programming a year; with around 25 per cent of content from independent production companies. Channel 4, on the other hand, is a statutory corporation under the licence from the UK regulator, Ofcom, with a remit to be both complimentary and different in programming to ITV1. It has no production facilities of its own and commissions all its programming (with S4C in Wales broadcasting in Welsh) of which 'Big Brother' is undoubtedly the most famous (or infamous). Channel 5 was rebranded as 'Five' in 2002 and was awarded its franchise in a competitive tender.

Overall, BB1 has the largest audience share at around 21 per cent followed by ITV1 with around 18 per cent, Channel 4 with 10 per cent, BBC2 at 9 per cent and Five with around 6 per cent. Of course, all these channels have lost out to the increasing time people spend on the Internet and not just competition with the multitude of new channels and often cannibalized by their digital clones available on the Freeview platform and Sky.

Direct Broadcasting by Satellite (DBS) is dominated by BSkyB multichannel packages which include the Disney Channel and Paramount TV. Transmissions are made through high powered satellites which send signals to household dishes (Sky also offers all the terrestrial and free digital channels). Ofcom calculates that just under a third of all homes in the UK (nearly 8 million) subscribe to BSkyB and BSkyB is currently the one channel to offer some broadcasts in HDTV format.

Cable has been slow to grow in the UK given the huge costs of laying cables and what has been considered by some as poor marketing compared to BSkyB, as well as little perceived advantage over aerial transmission as digital has unfolded. Cable reaches about 13 per cent of households in the UK representing over 3.3 million homes. The number of cable operators has rapidly reduced since the late 1990s and is now led by Virgin Media, formed in 2007 from the merger of the cable company NTL: Telewest and Virgin's mobile phone division. Having said this, cable offers significant potential to exploit interactive media and broadband (Virgin Media offers cable, video on demand, broadband, mobile and land line) and can offer some flexible packages to consumers, so continues to have considerable potential.

As noted above, digital TV may be part of the reason why Cable services have not taken-off as originally anticipated. Digital broadcasting was introduced in 1998 into the UK by BSkyB (then Sky) offering over 200 channels. There are many advantages to digital broadcasting as it offers superior sound and vision, and the ability to compress more channels into the same bandwidth compared to analogue along with a range of interactive options. On the downside, it is subject to occasional picture freeze and is not available to all parts of the UK. However, set-top converter boxes have come down in price significantly in the past 5 years (around £25 at the time of writing), and the UK Government plans to stop analogue broadcasting between 2008 and 2010, beginning with the borders region, putting the UK in line with trends in the US and Europe. Digital TV platforms include: digital terrestrial television (DTT), Digital Satellite and Cable, and Free Sat and Cable. For example, in the case of terrestrial, ITV introduced ITV2 as a free-to-air digital channel aiming at a younger audience in 1998; ITV3 was then introduced in 2004 aiming at older (35+) more upmarket audiences with a focus on movie repeats and drama scheduling and a year later, ITV4 was added to the portfolio aimed at younger men with a remit to cover sport, film and entertainment. ITV2 has proved one of the most watched of all the digital channels based on its spin-offs from ITV1's reality shows, according to Broadcasters' Audience Research Board (BARB) figures gaining just over 2 per cent of viewing in multichannels homes compared to Sky One with just under 2 per cent.

Most TV commercials are made by advertising agencies and shown on airtime purchased from the respective channel or network. Space has traditionally been purchased on TV by spots – short commercials placed into breaks *within* programmes or *between* programmes. They sell in incremental units of 10 seconds from 10 to 60. The majority of spots consists of 30 seconds but can occasionally run for several minutes in length (e.g. a recent commercial for Channel No. 5 featuring the Australian actress Nicole Kidman ran for 3 minutes).

To maximize revenues, TV companies offer a heavily discounted rate card for peak times; however, all spots can be 'pre-empted'. Imagine an auction where you have made your bid, then someone else comes along and makes a higher bid – so you lose. Thus, even if you have booked a spot, a contractor will sell the same spot to a higher bidder and unless you are prepared to counter with a higher offer the spot will be lost. In order to sell the less popular daytime spots, contractors offer packages of commercials across the week with some prime spots included. Another offer is a guaranteed home impression (GHI). A GHI is where the contractors sell the reaching of a particular size of audience rather than particular spots. Your commercial will be shown until the GHI has been reached.

In the US, the length of time allowed for commercials within programmes is unregulated being left to the market, and typically commercial breaks last for about 20 minutes or so per hour. Specific regulations differ across European broadcasters who, on the whole, tend to be restricted to 10–14 minutes of advertising per hour. In the UK, cable and satellite broadcasters are allowed to show an average of 9 minutes of advertising per hour; terrestrial broadcasters can show an average of 7 minutes per hour which increases to 8 minutes at peak times (7 to 9 am and 6 to 11 pm). The cost of a 30-second TV commercial on ITV1 across the whole network runs at somewhere over £100 000 which is about £7 per 1000 people. In order to maximize the audience, one of the main techniques used with TV commercials is to break shows into segments in places where the viewer is left in suspense, particularly with some kind of 'cliffhanger'. Quiz shows such as ITV1's 'Who Wants to be a Millionaire?' provide endless opportunities to leave viewers in anticipation and hence are highly popular with advertisers. However, technology such as TiVo and Sky + enables viewers to save programmes to their hard discs and to completely eliminate the advertising – leading advertisers towards product placement and heightening the importance of creativity. Furthermore, in the US there is an increasing use of the so-called 'banners' (or 'logo bugs') as with news cable or digital news broadcasts where 5–15 per cent of the screen is taken up with a commercial to 'force' the viewer to watch. With the clutter and fragmentation occurring on TV, the importance of spots is being diminished when compared to programme sponsorship and informercials. Research generally shows that about a third of the audience is 'lost' during commercial breaks. Studies dating back to Allen's pioneering 1965 work and other researchers who have filmed people watching television (e.g. Clancey, 1994) have observed that it is generally a chaotic affair involving conversation, playing with children, doing hobbies, reading, etc., such that only about a third of viewing can be described as 'pure'.

'Contextual' commercials appear to be the latest trend and are being pioneered in Japan with a partnership between Japan's second largest agency Hakuhodo and Yomiuri Telecasting, one of Japan's big four networks (*Wall Street Journal* online). In the contextual environment, commercials are identified closely to programmes to the extent of featuring the same actors and plot-lines which means devotees of a programme have to stay and watch them or miss the plot development. In one scene, a woman sits in a café longing for a family which leads her to imagine a specific Toyota minivan with her children and in the break a further scene is played out where she is seen researching the van online. Such developments are at the early stage, and the potential for audiences to switch-off and feel manipulated is clear. It is worth noting that this may be a purely TV phenomenon. De Pelsmacker *et al.* (2002) found in their study of context that television context ad content and brand recall were positively influenced by a positively appreciated context, but this was not the case for print.

Television audiences are measured by BARB (see Figure 18.3) which is owned by the BBC, ITV, Channel 4, BSkyB and the IPA. Their approach starts with a sample of 50 000 people who form the so-called 'establishment survey' from just over 5000 households chosen for fitting 'people meters'. These meters use remote detection and monitor TV and video usage each second that they are switched on with people recording on a handset when they are in/out of the room. The information is stored in the meter and remotely downloaded through the telephone line between 2 and 6 am and the data are provided electronically or in hard copy formats. They essentially show that, as you would expect, breakfast time is predominantly by child viewers, the daytime largely by housewives, unemployed and retired, and then a broader base appears after about 6 pm with the more affluent viewers coming in much later between 9 and 10 pm. The late night attracts TV addicts, people coming in late from the pub, etc. and followers of particular 'cult' programmes. Given the sample size, BARB has trouble coping with audience sizes for programmes gaining less than 1 per cent audience share and there are a variety of experiments underway to improve the technology involved. It is clear that in planning for TV you need more than just the quantitative data available and have to exercise considerable qualitative judgements as well.

Depending upon the creative work, TV commercials can be effective in cutting through the clutter and occasionally embedding themselves

WEEK ENDING: 21 January 2007

HOURS OF VIEWING, SHARE OF AUDIENCE AND REACH: Including Timeshift

Channel	Average Daily Reach		Weekly Reach		Average Weekly Viewing	Share
	000s	%	000s	%	Hrs: Mins per person	%
ALL/ANY TV	43,112	76.9	52,843	94.3	27:53	100.0
BBC 1 (inclu. Brkfast News)	30,025	53.6	47,514	84.8	6:00	21.5
BBC 2	17,051	30.4	37,825	67.5	2:24	8.6
TOTAL BBC1/BBC 2	33,165	59.2	48,876	87.2	8:24	30.1
ITV (inclu. GMTV)	25,266	45.1	44,208	78.9	5:32	19.8
CHANNEL 4/SAC	20,428	36.5	41,719	74.5	3:00	10.8
five	10,638	19.0	29,591	52.8	1:28	5.3
TOTAL/ANY COMM. TERR.Tv	33,483	59.8	49,449	88.2	10:00	35.9
Other Viewing	26,112	46.6	39,275	70.1	9:28	34.0

Figure 18.3 Example of BARB data
Source: BARB.

Figure 18.4 Ridley Scott's Apply commercial, 1984

into popular culture such as with McDonald's 'I'm lovin it' (incidentally McDonald's first global campaign) and Budweiser's 'Whassup' campaign. In the US, the Super Bowl football match is equally famous for its typically groundbreaking commercials which are shown between the game, the most famous being Ridley Scott's iconic commercial for the Apple Macintosh which was only ever aired the once during the Super Bowl in 1984 (see Figure 18.4). A plethora of factors have been found to affect the effectiveness of TV commercials. For example, Whipple and McManamon (2002) evaluated male and female voices in terms of their communication effectiveness. They found that men and women were judged equally effective as presenters for neutral products. For a female-gender-product, the sex of the spokesperson and the announcer significantly affected advertising evaluations, whereas for a male-gender- product the sex of the presenters had no impact on evaluations of the commercials.

Pop music has often been used in TV commercials since the 1980s. Previously, it had been largely limited to jingles and incidental music and the majority of performers regarded such commercialization as an anathema to their work. Gradually, the mood has changed and pop songs commonly accompany commercials mainly to add likeability and a 'feel good' factor rather than relevance to the music or song. Aretha Franklin, Michael Jackson, David Bowie, The Beatles, Iggy Pop, The Rolling Stones amongst many others have accompanied advertisers like Burger King, Pepsi-Cola and Microsoft. Apart from the royalties songs used as soundtracks for commercials have occasionally revitalized careers. Sometimes the trend has been reversed and an advertiser has had an unplanned success with a soundtrack such as with Levi's hit singles 'Inside', 'Spaceman' and 'Flat Beat' (Levi's does not welcome such hits and currently strives to produce commercials that will be remembered for the message rather than the music).

Web

The Internet user profile has changed greatly over its development since the late 1980s (the Internet, as we know it, dates back to 1969 with a computer connection between University of California, Los Angeles (UCLA) and Stanford). Early users were mainly young males, but of the 25 million or so Internet users in the UK, the ratio between male and female is now largely balanced. 25–35-year olds make up almost half of all users with 15–24 at just under a fifth. Just under a fifth of users aged 55+ and the so called 'grey surfers' in their 60s, 70s and 80s have greatly increased in number.

Over one-third of the people in the UK use the Internet every day. According to the TGI, most home users of the Web access travel sites (just over 25 per cent) followed by news (just under 20 per cent), event listings and music/MP3 (around 16 per cent each), then sport (15 per cent) and employment opportunities (13 per cent). Users tend to be higher earners and the top ISPs are BT (15 per cent) and AOL (10 per cent), but there has also been a tremendous growth amongst 'free' access ISP's (free but bundled with other subscribed services) such as TalkTalk and Orange. As to top sites: the top portal remains Google; the BBC are top for entertainment; commerce is dominated by eBay, Amazon, Tesco, Yahoo! and Argos, with Multimap.com and Expedia for travel. Books, music, DVD's and clothes are the primary products purchased online given the standardization of such products.

The Advertising Association estimates that just over £1350 million was spent on Internet advertising in the UK in 2005 with spending growing between nearly 80 and 140 per cent year-on-year since 2003 with the finance sector in the lead followed by travel & transport and entertainment & media. *Banner ads* are a new form of mass medium advertising and are used for creating awareness and recognition. They take on a wide variety of forms and names such as 'side panels', 'skyscrapers' and 'verticals'. It is not possible to be precise given the huge number of sites available, but the available evidence suggests response rates are (not surprisingly) extremely low at less than 1 per cent. Despite the general image of banner ads being irritating and irrelevant, research has suggested that they can be highly effective in gaining awareness and branding. There is evidence to suggest that, in relation to functional and expressive products, there are major differences between the performances of banner ads for the two product types. Dahlén and Bergendahl (2001) found that banner ads work better as 'transporters' to target ads for functional products, whereas banner ads for expressive products work better through ad impressions. They also found that consumers who click on banner ads for expressive products tend to be greater users of and be more positively disposed towards the brand. *Pop-ups* tend to be larger

than banner ads and appear when people access or sometimes leave particular sites. By their very nature, they have a greater potential to annoy than banner ads and all the leading browsers such as Explorer, Mozilla and Avant have blocking software so that they are less of a nuisance. However, there is evidence to suggest that the response to pop-ups depends on the attitude towards the ad (Aad) and their format, and they can be effective if they contain relevant information (Burns and Lutz, 2006). Finally, *interstitials* are ads that appear on screens while waiting for sites to download. Like pop-ups, interstitials have the potential to irritate because they appear while the site is loading but research suggests that people are more receptive to them.

Overall, the evidence suggests that people try and avoid advertising on the web. This has led to 'banner blindness' and extremely low click-through rates. Chang-Hoan and Cheon (2004) examined three latent variables of Web ad avoidance: perceived goal impediment, perceived ad clutter and prior negative experience and found that these constructs successfully explain why people cognitively, affectively and behaviourally avoid advertising messages on the Web, but perceived goal impediment was found to be the most significant antecedent. In essence, people avoid advertising on the Web whenever it gets in the way of what they have set out to do. One new development on the Web is the decision by ABC in the US to trial the streaming of TV shows online and for free which may go a small way to enhancing the impact of web advertising. Shows such as Lost and Desperate Housewives were posted by ABC the day after they aired on TV accompanied by regular and interactive commercials from the likes of Toyota and P&G. Given ABC controlled the rate of streaming, it was not possible for viewers to skip commercials. However, with the current infrastructure it is not possible to send individual video streams across the entire network to viewers and even those in the trial had to cope with a poor experience. Future development will undoubtedly open up the possibilities of web-TV.

Posters

Posters (billboards in the US and, commonly called so, in the UK) are large outdoor advertising structures normally cited close to high density/traffic areas in cities, roads or motorways, where regulations allow, aiming at passing pedestrians or drivers/passengers. For international advertisers, the medium is one of the most difficult to standardize for the sizes available vary greatly along with regulations and practices. Having said that, posters also vary greatly in the UK with difference sizes of boards, a huge variety of transport options (taxis, bus stations, tube stations, etc.) and formats (e.g. neon signs).

Posters can have a tremendous impact particularly if used with wit or intrigue. In many respects, their creative nature is most closely aligned to radio in the need for a short and sharp creative appeal along with repetition (aside from some transport media such as tube cards which can carry longer copy). Furthermore, it now offers the only truly flexible mass medium; being the only one that can deliver relatively centralized mass coverage in the way that TV used to be able to do; and at the other extreme, can be highly localized. For the most part, they have normally been regarded as a support medium for TV, but with the increasing inability of TV to provide a mass audience in a relatively straightforward manner (e.g. using a couple of commercial channels), there is a growing, albeit small, trend to use posters as the primary medium to great effect often generating considerable PR value as with the Bennetton, Wonderbra and fcuk campaigns. A survey by Taylor *et al.* (2006) revealed four primary reasons why posters are mainly used: visibility, media efficiency, local presence and tangible response. The study also identified eight executional factors that are principally associated with successful posters: name identification, location of the poster, readability, clarity of the message, used as a tool of integrated marketing communications (IMC), powerful visuals, clever creative and information provision.

The availability of posters has improved considerably over the past 20 years with the demise of the till countermanded (TC) system whereby the leading tobacco and drink companies had held prime sites across the UK on an agreement until they decided to give them up. Even before the banning of cigarette advertising, this convention had begun to decline and most sites are freely available by the contractors such as Clear Channel, JCDecaux, Primesight and Maiden. As such posters are largely booked *ad hoc* fortnightly and offered in packages equivalent to ISBA TV areas. The commission structure is frequently complex as agencies are entitled to the standard 15 per cent commission which is generally rebated, because it is a specialist area that often requires the use of a specialist outdoor agency and additional 5 per cent

can be levied from the site owner. At the year end specialist shops generally collect a further 5–8 per cent depending on the volume of space bought. Some specialist outdoor agencies such as Gen Outdoor have decided to introduce flat fees to simplify the whole system.

Poster panels are sold in 'sheets' primarily ranging from 4 (52.5 cm × 101.5 cm) through 6, 16, 32, 48 and 96 (12 m × 3 m) and there are around 115 000 panels in the UK with over half offered in the 6 sheet format (68 000). There are also several 'supersites' in London and some other parts of the country which are used for bespoke constructions using 3D imagery such as 'gluing' a Land Rover to the panel. In terms of prices, it is not possible to be precise given the range of options, locations, sizes and packages available. However, to give some indications of prices for a fortnight:

- £2 100 000 for 75 48-sheet posters at primary London sites.
- £260 000 for 100 6-sheet posters in Glasgow.
- £150 000 for a package of 2145 6-sheet posters within a national package.
- £93 000 for 1000 4-sheet posters on the London Underground.

Research is provided by Poster Audience Research (POSTAR) which assesses about 100 000 roadside panels. The data are continuously updated on a monthly basis that covers 31 demographic variables and includes not only who is passing, but also a scientific measure of the net impact based upon the visibility of each site and thus the genuine likelihood of seeing the poster. POSTAR provides a free planning tool at www.postar.co.uk to ascertain coverage and frequency for roadside planning and to estimate the number of panels required for a specific level of coverage.

Posters are normally purchased in a package to reach a specific gross rating point (GRP) level. The majority of posters are static. However, in extremely high density pedestrian or traffic areas, rotating billboards are often used that utilize triangular prisms to rotate three separate flat displays on strips of vinyl. Another mechanical option is the scrolling poster that carries up to 30 images on a roll and is normally backlit for night viewing (see Figure 18.5).

Digital technology is set to revolutionize the industry enabling posters to respond to movement such as people waving. Also, posters can be embedded with computer chips that interact with mobile phone web browsers to provide greater

Figure 18.5 Scrolling poster

product information such as the location of the nearest store to purchase a product or enable interact games to be played on a billboard using mobile phones. There is also the potential to link posters with radio advertising that will change during the day.

The so-called 'mobile posters' occur when a traditional poster is mounted to a trailer or lorry or when vehicles from taxis to buses are completely 'wrapped' in an advertising image. Posters are tightly regulated and limited for aesthetic and safety reasons in many countries including the UK. For example, before the Athens Olympics thousands of rooftop billboards were removed to improve the look of the city and views of historic sites. However, in the US there are 100 000 posters that play an integral role in signposting services such as restaurants and motels.

Radio

Unlike the US where radio has a long history dating back to the 1920s, terrestrial radio broadcasting (i.e. ignoring Radio Luxembourg and the so-called 'pirate' stations broadcasting off-shore in the 1960s) first began in the UK in 1974. Radio continues to be a lively and dynamic medium and takes many forms today including frequency modulation (FM) and amplitude modulation (AM) and digital (since 1998) and can be listened to through TV as well, web and devices such as mobiles and PDAs. Indeed, trials of digital services on mobiles have surprised researchers who found that digital radio is slightly more popular than mobile TV. It is radio's continued ability to transform and adapt itself to people's behaviour that has provided its underlying strength as, for example, with personal radio and in-car entertainment systems. This is reflected by there being over 200 independent stations which can be national like Classic FM (which has a weekly reach of about 12 per cent of the population) or highly localized such as Island FM which broadcasts to a population of 50 000 people in Guernsey and Alderney. However, Island FM tells us something about radio in that, although its broadcast population is

Figure 18.6   B-Live radio

small, it has a loyal audience and reaches about half of them on a weekly basis. Thus, radio remains a highly approachable medium that people relate to extremely well, particularly at the local level.

It is generally argued that radio differs from other media in that people are often doing other things while listening to the radio, such as eating, driving, working, writing, etc. However, there is a growing trend, particularly amongst younger people, for multiple media use at the same time such as watching TV, writing an e-mail and playing music while simultaneously doing homework. So this element of the medium, while still being a distinct feature, is less novel than previously. In respect of its creative appeal (as mentioned above), radio is probably most like posters in format in that you need short and sharp messages and lots of repetition to make your point. On the whole, it is not a medium that can provide a major impact in a few impressions as with TV, cinema or the press.

Radio audience research is produced by Radio Joint Audience Research Limited (RAJAR) which is owned by the independents and the BBC with the research being conducted by Ipsos MORI. The data are published quarterly and are based on

personal interviews and a survey of 130 000 respondents aged 15+ who provide their general media habits and fill out a listening diary for 1 week in 15-minute blocks between 06:00 and 24:00. Respondents also record where they listened, which is predominantly in the home, but there are significant shares outside the home during morning and evening commuting times. The latest figures can be seen at www.rajar.co.uk and it can be seen there that, at the time of writing, the BBC continues to dominate with its national, regional and local stations with about 54 per cent of the audience share in terms of hours listened to. The Web and mobile phones will likely further fragment audiences and allow a wide range of new entrants to radio broadcasting. For example, the UK arm of Bacardi-Martini has recently established its own commercial free radio station called 'B-Live', devoted to party anthems and DJs and promoted through Bacardi's existing music events (see Figure 18.6)

Part of radio's ability to redefine itself and prosper is that commercial production is arguably the most simple of all the mass media and it is often only the need to obtain clearance for a campaign that stops a commercial being aired within hours of being made. As to placement, it is possible to buy packages guaranteeing audience frequency and demographic coverage despite the lack of centralized selling systems. Most advertisers use media consultancies and sales houses which build the required audiences according to people's listening habits. Retailers and car companies tend to big advertisers given radio's ability to reach audiences close to the point of purchase, particularly in the mornings.

Cinema

The origins of cinema date back to the 1890s in London and it remained a powerful advertising medium until the advent of commercial television in the 1950s. Its demise has long been predicted but it has endured against competition from the small screen and, to a degree, re-invented itself with the introduction of multiplexes in the late 1980s which led to the doubling of the number of screens in the UK by the late 1990s and now around half of all cinemas are multi screen. Admissions have increased in line with these developments from around 75 millions to around 160 to 170 millions. Apart from widespread piracy, further challenges are underway with DVDs, the Web/broadband and the advent of large flat-screen plasma televisions which are becoming increasingly popular. The underlying difficulty for the cinema is that it is a destination medium as the audience needs to consciously decide to visit it and so it is dependent upon having appealing content. On the other hand, film production has become extremely expensive and risky and given it is a creative industry, there is no guaranteed consistency to the quality of output, much of which has been formulaic, and so the box office has suffered.

According to the Cinema Advertising Association (CAA), the cinema audience is fairly evenly split between male and female and predominantly younger than the audience at large (30 per cent of the audience is aged between 15 and 24, and 27 per cent between 25 and 34). It is also upmarket with around 65 per cent of the audience being ABC1 compared with just under of the population at large being so. On average, 15–24-year olds go to see around 2.5 films every couple of months. There is also a small art house group of cinemas within the mainstream (mainly in London and other major conurbations and University towns) with about 4 per cent of screens. Art house attract a slightly older audience (over 40 per cent of them are 40+) and tend to be more

female (58 per cent) and slightly more upmarket (over 70 per cent are ABC1). Less specific data are available on cinema audiences in the NRS and TGI, so it is possible to link cinema audiences, in general, to other media and buying behaviour.

Despite the smaller screens advertisers recognize that the cinema remains a high impact medium, that is also highly cost-effective at reaching the elusive younger audience. Prendergast and Wah (2005) found that cinema advertising offers a relatively less cluttered environment for advertisers to present their message to a captive audience. As opposed to previous studies, which utilized delayed recall, Prendergast and Wah interviewed audience members immediately after they had viewed a particular movie and they found that advertising exposure and recall rates were significantly related to various demographic variables, especially gender and age, and that the level of recall was found to be correlated with various situational stimuli in the cinema such as the larger-than-life screen, Dolby stereo sound, the silent environment, comfortable seats and audience members' expectations to focus on the screen.

Space is available from Carlton (see Figure 18.7), which has about 70 per cent of screens, and Pearl & Dean. Production costs tend to be high in order to gain impact and some advertisers use the same commercials shown on TV, but often they are bespoke and generally longer than the usual 30- or 60 second spots as they appreciate people have come to be entertained. Most advertisers buy packages sold in ISBA/ITV regions on a weekly basis (in line with how films are scheduled), though the option to buy individual cinemas remains. However, when you buy a region, you have to take all the cinemas included – you cannot pick and choose.

Summary

This chapter has examined the key trends, strategies in choice and major characteristics of mass communications media – press, television, the Web, posters, radio and cinema. From the news you would think that the new media, led by such sites as Google, MySpace and YouTube, were rapidly overtaking the so-called 'dinosaur' mass media. Certainly, seismic changes are afoot in the media landscape, but this chapter has argued that the mass media cannot be counted out as advertising tools yet. From a marketer's standpoint, the more mass communications media audiences

Figure 18.7   Carlton screen advertising

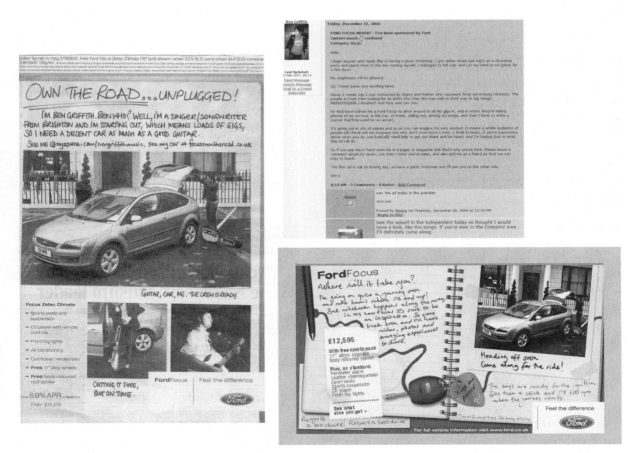

Figure 18.8   Ogilvy & Mather Ford campaign

fragment, the worse they seem to perform. In reality, the problem is that the media buying and, to some extent, the media planning model have been based on a three 'dimensional mindset' based on cost, reach and frequency, and generally the research techniques have not been effective at measuring small audiences. However, marketers are responding to the reality that the mass media audience is much more complex and multidimensional than it appears at first sight. For example, Figure 18.8 shows some examples from Ogilvy & Mather's 'Own the Road' campaign'. O&M loaned a Ford Focus to Ben Griffith, an aspiring young musician from Brighton, who in return is keeping a blog on MySpace and allowing the agency to monitor his progress. The press campaign features some selective information on the car and Ben Griffith as well as providing the address of his blog and Ford's website. People have posted comments on his blog. What this demonstrates is that media usage and research will increasingly focus on how people relate to media, the role that media plays in their lives and how they combine media usage rather than focus on a single medium. This will necessitate greater use of qualitative techniques, as with in-depth interviews and focus groups as pioneered by HCCL in their media planning for First Direct and Tango, rather than relying solely on audience measurement. Let us face it, against the size and power of the Tesco's and Boots loyalty cards, a lot of media data looks rather insignificant. Fragmentation will continue and formats will continue to evolve, but the mass communications media remain a potent force within marketing and will do so for the foreseeable future.

References

Abratt, R. and Cowan, D. (1999) Client-agency perspectives of information needs for media planning, *Journal of Advertising Research*, **39**(6), 37–52.

Ambler, T. and Hollier, E. A. (2004) The waste in advertising is the part that works, *Journal of Advertising Research*, **44**(4), 375–389.

Bluedorn, A. C., Carol, F. K. and Paul, M. L. (1992) How many things do you like to do at once? An introduction to monochronic and polychronic time, *Academy of Management Executive*, **6**(4), 17–26.

Broadbent, S. (1999) *When to Advertise*, NTC, Henley-on-Thames.

Burns, K. S. and Lutz, R. J. (2006) The function of format: consumer responses to six on-line advertising formats, *Journal of Advertising*, **35**(1), 53–63.

Chang, Y. and Thorson, E. (2004) Television and web advertising synergies, *Journal of Advertising*, **33**(2), 75–84.

Chang-Hoan, C. and Cheon, H. J. (2004) Why do people avoid advertising on the Internet? *Journal of Advertising*, **33**(4), 89–99.

Clancey, M. (1994) The television audience examined, *Journal of Advertising Research*, **34**(4), 76–87.

Dahlén, M. and Bergendahl, J. (2001) Informing and transforming on the web: an empirical study of response to banner ads for functional and expressive products, *International Journal of Advertising*, **20**(2), 189–205.

Dertouzoz, J. M. and Garber, S. (2006) Effectiveness of advertising in different media, *Journal of Advertising*, **35**(2), 111–122.

Leigh, J. H., George, M. Z. and Vanitha Swaminathan (2006) Dimensional relationships of recall and recognition measures with selected cognitive and affective aspects of print ads, *Journal Of Advertising*, **35**(1), 105–122.

McGrath, J. M. (2005) IMC at a crossroads: a theoretical review and a conceptual framework for testing, *Marketing Management Journal*, **15**(2), 55–66.

Moorman, M., Peter, C. N. and Smit, E. G. (2002) The effects of magazine-induced psychological responses and thematic congruence on memory and attitude toward the ad in a real-life setting, *Journal of Advertising*, **31**(4), 27–40.

De Pelsmacker, P., Geuens, M. and Anckaert, P. (2002) Media context and advertising effectiveness: the role of context appreciation and context/ad similarity, *Journal of Advertising*, **31**(2), 49–61.

Pilotta, J. J. and Schultz, D. (2005) Simultaneous media experience and synesthesia, *Journal of Advertising Research*, **45**(1), 19–26.

Prendergast, G. and Wah, C. L. (2005) The effectiveness of cinema advertising in Hong Kong, *International Journal of Advertising*, **24**(1), 79–93.

Ray, M. L. and Webb, P. H. (1986) Three prescriptions for clutter, *Journal of Advertising Research*, **26**(1), 69–77.

Speck, P. S. and Elliott, M. T. (1997) Predictors of advertising avoidance in print and broadcast media, *Journal of Advertising*, **26**(3), 61–77.

Taylor, C. R., George, R. F. and Hae-Kyong, B. (2006) Use and effectiveness of billboards, *Journal of Advertising*, **35**(4), 21–34.

Thomas Jr., G. M. (2004) Building the buzz in the hive mind, *Journal of Consumer Behaviour*, **4**(1), 64–72.

Vakratsas, D. and Ambler, T. (1999) How advertising works: What do we really know? *Journal of Marketing*, **63**(1), 26–44.

Whipple, T. W. and McManamon, M. K. (2002) Implications of using male and female voices in commercials: an exploratory study, *Journal of Advertising*, **31**(2), 79–91.

Recommendations for further reading

Belch, G. and Michael, B. (2007) *Advertising and Promotion: An Integrated Marketing Communications Perspective*, 7th edn, McGraw Hill, New York.

Fill, C. (2005) *Marketing Communications: Engagement, Strategies and Practice*, 4th edn, Financial Times/Prentice Hall, London.

FitzGerald, M. and Arnott, D. (2003) *Marketing Communications Classics*, 2nd edn, Thomson, Andover.

Hackley, C. (2005) *Advertising and Promotion: Communicating Brands*, Sage, London.

Percy, L. and Elliott, R. (2005) *Strategic Advertising Management*, 2nd edn, Oxford University Press, Oxford.

Pickton, D. and Broderick, A. (2005) *Integrated Marketing Communications*, 2nd edn, FT/Prentice Hall, London.

Roderick, W. (2000) *Advertising: What It Is and How to Do It*, 4th edn, McGraw-Hill, London.

Sargeant, A. and Douglas, W. (2001) *Direct and Interactive Marketing*, Oxford University Press, Oxford.

Shimp, T. A. (2007) *Integrated Marketing Communications in Advertising and Promotions*, 7th edn, Thomson, Southwestern.

CHAPTER 19

What do we mean by direct, data and digital marketing?

DEREK HOLDER

Since Lester Wunderman first coined the term 'direct marketing' in 1961, experienced marketing people are still arguing about what direct marketing is. From those early days we have seen the rise of new (or enhanced) methodologies bearing descriptions such as 'database marketing', 'relationship marketing', 'interactive marketing' and 'digital marketing'.

In this chapter we attempt to set the record straight and discuss the essential similarities and differences between direct marketing and these newcomers.

We look at the origins of direct marketing, its adoption by multi-channel users and how its disciplines underpin all that has followed its inception. We discuss the four basic principles of direct marketing: targeting, interaction, control and continuity (TICC).

Finally, we introduce the direct, data and digital marketer's information system, establishing its context within the company-wide information system.

What do we mean by direct marketing?

The origin of what came to be called direct marketing was the mail-order business: the classic example in the US was the Sears Roebuck catalogue. Later it came to include telephone marketing, magazine subscription selling, continuity book and music publishing, and other direct-to-consumer methods over and above catalogue-based mail order. As late as the 1980s Stan Rapp, a US pioneer, was still defining direct marketing as a means of distribution – not a definition that would be widely accepted today.

There must be as many definitions of direct marketing as there are writers on the subject. Rather than adding to them, here are two which you may find helpful:

> Direct marketing is a collection of methodologies for communicating a message to individuals with a view to obtaining a measurable, cost-effective response.
>
> FEDMA *Direct Marketing*, 1998

> Direct marketing is the process in which individual customers' responses and transactions are recorded… and the data used to inform the targeting, execution and control of actions … that are designed to start, develop and prolong profitable customer relationships.
>
> McCorkell, *Direct and Database Marketing*, 1997

The first lesson of both these definitions is that direct marketing is a *collection of methodologies* or a *process*. Direct mail, with which it is often confused, is only one *medium* used by many direct marketers – as are the telephone, catalogues and DRTV, etc.

The second lesson is that the primary job of direct marketing – as indeed of all marketing – is to convey a *message* – a message which is intended to provoke a *response*.

From mass marketing to digital marketing

For many years, until the 1990s, marketers loosely defined marketing as 'identifying and satisfying customer needs at a profit'. Up to the 1950s and 1960s mass marketing and mass communication dominated marketing practice. The technologies that drive marketing are information and communication. Twentieth century mass marketing was propelled by high-speed rotary printing, high-quality colour reproduction, film, radio and finally television broadcasting. These were the technologies of mass communication. In the 1970s and 1980s 'target' marketing grew rapidly as brands proliferated and extended to reach specific large market segments.

Marketing depends on information about markets and in those times decision making was aided by sample survey-based research. This provided media readership research, TV audience research, consumer panels, retail audits and *ad hoc* surveys. Media audience research answered the question, 'Who are we reaching with our advertising?' Consumer panels and retail audits answered the question, 'Is it working to create sales?'

At this stage in marketing's evolution many major companies were distant from the customer (apart from those companies who practised direct marketing). The company still controlled the key navigation tools – it decided the product, price, promotion and places (distribution channels). The company told its customers and prospects about its products and services when it wanted to, through which media channels it chose and dictated where and when the customers could obtain their products.

The champions of this form of marketing were Unilever and Proctor & Gamble. They researched their new products, test marketed and launched with brand advertising primarily through television. This was pre-BSkyB and the 100-plus channels available today, TV offered companies an unparalleled reach to market as well as low CPT (cost-per-thousand). Yet still consumers were anonymous buyers.

As Alan Mitchell, the well-known columnist and author has written, the pillars of marketing in these days were branding, advertising and research marketing. These he suggested were surrogates:

- Brands were a surrogate for a relationship between the company and the product.
- Advertising was a surrogate for the dialogue which a relationship brings.
- Marketing research was a surrogate for the learning that takes place with a dialogue.

Direct marketing grew rapidly in the 1980s and 1990s as it provided the missing dialogue between customers and company – it encouraged customers to respond and these responses were recorded and measured. Coupled with the cost of computer storage declining exponentially, it led to the creation of large customer databases containing full transactional, geographical and lifestyle information about their customers. This was particularly true in the service sector – financial services, travel and leisure, utilities and telecoms.

The information and technology revolution

The immense increase in affordable computer power now allows today's direct marketer to hold as much relevant information on *every* customer as the twentieth century mass marketer held on the *entire* market.

This represents nothing less than a revolutionary change to the marketing opportunity. Furthermore, the revolution is not over: computer power keeps on getting cheaper and marketing continues to become more sophisticated. Yet the communications technology revolution created by digital media may be of even greater significance.

Communications technology and digital marketing

Digital media represent the convergence of information and communications technologies. Through digital media, information is transferred from one computer to another. The information can be in the form of sounds or moving pictures. One of the computers can be a TV receiver, a phone, a smart card or soon, a refrigerator.

Now the marketer and customer each have a computer. And their computers can exchange information. The so-called dialogue of direct marketing can be turned into something approaching a real conversation in which information is exchanged and acted upon in real time.

It is useful to give a definition of digital marketing.

The first part of the definition illustrates the range of access platforms and communication tools that form the online channels which marketers

Digital marketing is:

- *Applying*: digital technologies which form online channels to market (web, e-mail, databases plus mobiles/wireless and digital TV);
- *To*: contribute to marketing activities aimed at achieving profitable acquisition and retention of customers (with a multi-channel buying process and customer life cycle);
- *Through developing*: a planned approach to improve customer knowledge (of their profiles, behaviour, value and loyalty drivers), then delivering integrated targeted communications and online services that match their individual needs.

use to build and develop relationships with customers. The access platforms or hardware include PCs, PDAs, mobile phones and interactive digital TV and these deliver content and enable interaction through different online communication tools such as websites, portals, search engines, affiliate and viral marketing, blogs, e-mail and text messaging. Some also include traditional voice telephone as part of digital marketing.

The second part of the definition shows that it should not be the technology that drives digital marketing, but the business returns from gaining new customers and maintaining relationships with existing customers. It also emphasizes how digital marketing does not occur in isolation, but is most effective when it is integrated with other communication channels such as phone, direct mail or face-to-face. Online channels should also be used to support the whole buying process from pre-sale to post-sale and further development of customer relationships.

The final part of the definition summarizes approaches to customer-centric marketing. It shows how it should be based on knowledge of customer needs developed by researching their characteristics, behaviour, what they value, what keeps them loyal and then delivering tailored web and e-mail communications.

In many ways the above is the same as the definition of direct marketing except it is limited to digital media. This is why many direct marketers see digital marketing as just adding a new front end by offering new media channels to market, whereas the back end – logistics, fulfilment and customer service – remains as before. If you think

about the old-fashioned mail-order catalogue, Sears Roebuck or Montgomery Ward, the modern-day equivalent is companies like Amazon and Direct Line. It is still direct to the customer but utilizes the new media channels.

Digital media has, however, permitted two further things of the utmost importance to marketing: they have revolutionized the cost structure of the functions they perform, and they have altered the balance of power between supplier and customer in ways that are only gradually playing themselves out.

Customers now can control the 'navigation' functions. They can build proprietary databases of their preferred suppliers, investigate products and services on the Internet at a time of their choosing, and in return expect an unprecedented level of customer service with goods delivered in first-class condition within 24–48 hours.

Direct marketing has become mainstream marketing

The Internet revolution is the first real progression in marketing since it originated in the mid-nineteenth century. It has changed the balance of power between companies and customers and created many new marketplaces such as online auctions like the global phenomenon of eBay. As we write online adverting spend annually is set to overtake radio and poster advertising combined reaching 10.5 per cent of all advertising spend. Google.co.uk is the most successful search engine in the world and the biggest issue many major brands are tackling today is how they get their brand up to the top of the Google search ranking. Meanwhile, mobile marketing is just set to explode. British Airways believes the future lies in ba.com and is directing its budgets to online. The concept of real-time one-to-one marketing is here.

Direct marketing has been at the forefront of this change. It has absorbed the technological advances faster than any other discipline. It has created the 'dialogue' with customers. It has always been based on measurable and accountable advertising. Today, as the disciplines of direct advertising, branding and sales promotion begin to blur, it is direct marketing which has led this change and is now considered as mainstream marketing. Direct marketing can build brands (Direct Line, MORE TH>N, Amazon and easyJet); it can target sales promotion, but at the same time collect the data and use it for future business planning, while combined with market research

Table 19.1 The direct model		
Features	*Benefits*	*Examples*
Online, fax, telephone and mail transactions Catalogues and websites	Lower overheads Cuts out middlemen Faster stock turn Facilitates exporting	First Direct easyJet Dell La Redoute

it can provide powerful customer insights. It continues to exemplify the rigour of measurable and accountable marketing. And to the effective twenty-first century marketer, it should be second nature to think first and foremost: direct, data and digital.

Firms that deal direct

In 1994, the year Michael Dell launched his first website, the Dell Direct call centre was already receiving nearly 50 000 calls from customers daily. Even then, Dell was the world's largest *direct* marketer of computers.

Like First Direct and easyJet, Dell is a pure direct marketer, dealing with its customers through its websites *and* call centres. Home-shopping companies, like La Redoute, provide another example.

The logic for dealing direct is based on efficiency – stripping out overheads or unproductive running costs. Such costs can include bricks-and-mortar outlets, sales forces, dealer margins, large stockholdings and so on. The direct model works for both business-to-consumer (B2C) and business-to-business (B2B) applications. In fact, Dell's customers range from large corporations, such as Barclays Bank, to individuals ordering from home. A particular advantage of the direct model is that it can reduce the cost of international expansion (Table 19.1).

A point to note is that it is not only producers of goods or services that conform to the direct model. First Direct, easyJet and Dell are all producers. But La Redoute is a pure retailer, not making any of the clothes or other items that it sells. The insurance company, Direct Line, is a producer. But direct insurance brokers, sourcing policies from a large number of insurers, are not producers.

Furthermore, Dell may sell software and peripherals that it does not produce. In fact Dell's chief production job is to assemble components made elsewhere. Thus the direct model can work for retailers providing that it increases retailing efficiency or makes buying easier or more attractive.

Interest in the direct model has been given a huge boost by the Internet, fostering the development of new types of direct business including:

Virtual exchanges: for example, Covisint, the world's largest B2B automotive marketplace; online auctions and reverse auctions, such as eBay and priceline.com; and infomediaries, search services and buying clubs.

These entirely new types of organization are not controlled by sellers. They are either neutral or working for buyers.

The Internet has the potential to increase the efficiency of the direct model exponentially through a reduction in transaction costs and materials sourcing costs, superior supply chain management and a greatly enhanced ability to tailor the product to the buyer's specification. In principle it is immaterial whether access is achieved through a PC, iTV or a mobile phone. In practice the 'front end' can affect the quantity and quality of the information that can be exchanged.

To the customer, the direct model is not always the answer. Many people prefer to go to the shops or send for a sales representative. Others will use the Internet as an information source, but complete their transaction through a traditional channel. In fact our channel preferences are likely to depend on what we are buying, as the chart at Figure 19.1 demonstrates. As a result, many companies find multi-channel marketing pays.

Multi-channel marketing

Multi-channel marketers also use direct marketing. GUS is a multi-channel retailer selling through websites and its retail stores, including Argos.

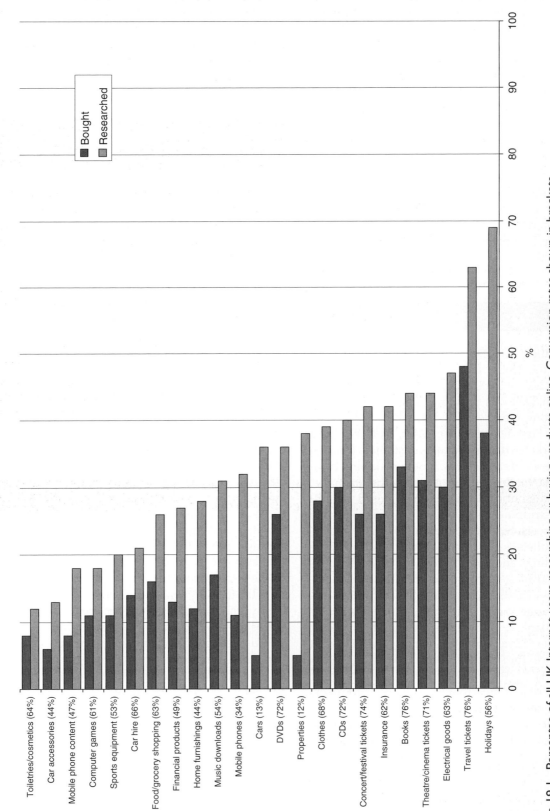

Figure 19.1 Percentae of all UK Internet users researching or buying products online. Conversion rates shown in brackets
Source: Mediascope Europe, Media Consumptions Study 2005, European Interactive Advertising Association (EIAA).

Tesco is a multi-channel retailer, although its website sales are dwarfed by its store-based sales. Producers, too, may use multiple sales channels. GM (Vauxhall) and Ford sell (a few) cars directly to private motorists on the web. IBM sells direct and through dealers. British Airways sells direct and through agents. Magazine publishers, such as *The Economist* and *Reader's Digest*, sell both through newsagents and through direct subscription. Charities raise funds through direct mail, through charity shops, through events and through street collections. Today, many charities are looking to online techniques such as viral marketing.

Some companies have spawned direct brands. Prudential insurance launched *egg* as a direct brand. First Direct is, of course, a subsidiary of HSBC. Direct Line is owned by the Royal Bank of Scotland.

Home-shopping catalogues have diversified both to website trading and to high street retailing – Lakeland and Past Times are examples. *Next* is an example of a high street retailer spawning a home-shopping business.

For most of these companies, the logic of stripping out costs by conforming exclusively to a direct model does not work. They do better by offering customers a wider choice of ways to deal with them. In a few cases differential pricing may be used – magazine subscription is a prime example – but in most cases the pricing is the same and the inventory is much the same.

Next believes that its catalogue and website assist shop sales and vice versa. By offering customers the widest possible choice of ways to browse and buy they maximize the return on their marketing investment.

Direct marketing is more than selling direct

All of the companies we have named use direct or digital marketing; not just when they are selling through their mailings, catalogues and websites. Direct marketing has come to mean more than just selling direct.

> Any company that uses direct response advertising, online or offline, and maintains a customer database, is using direct marketing.

Tesco would remain a major direct marketer if it scrapped its website tomorrow. Tesco maintains a huge customer database (Clubcard) and tailors offers to its customers, through personalized direct mail, based on their past purchasing behaviour (Table 19.2).

Table 19.2   Tesco Clubcard

History, operation and scale

Tested October 1993, launched nationally February 1995
Card applications in store, communications in store and direct mail
Over 200 million product purchases a day by over 10 million customers

Customer information and applications

Customer data:

Visit patterns	Spend levels
Departmental usage	Types of purchases
Coupon users/non-users	Profile/geographic data

Broad customer typologies:

Loyalists	Infrequent customers
Regulars	New customers

Applications include:

Recruitment	Lapsed and win back
Clubcard plus (savings card)	Helpline
Local marketing	

Magnetic strip cards like Clubcard enable retailers to link customer identities with purchases and use the data to offer the customer rewards offers, events and services which, to all intents and purposes, are tailored to the customer's needs and preferences. Although more than 10 million Clubcard statements are mailed quarterly, there are nearly nine million variations to these mailings reflecting customers' different shopping patterns.

Even though the vast majority of Clubcard members visit Tesco to do their shopping, this is still termed direct marketing because the programme is based on the collection of shop visit and purchase data and careful analysis of individual customer preferences. The activity may also be termed relationship marketing or even loyalty marketing. Of these terms, direct marketing is the most meaningful, being capable of precise definition.

Direct, data and digital marketing

Let us look again, a little more closely, at McCorkell's definition of direct marketing:

> Direct marketing is the process in which individual customers' responses and transactions are recorded . . .

McCorkell's definition does not specify the media through which customers' responses and transactions are invited or received. In fact a customer might spot a bargain on a website, make further enquiries by telephone and complete the transaction at a dealership. If the item purchased were a second-hand car, such a scenario would be very likely.

In this definition, *customers' responses are recorded*. If the car dealership did not bother to do this, then the process would not qualify as direct marketing. On the other hand, the form of response is not specified – for example, the data could include clickstream data as readily as phone calls or posted coupons.

> . . . and the data used to inform the targeting, execution and control of actions . . .

Note that the definition does not specify any interval between recording the data and using it. It may often apply to data stored on a customer database and used months later (as in the Tesco Clubcard example) but it can equally apply to data used in real time during a telephone call or website visit.

In fact the use of profile, preference and purchase data in real time was pioneered in call centre software before the World Wide Web was used for marketing. An early example was (still is) car insurance quotations. The quote given to the caller is driven by the answers to scripted questions. A later example is add-on offers triggered by home-shopping orders (e.g. matching accessories). In this case, no questions are asked to prompt the offer – it is driven by the content of the customer's order.

Again, the nature of the actions is not specified – they could include:

- Restricting a mailed invitation to the best customers.
- Targeting new customers who match the profile of the best established customers.
- Personalizing a website to make relevant offers to previous visitors. The purpose of the actions is clearly specified.

> . . . that are designed to start, develop and prolong profitable customer relationships.

This part of the definition excludes no business with expectations of success. However, the idea that customer data collection and analysis is the key to success was peculiar to direct marketing – although management consultancies and Customer Relationship Management (CRM) software vendors now also claim ownership of it.

Direct marketing and Pareto's Principle

If Thomas Jefferson (. . . all men are created equal) was the hero of mass marketing, Vilfredo Pareto is the hero of direct marketing. Pareto's Principle (of the distribution of incomes) was that 80 per cent would end up in 20 per cent of pockets however society attempted to regulate matters. To Pareto, whether all men are created equal or not, they certainly do not end up that way.

So it is with customers. Every direct marketer knows that some customers are much more valuable than others. Every astute direct marketer knows who the valuable ones are. The really smart direct marketer has a system for forecasting who the valuable ones are going to be.

Why is this so important? Let us consider two examples.

Figure 19.2 shows a real-life example of segmentation of charity donors based on their response to the last appeal made to them.

Customers who cost money

Typically, 75 per cent of new customers gained by a home-shopping business will have lapsed without providing enough business to recover the cost of recruiting them. All of the profit will be contributed by the remaining 25 per cent.

If the company learns which are the best sources of good customers, it can work to reduce the 75 per cent of loss-making intake. If it fails to learn, the 75 per cent will become 80 or 85 per cent, ensuring that the company loses money.

Again, typically, a bank will lose money on at least 80 per cent of its private customer base at any one time. By devoting special attention to the remaining 20 per cent, it can expect to satisfy more of them and so keep their custom. If it fails to differentiate between its good (and potentially good) customers and its loss-making customers, it is the good customers who are most likely to defect.

Figure 19.2 displays the result of applying a statistical model called CHAID (Chi-squared automatic interaction detector). This is also sometimes called tree segmentation. Here we are using CHAID to analyse the results of our last mailed appeal. We want CHAID to tell us how to recognize the differences between our most generous donors and our less generous donors. In particular, we would like to know who – if anyone – not to mail next time around.

CHAID splits the mailing base (all donors) into two, by picking out the most important of all the discriminatory variables that distinguish the best donors from the others. This variable turns out to be the number of previous gifts. The 36 per cent who have sent us two or more previous donations contributed 65 per cent of the money. This result is shown near the top of Figure 19.1.

Looking further down, we can see that CHAID keeps on dividing each segment into two, like an amoeba in a petri dish; each time it takes the most significant of the remaining discriminatory variables. What CHAID is answering each time is:

Of all the differences between the more generous and less generous donors in this segment, which is the most important single difference?

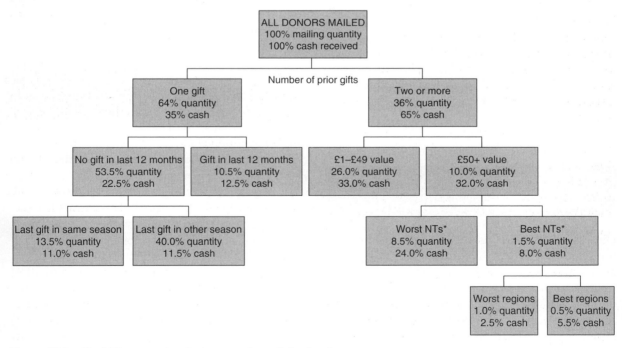

Figure 19.2   Real-life example of segmentation of charity donors
McCorkell, *Direct and Database Marketing*, 1997
*NT: geo-demographic neighbourhood type.

Looking at the left-hand side of the model, we see that the least generous 40 per cent of donors contributed only 11.5 per cent of the cash received. The model demonstrates that 88.5 per cent of the cash could have been raised from 60 per cent of the donors by not mailing single gift donors who had been inactive for over 12 months and who last gave at a different time of the year.

If we assume it cost £1 in mailing expense to raise £4 in cash, the overall result from 100 000 donors would be £400 000 raised at a cost of £100 000. However, the least responsive 40 000 would have cost £40 000 to mail and brought in only £46 000 cash. We might decide to send an appeal to these donors only once a year, at Christmas time, when they are most likely to respond. Meanwhile, the other 60 000 donors sent back £354 000 – almost £6 for every £1 of expense.

Sending our appeal to these donors only would improve our income to expense ratio by almost 50 per cent.

The direct marketer looks for solutions by listening to what the data says. As always in direct marketing, actions speak loudest. What people do matters more than their demographic, socio-economic or lifestyle profile.

B2B = Pareto × Pareto

However strongly Pareto's Principle applies to B2C marketing, the B2B scene is Pareto squared, one company having ten thousand times the purchasing power of another. So companies differentiate between larger (corporate) customers and smaller customers. Frequently call centres or contact centres deal with smaller business customers while field sales teams deal with larger customers.

Principles of direct, data and digital marketing: TICC

Direct marketing and its information systems focus on what the customer or prospect does. To put it another way, data about past behaviour is used to predict future behaviour. This data is processed on an individual basis and can be analysed and acted upon on an individual basis, even if the number of customers reaches millions. This does not render marketing research obsolete but, if we can rely only on marketing research information, we are forced to make assumptions about

Figure 19.3 Targeting, interaction, control and continuity

customer behaviour which may be generally right but will often be wrong in an individual case.

Successful direct marketing practice depends on four elements. These are: targeting, interaction, control and continuity.

Targeting, interaction, control and continuity

You will see from Figure 19.3 that the four elements of successful direct marketing can be looked at either as one triangle or alternatively as four triangles inside another one. *Interaction* is in the centre. Interaction includes the stimuli we marketers create in the hope of producing a response from the people in our target market. Their response is also included in the interaction triangle. In all cases we will attempt to attribute a response to the correct stimulus. Thus the results of our activities form the core of our information system and enable us to become progressively more efficient at *targeting, control* and *continuity*. That is because we are learning by experience.

Interaction takes centre stage in direct marketing's information system.

Targeting refers to our decisions on who will receive our message and includes our media selection: TV, banner ads, print advertising, direct mail, telemarketing, e-mail and so on. We may be targeting our established customers, identified prospects or a much larger audience of 'suspects'. In all of these cases our targeting decisions will generally outweigh in importance decisions about what to offer and how to frame our message. By examining the results of our previous attempts to target correctly, we can keep on refining our future targeting. All targeting is dependent on accurate data – whether it be external data such as circulation or

---

> ### Customer interactions
>
> These may not just be orders. They may be returns (of unwanted goods), queries, complaints, requests, suggestions, questionnaire responses and so on.

audience figures, or internal data about individual persons' characteristics and buying habits.

Control is the management of our marketing. It includes setting objectives, planning at the strategic and operational levels, budgeting and assessment of results. The process is cyclical, future planning being informed by past results.

Interaction is at the heart of direct marketing. The completeness and accuracy of our data within the interaction triangle will be crucial to the exercise of control. Interaction quantifies the *effects* of our marketing.

Continuity is about retaining customers, cross-selling other products to them and uptrading them. In the vast majority of business enterprises, the bulk of profit arises from dealings with established customers.

Our painstaking care in recording interactions enables us to communicate with customers, recognizing their interest and showing appreciation of their custom. The special challenge of e-commerce and of contact centre management is to respond to customers in real time.

All four of the TICC elements are critical. Direct marketing is not direct marketing unless they are all in place. Sometimes it is not possible to data capture the identity of every customer and sometimes it is necessary to record the transactions of a sample of customers only. These conditions apply in FMCG (fast moving consumer goods) markets. Nevertheless, if the four TICC elements are in place, it is possible to employ direct marketing methods in these markets.

What distinguishes digital marketing?

Digital marketing is essentially direct marketing through new media. The intention of direct marketing has always been interaction, if only in soliciting and receiving enquiries and orders by post and fulfilling these requests. Indeed, we have just discussed interaction as one of the four essential elements of direct marketing.

So why refer to new media direct marketing as anything but direct marketing?

There are two reasons. Firstly, digital marketing has already developed a language of its own because most of its pioneers never connected what they were doing with direct marketing. The thinking went, 'Here is a new medium, so we must invent a new way of marketing for it'. Most of those who did are no longer in business, whereas those who applied direct marketing principles and expertise to the new media have done much better.

To work effectively, the new media require the same disciplines that work in all direct marketing.

The advertising agency creative asks, 'How can I make this brand famous?'

The direct marketer asks, 'How can I make my next offer irresistible?'

There is no need to guess who will pull most customers in. We know from the results.

If you can remember them still, contrast the big dotcom spenders from 1998 and 1999 with the 1995 vintage cash burner, Amazon. The later entrants enriched the TV companies in senseless bids to make their names famous with ill-targeted and fatuous advertising that suggested no good reason to visit their websites.

Now what do you remember about Amazon? Here is a guess:

- Any book or CD you want
- Fast delivery
- 40 per cent off

What you remember is what Amazon offers. And what more could you want? Well, if you are really demanding, Amazon also gives you reviews, an easy site to negotiate, personalized (tailor-made) suggestions on what you might like to read next and easy ordering, etc.

Like the 'make my brand famous' dotcoms who blew millions on untargeted TV, Amazon's high spending days are behind it. With a still-growing business but a huge debt burden to carry, Amazon relies primarily on its affiliate marketing network to pull in new customers. You can visit amazon.co.uk to find out how to become an affiliate.

The affiliate marketing programme is all online, so less audience wastage. Many dotcoms have learned to their backers' cost that buying brand awareness on TV is not an affordable way to drive prospective customers to their websites: even now, many TV viewers lack access to the Internet. Furthermore, affiliate programmes allow payment by results.

Affiliate marketing programmes

Affiliates place links on their websites to drive traffic to the merchant. They are rewarded by commission payments – usually a percentage of sales. Premium affiliate sites (including portals such as MSN) demand a tenancy fee as well as commission.

A similar idea was pioneered in direct marketing under the name of *affinity group marketing*. Direct marketers also pioneered *PPI* (payment per inquiry) deals with media owners many years ago.

The case of Buy.com

Buy.com launched on TV in the UK with a massive TV campaign. But before being bought by the John Lewis Partnership, Buy.com was already using online promotion only. Buy.com reported that customer acquisition costs had fallen to £40.

But 38 per cent of site traffic (October 2000) was from Buy.com's affiliate marketing programme. The cost of acquiring customers from the volume affiliate programme (i.e. the part of the programme in which no tenancy fees are paid) was only £5.

Facts from *e.BUSINESS*, February 2001

Accurate targeting is one of the four elements of successful direct marketing.

The lessons learned by Buy.com from costly experience illustrate the importance of interaction, the second TICC element, as the chief supplier of actionable marketing information. The classic direct marketing method is to buy this experience quickly and cheaply through *testing* the most sensible-looking alternatives. It is only because direct marketers record and analyse the results of interaction that low cost testing is possible.

After its expensive TV experience, Buy.com started to exercise rigorous control of its customer acquisition costs. Control is the third TICC element.

Initially a company may not yet know how much it can afford to pay to acquire a new customer. The return on its new customer investment will be learned through continuity (the fourth TICC element) of customers' business. Forty pounds may be a reasonable price to pay for a new customer but it may well be too high. A lot

may depend on how successful Buy.com is in satisfying customers and encouraging them to come back for more.

Direct and digital marketing and lifetime value

The experienced direct marketer begins by making a calculation of how much he or she can afford to pay to acquire a new customer and this sets the target acquisition cost. The direct marketer then tracks the newly acquired customers to see if they are contributing the same amount of business as expected. The forecast of their lifetime value (LTV) will be adjusted on the basis of their first and second purchases.

> Lifetime value (LTV) – The lifetime value of a new customer is the net present value of all future contributions to profit and overhead from that customer.

Is Buy.com paying too much and, if so, can it reduce its costs? Time will tell.

If only 38 per cent of Buy.com site visitors have clicked through from affiliate sites, where have the others come from? Some will have come through recommendation or idle surfing. Many may have come from banners, interstitials, site registrations or keywords. All these terms apply strictly to digital media and describe opportunities that are exclusive to online marketing.

You will remember that one reason why digital marketing is distinguished from other direct marketing is that it has developed its own vocabulary, being widely regarded as an activity that is distinct from direct marketing.

Another reason why digital marketing deserves its own title is that the new media scene is technologically very different and offers the marketer challenges and opportunities that are without parallel. The impact of these changes is likely to transform marketing completely.

10 ways in which digital marketing is different

1 *The challenge of 24/7.* A trading website is always open. There is no downtime to restock, correct programming errors or repair broken links to other business systems.

2 *Marketing in real time.* A website deals with customers in real time, raising expectations of instant query resolution, immediate response to requests and even faster delivery. Furthermore customer interaction data is being gathered continuously.

3 *Personalization.* Personalization of a website is very different from personalized print. It must be based on a variety of data sources (e.g. clickstream, personal data and previous purchases) and used within a single site visit if appropriate.

4 *Data volumes and integration.* A website can collect much higher volumes of data of different types than can be collected from other reception points. (This poses a systems integration problem and a potentially crippling data volume problem, sometimes referred to as data overload.)

5 *Many-to-many communications.* Customers do not phone call centres just for a chat. But the Internet is different. It is open, democratic and even revolutionary. The plus side may be *viral marketing*. The downside could be *flaming* (abusive replies).

6 *Comparison shopping.* Never was comparison shopping so easy. The pricing policy may need to be changed for digital marketing. A new brand?

7 *Global reach.* The reach of the website is wide but logistical or legal constraints may apply. It may be necessary to restrict orders geographically.

8 *Keeping in touch.* Unlike direct mail, e-mail can be time sensitive, especially when sent to a business address. But, because e-mailing is so cheap, it is tempting to overuse it. It is easy to measure the response but not so easy to measure customers lost through irrelevant e-mailing.

9 *Low transaction costs.* The cost of handling online orders and information requests, as well as of e-mail solicitation, is much lower. This may permit lower ticket or lower margin transactions. However, credit card payment queries will be high and delivery costs will remain the same, wherever physical products that are not electronically transmissible are involved.

10 *A website is more like a shop than a catalogue.* Unlike a catalogue, a website cannot be sent to a list of prospective customers. Like a shop, it must wait for them to call in. Unlike a high street shop, it is not visible to passers-by. It needs promotion.

Can you think of any other ways in which a website is more like a shop than a catalogue? Here are two ideas:

1 Out-of-stock items (stock-outs) cannot be deleted from a printed catalogue. They continue

---

Lands' End: the cyber model

A home-shopping company for nearly 30 years and the world's most experienced Internet clothing retailer, Lands' End has found another way to make its website more like a shop. You can have your own personal cyber model try on the garments that interest you to ensure they will fit.

Lands' End will mail you its catalogue even if you buy from their website. Some people prefer to browse in a printed catalogue and shop online; others enjoy the interactive website but order by phone. See point 10 under '10 ways in which digital marketing is different'.

---

to occupy selling space and disappoint customers who try to order them. On the other hand, stock-outs can be deleted from websites almost as readily as the goods disappear from stores.

2 The direct marketer can measure the sales performance of each page and position in the catalogue. But the lessons cannot be applied until the next printing. Furthermore, the cataloguer cannot follow the customer's route through the catalogue, making it harder to explain the sales performance of individual items.

The website designer can use clickstream data to track customers' journeys through the site and can relate these patterns to sales. Then the site layout can be altered to optimize performance. The store can make similar adjustments although the data will rarely be so accurate or so complete.

A last word about digital jargon

Viral marketing is the turbocharged Internet version of the direct marketers' referral programme or MGM (member-get-member) scheme. As customers congregate in newsgroups or chat by e-mail, recommendations can spread like a forest fire.

Personalization has a similar meaning in both direct and digital marketing but the possibilities are more exciting in a dynamic environment than in print.

Cookies are the small text files stored on your computer to enable the website to recognize it when you call again and record your clickstream. This enables personalization. However, unless you register separately, the website will think that all users of your computer are the same person.

Permission marketing is a significant concept that underpins online CRM. Permission marketing is a term coined by Seth Godin to apply to e-mail marketing. It is best summarized in his book (Godin, 1999). Customers agree (opt in) to be involved in an organization's marketing activities, usually as a result of an incentive. It is now a legal requirement enforced by the UK Privacy and Electronic Communications Regulations 2003 that there must be a proactive agreement to receive electronic communications (see the detailed guidelines from the UK Information Commissioner at http://makeashorterlink.com/?X26862EA6, and also Chapter 12.2 below). This core principle of permission marketing is now a legal requirement throughout the EU. Unfortunately it has done little to reduce the flood of unwanted e-mails (spam) which largely originate from outside the EU.

Data: the direct and digital marketer's information system

It is essential that the direct and digital marketing information system includes customer history data. The minimum history required is a history of the customer's transactions. Often this will be summarized, showing us little more than the value of each transaction, the product or the merchandise category and when it occurred.

Without this minimum amount of data, we cannot practise efficient direct marketing because:

> Direct marketing is the process in which . . . individual customers' responses and transactions are recorded . . . and the data used to inform the targeting, execution and control of actions . . . that are designed to start, develop and prolong profitable customer relationships.

Figure 19.4 makes the point graphically.

The components of response, measurement and continuity are common to all direct marketing activity:

Response: A response is needed to acquire a customer and to begin compiling data relating to that customer. It is very unusual to hear of a direct marketing initiative that does not have response as a key stage in the communication programme.

Measurement: It has always been central to direct marketing. Before cheap computing power became available, it was already possible to record and measure the immediate results of marketing

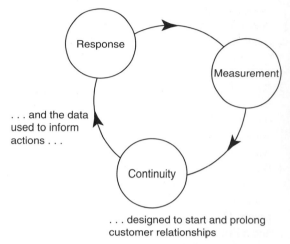

... customers' responses are recorded ...

... and the data used to inform actions ...

... designed to start and prolong customer relationships

Figure 19.4   Direct marketing is the process in which . . .

expenditures. Reply coupons and telephone numbers included codes to identify the source of responses. Cost-per-response (CPR) and cost-per-sale (CPS) were and still are useful measures. Now measurement is extended to individual customers' activity. Because each customer is identified, their buying behaviour can be tracked over time. This enables the eventual return on marketing investments to be measured and forecasting to be improved.

Continuity: It is the aim of every competent direct marketer who seeks to maximize the gearing on the customer acquisition investment by doing more business with the customer for a longer period.

The customer marketing database

An electronic library is needed to receive fresh data, keep it and make it accessible, so as to maintain the continuous learning loop that characterizes direct marketing.

This is the customer marketing database system. It brings together information from a variety of sources and links the information to customers (Figure 19.5).

The database enables marketing costs to be reduced. This is achieved through using information derived from:

- the cost, number and value of new customers obtained by source;
- the results of contacts with established customers.

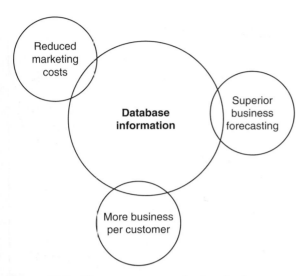

Figure 19.5   The customer marketing database

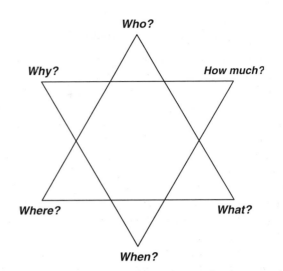

Figure 19.6   The customer marketing database answers six questions

For example, it may cost twice as much to acquire customers from advertising in *The Economist* as in *The Times*. But the database may reveal that *Economist* readers buy more and stay longer, increasing their LTV and making them more profitable.

More business per customer is achieved through using customer purchase histories, leading to:

- better identification and segmentation of customers;
- greater personalization and more relevant offers.

For example, customers giving high value orders and paying promptly may receive special treatment. Offers may reflect customers' specific interests.

Superior business forecasting is achieved by analysing campaign and customer history data, using past performance as a guide to future performance. Because the errors in past activities need not be repeated, efficiency should be subject to continuous improvement.

The database answers six questions

At its simplest, the database is the heart of an information system that answers the six simple questions shown in Figure 19.6 every time interaction occurs.

Who?

- Name and contact data
- Status (e.g. customer or prospect)

- Associations (i.e. same household or company as another customer)
- Credit status (if relevant)

What?

- Order or enquiry
- Items ordered
- Product category
- In stock/out of stock

Where?

- Sales channel
- Branch or media code

The system should allocate a unique reference number (URN) or alphanumeric code to each customer. This enables customer queries to be answered all the more quickly, the URN guiding service and sales staff to the customer record or transaction details.

The system will recognize whether an order is a repeat order from an established customer or a first order from a new customer.

How much?

- The price of each item
- Gross order value
- Fewer out-of-stocks
- Fewer returns

When?

- When last instruction/order received
- When last instruction/order fulfilled

Real-time data

Websites and contact centres can, with the right software, respond to purchase data in real time. When a customer puts a Manchester United Annual in the shopping basket this may trigger the offer of Ryan Gigg's autobiography.

Opportunistic marketing of this sort will be used in combination with offers or other special treatments that are driven by previously captured data.

Why?

- Response/non-response to last promotion
- Identifying code of promotion causing response

Not every system will contain transactional data because it will not always be available. For example, Lever Brothers would not have full transaction data for every Persil buyer, but would have promotional responses recorded on their database.

B2B customer marketing data is often more extensive and complex. A company may have a number of identities (branches, departments and divisions) and a good many individual buyers or decision makers. A business customer may also use multi-channels to secure supplies of different items. Purchases are increasingly likely to be automated, using EDI, Internet exchanges or an extranet.

Advantages of the database

A database exploiting transactional information tells the marketer everything about customers' purchases updated with each new response (and non-response).

For example, the transactional database:

- includes *all* customers, not just a sample or cross section;
- gives customer value data: Recency, Frequency, Monetary Value (RFM) of purchases culminating in the LTV of each customer;
- tells us about new customers: what they responded to and, perhaps, which creative treatment appealed to them;
- tells us about lost, lapsed and inactive customers;
- tells us about who buys which products and responds to which types of incentive or message;

Pareto and the database: American car rental market

- 20 per cent of American adults rent a car at least once a year;
- Only 5 per cent rent a car more than once;
- 0.2 per cent rent a car 10 or more times;
- This 0.2 per cent represents one in a hundred customers;
- One in a hundred customers provide car rental companies with one quarter (25 per cent) of their business.

Facts from *The One-to-One Future*, Peppers & Rogers

- gives continuous information which is automatically updated with each new transaction;
- reports upon, and analyses, marketing campaigns and tactics;
- facilitates controlled tests of alternatives (e.g. product and price comparisons);
- provides back data (historical data) which helps the process of predicting the future behaviour of each and every customer.

Correctly used, a transactional customer database gives a running commentary on the marketer's ability to serve the needs of customers, highlighting opportunities to increase efficiency.

At one time car rental advertising was almost untargeted. But the direct marketer differentiates between customers and non-customers, then between casual customers and regular customers and finally between regular customers and frequent customers. The example of the American car rental market shows why.

The top 25 per cent of customers are those who rent a car more than once. But within this exclusive group, 1 in 25 of them rents a car 10 times or more in a year. This group, amounting to one in a hundred customers (0.2 per cent of adults) is worth 25 times as much as the average customer. These extremely valuable customers provide car rental companies with a quarter of their business.

It would be cheaper to telephone these customers personally to thank them than it would to reach them all once with a TV commercial.

Recognizing the value of these 'super customers', car rental firms offered loyal users free rentals at weekends. But frequent business travellers want time with their families. When this idea

> The customer marketing database serves two functions:
>
> 1 It provides management information.
> 2 It facilitates one-to-one customer communications outbound and inbound.

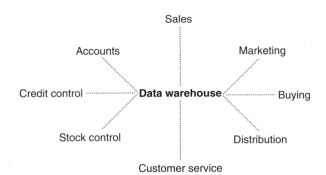

Figure 19.7   The data warehouse

failed, National Car Rental came up with a better idea. Targeting the tired, stressed and status-conscious business traveller, their answer was the Emerald Club, having its own aisle in National's car lot at the airport. Members could pick any car in the Emerald Aisle and drive off, pausing only to have their card 'swiped' at the checkout.

National's database enabled them to:

- recognize how much more valuable their best customers were than others;
- discover how much business was at risk if these customers were lost (it would take 33 average new customers to replace one lost top customer);
- recognize the circumstances of these customers, that is, frequent business travellers;
- send Emerald cards to the right customers.

Notice that the database is used to provide both management information and the means of communicating to customers.

The customer marketing database not only facilitates outbound communications but enables customers to be recognized when they telephone or visit the website. The contact centre agent (operator) can call up the customer's transaction record on screen so that the customer does not have to repeat information that the company should already know.

Data, CRM and eCRM

In recent years, many large companies have been dealing with the problem of integrating data from a multiplicity of management information systems. The ideal solution of bringing together all relevant customer information into one customer marketing database system was not available to these companies. The systems they used in different parts of the business were incompatible.

Looking at the captions in Figure 19.7: accounts, sales, marketing, buying, distribution,

---

The whole customer

As well as having a current account and a savings account, a bank customer may deal with the home loan division, the life and general insurance divisions, the credit card division and the personal investment management division. Since the average customer holds only 1.2 accounts, such a customer would be very valuable to the bank. Yet, before the creation of an enterprise-wide CRM system, the bank would not have recognized all of these different relationships as being with the same customer.

---

customer service, stock control and credit control, we can see these might all provide information for the marketing database.

Because some of these functions were seen as completely separate in many large businesses, and may have become computerized at different times, their systems are unlikely to be fully compatible. They will certainly not be compatible with e-commerce systems. Old systems are referred to as *legacy* systems.

However, if essential details, such as file formats, are harmonized, it is possible to store data that would otherwise simply be archived, in a data warehouse. Now, the data can be processed in such a way that it can be analysed by a competent person, using a PC.

The process of retrieving and analysing data from a data warehouse is called *data mining*. Data mining is often used in businesses with masses of transactional data, such as banks and airlines.

The idea of the data warehouse is to bring systems together to form an enterprise-wide management information system. In theory at least, this permits a CRM system to be employed. The idea behind CRM is that the whole of a customer's dealings with the company can be put together. Such systems are devised by outside software vendors and may need extensive adaptation.

In practice, company divisions or departments (including marketing) may find their needs better served by *data marts*. These are fed by the data warehouse but contain only information that is relevant to the departmental interest and are designed to make the data easier to interrogate and analyse.

Integrating eCRM

When the company's front office is a website, the volume of data being collected, processed and managed is very large. Some data, for example DNS (domain name system) and clickstream data, is peculiar to digital marketing. The latter, particularly, can overwhelm a system unless it is *summarized*. It is not necessary to keep this information for individual customers as long as customer preferences, either declared or implicit through transactional behaviour, are recorded.

> When human interaction is by e-mail or chat, there is a full, self-generated digital record of the contact – unlike a phone call or field sales visit. This record may be used to auto-generate e-marketing contacts.

Summary data

The transactional database needs historical data. Otherwise there can be no record of a customer's business relationship with the company. Usually, the data used to portray a customer history (or the results of a promotion) is summarized, so that it does not occupy too much space (memory) in the system.

While this is very sensible because it saves costs, the problem is that essential detail is sometimes lost. Generally speaking, the *number, value* and *dates* of a customer's transactions will be retained but the *merchandise categories* and, certainly, the actual *products purchased* will often be lost for all except the most recent transaction. Furthermore, companies are usually bad at keeping customer service records. A marketing analyst can waste hours or days looking at customer purchase profiles, seeking an explanation for why

some customers are disloyal. The true explanation may lie elsewhere. Perhaps the disloyal customers ordered goods that were out-of-stock or had to return defective items.

Meanwhile, the sharp reduction in data storage and retrieval costs has encouraged firms to keep more raw data for analysis instead of summarizing it and archiving old data. This is a major benefit of data warehousing.

CRM and database marketing

Although enterprise-wide CRM systems may have grown out of database marketing (some would say call centre operations), they have become distanced from the marketing function.

- CRM systems are essentially operational whereas marketing database systems can exploit data that is downloaded from operational systems without disturbing them. Marketing database needs may be supplied by a data mart within a CRM system.
- The CRM system is generally seen as the software that automates the front office. The front office includes the call or contact centre, the website and any other point of interaction between the company and its customers. Front office functions include service as well as sales.
- The impetus for the adoption of CRM has not necessarily been increased customer knowledge, but cost cutting. Cost cutting is achieved by increasing productivity of customer-facing staff and by diverting transactions down completely automated routes.
- The CRM system may work in tandem with an ERP (Enterprise Resource Planning) system that handles the back office functions. The emphasis is on operational efficiency.

CRM and relationship marketing

The very name 'customer relationship management' implies that customers are a resource that can be managed, like the supply chain and sales staff. Although CRM feeds off customer data, it is essentially neutral. It may be customer focused in a marketing sense or it may be enterprise focused, being employed to seek ways to save on customer service. It all depends who is extracting actionable data and for what purpose. However, the fact that a common information system is being used throughout the organization is clearly advantageous.

The customer as relationship manager

Two features that are apparent in all forms of interactive marketing are transparency and customer empowerment. The US software producer, MicroMarketing, has devised software that enables customers to pull information out of data warehouses in order to complete transactions by web or phone. This looks like the way of the future.

CRM should not be confused with *Relationship Marketing*, which is the title of an influential book first published in 1991. Its author was Regis McKenna, a marketing consultant known widely for his work with Apple Computers.

McKenna believes that marketing is everything and doing marketing is everyone's job.

The key elements of McKenna's notion are:

- Select a specific market segment and dominate through a superior understanding of customers' product and service needs. Integrate customers into the design process.
- Use monitoring, analysis and feedback to maintain 'dynamic positioning' that is always appropriate to the marketing environment.
- Develop partnerships with suppliers, vendors and users to help maintain a competitive edge.

Note that this concept of relationship marketing is also quite distinct from direct marketing, although direct marketers may be ideally placed to exploit it, especially in an e-commerce environment. One example of a direct and digital marketer apparently following McKenna's strategy to the letter is Dell.

Relationship marketing in action

- Dell sets out to develop and dominate the direct distribution segment of the PC market, a segment which (by value) consists primarily of business buyers.
- Dell customers 'build' their own computers on ordering from the Dell website. In practice, Dell believes they 'uptrade themselves' – specifying a higher performance machine than they could be 'sold' by a salesperson. By inviting customers' comments and suggestions and responding accordingly, Dell is also able to keep innovating in a relevant way. For example, DellHost allows customers to rent space for

their website from Dell, removing the necessity to buy, monitor and maintain servers. In this way Dell generates revenue by solving a known problem, not merely by selling hardware.
- Through opening up its order book on the extranet, Dell is able to make suppliers responsible for maintaining just-in-time parts deliveries. Suppliers can also meet on the extranet and collaborate to solve mutual problems. Superior supply chain management has given Dell a competitive edge.

Who is loyal; who is not

The database can often reveal whether a customer's purchase pattern indicates loyal or disloyal purchase behaviour. However, it cannot report directly on customers' use of competitive offerings. This can only be done on a sample basis, using marketing research. *Note*: The sample for this research can be taken from the database.

Limitations of the customer information system

The database is inward looking to the extent that it refers only to those customers that a business already has on its books.

Although it is possible to import external data to profile customers and compare them with the market at large, this is not a substitute for marketing research.

The database, however good, remains introspective.

It does not admit or report upon external influences. Disturbance to plans and forecasts may result from environmental influences, for example the economic situation, environmental concerns or other newsworthy preoccupations which affect purchase behaviour.

Worse, it does not report on customers' use of competitors or on the success or otherwise of competitive initiatives. Share of customer (or share of wallet) is a key success measure in direct marketing.

Unless marketers are in a monopolistic situation and have absolutely no competitors (and who is ever in that position?) they need to be fully alert to competitive influences. Competition and disruption may come not only from direct competitors, but also from indirect competitors.

Quantitative market research is required by all marketers, direct or otherwise. Qualitative research is also needed because the database can only reveal *what* customers are buying or not buying. It cannot say *why*, or suggest alternative new product avenues with much confidence. Data analysis relies on back data (customer history) to predict future behaviour. While this is generally the best guide, it is certainly not infallible. Circumstances and attitudes may change, causing sudden shifts in demand.

The database and research: the last word

In their report *The Machine that Changed the World*, Womack, Jones and Roos made clear how Toyota researched consumer preferences:

> Toyota was determined never to lose a former buyer . . . it could minimise the chance of this happening by using data on its consumer database to predict what Toyota buyers would want to do next . . . unlike mass producers who conduct evaluation clinics and other survey research on randomly selected buyers . . . Toyota went directly to its existing customers in planning new products . . . Established customers were treated as members of the Toyota family.

In one generation Toyota went from small producer to world's number one in the automotive market.

Clearly, if a manufacturer has 5 per cent of the market and a 70 per cent loyalty rate, it is more sensible for it to learn what its customers want than what other manufacturers' customers want. Yet few of Toyota's competitors accepted this obvious truth.

Toyota's success is a triumph for good marketing, not simply a testament to Japanese technology. While other manufacturers were obsessed with 'conquest sales' (sales made to competitors' customers) Toyota's understanding of the value of customer retention was and is central to the discipline of direct and digital marketing.

A competitor of Toyota estimated that it cost five times as much to make a conquest sale as a repeat sale. Collecting and acting on information like this is the hallmark of successful direct marketing.

Summary

As we enter 2007 whilst the term 'direct marketing' may still carry many prejudices and misunderstandings, the skill sets that direct marketers have honed over the years are even more vital to major businesses today. Direct marketing is still the most accountable form of marketing. Its concepts such as LTV help to determine the value of customer relationships and are as important as brand equity. Direct marketers are also better versed at managing the customer journey, understanding the touch points and building a one-to-one dialogue with customers. Equally, direct marketers understand profiling and customer value segmentation better than general marketers as it is based on the empirical customer data they maintain. Building, maintaining and utilizing customer databases are at the heart of direct marketing's strengths. While digital media has finally made one-to-one communications in real time possible. As Sir Martin Sorrell has quoted that direct and interactive marketing will be over 50 per cent of his global business income in the next 5 years. Direct marketing has come of age. It is increasingly difficult to differentiate direct marketing from marketing. As Mike Tildesley, Marketing Director of Direct Line, has said, 'Direct marketing is marketing – what's the difference'. In his case everything Mike does is direct marketing, from building the brand to servicing the customers via UK contact centres.

CHAPTER 20

A strategic approach to customer relationship management

ADRIAN PAYNE and PENNIE FROW

Introduction

Customer Relationship Management (CRM) is a management approach that seeks to create, develop and enhance relationships with carefully targeted customers in order to maximize customer value, corporate profitability and thus shareholder value. CRM is also concerned with utilizing information technology (IT) to implement relationship marketing strategies.

The market for CRM services is expanding, representing a significant growth sector. This is evident in both the take-up of CRM and the investment in CRM tools and techniques. The increased interest in CRM as a strategic business approach is a consequence of a number of trends. These include:

- The shift in business focus from transactional marketing to relationship marketing
- The transition in organizational structures from functions to processes
- The recognition of the benefits of using information proactively rather than solely reactively
- The greater utilization of technology in managing and maximizing customer insight.

However, there remains considerable confusion about what exactly CRM is. Confusion surrounding the definition and role of CRM may be explained by the following factors: its relatively recent arrival; the lack of a widely accepted and clear definition of its scope; an emphasis on IT aspects rather than its benefits in terms of building relationships with customers; and its associations with specific tools sold by IT vendors.

In this chapter, we outline a strategic framework for addressing CRM. This framework has been developed to clarify CRM's function and 'fit' within the organization, and to help optimize its use as a strategic management approach. This framework comprises five interrelated cross-functional processes:

1 the strategy development process
2 the value creation process
3 the multichannel integration process
4 the information management process
5 the performance assessment process.

While these processes have universal application in all organizations, the extent to which they need to be emphasized will vary according to each organization's unique situation.

This chapter provides a framework for understanding and implementing CRM as a means of ensuring the overall business strategy delivers increased shareholder results. The structure of the chapter is as follows: first, we briefly review the nature of CRM and provide a definition; second, a framework for understanding CRM at strategic level is outlined; third, five cross-functional processes that enable CRM to be adopted and implemented effectively are examined in turn; finally, we address four critical areas that need to be addressed for successful CRM implementation.

Defining CRM

The term 'Customer Relationship Management' emerged within the IT vendor community and practitioner community in the mid 1990s. It is typically used to describe technology-based customer solutions such as sales force automation. Within the academic community, the two terms 'relationship marketing' and 'CRM' are often used interchangeably (Parvatiyar and Sheth, 2001). CRM is, however, more commonly used in the context of technology solutions and has been described as 'information-enabled relationship marketing' by Ryals and Payne (2001).

A significant problem faced by many organizations deciding to adopt CRM stems from the fact that there is still a great deal of confusion about what constitutes CRM. In interviews with executives, which formed part of our research, we found a wide range of views regarding what is meant by CRM. To some, it meant direct e-mail, a loyalty card scheme or a data base, while others viewed it as a help desk or a call centre. Some said that it was about populating a data warehouse or undertaking data mining, while others saw CRM as an e-commerce solution such as the use of a personalization engine on the Internet, or a relational database for sales force automation. The lack of a widely accepted and appropriate definition of CRM can contribute to the failure of a CRM project where an organization views CRM from a limited technology perspective or undertakes CRM on a fragmented basis.

We believe that how CRM is defined is not merely a question of semantics. Its definition can have a significant impact on how CRM is accepted and practised by the entire organization. From a strategic standpoint, CRM is not simply an IT solution to acquiring and growing a customer base; rather, it involves a profound synthesis of strategic vision; a corporate understanding of the nature of customer value within a multichannel environment; the utilization of the appropriate information management and CRM applications; and high quality operations, fulfilment and service. Thus, we propose CRM, in any organization, should be viewed in a broad strategic context.

We define CRM as follows:

> CRM is a strategic approach concerned with creating improved shareholder value through the development of appropriate relationships with key customers and customer segments. CRM unites the potential of relationship marketing strategies and

IT to create profitable, long-term relationships with customers and other key stakeholders. CRM provides enhanced opportunities to use data and information to both understand customers and co-create value with them. This requires a cross-functional integration of processes, people, operations and marketing capabilities that is enabled through information, technology and applications (Payne and Frow, 2005).

This definition provided guidance for the development of the strategic framework we now outline.[1]

A strategic framework for CRM

Organizations large and small, across a variety of sectors, are increasingly embracing CRM as a major element of corporate strategy for two important reasons: new technologies now enable companies to target chosen market segments, micro-segments or individual customers more precisely and new marketing thinking has recognized the limitations of traditional marketing and the potential of more customer-focused, process-oriented perspectives.

However, CRM's recognized potential to deliver commercial improvement has been curtailed by a lack of clear guidance on what CRM is. what its component parts are and how the component parts can be integrated successfully within the organization. When an organization views CRM narrowly as a direct e-mail initiative, a loyalty card scheme or a call centre, it is likely to to develop its CRM activities on a piecemeal and fragmented basis.

In this chapter, we position CRM as a strategic set of activities that commence with a detailed review of an organization's strategy and conclude with an improvement in shareholder value. The notion that competitive advantage stems from the creation of value for the customer *and* for the company is key to the success of CRM, which demands that responsibility for value delivery is shared across functions and hierarchies. Because

[1] This chapter draws on material from:

Payne, A. and Frow, P. (2005) A strategic framework for CRM, *Journal of Marketing*, **69**(4), October, 167–176.

Payne, A. and Frow, P. (2006) Customer relationship management: from strategy to implementation, *Journal of Marketing Management*, **22**(1–2),135–168.

Payne, A. (2006) *The Handbook of CRM: Achieving Excellence in Customer Management*, Elsevier Butterworth Heinemann, Oxford.

CRM is a cross-functional activity and in large companies seeks to focus on potentially millions of individual customer relationships simultaneously, it can be unwieldy to implement and impossible to get right without a purposeful and systematic approach.

The *Strategic Framework for CRM* outlined in Figure 20.1 is based on the interaction of the five cross-functional business processes outlined above that deal with strategy development, value creation, multichannel integration, information management and performance assessment. These processes make a greater contribution to organizational prosperity collectively than individually and must, therefore, be treated as an integrated and iterative set of activities. A detailed consideration of each of the processes will help managers realize the benefits of CRM.

The framework is based on the premise that all five processes are critical to the business and that they need to be closely integrated with each other. The way in which the framework can be best considered is as a progression through each of the processes, approaching them essentially from left to right. It should start with a review of the organizations' strategic context and conclude with

improvement in shareholder value. The framework, as the arrows in both directions in Figure 20.1 suggest, is iterative and interactive. A review of a later process is likely to require a reconsideration of elements within processes examined earlier. Rather than be seen as a one-way linear progression, the framework should be viewed as an iterative feedback-driven progression aimed at continually enhancing the benefits of CRM. To understand what these benefits are and how they are manifested, it is necessary to consider each of the processes in turn.

The strategy development process

Where are we and what do we want to achieve?

Who are the customers that we want and how should we segment them?

Most companies today recognize that their future depends on the strength of their business relationships, and most crucially, their relationships with customers. In an effort to effect better CRM, many organizations are introducing technology solutions in an effort to break the bonds

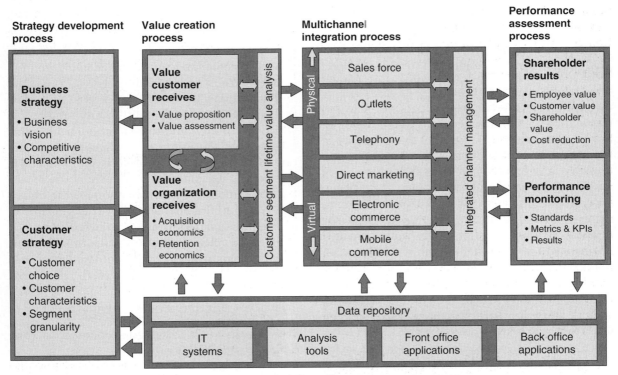

Figure 20.1 The strategic framework for CRM
Source: Based on Payne and Frow (2005).

of antiquated IT legacy systems – often with disappointing outcomes. CRM, however, is not simply an IT solution to the problem of getting the right customer base and growing it. CRM is much more.

Rather than immediately turning to such technology solutions, managers need to first consider CRM in the context of overall business strategy. CRM must actively reflect and reinforce the wider goals of the business if it is to be successful. The strategy development process requires a dual focus on the organization's _Business strategy_ and its _Customer strategy_, and how well the two interrelate and will fundamentally affect the success of the CRM strategy.

Business strategy

A comprehensive review of the business strategy will provide a realistic platform on which to construct the CRM strategy, as well as generate recommendations for general improvement. The area of business strategy is well known, so it requires little commentary here. An examination of industry and competitive characteristics (e.g. Porter, 1980) needs to be considered in terms of future possible structural change including creating challenges to traditional business models (e.g. Anderson _et al._, 1997).

Business vision and competitive characteristics

The organization needs to fully understand its own competencies within a competitive context in order to be able to transfer them to the customer as customer value. It is also vital that everyone in the organization is pulling in the same, strategic direction, and that they are alert to changes which might signal opportunity or disaster. This is especially important where the organization is in transition from a product orientation to customer orientation. Consideration of the following key business issues – present and future – will serve to re-affirm the appropriate course and direction for the organization.

Stage of industry evolution: What is the current state of your industry structure? What are the likely and possible future changes?

Competitors' profiles: What is the nature of your competitors? How do they compete? How will new competitors evolve in the future? Are there new entrants on the horizon that are not hindered by the same legacy architecture? Are there

new strategic alliances that may disrupt the value market?

Your company's profile: Where does your company fit within the industry structure? What are your organization's resources and competencies?

Business definition: What is your strategic intent? In the light of industry evolution and the competitive environment, how should you define your business scope? Have you developed a statement of business purpose or a mission statement that clearly communicates this to relevant stakeholders?

Channels of distribution: What is the current and future role of different distribution channels? What opportunities exist for disintermediation or re-intermediation? What opportunities exist for new forms of distribution and delivery in terms of electronic commerce and mobile commerce?

Information technology platform: What is the appropriate IT platform for serving present and future customers and corporate needs?

The value of such a review is that it will provide a realistic platform on which to construct the business's CRM strategy. A company needs to fully understand its own competencies in order to be able to transfer them to the customer as customer value. It is also vital that everyone within the organization is clear about the business's overall purpose and intent so that they can pull in the same, strategic direction. This is especially important where the organization is in transition from a product orientation to customer orientation.

As well as understanding its own capacities and limitations, the company needs to appreciate the nature of the competitive environment in which it operates, and to be alert to changes that might signal opportunity or disaster. A greater understanding of the external environment will also benefit the company's understanding of customers, of the opportunities and also the threats they face in the marketplace. The purpose of addressing business strategy as part of the CRM strategy development process is to determine how the organization's customer strategy should be developed and how it will evolve in the future.

Customer strategy

The other half of the strategy equation is deciding which customers the business wants most to attract and keep, and which customers it would prefer to be without. No firm can successfully be 'all things to all people', and thus finding the best potential customers and retaining them is vital.

Customer choice and customer characteristics

The prior review of business strategy will be instrumental in reaching a judgement on broad customer focus. A consideration of the following issues will assist the organization to determine more specifically its choice of customers and their characteristics when defining the role of CRM in the organization.

Nature of customer strategy: Do you have one? Is it flexible enough to withstand change in the competitive environment and strong enough to lead constructive change within the organization? What is the current nature of your dealings with customers? Are they basic transactions or more formalized relationships? Do you specialize in serving an elite clientele or is your focus more on the 'mass market'?

Status of customer strategy: Is your customer strategy considered important within the organization? Does the management of customers receive sufficient and appropriate support in terms of resource, recognition and real commitment? Is it working? If not, why not?

Customer segments: Who are your existing and potential customers? Which forms of segmentation are most appropriate rather than easiest to achieve? What are the major segments? What are the opportunities for micro segmentation, one-to-one marketing and mass customization?

Knowledge of customer base: Can you describe in detail the profile(s) of your customers? Can you identify patterns in their motivations and behaviours? If so, in a refined or basic way? Do you actively and proactively seek to build your customer 'intelligence'? Do you fully exploit the customer intelligence you have?

Product/service involvement and complexity of purchasing behaviour: Who constitutes the decision-making unit of your customers? How are your products/services purchased? How important are they to your customers? Is your average level of customer service quality exceptional/adequate/poor? Are you working to improve it/maintain it?

Customer relationships: What kinds of relationship do you have or want to have with your customers? How retainable are your customers? How do you 'remember' and 'reward' your customers? Do you feed customer communication back into the business so you can relate to customers on a one-to-one basis?

Value of customer base: Do you formally quantify the value of your customers? In what terms (loyalty, customer lifetime value (CLV) revenue, referrals, etc.)? Do you actively seek to select the most valuable customers and deselect the less or least valuable customers?

The organization will need to determine the amount and kind of customer information it requires, as well as how closely and through what channels it should interact with its customer base both now and in the future. Furthermore, while the ability to satisfy customers' existing needs is paramount, companies must also strive to pre-empt their future, often unexpressed, needs.

It is important to recognize that customers differ and thus relationships with customers will have to be managed differently if they are to be successful. This is a key principle of CRM. The aim of CRM is to build relationship strategies that refine relationships and in this way increase their value. Creating competitive advantage through the skilful management of customer relationships will normally require a reappraisal of the way in which customers are approached and segmented, and the way in which resources are allocated and used. To achieve this level of refinement requires a careful choice of the levels at which segmentation is undertaken.

Segment granularity

Creating competitive advantage through the skilful management of customer relationships will normally require a reappraisal of the way in which customers are approached and segmented, and the way in which resources are allocated and used. Customer strategy involves determining the appropriate level of *segmentation granularity* (including whether a macro-segmentation, micro-segmentation, or one-to-one is appropriate; e.g. Rubin, 1997), identifying key customer segments and building strategies to address these customers. If a company operates in an intermediated market, it will have a number of customer groups and each of them needs to be fully considered in terms of segmentation approach and granularity.

Decisions regarding segmentation need to be taken in the context of a number of considerations. These include the existing and potential profitability of different customer types, the information on customers that is available and that can be collected at a justifiable cost, the level of competition, and the existing and likely future use of channels.

Considerable attention has been directed at the potential for shifting from a mass market to a 'one-to-one' marketing environment (Peppers and Rogers, 1993). Exploiting e-commerce opportunities and the fundamental economic characteristics of the Internet can enable a much deeper level of segmentation granularity than is usually provided by other channels.

However, segment granularity needs to be examined in the company and industry context in which it is being considered. In some cases, especially in an e-commerce environment, an immediate migration to a 'one to one' or a 'one to few' may be undertaken. However, in more traditional businesses, more 'macro' forms of segmentation will be relevant. It is worth making the point that many companies have for a long time adopted one-to-one marketing through a key account management system, although it was not referred to as such.

An important point is that 'one-to-one' marketing does not imply adopting a 'one-to-one' approach with every single customer. Rather, it suggests understanding customers in terms of their economic importance and then adjusting the marketing approach to reflect the importance of different customer groups according to their existing and potential profitability. Peppers and Rogers make this point. However, it is sometimes disregarded when a discussion of one-to-one marketing is undertaken.

Thus, clear segmentation of the customer base and adopting the correct level of segment granularity is an important element of customer strategy. It is also a necessary pre-condition before considering the value creation process, as segmentation is crucial to this process.

The value creation process

How should we deliver value to our customers?

How should we maximize the lifetime value of the customers we want?

The value creation process is concerned with transforming the outputs of the strategy development process into programmes to deliver value to both the customer and the supplier organization. The *value creation process* consists of three key elements: (1) determining what value the company can provide to its customers (the 'value customer receives'), (2) determining the value of the organization received from its customers (the 'value organization receives') and (3) by successfully managing this value exchange, the organization then aims to maximize the lifetime value of desirable customer segments.

However, the emphasis in many companies is on the second element of value. To these companies, customer value means:

- how much money can we extract from the customer?
- how we can sell them more of the existing products and services they are buying?
- how we can cross-sell them new products and services?

Most companies do not consider, in sufficient detail, the value the company seeks to deliver to customers in clearly identified customer segments and micro-segments and *how* they are going to achieve this. Where both sides of the value exchange are not addressed in an integrated manner, it is not surprising that a supplier's offering to customers does not have a strong impact on key customer segments. Operating with a detailed understanding of the increased value a company can deliver to its customers is likely to significantly increase the value the organization subsequently receives from its key customer segments.

The value the customer receives

The value the customer receives from the supplier organization can be determined by developing value propositions and undertaking a value assessment. Here, customer value is seen as an inherent part of the product and one that can be managed actively by a company to benefit the customer. In fact, customers are not buying goods or services – they really buy specific benefits which solve problems. The value they attach to the offer is in proportion to the perceived ability of the offer to solve their problem. Product augmentation is a means of creating product differentiation and thus added value from the customer's perspective.

For managers wishing to review the existing 'offer' to customers and consider the potential for increasing the value they provide to their customers, some structured framework or methodology to do this is desirable. One useful approach is the value-proposition concept.

The value proposition

In recent years, managers have started to use the term 'value proposition' increasingly frequently. All businesses exist to deliver some form of value proposition which may be implicit or explicit. A company should aim to create a value proposition that is superior to and more profitable than those of competitors.

However, our discussions with many organizations suggest that they rarely develop a value proposition and where they do it is not usually underpinned by an analytical process.

The term 'value proposition' is used by organizations in two ways. In general terms, it is used to describe the notion of creating customer value in a very broad sense. In more specific terms, it is used to describe a particular approach to creating customer value first developed at consulting firm McKinsey & Co. (e.g. Lanning, 1998).

In this latter sense, the term 'value proposition' is used to describe an approach that formally defines:

- the target customers
- the benefits offered to those customers
- the price charged relative to the competition.

Value propositions provide an explanation of the relationship between the performance attributes of a product or service, the fulfilment of needs across multiple customer roles (e.g. acquiring, using and disposing of products) and the total cost. Thus, it should be based on an understanding of the total customer relationship life cycle.

Value assessment

Having developed a value proposition, the next step should be to undertake a value assessment. A value assessment seeks to determine if the value proposition that has been developed is likely to result in superior customer experience. Value assessment may be undertaken in a number of ways.

A frequent method is for a company to make an assessment based on subjective judgements about the attributes and benefits which are important to the customer. A frequent mistake made by companies is assuming customers attach the same importance to these attributes as does the supplier company. Experience suggests that companies often do not identify all the relevant attributes; and, even when a company correctly identifies those attributes which are most relevant to the customer, the ranking of these by the customer and the supplier may vary significantly.

The first step should be to identify the attributes of importance to given customer segments *from the perspective of the customer*. Once these attributes are defined, we can seek to identify the relative importance of each of them and the company's perceived performance on these attributes relative to the competition. There are various ways of discovering the importance that the customer attaches to each attribute. One method is to ask a representative sample of customers to rank them in importance on a five point scale. However, this is impractical when there is a large number of attributes as this gives little insight into their relative importance. Alternatively, rankings could be made on the attributes and a weight given to them.

A more sophisticated solution is to adopt an innovation developed in customer–market research: the use of conjoint analysis (e.g. Aaker *et al.*, 1998). Conjoint analysis is based on the concept of successively trading-off one of these attribute against another. Also known as trade-off analysis, it is now used more regularly by consulting firms, market research firms and advertising agencies.

Recognizing the differences between customer segments is critical. Trade-off analysis can also be used to identify customers that share common preferences in terms of attributes. Experience of researchers and consultants working in this area suggest that this form of analysis may often reveal substantial market segments with service needs that are not fully catered for by existing offers.

The value the organization receives

As indicated above, the value the company receives from the customer has the greatest association with customer value for most organizations. Customer value from this perspective of value is an output of, rather than an input to, value creation. As such, it focuses not on the creation of value for the customer but on the value outcome derived from providing and delivering superior customer value. Fundamental to the concept of customer value in this context is understanding the economics of customer acquisition and customer retention.

Customer acquisition and its economics

The importance of customer acquisition varies considerably according to a company's specific situation. For example, a new Internet entrant will primarily be concerned with customer acquisition, whilst an established manufacturing company operating in a mature market may be more concerned with customer retention.

The customer acquisition process is typically concerned with:

- acquiring customers at a lower cost
- acquiring more customers
- acquiring more attractive customers.

The starting point in understanding customer value is to determine the existing customer acquisition costs within the existing channels that are utilized and to determine how these vary across different segments or microsegments. The next step is to consider how acquisition costs may vary across different channels. The Internet has allowed many companies to create websites which have enabled customers to be acquired at a fraction of the costs of other more traditional channels.

Once a company has an understanding of how acquisition costs vary at both the segment and channel levels, they can then start to explore the issue of acquiring more customers and more attractive customers. For most marketing managers, acquiring more customers, within a given segment and channel, usually means using a better promotional approach in terms of more targeted direct e-mail, more effective advertising or an improved website. However, the opportunity of using existing customers to attract new customers should also be considered. This means creating 'advocacy' amongst your existing customers through delivering a superior value proposition that results in much better service than that of the competition.

In many instances, customer acquisition can be improved through insights from the analysis undertaken in developing the value proposition and value assessment outlined above. This should result in a better focus on key customer segments, adopting the appropriate level of segment granularity and creating propositions attractive to those target customers.

Customer retention and its economics

Many authors and researchers have suggested that it costs around five times more to get a new customer than to keep an existing one. Despite this finding, many companies have traditionally focused their marketing activity on acquiring

new customers, rather than retaining existing customers. This may be partly due to the historical convention in many companies that rewards customer acquisition to a much greater extent than customer retention.

Whilst most companies recognize that customer retention is important, relatively few of them understand the economics of customer retention within their own firm. Until relatively recently, there was little research that critically evaluated the relative financial benefits of customer acquisition versus customer retention. In 1990, a partner at consulting firm Bain & Co and a professor at the Harvard Business School published some revealing research findings, which demonstrated the financial impact of customer retention (Reichheld and Sasser, 1990). They found even a small increase in customer retention produced a dramatic and positive effect on profitability. Their research showed that a five percentage point increase in customer retention yielded a very high improvement in profitability in net present value (NPV) terms. Increasing the customer retention rate from, say, 85 to 90 per cent represented an NPV profit increase from 35 to 95 per cent amongst the businesses they examined.

Given these dramatic findings about the impact of improvement in customer retention and the explanations for them, there is a strong justification for companies to examine the economics of customer retention in their own businesses. However, our research suggests that managers have been slow to implement changes in marketing activities to emphasize customer retention.

Customer segment lifetime value analysis

A balance is needed between the marketing efforts directed towards existing and new customers. This balance will vary greatly depending on whether the business is a 'dotcom' startup or a mature 'bricks and mortar' company. However, in general, marketing expenditure is imbalanced with too much attention being directed at customer acquisition.

To enable a decision on the relative amount of emphasis that needs to be placed on them, an understanding of both acquisition and retention economics at the segment level is critical. To calculate a customer's real value, a company must look at the projected profit over the life of the account. This represents the expected profit flow over a customer's lifetime. The key metric used here is CLV, which is defined as the NPV of the future profit flow over a customer's lifetime.

It should not be assumed that companies will wish to retain *all* their customers. Some customers may cost too much money to service, or have such high acquisition costs in relation to their profitability that they will never prove to be worthwhile and profitable. Clearly, it would be inadvisable to invest further in such customer segments. It is likely that within a given portfolio of customers, there may be some segments that are profitable, some that are at break-even point and some that are unprofitable. Thus, increasing customer retention does not always yield increases in customer profitability. In some instances, increasing the retention of such unprofitable customers will decrease profitability. It should be recognized, however, that unprofitable customers may be valuable in their contribution towards fixed costs and considerable caution needs to be placed in the allocation of fixed and variable costs to ensure that customers who make a contribution are not simply discarded.

Advanced analytical models can help organizations determine customer value in terms of CLV. However, thoroughly understanding existing acquisition economics and retention economics at the segment and micro-segment levels is a stage relatively few organizations have advanced to. Once this stage has been reached, the organization should move to modelling *future profit potential* for each market segment. Modelling of future profit potential takes into account that individual consumers may be persuaded to buy other products, or more of an existing product, over time. Further, future profit potential may be significantly enhanced through creatively exploiting alternative channel structures, which we now consider.

The multichannel integration process

What are the best ways for us to get to customers and for customers to get to us?

What does the 'perfect customer experience', deliverable at an affordable cost, look like?

The multichannel integration process involves making decisions about the most appropriate combination of channels through which to interact with your customer base; how to ensure the customer experiences highly positive interactions within those channels; and, where customers interact with more than one channel, how to create a 'single unified view' of the customer experience. To determine the nature of the business's customer interface, it is necessary to consider the key issues underlying channel selection, the purpose of multichannel integration, the channel options available and the importance of integrated channel management in delivering an outstanding customer experience.

Issues in channel selection

Selecting the company's route to market (i.e. how to make its products or services available to the end consumer) involves considering a number of issues, which may be summarized under the headings of channel suitability and channel structure.

Channel suitability

The most appropriate choice of channel (or channels) for any company will be the one that is most attractive to the end consumers in the target market segment. The level of attraction will be determined by the company's ability to create customer value relevant to those customers' needs.

Thus, when developing channel strategy, a company must be equipped with an understanding of the benefits sought by the end consumer at the different stages of the buying process, from the customer's initial point of enquiry through to their ownership and use of the product or service.

Depending on the offer made, inherent benefits to the customer might include the ability to obtain information quickly, access the channel easily, communicate with the supplier effectively, physically inspect the product prior to purchase, have the product customized, and obtain service and support during the course of ownership. By identifying which benefits the customer seeks and the relative importance attributed to them, the company can evaluate channel suitability and determine which channel option would deliver these benefits to the greatest degree for the lowest cost. This emphasizes the point that creating a value proposition which will attract target customers does not simply rest with the design of the product or service, but it also relies on how the offer is made available to the end consumer in terms of route, presentation and sales support.

Channel structure

In addition to channel suitability, the way in which the channel is organized can seriously influence the success or failure of the channel. Besides considering target customers' current buying behaviours and motivations, the company should also consider how these might change over time, particularly with respect to the impact of developing technology. Over the last decade, the traditional channel structures of many industries have been dismantled and reconfigured in response to new technologies that have opened new paths to market. Managers responsible for channel strategy need to understand both the nature of their industry channel structure now and how it is likely to alter in the future. Valuable insights into emerging trends within channel structures can be gained from examining the experiences of other sectors or other industries on a global basis. Two types of structural behaviour are important:

1　disintermediation (where changes in the current business model or advances in technology mean that a company ceases to use intermediaries to create the value sought by end consumers).
2　re-intermediation (where changes in the current business model or advances in technology result in the emergence of new types of intermediary that can create more value than was possible in the previous channel structure).

Examples of *disintermediation* can be found in businesses that have adopted call centre technology and computer telephony integration (CTI) rather than utilizing traditional branch-based intermediaries. Direct Line Insurance, for example, was able to create additional customer value by offering customers the opportunity to deal directly, and thus more cost-effectively, with the company through the utilization of advances in call centre technology and IT. The removal of conventional and expensive brokerage networks enabled the company not only to offer lower premiums but also to gain a greater understanding of customers, which could be translated into the development of superior products and services.

A good example of *re-intermediation* exists on the Web in the form of so-called 'infomediaries', or web-enabled information agents. Rather than the consumer having to spend considerable time researching the alternatives available when considering purchasing a type of product, the infomediary performs that function on their behalf. For example, Autobytel, a Web-based car sales intermediary, was established to provide information about car prices, details of availability from dealers and even facilitate the purchase of cars.

Once macro-level decisions have been made regarding the most appropriate routes to market, the extent to which intermediaries are to be used and how these may change over time, the organization then needs to consider multichannel options and their combination in greater detail.

Multichannel integration

Faced with the necessity of offering consumers different channel types to meet their changing needs during the sales cycle (pre sale, sale, and post sale), it is increasingly imperative to integrate the activities in those different channels to produce the most positive customer experience and to create the maximum value. Competitive advantage today is not just about selling products and services to customers; it is about building long-term and profitable relationships with customers, which are founded on mutual benefit and trust. To succeed, therefore, the company must consistently seek to offer an individualized relationship in every customer interaction through whatever channel is being used. This will inevitably lead the company to undertake an ongoing review of *all* the possible means of interacting with customers. Whilst some businesses may choose a single channel strategy, many more will benefit from a strategy based on the integration of multiple channels.

Discussions on channels are usually dominated by those that are involved in making the sale. However, for strategic CRM the channels need to be considered in the context of the whole interaction over the life cycle of the customer relationship, not just in terms of the specific sales activity. The stages of a customer relationship can be considered under three broad headings: acquisition, consolidation and enhancement.

Within these typical stages, a great number of interactions occur between the customer and the organization across different channels. Understanding the nature of different customer encounters within a multichannel environment is essential if the organization's CRM activities are to be fully effective. Further, customers' needs during the customer relationship life cycle phases will vary according to the segment to which they belong and the product or service involved. Thus, determining the most appropriate forms of channel options for specific customer segments is also critical.

Channel options

The multichannel integration process involves a consideration of channel options. These options fall into six main channel categories, as shown in the strategic framework for CRM in Figure 20.1:

1   Sales force and personal representation
2   Outlets (including retail branches and kiosks)
3   Telephony (including telephone and facsimile contact and call centres)
4   Direct e-mail
5   E-commerce
6   M-commerce

Although there are many individual channel options, we have found it convenient to group them into these six categories. Thus, options such as retail branches and kiosks are included within 'outlets' and telephone contact, call centres and fax within 'telephony' and the Internet and digital TV within 'E-commerce'. E-commerce and M-commerce are addressed separately, as the ubiquity of the mobile device, future technology advances beyond existing wireless technology, and the ability to tailor information based on the customer's physical location, justify the latter being considered in its own right.

These channel categories can be represented as a continuum of forms of customer contact ranging from the physical (such as a face-to-face encounter with a company representative) to the virtual (such as an e-commerce or m-commerce transaction). Clearly, employing a combination of the channels most appropriate to the target customer base and company structure will provide the greatest commercial exposure and return. Over time, more of these channels will be used concurrently. For example, 'voice over IP' (voice over Internet protocol) integrates both telephony and the Internet.

Integrated channel management

Integrated channel management involves understanding what defines an outstanding customer experience, and being able to deliver it at an affordable cost to the organization. This raises two questions: What does an outstanding customer experience look like *within a given channel?*, and, Where customers may interact with more than one channel, how do we create the appropriate look, touch and feel *across different channels*, bearing in mind the inherent differences in the nature of these channels?

In tackling these issues, the organization needs first to consider what constitutes an outstanding customer experience for different customer segments in each of the channels being used (or considered), and to determine how such an experience might be delivered in a consistent manner and at an affordable cost within each channel.

Having established a set of standards for each channel, the organization can then work to integrate the channels, trying to optimize, but not compromise, the accepted channel standards. Achieving integration across the different channels will require attending to a myriad of areas in order to ensure that the multichannel service matches the individual needs of customers in different segments. A major objective will be to achieve brand consistency across these channels and this will require skilful channel management.

Modern customers expect to be served through a multitude of channels, for example through the Internet, face-to-face discussion, M-commerce applications, call centres and so on. At the same time, these customers are individuals who make their purchasing decisions according to the unique factors of each given situation. Therefore, customers may belong to a number of different customer segments, simultaneously. Taken together, these two aspects of customer nature present a considerable challenge: how to provide a high quality, multichannel service that satisfies the individual and the changing needs of increasingly empowered customers.

Providing services in both traditional and contemporary channels is a priority for companies that are seeking to meet, or indeed, to exceed, the expectations of discriminating customers. However, many companies do not seem to recognize the need to maintain equally high standards of service *across* multiple channels. Because the quality of a company's service provision is only as good as the weakest link in their multichannel service mix, successful channel integration demands that a company upholds the same high standard of service its customers have come to expect from the company in all of the channels being used. To succeed in integrated channel management, the company must be able to collect, analyse and utilize a wide range of customer information available from different channels as well as other sources. This is the role of the information management process.

The information management process

How should we organize information on customers?

How can we 'replicate' the mind of the customer?

The information management process is concerned with two key activities: the collection and collation of customer information from all customer contact points and the utilization of this information to construct complete and current customer profiles which can be used to enhance the quality of the customer experience. As companies grow and interact with an increasing number of customers through an increasing diversity of channels, the need for a systematic approach to organizing and employing information becomes ever greater. Where customer information is spread across disparate functions and departments, interactions with the customer may be based on partial or no knowledge of the customer, even though the customer may have been with the organization for years. This fragmentation of customer knowledge creates two major problems for the company. First, the customer is treated in an impersonal way, which may lead to dissatisfaction and defection. Second, there is no single unified view of the customer upon which to act and to plan.

A key role of the information management process is to 'replicate the mind of the customer'. Thus the emphasis in this process needs to be on how we can use this information in a proactive way to develop enhanced relationships with the customer, rather than on the elegance and sophistication of the technology solution. The traditional corner shop serves as a good example of successful CRM that replicates the mind of the customer.

The corner shop proprietor was often able to remember many details about his most valuable customers – those who returned to the shop again and again. Repeated interactions with the same customers would also lead to the formation of general impressions about customers, such as are they trustworthy and how valuable their custom was to the business. In other words, the shopkeeper knew which customers were most valuable and how to retain them by using this information to deliver increased customer value

that was tailored to the individual. However, as such businesses grew larger, it became easy to be overwhelmed by the amount of customer data that was generated and the ability to personalize the offer was greatly reduced.

In an effort to keep pace with escalating volumes of data, the tendency is for organizations to create more or bigger databases within functions or departments, leading to a wealth of disparate silos of customer information. Companies are thus left with a fragmented and often unwieldy body of information upon which to make crucial management decisions. The elevation of CRM from the level of a specific application such as a call centre, to the level of a pan-company strategy requires the integration of customer interactions across all communication channels, front- and back-office applications and business functions. What is required to manage this integration on an ongoing basis is a purposefully designed process that brings together data, computers, procedures and people. The key material elements of the information management process consist of the data repository, IT systems, analytical processes and front-office and back-office systems.

Data repository

To make an enterprise customer-focused, it is not sufficient simply to collect data about customers, or even to generate management information from individual databases, because they normally provide only a partial view of the customer. To understand and manage customers as complete and unique entities, it is necessary to have a powerful corporate memory of customers; an integrated enterprise-wide data store which can provide the data analyses needed to inform strategic and tactical decision-making processes. The approach best suited to providing such a resource is the use of a data repository together with appropriate analytical tools. In most cases, integration of information from different databases and departments will also be required.

The role of the data repository is to collect, hold and integrate customer information, and thus enable the company to develop and manage customer relationships effectively. In the simplest terms, the data repository comprises two main parts: the databases and the data warehouse, as shown in Figure 20.2.

Databases comprise a set of computer programs and software packages for storing data gathered

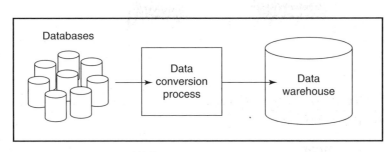

Figure 20.2   The data repository

from a source such as a call centre, the sales force, customer and market surveys, electronic points of sale (EPOS) and so on. Each database usually operates separately and is constructed to be user-specific, storing only that which is relevant to the tasks of its main users. Management and planning information drawn from a single database is therefore limited in value because it provides an incomplete view of customer-related activity.

The *data warehouse* is a collection of related databases that have been brought together so that the maximum value can be extracted from them. The basic idea of data warehousing is to gather as much data as possible in the hope that a meaningful picture will emerge.

An *enterprise data model* is used to manage this data conversion process model, in order to minimize data duplication and to resolve any inconsistencies between databases. As well as connecting to internal systems the data warehouse also often takes feeds from external sources. The data warehouse is organized to support the kinds of analyses performed at customer management and strategic planning levels. Analytical tools such as data mining can be used to reveal patterns in customer data, such as buying habits, which form the basis of improved customer understanding and relationship-building. End-users can access the data warehouse using online analytical processing (OLAP) tools.

Using a data warehouse has two key advantages. First, it stops complex data analysis from interfering with normal business activity by removing a heavy demand on the databases. Second, the data in a data warehouse changes only periodically (e.g. every 24 hours), allowing meaningful comparisons to be made on stable sets of data which exist in between updates of the data warehouse. If databases were used for analysis, analyses made at different times would produce different results, making it impossible to compare, for example, the sale of different products or the volume of sales in different regions.

Through the effective use of data analysis tools, the data warehouse can help answer questions about customers' behaviour and preferences, and the value they provide to the enterprise. The data warehouse is, therefore, instrumental to the CRM task of identifying the enterprise's best customers, and identifying ways to retain them and enhance their value.

More importantly, once firmly established, the data warehouse supports the monitoring of customers and provides a mechanism for testing and refining customer strategy. This capability is increasingly significant as markets become ever more dynamic, and personalized services and one-to-one marketing become more commonplace. In the world of e-business, especially, where the 'rules of the game' are not well understood, effective data analysis is critical.

Analytical tools

The analytical tools that enable effective use of the data warehouse can be found in general data mining packages and in specific software application packages. Data mining packages enable the analysis of large quantities of data to discover meaningful patterns and relationships. Each pattern and relationship explains something about customer behaviour and provides indications of how customer relationships can be improved. More specific software application packages include analytical tools that focus on such tasks as:

- Campaign management analysis
- Churn management
- Credit scoring
- Customer profiling
- Market segmentation analysis
- Profitability analysis

These task-specific software packages combine several of the general functions of data mining, with support for the task, that will not be found in general data mining software. Whether or not data analysis is performed using a general or task-specific package, the underlying data mining functions will be concerned with tasks which typically include segmentation analysis, prediction, deviation detection or finding associations between sets of data entries in a database.

IT systems

IT systems consist of the computer hardware and the related software and middleware used within the organization. Normally, organizations' IT structures are developed over a long period of time, and thus different, and often incompatible, computing systems – both hardware and software – are utilized in different parts of the business. Frequently, there is insufficient integration of these different systems and therefore technology integration is required before databases can be integrated into a data warehouse and user access can be provided across the company.

The driving consideration should be how to configure the organization's IT systems so that they deliver the information that is needed on customers both now and in the foreseeable future, as well as the other administrative systems that are required. In particular, as the number of customers and customer transactions escalate, how to scale existing systems or plan for the migration to larger systems without disrupting business operations is critical.

In terms of infrastructure development, a comment should be made on the nature of intranets and data warehousing. The highly structured nature of data stored in databases can be contrasted with the rich and diverse forms of information shared using intranets and knowledge management technologies, such as multimedia and video. This emphasizes that an effective CRM strategy must integrate data from significantly different systems across the entire information management process.

Front- and back-office applications

Front-office applications are the technologies used to support customer-facing activities and are ones where a great deal of current CRM emphasis has been placed. They encompass all those activities that involve direct interface with customers and include sales force automation, call centre management, product configuration tools and sales force and marketing automation. These applications are used to increase revenues by improving customer retention and raising sales closure rates. *Back-office applications* support internal administration activities and supplier relationships, involving human resources, procurement, warehouse management, logistics software and some financial processes.

Some activities, such as campaign management, are difficult to classify as either front-office or back-office because they are customer-facing, but do not directly support interactions with the customer. The growth of enterprise-wide systems and e-business is also blurring the distinction between front-office and back-office. Goods tracking, for example, has traditionally been a back-office system used by employees who do not have any interaction with the customers. Many companies are, however, providing customers with direct access to goods tracking software through the Internet so that they can track their own orders. In this case, goods tracking must be regarded as a front-office system because its performance affects the customer's perceptions of the organization.

The main concern about front- and back-office applications is ensuring that they are sufficiently coordinated and connected to optimize customer relations and workflow. They can represent a fault line in the company's ability to provide consistent customer value where communication and information functions are not integrated seamlessly. For instance, dozens of applications may be spread throughout an organization, or departments may be organized around products and services or business functions, rather than processes which support the customer relationship. For this reason, it is useful to review existing applications from the perspective of customer interaction, so that customer needs drive technology solutions, rather than the other way around.

Recently, much attention has been given to the implications of e-business strategies that put customers and business partners in direct contact with databases. This increased access to operational data can create new challenges for CRM, which may demand changes in the approach to data warehousing and the organization of front-office and back-office applications. One such challenge is the pressure that e-business creates for a 'real-time' marketing response, which requires all customer interactions to be conducted with an enterprise-wide view, rather than in terms of marketing planning activities. In some cases, this change may lead to the use of real-time data for data analysis, rather than a data warehouse that is only updated periodically.

Clearly, the information management process is playing an increasingly important role in CRM, supporting the collection and analysis of enormous volumes of complex customer data. Like other resources, data have a value in use, as well as a limited shelf life. It is therefore crucial that customer data are accumulated and deployed in an organized and integrated fashion to provide a comprehensive and current perspective of customers. Selecting appropriate IT hardware and software is a challenging task owing to the constraints of legacy systems and the enormous range of technology options. To ensure that technology solutions support CRM, it is important to conduct IT planning from a perspective of providing a seamless customer service, rather than planning for functional or product-centred departments and activities. Such a customer-centred approach to IT planning will ensure that customer information is used effectively to maximize customer value and the profitability of each customer. Furthermore, data analysis tools, such as those outlined above, make it possible to measure business activities to determine whether new ways of managing customer relationships might be advantageous in increasing shareholder value. This kind of analysis provides the basis for the performance assessment process.

The performance assessment process

How can we create increased profits and shareholder value?

How should we set standards, develop metrics, measure our results and improve our performance?

The performance assessment process involves an evaluation of the success of CRM. It is this process which ensures that the organization's strategic aims in terms of CRM are being delivered to an appropriate and acceptable standard and a basis for future improvement is established. The key actions involve understanding the drivers of shareholder value, identifying the appropriate metrics against which the various CRM activities can be measured, and establishing an effective performance monitoring system to apply these measures on an ongoing basis. The shareholder results element and performance monitoring element of this process have some overlap between them. However, the former involves a more 'macro' view of overall relationships which drive performance, whilst the latter is concerned with a much more detailed 'micro' view of metrics and key performance indicators.

Shareholder results

The ultimate objective of CRM for commercial organizations is to deliver shareholder results through an increase in shareholder value. Before a review of performance monitoring takes place, the organization should understand the specific drivers of shareholder results that ultimately determine CRM success. These drivers need to be considered in the context of the business strategy and the customer strategy set out in the strategy development process. There are four key drivers that impact on shareholder results: building employee value, building customer value, building shareholder value and reducing costs. The first three represent the main stakeholder groups from which shareholder results are obtained, while the latter impacts positively on the shareholder results process by lowering costs to improve profit margins.

Employee value, customer value and shareholder value

Many organizations acknowledge the importance of three key groups of stakeholders: employees, customers and shareholders that are critical to organizational success. These three groups clearly have a relationship with each other. However, the precise nature of the relationship between them has only recently been closely examined. This has led to the recognition of the need to adopt a more integrated approach across these groups and understand more deeply the linkages between them.

Managers readily agree that there is linkage, as shown in the performance 'linkage model' in Figure 20.3, between good leadership and management behaviour, improved employee attitudes, customer satisfaction and increased sales, profits and shareholder results. However, most managers have no idea of how much an improvement in one variable in this figure will lead to a measurable increase in another.

A few companies have now started to use such linkage models to explore these relationships more explicitly. The best known of these is

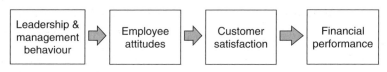

Figure 20.3   The performance linkage model

the 'service profit chain model' developed by researchers at the Harvard Business School (Heskett *et al.*, 1997) which illustrates the 'knock-on' effect between good leadership, strong and appropriate management, happy employees, satisfied customers and improved financial performance. This work provides, amongst other findings, strong evidence that profit is linked to customer loyalty, which is linked to consistent customer satisfaction. However, while few would argue with the logic of such a linkage model, only recently has any serious effort been made to investigate and identify quantitative relationships between variables in the model.

For example, Sears Roebuck and Co, the largest US department store chain, has been highly innovative in its efforts in this area. In addition to addressing more common elements of CRM such as the streamlining of their information systems, which previously involved 18 separate legacy databases into a single, integrated data warehouse, they also developed a linkage model to help manage shareholder results. They used a modified version of the service profit chain model to predict revenue growth and profitability. Using sophisticated causal pathway analysis, the company was able to identify 20 customer measures, 25 employee measures and 19 financial measures that together provided profit indicators. This illustrates how the specific metrics and key performance indicators can be derived from this more macro investigation of the drivers of shareholder value. For example, by applying these metrics in the evaluation of performance, the company discovered that a 5 unit increase in employee attitude drives a 1.3 unit increase in customer impression, a 0.5 increase in revenue growth and a quantifiable increase in profitability (Rucci *et al.*, 1998). With this knowledge and understanding, the company was able to effect a great improvement in performance and overall growth.

The development of linkage models such as the service profit chain has been a welcome development in enabling companies to evaluate the effectiveness of CRM at a strategic level in terms of improving shareholder results. More

companies are now starting to recognize the value of addressing these higher level drivers before determining standards, metrics and key performance indicators.

Cost reduction

The improvement of shareholder results through cost reduction is probably the area most often associated with managers' efforts to improve profitability. Cost reduction can be achieved through many ways. However, two ways are of special interest in the context of CRM: deploying electronic systems, such as automated telephony services, that lower costs by enabling reductions in terms of staff number and overheads and by utilizing new channels, such as online self-service facilities, that can lower the costs of customer acquisition, transaction and servicing.

The savings from automation and adoption of automated services and alternative channels are well documented. For example, replacing customer contact with branch-based employees with a centralized call centre or replacing a branch-base customer transaction with an Internet banking transaction that is many times cheaper. However, giving much concentration on cost reduction as a means of delivering shareholder results can be counterproductive if it decreases customer value. Companies need to determine what kinds of effect cost reduction will have on their customer base. Many individuals have had an increasing number of negative experiences with their bank as it continually seeks ways to implement cost reduction. Creating a central call centre not only will reduce costs but is also likely to disenfranchise customers who can no longer telephone their branches and have personalized contact with bank employees whom they know. Banks are losing many of their best customers as a result.

Achieving a productive balance between fiscal efficiency and profitability means understanding customer value that may be destroyed or enhanced as a result of such changes. Avoiding customer value destruction when reducing costs is a key element of successful CRM.

Performance monitoring

Despite the increasing focus on customer-facing activities, there is growing concern that metrics generally used by companies for CRM are not nearly as advanced as they should be. In particular, more detailed standards, measures and key performance indicators are needed to ensure that CRM activities are planned and practised effectively, and that a feedback loop exists to maximize performance improvement and organizational learning.

Standards

A set of CRM standards against which best practice is measured is needed so that companies can measure their performance against that of others. As yet, there is no such internationally recognized set of standards for CRM. However, a number of initiatives are under way in this area. Some, such as the Customer Operations Performance Center (COPC) Standard, have initially focused on specific aspects of CRM such as call centres. Others, such as a standards initiative at BT, are concerned with identifying key areas in which standards should be set across all the major areas of CRM.

In terms of CRM standards set in a specific context, the COPC-2000® Standard is a good example. This standard was developed in 1995 by a core group of users of call centre services and associated distribution fulfilment operations including American Express, Dell, Microsoft and L.L. Bean (COPC, 2004). The standard describes the performance measurement approaches that a customer service provider must establish and it defines the metrics it must use to evaluate the effectiveness and efficiency of its approaches. The Malcolm Baldrige National Quality Award criteria and framework were used as the basis for the standard. While COPC does not set specific performance objectives, such as a particular service level that every call centre must meet, it does require that all performance metrics be tracked, linked to drivers of customer satisfaction and used to improve overall call centre performance.

In terms of more universal CRM standards, the UK telecommunications company BT developed a set of standards, based on the concept of the COPC Standard, against which to measure best practice in the following areas (Chidley, 2000):

1   Does my organization demonstrate leadership in CRM? How do I compare with other organizations?
2   How satisfied are my customers with the products and services offered by my organization?
3   What is the lifetime value of my customers? How can I be more cost-effective in delivering customer service to them?
4   How effective and integrated is the access that my customers use to reach my organization?
5   How effective are the customer solutions and applications that enable my customers to obtain my products and services?
6   How do I manage the customer information used and generated at each customer contact to deliver the maximum value from my customers?
7   Do I have the skilled and motivated people to deliver my products and services to customers?
8   Does my organization have the appropriate customer-related processes to deliver quality products and services?
9   Does my organization have the appropriate Performance and Reporting procedures to measure the impact of CRM strategy and operations on the organization?

Each of these questions is translated into a set of standards that can be used by an organization to assess their CRM capabilities. Companies should consider developing a set of customer-related standards in all the major areas of the CRM framework and putting metrics and key performance indicators (KPIs) in place that permit a rigorous performance assessment to be undertaken.

Metrics, KPIs and results

Two main questions need to be addressed if CRM performance is to be measured and monitored successfully:

1   What metrics and KPIs should be used that adequately reflect the performance standards across the five major CRM processes?
2   How are these metrics and KPIs linked, and what opportunity do these linkages provide for improved results through better management of CRM across the organization?

The performance measurement systems adopted by organizations in the past have tended to be functionally driven. Thus, financial measures were mainly the concern of the finance department and the Board, marketing measures, the domain of the marketing department and people measures, the responsibility of the HR department. Such a functional separation of performance measures is clearly inappropriate for CRM which is a cross-functional and holistic management approach. Therefore, the measures used to appraise CRM performance must be selected on the basis that they interrelate and are applied together to give a complete view of the entire organization.

One of the most popular attempts to provide cross-functional measures is the 'balanced scorecard' developed by Kaplan and Norton (1996). This measurement device works by providing a cumulative view of several perspectives of the business: the customer perspective, the internal perspective, including internal performance measures, the growth perspective, including measures reflecting knowledge creation, innovation and learning and the financial perspective, which considers the shareholders' view of the organization. At a strategic level, it is concerned with issues relating to the shareholder results described above. At an implementation level, it is concerned with identifying appropriate metrics and KPIs. However, a drawback to using the 'balanced scorecard' approach is that there is no universally successful list of measures to use, as each organization's measurement criteria will require a different emphasis and mix of measures. Also, the 'balanced scorecard' does not address the linkages between the measures, which is crucial to understanding how to improve performance. The 'balanced scorecard' is, however, a significant development in focusing on the importance of non-financial measures that had been previously largely ignored in performance measurement systems.

The challenge for companies in evaluating and enhancing their CRM performance is, therefore, to identify the measures appropriate to the organization and to understand the linkages between them. As CRM has become increasingly critical to overall competitive performance, there is a great need to develop robust categories of metrics for measuring, monitoring and benchmarking good CRM practice.

Detailed research is now needed to identify these metrics and performance measures. However, in the absence of such research, we propose four key categories for consideration: strategic metrics, customer metrics, operational metrics and output metrics.

Strategic metrics measure the success of the organization's strategic approach to CRM. They measure, for example, the extent to which marketing information is used when developing the business strategy, the role of CRM in positioning the organization in the marketplace and whether the vision and objectives of the company focus sufficiently on the customer.

Customer metrics measure both the value delivered by the organization to the customer and the value that the customer provides to the organization. These set KPIs to measure, for example, levels of customer satisfaction and customer retention, customer acquisition costs and customer lifetime value.

Operational metrics measure both people and process performance. *People measures* include the appraisal, compensation, recognition, training and career progression of staff. Measures that are important here include employee retention, productivity, employee satisfaction and performance targets. *Process measures* include customer service levels, supplier performance targets and product and service development targets.

Output metrics measure the effectiveness of the CRM strategy on organizational performance by calculating the value delivered to each of the three main stakeholders: shareholders, employees and customers. Value is determined in terms of customer satisfaction, increased key segment profitability, reduction in operational costs and employee retention and productivity.

Inevitably, it is much easier to select which metrics to use than to determine how to monitor them in an integrated manner. It is, therefore, important not only to identify the appropriate standards of measurement but also to understand the relationship between the metrics so that the CRM processes can be refined, individually and collectively, to maximum effect.

Overall, the test of the performance assessment process lies in the organization's ability to respond confidently to the following fundamental questions:

1 Have we selected the most appropriate CRM performance standards? Do we benchmark our standards against 'best in class'?
2 Have we determined appropriate metrics and KPIs? Do we understand where these performance metrics are linked?
3 Can we determine the impact of each metric, individually and cumulatively, on our results?
4 Do we have appropriate feedback built into our CRM monitoring process so that there is continual improvement?

Organizing for CRM implementation

In the previous sections of this chapter, we examined five key processes that comprise the strategic framework for CRM. In this section, we examine the key issues involved in organizing for implementation of a CRM programme. The effective management of customer relationships involves many both different and interlinked aspects. However, simply addressing the processes is not enough to ensure that CRM is effectively implemented. Firms have to organize appropriately to ensure that they achieve satisfactory results from their CRM programmes.

Before a CRM strategy is developed, it is important to assess whether the organization is ready and willing to undertake all the needs to be done to successfully implement customer-focused strategies and CRM initiatives. CRM is not an appropriate strategy for a company to adopt if it does not have leadership support for CRM and a Board-level sponsor committed to its success. Thus, the cultural and leadership implications of CRM implementation must be fully understood and addressed if it is to have any chance of improving business results.

Research by the authors has identified four critical elements for successful CRM implementation. These include CRM readiness assessment,

CRM change management, CRM project management and employee engagement. These four implementation elements are shown in Figure 20.4 in relation to the five strategic processes of CRM.

We now consider how the four implementation elements in Figure 20.4 come together to support the organization's CRM strategy.

CRM readiness assessment

A CRM readiness assessment can help managers assess the overall position in terms of readiness to progress with CRM implementation and identify how well developed their organization is relative to other companies. Research by Ryals and Payne (2001) shows that there are identifiable stages of maturity in CRM development: pre-CRM planning, building a data repository, moderately developed, well developed and highly advanced. Each of these stages represents a level of CRM maturity characterized by the extent to which customer information is used to enhance the customer experience and customer-generated cash flows.

If an organization is in the early stages of CRM development, it is useful to start with an overview audit of the five key CRM processes to help get senior management understanding and buy-in at an early stage. The overview form of readiness audit can be used to rapidly form an initial view on the key CRM priorities, to define

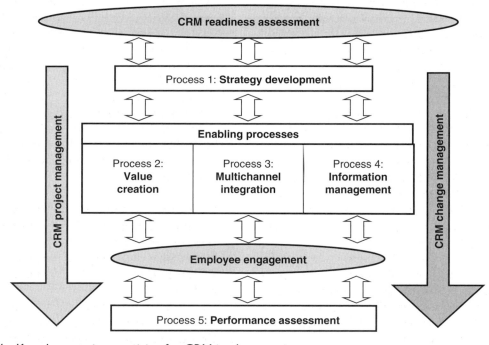

Figure 20.4   Key elements in organizing for CRM implementation
Source: Based on Payne and Frow (2006)

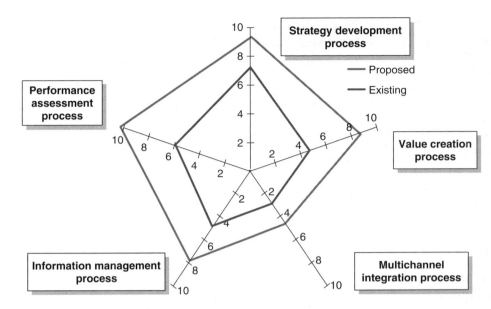

Figure 20.5   Overview audit of key CRM processes

the relative importance of those priorities and to determine where effort needs to be applied. Figure 20.5 shows the output of such an exercise for a major European bank. In the case of this bank, changes were considered to be necessary in all processes, with the greatest improvement needed in the value creation and performance assessment processes, as shown in Figure 20.5. A number of important new CRM initiatives were identified and project teams were formed to implement them. Other organizations have found this overview audit extremely helpful in identifying progress and challenges in their CRM initiatives. Such organizations typically found significant differences in the gap between the current position and the desired position and on the relative emphasis on each process.

Although simple in concept, we found that the completion of an overview audit and a structured discussion with a company's managers around the scorings was extremely valuable in highlighting areas on which an organization should concentrate in order to improve its CRM performance. To extend the response rate, it is possible to develop a simple web-based programme to collect and aggregate information from around the company.

Firms that are more advanced, or ones that wish to go into greater detail, can undertake a more comprehensive CRM audit. A number of CRM audit tools have also been developed, mainly by consulting firms. These audits vary greatly in detail and quality. Some are little more

than a quiz and others show little evidence of understanding all the strategic issues relevant to CRM. One of the few audits that is more robust is the customer management assessment tool (CMAT) (QCI, 2004). QCI have accumulated a substantial amount of data from a large number of businesses which enables comparisons to be made not only across all industries, but within specific industry sectors. However, such audits are not tailored to the specific circumstances of an organization or industry sector and are not weighted to reflect the relative importance of specific CRM issues to the organization. More work is needed in the area of comprehensive audit development.

CRM change management

To implement a large-scale and complex CRM initiative, companies will typically have to undergo substantial organizational and cultural change. A critical dimension of any large CRM programme, therefore, is an effective change management programme. (We make a distinction here between change management which is concerned with strategic organizational change and employee engagement which was seen as a more operationally-oriented set of activities. These activities are, however, closely entwined.)

Because CRM is potentially so wide-ranging in terms of the organizational ramifications, a robust analytical framework is needed to help CRM leaders identify the organizational change management issues in relation to a particular CRM programme. One well-known change management framework, the 'Seven S' framework (Peters, 1984), is a useful tool to help the organization identify those issues relevant to their business. This framework provides a means of viewing organizations as packages of key skills or skill gaps. Hence, it can be used as a tool for analysing organizational deficiencies, building on positive skills and identifying new skills needed. Child *et al.* (1995) illustrate the use of the 'Seven S' framework in a context relevant to CRM change management.

CRM project management

CRM project management has increasing importance as the size and complexity of CRM initiatives increase. There are two main types of CRM project: first, where a team of specialists is brought together on a temporary basis to address a particular project with a finite completion date and second, where a cross-functional team is assembled with a remit of ongoing management of part of the enterprise's CRM initiative. Successful CRM projects deliver against the CRM objectives derived from the corporate objectives and support the overall business strategy. Our research identified that CRM projects which overrun budgets and timescales create considerable damage to CRM credibility, hence effective CRM project management is essential.

Some organizations are adopting a large-scale and very comprehensive approach to CRM implementation. However, others found that an incremental and modular approach to CRM development or enhancement was more appropriate. These latter companies typically engaged in a series of smaller individual CRM projects, undertaken in an appropriate sequence, each with clearly defined objectives and return on investment (ROI) outcomes. These projects varied in the emphasis placed on analytical CRM, operational CRM and collaborative CRM (Meta Group, 2001).

As the CRM project plan is implemented, two further issues should be considered: creep in project scope and understanding the implications of scale. Ebner *et al.* (2002) point out that as a project grows in scope, the system's development can take on a life of its own, incorporating new features that do not support business objectives but add considerable complexity and cost. IT professionals have learnt that the bigger a project is, the harder it is to integrate and the more likely it is to

miss deadlines or be scrapped altogether. The business objectives that the CRM system was intended to achieve must be kept under constant scrutiny and any efforts to increase the scope of the project must be evaluated very carefully. Further, as a project is planned, it is critical that the implications of scale increase are understood. Point estimates of future demand should be replaced with estimates based on three levels of potential future demand: optimistic, most likely and pessimistic. As the numbers of users and customers grow, the system must be robust enough to accept higher possible increases in volume.

Employee engagement

The final of the four implementation elements is the engagement of employees to support the various initiatives that comprise the overall CRM programme. Employees have a crucial role to play within the CRM processes and implementation activities outlined in this chapter. An organization cannot develop and operate appropriately customer-focused systems and processes without motivated and trained employees.

Change management and project management are particularly dependent on engagement of employees for their success. Ensuring the delivery of a superior customer experience during times of unexpectedly high demand requires the active engagement and commitment of all customer-facing staff and is a hallmark of a well-planned CRM implementation. Increasingly, organizations are recognizing the significant value their employees contribute to the business, which extends well beyond the basic fulfilment of core duties. Employees are instrumental in implementing processes including customer service, improving efficiencies and nurturing consumer confidence and repeat purchase. The role of senior executives in facilitating employee engagement is also vital. However, at Board level, issues such as governance, finance, acquisitions and cost reduction may predominate over issues of customer management, marketing and employees.

Therefore, how all the company's human resources are engaged, but especially those who have any form of customer contact, is a key factor in determining CRM success. A wide body of research supports the claim that the surest way to enhance competitive performance is through recruiting and selecting the best employees, training and motivating them and providing effective leadership. This will maximize the likelihood of employees engaging effectively with both customers and their colleagues.

Summary

The strategic framework for CRM outlined in this chapter is a formal response to the confusion and frustration many companies are experiencing in their efforts to adopt CRM. Its purpose is to provide a comprehensive framework for the development of CRM strategy. By breaking CRM down into its key cross-functional processes, it is possible to communicate the underlying principles of CRM strategy, demonstrate the interdependence of CRM activities and plan CRM activity on a strategic and well-integrated basis.

The framework positions CRM as a strategic set of activities that commence with a detailed review of an organization's strategy (the strategy development process) and conclude with an improvement in business results and increased shareholder value (the performance assessment process). It is based on the proposition that creation of value for the customer *and* for the company (the value creation process) is the key to the success of relationships. CRM involves collecting and intelligently utilizing customer and other relevant data to generate customer insight (the information management process) to build a superior customer experience at each touch-point where the customer and supplier interact (the multichannel integration process).

Organizing for CRM implementation involves four elements that are critical to a successful CRM programme: CRM readiness assessment, CRM change management, CRM project management and employee engagement. Implementing CRM represents a considerable challenge in most enterprises. Any successful CRM implementation should be preceded by the development of a clear, relevant and well-communicated CRM strategy. Organizations also need to adopt a strategic definition of CRM that focuses on business issues rather than emphasizing IT issues.

Successful CRM demands coordination and collaboration, and most of all integration: integration of information and information systems to provide business intelligence; integration of channels to enable the development and delivery of a single unified view of the customer; integration of resources, functions and processes to ensure a productive, customer-oriented working environment and competitive organizational performance. CRM is admittedly a complex task, but by adopting a strategic approach, as outlined in this chapter, organizations should be able to realize the substantial benefits of effective CRM and make progress on the journey towards achieving excellence in customer management.

References

Aaker, D. A., Kumar, V. and Day, G. S. (1998) *Marketing Research*, 6th edn, John Wiley & Sons, New York, Chapter 22.

Anderson, E., Day, G. S. and Kasturi, V. (1997) Strategic channel design, *Sloan Management Review*, **38**, Summer, 59–69.

Chidley, J. (2000) *Setting Customer-Based Standards for CRM*, BT Internal document, London.

Child, P., Dennis, R. S., Gokey, T. C., McGuire, T., Shennan, M. and Singer, M. (1995) Can marketing regain the personal touch? *McKinsey Quarterly*, **3**, 112–125.

COPC (2004) Available at www.copc.com. (accessed 22 January 2004).

Ebner, M., Hu, A., Levitt, D. and McCory, J. (2002) How to Rescue CRM, *McKinsey Quarterly*, Special Edition, Technology, 49–57.

Heskett, J. L., Sasser Jr., W. E. and Schlesinger, L. A. (1997) *The Service Profit Chain*, The Free Press, New York.

Kaplan, R. S. and Norton, D. P. (1996) *The Balanced Scorecard*, Harvard Business School Press, Boston.

Lanning, M. J. (1998) *Delivering Profitable Value*, Perseus Publishing, Cambridge.

Meta Group (2001) *Integration: Critical Issues for Implementation of CRM Solutions*, Report by Meta Group Inc., February 15.

Parvatiyar, A. and Sheth, J. N. (2001) Conceptual Framework of Customer Relationship Management, in Sheth, J. N. Parvatiyar, A. and Shainesh, G. (eds), *Customer Relationship Management – Emerging Concepts, Tools and Applications*, Tata McGraw-Hill, New Delhi, pp. 3–25.

Payne, A. (2006) *The Handbook of CRM: Achieving Excellence in Customer Management*, Elsevier Butterworth Heinemann, Oxford.

Payne, A. and Frow, P. (2005) A strategic framework for CRM, *Journal of Marketing*, **69**(4), October, 167–176.

Payne, A. and Frow, P. (2006) Customer relationship management: from strategy to implementation, *Journal of Marketing Management*, **22**(1–2), 135–168.

Peppers, D. and Rogers, M. (1993) *The One to One Future: Building Business Relationships One Customer at a Time*, Piatkus Books, New York.

Peters, T. (1984) Strategy follows structure: developing distinctive skills, *California Management Review*, **26**(3), 111–125.

Porter, M. E. (1980) *Competitive Strategy*, Free Press, New York.

QCI (2004) CMAT available at www.qci.co.uk. (accessed 22 January 2004).

Reichheld, F. F. and Sasser Jr., W. E. (1990) Zero defections: quality comes to services, *Harvard Business Review*, September–October, 105–111.

Rubin, M. (1997) Creating customer-oriented companies, *Prism*, Arthur D. Little, **4**(4), 5–27.

Ryals, L. and Payne, A. (2001) Customer relationship management in financial services: towards information-enabled relationship marketing, *Journal of Strategic Marketing*, **9**, 1–25.

Rucci, A. J., Kirn, S. P. and Quinn, R. T. (1998) The employee-customer-profit chain at Sears, *Harvard Business Review*, January–February, 83–97.

Further reading

1 Christopher, M., Payne, A. and Ballantyne, D. (2002) *Relationship Marketing*, 2nd edn, Butterworth Heinemann, Oxford.

This newer edition of an earlier book focuses on the creation of stakeholder value and emphasizes how quality and customer service are critical foundations for long-term customer relationships.

2 Friedman, L. G. and Timothy, F. R. (1999) *The Channel Advantage: Going to Market with Multiple Sales Channels to Reach More Customers, Sell More Products, Make More Profit*, Butterworth Heinemann, Oxford.

A good treatment of issues relating to multichannel integration.

3 Greenberg, P. (2001) *CRM at the Speed of Light*, Osborne/McGraw Hill, Berkeley, CA.

This book contains a good discussion of industry and technical issues relating to CRM.

4 Peppers, D., Rogers, M. and Dorf, Bob. (1999) *One to One Fieldbook*, Doubleday, London.

This book, the third by Peppers and Rogers, provides a useful overview of the role of CRM, especially in the context of an 'online' environment. It also deals with the importance of dialogue and privacy issues as well as likely future developments in CRM.

5 Sheth, J N. and Parvatiyar, A. (2000) *The Handbook of Relationship Marketing*, Sage, Thousand Islands, CA.

An excellent academic treatment of the topic of relationship marketing. The editors have obtained contributions from virtually all the leading figures in the relationship marketing arena – a total of 23 contributions from leading scholars.

6 Swift, R. S. (2001) *Accelerating Customer Relationships: Using CRM and Relationship Technologies*, Prentice Hall, Upper Saddle River, NJ.

Swift's book provides an excellent introduction to CRM from a technological viewpoint. Of special value is its treatment of data warehousing and relationship technologies as well as specific studies of implementations.

CHAPTER 21

Marketing metrics

TIM AMBLER

Marketers have long felt marginalized or at least under pressure to justify their plans. They may not look for accountability but there is increasing acceptance that quantification, preferably in financial terms, of plans and performance is an increasing factor in marketing (e.g. Shaw and Mazur, 1997; Clark, 1999; Moorman and Rust, 1999; Marketing Science Institute, 2000; Schultz, 2000; Marketing Week, 2001). The Marketing Science Institute has rated marketing metrics as a top tier project in recent years (Marketing Science Institute, 2000; Lehmann and Reibstein, 2006).

Marketing performance measurement has traditionally focused on top line financial metrics such as sales and sales growth (Clark, 1999). More recently, financial attention has shifted to the bottom line expressed as net cash flow, profits or shareholder value (Lehmann and Reibstein, 2006). This chapter discusses whether using purely financial metrics is adequate or whether non-financial metrics are required as well. The US Institute of Management Accountants reports the growing use of non-financial measures (IMA, 1992, 1994, 1996). The biggest obstacle to measuring marketing performance is the assessment of the marketing asset, namely 'brand equity', although some ambiguity surrounds this term (Marketing Leadership Council, 2001).

This chapter deals with marketing in the company-wide sense (Webster, 1992), that is, what the company does to meet needs profitably (Kotler and Keller, 2006). In other words 'marketing' here refers to what the whole company does to satisfy customers and thereby maximize net cash flow. The performance of any marketing department, by contrast, can only be assessed against the goals they have been assigned and these vary from firm to firm. Most firms have no specialist marketing department at all and, of those that do, some have responsibility for pricing, for example, and some do not. The assessment of particular aspects of the marketing mix, such as advertising, also falls outside this chapter.

Managers are forced by time, financial constraints and environmental uncertainty to take a partial view of their environment (Day and Nedungadi, 1994). The goals they select and the metrics they use reflect that partial view. So metrics are more than just a scorecard for performance but influence plans made and actions implemented.

This chapter is structured as follows. After reviewing the theoretical, empirical and brand equity measurement literature, management practice is explored first in terms of its presumed evolution and then metrics usage. From this, some lessons for good and bad practice can be drawn and specifically in three areas: discounted cash flow (DCF), return on investment (ROI) and the benchmarks used for performance metrics comparison. DCF methods include customer lifetime value (CLV), customer equity and brand valuation. The metrics used for planning purposes, for example, are not necessarily suitable for performance evaluation. Brand equity needs to be formally measured but, on the other hand, searching for a single financial performance indicator ('the silver metric') is misguided. After suggesting where future research is needed, this chapter concludes with a summary of the findings.

Theoretical background

The marketing performance literature has been seen to provide little diagnosis (Day and Wensley, 1988), excessive focus on the short term (Dekimpe and Hanssens, 1995, 1999), too wide a variety with the consequential difficulties of comparison (Ambler and Kokkinaki, 1997; Clark, 1999). 'Perhaps no other concept in marketing's short history has proven as stubbornly resistant to conceptualization, definition, or application as that of marketing performance' (Bonoma and Clark, 1988, p. 1).

There are, arguably, four types of theory underlying the formal evaluation of marketing performance:

1 Control theory suggests that metrics can be used to minimize performance variances, that is, bring performance back to plan (Noble and Mokwa, 1999). The two principal dimensions of marketing control are outcome- versus behaviour-based measures and their degree of formality (Ouchi, 1979; Eisenhardt, 1985; Anderson and Oliver, 1987; Jaworski, 1988; Jaworski and MacInnis, 1989; Jaworski et al., 1993; Celly and Frazier, 1996). Outcome- versus behaviour-based forms of control have been particularly investigated in the study of sales control systems (e.g. Anderson and Oliver, 1987; Cravens et al., 1993; Oliver and Anderson, 1994; Babakus et al., 1996; Krafft, 1999).

2 Agency theory. Agents, whether middle managers reporting to their seniors or directors reporting to shareholders, expend considerable resources in supplying metrics to principals to provide reassurance that they are behaving in the interest of principals (Jensen and Meckling, 1976; Fama, 1980; Fama and Jensen, 1983). Again both outcome and behaviour measures are used (Nilakant and Rao, 1994) to reduce opportunist behaviour and therefore ensure that the agent will act in the principal's interest (Eisenhardt, 1989). Agency theory has been applied to, for example, sales force management, channel coordination and competitive signalling (see Bergen et al., 1992 for a review), but not specifically to metrics.

3 Institutional theory (Meyer and Rowan, 1977; Zucker, 1987; Eisenhardt, 1988) suggests that metrics will be selected, or perhaps evolve, according to the cultural norms of businesses and the sectors within which they operate. Chattopadhyay et al. (1999) carried out an extensive study to determine the factors that

influence the way executives think. They conclude that 'executives' beliefs are clearly influenced to a greater extent by the beliefs of other members of the upper-echelon team than by their past and current functional experience' (p. 781). Note that metrics selection here is driven internally and not by the market or by strategy. Selective attention may be deliberate or arise from past reinforcement (Dearborn and Simon, 1958).

4 Orientation theory suggests that the choice of metrics will be influenced by the way top management perceives its business. The extent to which top management is interested in assessing marketing, or market performance, may be explained by the extent to which they are market oriented (Kohli and Jaworski, 1990; Narver and Slater, 1990; Jaworski and Kohli, 1993; Day, 1994a). Market-driven firms need to gather and disseminate market intelligence within the organization (Kohli and Jaworski, 1990; Day, 1994b; Slater and Narver, 1995). Thus the choice of metrics reflects the relationship and the balance of power between functions within the firm (Workman, 1993; Fisher et al., 1997; Dawes et al., 1998; Homburg et al., 1999; Sarin and Mahajan, 2001). Numerous studies (e.g. Jaworski and MacInnis, 1989; Kohli and Jaworski, 1990; Glazer, 1991; Moorman et al., 1992; Moorman, 1995; Fisher et al., 1997; Dawes et al., 1998; Homburg et al., 1999; Hartline et al., 2000) show the effect of political issues on upward information flow.

A more extensive discussion of these four theories of metrics can be found in Ambler and Puntoni (2003). The theories overlap but note that the importance of metrics is not just due to the information they contain but for their reflection of what top management considers important.

Measuring brand equity

Ambler (2003) argues that marketing performance has two bottom-line components: short-term profit or net cash flow and a proxy for the changes in the out-years, namely the change in the marketing asset or brand equity. As already noted, the intangible marketing asset is a key indicator of business prospects (Jacobson, 1990; Balasubramanian et al., 2005). If a firm has built up large intangible assets it can expect a continuing flow of sales and profits without further investment, at least for a time.

Brand equity (Aaker, 1991, 1996) is a widely used term for the intangible marketing asset. Srivastava and Shocker (1991) define brand equity as 'a set of associations and behaviors on the part of a brand's customers, channel members and parent corporation that permits the brand to earn greater volume or greater margins than it could without the brand name and that gives a strong, sustainable and differential advantage' (p. 5). Brand equity reflects consumer loyalty and their willingness to pay a premium price for the brand and/or willingness to continue to purchase.

Brand equity is an asset owned by the marketing company and should not be confused with brand valuation, namely the financial net worth of the asset if, for example, it was sold. The value of my house is not the same as the house itself. The confusion is compounded by the ambiguity of the word 'value'. For example, Lehmann and Reibstein (2006, p. xii) ask 'Does brand equity refer to the value of the brand to the customer or the value of the brand to the firm (aggregated across customers)?'. Value in the former usage presumably refers to worthwhileness whereas the second use means financial net worth. Neither is correct.

Building brand equity 'provides sustainable competitive advantage because it creates meaningful competitive barriers' (Yoo *et al.*, 2000, p. 208), including the opportunity for successful extensions, resilience against competitors' promotional pressures, and creation of barriers to competitive entry (Farquhar, 1989; Keller, 1993).

Non-financial measures are of two types (Lehmann and Reibstein, 2006): consumer behavioural measures, such as loyalty and market share, and 'intermediate' measures such as awareness and intention to purchase (e.g. Keller, 1993; Park and Srinivasan, 1994). For example, Keller (1993) defines customer-based brand equity as 'the differential effect of brand knowledge on consumer response to the marketing of the brand' (p. 8) which separates intermediates from financial outcomes. Keller distinguishes two components of customer-based brand equity: brand awareness and brand image.

Agarwal and Rao (1996) found that 10 popular brand equity measures (such as perceptions and attitudes, preferences, choice intentions and actual choice) were convergent. Perceptions, preference and intentions (five in all) predicted market share but more dimensions of brand equity are needed to predict behaviour. 'It may not be necessary to subject respondents to difficult questions in order to obtain accurate measures of brand equity. Simple appropriately worded single-item scales may do just as well' (Agarwal and Rao, 1996, p. 246). Customer-based measures, however, are limited by consumer surveys failing to elicit accurate information about the store environment in terms of prices and promotions of different brands (Park and Srinivasan, 1994).

Valuing brand equity

It would clearly be convenient if brand equity could be measured with a single financial number because then that could be added to short-term net cash flow to give a single performance indicator, or 'silver metric'. In other words, it would be convenient if brand equity could simply be measured by its financial value. The difference in brand valuations from the beginning to the end of each period could be used to adjust the short-term performance (e.g. profits).

Simon and Sullivan (1993) separated the value of brand equity from the value of the firm's other assets. The result is an estimate of brand equity that is based on the financial market evaluation of the firm's future cash flow, that is, the difference between the financial market value of the firm and the value of its tangible assets. The theoretical approach is to use the future value of the present level of brand equity because current stock return are driven by expectation about the future based on current information (Lane and Jacobson, 1995). Perfect market theorists have never been able to explain how traders have better information about the firm's future than the firm itself but that is a discussion for another day.

Kerin and Sethuraman (1998) also employ the relationship between stock market prices and a firm's intangible assets: 'From a financial perspective, tangible wealth emanated from the incremental capitalized earnings and cash flows achieved by linking a successful, established brand name to a product or service' (p. 260).

A more sophisticated, utility, perspective deduces the value of brand equity from consumers' choices by formulating assumptions about the structure of the utility function at the individual level (Guadagni and Little, 1983; Kamakura and Russell, 1993; Swain *et al.*, 1993). The use of actual purchase behaviour is valid but the specification of the utility function is weak: 'our measure of intangible value is a residual and is conditioned on both the validity of the overall Brand Value measure and on the particular objective measures of physical features used' (Kamakura and Russell, 1993, p. 20).

Of the various ways of valuing brands, DCF is the most frequently used (Arthur Andersen, 1992; Perrier, 1997). Other methods include the cost of developing the brand, what the brand would fetch on the market, the capital value of the royalties if the brand were licensed and a 'formulary' approach that determines a multiple based on marketing variables which is applied to current brand profitability (Cravens and Guilding, 1999).

Ambler and Barwise (1998) draw attention to the confusion over whether the word 'brand' implies the inclusion or exclusion of the underlying product. In other words, should brand valuation be limited to the additional value of branding compared to the profit stream from the equivalent unbranded product? Since the question in this chapter is marketing performance as a whole, and the product must be part of that, it follows that brand valuation for marketing measurement purposes should include the profits attributable to the underlying product.

Ambler and Barwise also claim that brand valuation is flawed for the purpose of assessing marketing performance for eight reasons including the difficulty of distinguishing future cash flow due to past marketing actions from those due to future ones. Their other objections were subjectivity, coarse grain (brand valuation cannot be fine tuned enough to pick up short-term results), temporal shift of assumptions (the underlying forecast assumptions are not like for like), blinkered or narrow vision of the future, lack of theoretical underpinning or market comparability and the use of any single number for a multidimensional concept.

Criticism of only using financial indicators is also not new (Chakravarthy, 1986; Eccles, 1991; Bhargava *et al.*, 1994). Accounting measures are generally short term and fail to recognize the intangible marketing asset, here called brand equity. Yet for many companies, such as Coca Cola, intangible assets have become more valuable than tangible (Standard and Poor, 1996). Financial performance measures are therefore necessary but not sufficient in defining overall business performance and an exclusive use of financial measures may actually undermine long-term performance (Collins and Porras, 1995). The importance of brand equity as a performance driver has been underlined by the quantitative analysis provided by Balasubramanian *et al.* (2005). They found that greater intangible assets were linked with the creation of more shareholder value.

I conclude that quantifying the increase or decline in this intangible asset is a crucial part of assessing marketing performance since without that, short-term results can present a biased picture. On the other hand, brand valuation does not appear to provide the appropriate method.

Managerial metrics evolution

Success measures can be classified broadly as either financial or non-financial (Frazier and Howell, 1982; Buckley *et al.*, 1988). Although measurement of marketing performance was traditionally seen as being at the top line, that is, sales (Lehmann and Reibstein, 2006), some earlier work included profit and/or cash flow (Feder, 1965; Sevin, 1965; Day and Fahey, 1988).

In the 1980s, market share gained popularity as a strong predictor of cash flow and profitability (e.g. Buzzell and Gale, 1987). Later research, for example Gale (1994), showed however that both share and profits were driven by quality, although the interaction between perceived and actual quality was problematic. In the 1990s, other nonfinancial measures such as customer satisfaction (e.g. Ittner and Larcker, 1998; Szymanski and Henard, 2001), customer loyalty (Dick and Basu, 1994), and brand equity (see Keller, 1998 for review) became prominent. Ittner and Larcker (1998) found that 'the relationship between customer satisfaction and future accounting performance generally is positive and statistical significant' (p. 2).

This evolution is reflected within managerial practice. Clark (1999) showed financial measures (profit, sales, cash flow) being supplemented with non-financial indicators (market share, quality, customer satisfaction, loyalty, brand equity), input (marketing audit, implementation and orientation) and output (marketing audit, efficiency/ effectiveness, multivariate analysis) measures. Meyer (1998) claimed that 'firms are swamped with measures' (p. xvi) and that some have over 100 metrics. This variety makes comparison difficult between results of different studies (Murphy *et al.*, 1996). A literature search of five leading marketing journals yielded 19 different measures of marketing 'success', the most recurrent among which were sales, market share, profit contribution, purchase intention (Ambler and Kokkinaki, 1997).

The general pattern of evolution of marketing metrics appears to be:

- Little awareness of the need for marketing metrics at top executive level.
- Seeking the solution exclusively from financial metrics.
- Broadening the portfolio with a miscellany of non-financial metrics.
- Finding some rationale(s) to reduce the number of metrics to a manageable set of about 25 or less, for example Unilever (1998).

Managerial recognition of the excessive number of metrics has led to attempts to organize a limited number using 'dashboards' (Clark *et al.*, 2006), which bring together the multiple measures seen by senior management into a clear, integrated and concise package. Thus, management needs simultaneously to see a range of indicators metrics on a single page or screen giving an easy-to-read summary of key marketing metrics (McGovern *et al.*, 2004; Reibstein *et al.*, 2005).

Managerial metrics practice

From the preceding theoretical sections, it would appear that the selection of metrics is primarily driven by control and cultural (institutional and orientation) theory. Although agency theory would imply the selective use of metrics to influence higher levels of management or shareholders, this aspect barely appears in the literature and it seems likely that the different levels of the hierarchy share metrics less rather than more.

It would also appear that multiple measures of brand equity are an essential part of the package and cannot be replaced by a single financial indicator.

This section of the chapter compares two descriptions of UK practice (Davidson, 1999; Kokkinaki and Ambler, 1999) with that in the US (Marketing Leadership Council, 2001).

Davidson (1999) reduced an initial list of 47 to his preferred 10 metrics (Table 21.1). His four criteria for the selection of the short list were importance to analysts, practical ability to report, importance to management and economic importance.

Kokkinaki and Ambler (1999) used metric categories to structure their analysis of individual metric usage. Financial measures were reported as being seen by top management as significantly

Table 21.1   The 10 most valuable metrics according to Davidson (1999)

Market trend
Market share
Major brand trends
Customer retention levels
New products/services in the past 5 years as a percentage of sales
Unit volume trend (%)
R&D as a percentage of sales
Capex as a percentage of sales
Marketing as a percentage of sales
Distribution trend (%)

more important than all other (non-financial) categories (Table 21.2).

As far as the marketing asset is concerned, 62.2 per cent of the respondents reported the use of some term to describe the concept. The most common terms are brand equity (32.5 per cent of those who reported a term), reputation (19.6 per cent), brand strength (8.8 per cent), brand value (8.2 per cent) and brand health (6.9 per cent). Moreover, only 24.9 per cent of the firms regularly (yearly or more) value the marketing asset financially, whereas 41 per cent of them regularly quantify it in other ways, for example through customer/consumer-based measures. These findings suggest that a minority of companies (37 per cent of total sample) quantify their marketing assets, using any formulation, on a regular basis.

Kokkinaki and Ambler (1999) showed that customer orientation did not influence the regularity of tracking of financial and competitive measures, but that the regularity of collection of competitor measures was influenced by competitor orientation. The relation between orientation and measure importance is less clear. Customer orientation was positively related with the importance attached to most measures except financial and competitive measures. Competitor orientation also influenced the importance of competitor measures, but it was also a significant predictor of the importance attached to measures related to consumer behaviour, consumer thoughts and feelings and innovativeness.

The US study was a survey conducted amongst their members by the Marketing Leadership Council (2001). By far the greatest

Table 21.2 Importance of metric categories for assessing performance

	Mean	T	df	Sig. t
Financial	6.51			
Direct customer	5.53	−14.90	499	0.000
Competitive	5.42	−16.78	523	0.000
Consumer intermediate	5.42	−15.60	515	0.000
Consumer behaviour	5.38	−15.60	522	0.000
Innovativeness	5.04	20.13	524	0.000

Note: *t*-tests refer to the comparisons between financial measures and each of the other categories.
Source: Kokkinaki and Ambler (1999).

pressure for improved marketing metrics (66 per cent compared with 22 per cent for the next reason) was the need to demonstrate the financial impact of marketing; 71 per cent considered that the topic was more important than it had been a year before. This endorsed the Marketing Science Institute (2000) decision to keep marketing metrics at the top of their priorities.

The use of metrics across different sectors is shown in Table 21.3.

This shows a consistent number of metrics across sectors at around 21 but with considerable variation in selection across sectors although that may also owe something to small sector sample sizes.

The majority (63 per cent) of respondents were dissatisfied with their marketing metrics, the largest problem being the difficulty of measuring brand equity (49 per cent). Lack of data (58 per cent), inconsistency over time (52 per cent) and lack of expertise (50 per cent) were cited as the main reasons.

Good and bad practice

This section returns the spotlight to the question discussed earlier of silver metrics and the benchmarks used for performance assessment. Metrics are tools and, like any tool, are not necessarily useful except for their intended purpose. I will show why DCF, for example, is good practice as a planning metric but should be used with care for performance evaluation. ROI is a good tool for comparing capital investments but a bad tool for marketing planning and performance evaluation.

Discounted cash flow

DCF reduces the stream of forecast future cash flows to a single net present value using discount and risk factors to balance the time use and uncertainty of the forecasts with today's cash. As discussed above, it is the most popular method for brand valuation (Perrier, 1997) and is also the underlying methodology for CLV (Venkatesan and Kumar, 2004; Gupta and Lehmann, 2005), customer equity (Rust et al., 2004).

When planning and therefore comparing alternative marketing strategies, estimating the likely cash flows is good practice. Furthermore, the assumptions which need to be made for DCF can be standardized so that the differences arise from strategy rather than context such as market and economic growth.

We have established that performance can be assessed by adding the profits or cash flow for the period under assessment to the change in the marketing asset during the period. The question here, therefore, is whether a DCF silver metric can be used as proxy for the marketing asset.

While DCF is good practice for planning there are at least three problems with using DCF for performance evaluation in addition to the uncertainty about any forecasts being correct:

1   The managers whose performance is being judged are also usually responsible for the forecasts.

Metric	B2B	B2B Hi-tech	B2C Direct	B2C Telecoms	B2C Indirect	Packaged goods	Pharma	Total
Market share	100	100	77	100	100	92	100	93.3
Sales revenue	81	100	81	100	95	100	100	89.5
Market growth	85	70	65	100	90	92	80	80.8
Satisfaction	85	80	85	80	55	67	40	74.3
Price level	77	90	69	100	60	75	80	74.0
Market size	77	60	58	80	80	92	80	73.2
Aided awareness	62	60	69	100	90	75	80	73.1
Overall awareness	65	60	69	100	85	67	80	72.0
Unit volume	65	70	73	100	70	83	60	72.0
Sales by channel	69	70	65	100	75	83	60	71.9
Unaided awareness	62	60	65	80	90	75	80	71.2
Market share by segment	65	70	58	60	80	75	80	68.3
Customer complaints	50	50	73	60	55	75	20	58.6
Customer preference	58	50	62	60	65	58	20	57.8
Perceived quality	62	60	65	60	50	67		57.8
Customer service levels	50	50	58	40	60	83	40	56.8
Number of customers	50	40	81	80	40	42	40	54.9
Number of new customers	50	30	73	80	50	50	40	54.8
Perceived value	42	60	46	40	60	58	40	49.8
Attitude	46	60	39	20	60	58	60	49.1
Purchase intent	46	60	42	40	55	67	20	49.0
Brand equity	39	40	42	40	65	67	40	48.2
Likelihood to recommend	50	60	54	40	40	33	20	46.2
Recall of brand attributes	35	40	42	60	60	42	60	45.3
Churn rate	39	40	73	100	20	33		44.3
Customer profitability	35	30	46	60	45	50	40	42.4
Brand value	31	40	42	40	60	42	40	42.3
Number of products per customer	19	10	62	60	45	50	20	39.5
Customer gross margin	35	30	46	40	40	42	20	38.6
Percentage of sales at discount	35	30	19	40	50	50	80	37.5
Price premium/discount	27	20	27	20	50	58	40	34.6
Number of transactions per customer	12	10	46	20	45	42	40	31.8
Inclusion in consideration set	19	30	31	20	40	42	20	29.8
Customer acquisition cost	23	20	50	60	20	17	20	29.8
Average discount provided	27	30	15	20	35	42	60	28.8
Share of wallet	27	20	39	20	20	33		27.0
Cost to serve per customer	19	10	39	40	25	25	20	26.0
Price elasticity	15		27	40	30	50		24.0
Weight ratio (heavy/light users)	4		27	20	30	50	40	22.2
Customer lifetime value	12	10	35	40	10	8		17.5
n	26	10	26	5	20	12	5	104.0
Mean	45.8	46.9	52.7	57.7	54.0	56.6	49.0	52.7
Average measures per company	18.3	17.8	21.1	23.1	21.6	22.7	17.2	21.1

Table 21.3   Metrics usage reported by the Marketing Leadership Council (2001)

2   Difficulty with distinguishing forecasting from performance variance, for example is it good performance but a bad forecast?
3   Taking credit early for future marketing performance.

The difficulty of achieving independence in the forecasts used is very real since independent forecasters (e.g. finance) will still rely on marketers' knowledge about brand responses to marketing activities.

The unsuitability of forecasts as benchmarks is discussed later in this section but the point here is related. Suppose there has been no real change in the cash flow or marketing asset over the period but the forecasters have a better, as also more favourable, view of the cash outcome from that asset. The DCF estimate will have increased but that will be a forecasting, not a performance, variance. Yet in a silver metric evaluation it will look as if performance has improved.

The final problem area is taking performance credit before it is due. DCF includes future cash flows but it also includes assumptions about future marketing activities. In theory the DCF could be based on no future marketing activities but in practice that would be difficult as there would be no empirical data to ground it on. A DCF which assumes higher marketing performance in the out years will give the appearance of better marketing performance in the period under review. In other words, one cannot separate future improvements due to *future* activities from future improvements due to *past* activities.

The case for using DCF in planning is strong but in performance evaluation it is mixed. It should not be used as a silver metric but then no silver metric should be used. As noted above, the analysis of variance in changes in DCFs from period to period can be illuminating. Furthermore, if DCF is used in planning then executives will want to review performance against that same DCF, or perhaps the underlying forecasts and assumptions, when performance is reviewed.

Return on investment

ROI is a tool for comparing capital projects, ROI being the return divided by the investment or, more correctly, the net incremental cash received as a ratio of the net incremental cash outflow. Of course, marketing expenditure is not an 'investment' in that sense and is treated as a monthly expense in company accounts.

Srivastava and Reibstein (2005) drew attention to the logical flaw with using ROI for performance evaluation arising from *dividing* the profit by expenditure whereas all other net benefit metrics after *subtracting* expenditure. Division rather than subtraction creates a conflict between cash flow or profit (subtraction) and the ROI ratio (division). The profit or economic value added or increase in shareholder value from marketing all require the costs to be deducted from sales revenue along with the other costs.

The law of diminishing returns explains why pursuing ROI causes underperformance and suboptimal levels of activity. After ROI is maximized, further sales will still make profits but at a diminishing rate until the response curve crosses the line into incremental losses, that is, the point of maximum profitability. The exceptions are rare and arise only when demand is fixed and incremental costs do not increase.

A further problem with ROI, and a number of other evaluation methods, is knowing what the performance would have been without the marketing activity being considered. In other words, what is the baseline used for comparison? Apart from direct marketing where matching cells can be left as controls, baselines are hard to determine, likely to be subjective, and able to be manipulated by the marketer. A brand that is regularly promoted will have sub-normal (i.e. sub-baseline) sales in the non-promotional periods as retailers and consumers adjust their inventories and buying habits.

ROI has become a fashionable term for marketing productivity: marketers rarely mean ROI when they say 'ROI'. As the director general of the (UK) Institute of Public Relations observed, 'Ask 10 PRs to define ROI and you'll get 10 different answers' (Farrington, 2004, p. 15). The American Marketing Association White Paper (American Marketing Association, 2005, p. 8) on marketing accountability identifies six 'ROI Measures Currently Used' (Figure 8):

1   incremental sales revenue,
2   ratio of cost to revenue,
3   cost per sale generated,
4   changes of financial value of sales generated,
5   cost of new customer (sic),
6   cost of old customer retention.

None of these six is ROI.

Finally, ROI usually ignores the marketing asset (brand equity) and the longer term for which brand equity is a proxy. In theory brand valuations can be factored in but that is not usual ROI practice.

In summary, ROI is flawed as a silver metric both in theory and practical usage. It promotes underperformance and short termism. The term and the method should not be used.

Benchmarks

Most firms now operate in a rapidly changing environment in which uncertainty, complexity and risk are fundamental issues. There are four types of benchmarking activity: internal, functional, competitive and generic (Dence, 1995). Performance evaluation ideally involves multiple comparisons against past performance, business plan and goals set, performance and procedures of other units in the company, performance of similar units in other organizations, against specific competitors and other industries. Plan metrics are rarely used as comparators in academic research where performance tends to be evaluated against subjective criteria (Ambler and Kokkinaki, 1997) but they provide the most popular managerial benchmarks overall (Kokkinaki and Ambler, 1999) especially for financial and innovativeness measures. On the other hand, Kokkinaki and Ambler found that, market share apart, plan and external benchmarks were routinely used only by the minority of respondent firms.

Benchmarks (i.e. comparative figures) have a number of different uses. For example, when planning it is useful to establish benchmarks of what the outcomes would be without further marketing activity, that is, the baseline. This enables alternative plans to be compared with a zero base. When a plan is established, it may well become the benchmark against which actual performance is measured.

At the time the plan (what should happen) is agreed it may well be the same figures as the forecast (what will happen) but not necessarily. For reasons of motivation or bonuses or politics, the performance benchmark may differ from both forecast and plan.

Using forecasts as performance benchmarks has these drawbacks:

- Although there is typically just one formal plan, or budget, per year, large firms typically forecast and reforecast many times through the year in an effort to minimize surprises. Which forecast should be used?
- A forecast is an estimate of what will happen and therefore any forecast/actual variance indicates a poor forecast. The variance does not necessarily say anything about performance quality.

- As with other benchmarks, variance in outcomes need to be analysed between poor forecasting (the benchmark was wrong) and good or poor performance. Variances due to changing in market and environmental factors can be attributed to poor forecasting if the marketer could not have been expected to adapt to them or to performance if he could have adapted.

Considerable thought needs to be given to benchmarks both for planning and performance evaluation. In the latter case, the plan is conventionally used but see the research noted above. Once planning is complete, consideration should be given to whether it should be varied in any way before being used as the indicator of good or poor performance and how changes in exogenous factors, like market growth, should be treated in performance evaluation.

Future research

Theory and business practice shows that there can be no single set of metrics which suits all sectors and firms. Contextual determinants include the sector, the size and age of the business and the rate of change of the firms' commercial environment. To the extent that metrics represent milestones on the firm's chosen strategic path, the metrics will vary accordingly. In particular each firm will have, explicitly or implicitly, a business model linking the use of resources with performance. Within that, brand equity can be seen as a reservoir of unrealized cash flow. It increases when business is going well and cushions down turns. It allows marketing budgets to be cut in the short term without visible ill effect.

As discussed above, evidence seems to suggest that the evolution of marketing performance consciousness follows a sequence from non-awareness to scientific assessment (Kokkinaki and Ambler, 1999; Ambler, 2003). Further research is needed to test this evolutionary perspective on the measurement of marketing performance.

Probably of greater interest for practitioners is the relationship between metrics development and usage and performance. In other words, do sophisticated metrics users perform better than they otherwise would? In that case, causality could run either way: better performance could provide resources for more metrics development or more metrics development could drive better performance. Some limited research in that area (Clark *et al.*, 2004) showed no direct relationships between metrics, or use of metrics and performance but the relationship was mediated by organizational learning. In other words, metrics should be seen as part of learning which has long-term performance benefit even if it has short-term net cost. This is consistent with fast moving managers being reluctant radically to improve their metrics systems. This area for future research should be integrated with future dashboard research.

Swartz *et al.* (1996) showed that firms tend to perform better on those measures which are most visibly tracked. For whatever reasons, companies tend to get what they measure. Market share, for example, tends to increase where that is the dominant focus and customer satisfaction where that is the most actively tracked measure. If this is borne out by further research, then it would imply that firms need to monitor a represent set of metrics of the whole business model in order to maximize the bottom line: selective measurement leads to partial results.

Summary

Marketing performance measurement has traditionally focused on top-line financial metrics such as sales, market share and sales growth but increasing attention is being given to the bottom line expressed as net cash flow, profits or shareholder value with demands also to express that in a single financial indicator, or silver metric, such as ROI. This chapter has concluded that using purely financial metrics is inadequate because they do not express the multidimensional nature of the marketing asset, or brand equity. This asset is crucial in both planning and performance evaluation as it mediates marketing effects on ultimate cash flow. Since ultimate cash flow cannot be measured today, performance has to be judged by short-term profit, or cash flow, together with any change in brand equity.

This chapter dealt with marketing in the company-wide sense, that is, what the whole company does to satisfy customers and thereby maximize net cash flow. Departmental performance can only be assessed against the goals they have been assigned and these vary from firm to firm. Similarly, marketing mix performance should primarily be assessed for effectiveness against the assigned goals. Efficiency should be assessed, like marketing as a whole, it terms of profit contribution and any impact on brand equity.

There seem to be four types of theory underlying marketing metrics: control, agency, institutional and orientation. Control looks at variances with a view to keeping performance as close to plan as possible. Institutional and orientation theories overlap in considering the kinds of metrics which fit top management's approach to driving the business. Although agency theory has much to tell us about the selection of metrics by managers for higher levels or shareholders, that aspect has not been covered in this chapter.

Brand equity requires non-financial as well as financial metrics. It is a proxy for future cash flows and therefore the key brand equity metrics are those that predict those future cash flows. Brand equity is a relatively recent consideration for managers and is only just fitting in with the way metrics have evolved. The first attempts at metrics are usually financial followed by the recognition that non-financial metrics are needed too. This typically leads to excessive metrics in use and management being overwhelmed by data. The most sophisticated companies use quantitative techniques to refine the variety of metrics down to a dozen, or so, on a 'dashboard'. Variances can then be analysed in more detail.

Three examples of good and bad practice were drawn. DCF techniques are important for planning since they provide a means of comparing alternative forecasts. DCF methods include CLV, customer equity and brand valuation. It is certainly reasonable to retain the DCF for the chosen strategy to compare with actual results as they materialize. On the other hand, this chapter gave three reasons why DCF should not be used for performance evaluation and certainly not as a silver metric.

ROI is an inappropriate tool both for planning and performance evaluation. Its flaws include ignoring brand equity and dividing revenue by cost when they should be subtracted.

The third example of good and bad practice concerned the benchmarks used for performance comparison. Forecasts are likely to be poor comparators as they indicate what is expected to happen rather than what should happen as a result of the marketing activities. Forecast error is confounded with performance variation.

In looking forward to new research, perhaps the most important is the link between metrics usage, for planning and evaluation, and actual performance. Both practitioners and academics need reassurance all this is worthwhile. This chapter drew attention to two silver metrics that do not work and probably there is no silver metric that can work because the short and long terms are essentially separate considerations.

References

Aaker, D. A. (1991) *Managing Brand Equity*, Free Press, New York.

Aaker, D. A. (1996) *Building Strong Brands*, Free Press, New York.

Agarwal, M. K. and Rao, V. R. (1996) An empirical comparison of consumer-based measures of brand equity, *Marketing Letters*, **7**(3), 237–247.

Ambler, T. (2003) *Marketing and the Bottom Line*, 2nd edn, FT Prentice Hall, London.

Ambler, T. and Barwise, P. (1998) The trouble with brand valuation, *Journal of Brand Management*, **5**(5), May, 367–377.

Ambler, T. and Kokkinaki, F. (1997) Measures of marketing success, *Journal of Marketing Management*, **13**, 665–678.

Ambler, T. and Puntoni, S. (2003) Measuring Marketing Performance, Chapter 15, in Hart, S. (ed.), *Marketing Changes*, Thomson, London, pp. 289–309.

American Marketing Association (2005) *Marketing Accountability Study: White Paper*, American Marketing Association, Chicago.

Anderson, E. and Oliver, R. L. (1987) Perspectives on behavior-based versus outcome-based salesforce control systems, *Journal of Marketing*, **51**, October, 76–88.

Arthur Andersen (1992) *The Valuation of Intangible Assets*, Special Report No. P254, The Economist Intelligence Unit, London.

Babakus, E., Cravens, D. W., Grant, K., Ingram, T. N. and LaForge, R. W. (1996) Investigating the relationships among sales, management control, sales territory design, salesperson performance, and sales organization effectiveness, *International Journal of Research in Marketing*, **13**, 345–363.

Balasubramanian, S. K., Mathur, I. and Thakur, R. (2005) The impact of high-quality firm achievements on shareholder value: focus on Malcolm Baldrige and J. D. Power and Associates Awards, *Journal of the Academy of Marketing Science*, **33**(4), 413–422.

Bergen, M., Dutta, S. and Walker Jr., O. C. (1992) Agency relationship in marketing: a review of the implications and applications of the agency and related theories, *Journal of Marketing*, **56**, July, 1–24.

Bhargava, M., Dubelaar, C. and Ramaswami, S. (1994) Reconciling diverse measures of performance: a conceptual framework and test of a methodology, *Journal of Business Research*, **31**, 235–246.

Bonoma, T. V. and Clark, B. C. (1988) *Marketing Performance Assessment*, Harvard Business School Press, Boston.

Buckley, R., Hall, S., Benson, P. G. and Buckley, M. (1988) The impact of rating scale format on rater accuracy: an evaluation, *Journal of Management*, **14**(3), 415–423.

Buzzell, R. D. and Gale, B. T. (1987) *The PIMS Principles: Linking Strategy to Performance*, Free Press, New York.

Celly, K. S. and Frazier, G. L. (1996) Outcome-based and behavior-based coordination efforts in channel relationships, *Journal of Marketing Research*, **33**, May, 200–210.

Chakravarthy, B. S. (1986) Measuring strategic performance, *Strategic Management Journal*, **7**, 437–458.

Chattopadhyay, P., Glick, W. H., Miller, C. C. and Huber, G. P. (1999) Determinants of executive beliefs: comparing functional conditioning and social influence, *Strategic Management Journal*, **20**, 763–789.

Clark, B. H. (1999) Marketing performance measures: history and interrelationships, *Journal of Marketing Management*, **15**, 711–732.

Clark, B., Abela, A. and Ambler, T. (2004) Return on measurement: relating marketing metrics practices to firm performance, *American Marketing Association. Conference Proceedings*, Chicago, **15**, Summer, 46–47.

Clark, B., Abela, A. and Ambler, T. (2006) Behind the wheel, *Marketing Management*, **15**(3), May/June, 18–23.

Collins, J. C. and Porras, J. I. (1995) *Built to Last*, Century, London.

Cravens, D. W., Ingram, T. N., LaForge, R. W. and Young, C. E. (1993) Behavior-based and outcome-based salesforce control systems, *Journal of Marketing*, **57**, October, 47–59.

Cravens, K. S. and Guilding, C. (1999) Strategic brand valuation: a cross-functional perspective, *Business Horizons*, **4**(42), July/August, 53.

Davidson, J. H. (1999) Transforming the value of company reports through marketing measurement, *Journal of Marketing Management*, **15**, 757–777.

Dawes, P. L., Lee, D. Y. and Dowling, G. R. (1998) Information control and influence in emergent buying centers, *Journal of Marketing*, **62**, July, 55–68.

Day, G. S. (1994a) The capabilities of market driven organizations, *Journal of Marketing*, **58**, October, 37–52.

Day, G. S. (1994b) Continuous learning about markets, *California Management Review*, Summer, 9–31.

Day, G. S. and Fahey, L. (1988) Valuing market strategies, *Journal of Marketing*, **52**, July, 45–57.

Day, G. S. and Nedungadi, P. (1994) Managerial representations of competitive advantage, *Journal of Marketing*, **58**, April, 31–44.

Day, G. S. and Wensley, R. (1988) Assessing advantage: a framework for diagnosing competitive superiority, *Journal of Marketing*, **52**(2), 1–20.

Dearborn, D. C. and Simon, H. A. (1958) Selective perception: a note on the departmental identifications of executives, *Sociometry*, **21**, 140–144.

Dekimpe, M. G. and Hanssens, D. M. (1995) The persistence of marketing effects on sales, *Marketing Science*, **14**(1), 1–21.

Dekimpe, M. G. and Hanssens, D. M. (1999) Sustained spending and persistent response: a new look at long-term marketing profitability, *Journal of Marketing Research*, **36**, November, 397–412.

Dence, R. (1995) Best Practices Benchmarking, in Holloway, J., Lewis, J. and Mallory, G. (eds), *Performance Measurement and Evaluation*, Sage, London.

Dick, A. S. and Basu, K. (1994) Customer loyalty: towards an integrated conceptual framework, *Journal of the Academy of Marketing Science*, **28**(5), 5–16.

Eccles, R. G. (1991) The performance measurement manifesto, *Harvard Business Review*, **69**, January–February, 131–137.

Eisenhardt, K. M. (1985) Control: organizational and economic approaches, *Management Science*, **31**(2), 134–149.

Eisenhardt, K. M. (1988) Agency – and institutional – theory explanations: the case of retail sales compensation, *Academy of Management Journal*, **31**(3), 488–511.

Eisenhardt, K. M. (1989) Agency theory: an assessment and review, *Academy of Management Journal*, **14**(1), 57–74.

Fama, E. F. (1980) Agency problems and the theory of the firm, *Journal of Political Economy*, **88**(2), 288–307.

Fama, E. F. and Jensen, M. C. (1983) Separation of ownership and control, *Journal of Law and Economics*, **26**, June, 301–325.

Farquhar, P. H. (1989) Managing brand equity, *Marketing Research*, **1**, September, 24–33.

Farrington, C. (2004) The language barrier, *FT creative business*, **1**, June, 15.

Feder, R. A. (1965) How to measure marketing performance, *Harvard Business Review*, **43**, May–June, 132–142.

Fisher, R. J., Maltz, E. and Jaworski, B. J. (1997) Enhancing communication between marketing and engineering: the moderating role of relative functional identification, *Journal of Marketing*, **61**, July, 54–70.

Frazier, G. L. and Howell, R. D. (1982) Intra-industry marketing strategy effects on the analysis of firm performance, *Journal of Business Research*, **10**(4), 431–443.

Gale, B. T. (1994) The Importance of Market-Perceived Quality, in Stobart, P. (ed.), *Brand Power*, Macmillan, Basingstoke, London.

Glazer, R. (1991) Marketing in an information-intensive environment: strategic implications of knowledge as an asset, *Journal of Marketing*, **55**, October, 1–19.

Guadagni, P. M. and Little, J. D. C. (1983) A logit model of brand choice calibrated on scanner data, *Marketing Science*, **2**(3), 203–238.

Gupta, S. and Lehmann, D. R. (2005) *Managing Customers as Investments*, Wharton School Press, Upper Saddle River, NJ.

Hartline, M. D., Maxham, J. G. I. and McKee, D. O. (2000) Corridors of influence in the dissemination of customer-oriented strategy to customer contact service employees, *Journal of Marketing*, **64**, April, 35–50.

Homburg, C., Workman Jr., J. P. and Krohmer, H. (1999) Marketing's influence within the firm, *Journal of Marketing*, **63**, April, 1–17.

IMA (1992) *Cost Management Update*, **32**, October, US Institute of Management Accountants, Cost Management Group.

IMA (1994) *Cost Management Update*, **49**, March, US Institute of Management Accountants, Cost Management Group.

IMA (1996) *Cost Management Update*, **64**, June, US Institute of Management Accountants, Cost Management Group.

Ittner, C. D. and Larcker, D. F. (1998) Are nonfinancial measures leading indicators of financial performance? An analysis of customer satisfaction, *Journal of Accounting Research*, **36**, 1–35.

Jacobson, R. (1990) Unobservable effects and business performance, *Marketing Science*, **9**(1), 74–85.

Jaworski, B. J. (1988) Toward a theory of marketing control: environmental context, control types, and consequences, *Journal of Marketing*, **52**, July, 23–39.

Jaworski, B. J. and Kohli, A. K. (1993) Market orientation: antecedents and consequences, *Journal of Marketing*, **57**, July, 53–70.

Jaworski, B. J. and MacInnis, D. J. (1989) Marketing jobs and management controls: towards a framework, *Journal of Marketing Research*, **26**, November, 406–419.

Jaworski, B. J., Stathakopoulos, V. and Krishnan, H. S. (1993) Control combinations in marketing: conceptual framework and empirical evidence, *Journal of Marketing*, **57**, January, 57–69.

Jensen, M. C. and Meckling, W. H. (1976) Theory of the firm: managerial behavior, agency costs and ownership structure, *Journal of Financial Economics*, **3**, 305–360.

Kamakura, W. A. and Russell, G. J. (1993) Measuring brand value with scanner data, *International Journal of Research in Marketing*, **10**, 9–22.

Keller, K. L. (1993) Conceptualizing, measuring, and managing customer-based brand equity, *Journal of Marketing*, **57**, January, 1–22.

Keller, K. L. (1998) *Strategic Brand Management: Building, Measuring and Managing Brand Equity*, Prentice-Hall, Upper Saddle River, NJ.

Kerin, R. A. and Sethuraman, R. (1998) Exploring the brand value-shareholder value nexus for consumer goods companies, *Journal of the Academy of Marketing Science*, **26**(4), 260–273.

Kohli, A. K. and Jaworski, B. J. (1990) Market orientation: the construct, research proposition, and managerial implications, *Journal of Marketing*, **54**, April, 1–18.

Kokkinaki, F. and Ambler, T. (1999) *Marketing Performance Assessment: An Exploratory Investigation into Current Practice and the Role of Firm Orientation*, Report No. 00-500, Marketing Science Institute, Cambridge, MA.

Kotler, P. and Keller, K. L. (2006) *Marketing Management*, 12th edn, Pearson Prentice Hall, Upper Saddle River, NJ.

Krafft, M. (1999) An empirical investigation of the antecedents of sales force control systems, *Journal of Marketing*, **63**, July, 120–134.

Lane, V. and Jacobson, R. (1995) Stock market reactions to brand extension announcements: the effects of brand attitude and familiarity, *Journal of Marketing*, **59**, January, 63–77.

Lehmann, D. R. and Reibstein, D. J. (2006) *Marketing Metrics and Financial Performance*, Marketing Science Institute, Cambridge, Mass.

Marketing Leadership Council (2001) *Measuring Marketing Performance: Results of Council Survey*, August, Washington, DC.

Marketing Week (2001) Assessing marketers' worth, February, **1**, 42–43.

Marketing Science Institute (2000) *2000–2002 Research Priorities: A Guide to MSI Research Programs and Procedures*, Marketing Science Institute, Cambridge, MA.

McGovern, G. J., Court, D., Quelch, J. and Crawford, B. (2004) Bringing customers into the boardroom, *Harvard Business Review*, **82**(11), November, 70.

Meyer, J. W. and Rowan, B. (1977) Institutionalized organizations: formal structure as myth and ceremony, *American Journal of Sociology*, **83**, 340–363.

Meyer, M. W. (1998) Finding Performance: The New Discipline in Management, *Performance Measurement – Theory and Practice*, Vol 1, Centre for Business Performance, Cambridge, UK, pp. xiv–xxi.

Moorman, C. (1995) Organizational market information processes: cultural antecedents and new product outcomes, *Journal of Marketing Research*, **32**, August, 318–335.

Moorman, C. and Rust, R. T. (1999) The role of marketing, *Journal of Marketing*, **63**, Special Issue, 180–197.

Moorman, C., Zaltman, G. and Deshpande, R. (1992) Relationships between providers and users of market research: the dynamics of trust within and between organizations, *Journal of Marketing Research*, **29**, August, 314–328.

Murphy, G. B., Trailer, J. W. and Hill, R. C. (1996) Measuring performance in entrepreneurship research, *Journal of Business Research*, **36**, 15–23.

Narver, J. C. and Slater, S. F. (1990) The effect of a market orientation on business profitability, *Journal of Marketing*, **54**, October, 20–35.

Nilakant, V. and Rao, H. (1994) Agency theory and uncertainty in organizations: an evaluation, *Organization Studies*, **15**(5), 649–672.

Noble, C. H. and Mokwa, M. P. (1999) Implementing marketing strategies: developing and testing a managerial theory, *Journal of Marketing*, **63**, October, 57–73.

Oliver, R. L. and Anderson, E. (1994) An empirical test of the consequences of behavior- and outcome-based sales control systems, *Journal of Marketing*, **58**, October, 53–67.

Ouchi, W. G. (1979) A conceptual framework for the design of organizational control mechanisms, *Management Science*, **25**, September, 833–847.

Park, C. S. and Srinivasan, V. (1994) A survey-based method for measuring and understanding brand equity and its extendibility, *Journal of Marketing Research*, **31**, May, 271–288.

Perrier, R. (ed.) (1997) *Brand Valuation*, 3rd edn, Premier Books, London.

Reibstein, D., Norton, D., Joshi, Y. and Farris, P. (2005) *Marketing Dashboards: A Decision Support System for Assessing Marketing Productivity*, Wharton School Working Paper, Philadelphia, Penn.

Rust, R. T., Lemon, K. N. and Zeithaml, V. A. (2004) Return on marketing: using customer equity to focus marketing strategy, *Journal of Marketing*, **68**(1), 109–127.

Sarin, S. and Mahajan, V. (2001) The effect of reward structures on the performance of cross-functional product development teams, *Journal of Marketing*, **65**, April, 35–53.

Schultz, D. E. (2000) Understanding and measuring brand equity, *Marketing Management*, Spring, 8–9.

Sevin, C. H. (1965) *Marketing Productivity Analysis*, McGraw-Hill, New York.

Shaw, R. and Mazur, L. (1997) *Marketing Accountability: Improving Business Performance*, Financial Times, Retail and Consumer Publishing, London.

Simon, C. J. and Sullivan, M. W. (1993) The measurement and determinants of brand equity: a financial approach, *Marketing Science*, **12**(1), 28–51.

Slater, S. F. and Narver, J. C. (1995) Market orientation and the learning organization, *Journal of Marketing*, **59**, July, 63–74.

Srivastava, R. K. and Reibstein, D. J. (2005) *Metrics for Linking Marketing to Financial Performance*, Working Paper 05–200, Marketing Science Institute, Cambridge, Mass.

Srivastava, R. K. and Shocker, A. D. (1991) *Brand Equity: A Perspective on its Meaning and Measurement*, Working Paper 91–124, Marketing Science Institute, Cambridge, MA.

Standard and Poor (1996) *The Outlook*, Special Issue, **68**(17), 30 September, McGraw-Hill, New York, Section 2.

Swain, J., Erdem, T., Louvriere, J. and Dubelaar, C. (1993) The equalization price: a measure of consumer-perceived brand equity, *International Journal of Research in Marketing*, **10**, 23–45.

Swartz, G., Hardie, B., Grayson, K. and Ambler, T. (1996) Value for money? The relationships between marketing expenditure and business performance in the UK financial services industry, Cookham, Berkshire, UK, Chartered Institute of Marketing, April.

Szymanski, D. M. and Henard, D. H. (2001) Customer satisfaction: a meta-analysis of the empirical evidence, *Journal of the Academy of Marketing Science*, **1**, 16–35.

Unilever (1998) *Presentation to the Marketing Council Seminar on Measuring Marketing*, London, 2 December.

Venkatesan, R. and Kumar, V. (2004) A customer lifetime value framework for customer selection and resource allocation strategy, *Journal of Marketing*, **68**(4), 106–125.

Webster Jr., F. E. (1992) The changing role of marketing in the corporation, *Journal of Marketing*, **56**, October, 1–17.

Workman Jr., J. P. (1993) Marketing's limited role in new product development in one computer system firm, *Journal of Marketing Research*, **30**, November, 405–421.

Yoo, B., Donthu, N. and Lee, S. (2000) An examination of selected marketing mix elements and brand equity, *Journal of the Academy of Marketing Science*, **28**(2), 195–211.

Zucker, L. G. (1987) Institutional Theories of Organizations in Scott, W. R. (ed.), *Annual Review of Sociology*, Annual Reviews, Palo Alto, pp. 443–464.

CHAPTER 22

Implementing strategic change

LLOYD C. HARRIS

Introduction

Since the 1960s strategic marketers and those in allied disciplines have dedicated a significant amount of time and effort to generating a better understanding of the complex issues which surround the development and implementation of strategic marketing planning. During this period, planning theory has evolved from what we used to call 'long range planning' to 'strategic planning' to the present 'hybrid' of strategic marketing planning. The results of scholarly interest have been twofold; first, the development of innumerable and increasingly sophisticated planning models and second, various analyses of the difficulties of implementation. However, despite this level of academic attention, studies of practice continually find that very few strategic marketing plans are actually implemented successfully (the most common statistic cited being that fewer than 15 per cent of plans are actually implemented – see Hoskin and Wood, 1993). Somehow our grand plans and carefully crafted strategies are being wasted.

Despite these rather limited chances of success, practitioners and academics appear optimistically united in their agreement that the process of planning is beneficial to organizations. Not only is strategic marketing planning argued to assist in the identification of internal strengths and frailties but also help in generating insights into potentially lucrative 'strategic windows'; through which opportunities are identified to redefine the market or to capitalize on new technologies, segments and channels of distribution (Doyle, 1996).

Moreover, the process of planning is often forwarded as a means through which conflict is reduced, consensus is generated and ownership of plans is accomplished. Indeed, one of our academy's leading scholars, Nigel Piercy, has been quoted as saying that if planning is done well then 'it should be a gift from heaven' because planning should help managers to solve all their problems! Given these, undeniable, advantages of strategic marketing planning it is not surprising that theorists and practitioners continue to endeavour to understand better how and why the implementation of our change efforts so frequently degenerates into fiasco and failure.

The aim of this chapter is to analyse these problems and present some suggestions for overcoming them. First, we need to appreciate why implementation so commonly goes wrong and what obstacles prevent us from achieving our aims. This should be combined with an awareness of what factors assist our efforts and what levers exist for change. Focusing on the issue of organizational change, we need to get to grips with the whole issue of market-oriented culture change and develop an understanding of the unexpected consequences of change as well as the responses of individuals and groups to change efforts. These insights lead us towards the conclusion that, paradoxically, the development of an externally oriented market focus hinges on the astute management of internal-organizational dynamics. Thereafter, 10 levers for implementing strategic change are examined. To conclude, a brief overview of internal marketing is presented as a potential package for many of the levers of changes discussed.

Problems with implementating change

In order to generate insights into how to implement change successfully, we should first understand how and why planned changes fail to materialize. A useful framework for conceptualizing these issues is presented in Figure 22.1. The central aim of this figure is to highlight that it is crucial to understand *how* and *why* organizational members resist change efforts as well as the *impact* of such efforts.

The barriers to implementing change

Although some academics disagree, in my view, a genuine understanding of implementation is impossible without first considering how plans are formulated. My view is very much influenced by the work of Cespedes and Piercy (1996) who highlight the formulation–implementation dichotomy. They contend that much of the problems that we encounter during implementation occur because, so called, 'conventional' conceptions of marketing planning typically present formulation and implementation as separate (albeit sequential) stages of planning. This is argued to lead a myriad of potential difficulties that significantly reduce the probability that a given plan will actually happen. Problems include:

- The potential that the process of formulation ignores the idiosyncratic implementation skills and capabilities of the organization and, as such, tends

to disregard the notion that plans can emerge during the process.
- The assumption that the developed strategies and plans are capable of being implemented.
- The risk that planning formulation becomes myopically detached from the complex realities and contingencies of the context.
- The massive underestimation of the importance of the internal political and cultural infrastructure of the organization.

Consequently, while many writers have pondered the difficulties that occur within planning processes, a small number of studies have contended that formulation and implementation are interrelated, inseparable and at times indistinguishable. One of the most persuasive studies can be found in the work of Judson (1996) who discusses ten major potential problems in implementing marketing strategy and concludes that the first nine potential problems can be perceived as the 'upstream' flaws in the planning process which cause the final 'downstream' implementation problem (it can be argued that the reverse is also true). These 10 problems are presented in Figure 22.2.

In referring to conflicts with institutional controls and systems, Judson (1996) concentrates on conflicts between the developed plan and organizational budgets, information systems, reward structures and procedures of control. In my experience, Judson is right to highlight how the existing systemic architecture of a firm acts as a brake on implementation efforts. However, I would argue that merely 'fixing' these internal artefacts does rather smack of treating the symptoms of a problem rather than attempting to cure the underlying

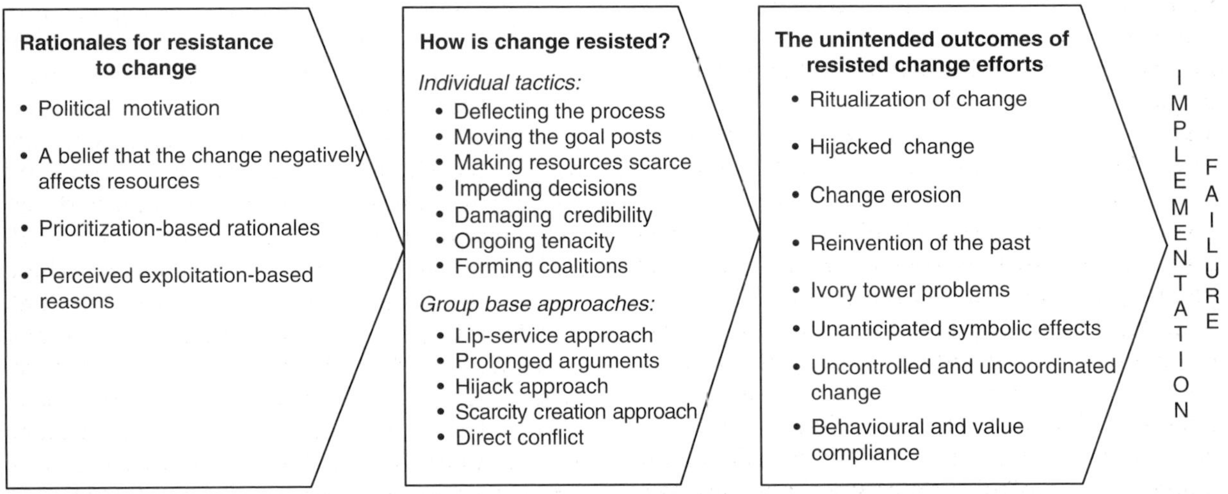

Figure 22.1 The Rationales, strategies, tactics and outcomes of resistance to change

disease (e.g. if we do not really believe that our reward systems based on levels of customer satisfaction rather than sales, how likely is it that managers will enthusiastically adopt this? how many employees will circumvent this change? and how many managers will simply disregard this after a few months?). My view is that the systems and structures of a firm are creations of that firm that reflect its underlying culture attitudes and beliefs. Thus, if we are to achieve long-lasting change, should not our efforts focus on *either* generating plans that are consistent with our intra-firm cultural beliefs (i.e. plans in which we believe) *or* driving our culture so that the strategically imperative becomes culturally acceptable? In this way, it seems logical that we accept that implementation hinges

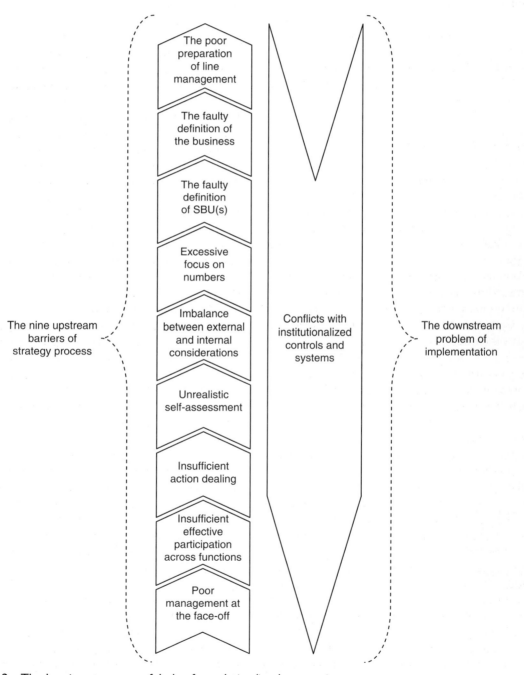

Figure 22.2   The barriers to successful plan formulation/implementation
Source: A diagrammatic representation of the list presented in Judson (1996, pp. 14–41).

on developing a realistic and coherent plan which is tailored to the internal cultural peculiarities of the firm.

Resisting the implementation of change efforts

So, the key challenge for us is to develop strategic marketing plans that are capable of being implemented or that overcome cultural barriers to change and, at the same time, meet the strategic requirements of the firm. Although this sounds deceptively simply, the evidence shows us that this is far from the case. Two issues need to be considered. First, *why*, and second, *how* do employees resist change efforts?

Why change is resisted

In Harris (2002a), people's justifications for resisting change were explicitly explored. The idea was to uncover the rationale behind the beliefs and actions of employees who (privately) admitted to resisting a management-espoused change effort. Four rationales for resisting market-oriented change emerged.

The first justification for resisting efforts to implement market orientation centres on the view that such enhancements are *politically motivated* to affect the authority or status of particular departments. This rationale was particularly prevalent among middle managers and executives and was rare among front-line staff. Unsurprisingly, where market-oriented change was perceived *negatively* to affect the status or authority of a manager's or executive's 'home' department, resistance was advocated whereas where change affected comparative power *positively*, change was encouraged and actively supported. Two interlinked varieties of this justification emerged. First, there were cases where market-oriented change was perceived as disproportionately enhancing the power of departments previously considered comparatively weaker. Second, there were cases where the change initiative was perceived directly to reduce the status, authority or power of an informant, an informal group, a department or even a business unit. Interestingly, in the first scenario, the emphasis is on relative departmental power while in the second, reduced power is perceived in both collective and individual terms. However, crucially, in both varieties of authority-justified resistance, such actions were consistently presented as deliberately

planned political manoeuvres. This perception (whether accurate or not) appeared cognitively to justify the view that resistance to market-oriented change was a logical, defensive action.

The second rationale for opposing market-oriented culture development initiatives centres on the argument that such change should be resisted since it *negatively affects the resources* available to particular departments. Such views were typically held by middle-to-top ranking managers whose resource-based arguments were common among those negatively affected and rare among those positively affected. Although a wide range of resources have been linked with market-oriented culture change (see Hooley *et al.* 1998), changes to scarce financial and human resource allocations appear to be the two most common triggers for resource-based justifications for opposing market-oriented change. In particular, where market-oriented change involved the establishment of new departments or functions that were perceived to increase the power of an existing function (typically the Marketing Department), resistance to such change was considered natural, rational and justified. In contrast to authority-based justifications, this rationale was not founded on beliefs that such changes were necessarily politically motivated but rather on the view that such alterations were fundamentally unfair.

Prioritization-based rationales for resisting market orientation initiatives focus on the belief that although an improved market orientation may be ultimately worthwhile in the long term, other more pressing objectives should be given a higher priority, at least in the short term. This view was more common at the lower management levels and among front-line staff, possibly reflecting their more operational focus. The range of alternative short-term priorities espoused by informants were understandably diverse given their range of perspectives. However, two main types of substitute priorities emerged. First, there were arguments that claimed that the espoused market-oriented change programme caused operational inefficiencies and impeded customer service. Second, resisting change was justified on the basis that such programmes would reduce short-term profit margins.

Finally, there was a *perceived exploitation-based* justification for opposing and resisting management-espoused, market-oriented change initiatives centred on beliefs that such changes entailed unreasonable, subjugating or emasculating demands. As such, this rationale was primarily found among front-line, customer-contact employees whose experience of the market-oriented change programmes was negative. In each of the companies studied, the market-oriented change initiative had, to varying degrees, led to an escalation of the labour process of front-line staff (see Gabriel, 1999). Such changes included increased expectations, responsibilities, stress, hours of work and higher standards of customer service.

How is change resisted?

Next we need to consider *how* change efforts are resisted. How do individuals and groups of individuals resist our efforts to implement change? Surely, these employees must recognize our right to dictate their working lives? Do they not know that we pay their wages? Well, probably, but in my experience it makes little difference; employees can adopt a wide range of tactics to disrupt our efforts. In a study (Harris, 1996), I found seven tactics commonly used to impede change.

First, managers and employees can *deflect the process* of implementation. This ploy hinges on deflecting the process of planning away from its original goals. In one company I looked at, a senior executive of the firm managed to derail a huge effort towards market-oriented culture change through forcing the change agents to focus on the financial issues of the change, effectively turning the planned change into a revised budgeting system! In this case, the individual resisting was a senior executive. However, this need not necessarily be the case. I am forever surprised with the extent to which even large organizations will hugely important boundary spanning roles to relatively junior or inexperienced employees.

Second, planned changes can be stopped if those resisting simply *move the goal posts* a sufficient number of times. A popular gambit here is to impede change through supplying a continuing (and if possible constant) barrage of alternative short-term goals. A good idea here is to identify areas of the company which you know senior executives or (even better) owners consider to be crucial to company success and in need of management attention. This is comparatively easy if you listened to the last few speeches given at the last annual company get-together. To conclude events, either the firm owner or some senior manager will have stood up and talked for rather too long about the 'future' and at this point thrown in a few fashionable management buzzwords. Once you are in possession of these, it is relatively simply

to either move the goal post yourself (or encourage others to do so) through numerous alternative suggestions for company 'crucial' short-term company targets.

Third, if the problem looks like people might actually succeed, a good tactic is to make *resources scarce*. Through the creation or identification of 'more pressing' short-term goals, you should be able to stop members of your department participating in planning efforts through the allocation or promotion of 'important' projects. A good ruse is to limit financial resources. In another company I looked at, a vociferous senior executive that I called 'the Anti-planner' held partial responsibility for organizational internal finance allocation. Thus, attempts at planning found severe limitations put on their ability to, for example commission external market research, significantly reducing their ability to elucidate strategic options. Similarly, constraints were put on off-the-job training, hampering efforts to educate and enthuse employees about the planned changes.

Fourth, a useful tactic at slowing down change is to *impede decisions*. This comes in a variety of forms. One form is what you could call *'agenda hijacking'*. That is, the tabling of a significant number of 'urgent' matters for each relevant meeting. This ploy is aided by concerted attempts to monopolize the avenues of discussion and devote considerable time to the debate of such issues. The idea here is that other managers and executives slowly being to feel that such tabled issues must be pressing and in need of attention thus diverting their attention away from planning and dissipating planning energy. Another variation can be called *'death by committee'*. This tactic is designed to attempt to delay decisions through allocating the responsibility of a decision to a special committee. Preferably, this special committee of working group or cross-functional team (use the one that sounds the best) will meet in many months time and agree to dedicate considerable effort in analysing the issues. If 'away days' in country hotels can be arranged this will happen and many working lunches will have to be taken. Eventually the hope is that a tentative suggestion that further research is needed will eventually be made (hopefully a good 6 months *after* the whole issue was important).

The fifth tactic centres on attempts to *damage the credibility* of strategic marketing planning. That is, the use of judicious rumour and innuendo to generate doubt in the minds of supporters and provide a focus for distrust. Without wishing to be negative about people in general, it really is surprising what people choose to believe. In mitigation, we are conditioned from an early age to trust each other and generally to believe what others tell us (particularly those in positions of authority). Thus, when a senior and well-respected colleague mentions over a cup of coffee that Jones-in-accounts is really a transvestite, pigeon fancier, eccentric millionaire with six toes, our first reaction is to accept this (albeit sceptically, 'I mean how do *you* know s/he's got six toes – I'd heard it was seven'). As a ruse to impede the implementation of change, this can be very effective. A huge amount of effort will need to be dedicated to counteracting rumours (with varying grains of truth) about our plans. Typically these rumours will focus on fears: concerns about job losses, de-layering, relocations, loss of privileges, the list is endless. The idea is to find out what colleagues care about (ranging from redundancy to the make of company cars). In one company I studied the sales department resolutely united against a proposed change until somebody mentioned that the suggestion that the company car scheme be changed was not going to happen (not least since the firm had just signed another 6 year contract) and so sales reps would not be told to drive Ladas rather than rather plush BMWs!

The sixth tactic that was found to be important in efforts to resist change is that of *ongoing tenacity*. That is, adopting ongoing efforts to restrict to possibility of meaningful change. Employees who truly believe that a proposed change is wrong are much more likely successfully to prevent things happening if they adopt multiple tactics and make sure that their efforts are pursued from the very start of the process right until the effort is officially given up as 'not feasible under the prevailing climate' (i.e. even when directors accept that the idea was a turkey and nobody did it anyway).

Finally, one (if not the) most effective way of resisting the implementation of change is to *form a coalition*. Given that those advocating change have often persuaded others of the importance of their support, those resisting change should also take the time to consider who in the firm is likely not to support this view and (more importantly) which individuals or groups does the change need to succeed. This analysis is likely to lead to the identification of two or three departments whose support is crucial. Thereafter, it is a relatively simply process of forming coalitions against this change using a variety of means: education, collaboration, coercion, political manoeuvring (the

choice is really context specific). The goal is to form a partnership of those who agree or who are willing to be seen to agree with your views. This alliance can persuade itself that their actions are for the good of the firm and then happily obstruct any implemented changes without feeling guilty (after all, 'it's not just me that thinks this, look at Jones-in-accounts he . . . err . . . she agrees with me').

In a subsequent study (Harris, 2002a) the whole issue of collective approaches for sabotaging market-oriented change efforts is examined in more depth. Here it is argued that calling the efforts of colleagues to prevent change, 'resistance' somehow created a falsely glamorous impression. Hence, it was argued that the term sabotage was more apt; referring to 'planned behaviours intentionally designed negatively to affect market-oriented change efforts'. This study reveals five collective approaches to impeding change. These efforts may be viewed as *largely* 'strategic' in nature, in that they represent a considered long-term plan but also 'tactical', in that, in some cases, such efforts are employed without such long-term objectives. Figure 22.3 presents a continuum of approaches that extends from the use of 'rational argument' to 'direct conflict' (a behaviour closer to 'lay' conceptions of sabotage – see Brown, 1977). The conceptualization of these phenomena as a continuum (rather than discrete activities) is intentionally used to suggest that the extent of sabotage is a matter of degree rather than a dichotomous activity.

The use of a *lip-service approach* to impede change entails the overt and public acceptance and oral agreement with the initiative, matched by the intentional obstruction of change by inactivity. In short, contributors acquiesce and publicly support the change but collectively continue to behave in whatever manner they see fit. This approach may be viewed as a form of instrumental compliance (see Legge, 1994) in that, in recognizing the legitimate authority of the hierarchy and the benefits of continued employment, employees overtly, orally conform but covertly resist change. In some respects, this can be viewed as a collective approach to impede decision making in a nonconfrontational manner. This approach was found to be particularly prevalent among front-line managers, supervisors and other customer-contact employees. For such employees, change is often manifested in disruption to operations including alterations to existing working patterns, procedures and policies. Consequently, for such employees more confrontational approaches are unnecessary and impractical.

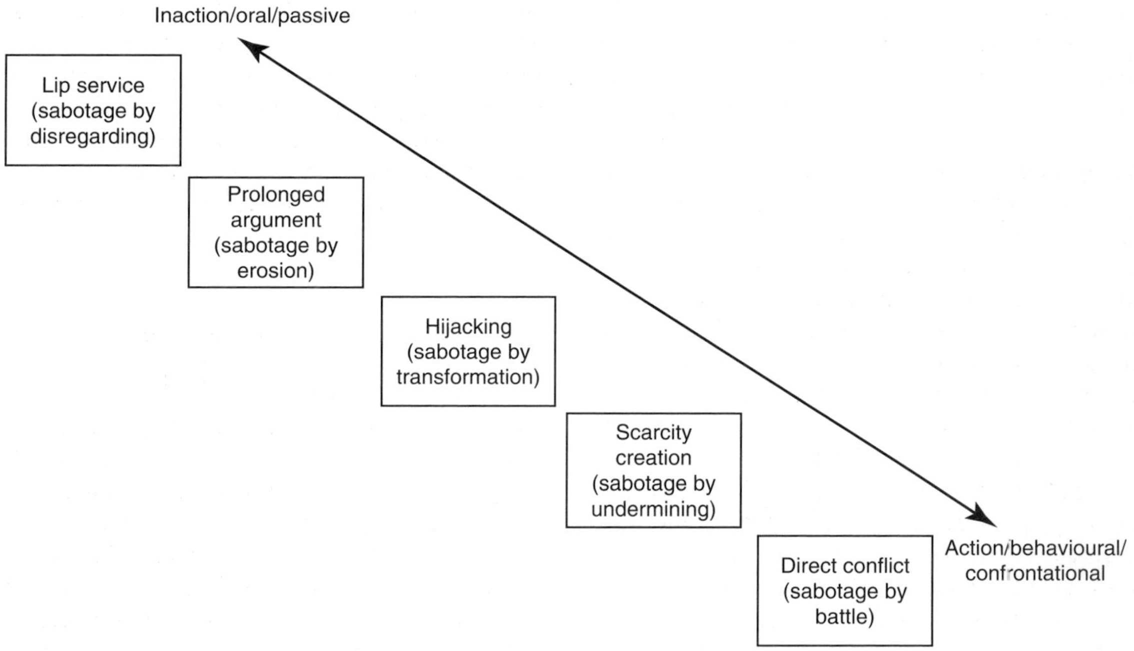

Figure 22.3　Collective efforts to sabotage change

The second strategy designed to obstruct the implementation of change focuses is that of *prolonged argument*. This approach involves the tenacious use of vociferous and protracted oral arguments *upon all possible occasions* to erode enthusiasm, support or agreement with the espoused change. In many ways this collaborative effort involves aspects of the individual tactics of tenacious, deflection the process of change aligned with efforts to damage the creditability of the change. This should be viewed as more active than the lip-service approach since the argumentative approach involves actively seeking opportunities orally to attack, deride or otherwise disparage the change programme. Although such actions may be viewed by top management and their supporters as dysfunctional (see Griffin et al., 1998) or 'counterproductive' (see Kolz, 1999), those employing this strategy consider their motives logical, justifiable and largely a byproduct of contemporary organizational politics (see Buchanan and Badham, 1999). This strategy of market-oriented culture change sabotage was primarily managerial and largely involved non-customer contact, middle managers. In essence, the strategy pivots on three issues. First, the approach depends on the ability of saboteurs to create opportunities orally to attack the logic, implementation, effectiveness or success of the espoused initiative. Second, the vociferousness,

persuasiveness and mental deviousness of arguers appears central to an effective argument approach. Finally, this style of resistance requires tenacity and perseverance and as such is often viewed as a long-term strategy.

The *hijack approach* to resisting a market-oriented culture change programme involves the intentional attempt to derail, refocus, reorient or subvert the content, processes or objectives of the market-oriented change initiative originally conceived. That is, opponents of the programme endeavour to transform the espoused change into something more 'acceptable' to their function, or simply something more personally palatable. In this sense, 'hijacking' can be viewed as a team effort by individuals employing the process deflection tactic. The hijack approach was employed, in a variety of forms, among managers and executives of all levels and was supported by a range of rationales. At the higher managerial level, a hijack approach was appreciably more sophisticated and larger in scale. Typically, the top managers endeavouring to resist market-oriented culture change using this approach attempted to derail the initiative at an early stage by transforming the espoused change into a less 'adventurous' change. However, managers at lower levels also used the hijack approach. The ways in which this transformation was attempted were diverse but commonly centred on the strict adherence to a particular 'tenet' (see Narver *et al.*, 1998) of change as a rationale for ignoring others.

The third approach focused on collective efforts of *scarcity creation*, in effect sabotaging by undermining the change effort. Whereas individuals often employ similar tactics, joint efforts to create scarcity of needed resources, if far more effective. All attempts to implement change require resources in the form of management time, finance, information, personnel and even office space. Consequently, through diverting, consuming or restricting access to particular resources, the effectiveness of market-oriented change may be severely restricted. The calculated nature of this approach to undermine espoused change constitutes purposeful behaviour of a more confrontational form. In this sense, the intentional creation of scarcity in vital resources represents an approach that is political in nature (see Harris, 1998) but that also demonstrates sensitivity to the capabilities and resources required during market-oriented change (see Day, 1999). This form of impeding change was typically adopted by middle-top managers whose functions were thought to be negatively affected by the change. Although a large range of (often context specific) resources were withheld, two main types of resources were most commonly made artificially scarce in an effort to obstruct change. First, in recognition that access to information constitutes power and that market orientation hinges on accurate information (see Jaworski and Kohli, 1993), saboteurs restricted access to information in numerous ways. Second, again recognizing the need for expertise in market-oriented change (see Nutt, 1998) and that expert power constitutes a particularly concentrated resource, managers with power over expertise resources, restricted access in an effort to obstruct change.

The final and most actively confrontational approach to obstructing change focuses on attempts to hinder the initiative through *direct conflict*. Direct conflict was more common during the earlier phases of change, although top managers frequently remained stalwarts of this approach long after the early phases. Such resistance to change reflects extremely pronounced personal opposition to change as well as strongly entrenched cultural values that remain orthogonal to the espoused initiative (see Harris, 1998) despite prolonged efforts of persuasion, education and communication. Middle-to-top managers adopting a conflictual strategy commonly evoked authority or resource-based justifications for their views. Those continuing a strategy of direct conflict at a junior level were either tacitly supported by direct superordinates or ignored as eccentrics. At senior levels, refusing to cooperate with change and constantly challenging the initiative was viewed as anachronistic behaviour that, ultimately, would abate.

The unintended outcomes of resisted change efforts

In discussing past planned changes with executives, it is common for them to refer to such efforts in quite black and white terms. Changes either happen or they do not and are quietly forgotten about until somebody writes a cliché filled memo explaining that such matters have been put on the back-burner until an appropriate strategic window of opportunity arises (management speak for 'it did not work, we are quite embarrassed we even thought of it, so let us all forget about it'). However, change rarely happens this way. Organizations can be incredibly complex and this complexity means that resistance to efforts to change more typically lead to unexpected consequences. In Harris and Ogbonna (2002) we uncovered eight common unintended consequences of change.

The first unintended consequence of culture change initiatives involved the effects of the *ritualization of change*. While the implementation programmes we studied varied tremendously in application, it emerged that the more sophisticated intervention efforts recognized that successful change efforts required ongoing interventions. A consequence of the recognition that frequent interventions were needed was the development of long-term plans for change, which when accounted for on the standard annual basis, became rituals which typically occurred but once-per-year. The difficulty here is organizations need to balance conflicting demands. On the one hand, successful change typically requires multiple and ongoing interventions. However, on the other hand, the more routinized the interventions become, the greater the likelihood that espoused changes will be ignored or that lip service will be paid.

The second unanticipated outcome of change centres on the extent to which the original aims and process become *hijacked* and the course of change diverted. Although those attempting to implement change expect to manage or manipulate the culture of their company, an unintended consequence of their actions is the generation of an opportunity for others to hijack this process for their own (often orthogonal) reasons. All of the change initiatives studied began with relatively clear and unsullied change aims and objectives. The setting of change targets was (in the first instance) most commonly undertaken by senior managements and sometimes specialist culture change teams. However, often during the planning process, these objectives tended to become adulterated by non-specialists or hijacked by individuals, departments or outlets for their own purposes. The impact of such interference was either the subversion of the process or the camouflaging of the process so that change programmes degenerated into cost cutting, customer service or de-layering initiatives.

Another management action resulting in unintended effects pivoted on the extent to which the intervention initiative took the inevitable *change erosion* into account (see Harrison and Carrol, 1991). That is, the extent to which the espoused ideals appeared eroded by subsequent events. While the over ritualization of change (often into a once-a-year, almost, ceremonial event) was potentially damaging, it is also the case that attention to the perpetuation of change was an important issue. In many cases, programmes for change will change what many employees do and also what some employees think. However, the continuance of such behaviours and the reinforcement of espoused beliefs tends not to happen over the long term. In the short-term, people can be enthused by proposed changes and change their behaviours and attitudes accordingly. However, while managements will take steps to sustain such changes, those against will also tenaciously resist and dampen enthusiasm, this combined with staff turnover effects, can quickly lead to an erosion of the change, sometimes into something entirely different from that which was originally intended.

In 8 per cent of the change programmes investigated, the change effort was subverted by *reinvention*. Cultural or change reinvention is used to denote instances when a change effort results in the espousal of attitudes and behaviours which whilst appearing 'new' merely camouflage the continued adherence to the old (and often more comfortable) culture. In other words, the change programme either intentionally or unintentionally repackages the 'old' culture under a veneer of the 'new'. Typically, old emphases on sales orientations become thinly veiled under the guise of

service quality programmes while customer loyalty schemes are camouflaged as relationship building programmes. This unintended consequence is especially prevalent at the outlet level where the change is closest to the demands of the customer interface but furthest from the control of culture change agents.

The fifth issue resulting in unexpected results has been (variously) called *ivory tower* effects. While cultural reinvention largely centres on the reinterpretations of outlet-level employees, unintended consequences also emerged where planners designed changes without sufficient awareness of the diversity of views throughout the organization. Highly linked to the previously discussed formulation–implementation dichotomy, intended changes often fail to happen since the developed plans are either divorced from organizational reality or incapable of meaningful implementation. Ivory tower planners are often ignorant of a series of 'realities' ranging from motivation and commitment levels through to practices and procedures. Given such limitations it is not surprising that the unrealistic and infeasible plans developed are resisted by individuals and groups who (often, rightly) seize on the flaws and inconsistencies to deride and derail the changes expected by planners.

Unintended outcomes also arise because those involved fail to pay sufficient attention to *symbolism during change*. Dandridge *et al.* (1980, p. 77) define symbols as '*those aspects of an organization that its members use to reveal or make comprehendible the unconscious feeling, images, and values that are inherent in that organization*'. We often talk of changing the behaviours and attitudes of employees but rarely acknowledge the importance of symbolic meaning. Nevertheless, such organizational myths and symbolic actions during change can have a profound effect on the change process. In particular, small actions and decisions, which inconsistent with the espoused change, can take on symbolic meaning and be quickly disseminated through the grapevine. While such symbols and symbolic impacts are obviously organizational specific, the symbols often focus on inconsistent management actions, customer service issues and reward systems.

The penultimate unanticipated outcome centres on the effects of *uncontrolled and uncoordinated change* efforts. Whilst in the majority of instances firms will be controlled or coordinated change by a central agency or group, in some cases unintended effects will be strongly linked to the lack of centralized control. Without control and coordination planned changes are unlikely to be implemented as conceived. Things will be interpreted in different ways, systems will be tailored to local idiosyncrasies, objectives will be given differing priorities, in other words, things may change, but not in the way planned. This is not necessarily a bad thing. Often, things can be implemented more effectively. However, if this is not coordinated and fed back into the system, efficiencies are lost and consistency eroded.

The final factor pivots on the issues of *behavioural and value compliance*. Ogbonna (1993) notes that many change interventions fail in their objective of value or attitudinal change but *do* influence the behaviours of organizational members. That is, they achieve the behavioural compliance objectives but fail change the values or attitudes of employees. This is dangerous for a variety of reasons (not least being that compliance only tends to occur when people are watching and when the managerial eye turns elsewhere, employees will quickly revert to their old habits). So, all too frequently, while our plans detail the long-term aims of changing the values, beliefs, opinions, all too often the implementation of such programmes degenerates into a farce where employees adhere to our behavioural rules (at least when we are watching) but blithely ignore the efforts to win their hearts and minds.

Getting changes implemented

In reviewing the literature on what factors lead to successful implementation it is comparatively simple to uncover numerous bullet-point lists that detail exactly what should be in place for a successful implementation effort. Typically, they look something like this:

- Sufficient resources should be available throughout the entire planning effort.
- The implementation effort should be led by an executive with good leadership skills.
- All employees should be enthusiastic supporters of the planned changes.
- Consideration should have been paid to issues of communication and coordination.
- The developed plan should recognize and deal with any issues of existing structure.
- The existing culture of the firm should be taken into account and any changes be well supported.
- The feedback systems for implementation should be rigorous and robust.

On first inspection, these factors seem both rational and deceptively, intuitively logical. While such lists tend to give us warm feelings and satisfy our need for a gratifying checklist against which we can evaluate our efforts, other than as a comfort blanket, such lists are not really much use.

In Harris (2002b) management approaches to change were scrutinized. Briefly, it emerged that five main emphases were stressed during change.

1 First, was an emphasis on '*Hearts and Minds*' during change was found where the focus is on the need fundamentally to change the existing attitudes and beliefs of employees to those values espoused by management. Typically such changes were initiated by identifying and establishing a series of management-espoused 'ideal' attitudes and beliefs. To degree, this approach reflects the Narver *et al.* (1998) programmatic learning approach in that it pivots on the establishment of appropriate principles.

2 Second, were approaches that centred on efforts to change the *behavioural and emotional display* of (largely) front-line staff to those display prescriptions espoused by management. In many regards, emphasizing behavioural and emotional display could be considered a less ambitious, or arguably a more realistic, emphasis than focusing on employees' values and beliefs.

3 Third, were change processes focusing on the initiation and/or maintenance of reciprocal, mutually beneficial *long-term relationships with customers* in order to enhance comparative customer orientation and improve responsiveness to buyer needs, wants and demands.

4 Fourth, in some firms developing an enhanced market orientation was found to centre on attempts to improve the organization's coordination of customer and competitor responsiveness largely (but not exclusively) through *political manoeuvring* designed to persuade, cajole or coerce adherence to espoused change.

5 Finally, were, effectively 'follower' type approaches to change that *focus on imitation* (often of sector leaders). Such an emphasis centres on the identification of the key success factors of competitors and the mimicking of such characteristics (often relying on the generation and appropriate use of market information).

These five approaches (and I am sure that are other context specific ones not listed) gives us some

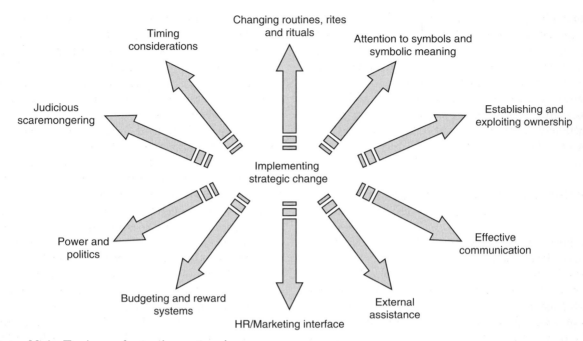

Figure 22.4   Ten levers for implementing change

insights into the approaches managements adopt and the emphases on which they focus. In this regard, this forms a categorization of the overall strategies for implementing change. However, what about the nitty-gritty tactics of change? For this, we need are insights into *how* changes are implemented at coalface. Unfortunately, the issue here are not simple. To my mind, there is not a magic wand, a checklist, an agenda that can be adopted and everything will suddenly happen (or, at least, is there is one, nobody has told me yet). In contrast, there are levers and tools that should be considered and can be employed, depending on the contingencies of the change. In other words, there is no 'quick fix' but there are tools and tactics that *can* help at different times. Although, there are an almost innumerable amount of tactics and levers for implementing change, 10 seem especially noteworthy (Figure 22.4).

Changing routines, rites and rituals

Routines, rites and rituals are akin to organizational-specific behavioural habits that reflect 'what we do around here'. These behavioural routines are incredibly ingrained in most organizations and act key barriers to change as managers grow ever more committed to the comfort of the *status quo* (see Geletkanycz, 1997). The behavioural patterns of employees at work serve a number of different functions (including security and as mechanisms

of control). However, most importantly such behaviours are manifestations of influence and status (see Ott, 1997), and as such are powerful levers for change. Not only does changing how people behave during work alter the 'way we do things around here', but some commentators believe that over time, what we do affects what we think. As previously mentioned, simply because employees are doing what management espouse, it does not mean that their attitudes have changed. However, a number of scholars have argued that enforced or compulsory changes to behaviours can act as a physical impetus to trigger reflective questioning of existing beliefs, values and even basic assumptions (see Hatch, 1993).

Although planners typically prefer to think about so called 'high level' strategy and leave the petty *minutiae* to subsequent stages of implementation, the folly of such a position has previously been highlighted during the discussion of the formulation–implementation dichotomy. Here it is emphasized that while planning should uncover the key success factors and aims of change, planners should also encompass operational issues which will involve alterations to the routines, rites, rituals and ceremonies of employees. It is at this level that a strategy is operationalized into changes that affect how things are done. So, two issues are imperative here. First, those at operational levels (or certainly intimate knowledge of this level) should be involved in the planning process to ground changes in organizational reality and identify the behavioural patterns that require changing. Second, that once changes are identified, individuals need to be given the responsibility of not only ensuring that the changes occur but also that the changes are maintained. Hence, the success of such changes are, in part, contingent on concurrent control and surveillance systems to monitor performance.

Attention to symbols and symbolic meaning

Symbols can be thought of artefacts, events or actions that connote meanings greater than their intrinsic content. That is, they are imbibed with subjective meaning which, in an organizational context becomes shared as a natural outcome of human social interaction. Such issues are important since symbols constitute an important means through which we form our beliefs, attitudes and even our basic assumptions about our working lives. Thus, from a symbolic perspective, Smircich and Morgan (1982) argue that *'the key challenge for a leader is to mange meaning in such a way that individuals orient themselves to the achievement of desirable ends'*. In this regard, symbols and the management of symbolic meaning form an important lever through which change can be implemented.

Turner and Spencer (1997) looked at just this issue in their conceptual examination of symbols could be employed to implement the marketing concept. They argued that while symbolic meaning can be found in a plethora of forms, language, stories, ceremonies and physical symbols were those that could most easily be employed to facilitate change. In terms of language, the terminology and tone used by planners and change agents sends out important and multi-layered signals about a desired change and can have a key impact of subsequent interpretations of change efforts. For example, many professional service providers go to extreme lengths to avoid the term 'customers' (they have 'clients', 'patrons' or 'patients'), image the symbolic impact of a CEO of a hospital banning the word 'patient' and replacing it with 'customer'. Second, language is not limited to the spoken word, the language of an espoused vision or mission should be designed to epitomize the values and aspirations of an organization. Stories are also a powerful lever for change. Theoretically based on true events (but more often devised by astute managers) stories convey meaning and can

serve as illustrations of the espoused values of a firm. Thus, shrewd storytelling via newsletters, bulletin boards or e-mails can be used to highlight and bring to life espoused corporate values. Organizational ceremonies are conscious celebrations of the beliefs and values inherent in a culture. As such, these events are ideal for communicating and reinforcing values and generating shared meaning. We tend to think of big events here (such as annual company meetings or regional get-togethers) but smaller more intimate occasions can also be useful ceremonies for instilling or reinforcing espoused virtues (induction and training sessions being good examples). Finally, physical symbols can also be used to trigger change. One company I studied recently was facing huge financial problems and was desperately trying to cut costs. Middle and Branch management were successfully avoiding doing so since it was widely (and inaccurately) believed that the current emphasis on cost cutting was merely a ploy to generate more profits for the owners. This position was reversed overnight when the owner of the firm publicly announced that the company Rolls Royce was to be sold and that in the future he would be using a second-hand Lada (incidentally, he did drive the Lada for 2 years but sensibly merely garaged the Rolls which, when conditions improved, was brought back with much ceremony).

Establishing and exploiting ownership

While I fully accept that leadership can aid the implementation of change (indeed, leadership could well be another lever for change), given the choice between a good leader and a whole bunch of folks believing in the change and feeling a sense of ownership over what is happening, I would always plump for ownership (somewhat spuriously since the generation of ownership should also lead to the identification of leaders). Although different academics define ownership in various ways, in this chapter, ownership refers to the extent to which those implementing a plan feel a sense of propriety over the plan. In this regard, a sense of ownership is considered a necessary precursor to a genuine sense of commitment by those who execute plans.

A consistent theme throughout this chapter is that during formulation, questions of implementation should be taken into account. One way to facilitate the simultaneous consideration of formulation and implementation issues is through broadening the base of involvement and ensuring that for each strategy, tactic, operational or action plan support already exists and an individual or group is ready and willing to champion or lead the process – not because we think that they should (although it helps) but because *they believe in what needs to be done and feel a sense of propriety over the change*. It is important to contextualize this before the matter of participation management is discussed. First, it is almost impossible to generate widespread ownership after a plan has been developed. It is *theoretically* possible that a developed plan will be so perfect that it will be universally approved throughout a firm and enthusiastically adopted by all; just not on this planet. Widespread ownership will not happen by chance or luck but requires careful design and management from the very start of the process. Unfortunately, executives and managers are typically unnerved with such ideas. As a rule, they find it more comfortable if a process if made more analytically sophisticated (preferably involving some form of computer modelling with 3D graphics accompanied by a pale, twitchy-look presenter who uses lots of mathematical notation that sounds really, really clever, and nobody really understands – after all if we do not understand it and we are *really* clever, then it must be good). Establishing ownership makes managers uneasy for a number of reasons. First, since it is based on participation (which involves testing ideas with those who will actually do them) mangers get jittery about security (after all, all our competitors really, really want to know what is going to happen to the accounts department) and loss of control (the problem here is that managers want to manage and tend to feel that participative decision making lessens their worth). Nevertheless, despite their misgivings managers need to be educated and cajoled into managing participation and generating ownership properly (that is, not just paying lip service). A few early successes here can make a big difference and serve as a symbolic illustration of the power of ownership.

As regards the management of the participation process, there are almost innumerable ways in which it can be achieved. A very effective way is for a core group of initial planners either to request input from particular groups as the process progresses and/or for the core group to divided issues amongst themselves, task each member with identifying others needed in implementation and drawing such people into the group by testing ideas via informal discussions or more formal means of data collection (e.g. surveys, etc.). Care should be taken to ensure that those participating represent a wide range of interests. If the aims are to reduce future resistance and increase the probability of implementation, we should include those with a vested interest, the culture carriers, the politically powerful as well as those functional groups or hierarchical levels who will be tasked with actually doing the work and (hopefully) taking leadership of each change.

Effective communication

In discussing the purpose and utility of communication programmes in leveraging change, many commentators will casually mention the need for systematic communications, largely on the basis that everyone will need to be told about the plan to garner their support. This makes me angry for a number of reasons. First, communication is supposed to be two-way – a dialogue wherein both parties exchange views *and* listen. I have nothing against autocratic management and am very fond of some dictator-like managers. However (and this is supposed to signify loud shouting) – *NOT DURING THIS PART OF PLANNING FORMULATION/IMPLEMENTATION!* Second, if the planning process has reached this stage without *already* communicating with those who will be tasked with implementing the plan, it is doomed to failure. The reason that communications programmes are important is that they should be fundamental to our efforts concurrently to consider both formulation and implementation. As highlighted earlier, without such an iterative process, developed plans are significantly less likely to be executed in a meaningful way. In this regard, it can be argued that, typically, planners misjudge (1) the need for communicating the necessity for change, (2) the need for communication to educate, illuminate and cajole support from others, and arguably the most important (3) facilitate the generation or plan ownership by those at the sharp end of change.

Given the idiosyncratic nature of most implementations, it is impossible to provide a quick fix, one-size-fits-all guide to effective communication. Nevertheless, there are some issue that should be considered in all cases. The first is the need for an ongoing programme of communication. As stated above, effective communication is needed from the very earliest stages of planning (to ensure that plans are implementable). However, at the other extreme, a communication programme is also needed long after the change has been implemented – for reasons for control. The means of communication should also be considered carefully. Although impersonal media (such as spam-like e-mails) have their uses, too much generalized, superficial information is likely to generate mistrust and erode ownership. Conversely, too much individualized information may cause overload and reinvention. In this sense, implementers need to tailor their communications according to the complexity or mundaneness of the change. Finally, there is often the need to allocate the responsibility of communication to an individual. This is far from an easy, enjoyable or even exciting role. Indeed, this places somebody at the forefront of conflicts and disagreements. Consequently, many firms give this to somebody nobody likes, with little power and frequently pretty lousy communication skills. This is not ideal. Preferably, a senior manager and executive with broad experience, social sensitivity and (if possible) personal charisma is really the individual who should be targeted.

External assistance

External personnel can also be employed as a useful lever for generating change. Unfortunately, when discussions about external personnel and implementing change begin, executives and managers seem to develop a strange disorder (increasingly known as David Brent Syndrome or DBS). This compels the poor sufferers to employ management-speak, jargon-riddled cliché (for other examples, please use a highlighter pen throughout this chapter). Immediately, someone will explain the need for a 'change agent' to 'maximize the synergistic returns' or more commonly the pressing need for a 'changemaster' (changemistresses simply not sounding as funky) to 'power our way' through 'old-timer thinking', targeting 'low-hanging fruit' into a 'blue sky mindset' (I actually heard a Professor of Strategy use all of these terms in one sentence). If this happens immediate action needs to be taken. First, your (by now) over-excited and slightly twitching management team need to be calmed down. It needs to be explained that an 'external agent' is neither (1) James Bond or Tom Cruise (it depends on the age of the executive) or (2) someone who is going to be hired to implement the unrealistic and unimplementable plan that has already been developed. In other words, an external agent is not going to be hired (a) to do the impossible bit at the end of planning (getting stuff to happen), (b) as a figurehead for

blame when things go wrong or (c) to be the poor soul that gets bossed around by everybody else and given 43 conflicting goals by 42 separate managers!

Once folks are past this 'mindset' we can really start addressing how external people can help us. First there are obvious benefits of employing external workers to fill specific skills gaps (by the way, this means really specialist tasks and not things like 'change management'; that is just a cop out). I accept that for some organizations, hiring firms and consultants to help in communicating change towards the end of a change process can be productive (although I cannot help thinking that if we have conducted the planning process with sufficient attention to context, should not we already know how to do this?). However, external personnel can also be (arguably) of more help during the start of the process. Those external to the firm should have no political bias and (hopefully) no cultural baggage to impede their analysis. Such they can generate unique and dispassionate insights into the internal dynamics of the firm. Hence, external personnel can be extremely useful in aiding planners to formulate implementable plans while questioning the utility and function of existing cultural attributes.

HR/Marketing interface

I once attended a conference where a presenter bemoaning the problems of implementing change, noted that getting changes to happen really all goes wrong because 'implementing changes involves people'. This, seemingly obvious insight, is not as superficial as you think. While, one would hope that those in strategic marketing functions are astute observers and managers of human nature (after all our job is largely to be focused on customers). Unfortunately our experience of, all too many, planning groups is that this is far from the case. These observations and arguments have led a large number of commentators to contend that the marketing/HR interface is crucial to successful implementation efforts (see e.g. Piercy, 1998). First, strategic marketers need specialized and specific skills in developing implementable plans and executing them efficiently. Second, the interaction and interface between HR and marketing functions represents the alignment of marketing strategies and workforce capabilities (see Chimhanzi, 2004).

Unfortunately, while there are a plethora of studies looking into the interaction of marketing with R&D, manufacturing, engineering and sales (see Chimhanzi, 2004), very few studies have concentrated on the marketing/HR relationship. Although many reasons have been forwarded for this gap, personally I think it is because (deep down) we are resentful that Personnel Departments got all posh on us and started calling themselves Human Resource Directorates (I have suggested previously that to redress this imbalance, I suggest that we re-brand ourselves as the Strategic Marketing Overlords – this has yet to meet universal acceptance). More realistically, if we accept that marketing's interaction with HR can assist in levering change, attention must be paid to this interface. Jackie Chimhanzi (2004) looks at just this issue. She theorizes that the extent of formal and informal connectedness, communication and conflict are linked with marketing strategy implementation effectiveness. While the empirical results were a little confused, the central argument appears valid; if we can improve this interface, then our skills are likely to improve and our HR systems and procedures are likely to assist our efforts to change rather than hindering them. As such HR systems can provide a useful and powerful mechanism to leverage change. The HR function in most firms forms a key channel of communication and education. New candidates can be screened for desired skills or espoused attitudes. Induction processes acculturize new employees into the espoused way of thinking and doing things. Training processes can be realigned or refocused to concentrate on the change objectives (ranging from encouraging a customer orientation to training customer-contact employees in how to be responsive to deviant consumer behaviour). Appraisal and mentoring systems can be used to gauge employee achievements and satisfaction. The opportunities are endless but are all contingent on ensuring that the HR function engages and collaborates with the implementation process. It is worth noting that the engagement of HR is significantly enhanced if this involvement and cooperation beings right at the very start of the planning process. In this sense, the utility of the HR interface in generating change is linked to the extent to which such issue are considered during the concurrent processes of plan formulation and implementation.

Budgeting and reward systems

A central argument to this chapter has been for plans to be implemented successfully, then congruence is needed with the existing context of the firm. The discussion has primarily focused on cultural attributes that form this context. Budgets and reward systems are particularly important artefacts of culture that can form monumental obstacles to change. Judson (1996, p. 183) addresses this topic and eloquently contends that budgets are often insufficiently considered during the development of plans, leading to post-formulation conflict where '*in most organizations, the budget is a more deeply entrenched and respected than strategic and operational planning. Thus it is the budget that prevails and the plan that suffers*'.

Consequently, Judson (1996) argues that firms should adopt the radical idea to base budgets on strategy. This may sound the obvious to students for marketing strategy, who will assume that corporations who bother to plan for their future will budget accordingly. Unfortunately, even today, this is often not the case. A strategy-based budgeting system entails setting a minimum baseline budget for each function/department followed by a process of costs and returns analysis for each action programme supporting the strategy and operating plans. Thereafter, for each strategy (and action programme), expenses and revenues are totalled for each department and layered on top of the baseline. This process should assist greatly in ensuring that functions have the resources needed for change and thus for getting change to happen.

Judson (1996) also highlights the importance of reward systems in facilitating the implementation of strategic change. Regrettably, strategic marketers, typically, think that 'reward systems' are entirely systems of financial compensation. Monetary rewards are important but should be considered merely an element of reward. There are much fewer forms of direct compensation (salaries, bonuses, stock options, profit sharing, etc.) that forms of intrinsic rewards (job enrichment, redesign, etc.) let alone indirect forms of compensation (largely preferred treatments). These forms or rewards are a potentially abundant source of rewards for those involved in planning and implementing change and as such form a powerful lever of bribes, enticements, sweeteners and incentives for encouraging (and this managing) the implementation of change.

Power and politics

Power can be defined as the latent ability of an individual or group to cause others to do things that otherwise they might not have done. In contrast, organizational politics centres on activities to increase power and pursue goals favourable to the individual or group. As such, the acquisition and employment of power via internal political manoeuvring constitutes a valuable mechanism for leveraging implementation. Piercy (1989) theorizes that the implementation of market-led strategic change can be achieved through the successful analysis and management of the corporate environment. He contends that corporate culture is a political phenomenon and that an organization's culture can be operationalized through power and politics (i.e. structure, information and process). Thus, the central thesis of Piercy (1989) is that implementation of market-oriented strategy is dependent upon the management of internal power and politics as symbols of culture.

The sources of power within organizations are well documented. Of particular interest is power derived from formal authority (also known as legitimate authority), information control, indispensability, control over rewards (including everything from career progression to remuneration to who decides the size of expense accounts), referent power, expertise and success (power accruing to winners). Each of these are sources of power that can be pursued, gained and subsequently employed to achieve our ends. This process necessarily involves an analysis of existing power structures and often illuminates the real powers in organization.

With regard to politics, numerous scholars have forwarded categorizations of organizational political strategies. Personally, I have always favoured Machiavelli's three principles. First, establish whether you are sufficiently strong to stand alone or need the help of others. Second, achieve successes to keep those around you uncertain and occupied. Third, cherish those with power but also ensure that the rabble do not hate you. These principles of politics give rise to innumerable political mechanisms to facilitate change. In a recent study, Harris and Ogbonna (2006), I looked at the tactics that can be applied for personal gain and have adapted them below to encompass individual and group gain. These tactics highlight how political manoeuvring can be used to construct power bases, overcome resistance and accomplish compliance.

- *Obligation creation and exploitation*: A focus on purposefully forming, maintaining and taking advantage of perceived indebtedness.
- *Personal-status enhancement*: The approach of intentionally improving the perceived standing or position of an individual, group or function relative to others.
- *Information acquisition and control*: The careful collection of pertinent and advantageous information and its judicious control to the perceived benefit of an individual, group or function.
- *Similarity exploitation*: A focus on deliberately taking advantage of similarities with others (almost exclusively influential superordinates) for the purpose of gain.
- *Proactive vertical alignment*: The deliberate search, identification, pursuit and development of close personal relations with individuals in positions of authority or influence to enhance individual, group or function gain.

These five tactics provide a starting point from which those seeking change can leverage their position to the point where implementation is not only politically desirable but also advantageous.

Judicious scaremongering

In part, judicious scaremongering can be viewed as the *riposte* of planners to the efforts of anti-planners to damage the credibility of change. This lever for implementing change is partly political in nature and involves an individual or group, overtly or surreptitiously promoting a series of future scenarios all of which are negative for the organization, groups or even particular individuals. However, this approach is also cleverly cultural in origin in that is focuses on the controlled creation/publicization of *crises*. Either through describing general scenarios applicable to all, or by tailoring their stories to the specific fears of individuals, scaremongerers can manufacture/highlight an atmosphere of impeding calamity or crises. This is massively culturally important. It was previously argued that most changes grind against the existing culture and climate of a firm. However, Martin (2002) builds on earlier work persuasively to note that cultures are especially susceptible to manipulation (even at the highest cognitive levels) during periods of crises (a number of different crises are mentioned including leadership turnover as well as financial predicaments).

Hence, the logic for creating/stressing crises is that (with appropriate and well-timed action) either the desired change will become highlighted as a solution (or part solution) to the crisis, a previously unacceptable change will become more palatable (and thus less resisted) or planners can suggest desired changes as potential resolutions to the looming predicament. Innumerable crises can be used in this way including, the prospective loss of major clients, plummeting customer satisfaction/loyalty levels (interestingly, the statistics for which should be generated and controlled by marketers), the probable loss of senior personnel, fears of sector-wide structural changes and the establishment or the expansion or failure of major competitors. Clearly, the successful use of judicious scaremongering as a tactical response was dependent on the skills (and deviousness) of the scaremongers concerned. Frequently, driven by the firm's planning evangelist, scaremongering tactics appear especially powerful where the advocate employed or played upon individual, group or organizational fears of collective or individual failure.

Timing considerations

It has previously been mentioned that the timing of change can have a big impact on the likelihood of implementation success. Earlier, it was noted that judicious scaremongering and other political ploys could be used to create crises, during which the successful implementation of change is more probable. However, other aspects of timing can also be important. While our goals and objectives are (hopefully) long term, the implementation of change is, more commonly, about the here-and-now. Assume that we are at the stage where we have generated implementable plans and that the organization is enthused about the planned change. At this juncture consideration should be given to the symbolic and practical impact of visible successes. Ultimately, the aim is implement all of the planned changes. However, during the early stages of change, attention should be paid to the need for achieving quick and noticeable successes. It is crucial that, as Judson (1996, p. 189) notes *'a planning group should not rely on serendipity to achieve early implementation successes. Rather, they should make a deliberate effort when developing action plans, to ensure that some early successes will indeed occur'*. In order, to maintain enthusiasm and counter those resisting change, it is imperative that conspicuous accomplishments are not only made but that the results of which are also disseminated across the organization. The aim here is *explicitly* to demonstrate that the planned changes are (1) achievable (thus raising the credibility of the plan and the moral authority of those involved in the change), (2) beneficial to the firm and (where

possible) employees, (3) directly linked to the implemented changes (added to the perceived value of the change programme). Such changes should be designed to provide symbols of the aims of change, generate focus and aid in the process of garnering commitment and gaining momentum.

Timing considerations should also encompass tactical issues regarding the scheduling or initiation of change. Marketers have long since recognized that there are some changes that, while desirable, are at certain times not politically expedient. Nigel Piercy and Ken Peattie back in (1988) refer to a number of tactics of implementation that involve judicious timing (one being waiting for eventual cultural change another being the application of political 'grease' as a precursor to change). In Harris (2000), evidence is also found that, for some firms, for some elements of change a wait-and-see or *laissez-faire* approach can be sensible. That is, rather than attempting to force change, where change is unlikely, pro-planning individuals wait for an appropriate moment to suggest the need for the desired change. This ploy was often used in anticipation that future events will supply a propitious time (such as the loss of a major client) for such a proposal. It is important that this tactic is not confused with not responding to change. A decision or course of 'action' which centres on simply ignoring the pressures for change is clearly unwise and likely to meet with failure. In contrast, the *laissez-faire* tactical response involves a conscious decision by an individual or group that responding to the pressures for change is inappropriate *at that current time* since the attempt at change would be *more* damaging. Hence, firms adopting a *laissez-faire* response frequently argued that change in the near future was needed but at present, environmental or organizational contingencies were not propitious. Consequently, the adoption of a *laissez-faire* response was commonly premised on the assumption that internal barriers could be eroded or removed over time and/or that future environmental conditions would prove a more appropriate context for change.

An internal marketing perspective

Many of the 10 levers for implementing change discussed previously can be argued to be from an internal marketing perspective, in that many of these suggestions attempt to identify and overcome, circumvent or acknowledge internal obstacles to change. In this sense, a convenient way of packaging these levers of change is via internal marketing programmes. Ahmed and Rafiq (2002) argue that, while there are numerous models of internal marketing, most can be considered to be grounded in the work of two original pieces. First, there are models which are largely based on the work of Leonard Berry (1981). This way of thinking about internal marketing centres on the assumption that if employees are treated as customers, this good treatment with increase employee satisfaction and thence their service mindedness. To do this means that we need to think of the tasks employees undertake as internal products while considering the needs, wants and demands of our internal customers (employees). This contrasts with the second way of thinking about internal marketing traceable back to the work of Christian Grönroos in (1985). This view argues that if service employees are to be genuinely customer conscious, the recruitment procedures, reward systems and management style of firms needs to be supportive of allowing customer-contact employees discretion during service encounters to capitalize on opportunities. This focus on interactive exchange is argued to lead to better-perceived service quality and ultimately higher sales and profits.

While both of these views have merit and although internal marketing has been argued to be different things by different people, the position that forwards internal marketing as the implementation for strategic marketing plans seems, by far, the most conceptually sound and (more importantly) pragmatic. Nigel Piercy and Neil Morgan, back in 1990, first presented this perspective through arguing that efforts to formulate marketing programmes for *external* customers should be developed alongside with programmes designed for *internal* customers. A good way of presenting this position is shown in Figure 22.5.

The idea is that programmes of external marketing are critically evaluated for necessary changes, and internal marketing activities put in place to maximize the probability of successful implementation. It is also suggested that internal marketing programmes supply grounded insights back into the process of planning.

Most marketers feel uncomfortable dealing with intra-organizational issues (after all, that is why we have – Personnel – stop it! – HR Departments). Historically, the perspective of strategic marketers has been (understandably) on the marketplace. Indeed, much of our training and most of our marketing education relentlessly expounds the virtues of outside-in perspectives, market focus and customer orientation while warning us of marketing myopia and other such perilous predelictations. While this has merit to a point, the consistently high levels of failed implementation do rather leave one with the impression that maybe, just maybe, marketers have become too hyperopically focused on extra-firm activities and grown scared of internal analysis and retrospection. Internal marketing is a direct challenge here. It requires us to turn our market-focused eye (at least briefly) away from external customers and to employ our marketing tools and techniques on those inside the organization. If we follow Piercy and Morgan's (1990) suggestion we can even package the programmes in similar ways and using terminology with which we are comfortable (product, place, etc.). In the final analysis nobody would argue that strategic marketers need to stop being focused on market needs and acting

Figure 22.5 An internal marketing perspective
Source: Adapted from Piercy and Morgan (1990).

as the voice of the customer inside the firm. However, there is a case to argue that marketers should stop themselves being oriented towards a merely external contexts and struggle to position themselves, Janus-esque, with a dual internal *and* external perspective.

Summary and conclusions

To begin I forwarded a series of observations and theories that developed the case that implementing strategic change was problematic and, all too frequently, prone to failure. In order to explore these issues, it was first highlighted that complications during implementation commonly stem from the mistaken assumption that the processes of plan formulation and implementation are separate. Accordingly, the arguments of a number of commentators were synthesized and formulation–implementation dichotomy highlighted as a serious cause of difficulties. Subsequently, in order to elucidate the main issues involved in implementing strategic change, we examined two broad issues. First, I focused on why and how attempts to implement change go wrong. Rather than assume that resistance to change is irrational, a range of rationales for resisting change was explored. This process revealed that many individuals resist change for logical and understandable reasons. This lead to a discussion of how both individuals and groups react behaviourally to change initiatives and consciously or unconsciously resist the efforts of planners. Finally, the outcomes of such efforts were examined and the range of unexpected or unanticipated outcomes of change highlighted. The second half of the chapter concentrated on identifying suggested levers for change. In this sense, the latter half of the chapter is an effort to supply marketers with tools to overcome or bypass the problems raised in the former half. Ten levers for change were suggested, each of which could be used to increase the probability of implementation success. Finally, it was argued that many of the levers discussed could be packaged within an internal marketing programme.

In conclusion, this chapter has attempted to identify and underscore both *how* and *why* change goes wrong. As a discipline I have long argued that we concentrate too much on the functional – what goes right, what should be the best way, etc.. This is okay and understandable. However, this focus is often detrimental to generating a genuine understanding of why we get things wrong, why our beautiful plans are rejected and our carefully computer-modelled changes are met with derision. If we are truly interested in success we must first delve into the less glamorous, less prestigious and definitely less comfortable world of failure.

In an effort to redress the imbalance between implementation success and failure, the latter half of this chapter forwards a series of levers for implementing change as well as a potential package for many of them. However, it must be stressed, these are only suggestions. There are no quick fix, universally applicable solutions. Each change is limited by context and each context is individual and idiosyncratic. Hence, levers for change *must* be tailored and customized for each, bespoke, individuality.

References

Ahmed, P. K. and Rafiq, M. (2002) *Internal marketing: Tools and Concepts for Customer-focused Management*, Butterworth Heinemann, Oxford.

Berry, L. L. (1981) The employee as customer, *Journal of Retailing Banking*, **3**, March, pp. 25–28.

Brown, G. (1977) *Sabotage: A Study in Industrial Conflict*, Spokesman Books, Nottingham.

Buchanan, D. A. and Badham, R. (1999) *Power, Politics, and Organizational Change: Winning the Turf Game*, Sage Publications, London.

Cespedes, F. V. and Piercy, N. F. (1996) Implementing marketing strategy, *Journal of Marketing Management*, **12**, 135–160.

Chimhanzi, J. (2004) The impact of marketing/ HR interactions on marketing strategy implementation, *European Journal of Marketing*, **38**(1/2), 73–98.

Dandridge, T. C., Mitroff, I and Joyce, W. F. (1980) Organizational symbolism: a topic to expand organizational analysis, *Academy of Management Review*, **5**(1), 77–82.

Day, G. S. (1999) *The Market Driven Organization: Understanding, Attracting and Keeping Valuable Customers*, The Free Press, New York.

Doyle, P. (1996) *Marketing Management and Strategy*, Prentice Hall, London.

Gabriel, Y. (1999) Beyond happy families: a critical reevaluation of the control-resistance-identity triangle, *Human Relations*, **52**(2), 179–203.

Geletkanycz, M. A. (1997) The salience of 'culture's consequences': the effects of cultural values on top executive commitment to the status quo, *Strategic Management Journal*, **18**(8), 615–634.

Griffin, R. W., O'Leary-Kelly, A. and Collins, J. (1998) Dysfunctional work behaviors in organizations, *Journal of Organizational Behavior, Trends in Organizational Behavior*, **5**, 66–82.

Grönroos, C. (1985) Internal marketing – theory and practice, *American Marketing Association's Services Conference Proceedings*, pp. 41–47.

Harris, L. C. (1996) The impediments to initiating planning, *Journal of Strategic Marketing*, **4**(2), 129–142.

Harris, L. C. (1998) Cultural domination: the key to a market oriented culture?, *European Journal of Marketing*, **32**(3/4), 354–373.

Harris, L. C. (2000) Getting professionals to plan: pressures, obstacles and tactical responses, *Long Range Planning*, **33**(6), 849–877.

Harris, L. C. (2002a) Sabotaging market-orientated culture change: an exploration of resistance justifications and approaches, *Journal of Marketing Theory and Practice*, **10**(3), 58–75.

Harris, L. C. (2002b) Developing market orientation: an exploration of management approaches, *Journal of Marketing Management*, **18**(7–8), 603–632.

Harris, L. C. and Ogbonna, E. (2006) Approaches to career success: an exploration of covert, clandestine, and concealed strategies, *Human Resource Management*, **45**(1), 43–66.

Harrison, J. R. and Carrol, G. R. (1991) Keeping the faith: a model of cultural transmission in formal organizations, *Administrative Science Quarterly*, **36**, 552–582.

Hatch, M. J. (1993) The dynamics of organizational culture, *Academy of Management Review*, **18**(4), 657–693.

Hooley, G., Möller, K. and Broderick, A. (1998) Competitive positioning and the resource-based view of the firm, *Journal of Strategic Marketing*, **6**, 97–115.

Hoskin, R. and Wood, S. (1993) Overcoming strategic planning disconnects, *Journal for Quality and Participation*, **16**(4), 50–58.

Jaworski, B. J. and Kohli, A. K. (1993) Market orientation: antecedents and consequences, *Journal of Marketing*, **57**, July, 53–70.

Judson, A. S. (1996) *Making Strategy Happening: Transforming Plans into Reality*. Blackwell, Oxford.

Kolz, A. R. (1999) Personality predictors of retail employee theft and counterproductive behavior, *Journal of Professional Services Marketing*, **19**(2), 107–114.

Legge, K. (1994) Managing Culture: Fact or Fiction, in Sisson, K. (ed.), *Personnel Management: A Comprehensive Guide to Theory and Practice in Britain*, Blackwell, Oxford, pp. 397–433.

Harris, L. C. and Ogbonna, E. (2002). The unintended consequences of culture interventions: a study of unexpected outcomes, *British Journal of Management*, **13**(1), 31–50, ISSN 1045–3172.

Martin, J. (2002) *Organizational Culture: Mapping the Terrain*. Sage, London.

Narver, J. C., Slater, S. F. and Tietje, B. (1998) Creating a market orientation, *Journal of Market Focused Management*, **2**, 241–255.

Nutt, P. C. (1997) Leverage, resistance and the success of implementation approaches, *Journal of Management Studies*, **35**(2), 213–240.

Ogbonna, E. (1993) Managing organizational culture: fantasy or reality? *Human Resource Management Journal*, **3**(2), 42–54.

Ott, J. S. (1997) *The Organizational Culture Perspective*, Dorsey Press, Chicago.

Piercy, N. F. (1989) Marketing concepts and actions: implementing market-led strategic change, *European Journal of Marketing*, **24**(2), 24–42.

Piercy, N. F. (1998) Marketing implementation: the implications of marketing paradigm weakness for the strategy execution process, *Journal of the Academy of Marketing Science*, **26**(3), 222–236.

Piercy, N. F. and Morgan, N. (1990) Internal marketing strategy: leverage for managing marketing-led strategic change, *Irish Marketing Review*, **4**(3), 11–38.

Piercy, N. F. and Peattie, K. J. (1988) Matching marketing strategies to corporate culture: the parcel and the wall, *Journal of General Management*, **13**(4), 33–44.

Smircich, L. and Morgan, G. (1982) Leadership: the management of meaning, *The Journal of Applied Behavioral Science*, **18**, 257–273.

Turner, G. B. and Spencer, B. (1997) Understanding the marketing concept as organizational culture, *European Journal of Marketing*, **31**(2), 110–121.

Further reading

Ahmed, P. K. and Rafiq, M. (2002) *Internal Marketing: Tools and Concepts for Customer-focused Management*, Butterworth Heinemann, Oxford. In interesting text that focuses on the concept of internal marketing. To my mind the first three chapters are the most conceptually illuminating, although there are also a number of case studies that are insightful. The authors go into detail about both of the two perspectives on internal marketing mentioned in the text and supply a hybrid version that seems logical, albeit, rather complex.

Harris, L. C. (2000) Getting professionals to plan: pressures, obstacles and tactical responses, *Long Range Planning*, **33**(6), 849–877. This is a study of the difficulties of getting planning started in the context of professional service firms. It provides some useful insights into the pressures, barriers and approaches that can be adopted to make planning happen.

Harris, L. C. (2002a) Sabotaging market-orientated culture change: an exploration of resistance justifications and approaches, *Journal of Marketing Theory and Practice*, **10**(3), 58–75. This is a qualitative study of how and why managers in firms attempt to resist efforts to develop a market oriented culture. The literature review provides a useful introduction to market orientation and also deals with issues of cultural manipulation.

Harris, L. C. and Ogbonna, E. (2000) The responses of front-line employees to market oriented culture change, *European Journal of Marketing*, **34**(3/4), 318–340. This is a qualitative study of how customer-contact employees react to efforts to change their ways of thinking about work and their ways of doing work. Plotting willingness to change and pre-existing subcultural strength on axes, nine reactions to change are described. A useful way of thinking about the probable responses of employees to change efforts.

Harris, L. C. and Ogbonna, E. (2006) The initiation of strategic planning: an empirical investigation of antecedent factors, *Journal of Business Research*, **59**(1), 100–111. This builds on two earlier qualitative studies both in the *Journal of strategic Marketing* in 1996. This later study presents the result of survey into the barriers to getting planning started. While this is not directly about the implementation of change, it seems to me that firms often have equal difficulties in starting the process.

Hatch, M. J. (1993) The dynamics of organizational culture, *Academy of Management Review*, **18**(4), 657–693. Although this article is a little dated, the perspective forwarded remains fresh and deeply illuminating. Much of this chapter has alluded directly or indirectly to the concept of organizational culture. In this paper, the components and dynamics of culture are identified and elucidated by one of the world's leading culture experts.

Judson, A. S. (1996) *Making Strategy Happening: Transforming Plans into Reality*. Blackwell, Oxford. A very good text with many practical insights into the formulation/implementation issue. The first four chapters are dedicated to explaining why plans fail and the remainder of text details a series of suggestion for how successful and implementable plans can be generated.

Piercy, N. F. (2002) *Market-led Strategic Change: Transforming the Process of Going to Market*, Butterworth-Heinemann, Oxford. This third edition of MLSC is an incredibly useful text that provides practitioners and students of marketing with useful and illuminating insights into the practical dynamics of getting marketing happening. This and earlier editions certainly shaped my perspective on what strategic marketing is and should be and definitely were important in shaping my early writing on planning initiation that is clearly grounded in this tradition.

Turner, G. B. and Spencer, B. (1997) Understanding the marketing concept as organizational culture, *European Journal of Marketing*, **31**(2), 110–121. This is a conceptual examination of how we can understand the concept of marketing as a multi-facetted organizational culture. Adopting an organizational symbolism perspective, this paper provides practical insights into how managers can use symbols to leverage change.

Part Four
The Application of Marketing

CHAPTER 23

Exit *services* marketing – enter *service* marketing

EVERT GUMMESSON

Introduction

Services marketing – and marketing in general – is in turbulent flux. This claim constitutes the vantage point for this chapter. The chapter is a synthesis of research, practical experience of marketer and consumer and personal ideas about where marketing is heading. For a more complete overview of concepts, models, authors and cases in services marketing, the reader is referred to textbooks and other overviews. (See Recommendations for Further Reading at the end of the Chapter).

When, in the 1970s, services immigrated to Marketingland and applied for citizenship, it was in protest against the hegemony of goods marketing. The initial sections of the chapter elaborate on the distinction between services and goods marketing, bearing in mind that goods (things) and services (activities) always appear together. So far, research in marketing and textbooks have not been able to integrate this insight with general marketing theory. The chapter proposes that the time is ripe for a merger on a higher level of validity and relevance.

Through the concept of the service-dominant logic (Vargo and Lusch, 2004a; Lusch and Vargo, 2006), a daring and constructive effort has been made to turn what we know so far into a tentative synthesis. Their logic opened up an international dialogue on the output of marketing as value propositions rather than as goods or services. By further appointing the customer co-creator of value, the roles of supplier and customer become blurred and require redefinition.

As Baker points out (2006, pp. 197–198), '. . . the distinction between success and failure in competitive markets may be reduced to two basic issues, first, an understanding of customer needs, and, second, the ability to deliver added value. . .' This is known as the marketing concept and is at least half a century old. It is increasingly referred to as customer-centricity but, despite its age, has only been partially implemented. We may now have the knowledge that allows us to turn the tide.

The chapter further brings in the marketing mix and what it stands for today. It considers the mix and the well-known value chain as primarily supplier-centric. It dethrones the mix to the second level of marketing and elevates networks of relationships in which we interact to the first level. So far, relational approaches – relationship marketing, customer relationship management (CRM) and one-to-one marketing – have been primarily focused on the dyad: the customer–supplier relationship. The chapter suggests a transition from customer-centricity to a balanced centricity of the interests of multiple parties. This requires a network, many-to-many, approach to marketing. The chapter ends with a summary and an epilogue.

'There is no such thing as services marketing!'

In the late 1960s, an American PhD student wanted to write his doctoral thesis on services marketing. His professor's response was instant: 'There is no such thing as services marketing!' There was very little written about services at that time; the spotlight was on goods and manufacturing.

If you were asked to write a chapter on services marketing in the late 1970s, you could draw on a limited number of research findings and practitioner cases. And there was resistance from the marketing establishment. 'Marketing services is the same as marketing goods', 'Services are non-important', and 'The service sector is retarded' were some of the frequently voiced objections.

Despite the resistance, there were enough stubborn pioneers who attracted a critical and rapidly growing mass of researchers and practitioners. Writing a chapter about services marketing in the late 1980s, therefore, required considerably more space and discernment than a decade before.

In the late 1990s, information technology (IT) entered the service arena with totally new infrastructures – notably e-mail, the Internet, powerful laptops and mobile telephony – but the service applications were more hype and odd cases than marketing reality. In the 2000s, although the bulk of services remain the same as basic customer needs have not changed dramatically, the ordering and production of many services have changed. IT applications have matured into working services and new services have spawned totally new markets and strategies, and will keep doing so.

When venturing to write a chapter on services marketing in 2007, the task is not that easy. In some way, we are back where we started. But we are back on a higher level of understanding and technology. We could add another lesson, which may stand out as shocking to some:

'There is no such thing as goods marketing!'

Together with the statement in the heading, this reflects a disturbing circumstance that has been there all along: How should we handle the dependency between goods and services? Take any service and there are goods elements; take any goods and there are service elements. Goods and services are destined to live together and to become competitive even to love each other. After having worked with marketing in organizations and done research in services for several decades, I dare now say with confidence that we begin to see the light:

'All marketing is about value propositions!'

This simply means that customers do not buy goods or services; they buy something that they perceive to be of value for them. As the proof of the pudding is in the eating, value only springs up in interaction with the customer and it does so in countless, individual ways. For example, buying a car is classified as the outcome of goods marketing, renting a car as the outcome of services marketing. For each customer, however, value is created in his or her interaction with the car. It is driving to a desired destination; driving the car well or badly; taking good care of it, or neglecting its maintenance; praising its convenience, or cursing traffic jams, absence of parking space, and the rising gas price; enjoying music and the privacy, or getting bored by long, lonely hours in the car; and so on.

The car remains a value proposition whether it is driver owned, owned by your employer, bought with borrowed money, leased, rented or owned by your parents. The actualization of value is in the hands of the consumer. In the current debate, the value proposition idea is gaining ground. First, it stresses that what you sell should add value to the customer, second that it is a proposition and not the final outcome of business and economic activity.

This may not be new, but eventually it seems to be catching the imagination of marketers. It could be the beginnings of a more general approach to marketing management based on better theory. Marketing theory today holds reminiscences of inadequate microeconomic theory; draws on sociology, psychology and other social sciences; and offers fragmented research, practitioner experiences, personal observations, success stories and sometimes hype. There is as yet too little effort in the direction of grand marketing theory and a higher level roadmap. Natural sciences strive to get deep into the secrets of nature, discovering galaxies, atoms, genes, and so on, which form the basis of life. Although knowledge of marketing has grown tremendously over the past half century, we have not [yet] found the marketing genome.

Tricks definitions play

One might conclude from the discussion so far that the terms 'goods' and 'services' should be abandoned. This is not so, but they should be used with more finesse.

Goods/services versus the service-dominant logic

There is no generally accepted and complete definition of services. Services could basically be referred to as dynamic activities and processes, while goods are static things. IBM, in their ongoing research programme *Services Science*, lists a random selection of efforts to define services from the literature and suggests that services are 'a provider-client interaction that creates and captures value'. Another approach is to list services, as is done in official statistics. Pauli (1987, pp. 33–34) suggested that '. . . perhaps it is not necessary to have a clear, once-and-for-all definition. After all, GATT (General Agreement on Tariffs and Trade) has never defined goods'. The following case exhibits the reality of this uncertainty and confusion in situations that we all experience as consumers.

> A visit to a supermarket reveals that goods are not well defined. For example, muesli can be anything from the original Swiss mixture of organically grown cereal, dried fruit and fibres, based on ideas about health, to a candy mix that sends your blood sugar to the moon for a brief spell of energy. Very few of the hundreds of 'yoghurt' variants on supermarket shelves and promoted as low-fat diet products have a living yoghurt culture in them. Further, food stores and restaurants offer the service of making food conveniently available. A restaurant offers the service of ready-to-eat food together with eating space and supportive equipment. It also offers ambiance – a certain atmosphere responding to a lifestyle – and there is any amount of variation of restaurants. Goods are of two types: consumption goods (food and drink) and durable goods (knives and forks, chairs and tables). The services appear as waiters and other staff, or it could be self-service, or a combination. A pleasant waiter (services) may or may not compensate for bad food (goods), and an unpleasant waiter may or may not destroy the pleasure of good food. So there is a contextually dependent trade-off between goods and services. However, you cannot run a restaurant without goods, notably the food. There are also hybrids of restaurants and food stores and physical stores, e-mail-order, Internet sales and direct selling (such as Tupperware home-parties) increasingly combine. For example, the same store may have a website allowing you to 'window-shop' on your computer screen, order from the website and get the goods in the mail, go to the store to buy it, or join a home-party hosted by the store.

Efforts have been made to get *product* accepted as a joint term for goods and services and to use *offering, package* or *solution* as all inclusive concepts for what the customer buys. It has not worked. When you read 'products' in a marketing text, it generally means goods, and the other concepts are only used in select cases.

The *service-dominant logic* suggests *service* (in the singular) as the core concept replacing both goods and services. A supplier offers a *value proposition*, but *value actualization* occurs in the usage and consumption process. Thus, value is the outcome of *co-creation* between suppliers and customers. This can be extended beyond the customer-supplier dyad. Consider the *complex* and *adaptive networks* in which we are embedded in society: intermediaries, competitors, friends, government, the media and so on. The co-creation also includes customer activities during the usage and consumption process. Although my current perception of marketing is not in conflict with the general ideas of the service-dominant logic, the chapter offers my own interpretation and combination of features.

The number of marketing situations are like the stars in the sky. We cannot really count them and allocate them to general categories which consider the necessary details. The situations are composed of both similarities and differences, of modules that can be shared in different configurations and customized or mass-customized to take care of situations that closely resemble each other.

When the terms 'goods' and 'services' are used in this text, they represent a certain *emphasis* or *perspectives*. They are used when either the *things aspect* or the *activities aspect* is in focus for analysis or action. We can also use the term 'services' in a loose sense when we talk about hotel services, railway services and so on. The term 'service' is used as synonymous with value. See also the discussion about the meaning of services in Grönroos (2007).

The service sector – fuzzy and fussy

Let us shift our view from the micro to the macro level. Like the unicorn in James Thurber's famous fable, the service sector is a mythical beast. In official statistics, economies consist of the service sector, the industrial (goods manufacturing) sector and the agricultural sector. These sectors are playgrounds for statisticians and economists who revel in ambiguous categories. In reality, these statistical 'boxes' are a procrustean compromise; the focal phenomenon does not fill up the box at the same time as part of it cannot be squeezed into it.

The sectors are fuzzy sets of things and activities. For example, when it is estimated that a company is getting 51 per cent of its revenue from the sales of manufactured goods, it is classified as a manufacturing company. If, instead, 51 per cent of its revenue comes from repairing and maintaining its products, it becomes a service company. If a manufacturing company turns its repair and maintenance department into a subsidiary, the service sector grows and the manufacturing sector drops. The upsurge in incorporating internal departments and outsourcing services gives the impression that the service sector grows. It is mainly the book-keeping of the sector that has changed, and reality has only changed marginally. These types of definitions have no validity and no relevance in marketing, academic research and practice alike. In addition, the statistics only count the part of our economy which is represented by money. It does not count when two people exchange goods or services for other goods or services, the work done in families and between friends and the black economy. The division in sectors may have some meaning for politicians and governments on a macro level, but I doubt it. It is more likely a hindrance to more informed and substantive understanding of the market and marketing situations.

Today's conventional truth is that the service sector has grown and keeps growing, that the goods sector is declining, and that the agricultural sector in many countries is vanishing. We allegedly left the agricultural era for the industrial era and have entered the post-industrial era, the information age, the knowledge-based society, or the service economy; there are many names that try to pinpoint our current situation. The statistics are based on cost, price and employment data but not on consumption as value for customers. The sector definitions are totally product-centric and the customer is non-existent.

In contrast, a customer-centric view shows us that we have never had as many products as we have today and there has been sustaining growth in shopping areas and Internet trade. For example, in the 1950s, well-off people had one car, and everybody had one radio set; two radios were for the wealthy. Today, people have any amount of radios, phones, computers, television sets and cameras, and two-car households are common. The fashion industry is booming, and leisure products like ski equipment become increasingly sophisticated and costly.

The alleged decline in food production is not reflected in stores or people. We have never been as fat as we are today. Obesity starts early, and increasingly children get type 2 diabetes, a disease which used to strike the elderly. We have never had so many agricultural products, but unfortunately these increasingly include artificial and chemical substances, which belong to manufacturing and are not linked to farming. Jamie Oliver in the UK, known worldwide as the Naked Chef on TV, has single-handedly managed to raise the awareness of the hazardous eating habits of schoolchildren – a case of social marketing extraordinaire.

We also use services which we could not afford before or that did not exist in their current form, like mobile telephony, entertainment and travel. Many of the most important services, however, are in short supply, such as proper education, legal assistance, security in the streets and homes, and not least health services. Home-care services are not affordable in many 'rich' countries because of tax and employment laws.

Many services are people intense and should remain so. However, the industrialization of services keeps going on, made possible through new or improved technology and systems. In his discussion on the industrialization of services, Levitt was too early in asserting that developments in service industries were hindered by inadequate concepts (1972, p. 43): 'Service thinks humanistically, and that explains its failures . . . Manufacturing thinks technocratically and that explains its success'. He was on to something but it is only in the third millennium that technology has become powerful enough to industrialize many service operations. Others, like transportation and electricity services, have been industrialized for a century or more, and keep finding new solutions.

One example of misguided statistics is the health-care sector, which is almost daily in the news reporting medical breakthroughs, shortage of doctors, skyrocketing costs and inefficient organization. However, the health-care sector is a nonsense category from the customer and marketer perspective. It harbours the most complex set of goods and services that you can think of. You can buy a band-aid in a pharmacy and use it if you cut yourself, or you can have trauma surgery after a traffic accident, or be struck by cancer that requires sophisticated treatment for years. In between these are thousands of health-related situations that require different value propositions. To make a credible generalization to health care, we need detailed, substantive cases and meticulous analyses – which we do not have.

Another myth is sector-related employment. We can read that the manufacturing and agricultural sectors in developed countries add no new net jobs. In relative terms, their employment has been going down for decades because of automation; it is all done by machines. It is further claimed that the new jobs come from the service sector, but the category is so diverse as to render such 'information' empty. Consider this case of new jobs and the interdependence between the manufacturing and service sectors (Mandel, 2006):

> In the early 2000s the housing boom in the US created a million new jobs subdivided between construction, building supplies, real estate and mortgage brokers, furniture and appliance manufacturing and distribution, home-supply stores, architects and interior designers. Simultaneously the IT bust lay off even more people. New jobs also came from health care services, but few from producers of pharmaceuticals and none from the medical equipment and supplies industry. Between 2001 and 2006 US health care added 1.7 million new jobs subdivided between private and government hospitals, physicians' offices, nursing facilities, health insurers, and diagnostic labs. The rest of the private service sector added none. The government sector (except hospitals) added 700 000 jobs of which over half a million were in education. These dramatic changes in service sub-sectors are not visible in aggregated statistics. To say that the service sector contributed all the new jobs is meaningless as changes up and down were caused by a few of its sub-sectors.

Goods, services, service, and the service sector have fuzzy definitions for a very trite reason: they represent fuzzy phenomena. It is time to put a halt to all the fuss that these statistics are creating in a wild goose chase and go for the real thing.

Goods/services differences – reality and myth

According to the mainstream literature, services can be defined by comparing them to goods – despite the fact that goods have not been generically defined. This is yet another wild goose chase. It is an unfortunate example of a non-scholarly stance and it is certainly not of help to the practising marketer.

Philosophical contributions from three centuries provided a set of 'characteristics' of services that have now been claimed to distinguish them from goods. The most famous are *intangibility, heterogeneity, inseparability* and *perishability*, now known as the IHIPs. In Scotland, Adam Smith (1723–1790) discussed perishability of services; in France, Jean-Baptiste Say (1767–1832) introduced intangibility (immateriality) and inseparability; and in England, Joan Robinson (1903–1983) brought in heterogeneity. Services seem, then, to have been dropped from the economics agenda, but the interest was revived in management and marketing. The earliest marketing references for these characteristics appeared in the beginning of the 1960s.

We shall take a critical but constructive look at the IHIPs from what we know today. We can, then, see that they do not discriminate between goods and services but offer characteristics which may sometimes be of interest for all value propositions and sometimes are irrelevant.

It is claimed that goods are tangible and services are *intangible*, and intangibility has since been used in the services marketing literature to 'explain' anything. I have rarely heard it in practitioner discussions, though, and there is no empirical evidence that the intangibility aspect has an impact on marketing strategy or market behaviour that separates a good from a service. You can argue for it in special cases, but there are equally intangible properties of goods such as a car brand and its symbolic value to an individual, and romantic dreams triggered by a perfume. Judge for yourself:

> Who, being personally exposed to surgery, will find it an intangible service? You are strapped to a bed and wheeled into a room packed with costly state-of-the-art technology, machines, tools and disposable products. They put spotlights on you like you were the star of a show – which in fact you may be; the room used to be called an operating theatre with future doctors and nurses watching from the stalls. In a dizzy condition as you have already been given sedatives through a syringe, you see a team of ghostlike people, totally covered in white except for the eyes. They are led by a guy with a knife in his hand. He cuts open your belly, messes around, even removes something. It may take hours. You are perhaps luckier than Humpty Dumpty and all the King's doctors and all the King's nurses can get you together again. Intangible, eh?

It is further claimed that goods are standardized, that goods quality can be tightly controlled and that the quality is easy to assess by the customer before purchase. Accordingly, services which are the other way around and are in part performed by human labour become *heterogeneous* and are of variable quality which is hard to control and assess before purchase. Again, there are such cases not only with services but also with goods, and it is easy to find cases that argue the opposite. For example, credit cards and cash machines offer standardized and tightly controlled services, or rather they are mass-customized because each customer has a different credit status and with-draws different sums of money.

Inseparability or simultaneity refers to the fact that with many services, production, marketing, purchasing, delivery and consumption are, at least in part, performed with the customer present and by the same employee. This aspect will be discussed later as the service encounter and inter-activity but is not limited to services. The general-ity of the inseparability property for services is limited, though. Many services are performed when the customer is not present, for example dry-cleaning, car repair or the transportation of goods to a store. Other examples are the police, the courts, the jails, the defence and road mainten-ance. We profit from their services, but most of us hope we will never get involved.

How about *perishability*? A prevalent idea is that services cannot be stored for later use, resold or returned. When a hairdresser has no cus-tomers, the unused capacity is wasted and if there are too many customers, they cannot be served and income opportunities are lost. But service companies store service capacity: a hotel is a store of rooms; a hospital is a store of medical know-ledge, equipment and procedures. When cus-tomers are few, time can often be spent on the maintenance of facilities and systems, adminis-tration and reading up on new developments. When demand follows predictable cycles, the size of staff can be adjusted accordingly. It is claimed that manufacturing does not have the perishabil-ity problem, which is not at all true. Fresh prod-ucts have a limited life. If the sales of garments are lower than manufacturing capacity, a plant can often go on producing and build inventory for later sales. However, there is a limit to this. One is financial; unsold products tie up capital and storage space, and demand maintenance, protection against damage and theft and insur-ance. Another is that the product cycle is quicker today because of both technology changes and fashion. A computer cannot be stored very long, and a dress made for the summer season has

lost most of its value when the autumn leaves are falling.

In textbooks and education, the IHIPs are presented as general for services, thus separating them from goods. As we have seen, it is easy to question them, as did Wyckham *et al.* in an article as early as 1975. They pointed out that intra-group variation (variation within the services and goods categories) could be greater than inter-group vari-ation (variation between the categories). Their suggestion was that a company's marketing strat-egy should be based on a function of all the fea-tures in the offering, irrespective of whether they were services or goods. This makes the distinc-tion goods-services immaterial and highlights the complete value proposition. It was not until recently, mainly through two articles by Lovelock and Gummesson (2004) and Vargo and Lusch (2004b), that this flawed generalization was exposed to a wider audience. Still, however, many textbooks continue to carry the IHIP message, thus misleading new generations of students.

The IHIPs can be used among a multitude of other properties of the value proposition, but they do not distinguish between goods and ser-vices. Other characteristics have been largely over-looked and one is the *rental* aspect and the *absence of ownership* in service purchases (Judd, 1964; Lovelock and Gummeson, 2004).

When and where marketing occurs

Services marketing developed the idea of the service encounter, which was mentioned in the paragraph on inseparability and simultaneity. The service encounter is characterized by interac-tion between providers and customers. It is often put forward in the mainstream literature as the core of services marketing. However, there are also the cases of no encounter. Then, there are numerous variations and degrees of intensity in between the close encounter and the no encounter.

To explain interactivity in the service encounter, the model in Figure 23.1 will be used (Gummesson, 2002). It shows different roles and interactions that are critical in marketing and it does so with the customer in focus. The service encounter is not only about marketing but also about production, delivery, innovation, com-plaints, administration and whatever you can think of. The same employee often fulfils several of these functions. To emphasize the employee's role

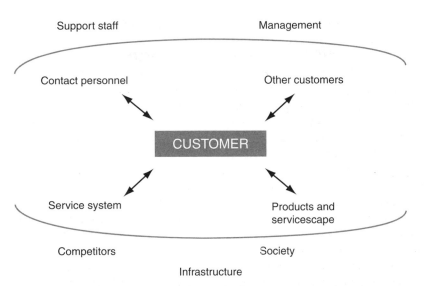

Figure 23.1 A service encounter model showing relationships and interaction between service providers and customers
Source: Adapted from Gummesson (2002), p. 68. Reproduced with permission.

in marketing, the concept of the part-time marketer will be discussed later.

The service encounter

Interaction between the customer and the contact person

The personal contact which service production often gives rise to is an important part of the customer's perception of the quality of the service. The customer interacts with contact staff – cashiers, flight attendants, craftsmen – for all or part of the time the service is being performed. At the same time, the customer partially consumes the service. The customer performs part of the work, for example, for a hospital service by calling to make an appointment, driving to the hospital and parking, or preparing for tests by fasting in the morning. During this personal encounter and the service production, the customer makes conscious and unconscious evaluations of the quality of the supplier and decides whether or not to remain a loyal customer. It is therefore important to make the encounter a positive experience as this case spells out.

> Christer Roth brought the local restaurant Ulla Winbladh in Stockholm, Sweden, to success. He was always there and his presence was felt. He kept a close watch on guests and employees and sensed the atmosphere, making sure that everything ran smoothly and that the food was top

class. He quickly got to know guests who came back, and he made them feel special. 'You must like your guests', he said. 'If you don't, the job is impossible'. He was not servile, constantly smiling to guests. He could argue with them but he did it in an open and sincere way that created respect. Before joining the restaurant he worked in a rehabilitation centre for drug-addicts. My immediate reaction was that this must have been very different. 'Not really', he said. 'In both cases you have to be interested in your customers and show a genuine concern'. He was right – both jobs are in the hospitality business. Commitment and a positive attitude is absolutely essential in business or government alike and Christer did not make a distinction between production, delivery and marketing; it was all there as value-adding activities.

Customer-to-customer interaction (C2C)

The individual customer is also influenced by other customers. A negative influence is queues which are usually experienced as a nuisance. Customers become an obstacle to each other in getting the service performed. On the positive side, customers can help each other (hospital), create a pleasant atmosphere (restaurant) and produce a service together (disco). C2C interaction and the customers' role in both the value proposition and value actualization is a growing area for research and practical applications. It will, therefore, be treated at more length in a later section of the chapter.

Customer interaction with physical products and servicescapes

The physical products include both *durable, capital goods* and *consumption goods* as was epitomized earlier. The literature stresses the significance of physical products in the services setting, the *servicescape* as Bitner (1992) calls it. The physical elements have, of course, a rational function such as escalators in an airport and easy-to-read signs. They also have a symbolic mission: an impression of tranquillity and dignity (funeral parlour) of professionalism (wigs on British judges), or youthfulness (IT start-up with young people in trendy offices).

Part of the industrialization of services is to replace staff with automation (machines and IT), generally with the objective of cost reduction but sometimes also to improve service quality. American psychologist Donald Norman (1988) estimated that we are in contact with 20 000 products in our daily lives. He talked of the 'psychopathology of everyday things', those that are wrongly designed from the user's viewpoint such as faucets in bathrooms that are difficult to turn if your fingers are wet and signs that can be misinterpreted.

Customer-to-system interaction

From a customer and competitor viewpoint, the service production system should be such that customers understand it, accept it and are attracted by it. This is especially important as customers increasingly operate the systems themselves, for example websites and ticketing machines. If the customers feel that a system is too complicated or feel insecure, they will avoid the purchase or find other ways. A severe problem today is customer-friendly websites and security in payment systems.

Provider internal operations

So far, customer–supplier interactions have been described. Within the provider system and organization, there are also *support staff (back office, backroom, backstage)* and *management*. They are not normally in contact with external customers but only interact with internal customers. Management is found on several levels but sometimes may be one of several roles that a person plays. A manager in a service company helps a contact or support person when needed, or switches between

tasks to balance capacity needs, for example a hotel manager checks out guests if the morning rush creates queues. In small service operations, the same person fulfils all the roles. To handle the many internal contacts in services firms, services marketing spawned the concept of internal marketing which is now thought to be applicable in all types of organizations (see Ballantyne, 2003).

The environment

The environment of the service production system is defined in the model as *competition, society* and *infrastructure*. Lack of competition is the definition of a monopoly. Until deregulation in the 1980s, railways, telecom, radio and television were often state monopolies. In several cases, the government sectors in practice have retained a monopoly on services, even though deregulation has been in progress for a long time. So have some private industries, for example banks that monopolize the money transaction infrastructure. Conjectured scarcity and waiting-lines are the most 'efficient' ways for politicians, government officials and service employees alike to boost power and keep up prices.

The infrastructure is crucial for a service company's opportunities. Infrastructure includes traditional elements like roads and waterways, postal systems, airline networks, and radio and television networks. A recent addition is broadband systems which increase the accessibility and speed of e-mail and the Internet.

Political decisions on the mega level may be of great importance to services. Here is a dilemma that the European Union (EU) is trying to get to grips with:

> In 1958 the Treaty of Rome, predecessor to the EU, put the Four Freedoms on the European trade agenda: free movement of goods, services, money and people across member state borders. The least successfully implemented freedom is services. It clashes with national culture, tradition, legislation, political power and local competition and consequently is tough to handle in practice. The service freedom has met with resistance and red tape to hold the 'foreign intruders' at bay. Eventually, on November 15, 2006, the EU Service Directive was agreed. Its aim is to have the stumbling-blocks removed by 2010. Until then, however, we will not know if the goal has been reached. However, the reference to 'services' is vague. The problem concerns certain, specific situations and it would make more sense to specify these than to speak of services in general.

The part-time marketer

Marketing cannot survive in isolation from other functions. That is general and not only so in services marketing and the service encounter. Marketing management usually does not address the dependency between functions, although many have over the years pointed to the inadequacy of functional silos. In practice, the marketing function is spread throughout the firm, and the marketing and sales departments may even play a limited role in the total marketing effort. Especially in small firms, there is not even a marketing and sales department. Instead, each and everyone is involved in marketing. This may be perceived as an organizational dilemma, but is also an opportunity to enhance marketing resources.

We can identify two types of marketers: *full-time marketers* (FTMs) and *part-time marketers* (PTMs).

Full-time marketers are those who are hired for working with marketing and sales tasks. They are found in *the marketing and sales departments* and among *external providers of marketing services.* Outsourcing of marketing activities has increased and these constitute reinforcements to the marketing function. Distributors offer transportation, wholesaling and retailing services, all strategic and crucial for success in marketing. The marketing function also engages external professionals such as advertising agencies, market research institutes and management consultants.

Part-time marketers are all others in the company and those in its environment that influence the company's marketing. That is obvious in the service encounter where, for example, a customer meets a flight attendant whose job is not marketing but whose behaviour influences the customer's perception of the airline. Customers are external PTMs; word-of-mouth is a traditional expression for this. But the customers' role in marketing has increased as has been pointed out already and will also be discussed later.

Note that *FTMs cannot be at the right place at the right time with the right customer contact and right knowledge, but the PTMs can.* Unsuccessful marketing is not solely to blame on the marketing and sales departments, but also on the marketing function as a whole, its PTMs and lack of integration between functions. To promote inter-functional cooperation, it would be beneficial for every marketer to learn about operations management as applied to services.

The distinction between FTMs and PTMs has extensive consequences for the approach to marketing. It makes it legitimate and imperative for everyone to influence customer relationships. Everybody is either an FTM or a PTM. Those employees who do not influence the relationships to customers full time or part time, directly or indirectly, are redundant.

Marketing and money: Quality, productivity and profitability

Marketing is not just about happy customers and the revenue they generate. It is also about the cost that is incurred and the bottom line, making sure that revenue minus cost leaves a profit. Marketers are often accused of not watching money closely enough, or being too ignorant of financial mechanics. This section is here to make sure that marketers see their role in the whole.

Quality has been mentioned several times. It had degenerated into an empty word but this changed during the 1980s. Services marketing became dominated by service quality issues, primarily defined as customer perceived quality which added a fresh angle to customer satisfaction and customer-orientation. The bulk of service researchers got engaged in questionnaire studies of customer satisfaction, and many keep doing so.

That was also the period when the West started to take goods quality more seriously, forced by the Japanese and their success in the markets for cars, television, cameras and a host of other products. Characteristic of the Japanese approach was that quality and productivity were approached simultaneously. It is nowhere as obvious as in the case of Toyota that has become the world leader in car quality, productivity, innovation and marketing. It has also extended its interest in quality and productivity to the customer and customer service. In 2007, Toyota overtook General Motors as the biggest car manufacturer in the world, and it is also the most profitable.

The following proposition forms the vantage point for the section: 'Quality, productivity and profitability are triplets; separating one from the other creates an unhappy family' (Gummesson, 1998, p. 6). The 'triplets' all serve the purpose of making operations efficient, both to the supplier and to the customer.

A misleading but recurrent statement claims that service productivity is lagging behind goods and manufacturing productivity. The statement is based on lack of understanding for service productivity, trying to manage and measure it on the terms of manufacturing. There is also a political and ideological debate on the productivity of the government sector as compared with the private service sector.

The interconnection between productivity, quality and profitability – the *triplets at play* – is graphically shown in Figure 23.2. At the top of the figure is quality, defined as 1 producing a defect-free product or service right from the beginning; and 2 producing a value proposition that customers need and want. If quality improves in this sense, it can have a positive impact on *revenue* (left section of the figure), *cost* (middle section) and *capital employed* (right section). When function and reliability improve, they boost the image in the market, customer retention and share of customer (i.e. the percentage of a customer's purchase of a certain product which is made from a specific supplier). These changes stimulate sales volume growth, differentiate a supplier from the competition and make the supplier less dependent on price competition. When sales and share of customer go up, the supplier can profit from scale economics (up to a certain level), and production costs per unit go down. This affects both productivity and profitability. Further, service costs for machinery go

down, and so do the costs of inspection, testing, rework, scrap, complaints and warranties. The capital employed is reduced as less inventory needs to be kept; accounts receivable go down because payment comes earlier and less payment is delayed because of complaints; and reduction of processing time frees resources. As the cash flow becomes quicker, the money can be used elsewhere and capital costs are reduced. Improved productivity becomes an antecedent to profitability.

The figure is conceptual and its interpretation goes as far as to conclude that something may go up or down. There is always a desire and need to measure, preferably precisely, the financial consequences of marketing strategies. This has been tried for at least 50 years without any remarkable progress. Currently, fresh efforts are being made (Ambler, 2000; Rust *et al.*, 2000) (See also, Chapter 21).

Re-casting supplier and customer roles

A legacy from economics states that there are sellers and buyers who enter into exchange. Mainstream marketing management considers the seller the active party persuading the passive

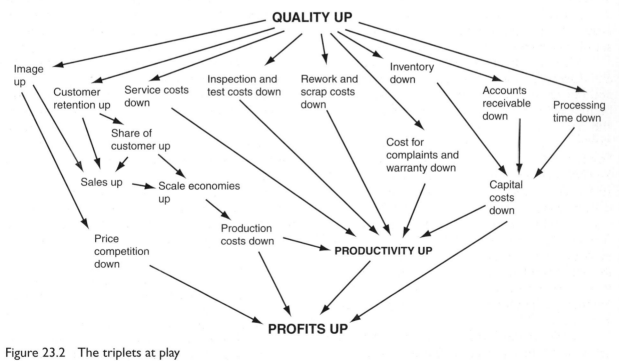

Figure 23.2   The triplets at play
Source: Adapted from Gummesson (1998), p. 6. Reproduced with permission.

customer. Relational approaches to marketing (see further below) have partially managed to change this view. In 1980, futurist Alvin Toffler minted the concepts 'prosumer' and 'prosumption' as composites of producer, consumer and consumption. The concepts say that the customer is an integral part of the production system and that the borderline between supplier and customer has been at least partly erased. It is not new; do-it-yourself is a big market and IKEA has built 60 years of unbroken success on customers doing transportation and assembly jobs.

However, the American Marketing Association's new definition of marketing from 2004 states that marketing delivers value *to* customers and *manages* customer relationships. So officially marketing is still locked in the supplier/customer and active/passive trap (see further a critical discussion in Grönroos, 2006).

Within the service-dominant logic, the customer is a prosumer and co-creator of value. The reality of this condition is progressively being demonstrated both in practice and theory. It has already been seen in Figure 23.1 and in the service encounter section. Two types of interaction were especially stressed there: contributions from the supplier and the customer in interaction and contributions from C2C interaction. There are also independent contributions from both the supplier and the customer. There is further individual customer interaction with the value proposition to arrive at value actualization and individual satisfaction. In all these instances, both customers and suppliers contribute to quality and productivity.

When quality and productivity are measured and displayed in statistics, only the supplier input and output are considered. This may sometimes be motivated from the supplier's point of view and especially in manufacturing. No wonder that service quality is mostly measured as the black box concept 'customer satisfaction' and technical aspects such as punctuality or relations aspects such as communication with customers. The productivity concept from manufacturing does not fit when activities are performed by customers. No wonder that engineers, statisticians and economists express frustration about service productivity and complain about it. However, they are locking themselves up in mental prisons and nothing – except their prejudices – stop them from getting out.

Goods manufacturing can also be interactive and is increasingly so through outsourcing and the building of networks organizations.

In business-to-business (B2B) marketing, companies may develop, produce and finance products in joint ventures.

We have already become familiar with C2C interaction. IT has expanded the opportunities for business customers and consumers to communicate with companies and with other customers. The Internet could be considered an enabler of C2C interaction. But C2C interaction occurs in a physical encounter in the marketplace as well as in the virtual IT-mediated encounter in marketspace.

Nicholls (2005) has classified physical C2C interaction by studying critical incidents of both positive and negative customer involvement in several services in Poland. He finds a great variety of events that can be related to time, place, conversation and need for information and help or turning down help. Most concern one-to-one, but some occur in a public environment and involve all those present. A context of many-to-many is created. This is also the case in a study by Harris and Baron (2004) who examined conversation between strangers on trains in England. In a model for C2C, they expose the consequences for consumers and providers. Among other things, they show that conversation between passengers on trains has a stabilizing effect on the mood of the passengers when, for example, delays occur. The results also show that when employees are not available, passengers perform their tasks. It can be information about the timetable or where to change trains. From the railway company's perspective, the passenger is an unsalaried part-time employee. The interaction can also be seen as a purely social act, for example, the joy of helping somebody or telling about something you know. Customers co-create the value of the service to the benefit of themselves and the service provider. Unfortunately, the providers may not see the contribution of this involvement and fail to support it.

How the customers' active involvement affects marketing is gradually being learnt. Even advertising agencies, who traditionally embody mass marketing, are rethinking (Creamer, 2007):

> Consumers were recently recognised to have a more influential role in marketing than the professional marketers. Every year the American journal *Advertising Age* nominates the best advertising agency. In 2006 the award did not go to a traditional agency but to the consumer! Through the Internet, email, mobile phones and other IT media, individual customers and C2C interaction

through communities reach out in the world. Consumers control the brands more than the legal brand owners do. Web-based chat groups, hate sites and fan clubs have been around for some time. Now we also have blogs and the TiVo (which keeps commercials off your TV). In an instant, YouTube, which lets anybody show their videos on the Internet, has become a smashing hit.

Gatarski and Lundkvist (1998) have analysed actors and interaction on the Internet where conversation, dialogue, and interaction – chatting – have become part of the social life. It can be chatting between a customer and a supplier, that is business-to-customer (B2C) interaction, or between customers C2C. An example of this is found in the next case, which is a modern – or perhaps postmodern, but true – success story. It is about the Linux operating system. It is about C2C interaction that develops Linux in a network context and customers who constitute an informal but highly efficient R&D department.

> In 2003, Linus Torvalds from Helsinki, Finland, became No. 3 on *Fortune's* list of the most influential people under 40 in the US, where he now lives. It began in 1991 with an e-mail to other computer geeks asking them to react to a new idea of an operating system for computers: . . .'just a hobby, won't be big and professional. . . Any suggestions are welcome, but I won't promise I'll implement them'.
>
> The Linux operating system was born. It was developed on cheap hardware through interaction between users, C2C. An operating system is a service infrastructure for the digital world. Bill Gates became the world's richest man on Microsoft's operating system, which in practice has had a monopoly and exists in every computer. Torvalds went another way through an open source code, free to anyone to enter the system, use it and influence it. He did not earn money on the system; his curiosity drove him.
>
> Linux did not just become a short-lived happening. Its market share in servers rose from 6.8 per cent in 1997 to 24 per cent in 2003 and it keeps rising. In 2005, it was almost everywhere. For example, Google, Motorola, and Volvo use it in some of their products and services, and Dell, HP, and IBM run it in servers and personal computers (PCs).
>
> What happens when such a network grows? The original community consisted of some hundred enthusiasts in a self-organizing system with Torvalds as the hub, keeping the network of contributors together. In 1999, the informal organization approached a critical tipping point. There were thousands of contributors to the system and Torvalds could not handle them all without big delays. He had to delegate. The former network captain now has a team of lieutenants. In 2005, IBM, HP, Intel and others contributed thousands of programmers. But Linux is still a network with no official headquarters, no CEO and no employees. Companies in the network profit from selling Linux packages, user manuals, updates and other services, and manufacturers preload Linux in servers and PCs.

The Linux case is a remarkable instance of C2C interaction creating a new computer service, performed in a way that defies all traditional theories of innovation processes and management. There is no plan but there is an obsession in the minds of the customers. Service design/engineering and service production/delivery work hand in hand. The considerable size of Linux today has not forced it into a traditional corporate structure. It stays a C2C network supplemented by alliances with different clusters of suppliers.

In B2B marketing, we cannot tell which B means supplier and which means customer. The design of the B2C acronym is plain, however; it is business-to-customer and not the other way around. To avoid falling back into the marketing management and mix ambush of considering the supplier active and the customer passive, I advocate an extension of the acronym to B2C/C2B.

The tech and human balance: High tech/high touch – and low tech

There is a strong trend in management and marketing to propose IT systems as a cure-all for economic ills. High tech is highly regarded; low tech has a lowly status. And the human being is too costly, too messy and too unreliable. Let us take a look at this trend. Traditional products like tabloids and hot dogs are bigger than ever in the marketplace – and they represent low tech. Basics needs and instincts such as love, social contact, sleep, nutrition and air cannot be taken over by high tech to the benefit of customers, even if efforts are made. The human being is instrumental in designing the smart systems and the software and controlling them. Consumers, we learn, are not buying products and services but experiences and dreams, driven in their choice of suppliers by something as mushy and woolly as brands and their symbolic value. So we have to look for a balance. Consider the case of Harley-Davidson (H-D), its general value proposition, its co-creation of value and the importance of C2C interaction. It is high tech/high touch.

Who wants a Harley-Davidson motorbike? The common idea seems to be that it is a younger man with an unconventional lifestyle. The classic movie *Easy Rider* with Jack Nicholson and Dennis Hopper inspired a whole generation of young people of the 1960s and Robert Pirsig's *Zen and the Art of Motorcycle Maintenance* became a cult book. Some bikers unfortunately form criminal gangs which have given rise to globally organized crime.

This widespread image is only marginally true for H-D, and the retailers should have understood it. Perhaps they knew, but nobody at the factory listened. H-D is expensive to buy and to maintain, and expensive to protect against theft. So the owner needs some money.

When the company finally studied its buyers systematically, they came up with a different picture. Those who really wanted an H-D were middle-aged males (and some females). They were married, had children, a good job and their own house. They wanted to hit the road and feel the freedom – but they wanted to do it in style. They could afford it. Perhaps it was a dream from younger days when they could not afford it. They hid their H-D in the garage where they served it and polished it. They hit the road sometimes when it was dark and the neighbours could not see them. But these enthusiastic customers missed something. They wanted company, they wanted to be with others who shared their interest in H-D, discuss motorbikes, feel the freedom, and do something thrilling which took them away from the responsibilities of the workday.

H-D management had to take some courageous decisions and expedite the implementation: upgrade the technical quality keeping the sound and other unique features; direct their marketing to the right target groups; and create opportunities for H-D owners to interact with H-D and between themselves.

Today, H-D is a profitable company which, in 2006, shipped 350 000 motorbikes. Harley Owners Group (H.O.G.) has one million members in 1200 local chapters '. . . united by a common passion: making the Harley-Davidson dream a way of life'. The club mission is 'to ride and have fun'. Through H.O.G., the H-D owner establishes a network of relationships with others with a shared lifestyle. We are reminded of the idea of the dream society where you buy a story, an experience, an identity, a lifestyle, and not in the first place a physical product even if the access to such a product is a necessary antecedent to all the others.

The conclusion is that *the customer does not buy an H-D, but a membership in a network where a motorbike is included and opens the opportunity for experiences and dreams. From this value proposition, customers co-create value to satisfy their individual needs and wants.* This is a general conclusion. Now consider a specific situation.

My colleague at Stockholm University, Ola Feurst, bought an H-D after a traffic accident and burnout. He needed to do something else than just work. It was also a dream from his teens which could now be fulfilled. The motorbike has become part of his brand identity. He bought a black leather suit and grew a beard; he already had a ponytail. He keeps the suit on in the classroom which helps maintain his brand. When Philip Kotler, the well-known marketing professor, at the age of 70 gave a guest lecture for us, we offered him a tour on Ola's H-D. He got excited and gave yet another reason for buying an H-D. 'I'd put it in my living room', he said. 'It's so beautiful. It's a sculpture'. It would add neatly to the large collection of glass sculptures already giving Kotler's living room a unique atmosphere.

The concept of high tech/high touch was launched by Naisbitt (1982) twenty-five years ago, but seems more topical than ever. Perhaps just tech/touch would be enough to leave space for low tech and less flashy human needs. To find this, optimal balance between technology and human aspects should be an important part of marketing strategy.

The marketing mix: The 4Ps are neither 4 nor Ps

The marketing mix consists of those marketing strategies that companies use to persuade and manipulate the market. An inventory of marketing mixes and their various applications show that there is a rich variety and little coherence (Constantinides, 2006) (See also Chapter 12). They are most popularly represented by the 4Ps: *product, price, promotion and place*. They offer an easy-to-remember simplification.

The 4P logic is straightforward. A supplier needs products, needs to price them, to promote them and distribute them to the place where the customer can buy them. The 4Ps have been extended into 5Ps by adding *people* (Judd, 1987), and 6Ps by adding *political power* and *public opinion formation* (Kotler, 1984). Booms and Bitner (1981) suggested the 7Ps for services marketing, the original ones plus *participants, physical evidence* and *process*. The three new service Ps stress that the customer is a participant in production and through this exposed to marketing, that goods influence services marketing, and that services are a series of activities and not static objects. This is an informed effort to adapt the Ps to services, but the pedagogical beauty of the P format may curb more visionary attempts to develop marketing theory.

There is a lot of truth in the 4Ps and other mixes, and they are a good start. The major problem is that they are supplier-centric first, and only secondarily consider customer needs.

Let us see what the marketing mix includes today. Every strategy is a large topic in itself and here I can only touch on some aspects. Pricing services is such an intricate and not well-researched area and so is the distribution of services (place). They deserve future attention. I will expand on the two Ps that I have studied more in depth – product and promotion. They are not so easy to tell apart.

Originally 'product' was *goods* and later *services* were added. Marketing makes many efforts to find a deeper meaning behind what we are buying and consuming. *Value proposition* has been advanced here, supported by the service-dominant logic. We are also known to seek *experiences, kicks*, and *dreams* through motorcycles, parties, diving in the Barrier Reef, or visiting the Vatican Museum to marvel at Michelangelo's paintings. The product can also be an international *event* like the European Song Contest or a local exhibition of roses. Their product is also defined through *storytelling*; we buy a story rather than the product itself. For example, all stories about the love lives of celebrities help build fame and sell tickets to theatres. The product today is also *information* where websites and search engines such as Google have opened up a new marketplace.

'Promotion' once consisted of *advertising, personal selling* and *sales promotion*. Today, the forms for promotion have become more sophisticated. Advertising pops into our homes through television, radio and computers. It enters music through music videos and movies through product placement. What car James Bond will drive in his next film and what mobile phone he will use to call his girlfriends depends on which manufacturer pays the most.

Advertising through the mass media and direct mail is supplemented by *public relations* (PR), with the aim to create a positive image of a company in the market and society, preferably through editorial text and documentaries to make it stand out as more credible. A lot is about *branding* and loading offerings with perceptions about the suppliers and their products. In a Formula 1 race, the cars are covered by logotypes and World Cup skiers are advertising pillars. Events are increasingly dependent on such *sponsorship*. A cultural or sports event gives the sponsoring companies an opportunity to expose themselves to the market and even get in personal contact with customers. They become associated with the event and the glory of the winner of an Olympic gold medal is reflected on them.

On a mega strategic level, *politics, lobbying* and *public opinion* come in. These means are used in both honest and dishonest form. Public opinion sometimes acts with common sense, sometimes not. For example, lobbyists can educate ignorant politicians but they can also corrupt them for selfish reasons and circumvent the democratic process.

Scientific research and *education* have also received growing attention by companies. The most obvious example is the pharmaceutical industry and their influence over medical research. Scientists are dependent on their sponsorship and pharmaceutical companies need the knowledge produced in research hospitals, but also to bask in the prestige of science, thus adding to their credibility in the public eye.

IT has given rise to *call centres* which companies themselves run as marketing concept and help desks or outsource to specialized call centre companies. *Telemarketing* has entered into a new phase. Both these operations require plenty of staff and add employment opportunities, but are equally dependent on IT. *E-mail* and *web sites, mobile phones* and *text messaging* have redesigned the marketing landscape. The dissolution of the boundaries between telephones, TV and computers is spawning a new world for marketers and customers. IT also causes problems. The Internet architecture is not built to protect against dishonesty and today 30 per cent of the cost of a computer and its software goes to patching unsafe systems and continuously developing new security programmes to curb criminality. Spam and pop-up windows are annoying elements, but even worse is the financial fraud that customers get exposed to.

The major criticism against the marketing mix is that it counteracts the customer concept and is more manipulative than oriented towards the real needs of the market. The marketing mix is supplier-centric with a half-hearted effort to adjust to customers.

Several of the marketing strategies listed above involve relational issues, and marketing increasingly is becoming recognized as dealing with relations in various forms rather than with mass exchange. This will be discussed in the next section.

The core of marketing: Relationships, networks and interaction

Relationship marketing, one-to-one marketing and *Customer Relationship Management (CRM)* – all with approximately the same essence but in part with different origin and emphasis – are established concepts today. Most commonly, relationship marketing is defined as a variant on the theme 'create long-term relationships with loyal customers'. My definition is broader and more abstract with the general purpose of trying to find the DNA of marketing. The definition is,

Relationship marketing is interaction in networks of relationships.

Relationships bring people or organizations together, temporarily or long term. From personal experience, we have an intuitive understanding of what relationships are. When relationships embrace more than two people, they quickly become complex *networks*; we talk about networks of relationships. What happens in relationships is *interaction* through communication and activities.

To make relationships more concrete and to emphasize their ubiquity and complexity – and in opposition to the simplistic 4Ps – I developed *the 30 relationships (the 30Rs)* (Gummesson, 2002). The 30 Rs organized themselves naturally into three groups. *Market relationships* embrace relationships and their properties in the market, primarily with customers, suppliers, intermediaries and competitors. We have noted that politics, lobbying, public opinion and scientific research also influence marketing; they offer *mega relationships*. These appear above the market relationships and marketing departments and are handled by the board of directors and top management. Among them are alliances, international relationships and the media. *Nano relationships* ('nano' means very small) embrace a company's inner relationships, how it is organized and how employees and departments interact. But all levels of relationships are interlinked. For example, the mega level determines certain conditions for the market and nano levels. Only considering market relationships – which is typical of most relational approaches – restricts marketing to tactics; overriding strategies, organizational structures and processes are lost.

The expression *one-to-one marketing* emphasizes that customers – people or organizations – are individuals with unique properties; there is even the expression *segment of one* (Peppers and Rogers, 1993). In opposition to reminiscences of microeconomics, it is time to recognize that an individual supplier is selling to an individual customer. The reigning strategy within the 4Ps is mass marketing and standardization. Customers are not statistics and grey masses. There is a myth about mass influence and mass distribution as cost-effective at the same time as the effect on the bottom line eludes measurement. Mass marketing will always be around in symbiosis with relational approaches, but it constitutes a limited part of all marketing. While mass marketing divides customers in markets, segments and niches, relationship marketing builds communities of individuals with similar needs and behaviour.

Customer Relationship Management is currently the most used concept. A comprehensive definition is provided by Payne (2006, p. 4) (See also, Chapter 20).

> CRM, also recently called customer management, is a business approach that seeks to create, develop and enhance relationships with carefully targeted customers in order to improve customer value and corporate profitability and thereby maximize shareholder value. CRM is often associated with utilizing information technology to implement relationship marketing strategies. As such, CRM unites the potential of new technologies and new marketing thinking to deliver profitable, long term relationships.

Customer Relationship Management is only partially successful. Too many companies believe that software and technology will solve all problems and have not understood the need for a high tech/high touch balance.

So far, relationships and interaction have been the focus for attention, but it is now time to take the step towards *networks*. Relationships in one-to-one and CRM are usually two-party supplier-customer relationships. But we live in complex networks which we influence and are influenced by. I, therefore, want to extend one-to-one to *many-to-many marketing* (Gummesson, 2006). The definition is,

Many-to-many marketing describes, analyzes and exploits the network properties of marketing.

The approach offered by many-to-many marketing and general network theory is equally applicable to all kinds of marketing situations. Here is a case of a B2B network organized by local hotels (von Friedrichs Grängsjö and Gummesson, 2006).

> In the beginning of the 1990s the hotel sector in Sweden suffered a reduction in room reservations. The hotels in the town of Östersund were hit hard and the managers of two of the largest hotels decided to start a local hotel network, the Hotel Group. There were 12 hotels and 2 guesthouses in Östersund varying in size from 7 to 177 rooms, all but one being privately owned, and 7 belonging to chains. All the hotels in town joined the Hotel Group. In addition, the Tourist and Congress Office, operated by the local government, became member of the group. The network has been successful in balancing the interests of its members to jointly market their town as a destination, but at the same time keeping individual freedom to compete for guests. The members agree that three basic principles are vital for the network: show enthusiasm, give time and participate actively, and contribute to financing. The outcome was increased reservations of available rooms from 48% in 1996 to 57% in 2002, considerably more than in the rest of Sweden. The Hotel Group was awarded the local prize 'Businessman of the Year' for attracting visitors to the benefit of not only the hotels but all local business.

The case shows how important relationships with competitors could be. Although competition is still the mantra of market economists, competition and cooperation have a yin and yang relationship – one cannot survive without the other. Like the hotels, companies in general can choose to compete on certain issues and cooperate on others. There is an optimum which is to the advantage of each company as well as to customers and society.

Despite its significance, network is a rare word in general marketing management textbooks, most of them founded on a consumer goods paradigm. There may be a word trap here; perhaps, networks are hidden behind other terms and concepts. In books on consumer behaviour, consumers are analyzed in the context of opinion leaders, reference groups and word-of-mouth. Consumers relate to family and friends, and to social, cultural, political, religious and ethnic belonging. They buy from many suppliers and live in a network of suppliers and others. They assume many roles, among them those of buyer, payer and user. So B2C/C2B networks exist, but in the traditional literature they are rarely analyzed through the many-to-many eye-glasses using network theory.

Customer, dyadic or network centricity?

The topic for the final sections concerns the viability of the marketing concept and customer-centricity. Does marketing need a new and more realistic credo? I will start with the traditional value chain and proceed with lean production and lean consumption to end up with the network approach and many-to-many marketing.

The value chain

Porter's (1985) value chain is unabashedly supplier-centric. It starts with inbound logistics (material), proceeds with operations (manufacturing and assembly) and outbound logistics (marketing and sales), and ends with service (spare parts with surrounding activities). The process is supported by the company infrastructure, human resource management, technology development and procurement.

The chain imposes several restrictions on marketing. It is limited to goods and manufacturing; value-added becomes a euphemism for cost-added; and its stages are sequential, while to produce a desired outcome an iterative mode is required. But most important: by ceasing when the customer enters, supplier operations become separated from the consumption context.

In the supplier value chain, a car is a manufactured product with fairly objective properties. For the customer, the car is an individually managed and subjectively interpreted phenomenon. The supplier chain is designed for standardized mass manufacturing, while the customer value process is characterized by individual flexibility with its shape and content varying from one moment to another.

The lean solution

Lean production has much in common with the value chain. It goes far back, but was especially brought to the fore in the car industry in the 1970s and 1980s. The Japanese had boosted productivity and quality and took the global lead in car design and manufacturing. Lean production is common-sensical and basic: Do not waste anything be it money, material, worker's time, or storage space, and apply hands-on strategies such as continuing improvements, do it right the first time, and man-agement commitment! What makes Toyota – the exemplar of lean production – continually suc-cessful is 'the brilliant focus on core processes' (Womack and Jones, 2005a, p. 1).

Lean production pioneers have begun to inquire about what happens at the customer end. One service to customers is respect. For example, customer time is not free, although it may seem so as customers are not on the payroll. Letting cus-tomers queue up at airports or on the telephone to speak to a computer supplier's help desk is rarely necessary; still it is standard procedure. The sup-plier process may have become lean, but how about *lean consumption*? And do the two processes provide a joint *lean solution*? Traditional service industries, such as the super-performing British retailer Tesco, are successfully trying the lean idea.

The new knowledge has emerged out of inductive empirical research and a trial and error process. From that, the following lean consump-tion principles have been derived (Womack and Jones, 2005b, p. 61):

1 Solve the customer's problem completely by ensuring that all the goods and services work, and work together.
2 Do not waste the customer's time.
3 Provide exactly *what* the customer wants.
4 Provide what is wanted exactly *where* it is wanted.
5 Provide what is wanted where it is wanted exactly *when* it is wanted.
6 Continually aggregate solutions to reduce the customers time and hassle.

Lean production worked because it was grounded in reality. So is lean consumption, and it fits the service-dominant logic and the customer's role as co-creator. That the lean solution is far from imple-mentation today became blatant in a study of car repair. Womack and Jones (2005a, pp. 43–45) found that for a service provider to repair a specific cus-tomer's car, 220 minutes were spent of which only 35 minutes represented value-creating time (16 per cent). Parallel to that, the customer had to spend 210 minutes, 58 being value-creating (28 per cent).

The lean solution implies that we question the realism of the marketing concept and customer-orientation. We cannot discard product-centricity because it is a reality that creates value proposi-tions, and new technology without any obvious links to customer needs and wants will continue to capture the minds of entrepreneurs. Confining suppliers and customers to separate research traditions such as operations management and consumer behaviour deprives them of their inter-dependent context.

We may, however, not stop here, but aim for a broader view as is spelled out in the next and final section.

Networks, many-to-many marketing and balanced centricity

Value-creation takes place in a network of activ-ities involving not just two, but multiple stakehold-ers. Among these are intermediaries, employees, shareholders, the media, citizens and society. Not only consumers should be good citizens but so should corporations. Today's wide-spread dogma that businesses are free-wheeling entities that can do anything to maximize shareholder value as along as they can get away with it does not add value in this stakeholder context.

This means that the degree of complexity of marketing theory increases. But reality *is* complex and we cannot just pretend it is not, if we want to develop marketing scientifically. Here network theory comes in handy. A network consists of nodes and relationships within which interaction takes place. It can accommodate movement in any direction; it allows iterations back and forth; it can change into any number of shapes; it is scale-free; it defines not only structure but also process and change. Its nodes can include people, organiza-tions, machines, events or activities. We can choose to focus on any of its parts without losing sight of the systemic context. A network can support a strict mode of operation which is cost-effective in mass production, but it can equally well be flex-ible to a customer's individual value-creation. I have found no theoretical and methodological alternative that can match network theory.

In adopting a network perspective, we leave the one-party orientation and the two-party bal-ance to arrive at a multiparty balance as the basis for marketing. By naming my effort to develop general, network-based marketing theory many-to-many marketing, the emphasis is put on inter-action between multiple parties.

Contrary to the recommendation by Shah *et al.* (2006) that customer-centricity can be implemented by the application of smarter strategies, my contention is that *customer centricity as the prime target for business is non-implementable and not fit to form the foundational credo of marketing.* Satisfied customers are not the only drivers of success. A balance of interests can only be actualized in a context of many stakeholders. We move to *balanced centricity.* It means that in long-term relationships and a well-functioning marketplace, all stakeholders have the right to satisfaction of needs and wants.

I am perhaps talking about the best of all worlds, a Utopia, but why not? Even if we never quite get there, moving in its direction seems to be the best of all strategies. Arming marketing with network theory, the service-dominant logic and the lean solution opens up for a possible breakthrough.

Summary

This has been an account of my travels and adventures in Marketingland. As the reader has probably noticed, the terminology and the logic are not yet sufficiently consistent and complete. However, the lookouts that we camped at during the journey offered fascinating sights waiting to be converted to insights and adapted to unique marketing situations, be it B2B or B2C/C2B.

During the journey we have encountered these issues:

- *Goods, services* and *the service sector* are ill-defined categories. The definitions become fuzzy for the very reason that they represent fuzzy phenomena. This has to be accepted as a springboard for creative and scholarly work, and the mock images of economic reality have to be weeded out. When the terms 'goods' and 'services' are used in this chapter, they represent *perspectives.* The focus can be on either the *things* or *activities* aspect.
- In alignment with *the service-dominant logic,* the term 'service' is used as synonymous with *value.* A supplier has a *value proposition,* but *value actualization* takes place during the customer's usage and consumption process. Suppliers and customers are *co-creators of value.*
- The *IHIPs* – intangibility, heterogeneity, inseparability and perishability – can be applied very well among a multitude of other properties

to characterize a value proposition. They may help to identify specific marketing situations, but they do not separate services from goods.
- What is labelled as *general marketing management* is both pseudo-general and pseudo-specific. Marketing is stuck in the middle. It is neither concrete enough to embrace the multiple details of real-world marketing situations, nor abstract enough to furnish theories that help uncovering the components of *the marketing genome* and a future *grand theory.*
- What we have learnt about interaction in the service encounter has been extended and becomes applicable to all marketing situations. *Relationships, networks* and *interaction* have been proposed at the top level of marketing with the *4Ps* and *the marketing mix* demoted to the next level. The marketing mix is *supplier-centric* and manipulative first and *customer-centric* second. It still has its mission as a set of strategies for the supplier to act.
- With quickly expanding *technology,* especially *IT,* and the prevailing idea that high-tech and integrated systems are more productive than people, attention to the *high tech/high touch balance* becomes progressively critical. Our fascination for high tech must not obscure the fact that our lives are dominated by human and social behaviour – and low tech. On the 'touch' side, marketing increasingly honours experiences, events, storytelling and brands as value propositions.
- The understanding of the customer's active involvement in value-creation is growing. Services marketing, the service-dominant logic, relational approaches to B2B marketing, developments on the Internet and increased understanding of C2C interaction all provide heavyweight empirical and conceptual evidence for *re-casting supplier and customer roles.*
- Marketing is the *revenue-generating function* of a firm. It is easily forgotten by practising marketers and marketing theorist alike that the ultimate test of success is a profit level that allows a firm to prosper in the long run. Therefore, marketing needs to focus not only on revenue but also on *cost* and *capital.* In this process, *quality,* or value as perceived by the customer, *productivity* and *profitability* become triplets. All this is reflected in the current boom in *marketing metrics.*
- *Complexity* must be recognized in marketing theory and research methodology. *Network theory* offers the most constructive attitude and manageable techniques for approaching

complexity. *Many-to-many* is a concept for merging network theory and marketing reality.

- The traditional *value chain* is blatantly supplier-centric. The developments of *lean solutions*, encompassing *lean production* and its extension into *lean consumption*, offer a balance between supplier and customer interests.

- The marketing concept and customer-orientation form a recurrent theme in the text. I have concluded that customer-centricity has not been well implemented simply because it is not implementable. A more realistic alternative is to leave *one-party centricity* – either *supplier-centricity* or *customer-centricity* – in favour of *two-party centricity* (supplier–customer win-win relationships), and eventually strive for *balanced centricity*, a stakeholder and network approach where the interests of multiple parties are mediated.

- Marketing as an academic discipline should provide *general strategies*. The *specific configuration of strategies* has to be adapted to each unique situation. Sometimes a marketing situation is 'uniquely unique' and sometimes marginally unique, but it is not differences between goods and services that determine the uniqueness.

- Although we have not yet got it conceptually and consistently together, I am prepared to say that *a paradigm shift* is taking place in marketing that needs to be reflected in research priorities, textbooks and education at a faster pace than today. *Time to market* is too long drawn out.

Epilogue

In writing this chapter, I recurrently found myself thriving on a process of tacit knowing. The outcome, tacit knowledge, can only be communicated and understood through first-hand experience and intuition. I have tried hard to find words and structures and offer something more coherent and elegant, even new theory. Our explicit knowledge is not adequate and the tacit touch is needed to make the marketing bumblebee fly.

The process of transforming services marketing into general marketing with service/value in focus rather than goods/services, and balanced centricity rather than customer-centricity, reminds me of Paulo Coelho's bestselling novel *The Alchemist* (1995). Just like the alchemist, the marketer tries to make gold. The book is about a shepherd who set out on a strenuous journey to find

a master alchemist with genuine knowledge. He learnt that the real gold of life was not the metal as such; gold represented value. The answer lay on his doorstep, but he needed the many aggravating experiences from the journey to see the obvious. And above all, he had learnt that you must listen to your heart, read the signs and follow your dreams.

Perhaps, we need all the detours of marketing models to find the genome of marketing. We have not arrived yet, but if we listen to our hearts, read the signs and follow our dreams rather than get stuck on received theories and methodological rituals, we may succeed to advance marketing.

References

Ambler, T. (2000) *Marketing and the Bottom Line*, Financial Times/Prentice Hall, London.

Baker, M. J. (2006) Editorial, *Journal of Customer Behaviour*, **5**(3), 197–200.

Ballantyne, D. (2003) A relationship mediated theory of internal marketing, *European Journal of Marketing*, **37**(9), 1242–1260.

Bitner, M. J. (1992) Evaluating service encounters: the effects of physical surroundings and employee responses, *Journal of Marketing*, **56**, April, 57–71.

Booms, B. H. and Bitner, M. J. (1981) Marketing Strategies and Organization Structures for Service Firms, in Donelly, J. H. and George, W. R. (eds), *Marketing of Services*, American Marketing Association, Chicago, IL.

Coelho, P. (1995) *The Alchemist*, Harper/Collins, London.

Constantinides, E. (2006) The marketing mix revisted: towards the 21st century marketing, *Journal of Marketing Management*, **22**(3–4), 407–438.

Creamer, M. (2007) Ad age agency of the year: the consumer, *Advertising Age*, **8**, January.

Gatarski, R. and Lundkvist, A. (1998) Interactive media face artificial consumers and must re-think, *Journal of Marketing Communications*, **4**, 45–59.

Grönroos, C. (2006) On defining marketing: finding a new roadmap for marketing, *Marketing Theory*, **6**(4), 395–417.

Grönroos, C. (2007) *Service Management and Marketing: Customer Management in Service Competition*, 3rd edn, Wiley, Chichester, UK.

Gummesson, E. (1998) Productivity, quality and relationship marketing in service operations, *International Journal of Contemporary Hospitality Management*, **10**(1), 4–15.

Gummesson, E. (2002) *Total Relationship Marketing*, 2nd edn, Butterworth-Heinemann, Oxford.

Gummesson, E. (2006) Many-to-Many Marketing as Grand Theory: A Nordic School Contribution, in Lusch, R. F. and Vargo, S. L. (eds), *Toward a Service-Dominant Logic of Marketing: Dialog, Debate, and Directions*, M.E. Sharpe, New York, pp. 339–353.

Harris, K. and Baron, S. (2004) Consumer-to-consumer conversations in service settings, *Journal of Service Research*, **6**(3), 287–303.

Judd, R. C. (1964) The case for redefining services, *Journal of Marketing*, **28**, January.

Judd, R. C. (1987) Differentiate with the 5th P: people, *Industrial Marketing Management*, November.

Kotler, P. (1984) Megamarketing, *Harvard Business Review*, March–April, 117–124.

Levitt, T. (1972) Production line approach to service, *Harvard Business Review*, September–October.

Lovelock, C. and Gummesson, E. (2004) Whither services marketing? In search of a paradigm and fresh perspectives, *Journal of Service Research*, **7**(1), 20–41.

Lusch, R. F. and Vargo, S. L. (2006) Service-dominant logic: reactions, reflections and refinements, *Marketing Theory*, **6**(3), 281–288.

Mandel, M. (2006) What's really propping up the economy, *Business Week*, **25**, September, 54–62.

Naisbitt, J. (1982) *Megatrends*, Warner Books, New York.

Norman, D. A. (1988) *The Psychology of Everyday Things*, Basic Books, New York.

Nicholls, R. (2005) *Interaction Between Service Customers*, The Poznan University of Economics, Poznan, Poland.

Pauli, G. A. (1987) *Services – The Driving Force of the Economy*, Waterlow Publishers, London.

Payne, A. (2006) *Handbook of CRM*, Butterworth-Heinemann, Oxford, UK.

Peppers, D. and Rogers, M. (1993) *The One to One Future*, Currency/Doubleday, New York.

Porter, M. E. (1985) *Competitive Advantage*, The Free Press, New York.

Rust, R. T., Zeithaml, V. A. and Lemon, K. N. (2000) *Driving Customer Equity*, The Free Press, New York.

Shah, D., Rust, R. T., Parasuraman, A., Staelin, R. and Day, G. S. (2006) The path to customer centricity, *Journal of Service Research*, **9**(2), 113–124.

Toffler, A. (1980) *The Third Wave*, William Marrow, New York.

Vargo, S. L. and Lusch, R. F. (2004a) Evolving to a new dominant logic for marketing, *Journal of Marketing*, **68**(1), January, 1–17.

Vargo, S. L. and Lusch, R. F. (2004b) The four service marketing myths: remnants of a goods-based, manufacturing model, *Journal of Service Research*, **6**, May, 324–235.

von Friedrichs Grängsjö, Y. and Gummesson, E. (2006) Hotel networks and social capital in destination marketing, *Service Industry Management*, **17**(1), 58–75.

Womack, J. P. and Jones, D. T. (2005a) *Lean Solutions*, Simon & Schuster, London.

Womack, J. P. and Jones, D. T. (2005b) Lean consumption, *Harvard Business Review*, March, 58–68.

Wyckham, R. G., Fitzroy, P. T. and Mandry, G. D. (1975) Marketing of services, *European Journal of Marketing*, **9**(1), 59–67.

Recommendations for further reading

Among the most comprehensive and widespread textbooks are (see also Grönroos 2007 in the Reference list above):

Lovelock, C. and Wirtz, J. (2007) *Services Marketing: People, Technology, Strategy*, 6th edn, Pearson/Prentice Hall, Upper Saddle River, NJ.

Palmer, A. (2004) *Principles of Services Marketing*, 4th edn, McGraw-Hill, London.

Zeithaml, V. A., Bitner, M. J. and Gremler, D. G. (2005) *Services Marketing*, 2nd edn, McGraw-Hill/Irwin, Boston, MA.

For a comprehensive review of the service-dominant logic with some fifty contributing authors, see:

Lusch, R. F. and Vargo, S. L. (eds) (2006), *Toward a Service-Dominant Logic of Marketing: Dialog, Debate, and Directions*, M.E. Sharpe, New York.

For accounts of the history of services marketing, see:

Berry, L. L. and Parasuraman, A. (1993) Building a new academic field–the case of services marketing, *Journal of Retailing*, **69**, Spring, 13–60.

Fisk, R. P., Brown, S. W. and Bitner, M. J. (1993) Tracking the evolution of the services marketing literature, *Journal of Retailing*, **69**, Spring, 61–103.

Fisk, R. P., Grove, S. J. and John, J. (eds) (2000) *Services Marketing Self Portraits: Introspections,*

Reflections, and Glimpses from the Experts, American Marketing Association, Chicago, IL.

Grönroos, C. (2007) *In Search of a New Logic for Marketing*, Wiley, Chichester, UK.

For the philosophy behind the earliest analyses on service, see:

Delaunay, J.-C. and Gadrey, J. (1992) *Services in EconomicThought*, Kluwer, Boston.

An early contributor to services was the late Richard Normann whose last book is a synthesis and legacy.

Normann, R. (2001) *Reframing Business: When the Map Changes the Landscape*, Wiley, Chichester.

The marketer needs to understand more about the development and production of services. See:

Edvardsson, B. *et al.* (eds) (2006) *Involving Customers in New Service Development*, Imperial College Press, London.

Johnston, R. and Clark, G. (2005) *Service Operations Management*, Financial Times/Prentice Hall, Harlow, UK.

CHAPTER 24

International marketing

ANGELA DA ROCHA and
JORGE FERREIRA DA SILVA

The forces of globalization have changed the ways in which companies compete. The opening of national borders during the last decades brought international competitors into almost every domestic market in the world, leaving local firms with the challenge of improving their operations, or disappearing. At the same time, firms from developed countries had to face competitors from emerging markets, which compete based on country-specific factor endowments. As a result, the configuration of world markets is changing, as well as the nature and direction of trade, investment and technology flows. In this new business geography, marketers are faced with huge opportunities in different parts of the world. More and more, domestic firms are internationalizing to take advantage of these opportunities.

However, to operate effectively in international markets is not a simple task. It requires managers with a global mind-set, prepared to understand and deal with different cultures and systems. It also demands specific marketing capabilities, which are not always available to the firm.

This chapter presents a discussion of this new environment, analysing some of the major trends and challenges faced by international marketers. The international expansion of firms is analysed, highlighting organizational motives and processes. Strategic aspects of international expansion are discussed, such as foreign market selection, and modes of entry and operation in foreign countries.

Finally, marketing strategies designed to serve foreign markets are examined.

The international environment: challenges and opportunities

The environment of international marketing is much more complex than the domestic one, both because of the heterogeneity of cultures and of the diverse economic, social, political and institutional systems. This complexity is the main reason why firms that internationalize face higher risks than those that remain only in their domestic market. But although this has also been true in the past, internationalization has become over the last decades less of an option and more of an imperative, at least for firms that do not want to play only a marginal role. The major force behind these changes is the phenomenon of globalization, which can be briefly conceptualized as an enlargement of the social space by economic and technological forces, in such a way that changes in one part of the world affect people and countries in another part.

This new international marketing environment is characterized by the action of global forces and poses new challenges as well as creates new opportunities for international marketers. Yet, to effectively respond to these challenges and exploit such opportunities, marketers need to develop a good understanding of these forces, and of how they are shaping the world we live.

The cultural environment

The cultural environment is probably the most important aspect of the macroenvironment to be understood when a firm enters international markets. Many marketing managers and firms have learned that the costs of not giving attention to cultural differences may be extremely high. In contrast, the advantages of being culturally sensitive can be enormous: successful products and services delivered to the marketplace, satisfied customers and higher profits. Ultimately, understanding cultural values can be the divide between success and failure in a foreign market.

Yet it is extremely difficult to understand people from other cultures, even if we master their language. This is because we lack the knowledge of the meanings behind their words. We suffer of cultural blindness; we are prisoners of our own values, beliefs, codes and norms, which cannot be successfully applied to different cultures. Worst of all, we are not aware of this limitation. Unless one is trained to understand cultural differences and respect them, the most typical reaction when faced with a different culture is to apply one's own cultural standards, which may result in rejection because it is considered to be threatening, strange, impossible to understand or even comic. This cultural bias is called ethnocentrism.

Culture defined

Culture has been referred to as a *web of meanings*, or, in a more operational way, as 'whatever it is one has to know or believe in order to operate in a manner acceptable to [a society's] members' (Goodenough apud Geertz, 1973). A business scholar conceptualized it as 'the collective programming of the mind, which distinguishes the members of one group [...] from another' (Hofstede, 1991).

- *Culture is learned*: People are socialized into a culture, which means that they have to learn values, beliefs, codes and symbols to be able to effectively operate in that culture. The process of cultural socialization is both formal and informal. Formal socialization is carried out by the family, schools and universities, churches, etc. Informal processes are embedded in everyday life; people learn by social interaction.

- *Culture is shared*: Culture is an in-group phenomenon, and it is thus shared by its members. As a consequence, meanings associated to attitudes and behaviours – the social structures of significance – are subconsciously apprehended by other members of the same group.
- *Culture is long standing*: Culture does not change easily. It can take generations to change cultural values, even when these values become ineffective and cannot serve the group well.
- *Culture is pervasive*: Culture encompasses every aspect of human life: work and leisure, love and war, industry and arts. It influences issues as diverse as food acquisition, clothing, sexual practices, division of labour, child raising, power and authority, communication and consumption.

Cultural dimensions

Several lists of cultural dimensions have been suggested, and there is no consensus among scholars of which list offers the most important dimensions. Table 24.1 presents two well-known lists, which have the advantage of combining several variables into more general factors. The two lists are very similar, although not exactly the same.

The first set of variables has to do with the emphasis society places on the satisfaction of individual or group needs. Collectivist societies prioritize group interests, based on the belief that individual welfare is a consequence of social welfare. Individualist societies, on the other hand, believe that social welfare is attained by serving individual interests. Most societies in the world are collectivist, and only in a few societies the interests of the individual prevail. In collectivist societies, group membership defines one's identity and social status. The most important group to which one belongs is often the extended family, or even the clan. The main function of the group is to protect its individual members. These groups are characterized by strong cohesion and lifetime loyalty of its members. Because of these obligations towards the group, one has to favour other group members (particularism) instead of applying general rules to them. In contrast, individualist societies favour general rules to be applied to all individuals (universalism). The degree of involvement one accepts in a relationship also varies from one society to the other. More individualist societies tend to see interactions among people as separate, specific events, while people in collectivist societies tend to engage in more diffuse relationships.

Table 24.1 The dimensions of culture	
Hofstede (1991)	*Trompenaars (1993)*
Individualism versus collectivism	Individualism versus collectivism
	Universalism versus particularism
	Specific versus diffuse
Power distance	Status attribution versus conquest
Uncertainty avoidance	Internal versus external control
Masculinity versus femininity	Neutral versus affective
Long-term versus short-term orientation	Past, present and future orientation

Source: Extracted from Hofstede, G. (1991) *Cultures and Organizations: Software of the Mind*, McGraw-Hill Book Company, London and Trompenaars, F. (1993) *Riding the Waves of Culture*, The Economist Books, London.

Another cultural dimension has to do with inequality, referring to issues such as power, authority and status. Hofstede's Power Distance dimension is defined as a measure of dependence relationships, including how people in a society deal with authority and power. Countries with small power distance consider it important to minimize inequalities among people and value interdependence, while those in countries with high power distance consider inequalities and dependence as a natural part of life, and could even have mechanisms to make social differences more obvious, such as the use of status symbols. Trompenaars looks at the status issue from a narrower but related perspective: whether one's status is attributed by the group (e.g. family, gender or ethnic status) or is based on personal achievement. He found evidence that Protestant cultures tend to favour achievement, while in Catholic, Buddhist and Hindu countries status attribution prevails.

Control issues are considered in another cultural dimension called uncertainty avoidance by Hofstede. This dimension captures how societies deal with uncertainty. Certain societies have high tolerance to uncertainty, while others do not. The latter tend to be less prone to adopt innovations, and more strict in terms of precision and punctuality. Mechanisms of control are important in a society with strong uncertainty avoidance. In a similar manner, Trompenaars sees the need for control under two categories: whether one is controlled by external events (external control) or one controls his own life (internal control). It seems that societies with lower uncertainty avoidance would tend to see life events as more internally controlled.

Affective behaviour is involved in yet another cultural dimension. Hofstede uses the terms masculinity–femininity to represent a continuum in which masculine cultures are more assertive, and value recognition, earnings, advancement and challenge, while feminine cultures tend to give more importance to relationships, cooperation, harmony, and security. Trompenaars uses the term neutral to designate cultures in which emotions are not easily displayed, and Affective, to represent those cultures in which people are stimulated to express their feelings. There seems to be some correspondence between neutral and masculine cultures, and between affective and feminine cultures.

Finally, both classifications consider time orientation. Hofstede looks at a society's time perspective, that is, whether it focuses on the short or the long term. Trompenaars recognizes that time assumes different meanings in different societies, and that people project themselves into the past, the present or the future in ways that differ from one group to the other.

These cultural dimensions can be found in social values and beliefs, but also in social practices. This is to say that culture encompasses every aspect of human life, from the most basic values expressing one's relationship to the world to everyday practices.

Cultural clusters

A number of studies have identified clusters of societies according to their cultural values. These studies can help marketers in various ways. One is the selection of international markets to enter.

	Cattell	Ronen and Shenkar	GLOBE
	Table 24.2 Cultural clusters		
Clusters	Catholic homeland	Latin European	Latin Europe
	Catholic colonial	Latin American	Latin America
	Nordic	Nordic	Nordic Europe
		Germanic	Germanic Europe
		Anglo	Anglo cultures
	Eastern European		Eastern Europe
	East Baltic		
	Islamic	Arabic	Arab Cultures
	Hamitic	Near Eastern	
			Sub-Saharan Africa
	Oriental (India, China)	Far Eastern	Southern Asia
			Confucian Asia
Countries not classified	France, Germany, UK, US, Soviet Union, Japan	Brazil, Japan, India, Israel	

Source: Extracted from Gupta, V., Hanges, P. J. and Dorfman, P. (2002) Cultural clusters: methodology and findings, *Journal of World Business*, **37**, 11–15.

For example, a company deciding to expand its international activities may consider entering markets that are more similar to its domestic market in terms of cultural values. Another application is the identification of countries in which standardized marketing strategies can be adopted, because their cultural values are congruent and relevant for the product the company sells. Correspondingly, it permits the identification of countries whose cultural values are dissimilar, thus inviting the adaptation of marketing strategies.

Country clusters vary according to the theoretical model and the methodology adopted in each study, but they tend to be consistent with each other. Table 24.2 presents three studies that identified cultural clusters using different types of country data. Differences are more often the result of inclusion of certain countries in one study but not in another. For example, Sub-Saharan countries (Namibia, Zambia, Zimbabwe, South Africa and Nigeria) were only included in the GLOBE study.

Not surprisingly, the examination of specific regions of the world in more detail may allow further identification of similarities and differences within a cluster. For example, one study formed clusters of Latin American countries (Lenartowicz

and Johnson, 2003). Three clusters were identified and three countries could not be classified in any cluster:

- *Southern Cone countries*: Argentina, Chile, Paraguay and Uruguay
- *Andean countries*: Bolivia, Ecuador and Peru
- *Northern South American countries*: Venezuela and Colombia
- *Not classified*: Brazil, Mexico and Puerto Rico.

European countries could also be clustered in more detail. A study identified six clusters, which were combined in two mega clusters (Brodbeck *et al.*, 2000):

- *Mega cluster 1*: Northern/Western European, combining Anglo, Nordic and Germanic countries
- *Mega cluster 2*: Southern/Eastern Europe, combining Latin European, Arab and Central/Eastern European countries.

Culture and international marketing

Culture can have a huge impact on marketing activities as a firm enters foreign markets (Box 24.1). Table 24.3 lists some marketing variables that can be strongly influenced by culture.

Box 24.1   A clash of cultures: the Danish cartoons and the Muslim reaction

Following the appearance in the Danish press of cartoons satirically depicting Prophet Muhammad, a number of Scandinavian companies faced a Muslim consumer boycott. In fact, firms such as the Arla Foods, a manufacturer of dairy products; Nodo Nordisk, an insulin maker and Lego, a toy-maker, reported a negative impact on their sales to the Middle East. Trying to avoid a consumer boycott that could escalate into political risk, other European companies adopted pre-emptive actions. For example, Carrefour voluntarily pulled products made in Denmark from its shelves in its Middle East stores, and Nestlé placed informative ads explaining that its products were not manufactured in Scandinavia.

A survey with consumers from four Muslim countries shortly thereafter showed that Denmark's reputation as a whole was affected. For example, while almost 50 per cent of Egyptians considered Danes trustworthy before the cartoons were published, the percentage of people holding the same opinion fell to only 19 per cent after the publication. Norway, a country that defended Denmark publicly, also suffered an impact on its image, although not as intense as Denmark's.

Sources: When markets melt away. *The Economist*, **378** (8464), 11 February, 2006, 56 and Global Market Insite. *Denmark's* international image. *The Anholt Nation Brands Index Special Report Q1 2006* (available at http://www.nationbrandindex.com/allreports.phtml, access on 13 January 2007).

Table 24.3   Examples of how culture impacts marketing practices

Marketing variable	Impacts on:	
	Consumer behaviour	*Firm behaviour*
Customer relationships	Emphasis on relationships versus transactions	Emphasis on relationships versus transactions
Marketing research	Intentional response bias	Preference for formal or informal methods
Product	Time for new product adoption Positioning issues Importance of warranties Brand loyalty	Product quality Delivery speed Service quality
Pricing	Price sensitivity Preference for credit	Emphasis on short- versus long-term profitability
Channels of distribution	Waiting lines Preference for retail formats	Emphasis on networking or contracts
Advertising	Advertising appeals (e.g. rational versus emotional; objective versus subjective) Ads length (longer versus shorter) Use of people (women, children) in ads	Preference for advertising versus personal selling
Personal selling	Preference for advertising versus personal selling Loyalty to salesperson versus firm	Length of salespeople contacts Conduct of meetings Negotiation styles Salespeople compensation

---

Box 24.2   Dos and don'ts in cross-cultural etiquette

Sebenius (2002) proposes the following list of dos and don'ts when negotiating with foreigners:

Greetings – How do people greet and address one another? What role do business cards play?

Degree of formality – Will my counterparts expect me to dress and interact formally or informally?

Gift giving – Do businesspeople exchange gifts? What gifts are appropriate? Are there taboos associated with gift giving?

Touching – What are the attitudes toward body contact?

Eye contact – Is direct eye contact polite? Is it expected?

Deportment – How should I carry myself? Formally? Casually?

Emotions – Is it rude, embarrassing or usual to display emotions?

Silence – Is silence awkward? Expected? Insulting? Respectful?

Eating – What are the proper manners for dining? Are certain foods taboo?

Body language – Are certain gestures or forms of body language rude?

Punctuality – Should I be punctual and expect my counterparts to be as well? Or are schedules and agendas fluid?

Source: Sebenius, J. K. (2002) The hidden challenge of cross-border negotiations, *Harvard Business Review*, March, 80.

This list does not intend to be complete, but to highlight to what extent cultural aspects may interfere in marketing practices. For example, in relational cultures marketing researchers have to be even more aware of intentional response errors, as a result of the respondent's concern in giving the 'right' answer. Also, firms may prefer to use more formal methods of marketing research, such as surveys, or adopt less formal methods, such as in-depth interviews, participant observation, etc. In Japan, for example, companies use interviews with salespeople in retail stores much more intensely than in the United States or in Western European countries. More relational or collectivist cultures may also favour longer contacts between customers and salespeople. Customers may be more loyal to the salesperson than to the store or firm selling the product.

Time orientation may also interfere in marketing practices. For example, tolerance for long waiting lines is higher among cultures that do not give an economic value to time. In Anglo cultures, people tend to believe that 'time is money' and thus be quite impatient when waiting for extended periods of time. Disney parks – owned by a US company – are known for their ability to create the illusion of shorter waiting lines.

Another area in which culture plays an important role in international marketing is negotiation. When two parties of different cultural background negotiate, misunderstandings can easily happen and jeopardize the whole process. To avoid misinterpretation, a manager has to master cross-cultural etiquette before he/she can really engage in international negotiations. Box 24.2 presents a series of Dos and Don'ts in cross-cultural negotiations.

Three types of influence strategies (assertive, persuasive and relationship based) can be used in negotiations. Assertive strategies comprise persistence, pressure and appeal to someone with higher authority; persuasive strategies include rational persuasion, emotional appeal and consultation; and relationship-based strategies consist of gift giving, informal engagement, personal appeal, socializing and offering something in exchange. The preference for a specific influence strategy is predisposed by cultural values and social beliefs, and thus varies across countries, as shown in Table 24.4.

The social and economic environment

The world population went up from 2.5 billion in the early 1950s to 6.5 billion in 2006, and is continuing to grow. This increase in population is happening mainly in the developing world, where 95 per cent of the growth occurs, while population in developed countries remains stable or declines. Nonetheless, the growth rate of the world population has been consistently falling in the last decades and will continue to fall. The following are some of the demographic trends that will shape the future of the global society and provide new opportunities for international marketers:

- Expected increase of the world's population to 9.1 billion by 2050, with population increases almost entirely concentrated in the developing world.

Table 24.4 Ranking of perceived effectiveness of influence strategies by countries

Country	Assertive	Persuasive	Relationship based
China	7	10	2
France	1	2	8
Hong Kong	3	8	7
India	4	3	4
Japan	2	5	12
Mexico	7	7	6
The Netherlands	8	6	11
New Zealand	10	4	10
Taiwan	5	9	1
Thailand	2	6	5
Turkey	9	1	9
United States	6	5	3

Source: Adapted from Fu, P. P. *et al.* (2004) The impact of societal cultural values and individual social beliefs on the perceived effectiveness of managerial influence strategies: a meso approach, *Journal of International Business Studies*, **35**, 284–305.

- Increase in life expectancy from 65 years in 2005 to 75 years in 2050 (82 years for developed countries and 74 years for developing countries), with a sharp rise in the proportion of the elderly in the total world population.
- Fall in mortality rates in many countries, creating a new generation of baby boomers, with more young people in the population than in the previous generation.
- Reduction in fertility rates, from 2.5 children born per woman in 2005 to about 2 by 2050, at the same time as women are faced with more education and job opportunities.
- Continued increase in the world's urban population, which will surpass the rural population by 2007 (Bloom and Canning, 2006). For example, around 150 million people have migrated from rural to urban areas in China during the last decade. It is expected that another 300 million will migrate during the next two decades.[1]

Social and demographic changes have been accompanied by changes in the economic and

[1] This is considered the fastest migration movement in history, although 800 million of the 1.3 billion Chinese are still living in rural areas. It has happened and continues to happen despite the existence of laws discouraging these movements.

financial systems. The forces of globalization are shaping the world economy in a way that radically differs from the past. Economies are now much more interdependent, and changes in one region of the world may severely impact countries in another region, as it was seen during the Asian 1997–1998 financial crisis.

The pace of economic growth has changed substantially during the last decades. In the years that followed World War II, the United States and Western European countries benefited from high growth rates, while the GDP of most Third World countries grew at much lower rates. Asian countries, in particular, were poor and backward, lacked critical natural resources and had high population growth rates. In contrast, resource-rich Latin America was the most developed region of the Third World, showing rapid increases in GDP per capita in the immediate post-war years (Elson, 2006).

In the last 50 years, Asia totally changed its economic importance in the world economy, growing at an average rate that almost doubled that of the rest of the world (Burton *et al.*, 2006). The first evidence of change in Asia was the transformation of Japan from a country devastated by war into the second largest economy in the world.

Table 24.5 Real GDP growth (per cent)			
Region	2005	2006	2007*
Asia and Australasia	5	5.4	4.6
Europe and Eurasia			
Commonwealth of independent states	6.4	7.0	6.3
Euro 12	2.1	2.2	2.1
EU25	2.1	2.2	2.2
South-Eastern Europe	4.8	5.9	5.1
The Americas			
Latin America	4.3	4.7	3.9
North America	3.2	3.2	3
Middle East and North Africa	6.0	5.8	5.9
Sub-Saharan Africa	5.6	4.3	4.7
World (at market exchange rates)	3.5	4.0	3.2
World (at parity purchasing power exchange rates)	5.0	5.4	4.7

* Forecasts.

Source: Economist Intelligence Unit (2006) http://www.eiu.com/site_info.asp? (accessed on 18 January 2007).

Following Japan's example, other Asian countries such as Hong Kong, South Korea, Singapore and Taiwan accelerated their growth rate in the 1960s and 1970s, followed by Thailand, Malaysia and Indonesia, and, more recently, by China and India. This extraordinary economic performance was temporarily halted at the end of the 1990s by the Asian financial crisis, but these economies have recovered as indicated by their real GDP growth rates in recent years (Table 24.5). In fact, Asian countries came out stronger of the financial crisis, thanks to a combination of thorough restructuring of their industrial and financial sectors and the adoption of sound macroeconomic policies.

Asia's growth is also a result of the region's integration into the global economy. Asia received a large share of the total net private capital flows to emerging markets, and it benefited more than any other region of the world from global trade. Another factor was the ability to take advantage of the globalization of production, due to its disciplined and low-cost labour force. Compared to Latin American countries, it is clear that Asian countries have developed a number of strong competitive advantages, including the ability to integrate into a regional supply chain, as well as extensive intraregional trade. Latin America, in contrast, was unable to sustain its earlier rates of economic growth. In fact, during the 1980s the region faced the so-called 'lost decade', with its real GDP per capita falling around 1 per cent (Elson, 2006). Latin American countries lagged behind in terms of technology, education, industrial competitiveness and integration with the global economy. Nonetheless, this picture seems to be changing in the last few years, with the region taking advantage of global trends.

Other changes are still underway. Africa, the lost continent, which has remained apart from the benefits of globalization until recently, is showing a few spots of success, with a number of countries appearing in the list of the 10 fastest-growing economies in the world, although others are in the list of the slowest growing (Table 24.6). Most of the African countries showing high economic growth, such as Angola, are benefiting from China's need for raw materials.

In fact, China's and India's accelerated growth rates have created huge opportunities for marketers all over the world. On one side, these countries can be seen as factories producing a diversified set of low-cost products to be exported to other

Table 24.6 Fastest- and slowest-growing economies in the world, 2006			
10 fastest-growing economies	*Real growth (%)*	*10 slowest-growing economies*	*Real GDP growth (%)*
Azerbaijan	18.0	Zimbabwe	−2.7
Sudan	11.8	Iceland	0.6
Angola	10.3	Italy	1.2
Mauritania	10.3	Côte d'Ivoire	1.4
Liberia	10.0	Germany	1.4
Kazakhstan	9.7	Portugal	1.4
China	9.6	Seychelles	1.5
Armenia	9.0	Swaziland	1.5
Estonia	8.9	France	1.8
United Arab Emirates	8.5	Malta	1.8

Source: Economist Intelligence Unit (2006).

countries, while on the other their accelerated growth is also creating new and large domestic markets, as millions of Chinese and Indians cross the poverty line and start to participate in the consumer market.

Trade flows

The 1990s saw a continuous increase of world trade, at an average rate that exceeded 6.0 per cent. This high performance did not continue in the early 2000s, although there was a significant recovery after 2003, mostly due to China's massive imports, which grew 40 per cent in 2003 alone. Developing countries have benefited unevenly from trade growth. Table 24.7 shows the evolution of exports and imports in the world since 1990.

The most interesting patterns of world trade in recent years are:

- Persistent growth of the US imports, and continued widening of its trade deficit.
- Weak export dynamism in developed countries.
- Continued expansion of the external trade of the transition economies (Central and Eastern European countries).
- Rapid increase of China's presence in international trade.
- Substantial increases in the price of certain commodities fuelled by China's needs for industrial raw materials, energy and food,

benefiting resource-rich countries in Asia, Latin America and Africa (oil).
- Substantial increase in intraregional trade in Asia, due to the formation of an intraregional supply chain, which has produced positive spillovers to other countries in the region.

Foreign direct investment flows

Foreign Direct Investment (FDI) is also accelerating the pace of globalization. There are three types of flows: equity investments, intracompany loans and reinvested earnings. In the last decade, equity investments have dominated, both from developed and developing countries' firms. In fact, FDI outflows from developing countries rose from 'a negligible amount' (UNCTAD, 2005) in the early 1980s to US $83 billion in 2004.

There are a number of reasons why companies make cross-border investments. Dunning (1994) classified firm motivations to FDI in four categories: market seeking, resource seeking, strategic asset seeking and efficiency seeking. All of them can explain the increase in FDI flows since the early 1990s. Competitive pressures are forcing corporations all over the world to move their plants to low-cost producing countries (efficiency seeking), and to resource-rich countries (resource-seeking motives). Strategic asset-seeking motives can be found in the need to have access to distribution networks, and market-seeking motives

Table 24.7 Growth rates in external trade, 1990–2003 (per cent)

Region and economic grouping	Export volume				Import volume			
	1990–2000*	2001	2002	2003	1990–2000*	2001	2002	2003
World	6	−0.2	2.6	4.9	6.7	−0.2	2.7	6.0
Developed economies of which:	5.3	−0.9	0.6	1.5	6.2	−1.3	1.4	3.5
Japan	2.6	−9.5	7.9	4.9	5.3	−2.0	2.0	7.1
United States	6.7	−5.7	−4.1	2.7	9.1	−2.9	4.6	5.5
Western Europe	5.4	1.8	0.6	0.8	5.0	−0.4	−0.5	2.0
Developing economies of which:	7.6	0.6	6.2	10.8	8.0	0.4	5.3	11.7
Africa	3.4	2.2	0.8	7.5	4.2	6.1	2.0	7.9
Latin America	9.3	2.7	0.2	5.2	11.6	1.3	−7.5	2.3
West Asia	5.3	3.3	−5.0	3.3	3.2	7.6	2.7	1.2
East and South Asia	8.1	−0.8	10.5	14.0	7.8	−1.7	9.8	15.9
Transition economies	6.6	8.2	8.1	12.4	6.0	15.0	7.3	11.0

Source: UNCTAD (United Nations Conference on Trade and Development) (2004) *Trade and Development Report*, Geneva, p. 45.
*Average.

convey the desire to take advantage of a rapidly growing middle class in emerging markets.

The main trends in FDI in recent years can be summarized as follows:

- Increased share of developing countries in world's FDI, reaching 11 per cent of the world's stock in 2004 (approximately US $1 trillion, of which 271 billion from Latin America and 718 billion from Asia), with Asia and Oceania becoming important sources of FDI.
- Substantial increase in FDI flows from the developed world to the developing countries.
- Decline of FDI flows to developed countries, with the US as the most important exception to this trend.
- Continued growth of international investments in services accounting for 63 per cent of total value of mergers and acquisitions in 2004.

The 2005 UNCTAD Survey on FDI Prospects asked FDI Experts and executives from transnational corporations to indicate the most attractive business locations in the world. The two groups agreed in 7 out of 10 countries. Four of the top five countries are located in the developing world (see Table 24.8), the only exception being the US,

which remains as one of the most attractive locations for FDI.

Although China appears as the most attractive country for FDI in both lists, some political analysts have claimed that China represents a high political risk, and that projections of the future of China should not be based on the past. They believe the probability of political unrest will increase in the future, as the country faces economic change and moves towards an open economy (Bremmer, 2005).

Social and economic trends and international marketing

Changes in demographics can create or increase the size of certain market segments, providing a whole set of new opportunities. Take for example the elderly market. The expected sharp increase in the percentage of older people in the population will be accompanied by an increase in the demand for several products and services related to health, retirement, leisure, etc. In developed countries, the elderly may present a new set of market opportunities to those firms that target this market segment. The huge increase in the

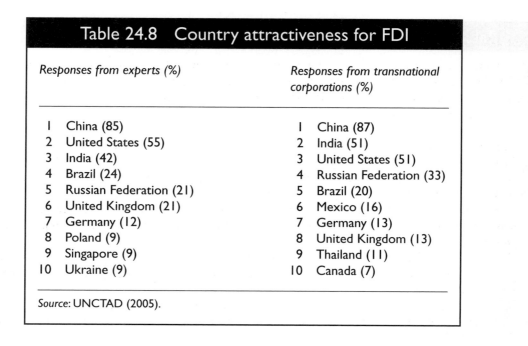

Table 24.8 Country attractiveness for FDI	
Responses from experts (%)	*Responses from transnational corporations (%)*
1 China (85)	1 China (87)
2 United States (55)	2 India (51)
3 India (42)	3 United States (51)
4 Brazil (24)	4 Russian Federation (33)
5 Russian Federation (21)	5 Brazil (20)
6 United Kingdom (21)	6 Mexico (16)
7 Germany (12)	7 Germany (13)
8 Poland (9)	8 United Kingdom (13)
9 Singapore (9)	9 Thailand (11)
10 Ukraine (9)	10 Canada (7)

Source: UNCTAD (2005).

number of consumers aged 45–65 will impact the consumption of luxury products, since this is the group with higher earnings in the population.

In addition, the fast aging of the population in the developed world may force countries to accept more immigrants to keep its labour force balanced in terms of age, thus reducing the negative impact of population aging on the cost of pension funds and health care. These fast-growing immigrant segments – such as Muslims in Europe, Hispanics in the US – will increase the market for ethnic products.

The demographic growth of developing countries is also a challenge for firms to adapt their marketing strategies to serve populous markets in which the average per capita income is much lower. Although sales per capita in these markets can be quite low, the numbers are impressive (see Figure 24.1). For example, forecasts show that 800 million people will be entering the consumer market in the next 10 years in the BRIC countries alone (Brazil, Russia, India and China).

In an often-quoted article, Prahalad and Hammond (2002) claim that most Western companies focus on the upper segment of the global population, which is quite restrictive in terms of the number of people, compared to the potential of the two other segments in the middle and bottom of the pyramid. Consider, for example, the Chinese market. Upper-class consumers represent approximately 5 per cent of urban consumers in China. They tend to buy luxury goods and to have

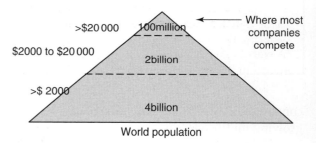

Figure 24.1   The global market pyramid
Source: Prahalad and Hammond (2002).

a preference for Western brands. Multinational firms selling their products in China tend to target this segment because of its similarity to middle-class consumers in developed countries, but this approach clearly limits their ability to tap into the full market potential of the Chinese market (Cui and Liu, 2001).

New marketing opportunities will come from developing products and services specifically designed to serve these poorer consumers in emerging markets (see Box 24.3).

This means not only developing affordable products and services that deliver value to the consumer, but also finding the right kind of distribution channels and designing credit systems to permit the access of the poor to financial services. Furthermore, consumer decision-making processes and cognitive preferences may differ because of lower education levels. For example,

---

Box 24.3   Creating products to serve the Indian market

The second largest country in population in the world, India faces the challenge of creating products and services to serve its domestic market, in which 70 per cent of the population is poor. Here are some examples of how domestic and multinational companies in India are serving this huge market segment.

- Tata Motors is developing a compact car to be sold for $2200, which is expected to be launched by 2008.
- Bajaj sells low-cost durable motorcycles, scooters and mopeds to Indian consumers, with a large service network available in every part of India.
- Tata Consultancy Services, another company of the Tata Group, developed computer-aided literacy programme, which permits illiterate adults to learn to sign their name and to read simple texts in 10 weeks.
- The Aravind Eye Care Centre of Marudai uses the equivalent of an assembly line to do cataract surgery in a large number of patients at a cost varying from $50 to $300, with a $5 domestically manufactured intraocular lens included.
- ICICI, the largest bank in India, reduced the cost of microfinance loans by securitizing them.
- Nokia India developed a customized mobile phone to serve specific Indian needs, including an in-built flashlight and a dust-resistant pad.
- Samsung washing machines come with a memory backup to face power outages, which are frequent in India, and its washing machines have special features to wash saris.
- Electrolux sells a refrigerator that keeps the food frozen even after 6 hours of power outage.

Sources: Getting the best to the masses, *Business Week*, 11 October 2004, 174–178 and Bharadwaj, V. T., Swaroop, G. M. and Vittal, I. (2005) Winning the Indian consumer, *The McKinsey Quarterly*, Special Edition, 42–51.

---

functionally illiterate consumers rely much more on concrete reasoning and pictographic information than literate adults, suggesting that companies should use pictorial depictions of product attributes, avoid changes in packaging and logos, and explain uses clearly (Viswanathan *et al.*, 2005). Table 24.9 presents alternative approaches to the marketing of products to poor consumers.

High-technology products provide an interesting example of how emerging markets represent attractive opportunities. Some emerging countries have already adopted high-technology products to an extent that is comparable to the leading developed countries. For example, in South Korea, 20 per cent of the transactions are online, 77 per cent of the homes have broadband and 85 per cent have access to the Internet. The four BRIC countries alone bought 17 per cent of all computers sold in the world in 2005.

To support digital inclusion and expand emerging markets potential, multinational corporations in the computer industry are investing in new marketing projects. Intel, for example, was planning to invest $1 billion starting in 2006 to support the production of low-cost personal computers and wireless access to the Internet. Microsoft was conducting a pilot project in Brazil, using the domestic retail chain Magazine Luiza, to test the selling of pre-paid computers to low-income consumers (Blecher, 2006).

In addition, to take advantage of local availability of large pools of engineers and scientists at much lower cost, multinational corporations are increasingly placing R&D facilities in selected emerging countries, such as Motorola's R&D centre in China, and Microsoft's and Intel's centres in India. This global displacement of R&D centres to emerging countries is reducing the costs and increasing the speed of innovation around the world.

The political and institutional environment

The success of a country in terms of attracting foreign business also seems to be related to a

Table 24.9 Marketing to the poor	
Marketing mix	*Alternative approaches*
Product	Simpler designs and models Smaller packages with less volume Larger packages Cheaper packages More efficient products Second brands
Pricing	Longer financing Pre-paid schema Rent instead of purchase Shared products
Channels of distribution	Microretailers Door-to-door Low-cost retailing chains
Communications	Pictorial depictions of product information Simple and clear instructions Consumer education

number of characteristics of its political and institutional environment. An attractive political and institutional environment has the following characteristics:

- Rule of law (extent of contract enforcement, property rights, punishment of theft and crime, etc.)
- Political stability (absence of social unrest, ethnic conflicts, terrorism, etc.)
- Adequate regulatory burden (low government intervention in the economy, fair taxes, limited restrictions to capital flows, etc.)
- Government effectiveness (effective bureaucracy, adequate public infrastructure, etc.)
- Low levels of corruption
- Voice and accountability (civil liberties, political rights, free press, etc.)
- Economic freedom (freedom in terms of trade, fiscal and monetary policies) (Globerman and Shapiro, 2003a).

In selecting a foreign market to export to or to open a branch or a subsidiary, these characteristics are very important in the firm's decision making. They have an impact on business practices, but they also impact business costs.

Legal system

The type of legal system is also part of a country's business attractiveness. Legal systems in the world can be classified in four different groups:

1 Legal systems based on Common Law, in which case law is dominant.
2 Legal systems based on Civil Law, which give primacy to written law.
3 Legal systems based on Muslim Law.
4 Mixed legal systems (Globerman and Shapiro, 2003b).

Countries such as the United Kingdom, the United States and Canada adopt legal systems based on the English Common Law. In this system, general legal statutes, common practice and tradition are applied to specific cases. Germany, Scandinavian countries, Latin European countries and many former Socialist countries adopt the Civil Law system, based on the Roman legal heritage, in which all possible foreseeable situations to which the law could apply are written. Some Muslim countries adopt exclusively Muslim Law, although most tend to mix it with elements of Civil or Common Law. The type of legal system adopted by a foreign country can have a number of implications for companies wishing to do business abroad, including the areas of intellectual property rights (patents, trademarks, logos, design), contracts with local agents and representatives, establishment of joint ventures, etc.

Regulatory issues

Other regulations may be of paramount importance to a foreign market operation. For example, quantitative restrictions to imports, such as quotas, limit the firm's export volume. Other regulations can include:

- Product specifications
- Content rules
- Requirements for packaging and labelling
- Procedures for product approval
- Need for safety checks, etc.

The international expansion of the firm

Internationalization has been defined as '... the process of increasing involvement in international operations' (Welch and Luostarinen, 1988), and an international enterprise as 'a firm which services foreign markets' (Dunning, 1980). Internationalization is a risky business. The firm leaves the well-known domestic environment to face realities that can substantially differ from those of the home country. Yet the rewards can be overwhelming.

But how and why do firms go international? This question has been extensively researched, although results are by no means convergent. Two types of explanations compete: objective or rational motives versus subjective or non-rational.

Economists claimed that business decisions are rational even if not all possible alternatives are necessarily considered in the decision-making process, which tends to be limited to a certain subset. Such 'bounded rationality' would result from cognitive limitations of the decision makers in their information processing and communications capabilities, even if they intended to be fully rational. Early work suggested that companies would invest in international production for at least three reasons: to neutralize competitors, to exploit unique competitive advantages and to diversify. Proponents of this explanation saw firms and markets as governance structures, with different transaction costs. Investment decisions

would result from a favourable position in terms of transaction costs when using a firm's own structure, as compared to the use of external partners or intermediaries. Many international business theorists followed this approach, and have developed extensive theoretical and empirical work in support of these views, among which the best known are internalization theory and the eclectic paradigm of international production. The eclectic paradigm suggests that in order to internationalize a firm must develop certain competitive advantages (ownership advantages), which can be better created, acquired or exploited by establishing itself (internalization advantages) in a foreign country that offers certain geographical advantages (location advantages) (Dunning, 1988).

Some empirical studies have shown, however, that companies often do not make foreign investment decisions in a rational and systematic way. Early research on FDI processes found that the FDI decision-making process could not be described by a careful and rational consideration of alternatives but rather as isolated decisions based on whether a given alternative was considered satisfactory. Scholars from the School of Uppsala proposed that internationalization is not 'the result of a strategy for optimum allocation of resources to different countries' but rather 'the consequence of a process of incremental adjustments to changing conditions of the firm and its environment' (Johanson and Vahlne, 1977). Managers would consider each problem as unique and make decisions based on the specific problem's context. When faced with a given foreign market opportunity, 'commitments to other markets are not explicitly taken into consideration, resource allocations do not compete with each other' (Johanson and Vahlne, 1977). Internationalization is seen as a gradual process by which a company increases its commitment to foreign markets based on ongoing influences and learning effects, as well as other situational influences. Internationalization proceeds by stages, starting with uncommitted exports, proceeding to active exporting and eventually moving to the establishment of subsidiaries abroad.

Neither perspective seems to fully apprehend the variety of internationalization processes. Some companies, especially large, multinational firms, tend to take more rational, objective decisions, following plans and making rigorous assessment of the economic outcomes of each entry decision, while others, such as smaller and less experienced firms, tend to follow the gradual approach.

More recent theoretical developments have explored two other possibilities in terms of motives in the internationalization process: network theory and the born-global approach.

Network theory was initially developed in the context of industrial marketing to explain how firms connect to each other and develop long-term relationships, in opposition to the traditional transaction-only approach dominant in marketing theory, and was later extended to explain how and why firms enter international markets. According to this perspective, many firms do not enter international markets as stand-alone actors, but are instead part of a network of other firms, which can help, stimulate or even make it mandatory to internationalize. For example, the auto parts industry was forced to internationalize following the globalization of the car industry. In fact, very often, when a firm is part of a supply chain, the internationalization of the leading firm in the supply chain forces suppliers to go international. Also, it is not uncommon that firms belonging to industrial clusters, such as many Italian and Brazilian firms, become exporters following the example of flagship firms in their clusters (Bonaccorsi, 1992). Belonging to a network can bring several benefits to a firm in its internationalization:

- *The network can provide physical facilities to a member firm*: For example, a smaller firm may use the offices of a large network member in its first steps in a foreign market.
- *The network can provide business contacts to the new entrant*: It is very difficult for an unknown firm to make initial business contacts in a new foreign market. Network members already operating in this market may facilitate these contacts.
- *The network can provide foreign market knowledge*: More experienced network members may deliver relevant market information to other members.
- *The network can attract foreign buyers*: As innovative firms in a network start to export, foreign buyers may be stimulated to search for other suppliers within the network.

The network approach is quite useful to understand how and why smaller firms, firms in an industrial cluster and even born-global firms start their internationalization process.

The born-global approach was the result of empirical observations that many firms see the world as their market since their inception. The increasing number of 'born globals' is apparently related to the phenomenon of globalization (Knight and Cavusgil, 1995; Madsen and Servais, 1996):

- The emergence of homogeneous market segments across the world, permitting increased specialization and segmentation.
- The reduction of costs to access international markets, such as travelling costs and telecommunication costs, making it easier to contact prospects and customers.
- Technological innovations, especially the Internet, permitting fast and cheap contacts with potential buyers, and customer contact.
- New production technologies, facilitating the production of smaller lots.
- The development of international supply chains, facilitating international business contacts.
- The globalization of financial markets, improving the access of smaller firms to cheaper venture capital.

These changes have allowed smaller and inexperienced firms to overcome the limitations of size and age, and enter international markets. Also, these firms are typically managed by new entrepreneurs, with a different profile from that of traditional firms: more internationally oriented, and often having personal networks in other countries. It is believed that such firms appear more often in small markets, because of a need to find global market segments, and in high-technology industries.

Selecting a foreign market

One of the most complex decisions in international marketing is the selection of a foreign market to enter, especially when a firm is starting its internationalization process. In fact, managers can be overwhelmed with the large number of attractive markets. To deal with this complexity, it is advisable to move in two steps: first, do a preliminary screening to filter a limited number of more interesting targets; second, develop a more detailed analysis for each pre-selected country.

Preliminary screening or 'which markets are attractive?'

Preliminary market selection can be based on various measures of country attractiveness, such as economic development indexes, investment

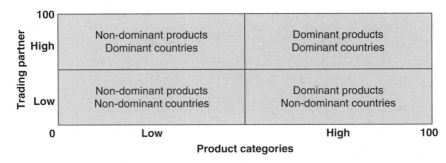

Figure 24.2 The dominant product–dominant country matrix
Source: Shankarmahesh *et al.* (2005).

attractiveness indexes, political risk indexes, etc. The choice of specific indexes and variables to be used in foreign market screening depends on the decision makers' understanding of what makes a country attractive for international business and on data availability. Methods based on macroindicators typically use the following procedure:

- Choose the relevant macrovariables (those that make a country attractive).
- Give weights to these variables, according to the perceived importance of each one in making a foreign market attractive.
- Compute an overall index for each country.
- Choose countries whose indexes better fit the company's offer.

Statistical techniques for data reduction and agglomeration can be used to facilitate this process. For example, if the number of variables considered in defining market attractiveness is too large, one solution is to reduce them to a smaller number of factors using factor analysis. Also, different market attractiveness variables can be combined to group target countries according to their similarities using cluster analysis. An interesting approach to the use of clustering and ranking methods to support preliminary marketing screening was recently developed by Cavusgil *et al.* (2004), who offered a detailed methodology to assess market attractiveness.

Foreign market selection can also benefit from evaluating how familiar customers are in a target country with product categories coming from certain source countries. One method, to be employed by industrial marketers, was developed by Shankarmahesh *et al.* (2005) using a 2 × 2 matrix. Figure 24.2 portrays the suggested matrix.

The matrix is based on two dimensions. The first dimension is called *product category*, and measures the share of distinct product categories in a country's export portfolio, ranging from 0 to 100 per cent. The second dimension is called *trading partner*, and measures the share of different trading partners in a country's export portfolio. These are combined in four quadrants. If a company's product is located in the upper-left quadrant, for example, it can benefit from the awareness of its country of origin in the target market, but if it is in the lower-left quadrant, the marketing task is much more complex. The easiest situation is the one in the upper-right quadrant, in which both the product and the country of origin are well known and accepted by customers in the target country.

Managers can also consider the stage in the product life cycle (PLC) to select in which markets to enter (Figure 24.3) and with what products. It is often the case that products facing a mature or saturated market in a developed country can find new markets in the introduction or early development phases in emerging markets. McDonald's entry in new markets such as Brazil, Russia and China is a good example of how a company whose original domestic market was saturated can benefit from global expansion to countries in earlier phases of the PLC. Interestingly, target customers in a country in an early life cycle stage may differ from those in a country in a more advanced stage. For example, when McDonald's entered the Brazilian market, it first attracted upper-middle-class urban consumers who already knew the chain when travelling to the US. After a rapid diffusion process, McDonald's broadened its customers' profile, reaching a wider range of different market segments.

Another consequence of entering markets at different life cycle stages is the need to adapt the marketing mix. For example, in the initial stages of the PLC it may be necessary to educate consumers to use the product, requiring specific instructions

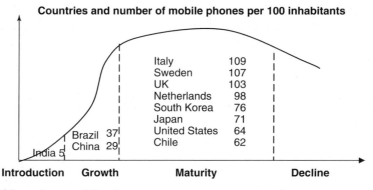

Figure 24.3 The global life cycle in mobile phones

in product packaging, more use of advertising to expand primary demand and a more intensive use of in-store personal selling to help consumers in the initial adoption stages. Also, the firm may need to use sales promotions to stimulate trial. During the market development stage, firms should focus their advertising efforts in building selective demand, and personal selling tends to be more directed towards obtaining market coverage. Once the market matures, advertising tends to concentrate in enhancing brand image, since consumers are already aware of the existence of the product and understand its attributes and functions, and personal selling is often restricted to in-store merchandising. Given these differences, if a company chooses to enter a market at a different stage of the PLC than its original market, it will be difficult to use the same marketing programme.

Detailed market analysis or 'how attractive is this market, really?'

Once a limited number of countries are selected in the preliminary screening phase, the next step includes detailed market analysis. This is often very expensive, because the data necessary to perform this type of analysis is not publicly available, and marketing research needs to be conducted. The following information should be gathered to take the final decision on the choice of foreign markets:

- *Market*: size and growth, product exports and imports, countries of origin;
- *Regulation*: tariff and non-tariff trade barriers, industrial regulations, product standards, other requirements;
- *Competition*: number, size, market share, strategies adopted, relations with government;

- *Consumers*: characteristics, differences from home country, made-in images;
- *Product*: competitive products, substitute products, packaging requirements, labelling;
- *Distribution*: number and levels of channels, physical distribution and logistics problems, distribution practices;
- *Promotion*: advertising and sales promotion practices, regulations, limitations;
- *Pricing*: competitors' prices, prices of substitute products, pricing practices in the industry, price controls, credit.

Psychic distance or 'how much affinity we feel towards this market?'

When a firm selects a new market to enter, this decision is often influenced by a phenomenon known as *psychic distance* (PD).

Economists have always considered distance as an important element in promoting or discouraging trade between nations, because of transportation costs. Since the 1950s, however, there has been a growing recognition that the choice of a given foreign market by a firm had less to do with the actual physical distance to that market, and more with the perception of similarities with the firm's domestic market. This phenomenon was called psychic distance (Beckerman, 1956) and defined as 'the distance between the home market and a foreign market resulting from the perception and understanding of cultural and business differences' (Evans *et al.*, 2000).

PD is both an individual and a collective phenomenon. It is an individual phenomenon because it refers to how an individual perceives the world. But it is also a group phenomenon since people belonging to the same culture tend to share similar perceptions of similarities and differences between their own country and foreign countries. This phenomenon can be explained by ethnocentrism, the social construction of stereotypes of other groups, due to common cultural filters. PD is then a culturally determined bias in the ways of seeing people belonging to other groups.

Although individual and national perceptions of PD tend to be closely related, they may differ because of specific international experiences accumulated by the individual during his life, such as cultural background, travel abroad and international experience, among other factors. For example, an American citizen of Japanese origin may perceive Japan as being psychically closer to the United States than a typical American without this cultural inheritance. A French manager who lived for many years in Brazil may feel closer to Brazil than his French counterparts that never visited the country.

If one looks at organizations as cultural groups, it can be expected that people from different firms may have different perceptions of other countries, given the firm's specific organizational culture, history and experiences. The organizational cultures in which managers are embedded influence their individual perceptions of similarities and differences with other countries. Also, relevant individuals within the firm (such as founders, owners or top managers) may transfer to the organization elements of their individual PD. Firms are repositories of individual and collective experiences of its members, which are filtered, selected, interpreted and stored in different ways, including in the firm's structure, processes, routines, policies and traditions. The international experiences acquired by a firm as well as the individual experiences of its members can therefore modify an individual's PD. Figure 24.4 summarizes this discussion.

The following are some aspects of the firm's or the manager's international experience that seem to influence PD:

- *Firm's direct experience in the specific foreign market or in similar markets:* When managers have direct experience in that market PD tends to be reduced, probably because of a better understanding of the 'true' distance between the domestic and the foreign market. This is followed by experience in similar markets, or markets within the same cultural cluster.
- *Firm's inward internationalization:* A firm's experience with inward international activities – such as importing, master franchising or

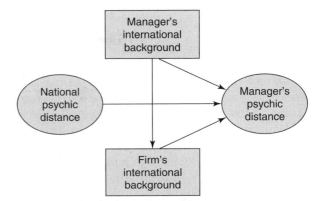

Figure 24.4 A conceptualization of national and manager's PD

licensing – tends to reduce PD to foreign markets where the firm has already developed these inward forms of business.
- *Manager's education and knowledge of foreign languages:* Education and knowledge of foreign languages tend to reduce PD, probably because these factors facilitate cross-cultural learning and understanding.
- *Manager's international business experience:* Managers' international business experience reduces PD, probably by developing the ability to understand other cultures.
- *Education abroad:* Overseas education or professional management training tends to reduce PD to the specific country, because of the contact with another culture.
- *Living abroad and trips overseas:* Living abroad and frequent trips overseas tend to reduce PD, probably by making managers feel more at ease with foreign locals.
- *International orientation:* Less ethnocentric managers are less influenced by PD considerations when choosing a new market to export.
- *Social ties in the foreign market:* Social ties between managers and individuals in foreign markets tend to reduce PD.

Choosing modes of entry and operation

A firm operating in an international market faces risks that do not exist in the domestic market, including, on the one hand, the possibility of losing control over its international marketing mix due to opportunistic behaviour of foreign partners, and, on the other, the risks of failure when operating

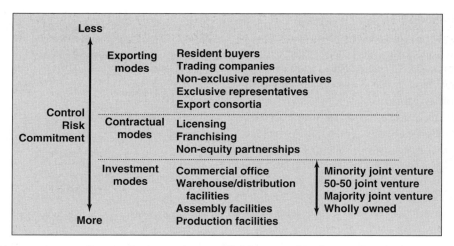

Figure 24.5   Entry and operation modes: a continuum of risk, control and commitment

directly in an unknown environment. Accordingly, the choice of modes of entry and operation by the international firm involves a trade-off between risk and control. The modes chosen to enter and operate in foreign countries can also be seen as an indication of the firm's commitment to international operations. Modes of entry and operation can thus be portrayed in a continuum from less to more control, risk and commitment (Figure 24.5).

Firms can move from one mode to another in their international trajectory. They can use simultaneously distinct types of modes of entry and operation in different markets. In addition, industry specificities can limit the mode choice. For example, firms in many service industries cannot export their products, because of the inseparability between production and consumption.

Exporting

Exporting is the most common way by which firms enter international markets, and it is the preferred mode of operation for many firms. There are a number of reasons why a firm may prefer exporting to other modes of entry and operation:

- The firm is a neophyte in international activities and this is the simplest and less risky way to learn about foreign markets and foreign operations.
- The firm is an experienced exporter, but its export intensity does not justify investments in foreign distribution or warehousing facilities.
- The firm is an experienced international marketer, but there are no competitive advantages in producing in a location other than the domestic due to country-specific advantages, such as the

access to low-cost or scarce raw materials, low-cost or highly skilled labour, or to the size of foreign markets.
- The firm has a number of production sites strategically located in different parts of the world, and exports from these areas to geographically close markets.
- The firm combines different modes of entry and operation depending on market specificities. Markets that are small or too risky are approached by exporting.

The firm can respond to unsolicited export orders, it can use export marketing intermediaries in the home country (indirect exporting) or joint export marketing groups (cooperative exporting) or it can send its products directly to the customer in the foreign market, using foreign agents, distributors or its own representative (direct exporting). A number of different types of intermediaries can be used in each type of exporting. Table 24.10 offers a list of the most common export marketing intermediaries that may be used by firms when exporting to a foreign market.

Firms often start exporting unintentionally responding to unsolicited orders coming from foreign countries. Although this would technically be a case of direct exporting, since the transaction is made without intermediaries, it actually implies less commitment and control over the export marketing mix. Ultimately, it can be said that a firm that only serves sporadic unsolicited export orders is not yet an exporter.

Nevertheless, unsolicited orders are frequently the first step in international business. They are often an indication of the export potential

Table 24.10	Principal marketing intermediaries in exporting	
Export intermediaries in the home country	*Export intermediaries in the foreign country*	*Distributors in the foreign country*
Resident foreign buyer Trading company Export management company Export consortia	Foreign agent /representative Company representative	Wholesaler Industrial distributor Retailing chain

Box 24.4   The role of foreign buying agents in the development of the International Footwear Industry in Brazil and China

In the 1970s, buying agents of US wholesalers searching for new suppliers of leather footwear established themselves in the Brazilian footwear cluster of the Sinos Valley, opening new export opportunities for small- and medium-sized local manufacturers. These agents played a crucial role in the cluster development, bringing product specifications, models, designs and styles. They helped these firms to improve their production processes and quality control practices. Two decades later, the cluster had expanded to become one of the largest in the world, supported by an integrated supply chain including suppliers of raw materials, machinery and all types of service providers. It was also characterized by the presence of large firms.

This tale of success was interrupted in the 2000s by low-price competition from Chinese firms. Chinese footwear exports threatened Brazilian manufacturers since the 1990s, but the devaluation of the Brazilian currency – the real – in the late 1990s helped firms to remain competitive, until new changes in exchange rates by 2004 made it very difficult for Brazilian firms to compete on price.

The rise of China as a major producer of footwear, on the other hand, was also stimulated by export agents, who played the same role in developing the Chinese footwear industry they had played decades before in Brazil. They developed these new suppliers, transferring technical know-how to Chinese firms.

of a product. If the firm receives repeated unsolicited orders from a given country, or from the same importer, this can call management's attention to foreign market opportunities.

Resident foreign buyers established in the source country are probably the easiest and less risky way in which a domestic firm can initiate its exporting activities, but it is also the one that permits less control over the export marketing mix. This is common practice in many industries, such as the footwear, apparel and furniture industries. These intermediaries have had a significant influence in starting many firms in exporting. In fact, these intermediaries have often the role of initiating a whole industry or industrial cluster in exporting (see Box 24.4). Typically these foreign buying agents have offices close to the production sites. They can perform many functions for the exporting firm and

for their foreign customers, including: to supply the exporting firm with product specifications, designs, models or prototypes; to negotiate prices and conditions with the exporting firm; to carry out quality checks before the product is shipped; to take care of all bureaucratic procedures and to ship the order to its final destiny.

International trading companies can be another valuable intermediary for companies that are starting to export, or to those that export to markets with very high political risk, or very high risk of default. They are also often used for the exporting of commodities. The most famous and reliable are the Japanese trading companies because of their long-term presence in world markets, but other trading companies have been established in other parts of the world following the Japanese model, or adopting indigenous models.

They can be general or specialized. General trading companies operate with a full range of products, while specialized companies have a narrow product focus (e.g. steel products, chemicals, agricultural commodities, etc.). Typically, these companies have detailed knowledge of market conditions, including the economic, political and institutional environment, changes in supply and demand, consumer tastes and preferences, etc. They are also often able to give access to export financing because of their connections with banks and other financial institutions.

Export management companies vary in size, but tend to be quite small, and are typically domestic. They offer international marketing services to non-competitive firms, substituting or complementing the activities of these firms' own export departments. Because of their smaller size and same country of origin as the exporting firm, their use permits the manufacturer to have more control over its international marketing activities than other types of intermediaries established in the home country.

Joint export marketing groups, or export consortia, cannot be characterized as indirect exporting, since these organizations are not part of the manufacturer's marketing organization; neither can they be considered direct exporting, since the manufacturer does not have full control over its export marketing activities. They can be conceptualized as an association of independent manufacturers with the purpose of jointly developing their export activities. Cooperative exporting is not a new concept, since producers of agricultural products have long used cooperatives to export their output. Yet the formal organization of export consortia by groups of manufacturing firms is relatively recent. Many national governments have promoted the formation of such groups. Some examples are Argentina, Brazil, Colombia, India, Israel and Kenya, among others. The results of these experiences are mixed; while some have been very successful, others have failed.

A firm increases control over its marketing activities when it takes the responsibility of managing its export operation by exporting directly to foreign customers. Even so, there are different degrees of control, depending on the specific type of intermediary used. Manufacturers may use a foreign agent or representative, non-exclusive or exclusive, or they can have their own representative abroad (e.g. a person working in a home office or a shared office in the target foreign country who is employed by the manufacturer in the home country). Manufacturers can also sell directly to wholesalers, distributors or large retailing chains in the foreign target market. Finally, it is also possible to export directly using mail order systems and the Internet.

Contractual modes

This type of entry and operation mode is characterized by a non-equity arrangement, by which firm-specific knowledge or capabilities are transferred from the firm in the home country to a partner in a foreign market. It differs from investment modes mainly because there is no investment involved.

Licensing involves the transfer by contract of products, technologies, expertise and/or patents to a foreign firm which has local market knowledge. Even though licensing requires very limited resources from the licensor, and thus is generally considered as less risky than foreign investment, ultimately it can threaten the firm's intangible assets, by transferring to a competitor firm-specific knowledge and capabilities that could be later used against the licensor. The reason for this is that even though licensing contracts have specific clauses to protect the licensor, it is not uncommon that national governments will allow domestic firms to end a licensing agreement and take advantage of the knowledge acquired. This type of situation has happened in Japan in the late 1970s and early 1980s, as the country moved from being a lower-quality imitator to become the marketer of products that were superior in quality, specifications and design to many of its international competitors. Licensees can also be less motivated than the licensor to invest in the development of the product's brand name in the target foreign market.

Franchising is a system by which a company (the franchisor) grants another (the franchisee) for a specified period of time and in a specified area the right to operate a business format. Franchising contracts allow rapid expansion with very limited investment, but the sales and profits are also much smaller than they would be if the company had started its own operations. In the case of international franchising it is common practice to establish a master franchisee in a foreign country, with the right to sign franchising contracts with other firms or individuals in that market. In a sense, the master franchisee acts almost as an intermediary between the franchisor in the home country and the group of individual franchisees in the target market. Franchising is often used by fashion retailers and fast food and restaurant chains, but it has also been used in a variety of services industries, mainly those that require a sales outlet. Among the firms that intensively used franchising as a mode of entry or operation in foreign markets are the American sandwich chain Subway, the Swedish furniture manufacturer and retailer Ikea, and the Italian fashion manufacturer and retailer Benetton.

Non-equity partnerships are contractual strategic alliances, in which partners intend to learn or acquire from each other technology, know-how, products or competencies, in order to create or sustain competitive advantage. Vertical strategic alliances are those between firms in different stages of the supply chain, and horizontal alliances are those between firms that have no supply or distribution relationship. Examples of vertical alliances are those in marketing, logistics or purchasing. Horizontal alliances are often related to technology and product development.

Investment modes

There are different types of foreign investment a firm can make: commercial offices or branches, warehousing and distribution, assembly and production facilities are the most common, but depending on the industry, specific types of investment may be necessary, such as stores in retailing, hotels and other facilities in the tourism industry, etc. Commercial offices or branches, warehousing and distribution facilities are often made by exporting firms, which need them to support their export operations. These firms may not consider assembly or production facilities because foreign markets may be too small or too risky, or because they can only manufacture their products in countries with specific factor endowments.

Regardless of the type of facilities, when a firm enters a foreign market by direct investment, it can choose between a greenfield (new) investment or an acquisition, and, in terms of ownership structure, between a sole venture or a joint venture.

A greenfield investment is a new operation, contrary to an acquisition, in which tangible and/or intangible assets are transferred to the acquiring company. The choice between green field investments or acquisitions depends on several factors. One is, of course, the availability of existing businesses to be acquired. In mature concentrated industries, such as the steel or the cement industry, acquisitions are the most common entry mode. Retailers are also forced to enter saturated markets by acquisition, since there are very few good locations available to open new stores. For

example, Wal-Mart entered Germany, Canada and the United Kingdom acquiring existing retailing chains, but started with green field investments in Brazil and Argentina. Another factor is the type of international strategy adopted by the firm. Multinational firms tend to use more acquisitions, while firms that follow a global strategy prefer greenfield investments. This is consistent with the fact that acquired firms tend to maintain some of its idiosyncratic behaviour, making it more difficult to standardize marketing and business practices.

A sole venture, or wholly owned subsidiary, is an international operation whose ownership is totally controlled by the mother company. A joint venture, on the other hand, is an independent operation in which two or more firms share the control. They can be majority, 50-50 or minority joint ventures, depending on the proportion of equity in the hands of a given partner. The choice of operating or not with a partner is sometimes a managerial decision, but it is often a result of environmental conditions.

Why do firms choose one mode over another?

Theorists have proposed a variety of reasons why firms prefer one entry mode over another, of which the most well known are:

- *Incremental*: Firms can follow an incremental pattern of internationalization, moving from lower-commitment entry modes (such as exporting) to higher-commitment (e.g. a wholly owned production subsidiary) as they acquire more experience in international markets (Johanson and Vahlne, 1977).
- *Case specific*: Firms may adopt a *zig-zag* pattern, choosing the most appropriate pattern according to the specific situation (Okoroafo, 1997).
- *Cultural*: Firms choose entry modes according to the perceived cultural or PD to the foreign target market. In general, the larger the cultural or PD, the higher the probability of choosing a joint venture instead of a wholly owned subsidiary as an entry mode (Kogut and Singh, 1988).
- *Transaction costs*: Firms may take entry mode decisions on more rational bases, seeking to balance control, risk and return issues, as is suggested by transaction-cost theorists. According to this perspective, transaction-specific assets, unpredictability of the external environment, unpredictability of the results to be obtained and the difficulty to verify compliance to agreements

affect the choice of entry modes (Anderson and Gatignon, 1986; Rindfleisch and Heide, 1997). Higher levels of uncertainty are associated with low-control FDI modes, especially for smaller firms, but increased uncertainty could take larger firms use high-control FDI entry modes (Erramilli and D'Souza, 1995).

- _Strategic:_ According to this perspective, the choice of entry mode is associated to the strategies adopted by the firm to manage its capabilities and geographic scope (Gomes-Casseres, 1989).
- _Organizational capabilities:_ This perspective suggests that the nature of organizational capabilities can explain why firms choose an entry mode over another. When a firm's know-how is easily copied, and when the probability of the know-how being imitated is perceived as larger than the difficulties to adapt to the host country, high-control entry modes are preferred. If firm advantages are country specific and cannot be easily transferred and when the motivation for entry is the development of future capabilities, then firms prefer cooperative (lower-control) modes, such as joint ventures (Madhoc, 1997).
- _Eclectic:_ Firms take entry mode decisions based on a combination of three sets of factors: strategic, environmental and transaction costs. Three strategic factors (industry concentration, global synergies and global strategic motivations) are considered. High levels of concentration in the global industry, the potential for global synergies among business units and global strategic motivations favour the choice of higher-control entry modes. As to environmental variables (country risk, location unfamiliarity, demand uncertainty and intensity of competition), when country risk is low, demand uncertainty is high, locations unfamiliar and the greater the intensity of competition in the host market, firms would tend to choose low-control modes. Also, the greater the value of firm-specific know-how and the greater the tacit component of such know-how, the higher the probability of choosing higher-control entry modes (Kim and Hwang, 1992; Hill _et al.,_ 1990).

Marketing strategy: global or local?

The adoption of global marketing strategies – strategies that are standardized across national markets – is very attractive for most firms, because of its cost advantages and coordination and simplification benefits. Many contend, however, that standardization of marketing strategies may be ineffective when markets are very dissimilar. Advocates of adaptation claim that it permits enhancement of the value delivered to customers, and gives flexibility to subsidiaries or local representatives to adjust to local needs.

When should a company decide in favour of adaptation or standardization? Although a very large number of factors can play a role in influencing one way or another, there are four sets of factors that need to be examined before a decision is made (Griffith _et al.,_ 2003; Alashban _et al.,_ 2002):

- _External environment similarity:_ Similarity between the cultural, social, economic, political and institutional aspects of the home country and the host country favours standardization.
- _Market similarity:_ The existence of homogeneous global segments, with similar attitudes and behaviour, favours standardization.
- _Industry structure:_ High levels of rivalry, large number of buyers, and large number and levels of distribution channels favour adaptation.
- _Organizational compatibility:_ Homogeneity in firm processes in different parts of the world and compatibility of the organizational structure are pre-conditions to adopt a standardization strategy.

Whether using standardization or adaptation, not necessarily all the elements of the marketing mix need to be standardized or adapted. Often companies choose to replicate some elements of a marketing strategy in its foreign markets, but to adapt others.

If the environment shapes to a large extent the standardization–adaptation decision in international marketing, the nature of the organization itself can play an important role in this decision. Solberg (2002) proposed that two variables – the headquarters' knowledge of foreign markets and the decision-making centre (local representatives or headquarters) – have an influence on whether the organization will favour standardization or adaptation. Four types of situations are portrayed in Figure 24.6, suggesting that depending on the combination of these two variables, the organization will adopt a different approach, with specific consequences on its level of learning and control. The adoption of centralized marketing decisions seemed to generate more conflict with intermediaries, while a more relaxed approach to standardization, leaving some decision power to local representatives seemed to be conducive to better relationships with them.

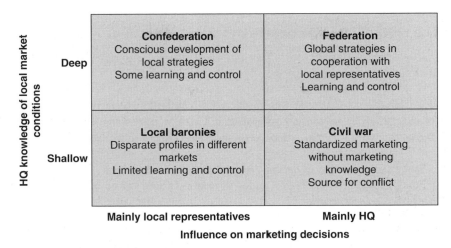

Figure 24.6 Typologies of governing strategies in international marketing decisions
Source: Solberg (2002).

The international marketing programme

Firms need to decide on the elements of the marketing programme, independently of whether they intend to standardize or adapt their marketing strategy, since even when taking the standardization decision, there are elements that need to be at least to some extent adapted.

International product policy

Firms may need to do adaptations on their products to be successful in certain markets. These adaptations can vary in degree, from simple adaptations in the packaging used for shipping the product to a complete redesign of the whole product line. The first step is, of course, to determine the extent to which products need to be adapted. Changes may include:

- breadth and scope of the product line;
- design;
- brand names;
- packaging and labelling.

Changes in the product line may imply the addition or elimination of specific sizes, changes in format and content. For examples, countries in which extended families live together may need larger sizes than countries in which nuclear families are dominant.

Brand names are a critical area for adaptation. When entering a new market, companies have a choice of using an existing brand name or creating a new one. Even when a company uses the same brand name, there are two alternatives: to make a direct translation in order to keep the meaning, or a phonetic translation for the pronunciation. Whatever the decision, brand name standardization can be problematic (see Box 24.5).

One reason to standardize the brand name is the desire of having a global brand that appeals to consumers in different countries. In fact, global brands today have a dominant share of international sales in many industries, such as consumer electronics, cars and cellular phones. A recent study with more than 17 000 highly profiled consumers worldwide investigated levels of brand recognition (Table 24.11) for the 15 leading consumer electronics brands. According to the study, Sony was the most popular brand, and Sanyo the least popular, but the levels of brand recognition were very high for all brands studied.

If the company uses the same brand name for its products all over the world, product standardization is a concern, because consumers will expect to find the same or similar products under the same brand name in different countries.

Another issue has to do with the country where the product is manufactured. In most markets in the world, products such as French perfumes, Italian shoes, Scottish whisky, Colombian coffee, Swiss chocolates, Japanese cars or Egyptian cotton have very high prestige, indicating that these countries are recognized for producing the best in the specific product category, to the point that consumers take the country of origin as an indicator of product quality. The 'Made in' information is

---

Box 24.5 The risks of international brand standardization

When transferring a brand name from a country to another, language problems may be a nightmare to standardization. Some examples:

- When entering China, Coca-Cola was translated as 'Ke-Kou-Kela', which had phonetic similarity with the original brand name, but an unusual translation in Chinese, something like 'a horse full of wax'.
- Chevrolet's Nova had an unfortunate association in Spanish with the expression 'no va', meaning 'it doesn't go'.
- Unilever's Le Sancy soap sounded in certain Asian dialect as 'death to you'.
- Volkswagen's Fox was launched in Mexico under the name Lupo to avoid confusion with Mexican President Vincent Fox's family name.
- Jolly Green Giant, a Pillsbury brand, was originally translated in Saudi Arabia as 'intimidating green ogre'.
- Hyundai had difficulty in making its brand name to be correctly pronounced by US and Brazilian consumers.

Source: Alashban *et al.* (2002) and *Exame*, 11 November 2004, 78.

Table 24.11 Brand recognition in consumer electronics

Brand	Recognition (%)
Microsoft	95.42
Sony	95.24
Canon	95.17
Panasonic	94.48
Philips	93.72
Toshiba	92.85
Nokia	92.40
HP	90.31
Casio	90.19
Sharp	88.48
Apple	86.51
Sanyo	85.04
Pioneer	84.61
Dell	84.09
Hitachi	74.11

Source: www. brandbarometer.com.

sometimes the only relevant information for consumers to make a decision about whether they should buy a product or not. Nation brands are also important in attracting investments, tourism and immigration.

The value of the 'Made in' is so important to certain products, that often domestic firms in emerging markets create brand names that mimic brands from other countries, trying to transfer this made-in effect to their own brands. This is the case of Romanson, a Korean brand of wristwatches, which tries to position itself as a Swiss-like watch, or the Hong Kong brand Giordano, which tries to capture the Italian fashion glamour (Han and Kim, 2003). Also, many Chinese apparel producers use Latin-like brand names, and Brazilian fast food chains adopt Americanized names.

Country-of-origin images reflect to some extent ethnocentric views of one's own country and others', cultural stereotypes and PD. For example, Americans tend to rate their own country as first in every regard, although this view is not shared by consumers in many other countries. The British rank themselves as the top nation brand, followed by other Anglo heritage countries (Canada, Australia, the United States and New Zealand). The French elect France as the most prominent country brand name, followed by Canada, Germany, Spain and Italy, showing some preference for the Latin European cluster (Global Market Insite).

Packaging and labelling are elements that frequently need some adaptation to accommodate to local needs and practices. Even when the product is the same, if the firm entered a market in the initial stages of the PLC, more information may be required in the packaging to educate consumers on product usage. Labels may have to follow local regulations.

Packages and labelling may also need to have their colours changed to fit local symbolism. Although there seems to be some universality in colour associations for certain products, more

Table 24.12   Association between colour perceptions and product packaging

Product packaging	Chinese	Korean	Japanese	American
The label on a can of vegetables	Green	Green	Green	Green
The wrapper of a bar of hand soap	Yellow	Yellow	Yellow	Yellow Green
A box of laundry detergent	Yellow	Blue	Yellow Green	Yellow Red
A box of candy	Yellow Red Purple	Yellow Red	Yellow Red	Yellow Brown
A soft drink label	Brown	Yellow Purple	Yellow	Red
A packet of cigarettes	Brown	Grey	Grey	Black Brown
A box of headache remedy	Grey	*	Grey Blue	Red

Source: Jacobs, L., Keown, C. and Worthley, R. (1991) Cross-cultural colour comparisons: global marketers beware! *International Marketing Review,* **8** (3), 21–30.
*No significant association.

typically the preference for the use of different colours, as well as their association with different products and meanings, vary from one culture to another. For example, although vegetables are naturally associated with green in most places, soft drinks are associated with different colours in different countries (Table 24.12).

Grey in Japan and China is associated with inexpensive products, while it is associated with high quality, dependable and expensive products in the US.

International pricing

International pricing may include: the decision on export prices, if the firm is an exporter; or the decision on prices to the customer in each foreign market, if the firm manufactures its products abroad. Pricing decisions should take into consideration:

- Consumers' price sensitivity.
- Prices of competitive and substitute products.
- Firm's strategic objectives, including market-share objectives and the desire of achieving slower or faster market penetration.

- Product positioning, taking into consideration the meanings of price to specific target segments.
- Costs, including production costs, shipping costs, tariffs, margins of various channel members, taxes and exchange rate effects.
- Firm pricing policies, including transfer prices and price coordination across foreign markets.

Even when prices are standardized, they may have disparate meanings to customers in different countries, due to factors such as differences in purchasing power, relative prices, relative perceptions of value of the product compared to others, etc. This is why pricing is the most difficult element of the mix to standardize.

International promotion

Two types of international promotion can be considered in international marketing. One has to do with promotional efforts to develop an export business; the other with promotional campaigns to consumers in target foreign markets.

The first type of promotion includes participation in international trade fairs and exhibitions, and sending product samples and promotional materials to potential foreign buyers. Trade fairs and exhibitions are a valuable marketing tool to smaller firms interested in developing foreign markets. For many, these events are extremely important, because of all that happens 'behind the scenes': networking, sales contacts and even contacts with potential foreign partners. The participation in international trade shows can bring the following benefits (Rice, 1992):

- Evaluate export marketing opportunities before investing heavily in exporting.
- Obtain feedback from potential customers on product potential.
- Evaluate reactions to a new product.
- Get information about competitors' product lines and new products.
- Develop relationships with potential customers.
- Identify joint venture partners.
- Improve the company's image.

Foreign catalogues are also used by firms to present their products to potential foreign buyers. Although most firms do have some sort of printed materials to send to foreign markets, these catalogues often lack the quality and care needed. Exporters should be reminded that sales materials are often the only clue a foreign buyer has to the company's reputation and capabilities. This also holds for exporters' sites in the Internet.

When a firm is established in a foreign market, it has to develop its promotional campaign, and the possibility of using the same materials and content developed for the domestic market or other foreign markets is often considered. When developing an advertising campaign or evaluating the adequacy of an existing one to a target foreign market, managers should give special attention to the following considerations:

- Language differences, not only in terms of which languages or dialects are spoken in the country, but also to differences when the language spoken is the same as in the home country – for example, when the Brazilian perfume company O Boticário entered the Portuguese market, it did not expect to find significant differences in the language spoken in Portugal compared to Brazil. After a number of problems, managers' finally understood that the same words in Portuguese could have different meanings in one country and another.
- Cultural preferences and limitations to the content of communication – Japanese ads tend to be much more subtle and indirect than Western ads.

- Cultural or religious taboos in the representation of human bodies – the use of female images in advertising is considered unacceptable in some Muslim countries, such as Iran.
- Regulatory limitations – many countries have regulations concerning children and teenagers advertising, and limit or restrict the advertising of certain products, such as medicines, tobacco, liquor and toys, among others. Truth in advertising is the object of regulation in most countries.
- Media availability – certain types of media may not be available, or space may be limited. This is typical of countries where the state owns and operates broadcast media. Literacy levels may also affect media availability.
- Media costs – media costs can vary substantially from one country to another.

As to sales promotion, differences can be expected in the use of certain types of incentives or special offers. For example, consumers may not be familiar with coupons and rebates, as in many Latin American countries. Point-of-purchase materials are often regulated.

The use of personal selling is a key element in a firm's effort to develop a foreign market. This is, however, an area were cross-cultural misunderstandings can easily occur, because a firm has to rely on uncontrollable personal interactions. The solution would be to employ local salespeople, whenever possible. Table 24.13 compares the advantages and disadvantages of using local salespeople or expatriates.

Local salespeople, besides the evident advantages of being part of the cultural setting, tend to be less expensive than to bring salespeople from the firm's home country. Nevertheless, the use of local salespeople should not be seen as a panacea. They can be more difficult to control, less loyal to the firm and may not have the required background (e.g. in many countries it may be difficult to hire sales engineers).

International distribution

We have already discussed in a previous section the alternatives available in terms of export channels to a manufacturer wishing to sell its products in a foreign market. But a firm that starts direct operations in a foreign market may have to face the challenge of developing its own distribution network.

When entering an international market, the first task in developing a distribution network is

Table 24.13   Using local salespeople versus expatriates

Locals	Expatriates
Better understanding of local business etiquette, practices and protocols	Better knowledge of firm's culture, business practices and protocols
Better knowledge of local language, including local meanings	Better knowledge of firm's products
More experienced with selling in the local market	More experienced with selling the firm's products
Already know distributors, retailers or industrial customers	Do not have local contacts
More difficult to control	Easier to control
Less loyal to the firm	More loyal to the firm
Less expensive	More expensive

to get a good understanding of the distribution systems in the foreign country. This requires the knowledge of:

- types of distributors available for the product;
- levels of distribution typically involved;
- relationships between manufacturer and other members of the distribution channel;
- reactions of distribution channel members to a foreign manufacturer;
- cultural aspects associated with the manufacturer–distributor relationship;
- commissions and margins applicable;
- legislation and regulation involving the manufacturer–distributor relationship.

Japan is an excellent example of how distribution can become a nightmare and a serious deterrent to a firm's ambitions to gain market share. Because of *keiretsu* practices in Japan, most wholesalers and distributors, as well as small retailers, are already part of the distribution network of an existing competitor. Since loyalty to the network is a sacred value in Japan, Western companies have had serious problems in penetrating the Japanese distribution system.

Once the firm decides on the type of channel it intends to use, the next step includes the selection of specific intermediaries. Typical selection criteria include:

- size of potential intermediaries;
- geographic coverage and market penetration;
- intermediaries resources and experience;
- commercial conditions offered.

It should be noted that conflict within the distribution channel is amplified by cultural differences. It can be extremely difficult for foreign manufacturers to build trust with local distributors, requiring a long period of investment to develop relationships.

Final considerations

Industries and markets are changing at an unprecedented pace, and there are no indications that this process will come to an end in the foreseeable future. As industry and market configurations change, there will be winners and losers. Winners will be those firms with the ability to adapt to global transformations, which adopt effective marketing and business strategies to deal with the new realities. Losers will be those that refuse to understand the long-term implications of present changes, and do not prepare themselves for the future.

To survive in the global marketplace companies need to develop sustained competitive advantages that will permit them to face domestic and foreign competition. In most cases, internationalization becomes an imperative for those firms that do not want to remain as marginal producers in the domestic market, filling small niches that are not attractive to larger ones. Exceptions are those industries in which globalization pressures are still low.

As a firm internationalizes, the complexity of its operations increases substantially. In fact, the more committed a firm is to internationalization, as measured by the amount of resources in international markets, the higher the level of its operational complexity. Marketing is no exception; a firm that operates in different markets faces the challenge of understanding these markets and developing effective marketing strategies to deal with each one of them. As a result, international marketers need to master not only the traditional marketing tools but also a new set of abilities, including cross-cultural sensitivity, negotiation skills and language capabilities.

References

Alashban, A. A., Hayes, L., Zinkhan, G. M. and Balazs, A. L. (2002) International brand-name standardization/adaptation: antecedents and consequences, *Journal of International Marketing*, **10**(3), 22–48.

Anderson, E. and Gatignon, H. (1986) Modes of foreign entry: a transaction cost analysis and propositions, *Journal of International Business Studies*, Fall, 1–26.

Beckerman, W. (1956) Distance and the pattern of intra-European trade, *The Review of Economics and Statistics*, **28**, 31–40.

Blecher, N. (2006) O alvo é a baixa renda, *Exame*, **40**(15), 26–30.

Bloom, D. E. and Canning, D. (2006) Booms, busts, and echoes: how the biggest demographic upheaval in history is affecting global development, *Finance & Development*, **43**(3), 8–13.

Bonaccorsi, A. (1992) On the relationship between firm size and export intensity, *Journal of International Business Studies*, **23**(4), 605–635.

Bremmer, I. (2005) Managing risk in an unstable world, *Harvard Business Review*, **83**(6), 51–60.

Brodbeck, F. C. *et al.* (2000) Cultural variation of leadership prototypes across 22 European countries, *Journal of Occupational and Organizational Psychology*, **73**, 1–29.

Burton, D., Tseng, W. and Kang, K. (2006) Asia's winds of change, *Finance & Development*, **43**(2), 9–13.

Cavusgil, S. T., Kiyak, T. and Yeniyurt, S. (2004) Complementary approaches to preliminary foreign market opportunity assessment: country clustering and country ranking, *Industrial Marketing Management*, **33**, 607–617.

Cui, G. and Liu, Q. (2001) Emerging market segments in an emerging economy: a study of urban consumers in China, *Journal of International Marketing*, **9**(1), 84–106.

Dunning, J. H. (1980) Toward an eclectic theory of international production: some empirical tests, *Journal of International Business Studies*, **11**(1), 9–31.

Dunning, J. H. (1988) The eclectic paradigm of international production: a restatement and some possible extensions, *Journal of International Business Studies*, **19**, 1–31.

Dunning, J. H. (1994) Re-evaluating the benefits of foreign direct investment, *Transnational Corporations*, **3**(1), 120–139.

Elson, A. (2006) What happened? *Finance & Development*, **43**(2), 37–40.

Erramilli, M. K. and D'Souza, D. E. (1995) Uncertainty and foreign direct investment: the role of moderators, *International Marketing Review*, **12**(3), 47–60.

Evans, J. A., Treadgold, A. and Mavondo, F. T. (2000) Psychic distance and the performance of international retailers – a suggested theoretical framework, *International Marketing Review*, **17**(4/5), 373–391.

Global Market Insite. How the world sees the world. *The Anholt Nation Brands Index Q3 Report 2005* (available at http://www.gmi-mr.com/gmipoll/docs/NBI_Q1_2005.pdf; access on 13 January 2007).

Globerman, S. and Shapiro, D. (2003a) Governance infrastructure and US foreign direct investment, *Journal of International Business Studies*, **34**(1), 19–39.

Globerman, S. and Shapiro, D. (2003b) Governance infrastructure and US foreign direct investment, *Journal of International Business Studies*, **34**(1), 19–39. Based on the University of Ottawa Faculty of Law classification.

Goodenough apud Geertz, C. (1973) *The Interpretation of Cultures*, Basic Books, New York, p. 11.

Gomes-Casseres, B. (1989) Joint ventures in the face of global competition, *Sloan Management Review*, Spring, 17–26.

Griffith, D. A., Chandra, A. and Ryans Jr., J. K. (2003) Examining the intricacies of promotion standardization: factors influencing advertising message and packaging, *Journal of International Marketing*, **11**(3), 30–47.

Han, C. M. and Kim, J. M. (2003) Korean marketing in China: an exploratory analysis of strategy-performance relationships, *Journal of International Marketing*, **11**(2), 79–100.

Hill, C. W. L., Hwang, P. and Kim, W. C. (1990) An eclectic theory of the choice of entry mode, *Strategic Management Journal*, **11**, 117–128.

Hofstede, G. (1991) *Cultures and Organizations: Software of the Mind*, McGraw-Hill, London, p. 5.

Johanson, J. and Vahlne, J. E. (1977) The internationalization process of the firm: a model of knowledge development and increasing foreign market commitments, *Journal of International Business Studies*, **8**(1), 23–32.

Kim, W. C. and Hwang, P. (1992) Global strategy and multinationals' entry mode choice, *Journal of International Business Studies*, **23**(1), 29–53.

Knight, G. A. and Cavusgil, S. T. (1995) The born global firm: a challenge to traditional internationalization theory, *Proceedings of the Third CIMaR Symposium*, Odense University, Odense, Denmark.

Kogut, B. and Singh, H. (1988) The effect of national culture on choice of entry mode, *Journal of International Business Studies*, Fall, 411–432.

Lenartowicz, T. and Johnson, J. P. (2003) A cross-national assessment of the values of Latin American managers: contrasting hues or shades of gray? *Journal of International Business Studies*, **34**(3), 266–281.

Madhoc, A. (1997) Cost, value and foreign market entry: the transaction and the firm, *Strategic Management Journal*, **18**, 39–61.

Madsen, T. K. and Servais, P. (1996) The internationalization of 'born globals' – an evolutionary process? *Proceedings of the Fourth CIMaR Symposium*, San Diego, California.

Okoroafo, S. C. (1997) Strategic and performance issues associated with mode of entry substitution patterns, *International Marketing Review*, **14**(1), 20–38.

Prahalad, C. K. and Hammond, A. (2002) Serving the world's poor, profitably, *Harvard Business Review*, **80**(9), 48–57.

Rice, G. (1992) Using the interaction approach to understand international trade shows, *International Marketing Review*, **9**(4), 32–45.

Rindfleisch, A. and Heide, J. B. (1997) Transaction cost analysis: past, present and future applications, *Journal of Marketing*, **61**, October, 30–54.

Shankarmahesh, M. N., Olse, H. W. and Honeycutt, D. A. (2005) Dominant product – dominant country framework of industrial export segmentation, *Industrial Marketing Management*, **34**, 203–210.

Solberg, C. A. (2002) The perennial issue of adaptation or standardization of international marketing communication: organizational contingencies and performance, *Journal of International Marketing*, **10**(3), 1–21.

UNCTAD (United Nations Conference on Trade and Development) (2005) *World Investment Report 2005: Transnational Corporations and the Internationalization of R&D*, United Nations, New York, p. 8.

Viswanathan, M., Rosa, A. J. and Harris, J. E. (2005) Decision making and coping of functionally illiterate consumers and some implications for marketing management, *Journal of Marketing*, **69**(1), 15–31.

Welch, L. S. and Luostarinen, R. (1988) Internationalization: evolution of a concept, *Journal of General Management*, **14**(2), 34–64.

CHAPTER 25

E-marketing

DAVE CHAFFEY

Introduction

In a short period of time, e-marketing has become a facet of marketing that cannot be ignored. With some enthusiastic adopters of digital technologies such as Cisco, easyJet and IBM now achieving the majority of their leads and customer service online, many organizations are actively examining how they can best make use of this new medium. However, the success of the early adopters has not gone unnoticed and competition is now fierce to gain visibility for a brand within the search engines and other online media sites. Consequently, marketers need to carefully assess the significance of e-marketing and assimilate it, as appropriate, into all aspects of marketing from strategy and planning to marketing research, objectives setting, buyer behaviour, marketing communications and the marketing mix. The key phrase here is *as appropriate*. The impact of new technologies such as the Internet will vary greatly according to the existing product, market, channel structure and business model of each organization.

This chapter outlines an approach to e-marketing planning, which can be applied to all organizations. The approach used will be a familiar one, based on careful assessment of the opportunities and threats, clearly defined objectives and strategies and selection of appropriate e-marketing tactical tools and resources to achieve these strategies. I will highlight the specific challenges and opportunities the Internet raises.

What is e-marketing?

E-marketing can be simply expressed as the use of electronic communications technology to achieve marketing objectives (see, e.g. McDonald and Wilson, 1999). The electronic communications technology refers to:

1. The use of Internet-based (TCP/IP) network technology for communications within an organization using an intranet; beyond the organization to partners such as suppliers, distributors and key account customers using password-based access to extranets and the open Internet where information is accessible by all with Internet access.
2. The use of web servers or websites to enable informational or financial exchanges as e-commerce transactions.
3. The use of other digital access platforms such as interactive digital TV, wireless or mobile phones and games consoles.
4. The use of e-mail for managing enquiries (inbound e-mail) and for promotion (outbound e-mail).
5. Integration of the digital access platforms and e-mail with other information systems such as customer databases and applications for customer relationship management and supply chain management.

To illustrate some of the opportunities of e-marketing, it is useful to re-apply the definition of marketing from the Chartered Institute of Marketing:

> e-marketing can identify, anticipate and satisfy customer needs efficiently.

Taking a website as a major part of e-marketing, consider how a website can fulfil these requirements of marketing. It can:

- *Identify* needs from customer comments, enquiries, requests and complaints solicited via e-mail and the website's contact facility, forums, chat rooms, online searches and sales patterns (seeing what is selling and what is not, recorded in the web log which reveals insights into interests determined by pages visited). Online surveys ask how to improve the site or products. Finally, there is a proliferation of online secondary sources of research, many of which provide free in-depth insights into customer needs.

- *Anticipate* customer needs by asking customers questions and engaging them in a dynamic dialogue built on the trust of opt-in e-mail. Collaborative filtering, as used by Amazon helps to identify and anticipate what customers might like given that buyers of similar books have similar interests. Profiling techniques allow many companies to perform data mining to discover and anticipate buyer's needs. Cookie-based profiling allows companies to analyse a visitor's interests without even knowing your name – courtesy of a piece of code sent to the visitors PC. It recognizes your PC and records which types of sites (interests) you have and can serve adverts and offers based on predicted interests.
- *Satisfy* needs with prompt e-mail responses, punctual deliveries, order status updates, helpful reminders, after sales services and added value services combine with the dynamic dialogue. The dialogue maintains permission to continue communicating and then adds value by delivering useful content in the right context (right time and right amount).
- *Efficiently* means in an automated way (or partially automated) ... an efficient, yet hopefully not impersonal, way (i.e. it allows tailor-made technology to improve service quality, increase the marketers memory to help maintain the customer relationship through time).

It is apparent from these applications, that e-marketing extends beyond the website to include all use of digital technology to manage the customer relationship. Databases are increasingly used to manage and record all interactions with customers, whether sales transactions, inbound enquiries via phone or e-mail and outbound communications such as a mail-shot or e-mail shot.

An alternative perspective on e-marketing is provided by the term 'Internet marketing' which has been described simply as '*the application of the Internet and related digital technologies to achieve marketing objectives*' (Chaffey *et al.*, 2006). In practice Internet-based marketing is a subset of e-marketing that will include the use of a company website in conjunction with promotional techniques such as banner advertising, direct e-mail and links or services from other websites to acquire new customers and provide services to existing customers that help develop the customer relationship.

Digital marketing is yet another term similar to Internet marketing. We reference it here, because it is a term increasingly used by specialist e-marketing agencies and the new media trade publications such as New Media Age (www.nma.co.uk) and Revolution (www.revolutionmagazine.com). The Institute of Direct Marketing has also adopted the term to refer to its specialist professional qualifications.

'Digital marketing' has a similar meaning to 'Electronic marketing' and is increasingly used by media agencies and their clients. To help explain the scope and approaches used for digital marketing I have developed a more detailed explanation of digital marketing:

> Digital marketing involves: Applying these technologies which form online channels to market: Web, e-mail, databases, plus mobile/wireless & digital TV)
>
> To achieve these objectives:
>
> Support marketing activities aimed at achieving profitable acquisition and retention of customers ... within a multi-channel buying process and customer lifecycle
>
> Through using these marketing tactics:
>
> Recognising the strategic importance of digital technologies and developing a planned approach to reach and migrate customers to online services through e-communications and traditional communications. Retention is achieved through improving our customer knowledge (of their profiles, behaviour, value and loyalty drivers), then delivering integrated, targeted communications and online services that match their individual needs.

The first part of the description illustrates the range of access platforms and communications tools that form the online channels which e-marketers use to build and develop relationships with customers.

The second part of the description shows that it should not be the technology that drives digital marketing, but the business returns from gaining new customers and maintaining relationships with existing customers. It also emphasizes how digital marketing does not occur in isolation, but is most effective when it is integrated with other communications channels such as phone, direct mail or face-to-face. Online channels should also be used to support the whole buying process from pre-sale to sale to post-sale and further development of customer relationships.

The final part of the description summarizes approaches to customer-centric e-marketing. It shows how success online requires a planned approach to migrate existing customers to online channels and acquire new customers by selecting the appropriate mix of e-communications and traditional communications. Retention of online customers needs to be based on developing customer insight by researching their characteristics, behaviour, what they value, what keeps them loyal and then delivering tailored, relevant web and e-mail communications.

Web 2.0

Since 2004, the *Web 2.0 concept* has increased in prominence amongst website owners and developers. The main technologies and principles of Web 2.0 have been explained in an influential article by Tim O'Reilly (O'Reilly, 2005). It is important to realize that Web 2.0 is not a new web standard or a 'paradigm shift' as the name implies, rather it is an evolution of technologies and communications approaches which have grown in importance since 2004–2005. The main characteristics of Web 2.0 are that it typically involves:

- Web services or interactive applications hosted on the web such as Flickr (www.flickr.com), Google maps (http://maps.google.com) or blogging services such as Blogger.com or Typepad (www.typepad.com).
- Supporting participation – many of the applications are based on altruistic principles of community participation.
- Encouraging creation of user generated content – blogs and sites like Myspace (www.myspace.com) and YouTube (www.youtube.com) are the best examples of this. Another is the collaborative encyclopaedia Wikipedia (www.wikipedia.com).
- Enabling rating of content and online services – services such as delicious (http://del.icio.us) and traceback comments on blogs support this. These services are useful given the millions of blogs that are available – rating and tagging (categorizing) content help indicate the relevance and quality of the content.
- Ad funding of neutral sites – web services such as Google Mail/GMail and many blogs are based on contextual advertising such as Google Adsense or Overture/Yahoo! Content Match.

- Involve data exchange between sites through XML-based data standards. RSS Feeds based on XML are used by sites such as the BBC to provide up-to-the-minute alerts on granular topics. An attempt by Google to facilitate this which illustrates the principle of structured information exchange and searching is Google Base (http://base.google.com). This allows users to upload data about particular services such as training courses in a standardized format based on XML. New classes of content can also be defined.
- Use rapid application development using interactive technology approaches known as AJAX (Asynchronous JavaScript and XML). The best known AJAX implementation is Google Maps which is responsive since it does not require refreshes to display maps.

E-marketing is undeniably the fastest moving area of marketing tactics, early adopters can gain competitive advantage. The authors' site, Dave Chaffey.com (www.davechaffey.com) shown in Figure 25.1, has regularly updated content available via blog, RSS feed and e-newsletter to help keep you up-to-date with e-marketing developments.

Digital media communications characteristics

Through understanding the key communications characteristics of the digital media we can exploit these media while guarding against their weaknesses. The six key changes in moving from traditional media to new media are:

1 *From push to pull*: Traditional media such as print, TV and radio are push media, a one-way street where information is mainly unidirectional, unless direct response elements are built-in. In contrast, the web is a pull medium. This is its biggest strength and its biggest weakness. It is a strength since pull means that prospects and customers only visit your site when it enters their head to do so – when they have a defined need – they are pro-active and self-selecting. But this is a weakness since online pull means we have less control than in traditional communications where the message is pushed out to a defined audience. What are the e-marketing implications of the pull medium? First, we need to provide the physical stimuli to encourage visits to websites. This may

Figure 25.1   DaveChaffey.com (www.davechaffey.com)

mean traditional ads, direct mail or physical reminders. Second, we need to ensure our site is optimized for search engines – it is registered and is ranked highly on relevant key word searches. Third, e-mail is important – this is an online push medium, it should be a priority objective of website design to capture customer's e-mail addresses in order that legal, opt-in, permission-based e-mail marketing can be used to push relevant and timely messages to customers.

2   *From monologue to dialogue*: Creating a dialogue through interactivity is the next important feature of the web and new media. A website, interactive digital TV and even a mobile phone enables us to enter dialogue with customers. These can be short term – perhaps an online chat to customer support, or long-term, lifelong dialogues discussing product and supply requirements. These dialogues can enhance

customer service, deepen relationships and trust and so build loyalty.

But digital dialogues have a less obvious benefit also – intelligence. Interactive tools for customer self help can help collect intelligence – clickstream analysis recorded using web analytics systems can help us build up valuable pictures of customer preferences. If we profile customers, placing them into different segments then build a more detailed picture that is used to refine our products and offers.

3   *From one-to-many to one-to-some and one-to-one*: Traditional push communications are one-to-many. From one company to many customers, often the same message to different segments and often poorly targeted. With new media 'one-to-some' – reaching a niche becomes more practical – e-marketers can tailor and target their message to different segments

through providing different site content for different audiences through mass customization. We can even move to one-to-one communications where personalized messages can be delivered according to customer preferences.

4 *From one-to-many to many-to-many communications*: New media also enable many-to-many communications. Hoffman and Novak (1996) noted that new media are many-to-many media. Here customers can interact with other customers via your website or in independent communities. The success of online auctions such as eBay also shows the power of many-to-many communications. However, online discussion groups represent a threat since it is difficult to control negative communications about a company. So, the e-marketing actions of many-to-many communications are to consider whether you should set up online communities on your site, or whether you can tap into other independent communities on specialist portals.

5 *From 'lean-back' to 'lean-forward'*: New media are also intense media — they are lean-forward media in which the website usually has the visitor's undivided attention. This intensity means that the customer wants to be in control and wants to experience flow and responsiveness to their needs. First impressions are important. If the visitor to your site does not find what they are looking for immediately, whether through poor design or slow speed they will move on, probably never to return.

6 *Integrated*: Although new media have distinct characteristics compared to traditional media, this does not mean we should necessarily concentrate our communications on new media. Rather we should combine and integrate new and traditional media according to their strengths. We can then achieve synergy — the sum is greater than their parts. Most of us still spend most of our time in the real-world rather than the virtual world, so offline promotion of the proposition of a website is important. It is also important to support mixed-mode buying through a 'web response' direct response approach. For example, a customer wanting to buy a computer may see a TV ad for a certain brand which raises awareness of the brand and then sees an advert in a print ad that directs him across to the website for further information. However the customer does not want to buy online, preferring the phone, but the site allows for this by prompting with a phone number at the right time. Here all the different communications channels are mutually supporting each other.

Similarly, inbound communications to a company need to be managed. Consider if the customer needs support for an error with their system. They may start by using the onsite diagnostics which do not solve the problem. They then ring customer support. This process will be much more effective if support can access the details of the problem as previously typed in by the customer to the diagnostics package.

E-marketing planning

Is a separate e-marketing plan necessary?

I have found when helping companies introduce a structured approach to e-marketing that if there is a specific resource for e-marketing activities such as an e-marketing or e-commerce manager, then they will be responsible for the e-marketing plan. However, where there is no identified responsibility for e-marketing, which is still the case in many small and medium organizations, there is likely to be a lack of a coherent e-marketing plan. This often occurs when marketing managers have limited resources or other priorities and a lack of recognition that a separate e-marketing plan is valuable. Is a plan still needed? I would argue yes, as a short-term device to ensure that the integration of the new channel is managed in a structured way. In the longer term, e-marketing will become Business As Usual and will be integrated into the normal marketing planning process. I say this because of these common and serious problems if there is not the focus that a separate e-marketing plan brings:

1 Customer demand for online services will be underestimated if this has not been researched and it is under-resourced and no or unrealistic objectives are set to achieve online marketing share.

2 Existing and startup competitors will gain market share if insufficient resources are devoted to e-marketing and no clear strategies are defined.

3 Duplication of resources will occur, for example, different parts of the marketing organization purchasing different tools or different agencies for performing similar online marketing tasks.

4 Insufficient resource will be devoted to planning and executing e-marketing and there is likely to be a lack of specific specialist e-marketing skills will make it difficult to respond to competitive threats effectively.

5 Insufficient customer data is collected online as part of relationship building and this data is not integrated well with existing systems.

6 Efficiencies available through online marketing will be missed, for example lower communications costs and enhanced conversion rates in customer acquisition and retention campaigns.

7 Opportunities for applying online marketing tools such as search marketing or e-mail marketing will be missed or the execution may be inefficient if the wrong resources are used or marketers do not have the right tools.

8 Changes required to internal IT systems by different groups will not be prioritized accordingly.

9 The results of online marketing are not tracked adequately on a detailed or high-level basis.

10 Senior management support of e-marketing is inadequate to drive what often needs to be a major strategic initiative.

What should an e-marketing plan contain?

Clearly e-marketing plans should be informed by, and integrate with the objectives and strategies of the marketing plan. Plans should be integrated such that developing the e-marketing plan may give insights that result in the other plans being updated. Smith and Chaffey (2005) use the SOSTAC® framework to suggest an approach to e-marketing planning, and a similar approach will be adopted here. SOSTAC stands for: Situation, Objectives and Strategy, Tactics, Action and Control.

When developing a plan, it should be remembered that e-marketing strategy is a channel marketing strategy which defines how a company should set channel-specific objectives and develop a differential channel-proposition and channel-specific communications consistent with the characteristics of the channel and consumer usage of it. The e-marketing strategy determines the strategic significance of the Internet relative to other communications channels which are used to communicate directly with customers at different customer touchpoints. Some organizations such as low-cost airlines will decide to primarily use virtual channels such as the website and e-mail marketing for

delivering services and communicating with customers. Others may follow a strategy where the use of face-to-face, phone or direct mail communications remain important.

So the focus of e-marketing strategy is decisions about how to use the digital channels to support existing marketing strategies and how to exploit its strengths and manage its weaknesses and to use it in conjunction with other channels as part of a multi-channel marketing strategy. This multi-channel marketing strategy defines how different marketing channels should integrate and support each other in terms of their proposition development and communications based on their relative merits for the customer and the company.

Situation analysis

Situation analysis is the first part of the e-marketing plan. It explains 'where are we now?' This includes analysis internally within the organization, and externally, of the business environment. These traditional analytical areas should also be assessed from an e-marketing perspective as follows:

- *KPIs*: Key Performance Indicators which identify the business success criteria, results and performance against targets and benchmarks.
- *SWOT analysis*: Identifying e-marketing specific internal Strengths, and Weaknesses, as well as external Opportunities and Threats. For instance are resources adequate, what are the SWOT elements for the current online presence compared with competitors.
- *PEST*: Political, Economic, Social and Technological variables that shape your marketplace. Legal constraints on e-marketing are particularly significant in controlling use of customer data for direct marketing, for example through e-mail and the introduction of new laws should be carefully monitored.
- *Customers*: How many are online, how many prefer different platforms such as iTV and mobile or wireless? Are there new channel segments emerging?
- *Competitors*: Who are they? What is their online proposition? How successful are they online? Are there new online adversaries?
- *Distributors*: They are new, online, intermediaries emerging while old offline distributors being wiped out (disintermediation)? What are the potential channel conflicts?

Naturally, the KPIs and marketplace dynamic will vary according to the type of online presence. Four of the major different types of online presence of which most sites have some components are:

1 *Transactional e-commerce site*: Stage models as described above. Examples: A car manufacturer such as Vauxhall (www.buypower.vauxhall.co.uk) or retailers such as Tesco (www.tesco.com).
2 *Services oriented relationship building website*: For companies such as professional services companies, online transactions are inappropriate. Through time these sites will develop increasing information depth and question and answer facilities. Examples: PricewaterhouseCooper (www.pwcglobal.com), Accenture (www.accenture.com) and Arthur Andersen KnowledgeSpace (www.knowledgespace.com).
3 *Brand building site*: These are intended to support the offline brand by developing an online experience of the brand. They are typical for low-value, high volume Fast Moving Consumer Goods (FMCG brands). Examples: Tango (www.tango.com), Guinness (www.guinness.com).
4 *Portal site*: Providing a gateway to other web content. Examples: Yahoo! (www.yahoo.com) and Vertical Net (www.e-consultancy.com).

External analysis

We will concentrate on the micro-environment factors of customers (demand analysis), competitors and distributors.

Demand analysis

For customers, market research should identify which customers are online – what are their profiles in terms of geo-demographics and for B2B their position in the decision making unit. To build demand estimates, we need to know the proportion of customers in each market and segment who:

1 *Have access to different channels*: Compilations show that e-channel adoption still varies markedly by media type and media. Important trends are the increased use of broadband, adoption of 3G for mobiles and the increase in digital TV.
2 *Are influenced by using which channel or channels?*: Although the proportion of e-commerce transactions for all purchases is low, the role of the Internet in influencing purchase is significant for high involvement purchases such as financial services, holidays or cars. For example, it is now estimated that nearly three quarters of the purchasers of new cars in some western

countries will research the purchase online even though the proportion purchasing entirely online is only in single figures. Understanding the reach of a website and its role in influencing purchase is clearly important in setting e-marketing budgets.
3 *Purchase using which channel or channels?*: The propensity to purchase online is dependent on different variables over which the marketer has relatively little control. However, factors which affect the propensity to purchase can be estimated for different types of products. De Kare-Silver (2000) suggests factors that should be considered include product characteristics, familiarity and confidence and consumer attributes. Typical results from the evaluation are: Groceries (27/50), Mortgages (15/50), Travel (31/50) and Books (38/50). De Kare-Silver states that any product scoring over 20 has good potential, since the score for consumer attributes is likely to increase through time. Given this, he suggests companies will regularly need to review the score for their products.

It is also important to understand the barriers and motivations that affect the use of digital media by consumers. The reasons, aspirations and expectations can then be reflected in your communications.

Competitor analysis

For competitors, benchmarking will reveal how digital media are being exploited. Criteria include ease of use, communication of value proposition, customer confidence, for example availability, depth, and breadth of customer service options, including phone, e-mail, and branch locations, onsite resources, relationship services and overall cost. The success of different companies in, and out of sector in achieving online sales should also be benchmarked.

Intermediary analysis

For distributors and intermediaries, a key influence of the Internet is its impact on channel structures. These marketplace phenomena should be assessed and then evaluated as part of strategy:

● *Disintermediation*: The removal of intermediaries such as distributors or brokers that formerly linked a company to its customers. A car manufacturer selling direct to customers rather than through a dealership is an example of this.

E-commerce maturity stage	Strategy process and performance improvement process	Structure: Location of e-commerce	Senior management buy-in	Marketing integration	Online marketing focus
Stage 1 Unplanned	Limited	Uncontrolled experimentation	Limited	Discrete	Content: Brochureware
Stage 2 Diffuse management	Low-level objectives	Diffuse	Aware	Common initiatives	Traffic: visitor acquisition
Stage 3 Centralized management	Specific organizational objectives	Centralized	Involved	Annual planning collaboration	Conversion and customer experience
Stage 4 Decentralized operations	Refined online channel improvement	Decentralized	Driving performance	Partnership	Retention
Stage 5 Integrated and optimized	Integrated multi-channel improvement	Integrated	Integral	Complete	Whole life cycle optimization

Figure 25.2 Stage model for e-channel capabilities

- *Reintermediation*: The creation of new intermediaries between customers and suppliers providing services such as supplier search and product evaluation. Many new brokers offering discounted cars have had a significant impact on the car market.
- *Countermediation*: A brand becomes part of an online intermediary through purchase, partnering or creation. Here an existing player or players form a new intermediary to compete against new intermediaries.

It is important for marketers to understand the dynamics and power of new and online intermediaries in any online marketplace and to create an e-marketplace map. The main intermediary types I identify when understanding the online marketplace are:

- Mainstream news media sites or portals (traditional, e.g. NYT.com, FT.co or Times or Pureplay, e.g. Google news an aggregator).
- Niche/vertical media sites, for example e-consultancy, ClickZ.com in B2B.
- Aggregators/price comparison sites, for example Kelkoo, Shopping.com, uSwitch, etc.
- Superaffiliates – second tier aggregators who are more focused than those above, but can be significant in any marketplace. Affiliates gain revenue from a merchant they refer traffic to using a commission-based arrangement based on

the proportion of sale or a fixed amount. They are important in e-retail markets, accounting for tens of percent of sales.
- Niche affiliates – typically individuals.

Internal analysis

Internal analysis involves assessment of the current status of e-marketing implementation. Figure 25.2 shows a stage model I developed for an E-consultancy (2005) report on managing an e-commerce team which can be used to assess evolution of e-marketing capabilities.

The internal analysis also looks at KPIs of e-marketing. Common KPIs used to assess online the significance of e-marketing activities include traditional measures such as:

- Enquiries
- Sales
- Market share
- ROI (return on investment)

Other KPIs are specific to e-marketing:

- *Online revenue contribution* (see section on objective setting).
- *Unique visitors*: The number of separate, individual visitors who visit the site (typically over a month).
- Total numbers of *sessions* or *visits* to a website (note that 'hits' are a spurious measure. Since when a web page is downloaded to the PC, a number of separate data transfers or hits take

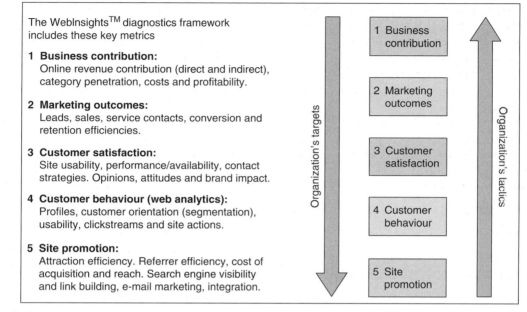

The WebInsights™ diagnostics framework includes these key metrics

1 Business contribution:
Online revenue contribution (direct and indirect), category penetration, costs and profitability.

2 Marketing outcomes:
Leads, sales, service contacts, conversion and retention efficiencies.

3 Customer satisfaction:
Site usability, performance/availability, contact strategies. Opinions, attitudes and brand impact.

4 Customer behaviour (web analytics):
Profiles, customer orientation (segmentation), usability, clickstreams and site actions.

5 Site promotion:
Attraction efficiency. Referrer efficiency, cost of acquisition and reach. Search engine visibility and link building, e-mail marketing, integration.

Organization's targets

1 Business contribution

2 Marketing outcomes

3 Customer satisfaction

4 Customer behaviour

5 Site promotion

Organization's tactics

Figure 25.3   Key metrics indicating the efficiency of web marketing in attracting and converting visitors to customers

place, usually one for each HTML and graphics file. Marketers should measure *page impressions* because they are a real measure of customer traffic to your site and for an advertiser, this equates with other familiar measures such as 'opportunities to view'). Attraction efficiency (Figure 25.3) indicates the proportion of your target audience you attract to site or its reach.

- *Repeat visits:* Average number of visits per individual. Total number of sessions divided by the number of unique visitors. Update your site more often and people come back more often. *Cookies* can help track repeat visits.
- *Duration:* Average length of time visitors spend on your site (but remember that for some areas of the site such as online sales or customer service you may want to minimize duration). A similar measure is number of pages viewed per visitor.
- Subscription rates numbers of visitors subscribing for services such as an opt-in e-mail and newsletters.
- *Conversion rates:* The percentage of visitors converting to subscribers (or becoming customers). This is critical to e-marketing, let us take an example. Say 2 per cent of 5000 visitors to a site in a month convert to 100 customers who place an order. £10 000 cost divided by 100 conversions = £100 cost per order. Now imagine you can double your conversion rate, or better still quadruple it to 8 per cent, you then get £25 cost per order. The leverage impact caused by

improved conversion rates is huge – revenues go up and percentage of marketing costs go down. Figure 25.3 provides a summary of different aspects of conversion from Chaffey (2001) which is adapted from Figure 2 in Berthon *et al.* (1998). It also highlights the importance of measuring return visitors to the site.

- Attrition rates through the online buying process.
- *Churn rates:* Percentage of subscribers withdrawing or unsubscribing.
- *Click Through Rates (CTR)* from a banner ad or web link on another site to your own.

E-marketing objectives

Objectives clarify the purpose and direction of e-marketing. Smith and Chaffey (2005) suggest there are five broad benefits, reasons or objectives of e-marketing. These can be summarized as the 5S's of e-marketing objectives. Marketers will decide whether all or only some will drive e-marketing:

1   *Sell:* Grow sales (through wider distribution to customers you cannot service offline or perhaps a wider product range than in local store, or better prices).
2   *Serve:* Add value (give customers extra benefits online: or product development in response to online dialogue).
3   *Speak:* Get closer to customers by tracking them, asking them questions, conducting online

interviews, creating a dialogue, monitoring chat rooms, learning about them.

4 *Save*: Save costs – of service, sales transactions and administration, print and post. Can you reduce transaction costs and therefore either make online sales more profitable? Or use cost savings to enable you to cut prices, which in turn could enable you to generate greater market share?

5 *Sizzle*: Extend the brand online. Reinforce brand values in a totally new medium. The Web scores very highly as a medium for creating brand awareness and recognition.

Specific objectives are created for each. Consider Sales – a typical objective might be:

> To grow the business with online sales e.g. to generate at least 10% of sales online. Within 6 months.

Or

> To generate an extra £100 000 worth of sales online by December.

These objectives can be further broken down for example to achieve £100 000 of online sales means you have to generate 1000 online customers spending on average £100 in the time period. If, say, your conversion rate of visitors to customers was a high 10 per cent then this means you have to generate 10 000 visitors to your site.

Objectives should also be set for the percentage of customers who are reached or influenced by each channel (*indirect online revenue contribution* or brand awareness in the target market). The online revenue contribution should also consider *cannibalization* – are online sales achieved at the expense of traditional channels? Another major online objective might be to consolidate relationships and increase loyalty from 50 to 75 per cent among a high-spending customer segments during the year.

Strategies

Strategy summarizes objectives and establishes how they will be achieved. Many of the key questions that an e-marketing strategy should answer are common to those for a marketing strategy, namely:

- Which *Segments*, and selected *Target Markets* are being targeted.
- *Positioning (P)* is a fundamental part of the overall customer proposition or offering for example what exactly is the product, its price and perceived value in the marketplace.

- Source of differentiation – what is the value proposition?
- Which access platforms should e-marketing be achieved through. For most organizations websites or e-mail marketing will be appropriate, but mobile marketing or interactive TV (iTV) are further options? For each platform, different stages of online services should be identified for future rollout as discussed in the section on situation analysis. For example, what level of interaction onsite – brochure, two-way interactive sales support, online sales or full e-CRM?
- Should new or existing products be sold into all existing segments and markets, or can specific or new segments and markets should be targeted?
- What resources are appropriate? For example, what is the split between online and offline e-marketing and budget and how are resources split between website design, website service and website traffic generation.

In this section some of the key strategic e-marketing decisions are outlined based on more detailed discussion in Chaffey *et al*. (2006):

Decision 1: Market and product development strategies

The Ansoff matrix is a useful analytic tool for assessing online strategies for manufacturers and retailers. It can help companies think about how online channels can support their marketing objectives, but also suggest innovative use of these channels to deliver new products and more markets. Options to review are summarized in Figure 25.4.

Decision 2: Business and revenue models

Evaluating new models is important since if companies do not review opportunities to innovate then competitors and new entrants certainly will. Andy Grove of Intel famously said: '*Only the paranoid will survive*' alluding to the need to review new revenue opportunities and competitor innovations. A willingness to test and experiment with new business models is also required. New revenue models, for a publisher, for example can include:

- advertising (on a fixed, cost per ad viewed or cost per click based);
- affiliate revenue (based on sales resulting from a site visit);

Market development strategies	Diversification strategies
Use Internet for targeting:	• Using the Internet to support:
• New geographic markets	• Diversification into related businesses
• New customer segments	• Diversification into unrelated businesses
	• Upstream integration (with suppliers)
	• Downstream integration (with intermediaries)
Market penetration strategies	**Product development strategies**
Use Internet for:	Use Internet for:
• Market share growth – compete more effectively online	• Adding value to existing products
• Customer loyalty improvement – migrate existing customers online and add value to existing products, services and brand	• Developing digital products (new delivery/usage models)
• Customer value improvement – increase customer profitability by decreasing cost to serve and increase purchase or usage frequency and quantity	• Changing payment models (subscription, per use, bundling)
	• Increasing product range (especially e-retailers)

*(Vertical axis: **Market growth** — New markets / Existing markets; Horizontal axis: **Product growth** — Existing products / New products)*

Figure 25.4   Using the Internet to support different growth strategies

- Pay Per View and bundling models;
- subscription models;
- e-mail list, data and audience research services.

Companies at the bleeding edge of technology such as Google and Yahoo! constantly innovate through acquiring other companies and internal research and development (Witness Google Labs (http://labs.google.com) and Yahoo! Research (http://research.google.com)).

Decision 3: Target marketing strategy

Deciding on which markets to target is a key strategic consideration for Internet marketing strategy in the same way it is key to marketing strategy. For e-channels, we select segments for targeting online that are most attractive in terms of growth and profitability. These may be similar or different according to groups targeted offline. Some examples of customer segments that are targeted online include:

- *the most profitable customers* – using the Internet to provide tailored offers to the top 20 per cent of customers by profit may result in more repeat business and cross sales;

- *larger companies (B2B)* – an extranet could be produced to service these customers, and increase their loyalty;
- *smaller companies (B2B)* – large companies are traditionally serviced through sales representatives and account managers, but smaller companies may not warrant the expense of account managers. However, the Internet can be used to reach smaller companies more cost effectively. The number of smaller companies that can be reached in this way may be significant, so although individual revenue of each one is relatively small, the collective revenue achieved through Internet servicing can be large;
- *particular members of the buying unit (B2B)* – the site should provide detailed information for different interests which supports the buying decision, for example, technical documentation for users of products, information on savings from e-procurement for IS or purchasing managers and information to establish the credibility of the company for decision makers;
- *customers who are difficult to reach using other media* – an insurance company looking to target younger drivers could use the Web as a vehicle for this;

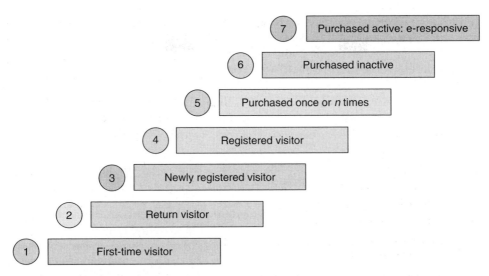

Figure 25.5   Customer lifecycle segmentation

- *customers who are brand loyal* – services to appeal to brand loyalists can be provided to support them in their role as advocates of a brand;
- *customers who are not brand loyal* – conversely, incentives, promotion and a good level of service quality could be provided by the website to try and retain such customers.

The segmentation and targeting approach used by e-retailers is based on five main elements which in effect are layered on top of each other.

1   *Identify customer lifecycle groups*: Figure 25.5 illustrates this approach. As visitors use online services they can potentially pass through seven or more stages. Once companies have defined these groups and setup the customer relationship management infrastructure to categorize customers in this way, they can then deliver targeted messages, either by personalized on-site messaging or through e-mails that are triggered automatically due to different rules.
2   *Identify customer profile characteristics*: This is a traditional segmentation based on the type of customer. For B2C e-retailers this will include age, sex and geography. For B2B companies, this will include size of company and the industry sector or application they operate in.
3   *Identify behaviour in response and purchase*: As customers progress through the lifecycle by analysis of their database, they will be able to build up a detailed response and purchase history which considers the details of recency, frequency, monetary value and category of products purchased.
4   *Identify multi-channel behaviour (channel preference)*: Regardless of the enthusiasm of the company for online channels, some customers will prefer using online channels and others will prefer traditional channels. Customers that prefer online channels can be targeted mainly by online communications such as e-mail, while customers who prefer traditional channels can be targeted by traditional communications such as direct mail or phone. We can use 'right channelling' to target customers using the combination of channels which is most efficient for the organization and consumer.
5   *Message tone, style and offer preference*: In a similar manner to channel preference, customers will respond differently to different types of message and offer. Some may like a more rational appeal in which case a detailed e-mail explaining the benefits of the offer may work best. Others will prefer an emotional appeal based on images and with warmer, less formal copy.

Decision 4: Positioning and differentiation strategy

Companies can position their products relative to competitor offerings according to four main variables: product quality, service quality, price and fulfilment time.

Strategies should review the extent to which increases in product and service quality can be balanced against variations in price and fulfilment time. Chaston (2000) argues that there are four options for strategic focus to position a company in the online marketplace. It is evident that these are related to the different elements of Deise *et al.* (2000). He says that online these should build on existing strengths, and can use the online facilities to enhance the positioning as follows:

- *Product performance excellence*: Enhance by providing online product customization.
- *Price performance excellence*: Use the facilities of the Internet to offer favourable pricing to loyal customers or to reduce prices where demand is low (e.g. British Midland Airlines uses auctions to sell underused capacity on flights).
- *Transactional excellence*: A site such as that of software and hardware e-tailer dabs.com offers transactional excellence through combining pricing information with dynamic availability information on products, listing number in stock, number on order and when they are expected.
- *Relationship excellence*: Personalization features to enable customers to review sales order history and place repeat orders. An example is RS Components (www.rswww.com).

The online value proposition

In an e-marketing context the differential advantage and positioning can be clarified and communicated by developing an online value proposition (OVP). Developing an OVP, involves:

- Developing messages which:
  - reinforce core brand proposition and credibility,
  - communicate what a visitor can get from an online brand that:
    - they cannot get from the brand offline?
    - they cannot get from competitors or intermediaries?
- Communicating these messages at all appropriate online and offline customer touch points in different levels of detail from strap lines to more detailed content on the website or in print.

Companies such as Dell, Kelkoo and Expedia have clearly defined value propositions.

Decision 5: Multi-channel distribution strategy

Decisions 5 and 6 relate to channel prioritization which assesses the strategic significance of the Internet and e-mail relative to other communications channels. In making this prioritization it is helpful to distinguish between customer communications channels and distribution channels.

Distribution channels refers to flow of products from a manufacturer or service provider to the end customer. These may be direct-to-consumer channels or more often, intermediaries such as retailers are involved. Internet distribution channel priorities have been summarized by Gulati and Garino (2000) as 'getting the right mix of bricks and clicks'. The relationships and partnering potential with different forms of online intermediary can be reviewed at this point.

Decision 6: Multi-channel communications strategy

As part of creating an Internet marketing strategy, it is vital to define how the Internet integrates with other inbound communications channels used to process customer enquiries and orders and outbound channels which use direct marketing to encourage retention and growth or deliver customer service messages. For a retailer, these channels include in-store, contact-centre, web and outbound direct messaging used to communicate with prospects and customers. Some of these channels may be broken down further into different media – for example, the contact-centre may involve inbound phone enquiries, e-mail enquiries or real-time chat. Outbound direct messaging may involve direct mail, e-mail media or web-based personalization.

- The multi-channel communications strategy must review different types of customer contact with the company and then determine how online channels will best support these channels. The main types of customer contact and corresponding strategies will typically be:
- Inbound sales-related enquiries (customer acquisition or conversion strategy).
- Inbound customer-support enquiries (customer service strategy).
- Outbound contact strategy (customer retention and development strategy).

For each of these strategies, the most efficient mix and sequence of media (a multi-channel touch or contact strategy) to support the business objectives must be determined. Typically the short-term objective will be conversion to outcome such as sale or satisfactorily resolved service enquiry in the shortest possible time with the minimum cost. However, longer-terms objectives of customer loyalty and growth also need to be considered. If the initial experience is efficient, but unsatisfactory to the customer, then they may not remain a customer!

Table 25.1	Online executions of different communications tools
Communications tool	*Online executions*
1 Advertising	Display ads, pay per click marketing, search engine optimization
2 Selling	Virtual sales staff, affiliate marketing, web rings, links
3 Sales promotion	Incentives, rewards, loyalty schemes
4 PR	Online editorial, ezines, newsletters, discussion groups, portals
5 Sponsorship	Sponsoring an online event, site or service
6 Direct mail	Opt-in e-mail and web response
7 Exhibitions	Virtual exhibitions
8 Merchandizing	Shopping malls, e-tailing, the interface
9 Packaging	Real packaging is displayed online and refers to websites
10 Word-of-mouth	Viral, affiliate marketing, e-mail a friend, web rings, links

Decision 7: Online communications budget and mix

The decision on the amount of spending on online communications and the mix between the different communications techniques such as search engine marketing, e-mail marketing and online advertising is closely related to the previous one. Varianini and Vaturi (2000) suggest that many e-commerce failures have resulted from poor control of media spending. They suggest that many companies spend too much on poorly targeted communications. They suggest the communications mix should be optimized to minimize the cost of acquisition of customers. It can also be suggested that optimization of the conversion to action onsite is important to the success of marketing. The strategy will also fail if the site design, quality of service and marketing communications are not effective in converting visitors to prospects or buyers. Traditional control techniques such as adopting a defined allowable cost per action (or acquisition), lifetime value modelling and media mix optimization can assist here.

In addition to campaign-based e-communications we also need continuous e-communications. Organizations need to ensure that there is sufficient investment in continuous online marketing activities such as search marketing, e-newsletters, affiliate marketing and sponsorship.

Decision 8: Organizational capabilities

A useful framework for reviewing an organization's capabilities to implement Internet marketing strategy is shown in Table 25.1 applied to Internet marketing. This 7S framework was developed by McKinsey consultants in the 1980s and summarized by Waterman *et al.* (1980).

Tactics

Tactics are the details of strategy. E-marketing tactics define the different e-marketing tools to be used and their sequence or stages. The main tools used to implement the e-marketing tactics are:

1 The website and ideally, an integrated database.
2 Customer relationship management tools, principally the integrated database.
3 Opt-in e-mail, again linked to the CRM database.
4 Online communication tools such as banner advertising, sponsorship, links and PR.
5 Traditional offline communication tools such as advertising and PR.

One approach to defining e-marketing tactics, which we will use here, is to re-examine the options that e-marketing provides through these tools for varying the marketing mix. We will focus on the '4Ps' of Product, Price, Place, Promotion defined around the start of the 1960s by Canadian Jerome McCarthy (McCarthy, 1960) together with the extended mix of the American academics, Booms and Bitner (1981). They considered the extra Ps crucial in the delivery of services – people, processes and physical evidence.

Some feel that for interactive marketing Pepper and Rogers 5Is (Pepper and Rogers, 1997) should replace the 7Ps in the information age. The 5Is do not supplant the 7Ps but rather are complementary to it since the 5Is defines the process needed, whereas the 7Ps are the variables which the marketer controls.

These are:

1 *Identification* – customer specifics.
2 *Individualization* – tailored for lifetime purchases.
3 *Interaction* – dialogue to learn about customers' needs.
4 *Integration* – of knowledge of customers into all parts of the company.
5 *Integrity* – develop trust through non-intrusion as in permission marketing.

Although the mix provides a useful framework for marketers, other factors also need to be considered. Decisions on the mix are not made until marketing strategy first determines target markets and required brand positionings. New marketers also need to know how to manage alliances or partnerships and build customer relationships to build lifetime value through using customer knowledge stored in databases. We will now review how the implications of the new media for the different elements of the marketing mix.

Product

The online world offers a host of new opportunities and prompts these product-related questions:

- What benefits do you deliver to your customers?
- Can they be delivered online?
- What other benefits might your customers like?
- Can these benefits be delivered online?
- What is your business? Can it be delivered online?

Ghosh (1998) suggested companies should consider how to modify product and add digital value to customers. These are huge questions that can reshape your whole business. Ghosh talks about developing new products or adding digital value to customers. He urged companies to ask:

- Can I afford additional information on or transaction services to my existing customer base?
- Can I address the needs of new customer segments by repackaging my current information assets or by creating new business propositions using the Internet?
- Can I use my ability to attract customers to generate new sources of revenue such as advertising or sales of complementary products?
- Will my current business be significantly harmed by other companies providing some of the value I currently offer?

He suggests you need to analyse each feature of your product or service and ask how can each of these features be improved or adapted online? Developing these online services should be customer-led by asking what information do my ideal target customers seek? 'How can I excel at giving them this online?' Communities of customers can be tapped into to help answer this question.

The different elements of extended product can also be highlighted or delivered online.

Often extended product contributes greatly to quality. Think about these aspects of extended product which can be highlighted or delivered online:

- Endorsements
- Awards
- Testimonies
- Customer lists
- Customer comments
- Warranties
- Guarantees
- Money back offers
- Customer service (see People and Process).

Extended product also includes incorporating tools to help users during their use of the product. For example, engineers can be provided with technical diagrams and updates on regulations to assist them with their work.

Price

The changes to pricing and price models introduced by the advent of the Internet have been significant.

New buying models require new pricing approaches which have forced marketers to radically rethink their pricing strategies. There have been many experiments, some successful, others less so. Examples include customer unions such as LetsBuyit (www.letsbuyit.com) and Name your price services such as Priceline (www.priceline.com), transparent pricing and global sourcing (particularly by giant procurement mergers like Ford and Chrysler). Kelkoo.com has survived from the Dot.com days and is now part of Kelkoo.

A growth in competition is caused partly by global suppliers and partly by globalized customers searching via the web to add further pressure on prices. Many online companies enjoy lower margins with more efficient web enabled databases and processes which cut out the middleman and his margin. These online cost savings which can be passed to customers to give further downward pressure.

Pricing is also under pressure through the trend towards *commoditization*. Once buyers can (a) specify exactly what they want (b) identify suppliers – they can run *reverse auctions*. *Price transparency* is another factor. As prices are published on the web, buyer comparison of prices is more rapid than ever before. Storing prices digitally in databases also enables shopping bots to find the best price. This customer empowerment creates further downward pressure on prices.

Prices are complex, options for the price package include:

- Basic price
- Discounts
- Add-ons and extra products and services
- Guarantees and warranties
- Refund policies
- Order cancellation terms
- Revoke action buttons.

A final consideration is the move from fixed prices to rental, and leasing prices. Cars, computers, flight simulators and now even music can be hired or leased.

Place

Place involves the place of purchase, distribution and in some cases, consumption. Some products exploit all three aspects of Place online, for example digitizable products such as software, media and entertainment. Esther Dyson has drawn this analogy with the electronic marketspace, she says:

> You put coke machines in places where you think people might want to drink a Coke. On the Internet you put Amazon buttons in places where there might be people inclined to buy books.

But it is not just digitizable products and services – all products and services can extend themselves online by considering their online representation for place of purchase and distribution. Other products, such as cars, are partially sold online and eventually bought offline using *mixed-mode buying* where some activities of the buying process are completed offline and some online.

Offline marketing communications and online marketing communications through the website should support channel switching as shown in Figure 25.6. Common buying modes include:

- *Online purchase*: Some customers want to search, compare and buy online. Does your website accommodate all stages of the buying process? Few products can be delivered online so fulfilment is usually offline.

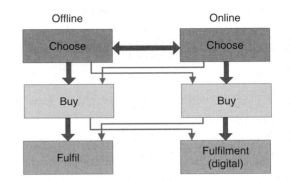

Figure 25.6   Alternative buying modes

- *Online browse and offline purchase*: Mixed-mode buying is when customers like to browse, look or research, *online* and eventually purchase *offline* in a real store or in a real meeting. Some of these customers might like to browse online but purchase via fax or telephone because of security and privacy issues. Does your site have fax forms and telephone numbers for placing orders or taking further enquiries? Does your site integrate with other communications channels? Some sites also have '*call back facilities*' which allow visitors to request a telephone call from a sales staff to complete the purchase.

Here are a few examples of other concepts of place which have been changed online:

- *Disintermediation*: This is removing the middleman to deal direct with customers instead of through agents, distributors and wholesalers. Note that this can create channel conflict as middlemen feel the squeeze. For example, Hewlett Packard (HP) sell a lot of equipment to hospitals. But, when hospitals started going directly to the HP site for firstly information and then secondly to place orders, it posed a big question: do we pay commission to the sales representative for this?
- *Re-intermediation*: This is the emergence of new types of middlemen who are brokers such as Bizrate that unite buyers with sellers.
- *Infomediation*: A related concept where middlemen that hold data or information to benefit customers and suppliers.
- *Channel confluence*: This has occurred where distribution channels start to offer the same deal to the end customer.
- *Peer-to-peer services*: Music swapping services such as Napster and Gnutella opened up an entirely new approach to music distribution with both supplier and middleman removed completely

providing a great threat, but also opportunity to the music industry.

- *Affiliation:* Affiliate programmes can turn customers into sales people. Many consider sales people as part of distribution. Others see them as part of the communications mix.

Excellent distribution requires a deep understanding of when and where customers want products and services. Partnership skills are also required as much distribution is externally sourced whether order fulfilment, warehousing, logistics or transport.

Promotion

The Internet can be used to extend and integrate all communications tools as summarized in Table 25.2.

Although websites can be considered a separate communications tool, they are, perhaps, best thought of as an integrator of all 10 tools shown in the table.

The following are offered as guidelines for effective promotion tactics:

1 *Mix:* E-marketers need to mix the promotional mix. This involves looking at the strengths and weaknesses of the promotional tools in the context of an organization and deciding on the optimum mix for different online promotional tools.
2 *Integration:* Both online and offline communications must be integrated. All communications should support the overall positioning and Online or Internet Value Proposition which the e-marketing strategy defines. A single consistent message and a single integrated database are needed – which recognizes and remembers customers' names and needs regardless of which access devices are being used (TV, telephone or PC).
3 *Creativity:* Today's marketer can exploit the creative opportunities presented by the Internet. For example, sending opt-in e-mails that make customers sit up and take notice, developing an online virtual exhibition or seminar.
4 *Interaction:* Next comes the extra layer of creativity – interaction. This enhances the experience and deepens the communications impact (and it also collects customer data).
5 *Globalization:* Then of course there are the added complications of a global audience. Websites open your window to the world. When global audience

look in (to your site) they may not like what they see.
6 *Resourcing:* The online communications opportunity is infinite. However resources to design and maintain the content, interactions and the database are not infinite. Resources are also needed to service customer enquiries whether online or offline (Table 25.3).

People

In services marketing, people or staff, are considered a crucial element of the marketing mix. As more products add online services to enhance their offerings 'People' become more important. In an online context, 'People' corresponds to customer service whether delivered through the website as 'customer self-service' or through interaction with staff. Automated self-service options include:

- *Autoresponders:* These automatically generate a response when a company e-mails an organization, or submits an online form.
- *E-mail notification:* Automatically generated by a companies' systems to update customers on the status of their order, for example, order received, item now in stock, order dispatched.
- *Call-back facility:* Customers fill in their phone number on a form and specify a convenient time to be contacted. Dialling from a representative in the call centre occurs automatically at the appointed time and the company pays which is popular.
- *Frequently Asked Questions (FAQ):* For these, the art is in compiling and categorizing the questions so customers can easily find (a) the question and (b) a helpful answer.
- *Onsite search engines:* These help customers find what they are looking for quickly are popular when available. Site maps are a related feature.
- *Virtual assistants:* They come in varying degrees of sophistication and usually help to guide the customer through a maze of choices.

Customer contact strategies also need to be considered we need to ask whether all customers want to conduct all their interactions online. Many companies use an inbound contact strategy of customer choice or *customer preferred channel* – offering customers a range of contact options. But a more cost-effective contact strategy may involve steering customers towards using the web as a contact tool.

Of course staff need to be trained and motivated whether they man the website, the telephones, the field sales, the reception. What

Table 25.2 The 7S strategic framework and its application to digital marketing management

Element of 7S model	Relevance to Internet marketing capability	Key issues
Strategy	The contribution of digital marketing in influencing and supporting organizations' strategy	• Gaining appropriate budgets and demonstrating/delivering value and ROI from budgets. Annual planning approach. • Techniques for using Internet marketing to impact organization strategy. • Techniques for aligning Internet marketing strategy with organizational and marketing strategy.
Structure	The modification of organizational structure to support Internet marketing.	• Integration of team with other management, marketing (corporate communications, brand marketing, direct marketing) and IT staff. • Use of cross-functional teams and steering groups. • Insourcing versus outsourcing.
Systems	The development of specific processes, procedures or information systems to support Internet marketing.	• Campaign planning approach integration. • Managing/sharing customer information. • Managing content quality. • Unified reporting of digital marketing effectiveness. • In-house versus external best-of-breed versus external integrated technology solutions.
Staff	The breakdown of staff in terms of their background, age and sex and characteristics such as IT versus marketing, use of contractors/consultants.	• Insourcing versus outsourcing. • Achieving senior management buy-in/involvement with digital marketing. • Staff recruitment and retention. Virtual working. • Staff development and training.
Style	Includes both the way in which key managers behave in achieving the organization's goals and the cultural style of the organization as a whole.	• Relates to role of the Internet marketing team in influencing strategy – is it dynamic and influential or conservative and looking for a voice.

Table 25.2   Continued

Element of 7S model	Relevance to Internet marketing capability	Key issues
Skills	Distinctive capabilities of key staff, but can be interpreted as specific skill-sets of team members.	• Staff skills in specific areas: supplier selection, project management, content management, specific e-marketing approaches (search engine marketing, affiliate marketing, e-mail marketing, online advertising).
Superordinate goals	The guiding concepts of the Internet marketing organization which are also part of shared values and culture. The internal and external perception of these goals may vary.	• Improving the perception of the importance and effectiveness of the digital marketing team amongst senior managers and staff it works with (marketing generalists and IT).

Table 25.3   Summary of the strengths and weaknesses of different communications tools for promoting an online presence

Promotion technique	Main strengths	Main weaknesses
Search engine optimization (SEO) – gaining visibility in the natural listings of search engines	Large online reach – used by a high proportion of web users Highly targeted – visitors are self-selecting and have high purchase intent. Relatively low cost, but increasing competition makes it difficult to appear on the all important first pages	Works best for specialist products rather than generic products for example insurance. Cost – search engine optimization is continuous as techniques change
Paid search marketing – gaining visibility in the sponsored listings sections of search engines or their content network. Typically, a pay per click arrangement with position based on amount bid and quality score indicated by CTR and other factors	Relatively low cost compared to some offline media with low wastage and again good targeting	Setting up and managing a large number of key words and effective copy is complex and can be time consuming. Increasing competition has led to bid inflation and reduced ROI. High dependence on Google

	Table 25.3 Continued	
Promotion technique	*Main strengths*	*Main weaknesses*
Affiliate campaigns	Payment is by results (e.g. 10 per cent of sale by merchant goes to referring site)	Further payment to affiliate network manager (network override) required for large-scale campaigns. Requires micro-management for best effect. Reputation on third party sites needs to be managed
Display advertising	Does offer a direct response model but achieves brand uplift also and can extend reach beyond other techniques	Response rates have declined historically to banner blindness
Sponsorship	Most effective if low-cost, long-term co-branding arrangement with synergistic site. Sponsorship of tools on media sites and tenancies possible also. Targeting by site and behavioural targeting possible	Relatively difficult to track brand impact. Traditionally expensive and low-response compared to search marketing, but new ad formats and pricing models such as ad networks have improved this
E-mail marketing	Push medium – cannot be ignored in users' in-box. Can be used for direct response link to website	Requires opt-in list for effectiveness. Best for customer retention rather than acquisition with cold lists. Message diluted amongst other e-mails and spam
Viral or buzz marketing	With effective creative possible to reach a large number at relatively low cost	Risks damaging brand since unsolicited messages may be received. If 'viral agent ineffective' then poor return on investment
Online PR	Relatively low-cost vehicle for PR. Many alternatives for innovation. Can benefit SEO	Offline PR may give higher impact and reach
Traditional offline advertising (TV, print, etc.)	Larger reach than most online techniques. Greater creativity possible leading to greater impact	Targeting arguably less easy than online. Typically high cost-of-acquisition

happens if a web transaction fails and the customer calls the centre – can call centre staff access the web database to complete the transaction, or do they have to collect all the details again – a seamless, integrated contact databases is required.

Physical evidence

When buying intangible services, customers look for physical evidence to reassure them. In the offline world this includes buildings, uniforms, logos and more. In the online world the evidence is digital – primarily through websites but also through e-mail. In the online world, customers look for other cues and clues to reassure themselves about the organization.

So firstly, a reassuring sense of order is required. This means websites should be designed with a consistent look and feel that customers feel comfortable (see Site Design Chapter in Smith and Chaffey (2005)). But onsite reassurance can extend far beyond this, particularly for an e-tailer by using:

- Guarantees
- Refund policies
- Privacy policies
- Security icons
- Trade body memberships
- Awards
- Customer lists
- Customer endorsements
- Independent reviews
- News clippings

Physical evidence can also help to integrate the online and offline world. Some white goods retailers use coupons printed out online which can be redeemed for a discount at a store. This helps conversion-to-sale rates and also tracks how the online presence is impacting offline sales.

Process

Process refers to the internal and sometimes external processes, transactions and internal communications that are required to run a business.

Excellent processes are devised as part of the move towards e-business. Un-integrated e-commerce sites create problems as witnessed by US online toy stores whose websites and associated processes did not link into an information system explaining to customers when stocks were unavailable. A well-managed process integrates into the business processes and systems which, in turn, shave costs and slash inventories.

Online services and their process of production are not as visible since much of the processes operate in systems unseen by the customer. Some of the process, or system, is on view, like menus, form filling, shopping baskets, follow up e-mails and of course the interactions on websites – are all visible. It is on this part of the process and its outputs that customers will judge service.

It seems that many companies have not yet learnt how to optimize these processes – 98 per cent of potential buyers exit before they make their purchase. This suggests ordering is too complicated or confusing or, the system simply does not work smoothly.

Optimization also involves minimizing the people involved with responding to each event and providing them with right information to serve the customer. Minimizing human resources can occur through redesigning the processes and/ or automating them through technology. Processes continue beyond the sale with feedback, upselling, cross selling, product development and improvement built in as part of the processes.

Controlling tactics

Who has control of these tactics and implementation is a big question and the e-marketer must win the ownership argument. Take the website: is it controlled by marketing or by technical or some other function. Many websites actually damage the brand with their broken links, dead ends, cumbersome downloads, out-of-date content, impossible navigation and unanswered e-mails. Regular reviews should not be devoted to reviewing the latest technology but rather, they should be focused on customer reviews.

Actions

Tactics break down into actions. In fact a series of actions, for example to build a website or run an online advertising campaign. Each tactic becomes a mini project.

Each tactical e-tool requires careful planning and implementation. Whether building a website, a banner ad, an iTV ad, a viral campaign or an opt-in campaign, good project management skills and diligent attention to detail is required.

These are typical actions that may be pursued for achieving different website objectives:

1 *Traffic building actions:* To generate visits and/or traffic to your website or portal or iTV channel – you will probably be using links or banners on other sites, sponsoring other online activities, possibly using competitions or creative content ideas to generate interest. You will need creative input and a budget to buy media space.
2 *Actions to achieve customer response:* To capture user enquiries – thus turning visitors into sales prospects, capturing data, using enquiry data to analyse customer needs, plan development – you will need a response mechanism for customers to enter their data online and a database logging and processing the data as it comes in.

3 *Actions to gain sales*: For collecting sales orders: use iTV or website to generate actual sales, handle money transaction, initiate order process system.
4 *Fulfilment actions*: Efficient data transfer to warehouse to get product off shelf and into the box for despatch ... Orders might be one off products or subscription services. More software and hardware solution to implement here: ideally, dovetail into parent's existing systems used for mail order and phone order businesses – then you know the processes which are invisible to the customer have been installed, tested and proven already.
5 *e-CRM actions*: To build better relationships by creating dialogue with customers ... you might be running online polls, using rewards and competitions to secure commitment and response; you could also set up and moderate an online user group: in this way you empower customers by means of interactivity – feedback, listen to customer response and visibly act on it.

Success in all these actions requires good implementation. It is possible to have a poor strategy but to mask it with outstanding actions which bring the company success; but the best strategy in the world will achieve nothing if it is not implemented well.

Action, or implementation, also requires an appreciation of what can go wrong from cyber libel to viruses, to mail bombs, hackers and hijackers to cyber squatting and much more . . . contingency planning is required. What happens when the server goes down or a virus comes to town? What happens if one of the e-Tools is not working, or is not generating enough enquiries? Something has to be changed. A risk management approach to e-marketing is useful, this involves:

- Brainstorming a list of all the things that could go wrong.
- Assessing their impact and likelihood.
- Taking actions to minimize the risk of the most highest impact, most probable risk.
- Revising and refining according to lessons learnt.

Control

Without control mechanisms, e-marketing depends on luck. It is a bit like playing darts in the dark. How do you know if you are hitting the target or are just shooting blindly and wildly? How do you know if you are targeting the right customers? Who are they? What do they like and not like?

How many of them become repeat customers? Which e-marketing tools work best? How much does each customer actually cost you? Control also includes monitoring your competitors – what they are doing; what they are repeating; what works for them; what they are stopping doing.

To answer these questions, an e-marketing performance measurement system is required. The requirements for this have been summarized by Chaffey (2001). These are:

1 A *performance measurement process*: This defines responsibilities for the different measurement activities such as objective setting, metrics collection and reporting, analysis, diagnosis and changing e-tactics, or even strategy through corrective action if necessary.
2 A *metrics framework*: You need to determine what data you will look at each day, each week, each month, each quarter. Time has to be made for a regular review of what is working and what is not – performance diagnosis. Performance is measured against detailed targets, based on the objectives and strategy. So you need to measure the KPIs which were detailed in the section on Situation Analysis and Figure 25.3.

So where do you get this information? Many of the metrics concerning visitor behaviour are available from web analytics tools such as Webtrends and Google Analytics which summarize the click-streams of different site visitors. Collection by other information systems or processes is required for key measures such as sales, subscriptions, conversion and attrition rates. Standard practise should ensure data from the different sources is compiled into a monthly or weekly report and is delivered *and* reviewed by the right people. Decide which metrics need to be reviewed daily, weekly or monthly and by whom. The e-marketer must know which tools are working that is why 'source of' sales or enquiries is useful – if, a particular banner ad does not pull customers drop it and try another until you find one that does.

Remember all forms of measurement – or metrics – cost money – you will have to factor in budgets and resources for the following mechanisms:

- monitoring customer awareness,
- monitoring customer satisfaction,
- monitoring customer attitudes.

Other forms of control like sales analysis require only that you allocate quality time. So how do you know if things are going well? Some objectives are easy to state and easy to measure: existing recording systems in the organization will produce the data to answer the question: so if the objective is to grow sales . . . well what was the target for growth and the timetable for achieving it . . . and did you make it?

Chaffey (2001) has suggested that control should consider the effectiveness of e-marketing in five key areas shown in Figure 25.3. Each e-marketing channel such as web or iTV should be considered separately against traditional channels using this framework.

Resourcing

A further question is what to outsource. For example, do you design the website or produce content in-house or contract out to an agency? And what balance should you strike between resources allocated to building the site and those required to maintain it on a regular basis and leaving a budget for a complete review and upgrade in 3, 6 or 9 months? Other resources to consider include promotion, telesales: additional staff required or can the in-house team do it? Who will do the e-marketing research? Who is going to analyse the data you get from the customer feedback, and, who is going to produce the recommendations. Is it the existing team, or a new position? If customers show there is need to change procedures, do we have the people to react and respond?

Summary

We have seen that well-established approaches to marketing strategy and planning can be applied to e-marketing. It can be argued that the main challenge of e-marketing is assessing its future significance to an organization and resourcing accordingly. Companies that have business models and products that can be readily migrated to the Internet have already successfully turned the Internet into their main sales, distribution and service channel. However, such organizations are in the minority. For the majority, the Internet simply represents another channel to market which must be integrated, but treated in a different way with new propositions and customer touch strategies. For these organizations, the difficulty is deciding how to resource it and mastering the new e-tools.

A further challenge for e-marketers is finding the staff or agency skills needed to select and deploy new e-marketing tools which may have a short-term future. For example, at the time of writing, viral marketing and e-mail marketing are in vogue, but new legislation and negative consumer reaction may reduce their effectiveness in future. Despite these challenges, the significance of e-marketing seems likely to increase in the future, regardless of industry or sector.

References

Ansoff, H. (1957) Strategies for diversification, *Harvard Business Review*, September–October, 113–124 .

Berthon, P., Lane, N., Pitt, L. and Watson, R. (1998) The World Wide Web as an industrial marketing communications tool: models for the identification and assessment of opportunities, *Journal of Marketing Management*, **14**, 691–704.

Berryman, K., Harrington, L., Layton-Rodin, D. and Rerolle, V. (1998) Electronic commerce: three emerging strategies, *The Mckinsey Quarterly*, **1**, 152–159.

Booms, B. H. and Bitner, M. J. (1981) Marketing Strategies and Organizational Structures for Service Firms, in Donnelly, J. and George, W. (eds), *Marketing of Services*, American Marketing Association, Chicago, pp. 477–451.

Chaffey, D. (2001) Optimising e-marketing performance – a review of approaches and tools, in *Proceedings of IBM Workshop on Business Intelligence and E-marketing*, Warwick, 6th December 2001.

Chaffey, D. (2007) *E-business and E-commerce Management: Strategy, Implementation and Practice*, 3rd edn, Financial Times-Prentice Hall, Pearson Education, Harlow, UK.

Chaffey, D., Mayer, R., Johnston, K. and Ellis-Chadwick, F. (2006) *Internet Marketing: Strategy, Implementation and Practice*, 3rd edn, Financial Times/Prentice Hall, Harlow, Essex, UK.

Chaston, I. (2000) *E-marketing Strategy*, McGrawHill, UK.

Deise, M., Nowikow, C., King, P. and Wright, A. (2000) *Executive's Guide to e-business. From Tactics to Strategy*, John Wiley and Sons, New York, NY.

DTI (2000) *Business In The Information Age – International Benchmarking Study 2000*, UK Department of Trade and Industry. Based on 6000 phone interviews across businesses of all sizes in eight countries. Statistics update: Available online at: www.ukonlineforbusiness.gov.uk.

E-consultancy (2005) Managing an E-commerce team. Integrating digital marketing into your organisation. 60 page report. Author: Dave Chaffey. Available from www.e-consultancy. com.

Ghosh, S. (1998) Making business sense of the Internet, *Harvard Business Review*, March–April, 126–135.

Gulati, R. and Garino, J. (2000) Getting the right mix of bricks and clicks for your company, *Harvard Business Review*, May–June, 107–114.

Hoffman, D. L. and Novak, T. P. (1996) Marketing in hypermedia computer-mediated environments: conceptual foundations, *Journal of Marketing*, **60**, July, 50–68.

Hoffman, D. L. and Novak, T. P. (2000) How to acquire customers on the web, *Harvard Business Review*, May–June, 179–188. Available online at: http://ecommerce.vanderbilt.edu/papers. html.

Kalakota, R. and Whinston, A. (1997) *Electronic Commerce. A Manager's Guide*, Addison Wesley, Reading, MA.

de Kare-Silver, M. (2000) *eShock 2000*, Macmillan, Basingstoke, UK.

Kumar, N. (1999) Internet distribution strategies: dilemmas for the incumbent. Financial Times Special Issue on Mastering Information Management, No 7. Electronic Commerce.

Macdonald, M. (2003) Strategic marketing planning: theory and practice, in Baker, M. (ed.), *The Marketing Book*, Butterworth Heinemann, Oxford.

McDonald, M. and Wilson, H. (1999) *e-Marketing: Improving Marketing Effectiveness in a Digital World*, Financial Times Management, Pearson Education, Harlow, UK.

McCarthy, J. (1960) *Basic Marketing: A Managerial Approach*, Irwin, Homewood, IL.

O'Reilly, T. (2005) What Is Web 2. Design Patterns and Business Models for the Next Generation of Software. Web article, 30/09/2005. O'Reilly Publishing, Sebastopol, CA.

Plant, R. (2000) *E-commerce strategy*, Financial Times, Pearson Publishing, Harlow, UK.

Pepper, D. and Rogers, M. (1997) *One to One Future*, 2nd edn, Doubleday, NY.

Porter, M. (2001) Strategy and the Internet, *Harvard Business Review*, March, 62–78.

Smith, P. R. and Chaffey, D. (2005) *eMarketing eXcellence: At the Heart of eBusiness*, Butterworth Heinemann, Oxford, UK.

Timmers, P. (1999) *Electronic Commerce Strategies and Models for Business-to-Business Trading*, John Wiley series in information systems, Chichester, England.

Varianini, V. and Vaturi, D. (2000) Marketing lessons from e-failures, *McKinsey Quarterly*, **4**, 86–97.

Waterman, R. H., Peters, T. J. and Phillips, J. R. (1980) Structure is not organisation, *McKinsey Quarterly* in-house journal, McKinsey & Co., New York.

Quelch, J. and Klein, L. (1996) The Internet and international marketing, *Sloan Management Review*, Spring, 61–75.

Queree, A. (2000) *Financial Times*, Technology supplement, 1 March.

CHAPTER 26

Marketing for nonprofit organizations

ADRIAN SARGEANT

Although historians have now taught us that the idea of applying marketing ideas to key nonprofit contexts such as fundraising has a tradition spanning centuries (Mullin, 1995), it was not until the late 1960s that academic interest in the topic first began to emerge. Kotler and Levy (1969) are credited with opening the academic debate on this issue arguing that marketing had for too long been regarded as a narrow business function and rebuking both academics and practitioners for ignoring the broader relevance of our ideas. At the time their perspective gave rise to much discussion, particularly in the early 1970s (see e.g. Luck, 1969; Ferber, 1970; Lavidge, 1970). Lovelock and Weinberg (1990) argued that this early debate 'fizzled-out' in the latter part of that decade as marketers became more concerned with other variants of their discipline and in particular turned their attention to the issue of whether service marketing might be any different from the marketing of products. By the end of the 1970s, Kotler and Levy's revised definition of marketing as 'serving human needs and wants sensitively' (p. 15) was no longer controversial.

A number of landmarks have been passed since then. In 1971, the *Journal of Marketing* provided an entire issue devoted to marketing's social/environmental role and the first empirical studies then followed (see e.g. Meade, 1974; Miller, 1974). In the early 1980s, the first generic nonprofit marketing textbooks appeared, with work by

Rados (1981), Kotler and Andreasen (1982) and Lovelock and Weinberg (1989) being particularly noteworthy. Textbooks also began to appear in the specific fields of healthcare (Cooper, 1979; Frederiksen *et al.*, 1984; Kotler and Clarke, 1986) education (Kotler and Fox, 1985), the Arts (Mokwa *et al.*, 1981) the marketing of ideas (Fine, 1981) social marketing (Manoff, 1985; Kotler and Roberto, 1989) and most recently, fundraising (Sargeant and Jay, 2004).

The 1980s and early 1990s saw the introduction of a number of scholarly journals, including the generic *Journal of Nonprofit and Public Sector Marketing* and the *International Journal of Nonprofit and Voluntary Sector Marketing*. Sector-specific journals also emerged including *New Directions in Philanthropic Fundraising*, *The Journal of Educational Advancement*, *Health Marketing Quarterly*, the *Journal of Health Care Marketing*, the *Journal of Marketing for Higher Education* and the *Social Marketing Quarterly*. It was also not unusual to find journals from other disciplines printing studies from the field of nonprofit marketing. Andreasen and Kotler (2004) note studies in fields as diverse as library science, art history and hospital management.

In this brief chapter, it would be impossible to do justice to the full range of this scholarly enterprise, but nor is it necessary to do so in a volume comprising the best of current marketing thought. Many marketing ideas, models and frameworks have as much relevance to the nonprofit as the for-profit domain. Indeed, the eminent marketer scholar Shelby Hunt (1977) argued that a profit/nonprofit dichotomy would only be valuable until:

- The broadening of the marketing concept was no longer regarded as controversial.
- The nonprofit sector and the issues that must be addressed therein was completely integrated into all marketing courses and not treated as a separate subject.
- Nonprofit managers perceived their organizations as having marketing problems.
- Nonprofits established marketing departments (where appropriate) and employed marketing personnel.

Since the adoption of marketing ideas in the nonprofit arena is no longer controversial and many nonprofits now employ marketing personnel to address marketing issues, the second of Hunt's tests seems the only area of difficulty. Nonprofit marketing has yet to be properly integrated into 'mainstream' marketing courses, quite possibly because it is seen as being of less interest to the majority of marketing students and/or employers. While this may seem intuitive, it fails to reflect the pattern of the majority of modern careers, where many individuals will now work for a variety of employers and quite possibly in a variety of different contexts. The need for a broader perspective on the subject has, therefore, never been greater.

That is not to say, however, that we should necessarily agree with Shelby Hunt that it is desirable that nonprofit and for-profit marketing be merged should this latter criterion be met. While greater coverage of nonprofit marketing in generic marketing modules would be applauded, the body of knowledge that comprises nonprofit marketing is beginning to develop to a point where it would be difficult to do more than merely scratch the surface of the topic in any generic course. The bodies of knowledge, in particular, for fundraising/volunteering and social marketing are now very well developed, as is the evidence that simply applying for-profit ideas to these contexts would be inappropriate. Nonprofit organizations share a number of characteristics that make the adaptation of marketing thought essential and in this chapter we will, therefore, conduct a review of these factors and suggest how marketing tools and ideas may be adapted to make them more suitable for the nonprofit context.

We begin, however, by defining what we mean by the term 'nonprofit'.

Defining the nonprofit sector

Over the years, many authors have developed widely differing terminology for what is ostensibly the same cohort of organizations. Labels such as the third sector, independent sector, not-for-profit sector, nonprofit sector, charitable sector and voluntary sector are used with varying frequency in different countries. Unfortunately, they are all too often used interchangeably and with a rather different emphasis on meaning, making it impossible to be clear, with any degree of certainty that any two writers are addressing the same facet of society. Our first task must, therefore, be to navigate a way through this complexity.

The notion of a third sector is illustrated in Figure 26.1. The third sector is distinguished by being somehow different from either government or the private sector. All three sectors are important facets of human society and all three have a role to play in the satisfaction of human need.

The private sector or 'market' caters for the majority of human need, certainly in the developed world, matching the supply of producers with consumer demand for goods and services. This market ensures that people can obtain much of what they want and need from others at a reasonable price – or at least those with money are facilitated in doing so! Economists argue that the market works since suppliers are prevented from charging excessive prices by the knowledge that others will enter the market to cater for the need if

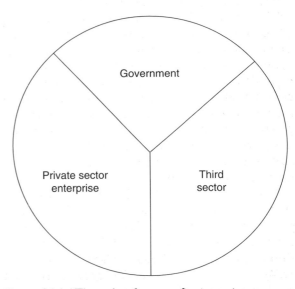

Figure 26.1   The role of nonprofits in society

they do so. Similarly, the market ensures that a multitude of different needs are met, by ensuring that a reasonable profit will be available to suppliers in each case. There is no philanthropy at work here. The market works purely on the notion of self-interest. As Smith (1776, p. 119) noted,

> It is not from the benevolence of the butcher, the brewer, or the baker that we expect our dinner, but from their regard to their own self-interest. We address ourselves, not to their humanity but to their self-love, and never talk to them of our own necessities but of their own advantages.

There are instances, however, where this market mechanism fails and where governments may be compelled to intervene to ensure that certain minimum standards of consumption are met for all individuals in a given society. During and immediately after the Second World War, many governments had to introduce food rationing to ensure that those on low incomes were not priced out of the market and starved as a consequence. Equally, the National Health Service established in the UK in the immediate post-war period had as its goal the provision of healthcare to all, irrespective of the ability to pay. The term 'public sector' is typically used to refer collectively to those institutions a society considers necessary for the basic well being of its members. Smith (1776, p. 122) defined the public sector as,

> ...those public institutions and those public works, which though they may be in the highest degree advantageous to a great society, are, however, of such a nature that the profit could never repay the expense to any individual, or small number of individuals; and which it, therefore, cannot be expected that any individual or small number of individuals, should erect or maintain.

Such institutions are both founded and funded by the State, both with its own interests in mind (to prevent civil unrest and to facilitate re-election) and those of its citizens. The funds to provide these institutions and works are derived from taxation (either local or national) and the funding each receives is a function of allocation, rather than the level of use *per se*. Thus, in State provided healthcare, it may be appropriate to allocate considerable funding to highly experimental and innovative forms of treatment that, if successful, will benefit only a very small number of people.

In the public sector, the State takes legal responsibility for institutions and the work they undertake. Indeed, as Chapman and Cowdell (1998, p. 2) note,

> it is one of the characteristics of public sector organizations that they are bounded by and operate within extensive legislation which creates an often creaking bureaucracy, much of which is concerned with the 'proper' use of public monies.

This notion of 'proper' use warrants elaboration. In a democracy, what may be deemed proper use will be subject to change. As various parties stand for election, they map out in their manifestos the role that government should play in all aspects of social life, but in particular in balancing the needs of society for the provision of public services, against the burden of the additional taxes that would be needed to pay for them. While it would be ideal for government to meet every basic human need, it is probably unrealistic to expect that wage earners in a given society would be willing to fund such comprehensive social provision through taxation and in practice a balance is, therefore, created with only the most widespread, popular and/or fundamental needs, being met in this way. Other facets of need are simply neglected.

It is within this neglected space, where neither government nor private sector enterprise is willing to engage, that the so-called third sector has a critical role to play. The Third Sector is distinctive since it comprises individuals or groups of individuals coming together to take 'voluntary' action. In other words, the sector comprises people electing to help other people resolve issues or concerns.

> The essence of voluntary action is that it is not directed or controlled by the State and that in the main it is financed by private, in contradistinction to public, funds. It embodies the sense of responsibility of private persons towards the welfare of their fellows; it is the meeting by private enterprise of a public need.
>
> (Nathan, 1952, p. 12)

It is the notion that the sector is not controlled by the State or by business that leads to the description of the sector in the US as the 'Independent Sector'. Whilst organizations in this sector may indeed be free of direct control, the difficulty with this terminology is that in financial terms, they can often be far from independent, drawing financial support from a plethora of government departments and/or private businesses. This has been a particular issue in the past 30 years as government has sought to withdraw progressively from many facets of social life leaving the third sector to shoulder the burden (albeit with support from often large government grants).

The fact that the sector occupies this third space means that the activities it undertakes can be quite unique. Third sector or 'voluntary sector' organizations often deal with local issues, politically unpopular issues, or with facets of life that attract little interest from politicians, often because few votes hang on the issue. Nevertheless, these can be critical issues for a society to address and the need is none the less pressing simply because the state or private sector enterprise fails to take an interest. In the UK alone, there are estimated to be well over 500 000 voluntary organizations, the label emphasizing the non-compulsory nature of participation.

The term 'charity' is also in common usage. Under English law, this has a very specific meaning and applies to that small subset of organizations whose work is considered so desirable by the State that a number of tax concessions are conferred to make it easier for these organizations to operate. Charities were first recognized in the Charitable Uses Act of 1601, the preamble to which delineated the following legitimate objects of charity:

> Some for the Relief of aged, impotent and poore people, some for Maintenance of sicke and maymed Souldiers and Marriners, Schooles of Learninge, Free Schooles and Schollers in Universities, some for Repair of Bridges, Ports, Havens, Causewaies, Churches, Seabanks and Highwaies, some for Educacion and preferment of Orphans, some for or towards Reliefe Stocke or Maintenance of Howses of Correccion, some for Mariages of poore Maides, some for Supportacion, Ayde and Help of younge tradesmen, Handicraftesmen and persons decayed, and others for releife or redemption of Prisoners or Captives, and for the aide or ease of any poore inhabitants concerning payment of Fifteens, setting out of Souldiers and other Taxes.'

It perhaps bears testimony to the quality of work undertaken by these early charity legislators that this Elizabethan Act was only recently repealed. English law now defines a charity as having one or more of the following purposes:

1   The prevention and relief of poverty
2   The advancement of education
3   The advancement of religion
4   The advancement of health
5   Social and Community advancement
6   The advancement of culture, arts and heritage
7   The advancement of amateur sport
8   The promotion of human rights, conflict resolution and reconciliation
9   The advancement of environmental protection and improvement
10 Other purposes beneficial to the community.

The notion of public benefit has also been made much more critical to the definition of charity by the Charities Act 2006, and organizations seeking to acquire charitable status must now demonstrate that they offer value to our wider society.

In the US, nonprofit organizations are defined by the Internal Revenue Code and largely section 501. Table 26.1 provides a summary and indicates the balance of organizations in each category. As the reader will appreciate 501(c)3 and 501(c)4, organizations predominate. Both categories are exempt from income and other forms of taxation, but only the 'public benefit' organizations that comprise 501(c)3 are able to receive tax-deductible contributions from individuals and corporations. To qualify for this additional benefit, organizations must operate to fulfil one of the following broad purposes: charitable, religious, scientific, literary or educational. A number of narrower purposes are also included: testing for public safety and prevention of cruelty to children or animals. The code also requires that no substantial part of an organization's activity should be focused on attempts to influence government, either directly or through participation in political campaigns. 501(c)4 organizations, by contrast, may contain advocacy groups and engage in substantial campaigning activities which 501(c)3 organizations are not permitted to do.

In this chapter, we adopt this latter term 'nonprofit' by virtue of the range of organizations it encompasses and the fact that it may usefully embrace a number of public sector organizations whose approach to marketing will also be distinctive in many of the ways described below. In employing this terminology, however, it is important to recognize two key weaknesses. First, it implies that this cohort of organizations will not make a profit. While this is technically true, many so called nonprofits can and do generate a very healthy surplus each year. What distinguishes them from businesses is merely that this surplus is ploughed back into the development of mission-related activities and not dispersed to the 'owners' or shareholders of the organization. Second, the term also suffers from an unfortunate predilection to define the sector by what it is not. Young (1983) famously asks 'if not for profit – for what?'

Table 26.1   Active entities on IRS Business Master File of Tax Exempt Organizations, 1998

Tax Code Number	Type of Tax Exempt Organization	Number in 1998
501(c)1	Corporations organized under an act of Congress	14
501(c)2	Totle Holding Companies	7125
501(c)3	Religious, charitable and similar organizations	733 790
501(c)4	Social welfare organizations	139 533
501(c)5	Labour and agricultural organizations	64 804
501(c)6	Business leagues	79 864
501(c)7	Social and recreational clubs	66 691
501(c)8	Fraternal beneficiary societies	84 507
501(c)9	Voluntary employees' beneficiary societies	14 240
501(c)10	Domestic fraternal beneficiary societies	21 962
501(c)11	Teachers' retirement fund	13
501(c)12	Benevolent life insurance associations	6423
501(c)13	Cemetery companies	9792
501(c)14	Credit unions	4378
501(c)15	Mutual insurance companies	1251
501(c)16	Corporations to finance crop operation	25
501(c)17	Supplemental unemployment benefit trusts	533
501(c)18	Employee-funded pension trusts	1
501(c)19	War veterans' organizations	35 682
501(c)20	Legal services organizations	56
501(c)21	Black lung trusts	28
501(c)23	Veterans' associations founded prior to 1880	2
501(c)24	Trusts described in section 4049 of ERISA	1
501(c)25	Holding companies for pensions and so on	1017
501(d)	Religious and apostolic organizations	118
501(e)	Cooperative hospital service organizations	43
501(f)	Cooperative service organizations of operating educational organizations	1
521	Farmer's cooperatives	1442
Total		1 273 336

Source: Weitzman *et al.* (2002) © Independent Sector. Used by permission of Jossey Bass & Sons Inc.

Is nonprofit marketing really different?

Having defined our terminology, we may now return to the central issue of this chapter, namely whether for-profit and not-for-profit marketing are in reality any different. Over the years, various authors have discussed this issue and there is considerable debate about whether any differences are as real as they might at first appear (Sargeant, 1999). Nevertheless the following eight characteristics of nonprofits may help explain some of the complexities the marketing function may encounter.

in a typical organization may encounter.

1 Two distinct markets
2 Multiple constituencies
3 Need for societal, not-market orientation
4 Non-financial objectives
5 Services and social behaviours rather than physical goods
6 Collaboration, not competition
7 Public scrutiny/non-market pressures
8 Higher ethical standards

We will consider each in turn.

Two distinct markets

In a for-profit context, the marketing function is concerned with developing goods and services which will, then, be sold to customers. This will generate revenue which can in turn be used to purchase the raw materials necessary to produce the next generation of goods and services, and so on. In short, there is only one primary constituency that needs to be addressed by the marketing function, namely the customers of the organization. In many nonprofits, however, there are two constituencies, since the funders of the organization are frequently not its service users. Funders merely pay for, or subsidize, the provision of benefits for others. Many nonprofits, therefore, have to employ marketing ideas in two distinct contexts: the market for resource attraction and the market for resource allocation.

Of course, one might argue that this difference between the two sectors is illusory. Some businesses draw income from a variety of sources, not necessarily just their primary customer group(s). Some may even attract significant government funding or seek occasionally to raise funds from a new issue of shares. Thus, marketers in business organizations can also find themselves dealing with multiple constituencies. It does seem safe to conclude, however, that the division between resource attraction and resource allocation is rarely so clear-cut as it is in the majority of nonprofit organizations.

This difference is highly significant for two key reasons. First, nonprofit managers have to balance their desire to provide mission-related products and services with their ability to sustain the income necessary to support them. Sadly, some activities may be highly relevant to the organization's mission, but they may be more difficult to fund than others that are perhaps more tangential. This makes the management of an appropriate portfolio of activities much more complex than would be the case in the for-profit environment.

Second, the majority of scholarly marketing thought has been focused on exchange of tangible goods or services. This tends to form the core of marketing thought taught in our business schools and reported in our textbooks. While understandable it neglects the growing body of work conducted into the market for resource attraction, much of which delivers real practical value for nonprofit managers, enhancing their understanding of the operation of this market and the manner in which it could best be approached.

We will examine each of these issues in turn.

1 *Nonprofit Portfolio Management*

While a variety of portfolio models have been employed over the years, these have largely been developed in the business context and are, thus, difficult to apply to the context of nonprofit marketing. In particular, nonprofit marketers should studiously avoid any portfolio model that has as its base the concept of market share (e.g. the Boston Box), since this notion cannot be meaningfully applied to the nonprofit context. This is the case for three reasons:

1 The sheer scale of the nonprofit sector and the fact that service and/or fundraising performance is usually reported in aggregate terms only means that it would be impossible to meaningfully quantify market share for most organizations.
2 Portfolio models employing market share assume that the performance of a product or service is related to market share (i.e. that there are economies of scale). This is simply not the case in most nonprofit contexts.
3 Finally, market share is employed in many portfolio models because it indicates the position of each competitor in a given market. Since many nonprofits do not compete, the use of such models is again problematic.

For these reasons, the portfolio model in Figure 26.2 is to be preferred. Its adoption would provide nonprofit managers with a clearer perspective on the overall health of their portfolio and offer general guidance in respect of where future investment and effort may be targeted.

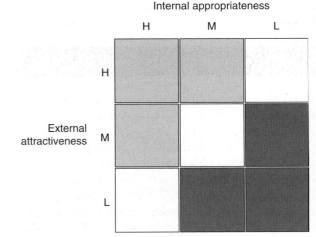

Figure 26.2 Nonprofit portfolio analysis

To utilize the model, it is necessary to begin by examining in detail the components of the two axes, namely external attractiveness and internal appropriateness. If we consider first the question of external attractiveness, this relates to a particular organization's ability to attract resources. Not all the services of an organization will be equally attractive to potential funders and whilst most charities would not exclude the provision of a service, simply because it was perceived by donors as unsavoury, few would argue that the ability to raise funds was not an issue. Whilst the specific factors will undoubtedly vary from one organization to another, the degree of support donors are willing to give a particular activity is likely to depend on

- the level of general public concern
- likely trends in public concern
- numbers of people aided
- immediacy of impact on beneficiary group.

It is important to recognize that this list is not exhaustive, and the beauty of this model is that organizations can utilize whatever factors they perceive as being relevant to their own environment and circumstances.

Turning now to the question of internal appropriateness, this relates to the extent to which the service 'fits' the profile of the organization providing it. In other words, is provision appropriate given the skills, expertise and resources available within the organization. Relevant factors here might include:

(a) The level of previous experience with the activity
(b) The perceived importance of the activity
(c) The extent to which the activity is compatible with the organization's mission

(d) The extent to which the organization has unique expertise to offer.

Once again this list can be expected to vary from context to context and an organization would look to identify those factors which are most pertinent to its particular circumstances.

Having now defined the components of internal appropriateness and external attractiveness, the reader will appreciate that not all the factors identified could be seen as having equal importance to a given organization. For this reason, it is important to weight the factors according to their relative importance. This is illustrated in Table 26.2. The reader will note that the weights for the components of each axis should all add up to 1. In the example given, the numbers of people the organization can aid is seen as being a more important determinant of external attractiveness than the question of how immediately the assistance can be provided. Donors to this organization do not appear to have any difficulty in taking a long-term view of the impact of their support.

The next step is to take each activity in which the organization is engaged and give it a score from 1 (Very Poor) to 10 (Excellent) in terms of how it measures up against each of the components listed. To make this process clear, a fictional example (let us call it Activity A) has been worked through in Tables 26.2 and 26.3. Considering first the question of how externally attractive this activity might be, it is clear that public support for it looks set to decline in the future and it is for this reason that a relatively low rating of 3 has been awarded against this factor. The activity does have the merit, however, of having an immediate and beneficial impact on a large number of people and somewhat higher ratings are, therefore, awarded for these factors. Multiplying the weights by the

Table 26.2 External attractiveness

Factor	Weight	Rating	Value
The general level of public concern	0.2	5	1.0
Likely trends in public concern	0.3	3	0.9
Number of people aided	0.4	8	3.2
Immediacy of impact on the beneficiary group	0.1	7	0.7
Total	1.0		5.8

Table 26.3 Internal appropriateness

Factor	Weight	Rating	Value
Level of previous experience with the activity	0.1	5	0.5
Perceived importance of the activity	0.2	2	0.4
Extent to which the activity is compatible with the organization's mission	0.5	6	3.0
Extent to which the organization has unique expertise to offer	0.2	7	1.4
Total	1.0		5.3

ratings assigned produces a value for each factor. Summing these values gives an overall score for (in this case) the external attractiveness axis of 5.8.

Similarly in the case of the internal attractiveness axis, each factor is assigned a weight. Each activity in which the organization is engaged is given a rating according to its performance in respect of each factor. Once again 1 = Very Poor, 10 = Excellent. Returning to our analysis of activity (A), Table 26.3 makes it clear that the charity has only moderate experience to offer and does not view its provision as being particularly important (even though it would appear to come within the organization's mission). The charity does, however, have fairly unique expertise which it could offer to recipients. The result is an aggregate score of 5.3 on the internal appropriateness axis.

These figures can now be plotted on the matrix in Figure 26.3, where the position of activity (A) has been clearly indicated. If it is conceptually useful, some organizations choose to progress the analysis one stage further and draw a circle around the plotted position, the diameter of which is directly proportional to the percentage of overall expenditure that is allocated to each activity. In this way, managers can see at a glance how funds are allocated between each of the services in the portfolio. Of course for this to happen, all the services that a particular organization provides would be plotted in this way and then an analysis undertaken of the health (and balance) of the portfolio as a whole. Depending on the location of each activity within the matrix, the organization can, then, either look to invest further in its development, divest the activity and use the resources elsewhere, or subject the activity to further evaluation if the position still remains unclear.

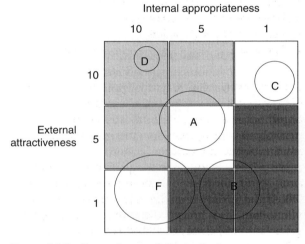

Figure 26.3 Example portfolio analysis

Activities falling in the top left hand corner of the matrix are clearly those which are perceived as fulfilling an important need in society and the attraction of funding is unproblematic. The organization also appears well placed to provide these services as it has the necessary expertise and/or experience in house. The activities are also more likely to be seen as being compatible with the organization's mission and are, hence, excellent candidates for continuing investment.

Activities falling in the bottom right hand corner, however, are clearly activities which could be causing an unnecessary drain on resources. They are not seen as being important by society and are not compatible with the organization's mission. Indeed, there may be other potential providers who could provide a much higher quality of service. Activities in this area of the matrix should then be scrutinized with a view to divestment. After all, if the activity is difficult to raise funds for, and the organization is not good at providing the service anyway, what could the rationale possibly be for continuing? Of course, this is only a model and the activity would have to be scrutinized very carefully before a divestment decision was taken, but the analysis has at least yielded considerable insight into the potential for valuable resources to be conserved and perhaps put to other, more appropriate use.

This leaves the question of activities falling within the central diagonal, such as the one in our fictional example. These should be carefully evaluated as they are only moderately appropriate for the organization to provide and they have only limited external attractiveness. It may be that there are very good strategic reasons for continuing to offer these services, or it may equally be that they could comfortably be left to another better qualified organization to supply. Further analysis would clearly be warranted.

2   *Understanding Donor Markets*
Nonprofits typically derive their voluntary income from one or more of the following sources:

- Individual donors
- Corporate donors
- Trusts/foundations

Government funds also form a significant source of income for the sector, but this is frequently in the form of a contractual relationship for the provision of specific goods or services and therefore not regarded as a 'voluntary' contribution. Gifts from living individuals form the majority of a typical organization's voluntary income. In the US, for example, total giving to the nonprofit sector in 2004 stood at US $248.52 billion. A staggering 90 per cent of Americans offered donations to nonprofits with people giving on average two percent of their income and contributing 76 per cent of the total income accruing to the sector (the balance coming from corporations, foundations and bequests) (AAFRC Trust, 2005).

Gift giving by individuals has, therefore, been the focus of much research, with contributions emerging from the fields of economics, clinical psychology, social psychology, anthropology and sociology. A key contribution from the discipline of nonprofit marketing has been the development of composite models of helping behaviour whose goal has been to explain the donation of money, time and even body parts. (Burnett and Wood, 1988; Guy and Patton, 1989; Bendapudi *et al.*, 1996; Sargeant, 1999). Sargeant and Woodliffe's (2007) model of individual giving is illustrated in Figure 26.4. It illustrates the wide range of factors

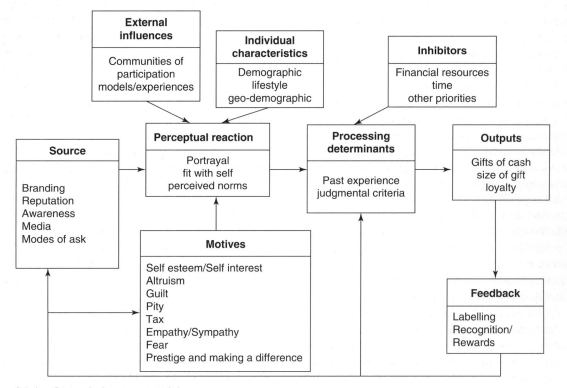

Figure 26.4   Giving behaviour model

with the potential to influence gift giving and speculates on the manner in which they may be interrelated. All such composite models make a valuable contribution in that they comprise literature reviews that open up the wealth of academic research to managers who may use it to inform their professional practice.

Source

As the model indicates, there are five key facets to donor communication that warrant consideration. Choices must be made about the media that will be used and the manner in which the appeal will be framed. The profile of donors recruited will reflect these choices. Donors recruited by direct e-mail tend to be older than those recruited from television advertisements and much older than those recruited through face-to-face solicitation on the High Street. Donors who agree to give one-off donations tend to be 10 years older on average than those who are willing to sign up for a regular monthly gift (Sargeant and Jay, 2004).

The model also recognizes that these solicitations are unlikely to take place in a vacuum. Whether it chooses to manage them or not, the organization's image and reputation will be communicated to a donor to a greater or lesser extent depending on their ambient level of awareness. There is a wealth of evidence that branding can impact on an organization's ability to successfully raise funds. As Tapp (1996, p. 335) notes, while 'charities do not describe much of what they do as "branding", organizations have long been concerned with maintaining a consistent style and tone of voice and conducting periodic reviews of both policies and actions to ensure that a consistent personality is projected". In his view, the clarity with which this 'personality' is projected will have a direct impact on an organization's ability to fundraise. Sargeant and Hudson (2005) argue that achieving this clarity is considerably more difficult in the charity context since many facets of charity personality are, in fact, shared by the sector as a whole. Charities are generally regarded, for example, as being caring, sympathetic and compassionate. Donors appear to start from this assumption unless and until evidence appears to the contrary. Only values characteristics linked to 'emotional stimulation', 'service', 'voice' and 'tradition' are capable of distinguishing between organizations. Organizations perceived as distinctive command a higher share of a donor's charitable wallet than those lacking such differentiation.

Perceptual reaction

Whether the solicitation will be perceived as relevant to the donor will be a function of these inputs and the fit of portrayal of the beneficiary group with a given individual's self image. Coliazzi *et al.* (1984) noted that individuals are more likely to help those that are perceived as being similar to themselves. They will, thus, tend to filter those messages from nonprofits existing to support disparate segments of society. There is also evidence that donors will filter messages on the basis of normative concerns (Morgan *et al.*, 1979). People appear to pay considerable attention to what others contribute within their respective societal group. The knowledge that others are contributing legitimizes contribution, and Reingen (1978) identified that showing prospective donors a fictitious list of previous donors led to higher donations and increased compliance. It is interesting to note that the length of the list of previous contributors is also an issue with longer lists outperforming shorter ones.

Processing determinants

The model, then, suggests that potentially relevant messages will be subjected to a further and perhaps more cognitive decision-making process. Two key factors warrant consideration here: an individuals past experience with an organization and the decision-making criteria they will apply.

In respect of the former, once a link is forged with a nonprofit, a given individual will be significantly more likely to help again in the future and to help in a variety of different ways (e.g. Kaehler and Sargeant, 1998). A good source of 'new' donors can, therefore, be individuals who have given in the past, or individuals who have been engaged in other ways, perhaps in campaigning/ lobbying, volunteering or even as service users of the organization. Of course, this pre-supposes that the individual's experience will have been a happy one, if they were dissatisfied in some way they are highly unlikely to wish to renew their association.

In respect of the conscious decision-making criteria that might be applied, there is a clear link between the individual's motives for support (which we shall discuss below) and whether the individual believes these personal needs are likely to be met. Individuals might also evaluate potential recipient organizations on the basis of the extent to which they believe that the organization is doing good work and having the promised impact on the beneficiary group. There is evidence that the perceived efficiency of the organization (i.e. not 'squandering' resources on fundraising and administration) can also have a role to play in deciding whether support will be offered (Sargeant and Jay, 2004).

Individual characteristics

A variety of demographic factors can influence giving. Variables such as age (Halfpenny, 1990; Nichols, 1992; Pharoah and Tanner, 1997), gender (Mesch *et al.*, 2002; Hall, 2004), social class (Jones and Posnett, 1991; Bryant *et al.*, 2003; McClelland and Brooks, 2004) and degree of religious conviction (Halfpenny, 1990; Pharoah and Tanner, 1997; Jackson, 2001) have all been shown to impact on giving behaviour. The core of charity donors tends to be aged between 55 and 70 with a higher percentage of women being prepared to give than men. The amounts donated, not surprisingly, have been shown to vary by socio-economic group, and Kottasz (2004) suggests that an individual's profession may also be associated with their giving behaviour. In her study of high-earning male professionals, lawyers tended to donate larger amounts of money to charity and on a more regular basis than respondents working in financial services. She speculates that this may be because the former group were significantly more empathetic than the latter, an empathetic disposition being positively associated with giving.

The utility of lifestyle variables in predicting giving behaviour has also been explored. Yankelovich (1985), for example, reported that the most important characteristics of the generous giver are all related to the donor's perceptions and values. Perceptions of financial security, discretionary funds, attendance at religious services and whether an individual volunteers time for charity were all shown to be good indicators of a propensity to give.

External influences

Schervish and Havens (1997) argue that models and experiences from one's youth shape future adult giving behaviour. Thus those growing up in a family with a strong tradition of charitable support will be significantly more likely to exhibit such behaviours themselves. Communities of participation are a further influence which Schervish (1993) defines as networks of formal and informal relationships entered into either by choice or by circumstance (e.g. schools, soup kitchens, soccer groups)

that bring an individual into contact with need. Schervish argues that a basic connection to a cause (e.g. being a graduate of a University) is not enough in itself to prompt subsequent donations to that University and that some degree of socialization is required. This, the author argues, is experienced through communities of participation and, thus, donors will be predisposed to give to causes connected in some way with these communities.

Motives

The wide variety of donor motives are also emphasized in the model and can assist donors in filtering out those charity appeals that are likely to be of most relevance and structuring the evaluation process that will subsequently be conducted to define the pattern of support exhibited. Historically, economists have attempted to explain giving by reference to the benefits that will accrue to the donor as a consequence of their gift. In this sense, the process is rational and the donor simply evaluates the costs and benefits of engaging in a particular donation. However, this fails to explain a large proportion of gifts where no direct benefit accrues to the individual and where perhaps the gift may be made anonymously (Walker and Pharoah, 2002). Economists such as Andreoni (2001) explain this by arguing that the utility deriving from a gift can take a variety of different forms including purely psychological utility resulting from the satisfaction of an emotional need. Donors, therefore, derive benefit from resolving the dissonance created when they experience feelings of guilt, pity, empathy, etc.

For many high value donors, the prestige associated with offering a major gift will be a significant issue. Harbaugh (1998) defines prestige as the utility that comes from having the amount of a donation made publicly known. Being seen to give may enhance a donor's social status, or serve as a sign of wealth or reliability. Donors may also wish to access a particular group, and thus desire to be defined by their philanthropic activity (Ostrower, 1996). Prestige is clearly about recognition and thus to respond to the motive of prestige, charities can create gift categories and then publicly disclose donors who achieve various levels of contribution. These categories normally carry titles, such as 'friend', 'fellow', or 'patron' depending on the size of the gift.

Finally, the issue of whether tax breaks may incentivize giving has received much attention. Although findings vary, the responsiveness of individual giving to changes in taxation appears relatively great. Okten and Weisbrod (2000), for example, calculate that a change in the price of donating of a given percentage results in a 24 per cent greater percentage change in donations. Tax relief is, therefore, considered by many to be an important motive for charitable support (Ostrower, 1996) although perhaps as Sargeant and Jay (2004, p. 100) note, no matter how great the relief 'it is important not to overstate the influence of taxation ... donors will always be better off not making a donation'.

Inhibitors

A number of factors have been shown to inhibit individual giving. Riecken *et al.* (1994) contend that lack of money, time or ego risks are the most notable of these. In respect of the latter, Steffey and Jones (1988) concur that some donors may experience anxiety over ridicule that may result from the support of unpopular or 'fringe' causes (see also Yavas and Riecken, 1985). A further notable barrier to giving has been shown to be doubts over the worthiness of the cause (Wagner and Wheeler, 1969) and in particular concerns in respect of how the donated resources will actually be used (Shuptrine and Moore, 1980).

Feedback

The impact of labels will be particularly potent when there are concrete prior behaviours to be labelled and when the label stresses the uniqueness of the donor's behavior (McGuire and Padawere-Singer 1976). Labels have been found to work only where the donor accepts the label (Allen 1982), emphasizing the need for the label to be credible and be supplied by a credible source. Having decided to offer a donation to a nonprofit, donors will typically be thanked by the respective organization in the hope that this will be the first stage in building an ongoing relationship with the individual concerned. The literature suggests that there are two significant components of this feedback process that fundraisers should seek to address. First, in thanking donors for their gift organizations often append labels to the donor such as kind, generous and/or helpful. Work by authors such as Swinyard and Ray (1977) have implied that this elicits a greater motivation to help and fosters favourable attitudes on the part of the donor (Moore *et al.*, 1985). The impact of labels will be particularly potent when there are concrete prior behavior to be labelled and when the label stresses the uniqueness of the donor's

behavior (McGuire and Padawer-Singer, 1976). Labels have been found to work only where the donor accepts the label (Allen, 1982), emphasizing the need for the label to be credible and be supplied by a credible source.

The fundraising literature is also replete with references to the need for adequate donor recognition (e.g. Warwick and Hitchcock, 2001; Irwin-Wells, 2002). Failure to provide adequate and appropriate recognition, it has been argued, will lead to either a lowering of future support or its complete termination (Boulding, 1973). Sargeant *et al.* (2001) provide the first empirical support for this proposition indicating a link between the perception of adequate recognition and the level of gifts/lifetime value.

Corporate giving

Business giving, too, has been the focus of much research, particularly in relation to the issue of their motives for the support of nonprofits. The literature suggests that there are broadly four categories of such motives, namely dual agenda motives, altruistic motives, taxation and the influence of the personal motives of the managers involved.

In respect of the former, Friedman (1970) argued that the business of business was to make a profit and that senior managers should leave the issue of how to disperse their earnings to the shareholders. Managers should simply serve the interests of business owners by making more money while playing by the basic rules of society.

Corporate giving from this perspective should be viewed as instrumental, in that it should be undertaken only to achieve specific business benefits. Inevitably there has been considerable academic interest in delineating what these might be and extant work has highlighted variables as diverse as brand differentiation, enhanced brand image, improved employee recruitment, morale and retention, enhanced government relations and the ability to reach new customer segments (e.g. Andreasen, 1996; Drumwright, 1996; Sagawa, 2001; Porter and Kramer, 2002; Wymer and Samu, 2003). Ricks (2005) also highlights increasing visibility, enhancing corporate image and thwarting negative publicity as important marketing reasons for corporate philanthropy.

Lee (1996), however, argued that genuine philanthropy lies at the heart of the majority of corporate charitable contributions. He based this on data from a survey of the top 400 donating companies in the UK which highlighted that

60 per cent of managers did not expect joint promotions to lead to higher sales, that only 40 per cent thought that donations would lead to increased public awareness and that 67 per cent of managers felt that there was no need for charities to be linked to the company's products in order to develop worthwhile relationships. Indeed, altruistic motives have been identified in many empirical studies (Neiheisel, 1995; Sharfman, 1994; Campbell *et al.*, 1999) and altruism is typically the most frequently cited reason for support (Meijer *et al.*, 2006).

Multiple constituencies

The second key difference between for-profits and nonprofits follows from the first. Although there are typically two primary markets to be addressed by nonprofit marketers, there are a much wider set of constituencies or 'publics' that a typical nonprofit must take account of in the design of strategy. Kotler and Andreasen (1991, p. 89) use the term 'publics' to refer to 'a distinct group of people, organisations, or both, whose actual or potential needs must in some sense be served'.

The term 'public' is, therefore, more general in its meaning than the concept of 'customer' and embraces every group whose needs must be taken account of by the focal organization. For a charity, this might typically include individual donors, corporate donors, trusts/foundations, legislators, the local community, the general public, local and national media, recipients of goods and services, the organization's own staff, volunteers, etc. While businesses, too, may serve a number of different publics, the power and relative significance of each is rarely so diffuse as it is in the nonprofit context. At a very practical level, the views of a much wider number of audiences must continually be addressed.

Societal not market orientation

A further key difference relates to the nature of some nonprofit missions. Many nonprofit organizations are compelled by their mission to take a long-term view of their relationships with their target markets. Health and welfare groups in the Third World, for example, may be promoting the use of contraception in direct conflict with the established patterns of local belief and culture. Similarly, many theatres and arts centres have a mission to explore a wide range of art forms, not just to provide those forms of entertainment that they know will be well patronized by their local community. There is, therefore, a tension between the satisfaction of current customer needs and the fulfilment of a particular organization's mission. Short-term customer satisfaction may often have to be sacrificed by nonprofits as they take a longer-term view of the benefit they can offer to society as a whole. This matters because it reveals a deep philosophical difference between the application of marketing in the for-profit context and the application of marketing in nonprofit organizations.

Since the 1950s, practitioners and academics have sought to explain what it means for an organization to fully grasp and implement the marketing concept. More recently, firms that successfully operationalize the marketing concept have come to be labelled 'market oriented' (Kohli and Jaworski, 1990; Narver and Slater, 1990). While perspectives on what this means in practice do vary, a number of common themes have now emerged including a focus on customers, a focus on competitors and the development of a culture that facilitates the sharing of market information around the organization to ensure it has the maximum possible influence on strategy. The level of market orientation attained matters because numerous studies have linked this with the level of performance (e.g. market share, performance, customer loyalty) that an organization is able to achieve (see e.g. Jaworski and Kohli, 1993).

One might, therefore, be tempted into arguing that the achievement of a market orientation would be a good thing for nonprofits and for-profits alike and, indeed, many studies have now explored market orientation in the nonprofit context (e.g. Bennett, 1998; Caruana *et al.*, 1998). There are, however, a number of good reasons why this assumption should be questioned.

First, the market orientation construct was an attempt to operationalize for-profit definitions of marketing that were developed in large commercial organizations in the mid 1960s. Very different definitions of marketing have been developed in the nonprofit context and attempting to operationalize Kotler and Levy's 'sensitively serving and satisfying human need', for example, is likely to have a very different outcome from operationalizing the definition of marketing provided by the Chartered Institute of Marketing.

Similarly, some of the terminology used in the for-profit context does not transfer well to the nonprofit arena. The very term 'market orientation' implies an orientation towards markets. Even though it has already been argued that nonprofits have a market for both resource acquisition and resource allocation, these are often not markets in the economic sense of the term. In fact, as Hansmann (1980) notes, nonprofits can often be seen as a response to a very particular form of market failure.

The second key argument for revising the terminology in this context is that the notion of 'market' implies some form of exchange which will take place between the supplier and the recipient of goods and services. There are a plethora of occasions when nonprofit organizations do exchange monetary value with the recipients of their goods or services (or even a warm feeling in return for donations); however, there are also many occasions when the notion of exchange has little meaning. The recipients of international aid exchange nothing except their need and gratitude with their supplying organization.

The components of market orientation are also problematic in the nonprofit context. Whilst a focus on customers is still important, in the nonprofit context (as was explained earlier) organizations are often less concerned with customer satisfaction *per se* than they are with the notion of longer-term benefit to society. It is, thus, necessary to broaden the focus on customers to address the needs of a wider range of stakeholders and perhaps even society as a whole.

Competition is also different in the nonprofit arena. Demand for nonprofit goods and services is often so insatiable that to regard other organizations as direct competitors would be ludicrous (Bruce, 1995). Naturally there are occasions when competition is of significance, as when, for example, organizations compete for funds, but it is often the case in relation to service delivery that potential collaboration between organizations is more of an issue than competition *per se*.

It has also been argued that to sensitively serve the needs of society, nonprofits must be responsive to such needs. Whilst businesses, too, must be responsive, in the nonprofit context it is the rapidity of this response that defines many organizations. This is accomplished because there is no requirement to consider either the political consequences of action or the financial returns that might accrue to shareholders. Nonprofits have the necessary freedom, flexibility and moral imperative to respond quickly to the dictates of social need and must ensure that they do so if the maximum benefit to society is to accrue (Jordan, 1964; Dahrendorf, 1997).

In recognition of these difficulties, Sargeant *et al.* (2002) propose the alternative framework of 'societal orientation' illustrated in Figure 26.5. The model is offered as an attempt to operationalize the Kotler and Levy definition of marketing referred to earlier. In this case, the authors have delineated the societal orientation construct itself and included what they regarded as the antecedents of a societal orientation and the benefits and consequences thereof.

Considering first the antecedents, the authors argue that nonprofits will only be able to achieve a societal orientation if they have a strong, clear mission that reflects the goals of the organization's key stakeholder groups. Similarly, these goals should be common (i.e. shared) across all the stakeholder groups and the nonprofit must have established appropriate systems and structures to ensure that they are in a position to be achieved.

In respect of consequences, the authors posit that societally oriented organizations will achieve significantly higher performance than those without such an orientation. In the nonprofit context, this means that nonprofits would be more

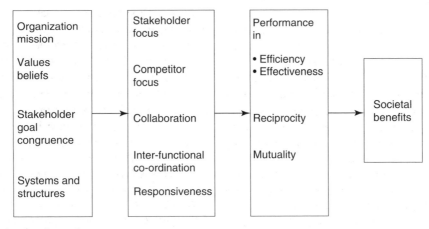

Figure 26.5 Societal orientation

effective in achieving their mission and make a more efficient use of resources in doing so.

According to the authors, however, these should not be viewed as the only outcomes from the successful attainment of a societal orientation. An additional dimension derives from the division between resource acquisition and resource allocation. Those individuals that supply an organization's funding are not necessarily those that will derive the primary benefit. One of the primary outcomes from the attainment of a societal orientation can, therefore, be the bringing together of these two groups, resulting in a mutual exchange of values, ideas and a shared sense of identity. The authors refer to this as reciprocity and mutuality.

Non financial objectives

Nonprofits also differ from their for-profit counterparts in that the derivation of appropriate organizational and thus marketing objectives is markedly more difficult. As Drucker (1990, p. 107) notes,

> performance is the ultimate test of any institution. Every non-profit institution exists for the sake of performance in changing people and society. Yet, performance is also one of the truly difficult areas for the executive in the non-profit institution.

Setting objectives which can then be used to monitor nonprofit performance is problematic because of the intangible nature of much of the service provided. It is also a problem because, as Drucker goes on to note, the results of a nonprofit institution are always outside the organization. Traditional internal measures such as return on investment (ROI) and profit have no meaning in this context. Their results are, therefore, inherently more difficult to measure. This is not to suggest, however, that nonprofit organizations should not at least try to set targets. As Drucker (1990, p. 107) makes clear,:

> In a non-profit organisation there is no such (thing as a) bottom line. But there is also a temptation to downplay results. There is the temptation to say: We are serving a good cause. We are doing the Lord's work. Or we are doing something to make life a little better for people and that's a result in itself. That is not enough. If a business wastes its resources on non results, by and large it loses its own money. In a non-profit institution though, it's somebody else's money – the donor's money. Service organisations are accountable to donors, accountable for putting the money where the results are, and for performance. So, this is an area that needs special emphasis for non-profit executives. Good intentions only pave the way to Hell!

Objective setting is also difficult because a nonprofit can have amorphous goals (Newman and Wallender, 1978). What Dahrendorf (1997) refers to as the creative chaos of the voluntary sector may well be a strength, but this feature complicates the delineation of appropriate measures of performance. Indeed, authors such as Weick (1977) have cautioned against the use of performance measures adopted from business, since if efficiency and production measures predominate, then the random 'deviant' behaviours that enhance an organization's ability to develop creative responses may be lost.

Work in this field has, therefore, suggested employing multiple measures of performance, considering both effectiveness and efficiency. An assessment of the former might begin with an analysis of 'mission directedness' or the extent to which an organization might be said to be fulfilling its mission (Sheehan, 1996). It could also be assessed by the extent to which specific operational objectives have been met or exceeded (Hall, 1978). These may be written in terms of maximizing inputs and outputs, but in respect of service delivery they may also be couched in terms of the quality of intervention achieved. Both are important. While a drug rehabilitation centre may have an objective to increase the throughput of clients, it will be at least, if not more concerned with the quality of care it is able to supply to these individuals. Increasing throughput at the expense of the quality of the intervention would ultimately be self-defeating.

Nonprofit efficiency is also very much an issue. Fundraising and administrative efficiency have generated a lot of interest of late, certainly in the popular press (Sargeant and Kaehler, 1998). Donors now appear to have a clear idea of what represents an acceptable percentage of income that may be applied to both administration and fundraising costs and organizations exceed these at their peril. Warwick (1994) identified that donors expect that the ratio between administration/fundraising costs and so-called charitable expenditure would be 20:80. It is interesting to note that, despite this expectation, most donors believe that the actual ratio is closer to 50:50. For example, Bennett and Savani's (2003) research shows that respondents perceived that only 46 per cent of the focal charities' expenditures reached beneficiaries, when in reality the average figure was 82 per cent. This matters because research has consistently shown a link between such perceptions, the longevity of the donor-nonprofit relationship and the percentage of an individual's charitable pot that they may be willing to give to a given organization. In objective writing, organizations may, therefore, want to concern themselves as much with perceptions of their performance as with the reality thereof. These concerns seem peculiar to the nonprofit context. Consumers in the commercial world rarely concern themselves with how well they perceive a manufacturer to be managed or issues such as the salaries of senior staff.

Services and social behaviours rather than physical goods

The majority of nonprofits produce services rather than physical goods. Day-to-day nonprofit marketing, therefore, has much more in common with the marketing of services than the marketing of consumer products. Nonprofit marketers, therefore, have to deal with the added complexities envisaged by Zeithaml (1996) including:

(a) *Intangibility:* When a customer purchases a physical item or service he/she can assess it by its appearance, taste, smell, etc. They can, therefore, 'confirm' their expectations about the properties of the product they are going to receive. With a service, however, the consumer has no way of verifying the claims of the producer until the service has actually been purchased. This is all the more problematic in the nonprofit context, because funders may well be purchasing services that will be consumed by an entirely different societal group.

(b) *Inseparability:* Physical goods are produced and then purchased by the customer. With services the process is the other way around. Services are sold first and then produced at the time of consumption by the customer. (In this sense, production and consumption are said to be inseparable). This means that producer and consumer have to interact to produce the service. Marketing a service, therefore, involves not only facilitating an exchange process, but also facilitating an often quite complex producer/ consumer interaction.

(c) *Heterogeneity:* Allied to the previous point, since production and consumption are inseparable, there are few chances for a service supplier to carry out pre-inspection or quality control in the same way that one can with physical goods. Indeed, monitoring and control processes are of necessity considerably more complex in the context of services.

(d) *Perishability:* Services cannot be stored in the same way that one can store food or electrical items in a retail outlet. If a theatrical performance begins with a half empty house, or there are last minute cancellations of a physician's appointments, those services have been lost forever. Marketers, therefore, have a more complex balancing operation to perform to ensure that their services remain as optimally utilized as possible.

Some nonprofits do not even produce a service that one could clearly define. They exist to attempt to alter some form of social behaviour either through direct communication with the target group, or indirectly through the lobbying of government. When it was first recognized in the 1970s that marketing tools could be applied equally well to the marketing of social ideas (Kotler and Zaltman, 1971), a new discipline of 'social marketing' was born.

Since then, Andreasen (1995) notes that social marketing has tended to be employed where individual members of the public engage in unsafe, resistant behaviours and where, as a consequence, behaviour change would improve their personal welfare and that of wider society. Much of the early research in this field focused on the promotion of products associated with such behaviour change and, thus, on the marketing of pharmaceuticals, condoms, oral rehydration tablets, etc. (Andreasen, 2002). More recently, work has focused on specific issues such as HIV infection and sexual responsibility (e.g. Cohen *et al.*, 1999; Reichert *et al.*, 2001; Moore *et al.*, 2002), smoking (e.g. McKenna *et al.*, 2000; Zucker *et al.*, 2000), drink driving (e.g. Braus, 1995), pollution/ business ethics (e.g. Abratt and Sacks, 1988), recycling/ energy conservation (McKenzie-Mohr, 1994), radon testing (DiPofi *et al.*, 2001), skin cancer prevention (Peattie *et al.*, 2001), and drug, solvent or alcohol abuse (e.g. Smith, 1992; Stanton *et al.*, 2000).

Other more generic work has focused on the development of frameworks and approaches drawn from successful professional practice (Goldberg, 1997; Rothschild, 1999), alternative consumer behaviour models (Hornik, 2001), market segmentation (Donovan, 1999) and the nature of successful communication messages (Maibach and Cotton, 1995; Pechmann and Reibling, 2000).

Collaboration, not competition

The fifth key difference between for-profit and nonprofit marketing has already been alluded to above. Competition is a key strategic issue for many nonprofits, but collaboration is an equally important facet of their relationship with other organizations. Many Third World agencies, for example, will share transportation channels to maximize the distribution and impact of aid, whilst minimizing cost. Indeed, in addition to other similar organizations, nonprofits may be able to identify suitable opportunities for collaboration with both public and private sector bodies (Andreasen and Kotler, 2004). In the fundraising context, it is also commonplace for nonprofits to share lists of lower value donors with other organizations, in the hope that every participant in the exchange will benefit from the sharing of these resources (Sargeant and Jay, 2004).

Thus in conducting a fundraising or marketing audit, it is instructive to consider examples of where organizations have collaborated successfully in the past and the factors that led to that success. The nonprofit should look to see what it could learn from these collaborations and whether there might be any way in which it itself could work in partnership with others. If this is felt to be desirable, it will be instructive to conduct background research into potential partners and to explore how such relationships might develop. An approach to one or more partners could then be included in the marketing strategy/tactics.

The content of a competitor analysis would also vary in the nonprofit context. When conducting an assessment of competitors, there are essentially three categories of organizations who are worthy of investigation.

Competitors For Resources – that is, other nonprofit organizations who seek to attract resources from the same sources as the nonprofit in question. Typically, nonprofits might look at the fundraising undertaken both by other organizations of a similar size *and* by organizations working with the same issue or cause. A brief examination of a third category, namely those engaged in new fundraising media, or with new donor audiences, would also be warranted.

Competitors for provision of nonprofit services – nonprofits may encounter competition from other organizations who seek to provide the same services as themselves. Increasingly this competition may come from for-profit organizations who may decide to compete for example, for government service contracts.

Organizations with competing missions – Many nonprofits now exist whose primary goal is to persuade society to adopt new forms of purchasing, smoking or sexual behaviours. Such nonprofits typically encounter opposition from other organizations which exist to further exactly the opposite forms of behaviour. In the US, for example, the campaigning organization Planned Parenthood frequently finds itself in competition for a share of the media voice with the Catholic church or 'pro-life' bodies opposed to its stance on abortion. In such circumstances, these organizations should clearly be regarded as competitors and subject to an equally detailed level of analysis.

Public scrutiny/non-market pressures

Certain categories of organization within the nonprofit sector are open to intense levels of public scrutiny. The emergency services, local authorities, hospitals and even universities are subject to regular public scrutiny. UK universities, for example, are comprehensively audited on the quality of their teaching and research every 4 years. In the healthcare sector, the government White Paper 'Working For Patients' introduced an independent body, the Audit Commission, into the UK healthcare framework. The commission (which had been performing a similar function for Local Authorities for some years) now has responsibility for ensuring that the National Health Service continues to provide 'value for money'.

The charity sector is also subject to enhanced scrutiny. In the UK, fundraisers must abide by the Codes of Professional Practice laid down by the Institute of Fundraising, and individual members of the public who are dissatisfied with a fundraising solicitation may now complain to a new Fundraising Standards Board, a self-regulatory body established by the industry in an attempt to bolster public trust and confidence in the profession. Fundraising, therefore, becomes one of the few forms of marketing singled out for enhanced public scrutiny.

It is interesting to note that the Fundraising Standards Board has felt it necessary to move beyond the baseline laid down by the Codes of Fundraising Practice and to offer donors a new 'Fundraising Promise', providing a number of enhanced rights, such as not to be subject to 'undue pressure' at the point of solicitation. This move has brought the UK closer to the model adopted in the US where the Association of Fundraising Professionals (AFP) has long committed to a Donor Bill of Rights.

The donor bill of rights

Philanthropy is based on voluntary action for the common good. It is a tradition of giving and sharing that is primary to the quality of life. To ensure that philanthropy merits the respect and trust of the general public, and that donors and prospective donors can have full confidence in the nonprofit organizations and causes they are asked to support, we declare that all donors have these rights:

(i) To be informed of the organization's mission, of the way the organization intends to use donated resources, and of its capacity to use donations effectively for their intended purposes.

(ii) To be informed of the identity of those serving on the organization's governing board, and to expect the board to exercise prudent judgment in its stewardship responsibilities.

(iii) To have access to the organization's most recent financial statements.

(iv) To be assured their gifts will be used for the purposes for which they were given.

(v) To receive appropriate acknowledgement and recognition.

(vi) To be assured that information about their donation is handled with respect and with confidentiality to the extent provided by law.

(vii) To expect that all relationships with individuals representing organizations of interest to the donor will be professional in nature.

(viii) To be informed whether those seeking donations are volunteers, employees of the organization or hired solicitors.

(ix) To have the opportunity for their names to be deleted from e-mailing lists that an organization may intend to share.

(x) To feel free to ask questions when making a donation and to receive prompt, truthful and forthright answers.

Reproduced by kind permission of the Association of Fundraising Professionals.

Nonprofits also have to contend with a variety of other non-market pressures. Whilst no one would claim for a moment that it is easy for a business organization to be able to forecast demand for its products, demand for the services of a nonprofit can fall away to nothing or literally double overnight.

The nature of Oxfam's work overseas with Third World countries can change radically from year to year depending on political, economic and climatic conditions. The very nature of a focus on the disadvantaged makes it almost impossible to know where future priorities might lie.

The instability of the environment in which many nonprofits operate, thus, contributes to the fact that such organizations often have less control over their own destiny than their counterparts in the for-profit sector. Marketers in nonprofits, therefore, have a much more complex role to perform.

Higher ethical standards

The final critical difference between the two sectors lies in the standards of professional behaviour that society has a right to expect. While it is undoubtedly true that ethical considerations are becoming increasingly important for business, the very nature of nonprofit organizations imposes additional moral responsibilities. Indeed, one of the distinguishing characteristics for many nonprofit organizations is the ethical nature of their operations. Since they do not have to seek to maximize profit, they can (and perhaps should) take decisions that seek to maximize the benefit that accrues to society as a whole. In other words, they are freed up to 'do the right thing' or take 'the right decision'. Of course, it is then necessary to decide what exactly the 'right' decision might be.

The study of ethics is essentially involved in determining right from wrong. Such decisions will be driven by an individual's own beliefs and values, those of the organization and those of the wider society in which they live. In Judeo-Christian society, for example, these values may be derived from respect and compassion for the individual and a wider concern for the impact of one's actions on others. Ethics operate at a different level from the laws of a particular society, since laws frequently provide for minimum standards of behaviour. They deal with the worst excesses of a society and with aspects of that society that are of wider interest and concern. They also reflect the prevailing view of the government, which one hopes in a democracy would in turn reflect the views of the majority of the members of that society.

Ethics by contrast operate at a 'higher' level. Whilst a particular action may not be illegal, it may nevertheless be regarded by a given individual as wrong because it indirectly harms others, or is not in the best interests of the organization that employs them. It is this grey area beyond the realms of the law that is the domain of ethical judgements and where the fundraising profession in particular has invested considerable time and effort to determine what does and does not constitute appropriate behaviour.

Since few donors are able to assess directly the impact their donation has had on the cause or beneficiary group, they must trust the nonprofit to deliver on its promises. The non-distribution clause requires nonprofit organizations and those associated with them to commit to the public good. Costs must be kept to a minimum and any surplus generated over operating costs must be ploughed back into the achievement of the organization's mission. Robert Payton suggests that those working in the nonprofit sector should regularly pose the question of themselves 'do we live for philanthropy, or do we live off philanthropy?' (Tempel, 2006, p. 33). Independent Sector (a leadership forum for charities, foundations and corporate giving programs in the US) is, no doubt, on this issue. Those who presume to serve the public good must assume the public trust and to achieve this, it argues, that nonprofit professionals should integrate nine commitments directly into their work.

1 Commitment to the public good
2 Accountability to the public
3 Commitment beyond the law
4 Respect for the worth and dignity of individuals
5 Inclusiveness and social justice
6 Respect for pluralism and diversity
7 Transparency, integrity and honesty
8 Responsible stewardship of resources
9 Commitment to excellence and to maintaining the public trust.

(*Source*: Independent Sector, 2007).

Organizations need to decide what constitutes appropriate behaviour and delineate what they are and are not prepared to do. Many nonprofits now enshrine this in an ethical policy which explicitly deals with the most common ethical issues likely to be encountered by staff. The document specifies both the general principles that will be applied and how staff should deal with specific examples. Many nonprofits also encourage their staff to join the relevant professional association and to adopt the code of ethics that their particular profession feels is appropriate. The ethical code developed by the AFP in the US for example is reproduced below.

AFP members aspire to:

● Practice their profession with integrity, honesty, truthfulness and adherence to the absolute obligation to safeguard the public trust.

● Act according to the highest standards and visions of their organization, profession and conscience.
● Put philanthropic mission above personal gain.
● Inspire others through their own sense of dedication and high purpose.
● Improve their professional knowledge and skills, so that their performance will better serve others.
● Demonstrate concern for the interests and well-being of individuals affected by their actions.
● Value the privacy, freedom of choice and interests of all those affected by their actions.
● Foster cultural diversity and pluralistic values, and treat all people with dignity and respect.
● Affirm, through personal giving, a commitment to philanthropy and its role in society.
● Adhere to the spirit as well as the letter of all applicable laws and regulations.
● Advocate within their own organizations, adherence to all applicable laws and regulations.
● Avoid even the appearance of any criminal offence or professional misconduct.
● Bring credit to the fundraising profession by their public demeanour.
● Encourage colleagues to embrace and practise these ethical principles and standards of professional practice.
● Be aware of the codes of ethics promulgated by other professional organizations that serve philanthropy.

Any readers interested in a further exploration of the topic of ethics in nonprofit management are advised to consult Anderson (1996) for a consideration of ethics in fundraising, Malaro (1994) for ethics in arts management and the Humanitarian Studies Unit (2001) for ethics in aid and development. The ethical literature in relation to healthcare and education are perhaps the most well developed. (see, for example, Weber, 2001; Nash, 2002).

Conclusions

In this brief review, we have focused on the key differences between for-profit and nonprofit marketing and used these as a vehicle for exploring the wider nonprofit literature. As the reader will by now be aware, the discipline of nonprofit marketing embraces a diverse range of contexts and categories of organization. Since its inception at the end of the 1960s, nonprofit marketing has come a long way. It has gained widespread acceptance as a distinctive sphere of marketing practice and the relevance of marketing ideas to the nonprofit domain is no longer in dispute. The critical issue that remains to be addressed is the dissemination of this body of knowledge to the professionals who may benefit. As this brief review has shown, blindly applying for-profit ideas is at best counter-productive and at worst may actually injure the organization the marketer is attempting to assist.

References

Abratt, R. and Sacks, D. (1988) The marketing challenge: towards being profitable and socially responsible, *Journal of Business Ethics*, **7**(7), 497–507.

Allen, C. T. (1982) Self-perception based strategies for stimulating energy conservation, *Journal of Consumer Research*, **8**(4), 381–390.

American Association of Fund-Raising Counsel (AAFRC) Trust for Philanthropy (2005) *Giving USA*, AAFRC, Indianapolis.

Anderson, A. (1996) *Ethics for Fundraisers*, Indiana University Press, Indianapolis.

Andreasen, A. R. (1995) *Marketing Social Change*, Jossey-Bass, San Francisco.

Andreasen, A. R. (1996) Profits for nonprofits: find a corporate partner, *Harvard Business Review*, **74**(6), 47–59.

Andreasen, A. R. (2002) Marketing social marketing in the social change marketplace, *Journal of Public Policy and Marketing*, **21**(1), 3–13.

Andreasen, A. R. and Kotler, P. (2004) *Strategic Marketing for Nonprofit Organizations*, 6th edn, Prentice Hall, Englewood Cliffs.

Andreoni, J. (2001) The Economics of Philanthropy, in Smelser, N. J. and Baltes, P. B. (eds), *International Encyclopedia of the Social and Behavioral Sciences*, Elsevier, London.

Bendapudi, N., Singh, S. N. and Bendapudi, V. (1996) Enhancing helping behavior: an integrative framework for promotion planning, *Journal of Marketing*, **60**(3), 33–54.

Bennett, R. (1998) Market orientation among small to medium sized UK charitable organizations: implications for fund-raising performance, *Journal of Nonprofit and Public Sector Marketing*, **6**(1), 31–45.

Bennett, R. and Savani, S. (2003) Predicting the accuracy of public perceptions of charity performance, *Journal of. Targeting, Measurement and Analysis for Marketing*, **11**(4), 326–342.

Boulding, K. E. (1973) *The Economy of Love and Fear: A Preface To Grants Economics*, Wadsworth, Belmont, CA.

Braus, P. (1995) Will baby boomers give generously? *American. Demographics*, **16**(7), 48–52, 57.

Bruce, I. (1995) Do not-for-profits value their customers and their needs? *International Marketing Review*, **12**(4), 77–84.

Bryant, W. K., Jeon-Slaughter, H., Kang, H. and Tax, A. (2003) Participation in philanthropic activities: donating money and time, *Journal of Consumer Policy*, **26**(1), 43–74.

Burnett, J. J. and Wood, V. R. (1988) A proposed model of the donation decision process, *Research in Consumer Behavior*, **3**, 1–47.

Campbell, L., Gulas, C. S. and Gruca, T. S. (1999) Corporate giving behavior and decision-maker social consciousness, *Journal of Business Ethics*, **19**(4), 375–383.

Caruana, A., Ramaseshan, B. and Ewing, M. T. (1998) The marketing orientation – performance link: some evidence from the public sector and universities, *Journal of Nonprofit and Public Sector Marketing*, **6**(1), 63–82.

Chapman, D. and Cowdell, T. (1998) *New Public Sector Marketing*, Financial Times Publishing, London.

Cohen, D. A., Farley, T. A., Bedimo-Etame, J. R. and Scribner, R. (1999) Implementation of condom social marketing in Louisiana, 1993–1996, *American Journal of Public Health*, **89**(2), 204–208.

Coliazzi, A., Williams, K. J. and Kayson, W. A. (1984) When will people help? The effects of gender, urgency and location on altruism, *Psychological Reports*, **55**, 139–142.

Cooper, P. D. (1979) *Healthcare Marketing: Issues and Trends*, Aspen Systems Corporation, Germantown, MD.

Dahrendorf, R. (1997) *Keynote Address to Charities Aid Foundation Conference*, QEII Conference Centre, October, London.

DiPofi, J. A., LaTour, M. S. and Henthorne, T. L. (2001) The new social marketing challenge to promote radon testing, *Health Marketing Quarterly*, **19**(1), 79–90.

Donovan, R. J. (1999) Targeting Male Perpetrators of Intimate Partner Violence: Western Australia's Freedom from Fear Campaign, Paper presented at the Fifth Innovations in Social Marketing Conference, University of British Columbia, Vancouver, BC.

Drucker, P. (1990) *Managing The Non-Profit Organization*, Butterworth Heinemann, Oxford.

Drumwright, M. E. (1996) Company advertising with a social dimension: the role of noneconomic criteria, *Journal of Marketing*, **60**(4), 71–87.

Ferber, R. (1970) The expanding role of marketing in the 1970s, *Journal of Marketing*, **34**(1), 29–30.

Fine, S. F. (1981) *The Marketing of Ideas and Social Issues*, Praeger, New York.

Frederiksen, L. W., Solomon, L. J. and Brehony, K. A. (1984) *Marketing Health Behavior*, Plenum, New York.

Friedman, M. (1970) The social responsibility of business is to increase it's profits, *New York Times Magazine*, SECT, 122–126.

Goldberg, M. (1997) Social marketing: are we fiddling while rome burns? *Journal of Consumer Psychology*, **4**(4), 347–370.

Guy, B. S. and Patton, W. E. (1989) The marketing of altruistic causes: understanding why people help, *Journal of Services Marketing*, **2**(1), 5–16.

Halfpenny, P. (1990) *Charity Household Survey 1988/9*, Charities Aid Foundation, Tonbridge, UK.

Hall, H. (2004) Gender differences in giving: going, going, gone? *New Directions for Philanthropic Fundraising*, **2004**(43), 71–72.

Hall, R. P. (1978) *Conceptual, Methodological and Moral Issues in the Study of Organizational Effectiveness*, Working Paper, Dept of Sociology, SUNY – Albany.

Hansmann, H. (1980). The role of the nonprofit enterprise, *Yale Law Review*, 89 (April), 835–899.

Harbaugh, W. (1998) What do donations buy? A model of philanthropy based on prestige and warm glow, *Journal of Public Economics*, **67**(2), 269–284.

Hornik, R. (2001) Remarks on the Occasion of the Andreasen Fellowship Lecture, Paper presented at the Social Marketing and Health Conference, Clearwater, FL, June 22.

Humanitarian Studies Unit (2001) *Reflections on Humanitarian Action: Principles, Ethics and Contradictions*, Pluto Press, London.

Hunt, S. D. (1977) The Three Dichotomies Model of Marketing: An Elaboration of Issues, in Slater, C. C. (ed.), *Macro-Marketing: Distributive Processes from a Societal Perspective*, University of Colorado, Boulder, pp. 52–56.

Independent Sector (2007) Member Code of Ethics, http://www.independentsector.org/Members/code_ethics.html (accessed 5 January 2007).

Irwin-Wells, S. (2002) *Planning and Implementing Your Major Gifts Campaign*, Jossey Bass, San Francisco.

Jackson, T. D. (2001) Young African Americans: a new generation of giving behavior, *International Journal of Nonprofit and Voluntary Sector Marketing*, **6**(3) 243–254.

Jaworski, B. J. and Kohli, A. K. (1993) Marketing orientation: antecedents and consequences, *Journal of Marketing*, **57**(3), July, 53–70.

Jones, A. and Posnett, J. (1991) Charitable giving by UK households: evidence from the family expenditure survey, *Applied Economics*, **23**(2), 343–351.

Jordan, W. K. (1964) *Philanthropy in England 1480–1660*, George Allen and Unwin, London.

Kaehler, J. and Sargeant, A. (1998) *Returns on Fund-Raising Expenditures in the Voluntary Sector*, Working Paper 98/06, University of Exeter.

Kohli, A. K. and Jaworski, B. J. (1990) Market orientation: the construct, research propositions and managerial implications, *Journal of Marketing*, **54**, April, 1–18.

Kotler, P. and Andreasen, A. (1982) *Strategic Marketing for Nonprofit Organizations*, Prentice Hall, Englewood Cliffs.

Kotler, P. and Andreasen, A. (1991) *Strategic Marketing for Nonprofit Organizations*, 4th edn, Prentice Hall, Englewood Cliffs.

Kotler, P. and Clarke, R. N. (1986) *Marketing for Health Care Organizations*, Prentice Hall, Englewood Cliffs.

Kotler, P. and Fox, K. F. A. (1985) *Strategic Marketing for Educational Institutions*, Prentice Hall, Englewood Cliffs.

Kotler, P. and Levy, S. J. (1969) Broadening the concept of marketing, *Journal of Marketing*, **33**(2), 10–15.

Kotler, P. and Roberto, E. L. (1989) *Social Marketing: Strategies for Changing Public Behavior*, The Free Press, New York.

Kotler, P. and Zaltman, G. (1971) Social marketing: an approach to planned social change, *Journal of Marketing*, **44**, Fall, 24–33.

Kottasz, R. (2004) How should charitable organizations motivate young professionals to give philanthropically? *International Journal of Nonprofit and Voluntary Sector Marketing*, **9**(1), 9–27.

Lavidge, R. J. (1970) The growing responsibilities of marketing, *Journal of Marketing*, **34**(1), 27.

Lee, S. (1996) *Philanthropy Still Has Its Place, Hollis Sponsorship and Donations Yearbook*, 4th edn, Hollis Directories Ltd, London.

Lovelock, C. H. and Weinberg, C. B. (1989) *Marketing for Public and Nonprofit Managers*, 2nd edn, The Scientific Press, Redwood City, CA.

Lovelock, C. H. and Weinberg, C. B. (1990) *Public and Nonprofit Marketing: Readings and Cases*, The Scientific Press, San Francisco.

Luck, D. J. (1969) Broadening the concept of marketing too far, *Journal of Marketing*, **33**(2), 53–55.

Maibach, E. and Cotton, D. (1995) Moving People to Behaviour Change: A Staged Social Cognitive Approach to Message Design, in Maibach, E. and Parrott, R. L. (eds), *Designing Health Messages*, Sage Publications, Newbury Park, CA, pp. 41–64.

Malaro, M. C. (1994) *Museum Governance: Mission, Ethics, Policy*, Prentice Hall, Englewood Cliffs.

Manoff, R. K. (1985) *Social Marketing*, Praeger, New York.

McClelland, R. and Brooks, A. C. (2004) What is the real relationship between income and charitable giving? *Public Finance Review*, **32**(5), 483–498.

McGuire, W. J. and Padawer-Singer, A. (1976) Trait salience in the spontaneous self concept, *Journal of Personality and Social Psychology*, **33**, 743–754.

McKenna, J., Gutierez, K. and McCall, K. (2000) Strategies for effective youth countermarketing program: recommendations from commercial marketing experts, *Journal of Public Health Management Practice*, **6**, May, 7–13.

McKenzie-Mohr D (1994) Social marketing for sustainability: the case for residential energy conservation, *Futures*, March, 224–33.

Meade, J. (1974) A mathematical model for deriving hospital service areas, *International Journal of Health Services*, **4**, 353–357.

Meijer, M.-M., de Bakker, F. G. A., Smit, J. H. and Schuyt, T. (2006) Corporate giving in the Netherlands 1995–2003: exploring the amounts involved and the motivations for donating, *International Journal of Nonprofit and Voluntary Sector Marketing*, **11**(1), 13–28.

Mesch, D. J., Rooney, P. M., Chin, W. and Steinberg, K. S. (2002) Race and gender differences in philanthropy: Indiana as a test case, *New Directions for Philanthropic Fundraising*, **2002**(37), 65–78.

Miller, S. J. (1974) Market Segmentation and Forecasting for a Charitable Health Organization, Paper presented to the Southern Marketing Association Conference, Atlanta, Georgia.

Mokwa, M. P., Dawson, W. D. and Priere, E. A. (eds) (1981) *Marketing The Arts*, Praeger, New York.

Moore, E. M., Bearden, W. O. and Teel, J. E. (1985) Use of labeling and assertions of dependency in appeals for consumer support, *Journal of Consumer Research*, **12**(1), 90–96.

Moore, J. N., Raymond, M. A., Mittelstaedt, J. D. and Tanner, J. F. (2002) Age and consumer socialisation agent influences on adolescents' sexual knowledge, attitudes and behaviour: implications for social marketing initiatives and public policy, *Journal of Public Policy and Marketing*, **21**(1), 37–52.

Morgan, J. N., Dye, R. F. and Hybels, J. H. (1979) *Results From Two National Surveys Of Philanthropic Activity*, University of Michigan Press, Michigan.

Mullin, R. (1995) *Foundations for Fundraising*, ICSA Publishing, London.

Narver, J. C. and Slater, S. F. (1990) The effect of a market orientation on business profitability, *Journal of Marketing*, **54**(4), 20–35.

Nash, R. J. (2002) *Real World Ethics: Frameworks for Educators and Human Service Professionals*, Teachers College Press, Boston.

Nathan, L. (1952) *Report to the Committee on Law and Practice Relating to Charitable Trusts*, HMSO, London.

Neiheisel, S. R. (1995) *Corporate Strategy and the Politics of Goodwill*, Peter Lang Publishing, New York.

Newman, W. H. and Wallender, H. W. (1978) Managing for nonprofit enterprises, *Academy of Management Review*, **3**(1), 24–32.

Nichols, J. E. (1992) Targeting older America, *Fund Raising Management*, **23**(3), 38–41.

Okten, C. and Weisbrod, B. (2000) Determinants of donations in private nonprofit markets, *Journal of Public Economics*, **75**(2), 255–272.

Ostrower, E. (1996) *Why the Wealthy Give: The Culture of Elite Philanthropy*, Princeton University Press, Princeton, NJ.

Peattie, K., Peattie, S. and Clarke, P. (2001) Skin cancer prevention: re-evaluating the public policy implications, *Journal of Public Policy and Marketing*, **20**(2), 268–279.

Pechmann, C. and Reibling, E. T. (2000) Planning an effective anti-smoking mass media campaign targeting adolescents, *Journal of Public Health Management Practice*, **6**, May, 80–94.

Pharoah, C. and Tanner, S. (1997) Trends in charitable giving, *Fiscal Studies*, **18**(4), 427–443.

Porter, M. and Kramer, M. (2002) The competitive advantage of corporate philanthropy, *Harvard Business Review*, **80**(12), 56–61.

Rados, D. L. (1981) *Marketing for Non-Profit Organizations*, Auburn House, Dover, MA.

Reichert, T., Heckler, S. E. and Jackson, S. (2001) The effects of sexual social marketing appeals on cognitive processing and persuasion, *Journal of Advertising*, **30**(1), 13–27.

Reingen, P. H. (1978) On inducing compliance with requests, *Journal of Consumer Research*, 5(2), 96–102.

Ricks Jr., J. M. (2005) An assessment of strategic corporate philanthropy on perceptions of brand equity variables, *Journal of Consumer Marketing*, 22(3), 121–134.

Riecken, G., Babakus, E. and Yavas, U. (1994) Facing resource attraction challenges in the nonprofit sector: a behaviouristic approach to fund-raising and volunteer recruitment, *Journal of Professional Services Marketing*, 11(1), 45–70.

Rothschild, M. L. (1999) Carrots, sticks and promises: a conceptual framework for the management of public health and social issues behaviours, *Journal of Marketing*, 63(4), 24–37.

Sagawa, S. (2001) New value partnerships: the lessons of denny's/save the children partnership for building high-yielding cross-sector alliances, *International Journal of Nonprofit & Voluntary Sector Marketing*, 6(3), 199–214.

Sargeant, A. (1999) *Marketing Management for Nonprofit Organisations*, Oxford University Press, Oxford.

Sargeant, A. and Hudson, J. (2005) Nonprofit brand or bland: an exploration of the structure of charity brand personality, *Proceedings of EMAC*, Università Bocconi, Milan, Italy, 24–27 May, CD-ROM.

Sargeant, A. and Jay, E. (2004) *Fundraising Management: Analysis, Planning and Practice*, Routledge, London.

Sargeant, A. and Kaehler, J. (1998) *Benchmarking Charity Costs*, Charities Aid Foundation, West Malling.

Sargeant, A. and Woodliffe, L. (2007) A Review of the Gift-Giving Literature, in Sargeant, A. and Wymer, W. (eds), *The Nonprofit Marketing Companion*, Routledge, London.

Sargeant, A., Foreman, S. and Liao, M. (2002) Operationalizing the marketing concept in the nonprofit sector, *Journal of Nonprofit and Public Sector Marketing*, 10(2), 41–65.

Sargeant, A., West, D. C. and Ford, J. B. (2001) The role of perceptions in predicting donor value, *Journal of Marketing Management*, 17(3/4), 407–428.

Schervish, P. G. (1993) Philosophy As Moral Identity of Caritas, in Schervish, P. G., Benz, O., Dulaney, P., Murphy, T. B. and Salett, S. (eds), *Taking Giving Seriously*, Center on Philanthropy, Indiana University, Indianapolis.

Schervish, P. G. and Havens, J. J. (1997) Social participation and charitable giving: a multivariate analysis, *Voluntas*, 8(3), 235–260.

Sharfman, M. (1994) Changing institutional rules: the evolution of corporate philanthropy, 1883–1953, *Business and Society*, 33(3), 236–269.

Sheehan, R. (1996) Mission accomplishment as philanthropic organizational effectiveness: key findings from the excellence in philanthropy project, *Nonprofit and Voluntary Sector Quarterly*, 25, 110–123.

Shuptrine, F. K. and Moore, E. M. (1980) The Public's Perceptions of the American Heart Association: Awareness, Image and Opinions, in Sumney, J. H. and Taylor, R. D. (eds), *Evolving Marketing Thought for 1980*, Southern Marketing Association, Atlanta.

Smith, A. (1776) *The Wealth of Nations*, Dent and Sons Ltd, Letchworth.

Smith, M. A. (1992) *Reducing Alcohol Consumption among University Students: Recruitment and Programme Design Strategies Based on Social Marketing Theory*, Unpublished Thesis, University of Oregon.

Stanton, A., Kennedy, M., Springarn, R. and Rotheram-Borus, M. J. (2000) Developing services for substance-abusing HIV positive youth with mental health disorders, *Journal of Behavioral Health Services Research*, 27(4), 380–389.

Steffey, B. D. and Jones, J. W. (1988) The impact of family and career planning variables on the organizational, career and community commitment of professional women, *Journal of Vocational Behavior*, 32(2), 196–212.

Swinyard, W. R. and Ray, M. L. (1977) Advertising-selling interactions: an attribution theory experiment, *Journal of Marketing Research*, 14, November, 509–516.

Tapp, A. (1996) Charity brands: a qualitative study of current practice, *Journal of Nonprofit and Voluntary Sector Marketing*, 1(4), 327–336.

Tempel, E. (2006) Ethical Frameworks for Fundraising, in *Principles and Techniques of Fundraising*, The Fund Raising School, Indianapolis, IN, pp. 31–43.

Wagner, C. and Wheeler, L. (1969) Model need and cost effects in helping behavior, *Journal of Personality and Social Psychology*, 12, 111–116.

Walker, C. and Pharoah, C. (2002) *A Lot of Give*, Hodder and Stoughton, London.

Warwick, M. (1994) *Raising Money by Mail: Strategies for Growth and Financial Stability*, Strathmoor Press, Berkeley, CA.

Warwick, M. and Hitchcock, S. (2001) *Ten Steps to Fundraising Success: Choosing the Right Strategy for your Organization*, Jossey Bass, San Fransisco.

Weber, L. (2001) *Business Ethics in Healthcare: Beyond Compliance*, Indiana University Press, Indianapolis, IN.

Weick, K. E. (1977) Re-Punctuating the Problem, in Goodman, P. S. and Pennings, J. (eds), *New Perspectives on Organizational Effectiveness*, Jossey Bass, San Fransisco, pp. 63–95.

Wymer Jr.,W. W. and Samu, S. (2003). Dimensions of business and nonprofit collaborative relationships, *Journal of Nonprofit & Public Sector Marketing*, **11**(1), 3–23.

Yankelovich, D. (1985) *The Charitable Behavior of Americans, Management Survey*, Independent Sector, Washington, DC.

Yavas, U. and Riecken, R. (1985) Can volunteers be targeted? *Journal of the Academy of Marketing Science*, **13**(2), 218–228.

Young, D. R. (1983) *If Not For Profit, For What? A Behavioural Theory of the Nonprofit Sector Based on Entrepreneurship*, Lexington Books, Lexington, KY.

Zeithaml, V. (1996) *Services Marketing*, McGraw-Hill, New York.

Zucker, D., Hopkins, R. S., Sly, D. F., Urich, J., Kershaw, J. M. and Solari, S. (2000) Florida's truth campaign: a countermarketing anti-tobacco media campaign, *Journal of Public Health Management Practice*, **6**(3), 1–6.

Further reading

Fundraising

Burnett, K. (2002) *Relationship Fundraising: A Donor Based Approach to the Business of Raising Money*, Jossey Bass, San Francisco.

Klein, K. (2005) *Fundraising for Social Change*, 5th edn, Jossey Bass, San Francisco.

Sargeant, A. and Jay, E. (2004) *Fundraising Management: Analysis, Planning and Practice*, Routledge, London.

Smith, G. (1996) *Asking Properly*, White Lion Press, London.

Warwick, M. (2004) *Revolution in the Mailbox: Your Guide to Successful Direct Mail Fundraising*, Jossey Bass, San Francisco.

Arts Marketing

Bernstein, J. S. and Kotler, P. (2006) *Arts Marketing Insights: The Dynamics of Building and Retaining Performing Arts Audiences*, Jossey Bass, San Francisco.

Colbert, F., Nantel, J., Bilodeau, S. and Rich, J. D. (2001) *Marketing Culture and the Arts*, Paul and Company Publishing Consortium, Concord.

Kerrigan, F., Fraser, P. and Ozbilgin, M. (2004) *Arts Marketing*, Butterworth Heinemann, London.

Kotler, P. and Bernstein, J. S. (2001) *Standing Room Only: Strategies for Marketing the Performing Arts*, Harvard Business School Press, Boston.

Education Marketing

Barnes, C. (1993) *Practical Marketing for Schools*, Blackwell Publishers, Oxford.

Foster, R. S. and Sauser, W. I. (1994) *Marketing University Outreach Programs*, Haworth Press, Binghamton.

Hayes, T. J. (2002) *New Strategies in Higher Education Marketing*, Haworth Press, Binghamton.

Kirp, D. L., Berman, E. P., Homan, J. T. and Roberts, P. (2004) *Shakespeare, and the Bottom Line: The Marketing of Higher Education*, Harvard University Press, Boston.

Kotler, P. and Fox, K. F. A. (1995) *Strategic Marketing for Educational Institutions*, Prentice Hall, Englewood Cliffs.

Healthcare Marketing

Berkowitz, E. N. (2003) *Essentials of Health Care Marketing*, Jones and Bartlett Publishers, Boston.

Fortenberry, J. L. (2005) *Marketing Tools for Healthcare Executives*, 2nd edn, Oxford Crest, Oxford.

Ginter, P. M., Duncan, W. J., Sappington, A. A. and Swayne, L. (2004) *Strategic Management of Health Care Organizations*, Blackwell Publishing, Boston.

Hillestad, S. G. and Berkowitz, E. N. (2003) *Health Care Market Strategy*, 3rd edn, Jones and Bartlett Publishers International, Sudbury, MA.

Public Sector Marketing

Bean, J. and Hussey, L. (1997) *Marketing Public Sector Services (Essential Skills for the Public Sector)*, HB Publications, London.

Chapman, D. and Cowdell, T. (1997) *New Public Sector Marketing*, Pitman Publishing, London.

Coffman, L. L. (1986) *Public Sector Marketing: A Guide for Practitioners*, Wiley, Chichester.

Kotler, P. and Lee, N. (2006) *Marketing in the Public Sector: A Roadmap for Improved Performance*, Wharton School Publishing, Philadelphia, PA.

Titman, L. G. (1995) *Marketing in the New Public Sector*, Financial Times and Prentice Hall, London.

Social Marketing

Andreasen, A. R. (1995) *Marketing Social Change: Changing Behavior to Promote Health, Service Development and the Environment*, Jossey Bass, San Francisco.

Andreasen, A. R. (2001) *Ethics in Social Marketing*, Georgetown University Press, Washington.

Andreasen, A. R. (2005) *Social Marketing in the 21st Century*, Sage Publications, Thousand Oaks.

Basil, D. Z. (2007) *Social Marketing: Advances in Research and Theory*, Haworth Press, Binghamton.

Kotler, P., Roberto, N. and Lee, N. R. (2002) *Social Marketing: Improving the Quality of Life*, Sage Publications, Thousand Oaks.

CHAPTER 27

Marketing ethics

ANDREA PROTHERO

Introduction

We are not proposing that marketers take the moral high ground on every issue. But when marketers are considered about as trustworthy as used-car salespeople, it would be a major step for marketers to lead the revolt against immoral practices and the cynical misuse of ethical policies. This way, the standing of the profession as a whole can be increased and we can work towards a fairer, more decent society – whilst still ensuring that the economy thrives.

(Chartered Institute of Marketing, 2004).

The most startling point from the above quote is not the quote itself, but rather its source – the Chartered Institute of Marketing, the professional body for marketers in the UK. In the twenty-first century, marketers themselves have recognized the importance of ethics to marketing practice. Consequently, the study of marketing ethics is important as society, business and marketers begin to further reflect on ethical issues of importance – be they global concerns over the warming of the earth and humans' responsibility for the destruction of our natural environment or more micro, firm-based issues which focus on unethical business and marketing practices. Trust for both business and marketing activities is declining, particularly following large corporate scandals such as the Arthur Andersen, Enron and WorldCom affairs. As such, it seems imperative in the twenty-first century that a text such as *The Marketing Book* focuses on the subject of marketing ethics. Indeed, marketing ethics is not a new topic and has been debated, contested and explored in detail since the 1950s in academic texts and articles (see, for example, Adler *et al.*, 1981; Tsalikis and Fritzsche,

1989; Jacobsen and Mazur 1995; Davidson, 2003; Murphy and Laczniak, 2006) as well as in more mainstream texts such as Vance Packard's critique of advertising, *The Hidden Persuaders* (1957) and critiques of consumer society (Fromm, 1955; Marcuse, 1964; Debord, 1977).

Marketing ethics in context

Before exploring marketing ethics and its implications for our understanding of both the theory and practice of marketing, it is firstly important to place it into a wider ethical context, as such it is necessary to briefly highlight the areas of ethics generally and more specifically business ethics and corporate social responsibility.

Ethics

Ethics itself has a deep, varied and rich history and focuses on questions of good and bad, right and wrong, and what it means to have or take responsibility, or promote human flourishing. Famous and influential philosophers, such as Plato, Aristotle, Immanuel Kant and John Stewart Mill, all felt that ethical questions were central to human life and human interactions, including public life. There are various ethical theories which have been developed over a long period of time ranging from absolutist theories – that focus on universal ethical principals regarding what everyone should do in all situations – to relativist theories focused upon subjective concerns in particular contexts and particular moments. Consequential ethical theories are concerned with the intended outcomes of actions and include utilitarian ethics that focus in various ways on the greatest good for the greatest number of people. Non-consequential theories consider the decision makers' motives and include deontological ethics' concern with one's 'duty' and the ethics of rights and justice. There are also contemporary ethical theories such as environmental ethics and feminist ethics, invoking values and concerns often ignored or left out of long-standing traditional views. Which perspective you decide to explore ethics from and what types of concerns you consider impact on the way you see the study and implementation of marketing ethics.

Business ethics and corporate social responsibility (CSR)

A key joke among students, at all levels, when taught business ethics and corporate social responsibility has been 'Business Ethics: I didn't know there were any'. It is, however, accepted that the ethical practices of business are under scrutiny now more than ever and ethical business practices and CSR are the ways of thinking for all businesses in the twenty-first century. Many have argued that ethics and CSR are fad topics and as such will move up and down the corporate agenda as ethics moves and sways in certain directions. However, most would argue that the ethical conduct of businesses and the people who make up those businesses are only going to increase in importance into the future. As Digby Jones, Director General of the CBI, emphasized in 2002, 'people like working for and buying from companies who are seen to be taking their responsibilities seriously'.

Thus, it is fair to suggest that business and ethics are intrinsically linked, and will remain so, well into the next century, and as such CSR, and the manner in which organizations conduct their activities, will continue to play an important role in society. This is not least because it has been well documented both academically and in the popular press that doing 'bad' is 'bad' for business. Nike's share price, for example, plummeted after it admitted abuse at its Indonesian plants in 2001. Newspapers themselves like nothing better than to criticize poor behaviour, as evidenced in coverage of the unethical practices of individuals such as Martha Stewart, Kenneth Lay and Jeffrey Skilling of Enron, as well as being critical of organizations, and the key individuals within these same companies, who market themselves as socially responsible.

For instance, criticisms against the Body Shop and its founder Anita Roddick were intense during the 1980s and early 1990s, at a time when it was generally recognized that the Body Shop's ethical and environmental actions were far superior to many others in the cosmetics industry, on a number of fronts. As well as popular press criticism of unethical practices, there are also a number of anti-corporation best sellers such as Naomi Klein's *No Logo*, which depict business in a bad light. Similarly, there has been a plethora of successful film documentaries criticizing business activity – see, for example, *Super Size Me*, *The Corporation* and most recently the award-winning *An Inconvenient Truth*. Movies themselves have also raised important issues about various ethical practices – recent examples include *Blood Diamond*, *The Insider* and *Erin Brockovich*. Companies are also targeted by pressure groups, consumers, lawyers and their employees who question the ethics of business strategies and practices. All of this public scrutiny has led organizations to continually redress their impact on society and all its stakeholders, at a time when ethical problems are also becoming more complex. Thus, all business activities can be subjected to public scrutiny – be they related to workplace, community, environmental or marketplace issues. Consequently, these issues have significant implications for marketing activities, an area of business, which has been seen to be responsible for significant unethical practices.

A key definition of business ethics has been provided by Crane and Matten (2004, p. 8).

> Business ethics is the study of business situations, activities, and decisions where issues of right and wrong are addressed.

It is these issues of right and wrong which have their roots in our understanding of the various ethical theories discussed above, which, then, transcend into our assessment of marketing ethics by focusing on issues of right and wrong in relation to marketing as a discipline and marketing as a practice. Indeed, these issues of 'good or bad' and 'right and wrong' often result in legal concerns alone.

Marketing ethics

Although in recent years many of the major ethical controversies in business have been related to the accountancy and finance areas, marketing has very often been the business function most associated with unethical behaviour (Tsalikis and Fritzsche, 1989; Armstrong and Sweeney, 1994; Nantel and Weeks, 1996). It is therefore imperative that a book such as this devotes attention to the study of marketing ethics. In their excellent text on marketing ethics, Laczniak and Murphy (2003) stress that from a marketing perspective we are exploring how ethical issues affect 'marketing decisions, behaviors and institutions' and to fully understand marketing ethics, we must explore these issues in a systematic manner. Consequently, all of the aspects of marketing covered in this book can and should be examined from an ethical perspective.

There have been a number of attempts to develop ethical marketing theories in the 1980s (Ferrell and Gresham, 1985; Hunt and Vitell, 1986; Dubinsky and Loken, 1989) and 1990s (Laczniak and Murphy, 1993) and more recently in the 2000s with an update of Hunt and Vitell's general theory of marketing ethics (Hunt and Vitell, 2006) and a normative offering from Laczniak and Murphy (2006). These theories explore marketing ethics from different theoretical perspectives and as such are dependent on how one views and examines ethics generally, as discussed in the ethics section above. In recent years, there have been some excellent texts and case studies focusing specifically on ethical marketing issues (Murphy *et al.*, 2005; Murphy and Laczniak, 2006) and also articles which consider ethical marketing across cultures (Nill and Shultz, 1997; Srnka, 2004) and the influence of ethical issues upon marketing students (Singhapakdi, 2004; Nill and Schibrowsky, 2005). Regardless of how one decides to explore ethics and which perspective is taken, from a practical viewpoint all exchanges have an impact on society and as such every transaction can be considered through an ethical lens (Laczniak and Murphy, 2006). Consequently, when one is exploring the various marketing strategies and practices detailed throughout the book, it is necessary to explore and assess these from an ethical perspective.

Macromarketing

When exploring marketing ethics, one can begin by asking two basic questions: First, what impact does marketing have on society and second, what impact does society have on marketing? By doing so, we are then able to explore marketing from a macro, societal, rather than a micro, firm level. As such we will then want to consider not only the ethical practices of marketers at a firm level, but also implications for marketing activities on a much wider, societal level. In this context, we can explore marketing from a macromarketing perspective and argue that marketing is not just a set of managerial practices or, indeed, an organizational philosophy, but moreover, a social institution. Macromarketing itself is a discipline that predates the term and has been a topic of investigation for as far back in time as the Greek philosophers Plato and Socrates. Terms such as 'marketing in/and society' are used regularly by academics and in essence we can substitute this term for macromarketing, a term first coined by George Fisk in 1962. When focusing on macomarketing, one is exploring issues relating to 'ethics, marketing systems, public policy, and social responsibility' (Hunt and Vitell, 2006). In order to explore marketing ethics, then it is important to consider ethical issues from a broad societal perspective, rather than a simple narrow firm perspective.

What is important is to begin to explore and ask questions concerning what are marketing's impacts on society and what are the ethical implications of this? With a macro focus, we can ask questions such as 'is marketing inherently bad', before focusing more specifically on the unethical strategies and practices of marketing departments and managers themselves. This allows us to consider marketing activities from both an absolutist and a relativist perspective.

Macromarketing sins

The use of marketing by businesses, and indeed governments and non-governmental organizations (NGOs), has been severely criticized by many in society for many decades now. One central key macro argument is that ultimately the use of marketing is inherently 'bad' for society and it is some of these macro arguments that are further explored below:

- *Marketing purports to the pursuit of happiness through consumption*: It is well documented in the literature that marketing is concerned with exchange relationships and the satisfaction of consumer needs and wants; and it these goals that marketers attempt to achieve. However, there have also been critical assessments of pursuing the notion of satisfying consumers, most notably as a result of such activities not necessarily leading to satisfied and happy consumers. It is argued that the pursuit of happiness through consumption ultimately leads to perpetual dissatisfaction, where consumers' needs are never fully met as there are always more goods to buy, or more services to be experienced. As Blackburn commented in 2004, 'At a time when materially "we've never had it so good", we feel more anxious and unhappy than ever', where it is suggested that the generation born in the 1970s are the unhappiest ever. Many of these criticisms are, indeed, a criticism not only of marketing but of business and the pursuit and capitalism. As such, when engaging in a critique of marketing principles and practices very often, this also leads to a debate of the role of capitalism in society.

- *Marketing leads to the pursuit of the ideal self through consumption, and this ideal self is promoted through marketing communications campaigns*: Recently there has much debate surrounding the ideal self and how marketers use notions of this ideal self to tempt consumers into buying more goods and services. This ideal self is then promoted through various marketing communications campaigns, such as 'buy this product and you will look/be like me', thus leading to much consumer dissonance when the ideal self is not achieved. Similarly, authors have questioned who determines what the 'ideal self' should look like, thus forming another contentious issue. It is argued that marketing communications leads to an idealized notion of what a 'good life' should be while at the same time also reinforcing social stereotypes.
- *By the use of various marketing activities marketing stereotypes consumers*: Connected to the discussion above, many have argued that marketers stereotype consumers in particular ways. For instance, in their advertising campaigns companies have been criticized for various stereotyping actions – for instance, an over-reliance on white-middle classed families; only using the 'traditional' family in ads; not using enough older consumers in ads; only showing beautiful, thin, 'perfect' consumers in ads, etc. Such stereotyping, it is argued, leads to dissatisfaction and isolation for those in society who do not conform to particular stereotypes.
- *Marketing targets vulnerable groups in society*: Companies have been criticized in many diverse product ranges for targeting vulnerable groups – for

instance, by promoting smoking or encouraging the use of formula rather than breast milk in developing nations. In developed nations, unscrupulous companies have also been criticized for targeting vulnerable groups – for instance, the use of door-to-door salespeople to encourage elderly people to buy expensive home security systems. Marketers have also been subject to much recent condemnation over its marketing campaigns to children and teenagers.
- *Marketing actively excludes potential customers from the marketplace*: In many situations, companies wish to maintain exclusivity about their products and as such actively discourage some groups from buying their products. An obvious way to do this is to price goods at a significantly high level to allow companies to maintain such exclusivity.

Micromarketing sins

At a firm, micro-level companies have been criticized for many unscrupulous marketing activities, both at a strategic and a tactical level. Activities at a micro level can also have long-term implications for society, and macro criticisms can also be applied at micro, firm level. Thus, it is imperative that both micro and macro concerns are considered together. Some examples of firm-level sins include:

- *Price fixing, excessive pricing, deceptive pricing*: Pricing irregularities are a common occurrence in business and many companies have been criticized for their pricing strategies. Sometimes, there is collective condemnation for a number of companies such as in the use of cartels, for instance. Recently, in the Republic of Ireland retailers were criticized by the Consumers' Association of Ireland following the removal of the countries Groceries Order. While prices of goods covered by the Order had fallen slightly, other products not covered, such as meat and fish, and fruit and vegetables, had actually increased in price. British Airways is currently being investigated by the Office of Fair Trading in the UK and the Department of Justice in the USA over alleged price fixing on its fuel surcharges. The company has seen a decrease in consumer confidence as a result and also saw both its Commercial Director and Head of Communications resign in 2006.
- *Selling dangerous products and product recalls*: For centuries, companies have been disparaged for

selling dangerous products ranging from cigarettes and alcohol, to the sale of weapons of mass destruction. There are also concerns over the sale of unsafe products. In the European Union (EU), product recalls have increased significantly recently, and it has been suggested that this is due to new legislation governing unsafe products. An average of two product recalls a day are listed on the European Commission website, with main offenders being children's toys and electrical goods. Details of product recalls in the UK are updated regularly on the Trading Standards website (http://www.tradingstandards.gov.uk/). A very visible recall in 2006 was the withdrawal of one million bars of chocolate by Cadbury's following a salmonella scare. Reports suggest the recall cost the company between twenty to thirty million pounds sterling as well as a temporary removal of the companies sponsorship of Coronation Street, the removal of other marketing communications activities and a temporary hold on the launch of new products within the company. Following the reintroduction of marketing communications, the company also increased its advertising spend by £7 million. Subsequent to the product recall there was an initial decrease in sales of Cadbury's products, but suppliers were soon reporting sales back to their pre-recall levels. There is still a possibility that the company will face prosecution in the UK and the EU for selling food unfit for human consumption and for not disclosing the food scare earlier.

- *Misleading consumers as to the benefits of their products*: Companies have long been said to exaggerate the benefits of their products to consumers. This may be in a very suggestive way, by perhaps alluding that using a particular product will make you more attractive, or more beautiful in some way, for instance; or a company can make unsubstantiated claims about their products, by suggesting that a diet product will make you thinner, for example without emphasizing that this has to be in conjunction with a change in diet and regular exercise.
- *Adopting dubious and unethical marketing communications strategies*: One of the biggest criticisms of marketing activities is in the use of company marketing communication strategies. These range from deception and negative advertising to the use of misleading advertising claims. Companies can be criticized by the general public or by competitors. The most complained about ad ever in the UK was a 2005 television

commercial from food company *KFC*. The ad showed people eating with their mouths full and drew complaints from 1671 consumers. The Advertising Standards Authority (ASA) did not uphold the complaint as it disagreed with the bulk of objections where people felt the ad encouraged bad manners in children. Complaints from competitor companies have included both Morrison's and Tesco complaints to the ASA about misleading pricing claims by rivals Asda, while at the same time Argos complained to the ASA about Tesco's price comparison claims with its electrical goods products, claiming Tesco's leaflets were misleading. Sometimes, government agencies and/or consumer watchdogs also make complaints to the ASA. Recently the food company Heinz had to remove press and poster ads for its '5-a-day the Heinz Way' campaign following complaints by the Food Commission. It was emphasized that Heinz's claims that its canned tomato soup contained two portion of the recommended five a day for fruit and vegetables was misleading. Negative advertising seems to be playing a significant role in the political campaigns of political parties, particularly in the lead up to a general election, and many have suggested that such negative campaigns are both damaging to the individual politicians and political parties involved, but also lead to negative consequences for society – through voter turn-off and a low election turn-out, for example.

One area of recent concern is over the use of food labelling and in particular the possibility of misleading and/or confusing consumers with information provided on food labels. Companies have been criticized for using terms such as 'fresh', 'natural', 'organic' and 'pure' inaccurately, as well as for the use of confusing labels highlighting a product's fat, sugar and salt contents. The Food Standards Agency (FSA) has introduced a voluntary traffic light system for the labelling of foods and a number of high profile retailers such as the Co-Op, Marks & Spencer, Sainsbury's and Waitrose have introduced the system. The FSA is hoping that with added pressure from consumers, other companies will also follow suit and help make labels easier for consumers to understand.

- *Intruding into people's lives via the use of database and direct marketing*: The use of data base and direct marketing has increased exponentially in recent years, and along with it so have the number of complaints about the use of these particular marketing strategies. Environmentalists, for example, complain about the waste of paper following direct market campaigns, while consumers complain about intrusion into their everyday lives by marketing activities – be this through cold calling on the telephone, or more recently through the use of spam e-mails selling various goods and services, for example.

Consumer sins

At the same time as considering marketing's impact on society, it is also important to recognize that consumers commit sins also. Consumer theft is a major issue for companies large and small and such theft can also occur on small or grand scales. Consumer frauds, such as Internet cons and telemarketing scams, are a major worry for consumers and companies alike and will ultimately have an impact on all consumers in the forms of higher prices to offset company losses. Whether consumer theft involves an individual stealing from a supermarket or a large-scale consumer fraud ultimately all agree it is the consumer who pays the price for the illegal activities of others. The increased use of online shopping and the use of the Internet for various exchange activities such as online banking has led to new ways in which consumers can be caught out by the actions of others – phishing, through the use of misleading e-mail and websites allows illegal access to online bank accounts and is the fastest growing form of consumer theft in the USA and such trends are set to continue.

The 'black' or 'underground' market is another example of unethical and illegal consumer activities. The selling of illegally acquired products or the counterfeiting of other companies products is a very lucrative business, particularly in developing nations. According to the International AntiCounterfeiting Coalition, the global counterfeit market is worth approximately US $600 billion annually and accounts for approximately 5–7 per cent of world trade sales. In the USA alone, the coalition states counterfeiting costs American businesses between US $200–250 billion a year and is responsible for the loss of over 750,000 jobs in the USA (see: http://www.iacc.org/counterfeiting/counterfeiting.php). Markets range from the selling of illegal drugs and prostitution through to the use of copyrighted media, such as music, movies and video games. Questions of ethics become important here, as does people's perceptions of what is ethical and what is not. For instance, many consumers will not think that they are doing anything wrong when purchasing an illegal copy of a movie, CD or DVD while on holidays, even though their actions are in fact illegal, and a significant number of British teenagers drink alcohol before the age of 18. It is when exploring areas such as consumer theft and underground markets that we can engage in interesting debates about ethics and 'right and wrong'. Very often individual opinion does not follow legislative requirements and *vice* versa and thus discussions can very quickly become both complex and controversial. For example, an individual might think that the use of cannabis is an illegal activity, but would make an exception for someone who is using the drugs to help with a medical illness such as Multiple Sclerosis, for example, even though this individual would be deemed in law to be acting illegally.

Consumer responses

Consumers themselves have responded to the unethical practices of business and marketers in many different ways. Perhaps the most significant has been the actions by some consumers to opt out of the marketplace, as a recognition of the fact that consuming goods and services does not necessarily lead to consumer happiness. There is much talk, for example, of consumer downsizing and voluntary simplicity in developed nations, as well as alternative consumer societies setting up (see, for example, McDonald *et al.*, 2006). Other examples of consumer resistance to the marketplace include groups who continue to work and live within society, but who opt out of the market in particular ways. For instance, in 2006 a small group in San Francisco called *The Compact*, one of whose founders was a marketing executive, took the decision to opt out of the retail rat race for the year. Other than food and health and safety products, the group decided not to make any other new purchases, but instead relied on borrowing, making themselves, or purchasing second-hand products. The group made national and international news and has set a new international trend in consumer behaviour. Other examples include consumers who engage in activities such as '*Buy Nothing Day*' or perhaps boycott particular products, as a result of company activities.

Consumer boycotts

One very visible way in which consumers can apply ethical principles to their everyday behaviour is to boycott the purchase of goods from particular companies and/or countries. This option has been available to consumers for hundreds of years and one of the first campaigns was organized by the National Negro Convention in the 1800s that called for the boycott of slave-produced goods. Consumer boycotts can range from small-scale local boycotts of companies products to much larger international boycotts. In 2004, it was estimated that boycotts cost UK firms £3.2 billion, up £600 million on 2003 estimates (Hickman, 2005). In some instance, the boycott can be where the company itself has not actually behaved unethically. Sales of dairy products made by the Arla Foods company of Denmark in the Middle East, for example, plummeted as a result of the boycotting of Danish products by Muslims, following the publishing of cartoons featuring Mohammed in a Danish newspaper. It has been estimated that sales of Danish goods worth over DKK 10 billion per annum could be at risk in Muslim countries (The Economist, 2006). Other recent boycotts of particular countries include the *Boycott Japan* campaign as a result of the countries policy on the killing of whales and a boycotting of French products in the USA because of the its stance on the Iraq war. Current boycotts in the UK include boycotts of Adidas, Asda and Wal-Mart, the Body Shop and L'Oreal, Boycott Bush (and companies who support the Republican Party Leader) and the Burma Campaign, UK (see http://www.ethicalconsumer. org/boycotts/boycotts_list.htm for details of individual campaigns). Boycotts themselves have mixed results, with some notable successes including the boycotting of various companies such as Barclays Bank in the 1980s, due to its dealings in the then Apartheid South Africa, and Shell's decision to not proceed with the sinking of its Brent Spar platform. As ethical issues continue to maintain a high prominence in society, one can expect boycotts to remain a visible and easy tactic for consumers to target unethical business practices.

Ethical consumers

An alternative to consumer boycotts is the purchase of ethical and fairly traded produce; both categories are increasing in significance in all developed nations. According to the Ethical Consumer organization (www.ethicalconsumer. org), the ethical market in the UK was worth £29.3 billion in 2005, up from approximately £8 billion in 1999, with more money spent on ethical products in 2005 than was spent on tobacco and alcohol. In 2004, the fair trade market was said to have a retail value of £140 million in the UK (Moore *et al.*, 2006), with sales in Europe reaching € 560 million (Connolly and Shaw, 2006), and as with ethical products this market is expected to continue to grow in the longer term. There are many who support such products, but they have also received criticism from some who suggest that many companies are jumping on the ethical bandwagon without substantially changing their activities. If implemented properly, however, many agree that the sales of ethical and fairly traded products will increase in the future and will be good for both business and the consumer. Ethical product ranges are diverse and range from banking and ethical investment products and services to beauty and cosmetics product ranges. Small ethical companies such as the *Innocent* fruit smoothie company and *Green and Black* chocolate company are very successful in the marketplace and hold a sizeable market share in their product categories. While ethical and fair trade spending is still comparatively low, many expect these niche markets to continue to grow as consumers become ever more conscious about what they spend their money on and also critical of companies who only pay lip-service to ethical issues, rather than embrace the concept into all business activities.

As with ethical activities, however, what it means to be an ethical consumer is contested. What is ethical consumption to one consumer may indeed be unethical to another. For example, one person may consider their consumption to be ethical because they recycle their products, whereas another consumer may question the need for the recycled products in the first instance. Does to buy ethical mean, for example, to buy local; to buy organic; to buy fair trade or to buy all of these – what then of conflicts? For instance, is a consumer being more ethical by buying only locally produced products and thus reducing transportation and environmental costs as a consequence, or by buying a fairly traded product from a developing nation? Barnett *et al.* (2005) suggest that 'ethical consumption, then, involves both a governing of consumption and a governing of the consuming self', and this is perhaps a good definition to help us begin to explore the complexities involved when attempting to understand what one means by ethical consumption. According the Ethical Consumer organization,

> Ethical purchasing put simply is buying things that are ethically by companies that act ethically. Ethical can be a subjective term both for companies and consumers, but in its truest sense means without harm to or exploitation of humans, animals or the environment. (http://www.ethical-consumer.org/aboutec/whybuyethically.htm)

Ethical products companies have also been successful in redefining their product ranges in other ethical ways. By far, the biggest success in this category was the relaunch of Dove skin care products in 2003 and 2004. Rather than change their products significantly, Dove took a risk and significantly changed the way in which beauty products for women are advertised. The company broke the mould in the cosmetics industry by using real women in their marketing communications campaigns and by doing so challenged the stereotypical view of the 'perfect' woman utilized by advertisers and as a result reignited an international debate on beauty. The company defined its beauty theory as,

> Dove makes it clear it sees beauty in imperfections and doesn't worship stereotypes. Dove's beauty is self-defined, beauty with brains, democratic. Dove recognizes not only the exterior, but also the woman within. There is a depth of character behind the eyes, a strength of vitality and personality showing through.
>
> (Johnson, 2005)

The initial campaign and subsequent ones which have followed have been hugely successful for the company that has seen significant increases in the sales for its products; its cleansing brand has become brand leader in the marketplace, and global sales of the product have increased from 13 to 25 per cent (Kolstad, 2007). The company's *Campaign for Real Beauty* has also been a universal success and illustrates how companies and consumers can work together in changing people's perceptions of what beauty means. Dove, owned by large multi-national Unilever, also made a number of other commitments by creating the Dove Self-Esteem Fund, a charity which helps various women's causes; the company even advertised the fund rather than the product range during the 2005 Super Bowl final, one of the most expensive global advertising slots. While the

company could have received criticism for ultimately selling beauty products, which some could consider unnecessary, by and large the publicity for its new efforts was mainly positive with many believing the company has successfully managed the relationship between a particular cause, in this case perceptions of beauty, and selling products.

Marketing's response – ethical and legal requirements, codes of practice

The reaction of businesses and marketers to their critics is that their activities are subject to both stringent professional codes of conduct and legislative requirements. There are many professional marketing associations and most will have their own codes of conduct, some of which will be subject to legislative requirements and others that are stipulated as best practice for marketers to follow. In the UK, the Chartered Institute of Marketing, for instance, has a professional code for its members. Many individual organizations also have a company wide ethical policy, which will include ethical marketing policies. Consequently, many of the unethical activities, such as direct marketing and misleading advertising, discussed above, are covered by codes of conduct and legal requirements. Marketers' response to such criticisms is that it is only a small minority who do not follow codes and/or legal requirements, and if they continue these practices, they will be punished in the long term.

Legislative acts enforced by trading standards officers, which marketers are affected by, include,

- Consumer Credit Act, 1974
- Consumer Protection Act, 1987
- Food Safety Act, 1990
- Prices Act, 1974 and 1975
- Trade Descriptions Act 1968.

Examples of marketing communications codes include the British Code of Advertising, Sales Promotion and Direct Marketing (2003) and more recently in Ireland the Children's Advertising Code, introduced by the Broadcasting Commission of Ireland in 2005. There are also independent bodies that regulate very specific business practices – for example, the Independent Committee for the Supervision of Standards of Telephone Information Services (ICSTIS) is responsible for premium rate telephone communication services. ICSTIS is currently investigating the overcharging for premium rate calls by a number of different television channels, including popular television programmes such as *ITVs X Factor* and the *Richard and Judy* show on *Channel 4*. There are also preference services available for mail, telephone and e-mail for people who do not wish to receive unsolicited direct marketing mail, telephone calls or e-mail messages.

Consequently, marketers argue that with government legislation, self-imposed regulatory bodies and individual company codes of ethics, it is only a small minority who damage reputation of marketing. Critics would counter that both legislation and self-imposed regulations do not always go far enough to protect consumers, animals and/or the environment.

Conclusions

There is no doubt that in today's business world, ethics and responsibility are core components for any business, small or large. While there is much debate and public controversy over how specific responsibilities are defined and played out in the marketplace, there is no doubting their importance. As such there are both challenges and opportunities for business in dealing with ethical issues in today's global marketplace. These opportunities and challenges can also be found in our exploration of marketing practices in the twenty-first century. While it is true to say that different companies will be affected in different ways, it is also true that no company will be immune to issues of ethical importance. Documentation for *Business in the Community, Ireland* sum up the importance of CSR as follows:

> The constantly challenging goal is to ensure that responsible business is integrated and embedded in the decision making culture rather than confined to a progressive individual, area or division.

Such a shift in business culture will have a profound effect on the marketing strategies and practices of all businesses for the foreseeable future.

References

Adler, R. D., Robinson, L. M. and Carlson, J. E. (1981) *Marketing and Society: Cases and Commentaries*, Prentice Hall, Englewood Cliffs, NJ.

Armstrong, R. and Sweeney, J. (1994) Industry type, culture, mode of entry and perceptions of international marketing ethics: a cross-cultural comparison, *Journal of Business Ethics*, **13**(4), 775–785.

Barnett, C., Cloke, P., Clarke, N. and Malpass, A. (2005) Consuming ethics: articulating the subjects and spaces of ethical consumption, *Antipode*, **37**(1), 23–45.

Blackburn, D. (2004) Dealing with the decade of anxiety, *Market Research Society Annual Conference*.

Chartered Institute of Marketing (2004) *New Year's Revolution: Morality in Marketing*,http://www.shapetheagenda.com/mediastore/_Insights/Morality_Agenda_Paper.pdf .

Connolly, J. and Shaw, D. (2006) Identifying fair trade in consumption choice, *Journal of Strategic Marketing*, **14**(4), 353–368.

Davidson, K. (2003) *Selling Sin: The Marketing of Socially Unacceptable Products*, 2nd edn, Quorum Books, Westport, CT.

Debord, G. (1977) *Society of the Spectacle*, Black and Rred: Detroit, MI.

Dubinsky, A. J. and Loken, B. (1989) Analysing ethical decision making in marketing, *Journal of Business Research*, **19**, 83–107.

Ferrell, O. C. and Gresham, L. G. (1985) A contingency framework for understanding ethical decision making in marketing, *Journal of Marketing*, **49**, Summer, 87–96.

Fromm, E. (1976) *To Have or To Be*, Routledge and Kegan Paul, London.

Hickman, L. (2005) Should I . . . . support a consumer boycott?, *The Guardian*, October 4, 12–13.

Hunt, S. D. and Vitell, S. J. (1986) A general theory of marketing ethics, *Journal of Macromarketing*, **8**, Spring, 5–16.

Hunt, S. D. and Vitell, S. J. (2006) The general theory of marketing ethics: a revision and three questions, *Journal of Macromarketing*, **26**(2), 143–153.

Jacobsen, M. F. and Mazur, L. A. (1995) *Marketing Madness*, Westview, Boulder, CO.

Johnson, O. (2005) How dove changed the rules of the beauty game, *Market Leader*, **31**, 43–46.

Kolstad, J. (2007) Unilever PLC: campaign for real beauty campaign, *Encyclopedia of Major Marketing Campaigns*, **2**, 1679–1686.

Laczniak, G. and Murphy, P. (2003) *Ethical Marketing Decisions: The Higher Road*, Prentice Hall, New York.

Laczniak, G. and Murphy, P. (2006) Normative perspectives for ethical and socially responsible marketing, *Journal of Macromarketing*, **26**(2), 154–177.

Laczniak, G. and Murphy, P. (1993) *Ethical Marketing Decisions*, Allyn and Bacon, Toronto.

McDonald, S., Oates C. J., Young, C. W. and Hwang K. (2006) Towards sustainable consumption: researching voluntary simplifiers, *Psychology and Marketing*, **23**(6), 515–534.

Marcuse, H. (1964) *One Dimensional Man*, Beacon, Boston.

Moore, G., Gibbon, J. and Slack, R. (2006) The mainstreaming of fair trade: a macromarketing perspective, *Journal of Strategic Marketing*, **14**(4), 329–353.

Nantel, J. and Weeks, W. A. (1996) Marketing ethics: is there more to it than the utilitarian approach?, *European Journal of Marketing*, **30**(5), 9–20.

Nill, A. and Schibrowsky, J. A. (2005) The impact of corporate culture, the reward system, and perceived moral intensity on marketing students' ethical decision making, *Journal of Marketing Education*, **27**(1), 68–80.

Nill, A. and Shultz II, C. (1997) Marketing ethics across cultures: decision-making guidelines and the emergence of dialogic idealism, *Journal of Macromarketing*, **17**(4), 4–19.

Packard, V. (1957) *The Hidden Persuaders*, David McKay, New York.

Srnka, S. J. (2004) Culture's role in marketers' ethical decision making: an integrated theoretical framework, *Academy of Marketing Science Review*, http://www.amsreview.org/articles/srnka01-2004.pdf.

Singhapakdi, A. (2004) Important factors underlying ethical intentions of students: implications for marketing education, *Journal of Marketing Education*, **26**(3), 261–270.

Tsalikis, J. and Fritzsche, D. J. (1989) Business ethics: a literature review with a focus on marketing ethics, *Journal of Business Ethics*, **8**(9), 695–743.

The Economist (US) (2006) When markets melt away; consumer boycotts, *The Economist*, **378**(8464), 56.

Further Reading Journals

There are a number of journals that focus specifically on issues relating to marketing ethics – the two most important are the *Journal of Macromarketing* and the *Journal of Public Policy and Marketing*. Both journals are a must for anyone wishing to get an up to date angle on marketing ethics topics. Look out for a special issue of the *Journal of Macromarketing* on marketing ethics due to be published in 2008. The *Journal of Business Ethics* has many articles with a marketing focus. There was also a special issue of the *Journal of Strategic Marketing* in 2006 focusing on fair trade – McDonagh, P. and Strong, C. (2006) Liberte, equalite, fraternite: reflections on the genesis and growth of fair trade for business strategy, *Journal of Strategic Marketing*, **14**(4).

Books and Journal Articles

Crane, A. and Matten, D. (2004) *Business Ethics*, Oxford University Press, Oxford – An excellent introductory student text to core business ethics issues. A second edition of the text is to be published in 2007.

Green, G. (2004) *Eight Theories of Ethics*, Routledge, London – An introduction to different ethical theories for those who wish to explore ethical theories in more detail.

Jones, C., Parker, M. and Ten Bos, B. (2005) *For Business Ethics*, Routledge, Abingdon, Oxford – An excellent insight into Business Ethics and how business ethics can be considered within the wider context of ethical theories.

Murphy, P. M. and Laczniak G. R. (eds) (2006) *Marketing Ethics: Cases and Readings*, Pearson Prentice Hall, Upper Saddle River, NJ – Provides interesting cases and readings on various marketing ethics issues; a good classroom resource for lecturers.

Murphy, P. M., Laczniak, G. R., Bowie, N. E. and Klein, T. A. (2005) *Ethical Marketing*, Pearson Prentice Hall, Upper Saddle River, N.J. – Excellent introductory text which examines the many in-depth marketing ethics issues.

Robinson, D. and Garratt, C. (2004) *Introducing Ethics*, Icon Books Ltd, Royston – Part of the excellent *Introducing* series of Icon Books; offers an illustrative introduction to key ethical issues.

Websites

http://adbusters.org/home/ – Website for the activist networking group Adbusters Media Foundation.

http://www.asa.org.uk –Website for the independent regulator for advertising, sales promotion and direct marketing.

http://www.campaignforrealbeauty.com – Dove's international campaign focusing on various beauty related issues.

http://www.ethicalconsumer.org – Website for the charitable organization The Ethical Consumer.

http://www.groups.yahoo.com/group/thecompact – Provides information on the San Francisco group who decided to opt out of the retail rat race.

http://www.iacc.org – The International Anti-Counterfeiting Coalition.

http://www.tradingstandards.gov.uk – Government-based website for the Trading Standards Institute which provides information on a variety of consumer protection and safety issues.

http://www.which.co.uk – Independent consumers' association in the UK.

CHAPTER 28

Green marketing

KEN PEATTIE

Introduction

It is 20 years since the publication of the Brundtland Report '*Our Common Future*' (WCED, 1987) brought the concept of 'Sustainable Development' into the mainstream of business and political debate. It put forward a convincing case that the economic growth that had characterized much of the twentieth century was not sustainable in environmental, social and ultimately economic, terms. In the wake of the Earth Summits at Rio in 1992 and Johannesburg in 2002, the World's governments and major corporations have generally adopted the pursuit of sustainability as a strategic goal. The challenge lies in turning these good intentions into meaningful progress in the face of powerful vested interests, an entrenched and environmentally hostile dominant social (and management) paradigm and a global economy with tremendous momentum on a trajectory that pursues conventional economic growth.

For marketing, the challenge is two-fold. In the short term, ecological and social issues have become significant external influences on companies and their markets. Companies have to react to changing customer needs, new regulations and a new social zeitgeist which reflects increasing concern about the socio-environmental impacts of business. In the longer term, the pursuit of sustainability will demand fundamental changes to the management paradigm which underpins marketing and other business functions (Shrivastava, 1994). This chapter aims to illustrate how the 'green challenge' is exerting an influence on current marketing practice, and how its implications will eventually require

a more profound shift in the marketing mindset, if marketers are to continue delivering customer satisfaction at a profit.

Green marketing in context

Management theory is firmly rooted in an economic and technical systems perspective which concentrates on exchanges, products, production and profits. Over time it has evolved to become more 'human' with the emergence of disciplines like organizational behaviour, human resource management, business ethics and societal marketing. The fact that businesses are physical systems existing within a finite and vulnerable natural environment has, until recently, been largely ignored as a management and marketing issue.

The emergence of the physical environment as a strategic marketing issue has evolved through several stages. In the 1970s a wave of environmental concern linked to the oil 'shocks' of the period, several major pollution incidents and evidence of the human and environmental impacts of chemicals such as DDT and pollutants such as airborne lead, spawned the concept of 'ecological marketing' (Hennison and Kinnear, 1976). This was largely concerned with those industries with the severest environmental impacts (including oil, cars and chemicals), and with the need for new technologies to alleviate particular environmental problems.

During the 1980s concern about the environmental impacts of business resurfaced following several major environmental incidents such as the Exxon-Valdez oil spill and the chemical plant explosion at Bhopal and mounting evidence of man-made stress in global environmental systems (including evidence of rainforest depletion, global warming and a hole in the stratospheric ozone layer). This concern led to consumer boycotts, new environmental legislation and a growing demand for 'green' products such as recycled paper, unleaded fuel, energy efficient appliances and organic food. These developments affected a much broader range of industries than during the 1970s, and there was widespread discussion about the implications of environmental concern for marketing using labels including 'green marketing', 'greener marketing' and 'environmental marketing'. This discussion was largely an extension of the societal marketing concept, with a focus on the responsibilities of marketers and the need to constrain and ameliorate the environmental impacts of marketing activities through product innovations and adapted production processes.

During the 1990s academics within the marketing discipline began to seriously discuss the physical implications and sustainability of marketing (e.g. O'Hara 1995; van Dam and Apeldoorn 1996), and to consider the environmental, social and economic dimensions of marketing in a more integrated way. The original 'managerialist' stream of research discussing how sustainability issues could be integrated into marketing practices was complemented by more critical and challenging work, which questioned some of the more fundamental assumptions about marketing (Kilbourne and Beckman, 1999). Moving into the new millennium, far more radical ideas about the integration of marketing and the environment began to emerge. Fuller's (1999) concept of 'sustainable marketing' examined marketing from the physical systems perspective of industrial ecology, and set out a practical approach to marketing as a closed-loop system that creates no waste and does not degrade natural systems or resources. Belz (2006) envisions the ultimate evolution of marketing towards 'transformational sustainability marketing' in which social and physical problems are as much a starting point of marketing thought processes as customer needs. The fundamental difference in such visions of marketing, is that they do not think in terms of social and environmental 'issues' that must be audited, understood and accommodated within the conventional marketing strategy process. Instead, sustainability represents a different approach to thinking about the economy, business, marketing, consumption and production.

The key differences between sustainability orientated concepts of green marketing (to choose and use one of the most popular labels) and the existing societal marketing concept lie in:

- an emphasis on the ultimate physical sustainability of the marketing process, as well as its social acceptability;
- a more holistic and interdependent view of the relationship between the economy, society and the environment;
- an open-ended rather than a long-term perspective;
- a treatment of the environment as something with intrinsic value over and above its usefulness to society;
- a focus on global concerns, rather than those of particular societies;
- an emphasis on socio-environmental issues as a potential source of innovation and opportunity for marketers, rather than just as a set of constraints and potential costs.

The concept of sustainability allows the apparently paradoxical integration of environmental concern (which traditionally involves encouraging conservation), with the discipline of marketing (which is based on seeking to stimulate and facilitate consumption). A sustainable approach to consumption and production involves enjoying a material standard of living today, which is not at the expense of the standard of living and quality of life of future generations. It is a deceptively simple concept involving two key principles:

1. Using natural resources at a rate at which environmental systems or human activity can replenish them (or in the case of non-renewable resources, at a rate at which renewable alternatives can be substituted in).
2. Producing pollution and waste at a rate which can be absorbed by environmental systems without impairing their viability.

The nature of green marketing can therefore be summarized as '*The holistic management process responsible for identifying, anticipating and satisfying the needs of customers and society, in a profitable and sustainable way*' (Peattie, 1995). Green marketing's key concepts of sustainability and holistic thinking are both apparently simple, but can be extremely difficult to translate into action. This is because conventional management wisdom emphasizes reductionalism and specialism, and is founded on

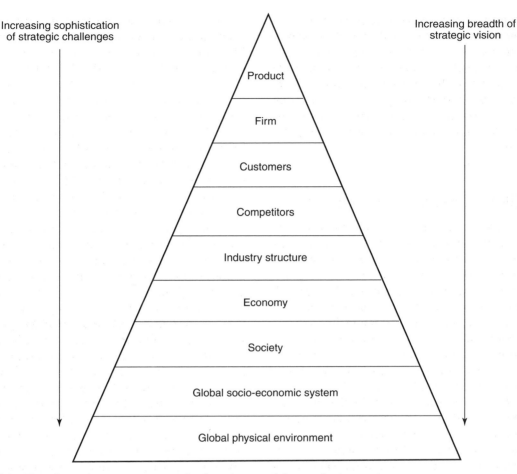

Figure 28.1   The physical environment as the foundation of the marketing environment

economic theories which mistakenly treat environmental resources as limitless, free (beyond the cost of extraction) or, for commodities like stratospheric ozone without a market, worthless. Green marketing attempts to relocate marketing theory and practice away from the economic hyperspace it has evolved in, and bring it back down to earth and reality.

Reconceputalizing the marketing environment

Companies benefit from a marketing orientation in many ways, one of the most important being the external focus on the marketing environment it encourages. However, marketing theory has followed the tradition of mechanistic economic models, which ignore the ecological contexts in which economic activity occurs (Capra, 1983). So the 'marketing environment' is frequently considered

in social, cultural, technological, economic and political terms, whilst ignoring the underlying natural environment. At best, the response to increased environmental concern has been to accommodate it within existing models of the environment (of the PEST type) by discussing it as a political pressure, an influence on the economics of business, a social trend or a technological challenge. The reality is that the physical environment is the foundation on which societies and economies are based. Figure 28.1 visualizes the marketing environment as composed of layers of issues and interactions.

The most immediate issues for marketing managers are typically internal ones related to product management and the internal company environment, and externally to customers. Beyond this, the analysis of the environment broadens out through different, but interwoven, levels of environment. Each level has important implications for marketing, but dealing with the deeper levels of the environment is perhaps a more difficult strategic challenge, due to their increasing breadth and complexity, and their decreasing proximity to the company itself. The physical global biosphere may seem distant to many companies' daily activities, but ultimately all business activity depends upon it, and its continuing stability and viability. Problems in the underlying global physical environment will impact firms, and their products and strategies, through interactions with each layer of the model.

Global physical environment

At the simplest level the environment affects businesses because it represents the physical space within which they and their customers exist, and it provides the resources upon which they depend. The human economy also ultimately depends upon the 'services' that the biosphere, and the ecosystems within it, provides. The UN's 'Millennium Ecosystem Assessment' provided an audit of scientific evidence concerning ecosystems. It showed that the unparalleled economic growth of the previous 50 years had *'resulted in a substantial and largely irreversible loss in the diversity of life on Earth'* and that *'gains in human well-being and economic development, . . . have been achieved at growing costs in the form of the degradation of many ecosystem services . . . and the exacerbation of poverty for some groups of people. These problems, unless addressed, will substantially diminish the benefits that future generations obtain from ecosystems'*.

For some companies there is a very direct relationship between the health of the environment and their business prospects. The fishing industry's agenda, for example, is dominated by the need to protect stocks from over-fishing. An authoritative international study published in *Science* during 2006 demonstrated that one-third of existing global fisheries had 'collapsed', and the impact of current fishing practices on marine ecosystems would destroy the others by 2050. In early 2007 the report of the *Intergovernmental Panel on Climate Change*, largely ended the debate about climate change and man's contribution to it, and demonstrated that carbon dioxide levels had rapidly climbed to their highest point in 650 000 years. The likely direct effects in terms of climate disruption now pose a serious threat to companies in tourism, agriculture, insurance or simply to those situated in coastal zones and on flood plains.

Although global issues such as climate change dominate the headlines, the green agenda contains a range of issues, each creating marketing opportunities and threats. Concerns about carbon dioxide emissions and climate change constitute a major threat for car and oil companies but an opportunity for those working in alternative fuels and energy efficiency devices. All of the other major industries in the world also face important environmentally related challenges. In tourism, destinations need to be developed sustainably to prevent them being degraded by their own success in attracting visitors, and to safeguard the cultures and lifestyles of the local population. Carbon emissions linked to holiday travel and cheap flights, and pollution impacts linked to the growing number of cruise ships visiting environmentally sensitive areas, are also placing the industry under pressure. For the car industry, air pollution, global warming and the fate of cars at the end of their working lives are key issues. For electronics companies end-of-life products (especially the export of e-waste to poor countries), energy consumption and the use of solvents are pressing issues. For agriculture, forestry and fishing, the consequences of unsustainable production in terms of loss of biodiversity, deforestation and soil erosion are crucial issues for the future. Even in the apparently abstract world of financial services there is increasing concern about environmental instability as a source of risk and insurance claims.

Global socio-economic system

The biosphere is effectively a single complex global system that transcends geo-political boundaries. Recent decades have also seen a more global social perspective reflected in global companies, markets, technologies and socio-cultural trends. The political response to the green challenge has also become more globalized through international environmental legislation and agreements (such as the Montreal Protocol to reduce CFC use, or the resolution on climate change signed by 20 of the largest countries early in 2007), and intergovernmental conferences. Although issues of social concern vary over time and between countries, survey data reveals that concern about the state of the environment is spread across the planet, and (contrary to many peoples' expectations) is shared by the populations (if not always the governments) of the less-industrialized as well as the industrialized nations.

There is also growing concern about the power, influence and accountability of global corporations. In a world still largely governed through national laws, it is a considerable challenge to ensure that the behaviour of trans-national corporations, of which over 60 000 now exist, does not sacrifice the social and environmental interests of citizens in some countries for the benefits of shareholders and consumers others.

The global socio-economic system is highly complex and has a complex relationship with the physical environment. Initiatives aimed at tackling one problem can often exacerbate another. During 2006 many American farmers took advantage of a growing demand for alternative fuels by selling their corn crop for ethanol production. This led to a shortage on the corn market which pushed up the prices of tortillas, the staple food for the poor within Mexico, by over 400 per cent sparking widespread social protests. The relationship between global trade liberalization, poverty alleviation and environmental degradation is complex, controversial and goes beyond the scope of this chapter. What is clear is that the economies of countries such as India and China are expanding rapidly. The Goldman Sachs Group forecast per capita GDP in China to rise from US $1324 in 2005 to $4965 by 2020, and in India from $559 to $1622 by 2020. These increases of 375 and 290 per cent respectively in per capita consumption growth, within countries that are also experiencing rapid population expansion, will be environmentally disastrous if the systems of consumption and production they develop mirror those that have emerged in recent decades in industrialized economies such as the UK and USA.

Society

Concern about the socio-environmental impacts of business is generally increasing, and is being reflected in a number of ways including:

- *Changing values and attitudes*: There is increasing public concern about the environment and declining levels of trust placed in companies and other institutions. A 2005 TNS/6th Dimension survey of European countries showed that almost 60 per cent of Europeans favoured tough international legislation to restrict environmental damage by companies, and only 6 per cent believed environmental threats had been 'overhyped'.
- *Pressure group activity*: The size, budgets and sophistication of pressure groups concerned with the socio-environmental impacts of businesses have increased significantly over the past 20 years.

Many of their communications campaigns are now produced by the same agencies that work for major corporations. As the experience of companies like Nike and Gap has shown in relation to international labour standards, companies with the most famous brand names are the most likely to be targeted, even though they may not be the worst offenders. There has also been a recent trend towards partnership approaches between pressure groups and companies, often as part of cause-related marketing initiatives. The Marine Stewardship Council (MSC) scheme to manage the world's fish stocks more sustainably was established in 1995 through a partnership between Unilever and the World Wide Fund for Nature (WWF).

- *Media interest*: News stories relating to current or impending crises such as climate change, deforestation or global poverty can increase levels of awareness, perceived salience and urgency amongst the public. Entertainment through factual films such as Al Gore's 'Inconvenient Truth' and fiction such as 'The Day After Tomorrow' have also raised awareness about climate change amongst audiences unlikely to take an interest in the scientific debate. However, there is a tendency for 'boredom' to set in regarding an issue, and the media's supportive interest in the emergence of an alternative green business or product will often change to destructive criticism once it is established (Thrørgersen, 2006).
- *Political and legal interest*: Government policies across the world are seeking to promote the development of more sustainable production and consumption systems. The quantity and complexity of social and environmental legislation faced by companies therefore continues to grow. Businesses in Europe are now affected by over 80 EU environmental directives and regulations. Regulations in several industries are imposing extended producer responsibility and requiring companies to undertake collection and responsible reuse or disposal of end-of-life products. Examples such as the End-of-Life Vehicles (ELV) Directive or the Waste Electronic and Electrical Equipment (WEEE) Directive are profoundly affecting the automotive and electronics industries. Companies that rely on mere compliance risk being left behind by the upward 'ratcheting' of legislation. In the USA, the trend towards forcing the CEOs of polluters to make personal court appearances, and in some cases jailing them, has helped to focus corporate minds.

The economy

Investments in environmental protection were conventionally viewed as involving a trade-off with economic growth and competitiveness (Porter and van der Linde, 1995). Recognition is growing that these issues are interlinked in complex ways, and that long-term economic growth will be dependent on better environmental protection. Many business opportunities are now emerging for technologies, goods and services that address environmental problems, or at least make less of a contribution towards them. The European Commission estimates that by 2010 'environmental industries' will be worth $640 billion, and that their growth will provide an additional half million European jobs.

Key areas where environmental concern is influencing economic issues include:

- *Production economics*: Environmental considerations are radically altering the production economics of 'front-line' industries such as cars, electronics, chemicals and power generation. Rising landfill costs, and tougher regulations on emissions mean that production costs are increasingly influenced, not by what has gone into a product, but by what is discarded when making it.
- *Investor interest*: Interest in ethical and environmental investment has grown with initiatives such as the FTSE4Good index of socially responsible companies, and changes to legislation requiring institutional investors to focus more on the social and environmental performance of holdings. According to the Social Investment Forum the total value of socially responsible investments in the UK rose from £23 billion in 1997 to £225 billion in 2001, whilst in the USA it had reached over $2.3 trillion.
- *Green taxes*: A new generation of environmentally related taxes including landfill taxes, climate change levies, air passenger duties and road pricing are being introduced in many countries. There are also product specific taxes being used to encourage particular changes in consumer behaviour. In 2002 the Republic of Ireland introduced a plastic bag tax of €0.15 which resulted in a 90 per cent drop in shopping bag consumption (with around one billion fewer bags consumed annually), which also raised around $9.6 million for investment in environmental technologies (a surprising result from changing one small marketing variable in one country).
- *Access to capital*: Environmental performance is seen by lenders and investors as an important influence on risk in many industries. An effective environmental strategy is becoming important to guarantee access to capital and insurance in a number of environmentally sensitive industries. There are also growing examples of private equity being used to back environmental technologies, such as Bill Gates' $84 million investment in alternative fuels businesses.

Industry structure

Industry structures are conventionally visualized as composed of linear exchanges and value chains. The green challenge is one of many forces encouraging a more relationship-based view of industry structures, particularly through an emphasis on recycling and supply loops. These feature relationships in which the customer returns products or packaging to the manufacturer, and in the process become another form of supplier. Fuji Xerox are recycling veterans having begun the routine reuse of components in 1968. Their 2006 Sustainability Report cited 20 000 end-of-life products collected, with 99.2 per cent of their components being recycled, avoiding 900 tons of landfill waste.

The changes that greening is bringing to industry structures include:

- *The threat of substitutes*: Products with a relatively poor eco-performance can become targets for new substitutes. Concern about the destruction of peat wetlands has led to a number of products such as ground coconut husks being launched to act as a peat substitute for gardeners. In the future a more radical set of substitutions may emerge, as markets which were traditionally based around purchase and ownership of products move towards greater use of services, hire and leasing (Cooper and Evans, 2000).
- *Supplier relationships*: Greening is forcing many companies to reconsider supplier relationships, since their total environmental impact will be strongly influenced earlier in the supply chain. Tools like 'life cycle analysis' and social/ environmental supplier audits are being used by companies to monitor, and often to work in partnership to improve, their suppliers' social and environmental performance (or eco-performance).
- *Market entry barriers*: Strict national environmental laws can act as an entry barrier. Recent years has witnessed friction between the USA and the EU over the EU's resistance to genetically modified (GM) food. The EU's concern about the health and

environmental safety of GM crops being interpreted by the USA as a disguised market entry barrier. For some companies, good environmental performance can act as a key to gain entry into a new market. Varta batteries had failed in several attempts to translate their European market strength into penetration of the UK market, but this was achieved very rapidly with the introduction of their innovative mercury-free battery range.

Competitors

Over the last 20 years, in a wide range of markets, including detergents, retailing, ice cream, batteries, white goods, cars, toilet paper and banks, companies have used eco-performance as a basis on which to compete. Global competition and continuous improvement philosophies have narrowed the differences between products to the extent that 'softer' issues such as perceived social and environmental impacts can act as a 'tie-breaker' for the consumer trying to choose brands (Christensen, 1995). The Cooperative Bank for example adopted an explicit ethical policy, which it has since used to differentiate itself and encourage customer loyalty, gaining over 200 000 customers as a result (Hedstrom *et al.*, 2000).

Experience shows that environmental disasters such as oil or chemical spills put all players in an industry under increased stakeholder pressure, and not just the culprits. This suggests that as the green challenge deepens, it may reduce the intensity of competitive rivalry, instead of acting as a new arena for it to be played out in. Many key environmental problems confront entire industries and require industry-wide responses. Alliances are emerging between former rivals to address common environmental challenges and to develop greener technologies. In the USA, Ford, Chrysler and GM have collaborated in an effort to develop low-emission vehicles (and less proactively in pooling millions of dollars to lobby against stricter greenhouse gas restrictions).

Customers

The world-wide boycott of CFC driven aerosols in the late 1980s first demonstrated the potential of consumers to unite behind an environmental issue that they understood and could relate to, in a way that enforced rapid change to an entire industry throughout its supply chain. UK research by the Co-operative Bank suggested that around one in

three Britons make some purchases on the basics of ethics and environment, and that at least 5 per cent consistently search for ethical labelling, recycle, participate in boycotts and discuss green issues in relation to the brands they buy. Social and environmental concerns are also becoming increasingly integrated into business-to-business marketing and purchasing (Drumwright, 1994), and governments are increasingly using their own purchasing power to aid in the development of green markets. The EU's Green Public Procurement programme is promoting the integration of environmental criteria into the 1000 billion Euros of European public sector spending (representing 16 per cent of total GDP).

Firms

As external concern about their socio-environmental impacts grows, so companies large and small are responding with organizational changes. The establishment of directorial responsibilities and management positions for corporate social responsibility (CSR) and/or environment; the introduction of green auditing and reporting systems; and changes to company policies and facilities to reduce waste and pollution are common responses. Corporate strategies and cultures are increasingly seeking to address green issues, often to reflect external stakeholder pressure, but also to reflect the concerns of employees and investors. For marketers, pressure to improve the eco-performance of the products that they manage may stem from external customer or regulatory requirements, or it may reflect internal requirements to pursue sustainability as a corporate goal. In the wake of the Enron scandal, and a number of other high-profile failures of corporate governance, there has been renewed interest in concepts such as CSR and corporate citizenship. In progressive companies, what began as environmentally orientated green strategies have become integrated with other CSR and governance issues to create a more balanced approach to the management and reporting of sustainability issues.

Products

Environmental concern is creating demands for new products (such as pollution control equipment) and is causing existing products to be reconsidered and in many cases redesigned, reformulated or produced differently. It can also lead to product repositioning, for example health concerns about increased ultra-violet radiation levels and the risk of skin cancer, has led to the marketing of sun tan lotions changing from an emphasis on sun exposure and beauty to an emphasis on sun protection. The impact on products varies across markets. In some, such as cars, cleaning products or paper products, changes are widespread. In others, such as food, financial services or computers, examples of change are more sporadic. There was a flurry of green product introductions in the late 1980s and early 1990s, although this later decelerated, mainly in response to concerns about the validity of some of the green claims involved (Carlson *et al.*, 1993), increased levels of media and NGO scrutiny, and mounting consumer scepticism. By 1997 products marketed on the basis of green attributes accounted for 9.5 per cent of all new US product introductions, with the highest proportion in the 'household products' category, accounting for 29.5 per cent of product introductions (Fuller, 1999).

The greening of marketing strategy

The growing importance of environmental and social issues throughout the marketing environment has been reflected in their consideration in marketing strategy development. Reactive and defensive strategies based on legislative compliance and bolting on 'end-of-pipe' technologies to alleviate pollution problems have gradually given way to more proactive and opportunistic strategies, with new products being developed and positioned as 'solutions' to social and environmental problems. During the 1990s the argument that greening can act as a source of competitive advantage emerged from authors such as Elkington (1994), Azzone and Bertele (1994) and Porter and van der Linde (1995). Porter and van der Linde's argument is that the search for environmentally superior solutions leads to innovation and the creation of more efficient and effective technologies. Their logic is that tough environmental legislation (often vigorously opposed by companies) creates new challenges for companies, which prompts them to innovate and secure improvements in competitive, as well as environmental, performance. This is what Varadarajan (1992) termed 'enviropreneurial marketing'.

Others have argued that it is difficult in practice to achieve and sustain competitive advantage from good eco-performance (e.g. Walley and Whitehead, 1994; Wong *et al.*, 1996). The issues have often proved complex and costly to address; customers have often proved difficult to convince; greener product offerings have sometimes struggled to compete on technical merits against conventional products, and the media has often proved more critical of those attempting to improve their eco-performance and capitalize on it, than of the most polluting and wasteful companies. Ottman *et al.* (2006) describe this as a new form of 'marketing myopia' in which the enthusiasm for a product's environmental credentials lead the company to lose sight of its match with consumer needs and perceptions. Despite this, it is clear that poor eco-performance can put a company at a massive competitive disadvantage. Exxon's combined bill for clean up costs, fines and legal costs estimated at over \$3 billion in the immediate aftermath of the Exxon-Valdez disaster, which also left 41 per cent of Americans describing themselves as *'angry enough to boycott Exxon products'* (Kirkpatrick, 1990).

For the marketing strategist it is vital to understand the potential impact of the green agenda on their business and its customers, and the relative strengths and weaknesses of their company's eco-performance because it can provide:

- *New market opportunities:* Through access to growing green markets. At the beginning of the new millennium, the total market for 'LOHAS' (lifestyles of health and sustainability) involved 68 million consumers and was worth \$230 billion in the USA alone, according to the Center for Fair and Alternative Trade Studies at Colorado State University. In markets such as financial services and tourism, green products represent the fastest growing area for new business.
- *Differentiation opportunities:* AEG increased their sales by 30 per cent within an otherwise static white goods market, following an advertising campaign stressing the relative energy and water efficiency of their products.
- *Opportunities for cost advantages:* Although conventional wisdom associates good eco-performance with investment and increased costs, this is partly a reflection of the 'end-of-pipe' methods used (since adding a catalytic converter onto a car can only increase its costs). Investments using a more radical, clean technology approach are capable of reducing material and energy inputs, and cutting inefficient pollution and waste. Among 181 waste reduction projects

within 29 chemical industry plants studied by Porter and van der Linde (1995), only one led to a net cost increase and the average annual savings (on the projects where this could be meaningfully measured) was $3.49 per dollar spent.

- *Niche opportunities*: In the short term, greener products such as organic food and cruelty-free cosmetics have succeeded within market niches comprised of the most environmentally aware consumers. There is, however, a danger that the success of green niche products could effectively hold back the greening of markets. This could occur if by satisfying the most environmentally aware consumers, pressure to green the market becomes diluted and the momentum of change falters. In many industries it will require the greening of the mass market to make a substantive contribution to sustainability (Belz, 2006).

Although controversial, there is growing evidence from investment returns that good eco-performance can generate financial out-performance. For example during 2006 the Co-operative Insurance Sustainable (CIS) Leaders trust, a fund that invests only in ethical and green companies, outperformed all other unit trusts in the UK All Companies sector.

The green consumer

The 'green consumer' has been the focal point of both new marketing theories and changes to marketing practice aiming to respond to measurable increases in environmental and social concern amongst the population. Marketers have sought to identify, segment and target green consumers by understanding their characteristics, motivations, behaviour and willingness to purchase greener products (preferably at premium prices). If this can be done, and appropriate market offerings created in response, then the competitive advantage outlined by Porter and others can be achieved.

Academic researchers and market research agencies have striven to define and understand the relationship between peoples' environmental concern and their purchasing behaviour. Many factors have been proposed as influences on green consumer behaviour such as changing consumer values, demographic factors, knowledge of environmental problems and alternative products, perceived personal relevance and the ability of the individual to make an effective contribution (for a model which integrates the majority of these,

see Dembkowski and Hanmer-Lloyd, 1994). All of these efforts have sought to discover a reliable basis to define and target green consumer segments. Socio-demographic criteria such as gender, age and income have often been used, but as Wagner (1997) comments '*Socio-demographic attempts to profile the green consumer have not always yielded strongly indicative results, and the results produced in one study have been repeatedly contradicted in another.*' Other segmentation attempts have used environmental attitudes, environmental knowledge, level of education, social consciousness or related behaviours to develop categorizations of consumers of different shades of green. However, once again '*results of these studies were frequently inconclusive and sometimes contradictory*' (Kilbourne and Beckmann, 1998).

The difficulties in isolating green consumers reflect several factors:

- It overlooks the point made by Kardash (1974) that all consumers (barring a few who enjoy contrariness for its own sake) are '*green consumers*' in that, faced with a choice between two products that are identical in all respects except that one is superior in terms of its eco-performance, they would differentiate in terms of the environmentally superior product.
- By attempting to relate a consumer's environmental concern to purchases, marketing researchers may be looking in the wrong place. Many of the most significant contributions that consumers can make towards environmental quality come in product use, maintenance and disposal or in delaying or avoiding a purchase through a 'make do and mend' mentality.
- Environmental improvements in products are often entangled with economic or technical benefits. Energy-saving products provide economic and environmental benefits, and people may choose organic food for reasons of environmental concern, personal health concern or simply for the taste benefits.
- General environmental concern amongst consumers is not matched by good levels of 'environmental literacy' or a clear understanding of how specific consumption decisions relate to particular environmental or social problems.

The answer to understanding green purchasing behaviour, may lie in considering the purchase rather than the purchaser. If we accept Kardash's proposal that, all other things being equal, most customers would differentiate in favour of greener products, then understanding green purchasing behaviour (and often the lack of it), is explained by the extent to which other things are not 'equal'. Many green purchases involve some form of compromise over conventional purchases such as:

- *Paying a green premium*: This can be imposed by economic necessity where improving eco-performance increases production costs. Alternatively it can be created by marketing strategies in which greener products aimed at green market niches are given a premium price irrespective of production costs.
- Accepting a lower level of technical performance in exchange for improved eco-performance (e.g. rechargeable batteries provide less power but are ultimately more cost effective and greener).
- Travelling to non-standard distribution outlets (e.g. Ecover detergents were originally marketed through health-food shops, and alternatively fuelled cars need to access suitably equipped service stations).

Where there is a compromise involved in making a greener purchase, a key factor which will determine whether or not this is acceptable to customers, is the confidence they have in the social or environmental benefits involved. Customers will need to be confident that:

- the issue(s) involved are real problems;
- the company's market offering has improved eco-performance compared to competitor or previous offerings;
- purchasing the product will make a material difference.

Analysing green purchases in terms of the compromises involved and confidence engendered can help to explain some of the inconsistencies in the research findings into green consumer behaviour. The majority of consumers profess environmental concern, a desire to buy greener products and a willingness to pay more for them or to accept technical performance reductions. Far fewer consumers are measurably changing their purchasing behaviour, and this has been interpreted as a failure to back up purchase intentions and a tendency to over-report social and environmental concerns (Wong *et al.*, 1996). This undoubtedly explains part of the discrepancy, but the missing element is the scepticism exhibited by customers relating to companies' green marketing offerings and their motivations (Mohr *et al.*, 2001). Reducing the compromises involved in green consumption,

whilst increasing consumer confidence in the environmental and ethical value in the green products they are offered, will be crucial for the development of green markets in future. The success of the FairTrade brand Café Direct in becoming the UK's third largest roast and ground coffee brand is based upon a balance of competitively priced and excellent tasting coffee, made available through mainstream retailers, and marketing that communicates the social worth of the products, backed by a trusted certification scheme.

In relating environmental knowledge to green consumption, researchers assume that increasing environmental knowledge will increase the desire to purchase greener products. The reverse may be true, in that increasing environmental knowledge may reduce a consumer's confidence in the effectiveness of market-based solutions for environmental challenges, and may make them more aware of the short-comings of products being marketed on a green platform (Peattie, 2001). There has been a tendency for green consumer behaviour to be understood by grafting social and environmental concerns onto conventional models of consumer behaviour such as the 'Theory of Planned Behaviour' or the 'Theory of Reasoned Action'. In an extraordinarily thorough review of the challenge of promoting sustainable consumer behaviour, Jackson (2005) demonstrates the limitations of such an approach and the need to move beyond models and theories that concentrate on consumers as individuals and consumption as a very rational and conscious process of satisfying individual wants. Jackson's analysis demonstrates the importance of the social aspects of consumption including the influence of families, of lifestyles, of the social meanings of products, and of habit on consumers' purchasing behaviour.

Eco-performance

Sustainability is the underlying principle of green marketing, and a company can justifiably claim green credentials if it is demonstrably and consistently moving towards it. Achieving sustainability is not a prerequisite for a valid claim to be green, just as 100 per cent customer satisfaction is not a prerequisite to claim a marketing orientation. In many markets, economic and technical considerations preclude sustainability as a short-term objective for green companies, even though sustainability can be their ultimate goal.

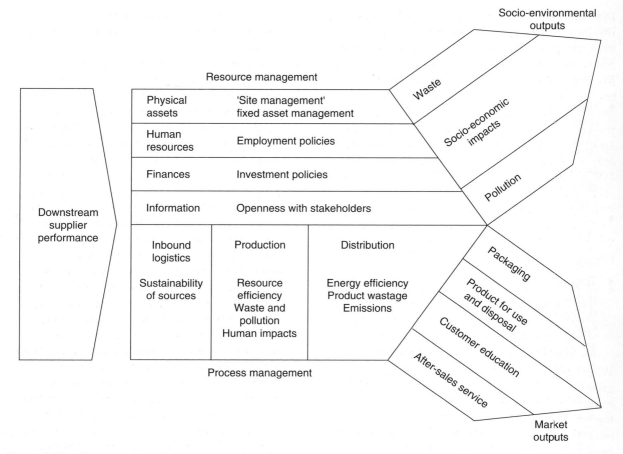

Figure 28.2   Components of environmental performance

Consumers' ability to discriminate in favour of responsible companies and to avoid the irresponsible will depend upon the existence and communication of meaningful measures to compare the relative 'eco-performance' of products, technologies and companies. This is far from straightforward. A question like *'What constitutes a green product?'*, has no simple answer. Is it one that has achieved sustainability? One that is better than its competitors? One that is less harmful than the product it replaces? Or one produced by a company with a good environmental management system? How can we compare the importance of different types of social and environmental impact? Such dilemmas are exemplified by the consumer in the supermarket seeking to make responsible choices amongst the produce on offer. Does the locally produced, low food-miles option, the Fair trade product from a poor country or the organically grown produce represent the 'best' choice? An important new frontier for business academics and practitioners will be to try to develop eco-performance measures that allow meaningful

comparisons of companies, products and technologies to be made by, and on behalf of, consumers and organizational buyers (see e.g. Epstein and Roy, 2001).

Developing a holistic understanding of eco-performance, requires an appreciation of how the external environment (and workforce) is impacted by the product throughout its physical life cycle, the production system, the organization and the supply chain of which it is a part. Even for companies with little interest in competing on a social or environmental basis, these issues are important to understand, if only in terms of identifying potential strategic vulnerabilities and risks. This process is analogous to Porter's Value Chain approach, as shown in Figure 28.2.

Going green: the philosophical challenge

If green marketing is viewed as the process of responding to socio-environmental concerns in the marketing environment, and producing products with superior eco-performance to meet customers' needs and to generate competitive advantage, it simply represents a variant of existing marketing thinking and practice. The more profound differences between conventional and green marketing are reflected in the values and philosophies which underpin a green marketing strategy, and the ways in which particular elements of marketing are conceptualized (Peattie, 1999). Integrating sustainability into marketing will require more than an emphasis on the development of new greener products and cleaner production processes. It will require a re-evaluation of some fundamental marketing assumptions and concepts (Kilbourne *et al.*, 1997), including:

- *Marketing's legitimacy*: Marketing's role in driving forward economic growth by stimulating demand, and its role in satisfying customer wants have always legitimized marketing, to the extent that the benefits of ever increasing consumer choice and economic growth have gone largely unquestioned. A sustainability perspective raises questions about the legitimacy and ethics of marketing as it is currently practiced. Conventional marketing has a focus on the wants and needs of the current generation of consumers, with little consideration of the impact of their consumption activities on the consumption and quality of life opportunities of future generations of consumers. Marketing is largely concerned with addressing the wants of those within wealthy countries in a world where UN figures reveal three billion people whose basic needs are not met because they live on less than $2 a day. They also live outside the consumer economy because they have little or no disposable income. According to United Nations Development Programme figures by the turn of the century, the richest 20 per cent of the global population within the industrialized nations were consuming 86 per cent of global resources, whilst the poorest 20 per cent of the global population shared only 1.4 per cent of the planet's resources. Ecological footprint research demonstrates that the lifestyle of the average UK consumer would require three Earth's worth of resources to extend it to the entire planet (and five Earths to globalize the American consumer lifestyle). The ethics of such imbalances and the continued pursuit of economic growth when evidence demonstrates that existing patterns of consumption and production cannot be sustained

by the planet are rarely questioned or even acknowledged as an issue in marketing books or discussions.
- *Consumers*: Henri Fayol once quipped about sending out for workers, but human beings turning up instead. Similarly, green marketers need to reconsider their approach to consumers. The word 'consumer' epitomises a view of customers, not as people, but as a means of consumption. In marketing a very limited number of consumer wants or needs are considered at a time, yet peoples' needs and wants are many, varied and often potentially incompatible. One may yearn to live in an area free from the pollution, congestion and danger posed by cars, and yet be unwilling to give up the personal mobility benefits that car ownership provides. Just as a product is more accurately analysed as a 'bundle of benefits', a customer should be considered as possessing a 'bundle of wants and needs'. By contributing to reduced environmental degradation, green consumer behaviour addresses an inherent human need for a viable environment, which may sometimes be at the expense of more explicit material wants. Recent years have witnessed an increasing range of conservation-orientated behaviour among consumers, from the recycling of cans and bottles to the boom in returning consumer durables to the supply chain through eBay or car boot fairs.
- *Customer satisfaction*: In the past, customer satisfaction has been judged in terms of the performance of the product at the moment (or during the period) of consumption. A green consumer may reject a product because they become aware of the environmental harm that the product causes in production or disposal. They may also avoid a product because they disapprove of the activities of the producer, its suppliers or investors. Even the concept that real satisfaction is derived from material consumption may need to be challenged. Ironically marketing assumes that consuming products produces satisfaction, yet economics, a discipline that marketing leans heavily upon, assumes that human needs are insatiable. Research from psychology has demonstrated a complex and loose relationship between material consumption and happiness, and that beyond a certain level of material consumption; we derive little additional satisfaction from further consumption. Robert Lane (2000) in his book '*The Loss of Happiness in Market Economies*' outlines the risk that societal pressures to maintain levels of material

consumption (including commercial marketing) actually keep us away from more intrinsically satisfying activities such as spending time with friends and family. One challenge to the conventional approach to consumption is the trend towards 'downshifting', the stepping out of a hard-working, high-earning, consumption-intensive lifestyle and into one that is less materially rewarding, but ultimately more satisfying (Andrews and Holst, 1998). Research in 2004 by Prudential Insurance revealed that some 1.4 million Britons had purposefully reduced their incomes in exchange for a better quality of life, with a further 600 000 hoping to downshift within the next 2 years.

- *The product concept:* If customer satisfaction is increasingly dependent upon the production process and on all the activities of the producer, we are approaching the situation where the company itself is becoming the product consumed. Drucker's (1973) famous concept that *'Marketing is the whole business seen from its final result, that is from the customers' point of view'*, seems set to become an enforced reality for many businesses, because the green movement means that customers (or those who influence them) are now actively looking at all aspects of their company.
- *Producer responsibility:* The responsibilities of the producer were conventionally seen in terms of ensuring that products were fit for purpose, fairly represented, safe and not priced or promoted in a way that exploited customers. Environmental concern has added a new layer of responsibility concerned with the fate of the product at the end of its life-span (and increasingly enshrined in extended producer responsibility legislation such as the European ELV and WEEE Directives), an issue which was previously irrelevant to marketers beyond signalling the possibility of a new purchase. For consumer durables such as cars, white goods and consumer electronics, these new responsibilities will have considerable impacts on product design and supply chain management.
- *Criteria for success:* Conventional marketing theory implies that if the enduring four Ps of the mix are right, then success will follow in the form of a fifth P- 'Profits'. Success in green marketing involves ensuring that the marketing mix and the company also meet four 'S' criteria (Peattie, 1995):
  - Satisfaction of customer needs.
  - Safety of products and production processes for consumers, workers, society and the environment.
  - Social acceptability of the products, their production and the other activities of the company.
  - Sustainability of the products, their production and the other activities of the company.
- *Demarketing:* One unavoidable conclusion of green marketing logic, is that where a product is being consumed and produced in an unsustainable way, it may have to be demarketed (either voluntarily or forcibly) to reduce consumption. Consumption reduction was explored by Fisk in his *'Theory of Responsible Consumption'* (1973), but is a concept which most politicians, economists and business practitioners would prefer not to contemplate. However, in tourism and energy markets, changes in pricing or access to products have been used to try to reduce the level of consumption.

Going green: the management challenge

The majority of green marketing activity that emerged during the late twentieth century was not radically different to existing conventional marketing, and did not reflect a revolution in marketing practice or philosophy in adopting sustainability principles. Some alternative brands which were founded on social, ethical and environmental principles such as Body Shop and Ben & Jerry's emerged and expanded from market niches into global businesses. More typically greening involved evolutionary changes in which existing brands improving the material and energy efficiency of their products and production processes, and sought to reduce pollution and waste. More recently even those pioneering alternative companies and brands have been absorbed by the mainstream global companies that they were originally established as an alternative to: Body Shop's absorption into L'Oreal, Green & Black's into Cadburys, Ben & Jerry's into Unilever, and the purchase of the Ethos ethical water brand by Starbucks are all examples of this trend. Whether this represents the increasing ethical orientation of the mainstream companies, or represents them seeking to acquire their way into growing market segments, and simultaneously neutralizing a perceived strategic threat from alternative green brands, remains to be seen.

Marketers' becoming interested in measuring and managing their eco-performance may reflect external drivers of legislation, customer demand, competitor initiatives and public opinion, or internal drivers relating to top management commitment, corporate strategy or the pursuit of competitive advantage (Bannerjee, 1999). Whatever the motivation, making a commitment to improve or compete on eco-performance can be challenging. Even among those companies well-known for good eco-performance, greening programmes have often been prone to hitting what Robert Shelton of Arthur D. Little described as a 'Green Wall'. Here the management responsible for environmental improvement, and their strategies, come into conflict with entrenched corporate power balances and values once the 'low-hanging fruit' represented by initiatives such as energy savings and packaging reductions have been 'picked' (Shelton, 1994). Such evolutionary improvements in efficiency and environmental performance are easily accepted by organizations. The development of more radical 'clean' technologies, changes to existing market structures and relationships, or more radical changes to elements of the marketing mix, are more likely to meet corporate resistance. It is clear that for managers seeking to promote corporate social and environmental improvement, there is also a significant internal marketing task to address. Evidence suggests that the most successful corporate social and environmental improvement programmes are those which reflect both a belief in the business benefits of such programmes and the underlying values of the company (Weaver *et al.*, 1999).

Adopting a holistic perspective

As social and environmental pressures on, and expectations of, businesses grow, so marketers need to have a greater appreciation of, and input into, all aspects of a business, its products and its production system. How energy efficient is our production process? Where are raw materials sourced from? Where is spare capital being invested? How well do we treat our workforce and suppliers? Such questions were once not the concern of marketers, but today they are increasingly likely to influence the perceptions of important stakeholders including customers, and are therefore strategic marketing issues. Addressing such questions, and the demands for answers to them, requires new information for marketers and new approaches to the management of that information. Initially many companies have sought to integrate social and environmental issues into existing approaches

to quality management through the implementation of environmental management standards and systems such as the ISO 14000 standards. A range of new auditing services are now available to companies so that their conventional financial, strategic and marketing audits can be complemented by social and environmental audits.

Embracing a stakeholder approach

A 'stakeholder approach' is vital for the development of appropriate and holistic green philosophies, strategies and policies (Polonsky and Ottman, 1998). Internally and externally organizations face growing interest in their eco-performance from an increasing range of interested parties. Table 28.1 highlights a range of stakeholders and examples of socio-environmental issues that could be associated with the development, manufacture and marketing of a particular product.

New management responsibilities

The conventional marketing paradigm emphasizes consumer sovereignty and casts the marketer as a relatively passive servant pledged to do the consumer's bidding. A sustainability perspective includes a greater emphasis on considering the welfare as well as the wants of customers, and also the welfare of those beyond the market. This requires a greater emphasis on companies taking responsibility for their customers and products and is reflected in the idea of 'Product Management' evolving into 'Product Stewardship', in which managers seek to manage and minimize the negative impacts of products throughout their life from design through to disposal. In agro-chemicals markets where difficulties with correct product use often occur in countries with low-literacy rates among farmers, some companies are using the concept of product or brand stewardship to ensure correct product use. Dow Corning, for example, demands that its agro-chemical sales staff:

- inform customers about known hazards relating to the products;
- advise customers to use products in accordance with label recommendations;
- insist that distributors pass on handling, use and disposal information to their customers;
- report and respond vigorously against cases of misuse;
- co-ordinate visits by company staff to customer sites, to ensure safe use and disposal of products.

Table 28.1   Stakeholder interest in product impacts

Stakeholder	Potential issue	Indicator
Company shareholders and managers	Product safety and acceptability	Prosecutions Inclusion rate in ethical funds
Employees	Harmful processes and substances	Accident rate; time lost due to injury
Customers	Labelling	Customer satisfaction; breaches of government/industry guidelines.
Business partners	Product recall handling	Efficiency, speed and success of product recalls
Suppliers	Involvement in research and development	Results of supplier element of life cycle analysis and use of results in the design process
Competitors	Health and safety performance and effect on industry reputation	Performance against industry benchmarks and guidelines
Government and regulators	Product stewardship	Quantity of hazardous non-product output (NPO) returned to process or market by reuse/recycling
NGOs, pressure groups and other influencers	Product safety and socio-environmental impacts	Incidence of NGO/regulatory targeting
Communities	Harmful substances	Releases to air, land and water of NPO

Source: Adapted from WBCSD (2000) *Corporate Social Responsibility: Making Good Business Sense*, Geneva, Switzerland.

Changing the marketing timeframe

The need to look beyond the interests of the current generation of consumers is one time-based challenge for the green marketer operating in a business culture characterized by increasingly short-term shareholder expectations and time horizons. Even within conventional time-frames, although production and consumption is a multi-stage process, it is the actual purchase which is the focus of marketers' attention, and which is still the focus of the majority of the literature dedicated to marketing (Kotler and Armstrong, 2004). Greening requires a new time perspective incorporating a 'cradle-to-grave' view of products that considers their performance through all the stages of their physical life cycle. In the case of consumer durables

this could be many years and the question of actual durability assumes a new importance. Evidence suggests that many products currently exist only as semi-durables, and creating more durable products can form an important part of a green strategy. Agfa Gevaert switched from a policy of selling photocopiers, to leasing them on a full service basis. This led to a product redesign brief based around durability, and the upgrading of the copy drums from a lifespan of under 3 million to over 100 million copies. For marketers this can represent a significant departure from previous strategies since it effectively reduces rates for product replacement, and may require a switch of emphasis in strategy away from purchase and towards leasing or towards the marketing of complementary products and services.

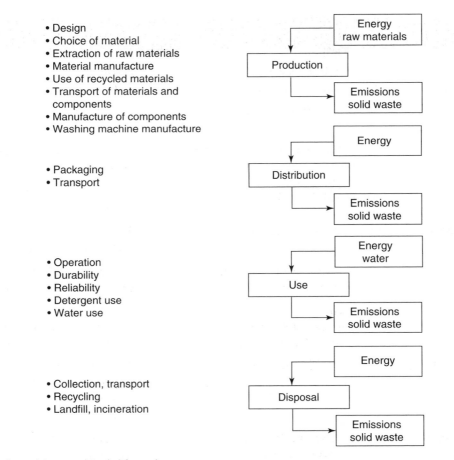

- Design
- Choice of material
- Extraction of raw materials
- Material manufacture
- Use of recycled materials
- Transport of materials and components
- Manufacture of components
- Washing machine manufacture

- Packaging
- Transport

- Operation
- Durability
- Reliability
- Detergent use
- Water use

- Collection, transport
- Recycling
- Landfill, incineration

Energy raw materials

Production

Emissions solid waste

Energy

Distribution

Emissions solid waste

Energy water

Use

Emissions solid waste

Energy

Disposal

Emissions solid waste

Figure 28.3   A washing machine's life cycle

The need to examine the impact of products from cradle-to-grave, is leading towards the concept of remarketing or even closed-loop (waste-free) marketing. Various tools are being developed to aid the green marketer to assess the full environmental impact of products, the best known being Life cycle Analysis and Eco-balance Analysis. The greatest difficulty for the marketer is to know how far forward or back, and down how many of the branches of the supply chain, such an analysis should go. An example of a cradle-to-grave life cycle is provided in Figure 28.3.

The practical challenge: greening the marketing mix

Green product management

To create a significantly greener economy, there will need to be a range of new and greener products and technologies. Instead of seeking to ameliorate environmental and social impacts of existing products and technologies through 'end-of-pipe' initiatives, there is a growth in more innovative 'clean technology' solutions. This is reflected in the inclusion of eco-performance criteria in the new product development processes of many industries through concepts like 'Design for Environment'. Successful development of new green products requires high levels of internal cross-functional communication and integration, good information, early consideration of green issues, strong support from top management and a specific approach to measurement and benchmarking (Pujari *et al.*, 2002). Guidelines for conducting product-specific marketing audits that summarize the relative socio-environmental impacts of products are now available to help marketers tackle these issues (see for example Fuller, 1999).

Green product attributes fall into two general categories. Firstly, there are those relating to the social and environmental impacts of the tangible product (or service encounter) itself. For a car manufacturer, these attributes would include issues like fuel efficiency, longevity and safety during use and recyclability once the vehicle reaches the end of its working life. A key product management and design challenge that a green perspective introduces, is the emphasis on the product's post-use fate. Improving the post-use eco-performance of products can be achieved through a modular design approach and good after sales service provision to make repairing products cost effective. Alternatively systems can be set up to collect post-use product (as is now mandatory in Europe for cars and electronics) for reuse in other markets, remanufacture, or for the recycling of valuable components and materials.

The second category of attributes relates to the processes by which the product is created, and the policies and practices of the company that produces it. Conventional marketing talks about the core product, the tangible product (which includes packaging and other physical dimensions) and the augmented product (including service dimensions). Since green marketing requires an approach to product management which incorporate how the product is made as a product attribute, it is helpful to think of this as the 'total product' concept (Peattie, 1995). Fair trade or organic produce, recycled or non-chlorine bleached paper, 'green' energy from renewable sources or cruelty-free cosmetics are all examples of products marketed on the merits of the means of production or the organization behind the products.

Green packaging

Discarded packaging accounts for a large proportion of waste in industrialized economies and a good deal of the environmental impact of many products. For the UK data from Biffa Waste Services shows that packaging accounts for 3 per cent of the total resources consumed within the UK economy and 40 per cent of all the plastic consumption in Europe. Packaging waste also grew in the UK by 12 per cent between 1997 and 2005. Packaging has therefore been an obvious starting point for many companies' green marketing efforts, since it can often be safely and cost-effectively reduced without expensive changes to core products or production processes and without a risk of disaffecting customers. For

example Marks and Spencer successfully made their ready meal packaging 30 per cent lighter and Boots redesigned their Botanics shower gel range to require 18 per cent less packaging materials.

As with many dimensions of green marketing, success in practice can be more difficult than some of the prescriptive advice available for marketers suggests. When Sony experimented with reclaiming and reusing packaging materials for its television sets, it led to a customer misconception that the product inside the packaging was also not new. For the reuse and recycling of packaging materials to make a meaningful difference, manufacturers need to ensure that efforts are supported by the infrastructure of collection systems and customer information and education.

Green promotion

Many companies have sought to promote themselves and their products through explicit or implicit association with environmental or social issues. However promotion has been one of the most controversial areas of the green marketing agenda. Conventional advertising has been criticized for presenting green products as oversimplified solutions to complex environmental problems at best or prone to 'Greenwashing' and 'Green Hype' at worse (Carlson *et al.*, 1993). The result of such concerns has been the emergence of the concept of 'sustainable communications' rather than the more narrowly defined concept of green promotion. Sustainable communications strongly stress a dialogue with stakeholders, particularly customers, aimed at informing and educating those customers, and seeking to establish the social and environmental credentials of the company and its products. Often this has been addressed through an emphasis on corporate-level communication campaigns, and through partnerships and alliances. MORI survey results indicated that 30 per cent of British adults had recently bought a product or service because of the company's link to a charitable organization.

Ottman *et al.* (2006) propose that the secret to successful communications for green product is to effectively connect the product's attributes and the brand message with the value desired by consumers. Some of the examples they highlight are summarized in the table (p. 579).

Desired consumer value	Message and business/product
Efficiency and cost effectiveness	'Did you know that between 80 and 85 per cent of the energy used to wash clothes comes from heating the water? Tide Coldwater – The Coolest Way to Clean.' Tide Coldwater Laundry Detergent 'mpg:)' – Toyota Prius
Health and safety	'20 years of refusing to farm with toxic pesticides. Stubborn, perhaps. Healthy, most definitely.' – Earthbound Farm Organic
Performance	'Fueled by light so it runs forever. It's unstoppable. Just like the people who wear it.' – Citizen Eco-Drive Sport Watch
Symbolism	'Make up your mind, not just your face.' – The Body Shop
Convenience	'Long life for hard-to-reach places.' – General Electric's CFL Flood Lights
Bundling	'Performance and luxury fueled by innovative technology. – Lexus RX400h Hybrid Sports Utility Vehicle

Different communications issues will arise depending upon the nature of the media that marketers use. Advertising brings with it the danger that the company will be accused of green hype or trivializing or exploiting serious social and environmental issues. On-pack promotion appears a useful and effective means to influence consumer decisions, but it can be difficult to explain a complex issue on a package that you are also trying to reduce in size. Direct mail may seem like an effective way to target the most environmentally concerned consumers, but creates the danger of being perceived as a 'junk mailer'. Sales promotions or sponsorships linked to social or environmental causes have been shown to be very effective, but they need to be selected carefully to ensure that there is synergy with the product being promoted. Otherwise customer evaluations of the company can actually deteriorate (Mohr *et al.*, 2001). Personal selling in non-consumer markets is often important and requires the sales force to be aware of the environmental implications of the company and its products and processes (Drumwright, 1994). Public relations has also been a key communications channel for companies to put across messages relating to good eco-performance, both in relation to brands and to corporate-level communications aimed at building corporate reputation and identity. Given the scepticism consumers are increasingly exhibiting in relation to green messages using conventional marketing communications media, Ottman *et al.* (2006) recommend innovative usage of word-of-mouth, e-mail and online 'word-of-mouse' to create a credible 'buzz' about new green products.

Integrated communications is increasingly viewed as a key ingredient to marketing success. It is particularly important when companies are attempting to promote themselves, or protect themselves, in relation to social and environmental issues. If one part of a company is attempting to gain competitive advantage on the basis of eco-performance, then competitors, NGOs, the media and regulators will be forming an orderly queue to attack the company if another part of that company is seen to be failing to live up to the image. The key is to understand the concerns of stakeholder audiences and then to communicate effectively and efficiently.

Green pricing

Pricing represents the crux of the green marketing challenge. If the external social and environmental costs of production were reflected in the prices that customers pay, then there would be considerable incentives for manufacturers to reduce those costs and become more sustainable. Companies seeking to absorb those costs and pass them onto the consumer, are vulnerable both to accusations of exploiting customer interest in green products, and to undercutting from competitors still effectively subsidized by the environment. The 'win–win' argument for greening proposed by the like of Porter and van der Linde (1995) suggest that consumer demand for green products can allow for the addition of a green price premium, as applies to free-range eggs and dolphin friendly (rod and line caught) tuna.

Greening strategies can affect the cost structures of a business with a knock-on effect on prices, particularly if pricing is on a 'cost plus' basis. Developing new sustainable raw material sources, complying with legislation, writing off old, 'dirty' technologies, capital expenditure on clean technology and the overheads associated with greening the organization can impose a cost burden. However, this can be counterbalanced by the savings made by reducing raw materials and energy inputs, by reducing packaging, cutting waste disposal costs and by finding markets for by-products. If costs are looked at holistically and managed on a portfolio basis, then wider eco-efficiency process benefits, when added to premium demand benefits, can counterbalance the costs of greening to make a positive contribution to profitability. Electrolux's 'Green Range' of white goods, for example has a lower environmental impact than the company's standard range, and has also achieved a 3.5 per cent higher gross margin.

Progress towards sustainability may be aided if the focus on 'purchase price' within marketing could be reduced in favour of a focus on 'total cost' and 'pay-per-use'. Low energy light bulbs, for example, have a higher purchase price, but a lower overall running cost for consumers. Buildings are also built to a price, rather than built to deliver a certain level of overall usage costs. A total cost focus would result in buildings which were more expensive to purchase, but which were economical in the long term and which would reduce a significant element of society's environmental impact. So far consumers have often been resistant to changes to pricing and payment schemes even when they are cost-beneficial (Electrolux's experiments with pay-per-wash pricing for washing machines failed to win over consumers, although Ottman *et al.* (2006) blame this on a misplaced promotional strategy). Better information about the social and environmental costs attached to products might also give consumers more complete information and more incentive to change their behaviour. It is quite common for consumers of veal for example, to enjoy it far less once they discover exactly how it is produced.

Green logistics

The environmental impact of many products is strongly determined by the fuel consumed and materials used in transporting them to customers. Early efforts in developing greener logistics have centred around the reduction and recycling of transit packaging and the optimization of distribution routes and driving practices for fuel efficiency. Getting the optimal environmental performance in distribution can be difficult. Reducing package thickness, for example, can reduce the resources consumed and the energy used in distribution, but increase the level of in-channel waste due to the reduced level of protection for the product. Similarly, larger trucks reduce the amount of fuel consumed per product unit moved, but have a greater negative impact on roads and the communities they pass through.

In the future the implementation of 'carbon taxes' on fossil fuel consumption and congestion charges will affect the economics of distribution. This could ultimately encourage industries to replace global production and distribution chains with global networks of operations producing and distributing on a more regional or local scale. The growing ability of 'smart' production systems to produce customized production batches at competitive unit costs may allow economies of distance to outweigh economies of scale. The new requirements for companies to take back products and discarded packaging will also require a significant redesign of distribution channels to handle the 'reverse logistics' involved in reusing containers, and reclaiming waste and end-of-life products.

Labelling

Labelling has been a particularly important issue within green marketing, with relevance to both promotion and logistics. As a promotional device, green labels are often important to provide customers with a simple and trustworthy signal of a product's social and environmental credentials (Ottman *et al.*, 2006). There are long-standing national labelling schemes such as the German 'Blue Angel' scheme which are extensively trusted and used by consumers. There are also more specific schemes which relate to particular industries or products (e.g. Rug-mark carpets made without child labour); or to particular methods of production (e.g. organic certification from the Soil Association) or business conduct (e.g. the Fair Trade mark). Labelling can also support consumer recycling behaviour, for example by labelling plastic containers by type to simplify sorting and recycling.

Labelling programmes vary in terms of whether or not they are mandatory or voluntary within a particular industry, whether they involve single or multiple issues, the level of information they provide and the level and style of verification that underpins them. Each of these dimensions has provided ample opportunity for controversies about labelling schemes within industries and between companies, regulators and NGOs (as befell the troubled EU Eco-label scheme).

The evolving agenda: from green products to sustainable value

The early years of green marketing, much like the early years of industrial growth after the Second World War, have been dominated by a focus on products. Initially greening centred on specific physical products such as lead-free fuel, recycled paper, organic food or cruelty-free cosmetics. The key difference lay in the emphasis on how the product was made, both as a product attribute, and as an influence on consumer demand.

Gradually the focus in green marketing has broadened to include services such as tourism and financial services. Globally, services account for the majority of economic activity, and of economic growth, yet there is little research on the sustainability impacts of services, coupled with a lack of methodologies to pursue sustainable service design and development. Yet some elements of the service economy such as transport, travel and hospitality have considerable social and environmental impacts. Typically, services are a combination of intangible elements (services), physical elements (products) supported by an infrastructure (systems). Viewing the delivery of value to customers holistically as a Product Service System (PSS) is an increasingly common approach in research communities, but it is an approach which most businesses are, as yet, unfamiliar with.

Taking a holistic PSS-based view is important, because increasingly there is a blurring of the edges as to what exactly represents a 'service'. Also, the extensive use of outsourcing as a service in many industries can also obscure the nature and distribution of the socio-environmental impacts of production. To make progress towards sustainability, supply chain management and service design will become an increasingly important business process. It is important for people involved in the design of any product, service or PSS (including marketers, design engineers, industrial designers, procurers, supply chain managers and entrepreneurs) to take account of life cycle impacts to determine environmental and social impacts, and to seek strategies to minimize negative impacts.

The blurring of the distinction between products, services and systems means that for the future of green marketing, perhaps we should be thinking more in terms of 'sustainable solutions'. Sustainable solutions are products, services or system changes that minimize negative (and maximize positive) sustainability impacts throughout and beyond the life cycle of existing products or solutions, while fulfilling acceptable societal demands and needs. In improving these aggregate impacts, these solutions are delivering 'sustainable value'. These concepts allow us to take a more holistic view of the economy and its outputs, process and goals. Sustainable solutions (whether products, services or PSS), represent the outputs, and green marketing and sustainable design represent the processes which aim to deliver those outputs. However, the ultimate goal should be to deliver higher levels of net sustainable value (that satisfy customers and other stakeholders) through those outputs (Charter and Clark, 2002).

The future of green marketing

Sustainability as a concept can be controversial, open to multiple interpretations, hard to measure and difficult to translate into meaningful action amongst the very real political, economic and technological constraints faced by companies and governments. The underlying reality is very simple. Any system or activity that is not sustainable ultimately cannot be sustained. Although this can be dismissed as a truism, it is a point that often seems to be missed. The last 50 years have witnessed some extraordinary developments in technologies, products, markets and marketing. It has also witnessed a doubling of world population from around three billion to over six and a half billion. Without becoming more sustainable, over the next 50 years, marketing will struggle to do more than to deliver an increasingly mixed and short term set of blessings, to a shrinking proportion of the world's population.

The dangers of unsustainable growth have rarely been more clearly illustrated than during the boom and bust of the 'Dot com' financial bubble. It demonstrated a lot of simple truths about the need for businesses to deliver real benefits and generate real and sustainable income streams, and also the dangers of profligate spending today on the promise of the wealth that new technologies will deliver tomorrow. These truths also apply to the industrialized economies as a whole. Many of the environmental costs of production and consumption are not being fully reflected (either directly or indirectly via taxation) in the cost structures of companies and the prices paid by their customers. This means that society and the environment are currently subsidizing our consumption and production. Our businesses are environmentally 'over-trading' and this is not a position that can be maintained indefinitely. Companies can grow and apparently prosper while running up huge financial debts (as Enron and Parmalat did). The danger is that the longer a debt accumulates, the more destructive the crash then becomes. While our businesses continue to consume the Earth's natural capital at an unsustainable rate, the risks grow that this environmental debt will create significant social and environmental consequences. The world cannot maintain its recent trends of growth in consumption and production without future consumers, and the billions living outside the consumer economy, bearing the cost.

The role that marketing can, and should, play in the development of a more sustainable economy has been the subject of some debate. Marketing has often been presented as part of the problem in stimulating unsustainable levels of consumption, and in using public relations and other means of communication to obscure or deny the negative consequences of that consumption. Marketing is also frequently presented as an important part of the solution in the context of market mechanisms being used to encourage more sustainable consumption. It is certainly true that marketing as a tool can be used to help or hinder the sustainability agenda. Some environmentalists have criticized green marketing on the basis that 'Changing our shopping habits will not save the world'. This is true, but if it creates improvement in the eco-performance of businesses, it will buy much needed time in which to understand how to make the more important changes to our economic, technical and political systems, in order to manage our environment in a sustainable way. It is clear that the greening of marketing and market forces will only have real meaning if accompanied by changes to corporate values and strategies, regulations, investment processes, political systems, education and trade. Belz's (2006) vision of 'transformational sustainability marketing' sees companies and marketers working to help create changes to the framework conditions for marketing through

. . . the active participation of companies in public and political processes to change the existing framework in favour of sustainability . . . Within the present institutional framework the successful marketing of sustainable products is possible, but limited. The institutional design fails to set positive incentives for sustainable behaviour, both for producers and consumers . . . Changes in institutions are necessary to expand the intersection between socio-ecological problems and consumption, and to set up the conditions for the successful marketing of sustainable products beyond niches.'

Another important role that will need to be played by marketing in the future, is to promote more sustainable ways to live and consume. In addition to the marketing of new products, technologies and services we will need the social marketing of many ideas, old and new, in order to make our economies more sustainable. These will include recycling, fair trade, product–service substitutions, composting, frugality, energy efficiency and less materialistic ways of life. The concept of sustainability itself will also need to be marketed.

Despite the human tendency to desire a life that is similar to the life we know, only better, and despite the many uncertainties about what a sustainable future might look like, research findings consistently show that most people would like to buy greener products from greener companies. For companies that choose to ignore this customer demand (whether explicit or latent) it is questionable whether they are practising marketing at all. Creating more sustainable marketing strategies will remain an uphill battle whilst general understanding of the sustainability challenge and how it relates to our consumption and lifestyles remains vague, and scepticism about the ability of companies to contribute to it endures. Winning this battle will be a key challenge for marketers in this new millennium, and the outcome will have a significant impact on the quality of life of consumers and citizens for generations to come.

References

Andrews, C. and Holst, C. B. (1998) The real meaning of 'inwardly rich', *Journal of Voluntary Simplicity*, May 28.

Azzone, G. and Bertele, U. (1994) Exploiting green strategies for competitive advantage, *Long Range Planning*, **27**(6), 69–81.

Bannerjee, S. B. (1999) Corporate Environmentalism and the Greening of Marketing: Implications for Theory and Practice, in Charter, M. J. and Polonsky, M. J. (eds), *Greener Marketing*, 2nd edn, Greenleaf Publishing, Sheffield.

Belz, F.-M. (2006) Marketing in the 21st Century, *Business Strategy and the Environment*, **15**(2), 139–144.

Capra, F. (1983) *The Turning Point*, Bantam, New York.

Carlson, L., Grove, S.J. and Kangun, N. (1993) A content analysis of environmental advertising claims: a matrix method approach, *Journal of Advertising*, **22**(3), 27–39.

Charter, M. and Clark, T. (2002) *Sustainable Value*, Greenleaf Publishing, Sheffield.

Christensen, P. D. (1995) The environment: it's not time to relax, *McKinsey Quarterly*, **4**, 146–154.

Cooper, T. and Evans, S. (2000) *Products to Services*, Friends of the Earth, London.

Dembkowski, S. and Hanmer-Lloyd, S. (1994) The environmental-value-attitude-system model: a framework to guide the understanding of environmentally conscious consumer behaviour, *Journal of Marketing Management*, **10**(7), 593–603.

Drucker, P. F. (1973) *Top Management*, Heinemann, London.

Drumwright, M. (1994) Socially responsible organizational buying: environmental concern as a noneconomic buying criterion, *Journal of Marketing*, **58**(3), 1–19.

Elkington, J. (1994) Toward the sustainable corporation: win-win-win business strategies for sustainable development, *California Management Review*, **36**(2), 90–100.

Epstein, M. J. and Roy, M. J. (2001) Sustainability in action: identifying and measuring the key performance drivers, *Long Range Planning*, **34**(5), 585–604.

Fisk, G. (1973) Criteria for a theory of responsible consumption, *Journal of Marketing*, **37**(2), 24–31.

Fuller, D. A. (1999) *Sustainable Marketing*, Sage Publications, Thousand Oaks, CA.

Hedstrom, G., Shopley, J. and LeDuc, C. (2000) *Realising the Sustainable Development Premium*, Prism/Arthur D. Little, Q1, 5–19.

Hennison, K. and Kinnear, T. (1976) *Ecological Marketing*, Prentice Hall, NJ.

Jackson, T. (2005) Motivating sustainable consumption: a review of evidence on consumer behaviour and behavioural change, Centre for Environmental Strategy, University of Surrey, Surrey.

Kardash, W. J. (1974) Corporate Responsibility and the Quality of Life: Developing the Ecologically Concerned Consumer, in Henion, K. E. and Kinnear, T. C. (eds), *Ecological Marketing*, American Marketing Association, Austin.

Kilbourne, W. E. and Beckman, S. (1999) Review and critical assessment of research on marketing and the environment. *Journal of Marketing Management*, **14**(6), 153–532.

Kilbourne, W. E. and Beckmann, S. C. (1998) Review and critical assessment of research on marketing and the environment, *Journal of Marketing Management*, **14**(6), 513–532.

Kilbourne, W. E., McDonagh, P. and Prothero, A. (1997) Sustainable consumption and the quality of life: a macromarketing challenge to the dominant social paradigm, *Journal of Macromarketing*, **17**(1), 4–24.

Kirkpatrick, D. (1990) Environmentalism: the new crusade, *Fortune*, 12 February, 44–52.

Kotler, P. and Armstrong, G. (2004) *Principles of Marketing*, 10th edn, Pearson Education, Harlow.

Lane, R. (2000) *The Loss of Happiness in Market Economies*, Yale University Press, New Haven.

Mohr, L. A., Webb, K. J. and Harris, K. E. (2001) Do consumers expect companies to be socially responsible? The impact of corporate social responsibility on buying behavior, *Journal of Consumer Affairs*, **35**(1), 45–72.

O'Hara, S. U. (1995) The baby is sick/the baby is well: a test of environmental communication appearls, *Journal of Advertising*, **24**(2), 55–70.

Ottman, J. A., Stafford, E. R. and Hartman, C. L. (2006) Green marketing myopia, *Environment*, **48**(5), 22–36.

Peattie, K. (1995) *Environmental Marketing Management: Meeting the Green Challenge*, Pitman Publishing, London.

Peattie, K. (1999) Trappings versus substance in the greening of marketing planning, *Journal of Strategic Marketing*, **7**, 131–148.

Peattie, K. (2001) Golden goose or wild goose? The hunt for the green consumer, *Business Strategy and the Environment*, **10**(4), 187–199.

Polonsky, M. and Ottman, J. (1998) Stakeholders in green product development process, *Journal of Marketing Management*, **14**, 533–557.

Porter, M. E. and van der Linde, C. (1995) Green and competitive: ending the stalemate, *Harvard Business Review*, September–October, 120–133.

Pujari, D., Wright, G. and Peattie, K. (2002) Green and competitive: influences on Environmental

New Product Development (ENPD) performance, *Journal of Business Research*, **56**(8), 657–671.

Shelton, R. D. (1994) Hitting the green wall: why corporate programs get stalled, *Corporate Environmental Strategy*, **2**(2), 5–11.

Shrivastava, P. (1994) CASTRATED environment: GREENING organizational studies, *Organization Studies*, **15**(5), 705–726.

Thrørgersen, J. (2006) Media attention and the market for 'green' consumer products, *Business Strategy and the Environment*, **15**(3), 145–156.

van Dam, Y. K. and Apeldoorn, P. A. C. (1996) Sustainable marketing, *Journal of Macromarketing*, **16**(2), 45–56.

Varadarajan, P. R. (1992) Marketing's contribution to strategy: the view from a different looking glass, *Journal of the Academy of Marketing Science*, **20**, 323–343.

Wagner, S. A. (1997) *Understanding Green Consumer Behaviour*, Routledge, London.

Walley, N. and Whitehead, B. (1994) It's not easy being green, *Harvard Business Review*, **72**(3), 46–52.

WCED (1987) Our Common Future (The Brundtland Report), World Commission on Environment and Development, Oxford University Press, Oxford.

Weaver, G. R., Trevino, L. K. and Cochran, P. L. (1999) Corporate ethics practices in the mid 1990s: an empirical study of the Fortune 1000, *Journal of Business Ethics*, **18**(3), 283–294.

Wong, V., Turner, W. and Stoneman, P. (1996) Marketing strategies and market prospects for environmentally-friendly consumer products, *British Journal of Management*, **7**, 263–281.

Further reading

Business Strategy and the Environment (2006) *Special Issue on Sustainability Marketing*, **15**(3). Includes six papers on different aspects of achieving sustainability in marketing including an analysis of the role played by the media, the promotion of recycling amongst consumers, eco-labelling schemes, consumer advice and the marketing of products to the poorest 'bottom-of-the pyramid' consumers (which poses as interesting dilemma between the social value of bringing products to the three billion consumers currently excluded from the market economy and the environmental consequences of successfully doing so).

Journal of Marketing Management (1998), Special Issue on Contemporary Issues in Green Marketing, **14**(6). This issue pulled together eight papers from leading experts in the field of green marketing, covering theoretical contributions, a critical review of research in the field, and papers relating to product development, recycling, sustainable communications and green alliances. An invaluable starting point for anyone seeking to understand green marketing from an academic perspective.

Jackson, T. (2004) Motivating sustainable consumption: a review of evidence on consumer behaviour and behavioural change, Centre for Environmental Strategy, University of Surrey, Surrey. A *tour de force* covering the history of attempts to market to consumers on social, environmental and ethical grounds and exploring the different research traditions in green consumer behaviour research. It develops an integrated approach to understanding consumption and sustainability combining conventional marketing research with insights from sociology and psychology and sets out the challenges involved in motivating behavioural change for policy makers and businesses.

Charter, M. and Polonsky, M. J. (1999) *Greener Marketing*, 2nd edn, Greenleaf Publishing, Sheffield. An edited collection which provides detailed coverage of the strategic implications of the greening of marketing, and the implications of this for the management of an extended marketing mix. The themes of the text are reinforced through a collection of detailed case studies covering a wide range of organizations.

Fuller, D. A. (1999) *Sustainable Marketing*, Sage Publications, Thousand Oaks, CA. An excellent exploration of marketing from a physical systems and sustainability perspective. For anyone who suspects that green marketing is in some way 'wooly' this book provides a very specific and factual guide to the forces promoting the greening of marketing and the processes by which it can be achieved.

McDonagh, P. and Prothero, A. (1997) *Green Management: A Reader*, Dryden Press, London. An excellent edited collection of papers combining the deeply philosophical with the highly practical. The practical papers have a strong marketing bias, and the entire collection is invaluable for putting marketing and the environment clearly in its organizational, social and global context.

Menon, A. and Menon, A. (1997) Enviropreneurial marketing strategy: the emergence of corporate environmentalism as market strategy, *Journal of Marketing*, **61**(1), 51–67. Analyses the evolution of the relationship between marketing and the environment and in particular at the emerging of 'enviropreneurial marketing'. Provides a useful discussion of the driving forces behind the greening of marketing, the opportunities that it provides, and the relationship with corporate strategy.

Peattie, K. (1995) *Environmental Marketing Management: Meeting the Green Challenge*, Financial Times Pitman, London. A book which attempts to pull together much of what was written about marketing and the environment in the late 1980s and early 1990s to develop a comprehensive picture of what the green challenge means for marketing. Discusses the environment as a philosophical, strategic and practical challenge for marketing management, and illustrates the issues with short case studies at the end of most chapters.

Ottman, J. A., Stafford, E. R. and Hartman, C. L. (2006) Green marketing myopia, *Environment*, **48**(5), 22–36. A useful article that uses numerous examples to show how some green marketing initiatives failed because they did not strike the right balance between environmental concern and customer focus. Explores the inescapable nature of a greener and more materially efficient future for marketing and the steps to successfully integrating environmental product attributes with perceived consumer value.

Shrivastava, P. (1994) CASTRATED environment: GREENING organizational studies, *Organization Studies*, **15**(5), 705–726. An astonishing article which deconstructs the existing management paradigm to detail exactly how and why it is inherently incompatible with the physical environment within which it exists. Outlines a new environmental management paradigm and points the way forward towards a more sustainable way of managing businesses.

CHAPTER 29

Marketing in emerging economies

PIYUSH KUMAR SINHA and PRATHAP OBURAI

Introduction

Emerging economies have become known as markets that are creating a few surprises for marketers. They are not only turning out to be difficult for many leading brands, but are developing their own brands and world leaders. Once called the Third World these countries are changing the rules of the marketing game. These countries show a different cultural pattern as compared to the developed economies. They also reflect differing consumption patterns. Most of these countries have witnessed a communication revolution before developing economically, leading to high awareness about products and practices across the world. These markets are not only witnessing the entry of large brands and retailers, but several local companies are becoming multinational corporations (MNCs) in their own right.

This chapter aims to:

(a) Establish the nature of the different terrain that marketers in the emerging economies have to deal with.
(b) Describe the phenomenon of emerging economies.
(c) Discuss their characteristics.
(d) Highlight the difference between emerging and emergent economies as well as among the emerging economies.
(e) Postulate a different development route using the case of India.
(f) Suggest an approach to marketing in such economies.

Defining emerging economies

Emerging economies is a term coined in 1981 by Antoine W. van Agtmael of the International Finance Corporation of the World Bank. He defined an emerging or developing market economy (EME) as an economy with low-to-middle per capita income. Although a loose definition, countries whose economies fall into this category, varying from very big to very small, are usually considered emerging because of their developments and reforms. Hence, even though China is deemed one of the world's economic powerhouses, it is clubbed into the category alongside much smaller economies like that of Tunisia with a great deal less resources. Both China and Tunisia belong to this category because both have embarked on economic development and reform programmes, and have begun to open up their markets and 'emerge' onto the global scene. EMEs are considered to be fast growing economies. EMEs are characterized as transitional, meaning they are in the process of moving from a closed to an open market economy while building accountability within the system. Examples include the former Soviet Union and Eastern bloc countries. As an emerging market, a country is embarking on an economic reform programme that will lead it to stronger and more responsible economic performance levels, as well as transparency and efficiency in the capital market. An EME will also reform its exchange rate system because a stable local currency builds confidence in an economy, especially when foreigners are considering investing. Exchange rate reforms also reduce the desire for local investors to send their capital abroad (capital flight). Besides implementing reforms, an EME is also most likely to be receiving aid and guidance from large donor countries and/or world organizations such as the World Bank and International Monetary Fund (Heakal, 2003).

Another research study has defined emerging economies as low-income, rapid-growth countries using economic liberalization as their primary engine of growth. They fall into two groups: developing countries in Asia, Latin America, Africa and the Middle East, and transition economies in the former Soviet Union and China. In the early 1980s, the term newly industrializing countries was applied to a few fast growing and liberalizing Asian and Latin American countries. Because of the widespread liberalization and adoption of market-based policies by most developing countries, the term 'newly industrializing countries' has now been replaced by the broader term 'emerging market economies'. An emerging economy can be defined as a country that satisfies two criteria: a rapid pace of economic development, and government policies favouring economic liberalization and the adoption of a free-market system (Hoskisson *et al.*, 2000).

According to Arnold and Quelch (1998) the phrase 'emerging markets' (EMs) is being adopted in place of the previous lexicon of 'less developed countries,' 'newly industrializing countries' or even 'Third World countries', which emphasized the countries' sources of cheap raw materials and labour rather than their markets. Emerging markets constitute the major growth opportunity in the evolving world economic order.

Frost & Sullivan use a variety of parameters to define emerging economies, including size of the economy, GDP growth rates, stability of financial markets, degree of openness in the economy, government efficiency and infrastructure. Accordingly all areas outside of North America, Western Europe, Australia, Japan and some parts of the Asia Pacific region such as Singapore are defined as emerging markets. Examples of some emerging market countries are Brazil, Russia, India, China (BRIC), Argentina, Chile, Venezuela, Poland, Czechoslovakia, Russia, Hungary, Greece, South Africa, Turkey, Egypt, Israel, Indonesia, Korea, Malaysia, Taiwan and Philippines (Kommineni, 2005).

The emerging economies, or more precisely, EMEs are generally identified on three criteria, viz., (i) low-income or 'developing country' status,

(ii) high economic growth and (iii) government policies leading to greater opening of the economy to domestic and global market forces (Arnold and Quelch, 1998; Hoskisson *et al.*, 2000). One more criteria for defining emerging market economies was of size as cited in Dholakia and Kumar (2004). In 1999, it had suggested grouping of countries into 'paralysed' (the poor economies), 'progressing' (the emerging economies), and 'paranoid' (the rich countries terrified by competition from the progressives). (The Economist, 1999). However, it soon realized that these groupings would not remain stable over time, given the ever-changing nature of the global forces. It, therefore, decided to identify two sets based on economic expansion through sound policies followed by countries with absolute size of the economy playing an important role. The International Finance Corporation (1999) identified 51 rapidly growing developing countries as emerging economies and Hoskisson *et al.* (2000) added 13 transition economies in the former USSR to make a list of 64 EMEs. All developed countries were excluded from their list. A research study (Dholakia and Kumar, 2004) has made an attempt to enumerate a set of relevant indicators of economic performance over a decade that includes Growth of Imports (Gimpgs), Growth of Foreign Direct Investment (Gfdi), Growth of Gross Capital Formation (Ggcf), Growth of Per Capita Gross Domestic Product (Ggdppc), Inflation (INF), Growth of Forex Reserves (Gfr) and Human Development Index (HDI). The data suggest that emerging economies are as good as developed economies (Figure 29.1).

The nature of emerging markets

Emerging economies are seen as fast-growing markets that provide significant market opportunities for companies. It is also noticed that the consumption patterns in emerging economies are changing discernibly. Moreover, technological differences between emerging economies and developed economies are narrowing rapidly. Therefore, the business and commercial world have started to view the former not just as export destinations, but as markets with high business potential and growth prospects.

All developing countries, including the East Asian and Latin American countries, are different from each other in culture, structure, size, stage of

	High-income countries			Developing countries			World statistics		
	2006	2007	2008	2006	2007	2008	2006	2007	2008
Real GDP	3.0	2.8	2.8	6.3	6.0	5.9	3.7	3.5	3.5
Real GDP, PPP	2.9	2.8	2.8	6.7	6.5	6.4	4.6	4.5	4.5
Exports	6.5	6.4	6.8	10.6	10.4	10.5	7.6	7.6	7.8
Imports	6.7	5.9	6.2	11.9	11.7	11.0	8.0	7.5	7.6
CA (% GDP)	−1.4	−1.3	−1.2	2.7	1.8	1.1	NA	NA	NA

Source: World bank.

Figure 29.1   Forecast summary, 2006–2008 (%)

development, history and political organization. Singapore, for example, is a city-state with an autocratic type of regime and a predominantly Chinese population although there is a recognizable South Indian population. It was a former colony of Great Britain. Korea is bigger in size but has a homogenous population and was in the past colonized by the Japanese. Indonesia is a multicultural society, mostly agricultural, endowed with oil, and was a colony of the Dutch. China is different in many ways. Size alone places it in a different category along with India. But then India in terms of culture and history is vastly different from China. Most of these countries have emerged from colonialism, feudalism and autocratic planning.

Emerging markets have unique features in comparison with developed markets and these are manifested in the many areas such as cultural, political and legal, economic and education. There is a high sensitivity to social norms, appeal to local tastes and preferences and conformity to religious mores and standards of behaviour.

Population characteristics

The emerging economies are young. The populations are youthful and growing. While Japan, Europe and the US are worried about pensions and the rapid aging of their populations where Peter Drucker has declared that the 'youth market is over', but in the developing world, the youth market is just beginning. While only 21 per cent of the US population is under the age of 14, this figure is 33 per cent in India, 29 per cent in Brazil and 33 per cent in Iran. These percentages are on a much larger population base. Most of the world's population growth will take place in developing countries (Banga and Mahajan, 2005). More than 90 per cent of the world's net new population will come from emerging nations as a consequence of

rapidly aging population in advanced countries (Figure 29.2).[1]

Incomes and cash flows in the developing world are much lower. In rural and poor segments, low income limits purchases. But even in more affluent sectors, there is a tendency to limit purchase size. In environments of past or present scarcity, cash is kept liquid rather than being tied up in household inventory. Saving rates in China and nine other rapidly developing countries climbed from 20 per cent to 34 per cent between the early 1970s and early 1990s, at the same time that savings in industrialized countries fell. Developing markets are highly fragmented, with few national brands that have a commanding presence. Customers in these markets also have not yet developed a culture of consumerism. While consumers are buying 'super size' or 'economy size' in the developed world, single sachets of shampoo and other products are accounting for billions of dollars of revenue in the developing world. However, one needs to be careful in interpreting these figures. As can be seen from Figure 29.3, each of these countries shows a unique characteristic with regard to consumption. While the higher expenditure on food and non-alcoholic expenditure can be explained by the lower GDP and emerging consumption, a high ratio of transportation is in line with the developed economies. In the case of Malaysia, it is higher than all developed countries. Similarly, the expenditure on communication is higher than in developed economies. In the case of China it stands at 14 per cent which is much higher than in developed countries. It is evident in terms of expenditure on clothing too. Malaysia spends in the same proportion as developed economies in the case of housing and hotels and catering. For

[1] Presentation by Prof. Jagdish Sheth during the 1st IIMA International Conference on Marketing Paradigms for Emerging Economies, Ahmedabad, India, January 2005.

Country name	Babies	Infants	Children	TW	TE	SA	YA	MAA	BB	PE
Emerging countries										
Croatia	0.92	1.9	9.01	5.71	8.6	6.64	19.82	41.2	27.85	22.36
India	2.12	4.26	17.37	10.52	14.12	9.47	27	32.89	18.62	7.95
Pakistan	3.26	6.39	22.2	12.28	15.7	9.87	27.44	25.92	14.61	5.76
China	1.04	1.83	9.35	8.36	13.16	7.62	23.34	45.57	26.18	11.56
Philippines	2.3	4.62	18.99	11.54	14.92	9.64	27.55	30.86	17.17	6.44
Malaysia	2.43	4.85	17.64	10.12	13.79	9.43	26.88	33.91	19.52	6.59
South Africa	2.02	3.94	15.46	10.87	15.46	10.93	29.87	32.37	18.03	7.48
Brazil	1.86	3.7	14.38	8.89	12.82	9.45	27.84	36.79	21.48	8.4
Russia	1	1.98	7.31	5.84	11.1	8.6	24.18	29.47	17.54	17.54
Average	1.88	3.72	14.63	9.35	13.30	9.07	25.99	34.33	20.11	10.45
Developed countries										
Australia	1.19	2.39	10.11	6.77	9.51	6.92	20.79	42.42	27.54	17.52
Japan	0.9	1.8	7.42	4.75	7.08	5.75	17.99	42.07	27.31	25.97
UK	1.14	2.27	9.26	6.35	9.15	6.44	19.03	41.72	27.04	21.36
US	1.4	2.78	10.73	7.18	10.28	7.18	20.72	41.84	28.47	16.74
France	1.29	2.57	9.96	6.16	6.45	19.18	41.73	27.52	20.4	8.44
Germany	0.87	1.75	7.6	5.24	8.13	5.93	17.9	43.17	28.27	24.33
Average	1.13	2.26	9.18	6.08	8.43	8.57	23.03	39.79	26.51	19.06

TW: Tweenagers; TE: Teenagers; SA: Studying age; YA: Young adults; MAA: Middle aged adults; BB: Baby.
Source: Compiled from Euromonitor Reports.

Figure 29.2   Classification and distribution of population in emerging and developed countries in 2005

	Emerging markets								Developed markets					
	IN	MY	CN	BR	PH	SA	RU	Average	US	UK	FR	JN	GR	Average
Food and non-alcoholic beverages	43.4	22.37	28.89	12.5	37.43	18.79	39.07	28.93	7.08	9.15	14.6	14.48	11.96	11.45
Alcoholic beverages and tobacco	3.09	2.65	2.39	3.24	1.62	8.81	10.98	4.68	2.18	3.95	3.45	3.36	4.15	3.42
Clothing and footwear	4.72	3.58	7.84	6.48	2.74	4.92	9.34	5.66	4.06	5.93	4.55	4.8	5.87	5.04
Housing	10.8	21.14	9.91	20.63	22.48	12	13.78	15.82	18.32	18.1	23.5	25.63	24.98	22.11
Household goods and service	2.92	5.32	6.37	8.67	4.92	9.62	5.41	6.18	4.68	6.46	5.84	4.43	6.78	5.64
Health goods and medical services	7.87	2.31	5.21	5.95	1.57	7.87	2.28	4.72	19.31	1.74	3.8	4.02	4.32	6.64
Transport	12.7	16.09	2.7	9.82	7.86	16.93	8.02	10.59	10.87	15.2	15	10.64	14.53	13.25
Communications	0.98	3.02	14.53	8.13	0.84	1.95	1.32	4.40	1.77	2.37	2.35	2.68	2.99	2.43
Leisure and recreation	1.41	4.09	4.33	6.79	0.47	4.57	4.86	3.79	9.01	12	9.21	9.95	9.21	9.87
EducationHotels	2.34	1.86	6.64	5.6	3.85	2.5	0.12	3.27	2.6	1.4	0.61	2.2	0.7	1.50
and catering	1.45	13.07	5.07	4.64	5.19	2.58	2.47	4.92	6.1	12	7.58	7.37	4.4	7.49
Misc goods and services	8.28	4.51	6.13	7.57	11.05	9.46	2.35	7.05	14.01	11.7	9.54	10.44	10.11	11.16

IN: India; MY: Malaysia; CN: China; BR: Brazil; PH: Philippines; SA: South Africa; RU: Russia; US: United States; FR: France; JN: Japan; GR: Germany.
Source: Compiled from Euromonitor Reports, Figure in %.

Figure 29.3   Consumer expenditure in emerging and developed markets in 2005

% retail value rsp	Emerging markets							Developed markets				
	CN	IN	MY	PH	RU	BR	Average	JP	GR	FR	UK	Average
Baby care	1.6	1.6	5.0	5.4	1.9	2.6	3.1	0.7	1.3	1.9	1.6	1.4
Bath and shower products	12.5	38.5	16.6	9.8	10.4	8.2	17.6	5.9	7.9	7.3	10.6	7.9
Deodorants	0.2	1.0	2.5	4.6	5.4	8.1	2.7	0.9	5.3	5.5	7.8	4.9
Hair care	19.5	23.4	19.5	23.1	19.9	28.7	21.1	18.5	21.2	17.8	21.7	19.8
Colour cosmetics	11.3	2.5	9.8	4.0	13.1	8.1	8.1	18.9	12.1	10.9	13.7	13.9
Men's grooming products	1.0	7.3	6.7	4.5	7.5	9.0	5.4	5.3	8.2	8.3	11.4	8.3
Oral hygiene	14.1	15.4	13.6	20.7	10.1	9.3	14.8	6.4	9.6	6.6	9.7	8.1
Fragrances	1.7	1.3	6.7	8.6	18.7	16.1	7.4	1.9	13.1	15.4	10.0	10.1
Skin care	36.8	9.3	23.4	20.7	14.1	11.4	20.9	42.9	21.5	25.5	14.7	26.2
Depilatories	–	0.4	0.4	0.1	0.3	0.4	0.3	1.3	1.3	1.4	1.9	1.5
Sun care	1.9	0.4	0.3	0.2	0.7	1.8	0.7	0.9	1.5	2.3	3.2	2.0
Premium cosmetics	7.1	4.5	17.2	8.5	9.4	2.0	9.3	43.2	18.6	34.9	25.2	30.5
Cosmetics and toiletries	100	100	100	100	100	100	100	100	100	100	100	100

Note: Figures do not sum up due to the inclusion of men's grooming products in other subsectors.
CN: China; IN: India; MY: Malaysia; JP: Japan; PH: Philippines; BR: Brazil; RU: Russia; GR: Germany; FR: France; UK: United Kingdom.
Source: Compiled from Euromonitor Reports.

Figure 29.4   Sales of cosmetics and toiletries: % value 2004

cosmetics and toiletries, developed economies spend on premium cosmetics (30 per cent), skin care (26 per cent) and hair care (20 per cent), whereas emerging economies spend skin care (21 per cent), hair care (21 per cent), and bath and shower products (18 per cent) (Figure 29.4). Homes are much smaller, so furnishings and other products need to be scaled accordingly. India, with 342 people per square kilometre, is more than eleven times as densely populated as the US (31), and China is more than four and a half times as densely populated (135) (Banga and Mahajan, 2005).

Cultural characteristics

Culture, by defining socially correct behaviour, acts as a co-ordinating mechanism for regulating transactions. In these circumstances it may be preferable that the message to be communicated focuses on cultural universals such as cleanliness, training and general manifestations, rather than culturally specific practices (Fletcher and Melewar, 2001). In emerging markets, however, social structure has a major impact on purchasing decisions because the majority of people in these markets are not subject to global or even external influences outside their village community. The research studies by Hofstede and Trompenaars and Hampden-Turner

illustrate some major cultural differences between emerging and developed markets. Of the countries studied, the 14 most developed countries are compared with the 14 least developed countries (Fletcher and Melewar, 2001). Based on a study of 53 cultures, Hofstede (1980) identified five dimensions of cultural variation: power distance, uncertainty avoidance, individualism, masculinity and long-term orientation (Veiga et al., 1995).

1 Power distance: The degree to which people of a country accept inequality among people. High power distance reflects the acceptance of great distance between those with power and those without power, such as senior managers versus the rank and file.
2 Uncertainty avoidance: The degree to which people of a country prefer structured over unstructured situations. High uncertainty avoidance leads to rule-oriented, ideological behaviours.
3 Individualism: The degree to which people of a country learn to act as individuals rather than as members of a cohesive group. It reflects the extent to which people emphasize personal goals over group goals.
4 Long-term orientation: The degree to which people of a country are oriented to the future rather than to the past or present. It reflects an emphasis on thrift, persistence and change, as

opposed to a here-and-now perspective that places a higher value on tradition.

5 *Entrepreneurialism*: The degree to which people of a country are oriented toward investing in new ways of doing things. A high degree of entrepreneurialism reflects a willingness to take risk.

6 *Concern for people*: The degree to which the people of a country place importance on building personal relationships. A high concern for people results in a major emphasis being placed on employees' quality of life.

The four dimensions of Trompenaars and Hampden-Turner were 'particularism versus universalism', 'affective versus neutral', 'specific versus diffuse' and 'achievement versus ascription'. Research findings indicated that with Hofstede's dimensions, these markets exhibit a much greater degree of peer distance. Emerging markets also display a much greater degree of collectivism as opposed to individualism. With the Trompenaars dimensions emerging markets tend to be particularistic rather than universalist with obligations and particular circumstances taking precedence no matter what the rules say. Emerging markets also tend to be specific rather than diffuse as reflected in their being characterized by cultures that are highly contextual.

Political environment

Emerging markets are more likely to be characterized by a greater degree of control over the freedom of their citizens and these markets are run by one party. Communication is largely for government propaganda. Communication messages are developed keeping in mind the government. Bureaucrats are somewhat capricious in what they will and will not allow to be disseminated to the citizens of the country (Fletcher and Melewar, 2001). The consequence for communication is that more emphasis will need to be placed on endorsements, testimonials and encouraging adoption, not by early adopters as in the developed world, but by influence figures in these regimes.

Legal framework

In emerging markets, the legal framework is usually underdeveloped and in many cases, has received little revision since the colonial era. These regulations relate product quality, distribution,

flexibility in pricing, tax structure as well as communication. They control who can deliver the message, what the message can contain, when the message can be communicated, where the message can be communicated, who the message can be communicated to, the frequency with which the messages can be communicated and how the message should be communicated. This subjectivity can also relate to forms of promotion other than advertising such as premium offers, money-off promotions, coupons and contests (Fletcher and Melewar, 2001). Regulations are enforced selectively and are subject to negotiation.

Economic status

Emerging markets are characterized by low rates of mobilizing savings that in turn impact on the ability to acquire the infrastructure to receive communication messages. Therefore, the use of television and the Internet as communication vehicles is likely to be restricted and messages received via these media are more likely to be received in a community setting rather than individual environment.

Emerging markets are often characterized by shortages (Aiyeku and Nwankwo, 1997). In such markets the focus is on meeting production targets and good performance is not rewarded nor is poor performance penalized. Being driven by planner rather than by consumer sovereignty, the pressure to identify and meet consumer needs is constrained (Aiyeku and Nwankwo, 1997). This leads to a short-term focus rather than to a long-term focus for managers who are not likely to respond to communications appeals offering long-term gain – rather they will respond to appeals promising short-term benefit.

Educational status

Research studies have indicated a strong correlation between educational levels and economic development (Terpstra and Sarathy, 2000). Literacy rates in emerging markets can be as low as 20 per cent. Even in China where improving literacy has been a development objective for decades, 27 per cent are still illiterate (Shao and Wong, 1996). As a result, communication messages may need to be conveyed via aural or visual rather than via print media. Where print media are used, the emphasis will need to be more on pictorial rather than on verbal. Where demonstration is required, this is more likely to occur on a face-to-face basis rather than via the media. This increases the emphasis on seminars and training programmes.

Collectively, differences in culture, politics, law and its application, economic circumstances and education account for the time gap between innovation creation and innovation adoption being greater in emerging than in developed economies. This has implication for communication and promotion.

High rates of emigration to the developed world

The developing world is exporting not only products and services to the developed world, but also people. The foreign-born population in the US rose to 31 million people in the last census in 2000, up 57 per cent from 1990. These immigrants are in touch with family and friends back home. Globally, immigrants sent home an estimated $93 billion in 2003, second only to foreign direct investment as the largest financial flow from the developed to the developing world. While immigrants are formally a part of developed markets, they are part of something much bigger. These global diasporas are redefining the borders of markets and creating social networks that stretch across the developed and developing world.

Unofficial elements

Unofficial market activities account for much greater percentages of international trade in emerging markets resulting in unreliable import/export figures. Smuggling is the most common manifestation of illegal markets and is often due to restrictions imposed for balance of payments reasons (Gillespie and McBride, 1996). Arnold and Quelch (1998) pointed out that emerging markets are marked by high levels of product diversion between countries and widespread counterfeiting of products both of which require customized initiatives undertaken by locally based operating units. Hence, effective communication with emerging markets should cater for those who patronize unofficial as well as official channels (Fletcher and Melewar, 2001).

Interference factors

Interference may disrupt communication to a greater extent in international than in domestic marketing because of the complexity of the international environment. The more important of these interference factors are socio-cultural, distribution channel related and government controls. Socio-cultural factors in emerging markets include tribalism and allegiance to ethnic affiliations. Effective promotion in such circumstances must be directed to these powerful groups. In many emerging markets the distribution channels are vastly different from those in developing countries. The retail sector is often underdeveloped which results in an emphasis on direct selling to the customers. In a number of emerging markets, the co-operative movement is very strong and is the vehicle for indigenous elements of the local population to engage in business. In Indonesia, it is the backbone of the country even though co-operatives account for less than 5 per cent of GDP (Towie, 1997). Government is another source of interference. Emerging markets are more likely to be run by authoritarian regimes either of the right (military dictatorships) or of the left (socialist regimes) and such regimes can more easily create interference than democratically elected governments. Also, in emerging markets there is greater likelihood that there will be a need to deal with state owned enterprises and, in many cases, they may be the only conduit for entering goods into the market. This situation is more likely in those emerging markets that are collectivist rather than individualist in cultural orientation.

Infrastructure availability

Most of the rural population of the 86 per cent markets is inaccessible by motor vehicles, and they lack good sanitation and electricity. At the same time, the cities are growing very rapidly, and this fast urbanization has placed tremendous strains on the urban infrastructure. Infrastructure everywhere in the developing world is fragile or underdeveloped. Transportation networks are non-existent. Power failures are frequent. Clean water and sanitation are often lacking. Underdeveloped economic systems and restrictive regulations have created thriving informal or parallel economies in developing nations. It is estimated that the informal economy accounts for at least 40 per cent of the GNP of low-income nations.

Distribution channels

Developing nations have poor distribution systems. In large cities, distribution is often through small, hole-in-the-wall shops such as the paan-walla shops in India, the tiendas de la esquinas in Mexico and sari-sari stores in the Philippines. A market of 600 million is locked in India's villages, 42 per cent of which have populations of less than 500, with weak connections to the outside world. The lack of media, roadways and electricity creates seemingly impenetrable barriers. Some villages do not have retail outlets at all, and some distribution opportunities, such as market days or carnivals, are temporary in nature (Banga and Mahajan, 2005). The distribution channels are not only longer but also not very effective. Also with fill rate of less than 75 per cent, the distribution cost is higher and stock outs are commonplace. There is a lack of a cold chain. Consequently, perishable products do not fetch desired value due to loss in quality during distribution and they need to be sold as near the farm as possible. The customers also end up paying more for these products.

Marketing communication

Emerging markets vary in both the availability of certain media and the extent to which the media are controlled by the government and hence are available for the use by advertisers. According to Quelch and Austin (1993), this depends on the stage of economic development, literacy rates, urbanization and levels of government control. In addition, the marketing conventions that are taken for granted in developed countries are often absent in emerging markets. Authorities display a greater tendency to change regulations governing media usage for promotion frequently and often do so in an unpredictable fashion. Among advertising media, radio is the most popular for reaching audiences in small towns and rural areas. In many emerging markets such as those in West Africa, radio reaches more than 90 per cent of urban and more than 70 per cent of rural areas (Aiyeku and Nwankwo, 1997). Although the use of colour television is increasing in many urban areas of emerging markets, black and white televisions are often

in widespread use in rural areas. If complex messages need to be conveyed then newspapers are used. Literacy levels may, however, restrict this medium, especially in countries where literacy rates are much lower for females than males. Personal communication in emerging economies in emerging markets is very important from business-to-business marketing especially where demonstration and product usage education is required. In addition, out of home media are important such as buses, cinemas and mobile units.

The medium employed is more likely to be the direct salesperson. This is because of the relative lack of distribution and communication infrastructure. This is also facilitated by the low cost of salespersons. The focus on direct selling as a marketing strategy may also reflect the limited availability of publicity media in emerging markets. Examples of companies that have taken advantage of this situation are Avon, Amwy, Mary Kay Cometics and Tupperware.

In general, media penetration varies widely among emerging markets. Aiyeku and Nwankwo (1997) argue in respect of African countries that, for the message to be well received, advertising materials must be sensitive to both national and regional beliefs and customs, and the media mix should combine traditional and western methods of conveying information. Another factor will be the extent of previous exposure to promotion. Whereas in developed markets exposure has been continuous for decades, in emerging markets this exposure has been limited and promotion may be still a novelty in itself. This was found to be the case with public relations activity in China (Shao and Wong, 1996).

As previously mentioned, emerging markets tend to value collectivism, accept power distance and may be characterized as high context. Therefore, the type of commercial, the spokespersons and the storyline are likely to cause a different emotional response and will require any standard advertisement or promotional form to be adjusted accordingly (Fletcher and Melewar, 2001).

India: a case of defiance and conformity

India has been classified as a developing economy and is expected to become the third most powerful country in the world by 2035 with a GDP of US $7854 (BRIC Report, 2003). With a protectionist regime until the late 1980s, the impact of liberalization was becoming evident by the early 1990s and by the end of the century it was operating like a free economy, though restrictions exist in some sectors. The high GDP growth is becoming a cause of concern for many as they feel that the country does not have the infrastructure to support the growth. But the fact remains that it is growing with a population that is second only to China.

Route to economic development

Indian economic development is being fuelled by development in all sectors. The country has taken a parallel process route to development. While the growth in developed economies has happened in a linear fashion, India is growing differently, even when compared to most other remerging economies, with perhaps an exception of China. The diversity within the country is very vivid. The country has 26 states, 14 scheduled languages, about 100 dialects. Barring a few states, most have their own language, varied cultural and social practices. Variation in food as well as clothing is also very evident.

Almost all of the states have a differing contribution of economic activity to the State Domestic Product. Some states still show a very high proportion of agriculture. There are states where the contribution of tourism is high. It is been witnessed that states are finding their own way to prosper.

The classic development theory suggests that economies develop using the Agriculture – Industrial – Service – Knowledge – Experience route. A country like India, with diversity in resources and practices, is witnessing growth in each of them simultaneously. Urban conglomerates such as Mumbai, Delhi, Kolkata and Chennai followed the conventional route. Bangalore took the knowledge route to development. The State of Andhra Pradesh was primarily agrarian. In the last decade the dotcom explosion has brought money into the state and its smaller towns and rural area through remittances. Goa has chosen tourism to build its economy, again money being generated due to spending by visitors (i.e. foreign sources). Kerala has taken the path from Agriculture to Experience (tourism). The development of smaller cities is also being supported by the BPO/KPO enterprises that use the local resources but the source of money is from outside the country. This has created different earning patterns and levels.

Manufacturers and retailers are venturing into agriculture. Companies like ITC have ventured into corporate farming after being in manufacturing for several years. Retailers like Reliance and Bharati have plans to venture into farming to provide good value to their customers. Services are driving manufacturing and agriculture. According to the Telecom Regulatory Authority of India (TRAI), India added close to 74 million new mobile telephone subscribers in the year 2006. A high adoption of mobile services has paved the way for multinational wireless equipment makers like Nokia, LM Ericsson and Motorola to set up manufacturing units in this country. Similarly, McDonald has helped farmers in enhancing their production of potatoes and other ingredients. The Internet has also been a single driver of many services, such as gifting and e-commerce (Figure 29.5).

Product penetration

Penetration of some products like detergent, washing powder, toilet soaps and cooking oil is more than 90 per cent in both rural and urban India (Figure 29.6). However, brand penetration is comparatively low. In 2005, four out of five households in India used at least one Hindustan Unilever (a Unilever Subsidiary) product (Chatterjee, 2006). As can be seen from Figure 29.7, Hindustan Lever has the highest penetration with a reach of 166 million households. Colgate Palmolive is positioned in the second position with 85 million households. Philips India is the number one among durable companies in India and reaches 19 million households. According to FICCI Consumer Durable Goods Survey (2005) white goods penetration was low in India. Especially in rural India penetration in the case of refrigerators was 2 per cent and for washing machines the figure stood at 0.5 per cent.

Remittance increase penetration

Besides the increased generation and flow of money from domestic sources, the growth in India is also being fuelled by foreign money. Consumer spending in developing economies is affected by remittances[2]. According to the World Bank's annual

---

[2] Remittances are transfers of money by foreign workers to their home countries.

Personal disposable income, household sector saving and GDP across all India, 2003–2004					
	Personal disposable income (Rs Billion)	Saving (Rs Billion)	Per capita income (Rs)	Per capita saving (Rs)	Per household income (Rs)	Per household saving (Rs)
I (lowest)	471.25	32.62	3813	264	22 806	1579
2	752.21	80.8	6437	691	36 167	3885
3	968.19	130.33	8806	1185	49 537	6668
4	1281.29	209.09	11 066	1806	59 909	9776
5	1465.41	263.56	13 750	2473	75 990	13 667
6	2083.93	423.65	17 034	3463	89 123	18 118
7	1992.33	413.51	21 061	4371	115 168	23 903
8	2809.31	645.99	26 910	6188	137 889	31 707
9	3725.28	971.78	37 602	9809	183 476	47 862
10 (highest)	8035.84	2627.84	88 940	29 085	395 551	129 351
Total	23 585.03	5799.17	21 767	5352	115 981	28 518
Top 20%	11 761.12	3599.61	62 090	19 003	289 544	88 618
Top 5%	5365.25	1818.12	124 642	42 237	527 731	178 832
Top 1%	2038.44	732.12	257 041	92 318	1 017 456	365 425

Source: BW Marketing Whitebook (2006, p. 108).

Growth of key durable categories in India						
	Unit growth		Value growth		Price change	
Category	2003/2002	2004/2003	2003/2002	2004/2003	2003/2002	2004/2003
Colour TV	8.1	9	0.1	1.4	−7.4	−6.9
Flat CTV	97.9	125.3	63.6	96.3	−17.3	12.9
Refrigerator	4.4	6.4	−1.9	3.1	−6.1	−3.1
Frost free	17.4	33.2	9.9	27.1	−6.4	−4.6
Washing machine	9.3	11	3.4	9.9	−5.4	−1
Fully automatic	18.2	48.4	12.3	39.7	−5.1	−5.9
Microwaves	39.7	58.3	27.6	37.3	−8.7	−13.2
Convection	60.6	65.4	51.8	49.4	−5.5	−9.7
Hi-fi music system	−12.7	50.8	−14.5	50.7	−2	−0.1
Mini-7.1	51.4	−12.3	45.6	−5.6	−3.9	
All Figures in %						

Source: BW Marketing Whitebook (2006).

Figure 29.5 The different routes to economic development

Global Economic Prospects (GEP) report for 2006, in 2004, India was the country with the largest inflow of remittance in the world at $21.7 billion, followed by China and Mexico at $21.3 billion and $18.1 billion, respectively. Of the other South Asian countries, Pakistan received $3.9 billion and Bangladesh $3.4 billion in 2004. Remittance inflows into India had surged to $20 billion in 2003 from a level of $13 billion in 2001 – mainly on the back of sharp increase in the number of migrants and good response from the non-resident Indians community to several attractive deposit schemes and bonds. This amount is about 10 per cent of the total world remittances (*The Hindu Business line*, 2005).

As a percentage of GDP, however, remittances in India account for just 3 per cent of GDP as compared to Lebanon (25 per cent) and the Philippines (15 per cent). It is estimated to increase rapidly due to the change in the profile of Indians going abroad. This trend is already evident, not only in the growing volume of IT and ITeS export earnings

					Category-wise spends in India					
Year	PFCE per capita (current prices)	FB & T	C & F	GRF & P	FA & S	MCH	T & C	RE & C	Total spending	Growth rate (%)
1992–1993	5745	3106	330	724	176	201	647	183	11113	12.3
1993–1994	6444	3534	392	765	197	219	729	198	12478	13.4
1994–1995	7315	3956	446	829	218	306	846	230	14146	12.5
1995–1996	8252	4420	521	873	262	355	958	267	15908	15.9
1996–1997	9552	5270	543	942	282	395	1160	294	18437	6.5
1997–1998	10183	5370	594	1051	305	477	1303	345	19628	13.9
1998–1999	11591	6240	530	1151	338	665	1458	388	22362	8.6
1999–2000	12641	6506	618	1279	356	834	1589	450	24274	3.9
2000–2001	13160	6324	645	1494	400	963	1755	484	25226	9.0
2001–2002	14396	6783	582	1658	417	1104	2053	489	27483	4.4
2002–2003	15082	6757	664	1780	440	1216	2235	513	28686	

FB & T: Food, beverages and tobacco; C& F: Clothing and footwear; GRF & P: Gross rent, fuel and power; FA & S: Furniture appliances and services; MCH: Medical care and health; T & C: Transportation and communication; RE & C: Recreation, education and culture.
Source: BW, Marketing Whitebook (2006).

Figure 29.5 Continued

but also in the changing composition of workers' remittances. In the early 1980s, most remittances were from the Gulf and were essentially meant to meet maintenance expenses of families in India. Today North America has replaced the Gulf as the most important source of workers' remittances, accounting for 44 per cent of total remittances, a significant part of which goes towards savings and investment. A large part (52 per cent) of the total remittance of $20 billion is accounted for by high-value remittances exceeding $1000. Technology is also helping this transaction happen quickly and free of hassles (*Economic Times*, 2006).

The young population is seen as having more disposable income to fuel the growth of consumable and luxury products. The median age of the country is 27 years, which is similar to the median age of the software professionals at 27.5 years (George, 2005). An entry level IT professional is offered an average salary of approximately Rs 240 000 per annum. India recorded the highest average salary rise, of 13.8 per cent, in the South-East Asian region in 2006. This increase in the service and manufacturing sectors is expected to be around 15 per cent in 2007. At present, there are now about 1.6 million Indian households that spend an average of $9000 a year on luxury goods (Narayan, 2006).

Conclusion

The easy route to exporting or dumping in developing countries is long gone. These economies are growing on their own strength and not just on the back of borrowed funds, products and technologies. These countries are not only emerging as large exporters but are also buying companies in the developed economies to expand, as had been demonstrated by companies like TATA and Ranbaxy. The problem is that success in one market blinds the marketers and for the sake of 'economizing' they try to follow the same formula. In many cases the failure has been caused by the lack of initial market research and dependence on macrolevel data (Helen *et al.*, 2005).

Marketing orientation (Kohli *et al.*, 1993; Farley and Deshpandé, 2005) would need to be practiced in its true sense for building a sustainable competitive advantage. Companies would have to sense customer requirements, disseminate this information across the organization, and respond to it with honesty and diligence. Companies may have to integrate market with non-market strategies (Yuanqiong, 2006). The marketing planning may also require changes. Due to a fast changing

Products	All India Urban	All India Rural	North		East		West		South	
			Urban	Rural	Urban	Rural	Urban	Rural	Urban	Rural
Detergents/ washing soaps	96.4	90.7	99.2	94.3	80.6	74.3	98.8	95.2	99.4	99.2
Washing powder/liquid	99.1	95.2	99.4	96.4	99.9	99.8	98.7	93.3	99	91.2
Toilet soap	99.6	97.8	99.7	97.4	99.8	99.3	99.2	94.3	99.9	99.7
Shampoos	89	73.4	90.8	75.1	94.2	69.3	83.9	66.2	90.4	81.4
Tooth paste/ tooth powder	99.3	83.4	99.5	80	98.9	74.8	98.8	86.4	99.8	92.2
Tooth paste	95.4	65.7	95.1	60.6	95.5	55.1	95.9	69.2	94.9	77.6
Tooth powder	45.6	50	38.9	45.9	37.1	39.9	51.5	62.2	48.9	53.3
Talcum powder	65	37.7	50.9	15.9	63.9	32.3	67.1	48.1	74.7	54.8
Milk food drinks	31.9	5.9	15.7	0.8	48	6.5	18.2	0.9	51.2	14.3
Coffee	38.1	13.4	20.6	0.5	23.3	0.7	23.9	3.2	74.5	45.6
Noodles/pasta/ macroni	40.8	2.6	42.9	2.9	60.4	2.4	33.4	0.9	37.1	3.9
Squashes/ powders	19.9	2.3	22.7	1.3	20.9	0.9	19.5	1.8	17.7	4.8
Pre-/post-wash	66.4	47.5	75.8	41.4	76.7	47.3	50.1	42	71.1	58
Tea	97.3	89.7	99.7	93	97.2	86.5	99.3	96.2	93.3	84.3
Food cleaner	23.3	1.5	19.9	0.2	24.9	0.3	24.2	1.2	24.3	4
Toilet/bathroom cleaners	42.3	3.5	37.7	1.2	33.9	1.6	40.7	3	51.7	7.7
Oil/ghee/ vanaspati	99.7	97.2	99.9	95.2	100	98.2	99.3	95.6	100	99.5
Spices	83.2	48	84.6	52	91	45.4	76.3	36.6	85.6	56.1
Soft drink	33.6	7.5	48.9	5.9	38.4	3.7	17.4	2.5	36.2	16.6
Hair oil and dressings	90.9	81.3	81.8	56.6	97.3	96.1	96.8	92.1	88.8	81.7
Insecticides	73.3	17	63.8	16.7	88.3	15.4	64.7	10	82.6	24.5
Cold rubs/pain balms	52.2	25.1	24.3	5.9	28.1	9.6	59.9	31.2	78.5	52.9
Glucose powder	21.2	7.8	17.5	3.4	37.5	12.5	14.1	1.9	23.6	12.4
Atta/wheat	90.9	58.7	88.8	32	96.8	74.7	84.6	48	96.3	77.3
Salt	99.5	98.2	99.8	98.5	99.9	99.8	98.6	95.2	99.9	98.9
Antiseptic liquids/creams	28.7	11.6	30	12.5	48.9	16.5	27.2	15.1	19	3.4
Skin cream	75	60.3	77.7	54.7	80.4	69.1	74	59.3	71.2	58.1
Butter	22.1	1.3	29.9	0.2	27.2	0.2	18	1.1	17.6	3.6

All figures are in per cent, period January–August 2005.
Source: Compiled from BW Marketing Whitebook (2006).

Figure 29.6   Product penetration in India

Company name	Category	Year	
		2000	2005
HLL	FMCG	150	166
Colgate Palmolive	FMCG	78	85
Nirma	FMCG	–	40
Dabur	FMCG	–	15
Marico	FMCG	22	32
Philips	Durable	22	19
BPL	Durable	11	14
Videocon Industries	Durable	11	18

Source: Chatterjee (2006).

Product penetration in emerging and developed countries in 2005

	PC[1]	Television				Internet	
		BTV[1]	CTV[1]	Cable TV[1]	Satellite TV[1]	Penetration (%)	Usage growth (%), 2000–2006
Developing market							
India	1	40.74	36.48	15.1	1.35	5.4	1100
China	15.8	36.83	46.77	19.69	3.5	9.4	446.7
Brazil	28	7.2	87.86	8.12	19.7	14.1	418
Philippines	2.9[2]	26.25[2]	66.3[2]	6.58[2]	2.28[2]	9.1	291
Malaysia	26.4	2.29	90.23	7.59	9.12	40.2	197.7
South Africa	9.4	4	66.14	34.07	34.07	10.4	112.5
Russia	9	16.75	75.73	34.46	NA	16.5	664.5
Average	14.93	17.97	67.20	19.84	13.55	15.01	461.49
Developed market							
US	74.2	0.8	99.65	73.1	26.58	69.3	117.3
UK	50.2	0.69	98.35	22.11	29.71	62.5	144.2
France	41.7	8.5	95.94	28.02	63.08	48.4	247.3
Japan	52.6	1.63	99	49.35	37.36	67.2	83.3
Germany	43	4.07	97.4	60.97	39.57	61.3	110.9
Average	46.88	3.72	97.67	40.11	42.43	61.74	140.60

[1]Penetration per 100 households.
[2]All the figures are in 2003.
Source: Compiled from Euromonitor Reports and Internetworldstats.com.

Percentage of household having access to banking services and other assets in India

	Household using banking services	Radio, transistor	Television	Telephone	Bicycle	Scooter, motorcycle, moped	Car, jeep, van	None of the specified assets
All India	35.5	35.1	31.6	9.1	43.7	11.7	2.5	34.5
Rural	30.1	31.5	18.9	3.8	42.8	6.7	1.3	40.5
Urban	49.5	44.5	64.3	23	46	24.7	5.6	40.5

Source: BW Marketing Whitebook (2006, p.45).

Figure 29.7   Million households in India using brands/products

Categories	Ad spends in India (in Rs crore)						
	Year 2002	Growth	2003	Growth	2004	Growth	2005
TV	3909	10.0	4300	13.0	4860	11.4	5412
Press	4400	8.0	4752	14.7	5450	16.0	6322
Radio	150	20.0	180	22.2	220	44.1	317
Cinema	108	8.3	117	14.5	134	8.2	145
OOH	690	14.5	790	7.6	850	5.5	897
Internet	30	33.3	40	50.0	60	75.0	105
Ad industry size	9287	31.2	12182	−5.0	11574	14.0	13198

Source: Compiled from BW marketing WhiteBook (2006).

Figure 29.7   Continued

market, the formal and the informal approaches may have to be merged. Competitive assessment may require to be conducted at several hierarchical levels and locations and be founded primarily on anticipated responses of the customers rather than the competitors (Wilson, 1999). Companies would need to encourage a good analysis of the traditional methods and adopt different and innovative methods of analysis and planning.

Mass is dead, but no market is small. Conventional segmentation variables have become simply profiling dimensions. As the profiles are also changing fast, the only long-term stable variable is customers' values. Businesses would have to be built around customer values. Customers are individuals but are an integral part of a larger system. A successful marketer would need to understand the larger system and then the individual. Values are formed by the systems such as family, friends, teachers, colleagues and not the individuals. Most of the values we cherish are instilled before we recognize them. Social science knowledge would bring better understanding of customer value.

Top-down segmentation, and hence sampling, would not help in getting growth; a Bottom-up approach would be required. The study and the marketing effort would start with one customer and then build it from there. The focus of research would be to know more about the customers than knowing about more customers. The study would need to build a – Quantitative – Qualitative research paradigm.

Given this context, there is a need to develop a deeper understanding of marketing phenomena in emerging economies based on the empirical realities of those markets. If business is to succeed in emerging markets, then their strategies and action plans need to be based on in-depth contextual understanding of the marketing phenomena in these markets. This implies the need to develop an adequate knowledge base. Hence the urgency to test, adapt, modify and develop concepts, frameworks and theories relating to marketing based on empirical research anchored in the context of emerging economies.

Acknowledgements

Authors gratefully acknowledge the research support provided by Mr Sanjay Kumar Kar, Academic Associate, IIMA and Ms Vandana Sood, Research Associate, IIMA.

References

Aiyeku, J. F. and Nwankwo, S. (1997) Marketing strategies and implications for transitory economies of less developed countries: a case study of Sub-Sahara Africa, *Journal of International Marketing and Exporting*, **2**(1), 16–24.

Arnold, D. J. and Quelch, J. (1998) New strategies in emerging markets, *Sloan Management Review*, Fall, **40**(1), 7–20.

Banga, K. and Mahajan, V. (2005) The Lands of Opportunity, available at http://www.whartonsp.com/articles/article.asp?p=404802&seqNum=4&rl=1 (accessed on 18 December 2006).

BRIC Report (2003) Dreaming With BRICs: The Path to 2050, Global Economics Paper No. 99.

BW Marketing Whitebook (2006) *The Essential Handbook for Marketers.*

Chatterjee, P. (2006) The reach of brands, *The Hindu Business Line*, 11 May, Online Edition, available at http://www.thehindubusinessline. com/ catalyst/2006/05/11/stories/ 2006051100190300.htm (accessed on 15 December 2006).

Dholakia, R. H. and Kumar, A. S. (2004) Identification of top performing economies, *Vikalpa*, **29**(2), 17–25, 39–53.

Economic Times (2006) Remittance: dollar dreams coming true, *Times News Network*, Tuesday, 05 December, available at http://economictimes. indiatimes.com/articleshow/712359.cmswww. indiatimes.com (accessed on 17 December 2006).

Economist (1999) Feeling left out. *Economist*, **350**(8100), 2 January, 17.

Farley, J. U. and Deshpandé, R. (2005) Charting the evolution of Russian firms from Soviet 'producer orientation' to contemporary 'market orientation', *Journal of Global Marketing*, **19**(2), 7–26.

FICCI Consumer Durable Goods Survey (2005) October, New Delhi, available at http://www. ficci.com/surveys/consumer-durable.pdf (accessed on 15 December).

Fletcher, R. and Melewar, T. C. (2001) The complexities of communicating to customers in emerging markets, *Journal of Communication Management*, **6**(1), 9–23.

George, I. (2005), India's top 10 IT employers, 10 June, available at http://www.rediff.com/ money/2005/jun/10bspec.htm (accessed on 15 December 2006).

Gillespie, K. and McBride, J. B. (1996) Smuggling in emerging markets: global implication, *Columbia Journal of World Business*, Winter, 41–54.

Heakal, R. (2003) What Is An Emerging Market Economy?, available at http://www.investopedia.com/articles/03/073003.asp (accessed on 16 December 2006).

Helen, R., Parvez, G. and Catherine, G. (2005) The impact of marker orientation on internationalisation of retailing firms: Tesco in Eastern Europe, *International Review of Retail Distribution and Consumer Research*, **13**(1), 53–74.

Hofstede, G. H. (1980) *Culture Consequences: International Differences in Work-related Values*, Sage Publications, London.

Hoskisson, R. E., Eden, L., Lau, C. M. and Wright, M. (2000) Strategy in emerging economies, *Academy of Management Journal*, **43**(3) June, 249–267.

International Finance Corporation (IFC) (1999) http://www.ifc.org/EMBD/SLIDES/img009.gif

Kohli, A., Jaworski, B. and Kumar, A. (1993) MARKOR: a measure of market orientation, *Journal of Marketing Research*, **30**, 467–77.

Kommineni, V. (2005) Interactive Kiosks in Emerging Economies Loss or Lots of Relevance? Paper presented in ICMPEE, IIMA, India.

Narayan, S. (2006) India's Lust for Luxe, Monday, 03 April, available at http://www.time.com/ time/magazine/article/0,9171,1179415,00.html.

Quelch, J. and Austin, J. (1993) Should multinationals invest in Africa? *Sloan Management Review*, Spring, 107–119.

Shao, A. T. and Wong, Y. M. (1996) Public relations in China: a status report, *Journal of Asia Pacific Business*, **1**(4), 43–66.

Terpstra, V. and Sarathy, R. (2000) *International Marketing*, Dryden Press, Fort Worth.

The Hindu Business Line (2005) India tops in remittance inflow, Internet Edition, Friday, 9 December, available at http://www.thehindubusinessline.com/2005/12/09/stories/2005120902961100.htm (accessed on 15 December 2006).

Towie, M. (1997) A plant investment with a fresh dividend, *Business Review Weekly*, 24th March, 52.

Wilson, D. F. (1999) Competitive marketing strategy in a volatile environment: theory practice and research priorities, *Journal of Strategic Marketing*, **7**, 19–40.

Veiga, J. F., Yanouzas, J. N. and Buchholtz, A. K. (1995) Emerging cultural values among Russian managers: what will tomorrow bring? *Business Horizons*, **38**(4) July–August, 20–277.

Yuanqiong, He (2006) How firms integrate non-market strategy with market strategy: evidence from mainland of China, *The Journal of American Academy of Business*, **10**(1), 357–361.

Further reading

Pelle, S. (2007) *Understanding Emerging Markets: Building Business BRIC by Brick*, Response Books. A must read for those interested in emerging markets. Provides a good deal data, relevant theoretical concepts and balanced business advice.

van Agtmael, A. (2007) *The Emerging Markets Century: How a New Breed of World-Class Companies is Overtaking the World*, Free Press, New York. This is a contribution by the pioneer who coined the term 'emerging markets', and details the growth and emergence of large and small world-class firms from the emerging markets. This book provides information on investment strategies and policies that developed markets' firms can use.

Shenker, O. (2005) *The Chinese Century: The Rising Chinese Economy and Its Impact on the Global Economy, the Balance of Power, and Your Job*, Wharton School Publishing, New Delhi. This is a valuable academic source for those who wish to get a good understanding China. While there are now a great number of books on China, many of them contain anecdotal material and provide partial understanding of recent developments or focus too much on past political climate; this book takes an unbiased view of China and business climate and its likely impact on both the developing and developed parts.

Prahalad, C. K. (2005) *The Fortune at the Bottom of the Pyramid: Eradicating Poverty through Profits*, Wharton School Publishing, New Delhi. This book has a wealth of case studies and provides a detailed examination of the strategies that companies that have captured low end of many emerging markets such as Brazil and India.

Mahajan, V. and Banga, K. (2005) *The 86% Solution: How to Succeed in the Biggest Market Opportunity of the 21st Century*, Wharton School Publishing, New Delhi. This book complements Prahalad's book cited above, and has practical strategies and implementation tactics.

Prestowitz, C. (2005) *Three Billion New Capitalists: The Great Shift of Wealth and Power to the East*, Basic Books, New York. Details the rise of Asia, and suggests that nations and firms around the world may have to refocus and adjust strategies.

Sheth, N. J. and Sisodia, S. R. (2006) *Tectonic Shift: The Geo-economic Realignment of Globalising Markets*, Response Books. This book is a good attempt by marketing academics to look at the globalization of markets and its likely impact on the world trade. Posits the emergence of new trading blocks and centres of growth.

www2.goldmansachs.com web site has research material on emerging markets available in the public domain for free access and use.

Barkley, R. J. and Marina, R. V. (2004) *Comparative Economics in a Transforming World Economy*, 2nd edn, MIT Press, Cambridge. An excellent treatment that provides summaries on key countries from around the world. The chapter on former Soviet Union and eastern Bloc nations are especially relevant.

CHAPTER 30

Retailing

LEIGH SPARKS

Introduction

The retail industry has huge economic and social significance. It improves the standard of living and increases employment, it invests, it innovates, is responsible for anchoring urban regeneration in many parts of the country and – of huge importance – embodies the spirit of competition.

Tony DeNunzio, then CEO of Asda,
in Department of Trade and Industry (2004)

Retailing (traditionally defined as the sale of articles, either individually or in small numbers, directly to the consumer) is a distinct, diverse and dynamic sector of many economies. The ubiquitous presence and nature of the organizational structure of many retail outlets – large numbers of small local, independent shops – has however for a long time blinded many to the challenges and opportunities in retailing. With the emergence of modern techniques of retailing and retail marketing and the emergence of huge international retail corporations and new retail forms and formats including the Internet, retailing has become much more visible and central to consumers' and governments' concerns (Dawson, 2001). Reflecting as it does, cultures and consumers, retailing is the primary conduit for production and consumption linkages in economies. Virtually everyone experiences retailing, as virtually everyone shops! The closeness of these retailer and consumer linkages demands retail engagement in marketing. Indeed many retailers could be judged to be consummate marketers, often at the forefront of the discipline.

Retailing is a huge part of many economies. Perhaps 25 per cent of all enterprises in the European Union (EU 2006) are involved in retailing. About 12 per cent of the total working population in the EU are engaged in retailing. There are over 3.5 million shops in the EU and a large retail Internet presence in many EU countries. In the UK, the retail sector constitutes an important part of the economy, contributing c16 per cent of GDP and is worth c£150 billion. It employs around 3 million people or 1 in 9 of the workforce and involves over half a million retail premises. Retail property dominates UK institutional investment, accounting for over half of the capital value of direct property assets held by institutions and property companies. UK retailers are involved in global sourcing and retailing activities. The global success of UK retailers is enhanced by a positive retail environment within the UK, with non-UK based retailers being strongly represented in the country.

The retail sector is enormous and influential. It contains however massive contrasts. Retailing is operated through many single shop entrepreneurial businesses, but the sector also contains some of the world's largest companies. There are large and small fixed shops, mobile shops and virtual shops. Retailing is a local affair with local demands: but some retailers are increasingly international and indeed 'global retail brands' such as IKEA are significant. Retail sales are increasing, although the number of shops is falling and their format is changing. Low employee pay characterizes much of the sector, but managerial pay is above average. Executive rewards can be enormous; in 2006, five of the six executive directors of Tesco, which is arguably Britain's most successful business, received a remunerations package of at least £2.2 million.

For some consumers, the development of large retail outlets and large retail businesses simply provides a more convenient place and way in which to shop. For others, the rise of the retail corporation has sanitized and standardized towns making them clones or 'bland identikits dominated by a few retail behemoths' (Simms *et al.*, 2005). The seemingly irresistible rise of Wal-Mart in the USA (Brunn, 2006) and Tesco in the UK (Burt and Sparks, 2003) has provoked reactions over the use of retail power and the practices 'imposed' by such retailers on farmers, suppliers, distributors and consumers. In the UK this concern has lead to another investigation of the grocery sector (due to report in 2007), only a few years after the last one (Competition Commission, 2000). But, whilst there is a wave of sentiment against such retailers in some of the media and local opposition groups have utilized the Internet in particular to co-ordinate resistance to proposed developments, consumers continue to flock to such stores and to spend even more on a wider range of product and services. Retailing is centre stage in considerations of economies, societies and the patterns of how we want to live our lives. We all need food and clothing and for some, the latest iphone; the question is how best to organize the distribution of the products that are demanded.

This chapter examines the key components of the practice of retailing and seeks to show the distinctive and changing nature of the retail sector. As befits a chapter in a book on marketing, it begins with the cultural and consumer aspects of the retail environment. It then moves to the places and locations where retailing occurs. Interrelationships linking retail businesses with other organizations are examined before a consideration of the internal operations of retailers themselves are presented. The people who take on the running of retail businesses and individual shops, the nature of the selling and retailing processes and the supply and sale of goods are introduced and discussed. This chapter concludes by summarizing the state of the retail industry today and considering briefly some of the challenges for the future.

Culture and retail consumers

Any consideration of retailing should begin with the country or local environments in which, and the consumers with which, retailing interacts. The very specific relationships retailing has with culture

and consumers are crucial to the distinctiveness and operation of the sector. Retailing must be responsive to the culture within which it operates. Internationally, this creates a great diversity in terms of regulatory and shopping environments, service standards and store formats and layouts. For example Japanese culture and societal behaviours are fundamentally different to the cultural norms and values of for example Saudi Arabia or the southern US. Some aspects of a global culture are emerging and there will be similarities in some of the retailing across these locations. In the main however, retailing mainly adapts to the *local or national* situation and norms. Considerable differences in approaches and operations may thus be found, though the core process – making products available for consumers to buy – is the same.

These cultural norms are derived from societal and economic situations. Retailing is an economic transaction, but also in many cases is fundamentally a social interaction. The norms of economic and social behaviour permeate, inform and on occasions, constrain, retail operations. The restrictive German shop opening hours are a legal recognition of cultural dimensions to the organization of society, and have long-standing roots. The limitation of alcohol sales to government-owned shops in Sweden and Canada reflects societal concerns over the use and abuse of alcohol. The persistence of fresh produce markets in Mediterranean Europe and wet markets in East Asia derives from traditional patterns of food preparation and consumption. The advertising of retail products through weekly newspaper 'fliers' or inserts in Denmark and the US have different origins and obligations, but nonetheless inform and constrain the retailer and retail practice. Such advertising and promotional offers would be deemed wasteful, inappropriate or ineffective in other societies and economies. Limits on what can be advertised or sold in Islamic countries, or what advertisements or catalogues can contain, reflect cultural and religious norms of these societies.

It is tempting to use these examples to suggest that there are uniform national cultures and thus retailers' responses to culture work best on the national level. But, culture is a complex, multi-dimensional concept that derives from a range of personal and group values and attitudes. Culture may be learnt and can be passed from generation to generation. Culture is also a social phenomenon. The notion of culture suggests behaviours, desires and needs that can be stated. It is also adaptive in that culture can change to meet circumstances or outside stimuli. As the world becomes more inter-connected and perhaps standardized, so perhaps the cultural influences from outside (e.g. American influences) come to play a bigger role. This however can be overstated. Local differences in taste, demands, brands and behaviours and attitudes still persist and 'force' retailers to work with the local cultures rather than against them.

For retailers, there are a number of implications of culture and its component aspects. First, as culture is absorbed, learned and transmitted from generation to generation, certain aspects of culture may become deep rooted and thus hard to change. There are therefore boundaries on what, how or when products can be promoted or retailed. What is acceptable within societies varies.

Secondly, a shared culture binds some groups together and thus can provide the basis for identifying markets or market segments. The presence of different communities and particular consumer behaviour patterns in large cities across the world demonstrate the potential for group or local segmentation. Little Italy in Toronto and the various Chinatowns globally illustrate this point, but there are many smaller enclaves and groups based around a number of nationalities. In response to the increasing presence and role of an Hispanic population in southern Florida, food retailers have begun to develop more Spanish or Mexican themed, designed and run stores. Publix, a leading Florida-based supermarket chain is experimenting with Publix Sabor a supermarket developed with Hispanic influences. Shopping Centres Today (2006) notes 'the environment within a Publix Sabor is very different from a regular Publix supermarket. The stores have salsa and meringue music piped in, and they feature bright colours, ceramic tiles and wrought iron. The shelf signs are written in English with the Spanish translation below. All employees are bilingual and the store advertising is in both languages.' It is not only ethnicity that can form a cultural segmentation. Aspects of 'youth culture' have proved attractive to retailers trying to target the young market. Top Shop would be a UK example, as would Legit, a South African black urban fashion focused discount retail chain, that is highly adapted to its target market.

Thirdly however, whilst retailing operates mainly within cultural norms and thus reflects these, retailers can also shape these cultural norms in many ways. Retail stores, operations and environments are not neutral entities but rather can condition and structure consumer moods and behaviours and in some cases over the long-term

influence cultural norms. The approaches of some stores 'develop' consumers by requiring them, implicitly or explicitly to rethink aspects of their beliefs and attitudes. What was once probably unthinkable can become commonplace, as for example with the presence of Ann Summers stores in high streets and shopping centres.

Further examples of this in the UK include the design revolution sparked by Terence Conran's Habitat stores from the 1960s, the critical, unique and long-term importance of Marks and Spencer to British clothing manufacturing and retailing and the campaigning and ethical sensibilities overtly used by Anita Roddick and The Body Shop. These three retailers changed British society and aspects of British consumer and retail culture. IKEA, Louis Vuitton, McDonalds, Starbucks, Wal-Mart, Tesco, Zara and H&M are doing the same thing today, albeit in different ways and sectors and on an international basis. For example, Tesco has revolutionized the way in which food retailers are thought of and defined in the UK and the products and services that can be offered. By extending its brand into financial services, Tesco altered the perceptions of insurance and other financial and service products and the ways in which they could be priced and sold.

This emphasis on culture demands that retailers be embedded in the culture of the economy and society in which they operate. This may be best achieved by being part of that economy and society, or at least understanding it, and is thus mainly accomplished through an understanding of local consumers. Knowledge of what drives local consumers and what they need and want (in product and service terms) is fundamental to the operation of retailing. This embeddedness may be derived from the local operations, companies or managers or may be achieved by a thoroughly researched knowledge of the local consumer base. Whichever, there is a radical difference in retailing, when compared to most other management activities and industrial sectors. In retailing the issues of consumer knowledge intrude directly into the business day in and day out. Retailing is dependent on people, both because it employs a lot of them to serve customers in stores, but also because an understanding of peoples' behaviours, attitudes and psychology are critical in most retail businesses. Failure to understand consumers and the local market means failure, period.

One basic constraint on the development of retailing is the demographic structure of any market. At its most simple, demographic change relates to features such as the number, age structure and location of individuals and households. For retailers, changes in these dimensions are fundamental as they affect the size and the location of their target markets. An examination of some demographic issues in Europe immediately identifies far-reaching changes in recent decades, which have major implications for the development of retailing.

First, whilst growth continues in the number of people in most countries, the rate of growth has reduced substantially over the last half-century. This can be attributed to lower birth rates, fertility levels and socio-economic changes, such as the full participation of women in the paid labour force. For retailers it means that they can no longer rely on previous assumptions of 'natural' population growth to increase market size. The battle for market share is thus much harder now as natural growth is that much slower. Where there is population growth, this may be of particular demographic origins for example immigration, and the consumer behaviour patterns may be very different to the local population.

Secondly, whilst the population may (just) still be growing, there has been a fundamental shift in its age composition. The decline in the birth rate, coupled with reduction in child mortality, longer life expectancy and improved medical care have resulted in a much more 'elderly' population structure than before. Even though large numbers of this elderly population are more affluent and active than previous generations, retailers still have to consider how they respond to this and other population segments. The retail offer has to be adjusted to meet the changing numbers in different target markets. These different age segments have of course very different attitudes. Retailers have to understand these generations and their behaviours and attitudes, and adjust their retail formats, locations, products and offers accordingly.

Thirdly, consumer change can be considered at the household as well as the individual level. Demographic changes have been allied with socio-economic and lifestyle changes, such as later age of marriage and higher divorce rates, to radically restructure both the number and structure of households in most countries. There are now far more households in Europe than before, but there are fewer people (often only one person) in each of them. For retailers, this can provide selected opportunities and market growth (e.g. in furnishings) but also requires other retailers to adapt their product sizes and ranges for example introduce packet sizes suitable for individual consumption.

These basic demographic changes are combined with further changes in socio-economic status and lifestyle. How people live their lives has changed dramatically. Teenage behaviour hopefully bears little resemblance to many activities carried out by previous generations of teenagers. For many groups, of all ages, there are more opportunities, more choices and in some cases more affluence to enable satisfaction of needs. These needs themselves have of course altered fundamentally.

Examples of some of these changes include the different occupational structure of economies, together with an altered gender balance of the workforce. The distribution of income has changed both generally and between the sexes. More women are in paid employment than before and many have much greater economic power and freedom. Consumers are more educated and informed and have access to more data on choices than ever before. These changing situational factors of course have implications for attitudes and values and affect life cycles and stages. The UK traditional certainty of marriage by 21, children by 25, the housewife staying at home while the male breadwinner works, has gone. Holidays are more likely to be in Spain or Florida than Blackpool. Curry is more commonly eaten than fish and chips. Such behaviours reflect the changed realities of living in the twenty-first century.

One particular certainty that has disappeared is the idea that whole swathes of the country would be doing the same things at the same times. Meal times previously were common. Television programmes (on three channels) were watched in huge numbers. People all dressed basically the same, often from Marks and Spencer, or worse C&A. Football matches took place at 3 pm on a Saturday. Telephone calls were made from home or a public phone box (for which you queued). Holidays were taken at the same time and often to the same place (Glasgow Fair in Blackpool). Now, families eat together far less often. Satellite TV has multiplied the choice of programmes to watch. Other media bombard the marketplace with choice and options. Football occurs anytime, anyday and is broadcast live. Mobile phones ring on trains and in lectures! Countries are fragmented, sectionalized and highly differentiated. However they increasingly contain a mobile but connected society, though the connections are very different of those of previous generations. For example, Finland contains as many active mobile phones as it does people. Retailers have to work much harder to identify the group commonalities that may exist and to react quickly to changing patterns, which themselves may be more diffuse and transient.

Consumers are a dynamic grouping. Consumers change and consumer behaviour develops over time. Norms of consumer behaviour that were once thought to be inviolate or immutable have altered considerably. As economies and societies have grown, so have consumer desires. What is important to the society or to groups of consumers has evolved. The way in which time and money are inter-related is one illustration of the process. Consumers in many economies use time very differently to previous generations. The economy increasingly operates 365/24/7. Consumers have a different potential for, and perception of time and travel, both generally and for shopping. The implications of this for retailing are fundamental. Consumers' needs and their ability to satisfy these needs, have altered dramatically; giving rise to retailing concepts such as organic superstores, lifestyle shopping, farmers' markets, outlet malls, convenience stores, discounters and fast food. At the product level, changing attitudes towards vegetarianism, meat consumption, ready meals or the acceptability of fur or products based on animal testing are equivalent examples. More recently as environmental concerns have continued to develop, some consumers expect retailers to act in a socially responsible and preferably sustainable way. For some, ethical retailing can be found only in small-scale local retail operations utilizing local sourcing and products, but for others Fairtrade or (RED) and other labels are acceptable compromises. Some of the compromises (or the need to engage as a starting point as it would be seen by others) are clear in the description of (RED):

> (RED) was created by Bono and Bobby Shriver, Chairman of DATA to raise awareness and money for The Global Fund by teaming up with the world's most iconic brands to produce (PRODUCT)^{RED} branded products. A percentage of each (PRODUCT)^{RED} product sold is given to The Global Fund. The money helps women and children affected by HIV/AIDS in Africa.
>
> What's the meaning of the parentheses or brackets? Well, we call them 'the embrace'. Each company that becomes (RED) places its logo in this embrace and is then elevated to the power of red. Thus the name – (PRODUCT)^{RED}.
>
> You, the consumer, can take your purchase to the power of (RED) simply by upgrading your choice. Thus the proposition: (YOU)^{RED}. Be embraced, take your own fine self to the power of (RED). What better way to become a good-looking samaritan?!
>
> http://www.joinred.com/more.asp – accessed 14th January 2007

From these various cultural and consumer changes (see also Miller *et al.*, 1998; Bowlby, 2000) a range of implications for retailers can be identified.

First, there are trends in *consumption* that is, the general structure of demand and the amount of specific goods consumed. A good example is the modern supermarket. Here, the increased product ranges in areas of ready meals and prepared foods reflect changing demand patterns. The segmentation of products by price or by other attributes for example organic, gluten-free, healthy living or children's meals is a reaction to wider trends in the market. The extension of retailing into banking, insurance, health care and services such as Internet provision, mobile phone plans and top-up phone cards also illustrates the shift in consumption towards services.

There are then implications for *consumer behaviour* that is, consumer decisions as to which of their wants they wish to satisfy and how, when and where they are going to obtain satisfaction. The most obvious change for retailers in this area has been the increasing demand for convenience. Convenience in terms of time and location has becoming increasingly important, giving rise to 24 hour trading, petrol station convenience stores, home and workplace delivery and supermarkets at railway stations amongst a range of reactions. Convenience however also requires retailers to make it easier and simpler for consumers to obtain what they want; it may be here that the Internet is having most success.

Thirdly, there are changes in *shopping behaviour* that is, the consumer process during the shopping activity itself. As consumers have changed, so the elements of the retail offer that attracts them and encourages them to purchase or consume have changed. Much more attention has had to be paid by retailers to elements of store design, ambience and atmospherics generally as well as issues to do with the balance between price, service and quality. For many, going shopping on occasions has become more of a leisure activity. Consumers expect to be more in control of the trip and to be on occasions entertained. The development of cafes in bookshops such as Borders, or a total redesign of the selling of a product as in Sephora, or involvement in production as in Build-A-Bear

Table 30.1 Types of shopping trips			
Purpose	*Reason*	*Product example*	*Format and retailer example*
Essential	Replenishment of stock items; primary shopping trip	Food and household items	Food superstore (Tesco)
Purposive	Clear purpose to trip; major item purchase	Electrical items	Retail park (B&Q, Comet, etc.), shopping centre with department stores (House of Fraser)
Leisure (or fun)	Social activity, occasionally ancillary to visit	General purchases, gifts, services	Town centre, shopping centre or mall (e.g. Bluewater), leisure activity focus (museum shop, HMV, JJB Sports, Manchester United Superstore)
Convenience	Time constrained, top-up trip, everyday purchases	Ready meals, milk, newspapers	Convenience store (Spar), petrol station store (Shell Select), transport node store (Marks and Spencer Simply Food)
Experimental	Unusual product or innovative method	Tickets, home delivery of large items, local or specialist produce	Ticketmaster.com, Argos, farm shop

are illustrations that shopping behaviours are not solely functional activities.

Combining these various strands of consumer change, it can be suggested that there are now different reasons behind different shopping trips and that consumers satisfy their desires in different ways and different times (Table 30.1). At some times, consumers need to replenish basic items and the trip is a highly functional one. At other times, similar items may be purchased using a different format for example the same consumer might buy the same goods from a Tesco superstore, a Tesco Metro or Tesco.com, but at different times. Other shopping trips are focused on the trip itself more than the shopping. Leisure in its broadest sense is critical to the experience of the trip and of the shopping. Table 30.1 suggests that retailers have to be able to focus on consumers and their changing behaviours in order to continue to develop their businesses. This is much more complex than it has been in the past as the direction, pace and dimensions of change have fragmented.

Retail locations and outlets

This emphasis on culture and consumers is reflected in the importance that is afforded by retailers to the places where retailing takes place – the locations of retailing. This is in itself a distinctive dimension of the retail industry, as few industries involve managing and operating such a diverse and dispersed outlet network. There are for example over 31 000 Seven-Eleven convenience stores across the world, with over 11 500 in Japan alone. The Body Shop operates over 2100 outlets in 55 countries. Inditex (the parent company for Zara) has over 3000 stores in 64 countries. It is hard to conceive of other businesses outside retailing having to organize and control such extensive branch networks. Whilst the old adage 'location, location, location' has probably been overplayed, it has some truth, and above all it is an identifying characteristic of the retail trade. Retailers must understand the spaces within which consumers operate and try to match these in terms of their locational and operational decisions. Retailers thus manage the macro-location (the country, region or city) and the micro-location (the store location and internal environment). In this section the macro-locational issues are considered, leaving store design and other internal store-based issues to later.

Retailing not only has a distinctive locational dimension, but is further distinguished by its diversity of retail location. Furthermore, locations are dynamic. Some shop locations seem fixed in the most visible of ways as with Harrods in London, Galeries Lafayette and Printemps in Paris or Bloomingdales in New York. Others are more transient, such as street, wet or night markets, car-boot sales, farmers markets and other similar activities. Whilst some street locations clearly have a retail premium such as Ginza in Tokyo, Oxford Street in London or Fifth Avenue in New York, others come and go from retail activity. Town centres and city centres are for many economies the main place of concentration of retailing and the centre of this economic and social interaction. Market spaces in British historic cities such as Carlisle and York or Nice and many other towns and cities in France illustrate this well. In some economies, most notably the US, this town centre and central emphasis has been disturbed by the decentralization of most retail activity (e.g. Longstreth, 1997, 1999), driven by the introduction of the car as the main mode of shopping transport.

The most developed car-borne and thus decentralized-retail economy is the US. In many town and city centres, particularly in the southern part of the US, the central area (the downtown) is a desolate, retail-free zone. The retail activity mainly occurs in regional and suburban malls and strip and power centres along important highways or at key road intersections. The historical location for retailing has thus been (often totally) replaced over time by locations that better reflect transport movements, modes and patterns, consumer preferences and retailer formats and cost structures.

This locational shift has had important implications for the form of much of the retail infrastructure. Large hypermarkets, power centres, strip malls and covered shopping centres with huge car parks are a result of this process (Kowinski, 2002). The internalization and privatization of retail space, as in a shopping mall, is a further outcome of this transformation of previously public retail space.

In the UK, this process of locational decentralization is seen quite clearly, though it is not as extensive as in the US, primarily due to more restrictive controls on retail development and a different attitude to the use of a more scarce resource, land. Retailing was for a long time a city or town centre activity, but since the Second World War, and the latter part of the twentieth century in particular, it has become more decentralized. This decentralization is often portrayed as a series of 'waves' of types of retailing moving out-of-town (Schiller, 1987; Hallsworth, 1994; Fernie, 1998; Thomas, 2006). When people 'go shopping' now, they are as likely to be thinking of an off-centre superstore, a retail warehouse park, a regional shopping centre or a factory outlet centre as they are of the high street in the local town. Nonetheless town and city centres remain important shopping destinations in the UK.

This movement away from central locations has been encouraged by a number of factors, including:

- the growth of an affluent and mobile population in suburban areas in contrast to a declining less affluent and less mobile town and city centre population;
- the development of strong corporate chains with fewer ties to a locality and more willingness and need to move shops to areas of demand and opportunity;
- changes in the methods of selling which have seen a demand for larger stores and associated parking. Such stores are harder to accommodate in built-up areas as unit sizes and shapes have become less appropriate. It has been cheaper to build and easier to operate shops in decentralized purpose-built locations.

This decentralization has been controversial as it utilizes greenfield land in many instances, often has an adverse aesthetic impact and expands the reliance on private transport. Consumers have embraced it however. As a consequence, some locations including in both urban and rural situations

Table 30.2 Types of shopping centre development		
Type of shopping centre	*Provision*	*Example (all Glasgow)*
Major city-centre renewal schemes	Provide a wide range of shopping facilities adding to the provision of the existing town or city centre	Buchanan Galleries
Small in-town schemes	Usually provide specialist shopping facilities	Princes Square
Non-central-city centres (district and neighbourhood centres)	Comprise several stores and sometimes a superstore or hypermarket targeted at everyday consumption needs	Bearsden Shopping Centre
Edge-of-town and out-of-town centres (retail parks, factory outlet centres)	Typically based around one or two large superstores and containing retailers in a variety of product areas	The Forge; Glasgow Fort
Large out-of-town regional shopping centres	Create the equivalent of a new city centre outside the city	Braehead Shopping Centre; Silverburn
Centres associated with transport nodes	Built, for example, at sites such as railway stations (often within the urban area) and airports (outside it)	Central Station Concourse; Glasgow Airport

have seen a huge reduction in retail outlets and subsequent problems of accessibility and choice for consumers who are not mobile (economically or physically). Land-use planners have therefore been increasingly concerned to integrate retail development within existing towns and cities. Nonetheless, the planning policies of the 1980s and 1990s resulted in large numbers of decentralized food and non-food superstores and some regional shopping centres. More recently policy has sought to control and limit out-of-town development and focus new retail space into town centres (Guy, 2006).

There is a distinction between managed and unmanaged shopping locations. Individual shops are obviously managed. A shopping street however is basically a loose un-managed collection of individual stores and thus provides a general node for shopping. Town centres are unmanaged amalgams of several such streets. However there are also managed shopping environments. Some of

these for example arcades in city centres or town markets are long standing, albeit relatively small components of the shopping panorama. Others however (e.g. regional shopping centres), and particularly those built more recently are major retail destinations in their own right. As with other retail formats, shopping centres or malls have been getting larger. Nine of the ten largest shopping centres in the world are in Asia, with particular recent expansion in China. Scale however is no protection against market changes and some very large shopping centres have closed, particularly in the US (see www.deadmalls.org; www.mallofmemphis.org).

Many cities have various forms of planned shopping centres within their boundaries (Table 30.2). For example Buchanan Galleries in the centre of Glasgow is a major retail attraction. But there are also decentralized locations containing shopping centres, which can draw people from large distances, and other planned environments serving a variety of functions. Gateshead's Metro

Centre is an early UK off-centre regional shopping centre. The Mall at Cribbs Causeway in Bristol and Cheshire Oaks Factory Outlet Centre in the North West of England are other examples of planned decentralized retail environments. These centres are designed, planned, branded, marketed and managed as distinctive retail locations (e.g. Bluewater in Kent). Given the recent restrictions via planning policy on out-of-town developments, some of the most modern planned shopping centres are in major city centres such as Bullring in Birmingham.

Across many western countries, the twin processes of decentralization and managed environments have transformed the retail landscape (Ruston, 1999). The impact on existing locations has been considerable. As a consequence of this, there is increasing interest in whether management techniques from planned shopping centres can be applied to unplanned town centres. Many UK towns now have town centre managers who engage in active place marketing to attract and retain consumers. Town centre management aims to market the whole of a town as a destination, including its competing retailers. Locations rather than individual shops are thus also in competition.

Some retailers have become clear destinations in their own right and as a result transform the locational landscape wherever they develop. For example in the UK it used to be the case that towns fought hard to get a Marks and Spencer store because of the spin-off benefit in increased consumer visits and prestige it brought. Marks and Spencer would receive favourable rental agreements to participate in a shopping centre scheme, whilst other retailers would then pay higher rents to locate next to the Marks and Spencer store. IKEA's arrival has the same impact in many countries. Wal-Mart Supercenters have become destination stores in the USA. The company has such a reputation that consumers will travel to it almost no matter where in a town or city it is located. The store becomes a desired destination, and if it moves, then customers follow. The hundreds of Wal-Mart stores in the US that have been closed as the company's locational and format demand has evolved, bear silent witness to their extensive construction and de-construction of locational landscapes. These closed stores illustrate the volatility of retail demand and supply, but also the way in which some retailers can manipulate demand and consumer decision making. They also demonstrate the difference between the US and Europe in that in the former land is treated as a disposable asset.

Shopkeepers and retail managers

The nature of retail business is also distinctive and diverse in terms of those who take on the management and operation of retail businesses – shopkeepers and retail managers. The method of business organization and firm-type chosen has implications for resources, the scope of operations and decision-making roles and capabilities. Retailing remains numerically dominated in almost every country by independent retailers (i.e. retailers who operate single stores) with shopkeepers who are the owner and/or manager. This local form of retailing has been central to retail operations throughout history. Retailing has low entry and exit barriers. However, the independent retailer is but one form of business organization in retailing. Five forms are generally identified (Table 30.3). The local shop run as an independent business is the mainstay in numerical terms of most retail sectors. They are located everywhere and could retail almost anything. Some are generalist shops (e.g. the corner store) whereas others are very specialist (e.g. second hand wedding dresses).

In some countries, the government has been a major retailer controlling and operating many stores (e.g. as in the past in communist Poland) or reserving control for particular product lines (e.g. quasi-government liquor stores – the LCBO – in Ontario, Canada). Generally however such direct government involvement in the running of shops is rare.

More commonly, there are corporate or multiple retailers. These are businesses operating several (or 'multiple') shops as a company entity, and thus gain from economies of scale, scope and replication. Such companies dominate the trading component of retailing in many countries and can be enormous businesses (e.g. Wal-Mart), sometimes with operations in many countries across the globe (e.g. Carrefour, Metro or IKEA). Corporate retailers can be found operating large retail outlets such as superstores, small stores in town centres and shopping malls and even concessions within department stores. They may be focused on particular lines of trade (e.g. JJB Sports or New Look).

Historically, consumer co-operatives have been strong in many countries and remain important in some (e.g. Finland, Denmark, Switzerland and Japan). These businesses are owned by members and typically are run for mutual benefit not shareholder profit. The Co-operative Group with

Table 30.3	Retail organizational types
Type	*Examples*
Independent retailing	Single local shop
Government shops	LCBO (Liquor Control Board of Ontario Stores), Royal Mail
Corporate retailers	Marks and Spencer (public) Arcadia Group (private)
Consumer co-operatives	Co-operative Group
Contractual chains	Body Shop (franchise) Spar (affiliated group) NISA (buying group)

thousands of shops dominates the Co-operative Movement in the UK, although some smaller single shop societies do still exist (e.g. Grosmont in Yorkshire). In some local communities, often as a response to the lack of retail facilities in an area, residents have grouped together to run a community-based shop, which may obtain logistical and other support from larger co-operatives.

Finally, many previously independent retailers have given up some degree of independence by becoming part of a contractual chain or a franchise that is, they are independent businesses but are supplied by, or legally linked, to a larger 'umbrella' organization. The contractual forms vary from operation to operation (e.g. Spar, Seven-Eleven Japan, Body Shop, Musgraves). All attempt to collectively maximize buying, marketing and other activities to improve overall performance, in the belief that working together, combined with independent shop ownership and its local knowledge, enhances their competitive position. In essence they seek the organizational benefits of the larger corporate chains, alongside the flexibility and entrepreneurial flair of the independent trader.

There are many examples of the development of franchise systems in retailing and it has become a relatively common approach to internationalization, particularly in the non-food sector. Some of the largest businesses in retailing contain within them considerable franchise operations. For example, Seven-Eleven Japan operates its over 11 500 stores in Japan on the basis of a form of franchise. In Ireland, Musgraves, a wholesaler, has used a franchise system with two formats (SuperValu and Centra) to expand significantly

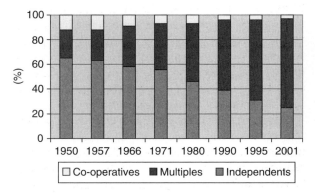

Figure 30.1 Market share by organizational type in the UK (1950–2001)

and to become the market leader in food retailing. Musgraves' recent purchases in the United Kingdom of Budgens and Londis are providing them with an opportunity to attempt to replicate the franchise model and its success.

The balance of power amongst these business organizational forms varies from country to country and has altered over time. As a general rule, centrally controlled large organizations (running chains of large and small stores) have gained power and market share from other forms and particularly from independent and co-operative retailers (Figure 30.1). Corporate retailers have become the dominant commercial form in many countries. This power has been gained because of the cost and efficiency advantages of operating larger businesses under central control (e.g. in advertising, branding and in operational consistency) (Clarke *et al.*, 2002). This illustrates the economies of scale and scope available to retailers, but also suggests more distancing of the business from the local situation. The role and function of store management in a chain organization has consequently become more critical over time, though the boundaries of central versus local control remain flexible and variable amongst multiple retailers. Independent local retailers with local knowledge and an ability to satisfy local needs and wants can be successful over a long period. However, succession can be a problem for such retailers.

The scale of some of the leading corporate retailers is now almost hard to comprehend. Wal-Mart is the world's largest retailer. It had sales in 2005 (i.e. financial year ending 31 January 2006) of $312 billion, operated over 6600 stores, employed over 1.8 million associates, and achieved over $18.5 billion operating profit and $11.2 billion net profit. Wal-Mart reached the landmark of $1 billion annual sales in 1979, then achieved $1 billion sales in a week in 1993, before taking $1 billion in sales *in a day* in 2001. Given these sales figures Wal-Mart must be doing things right in the eyes of its customers. Nonetheless Wal-Mart as a retailer is increasingly polarizing opinion (Brunn, 2006), with its detractors accusing it of many poor business practices and behaviours, which permit its low prices. Others believe it has been a driving force in the productivity growth in the US since the mid-1990s and has allowed lower income American consumers in particular to improve their standards of living.

In the UK, the largest and most successful retailer in recent times has been Tesco which has achieved sales of over £40 billion and profits of more than £2.2 billion. Its remarkable growth since the 1970s has seen it take over as the number one retailer in the country and in food retailing extend its market share lead over its rivals to an unprecedented extent (Seth and Randall, 1999, 2005). This growth has in recent years come at the cost of a backlash against the company however. Its critics see it as too dominant in the country, stifling competition and forcing farmers and suppliers out of business as Tesco use their power to extract extra margin and to make unreasonable demands. They also believe that the company drives local retailers out of business and makes retailing a standardized homogeneous experience (www.tescopoly.org). However the company continues to grow. This is mainly due to the willingness of consumers to continue to use the company and to expand their purchases with them (e.g. into non-food items).

It should be clear from the discussion thus far that retailing is now big business. This retail transformation necessarily extends to the management of retail businesses. As the scale of the retail store has increased, and as the scale of the retail business has grown, so too the need for professional, well-trained management has expanded. The types of skills and demands that a store manager in any organizational type has to exhibit are now very different to the shopkeepers of old. Independent shopkeepers compete in a massively competitive industry, where store management and business control principles and techniques have developed strongly in corporate and other chain businesses. Retail management skills are thus critical for success at all levels.

A large food superstore or hypermarket (of which there are many in the UK) could take over £100 million in a year in sales. The store could be open 24 hours a day, 7 days a week. There might be over 600 employees on the site working a variety of shift patterns and at many different grades. The amount of product and consumers passing in and out of the store in a day is huge. The technology in the store is highly advanced and sophisticated. Yet this store is only one part of a business that could have £42 billion worth of sales in a year and employ almost 275 000 people. Its shops, marketing, buying and logistics operations are all professional and dynamic environments.

It is one of the facets of retailing however that the picture painted above of corporate management is but one aspect of the business. At the same time, others find their role in retailing by setting up companies, running small selective stores or small chains and thus satisfying their own entrepreneurial and personal drive. In the UK, companies such as Sock Shop, Body Shop, JJB Sports, Cotton Traders, Carphone Warehouse, Lush and sweatyBetty have come from personal ambitions and drive to produce a better retail offer in a field that interests them. Retailing is one of the few sectors that can accommodate, and indeed needs, a variety of forms of operation and where a specialist can make a difference. Such businesses however still require a variety of retail skills to succeed, including management, marketing, buying and operations.

One such personal business is sweatyBetty, a small, London-based women-only high street retailer ('activewear boutique'). It can be described as a highly targeted contemporary fusion of sportswear, swimwear, outdoorwear and gymwear. The founders believe that they have identified a gap in the market for women-only activewear, arguing that current sports retailers are not meeting women's needs and that women want particular things from a sports store. For many women, they feel, the feel-good factor and the overall health and well-being aspects of keeping fit are more important than winning. Their first store opened in November 1998. There are now 24 small stores including in-store concessions at Selfridges and Harrods, and a transactional website (www.sweatybetty.com). Its values and beliefs encapsulate the company's sense of difference, the founder's personal credo and their sense of business as fun, with the aim of 'building an amazing company, run by women for women to be the best'.

Product sourcing, branding and distribution

> The challenge in retailing is that your customers experience your product directly … What they experience in the store is the brand. So stores have to be both internally and externally coherent. The way the brand is projected and advertised reflects the way it lives and works internally.
>
> Norman (1999, p. 29)

The growth of large retail companies such as Wal-Mart, Tesco, Metro, Seven & I or Carrefour also illustrate another fundamental difference between retailing and other forms of business. To a much greater extent, than for example manufacturing, retailers have to construct strategies for developing and managing multi-plant operations with much greater variety and variability in concepts and transactions (Reynolds and Cuthbertson, 2004). Retail management at the highest level is very different to other production-based businesses and is at the local level much more open to local demand vicissitudes. The role of computer technology and systems in data capture and transmission and in chain control has therefore increased substantially.

The business of retailing involves the selection and assembly of goods for sale to customers (i.e. the process of product sourcing and distribution). This process is also one dominated by variety – of types of goods, sourcing strategy and product mix. Retailers sell a wide variety of items. Some are concentrated in a narrow line of business (specialist stores e.g. Lush, Sephora, Dr & Herbs, New Look) whereas others are much wider in

their scope (general stores e.g. Asda/Wal-Mart, Debenhams). In any event, retailers have to source products for their product range. This involves dealing with particular suppliers (perhaps local suppliers), with wholesalers or other forms of intermediary.

The products that are sourced have changed over time. Whilst there always has been a market for exotic and non-local products, the expectations of many consumers and the abilities of many retailers have transformed the supply position. A reliance on local (i.e. immediate area) sourcing is now not the normal relationship. For many retailers, products from around the world are standard elements to be included in the product mix. Some would question the economic, cultural and environmental impacts of this to both the origin and the destination countries (e.g. Klein, 1999) and there is rising concern over the desirability and sustainability of such practices. The concept of 'food miles' (the mileage of food before it reaches the consumer or the plate) has become synonymous with unsuitable and out-of-season sourcing of food and environmentally unsustainable practices. Retail opportunities focused on local food arise as a consequence of this for example farmers' markets and independent local operations such as Weetons (www.weetons.com). However as yet there is only limited evidence of mass consumers factoring such issues into their purchasing patterns, though this may change.

As retailers have become larger and as their abilities have increased, they have been better able to exploit international product sourcing and buying opportunities. For many non-food products, the costs of production are much lower in countries outside the developed world and it therefore makes economic sense to manufacture abroad (e.g. in Bangladesh, Laos, Vietnam and of course China) and transport the product. Thus many clothing manufacturers in many countries have re-located factories to the Far East or elsewhere to meet the needs of consumers and retailers for cheap products. The management and logistics problems this creates are resolvable by retailers, but there has been consumer concern over exploitation of cheap labour in some locations and the loss of indigenous jobs, as well as recently over environmental issues. Concerns arise mainly over the conditions in which products are manufactured and the use of, for example child labour in 'sweat shops'. Environmental and social rising concerns may in due course spark a wider re-evaluation by consumers of what they value, but this would require in most cases a need to look beyond obtaining products at the lowest price. Retailers therefore are under pressure both to make sure they act appropriately and to remain aware of changing consumers feelings on these issues, but at the same time to keep prices at a level their customers accept.

Clothing production is the obvious example of products being sourced from far afield, but the same is also true of food. Any British supermarket contains many non-UK or non-EU products. Control of the supply chain is thus vital to get products to the stores in good condition. This process of retailer control of supply systems and the use of computer technology for control of central distribution have been key features of recent years. In this respect British logistics systems are amongst the most economically efficient in the world as a consequence (Fernie and Sparks, 1998; Gustafsson *et al.*, 2006).

In addition to control over the range and location of products, retailers have extended their influence over the contents of the product. Claims for organic production, sustainable forests and Fairtrade origins require control, often extending to audited codes of conduct for supplier inputs and methods of production. As societal and consumer concerns change, the retailer needs to source, manage and guarantee products which meet these needs. There is now evidence that organic products have become 'mainstream' in retailing as consumer demand has expanded. Specialist retailers such as Whole Foods Market in the US have had tremendous success, even forcing retailers such as Wal-Mart to develop its organic range. In the UK and the rest of Europe, organic products have grown strongly and become a standard part of the food retailer's range. There remain

issues however over the use of organics as a marketing message by some retailers, particularly when the products are imported or travel long distances rather than being locally produced and sourced.

In obtaining products, retailers have choices to make over what products to sell, but also under what name to sell them. Many products carry the manufacturer's name or brand. Retailers however have become increasingly aware of the potential in supplying products produced under their own control and specification. The approach to retailer branding varies across the globe, but many retailers are becoming much more involved in managing and marketing their own retail names or brands. For a retailer, the name used on the product could have limited direct meaning, but increasingly retailers sell products that carry their own name (e.g. Asda, Marks and Spencer) or a brand they own and have developed (e.g. George, Per Una), recognizing the potential for promotion, advertising and market positioning. Retail branding is extensive in clothing. Next, Mango, Gap, Zara, Benetton and H&M retail brands are well known. Retail branding is now becoming more extensive in other retail product sectors and some retail businesses are effectively collections of brands (e.g. Baugur).

Retail branding in the UK is generally recognized to be more extensive than in other countries and to take a larger share of sales (Burt, 2000). In food retailing a core product branding strategy has emerged that involves the development of three price and quality points. As Table 30.4 shows all the leading food retailers have followed this approach. Initially, retail product branding was low-quality, sometimes even generic product, designed to capture the attention of very price

Table 30.4 Retailers product brand segmentation strategies in the UK food sector

	Exclusive	Standard	Value
Tesco	Finest	Tesco	Value
Morrisons	The best	Morrisons	Bettabuy
Sainsbury	Taste the difference	Sainsbury's	Economy
Asda	Extra special	Asda	Smart price

conscious consumers. This was followed by a movement slightly upmarket to target the leading manufacturer brands with a product of almost similar quality, priced just below the manufacturer's prices. In time retail product developers began to copy the leading brands a little too closely, but by this time retailers had also become aware that consumers were reacting well to their own branded products. It is from this base that the tri-position (good, better, best in the words of the retailers!) brand strategy has emerged. As the table shows, products are priced and positioned at three levels to attract the economy consumer (e.g. Value lines), the mainstream consumer (e.g. Tesco) and the 'luxury' or high quality consumer (e.g. Finest). This approach has been very successful. Most of these retailers have also added to this brand approach by segmenting markets on dimensions other than price. Examples in Tesco include healthy living, organic, ingredients, free from, for one and mega deals. This tri-position brand strategy has also been extended into non-food and service lines (e.g. finest credit card and value mobile phone plan).

Retailers have also learned that as consumers have recognized and trusted their product branding so there is an opportunity to extend the brand in other different ways. This is seen most clearly in the developments in financial and other services. Retailers have thus become banks, investment houses, lifestyle helpers, telecoms and Internet solution providers and so on. At the store level some retailers have segmented the market and adjusted store sizes and locations to meet perceived shopping needs. In Tesco's case the store portfolio is branded under the core brand of Tesco and attempts to live up to its strapline 'Every Little Helps', through formats such as Extra, Express, Metro and Homeplus. In essence this business and others like it are attempting to move away from thinking about product branding to think about corporate branding (Burt and Sparks, 2002) and to ensure all their activities reflect well on this corporate brand (Table 30.5).

The importance of the perception of quality in the eyes of the British consumer in terms of retail product brands should not be underestimated. There has been phenomenal growth in the premium level products identified in Table 30.4. British consumers seem to trust and value these retail brand premium products. To some extent this has always been the case, with the prime example being the St Michael brand from Marks and Spencer. However after the problems of Marks and Spencer in the late 1990s, the company quietly dropped St Michael as the only brand in the store and instead are using a segmentation strategy based around the name Marks and Spencer and other specialist in-house brands such as Per Una. In a different way, the experience in the UK of Aldi, the German discount retailer, makes the same point. Aldi's strategy has been based around in-house brands and product names with limited if any co-ordination. The packaging and approach, including perhaps of quality, reflected the hard discount emphasis. For UK consumers there was considerable resistance to purchasing products with unknown and often foreign sounding names. In 2006 Aldi introduced a co-ordinated and well-designed brand position across parts of their range, using a colour scheme that mimics Tesco's Finest and other retailers, and entitled Specially Selected. This has received strong consumer acceptance.

Business relationships and loyalty

> Sainsbury, which has tried loyalty cards to attract customers to new stores, yesterday dismissed them as 'electronic Green Shield stamps' that represented poor value for money. It has no plans to introduce them nationally, it said.
>
> *The Independent*, 11 February 1995, p. 6

As has been emphasized, the process of retailing involves relationships with other businesses and groups. These too have their own distinctive characteristics arising from the nature of retailing. The requirement to source products, combined as with issues over branding, inevitably means that retailers are concerned with relationships with business partners, as well as relationships with employees and consumers. These business relationships can take many forms and many variants, but essentially retailers can choose to have either collaborative or transactional (sometimes conflictual) relationships. In short, retailers can either work with partners to achieve shared objectives, or they can use their position alone to operate their business to achieve their own ends.

For example product sourcing involves a number of elements, but retailers are attempting to purchase and obtain product at a given price and quality position. For some retailers price is the over-riding concern and retailers will always seek the lowest price for products they know their customers will purchase. This means that the relationships they have with individual suppliers are

Table 30.5   Tesco corporate brand relationship extension

Activity	Example	Tesco example
Building transaction and information linkages	POS, Loyalty cards	Tesco Clubcard, Tesco Personal Finance, Cashback, Location Maps
Extending and deepening infrastructure links	In-store branding, new store formats, new infrastructure	Tesco Extra, Metro, Express etc formats, Tesco.net, Tesco Direct, Tesco.com
Operational links for customers	Consistency of high-service performance	'One in front' campaign, 'Every Little Helps', First Class Service
Personal/face-to-face links	Staff interaction with customers	Service areas for example butchers, customer service desks, customer panels and question time
Service or expertise links	0800 lines, development of clubs	Baby Club, Wine Club, Pharmacy, Recipe Cards
Cementing financial links	Direct financial services	Tesco personal Finance, including insurance, pensions, credit cards, Tesco banking
Building emotional links	Lifestyle advertising, customer information, trust	Television advertising, finest products, healthy eating leaflets, computers for schools, championing 'Grey' market goods and reduced brand prices, bag for life
Searching for event links	In-store activities, sponsorship of events, local charity activity	Collection schemes, for sale wall, local event details in store, Millennium Dome sponsorship
Have usage links	Convenience products	'Grab and Go' areas, newspaper and lottery areas, 24-hour opening
Media communications links	Traditional and Internet	Corporate affairs activities
Distribution and availability links	Format development, home delivery, catalogues	Tesco Direct, Tesco Clothing Catalogue, Tesco specialist magazines for example vegetarian, Internet cafes in-store, Tesco ISP

Source: Burt and Sparks (2002).

often transient and focus on transactional price components alone. The relationship in that sense is straightforward, but often comes down to a conflict about price.

More complex, but of importance to many retailers, is the notion of a collaborative relationship with suppliers which involves all parties in something rather more than simply a transaction based on price. The relationship might be to secure a source of supply or to obtain a given quality and quantity of a product. It might be to develop a product line, to ensure product consistency and quality, to enable flexibility of supply or to allow access to a unique product. If a retailer is branding the product then the collaborative arrangement may be about ensuring certain quality standards. For many retailers therefore, whilst price will be very important, there could well be other aspects of the business relationship which need to be in place. Some of these relationships or partnerships are of long standing and have involved extensive product development and consequent growth of both partners.

Retailers of course have business relationships beyond product sourcing. Relationships exist with an array of service providers. Finance is one example, with independent retailers seeking bank finance and multiple or corporate retailers searching for institutional finance to enable them to develop their store portfolios. With retail sites being highly expensive to rent, buy or develop, retailers need to secure such institutional funding. One of the most important relationships occurs in the physical supply of products to the retailer. Product sourcing in a transactional sense has been identified above, but products have to be delivered to the retail store to be available for merchandizing and for sale. Logistics systems and logistics providers therefore may be key components of another set of business relationships (Fernie and Sparks, 1998). As might be imagined, with product sourcing complexities, expansion in the number of stores and spatial breadth in many companies and the increased expectations of consumers with respect to product quality and availability, supply chain management has become more and more important. For many retailers, being in retailing is sufficient, and logistics systems are often outsourced to these logistics services providers. Whilst many vehicles are seen on roads carrying retailer logos and livery, most of them are owned and operated by contractual logistics services partners such as DHL Exel.

These relationships in the supply chain can be critical to the nature of the retail performance. In recent years companies such as Zara and H&M, and in different ways Asos.com and Primark, have redefined the parameters of the fashion supply chain. The advent of 'fast fashion' with an emphasis on speed through the supply chain from design to production to purchase has forced relationships and competitors to change. When Zara's supply chain is measured in days and weeks, other retailers with slower chains (e.g. months and years) will inevitably fall behind in consumer popularity (Figure 30.2).

Customer relationships have become increasingly important to retailers. Historically, whilst retailers were in competition with each other on a local level, customers were less mobile and less volatile or promiscuous in their patronage. As a result there was a degree of certainty or relationship with the local store or local co-operative. As consumers changed behaviours and utilized their increased mobility and choice, so retailers have been less able to depend on certainty of demand. In such circumstances large retailers have tried to identify, brand and get to know their customers.

One of the main mechanisms for the development of this relationship has been the 'loyalty' card or scheme. These have been enormously popular with some retailers and attempt to build a relationship with individual customers. The depth of this relationship may often be exaggerated, but retailers hope that by possessing a loyalty card for a company, the customer will behave more loyally and shop around less. In turn the retailer gains data on which to base strategic and tactical decision making. For this knowledge and potential change in behaviour, retailers give customers some reward, usually a small dividend on purchase volume, but occasionally rights to buy products from a catalogue or to use their points in other ways. The modern loyalty card is a product both of consumer change and technology development. In essence large retailers are using systems to identify customers. This is a practice or advantage that the best local retailers have almost instinctively. But the advent of cheap but large computer systems has enabled large retailers to replicate these advantages.

There are many large loyalty card schemes across the world. In the UK, Boots the Chemist's Advantage Card has almost 15 million active cardholders and is used in 70 per cent of sales transactions in the company. The Tesco Clubcard scheme (Humby *et al.*, 2003) has probably 13 million members and has been credited with helping the retailer reach its current dominant market position. The information received on purchase patterns has been vital in adjusting the product, store and other offers and in targeted and micro-marketing activities. The data to some extent is the heart of the business strategy.

Other retailers have not been so convinced by the idea or practice of loyalty cards. Their argument is that it is an expensive way to learn about consumer behaviour, provides only partial data and does not really engender loyalty *per se*. Businesses such as Sainsbury, Asda and the Co-operative Group have at different times switched their views on the value of such schemes.

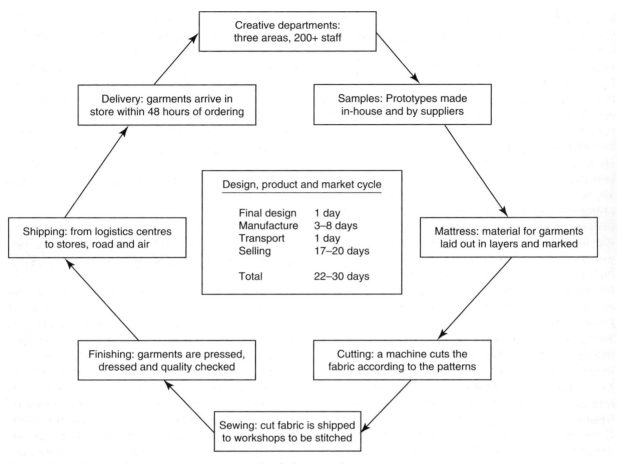

Figure 30.2 Zara: time-based competition in the fashion market

The evidence however would seem to point to loyalty schemes being successful when managed and integrated fully with the business. As the retail analysts Cazenove note: 'we believe that Clubcard, which conveys an array of material benefits across virtually every discipline of its business, is Tesco's most potent weapon in the ongoing battle for market share' (quoted in Rigby, 2006).

The consumer focus that a loyalty scheme can bring retailers to track mobile consumers as they shop in different ways across the company. Thus for example as Tesco have developed their various formats and channels (e.g. Metro, Express, Extra, Direct, Homeplus, Telecoms, etc.) so the Clubcard can be used as the connective mechanism to track consumers and their patterns of shopping. Such data, whilst somewhat problematic in both privacy and practical terms at the individual level (e.g. see Smith and Sparks, 2004) does allow a strong degree of segmentation and a fuller understanding of actual and potential behaviours (Humby *et al.*, 2003).

Merchandizing and selling

For many outside retailing, selling is often viewed as the same as retailing; selling is however one component of the retail operation. Selling itself varies of course, with the move to self-service in many product categories and retailers reducing the role of direct sales personnel in the store. In other retailers, the product knowledge and sales skills of the staff are critical in the delivery of customer service and the repeat patronage of consumers. The art and science of selling and the quality of the sales staff are of fundamental importance for much business success. In other situations, the lack of quality or knowledge of the staff acts as a negative influence on consumers.

Store and selling design varies enormously by situation (Underhill, 1999). The emphasis on design, staff knowledge and staff competency may be vital in some situations, but of no consequence in others. The retail offer has become more disparate overall as retailers have attempted to match their offer to the demands of the customer. Some stores are dramatic (e.g. Sephora, Girl Heaven), some are functional (e.g. Aldi or Lidl) others playful (e.g. Build-A-Bear, Disney or REI). Some have many staff selling; others simply have takers of money. All however, are based on retailers' understanding of what works with their customers.

Store-based selling has its own distinctive characteristics. How the product is merchandized and the ways in which design and display interact are important to attracting consumers and obtaining their custom. As a result much effort is expended in laying out the store and in ensuring that products are presented appropriately. This presentation includes aspects of visual display, as well as essential product information. Depending on the product lines involved and the approach of the retailer, such merchandizing may be of lesser or greater importance. Even in supposedly simple retailer situations (e.g. markets) product display can be sophisticated and help consumers make choices amongst 'stores' and products. Mail order or catalogue retailers (e.g. Argos) have similar selling objectives, but a different set of tasks and expectations to manage, through a one-dimensional page in a paper catalogue (although the Internet opens up other possibilities for them).

Store merchandizing and display techniques condition the retail environment in every store. Some of the techniques are rather obvious and relatively easy to identify, whereas others are far more subtle and difficult to discern (Underhill, 1999). Visual merchandizing and design direct attention and movement by leading customers around and through the merchandize. 'Hot Spots' in the store are created to 'drag' people through the shop and grab their attention. Lighting and music are used in some stores to alter the mood of sections of shops. Colour is used to create an environment or an image. Touch is encouraged to exploit the tactile senses. Even smells are used to evoke responses, whether perfume, cosmetics or coffee and fresh bread. Some design and display may be organized to recreate remembered activities or past situations and provoke positive responses. In short, stores are not abstract collections of products, but managed selling environments, designed to stimulate customer reactions and purchase.

Possibly some of the most managed yet involving retail environments are found in flagship stores (Kozinets *et al.*, 2002) such as Nike Town. Here, all aspects of the environment are managed to create a mix of a store, museum and interactive playzone (Sherry, 1998; Peñaloza, 1999). To fit with such an approach employees and design have to support the brand marketing at every stage. A similar approach, though on a different scale, underpins a recent move by Halfords to experiment with a stand-alone Bikehut store. This is merchandized, designed and staffed with the specialist bike customer in mind, with all activities and design aligned with customer expectations. This is in contrast to the current use of the sub-brand as an in-house operation as part of the larger store, staffed by Halfords employees.

The state of the retail world

The description so far of the process of retailing has pointed both to the major functional areas of retail business activity and to some of the changes that have been taking place in the sector and their implications for consumers (see also Clarke, 2000; Clarke *et al.*, 2006; Jackson *et al.*, 2006). These can be summarized into a number of key issues.

First, recent decades have seen an enormous change in the location of retailing. Retailing takes place now in very different locations than previously. There has been a broad trend of decentralization of retail locations and the rise of superstores and shopping centres. Other emerging retail locations include sports stadia (e.g. Manchester United Superstore), hospitals, airports (e.g. Heathrow) and museums or heritage sites (e.g. Britannia shop at Ocean Terminal, Leith). Less-planned activities occur in open-air markets, car-boot sales, farmers markets, some charity shops (Horne and Maddrell, 2002) and other, sometimes, transient events. Retailing today has been locationally transformed away from the high street and even the shopping centre.

Secondly, there has been an alteration in the formats through which retailing takes place. Shops today are not like shops of previous times and retailer strategies have become more segmented. Sainsbury amongst others has reacted to consumer change by developing and operating a range of format/locational store types. They differ in scale, design, technique and approach. Halfords has three store formats and sizes (Super, High St, Metro) to capture different consumers and/or different shopping patterns. Much effort has been expanded by large retailers to develop and transform the small shop as part of their corporate approach to retailing, as for example in Tesco.

Even in catalogue retailing this format change has occurred with the decline of the huge, agency, Grattans-style catalogue and its replacement by narrowly targeted 'specialogues' for example, Artigiano, Toast, Cotton Traders or retailer brand channels (e.g. Next Directory).

Thirdly, retailers have increased in scale and power. They have grown enormously in size and many are now significant businesses in their own right, often being larger than the manufacturers who supply them. Even in a short span of time, the scale of growth is remarkable (Table 30.6). In the UK retailing is dominated by these large and often food-based businesses. Through their scale, they can reorganize various relationships to suit themselves. This scale of operation brings practical and financial benefits to the business. Recently, the scale has increased to another level with major mergers or takeovers on the international stage for example Wal-Mart of Woolco in Canada and Asda in the UK; the merger of Carrefour and

Promodès in France; and the expansion of other retailers across the world. The world's leading retailers are now amongst some of the biggest organizations around and have an increasingly international approach (Dawson et al., 2003, 2006). It is not just the scale of these retail organizations that is remarkable, but the breadth of their business in spatial terms.

This is shown in Table 30.7 which lists the largest retailers in the world in 2005 (the latest date for comparable data) and the fastest growing over the last 5 years. The scale of Wal-Mart is immediately notable, as is the dominance of US-based retailers in the listing of largest retailers. This reflects the size of their national market. This table also shows the different approach to internationalization adopted by the US and European firms. Ten years has seen quite considerable change in the listing, arising from organic growth, mergers and takeovers (e.g. Carrefour) and failure (e.g. Ahold). The listing of fastest growing retailers is

Table 30.6   The UK's largest retailers 1990/1991 and 2004/2005

(a) 2004/2005

Rank	Name	UK sales (billion pounds)	UK stores (number)	UK sales area (million sq.ft)	Store fascias
1	Tesco	27.15	1780	24.19	Tesco
2	J. Sainsbury	15.05	901	16.60	Sainsbury's, Bells, Jackson
3	ASDA*	14.16	263	11.46	Asda, Asda Wal-Mart
4	Morrisons	12.12	498	12.47	Morrisons, Safeway
5	Marks and Spencer	7.03	399	12.90	Marks and Spencer
6	Argos	5.54	879	n/a	Argos, Homebase
7	Boots	4.83	1428	n/a	Boots
8	Dixons	4.82	1031	7.62	Currys, PC World, Dixons, The Link
9	John Lewis Partnership	4.78	192	7.23	Waitrose, John Lewis
10	Somerfield	4.68	1308	10.64	Somerfield, Kwik Save

* Owned by Wal-Mart.

Table 30.6 Continued

(b) 1990/1991

Rank	Name	UK sales (billion pounds)	UK stores	UK sales area (million sq.ft)	Store fascias
1	J. Sainsbury	6.84	369	10.06	Sainsbury's, Savacentre, Homebase
2	Tesco	6.35	384	9.66	Tesco
3	Marks and Spencer	4.89	288	9.47	Marks and Spencer
4	Argyll Group[1]	4.49	1113	8.37	Safeway, Presto. Lo-Cost, Galbraith
5	ASDA	4.34	365	10.27	Asda, Allied Maples, Allied, Maples, Waring and Gillow
6	Isosceles[2]	3.11	758	7.31	Somerfield, Gateway, Wellworth, Food Giant
7	Kingfisher	3.11	2095	19.20	B&Q, Comet, Superdrug, Woolworths, Titles, Gifts and Treats, Depot, Charlie Brown's
8	Boots the Chemist	2.98	2266	n/a	Boots, Halfords, Children's World, Fads, Do It All (50%)
9	John Lewis Partnership	1.97	116	3.51	John Lewis and other department stores, Waitrose
10	Sears	1.87	3432	n/a	Shoe City, Freeman Hardy Willis, Dolcis, Saxone, Roland Cartier, Manfield, Cable & Co. Warehouse, Fosters, Your Price, Wallis, Miss Selfridge, Adams, Olympus, PRO Performance Shoes, Sportsave, Millets, Selfridges, Freemans, Stage One

[1] Argyll Group became Safeway; [2] Isosceles became Somerfield
Source: Calculated from Retail Intelligence/Mintel *The UK Retail Rankings*, 1992 and 2006 editions, Corporate Intelligence Group, London.

much more diverse, with retailers from many countries. Again much growth arises from takeover (e.g. Morrisons and Safeway). This listing shows also that at this level convenience and drug store chains have been developing rapidly.

Table 30.8 examines two retailers to illustrate the international operations that can occur in retailing and the way in which these are managed through format and brand development. Carrefour, the world's second largest retailer has been an international business for many years (Dawson *et al.*, 2006), but its spread of food operations is

still impressive. Iceland-based Baugur is a much less well-known retailer but as Table 30.7 shows, it has been growing rapidly. Its growth has been through acquisition of brand retailers in the main and a concentration on the UK and parts of Scandinavia, as well as its small home market. The breadth of brand is of interest as is the potential for developing these internationally.

However, it needs to be noted that internationalization is not always easy and successful. Indeed failures and market exits are surprisingly common (Burt *et al.*, 2004), even with high profile

Table 30.7 World's largest and fastest growing retailers

(a) Largest in 2005

Rank	Company	Country of origin	Retail sales (billion US $ in 2005)	Number of countries with stores	Rank in 1996
1	Wal-Mart	USA	312.43	9	1
2	Carrefour	France	92.78	31	8
3	Home Depot	USA	81.51	3	24
4	Metro	Germany	69.13	30	4
5	Tesco	UK	68.87	13	18
6	Kroger	USA	60.55	1	13
7	Target	USA	52.62	1	12
8	Costco	USA	51.86	6	23
9	Sears	USA	49.12	2	7
10	Schwarz	Germany	45.89	22	33

(b) Fastest growing 2000–2005

Rank	Company	Country of origin	Retail sales (billion US $ in 2005)	Sales rank 2005
1	Baugur	Iceland	12.55	51
2	Couche-Tard	Canada	10.16	69
3	Kintetsu	Japan	2.69	239
4	Tokyu	Japan	6.00	112
5	AS Watson	Hong Kong SAR	11.42	60
6	Jean Coutu	Canada	9.51	73
7	GameStop	USA	3.10	201
8	Katz	Canada	3.84	166
9	Dirk Rossman	Germany	3.36	189
10	Morrisons	UK	21.84	33

Source: Extracted from Deliotte/NRF Stores (2007) 2007 Global Powers of Retailing, downloaded from www.nxtbook.com/nxtbooks/nrfe/stores-globalretail07/ (accessed on 18 January 2007).

Table 30.8   Multi-format and multi-brand international retailing

(a) Carrefour Group 2005

Country	Hypermarkets	Supermarkets	Hard discount	Other	Total
France	179	595	782	108	1664
Belgium	56	79			135
Spain	136	143	1891		2170
Greece	19	148	267	52	486
Italy	50	238		171	459
Poland	32	71			103
Portugal	7		292		299
Czech Republic	11				11
Slovakia	4				4
Switzerland	9				9
Turkey	12	86	339		437
Argentina	28	114	319		465
Brazil	99	35	201		335
Colombia	21				21
China	70	8	225		303
Korea	31				31
Indonesia	20				20
Malaysia	8				8
Singapore	2				2
Taiwan	37				37
Thailand	23				23
Franchises/Partners (UAE, Qatar, Santo Dominguo, Tunisia, Egypt, Oman, Saudi Arabia, Japan, Algeria)	36	110		56	202
Total	890	1627	4316	387	7220

Source: Constructed from www.carrefour.com (accessed 17 January 2007)

Table 30.8   Continued

(b) Baugur Group

'The Baugur Group Retail Division is based on the strategy of acquiring companies possessing strong brands with potential for further strengthening and development inside and outside their home market'

Company/brand	Sector	Number of stores	Countries
Mosaic (Karen Millen, Coast, Shoe Studio Group, Whistles, principles, warehouse, Oasis, Odille Oasis)	Womanswear fashion clothing and shoes	1581	UK
MKOne	Fashion clothing	174	UK
Jane Norman	Womens fashion	130	UK, Iceland, Denmark
All Saints	Design-led fashion brand (men and women)	49	UK, Iceland, Denmark, Spain
House of Fraser	Department store	61	UK
Hamleys	Toy retailer	13	UK
Iceland	Frozen food	667	UK, Ireland
Booker	Wholesaler cash and carry	170	UK
Woodward Foodservice	Foodservice	28	UK
Julian Graves/Whittard of Chelsea	Speciality foods	422	UK
Goldsmith/Mappin and Webb	Jewellers	195	UK
Wyevale Garden Centres	Garden centres	114	UK
Hagar	Supermarkets, sporting goods and operation of international franchises	81	Iceland, Sweden, Denmark
Húesasmiðjan	Building materials and home products	31	Iceland
SMS	Supermarkets	8	Faroe Islands
ILLUM	Department store	1	Denmark
Magasin du Nord	Department store	6	Denmark
Day Birger et Mikkelsen	Product design	9	19 countries (various distribution points)
Merlin	Electronics (including online)	48	Denmark
Total		3788	

Source: Baugur Group Corporate Brochure, downloaded from www.baugurgroup.com (accessed on 22 January 2007).

businesses. Wal-Mart for example in 2006 pulled out of Korea and Germany. Marks and Spencer endured a torrid exit from various markets in the early 2000s (Burt *et al.*, 2002). Ahold, once one of the major 'stars' of grocery retailing internationalization has been forced to divest several markets (Wrigley and Currah, 2003). Various reasons behind these failures and exits can be put forward but common themes include consumer acceptance of the transferability of store image across national boundaries and the required degree of format and product standardization or adaptation (Salmon and Tordjman, 1989).

Finally, there are obviously impacts of these trends. These impacts are felt at different levels. International activity affects the retail landscape at the local level. The nature of competition and availability is such that all elements of the retail sector interact and affect consumers everywhere. Who gains and loses from this local, national and international reconstruction of the retail landscape? There has to be concern about the quality of products available for people to buy, both in terms of what is available to them, but also in terms of where it is made and under what conditions. What future is there for the local, indigenous retailers and should they be protected from multinational retail entries? Retailing has changed, and whilst there have been major benefits of the new system; there are dangers and problems as well.

Future retailing

DSG international's market leadership is due to our success in keeping close to the needs of our customers, keeping close to the latest developments in consumer technology and leading the market in innovation. With these changes (*the change of Dixons from a physical shop presence to be an Internet business*) we now intend to become the most successful electrical retailer on the web, alongside our leadership position in bricks and mortar electrical retailing.

John Clare, Group Chief Executive, DSG International, 5 April 2006, press release downloaded from www.dsgiplc.com on the 17 January 2007

The increasing scale of leading retailers is a good place to start any consideration of the future of retailing (Dawson, 2000; Sparks and Findlay, 2000; Krafft and Mantrala, 2006). Scale provides big benefits to retailers – if it is managed correctly. There are however dangers to huge scale. In particular

the management of retailing across continents and businesses is not a simple task. The pursuit of scale in retailing is likely to continue, but management has to be careful of how the organization operates and relates to local consumers.

Retailing in many countries may also be challenged by an over-supply of retail floorspace and by turbulence in the environment. Retailing has gone through a period of major change. This process is not complete and competition and volatility is ever present in the market. For retailers this is a major challenge. It is not helped by the tendency in recent decades to build more and more new stores in new locations. The retailing this 'replaces' remains to some degree. Some of the new developments were not well sited and/or were speculative development. Some of the 'old' space is simply left derelict. There is thus too much retail space, though conversely not enough high-quality locations. Being in the right place at the right cost is a management headache.

Retail management and marketing is also concerned about the activities the company undertakes. The impact of these activities is now becoming a major consumer and governmental concern. Retailers are under pressure to improve their environmental and social awareness activities and to minimize adverse affects of their business. Concerns about global production and sourcing, labour practices and the need for adaptation to local situations are increasing. Ethical and environmental concerns are increasing and in some cases have resulted in legislation. Some environmental actions are clearly beneficial for retailers (e.g. energy reduction) with companies striving to build the most energy-efficient stores. Other actions for example reduction of food miles, labelling of 'unhealthy' food, western wages in eastern factories are more problematical. Retailers such as Tesco and Marks and Spencer have started 2007 however with Green Manifestos, setting challenging ambitions and targets in this area. One thing is clear; the environmental issues of retailing and consumers' use of retailers is going to remain high on the future retail agenda.

Finally, any discussion of the future of retailing has to consider the issue of e-retailing or Internet shopping (Kornum and Bjerre, 2005). In the run-up to 2000 there was both spectacular hype and then the equally spectacular fall of many Internet operations. Both the hype and the fall were probably overdone. Profitable Internet retailers exist and the sector continues to develop strongly. Two of the most visited UK retail Internet

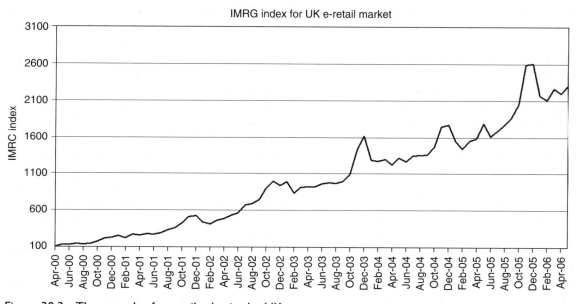

Figure 30.3 The growth of e-retail sales in the UK
Source: IMRG (www.imrg.org) (Reproduced with permission).

sites are Tesco and Argos both of whom have added e-retailing to their existing channels of operations, enabling them to increase their product and customer range. Some specialist operators, including quite small and local businesses, are doing well. The movement of Dixons to become an Internet-only operation is another signifier of the expansion and acceptance of the channel. Indeed many retailers would now describe themselves as multi-channel. Whilst there seems to be an appetite in the UK and elsewhere for the Internet as a shopping medium, the true extent to which it will eventually challenge or complement existing retailing remains open to question.

One of the reasons why the impact of e-retailing is as yet undecided is that there remain issues about the form and functions that need to be performed and the costs of these. Some have developed pure Internet-based operations (e.g. Amazon.co.uk). Others have developed an Internet operation on the back of existing activity, but with specialist picking facilities (e.g. Sainsbury). Tesco however chose to add the Internet channel to their existing store-based operation and to initially focus picking of orders and delivery from local stores. With the expanded ranges now provided online, they now also use their distribution network for picking and delivery of non-store carried products. These different models may be suitable in different circumstances, though concern in all cases remains about the mechanics of delivery and whether huge

volumes of home delivery is actually economically or environmentally desirable (Foresight Retail Logistics Task Force, 2000).

The Internet is becoming a factor in shopping and retailing in the UK and elsewhere. Internet retail sales in the UK according to IMRG reached £7.66 billion in the 10-week run-up to Christmas 2006, as Britain's 25 million online shoppers engaged in online Christmas shopping. This was approximately 54 per cent more than in the same period in 2005, which itself was 41 per cent more than in 2004. IMRG which have tracked and indexed Internet retail sales in the UK since 2000 show clearly (Figure 30.3) that the growth has been spectacular and consistent. It is also true that as the Internet increases as a media outlet and channel of information and product delivery, so retailers are looking to drive traffic to their websites and to convert intention or visits into purchases. More advertising and promotional spend may thus go into the Internet and away from some other channels. It has to be remembered though, that Internet sales, even with recent growth, are only 3–5 per cent of total UK retail sales, so there is a long way to go before it is a dominant channel.

Summary

This chapter set out to introduce the subject and context of retailing. Retailing has undergone major change in form and to some extent function in recent decades. Components of this include:

- growth of particular organizational types;
- dominance of the market by major multiple retailers who continue to grow in scale;
- increasing internationalization of retailing activity;
- a variety of responses to the changing consumer patterns of demand;
- an increasing professionalization of management, including marketing, in many retail businesses.

Retailing is a major component of the economies of many countries. Individuals experience retailing every day through their shopping activity. It has come to hold a higher place in people's minds as it has been transformed from a functional sector providing necessities to one that provides a range of experiences and opportunities. With its close understanding of consumers, retailing continues to change and fascinate in equal measure. Retailers' practice of marketing has similarly to adapt to these new realities.

References and further reading

Bowlby, R. (2000) *Carried Away: The Invention of ModernShopping*, Faber and Faber, London.

Brunn, S. (ed.) (2006) *Wal-Mart World: The World's Biggest Corporation in the Global Economy*, Routledge, New York.

Burt, S. L. (2000) The strategic role of retail brands in British grocery retailing, *European Journal of Marketing*, 34(8), 875–890.

Burt, S. L. and Sparks, L. (2002) Corporate branding, retailing and retail internationalisation, *Corporate Reputation Review*, 5, 194–212.

Burt, S. L. and Sparks, L. (2003) Power and competition in the UK retail grocery market, *British Journal of Management*, 14, 237–254.

Burt, S. L., Dawson, J. A. and Sparks, L. (2004) The international divestment activities of European grocery retailers, *European Management Journal*, 22, 483–492.

Burt, S. L., Mellahi, K., Jackson, T. P. and Sparks, L. (2002) Retail internationalisation and retail failure: issues from the case of Marks and Spencer, *International Review of Retail, Distribution and Consumer Research*, 12, 191–219.

Clarke, I. (2000) Retail power, competition and local consumer choice in the UK grocery sector, *European Journal of Marketing*, 34, 975–1002.

Clarke, I., Hallsworth, A., Jackson, P., de Kervenoael, R., Perez del Aguila, R. and Kirkup, M. (2006) Retail restructuring and consumer choice. 1. Long term changes in consumer behaviour: Portsmouth 1980–2002, *Environment and Planning A*, 38, 25–46.

Clarke, R., Davies, S., Dobson, P. and Waterson, M. (2002) *Buyer Power and Competition in European Food Retailing*, Edward Elgar, Cheltenham.

Competition Commission (2000) *Supermarkets*, Cm 4842, Stationery Office, Norwich.

Dawson, J. A. (1995) Retail Change in the European Community, Chapter 1 in Davies, R. L. (ed.), *Retail Planning Policies in Western Europe*, Routledge, London.

Dawson, J. A. (2000) Retailing at century end: some challenges for management and research, *International Review of Retail, Distribution and Consumer Research*, 10, 119–148.

Dawson, J. A. (2001) Is there a new commerce in Europe? *International Review of Retail, Distribution and Consumer Research*, 11, 287–299.

Dawson, J. A. and Burt, S. L. (1998) European Retailing: Dynamics, Restructuring and Development Issues, Chapter 9 in Pinder, D. (ed.), *The New Europe: Economy, Society and Environment*, Wiley, Chichester.

Dawson, J. A., Mukoyama, M., Choi, S. C. and Larke, R. (eds) (2003) *The Internationalisation of Retailing in Asia*, Routledge Curzon, London.

Dawson, J. A., Larke, R. and Mukoyama, M. (eds) (2006) *Strategic Issues in International Retailing*, Routledge Curzon, London.

Department of Trade and Industry (2004) *The Retail Strategy Group – Driving Change*, Department of Trade and Industry, London.

Fernie, J. (1998) The breaking of the fourth wave, *International Review of Retail Distribution and Consumer Research*, 8, 303–317.

Fernie, J. and Sparks, L. (eds) (1998) *Logistics and Retail Management*, Kogan Page, London.

Foresight Retail Logistics Task Force (2000) *At Your Service: future models of retail logistics*, DTI, London.

Gustafsson, K., Jönson, G., Smith, D. L. G. and Sparks. L. (2006) *Retailing Logistics and Fresh Food Packaging*, Kogan Page, London.

Guy, C. (1994) *The Retail Development Process*, Routledge, London.

Guy, C. (2006) *Planning for Retail Development*, Routledge, London.

Hallsworth, A. (1994) The decentralization of retailing in Britain – the breaking of the third wave, *Professional Geographer*, 46, 296–307.

Horne, S. and Maddrell, A. (2002) *Charity Shops*, Routledge, London.

Humby, C., Hunt, H. and Phillips, T. (2003) *Scoring Points: How Tesco is Winning Customer Loyalty*, Kogan Page, London.

Jackson, P., Perez del Aguila, R., Clarke, I., Hallsworth, A., de Kervenoael, R. and Kirkup, M. (2006) Retail restructuring and consumer choice 2: understanding consumer choice at the household level, *Environment and Planning A*, **38**, 47–67.

Klein, N. (1999) *No Logo*, Picador, New York.

Kornum, N. and Bjerre, M. (eds) (2005) *Grocery E-commerce: Consumer Behaviour and Business Strategies*, Edward Elgar, Cheltenham.

Kowinski, W. S. (2002) *The Malling of America*, Updated 2nd edn, Xlibris Corporation, Philadelphia, PA.

Kozinets, R. V., Sherry, J. F., Deberry-Spence, B., Duhachek, A., Nuttavuthisit, K. and Storm D. (2002) Themed flagship brand stores in the new millennium: theory, practice, prospects, *Journal of Retailing*, **78**, 17–29.

Krafft, M. and Mantrala, M. K. (2006) *Retailing in the 21st Century*, Springer, Berlin.

Longstreth, R. (1997) *City Center to Regional Mall*, MIT Press, Cambridge, MA.

Longstreth. R. (1999) *The Drive-In, the Supermarket and the Transformation of Commercial Space in Los Angeles 1914–1941*, MIT Press, Cambridge, MA.

Miller, D., Jackson, P., Thrift, N., Holbrook, B. and Rowlands, M. (1998) *Shopping, Place and Identity*, Routledge, London.

Norman, A. (1999) Asda: the Accelerated Repositioning of a Brand, in Gilmore, F. (ed.), *Brand Warriors*, Harper Collins, London, pp. 25–35.

Peñaloza, L. (1999) Just doing it: a visual ethnographic study of spectacular consumption behaviour at Nike Town, *Consumption, Markets and Culture*, **2**, 337–400.

Reynolds, J. and Cuthbertson, C. (eds) (2004) *Retail Strategy: The View From the Bridge*, Elsevier, Oxford.

Rigby, E. (2006) Technology special, Financial Times Weekend Edition, 11 November, p. 16.

Ruston, P. (1999) *Out-of-Town Shopping: The Future of Retailing*, British Library, London.

Salmon, W. J. and Tordjman, A. (1989) The internationalization of retailing, *International Journal of Retailing*, **4**(2), 3–16.

Schiller, R. (1987) Out of Town Exodus, in McFadyen, E. (ed.), *The Changing Face of British Retailing*, Newman Books, London, pp. 64–73.

Seth, A. and Randall, G. (1999) *The Grocers:The Rise and Rise of the Supermarket Chains*, Kogan Page, London.

Seth, A. and Randall, G. (2005) *Supermarket Wars: Global Strategies for Food Retailers*, Palgrave Macmillan, Basingstoke.

Sherry, J. F. (1998) The Soul of the Company Store, Nike Town, Chicago and the Emplaced Landscape, in Sherry, J. F. (ed.), (1998) *Servicescapes: The Concept of Place in Contemporary Markets*, NTC Business Books, Lincolnwood, IL, pp. 109–146.

Shopping Centres Today (2006) Publix Expands Hispanocentric Sabor Supermarkets, downloaded from www.icsc.org/srch/sct/sct0706/retail_publix.php (accessed on 17 January 2007).

Simms, A., Kjell, P. and Potts, R. (2005) *Clone Town Britain: The Survey Results on the Bland State of the Nation*, New Economics Foundation, London.

Smith, A. P. and Sparks, L. (2004) All about Eve? *Journal of Marketing Management*, **20**, 363–385.

Sparks, L. and Findlay, A. (2000) *The Future of Shopping*, RICS 2020: Visions of the Future, London.

The Independent (1995) Tesco offers loyalty bonus with discount card, *The Independent*, 11 February, p. 6.

Thomas, C. J. (2006) New 'high streets' in the suburbs? The growing competitive impact of evolving retail parks, *International Review of Retail Distribution and Consumer Research*, **16**, 43–68.

Underhill, P. (1999) *Why we Buy: The Science of Shopping*, Orion, London.

Wrigley, N. and Currah, A. (2003) The 'stresses' of retail internationalisation: lessons from Royal Ahold's experience in Latin America, *International Review of Retail, Distribution and Consumer Research*, **13**, 221–243.

Index